COPYRIGHT, PATENT, TRADEMARK

AND

RELATED STATE DOCTRINES

CASES AND MATERIALS ON THE LAW

OF

INTELLECTUAL PROPERTY

FIFTH EDITION

by

PAUL GOLDSTEIN
Lillick Professor of Law
Stanford University

NEW YORK, NEW YORK
FOUNDATION PRESS

2002
Mat #18342588

COPYRIGHT © 1973 CALLAGHAN & COMPANY
COPYRIGHT © 1981, 1990, 1993, 1997, 1999 FOUNDATION PRESS
COPYRIGHT © 2002 By FOUNDATION PRESS
                 395 Hudson Street
                 New York, NY 10014
                 Phone Toll Free 1–877–888–1330
                 Fax (212) 367–6799
                 fdpress.com
All rights reserved
Printed in the United States of America

ISBN 1–58778–166–2

To
My Mother

*

PREFACE

At a meeting of the American Bar Association's Section on Patents, Trademarks and Copyrights, a seasoned copyright practitioner introduced his remarks with the observation that section members "are exposed to many occupational hazards.... One of the less serious ones—but still an obstacle faced almost daily—is the fact that most people do not understand the difference between patents, trademarks and copyrights. This applies to clients, other lawyers and at times even judges. When I tell a general practitioner that I am a copyright lawyer, he immediately corrects me: 'You mean patents!' He then says: 'Well, anyway, as a patent lawyer, you can copyright a name for me can't you?'"* (The inside joke was that trademark law, not copyright law, protects names.)

Why the confusion between copyright, patent and trademark law? One reason is that these federal laws occupy a common ground, each seeking to stimulate investment in information through the award of property rights. The information produced, and the specific intellectual property rights that attach, are sometimes hard to separate. Adding to the confusion is the fact that state laws—principally trade secret law, unfair competition law and the right of publicity—also qualify as intellectual property.

Because these laws occupy a common field, they invite comparison. How, and how efficiently, does each law allocate costs and benefits among producers, distributors and consumers of information? The field also invites less theoretical inquiry. A lawyer must be prepared to pick out not only a single thread of protection for a client's project (one consisting, say, of trade secret and patent protection), but possibly a more ample fabric (a combination of trade secret, patent, copyright and trademark). And, although the lawyer will move easily from state to federal law, the lines between, like so many other lines in a federal system, bristle with conflict—often of a constitutional dimension.

In the years since publication of the Fourth Edition, the perceived importance of intellectual property continues to grow dramatically—in Congress and in the courts, in boardrooms and in law firms. Congress has repeatedly amended the copyright, patent and trademark acts in important respects, and cases arising under these acts increasingly crowd the judicial docket. The question of intellectual property on the Internet, just begin-

---

*Alan Latman, Preliminary Injunctions in Patent, Trademark and Copyright Cases, 60 Trademark Rep. 506 (1970).

ning to ramify at the time of the Fourth Edition, has since become one of the legal system's hottest topics. Also, as the importance of intellectual property to the nation's balance of trade has come into clearer focus, Congress has moved to bring U.S. law into line with international treaty requirements and has employed trade measures to stimulate world-wide protection for intellectual goods originating in the United States.

The Fifth Edition reflects suggestions made by many teachers who used the Fourth. For their good advice, I am grateful to Joseph P. Bauer, Joseph J. Beard, Andrew Beckerman-Rodau, Michael H. Davis, Graeme B. Dinwoodie, William T. Fryer, III, David Allen Hall, I. Trotter Hardy, Robert A. Kreiss, R. Anthony Reese, Edward B. Samuels, Jeffrey M. Samuels, Edmund J. Sease and Geri J. Yonover. I am also grateful to my colleagues in the intellectual property practice at Morrison & Foerster for continually challenging me with questions at the law's cutting edge.

Stanford Law School, where I completed the first four editions of this book, continued to provide a congenial setting for work on the fifth. I am particularly indebted to Dean Kathleen Sullivan for her generous support, and to the staff of the Robert Crown Law Library for helping so many times in so many ways. I am grateful to Nicole Acton, a student at the Law School, for cite-checking and proofreading the text and for preparing the index. Her work was supported by the Claire and Michael Brown Memorial Fund at the Law School. Finally, I am indebted to my assistant, Lynne Anderson, for so cheerfully and efficiently overseeing production of the manuscript.

Note on Style. The articles and many of the cases appearing in these pages have been edited. The deletion of sentences and paragraphs is indicated by ellipses. The deletion of string citations is not indicated. Most footnotes have been excised. Those that remain have not been renumbered. Parallel citation to federal, state and regional reporters and to the United States Patent Quarterly has been employed where appropriate.

P.G.

Stanford, California
May, 2002

SUMMARY OF CONTENTS

PREFACE v
TABLE OF CASES xxvii

PART ONE INTELLECTUAL PROPERTY LAW IN CONTEXT 1

  I. The Sources and Limits of Intellectual Property Law 1
  II. The Nature and Functions of Intellectual Property Law 6
    A. Copyright Law 8
    B. Patent Law 13
    C. Trademark Law 20

PART TWO STATE LAW OF INTELLECTUAL PROPERTY 25

  I. Rights in Undeveloped Ideas 25
    A. Theories of Protection 32
    B. Limits of Protection: The Place of Ideas in the Competitive
       Plan 50
  II. Unfair Competition 57
    A. Theory of Protection 58
      1. Passing Off and Secondary Meaning 58
      2. Zone of Expansion 65
      3. Dilution 72
      4. Misappropriation 81
    B. Limits of Protection 90
      1. Personal Interests: Rights in Names 90
      2. Economic Interests: The Place of Unfair Competition in
         the Competitive Plan 96
  III. Trade Secrets 108
    A. Theory of Protection 108
    B. Limits of Protection 133
      1. Personal Interests: Restraints on Post–Employment Com-
         petition 133
      2. Economic Interests: The Place of Trade Secrets in the
         Competitive Plan 151
  IV. Right of Publicity 167
    A. Theory of Protection 167
    B. Limits of Protection 191

PART THREE FEDERAL LAW OF INTELLECTUAL PROPERTY 205

  I. Trademark Law 209
    A. Requirements for Protection 211
      1. Use and Use in Commerce 211
      2. Distinctiveness and Related Statutory Standards 229
      3. Statutory Subject Matter 256

B. Administrative Procedures --- 283
C. Rights and Remedies --- 288
   1. Rights --- 288
D. Limitations on Rights --- 314
   2. Remedies --- 329
   3. Secondary Liability -- 339
E. Infringement -- 347
F. Federal Unfair Competition Law: Lanham Act § 43(a) --------------- 368
II. Patent Law --- 386
  A. Requirements for Protection -------------------------------------- 389
    1. Statutory Subject Matter ------------------------------------- 389
    2. Statutory Standards -- 407
  B. Administrative Procedures --------------------------------------- 484
    1. Application -- 485
    2. Prosecution --- 489
    3. Judicial Review --- 496
  C. Rights and Remedies -- 505
    1. Rights --- 505
    2. Remedies --- 525
  D. Infringement --- 542
III. Copyright Law --- 568
  A. Requirements for Protection ------------------------------------- 569
    1. Formalities --- 569
    2. Statutory Subject Matter ------------------------------------ 587
    3. Originality --- 601
  B. Ownership --- 620
    1. Works for Hire and Joint Works ------------------------------ 620
    2. Transfer and Term -- 639
  C. Rights and Remedies -- 657
    1. Rights --- 657
    2. Remedies --- 737
  D. Infringement --- 750
    1. Literature -- 753
    2. Music -- 759
    3. Visual Arts --- 767
  E. Rights Beyond Copyright: Moral Right --------------------------- 778
  F. Preemption of State Law -- 793

PART FOUR INTELLECTUAL PROPERTY PROTECTION OF COMPUTER
    PROGRAMS -- 803

I. Copyright Law -- 805
  A. Scope of Protection -- 805
    1. Computer Code -- 805
    2. User Interfaces -- 826
  B. Limits of Protection --- 841
    1. Statutory Exemptions --------------------------------------- 841
    2. Fair Use -- 855
    3. First Amendment -- 873

II. Patent Law -- 894
III. Trade Secret Law -- 932

PART FIVE Intellectual Property Protection of Industrial
Design --- 940

I. Design Patent Law --- 941
II. Copyright Law -- 955
III. Trademark and Unfair Competition Law --------------------------------- 980
IV. Federal Preemption -- 999

Appendix -- 1009
Index --- 1019

*

TABLE OF CONTENTS

PREFACE v
TABLE OF CASES xxvii

PART ONE INTELLECTUAL PROPERTY LAW IN CONTEXT 1

I. The Sources and Limits of Intellectual Property Law 1
II. The Nature and Functions of Intellectual Property Law 6
   A. Copyright Law 8
      Paul Goldstein, Copyright's Highway: From Gutenberg to the
        Celestial Jukebox 8
   B. Patent Law 13
      "To Promote the Progress of . . . Useful Arts" 13
      Fritz Machlup, An Economic Review of the Patent System 14
   C. Trademark Law 20
      Nicholas S. Economides, The Economics of Trademarks 20

PART TWO STATE LAW OF INTELLECTUAL PROPERTY 25

I. Rights in Undeveloped Ideas 25
   Sellers v. American Broadcasting Co. 25
   Harry R. Olsson, Jr., Dreams for Sale 28
   A. Theories of Protection 32
      Lueddecke v. Chevrolet Motor Co. 32
      Nadel v. Play-By-Play Toys & Novelties, Inc. 38
   B. Limits of Protection: The Place of Ideas in the Competitive
      Plan 50
      Aronson v. Quick Point Pencil Co. 50
II. Unfair Competition 57
   A. Theory of Protection 58
      1. Passing Off and Secondary Meaning 58
         William R. Warner & Co. v. Eli Lilly & Co. 58
      2. Zone of Expansion 65
         Sample, Inc. v. Porrath 65
      3. Dilution 72
         Mead Data Central, Inc. v. Toyota Motor Sales, U.S.A.,
          Inc. 72
      4. Misappropriation 81
         Board of Trade of City of Chicago v. Dow Jones & Co. 81
   B. Limits of Protection 90
      1. Personal Interests: Rights in Names 90
         David B. Findlay, Inc. v. Findlay 90
      2. Economic Interests: The Place of Unfair Competition in
        the Competitive Plan 96
        Crescent Tool Co. v. Kilborn & Bishop Co. 96
        Sears, Roebuck & Co. v. Stiffel Co. 98
        Compco Corp. v. Day–Brite Lighting, Inc. 101

III. Trade Secrets 108
    A. Theory of Protection 108
        Metallurgical Industries Inc. v. Fourtek, Inc. 108
        E. I. duPont deNemours & Co. v. Christopher 124
    B. Limits of Protection 133
        1. Personal Interests: Restraints on Post–Employment Competition 133
            PepsiCo, Inc. v. Redmond 134
            Reed, Roberts Associates, Inc. v. Strauman 144
        2. Economic Interests: The Place of Trade Secrets in the Competitive Plan 151
            Kewanee Oil Co. v. Bicron Corp. 151

IV. Right of Publicity 167
    A. Theory of Protection 167
        Carson v. Here's Johnny Portable Toilets, Inc. 167
        White v. Samsung Electronics America, Inc. 176
    B. Limits of Protection 191
        Comedy III Productions, Inc. v. Gary Saderup, Inc. ... 191

PART THREE   Federal Law of Intellectual Property 205

I. Trademark Law 209
    A. Requirements for Protection 211
        1. Use and Use in Commerce 211
            Blue Bell, Inc. v. Farah Mfg. Co. 214
            WarnerVision Entertainment, Inc. v. Empire of Carolina, Inc. 219
        2. Distinctiveness and Related Statutory Standards 229
            a. "Trademark by Which the Goods of the Applicant May Be Distinguished From the Goods of Others" 230
                King–Seeley Thermos Co. v. Aladdin Industries, Inc. 230
            b. "Deceptive . . . Matter" 239
                In re Budge Manufacturing Co. 239
            c. Confusing Similarity to Prior Marks 242
                In re N.A.D., Inc. 242
            d. "Merely Descriptive or Deceptively Misdescriptive" 245
               Application of Sun Oil Co. 245
            e. "Primarily Geographically Descriptive or Deceptively Misdescriptive" 248
               In re Loew's Theatres, Inc. 248
            3. Statutory Subject Matter 256
            a. Types of Marks 256
              (i.) Trademarks and Service Marks 256
                In re Advertising & Marketing Development, Inc. ... 256
              (ii.) Certification Marks and Collective Marks 261
                 Midwest Plastic Fabricators, Inc. v. Underwriters Laboratories Inc. 261
                Frederick Breitenfeld, Collective Marks—Should They Be Abolished? 266

b. Content 270
    Qualitex Co. v. Jacobson Products Co., Inc. 270
B. Administrative Procedures 283
C. Rights and Remedies 288
  1. Rights 288
    a. Geographic Boundaries 288
      Dawn Donut Co. v. Hart's Food Stores, Inc. 289
    b. Product and Service Boundaries: Dilution 299
      Ringling Bros.–Barnum & Bailey Combined Shows,
      Incorporated v. Utah Division of Travel Development 299
D. Limitations on Rights 314
  New Kids on the Block v. News America Publishing, Inc. 314
  2. Remedies 329
    Maltina Corp. v. Cawy Bottling Co. 329
  3. Secondary Liability 339
    Hard Rock Cafe Licensing Corp. v. Concession Services,
    Inc. 339
E. Infringement 347
  Pikle–Rite Co. v. Chicago Pickle Co. 347
  McGregor–Doniger, Inc. v. Drizzle, Inc. 353
F. Federal Unfair Competition Law: Lanham Act § 43(a) 368
  Two Pesos, Inc. v. Taco Cabana, Inc. 368

II. **Patent Law** 386
A. Requirements for Protection 389
  1. Statutory Subject Matter 389
    Diamond v. Chakrabarty 389
    State Street Bank & Trust Co. v. Signature Financial
    Group, Inc. 395
  2. Statutory Standards 407
    a. Section 102: Novelty and the Statutory Bars 407
      Application of Borst 407
      Pfaff v. Wells Electronics, Inc. 410
      TP Laboratories, Inc. v. Professional Positioners, Inc. ... 416
    b. Section 103: Nonobviousness 434
      Graham v. John Deere Co. 434
      Stratoflex, Inc. v. Aeroquip Corp. 442
    c. Sections 102 and 103 in Concert: What Is Prior Art? 460
      Hazeltine Research, Inc. v. Brenner 460
    d. Utility 468
      Brenner v. Manson 469
    e. Inventorship 477
    f. Enabling Disclosure 479
      W.L. Gore & Associates v. Garlock, Inc. 479
B. Administrative Procedures 484
  1. Application 485
    a. Claims 485
    b. Specification 486
    c. Drawings 488
  2. Prosecution 489
  3. Judicial Review 496
    Calmar, Inc. v. Cook Chem. Co. 496

C. Rights and Remedies --- 505
   1. Rights -- 505
      Paper Converting Machine Co. v. Magna–Graphics Corp..... 505
      Wilbur–Ellis Co. v. Kuther -------------------------------------- 514
   2. Remedies -- 525
      Rite–Hite Corp. v. Kelley Company, Inc. -------------------- 525
D. Infringement --- 542
   Floyd H. Crews, Patent Claims and Infringement ----------------- 542
   Graver Tank & Mfg. Co. v. Linde Air Products Co. -------------- 543
   Warner–Jenkinson Company, Inc. v. Hilton Davis Chemical Co. --- 550
   Festo Corporation v. Shoketsu Kinzoku Kogyo Kabushiki Co., Ltd. -- 561
   Floyd H. Crews, Patent Claims and Infringement ----------------- 561

III. **Copyright Law** --- 568
   A. Requirements for Protection -- 569
      1. Formalities --- 569
         a. Notice-- 569
            Hasbro Bradley, Inc. v. Sparkle Toys, Inc. ------------- 570
         b. Registration and Deposit -------------------------------- 580
            Benjamin Kaplan, The Registration of Copyright -------- 580
      2. Statutory Subject Matter -- 587
         Copyright Law Revision, H.R. Rep. No. 94–1476 ------------- 587
         Baker v. Selden -- 591
      3. Originality--- 601
         Bleistein v. Donaldson Lithographing Co.------------------ 601
         Feist Publications, Inc. v. Rural Telephone Service Co. ------ 606
   B. Ownership --- 620
      1. Works for Hire and Joint Works ---------------------------------- 620
         Copyright Law Revision, H.R. Rep. No. 1476 --------------- 620
         Community for Creative Non–Violence v. Reid-------------- 622
         Erickson v. Trinity Theatre, Inc. --------------------------- 629
      2. Transfer and Term -- 639
         New York Times Company, Inc. v. Tasini ----------------- 639
         Copyright Law Revision, H.R. Rep. No. 1476 -------------- 648
   C. Rights and Remedies -- 657
      1. Rights --- 657
         a. The Statutory Rights----------------------------------- 657
            Copyright Law Revision, H.R. Rep. No. 94–1476---------- 657
            Mirage Editions, Inc. v. Albuquerque A.R.T. Co. --------- 662
            Lee v. A.R.T. Company----------------------------------- 664
            Columbia Pictures Industries, Inc. v. Redd Horne, Inc. 668
         b. Secondary Liability----------------------------------- 678
            Fonovisa, Inc. v. Cherry Auction, Inc. --------------------- 678
         c. Fair Use --- 685
            Harper & Row Publishers, Inc. v. Nation Enterprises --- 685
            Campbell v. Acuff–Rose Music, Inc. ---------------------- 697
         d. Exclusive Rights and New Technologies ------------------- 716

C. Rights and Remedies—Continued
    *Sony Corporation of America v. Universal City Studios,
    Inc.* 717
    2. Remedies 737
       Copyright Law Revision, H.R. Rep. No. 1476 737
       Stevens Linen Associates v. Mastercraft Corp. 740
       Cream Records, Inc. v. Jos. Schlitz Brewing Co. 744
D. Infringement 750
    1. Literature 753
       Nichols v. Universal Pictures Corp. 753
    2. Music 759
       Selle v. Gibb 759
    3. Visual Arts 767
       Steinberg v. Columbia Pictures Industries, Inc. 767
       Gross v. Seligman 775
E. Rights Beyond Copyright: Moral Right 778
    Gilliam v. American Broadcasting Companies, Inc. 779
F. Preemption of State Law 793

PART FOUR Intellectual Property Protection of Computer
    Programs 803

I. **Copyright Law** 805
  A. Scope of Protection 805
    1. Computer Code 805
       Computer Associates International, Inc. v. Altai, Inc. 805
    2. User Interfaces 826
       Lotus Development Corp. v. Borland International, Inc. 826
  B. Limits of Protection 841
    1. Statutory Exemptions 841
       Vault Corporation v. Quaid Software Limited 841
    2. Fair Use 855
       Sega Enterprises Ltd. v. Accolade, Inc. 855
    3. First Amendment 873
       Universal City Studios, Inc. v. Corley 873
II. **Patent Law** 894
  Diamond v. Diehr 894
  *United States Patent and Trademark Office, Examination Guide-
  lines for Computer–Related Inventions* 910
  State Street Bank & Trust Co. v. Signature Financial Group, Inc. 920
  AT&T Corp. v. Excel Communications, Inc. 920
III. **Trade Secret Law** 932
  Computer Associates International, Inc. v. Altai, Inc. 932

PART FIVE Intellectual Property Protection of Industrial
    Design 940

I. **Design Patent Law** 941
  In re Nalbandian 941
  Avia Group International, Inc. v. L.A. Gear California, Inc. ... 947

II. Copyright Law ---- 955
Mazer v. Stein ---- 955
Carol Barnhart Inc. v. Economy Cover Corp. ---- 962
III. Trademark and Unfair Competition Law ---- 980
In re Morton–Norwich Products, Inc. ---- 980
Two Pesos, Inc. v. Taco Cabana, Inc. ---- 984
Ferrari S.P.A. Esercizio v. Roberts ---- 984
IV. Federal Preemption ---- 999
Bonito Boats, Inc. v. Thunder Craft Boats, Inc. ---- 999

APPENDIX   *Festo Corporation v. Shoketsu Kinzoku Kogyo Kabushiki Co., Ltd.* ---- 1009
INDEX ---- 1019

TABLE OF CASES

Principal cases are in bold type. Non-principal cases are in roman type. References are to Pages.

Abend v. MCA, Inc., 863 F.2d 1465 (9th Cir. 1988), 655

Academy of Motion Picture Arts and Sciences v. Creative House Promotions, Inc., 944 F.2d 1446 (9th Cir.1991), 580

Academy of Motion Picture Arts and Sciences v. Creative House Promotions, Inc., 728 F.Supp. 1442 (C.D.Cal.1989), 579

A.C. Aukerman Co. v. R.L. Chaides Const. Co., 960 F.2d 1020 (Fed.Cir.1992), 541

Adkins v. Lear, Inc., 67 Cal.2d 882, 64 Cal. Rptr. 545, 435 P.2d 321 (Cal.1967), 522

Advertising & Marketing Development, Inc., In re, 821 F.2d 614 (Fed.Cir.1987), **256**

A.F. Stoddard & Co., Ltd. v. Dann, 564 F.2d 556 (D.C.Cir.1977), 479

Alappat, In re, 33 F.3d 1526 (Fed.Cir.1994), 929

A. Leschen & Sons Rope Co. v. American Steel and Wire Co., 55 F.2d 455 (Cust. & Pat.App.1932), 210

Alfred Bell & Co. v. Catalda Fine Arts, 191 F.2d 99 (2nd Cir.1951), 619

Alfred Dunhill Ltd. v. Interstate Cigar Co., Inc., 364 F.Supp. 366 (S.D.N.Y.1973), 385

Alfred Dunhill of London v. Dunhill Shirt Shop, 3 F.Supp. 487 (S.D.N.Y.1929), 80

Allen v. National Video, Inc., 610 F.Supp. 612 (S.D.N.Y.1985), 189

Allen v. Standard Crankshaft and Hydraulic Co., 323 F.2d 29 (4th Cir.1963), 457

Allen, Ex parte, 2 U.S.P.Q.2d 1425 (Bd.Pat. App & Interf.1987), 404

Alva Studios, Inc. v. Winninger, 177 F.Supp. 265 (S.D.N.Y.1959), 619

Amazon.com, Inc. v. Barnesandnoble.com, Inc., 239 F.3d 1343 (Fed.Cir.2001), 930

American Enka Corp. v. Marzall, Comr. Pats, 82 U.S.P.Q. 111 (D.D.C.1952), 280

American Geophysical Union v. Texaco Inc., 60 F.3d 913 (2nd Cir.1994), 714

American Home Products Corp. v. Johnson & Johnson, 577 F.2d 160 (2nd Cir.1978), 383

American Red Cross v. Palm Beach Blood Bank, Inc., 143 F.3d 1407 (11th Cir.1998), 149

American Steel Foundries v. Robertson, 269 U.S. 372, 46 S.Ct. 160, 70 L.Ed. 317 (1926), 210

American Trading Co. v. Heacock Co., 285 U.S. 247, 52 S.Ct. 387, 76 L.Ed. 740 (1932), 210

American Travel & Hotel Directory Co. v. Gehring Publishing Co., 4 F.2d 415 (S.D.N.Y.1925), 753

American Washboard Co. v. Saginaw Mfg. Co., 103 F. 281 (6th Cir.1900), 382, 383

A&M Records, Inc. v. Napster, Inc., 239 F.3d 1004 (9th Cir.2001), 717, 733

Amsterdam v. Triangle Publications, 189 F.2d 104 (3rd Cir.1951), 617

Anderson's–Black Rock v. Pavement Salvage Co., 396 U.S. 57, 90 S.Ct. 305, 24 L.Ed.2d 258 (1969), 459

Anheuser–Busch, Inc. v. Balducci Publications, 28 F.3d 769 (8th Cir.1994), 324

Anthony, In re, 414 F.2d 1383 (Cust. & Pat. App.1969), 476

Anti–Monopoly, Inc. v. General Mills Fun Group, Inc., 684 F.2d 1316 (9th Cir.1982), 236

Apple Computer, Inc. v. Franklin Computer Corp., 714 F.2d 1240 (3rd Cir.1983), 596, 823, 824, 825, 930

Apple Computer, Inc. v. Microsoft Corp., 799 F.Supp. 1006 (N.D.Cal.1992), 596, 839

Application of (see name of party)

Arnstein v. Porter, 154 F.2d 464 (2nd Cir. 1946), 750

Aro Mfg. Co. v. Convertible Top Replacement Co., 365 U.S. 336, 81 S.Ct. 599, 5 L.Ed.2d 592 (1961), 516

Aronson v. Quick Point Pencil Co., 440 U.S. 257, 99 S.Ct. 1096, 59 L.Ed.2d 296 (1979), **50,** 56, 104, 165, 522, 1008

Associated Film Distribution Corp. v. Thornburgh, 614 F.Supp. 1100 (E.D.Pa.1985), 802

Atari, Inc. v. North American Philips Consumer Electronics Corp., 672 F.2d 607 (7th Cir.1982), 840

Atlas v. Eastern Air Lines, Inc., 311 F.2d 156 (1st Cir.1962), 427

Atlas Powder Co. v. Ireco Chemicals, 773 F.2d 1230 (Fed.Cir.1985), 539

AT&T Corp. v. Excel Communications, Inc., 172 F.3d 1352 (Fed.Cir.1999), **920**

Automatic Radio Mfg. Co. v. Hazeltine Research, 339 U.S. 827, 70 S.Ct. 894, 94 L.Ed. 1312 (1950), 522, 523

Avco Corp. v. Precision Air Parts, Inc., 1980 WL 1173 (M.D.Ala.1980), 800

Avia Group Intern., Inc. v. L.A. Gear California, Inc., 853 F.2d 1557 (Fed.Cir. 1988), **947**

Aymes v. Bonelli, 47 F.3d 23 (2nd Cir.1995), 853

Baker v. Selden, 101 U.S. 99, 11 Otto 99, 25 L.Ed. 841 (1879), **591,** 595, 596

Baltimore Orioles, Inc. v. Major League Baseball Players Ass'n, 805 F.2d 663 (7th Cir. 1986), 799

Barrus v. Sylvania, 55 F.3d 468 (9th Cir. 1995), 384

Basic Books, Inc. v. Kinko's Graphics Corp., 758 F.Supp. 1522 (S.D.N.Y.1991), 714

Bass, In re, 474 F.2d 1276 (Cust. & Pat.App. 1973), 465, 466

Bassett v. Mashantucket Pequot Tribe, 204 F.3d 343 (2nd Cir.2000), 206

Bayer Co. v. United Drug Co., 272 F. 505 (S.D.N.Y.1921), 235

Beacon Looms, Inc. v. S. Lichtenberg & Co., Inc., 552 F.Supp. 1305 (S.D.N.Y.1982), 578

Beatrice Foods Co., Application of, 429 F.2d 466 (Cust. & Pat.App.1970), 297, 298

Beauregard, In re, 53 F.3d 1583 (Fed.Cir. 1995), 930

Belcher v. Tarbox, 486 F.2d 1087 (9th Cir. 1973), 599

BellSouth Advertising & Pub. Corp. v. Donnelley Information Pub., Inc., 999 F.2d 1436 (11th Cir.1993), 615

Bernard Food Industries v. Dietene Co., 415 F.2d 1279 (7th Cir.1969), 383

B.F. Goodrich Co. v. Wohlgemuth, 117 Ohio App. 493, 192 N.E.2d 99 (Ohio App. 9 Dist.1963), 150

Big O Tire Dealers, Inc. v. Goodyear Tire & Rubber Co., 561 F.2d 1365 (10th Cir. 1977), 65, 70, 79

Bissell, Inc. v. Easy Day Manufacturing Company Doing Business as Suburbanite Mop Company, 130 U.S.P.Q. 485 (Trademark Tr. & App. Bd.1958), 279

Bleistein v. Donaldson Lithographing Co., 188 U.S. 239, 23 S.Ct. 298, 47 L.Ed. 460 (1903), **601,** 615, 618, 953

Blisscraft of Hollywood v. United Plastics Co., 294 F.2d 694 (2nd Cir.1961), 953

Blonder–Tongue Laboratories, Inc. v. University of Illinois Foundation, 402 U.S. 313, 91 S.Ct. 1434, 28 L.Ed.2d 788 (1971), 566

Blue Bell, Inc. v. Farah Mfg. Co., Inc., 508 F.2d 1260 (5th Cir.1975), 213, **214,** 223

Blue Bell, Inc. v. Jaymar–Ruby, Inc., 497 F.2d 433 (2nd Cir.1974), 223, 224

Board of Trade of City of Chicago v. Dow Jones & Co., 98 Ill.2d 109, 74 Ill. Dec. 582, 456 N.E.2d 84 (Ill.1983), **81,** 87, 88, 89, 321, 801

Bonito Boats, Inc. v. Thunder Craft Boats, Inc., 489 U.S. 141, 109 S.Ct. 971, 103 L.Ed.2d 118 (1989), 105, 997, **999,** 1008

Bookbinder's Restaurant, Application of, 240 F.2d 365 (Cust. & Pat.App.1957), 224

Booth v. Haggard, 184 F.2d 470 (8th Cir. 1950), 577

Borden, Inc., 92 F.T.C. 669 (1976), 338

Borden Ice Cream Co. v. Borden's Condensed Milk Co., 201 F. 510 (7th Cir.1912), 79

Borden, Inc. v. Federal Trade Commission, 711 F.2d 758 (6th Cir.1983), 338

Borst, Application of, 345 F.2d 851 (Cust. & Pat.App.1965), **407,** 427, 432

Boutell v. Volk, 449 F.2d 673 (10th Cir.1971), 567

Brandir Intern., Inc. v. Cascade Pacific Lumber Co., 834 F.2d 1142 (2nd Cir.1987), 977

Breed v. Hughes Aircraft Co., 253 F.3d 1173 (9th Cir.2001), 207

Brenner v. Manson, 383 U.S. 519, 86 S.Ct. 1033, 16 L.Ed.2d 69 (1966), **469,** 476, 477

Broadcast Music, Inc. v. Columbia Broadcasting System, Inc., 441 U.S. 1, 99 S.Ct. 1551, 60 L.Ed.2d 1 (1979), 736

Broadview Chemical Corp. v. Loctite Corp., 311 F.Supp. 447 (D.Conn.1970), 539

Brose v. Sears, Roebuck & Co., 455 F.2d 763 (5th Cir.1972), 541

Brown Chemical Co. v. Meyer, 139 U.S. 540, 11 S.Ct. 625, 35 L.Ed. 247 (1891), 94

Brown Sheet Iron & Steel Co. v. Brown Steel Tank Co., 198 Minn. 276, 269 N.W. 633 (Minn.1936), 94

Brulotte v. Thys Co., 379 U.S. 29, 85 S.Ct. 176, 13 L.Ed.2d 99 (1964), 521, 522

Budge Mfg. Co., In re, 857 F.2d 773 (Fed. Cir.1988), **239,** 255

Burmel Handkerchief Corporation v. Cluett, Peabody & Co., 127 F.2d 318 (Cust. & Pat.App.1942), 280

Burroughs Wellcome Co. v. Barr Laboratories, Inc., 40 F.3d 1223 (Fed.Cir.1994), 431

Burrow–Giles Lithographic Co. v. Sarony, 111 U.S. 53, 4 S.Ct. 279, 28 L.Ed. 349 (1884), 615

Cain v. Universal Pictures Co., 47 F.Supp. 1013 (S.D.Cal.1942), 597

Callaghan v. Myers, 128 U.S. 617, 9 S.Ct. 177, 32 L.Ed. 547 (1888), 618

Calmar, Inc. v. Cook Chemical, Inc., 383 U.S. 1, 86 S.Ct. 684, 15 L.Ed.2d 545 (1966), **496**

Campbell v. Acuff–Rose Music, Inc., 510 U.S. 569, 114 S.Ct. 1164, 127 L.Ed.2d 500 (1994), **697,** 710, 712, 713

Car–Freshner Corp. v. S.C. Johnson & Son, Inc., 70 F.3d 267 (2nd Cir.1995), 321

Carol Barnhart Inc. v. Economy Cover Corp., 773 F.2d 411 (2nd Cir.1985), **962,** 976, 978

Carson v. Here's Johnny Portable Toilets, Inc., 698 F.2d 831 (6th Cir.1983), **167,** 186, 188

Carter v. Helmsley–Spear, Inc., 71 F.3d 77 (2nd Cir.1995), 792

Carter Products, Inc. v. Colgate–Palmolive Co., 130 F.Supp. 557 (D.Md.1955), 429, 497

Castrol Inc. v. Pennzoil Co., 987 F.2d 939 (3rd Cir.1993), 383

CCC Information Services, Inc. v. Maclean Hunter Market Reports, Inc., 44 F.3d 61 (2nd Cir.1994), 616

Champion Spark Plug Co. v. Sanders, 331 U.S. 125, 67 S.Ct. 1136, 91 L.Ed. 1386 (1947), 322

Chanel, Inc. v. Smith, 1973 WL 19871 (N.D.Cal.1973), 64

Charcoal Steak House of Charlotte, Inc. v. Staley, 263 N.C. 199, 139 S.E.2d 185 (N.C. 1964), 61

Chicago Lock Co. v. Fanberg, 676 F.2d 400 (9th Cir.1982), 129

Childress v. Taylor, 945 F.2d 500 (2nd Cir. 1991), 638, 639

Christianson v. Colt Industries Operating Corp., 486 U.S. 800, 108 S.Ct. 2166, 100 L.Ed.2d 811 (1988), 206

Chrysler Corp. v. Brown, 441 U.S. 281, 99 S.Ct. 1705, 60 L.Ed.2d 208 (1979), 132

Clarke, In re, 17 U.S.P.Q.2d 1238 (Trademark Tr. & App. Bd.1990), 277

Cliffs Notes, Inc. v. Bantam Doubleday Dell Pub. Group, Inc., 886 F.2d 490 (2nd Cir. 1989), 325

Clinton E. Worden & Co. v. California Fig Syrup Co., 187 U.S. 516, 23 S.Ct. 161, 47 L.Ed. 282 (1903), 254

Cloth v. Hyman, 146 F.Supp. 185 (S.D.N.Y. 1956), 749

Coca–Cola Co. v. Koke Co. of America, 254 U.S. 143, 41 S.Ct. 113, 65 L.Ed. 189 (1920), 254

Coca–Cola Co. v. Victor Syrup Corp., 218 F.2d 596 (Cust. & Pat.App.1954), 337

Cole v. Phillips H. Lord, Inc., 262 A.D. 116, 28 N.Y.S.2d 404 (N.Y.A.D. 1 Dept.1941), 45

Colligan v. Activities Club of New York, Limited, 442 F.2d 686 (2nd Cir.1971), 384

Columbia Broadcasting System, Inc. v. Zenith Radio Corp., 391 F.Supp. 780 (N.D.Ill. 1975), 567

Columbia Pictures Industries, Inc. v. Professional Real Estate Investors, Inc., 866 F.2d 278 (9th Cir.1989), 674

Columbia Pictures Industries, Inc. v. Redd Horne, Inc., 749 F.2d 154 (3rd Cir.1984), **668,** 674

Comedy III Productions, Inc. v. Gary Saderup, Inc., 106 Cal.Rptr.2d 126, 21 P.3d 797 (Cal.2001), **191,** 202

Community for Creative Non–Violence v. Reid, 490 U.S. 730, 109 S.Ct. 2166, 104 L.Ed.2d 811 (1989), **622,** 637, 638

Compco Corp. v. Day–Brite Lighting, Inc., 376 U.S. 234, 84 S.Ct. 779, 11 L.Ed.2d 669 (1964), 4, **101,** 104, 105, 106, 163, 381, 997, 1008

Computer Associates Intern., Inc. v. Altai, Inc., 982 F.2d 693 (2nd Cir.1992), **805,** 824, 839, 929, 931, **932**

Consumers Union of United States, Inc. v. Theodore Hamm Brewing Co., 314 F.Supp. 697 (D.Conn.1970), 383

Contico Intern., Inc. v. Rubbermaid Commercial Products, Inc., 665 F.2d 820 (8th Cir. 1981), 953

Cream Records, Inc. v. Jos. Schlitz Brewing Co., 754 F.2d 826 (9th Cir. 1985), **744,** 748

Crescent Tool Co. v. Kilborn & Bishop Co., 247 F. 299 (2nd Cir.1917), **96,** 105

Crocker National Bank v. Canadian Imperial Bank of Commerce, 223 U.S.P.Q. 909 (Trademark Tr. & App. Bd.1984), 226

Crossbow, Inc. v. Dan–Dee Imports, Inc., 266 F.Supp. 335 (S.D.N.Y.1967), 383

Dan River Mills, Incorporated v. Danfra, Ltd., 120 U.S.P.Q. 126 (Trademark Tr. & App. Bd.1959), 279

David B. Findlay, Inc. v. Findlay, 271 N.Y.S.2d 652, 218 N.E.2d 531 (N.Y.1966), **90,** 94, 95

Davies v. Krasna, 121 Cal.Rptr. 705, 535 P.2d 1161 (Cal.1975), 47

Dawn Donut Co. v. Hart's Food Stores, Inc., 267 F.2d 358 (2nd Cir.1959), **289,** 298, 299, 336

Dawson Chemical Co. v. Rohm & Haas Co., 448 U.S. 176, 100 S.Ct. 2601, 65 L.Ed.2d 696 (1980), 520

DC Comics, Inc., In re, 689 F.2d 1042 (Cust. & Pat.App.1982), 281

De Acosta v. Brown, 146 F.2d 408 (2nd Cir. 1944), 753

Deepsouth Packing Co. v. Laitram Corp., 406 U.S. 518, 92 S.Ct. 1700, 32 L.Ed.2d 273 (1972), 516, 518, 519

Delaware & Hudson Canal Co. v. Clark, 80 U.S. 311, 20 L.Ed. 581 (1871), 229

Dennison Mfg. Co. v. Panduit Corp., 475 U.S. 809, 106 S.Ct. 1578, 89 L.Ed.2d 817 (1986), 458

Deuel, In re, 51 F.3d 1552 (Fed.Cir.1995), 453

Diamond v. Chakrabarty, 447 U.S. 303, 100 S.Ct. 2204, 65 L.Ed.2d 144 (1980), **389,** 403, 404, 406, 407

Diamond v. Diehr, 450 U.S. 175, 101 S.Ct. 1048, 67 L.Ed.2d 155 (1981), **894**

Diamond Scientific Co. v. Ambico, Inc., 848 F.2d 1220 (Fed.Cir.1988), 523

Dickinson v. Zurko, 527 U.S. 150, 119 S.Ct. 1816, 144 L.Ed.2d 143 (1999), 501

Distinguished Coffee v. Guerrant, 3 App.D.C. 497 (App.D.C.1894), 475

Donald Frederick Evans & Associates v. Continental Homes, Inc., 785 F.2d 897 (11th Cir.1986), 801

DSC Communications Corp. v. DGI Technologies, Inc., 81 F.3d 597 (5th Cir.1996), 872

Dubilier Condenser Corporation, United States v., 289 U.S. 178, 53 S.Ct. 554, 77 L.Ed. 1114 (1933), 149

Dun v. Lumbermen's Credit Ass'n, 209 U.S. 20, 28 S.Ct. 335, 52 L.Ed. 663 (1908), 750

Duo–Tint Bulb & Battery Co., Inc. v. Moline Supply Co., 46 Ill.App.3d 145, 4 Ill.Dec. 685, 360 N.E.2d 798 (Ill.App. 3 Dist.1977), 105

Duraco Products, Inc. v. Joy Plastic Enterprises, Ltd., 40 F.3d 1431 (3rd Cir.1994), 995, 996

Edison v. Thomas A. Edison, Jr., Chemical Co., 128 F. 957 (C.C.D.Del.1904), 94, 95

Egbert v. Lippmann, 104 U.S. 333, 14 Otto 333, 26 L.Ed. 755 (1881), 429

Eibel Process Co. v. Minnesota & Ontario Paper Co., 261 U.S. 45, 43 S.Ct. 322, 67 L.Ed. 523 (1923), 543

E.I. duPont deNemours & Co. v. Christopher, 431 F.2d 1012 (5th Cir.1970), **124,** 129, 163

Eldred v. Reno, 239 F.3d 372 (D.C.Cir.2001), 2

Electric Smelting & Aluminum Co. v. Carborundum Co., 189 F. 710 (C.C.W.D.Pa. 1900), 538

Eli Lilly & Co. v. Medtronic, Inc., 496 U.S. 661, 110 S.Ct. 2683, 110 L.Ed.2d 605 (1990), 518

Elsmere Music, Inc. v. National Broadcasting Co., 482 F.Supp. 741 (S.D.N.Y.1980), 711

Erickson v. Trinity Theatre, Inc., 13 F.3d 1061 (7th Cir.1994), **629,** 638

Erie R. Co. v. Tompkins, 304 U.S. 64, 58 S.Ct. 817, 82 L.Ed. 1188 (1938), 207

Esquire, Inc. v. Ringer, 591 F.2d 796 (D.C.Cir.1978), 976, 977

Farnum v. G.D. Searle & Co., 339 N.W.2d 384 (Iowa 1983), 131

Federal–Mogul–Bower Bearings, Inc. v. Azoff, 313 F.2d 405 (6th Cir.1963), 382

Feist Publications, Inc. v. Rural Telephone Service Co., 499 U.S. 340, 111 S.Ct. 1282, 113 L.Ed.2d 358 (1991), 2, **606,** 615, 616, 618, 619, 825

Ferrari S.P.A. Esercizio v. Roberts, 944 F.2d 1235 (6th Cir.1991), 367, **984,** 994, 996, 997

Festo Corp. v. Shoketsu Kinozoku Kogyo Kabushiki Co., Ltd., 2002 WL 1050479 (2002), 561

Fleischmann Distilling Corp. v. Maier Brewing Co., 386 U.S. 714, 87 S.Ct. 1404, 18 L.Ed.2d 475 (1967), 337

Flintkote Co. v. Tizer, 158 F.Supp. 699 (E.D.Pa.1957), 366

Florida Prepaid Postsecondary Educ. Expense Bd. v. College Sav. Bank, 527 U.S. 627, 119 S.Ct. 2199, 144 L.Ed.2d 575 (1999), 3

FMC Corp. v. Manitowoc Co., Inc., 835 F.2d 1411 (Fed.Cir.1987), 504

Fogerty v. Fantasy, Inc., 510 U.S. 517, 114 S.Ct. 1023, 127 L.Ed.2d 455 (1994), 749

Folsom v. Marsh, 9 F.Cas. 342 (C.C.D.Mass. 1841), 568

Fonovisa, Inc. v. Cherry Auction, Inc., 76 F.3d 259 (9th Cir.1996), **678,** 684, 732

Food Center, Inc. v. Food Fair Stores, Inc., 356 F.2d 775 (1st Cir.1966), 70

Foster, Application of, 343 F.2d 980 (Cust. & Pat.App.1965), 463, 465, 467, 468

Foster, Ex parte, 90 U.S.P.Q. 16 (Pat.& Tr. Office Bd.App.1951), 406

Franklin Mint Corp. v. National Wildlife Art Exchange, Inc., 575 F.2d 62 (3rd Cir. 1978), 777

Frank Music Corp. v. CompuServe, Inc., No. 93 Civ. 8153 (S.D.N.Y.), 732

Frederick Warne & Co. v. Book Sales Inc., 481 F.Supp. 1191 (S.D.N.Y.1979), 598

Fred Fisher Music Co. v. M. Witmark & Sons, 318 U.S. 643, 63 S.Ct. 773, 87 L.Ed. 1055 (1943), 655

FTC v. Formica Corporation, 200 U.S.P.Q. 182 (Trademark Tr. & App. Bd.1978), 238

Galt House, Inc. v. Home Supply Co., 483 S.W.2d 107 (Ky.1972), 63

Gastown, Inc., Application of, 51 C.C.P.A. 876, 326 F.2d 780 (Cust. & Pat.App.1964), 224, 225

Gay Toys, Inc. v. Buddy L Corp., 522 F.Supp. 622 (E.D.Mich.1981), 978

General Instrument Corp. v. Hughes Aircraft Co., 399 F.2d 373 (1st Cir.1968), 565

General Motors Corp. v. Toyota Motor Co., 667 F.2d 504 (6th Cir.1981), 479

Gilliam v. American Broadcasting Companies, Inc., 538 F.2d 14 (2nd Cir.1976), **779,** 791

Girl Scouts of United States of America v. Personality Posters Mfg. Co., 304 F.Supp. 1228 (S.D.N.Y.1969), 385

Gold Seal Co. v. Weeks, 129 F.Supp. 928 (D.D.C 1955), 255

Goldstein v. California, 412 U.S. 546, 93 S.Ct. 2303, 37 L.Ed.2d 163 (1973), 104, 801, 1008

Gottschalk v. Benson, 409 U.S. 63, 93 S.Ct. 253, 34 L.Ed.2d 273 (1972), 803

Graham v. John Deere Co., 383 U.S. 1, 86 S.Ct. 684, 15 L.Ed.2d 545 (1966), **434,** 456, 458, 497

Graver Tank & Mfg. Co. v. Linde Air Products Co., 339 U.S. 605, 70 S.Ct. 854, 94 L.Ed. 1097 (1950), **543,** 564, 565, 566

Gross v. Seligman, 212 F. 930 (2nd Cir. 1914), **775,** 777

Haig & Haig Limited, Ex parte, 118 U.S.P.Q. 229 (Com'r Pat. & Trademarks 1958), 280, 281

Halliburton Oil Well Cementing Co. v. Walker, 329 U.S. 1, 67 S.Ct. 6, 91 L.Ed. 3 (1946), 484

Hamilton, United States v., 583 F.2d 448 (9th Cir.1978), 617, 618

Hamilton Nat. Bank v. Belt, 210 F.2d 706 (D.C.Cir.1953), 48

Hanover Star Milling Co. v. Metcalf, 240 U.S. 403, 36 S.Ct. 357, 60 L.Ed. 713 (1916), 71

Hard Rock Cafe Licensing Corp. v. Concession Services, Inc., 955 F.2d 1143 (7th Cir.1992), **339,** 346

Harjo v. Pro–Football Inc., 50 U.S.P.Q.2d 1705 (Trademark Tr. & App. Bd.1999), 255

Harper & Row Publishers, Inc. v. Nation Enterprises, 471 U.S. 539, 105 S.Ct. 2218, 85 L.Ed.2d 588 (1985), **685,** 711, 715

Harper & Row Publishers, Inc. v. Nation Enterprises, 723 F.2d 195 (2nd Cir.1983), 600

Hartford House, Ltd. v. Hallmark Cards, Inc., 846 F.2d 1268 (10th Cir.1988), 381

Hartop, Application of, 311 F.2d 249 (Cust. & Pat.App.1962), 476

Hasbro Bradley, Inc. v. Sparkle Toys, Inc., 780 F.2d 189 (2nd Cir.1985), **570,** 578, 585

Hazeltine Research, Inc. v. Brenner, 382 U.S. 252, 86 S.Ct. 335, 15 L.Ed.2d 304 (1965), **460,** 465

Henri's Food Products Co. v. Kraft, Inc., 717 F.2d 352 (7th Cir.1983), 367

Herbert Rosenthal Jewelry Corp. v. Kalpakian, 446 F.2d 738 (9th Cir.1971), 596

Hess v. Advanced Cardiovascular Systems, Inc., 106 F.3d 976 (Fed.Cir.1997), 477

Hormel Foods Corp. v. Jim Henson Productions, Inc., 73 F.3d 497 (2nd Cir.1996), 325

How J. Ryan & Associates v. Century Brewing Ass'n, 185 Wash. 600, 55 P.2d 1053 (Wash.1936), 30

Illinois High School Ass'n v. GTE Vantage Inc., 99 F.3d 244 (7th Cir.1996), 237

Industria Arredamenti Fratelli Saporiti v. Charles Craig, Ltd., 725 F.2d 18 (2nd Cir. 1984), 996

In re (see name of party)

Intel Corp. v. Terabyte Intern., Inc., 6 F.3d 614 (9th Cir.1993), 322

International News Service v. Associated Press, 248 U.S. 215, 39 S.Ct. 68, 63 L.Ed. 211 (1918), 87, 88, 799

International Star Class Yacht Racing Ass'n v. Tommy Hilfiger, U.S.A., Inc., 80 F.3d 749 (2nd Cir.1996), 283

Inwood Laboratories, Inc. v. Ives Laboratories, Inc., 456 U.S. 844, 102 S.Ct. 2182, 72 L.Ed.2d 606 (1982), 105, 346, 996

Iowa State University Research Foundation, Inc. v. American Broadcasting Companies, 621 F.2d 57 (2nd Cir.1980), 711

I.P. Lund Trading v. Kohler Co., 163 F.3d 27 (1st Cir.1998), 313

Irons & Sears v. Dann, 606 F.2d 1215 (D.C.Cir.1979), 166

Isenstead v. Watson, 157 F.Supp. 7 (D.D.C 1957), 476

J.E.M. AG Supply, Inc. v. Pioneer Hi–Bred Intern., Inc., 534 U.S. 124, 122 S.Ct. 593, 151 L.Ed.2d 508 (2001), 407

Jet Spray Cooler, Inc. v. Crampton, 377 Mass. 159, 385 N.E.2d 1349 (Mass.1979), 123

Joshua Meier Co. v. Albany Novelty Mfg. Co., 236 F.2d 144 (2nd Cir.1956), 382

J.T. Healy & Son, Inc. v. James A. Murphy & Son, Inc., 357 Mass. 728, 260 N.E.2d 723 (Mass.1970), 121

Juicy Whip, Inc. v. Orange Bang, Inc., 185 F.3d 1364 (Fed.Cir.1999), 474

Kellogg Co. v. National Biscuit Co., 305 U.S. 111, 59 S.Ct. 109, 83 L.Ed. 73 (1938), 236, 238

Kepner–Tregoe, Inc. v. Carabio, 203 U.S.P.Q. 124 (E.D.Mich.1979), 759

Kewanee Oil Co. v. Bicron Corp., 416 U.S. 470, 94 S.Ct. 1879, 40 L.Ed.2d 315 (1974), 104, **151,** 163, 165, 1008

Kieselstein–Cord v. Accessories by Pearl, Inc., 632 F.2d 989 (2nd Cir.1980), 978

Kingsdown Medical Consultants, Ltd. v. Hollister Inc., 863 F.2d 867 (Fed.Cir.1988), 504

King–Seeley Thermos Co. v. Aladdin Industries, Inc., 321 F.2d 577 (2nd Cir. 1963), 229, **230,** 235

Kleinman v. Kobler, 230 F.2d 913 (2nd Cir. 1956), 457

Kori Corp. v. Wilco Marsh Buggies & Draglines, Inc., 761 F.2d 649 (Fed.Cir.1985), 539

Kotzin, Application of, 276 F.2d 411 (Cust. & Pat.App.1960), 278

Krimmel, In re, 292 F.2d 948 (Cust. & Pat. App.1961), 476

Lahr v. Adell Chemical Co., 300 F.2d 256 (1st Cir.1962), 188

L'Aiglon Apparel v. Lana Lobell, Inc., 214 F.2d 649 (3rd Cir.1954), 382

LaMacchia, United States v., 871 F.Supp. 535 (D.Mass.1994), 734

Lamothe v. Atlantic Recording Corp., 847 F.2d 1403 (9th Cir.1988), 383, 791

Larry Harmon Pictures Corp. v. Williams Restaurant Corp., 929 F.2d 662 (Fed.Cir. 1991), 225

Lasercomb America, Inc. v. Reynolds, 911 F.2d 970 (4th Cir.1990), 873

L. Batlin & Son, Inc. v. Snyder, 536 F.2d 486 (2nd Cir.1976), 619

Lear, Inc. v. Adkins, 395 U.S. 653, 89 S.Ct. 1902, 23 L.Ed.2d 610 (1969), 522

Lee v. A.R.T. Co., 125 F.3d 580 (7th Cir. 1997), **664**

Lee v. Runge, 404 U.S. 887, 92 S.Ct. 197, 30 L.Ed.2d 169 (1971), 620

Levi Strauss & Co., In re, 165 U.S.P.Q. 348 (Trademark Tr. & App. Bd.1970), 278

Levi Strauss & Co. v. Blue Bell, Inc., 778 F.2d 1352 (9th Cir.1985), 278

Levi Strauss & Co. v. Blue Bell, Inc., 632 F.2d 817 (9th Cir.1980), 278

Levitt Corp. v. Levitt, 593 F.2d 463 (2nd Cir.1979), 95, 96

Lincoln Park Van Lines, In re, 149 U.S.P.Q. 313 (Trademark Tr. & App. Bd.1966), 280

L.L. Bean, Inc. v. Drake Publishers, Inc., 811 F.2d 26 (1st Cir.1987), 79

Loew's Theatres, Inc., In re, 769 F.2d 764 (Fed.Cir.1985), **248**

Lotus Development Corp. v. Borland Intern., Inc., 49 F.3d 807 (1st Cir.1995), **826,** 838, 839

Lowell v. Lewis, 15 F.Cas. 1018 (C.C.D.Mass. 1817), 468, 474

Lowry, In re, 32 F.3d 1579 (Fed.Cir.1994), 930

Lucent Information Management, Inc. v. Lucent Technologies, Inc., 186 F.3d 311 (3rd Cir.1999), 224

Lueddecke v. Chevrolet Motor Co., 70 F.2d 345 (8th Cir.1934), **32,** 44, 45, 46, 47

Lugosi v. Universal Pictures, 160 Cal.Rptr. 323, 603 P.2d 425 (Cal.1979), 187

Maltina Corp. v. Cawy Bottling Co., Inc., 613 F.2d 582 (5th Cir.1980), **329,** 335, 336

M.A. Mortenson Co. v. Timberline Software Corp., 140 Wash.2d 568, 998 P.2d 305 (Wash.2000), 854

Manhattan Industries, Inc. v. Sweater Bee by Banff, Ltd., 627 F.2d 628 (2nd Cir.1980), 228

Marcus Advertising, Inc. v. M. M. Fisher Associates, Inc., 444 F.2d 1061 (7th Cir. 1971), 30

Markman v. Westview Instruments, Inc., 517 U.S. 370, 116 S.Ct. 1384, 134 L.Ed.2d 577 (1996), 562, 563

Martinetti v. Maguire, 16 F.Cas. 920 (C.C.D.Cal.1867), 598

Masline v. New York, N. H. & H. R. Co., 95 Conn. 702, 112 A. 639 (Conn.1921), 45, 46

Matarese v. Moore–McCormack Lines, 158 F.2d 631 (2nd Cir.1946), 47

Maternally Yours v. Your Maternity Shop, 234 F.2d 538 (2nd Cir.1956), 207

Matthew Bender & Co., Inc. v. West Pub. Co., 158 F.3d 693 (2nd Cir.1998), 618

Mazer v. Stein, 347 U.S. 201, 74 S.Ct. 460, 98 L.Ed. 630 (1954), **955,** 976

McGinley, In re, 660 F.2d 481 (Cust. & Pat. App.1981), 256

McGregor–Doniger Inc. v. Drizzle Inc., 599 F.2d 1126 (2nd Cir.1979), **353,** 367

McKenzie v. Cummings, 24 App.D.C. 137 (App.D.C.1904), 475

Mead Data Cent., Inc. v. Toyota Motor Sales, U.S.A., Inc., 875 F.2d 1026 (2nd Cir.1989), **72,** 78, 106

Mead Digital Systems, Inc. v. A.B. Dick Co., 723 F.2d 455 (6th Cir.1983), 564

Meredith Corp. v. Harper & Row, Publishers, Inc., 378 F.Supp. 686 (S.D.N.Y.1974), 711

Metallurgical Industries Inc. v. Fourtek, Inc., 790 F.2d 1195 (5th Cir.1986), **108,** 119, 121

Metropolitan Opera Ass'n v. Wagner–Nichols Recorder, 199 Misc. 786, 101 N.Y.S.2d 483 (N.Y.Sup.1950), 88

Mid America Title Co. v. Kirk, 59 F.3d 719 (7th Cir.1995), 617

Midler v. Ford Motor Co., 849 F.2d 460 (9th Cir.1988), 188

Midway Mfg. Co. v. Strohon, 564 F.Supp. 741 (N.D.Ill.1983), 824

Midwest Plastic Fabricators, Inc. v. Underwriters Laboratories Inc., 906 F.2d 1568 (Fed.Cir.1990), **261**

Miller v. Universal City Studios, Inc., 650 F.2d 1365 (5th Cir.1981), 616

Mills Music, Inc. v. Snyder, 469 U.S. 153, 105 S.Ct. 638, 83 L.Ed.2d 556 (1985), 656

Milprint, Inc. v. Curwood, Inc., 562 F.2d 418 (7th Cir.1977), 206

Minnesota Mining & Manufacturing Co., Ex parte, 92 U.S.P.Q. 74 (Chief Examiner 1952), 280

Mirage Editions, Inc. v. Albuquerque A.R.T. Co., 856 F.2d 1341 (9th Cir.1988), **662**

Mitchell Bros. Film Group v. Cinema Adult Theater, 604 F.2d 852 (5th Cir.1979), 598, 599

Mobil Oil Corp. v. Pegasus Petroleum Corp., 818 F.2d 254 (2nd Cir.1987), 368

Morton v. New York Eye Infirmary, 17 F.Cas. 879 (C.C.S.D.N.Y.1862), 405

Morton–Norwich Products, Inc., In re, 671 F.2d 1332 (Cust. & Pat.App.1982), **980**

Mosler Safe Co. v. Ely–Norris Safe Co., 273 U.S. 132, 47 S.Ct. 314, 71 L.Ed. 578 (1927), 382

Muller, Ex parte, 81 U.S.P.Q. 261 (Pat.& Tr. Office Bd.App.1947), 405

Murray v. National Broadcasting Co., 844 F.2d 988 (2nd Cir.1988), 47

Musto v. Meyer, 434 F.Supp. 32 (S.D.N.Y. 1977), 759

Mutation Mink Breeders Ass'n v. Lou Nierenberg Corp., 23 F.R.D. 155 (S.D.N.Y. 1959), 383

Mutual of Omaha Ins. Co. v. Novak, 836 F.2d 397 (8th Cir.1987), 325

Nabisco, Inc. v. PF Brands, Inc., 191 F.3d 208 (2nd Cir.1999), 311, 313

Nadel v. Play–By–Play Toys & Novelties, Inc., 208 F.3d 368 (2nd Cir.2000), **38**, 45, 46, 47, 48

N.A.D. Inc., In re, 754 F.2d 996 (Fed.Cir. 1985), **242**

Nalbandian, In re, 661 F.2d 1214 (Cust. & Pat.App.1981), **941**, 953

Nantucket, Inc., In re, 677 F.2d 95 (Cust. & Pat.App.1982), 230

National Basketball Ass'n v. Motorola, Inc., 105 F.3d 841 (2nd Cir.1997), 106

National Comics Publication v. Fawcett Publications, 191 F.2d 594 (2nd Cir.1951), 578

National Conference of Bar Examiners v. Multistate Legal Studies, Inc., 692 F.2d 478 (7th Cir.1982), 587

National Football League Properties, Inc. v. Consumer Enterprises, Inc., 26 Ill.App.3d 814, 327 N.E.2d 242 (Ill.App. 1 Dist.1975), 104

New Kids on the Block v. New America Pub., Inc., 971 F.2d 302 (9th Cir.1992), 314, 321

New York Times Co., Inc. v. Tasini, 533 U.S. 483, 121 S.Ct. 2381, 150 L.Ed.2d 500 (2001), **639**, 651

Nichols v. Universal Pictures Corporation, 45 F.2d 119 (2nd Cir.1930), 597, **753**, 777

Ocumpaugh v. Norton, 25 App.D.C. 90 (App. D.C.1905), 431

OddzOn Products, Inc. v. Just Toys, Inc., 122 F.3d 1396 (Fed.Cir.1997), 466

Olan Mills, Inc. v. Linn Photo Co., 23 F.3d 1345 (8th Cir.1994), 732

Onassis v. Christian Dior–New York, Inc., 122 Misc.2d 603, 472 N.Y.S.2d 254 (N.Y.Sup.1984), 189, 190

On Command Video Corp. v. Columbia Pictures Industries, 777 F.Supp. 787 (N.D.Cal.1991), 674

Original Appalachian Artworks, Inc. v. Toy Loft, Inc., 684 F.2d 821 (11th Cir.1982), 584

Pagliero v. Wallace China Co., 198 F.2d 339 (9th Cir.1952), 996

Pallin v. Singer, 36 U.S.P.Q.2d 1050 (D.Vt. 1995), 405

Palmquist, Application of, 319 F.2d 547 (Cust. & Pat.App.1963), 467

Panavision Intern. v. Toeppen, 141 F.3d 1316 (9th Cir.1998), 314, 328

Panduit Corp. v. Dennison Mfg. Co., 810 F.2d 1561 (Fed.Cir.1987), 458

Paper Converting Machine Co. v. Magna–Graphics Corp., 745 F.2d 11 (Fed. Cir.1984), **505**, 516, 518

Park 'N Fly, Inc. v. Dollar Park and Fly, Inc., 469 U.S. 189, 105 S.Ct. 658, 83 L.Ed.2d 582 (1985), 287, 288

Paulik v. Rizkalla, 760 F.2d 1270 (Fed.Cir. 1985), 424

Pentec, Inc. v. Graphic Controls Corp., 776 F.2d 309 (Fed.Cir.1985), 457

PepsiCo, Inc. v. Redmond, 54 F.3d 1262 (7th Cir.1995), **134**, 148

Perfect Fit Industries, Inc. v. Acme Quilting Co., Inc., 646 F.2d 800 (2nd Cir.1981), 64

Pfaff v. Wells Electronics, Inc., 525 U.S. 55, 119 S.Ct. 304, 142 L.Ed.2d 261 (1998), **410**, 426, 431

Pikle–Rite Co. v. Chicago Pickle Co., 171 F.Supp. 671 (N.D.Ill.1959), **347**, 366

Pioneer First Federal Sav. & Loan Ass'n v. Pioneer Nat. Bank, 98 Wash.2d 853, 659 P.2d 481 (Wash.1983), 107

Prestonettes, Inc., v. Coty, 264 U.S. 359, 44 S.Ct. 350, 68 L.Ed. 731 (1924), 321

ProCD, Inc. v. Zeidenberg, 86 F.3d 1447 (7th Cir.1996), 855

Qualitex Co. v. Jacobson Products Co., Inc., 514 U.S. 159, 115 S.Ct. 1300, 131 L.Ed.2d 248 (1995), **270**, 379, 380

Raxton Corp. v. Anania Associates, Inc., 635 F.2d 924 (1st Cir.1980), 71

Reddy Communications, Inc. v. Environmental Action Foundation, 477 F.Supp. 936 (D.D.C.1979), 323, 324

Reed, Roberts Associates, Inc. v. Strauman, 386 N.Y.S.2d 677, 353 N.E.2d 590 (N.Y.1976), **144**, 165

Religious Technology Center v. Netcom On–Line Communication Services, Inc., 907 F.Supp. 1361 (N.D.Cal.1995), 731

Republic Pictures Corp. v. Security–First Nat. Bank of Los Angeles, 197 F.2d 767 (9th Cir.1952), 206

Richter v. Westab, Inc., 529 F.2d 896 (6th Cir.1976), 30

Ringgold v. Black Entertainment Televison, Inc., 126 F.3d 70 (2nd Cir.1997), 716

Ringling Bros.–Barnum & Bailey Combined Shows, Inc. v. Utah Div. of Travel Development, 170 F.3d 449 (4th Cir.1999), **299**, 310, 311

Rite–Hite Corp. v. Kelley Co., Inc., 56 F.3d 1538 (Fed.Cir.1995), **525**, 537

Rivera Watch Corporation, Ex parte, 106 U.S.P.Q. 145 (Com'r Pat. & Trademarks 1955), 253

Roberts v. Sears, Roebuck & Co., 723 F.2d 1324 (7th Cir.1983), 460

Roche Products, Inc. v. Bolar Pharmaceutical Co., 733 F.2d 858 (Fed.Cir.1984), 517

Rogers v. Grimaldi, 875 F.2d 994 (2nd Cir. 1989), 382

Rohauer v. Killiam Shows, Inc., 551 F.2d 484 (2nd Cir.1977), 655

Rohm & Haas Co. v. Crystal Chemical Co., 736 F.2d 688 (Fed.Cir.1984), 540

Rosemont Enterprises, Inc. v. Choppy Productions, Inc., 74 Misc.2d 1003, 347 N.Y.S.2d 83 (N.Y.Sup.1972), 203

Rosemont Enterprises, Inc. v. McGraw–Hill Book Co., 85 Misc.2d 583, 380 N.Y.S.2d 839 (N.Y.Sup.1975), 203

Rosemont Enterprises, Inc. v. Random House, Inc., 58 Misc.2d 1, 294 N.Y.S.2d 122 (N.Y.Sup.1968), 203

Rosemont Enterprises, Inc. v. Urban Systems, Inc., 72 Misc.2d 788, 340 N.Y.S.2d 144 (N.Y.Sup.1973), 203

Roth v. Pritikin, 710 F.2d 934 (2nd Cir.1983), 639

Ruckelshaus v. Monsanto Co., 467 U.S. 986, 104 S.Ct. 2862, 81 L.Ed.2d 815 (1984), 132

Russell v. Price, 612 F.2d 1123 (9th Cir. 1979), 674

Sakraida v. Ag Pro, Inc., 425 U.S. 273, 96 S.Ct. 1532, 47 L.Ed.2d 784 (1976), 459

Salinger v. Random House, Inc., 811 F.2d 90 (2nd Cir.1987), 711

Sallen v. Corinthians Licenciamentos LTDA, 273 F.3d 14 (1st Cir.2001), 329

Sample, Inc. v. Porrath, 41 A.D.2d 118, 341 N.Y.S.2d 683 (N.Y.A.D. 4 Dept.1973), **65,** 70, 71, 80

Sandoval v. New Line Cinema Corp., 147 F.3d 215 (2nd Cir.1998), 716

San Francisco Arts & Athletics, Inc. v. United States Olympic Committee, 483 U.S. 522, 107 S.Ct. 2971, 97 L.Ed.2d 427 (1987), 325

Sarkar, Application of, 575 F.2d 870 (Cust. & Pat.App.1978), 165

Sawin v. Guild, 21 F.Cas. 554 (C.C.D.Mass. 1813), 517

Schrader, In re, 22 F.3d 290 (Fed.Cir.1994), 930

SCM Corp. v. Langis Foods Ltd., 539 F.2d 196 (D.C.Cir.1976), 225

Sears, Roebuck & Co. v. Stiffel Co., 376 U.S. 225, 84 S.Ct. 784, 11 L.Ed.2d 661 (1964), 4, **98,** 104, 105, 106, 163, 381, 997, 1008

Sega Enterprises Ltd. v. Accolade, Inc., 977 F.2d 1510 (9th Cir.1992), **855,** 870, 871, 872, 929, 931

Selchow & Righter Co. v. McGraw–Hill Book Co., 580 F.2d 25 (2nd Cir.1978), 237

Selle v. Gibb, 741 F.2d 896 (7th Cir.1984), **759**

Sellers v. American Broadcasting Co., 668 F.2d 1207 (11th Cir.1982), **25,** 30

Seminole Tribe of Florida v. Florida, 517 U.S. 44, 116 S.Ct. 1114, 134 L.Ed.2d 252 (1996), 3

Senza–Gel Corp. v. Seiffhart, 803 F.2d 661 (Fed.Cir.1986), 521

Serbin v. Ziebart Intern. Corp., 11 F.3d 1163 (3rd Cir.1993), 384

Servo Corp. of America v. Kelsey–Hayes Co., 289 F.2d 957 (Cust. & Pat.App.1961), 279

Servo Corp. of America v. Servo–Tek Products Co., 289 F.2d 955 (Cust. & Pat.App. 1961), 279

Sheldon v. Metro–Goldwyn Pictures Corporation, 309 U.S. 390, 60 S.Ct. 681, 84 L.Ed. 825 (1940), 748

Sheldon v. Metro–Goldwyn Pictures Corporation, 81 F.2d 49 (2nd Cir.1936), 601, 615, 618

Shellmar Products Co. v. Allen–Qualley Co., 87 F.2d 104 (7th Cir.1936), 122

Sid & Marty Krofft Television Productions, Inc. v. McDonald's Corp., 562 F.2d 1157 (9th Cir.1977), 747, 748

Silenus Wines, Inc., Application of, 557 F.2d 806 (Cust. & Pat.App.1977), 225

Silverman v. CBS Inc., 870 F.2d 40 (2nd Cir.1989), 227, 228

Skil Corp. v. Rockwell Intern. Corp., 375 F.Supp. 777 (N.D.Ill.1974), 384

Smith, In re, 714 F.2d 1127 (Fed.Cir.1983), 430

Smith v. BIC Corp., 869 F.2d 194 (3rd Cir. 1989), 131

Smith v. Chanel, Inc., 402 F.2d 562 (9th Cir.1968), 63, 64

Smith v. Montoro, 648 F.2d 602 (9th Cir. 1981), 383, 791

Societe Comptoir De L'Industrie Cotonniere Etablissements Boussac v. Alexander's Dept. Stores, 299 F.2d 33 (2nd Cir.1962), 385

Solomons v. United States, 137 U.S. 342, 26 Ct.Cl. 620, 11 S.Ct. 88, 34 L.Ed. 667 (1890), 148

Sony Corp. of America v. Universal City Studios, Inc., 464 U.S. 417, 104 S.Ct. 774, 78 L.Ed.2d 574 (1984), 685, 710, 715, **717,** 730, 750

South Corp. v. United States, 690 F.2d 1368 (Fed.Cir.1982), 207

Special Equipment Co. v. Coe, 324 U.S. 370, 65 S.Ct. 741, 89 L.Ed. 1006 (1945), 524

Standard Oil Co. v. American Cyanamid Co., 774 F.2d 448 (Fed.Cir.1985), 457

Standard & Poor's Corp. v. Commodity Exchange, Inc., 683 F.2d 704 (2nd Cir.1982), 89

Standard Pressed Steel Co. v. Midwest Chrome Process Company, 183 U.S.P.Q. 758 (Trademark Tr. & App. Bd.1974), 223

Stanley v. Columbia Broadcasting System, 35 Cal.2d 653, 221 P.2d 73 (Cal.1950), 46

State Street Bank & Trust Co. v. Signature Financial Group, Inc, 149 F.3d 1368 (Fed.Cir.1998), **395,** 403, 920, 930

Steinberg v. Columbia Pictures Industries, Inc., 663 F.Supp. 706 (S.D.N.Y. 1987), **767**, 777

Stephano v. News Group Publications, 485 N.Y.S.2d 220, 474 N.E.2d 580 (N.Y.1984), 202, 203

Step–Saver Data Systems, Inc. v. Wyse Technology, 939 F.2d 91 (3rd Cir.1991), 854

Sterling Brewing, Inc. v. Cold Spring Brewing Corp., 100 F.Supp. 412 (D.Mass.1951), 298

Stern Electronics, Inc. v. Kaufman, 669 F.2d 852 (2nd Cir.1982), 840

Stevens Linen Associates v. Mastercraft Corp., 656 F.2d 11 (2nd Cir.1981), **740**

Stewart v. Abend, 495 U.S. 207, 110 S.Ct. 1750, 109 L.Ed.2d 184 (1990), 655, 656

Stone & McCarrick v. Dugan Piano Co., 220 F. 837 (5th Cir.1915), 598

Stratoflex, Inc. v. Aeroquip Corp., 713 F.2d 1530 (Fed.Cir.1983), **442**, 455, 456, 459, 516

Straus v. Notaseme Hosiery Co., 240 U.S. 179, 36 S.Ct. 288, 60 L.Ed. 590 (1916), 337

Structural Rubber Products Co. v. Park Rubber Co., 749 F.2d 707 (Fed.Cir.1984), 427

Sugar Busters LLC v. Brennan, 177 F.3d 258 (5th Cir.1999), 299

Sun Oil Co., Application of, 426 F.2d 401 (Cust. & Pat.App.1970), **245**

Suntrust Bank v. Houghton Mifflin Co., 268 F.3d 1257 (11th Cir.2001), 710

Suntrust Bank v. Houghton Mifflin Co., 252 F.3d 1165 (11th Cir.2001), 715

Superior Form Builders, Inc. v. Dan Chase Taxidermy Supply Co., 74 F.3d 488 (4th Cir.1996), 978

Taylor v. Meirick, 712 F.2d 1112 (7th Cir. 1983), 748

T.B. Harms Co. v. Eliscu, 339 F.2d 823 (2nd Cir.1964), 205, 206

Ted Arnold Limited v. Silvercraft Co., 259 F.Supp. 733 (S.D.N.Y.1966), 977

Telex Corp. v. International Business Machines Corp., 510 F.2d 894 (10th Cir. 1975), 123

The Frito Company v. Buckeye Foods, Inc., 130 U.S.P.Q. 347 (Trademark Tr. & App. Bd.1961), 279

The Telephone Cases, 126 U.S. 1, 8 S.Ct. 778, 31 L.Ed. 863 (1888), 431

Thomas Wilson & Co. v. Irving J. Dorfman Co., 433 F.2d 409 (2nd Cir.1970), 747

Tiffany & Co. v. Tiffany Productions, 147 Misc. 679, 264 N.Y.S. 459 (N.Y.Sup.1932), 80

Tilghman v. Proctor, 102 U.S. 707, 12 Otto 707, 26 L.Ed. 279 (1880), 428

T.J. Hooker v. Columbia Pictures Industries, Inc., 551 F.Supp. 1060 (N.D.Ill.1982), 188

TP Laboratories, Inc. v. Professional Positioners, Inc., 724 F.2d 965 (Fed.Cir. 1984), **416**, 426, 430

Trade–Mark Cases, In re, 100 U.S. 82, 10 Otto 82, 25 L.Ed. 550 (1879), 209, 615

TrafFix Devices, Inc. v. Marketing Displays, Inc., 532 U.S. 23, 121 S.Ct. 1255, 149 L.Ed.2d 164 (2001), 238, 380, 381

Triad Systems Corp. v. Southeastern Exp. Co., 64 F.3d 1330 (9th Cir.1995), 872

Truck Equipment Service Co. v. Fruehauf Corp., 536 F.2d 1210 (8th Cir.1976), 105

Twin Peaks Productions, Inc. v. Publications Intern., Ltd., 996 F.2d 1366 (2nd Cir. 1993), 382

Two Pesos, Inc. v. Taco Cabana, Inc., 505 U.S. 763, 112 S.Ct. 2753, 120 L.Ed.2d 615 (1992), **368**, 378, 379, 382, 984, 995

Underwater Devices Inc. v. Morrison–Knudsen Co., 717 F.2d 1380 (Fed.Cir.1983), 540

Union Carbide & Carbon Corp. v. Graver Tank & Mfg. Co., 196 F.2d 103 (7th Cir. 1952), 566

Union Carbide Corp. v. Graver Tank & Mfg. Co., 345 F.2d 409 (7th Cir.1965), 540

Uniroyal, Inc. v. Rudkin–Wiley Corp., 837 F.2d 1044 (Fed.Cir.1988), 456

United Drug Co. v. Theodore Rectanus Co., 248 U.S. 90, 39 S.Ct. 48, 63 L.Ed. 141 (1918), 288

United States v. _____ (see opposing party)

United States Golf Ass'n v. St. Andrews Systems, Data–Max, Inc., 749 F.2d 1028 (3rd Cir.1984), 89

Universal City Studios, Inc. v. Corley, 273 F.3d 429 (2nd Cir.2001), 735, **873**

University of Illinois Foundation v. Blonder–Tongue Laboratories, Inc., 422 F.2d 769 (7th Cir.1970), 428

USM Corp. v. Marson Fastener Corp., 379 Mass. 90, 393 N.E.2d 895 (Mass.1979), 121

USM Corp. v. SPS Technologies, Inc., 694 F.2d 505 (7th Cir.1982), 521

Vacheron & Constantin–Le Coultre Watches, Inc. v. Benrus Watch Co., 260 F.2d 637 (2nd Cir.1958), 586

Valco Cincinnati, Inc. v. N & D Machining Service, Inc., 24 Ohio St.3d 41, 492 N.E.2d 814 (Ohio 1986), 122

Van Products Co. v. General Welding & Fabricating Co., 419 Pa. 248, 213 A.2d 769 (Pa.1965), 164

Vault Corp. v. Quaid Software Ltd., 847 F.2d 255 (5th Cir.1988), 716, **841**, 854, 855

Vocational Personnel Services, Inc. v. Statistical Tabulating Corp., 305 F.Supp. 701 (D.Minn.1969), 64

Vuitton et Fils S.A. v. J. Young Enterprises, Inc., 644 F.2d 769 (9th Cir.1981), 996

Waits v. Frito–Lay, Inc., 978 F.2d 1093 (9th Cir.1992), 186, 190

Wall v. Rolls–Royce of America, 4 F.2d 333 (3rd Cir.1925), 80

Wallace Intern. Silversmiths, Inc. v. Godinger Silver Art Co., 916 F.2d 76 (2nd Cir.1990), 997

Wal–Mart Stores, Inc. v. Samara Bros., Inc., 529 U.S. 205, 120 S.Ct. 1339, 146 L.Ed.2d 182 (2000), 379, 380, 995

Walt Disney Productions v. Air Pirates, 581 F.2d 751 (9th Cir.1978), 598

Warmerdam, In re, 33 F.3d 1354 (Fed.Cir. 1994), 930

Warner Bros. Inc. v. American Broadcasting Companies, 720 F.2d 231 (2nd Cir.1983), 777

Warner–Jenkinson Co., Inc. v. Hilton Davis Chemical Co., 520 U.S. 17, 117 S.Ct. 1040, 137 L.Ed.2d 146 (1997), **550,** 565

Warner–Lambert Pharmaceutical Co. v. John J. Reynolds, Inc., 178 F.Supp. 655 (S.D.N.Y.1959), 164, 165

WarnerVision Entertainment Inc. v. Empire of Carolina, Inc., 101 F.3d 259 (2nd Cir.1996), **219**

Weiner King, Inc. v. Wiener King Corp., 615 F.2d 512 (Cust. & Pat.App.1980), 298

Wendt v. Host Intern., Inc., 125 F.3d 806 (9th Cir.1997), 187

Werlin v. Reader's Digest Ass'n, Inc., 528 F.Supp. 451 (S.D.N.Y.1981), 47

West Pub. Co. v. Mead Data Cent., Inc., 799 F.2d 1219 (8th Cir.1986), 618

Wexler v. Greenberg, 399 Pa. 569, 160 A.2d 430 (Pa.1960), 133

White v. Samsung Electronics America, Inc., 989 F.2d 1512 (9th Cir.1993), 189

White v. Samsung Electronics America, Inc., 971 F.2d 1395 (9th Cir.1992), **176,** 185, 187, 321

White–Smith v. Apollo Co., 209 U.S. 1, 28 S.Ct. 319, 52 L.Ed. 655 (1908), 716

Whittemore v. Cutter, 29 F.Cas. 1120 (C.C.D.Mass.1813), 517

Wilbur–Ellis Co. v. Kuther, 377 U.S. 422, 84 S.Ct. 1561, 12 L.Ed.2d 419 (1964), **514,** 516

William R. Warner & Co. v. Eli Lilly & Co., 265 U.S. 526, 44 S.Ct. 615, 68 L.Ed. 1161 (1924), **58,** 346

William Skinner & Sons, Ex parte, 82 U.S.P.Q. 315 (Com'r Pat. & Trademarks 1949), 280

Williams & Wilkins Co. v. United States, 487 F.2d 1345 (Ct.Cl.1973), 712, 717

Winans v. Denmead, 56 U.S. 330, 15 How. 330, 14 L.Ed. 717 (1853), 563

Windsurfing Intern. Inc. v. AMF, Inc., 782 F.2d 995 (Fed.Cir.1986), 456

W.L. Gore & Associates, Inc. v. Garlock, Inc., 721 F.2d 1540 (Fed.Cir.1983), **479**

Worden v. Fisher, 11 F. 505 (C.C.E.D.Mich. 1882), 478

Yadkoe v. Fields, 66 Cal.App.2d 150, 151 P.2d 906 (Cal.App. 2 Dist.1944), 50

Yardley, In re, 493 F.2d 1389 (Cust. & Pat. App.1974), 979

Zatarains, Inc. v. Oak Grove Smokehouse, Inc., 698 F.2d 786 (5th Cir.1983), 321

Zippo Mfg. Co. v. Rogers Imports, Inc., 216 F.Supp. 670 (S.D.N.Y.1963), 105

COPYRIGHT, PATENT, TRADEMARK

AND

RELATED STATE DOCTRINES

*

PART ONE

Intellectual Property Law in Context

I. The Sources and Limits of Intellectual Property Law

UNITED STATES CONSTITUTION
   Article 1, Section 8

The Congress shall have power ...

   (3) To regulate Commerce with foreign Nations, and among the several States, and with the Indian Tribes....

   (8) To promote the Progress of Science and useful Arts, by securing for limited Times to Authors and Inventors the exclusive Right to their respective Writings and Discoveries....

Article 6

   ... This Constitution, and the Laws of the United States which shall be made in Pursuance thereof; and all Treaties made, or which shall be made, under the Authority of the United States, shall be the supreme Law of the Land; and the Judges in every State shall be bound thereby, any Thing in the Constitution or Laws of any State to the Contrary notwithstanding....

NOTES

1. *Constitutional Structure.* Article 1, section 8, clause 3 describes the congressional commerce power and is the constitutional source of federal trademark and unfair competition legislation. Article 1, section 8, clause 8 is the source of federal copyright and patent legislation. Colonial usage and syntax indicate that the Constitution's framers, in speaking of "Science" in clause 8, were referring to the work of authors, and by "useful Arts" meant

1

the work of inventors. Structurally the clause is a balanced sentence—a style common to the period—and can be reworked to read:

(8)(a) To promote the Progress of Science ... by securing for limited Times to Authors ... the exclusive Right to their ... Writings.

(b) To promote the Progress of ... useful Arts, by securing for limited Times to ... Inventors the exclusive Right to their ... Discoveries.

See Karl B. Lutz, Patents and Science: A Clarification of the Patent Clause of the U.S. Constitution, 18 Geo.Wash.L.Rev. 50 (1949).

2. *Constitutional Constraints.* To what extent does the constitutional preamble, "To promote the Progress of Science and Useful Arts," operate to limit Congress's power under Article 1, section 8, clause 8? The Copyright Term Extension Act of 1998, Pub. L. No. 105–298, 112 Stat. 2827 (1998), added twenty years to the term of copyright, not only prospectively, but retrospectively. Can it promote the progress of science to extend the term of protection for works that have already been created? If not, is the Act's retrospective extension of term unconstitutional? In Eldred v. Reno, 239 F.3d 372, 377, 57 U.S.P.Q.2d 1842 (D.C.Cir.2001), *cert. granted, sub nom. Eldred v. Ashcroft,* ___ U.S. ___, 122 S.Ct. 1062, 151 L.Ed.2d 966 (2002), the court acknowledged that under the "limited times" provision, "[i]f the Congress were to make copyright protection permanent, then it surely would exceed the power conferred upon it by the Copyright Clause," but concluded that the preamble did not circumscribe the limited times provision.

To what extent does Article 1, section 8, clause 8 constrain Congress when it acts under some other constitutional power, such as Article 1, section 8, clause 3's commerce power? Some databases may lack the level of originality that the Supreme Court has said is constitutionally required of copyrightable works. Feist Publications, Inc. v. Rural Telephone Service Co., 499 U.S. 340, 111 S.Ct. 1282, 113 L.Ed.2d 358, 18 U.S.P.Q.2d 1275 (1991). Can Congress instead protect these databases under the commerce power? Can it employ the commerce power to protect databases in perpetuity rather than for "limited times"?

See generally, Michael H. Davis, Extending Copyright and the Constitution: "Have I Stayed Too Long?", 52 Fla. L. Rev. 989 (2000); Paul J. Heald & Suzanna Sherry, Implied Limits on the Legislative Power: The Intellectual Property Clause as an Absolute Constraint on Congress, 2000 U. Ill. L. Rev. 1119 (2000).

3. *Takings.* Does the federal government "take" property for public use, requiring payment of just compensation under the Fifth Amendment to the Constitution, when, without permission, it practices a patented invention or discloses trade secret information submitted to a federal regulatory agency? One writer has noted that the question has "evoked wildly differing responses, ranging from the view that virtually all government uses of intellectual property constitute takings to the view that virtually none of them do," and concluded that "on balance, most federal uses of patents and copyrights probably do implicate the Takings Clause, but that noninfringing uses of trademarks and some other forms of unfair competition probably do not." Thomas F. Cotter, Do Federal Uses of Intellectual Property Implicate the Fifth Amendment?, 50 Fla. L. Rev. 529, 532–33 (1998).

4. *Sovereign Immunity.* Can Congress, acting under Article 1, section 8, clause 8, or some other constitutional authority, annul states' sovereign immunity from liability for copyright or patent infringement? In Florida Prepaid Postsecondary Education Expense Board v. College Savings Bank, 527 U.S. 627, 119 S.Ct. 2199, 144 L.Ed.2d 575 (1999), the Supreme Court overturned amendments to the Patent Act that aimed at abrogating sovereign immunity and were explicitly founded on the Copyright–Patent Clause, the Commerce Clause and section 5 of the Fourteenth Amendment. Following its earlier decision in Seminole Tribe of Florida v. Florida, 517 U.S. 44, 116 S.Ct. 1114, 134 L.Ed.2d 252 (1996), that Congress may not abrogate state sovereign immunity pursuant to its Article I powers, the Court further held that the measure could not be sustained as legislation enacted in support of the Fourteenth Amendment's Due Process Clause. Recognizing that patents constitute property, "of which no person may be deprived by a State without due process of law," the *Florida Prepaid* Court observed that "a State's infringement of a patent, though interfering with a patent owner's right to exclude others, does not by itself violate the Constitution. Instead, only where the State provides no remedy, or only inadequate remedies, to injured patent owners for its infringement of their patent could a deprivation of property without due process result." 527 U.S. at 642–44. The Supreme Court has repeatedly held that, under the Constitution's Supremacy Clause, the federal patent and copyright statutes preempt state laws that have equivalent reach and effect. What impact do these decisions have on the question raised in *Florida Prepaid* whether "the State provides no remedy, or only inadequate remedies, to injured patent owners for its infringement of their patent"?

The Eleventh Amendment, even as applied in *Florida Prepaid*, does not leave intellectual property owners entirely without remedy in the face of state-authorized infringements. Injunctive and declaratory relief is available against infringements committed by state employees acting in their official capacity, and the full battery of statutory remedies is available against state employees acting in their individual capacity.

See generally, Mitchell N. Berman, R. Anthony Reese & Ernest A. Young, State Accountability for Violations of Intellectual Property Rights: How to "Fix" *Florida Prepaid* (And How *Not To*), 79 Tex. L. Rev. 1037 (2001); Eugene Volokh, Sovereign Immunity and Intellectual Property, 73 So. Cal. L. Rev. 1161 (2000).

NOTE: A ROAD MAP TO INTELLECTUAL PROPERTY LAW

Intellectual Property in the Federal System. A road map to U.S. intellectual property law drawn today would look very different from one drawn two centuries ago. State courts and legislatures had a far greater say in the protection of intellectual products at the beginning of the nineteenth century than they do at the beginning of the twenty-first century. State unfair competition law was long the only source of protection for the commercial goodwill embodied in brand names. The first federal trademark act was not passed until 1870 and, even then, provided only for the registration of marks protected under state common law. State and federal governments divided responsibility for protecting literary works: state common law copyright protected a work before its publication, and federal statutory copyright protection attached only upon publication. Protection for inventions followed roughly the same division. State trade secret law protected a technological discovery so long as the inventor kept it secret. If the inventor applied for a patent, and if the invention met the federally-prescribed statutory standards, a patent would issue and the invention would become public.

Two centuries later, the balance of power over intellectual property has shifted decisively to Congress and the federal courts. The federal Trademark Act is today the principal vehicle for registering marks used on goods and services and is the main source of substantive rights in marks; section 43(a) of the Act has also substantially displaced state unfair competition law in importance. The 1976 Copyright Act preempts all but the narrowest corner of state common law copyright, and today protects all tangibly fixed literary and artistic works, whether published or unpublished. Only state trade secret law has retained its early scope and vitality.

While federal law has eclipsed some of the traditional forms of state law intellectual property protection, newer forms continue to emerge and to flourish. Beginning in the 1950's, state courts conceived and nurtured a new "right of publicity" to protect against the commercial appropriation of an individual's name or likeness. More recently the doctrine of trespass to chattels has been invoked to regulate poaching on the Internet. In 1979, the National Conference of Commissioners on Uniform State Laws promulgated the Uniform Trade Secrets Act, now in force in one form or another in the great majority of the states. In 1993 the American Law Institute adopted and promulgated its long-awaited Restatement of the Law Third, Unfair Competition.

Doctrinally the most significant development for the nationalization of intellectual property law in the United States has been federal preemption doctrine under which, by force of the U.S. Constitution's Supremacy Clause, federal law will sometimes preempt state law. The United States Supreme Court has addressed the possibility of preemption in no fewer than six decisions since its seminal 1964 decisions in Sears, Roebuck & Co. v. Stiffel Co., and Compco Corp. v. Day–Brite Lighting, Inc., pages 98 and 101, below, holding that states cannot protect subject matter that comes within Congress's copyright-patent power but fails to qualify for federal copyright or patent protection. Congress has also acted preemptively. Section 301(a) of the 1976 Copyright Act preempts state law if three conditions are met: the state right in question is "equivalent to any of the exclusive rights within the general scope of copyright as specified by section

106" of the Act; the right is in a work of authorship that is fixed in a tangible medium of expression; and the work comes within "the subject matter of copyright as specified by sections 102 and 103" of the Act.

Intellectual Property in the Global Arena. Intellectual property law is territorial, which means that American copyrights, patents and trademarks have no force outside the United States. However, treaty relations exist today between the United States and other countries that enable American intellectual property owners to obtain protection for their intellectual goods under the laws of most other countries.

For more than a century, two multilateral treaties, the Berne Convention for the Protection of Literary and Artistic Works and the Paris Convention for the Protection of Industrial Property, have been the principal source of international obligations respecting protection of foreign works—the Berne Convention for copyright, and the Paris Convention for patents and trademarks. Both conventions follow the principle of national treatment buttressed by minimum standards. *National treatment* obligates each treaty member to protect the creations of nationals of other treaty members on the same terms as it protects the creations of its own nationals. *Minimum standards* means that, where the treatment a country gives to its own nationals falls below the standards prescribed by the treaty, the country must give the foreign national no less than the treaty standard requires. So, for example, since the United States and Germany both belong to the Berne Convention, a German national suing for infringement of the copyright in her novel in the United States would get at least the same rights and remedies that the United States gives its own nationals under the 1976 Copyright Act. But, since the Berne Convention bars formalities as a condition to protection, the German national could not be required to register her claim to copyright in the United States Copyright Office as a condition to filing her lawsuit, even though a U.S. national must comply with this formality.

As the world's largest exporter of intellectual goods, the United States has taken the lead in pressing for trade arrangements that will secure profits abroad more effectively than intellectual property treaties alone. By far the most significant of these trade arrangements is the Agreement on Trade–Related Aspects of Intellectual Property Rights (TRIPs), which is part of a larger agreement amending the General Agreement on Tariffs and Trade finalized at Marrakesh, Morocco on April 15, 1994. TRIPs incorporates by reference the main parts of the Berne and Paris Conventions, but also adds minimum standards of its own. Most significantly, TRIPs augments the creaky enforcement procedures of the Berne and Paris Conventions with a more practicable enforcement alternative, entitling a member country whose nationals are injured by a foreign practice to file a complaint against the offending country before a World Trade Organization panel. A country that fails to comply with a panel order faces the prospect of legitimate trade retaliation by the victim country to compensate for the economic injury caused by the offense.

II. THE NATURE AND FUNCTIONS OF INTELLECTUAL PROPERTY LAW

"If nature has made any one thing less susceptible than all others of exclusive property, it is the action of the thinking power called an idea, which an individual may exclusively possess as long as he keeps it to himself; but the moment it is divulged, it forces itself in to the possession of every one, and the receiver cannot dispossess himself of it. Its peculiar character, too, is that no one possesses the less, because every other possesses the whole of it. He who receives an idea from me, receives instruction himself without lessening mine; as he who lights his taper at mine, receives light without darkening me. That ideas should freely spread from one to another over the globe, for the moral and mutual instruction of man, and improvement of his condition, seems to have been peculiarly and benevolently designed by nature, when she made them, like fire, expansible over all space, without lessening their density in any point, and like the air in which we breathe, move, and have our physical being, incapable of confinement or exclusive appropriation. Inventions then cannot, in nature, be a subject of property. Society may give an exclusive right to the profits arising from them, as an encouragement to men to pursue ideas which may produce utility, but this may or may not be done, according to the will and convenience of the society, without claim or complaint from any body."

> Letter from Thomas Jefferson to
> Isaac McPherson, August 13, 1813,
> Writings of Thomas Jefferson 1286,
> 1291–1292 (Library of America
> 1984).

The principal object of intellectual property law in the United States is to ensure consumers a wide variety of intellectual goods at the lowest possible price. Intellectual property law aims to achieve this end by giving individuals and businesses property rights in the information they produce and, through the opportunity to profit from the information, the economic incentive to produce it.

Copyright attracts investment to the production and distribution of literary and artistic works by promising authors and artists exclusive rights for a limited period. Patent law uses property rights to stimulate private investment in new, useful and nonobvious technologies. Trademark law encourages businesses to invest in the names and slogans that signify the source of their goods and services by prohibiting competitors from using these same symbols on their own wares. More recently, the right of publicity gives individuals the ability to capture the value of their celebrity in the marketplace. Common law copyright, trade secret law and unfair competition law have historically served an auxiliary function, granting protection under state law until information has been sufficiently developed to qualify for federal protection under the copyright, patent or trademark statutes. As a rule, intellectual property rights are freely alienable so that the author or inventor can transfer his rights to a business that is better positioned to exploit the right and realize its value in the marketplace.

Information is intangible, and the need for private property rights in intellectual goods is comparatively more pressing than the need for private property rights in tangible objects such as land or cattle. In a world without property rights, a rancher could fend off rustlers by surrounding her land with an impenetrable fence and bringing the cattle to market under armed guard. It is, however, the unusual creator of information who can fence in his product by keeping it secret and at the same time reap economic rewards from the information in the marketplace; the few revenues to be earned will rarely repay the cost of maintaining secrecy, much less the cost of creating the information.

In economist's terms, investment in information suffers special problems of appropriability. The fact that information is intangible means that, absent property rights, a producer of information will find it difficult to appropriate to herself the information's value in the marketplace. While most information will have little value to its producer unless she can sell it, sale will expose the information to competitors who, absent property rights, will be able freely to replicate the information and sell it at a price lower than what the first producer must charge to recoup her investment in producing the information. The critical point is that, unable to appropriate the value of her information, the producer will from the start be disinclined to invest in producing information.

The economic problem of information as the object of private property rights does not end with appropriability. The fact that information is intangible also means that it is indivisible: an unlimited number of users can consume a piece of information without depleting it. (Think of a motion picture: after it is "consumed" by one person, or one million, it still exists; the same could not be said of a loaf of bread.) Another way of saying this is that, once information has been produced, its use may benefit an indeterminate number of users without imposing any additional costs on the producer. This unique characteristic of intellectual goods—that anyone can use them without diminishing their availability to anyone else—leads to a powerful moral intuition against intellectual property law: since intellectual property law enables information producers to charge for access to their information, it inescapably withholds information from people who cannot, or will not, pay the price of admission, even though giving them free or lower-cost access would harm no one else. When a life-saving drug for which the patent owner charges $500 a dose can be sold profitably at $5 a dose, patients, particularly in economically less developed countries, can be expected to complain that something is wrong with the system. This may explain why legal systems around the world tend to allow more extensive inroads into intellectual property than into property in land or goods.

It should by now be evident that the intellectual property solution to the problem of inappropriability—property rights as private incentive—inevitably conflicts with the social benefits of indivisibility—unrestricted public access. Intellectual property as a solution to inappropriability implies that, to recover its investment, an information producer will use its property rights to charge consumers for access to its work. Yet indivisibility implies that, once information has been produced, its use may confer a benefit on the consumer without imposing any additional cost on the producer. If the producer charges for access to the information, consumers who are unable or unwilling to pay the price will be deprived of the information, leaving them worse off than they would have been in the absence of property rights. "Put succinctly, the dilemma is that without a legal monopoly not enough information will be produced but with the legal monopoly too little of the information will be used." Robert Cooter & Thomas Ulen, Law and Economics 135 (2d ed. 1997).

An essentially utilitarian balance between the competing demands of appropriability and indivisibility dominates intellectual property law in the United States and, to varying degrees, in the rest of the world. Nonetheless, other rationales have historically been offered for intellectual property law. Natural rights theory, rooted in the writings of John Locke and Immanuel Kant, is the principal complement, and sometimes competitor, to the utilitarian rationale; it holds that producers of intellectual goods should receive protection for their creations, not because they require protection as an inducement to their efforts but because they deserve it as an inherent natural right. On natural rights and other rationales—and critiques—of intellectual property law, see Justin Hughes, The Philosophy of Intellectual Property, 77 Geo. L.J. 287 (1988); Stewart E. Sterk, Rhetoric and Reality in Copyright Law, 94 Mich. L. Rev. 1197 (1996); Wendy J. Gordon, A Property Right in Self–Expression: Equality and Individualism in the Natural Law of Intellectual Property, 102 Yale L.J. 1533 (1993); Tom G. Palmer, Intellectual Property: A Non–Posnerian Law and Economics Approach, 12 Hamline L. Rev. 261 (1989); A. Samuel Oddi, Un–Unified Economic Theories of Patents—The–Not–Quite–Holy Grail, 71 Notre Dame L. Rev. 267 (1996).

A.   COPYRIGHT LAW

Paul Goldstein, Copyright's Highway: From Gutenberg to the Celestial Jukebox
173–179 (1994).

[Adam] Smith rejected the idea of writers' having an unfettered natural right to their published works, but nonetheless believed that some limited form of statutory protection was justified "as an encouragement to the labours of learned men." He understood that copyright was a monopoly, not in the baleful sense of a businessman's cartel, such as the Stationers' Company, bent on controlling book production and driving up prices, but as a highly constrained property right that exposed the works it protected to competition with other works in the marketplace. Copyrights thus stood apart from institutional or industry-wide monopolies. "As they can do no harm and may do some good," he wrote, they "are not to be altogether condemned."

Adam Smith's lukewarm endorsement hardly amounted to a full-scale rationale for copyright. And he left many questions unanswered. What did he mean when he said that copyright does "no harm" and "may do some good"? Was it that the public is getting something—a new book of poems, or a gazetteer—that it would not have had otherwise? What evidence was there that writers and publishers needed copyright to encourage the required labor and investment? Was there any reason to believe that a twenty-eight-year term of copyright, neither more nor less, was the correct incentive?

Jeremy Bentham took up the task of making an affirmative case for copyright. He focused on the question of incentives, on whether, without copyright, writers would write and publishers publish. Starting from the observation "that which one man has invented, all the world can imitate," he concluded that in a competitive marketplace only laws can deter such imitation, and that, otherwise, creative individuals would find themselves driven out of the market by rivals who, "without any expense, in possession of a discovery which has cost the inventor much time and expense, would be able to deprive him of all his *deserved* advantages, by selling at a lower price." In short, "he who has no hope that he shall reap, will not take the trouble to sow."

The great essayist, politician, and historian Thomas Babington Macaulay accepted Bentham's point about the need for incentives, but he challenged Bentham's—and Smith's—evident assumption that copyright did little or no harm. The occasion for Macaulay's observations was an 1841 House of Commons debate on the nagging question of the proper length of the copyright term. (From the time of the first English copyright act, publishers had continued to press for longer ones.) The Commons was considering whether to extend the term from twenty-eight years to one that, like the French law, would end at a prescribed period—sixty years after the author's death.

Macaulay opposed this, but he started with a debater's ploy, painting the positive case for copyright. "It is desirable that we should have a supply of good books," he began, and copyright is far more reliable than royal or aristocratic patronage in ensuring that supply. "We cannot have such a supply unless men of letters are liberally remunerated; and the least objectionable way of remunerating them is by means of copyright." But, Macaulay added, monopoly is an evil; it is "a tax on readers for the purpose of giving a bounty to writers." Consequently, and here was the pivot of his argument, "the evil ought not to last a day longer than is necessary for the purpose of securing the good."

Macaulay cited the example of Samuel Johnson. "Dr. Johnson died fifty-six years ago. If the law were what my honourable and learned friend wishes to make it, somebody would now have the monopoly of Dr. Johnson's works." But, Macaulay asked, "would the knowledge that this copyright would exist in 1841 have been a source of gratification to Johnson? Would it have stimulated his exertions? Would it have once drawn him out of his bed before noon?" While the added incentive to Johnson would have been small, the added cost to readers would have been high. "Considered as a reward to him, the difference between a twenty years' term and sixty years' term of posthumous copyright would have been nothing or next to nothing. But is the difference nothing to us? I can buy *Rasselas* for sixpence; I might have had to give five shillings for it . . . Do I grudge this to a man like Dr. Johnson? Not at all . . . But what I do complain of is that my circumstances are to be worse, and Johnson's none the better; that I am to give five pounds for what to him was not worth a farthing."

Macaulay's insight about copyright's drawbacks applied not only to the duration of a copyright term—the House of Commons voted down the proposed extension—but also to copyright's scope. What uses of a given text should copyright be allowed to control? Should the "evil" of copyright extend to uses whose control was more than was "necessary for securing the good"? . . . .

It remained for Kenneth Arrow (who later won the Nobel Prize in Economic Science) to bring the moral and practical intuitions of Smith, Bentham, and Macaulay to hard economic ground in an essay published in 1962. Like Bentham, he observed that creative individuals, and the business enterprises to which they entrust the dissemination of their works, will not sow where they cannot reap; to this he added the economist's point that free markets have no effective mechanism for getting users to join together to share in the costs of production. Arrow also observed that, once information has been produced, there is no cost to give it to any additional user. When a pay television company charges a subscriber seven dollars to view a certain motion picture, many people who might have gladly paid a smaller sum will choose not to see the film. In the crisp calculus of twentieth-century economics, this is undesirable because it decreases the welfare of one class of consumers—the excluded viewers—without increasing the welfare of another—those willing and able to pay the asking price.

The dilemma for public policy is that if society withholds property rights from creative work, the price that its producers can charge for access to it will begin to approach zero; their revenues will diminish and, with them, their incentives to produce more. But if society confers property rights on creative works, prices will rise and the information produced will reach smaller, wealthier (or more profligate) audiences, even though it might be that the work could be disseminated to everyone else at no additional cost.

At bottom, the problem is that, in many instances in intellectual, literary, and educational life, information and entertainment are costly to produce but cheap to distribute. One solution to the problem is to have governments subsidize the creative work it believes the public wants, and then distribute free copies of the works produced. The public would of course pay in the form of higher taxes, but these payments would be unconnected to any particular value a work might have for any particular taxpayer. For example, if the income tax was used to pay for these subsidies, the rich would effectively pay a greater share of the cost than the poor. (The U.S. Copyright Act in fact approximates this subsidy solution by withholding copyright from works of the U.S. government, such as Commerce Department census reports.)

Few disagree with Arrow's analysis of the public policy problem that intellectual property presents. But one economist, Harold Demsetz, bristled at the suggestion that government subsidies could solve the problem. For Demsetz, an economics professor at the University of Chicago, it is not sufficient to lament, as Arrow did, the failings of free markets. Market failures must be weighed against the shortcomings of government subsidy, and for Demsetz, the deficiencies of private property rights are less baleful than the hazards of public intervention. Demsetz started from the by now familiar point that, as he put it, "it is hardly useful to say that there is 'underutilization' of information if the method recommended to avoid 'underutilization' discourages the research required to produce the information." But he gave the argument a distinctive twist. The production and consumption of information, he argued, cannot be judged independently of each other. Producers produce what consumers will pay for, in the case of intellectual goods no less than in the case of breakfast cereals and automobiles. While charging for access to these goods might seem a bad thing to Arrow, prices do have the salutary effort of signaling consumer preference and channeling private investment in the right directions.

Demsetz's disagreement with Arrow was not that he reached the wrong conclusions but that he did not reach far enough; he failed to pin his conclusions to marketplace realities. Whatever the theoretical failings of private property rights in intellectual goods, they do have the virtue of revealing at least some information about consumer preferences, information that government subsidy systems at best imperfectly collect. The logic of property rights dictates their extension into every corner in which people derive enjoyment and value from literary and artistic works. To stop short of these ends would deprive producers of the signals of consumer preference that trigger and direct their investments.

NOTES

1. *The Uneasy Case for Copyright?* In a provocative article published in 1971, Professor (now Supreme Court Justice) Stephen Breyer attacked the natural rights argument for copyright that an author's labor entitles her to appropriate the value of the work. Against the claim that authors should be paid according to the value of their work to society, Breyer observed that "few workers receive salaries that approach the total value of what they produce." Nor, he wrote, is there anything inherently immoral about this, since the difference between the value of a worker's effort and the amount she is paid for it is passed on to the consumer in the form of a lower price for the product. Breyer thus dismissed the "intuitive, unanalyzed feeling" that an author's work is her property. "We do not ordinarily create or modify property rights, nor even award compensation, solely on the basis of labor expended." The Uneasy Case for Copyright: A Study of Copyright in Books, Photocopies and Computer Programs, 84 Harv. L. Rev. 281, 285–89 (1970).

Breyer devoted the remaining sixty of his article's seventy pages to questioning the foundational economic premise of American copyright law: that copyright is needed as an incentive to produce and distribute creative works. Two arguments stand out: that, even without copyright, an original publisher can ward off unauthorized copies of a written work by threatening to issue a "fighting edition" priced even lower than the pirate's; and that, although it costs a pirate less to publish a book than it costs the original publisher, the original publisher has a lead-time advantage that enables it to recoup its costs. Breyer estimated that "by the time a copier chooses a book, prints it, and distributes it to retailers, he may be six to eight weeks behind, by which time the initial publisher will have provided retailers with substantial inventories. It is unlikely that a price difference of less than a dollar will lead many retailers or customers to wait for a cheaper edition, for hardbound book customers do not seem to respond readily to price reductions. They are not willing, after all, to wait for a cheaper paperbound edition." *Id.* at 300.

Barry W. Tyerman, a third-year student at UCLA Law School, took on Breyer's uneasy case for copyright in an article published the following year, The Economic Rationale for Copyright Protection for Published Books: A Reply to Professor Breyer, 18 U.C.L.A. L. Rev. 1100 (1971). Tyerman questioned whether the initial publisher will enjoy the lead time advantage claimed by Breyer. "Advances in book publishing technology have seriously diminished the time (and cost) that would be required to copy a given book." Further, "the alleged price insensitivity of book *consumers* may be largely irrelevant since to a great degree it is book *distributors* ... who actually determine the character of the retail market for most books. Thus, if a copier could offer copies of a particular book at a price significantly below that offered by the initial publisher, many retailers would be willing to tolerate a slight delay in stocking that book in return for the prospect of a greater profit margin on the eventual sale to the public." *Id.* at 1109–1111. (Emphasis in original.)

As to fear of retaliation, Tyerman noted that "any stigma that might once have attached to book 'pirating' would probably be removed by the legislature's act of repealing copyright protection. Under these circumstances, it is unlikely that 'fighting editions' would prove to be the significant deterrent to book copying that they might have been in the nineteenth century." In Tyerman's view, the important question was "how many times could a publisher sell drastically below his costs to drive out a copier and still remain financially solvent?" In a world without copyright, "there would be no safe haven in which the initial publisher could produce a book free from competition in that title and make the profits necessary to finance the production and sale of 'fighting editions' of other titles." *Id.* at 1113.

2. Breyer and Tyerman focused on copyright's effects on the *quantity* of books produced. What are copyright's effects, if any, on the *quality* of published books? The quality of works produced under copyright is significantly connected to the rule that copyright protects expression—lines of prose, for example, or musical melodies or landscapes—but not elemental plots or themes or colors. Because copyright does not protect ideas or other such fundamental elements of creativity, it offers no incentive to invest in their production or dissemination; the incentive will instead be to come up with new ways of expressing old ideas. The result is a marketplace crowded with works that, though different in their expressions, are redundant in their ideas. Is this result desirable in the case of fiction, musical composition, paintings and graphics? In the case of technical works, maps and computer programs?

3. *Copyright and Technology.* Until the printing press, a pirate who copied an author's manuscript had to invest the same physical labor as the author or scribe who penned the original; the cost advantage of piracy was nil. The printing press brought cheap copies, and as copies grew cheaper still, the worth of each copy's creative content increased relative to the cost of reproduction, raising the question of who—author, user or the technology's inventor—should be entitled to share in the newly created value. The history of copyright in the centuries since reveals the repeated extension of exclusive rights to domains far from the printing of texts—reproduction in photographs, phonorecords, films, videotapes and computers, as well as technologically diverse forms of distribution, performance and display. As the copyright pie grows larger, should it be sliced any differently than before?

4. For a general analysis of copyright economics, see William M. Landes & Richard A. Posner, An Economic Analysis of Copyright Law, 18 J. Legal Studies 325 (1989). See also Tom G. Palmer, Intellectual Property: A Non–Posnerian Law and Economics Approach, 12 Hamline L. Rev. 261 (1989). For an historical overview of economic thought about copyright, see Gillian K. Hadfield, The Economics of Copyright: An Historical Perspective, 38 Copyright L. Symp. (ASCAP) 1 (1992); Arnold Plant, The Economic Aspects of Copyright in Books, 1 Economica 167 (n.s. 1934).

B. PATENT LAW

"To Promote the Progress of . . . Useful Arts"

Report of the President's Commission on the Patent System 1–3 (1966).

The United States patent system is an institution as old as the Nation itself. Stemming from a Constitutional mandate, patent acts were passed in

1790, 1793, and 1836. The Act of 1836 established the pattern for our present system by providing statutory criteria for the issuance of patents and requiring the Patent Office to examine applications for conformance thereto. Although the law has been amended on numerous occasions—and even rewritten twice since 1836—no basic changes have been made in its general character in the succeeding one hundred and thirty years.

However, during this period of few statutory changes, major developments have occurred in the social and economic character of the country. The United States has undergone a dramatic transformation, creating and utilizing an enormously complex technology, to emerge as the world's most productive industrial community. . . .

Agreeing that the patent system has in the past performed well its Constitutional mandate "to promote the progress of . . . useful arts," the Commission asked itself: What is the basic worth of a patent system in the context of present day conditions? The members of the Commission unanimously agreed that a patent system today is capable of continuing to provide an incentive to research, development, and innovation. They have discovered no practical substitute for the unique service it renders.

First, a patent system provides an incentive to invent by offering the possibility of reward to the inventor and to those who support him. This prospect encourages the expenditure of time and private risk capital in research and development efforts.

Second, and complementary to the first, a patent system stimulates the investment of additional capital needed for the further development and marketing of the invention. In return, the patent owner is given the right, for a limited period, to exclude others from making, using, or selling the invented product or process.

Third, by affording protection, a patent system encourages early public disclosure of technological information, some of which might otherwise be kept secret. Early disclosure reduces the likelihood of duplication of effort by others and provides a basis for further advances in the technology involved.

Fourth, a patent system promotes the beneficial exchange of products, services, and technological information across national boundaries by providing protection for industrial property of foreign nationals.

Fritz Machlup, An Economic Review of the Patent System

Study No. 15, Subcommittee on Patents, Trademarks and Copyrights, Senate Committee on the Judiciary, 85th Cong., 2d Sess. 44–45, 50–52, 54–55 (1958).

Patents, by giving their owners exclusive rights to the commercial exploitation of inventions, secure to these owners profits (so-called "quasi rents") which are ultimately collected from consumers as part of the price paid for goods and services. The consumers pay; the patent owners receive. Are the consumers—the non-patent-owning people—worse off for it?

"No; they are not," says one group of economists. Patents are granted on inventions which would not have been made in the absence of a patent system; the inventions make it possible to produce more or better products than could have been produced without them; hence, whatever the consumers pay to the patent owners is only a part of the increase in real income that is engendered by the patent-induced inventions.

"Wrong," says another group of economists. Many of the inventions for which patents are granted would also be made and put to use without any patent system. The consumers could have the fruits of this technical progress without paying any toll charges. Even if *some* inventions are made and used thanks only to the incentives afforded by the patent system, consumers must pay for *all* patented inventions and, hence, lose by the bargain. Moreover, if patents result in monopolistic restrictions which hold down production and hinder the most efficient utilization of resources, it is possible that total real income is less than what it would be without the patent system. Of course, there is impressive technical progress and a substantial growth of national income under the patent system, yet perhaps less so than there would be without patents.

This is but one of the fundamental conflicts in the economics of the patent system. There is another, which is quite independent of any profits collected by the patent owners and of any monopolistic restrictions imposed on production. This second basic problem relates to the overall allocation of productive resources in a developing economy, and to the question whether at any one time the allocation to industrial research and development is deficient, excessive, or just right. . . .

Competition among rival firms which takes the form of a race between their research teams—a race, ultimately, to the patent office—may have various objectives: (a) To be the first to find a patentable solution to a problem posed by the needs and preferences of the customers—a better product—or by the technological needs and hopes of the producers—better machines, tools, processes; (b) after a competitor has found such a solution and has obtained exclusive patent rights in its exploitation, to find an alternative solution to the same problem in order to be able to compete with him in the same market—in other words, to "invent around" the competitor's patent; and (c) after having found and patented the first solution, to find and patent all possible alternative solutions, even inferior ones, in order to "block" the competitor's efforts to "invent around" the first patent.

These forms of "competitive research" were described and discussed by antipatent economists during the patent controversy of the 19th century. Concerning the first form, there was much complaint that other inventors who discovered practically simultaneously "the same utility," but were not the first in the race to the patent office, had to forego their "natural privilege of labor" and were barred from using their own inventions. The fact that there was competition in making new inventions was found to be healthy. But that he who lost the race to the patent office should be barred from using his own invention, and should have to search for a substitute invention, was found to be absurd.

What may appear absurd to a disinterested observer, or unjust and unfair to one who lost the right to use the fruit of his own labor and investment, must to an economist appear as sheer economic waste. Of course, one may regard this as an incidental expense of an otherwise beneficial institution, an unfortunate byproduct, an item of social cost, which, perhaps, is unavoidable and must be tolerated in view of the social advantages of the system as a whole. However, from merely defending the need of "inventing around a patent" as a minor item of waste, the discussion has recently proceeded to eulogize it as one of the advantages of the system, indeed as one of its "justifications."

The advantage is seen in the additional "encouragement" to research. If the competitors were given licenses under the patent of the firm that won the race, they would have to pay royalties but would not be compelled to "invent around" it. Exclusivity, however, forces some of them to search for a "substitute invention." But why should this be regarded as an advantage? The idea is probably that, if industrial research is desirable, more research is more desirable, and that it does not matter what kind of knowledge the research effort is supposed to yield. From an economic point of view, research is costly since it absorbs particularly scarce resources which could produce other valuable things. The production of the knowledge of how to do in a somewhat different way what we have already learned to do in a satisfactory way would hardly be given highest priority in a rational allocation of resources.

This same, or a still lower, evaluation must be accorded to the third form of "competitive research"—inventive effort for the purpose of obtaining patents on all possible alternatives of an existing patented invention just in order to "block" a rival from "inventing around" that patent. In this case inventive talent is wasted on a project which, even (or especially) if it succeeds exactly in achieving its objective, cannot possibly be as valuable as would be other tasks to which the talent might be assigned. When thousands of potential inventions are waiting to be made—inventions which might be of great benefit to society—how can one seriously justify the assignment of a research force to search for inventions that are not intended for use at all—but merely for satisfying a dog-in-a-manger ambition?

There is, however, another "justification" for this kind of "competitive research": it can be summarized in the colorful word "serendipity." This means "the faculty of making happy and unexpected discoveries by accident." The idea is that the research teams engaged in "inventing around patents," or in inventing to obtain patents to "block" other people's efforts to "invent around patents," might by sheer accident hit upon something really useful. In other words, the work of these research forces is justified by the possibility or probability that they might find something which they did not set out to find.

There is no doubt that these happy accidents occur again and again. But can one reasonably let an effort to produce something without social value take the credit for accidental byproducts that happen to be useful? Can one reasonably assert that research not oriented toward important objectives is more likely to yield useful results than are research efforts that are so oriented? Is it easier to find the important by seeking the unimportant? ...

The most perplexing and disturbing confusions occur in discussions about the "value of patents." This is no wonder, what with the large number of possible meanings in the minds of the writers on the subject: they may be talking about (a) the value of patents to their owners, (b) the value of patents to society, (c) the value of the patent system to society, (d) the value of patented inventions to their users, (e) the value of patented inventions to society, (f) the value of patent-induced inventions to society. But even this is not all, because the social value of inventions may depend on the degree to which they are used, and the value of patents to their owners on the way they are exploited.

Singling out, from this long list, (b) the value of patents to society— and making quite sure that this refers neither to the social benefits of the patent system nor to the social value of the inventions, which are altogether different matters—it is worth pointing out that existing domestic patents held by domestic owners cannot be reasonably regarded as parts of the national wealth or as sources of real national income. To regard them so is as fallacious as it would be to include in national wealth such things as the right of a businessman to exclude others from using his trade name, or the right of a (domestic) creditor to collect from his (domestic) debtors, or to include such things as (domestic) money, securities, damage claims, and lottery tickets. The right of a person to keep others from doing something is no social asset and, again, somebody's right to keep others from using his invention should not be confused with the invention itself. To confuse an important invention with the patent that excludes people from using it is like confusing an important bridge with the tollgates that close it to many who might want to use it. No statistics of national wealth would ever include (domestic) "patent property." And the "destruction of patent property"—though it may affect the future performance of the economy— would leave the Nation's wealth, as it is now understood in social accounting, unimpaired. (An exception must be noted concerning foreign patent rights. One may regard domestic holdings of foreign patents as claims to future royalties and profits earned abroad and, hence, as assets; of course, foreign holdings of domestic patents, establishing foreign rights to future royalties and profits earned here, would then have to be counted among the liabilities and, therefore, as deductions from national wealth.)

NOTES

1. Patent law denies protection to abstract, fundamental ideas. Patent law also imposes comparatively high standards for protection—nonobviousness, novelty and utility. Taken together, these rules aim to steer private research and development away both from the discovery of fundamental ideas and from inventions that make only obvious or non-novel leaps over the prior art. These twin pressures are not, however, alone in defining patent law's incentive structure, for the grant of a patent to *A* will characteristically impair *B*'s incentives to invent in the same field, including his incentive to invest in improvements on *A*'s invention. For examination of this phenomenon in the field of biomedical research, see Rebecca S. Eisenberg & Michael A. Heller, Can Patents Deter Innovation? The Anticommons in Biomedical Research, 280 Science 698 (1998); Clarisa Long, Patents and Cumulative Innovation, 2 Wash. U.J. L. & Policy 229 (2000).

2. *A World Without Patents?* Patent laws are today well entrenched in legislation around the world. Nonetheless, over a century ago several countries questioned the desirability of having patent legislation at all. Fueled by free trade sentiments that viewed patents as baleful protectionist measures, the attack on patent legislation was particularly severe in Europe. The Netherlands repealed its patent law in 1869. Switzerland, which had so far failed to adopt a patent system, consistently rejected proposals to enact patent legislation. In England, speakers in both houses of Parliament proposed the abolition of patents, and a bill passed by the House of Lords proposed to cut back the patent term and to introduce compulsory licensing and other restrictions on patent rights. By the 1870's, the anti-patent movement had mostly dissipated. (Switzerland, however, did not adopt a patent law until 1887 and the Netherlands did not reintroduce a patent law until 1910.) The residues of the anti-patent movement remain evident today in the compulsory license requirements and other limitations introduced into many national laws.

For an incisive analysis of the anti-patent movement in nineteenth-century Europe, see Fritz Machlup & Edith Penrose, The Patent Controversy in the Nineteenth Century, 10 J. Econ. Hist. 1 (1950).

3. *The Subsidy Alternative.* Patent law is only one of several public policy mechanisms for stimulating technological advance. The most prominent alternative—and supplement—is government subsidy. Cash from the federal government supports much of the basic research conducted in universities, government institutes and even private firms. Subsidies do not necessarily end with basic research. Government may also pay producers to implement inventions and consumers to acquire them. Agriculture and instructional technology are two fields in which consumers have been unwilling to bear by themselves the risk and expense associated with adopting new technologies. The federal government has deployed county agents and regional educational laboratories to overcome the last hurdles to innovation posed by consumer ignorance or indifference in these fields.

Subsidies may also take the form of prizes. One bill before the United States Senate would have authorized a National Science and Technology Awards Council to publish annually a list of no more than ten "most wanted scientific breakthroughs," and to award prizes ranging from $5,000 to $150,000 to the first person to meet the performance criteria established by the Council for each category. S. 1480, 94th Cong., 1st Sess., 121 Cong.Rec. 10832–34 (1975). Federal and state income tax incentives can be used to allow investors to write off research and development costs as deductible current expenses rather than as expenditures that must be capitalized and then amortized over the life of the invention.

If the federal government supports work that the researcher later develops into a working invention, should the researcher be denied a patent on the ground that, since the work was publicly financed, its fruits should belong to the public without charge? Is it unfair or inefficient to give monopoly rewards to a private entrepreneur who has paid nothing for the basic research, and to require the public to pay for it twice—first in the tax revenues allocated to the research program, and a second time in increased prices paid for the goods produced? Some expenditure, private or public, will always be needed to put an invention into practice. This means that the public will pay a second time in any event—either through higher prices paid for private distribution or for subsidies to dissemination. Is the real question whether the private or public sector represents the more efficient vehicle for dissemination? See Wassily Leontief, On Assignment of Patent Rights on Inventions Made Under Government Research Contracts, 77 Harv. L. Rev. 492 (1964).

Should federally-funded inventions such as patented pharmaceuticals be subjected to price controls in the public interest? See Peter S. Arno & Michael H. Davis, Why Don't We Enforce Existing Drug Price Controls? The Unrecognized and Unenforced Reasonable Pricing Requirements Imposed Upon Patents Deriving in Whole or in Part from Federally Funded Research, 75 Tulane L. Rev. 631 (2001). For an exploration generally of the advantages and pitfalls of direct government awards as an alternative or adjunct to patents, see Steve P. Calandrillo, An Economic Analysis of Intellectual Property Rights in Information: Justifications and Problems of Exclusive Rights, Incentives to Generate Information, and the Alternative of a Government–Run Reward System, 9 Fordham Intellectual Prop. Media & Ent. L.J. 301 (1998).

4. On the economics of invention, see Kenneth J. Arrow, Economic Welfare and the Allocation of Resources for Invention, in The Rate and Direction of Inventive Activity : Economic and Social Factors 609 Nat'l Bureau of Econ. Research ed., (1962); William D. Nordhaus, Invention, Growth and Welfare: A Theoretical Treatment of Technological Change (1969). On the economics of the patent system, see John W. Schlicher, Patent Law: Legal and Economic Principles (1995). See also Kenneth W. Dam, The Economic Underpinnings of Patent Law, 23 J. Legal Stud. 247 (1994). For a critical review of recent economic approaches to patent law, see A. Samuel Oddi, Un–Unified Economic Theories of Patents—The Not–Quite–Holy Grail, 71 Notre Dame L. Rev. 267 (1996).

C. Trademark Law

Nicholas S. Economides, The Economics of Trademarks

78 Trademark Rep. 523, 526–531 (1988).*

The primary reasons for the existence and protection of trademarks are that (1) they facilitate and enhance consumer decisions and (2) they create incentives for firms to produce products of desirable qualities even when these are not observable before purchase. Both of these effects are a consequence of the fact that trademarks permit consumers to distinguish between goods which look identical in all features that are observable before purchase.

From an economic standpoint, the argument for trademarks is simple. In many markets, sellers have much better information as to the unobservable features of a commodity for sale than the buyers. This is known as information asymmetry. Unobservable features, valued by the consumer, may be crucial determinants of the total value of the good. Observable features can often be imitated to the smallest detail, even though huge differences remain in the unobservable features of the product. In the absence of trademarks, faced with the choice between goods which look identical, the consumer will only by chance pick the one with the desirable unobservable qualities. Further, firms would produce products with the cheapest possible unobservable qualities, because high levels of unobserved qualities would not add to a firm's ability to sell at a higher price and realize higher profits. However, if there is a way to identify the unobservable qualities, the consumer's choice becomes clear, and firms with a long horizon have an incentive to cater to a spectrum of tastes for variety and quality, even though these product features may be unobservable at the time of purchase.

The economic role of the trademark is to help the consumer identify the unobservable features of the trademarked product. This information is not provided to the consumer in an analytic form, such as an indication of size or a listing of ingredients, but rather in summary form, through a symbol which the consumer identifies with a specific combination of features. Information in analytic form is a complement to, rather than a substitute for, trademarks.

Trademarks were originally used to identify the makers of jewelry in the middle ages, but craftsmen's marks were used in pottery since ancient times. Although their original intent may have been to identify the maker for possible fraud regarding the assigned quality of the alloy, soon trademarks were utilized to identify the quality standard of particular makers. By the beginning of the twentieth century trademarks were understood not to be useful in identifying the source, but rather as identifying a quality standard. Presently the trademark typically identifies the product (the full combination of features that constitute the product), and its role of identifying the source is secondary in the minds of consumers. The consumer of NABISCO WHEAT THINS knows and cares little about source (manufacturer). Rather the consumer identifies the trademark with the features of the commodity, including crispness, sweetness or lack thereof, color, and the like. The trademark identifies both quality and variety features of the product, i.e., both features like freshness, more of which is desirable by all, and features like sweetness, over which consumers have varying preferences, some preferring little of it, and some desiring lots of it. Thus, although trademarks and trade names typically identify quality standards, often trademarks identify the full features of the product.

Moreover, the existence of trademarks allows firms to differentiate products in their unobservable features and to efficiently convey these differences to consumers. The tendency of firms to produce products that are not identical is natural in an environment where firms strive to maximize profits. The existence of trademarks allows this tendency to manifest itself with respect to unobservable characteristics of the products. The consumer is thus afforded a wider quality/variety spectrum....

The degree to which a trademark is successful in conveying to the consumer unobservable features of the product before purchase depends on the underlying market conditions, the product, the frequency of purchase, the ease of information diffusion across consumers, and the ability of recall of consumers.

For products which are frequently purchased by the same consumer, trademarks function directly through the previous experience of the consumer. Consider an experience good (which the average consumer buys often). Assume further that there are certain features of the product which are unobservable at the time of purchase. A typical example of such a product is a bottle of diet COKE, the cola beverage. Information on the bottle and label give little indication of the taste. The trademark identifies the product. A consumer is typically offered a free introductory bottle, or buys the first bottle to sample it. From his experience he is then able to decide rationally as an informed consumer about his future choices between diet COKE and all other goods.

The crucial requirements for this mechanism to work are, first, that the consumer has a sufficiently good memory; second, that the consumer is able to identify the full features of the product with the trademark; and third, that the features of the product do not change between the first and subsequent consumption decisions. In the case of experience goods, the trademark has a reputation with the old customer which identifies its features. In this case, social interactions and information transfer among consumers are not necessary for the trademark to facilitate efficient choice.

For the trademark to fulfill its function all three requirements mentioned above are necessary. It can be fairly assumed that the consumer is endowed with a good memory. The second condition is likely to hold because the law protects the identification of trademarks with particular products by disallowing the use of similar symbols, words or designs on any other product in a manner likely to cause confusion. Preventing confusion is an important function of trademarks. Even in cases of no likelihood of confusion, similar trademarks have been disallowed because of the possible "dilution" of the mental association between a trademark (or trade name) and a particular product (or firm).

The last requirement is that the manufacturers do not change the features of the product between purchases. Under conditions of stability in the market, prosperity of the firm is guaranteed by its adherence to a high quality level for goods bearing its trademark or trade name. If, however, the horizon of the firm is short, it may opt to cash-in on its trade name reputation by selling lower quality goods. Events which can shorten the horizon of the firm and force it to emphasize the short run can be severe financial constraints which follow a leveraged buy-out, or a dramatic fall in the demand for the product because of innovation in competing products, or a severe economic shock. . . .

In the case of experience goods where the consumer identifies the trademark with the product before purchase, it appears that there is no other mechanism which would work as efficiently. In the absence of trademarks, it could be argued that quality regulation, say through minimum quality standards, enforced through laws on fraud, could conceivably create a similar level of efficiency in the market place. Although quality minimums might be upheld through regulation, it is practically impossible to regulate variety efficiently. Given the consensus among consumers on the desirability of a quality feature, a regulatory board can set minimum quality standards. Variety features, where unanimity in the direction of preference is lacking, are very difficult and very costly to regulate. To achieve efficient regulation, estimation of the demand for each combination of variety features is needed—a very difficult task. Thus any regulatory system will most likely fail to provide the appropriate combinations of features which constitute the efficient mixture of desired varieties. . . .

For products which are consumed infrequently by the same individual, such as washing machines, refrigerators, television sets, video cassette recorders, and the like, trademarks work in an indirect way. Assume again that there are unobservable features. Lacking previous consumption, a consumer is unable to identify the trademark with the product. To be able to associate the trademark with the features of the product he has to rely on information diffused informally through friends or from evaluations disseminated centrally through magazines, radio or television. It is clear that, because of differences of interpretation as well as differences of opinion and preference across consumers, the information on which the choice will be based is most likely to be much more vague than in the case of experience goods. Most relevant information reaches the consumer in summary form. Information gathered through this process is likely to be incomplete and the consumer has little hope of more complete information on product features.

However, firms may use trade names to help the consumer identify the quality level of products. Even though the consumer is an infrequent buyer of a particular kind of electronic product, he may be a frequent buyer of the overall category of electronic products, and thus he is likely to have previous experience in the consumption of goods with the same trade name. Choosing a high quality standard in the category of electronic products, a manufacturer can use his trade name to transmit information on quality through the direct previous experience of consumers.

NOTES

1. *Trademarks as Prestige.* Advertising does more than inform and persuade. Advertising sometimes becomes an element of the product or service itself. In an important article, Advertising and the Public Interest: Legal Protection of Trade Symbols, 57 Yale L.J. 1165, 1181 (1948), Professor Ralph S. Brown observed, "The buyer of an advertised good buys more than a parcel of food or fabric; he buys the pause that refreshes, the hand that has never lost its skill, the priceless ingredient that is the reputation of its maker. All these may be illusions, but they cost money to create, and if the creators can recoup their outlay, who is the poorer? Among the many illusions which advertising can fashion are those of lavishness, refinement, security, and romance. Suppose the monetary cost of compounding a perfume is trivial; of what moment is this if the ads promise, and the buyer believes, that romance, even seduction, will follow its use? The economist, whose dour lexicon defines as irrational any market behavior not dictated by a logical pecuniary calculus, may think it irrational to buy illusions; but there is a degree of that kind of irrationality even in economic man; and consuming man is full of it."

Should trademark law protect marks, particularly prestige marks like "Rolex" or "Ralph Lauren," that do more than inform and persuade? Professor Glynn S. Lunney, Jr. has observed a contemporary expansion in trademark law focusing "on a trademark's value not merely as a device for conveying otherwise indiscernible information concerning a product ('deception-based trademark'), but as a valuable product in itself ('property-based trademark')," and noted that, "unlike deception-based trademark, property-based trademark has only a tenuous relationship to consumer deception, and therefore lacks the offsetting efficiency advantages associated with deception-based trademark's quality control and certification functions. As a result, property-based trademark appears presumptively anti-competitive—it generates market power and associated efficiency losses without the offsetting efficiency gains that are thought to justify deception-based trademark." Nor, in Lunney's view, do the property rights given under copyright and patent law offer a valid analogy: "Unlike patent and copyright, trademark law neither ties its prerequisites for protection to a need for additional incentive, nor defines its protection to ensure an appropriate incentive level. As a result, trademark's expansion risks creating an incentive structure fundamentally at odds with social welfare."

Glynn S. Lunney, Jr., Trademark Monopolies, 48 Emory L.J. 367, 371–73 (1999).

For the suggestion that more extensive, property-like protection of marks can best be evaluated by differentiating among the nature of the mark and the standards to be applied—moral claims, utilitarian claims, negative goodwill and the need to refer to the mark in public discourse— see Alex Kozinski, Trademarks Unplugged, 68 N.Y.U. L. Rev.960 (1993). See also Stephen L. Carter, The Trouble with Trademark, 99 Yale L.J. 759 (1990).

2. For a review of trademark law's legal, intellectual and economic history, see Daniel M. McClure, Trademarks and Unfair Competition: A Critical History of Legal Thought, 69 Trademark Rep. 305 (1979). On the economics of trademark law generally, see William M. Landes & Richard A. Posner, Trademark Law: An Economic Perspective, 30 J.L. & Econ. 265 (1987); Jules Backman, The Role of Trademarks in Our Competitive Economy, 58 Trademark Rep. 219 (1968).

PART TWO

State Law of Intellectual Property

I. Rights in Undeveloped Ideas

Sellers v. American Broadcasting Co.

United States Court of Appeals, Eleventh Circuit, 1982.
668 F.2d 1207, 217 U.S.P.Q. 41.

JOHNSON, Circuit Judge:

Plaintiff, Larry L. Sellers, filed a three-count complaint against defendants American Broadcasting Co. (ABC) and Geraldo Rivera, alleging breach of contract, copyright infringement and misappropriation. The district court granted summary judgment in favor of the defendants and plaintiff appeals. We affirm.

In June 1978, Sellers informed Rivera, an investigative reporter occasionally employed by ABC, that he had an "exclusive story" concerning rock-and-roll singer Elvis Presley's death. Before revealing the details, however, Sellers demanded that Rivera sign an agreement guaranteeing him all copyright privileges to the story and requiring ABC to publicly credit him with uncovering the true cause of the singer's death.[1] In return,

---

[1] The entire agreement states:

I, Larry L. Sellers, do hereby agree not to release this exclusive story to any reporter other than Geraldo Rivera or any network other than ABC until the network has first released said story within a reasonable period of time or thirty days. Once the story has been released, other media forms may be contracted by Larry Sellers.

I, Geraldo Rivera, do hereby agree to grant Larry Sellers all copy-write [sic] privileges of the exclusive Elvis Presley story and full claim for the discovery of the story by acknowledgement in any media use made of it from this day forth.

If the story is accepted for further investigation, all expenses incurred by Larry Sellers will be reimbursed by ABC.

Should the story be proven false, this contract is hereby null and void.

Sellers agreed to provide ABC and Rivera with the "exclusive story" and further agreed not to release the story to any other network or reporter. Upon execution of the contract, Sellers proceeded to articulate his theory. Sellers recorded the entire conversation and a transcript of the meeting has been made part of the record in this case.

According to Sellers, cortisone was prescribed for Presley during the three-year period prior to his death. Presley's personal physician and personal bodyguard replaced the cortisone with placebos. Deprivation of the cortisone caused a collapse of Presley's cardiovascular system, resulting in death. Sellers hypothesized that the physician and the bodyguard committed the murder in order to prevent Presley from seeking the repayment of a $1.3 million loan to them to be used for the construction of a racketball center. As an alternative theory, Sellers postulated that the singer might have been suffocated by either the physician or the bodyguard.

Rivera informed the plaintiff that the story could not be used unless verified. He suggested that plaintiff investigate the matter further and contact him in the event that verification was obtained. Following the conversation with Rivera, Sellers traveled to Memphis on two occasions, apparently in an effort to obtain the needed support for his theory. During the second trip, Sellers called Mrs. Rivera and informed her that he had uncovered proof of his theory but refused to relate to her the nature of the new evidence. The phone call constituted the last time Sellers contacted either Rivera or ABC concerning the story.

More than nine months after signing the agreement with Sellers, Rivera and producer Charles Thomsen decided to do a feature story on Presley's death. After a two-month investigation, it was determined that Presley died of polypharmacy (interaction of prescription drugs) and not cardiac arrhythmia as officially listed. ABC broadcast an hour-long special concerning the information uncovered during the "Rivera–Thomsen" investigation. Geraldo Rivera appeared on the program as a correspondent. ABC also did a number of follow-up stories on Presley's death. In neither the hour-long special nor the follow-up stories did the network suggest that Presley was murdered by a withdrawal of cortisone or by suffocation.

Sellers brought suit contending that ABC and Rivera misappropriated his "exclusive story" concerning the singer's death. Sellers also asserted claims for breach of contract and copyright infringement. The district court entered summary judgment for defendants. The court determined that plaintiff's "exclusive story" consisted of the theory that Presley had been murdered by his bodyguard and his personal physician through a deprivation of cortisone. Since ABC and Rivera did not use Sellers' "exclusive story" in any of their broadcasts, the court concluded that there had not been any misappropriation or breach of the written agreement.

On appeal, Sellers contends that a dispute of material fact exists concerning the precise scope of his "exclusive story" and, accordingly, summary judgment was improvidently granted. Sellers asserts that he informed Rivera not only of the possibility that Presley might have been murdered through a deprivation of cortisone, but also that the cause of death might have been the interaction of numerous prescription drugs, that the singer's personal physician may have been grossly negligent in over-prescribing drugs for Presley and that there had been a cover-up of the true cause of death. Assuming without deciding that Sellers did present these additional theories to Rivera, we nonetheless conclude that they are so vague and uncertain as to be unenforceable as a matter of law.

Under New York law,[4] a contract will not be enforced if an essential element is vague, indefinite or incomplete. A complete review of the transcribed meeting between the parties shows that at best Sellers made broad, general statements concerning the possibility of overdose, gross negligence by the personal physician and a cover-up. The transcript demonstrates that plaintiff failed to provide any substantiating details for these vague allegations. He did not make clear whether Presley's death resulted from a single drug or a combination of drugs. He made no effort to provide the name of any specific drug that had been overprescribed by the personal physician. Nor did plaintiff show that medication unnecessary for the treatment of the singer's illnesses was prescribed for Presley. Finally, references to books and newspaper articles[5] constituted the only support for these vague and uncertain statements. Sellers' theory that Presley was murdered by a withdrawal of cortisone may well have been specific enough to give rise to an enforceable agreement. The district court, however, concluded that the defendants did not utilize the cortisone-murder theory in any of their broadcasts and did not, therefore, breach the agreement. Plaintiff does not challenge this conclusion on appeal.

As to plaintiff's remaining claim, New York courts will permit recovery for the misappropriation of an idea or theory if (1) the idea is novel; (2) the idea is in a concrete form; and (3) the defendant makes use of the idea. We conclude that Sellers' theory that Presley died of an interaction of prescription drugs was neither novel, unique nor original. Plaintiff's own exhibits show that a number of newspapers had speculated that Presley's death might have been drug-related long before the meeting between Sellers and Rivera. As to Sellers' other vague theories, we conclude that they were not sufficiently concrete to give rise to a cause of action for misappropriation.[7]

---

4. The district court concluded that New York law controlled the interpretation of the contract. Neither party disputes this conclusion.

5. We note that at least a portion of plaintiff's "exclusive story", particularly the theory that Presley died from an interaction of drugs, appeared in a number of newspaper articles prior to his discussion with Rivera. Under New York law, an idea or theory does not constitute property and will not support the right to recover in contract unless original. Thus, to the extent plaintiff's "exclusive story" was already widely disseminated and in the public domain, he cannot recover in contract for the use of his theory by the defendants.

7. The only portion of plaintiff's "exclusive story" that may have been sufficiently concrete to sustain a cause of action for misappropriation was his theory that Presley died from a withdrawal of cortisone. The district court, however, found that the defendants did not use the theory in any of their broadcasts. Plaintiff does not challenge this conclusion on appeal.

For the reasons stated herein, judgment for the defendants is AF-FIRMED.

Harry R. Olsson, Jr., Dreams for Sale

23 Law & Contemp. Probs. 34–35, 54–55 (1958).*

Idea submission claims have been a real plague for many years, but, as an attorney writing about idea submitters and advertisers has observed, things have taken a turn for the worse in the past quarter century, as courts now have a tendency to allow recovery where they would not earlier have done so. Consequently, reward is being given prematurely to those who otherwise might turn their mere "ideas" into finished works, and the commercial users of ideas are exposed to danger by the law in some American jurisdictions if they depart from well-worn idea channels. The battlefield in these cases is generally that of the submitted idea for which the submitter later claims that compensation is due him as the result of a use allegedly made by the recipient of the idea.

Such a claim takes one of several guises: that the recipient expressly promised to pay the submitter if he used the idea; that he impliedly promised to pay if he used the idea; that the law imposes an obligation to pay on quasi-contractual unjust enrichment grounds if the idea is used; that the recipient took a property—the idea—belonging to the submitter and used it, thus committing a tort in the nature of a conversion; or, finally, that a fiduciary relationship was violated by the recipient.

Occasionally, the claim is made seriously that a statutory or common law copyright infringement has been committed by the recipient; but copyright lawyers, as we shall see, have had little difficulty, except for a time in opportunity-rich California, in disposing of that contention. It is sometimes claimed that the act of use constitutes unfair competition; and in this area, all lawyers have difficulty, for unfair competition has been made the bridge between law and morality, and all sorts of baggage has been trundled across it since the historic International News Service v. Associated Press case [248 U.S. 215, 39 S.Ct. 68, 63 L.Ed. 211 (1918)]. . . .

Some Statistics

Robert W. Sarnoff, president of National Broadcasting Company, recently said: "In the year now ending, NBC headquarters, its stations, its field offices, its artists, and its producers will have received some three million letters from the viewing public. In New York alone, we will have had more than 41,000 telephone calls praising or criticizing our shows, and more than 100,000 telegrams." Dore Schary, one of the motion picture industry's outstanding producers, told recently on a television program that a large studio receives 20,000 stories or ideas a year, of which but twenty are made into motion pictures.

* Copyright 1958 by Duke University.

Of the three national TV networks, one, NBC, currently is receiving 30,000 to 40,000 suggestions of all types every year. These figures include everything from letter outlines to pilot films. One department alone received from 7,000 to 10,000 "approaches" a year. From 2,000 to 3,000 get some serious study. Ten thousand story submissions of all types are offered. The effect of this tremendous influx is obvious. At the present time, the idea-submission lawsuits confronting the networks probably account for sixty-five percent of all suits against them in the area of copyright, defamation, right of privacy, and unfair competition.

The extraordinary and multiple claims that result from idea protection are perhaps illustrated best by citing a case of a new program coming on the air and what happened to the network—NBC in this case—that put it on:

On March 1, 1954 the program "Home" was first presented on the NBC Television Network. Prior to its date of first broadcast, NBC had received six idea submission claims relating thereto. The six claims were entirely independent of one another, and each claimant claimed that his idea submission would form the basis of the series to be broadcast. Advance publicity about the program, the only information probably available on which each of the claims could have been based, said little more than that "Home" would be a service-type (as opposed to entertainment-type) program, like a magazine-of-the-air. But this was not the end of our trouble, for following the first broadcast of the program three more claims came in. Two of them became lawsuits. The program went off the air following its broadcast on August 9, 1957. Two of the three idea submission lawsuits concerning it are still pending. As late as July 31, 1957, a motion was noticed for an order enjoining the series three days prior to its going off the air.

The fact that the idea was old was no deterrent to the claims made regarding the "Home" program. A brief search of the exhaustive files maintained by NBC revealed that the network had received submissions of the basic "home" idea since 1929—prior to the earliest of the nine claimants' alleged submissions.

RICHTER v. WESTAB, INC., 529 F.2d 896, 902, 189 U.S.P.Q. 321 (6th Cir.1976). WEICK, J.: The law does not favor the protection of abstract ideas as the property of the originator. An idea should be free for all to use at least until someone is able to translate such idea into a sufficiently useful form that it may be patented or copyrighted. Thus competition in the use of ideas is a social good, hastening the process of invention.

When a design firm suggests that a particular product be decorated with thematic designs, this act of suggesting should not establish an exclusive right to exploit the idea. Perhaps the design firm will not be sufficiently competent to produce good designs based upon the concept. A concept is of little use until solidified into a concrete application. The idea of fashion designs is useless unless good designs are obtained. If the design firm is incapable of producing good designs the public should not be denied the benefit of the idea if another designer could produce good designs. Thus the principle denying legal protection to abstract ideas has important social interests behind it.

NOTES

1. Is the passage excerpted from Richter v. Westab correct that a "concept is of little use until solidified into concrete application"? What assumptions does this statement make about the efficient division of labor in information industries? Is it correct to assume that workers who come up with good ideas are also best placed to execute them? That those who are well placed to execute good ideas are also capable of originating them? Does it follow from decisions like *Sellers* that a division of labor between idea origination and idea development will occur only within firms? Can contracts effectively bridge the efforts of idea originators and idea developers?

What are the likely effects of a rule that denies property protection to ideas? Will it spur firms to originate and develop new ideas, or will firms merely take old ideas and develop them into new, concrete forms? Note that the elaboration of an idea into concrete form will not gain protection for the idea itself, but only for the specific form in which the idea is elaborated.

For an analysis of organizational problems surrounding the development of ideas, and some suggestions for institutional innovation, see Gerald G. Udell, The Essential Nature of the Idea Brokerage Function, 57 J. Pat. Off. Soc'y 642 (1975).

2. *Professional and Amateur Submitters.* Should recovery for use of an idea ever turn on the status—amateur or professional—of the submitter? What are the respective expectations, bargaining positions and long-run interests of amateur and professional idea submitters?

Lawyers usually think of their compensation as payment for services rendered. To what extent do these services embody anything more than submitted ideas? The overlap between services rendered and ideas submitted is well illustrated by cases involving an advertising agency's submission of a commercial slogan to its client. Some courts focus on the act of submission and permit recovery on the basis of professional services rendered, without regard to the slogan's novelty or concreteness. See, for example, How J. Ryan & Assocs. v. Century Brewing Ass'n, 185 Wash. 600, 55 P.2d 1053 (1936). Other courts ignore the service aspect, weigh the slogan's novelty and concreteness, and deny recovery if these requisites are not met. See, for example, Marcus Advertising, Inc. v. M.M. Fisher Assocs., Inc., 444 F.2d 1061, 170 U.S.P.Q. 244 (7th Cir.1971). Generally, cases in the first category involve established, professional advertising agencies while those in the second involve amateur submitters.

3. *Company Submission Policies.* Two marketing professors at the University of Oregon have surveyed how different companies treat unsolicited ideas. Most respondents said that they will evaluate an unsolicited idea, particularly if the idea looks promising. Slightly under one-half of the respondents indicated that they require the submitter to sign a waiver before they will examine an unsolicited idea. Approximately one-half of the firms said that they ignore unsolicited ideas, at least in some cases. One firm responded with unusual candor: "most of these [unsolicited ideas] are thrown in the waste basket after we examine them. If we are interested, we proceed [to secure a waiver]."

Some companies return submitted ideas together with a waiver form:

Your letter was opened in our mail department. It apparently pertains to a new product suggestion. It is the policy of our company not to accept suggestions from outside sources without first receiving a signed copy of our disclosure form.

Enclosed you will find the material you submitted as well as a copy of our policy statement on unsolicited ideas. A disclosure agreement form is also enclosed for your use if you wish to submit your idea to our company under the terms stated in the enclosed policy statement.

Other companies retain the idea while awaiting receipt of an executed waiver:

I do not have a technical background, and one of the obligations of my position is to insure that any information submitted such as yours is neither reviewed by me nor presented for review to anyone else in the company unless and until we have received the non-confidential disclosure agreement I have referred to above. I trust that you will sign the agreement and return it, at which point I will forward the material you sent me to the appropriate personnel for evaluation. Otherwise those materials will be returned to you by me without having been examined or reviewed by anyone. . . .

The waiver forms themselves contain a variety of conditions: that review of the idea imposes no obligation of any kind on the firm; that any review and offer to negotiate is not an admission of novelty, priority or originality; that review of the idea does not impair the firm's right to contest existing or future patents on the idea; that acceptance and review of an idea does not create a confidential relationship; and that the submitter waives all rights except those that may be acquired under patent law.

The study is reported in Del I. Hawkins & Gerald G. Udell, Corporate Caution and Unsolicited New Product Ideas: A Survey of Corporate Waiver Requirements, 58 J. Pat. Off. Soc'y 375 (1976).

4. *Invention Promoters.* Many who seek to profit from their ideas have turned to professional idea brokers and invention promoters who, for a fee and sometimes part of the profits, agree to develop the idea and place it with an appropriate manufacturer. Few of these entrepreneurs enjoy success. One promoter has disclosed that for every 586 of its customers only four received more income from their inventions than they paid in fees; another indicated a success rate of two out of 3,200, and another, 3 out of 30,000. Robert J. Thomas, Invention Development Services and Inventors: Recent Inroads on Caveat Inventor, 60 J.Pat.Off.Soc'y 355, n. 3 (1978).

Starting in the mid–1970's, the widespread perception of abuses by invention promoters sparked a fusillade of regulatory efforts. The Federal Trade Commission obtained early consent decrees with several major firms. See, generally, Gerald G. Udell & Michael F. O'Neil, The FTC in the Matter of IRD, Inc.: An Analysis of Recent FTC Action Against Invention Promoters, 58 J.Pat.Off.Soc'y 442 (1976). State attorneys general and state legislatures have also acted. California's pioneer law regulating invention development contracts requires developers to maintain a bond of at least $25,000 and provides for cancellation by either party within seven days of the contract's execution; clear and conspicuous disclosure of fees; and recovery of treble damages, or at least $3,000, by injured customers. Cal.Bus. & Prof.Code §§ 22370 et seq. (West 1997). The federal Inventors' Rights Act of 1999, Pub. L. No. 106–113, codified at 35 U.S.C. § 297, requires the U.S. Patent and Trademark Office to act as a clearinghouse of sorts for complaints about invention promoters.

5. An idea submission will typically fall into one of four postures: (a) X submits her idea to Y upon Y's express solicitation; (b) X informs Y that she would like to submit an idea of possible value to Y and Y does nothing to block the submission; (c) X thrusts upon Y a full disclosure of her idea before Y has the opportunity to block the submission; (d) X makes no submission at all but charges that Y has copied her idea. As you read the materials in the next section outlining the theories on which recovery for the use of ideas can be based—express contract, implied in fact contract, quasi contract, property—consider whether one of the four theories is particularly well suited to resolve the interests at stake under each of the four postures.

A. THEORIES OF PROTECTION

Lueddecke v. Chevrolet Motor Co.

United States Circuit Court of Appeals, Eighth Circuit, 1934.
70 F.2d 345.

WOODROUGH, Circuit Judge.

Mr. H.W. Lueddecke brought this action at law, as plaintiff, against Chevrolet Motor Company and other corporations (all referred to herein as companies), as defendants, to recover on an alleged implied contract on the part of the defendant companies to pay plaintiff the reasonable value of an idea and suggestion which he alleges he furnished to them. Demurrers were interposed to the petition and were sustained. Plaintiff having declined to plead further, the case was dismissed, and the plaintiff appeals.

The petition alleges that the plaintiff sent the following letter to the companies:

"Dear Sirs: As the proud owner of a Chevrolet Sedan, and also with the knowledge of a man who knows automobiles, I am asking you a few questions and then making you a proposition.

"Do you know that a very serious error has been made in the general location of several of the individual units or mechanisms of the Chevrolet car? Do you also know that within another year or so this very error (unless corrected) will reduce Chevrolet sales by possibly a million or even several million dollars? And again, while I, as well as many others, have had and will still have this error of your designers overcome at considerable expense, it will within a short space of time possibly cause some other low-priced car to become more popular than the Chevrolet.

"While many car owners have gone to the trouble of correcting this defect, I have found neither an owner nor a mechanic who was able to discover the cause of the defect. And, unless corrected, the defect will mean considerable annual expense to the owner of the car, for which there is really no excuse at all.

"The cost of overcoming this defect in a car should not be over 20to 30you as you build the car if you take the easiest and shortest way out of the difficulty. To the owner who has purchased his car the cost will vary from $3.00 to $7.00 depending on where he lives, in city or country.

"The best way out of the difficulty, however, would necessitate a change of design as suggested above, and that can be done without great expense or without sacrificing the essential features of the design of the car.

"Now, I shall not ask you for a one-eighth royalty on $500,000 or $1,000,000 of sales, but I would like to have you make me an offer stating what such information would be worth to you?or how much you could offer and would pay for the same. Upon receipt of your reply, if your offer is satisfactory, I will give you complete information of the above mentioned changes for the Chevrolet car.

"An early reply will be appreciated.

"Yours truly,"

That reply was made as follows:

"Dear Sir: Your letter of June 27, to the Chevrolet Motor Company, regarding your suggestion to change the design of Chevrolet cars, has been forwarded to the New Devices Committee for attention.

"We have this Committee in General Motors, composed of some of our most important executives and engineers, to review all new inventions submitted direct to the Corporation or through any of its divisions or executives.

"It is against the policy of the Corporation to make any agreement for inventions until we know exactly what they are and have sufficient information to place them before the New Devices Committee for consideration.

"If you care to send us drawings and a description of your ideas, the Committee will be very glad to examine them and let you know whether or not General Motors is interested.

"We always insist, however, that everything submitted to us be protected in some way and would suggest, if you have not applied for patents, that you establish legal evidence of ownership and priority of your idea by having your original drawing signed, dated and witnessed by two or more competent persons or notarized.

"We assure you that, if we find the design of sufficient interest to warrant further investigation, some mutually satisfactory agreement will be made.

"Yours very truly,

"New Devices Committee."

That plaintiff then answered:

"Dear Sirs: I have Mr. T.O. Richards' reply (dated July 15th) to my letter of June 27th. Referring to my previous letter you will find that I said that your designers of the Chevrolet car had made a very serious blunder in the location of several of the individual units of the car. I also stated that many car owners have gone to the trouble of correcting the defect, either temporarily or permanently, at considerable expense to themselves. But I have never found either a mechanic or a car owner who knew the cause of the trouble drivers were having with their cars. Because of this fact I thought it expedient and profitable to take the matter up directly with your company.

"Now the matter that I have to present is this: You will find that the body of all Chevrolet cars that have been driven 200 miles or more is from one inch to three inches lower on the left side of the driver than on his right side. Because of this the left rear fender especially, in driving over fairly rough or wavy streets or in rounding corners to the right, will quite often strike against the tires. This has been the cause of tearing up tires or of suddenly slowing down the car—thereby making accidents likely. The experience is also annoying to the driver and occupants of the car.

"Many drivers seem to think that the springs on the left side were naturally weak and not so good; others seem to think that they struck a bad place in the road and that the springs lost their elasticity as a result. But the fact of the case is that the car is not properly balanced—right side against left side. On the left side you have the steering mechanism, the starter, the generator, and the storage battery. This, together with a one hundred fifty pound (150#) driver, when one drives by himself, throws approximately three hundred pounds (300#) more weight on the left side than on the right side of the car.

"After I had driven my car about 2,800 miles the body was exactly two and three-quarters inches lower on the left side than on the right side. In order to level the body of the car I had an extra spring leaf put into both the front and rear springs on the left side, and that straightened the body up perfectly. My plan is that you either put in this extra spring leaf in both front and rear springs on the left side of the car when you build the car, or else you should change the location of some of the individual units—shifting those units which could be most conveniently moved to the right side of the car or motor. It is my idea that the battery should be moved from the left side to the right side. This would take about fifty pounds from the heavy side and add it to the light side. Then either or both the starter and generator should be moved to the right side of the motor—they would just about balance the weight of the steering unit and the usual excess weight of the driver over his front seat mate.

"The facts given above cannot be denied, and the remedy is simple and clear. I hope you will find them of profit to your firm. I would appreciate a reply at your earliest convenience.

"Respectfully submitted."

To which the New Devices Committee replied:

"Dear Sir: This will acknowledge your letter of July 22 regarding a system for balancing the weight of cars.

"The Committee, at its last meeting, thoroughly discussed your suggestion but decided, unfortunately, that it would not be advisable to redesign our springs in this manner at the present time. We cannot therefore, see our way clear to go into the matter with you further.

"We appreciate your interest in General Motors and regret that we cannot reply to you more favorably.

"Yours very truly,

"New Devices Committee."

It is then alleged in the petition that the plaintiff, by and through these letters, did sell and convey to the defendants ideas as to how to balance a Chevrolet car so that the fenders would not strike the wheels, and more particularly to balance the car so that the weight would be more evenly divided on both sides, and that he forwarded his ideas in the form that defendants had requested, and that thereafter the defendants had put into force and effect the ideas so submitted by the plaintiff, or a portion thereof, and that the defendants had, since the plaintiff's ideas were presented to them, used the same or substantial portions thereof on all Chevrolet motorcars manufactured by the defendants, and by the defendants' request that the plaintiff forward his ideas to them, and by using the same, or portions thereof, there was an implied contract on the part of the defendants to pay to the plaintiff the reasonable value of said ideas, which said reasonable value it is alleged was $2,500,000.

We are of the opinion that the demurrers were properly sustained by the trial court. In the first place we are not persuaded that the idea communicated in the letters of the plaintiff was a novel and useful idea in which plaintiff could successfully assert a property right. In the second place, the correspondence and alleged conduct of the companies controvert the claim that there was a promise to pay plaintiff for the ideas or

suggestions which he transmitted, and there are no circumstances presented from which the law implies such a promise.

It appears from plaintiff's first letter to the companies that it was then
known to many others besides the plaintiff that there was a defect in the
Chevrolet car as it was being manufactured and sold. Plaintiff did not claim
to be the discoverer of this defect in the car. He says: "I, as well as many
others, have had and will still have this error of your designers to overcome
at considerable expense." "Many car owners have gone to the trouble of
correcting this defect." The plaintiff's second letter discloses that the defect
he had in mind was that the body of the car was not held suspended in
balance by the springs with sufficient strength to maintain a constant
equilibrium, but that when the car was used the body would sag down on
the left side. The remedy availed of by himself and others was to reinforce
the springs on the side where the body sagged. This much of the idea being
generally known and common property, the only other idea which the
plaintiff conveyed to the defendants is in the suggestion that the defendants relocate some of the individual units contained in the body of the car
with reference to the center of gravity of the car, "Shift those units which
could be most conveniently moved to the right side of the car or motor."
Plaintiff says: "It is my idea that the battery should be moved from the left
side to the right side. This would take about fifty pounds from the heavy
side and add it to the light side. Then either or both the starter and
generator should be moved to the right side of the motor—they would just
about balance the weight of the steering unit and the usual excess weight
of the driver over his front seat mate."

From these statements it is apparent that the plaintiff did not claim to
know just what shifting of individual units from one side of the car to the
other would be necessary or practicable to effect the proper balance of the
car in use. He recognizes cases when "one is driving by himself and thereby
puts the weight of his body on one side of the car." He reflects the thought
that there is a "usual excess weight of the driver over his front seat mate."
In other words, that, when several passengers are riding in a car, the
weight may not bear evenly on both sides of the center of gravity of the
body of the vehicle. Plaintiff's suggestion really was that the companies
should make experiments in redisposing some of the readily movable units
mounted on the car body and in shifting them from the left to the right
side of the car until a balance was effected which would turn out to be
enduring in use. The plaintiff said, in effect: It is known that your car body
sags lopsidedly to the left when it is being used. I suggest that you try
shifting the units which can be most conveniently moved until you get a
better balance.

Plaintiff did not say that he had made any such experiments himself or
that he knew through experiments what the effect of the suggested shifting
of units would be upon a car when the car was used. Plaintiff alleges that
what the companies did after they got this letter was to shift the battery
from the left side to the right side of the car and also other equipment as
set out in the letter "or a portion thereof." That is, the defendants,

knowing as others knew that the body of their car when the car was used sagged lopsidedly to the left, transposed fifty pounds of batteries to the opposite side and such other movable equipment as they found from experiment (or engineering calculations) sufficed to produce a more effective balance of the car body when the car was in use. The matter would be no clearer or simpler if we had to do with spring wagons or buggies rather than Chevrolet automobiles. The springs of either vehicle have to be strong enough to offset some uneven disposal of weights on the body. The mere idea of experimenting with the disposal of the weights was not novel and useful, and plaintiff had no property right therein.

In Masline v. New York, etc., R. Co., 95 Conn. 702, 112 A. 639, 641, the court stated: "An idea may undoubtedly be protected by contract. But it must be the plaintiff's idea. Upon communication to the defendant it at once did appear that the idea was not original with the plaintiff, but was a matter of common knowledge, well known to the world at large. He had thought of nothing new, and had therefore no property right to protect which would make his idea a basis of consideration for anything. His valuable information was a mere idea, worthless so far as suggesting anything new was concerned, known to every one, to the use of which the defendant had an equal right with himself."

In the second place, the letter of the New Devices Committee of the companies to the plaintiff contains no promise to pay for any mere suggestion or idea which the plaintiff might choose to send them. They said it was against the policy of the companies to make any agreement for inventions until they knew exactly what they were. They suggested that plaintiff establish legal evidence of his ownership of his ideas by having his original drawing notarized. In the first letter plaintiff said: "I, as well as many others, have had and will still have this error of your designers overcome at considerable expense." "The best way out of the difficulty would necessitate a change of design." And, therefore, the committee suggested that plaintiff send drawings and a description of his ideas, and that he establish legal evidence of ownership and priority of his ideas by having his original drawing signed or notarized, and that, if they found the design of sufficient interest to warrant further investigation, some mutually satisfactory agreement would be made.

The clear implication is that the companies did not make any agreement to pay for merely pointing out some defect in the Chevrolet car or for any mere suggestion that they perfect the car by experimentation or improvement of their own working out, but if the plaintiff should submit a design with drawings and descriptions of his ideas, then, if the design was of sufficient interest to warrant investigation, an agreement would be made. As the plaintiff did not submit any "design" or "drawings and description of his ideas" or bring himself within the committee's proposal or offer, he cannot successfully claim a contract, even if he had an idea in which he had a property right and which he could make a subject of barter and sale. The correspondence shows that the minds of the parties never met on any proposed sale of plaintiff's ideas. The law will not imply a promise on the part of any person against his own express declaration. Municipal Waterworks Co. v. City of Ft. Smith (D.C.) 216 F. 431; Landon v. Kansas City Gas Co., 300 F. 351 (D.C.); Boston Ice Co. v. Potter, 123 Mass. 28, 25 Am.Rep. 9; Earle v. Coburn, 130 Mass. 596. In the latter case it is stated: "As the law will not imply a promise, where there was an express promise, so the law will not imply a promise of any person against his own express declaration; because such declaration is repugnant to any implication of a promise."

If, in fact, the defendants did derive benefit from the plaintiff's ideas that the units on their Chevrolet car should be shifted, and if their subsequent redisposal of some of the units to the other side of the car body was in any wise inspired by the plaintiff's idea, nevertheless, they are not indebted to the plaintiff, because they did not offer to make any agreement to pay for such mere suggestion as the plaintiff made, and their correspondence did not invite such a suggestion. When plaintiff voluntarily divulged his mere idea and suggestion, whatever interest he had in it became common property, and, as such, was available to the defendants. In Bristol v. Equitable Life Assur. Soc'y [132 N.Y. 264, 267, 30 N.E. 506, 507] the court stated: "Without denying that there may be property in an idea or trade secret or system, it is obvious that its originator or proprietor must himself protect it from escape or disclosure. If it cannot be sold or negotiated or used without a disclosure, it would seem proper that some contract should guard or regulate the disclosure; otherwise, it must follow the law of ideas, and become the acquisition of whoever receives it."

The judgment is affirmed.

Nadel v. Play-By-Play Toys & Novelties, Inc.

United States Court of Appeals, Second Circuit, 2000.
208 F.3d 368, 54 U.S.P.Q.2d 1810.

SOTOMAYOR, Circuit Judge

Plaintiff-appellant Craig P. Nadel ("Nadel") brought this action against defendant-appellee Play–By–Play Toys & Novelties, Inc. ("Play–By–Play") for breach of contract, quasi contract, and unfair competition. The thrust of Nadel's complaint was that Play–By–Play took his idea for an upright, sound-emitting, spinning plush toy and that, contrary to industry custom, Play–By–Play used the idea in its "Tornado Taz" product without paying him compensation. Play–By–Play also filed several counterclaims against Nadel, alleging that Nadel falsely told other members of the toy industry that Play–By–Play had stolen his idea, thereby harming its ability to receive toy concepts from toy industry members.

For the reasons that follow, we vacate that part of the district court's order granting Play–By–Play's motion for summary judgment and dismissing Nadel's complaint and affirm that part of the district court's order dismissing Play–By–Play's counterclaims.

BACKGROUND

Nadel is a toy idea man. Toy companies regularly do business with independent inventors such as Nadel in order to develop and market new toy concepts as quickly as possible. To facilitate the exchange of ideas, the standard custom and practice in the toy industry calls for companies to treat the submission of an idea as confidential. If the company subsequently uses the disclosed idea, industry custom provides that the company shall compensate the inventor, unless, of course, the disclosed idea was already known to the company.

In 1996, Nadel developed the toy concept at issue in this case. He transplanted the "eccentric mechanism"[1] found in several hanging Halloween toys then on the market—such as "Spooky Skull" and "Shaking Mutant Pumpkin"—and placed the mechanism inside of a plush toy monkey skin to develop the prototype for a new table-top monkey toy. This plush toy figure sat upright, emitted sound, and spun when placed on a flat surface.

In October 1996, Nadel met with Neil Wasserman, an executive at Play–By–Play who was responsible for the development of its plush toy line. According to Nadel, he showed his prototype monkey toy to Wasserman, who expressed interest in adapting the concept to a non-moving, plush Tazmanian Devil toy that Play–By–Play was already producing under license from Warner Bros. Nadel contends that, consistent with industry custom, any ideas that he disclosed to Wasserman during their October 1996 meeting were subject to an agreement by Play–By–Play to keep such ideas confidential and to compensate Nadel in the event of their use.

Nadel claims that he sent his prototype monkey toy to Wasserman as a sample and awaited the "Taz skin" and voice tape, which Wasserman allegedly said he would send, so that Nadel could make a sample spinning/laughing Tazmanian Devil toy for Play–By–Play. Wasserman never provided Nadel with the Taz skin and voice tape, however, and denies ever having received the prototype monkey toy from Nadel.

Notwithstanding Wasserman's denial, his secretary, Melissa Rodriguez, testified that Nadel's prototype monkey toy remained in Wasserman's office for several months. According to Ms. Rodriguez, the monkey toy was usually kept in a glass cabinet behind Wasserman's desk, but she remembered that on one occasion she had seen it on a table in Wasserman's office. Despite Nadel's multiple requests, Wasserman did not return Nadel's prototype monkey toy until February 1997, after Play-by-Play introduced its "Tornado Taz" product at the New York Toy Fair.

The parties do not dispute that "Tornado Taz" has the same general characteristics as Nadel's prototype monkey toy. Like Nadel's toy, Tornado Taz is a plush toy that emits sounds (including "screaming," "laughing,"

---

1. An eccentric mechanism typically consists of a housing containing a motor with an eccentric weight attached to the motor shaft. When the motor is activated, the motor rotates the weight centrifugally, causing the housing to shake or spin.

"snarling," and "grunting"), sits upright, and spins by means of an internal eccentric vibration mechanism.

Nadel claims that, in violation of their alleged agreement, Play–By–Play used his idea without paying him compensation. Play–By–Play contends, however, that it independently developed the Tornado Taz product concept and that Nadel is therefore not entitled to any compensation. Specifically, Play–By–Play maintains that, as early as June or July of 1996, two of its officers—Wasserman and Slattery—met in Hong Kong and began discussing ways to create a spinning or vibrating Tazmanian Devil, including the possible use of an eccentric mechanism. Furthermore, Play–By–Play claims that in late September or early October 1996, it commissioned an outside manufacturing agent—Barter Trading of Hong Kong—to begin developing Tornado Taz.

Play–By–Play also argues that, even if it did use Nadel's idea to develop Tornado Taz, Nadel is not entitled to compensation because Nadel's concept was unoriginal and non-novel to the toy industry in October 1996. In support of this argument, Play–By–Play has submitted evidence of various toys, commercially available prior to October 1996, which used eccentric motors and allegedly contained the same characteristics as Nadel's prototype monkey toy. . . .

DISCUSSION

I. NADEL'S CLAIMS

On January 21, 1999, the district court granted Play–By–Play's motion for summary judgment dismissing Nadel's claims for breach of contract, quasi contract, and unfair competition. Interpreting New York law, the district court stated that "a party is not entitled to recover for theft of an idea unless the idea is novel or original." Nadel v. Play By Play Toys & Novelties, Inc., 34 F.Supp.2d 180, 184 (S.D.N.Y.1999). Applying that principle to Nadel's claims, the district court concluded that, even if the spinning toy concept were novel to Play–By–Play at the time Nadel made the disclosure to Wasserman in October 1996, Nadel's claims must nonetheless fail for lack of novelty or originality because "numerous toys containing the characteristics of [Nadel's] monkey were in existence prior to [ ] October 1996." Id. at 185. In essence, the district court interpreted New York law to require that, when a plaintiff claims that a defendant has either (1) misappropriated his idea (a "property-based claim") or (2) breached an express or implied-in-fact contract by using such idea (a "contract-based claim"), the idea at issue must be original or novel generally. Thus, according to the district court, a finding that an idea was novel as to Play By Play—i.e., novel to the buyer—cannot suffice to sustain any of Nadel's claims.

On appeal, Nadel challenges the district court's conclusion that a showing of novelty to the buyer—i.e., that Nadel's idea was novel to Play–By–Play at the time of his October 1996 disclosure—cannot suffice to sustain his claims for breach of contract, quasi contract, and unfair competition under New York law. Nadel claims, moreover, that the record contains a genuine issue of material fact concerning whether his toy idea was novel to Play–By–Play at the time of his October 1996 disclosure to Wasserman and that the district court therefore erred in granting Play–By–Play's motion for summary judgment.

Nadel's factual allegations present a familiar submission-of-idea case: (1) the parties enter into a pre-disclosure confidentiality agreement; (2) the idea is subsequently disclosed to the prospective buyer; (3) there is no post-disclosure contract for payment based on use; and (4) plaintiff sues defendant for allegedly using the disclosed idea under either a contract-based or property-based theory. For the reasons that follow, we conclude that a finding of novelty as to Play–By–Play can suffice to provide consideration for Nadel's contract claims against Play–By–Play. Accordingly, because we also find that there exists a genuine issue of material fact as to whether Nadel's idea was novel to Play–By–Play at the time of his October 1996 disclosure, we vacate the district court's grant of summary judgment on Nadel's contract claims. With respect to Nadel's misappropriation claim, we similarly vacate the district court's grant of summary judgment and remand for further proceedings to determine whether Nadel's idea was original or novel generally.

A. Submission-of-Idea Cases Under New York Law

Our analysis begins with the New York Court of Appeals' most recent discussion of the law governing idea submission cases, Apfel v. Prudential–Bache Securities, Inc., 81 N.Y.2d 470, 600 N.Y.S.2d 433, 616 N.E.2d 1095 (1993). In *Apfel*, the Court of Appeals discussed the type of novelty an idea must have in order to sustain a contract-based or property-based claim for its uncompensated use. Specifically, *Apfel* clarified an important distinction between the requirement of "novelty to the buyer" for contract claims, on the one hand, and "originality" (or novelty generally) for misappropriation claims, on the other hand.

Under the facts of *Apfel*, the plaintiff disclosed his idea to the defendant pursuant to a confidentiality agreement and, subsequent to disclosure, entered into another agreement wherein the defendant agreed to pay a stipulated price for the idea's use. The defendant used the idea but refused to pay plaintiff pursuant to the post-disclosure agreement on the asserted ground that "no contract existed between the parties because the sale agreement lacked consideration." The defendant argued that an idea could not constitute legally sufficient consideration unless it was original or novel generally and that, because plaintiff's idea was not original or novel generally (it had been in the public domain at the time of the post-disclosure agreement), the idea provided insufficient consideration to support the parties' post-disclosure contract.

In rejecting defendant's argument, the Court of Appeals held that there was sufficient consideration to support plaintiff's contract claim because the idea at issue had value to the defendant at the time the parties concluded their post-disclosure agreement. The *Apfel* court noted that "traditional principles of contract law" provide that parties "are free to make their bargain, even if the consideration exchanged is grossly unequal or of dubious value," and that, so long as the "defendant received something of value" under the contract, the contract would not be void for lack of consideration.

The *Apfel* court explicitly rejected defendant's contention that the court should carve out "an exception to traditional principles of contract law" for submission-of-idea cases by requiring that an idea must also be original or novel generally in order to constitute valid consideration. In essence, the defendant sought to impose a requirement that an idea be novel in absolute terms, as opposed to only the defendant buyer, in order to constitute valid consideration for the bargain. In rejecting this argument, the *Apfel* court clarified the standards for both contract-based and property-based claims in submission-of-idea cases. That analysis guides our decision here....

Moreover, *Apfel* made clear that the "novelty to the buyer" standard is not limited to cases involving an express post-disclosure contract for payment based on an idea's use. The *Apfel* court explicitly discussed the pre-disclosure contract scenario present in the instant case, where "the buyer and seller contract for *disclosure* of the idea with payment based on use, but no separate postdisclosure contract for the *use* of the idea has been made." In such a scenario, a seller might, as Nadel did here, bring an action against a buyer who allegedly used his ideas without payment, claiming both misappropriation of property and breach of an express or implied-in-fact contract. The *Apfel* court recognized that these cases present courts with the difficult problem of determining "whether the idea the buyer was using was, in fact, the seller's." Specifically, the court noted that, with respect to a misappropriation of property claim, it is difficult to "prove that the buyer obtained the idea from [the seller] and nowhere else." With respect to a breach of contract claim, the court noted that it would be inequitable to enforce a contract if "it turns out upon disclosure that the buyer already possessed the idea." The court then concluded that, with respect to these cases, "[a] showing of novelty, at least novelty as to the buyer" should address these problems.

We note, moreover, that the "novelty to the buyer" standard comports with traditional principles of contract law. While an idea may be unoriginal or non-novel in a general sense, it may have substantial value to a particular buyer who is unaware of it and therefore willing to enter into contract to acquire and exploit it....

In contrast to contract-based claims, a misappropriation claim can only arise from the taking of an idea that is original or novel in absolute terms, because the law of property does not protect against the misappropriation or theft of that which is free and available to all.

Finally, although the legal requirements for contract-based claims and property-based claims are well-defined, we note that the determination of novelty in a given case is not always clear. The determination of whether an idea is original or novel depends upon several factors, including, *inter alia,* the idea's specificity or generality (is it a generic concept or one of specific application?), its commonality (how many people know of this idea?), its uniqueness (how different is this idea from generally known ideas?), and its commercial availability (how widespread is the idea's use in the industry?). Thus, for example, a once original or novel idea may become so widely disseminated over the course of time that it enters the body of common knowledge. When this occurs, the idea ceases to be novel or original.

Moreover, in assessing the interrelationship between originality and novelty to the buyer, we note that in some cases an idea may be so unoriginal or lacking in novelty that its obviousness bespeaks widespread and public knowledge of the idea, and such knowledge is therefore imputed to the buyer. In such cases, a court may conclude, as a matter of law, that the idea lacks both the originality necessary to support a misappropriation claim and the novelty to the buyer necessary to support a contract claim....

B. Nadel's Misappropriation Claim

In this case, the district court did not decide whether Nadel's idea—a plush toy that sits upright, emits sounds, and spins on a flat surface by means of an internal eccentric motor—was inherently lacking in originality. We therefore remand this issue to the district court to determine whether Nadel's idea exhibited "genuine novelty or invention" or whether it was "a merely clever or useful adaptation of existing knowledge." *Educational Sales Programs [v. Dreyfus Corp.]*, 317 N.Y.S.2d at 844.

C. Nadel's Contract Claims

Mindful that, under New York law, a finding of novelty as to Play–By–Play will provide sufficient consideration to support Nadel's contract claims, we next consider whether the record exhibits a genuine issue of material fact on this point.

Reading the record in a light most favorable to Nadel, we conclude that there exists a genuine issue of material fact as to whether Nadel's idea was, at the time he disclosed it to Wasserman in early October 1996, novel to Play–By–Play. Notably, the timing of Play–By–Play's development and release of Tornado Taz in relation to Nadel's October 1996 disclosure is, taken alone, highly probative. Moreover, although custom in the toy industry provides that a company shall promptly return all samples if it already possesses (or does not want to use) a disclosed idea, Play–By–Play in this case failed to return Nadel's prototype monkey toy for several months, despite Nadel's multiple requests for its return. According to Wasserman's secretary, Melissa Rodriguez, Nadel's sample was not returned until after the unveiling of "Tornado Taz" at the New York Toy Fair in February 1997. Ms. Rodriguez testified that from October 1996 through February 1997, Nadel's sample was usually kept in a glass cabinet behind Wasserman's desk, and on one occasion, she remembered seeing it on a table in Wasserman's office. These facts give rise to the reasonable inference that Play–By–Play may have used Nadel's prototype as a model for the development of Tornado Taz.

None of the evidence adduced by Play–By–Play compels a finding to the contrary on summary judgment. With regard to the discussions that Play–By–Play purportedly had in June or July of 1996 about possible ways to create a vibrating or spinning Tazmanian Devil toy, those conversations only lasted, according to Mr. Slattery, "a matter of five minutes." Play–By–Play may have "discussed the concept," as Mr. Slattery testified, but the record provides no evidence suggesting that, in June or July of 1996, Play–By–Play understood exactly *how* it could apply eccentric motor technology to make its Tazmanian Devil toy spin rather than, say, vibrate like Tickle Me Elmo. Similarly, although Play–By–Play asserts that it commissioned an outside manufacturing agent—Barter Trading of Hong Kong—to begin developing Tornado Taz in late September or early October of 1996, Play–By–Play admits that it can only "guess" the exact date. Play–By–Play cannot confirm that its commission of Barter Trading pre-dated Nadel's alleged disclosure to Wasserman on or about October 9, 1996. Nor has Play–By–Play produced any documents, technical or otherwise, relating to its purported business venture with Barter Trading or its independent development of a spinning Tornado Taz prior to October 1996. Based on this evidence, a jury could reasonably infer that Play–By–Play actually contacted Barter Trading, if at all, *after* learning of Nadel's product concept, and that Play–By–Play's development of Tornado Taz is attributable to Nadel's disclosure.

We therefore conclude that there exists a genuine issue of material fact as to whether Nadel's idea was, at the time he disclosed it to Wasserman in early October 1996, novel to Play–By–Play. . . .

CONCLUSION

For the foregoing reasons, we affirm that part of the district court's judgment dismissing Play–By–Play's counterclaims. We vacate that part of the district court's judgment granting Play–By–Play's motion for summary judgment and dismissing Nadel's complaint and remand for further proceedings consistent with this opinion.

NOTES

1. *Property.* *"In the first place we are not persuaded that the idea communicated in the letters of the plaintiff was a novel and useful idea in which plaintiff could successfully assert a property right."* [*Lueddecke,* 70 F.2d at 347.]

Idea submitters rarely succeed on a property theory. Any expression of an idea that is sufficiently novel and concrete to qualify for protection as property could probably also qualify for protection under one of the more developed and traditional intellectual property systems such as trade secret or patent law. When courts invoke property doctrine in idea cases it is usually as a gentle way of telling the submitter that he will not recover in his action.

Can trade custom create property rights in ideas? Consider the following passage from Cole v. Phillips H. Lord, Inc., 262 App.Div. 116, 117, 120, 28 N.Y.S.2d 404, 406, 407 (1st Dept.1941), in which plaintiff, who had conceived and communicated to defendant production company the format for a radio series, "Racketeer and Co.," sought to recover a share of the profits from defendant's sale of the series idea under the title, "Mr. District Attorney," to a radio network:

> Plaintiff's testimony and that of the witness Titterton, who was not only disinterested but might have been partial to the defendant by reason of the fact that his employer, National Broadcasting Company, had purchased the rights to defendant's alleged creation, established that in the radio field there is a well recognized right to an original idea or combination of ideas, set forth in a formula for a program. Such program contemplates an indefinite number of broadcasts in a series. Each broadcast has a script which represents a dialogue and 'business' of that particular broadcast. The idea or the combination of ideas formulated into a program remains constant whereas, of course, the script varies in each separate broadcast.
>
> That a property right exists with respect to a combination of ideas evolved into a program as distinguished from rights to particular scripts, finds support in defendant's own course of conduct. When it transferred any rights to Mr. District Attorney, it sold not scripts but the basic idea.

Special trade assumptions can of course also be construed to permit recovery on an implied contract basis as in the *Nadel* case.

On ideas as the subject of property rights, see Andrew Beckerman–Rodau, Are Ideas Within the Traditional Definition of Property?: A Jurisprudential Analysis, 47 Ark. L. Rev. 603 (1994).

2. *Express Contract. "He had thought of nothing new, and had therefore no property right to protect which would make his idea a basis of consideration for anything."* [*Lueddecke,* 70 F.2d at 348, quoting from Masline v. New York, N.H. & H. R. Co., 95 Conn. 702, 112 A. 639 (1921).]

Under the facts of *Masline,* plaintiff, a brakeman and baggage-master on defendant's line, informed defendant "that he had information of value in the operation of the defendant's road by which, if applied by the defendant, it could earn at least $100,000 a year therefrom without any expense on the part of the defendant, and that the plaintiff would furnish the defendant this information for a valuable consideration." Subsequently, plaintiff and defendant orally "agreed that, if the plaintiff would submit his proposition, and if said proposition was adopted and acted upon by the defendant, the plaintiff should receive as compensation for imparting such information," five percent of the receipts. Plaintiff then disclosed the idea that defendant sell advertising space in its cars and railway depots. Defendant promptly implemented the idea but refused to compensate plaintiff. Although the court found that, before plaintiff's disclosure, defendant had never used this type of plan, it found, too, that the idea "was not new . . .

but was perfectly obvious to all men." From this, the court reasoned, the idea "could have no market value so as to form the consideration for a contract ... and that the idea was not property nor did it constitute consideration for a promise." 112 A. at 639, 640.

Should the fact that an idea is insufficiently novel and concrete to qualify as property also disqualify it as contract consideration? Could consideration have been found in plaintiff's bargained-for act of disclosure?

Nadel interpreted New York law to require a limited degree of novelty—novelty to the buyer—for a contract to be enforceable. Should this requirement be confined to implied in fact contracts, as under the facts of *Nadel*, or should it be extended to express contracts as well? Consider the observation by Justice Roger Traynor, dissenting in Stanley v. Columbia Broadcasting System, Inc., 35 Cal.2d 653, 675, 221 P.2d 73, 86 U.S.P.Q. 520 (1950) that even a widely-known idea "may be protected by an express contract providing that it will be paid for regardless of its lack of novelty. An implied-in-fact contract differs from an express contract only in that the promise is not expressed in language but implied from the promisor's conduct. It is not a reasonable assumption, however, in the absence of an express promise, or unequivocal conduct from which one can be implied, that one would obligate himself to pay for an idea that he would otherwise be free to use.... If the idea is not novel, the evidence must establish that the promisor agreed expressly or impliedly to pay for the idea whether or not it was novel."

Could *Masline* have reached the same result by implying into the contract a condition that compensation would be paid only if the disclosed idea were concrete and novel? By finding that defendant had acted not on plaintiff's disclosure but rather on its own general knowledge and initiative?

3. *Contract Implied in Fact. "The correspondence shows that the minds of the parties never met on any proposed sale of plaintiff's ideas. The law will not imply a promise on the part of any person against his own express declaration." [Lueddecke, 70 F.2d at 348.]*

The relationship between the parties is the fact most often examined in determining whether a contract will be implied. If the submitter can show a confidential relationship with the recipient, she has gone far toward making out a case for recovery. Proof of a confidential relationship forms the basis for a series of inferences that can lead logically to the implication of a contract: disclosure of an idea within a confidential relationship indicates that the idea is disclosed in confidence; that the idea is disclosed in confidence indicates that the originator does not intend to divest her rights in it by publication, at least not without compensation; acceptance of the idea by the recipient in confidence suggests his understanding that he is not to publish or otherwise use it without the originator's consent, at least not without compensating her for the use.

Are actions for breach of confidence respecting disclosed ideas properly classified as actions for breach of an implied contract or as tort actions for breach of a confidential relationship? The distinction may be important when it comes to determining the appropriate statute of limitations. See, for example, Davies v. Krasna, 14 Cal.3d 502, 121 Cal.Rptr. 705, 535 P.2d 1161 (1975).

4. *Quasi Contract. "If, in fact, the defendants did derive benefit from the plaintiff's ideas ... nevertheless, they are not indebted to the plaintiff because they did not offer to make any agreement to pay for such mere suggestion as the plaintiff made...."* [*Lueddecke,* 70 F.2d at 348.]

Compare Matarese v. Moore–McCormack Lines, 158 F.2d 631, 71 U.S.P.Q. 311 (2d Cir.1946), which raised the issue "whether a corporation may be required to pay the reasonable value of the use of certain inventive ideas disclosed by an employee to an agent of the corporation in the expectation of payment where an express contract fails for want of proof of the agent's authority." 158 F.2d at 632. The court answered in the affirmative. The agent's "promise of compensation, the specific character, novelty and patentability of plaintiff's invention, the subsequent use made of it by defendants, and the lack of compensation given the plaintiff—all indicate that the application of the principle of unjust enrichment is required." 158 F.2d at 634. The court was careful to distinguish *Lueddecke:* "Courts have justly been assiduous in defeating attempts to delve into the pockets of business firms through spurious claims for compensation for the use of ideas. Thus to be rejected are attempts made by telephoning or writing vague general ideas to business corporations and then seizing upon some later general similarity between their products and the notions propounded as a basis for damages...." 158 F.2d at 634. See also Werlin v. Reader's Digest Ass'n, Inc., 528 F.Supp. 451, 213 U.S.P.Q. 1041 (S.D.N.Y. 1981).

5. *"Novelty" and "Concreteness".* The words "novel" and "concrete" appear in virtually all idea cases and have assumed almost talismanic significance. The terms have nonetheless gained little specific content. Presumably "novel" means the opposite of "common" or, perhaps, "old." "Concrete" is probably the antithesis of "abstract." Beyond this, the decisions offer little guidance. One reason may be that courts apply the two requirements differently depending on the plaintiff's theory of action. Courts apply the novelty and concreteness requirements least rigorously when the cause of action is for breach of an express contract, somewhat more rigorously in implied in fact contract actions, and more rigorously still in quasi-contract and property actions.

Novelty. Nadel listed several factors for the trial court to consider in determining whether the submitted idea was novel: the idea's specificity, commonality, uniqueness and commercial availability. In Murray v. National Broadcasting Co., 844 F.2d 988, 6 U.S.P.Q.2d 1618 (2d Cir.), cert.den., 488 U.S. 955, 109 S.Ct. 391, 102 L.Ed.2d 380 (1988), the Second Circuit Court of Appeals applied New York law to affirm dismissal of a complaint based on the claim that, four years before defendant's introduction of the highly popular "Cosby Show," plaintiff had proposed a similar show starring Cosby to the network. "While NBC's decision to broadcast *The*

Cosby Show unquestionably was innovative in the sense that an intact, nonstereotypical black family had never been portrayed on television before, the mere fact that such a decision had not been made before does not necessarily mean that the idea for the program is itself novel." 844 F.2d at 992. Judge Pratt dissented: "To say, as a matter of law, that an idea is not novel because it already exists in general form, would be to deny governmental protection to any idea previously mentioned anywhere, at any time, by anyone." 844 F.2d at 997.

To the extent that the term "novel" is intended to refer to a specific attribute, such as newness, how well equipped are courts to measure the attribute? Patent law uses the term "novel" in a very precise sense, and assumes that novelty will be determined through systematic searches of prior art in the Patent and Trademark Office and in the relevant technical literature. See pages 407 to 434. Are similar searches possible, or desirable, in the context of submitted ideas?

Concreteness. "The law shies away from according protection to vagueness, and must do so especially in the realm of ideas with the obvious dangers of a contrary rule." Hamilton Nat'l Bank v. Belt, 210 F.2d 706, 708, 99 U.S.P.Q. 388 (D.C.Cir.1953). Plaintiff in *Hamilton* sought to recover for the bank's use of an idea he had submitted for organizing and sponsoring radio broadcasts of student talent shows. In the court's view, "If the idea had been merely to broadcast programs of selected student talent it would have been too general and abstract and perhaps would also have lacked newness and novelty. On the other hand, had the plan been accompanied with a script for each broadcast it would have been sufficiently concrete." 210 F.2d at 709. The court observed that plaintiff's submission fell somewhere between these two poles and affirmed a judgment for plaintiff: "where the plan is for a series of broadcasts the contents of which depend upon selection of talent at different times, a detailed program cannot be presented at the preliminary stages of negotiation." 210 F.2d at 709.

A finding that the submitted idea is novel and concrete will not guarantee recovery even if the other required contract elements are found. For the submitter to recover, the court must also find that the recipient used the idea in its concrete form. Hamilton Bank probably would have escaped liability if it had used Belt's basic idea—a weekly broadcast of student talent—but had varied the trappings from those described in Belt's presentation.

6. *Damages.* The theory of action pursued will determine the measure of damages for idea appropriations. If an express contract is proved, its terms on compensation will govern. For a factually implied contract, the measure will be what the defendant is presumed to have agreed to pay, or the reasonable value of the idea. If recovery is based on quasi contract, recovery will be measured by the defendant's unjust enrichment—its actual profit from the use of the idea. If, on the remand in *Nadel,* plaintiff prevailed on either or both of its claims, what would the measure of recovery have been?

7. *You Can't Cheat an Honest Man.* Since rights to an idea may be lost upon the idea's unguarded communication, an idea submitter is well advised to obtain, prior to disclosure, the recipient's agreement to compensate for use of the idea. But recipients are also—and more often-well-advised. If they encourage the submission of ideas at all, they typically condition receipt upon a release from any obligation to pay for the ideas, whether used or not. Competing considerations of insulation from suit and good public relations make drafting the relevant documents a particularly sensitive task. Consider how one layman botched the job:

> 43 Bock Ave. Aug. 8th 1938
> Newark, N.J., Newark, N.J.

Mr. W.C. Fields:

Dear Bill:

Enclosed find a radio script which I think suits your inimitable style of super-comedy.

To say that I rate you as the greatest of comedians is putting it mildly you old rascal you.

There isn't a greater master of mimicry, buffoonery, or what have you on the stage, radio, or screen.

When you open up your hocus pocus, hipper dipper, strong men weep and pay their income tax.

When I read in a daily paper that a medico tried to limit your liquid refreshment I knew the millenium was here.

Bill without his nourishment.

Egad! What next? Is there no Justice? Gazooks! Must an old Indian fighter turn squaw.

When Goofus, Gufus, Hoofus and Affadufus are allegedly doing comedy on the "air," your very absence and silence is "funny."

You "Old Reprobate."

When are you coming back to us over the "ether" without an operation except on our funny bone.

What's that? "Bill Cody" Fields has retired from the "Fields" of comedy.

Preposterous! Idiotic! Fantastic! Whatever you think the enclosed radio script is worth is O.K. with me "Bill."

Pardon a young man's brashness in addressing you so familiarly, but I know you'll understand.

With sincerest best wishes to you for a long life and happy days.

I remain

> Sincerely yours,
>
> Harry Yadkoe

43 Bock Ave.
Newark, N.J.
September 9, 1938

To which Fields replied:

Mr. Harry Yadkoe
43 Bock Ave.
Newark, N.J.

Dear Harry Yadkoe:

I liked your wheezes and your treatment, which follows along the line I have been giving our dear customers. Thanks for your gay compliments and thanks for the snake story. I shall use it in conjunction with one I have either on the radio or in a picture. I am about to embark on a new radio series and if you would like to submit a couple of scripts gratis and I am able to use them, who knows, both parties being willing, we might enter into a contract. My reason for injecting the vile word "gratis" is that we get so many letters from folks who if we even answer in the negative, immediately begin suit for plagiarism. Whilst we have never had to pay off, they sometimes become irritating no end.

Very truly yours,

W.C. Fields (signed)

W.C. Fields
c/o Beyer & MacArthur Agents Taft Bldg.,
Cor. Hollywood Blvd. & Vine Sts.,
Hollywood Calif.

Plaintiff, who claimed that Fields used several of the submitted gag ideas, received an $8,000 judgment for breach of an implied contract to pay for the reasonable value of the use of his material. Appropriately enough, the movie in which plaintiff's material was used was "You Can't Cheat an Honest Man." Yadkoe v. Fields, 66 Cal.App.2d 150, 151 P.2d 906 (1944).

Reread the form letter involved in Lueddecke v. Chevrolet Motor Co., above, and consider whether, as house counsel for defendant, you would have approved its attempt at courtesy—"it would not be advisable to redesign our springs in this manner at the present time."

B.   LIMITS OF PROTECTION: THE PLACE OF IDEAS IN THE COMPETITIVE PLAN

Aronson v. Quick Point Pencil Co.

Supreme Court of the United States, 1979.
440 U.S. 257, 99 S.Ct. 1096, 59 L.Ed.2d 296, 201 U.S.P.Q. 1.

Mr. Chief Justice BURGER delivered the opinion of the Court.

We granted certiorari to consider whether federal patent law pre-empts state contract law so as to preclude enforcement of a contract to pay royalties to a patent applicant, on sales of articles embodying the putative invention, for so long as the contracting party sells them, if a patent is not granted.

(1)

In October 1955 the petitioner Mrs. Jane Aronson filed an application, Serial No. 542677, for a patent on a new form of keyholder. Although ingenious, the design was so simple that it readily could be copied unless it was protected by patent. In June 1956, while the patent application was pending, Mrs. Aronson negotiated a contract with the respondent, Quick Point Pencil Company, for the manufacture and sale of the keyholder.

The contract was embodied in two documents. In the first, a letter from Quick Point to Mrs. Aronson, Quick Point agreed to pay Mrs. Aronson a royalty of 5% of the selling price in return for "the exclusive right to make and sell keyholders of the type shown in your application, Serial No. 542677." The letter further provided that the parties would consult one another concerning the steps to be taken "[i]n the event of any infringement."

The contract did not require Quick Point to manufacture the keyholder. Mrs. Aronson received a $750 advance on royalties and was entitled to rescind the exclusive license if Quick Point did not sell a million keyholders by the end of 1957. Quick Point retained the right to cancel the agreement whenever "the volume of sales does not meet our expectation." The duration of the agreement was not otherwise prescribed.

A contemporaneous document provided that if Mrs. Aronson's patent application was "not allowed within five (5) years, Quick Point Pencil Co. [would] pay two and one half percent (2½%) of sales ... so long as you [Quick Point] continue to sell same."

In June 1961, when Mrs. Aronson had failed to obtain a patent on the keyholder within the five years specified in the agreement, Quick Point asserted its contractual right to reduce royalty payments to 2½% of sales. In September of that year the Board of Patent Appeals issued a final rejection of the application on the ground that the keyholder was not patentable, and Mrs. Aronson did not appeal. Quick Point continued to pay reduced royalties to her for 14 years thereafter.

The market was more receptive to the keyholder's novelty and utility than the Patent Office. By September 1975 Quick Point had made sales in excess of seven million dollars and paid Mrs. Aronson royalties totalling $203,963.84; sales were continuing to rise. However, while Quick Point was able to pre-empt the market in the earlier years and was long the only manufacturer of the Aronson keyholder, copies began to appear in the late 1960's. Quick Point's competitors, of course, were not required to pay royalties for their use of the design. Quick Point's share of the Aronson keyholder market has declined during the past decade.

(2)

In November 1975 Quick Point commenced an action in the United States District Court for a declaratory judgment, pursuant to 28 U.S.C.A. § 2201, that the royalty agreement was unenforceable. Quick Point asserted that state law which might otherwise make the contract enforceable was preempted by federal patent law. This is the only issue presented to us for decision.

Both parties moved for summary judgment on affidavits, exhibits, and stipulations of fact. The District Court concluded that the "language of the agreement is plain, clear and unequivocal and has no relation as to whether or not a patent is ever granted." Accordingly, it held that the agreement was valid, and that Quick Point was obliged to pay the agreed royalties pursuant to the contract for so long as it manufactured the keyholder.

The Court of Appeals reversed, one judge dissenting. It held that since the parties contracted with reference to a pending patent application, Mrs. Aronson was estopped from denying that patent law principles governed her contract with Quick Point. Although acknowledging that this Court had never decided the precise issue, the Court of Appeals held that our prior decisions regarding patent licenses compelled the conclusion that Quick Point's contract with Mrs. Aronson became unenforceable once she failed to obtain a patent. The court held that a continuing obligation to pay royalties would be contrary to "the strong federal policy favoring the full and free use of ideas in the public domain," Lear Inc. v. Adkins, 395 U.S. 653, 674, 89 S.Ct. 1902, 1913, 23 L.Ed.2d 610 (1969). The court also observed that if Mrs. Aronson actually had obtained a patent, Quick Point would have escaped its royalty obligations either if the patent were held to be invalid, see id., at 674, 89 S.Ct. at 1913, or upon its expiration after 17 years, see Brulotte v. Thys Co., 379 U.S. 29, 85 S.Ct. 176, 13 L.Ed.2d 99 (1964). Accordingly, it concluded that a licensee should be relieved of royalty obligations when the licensor's efforts to obtain a contemplated patent prove unsuccessful.

(3)

On this record it is clear that the parties contracted with full awareness of both the pendency of a patent application and the possibility that a patent might not issue. The clause de-escalating the royalty by half in the event no patent issued within five years makes that crystal clear. Quick Point apparently placed a significant value on exploiting the basic novelty of the device, even if no patent issued; its success demonstrates that this judgment was well founded. Assuming, *arguendo,* that the initial letter and the commitment to pay a 5% royalty was subject to federal patent law, the provision relating to the 2½% royalty was explicitly independent of federal law. The cases and principles relied on by the Court of Appeals and Quick Point do not bear on a contract that does not rely on a patent, particularly where, as here, the contracting parties agreed expressly as to alternative obligations if no patent should issue.

Commercial agreements traditionally are the domain of state law. State law is not displaced merely because the contract relates to intellectual property which may or may not be patentable; the states are free to regulate the use of such intellectual property in any manner not inconsistent with federal law. Kewanee Oil Co. v. Bicron Corp., 416 U.S. 470, 479, 94 S.Ct. 1879, 1885, 40 L.Ed.2d 315 (1974); see Goldstein v. California, 412 U.S. 546, 93 S.Ct. 2303, 37 L.Ed.2d 163 (1973). In this as in other fields, the question of whether federal law pre-empts state law "involves a consideration of whether that law 'stands as an obstacle to the accomplishment and execution of the full purposes and objectives of Congress.' Hines v. Davidowitz, 312 U.S. 52, 67 (1941)." *Kewanee Oil Co.,* supra. If it does not, state law governs.

In *Kewanee Oil Co.,* supra, 416 U.S. at 480–481, 94 S.Ct. at 1885–1886, we reviewed the purposes of the federal patent system. First, patent law seeks to foster and reward invention; second, it promotes disclosure of inventions, to stimulate further innovation and to permit the public to practice the invention once the patent expires; third, the stringent requirements for patent protection seek to assure that ideas in the public domain remain there for the free use of the public.

Enforcement of Quick Point's agreement with Mrs. Aronson is not inconsistent with any of these aims. Permitting inventors to make enforceable agreements licensing the use of their inventions in return for royalties provides an additional incentive to invention. Similarly, encouraging Mrs. Aronson to make arrangements for the manufacture of her keyholder furthers the federal policy of disclosure of inventions; these simple devices display the novel idea which they embody wherever they are seen.

Quick Point argues that enforcement of such contracts conflicts with the federal policy against withdrawing ideas from the public domain and discourages recourse to the federal patent system by allowing states to extend "perpetual protection to articles too lacking in novelty to merit any patent at all under federal constitutional standards," Sears, Roebuck & Co. v. Stiffel Co., 376 U.S. 225, 232, 84 S.Ct. 784, 789, 11 L.Ed.2d 661 (1964).

We find no merit in this contention. Enforcement of the agreement does not withdraw any idea from the public domain. The design for the keyholder was not in the public domain before Quick Point obtained its license to manufacture it. In negotiating the agreement, Mrs. Aronson disclosed the design in confidence. Had Quick Point tried to exploit the design in breach of that confidence, it would have risked legal liability. It is equally clear that the design entered the public domain as a result of the manufacture and sale of the keyholders under the contract.

Requiring Quick Point to bear the burden of royalties for the use of the design is no more inconsistent with federal patent law than any of the other costs involved in being the first to introduce a new product to the market, such as outlays for research and development and marketing and promotional expenses. For reasons which Quick Point's experience with the Aronson keyholder demonstrate, innovative entrepreneurs have usually found such costs to be well worth paying.

Finally, enforcement of this agreement does not discourage anyone from seeking a patent. Mrs. Aronson attempted to obtain a patent for over five years. It is quite true that had she succeeded, she would have received a 5% royalty only on keyholders sold during the 17–year life of the patent. Offsetting the limited terms of royalty payments, she would have received twice as much per dollar of Quick Point's sales, and both she and Quick Point could have licensed any others who produced the same keyholder. Which course would have produced the greater yield to the contracting parties is a matter of speculation; the parties resolved the uncertainties by their bargain.

(4)

No decision of this Court relating to patents justifies relieving Quick Point of its contract obligations. We have held that a state may not forbid the copying of an idea in the public domain which does not meet the requirements for federal patent protection. Compco Corp. v. Day–Brite Lighting, Inc., 376 U.S. 234, 84 S.Ct. 779, 11 L.Ed.2d 669 (1964); Sears, Roebuck & Co. v. Stiffel Co., 376 U.S. 225, 84 S.Ct. 784, 11 L.Ed.2d 661 (1964). Enforcement of Quick Point's agreement, however, does not prevent anyone from copying the keyholder. It merely requires Quick Point to pay the consideration which it promised in return for the use of a novel device which enabled it to preempt the market.

In Lear, Inc. v. Adkins, 395 U.S. 653, 89 S.Ct. 1902, 23 L.Ed.2d 610 (1969), we held that a person licensed to use a patent may challenge the validity of the patent, and that a licensee who establishes that the patent is invalid need not pay the royalties accrued under the licensing agreement subsequent to the issuance of the patent. Both holdings relied on the desirability of encouraging licensees to challenge the validity of patents, to further the strong federal policy that only inventions which meet the rigorous requirements of patentability shall be withdrawn from the public domain. Accordingly, neither the holding nor the rationale of *Lear* controls when no patent has issued, and no ideas have been withdrawn from public use.

Enforcement of the royalty agreement here is also consistent with the principles treated in Brulotte v. Thys Co., 379 U.S. 29, 85 S.Ct. 176, 13 L.Ed.2d 99 (1964). There, we held that the obligation to pay royalties in return for the use of a patented device may not extend beyond the life of the patent. The principle underlying that holding was simply that the monopoly granted *under a patent* cannot lawfully be used to "negotiate with the leverage of that monopoly." The Court emphasized that to "use that leverage to project those royalty payments beyond the life of the patent is analogous to an effort to enlarge the monopoly of a patent...." Id., at 33, 85 S.Ct., at 179. Here the reduced royalty which is challenged, far from being negotiated "with the leverage" of a patent, rested on the contingency that no patent would issue within five years.

No doubt a pending patent application gives the applicant some additional bargaining power for purposes of negotiating a royalty agreement.

The pending application allows the inventor to hold out the hope of an exclusive right to exploit the idea, as well as the threat that the other party will be prevented from using the idea for 17 years. However, the amount of leverage arising from a patent application depends on how likely the parties consider it to be that a valid patent will issue. Here, where no patent ever issued, the record is entirely clear that the parties assigned a substantial likelihood to that contingency, since they specifically provided for a reduced royalty in the event no patent issued within five years.

This case does not require us to draw the line between what constitutes abuse of a pending application and what does not. It is clear that whatever role the pending application played in the negotiation of the 5% royalty, it played no part in the contract to pay the 2½% royalty indefinitely.

Our holding in *Kewanee Oil Co.,* supra, puts to rest the contention that federal law pre-empts and renders unenforceable the contract made by these parties. There we held that state law forbidding the misappropriation of trade secrets was not preempted by federal patent law. We observed:

> Certainly the patent policy of encouraging invention is not disturbed by the existence of another form of incentive to invention. In this respect the two systems [patent and trade secret law] are not and never would be in conflict. Id., 416 U.S., at 484, 94 S.Ct., at 1887.

Enforcement of this royalty agreement is even less offensive to federal patent policies than state law protecting trade secrets. The most commonly accepted definition of trade secrets is restricted to confidential information which is not disclosed in the normal process of exploitation. See Restatement of Torts § 757, comment b (1939). Accordingly, the exploitation of trade secrets under state law may not satisfy the federal policy in favor of disclosure, whereas disclosure is inescapable in exploiting a device like the Aronson keyholder.

Enforcement of these contractual obligations, freely undertaken in arm's length negotiation and with no fixed reliance on a patent or a probable patent grant, will:

> encourage invention in areas where patent law does not reach, and will prompt the independent innovator to proceed with the discovery and exploitation of his invention. Competition is fostered and the public is not deprived of the use of valuable, if not quite patentable, invention. [Footnote omitted.] Id., at 485, 94 S.Ct., at 1888.

The device which is the subject of this contract ceased to have any secrecy as soon as it was first marketed, yet when the contract was negotiated the inventiveness and novelty were sufficiently apparent to induce an experienced novelty manufacturer to agree to pay for the opportunity to be first in the market. Federal patent law is not a barrier to such a contract.

Reversed.

Mr. Justice BLACKMUN, concurring in the result.

For me, the hard question is whether this case can meaningfully be distinguished from Brulotte v. Thys Co., 379 U.S. 29, 85 S.Ct. 176, 13

L.Ed.2d 99 (1964). There the Court held a patent licensor could not use the leverage of its patent to obtain a royalty contract that extended beyond the patent's 17–year term. Here Mrs. Aronson has used the leverage of her patent application to negotiate a royalty contract which continues to be binding even though the patent application was long ago denied.

The Court asserts that her leverage played "no part" with respect to the contingent agreement to pay a reduced royalty if no patent issued within five years. Yet it may well be that Quick Point agreed to that contingency in order to obtain its other rights that depended on the success of the patent application. The parties did not apportion consideration in the neat fashion the Court adopts.

In my view, the holding in *Brulotte* reflects hostility toward extension of a patent monopoly whose term is fixed by statute, 35 U.S.C.A. § 154. Such hostility has no place here. A patent application which is later denied temporarily discourages unlicensed imitators. Its benefits and hazards are of a different magnitude from those of a granted patent that prohibits all competition for 17 years. Nothing justifies estopping a patent application licensor from entering into a contract whose term does not end if the application fails. The Court points out that enforcement of this contract does not conflict with the objectives of the patent laws. The United States, as *amicus curiae*, maintains that patent application licensing of this sort is desirable because it encourages patent applications, promotes early disclosure, and allows parties to structure their bargains efficiently.

On this basis, I concur in the Court's holding that federal patent law does not pre-empt the enforcement of Mrs. Aronson's contract with Quick Point.

NOTES

1. Is *Aronson* a blanket endorsement of state idea protection? What if, instead of express contract, the state law ground for recovery had been contract implied in fact? Quasi contract? Property? What are the different market effects of each of these doctrines? Did the Court's rationale indicate a line between those state doctrines whose market effects are tolerable and those that are not?

2. Section 301 of the Copyright Act will preempt a state law if three conditions are met: the work protected by the state law is "fixed in a tangible medium of expression;" the work comes "within the subject matter of copyright;" and the state law grants a right that is "equivalent to any of the exclusive rights within the general scope of copyright." State law protection of ideas characteristically escapes preemption under section 301. If the idea's creator communicated the idea orally, the work will not have been fixed in a tangible medium of expression. Even if the idea is tangibly fixed, ideas fall outside the subject matter of copyright. Finally, state contract rights are not equivalent to any of the rights conferred by the Copyright Act.

Section 301 is discussed in detail at pages 793 to 802, below.

II. UNFAIR COMPETITION

Unfair competition law embraces a continuum of deceptive conduct, from passing off to trademark infringement. When a customer orders Coca-Cola at a lunch counter and is instead served a glass of Brand X cola, the tort committed by the server is passing off. When X Company bottles its Brand X drink in containers bearing the Coca-Cola name, the tort is trademark infringement. These two doctrines, passing off and trademark infringement, are closely and sometimes inseparably connected, and both address essentially the same injuries: the injury to consumers who get a product different from the one they expected, and the injury to producers—Coca Cola in the example—that lose sales they would otherwise have made. The differences between the two doctrines are primarily historical and jurisdictional.

Historically, passing off is the seminal doctrine. The starting point was the common law of deceit, from which courts in both England and the United States gradually evolved a distinct tort of passing off. An action for passing off would lie if the plaintiff could prove that the defendant had used plaintiff's name or brand to deceive consumers into thinking that plaintiff was the source of defendant's goods. Intent to deceive was the gravamen of passing off and remains so today in unfair competition cases in which the plaintiff's symbol is descriptive or otherwise weak. In cases where plaintiff's symbol was arbitrary or otherwise highly distinctive, courts came to insist less on proof of fraudulent intent; the fact that defendant had copied a distinctive mark was itself evidence of an intent to deceive. State common law was the source of substantive protection for these distinctive marks, and the first United States trademark statute, Act of July 8, 1870, ch. 230, 16 Stat. 198, provided for their registration on a single federal register.

Unfair competition remained the province of state law, while trademark became mainly the province of federal law. By the mid-twentieth century, however, most states had enacted their own trademark registration statutes, and many have enacted antidilution statutes giving trademark-like protection to distinctive symbols apart from evidence of consumer confusion as to source. The federal Lanham Act, enacted in 1946, created a federal law of unfair competition that substantially parallels state unfair competition law. State antidilution laws are discussed beginning at page 72, below. The Lanham Act's unfair competition provision, section 43(a), is discussed beginning at page 368, below. Part 3, Chapter I covers the federal law of trademarks and their statutory companions—service marks, collective marks and certification marks.

Unfair competition is today both a supplement to federal trademark law (it is the rare trademark lawsuit that does not have at least one count for unfair competition) and a significant doctrine in its own right. State unfair competition law has been an important source of restitutionary measures not recognized under federal law—misappropriation doctrine, page 81, below is the most prominent example. On May 11, 1993, the American Law Institute adopted and promulgated its Restatement of the Law Third, Unfair Competition. The Unfair Competition Restatement encompasses not only the traditional rubrics—passing off and trademark infringement—but also deceptive advertising, trade secret theft and infringement of the right of publicity.

Bibliographic Note. J. Thomas McCarthy, McCarthy on Trademarks and Unfair Competition (4th ed. 1996) and Rudolf Callmann, The Law of Unfair Competition, Trademarks and Monopolies (L. Altman, 4th ed. 1981) are the leading treatises on unfair competition law. State Trademark and Unfair Competition Law (1989), edited by the International Trademark Association, compiles the trademark and unfair competition laws of all fifty states and the District of Columbia and Puerto Rico.

The history of unfair competition law is summarized in Zechariah Chafee, Jr. Unfair Competition, 53 Harv. L. Rev. 1289 (1940) and is exhaustively considered in Frank I. Schechter, The Historical Foundations of the Law Relating to Trade–Marks (1925).

A.   Tʜᴇᴏʀʏ ᴏꜰ Pʀᴏᴛᴇᴄᴛɪᴏɴ

1.   PASSING OFF AND SECONDARY MEANING

William R. Warner & Co. v. Eli Lilly & Co.

Supreme Court of the United States, 1924.
265 U.S. 526, 44 S.Ct. 615, 68 L.Ed. 1161.

Mr. Justice SUTHERLAND delivered the opinion of the Court.

Respondent is a corporation engaged in the manufacture and sale of pharmaceutical and chemical products. In 1899 it began and has ever since continued to make and sell a liquid preparation of quinine, in combination with other substances, including yerba-santa and chocolate, under the name of Coco–Quinine.

Petitioner also is a pharmaceutical and chemical manufacturer. The Pfeiffer Chemical Company, Searle & Hereth Company and petitioner are under the same ownership and control. The first named company in 1906 began the manufacture of a liquid preparation which is substantially the same as respondent's preparation and which was put upon the market under the name of Quin–Coco. Two years later the Searle & Hereth Company engaged in the manufacture of the preparation, which ever since has been sold and distributed by petitioner.

This suit was brought in the Federal District Court for the Eastern District of Pennsylvania by respondent to enjoin petitioner from continuing to manufacture and sell the preparation if flavored or colored with chocolate; and also from using the name Quin–Coco, on the ground that it was an infringement of the name Coco–Quinine, to the use of which respondent had acquired an exclusive right. The District Court decided against respondent upon both grounds. On appeal the Court of Appeals ruled with the District Court upon the issue of infringement but reversed the decree upon that of unfair competition.

The entire record is here and both questions are open for consideration.

First. We agree with the courts below that the charge of [trademark] infringement was not sustained. The name Coco–Quinine is descriptive of the ingredients which enter into the preparation. The same is equally true of the name Quin–Coco. A name which is merely descriptive of the ingredients, qualities or characteristics of an article of trade cannot be appropriated as a trademark and the exclusive use of it afforded legal protection. The use of a similar name by another to truthfully describe his own product does not constitute a legal or moral wrong, even if its effect be to cause the public to mistake the origin or ownership of the product.

Second. The issue of unfair competition, on which the courts below differed, presents a question of more difficulty. The testimony is voluminous, more than two hundred witnesses having been examined; but, since the question with which we are now dealing is primarily one of fact, we have found it necessary to examine and consider it. Nothing is to be gained by reviewing the evidence at length, and we shall do no more than summarize the facts upon which we have reached our conclusions.

The use of chocolate as an ingredient has a three-fold effect: It imparts to the preparation a distinctive color and a distinctive flavor, and, to some extent, operates as a medium to suspend the quinine and prevent its precipitation. It has no therapeutic value; but it supplies the mixture with a quality of palatability for which there is no equally satisfactory substitute. Respondent, by laboratory experiments, first developed the idea of the addition of chocolate to the preparation for the purpose of giving it a characteristic color and an agreeable flavor. There was at the time no liquid preparation of quinine on the market containing chocolate, though there is evidence that it was sometimes so made up by druggists when called for. There is some evidence that petitioner endeavored by experiments to produce a preparation of the exact color and taste of that produced by respondent; and there is evidence in contradiction. We do not, however, regard it as important to determine upon which side lies the greater weight. Petitioner, in fact, did produce a preparation by the use of chocolate so exactly like that of respondent that they were incapable of being distinguished by ordinary sight or taste. By various trade methods an extensive and valuable market for the sale of respondent's preparation already had been established when the preparation of petitioner was put on the market. It is apparent, from a consideration of the testimony, that the efforts of petitioner to create a market for Quin–Coco were directed not so much to showing the merits of that preparation as they were to demonstrating its practical identity with Coco–Quinine, and, since it was sold at a lower price, inducing the purchasing druggist, in his own interest, to substitute, as far as he could, the former for the latter. In other words, petitioner sought to avail itself of the favorable repute which had been established for respondent's preparation in order to sell its own. Petitioner's salesmen appeared more anxious to convince the druggists with whom they were dealing that Quin–Coco was a good substitute for Coco–Quinine and was cheaper, than they were to independently demonstrate its merits. The evidence establishes by a fair preponderance that some of petitioner's salesmen suggested that, without danger of detection, prescriptions and orders for Coco–Quinine could be filled by substituting Quin–Coco. More often, however, the feasibility of such a course was brought to the mind of the druggist by pointing out the identity of the two preparations and the enhanced profit to be made by selling Quin–Coco because of its lower price. There is much conflict in the testimony; but on the whole it fairly appears that petitioner's agents induced the substitution, either in direct terms or by suggestion or insinuation. Sales to druggists are in original bottles bearing clearly distinguishing labels and there is no suggestion of deception in those transactions; but sales to the ultimate purchasers are of the product in its naked form out of the bottle; and the testimony discloses many instances of passing off by retail druggists of petitioner's preparation when respondent's preparation was called for. That no deception was practiced on the retail dealers, and that they knew exactly what they were getting is of no consequence. The wrong was in designedly enabling the dealers to palm off the preparation as that of the respondent. One who induces another to commit a fraud and furnishes the means of consummating it is equally guilty and liable for the injury.

The charge of unfair competition being established, it follows that equity will afford relief by injunction to prevent such unfair competition for the future. Several acts of unfair competition having been shown, we are warranted in concluding that petitioner is willing to continue that course of conduct, unless restrained. It remains to consider the character and extent of this relief.

Respondent has no exclusive right to the use of its formula. Chocolate is used as an ingredient not alone for the purpose of imparting a distinctive color, but for the purpose also of making the preparation peculiarly agreeable to the palate, to say nothing of its effect as a suspending medium. While it is not a medicinal element in the preparation, it serves a substantial and desirable use, which prevents it from being a mere matter of dress. It does not merely serve the incidental use of identifying the respondent's preparation, and it is doubtful whether it should be called a non-essential. The petitioner or anyone else is at liberty under the law to manufacture and market an exactly similar preparation containing chocolate and to notify the public that it is being done. But the imitator of another's goods must sell them as his own production. He cannot lawfully palm them off on the public as the goods of his competitor. The manufacturer or vendor is entitled to the reputation which his goods have acquired and the public to the means of distinguishing between them and other goods; and protection is accorded against unfair dealing whether there be a technical trademark or not. The wrong is in the sale of the goods of one manufacturer or vendor as those of another. If petitioner had been content to manufacture the preparation and let it make its own way in the field of open and fair competition, there would be nothing more to be said. It was not thus content, however, but availed itself of unfair means, either expressly or tacitly, to impose its preparation on the ultimate purchaser as and for the product of respondent.

Nevertheless, the right to which respondent is entitled is that of being protected against unfair competition, not of having the aid of a decree to create or support, or assist in creating or supporting, a monopoly of the sale of a preparation which everyone, including petitioner, is free to make and vend. The legal wrong does not consist in the mere use of chocolate as an ingredient, but in the unfair and fraudulent advantage which is taken of such use to pass off the product as that of respondent. The use dissociated from the fraud is entirely lawful, and it is against the fraud that the injunction lies. But respondent being entitled to relief, is entitled to effective relief; and any doubt in respect of the extent thereof must be resolved in its favor as the innocent producer and against the petitioner, which has shown by its conduct that it is not to be trusted. Clearly, the relief should extend far enough to enjoin petitioner, and its various agents from, directly or indirectly, representing or suggesting to its customers the feasibility or possibility of passing off Quin–Coco for Coco–Quinine. The Court of Appeals held that petitioner should be unconditionally enjoined from the use of chocolate. We think this goes too far; but, having regard to the past conduct of petitioner, the practices of some druggists to which it has led, and the right of respondent to an effective remedy, we think the decree fairly may require that the original packages sold to druggists shall not only bear labels clearly distinguishing petitioner's bottled product from the bottled product of respondent, but that these labels shall state affirmatively that the preparation is not to be sold or dispensed as Coco–Quinine or be used in filling prescriptions or orders calling for the latter. With these general suggestions, the details and form of the injunction can be more satisfactorily determined by the District Court. The decree of the Court of Appeals is reversed and the cause remanded to the District Court for further proceedings in conformity with this opinion.

Reversed.

CHARCOAL STEAK HOUSE OF CHARLOTTE, INC. v. STALEY, 263 N.C. 199, 139 S.E.2d 185, 144 U.S.P.Q. 241 (1964). SHARP, J.: Although a generic word or a geographic designation cannot become an arbitrary trademark, it may nevertheless be used deceptively by a newcomer to the field so as to amount to unfair competition, and the prohibition against any right to the exclusive use of such a word or designation has been modified by the "secondary meaning" doctrine. This was fashioned to protect the public from deception, and is but one facet of the law of unfair competition.

When a particular business has used words publici juris for so long or so exclusively or when it has promoted its product to such an extent that the words do not register their literal meaning on the public mind but are instantly associated with one enterprise, such words have attained a secondary meaning. This is to say, a secondary meaning exists when in addition to their literal, or dictionary, meaning, words connote to the public a product *from a unique source*. It has been suggested, however, that when a descriptive word or phrase has come to mean a particular entrepreneur, the term *secondary meaning* is inaccurate because, in the field in which the phrase has acquired its new meaning, its so-called secondary meaning has become its primary, or natural, meaning.

The law will afford protection against the tortious appropriation of trade names and trademarks alike. To establish a secondary meaning for either, a plaintiff must show that it has come to stand for his business in the public mind, that is, "that the primary significance of the term in the minds of the consuming public is not the product but the producer." Kellogg Co. v. Nat. Biscuit Co., 305 U.S. 111, 118, 59 S.Ct. 109, 113, 83 L.Ed. 73, 78, 39 U.S.P.Q. 296, 299. But even though generic, or descriptive, words, when used alone, have come to have a secondary meaning, "a competitor may nevertheless use them if he accompanies their use with something which will adequately show that the first person or his product is not meant." Union Oyster House v. Hi Ho Oyster House, supra, 316 Mass. at 544, 55 N.E.2d at 943, 62 U.S.P.Q. at 218.

NOTES

1. *The Calculus of Passing Off.* Unfair competition law seeks to accommodate the interest of businesses in choosing and investing in symbols that will capture their goodwill, and the interest of consumers in being free from confusion about the source of goods and services, by protecting (a) the first to use a name, brand or other symbol in connection with the sale of goods or services against (b) another competitor whose subsequent use of the symbol (c) confuses, or is likely to confuse, consumers into believing that the first user, rather than the competitor, is the source of the goods or services. The three elements are matters of degree, and each reciprocates the other two. Some typical unfair competition cases will illustrate this reciprocal relationship.

In the first case, *A*'s symbol or device has, because of its descriptiveness or brevity of use, acquired no secondary meaning—no capacity to identify *A* as a source of goods or services. For *A* to prevail, it must prove that competitor *B* actively palmed off its goods or services as coming from *A* and, by word or deed, deceived consumers as to source. *A* must also show that this conduct in fact confused consumers as to the source of the goods or services.

In the second case, *A*'s symbol or device, though descriptive or otherwise common, also possesses secondary meaning. Neither *B*'s conscious intent to deceive, nor actual deception of consumers need be shown in this case, only the likelihood that *B*'s use of the symbol or device will deceive consumers as to source.

In the third case, *A* has adopted a distinctive, nondescriptive symbol or device that functions exclusively to identify *A* as the source. Here courts will conclusively presume that *B's* use of the symbol was intended to—and did—cause consumer confusion. Given the abundance of alternative symbols and other insignia available for adoption by *B*, courts will presume that *B's* use of a facsimile could only have been motivated by an intent to deceive and was in fact successful in accomplishing the deception.

In any of these three situations, the symbol or device used by competitor *B* need not be identical to the first user *A's* symbol or device. However, the closer the similarity between the two, the greater is the probability that a court will infer deception.

2. *Use*. To obtain and maintain protection under unfair competition law, a name or other symbol must actually be used in business. Names cannot be reserved for future use. In one case, for example, a court refused to enjoin the use of "Galt House" as the name of a hotel in Louisville, Kentucky since plaintiff, incorporated a few years earlier as Galt House, Inc., had taken no steps to use the name on a hotel or, indeed, on any other operating business. Galt House, Inc. v. Home Supply Co., 483 S.W.2d 107, 174 U.S.P.Q. 268 (1972). More typically, the use requirement will constrain a business that uses a name or symbol in one geographic or product market from securing rights in markets it has not yet entered.

The rationale for the use requirement is that since a business's name or symbol does not identify it in markets it has not yet entered, the use of the name or symbol in those markets by a later user would not confuse consumers as to source nor would it divert trade from the business. Indeed, one consequence of the use requirement is that the later user would gain exclusive rights to the symbol in these markets. How can the use requirement be administered in a world of highly mobile consumers and Internet users who transport symbols, goods and services from one region to another? In a world in which firms, seeking to capitalize on the symbols and goodwill associated with one line of goods or services, plan to use the same symbol in connection with different goods or services? These questions lie at the heart of two doctrinal departures from unfair competition law's traditional reliance on the use requirement, the zone of expansion doctrine and dilution doctrine, considered respectively at pages 65 and 72 below.

3. *Nondeceptive References*. Can a competitor that has lawfully copied a product refer to that product's trademark in its own advertising for the purpose of identifying the content of its product? In Smith v. Chanel, Inc., 402 F.2d 562, 159 U.S.P.Q. 388 (9th Cir.1968), the court held that appellant, which advertised its less costly fragrance as an exact duplicate of plaintiff's "Chanel No. 5," could use the trademark for this purpose "and that such advertising may not be enjoined under either the Lanham Act, 15 U.S.C.A. § 1125(a), or the common law of unfair competition, so long as it does not contain misrepresentations or create a reasonable likelihood that purchasers will be confused as to the source, identity, or sponsorship of the advertiser's product." 402 F.2d 562, 563. On remand, the district court found that defendant's fragrance was not in fact an exact duplicate of Chanel No. 5 and concluded that his advertising thus involved a misrepresentation. Chanel, Inc. v. Smith, 178 U.S.P.Q. 630 (N.D.Cal.1973), aff'd, 528 F.2d 284 (9th Cir.1976).

Why would a consumer pay for a prestige product when an exact duplicate, identified as such, is available for half the price? Is the rule of Smith v. Chanel a complete response to critics who argue that unfair competition and trademark law improperly grant protection to prestige values that have nothing to do with product information? See page 23, above.

4. *Injunctions.* Unfair competition injunctions are limited only by the judicial imagination. A court may enjoin the defendant from making any use of the plaintiff's trade insignia, or only require the defendant to include disclaimers indicating the true source of its goods or services. One court order called for the local telephone company to delete defendant's name from future directories and to place intercepts on its present telephone number so that operators could query callers as to whether they were interested in the services of plaintiff or defendant, and relay calls accordingly. Vocational Personnel Services, Inc. v. Statistical Tabulating Corp., 305 F.Supp. 701, 163 U.S.P.Q. 55 (D.Minn.1969). Another court required the defendant not only to deliver up for destruction offending materials in its own possession, but also to recall offending materials from distributors. The court recognized that the recall provision was "an unusual, and perhaps unprecedented, remedy for a violation of New York's law of unfair competition," but concluded that it was "well within the district court's broad powers as a court of equity." Perfect Fit Industries, Inc. v. Acme Quilting Co., Inc., 646 F.2d 800, 805, 210 U.S.P.Q. 175, 179 (2d Cir.1981), cert. denied, 459 U.S. 832, 103 S.Ct. 73, 74 L.Ed.2d 71 (1982).

5. *Monetary Awards.* Courts will usually award monetary relief—damages and accounting of profits—against unfair competition only if the defendant acted willfully or fraudulently. The formula for each remedy is relatively straightforward. The accounting measure entitles the plaintiff to all profits that the defendant earned from its unfair conduct. The defendant has the burden of apportioning its total profits between those that were consequential and those that it earned independent of its unfair competition; the defendant also bears the burden of proving deductions from profits such as manufacturing and selling costs. Under the damage measure, the plaintiff bears the burden of proving losses attributable to defendant's conduct— losses, for example, resulting from reductions in sales or prices, or from injury to its business reputation.

The general rule, that if a plaintiff is entitled to one of these two measures it is entitled to both, creates a risk of overcompensation. If plaintiff and defendant are direct competitors, an award of defendant's profits as well as damages for plaintiff's lost profits would give the plaintiff a punitive double recovery. Recognizing this, courts have in these cases allowed the accounting but confined damages to items independent of lost sales, such as price reductions and advertising outlays required to combat the defendant's activity. Where the defendant's conduct has been notably oppressive, courts may separately award punitive damages.

In a small number of cases, courts have given successful unfair competition plaintiffs an award measured by the cost of advertising that the plaintiff would have to undertake to dispel the consumer confusion created by the defendant's conduct. The leading case, Big O Tire Dealers, Inc. v. Goodyear Tire & Rubber Co., 561 F.2d 1365, 195 U.S.P.Q. 417 (10th Cir.1977), cert. dismissed, 434 U.S. 1052, 98 S.Ct. 905, 54 L.Ed.2d 805 (1978), held that the plaintiff was entitled to compensatory damages restoring it to its economic position before the defendant began its advertising campaign. The court computed these damages by multiplying the amount ($9,690,029) that defendant had spent on its national advertising campaign by a fraction (28%) representing the proportional number of states (14 out of 50) in which plaintiff sold its goods. The court then reduced this figure by 75%, following a rule of thumb employed by the Federal Trade Commission in corrective advertising cases, on the theory that every dollar spent in misleading advertising requires no more than a 25% outlay to dispel its effects. 561 F.2d at 1375–76.

6. *Unfair Competition Abroad.* Foreign legal systems, most notably on the European Continent, have been far more adventurous than the American legal system in evolving a general theory of unfair competition. The late Eugen Ulmer identified the goal in continental jurisprudence of protecting "the honest trader in having the right to restrain his competitors from causing him injury by unfair conduct. The test was whether a competitor's conduct complied with 'honest usages' of the trade, the 'usages honnêtes' (Article 10*bis* Paris Convention), the 'correttezza professionale' (Article 2598 Codice Civile) or the 'bonos mores' ('gute Sitten') in the course of trade (Article 1, German Law against Unfair Competition 1909)." Friedrich–Karl Beier, The Law of Unfair Competition in the European Community—Its Development and Present Status, 7 E.I.P.R. 284 (1985).

Under the general rubric of "honest usages" of trade, European courts have barred not only passing off and misrepresentation, but comparative advertising such as encouraging Opel owners to trade in their "good old Opels" for "a comfortable Granada" (Germany); sales below cost plus a reasonable mark-up (Italy); sales of software designed to circumvent anti-copying protection embodied in other software (France); and sale of decoders for subscription television. (Netherlands). See Aidan Robertson & Audrey Horton, Does the United Kingdom or the European Community Need an Unfair Competition Law? 17 E.I.P.R. 568, 575 (1995).

2. ZONE OF EXPANSION

Sample, Inc. v. Porrath

Supreme Court of New York, Appellate Division, Fourth Department, 1973.41 A.D.2d 118, 341 N.Y.S.2d 683, 178 U.S.P.Q. 365, aff'd on opinion below.
33 N.Y.2d 961, 353 N.Y.S.2d 733, 309 N.E.2d 133, 181 U.S.P.Q. 850.

GOLDMAN, Presiding Justice.

In this action appellants, The Sample, Inc. and The Sample of Buffalo, Inc., appeal from a judgment denying their application for a declaratory judgment permitting them to use the trade name "Sample" in connection with a proposed new retail outlet in the Town of Wheatfield, Niagara County, New York. The order denying appellants this requested relief granted the respondents, Theresa Porrath, Samuel Porrath, Dorothy Gellman and Samuel Gellman, copartners doing business under the firm name of The Sample Shop, a permanent injunction restraining appellants from using the name "Sample" in any business operation to be conducted within the City of Niagara Falls and the Towns of Niagara, Wheatfield, Lewiston and Porter in the County of Niagara.

The history of the business activities of the parties, their methods of operation, the territorial markets they serve and much pertinent data were fully presented to the trial court. It appears from the proof that the Buffalo based "The Sample, Inc." was established in 1929 and has advertised in Buffalo papers under the trade name "The Sample" since its founding. In its early days it specialized in the sale of women's apparel but over the years has expanded greatly the variety of merchandise offered for sale and now includes men's as well as women's clothing and in addition thereto operates other departments such as jewelry, ladies' shoes and fabrics, children's wear and many other commodities. "The Sample, Inc." opened its first branch store outside of Buffalo in the City of Lockport, Niagara County, in 1946 and now operates in nine locations in Western New York, two of which are in Niagara County. Each branch store is a separate, wholly-owned subsidiary corporation. The parent corporation had net sales in 1971 in excess of $10,600,000 with more than $1,350,000 produced by the two Niagara County stores. Over 61,500 persons hold charge accounts with "The Sample, Inc." and 7,200 of these customers live in Niagara County. Appellants have spent $2,165,461 for advertising under the name "The Sample", spending almost as much in 1971 as respondents have in the last 23 years. This advertising has appeared primarily in two large Buffalo newspapers, which have a circulation of over 25,000 in Niagara County and appellants have also advertised extensively in the Lockport Union Sun and Journal and the Tonawanda News, both of which are largely distributed throughout Niagara County.

Respondents operate two stores, the first of which was opened in 1934 in Niagara Falls under the name "Sample Dress Shop". These stores which had net sales of $678,000 in 1971 stock primarily women's apparel and do not offer for sale such items as men's wear and the various other merchandise which is sold in "The Sample, Inc." stores. Since 1948 respondents have spent a total of $311,000 in advertising, almost entirely in the Niagara Falls Gazette. The primary market of the two stores is in the City of Niagara Falls and the four towns surrounding the city.

The store which appellants desire to open would be located in the Summit Park Mall in the Town of Wheatfield in Niagara County, one and a half miles from one of respondents' stores. They propose to name it "The Sample Shop of Buffalo, Inc.". Appellants have offered to call the store by any other name, which includes the word "Sample", such as the "Bunis (family name of principal stockholders) Sample Shop", or any reasonable and distinguishing name so long as it includes the word "Sample". Appellants have demonstrated a willingness to select a name which will eliminate any conflict with respondents' "The Sample Shop".

An in-depth market survey by National Marketing Associates, Inc. was put into evidence by appellants. It indicates that women in the 18–50 years age group who live within a five mile radius of the Summit Park Mall are more likely to associate the word "Sample" with a store operated by appellants than one owned by respondents. The market data contained in the survey clearly show that a substantial majority of persons interviewed, when asked to identify a store operated under the names "The Sample" or "Sample Shops", responded by indicating the store owned by appellants.

The trial court found that respondents' name, "The Sample Shop", has "acquired a secondary meaning identifying in the minds of the public" the two stores operated by respondents in the City of Niagara Falls. It further found "that the public would be confused and deceived by plaintiffs' use of the word 'Sample'" and that there "is a likelihood of dilution of the distinctive quality of defendants' trade name by plaintiffs' use of the word 'Sample' as a part of a corporate or assumed name". The trial court concluded from its findings that appellants are not entitled to judgment declaring their right to operate the new store under the name "The Sample of Buffalo, Inc." and granted judgment to respondents restraining and enjoining appellants from the "use of the word 'Sample' as part of a corporate or assumed name". We find this determination to be against the weight of the evidence.

The preponderance of the evidence supports appellants' contention that a majority of potential customers of both parties are more likely to associate the word "Sample" with a store operated by appellants rather than one operated by respondents. The uncontradicted data of the market survey and the history of the business activities of both parties show that respondents' business name has not acquired a secondary meaning and that the greater likelihood is that appellants' name, "The Sample, Inc.", has gained such a secondary meaning in the minds of the purchasing public.

In the determination of the issue here presented, the overriding objective is to promote and protect the concept of commercial fairness. Unfair competition and trademark infringement are all unique in their particular factual patterns and each case should be decided "on its facts", and because of incompatibility there cannot be strict adherence to precedents.

The principle of commercial fairness is well enunciated by the United States Court of Appeals of the First Circuit in Food Center v. Food Fair Stores, 356 F.2d 775, 148 U.S.P.Q. 621. In that case a Massachusetts retail supermarket carried on business under the name "New England Food Fair". It sought to enjoin the defendant, the nation's fifth largest chain of grocery supermarkets operating in 15 States under the name "Food Fair", from operating under its name in the Massachusetts area. The District Court found that the plaintiff's name had acquired a secondary meaning in greater Boston and to some extent in other parts of Eastern Massachusetts. In vacating the judgment of the District Court the Circuit Court said "In attempting to apply principles and precedents to the facts of this case, we recognize at the outset that the field of protection of trade names is part of the wider domain of the law relating to unfair competition, where the overriding objective of courts and legislatures is that of commercial fairness". As in the case at bar in the use of the word "Sample", the court found that the name "Food Fair" was not of the strongest order of originality. The Federal court concerned itself, as we should, that the public be not disadvantaged by confusion of names and set forth specific recommendations as to territory and operation to avoid confusion. In the case at bar all that is required is the adoption of a name by appellants which will clearly identify appellants' store and distinguish it, in the minds of the public, from respondents' stores. This we believe is accomplished by using the word "Buffalo" in appellants' name.

Succinctly stated, the paramount question is whether the acts complained of are fair or unfair. No longer is it the law that the protection of a business name depends primarily upon whether that name has acquired a secondary meaning. If it is demonstrable and clear from the record that the acts of one charged with usurpation of another's commercial name are actually unfair, equitable principles become operative. What equity will not tolerate is the appropriation of another's business name together with the exploitation and the grasping for enjoyment of the benefits of another's labor and effort, when the latter has culminated in a special quality being attached to the particular name.

The issue of trade name infringement was not decided by the trial court because neither party had taken any action concerning the matter for many years. The court found that there were two separate and distinct market areas; that the trade name of both parties had acquired a secondary meaning in their particular area; each entity was entitled to protection in its own specialized area; the public would be confused and deceived by the appellants' use of the word "Sample" at the store at Summit Park Mall; there was a likelihood of diluting the distinctive quality of the respondents' trade name; there would be little disadvantage to the appellants if they were unable to use the word "Sample" in the name of their new store; and by using the name the appellants would be taking advantage of the goodwill associated with the word "Sample" and established by the respondents.

Secondary meaning has been defined as the trade meaning which may attach to a particular mark because its user has expended time and money in the promotion of the mark. Where a business name acquires a special significance pointing to only one business enterprise in a certain locality, it is protected from use by another in the same area. The concept of secondary meaning is that a name has become so identified with a particular business that it exclusively signifies only that one particular business.

Priority of use alone is not equivalent to acquisition of that special significance which entitles a trade name to protection against infringement.

The respondents have not met the burden of establishing the existence of a secondary meaning for their trade name "The Sample Shop" and this they must do in order to restrain appellants from using that trade name. The results of the consumer attitude study conducted at the request of appellants are entitled to probative weight. This study demonstrated that many more consumers were aware of the appellants' name than that of the respondents. This awareness no doubt emanates from the considerable advertising carried on by the appellants in and by all of the media. This awareness also mitigates against a finding that the business name of respondents has acquired a secondary meaning either in the respondents' limited geographical area or within the metropolitan area constituting Buffalo and Niagara Falls in Erie and Niagara Counties.

The finding that the appellants will be taking advantage of the goodwill associated with the name "Sample" and established by the respondents is not supported by the record. The consumers in the Summit Park Mall area relate the name "Sample" to the Buffalo based retail stores more than to the Niagara Falls based stores. This identification probably stems from the advertising of the word "Sample" in connection with appellants as early as 1929.

The record fails to establish that the appellants' use of the word "Sample" would deceive the public and dilute the distinctive quality of respondents' name. The facts are that the public identifies the name "Sample" with the appellants rather than with the respondents or at least it cannot be said on this record that the identification is more in favor of respondents than appellants.

Finally, a finding that the use of a different name would result in little disadvantage to appellants is not valid. The name associated with the Buffalo stores has acquired singular significance through substantial advertising expenditures. That the new store would be deprived of that name is of no little consequence and would be detrimental to successful operation.

There is no inkling of bad faith on the part of the appellants or of any intention to deceive and confuse the public and to identify the respondents' products with the appellants.

Of course, an injunction will issue to prevent any activity calculated to impair the value of a trade name or to deceive the public. The appellants are not attempting to trade on the goodwill of the respondents' distinctive name so that there is a misappropriation of a property right belonging to another. There may possibly be some confusion as a result of the use of appellants' name in the Summit Park Mall but we must look at the over-all picture, and it is quite clear that neither party has any manifestly superior claim to the name "Sample". The most equitable solution to this controversy is to allow the use of similar but not identical names so that both stores may use the word "Sample". By such a disposition the interests of all parties will be protected and commercial fairness will be achieved.

The judgment below should be reversed and judgment entered declaring that the appellants may operate a retail store in the Summit Park Mall, in the Town of Wheatfield, Niagara County, New York, under the name "The Sample of Buffalo, Inc.".

NOTES

1. Did the fact in *Sample* that "many more consumers were aware of the appellants' name than that of the respondents," necessarily mean that respondent's name had acquired *no* secondary meaning, even in its own limited geographical area? If so, would appellants have succeeded in an action to enjoin respondents from using the "Sample" name on their present stores? If not, would appellant's use of the "Sample" name in the Summit Park Mall necessarily produce some consumer confusion?

In Food Center, Inc. v. Food Fair Stores, Inc., relied on in *Sample*, the court observed that "as for the public, there would be confusion in areas served by both enterprises, but, at least at present, we see no evidence that it would suffer in quality of service or that the reputation of either party would suffer in the process." 356 F.2d 775, 782. What relief would, or should, be available to the parties and to the public in the event that the quality of either firm's goods and services later declined?

2. *Reverse Confusion.* What if appellant's advertising in *Sample* had been so extensive that it obliterated any goodwill that respondent had developed for its own stores, with the result that customers at respondent's stores believed the stores were part of appellant's chain? The confusion of source in this case would be just the opposite of the confusion that ordinarily occurs in unfair competition cases: instead of consumers being confused into thinking that the second user's goods and services come from the first user, they would be confused into thinking that the first user's goods and services come from the second user.

Big O Tire Dealers, Inc. v. Goodyear Tire & Rubber Co., 561 F.2d 1365, 195 U.S.P.Q. 417 (10th Cir.1977), cert. dismissed, 434 U.S. 1052, 98 S.Ct. 905, 54 L.Ed.2d 805 (1978), held that under Colorado law the first user would in these circumstances be entitled to relief against the second user on a theory of "reverse confusion." Plaintiff in *Big O* had begun selling tires under the mark "Bigfoot" in fourteen states in April, 1974. In September, 1974, over plaintiff's objections, defendant launched a national advertising campaign using the term "Bigfoot" to promote the sale of its newly introduced tire. One result of the campaign was that customers came to plaintiff's stores to buy defendant's tires and were disappointed when they found that they could not.

The court rejected the defendant's argument that there could be no liability for unfair competition without a showing that defendant, Goodyear, intended to trade on the goodwill of plaintiff, Big O. The court relied in part on the district court's reasoning: " 'The logical consequence of accepting Goodyear's position would be the immunization from unfair competition liability of a company with a well established trade name and with the economic power to advertise extensively for a product name taken from a competitor. If the law is to limit recovery to passing off, anyone with adequate size and resources can adopt any trademark and develop a new meaning for that trademark as identification of the second user's products. The activities of Goodyear in this case are unquestionably unfair competition through an improper use of trademark and that must be actionable.' 408 F.Supp. at 1236." 561 F.2d at 1372.

3.   *Zone of Expansion*. Can a firm ever have rights in a region in which it does no business? In which its name has no secondary meaning? Under the so-called zone of expansion doctrine, traditionally identified with dicta in Hanover Star Milling Co. v. Metcalf, 240 U.S. 403, 36 S.Ct. 357, 60 L.Ed. 713 (1916), a prior user can preempt the right to use its name and symbols in territories "that would probably be reached by the prior user in the natural expansion of his trade." 240 U.S. at 420, 36 S.Ct. at 363. Some cases, including *Sample*, suggest that larger, more aggressive firms will receive more commodious zones of expansion than smaller firms. Is it relevant that large retailers have been known to fail? That small firms are sometimes acquired by larger ones?

Several courts have limited the zone of expansion doctrine to situations in which the second user adopted the first user's name or symbol in bad faith—knowing of the prior use—or in which the first user's name or symbol had acquired secondary meaning in the relevant market. See Raxton Corp. v. Anania Assocs., Inc., 635 F.2d 924, 930, 208 U.S.P.Q. 769 (1st Cir.1980):

> A 'natural expansion' doctrine that penalized innocent users of a trademark simply because they occupied what for them would be a largely undiscoverable path of some remote prior user's expansion strikes us as at once unworkable, unfair, and, in the light of statutory protection available today, unnecessary. Such a doctrine would have to weigh the remote prior user's intangible and unregistered interest in future expansion as more important than the subsequent user's actual and good faith use of its name. Besides involving the obvious practical difficulties of defining the 'natural expansion path' of a business, this doctrine would also allow trademark owners to 'monopolize markets that [their] trade ha[d] never reached.' *Hanover*, 240 U.S. at 416, 36 S.Ct. at 361.

> The unfairness of this doctrine vanishes if the hypothesis of an *innocent* subsequent user is dropped, or if it is shown that the disputed trademark is known to consumers in the area of subsequent use prior to the subsequent user's adoption. In these cases it can be presumed unless demonstrated to the contrary that the subsequent user knowingly copied a mark. At the least, this suggests that the subsequent user should have been more careful to select a name free of prior rights and should be held to assume the risk of its negligence. At worst, this indicates a design to appropriate the goodwill of another.

Raxton's reference to the "statutory protection available today" was to section 22 of the Lanham Act, 15 U.S.C.A. § 1072, under which a mark's registration on the Principal Register in the Patent and Trademark Office will put subsequent users anywhere in the United States on constructive notice of the registrant's ownership of the mark, thus depriving them of a good faith defense and assuring the registrant of exclusive rights in markets not yet entered.

3. DILUTION

Mead Data Central, Inc. v. Toyota Motor Sales, U.S.A., Inc.

United States Court of Appeals, Second Circuit, 1989.
875 F.2d 1026, 10 U.S.P.Q.2d 1961.

VAN GRAAFEILAND, Circuit Judge:

Toyota Motor Sales, U.S.A., Inc. and its parent, Toyota Motor Corporation, appeal from a judgment of the United States District Court for the Southern District of New York (Edelstein, J.) enjoining them from using LEXUS as the name of their new luxury automobile and the division that manufactures it. The district court held that, under New York's antidilution statute, N.Y.Gen.Bus.Law § 368–d, Toyota's use of LEXUS is likely to dilute the distinctive quality of LEXIS, the mark used by Mead Data Central, Inc. for its computerized legal research service. On March 8, 1989, we entered an order of reversal, stating that an opinion would follow. This is the opinion.

THE STATUTE

Section 368–d of New York's General Business Law, which has counterparts in at least twenty other states, reads as follows:

Likelihood of injury to business reputation or of dilution of the distinctive quality of a mark or trade name shall be a ground for injunctive relief in cases of infringement of a mark registered or not registered or in cases of unfair competition, notwithstanding the absence of competition between the parties or the absence of confusion as to the source of goods or services.

THE PARTIES AND THEIR MARKS

Mead and Lexis

Mead is a corporation organized under the laws of Delaware with its principal place of business in Miamisburg, Ohio. Since 1972, Mead has provided a computerized legal research service under the trademark LEXIS. Mead introduced evidence that its president in 1972 "came up with the name LEXIS based on Lex which was Latin for law and I S for information systems." In fact, however, the word "lexis" is centuries old. It is found in the language of ancient Greece, where it had the meaning of "phrase", "word", "speaking" or "diction". "Lexis" subsequently appeared in the Latin where it had a substantially similar meaning, i.e., "word", "speech", or "language".

Like many other Latin words, "lexis" has been incorporated bodily into the English. It can be found today in at least sixty general dictionaries or other English word books, including Webster's Ninth New Collegiate Dictionary and Webster's New World Dictionary. Moreover, its meaning has not changed significantly from that of its Latin and Greek predecessors; *e.g.,* "Vocabulary, the total set of words in a language" (American Heritage Illustrated Encyclopedic Dictionary); "A vocabulary of a language, a particular subject, occupation, or activity" (Funk & Wagnalls Standard Dictionary). The district court's finding that "to establish that LEXIS is an English word required expert testimony at trial" is clearly erroneous. Anyone with a rudimentary knowledge of English can go to a library or bookstore and find the word in one of the above-mentioned standard dictionaries.

Moreover, the record discloses that numerous other companies had adopted "Lexis" in identifying their business or its product, *e.g.,* Lexis Ltd., Lexis Computer Systems Ltd., Lexis Language and Export Information Service, Lexis Corp., Maxwell Labs Lexis 3. In sum, we reject Mead's argument that LEXIS is a coined mark which originated in the mind of its former president and, as such, is entitled per se to the greater protection that a unique mark such as "Kodak" would receive.

Nevertheless, through its extensive sales and advertising in the field of computerized legal research, Mead has made LEXIS a strong mark in that field, and the district court so found. In particular, the district court accepted studies proffered by both parties which revealed that 76 percent of attorneys associated LEXIS with specific attributes of the service provided by Mead. However, among the general adult population, LEXIS is recognized by only one percent of those surveyed, half of this one percent being attorneys or accountants. The district court therefore concluded that LEXIS is strong only within its own market.

As appears in the Addendum to this opinion, the LEXIS mark is printed in block letters with no accompanying logo.

Toyota and Lexus

Toyota Motor Corp. has for many years manufactured automobiles, which it markets in the United States through its subsidiary Toyota Motor Sales, U.S.A. On August 24, 1987 Toyota announced a new line of luxury automobiles to be called LEXUS. The cars will be manufactured by a separate LEXUS division of Toyota, and their marketing pitch will be directed to well-educated professional consumers with annual incomes in excess of $50,000. Toyota had planned to spend $18 million to $20 million for this purpose during the first nine months of 1989.

Before adopting the completely artificial name LEXUS for its new automobile, Toyota secured expert legal advice to the effect that "there is absolutely no conflict between 'LEXIS' and 'LEXUS.'" Accordingly, when Mead subsequently objected to Toyota's use of LEXUS, Toyota rejected Mead's complaints. The district court held correctly that Toyota acted without predatory intent in adopting the LEXUS mark.

> [T]he absence of predatory intent by the junior user is a relevant factor in assessing a claim under the antidilution statute, ... since relief under the statute is of equitable origin....

Sally Gee, Inc. v. Myra Hogan, Inc., 699 F.2d 621, 626 (2d Cir.1983).

However, the district court erred in concluding that Toyota's refusal to acknowledge that its use of LEXUS might harm the LEXIS mark, deprived it of the argument that it acted in good faith. If, as we now hold, Toyota's mark did not dilute Mead's, it would be anomalous indeed to hold Toyota guilty of bad faith in proceeding in reliance on its attorney's correct advice to that effect. Indeed, even if the attorney's professional advice had been wrong, it does not follow that Toyota's reliance on that advice would have constituted bad faith.

The LEXUS mark is in stylized, almost script-like lettering and is accompanied by a rakish L logo.

THE LAW

The brief legislative history accompanying section 368–d describes the purpose of the statute as preventing "the whittling away of an established trade-mark's selling power and value through *its* unauthorized use by others upon dissimilar products." 1954 N.Y.Legis.Ann. 49 (emphasis supplied). If we were to interpret literally the italicized word "its", we would limit statutory violations to the unauthorized use of the identical established mark. This is what Frank Schechter, the father of the dilution theory, intended when he wrote The Rational Basis of Trademark Protection, 40 Harv.L.Rev. 813 (1927). However, since the use of obvious simulations or markedly similar marks might have the same diluting effect as would an appropriation of the original mark, the concept of exact identity has been broadened to that of substantial similarity. Nevertheless, in keeping with the original intent of the statute, the similarity must be substantial before the doctrine of dilution may be applied.

Indeed, some courts have gone so far as to hold that, although violation of an antidilution statute does not require confusion of product or source, the marks in question must be sufficiently similar that confusion may be created as between the marks themselves. We need not go that far. We hold only that the marks must be "very" or "substantially" similar and that, absent such similarity, there can be no viable claim of dilution.

The district court's opinion was divided into two sections. The first section dealt with Toyota's alleged violation of the Lanham Act, and the second dealt with the alleged dilution of Mead's mark under New York's antidilution statute. The district court made several findings on the issue of similarity in its Lanham Act discussion; it made none in its discussion of section 368–d. Assuming that the district court's finding of lack of physical similarity in the former discussion was intended to carry over into the latter, we would find ourselves in complete accord with it since we would make the same finding. However, if the district court's statement in its Lanham Act discussion that "in everyday spoken English, LEXUS and LEXIS are virtually identical in pronunciation" was intended to be a finding of fact rather than a statement of opinion, we question both its accuracy and its relevance. The word LEXUS is not yet widely enough known that any definitive statement can be made concerning its pronunciation by the American public. However, the two members of this Court who concur in this opinion use "everyday spoken English", and we would not pronounce LEXUS as if it were spelled LEXIS. Although our colleague takes issue with us on this point, he does not contend that if LEXUS and LEXIS are pronounced correctly, they will sound the same. We liken LEXUS to such words as "census", "focus" and "locus", and differentiate it from such words as "axis", "aegis" and "iris".[2] If we were to substitute the letter "i" for the letter "u" in "census", we would not pronounce it as we now do. Likewise, if we were to substitute the letter "u" for the letter "i" in "axis", we would not pronounce it as we now do. In short, we agree with the testimony of Toyota's speech expert, who testified:

> Of course, anyone can pronounce "lexis" and "lexus" the same, either both with an unstressed I or both with an unstressed U, or schwa—or with some other sound in between. But, properly, the distinction between unstressed I and unstressed U, or schwa, is a standard one in English; the distinction is there to be made in ordinary, reasonably careful speech.

In addition, we do not believe that "everyday spoken English" is the proper test to use in deciding the issue of similarity in the instant case.... When Mead's speech expert was asked whether there were instances in which LEXUS and LEXIS would be pronounced differently, he replied "Yes, although a deliberate attempt must be made to do so.... They can be pronounced distinctly but they are not when they are used in common parlance, in everyday language or speech." We take it as a given that television and radio announcers usually are more careful and precise in their diction than is the man on the street. Moreover, it is the rare television commercial that does not contain a visual reference to the mark and product, which in the instant case would be the LEXUS automobile. We conclude that in the field of commercial advertising, which is the field subject to regulation, there is no substantial similarity between Mead's mark and Toyota's.

There are additional factors that militate against a finding of dilution in the instant case. Such a finding must be based on two elements. First, plaintiff's mark must possess a distinctive quality capable of dilution. Second, plaintiff must show a likelihood of dilution. As section 368–d expressly states, a plaintiff need not show either competition between its

---

2. Similarly, we liken LEXUS to NEXX-US, a nationally known shampoo, and LEXIS to NEXIS, Mead's trademark for its compu-terized news service. NEXXUS and NEXIS have co-existed in apparent tranquility for almost a decade.

product or service and that of the defendant or a likelihood of confusion as to the source of the goods or services.

Distinctiveness for dilution purposes often has been equated with the strength of a mark for infringement purposes. It also has been defined as uniqueness or as having acquired a secondary meaning. Allied Maintenance Corp. v. Allied Mechanical Trades, Inc., 42 N.Y.2d at 545, 399 N.Y.S.2d 628, 369 N.E.2d 1162. A trademark has a secondary meaning if it "has become so associated in the mind of the public with that entity [Allied] or its product that it identifies the goods sold by that entity and distinguishes them from goods sold by others." Id. In sum, the statute protects a trademark's "selling power." However, the fact that a mark has selling power in a limited geographical or commercial area does not endow it with a secondary meaning for the public generally.

The strength and distinctiveness of LEXIS is limited to the market for its services—attorneys and accountants. Outside that market, LEXIS has very little selling power. Because only one percent of the general population associates LEXIS with the attributes of Mead's service, it cannot be said that LEXIS identifies that service to the general public and distinguishes it from others. Moreover, the bulk of Mead's advertising budget is devoted to reaching attorneys through professional journals.

This Court has defined dilution as either the blurring of a mark's product identification or the tarnishment of the affirmative associations a mark has come to convey. Mead does not claim that Toyota's use of LEXUS would tarnish affirmative associations engendered by LEXIS. The question that remains, therefore, is whether LEXIS is likely to be blurred by LEXUS.

Very little attention has been given to date to the distinction between the confusion necessary for a claim of infringement and the blurring necessary for a claim of dilution. Although the antidilution statute dispenses with the requirements of competition and confusion, it does not follow that every junior use of a similar mark will dilute the senior mark in the manner contemplated by the New York Legislature.

As already stated, the brief legislative history accompanying section 368–d described the purpose of the statute as preventing "the whittling away of an established trademark's selling power and value through its unauthorized use by others upon dissimilar products." The history disclosed a need for legislation to prevent such "hypothetical anomalies" as "Dupont shoes, Buick aspirin tablets, Schlitz varnish, Kodak pianos, Bulova gowns, and so forth", and cited cases involving similarly famous marks. 1954 N.Y.Legis.Ann. 49–50.

It is apparent from these references that there must be some mental association between plaintiff's and defendant's marks.

> [I]f a reasonable buyer is not at all likely to link the two uses of the trademark in his or her own mind, even subtly or subliminally, then there can be no dilution.... [D]ilution theory presumes *some kind of*

mental association in the reasonable buyer's mind between the two party's [sic] uses of the mark.

2 J. McCarthy, Trademarks and Unfair Competition § 24.13 at 213–14 (2d ed. 1984).

This mental association may be created where the plaintiff's mark is very famous and therefore has a distinctive quality for a significant percentage of the defendant's market. However, if a mark circulates only in a limited market, it is unlikely to be associated generally with the mark for a dissimilar product circulating elsewhere. As discussed above, such distinctiveness as LEXIS possesses is limited to the narrow market of attorneys and accountants. Moreover, the process which LEXIS represents is widely disparate from the product represented by LEXUS. For the general public, LEXIS has no distinctive quality that LEXUS will dilute.

ADDENDUM

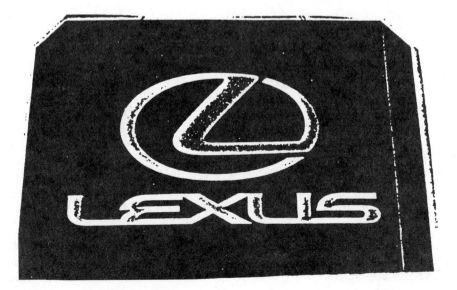

The possibility that someday LEXUS may become a famous mark in the mind of the general public has little relevance in the instant dilution analysis since it is quite apparent that the general public associates nothing with LEXIS. On the other hand, the recognized sophistication of attorneys, the principal users of the service, has substantial relevance. Because of this knowledgeable sophistication, it is unlikely that, even in the market where Mead principally operates, there will be any significant amount of blurring between the LEXIS and LEXUS marks.

For all the foregoing reasons, we hold that Toyota did not violate section 368–d. We see no need therefore to discuss Toyota's remaining arguments for reversal.

The opinion of SWEET, District Judge, concurring, is omitted.

NOTES

1. Judge Sweet, concurring in Mead v. Toyota, complained that "the majority has failed adequately to define the likelihood of dilution concept." Observing that the "tarnishing" concept "is helpful because that principle can be applied in practice," Judge Sweet observed that the "blurring" concept "offers practitioners and courts only marginally more guidance than 'likelihood of dilution.'" 875 F.2d at 1034–35. In his view, "blurring sufficient to constitute dilution requires a case-by-case factual inquiry" focused on six judicially-recognized factors:

(1) similarity of the marks

(2) similarity of the products covered by the marks

(3) sophistication of consumers

(4) predatory intent

(5) renown of the senior mark

(6) renown of the junior mark

Only the sixth factor gave Judge Sweet any serious pause: "This case raises an issue that is likely to arise rarely in dilution law—the prospect that a junior mark may become so famous that it will overwhelm the senior mark. Dilution under this theory might occur where the senior user's advertising and marketing have established certain associations for its product among a particular consumer group, but the junior mark's subsequent renown causes the senior user's consumers to draw the associations identified with the junior user's mark. Here, for example, Toyota seeks to associate LEXUS with luxury and the carriage trade, which Mead fears may overwhelm LEXIS's association with indispensability and economy." 875 F.2d at 1038.

Nonetheless, Judge Sweet concluded that no blurring was likely to occur: "First, section 368–d protects a mark's selling power among the consuming public. Because the LEXIS mark possesses selling power only among lawyers and accountants, it is irrelevant for dilution analysis that the general public may come to associate LEXIS or LEXUS with Toyota's automobile rather than nothing at all. Second, the district court offered no evidence for its speculation that LEXUS's fame may cause Mead customers to associate 'lexis' with Toyota's cars. It seems equally plausible that no blurring will occur—because many lawyers and accountants use Mead's services regularly, their frequent association of LEXIS with those services will enable LEXIS's mark to withstand Toyota's advertising campaign." 875 F.2d at 1039–40.

Would Mead have an unfair competition action against Toyota if Toyota's widely advertised mark in fact swamped Mead's mark so that Mead customers would first think of Toyota's car when they hear the term, Lexis? See Big O Tire Dealers, Inc. v. Goodyear Tire & Rubber Co., discussed at page 70, note 2, above.

2. *Tarnishment.* Dilution doctrine's prohibition against tarnishment can be applied broadly or narrowly. Applied broadly, the prohibition encompasses any unauthorized use of a mark in any context, commercial or noncommercial, that diminishes the mark's positive associations. Applied narrowly, the prohibition encompasses only unauthorized commercial uses of the mark in connection with shoddy goods or with goods that lack the prestige associated with the mark.

The choice between a broad and a narrow approach to tarnishment may have constitutional implications. In L.L. Bean, Inc. v. Drake Publishers, Inc., 811 F.2d 26, 1 U.S.P.Q.2d 1753 (1st Cir.1987), cert. denied, 483 U.S. 1013, 107 S.Ct. 3254, 97 L.Ed.2d 753 (1987), the court reversed the grant of an injunction against a sexual parody of plaintiff's famous catalogue that incorporated a facsimile of plaintiff's trademark. In the court's view, the Maine antidilution statute, as applied, violated the first amendment's free expression guarantees. The core of the court's concern was the application of the statute to noncommercial conduct. "Drake has not used Bean's mark to identify or market goods or services; it has used the mark solely to identify Bean as the object of its parody." Further, to deny "parodists the opportunity to poke fun at symbols and names which have become woven into the fabric of our daily life, would constitute a serious curtailment of a protected form of expression." 811 F.2d at 33, 34. Dicta throughout the opinion indicate that the court would have upheld an application of the statute limited to use of the mark in connection with the marketing of goods or services.

3. *Common Law and Statutory Relief.* Dilution doctrine has a long common law history. Borden Ice Cream Co. v. Borden's Condensed Milk Co., 201 Fed. 510 (7th Cir.1912), reflects the early view that noncompetitive poaching is not actionable. The court there denied plaintiff, a condensed milk company, an injunction against defendant's use of the name, "Borden," in connection with the sale of ice cream on the ground that plaintiff was not engaged in the ice cream business. But, soon after, the Tiffany jewelry firm, the Rolls–Royce automobile firm and the Dunhill pipe firm were respectively held entitled to injunctive relief against defendants who had used the name, "Tiffany" in connection with motion pictures, "Rolls–

Royce" in connection with radio tubes, and "Dunhill" in connection with shirts. Tiffany & Co. v. Tiffany Productions, 147 Misc. 679, 264 N.Y.S. 459 (Sup.Ct.1932), aff'd, 262 N.Y. 482, 188 N.E. 30 (1933); Wall v. Rolls–Royce of America, 4 F.2d 333 (3d Cir.1925); Alfred Dunhill of London v. Dunhill Shirt Shop, 3 F.Supp. 487 (S.D.N.Y.1929).

Common law courts usually rationalize decisions for plaintiff in dilution cases on a deception ground. Where, as in *Rolls-Royce,* there is some likelihood that consumers will believe that plaintiff manufactured defendant's goods, the deception relied on is of the usual passing off variety. Where, as in *Dunhill,* the likelihood of confusion as to source is more attenuated, confusion of sponsorship may be employed as the ground for decision. Only in cases, like *Tiffany,* where likelihood of confusion as to source or sponsorship is hardly colorable, do courts tend to avoid the deception ground entirely and rely instead on a misappropriation ground.

The Unfair Competition Restatement, which categorically rejects an independent tort of misappropriation, also constrains the common law of dilution by making antidilution statutes the exclusive source of liability for non-confusing uses of another's designation. Restatement of the Law, Third, Unfair Competition § 25(1) (1995). In 1947, Massachusetts became the first state to enact an antidilution statute, and these statutes, modeled on the U.S. Trademark Association's Model State Trademark Bill, are now in force in more than half the states.

4. *Should* courts and legislatures detach protection for names and symbols from its historic roots in the requirement of consumer deception? To what extent do the traditional economic arguments for trademark and unfair competition protection, summarized in the Economides excerpt at page 20, above, also support dilution doctrine? Can protection for a symbol's selling power be justified on the grounds of economic incentive or natural right offered in support of copyrights and patents? What reasons are there to withhold from a popular symbol like McDonald's Golden Arches or the name Coca–Cola, the same broad scope of protection given to a popular, copyrighted song? Should the answer turn on whether the law imposes other limitations on protection, for example, a limited term?

Underlying every dilution decision is the question whether a brand owner should have rights in a product or service market it has not yet entered. How, if at all, does this question differ from the question that underlies zone of expansion cases, like *Sample,* page 65 above, in which the battleground is unoccupied geographic, rather than product or service, markets?

5. Frank I. Schechter, The Rational Basis of Trademark Protection, 40 Harv. L. Rev. 813 (1927), is the seminal article arguing for protection against trademark dilution. On the Restatement's treatment of dilution, see Miles J. Alexander & Michael K. Heilbronner, An Analysis of the Dilution Section of the Restatement (Third) of Unfair Competition, 47 S.C. L. Rev. 629 (1996).

For a variety of contemporary views on dilution doctrine, see Symposium, Dilution Law: At a Crossroads?, 83 Trademark Reporter 107 (1993). On the federal law of dilution, see page 299, below.

4. MISAPPROPRIATION

Board of Trade of City of Chicago v. Dow Jones & Co.

Supreme Court of Illinois, 1983.
98 Ill.2d 109, 74 Ill.Dec. 582, 456 N.E.2d 84.

GOLDENHERSH, Justice:

Defendant, Dow Jones & Company, Inc., appealed from the judgment of the circuit court of Cook County entered in favor of plaintiff, the Board of Trade of the city of Chicago, in its action for declaratory judgment. Plaintiff sought a declaration that its offering of a commodity futures contract utilizing the Dow Jones Industrial Average as the underlying commodity would not violate defendant's legal or proprietary rights. The appellate court reversed and we allowed plaintiff's petition for leave to appeal.

The opinion of the appellate court adequately sets forth the facts, and they will be restated here only to the extent necessary to discuss the issues. Defendant, a Delaware corporation with its principal office in New York City, publishes the Wall Street Journal, Barrons, a weekly business magazine, and the Asian Wall Street Journal. It also maintains the Dow Jones News Service, through which it distributes financial news to subscribers. It produces several stock market indexes, the Dow Jones Industrial Average, Transportation Average, and Utilities Average, which are computed on the basis of the current prices of stocks of certain companies selected by defendant's editorial board.

The financial news furnished by defendant is disseminated in a variety of ways. It is distributed to brokerage houses, banks, financial institutions, individual investors, and others who are interested in stock market news. This information is transmitted to teleprinters, cathode-ray-tube receivers, and other devices, such as wall displays in brokerage houses. Subscribers desiring the averages can extract them from the news service or arrange with defendant to deliver the averages directly to them by teleprinter. Through special contracts, others receive the averages through entities which are licensed by defendant to sublicense the distribution of the averages. Plaintiff has a "Subscription Agreement" under which it pays defendant for its News Service and is allowed to compute and display the Dow Jones Averages on plaintiff's trading floor on a continuous, "real time" basis.

Plaintiff is the oldest and largest commodities exchange market in the United States. It was organized in 1848, and in 1859 the General Assembly granted plaintiff a special charter which incorporated it as a not-for-pecuniary-profit organization. Over the years plaintiff has added different types of futures contracts and now offers these contracts in a variety of fields, including agricultural products, precious metals and financial instruments. All commodities exchanges in the United States are regulated by the Commodities Futures Trading Commission (CFTC), and no exchange may trade a futures contract until the CFTC approves the futures contract and designates the exchange as a contract market for that contract.

A futures contract is a contract traded on a commodities exchange which binds the parties to a particular transaction at a specified future date. A stock index futures contract is a futures contract based upon the value of a particular stock market index. Dr. James H. Lorie, stipulated by the parties to be an expert, called by plaintiff, testified that these contracts have been traded since February 1982. At the time of trial they were traded on the Kansas City Board of Trade based on the Value Line Average, on the Chicago Mercantile Exchange based on the Standard & Poor's 500 Stock Index and on the New York Futures Exchange based on the New York Stock Exchange Composite Index. He stated that their "overriding purpose is the management of risk." Unlike other futures contracts, no underlying commodity exists to be delivered at the future date, but rather the transaction is settled by the delivery of a certified promissory note in lieu of cash. He explained that the total risks of investing in the stock market are divided into two parts. One part is the "nonsystematic risk," which occurs when an individual company encounters problems such as strikes, changing consumer attitudes or other problems which would devalue that company's stock. "Nonsystematic risk" can be controlled by an investor through the use of a diversified portfolio. The other type of risk is "systematic risk," which is the risk associated with the broad general movements of the stock market as a whole. Diversification of one's stock portfolio will not provide protection against sharp declines in the stock market. He explained that there are only two ways to protect against systematic risk. The most direct way is for an investor to sell his stocks. This method is rather costly because of the transactional costs in selling and buying stocks, such as brokerage fees. Additionally, if capital gains are realized, the transactions become even more costly. The second method of protecting against systematic risk is to deal in stock market futures contracts. This method is more efficient, Professor Lorie explained, since an investor holding a hypothetical $100,000 portfolio could purchase two futures contracts in the Chicago Mercantile Exchange for one-fifteenth the cost of selling his stocks.

An investor who holds a diversified stock portfolio may "hedge" against systematic risk by entering into a stock index futures contract predicting that the market index would decline. Dr. Lorie testified that this was the most effective method of "hedging" of which he was aware.

Plaintiff, desiring to be designated as a contract market for stock index futures contracts, devoted more than two years to developing its own index to be used as the basis for its stock index futures contract. During the greater part of this period, the Securities and Exchange Commission (SEC) and the CFTC were in a dispute concerning which agency had jurisdiction to regulate stock index futures contracts. In December 1981, the two

Federal agencies agreed on the scope of their respective jurisdiction and on recommendations to Congress for regulatory legislation. They agreed that the CFTC would regulate trading in stock market index contracts and that such trading would be permitted only if the contracts were based on widely known and well-established stock market indexes. This jurisdictional agreement effectively precluded CFTC approval of a contract based on the index developed by plaintiff.

On February 26, 1982, plaintiff submitted an application to the CFTC asking that it be designated as a contract market for Chicago Board of Trade Portfolio Futures Contracts. The application proposed the use of three indexes, the stock market index, transport index, and the electric index portfolio contracts. It was explained:

> Each index covers a significant portion of the overall stock market. The stock market index covers industrial firms, the Transport Index covers air, rail, and trucking firms, and the Gas and Electric Index covers utility companies. This division is similar to the way other major market indices divide the stock market.

No mention of the Dow Jones name appeared in the application, but the stocks used in each of the indexes were identical to those used in the Dow Jones averages. In a draft proposal to the CFTC for trading "CBT indexes," the Dow Jones averages stock lists were cut out of the Wall Street Journal and pasted into the proposals. The CFTC advised plaintiff that the CBT indexes were not just similar to, but were identical to the Dow Jones averages and that this should be explicitly stated in its application. On May 7, 1982, plaintiff amended its application to state that the CBT indexes were identical to Dow Jones averages and that when Dow Jones changed a component stock or revised the divisor, plaintiff would make the same change so that the CBT indexes would remain identical to the Dow Jones averages. Plaintiff also added a disclaimer to the application disclaiming any association with Dow Jones. On May 13, the CFTC approved plaintiff's use of the stock market index portfolio contract, but did not rule concerning the use of the transportation or utility index portfolio contracts.

The circuit court held that the burden of producing evidence and the burden of persuading the trier of fact fell upon defendant and found that defendant had a "property right and valuable interest in the Dow Jones averages" but that plaintiff's use of the averages in the manner proposed did not violate those rights. The order, however, required that there be imprinted upon the CBT index contract a disclaimer disavowing any association with or sponsorship by defendant, Dow Jones. The appellate court reversed, holding that plaintiff had the burden of production and persuasion, and that plaintiff's use of the averages constituted commercial misappropriation "of the Dow Jones index and averages."

... Plaintiff argues that the appellate court's holding erroneously expands the tort of misappropriation and that its decision contravenes public policy. Citing Capitol Records, Inc. v. Spies (1970), 130 Ill.App.2d 429, 264 N.E.2d 874, Metropolitan Opera Association v. Wagner–Nichols Recorder Corp. (199 Misc. 786, 101 N.Y.S.2d 483, aff'd (1951)), 279 A.D.

632, 107 N.Y.S.2d 795, Standard & Poor's Corp. v. Commodity Exchange, Inc. (2d Cir.1982), 683 F.2d 704, and International News Service v. Associated Press (1918), 248 U.S. 215, 39 S.Ct. 68, 63 L.Ed. 211, plaintiff argues that competitive injury is a fundamental prerequisite essential to a finding of misappropriation. It argues that the facts of this case are analogous to National Football League v. Governor of Delaware (D.Del.1977), 435 F.Supp. 1372, and Loeb v. Turner (Tex.Civ.App.1953), 257 S.W.2d 800, in which the courts refused to find misappropriation because, *inter alia,* the parties were not in competition with each other. It argues that it has done nothing immoral or unethical but has merely created a "new product" which is "outside the primary market which the producer of the original product originally set out to satisfy * * *." Finally, plaintiff argues that the appellate court's decision is against public policy in that it grants what amounts to a common law patent monopoly to defendant which permits it to exclude others from using its product for any purpose "regardless of whether the producer is being injured or intends to exploit the product itself."

Defendant responds that the tort of misappropriation should be flexible so that, by carefully tailoring their misappropriation to avoid the strict rules of the tort, "enterprising pirates" cannot avoid the application of the doctrine. Citing Sims v. Mack Truck Corp. (3d Cir.1979), 608 F.2d 87, 95, cert. denied, (1980), 445 U.S. 930, 100 S.Ct. 1319, 63 L.Ed.2d 764, defendant argues that under the doctrine of misappropriation direct competition is not essential to tort liability. Defendant argues that plaintiff seeks to exploit defendant's reputation for accuracy and impartiality without compensating it for its good will. Finally, in response to plaintiff's argument that the appellate court's opinion is against public policy, defendant argues that the appellate court's opinion is consistent with public policy in that it maintains the incentive for the creation of intellectual property. Defendant argues that if its rights in the averages are not protected, there will be a diminished incentive for it to continue to provide the averages. Defendant points out that it does not seek to monopolize the production of stock indexes and that plaintiff is free to develop its own, but that it desires to protect its rights in the averages which it created and continues to produce.

None of the many cases cited by the parties presents facts sufficiently similar to serve as definitive authority for the decision of the issue presented here. The rationales applied in developing a basis for the tort of misappropriation appear to be as diverse as the factual situations out of which the issues in those cases arose.

The doctrine of misappropriation as a form of unfair competition was first enunciated by the Supreme Court in International News Service v. Associated Press (1918), 248 U.S. 215, 39 S.Ct. 68, 63 L.Ed. 211. In that case, INS was copying news stories from bulletin boards of members of AP and transmitting the fresh news contained on those bulletin boards to its own members. Thus, INS could obtain information collected by AP at great expense and transmit this information to its midwestern and west coast members, who could then print the news at the same time as the competing

AP members or, in some instances, earlier. In affirming the decree enjoining the practice the majority opinion suggested that without the revenues derived from this exclusive, timely presentation of the news, AP or other news services would not have sufficient incentive to continue performing their services.

The tort of misappropriation was recognized in Illinois for the first time in Capitol Records, Inc. v. Spies (1970), 130 Ill.App.2d 429, 264 N.E.2d 874. There the defendant purchased records and magnetic tapes sold by the plaintiff and recorded them on magnetic tapes. He then sold these re-recordings to his customers. A disclaimer was placed on the cassette tapes disclaiming any relationship between the defendant and plaintiff or the recorded artists. Defendant was able to sell his product at a lesser price than plaintiff since he avoided the costs of contracting with the performers, producing the master recordings, paying royalty fees, and advertising. Relying on the rationale of Schulenburg v. Signatrol, Inc., (1964), 50 Ill.App.2d 402, 411–12, 200 N.E.2d 615, affirmed in part and reversed in part (1965), 33 Ill.2d 379, 212 N.E.2d 865, the court reasoned that the manner of competition was "unfair" since the defendant was able to compete on equal terms by avoiding those costs normally associated with producing such recordings. Underlying the court's reasoning is the premise that the plaintiff's pecuniary reward for producing its intangible product would be severely reduced if other competitors could avoid production costs by merely waiting until a record became popular and then recording the work for resale.

Competing with the policy that protection should be afforded one who expends labor and money to develop products is the concept that freedom to imitate and duplicate is vital to our free market economy. Indeed, when the doctrine of misappropriation was first enunciated, Justice Brandeis recognized this competing policy:

> He who follows the pioneer into a new market, or who engages in the manufacture of an article newly introduced by another, seeks profits due largely to the labor and expense of the first adventurer; but the law sanctions, indeed encourages, the pursuit. (International News Service v. Associated Press (1918), 248 U.S. 215, 259, 39 S.Ct. 68, 79, 63 L.Ed. 211, 229 (Brandeis, J., dissenting).)

Similarly, Professor Rahl reasons:

> Substantial similarity of alternatives can come about in only one of two ways—by independent development or by imitation. While there are many instances of simultaneous independent innovation, our economy would still be in the Dark Ages if this were the only circumstance under which competing alternatives could be offered. Imitation is inherent in any system of competition and it is imperative for an economy in which there is rapid technological advance. Rahl, The Right to "Appropriate" Trade Values, 23 Ohio St.L.J. 56, 72 (1962).

In balancing the factors that should determine which of the competing concepts should prevail, it appears unlikely that an adverse decision will cause defendant to cease to produce its averages or that the revenue it currently receives for the distribution of those averages will be materially affected. Defendant correctly asserts that it will lose its right to prospective licensing revenues in the event that in the future it elects to have its name associated with stock index futures contracts, but reliance upon the existence of a property right based upon the ability to license the product to prospective markets which were not originally contemplated by the creator of the product is somewhat "circular." Williams & Wilkins Co. v. United States (1973) 203 Ct.Cl. 74, 487 F.2d 1345, 1357 n. 19.

Alternatively, holding that plaintiff's use of defendant's indexes in the manner proposed is a misappropriation may stimulate the creation of new indexes perhaps better suited to the purpose of "hedging" against the "systematic" risk present in the stock market.

Whether protection against appropriation is necessary to foster creativity depends in part upon the expectations of that sector of the business community which deals with the particular intangible. If the creator of an intangible product expects to be able to control the licensing or distribution of the intangible in order to profit from his effort, and similarly those who would purchase the product expect and are willing to pay for the use of the intangible, a better argument can be made in favor of granting protection. The record shows that the plaintiff sought to develop its own index prior to the CFTC's requirement that the contracts be based on well-known, well-established indexes. It then offered defendant 10 cents per transaction, which it estimated would be somewhere between $1 million and $2 million per year, for the use of its name and averages. While there appears to be some dispute as to whether this offer of payment was primarily for the use of defendant's name or for the use of the averages, the offer of money is relevant to the extent that it acknowledges the value of the association of defendant's name and good will with the averages it produces.

To hold that defendant has a proprietary interest in its indexes and averages which vests it with the exclusive right to license their use for trading in stock index futures contracts would not preclude plaintiff and others from marketing stock index futures contracts. The extent of defendant's monopoly would be limited, for as defendant points out, there are an infinite number of stock market indexes which could be devised. As one commentator notes, the effect of granting a "monopoly" at the base of the production pyramid is much less objectionable than granting a monopoly at the top of the pyramid:

> Social cost assumes more manageable size and so less significance near the base of the pyramid. Exclusive rights in a special kind of typewriter key are far less objectionable than a monopoly in the lever, because far less is swept into the monopolist's control. Developments In the Law: Competitive Torts, 77 Harv.L.Rev. 888, 938 (1964).

We conclude that the possibility of any detriment to the public which might result from our holding that defendant's indexes and averages may not be used without its consent in the manner proposed by plaintiff are outweighed by the resultant encouragement to develop new indexes specifically designed for the purpose of hedging against the "systematic" risk present in the stock market.

We have considered plaintiff's contention that defendant has failed to prove that the proposed use of the averages would cause it injury. The publication of the indexes involves valuable assets of defendant, its good will and its reputation for integrity and accuracy. Despite the fact that plaintiff's proposed use is not in competition with the use defendant presently makes of them, defendant is entitled to protection against their misappropriation. . . .

For the reasons stated, the judgment of the appellate court is affirmed.

Judgment affirmed.

The opinion of SIMON, J., dissenting is omitted.

NOTES

1. *International News Service v. Associated Press.* I.N.S. v. A.P., cited in the *Dow Jones* case, is a landmark. Defendant, I.N.S., had circulated news releases taken from A.P. bulletin boards and early editions of A.P. member newspapers, in some instances distributing the items to its customers verbatim, in others rewriting the reports before selling them. Drawing on common law principles of unfair competition, the Supreme Court condemned both forms of piracy and ruled as a matter of federal common law that, as between the competing news agencies, A.P. possessed a "quasi property" in the news it gathered that I.N.S. could not lawfully appropriate as its own. Justices Holmes and Brandeis dissented in separate opinions.

Justice Pitney's opinion for the *I.N.S.* majority rested the new misappropriation tort on both utilitarian considerations—to allow I.N.S. to continue poaching A.P.'s news reports "would render publication profitless, or so little profitable as in effect to cut off the service by rendering the cost prohibitive in comparison with the return"—and natural rights principles—"he who has fairly paid the price should have the beneficial use of the property." The protected interest was only a "quasi property," however, because "we may and do assume that neither party has any remaining property interest as against the public in copyrighted news matter after the moment of its first publication." 248 U.S. 215, 236, 240–41, 39 S.Ct. 68, 63 L.Ed. 211 (1918).

Justice Holmes would have confined the application of unfair competition doctrine to a claim that I.N.S. had passed off A.P. releases as its own: "[A]s in my view, the only ground of complaint that can be recognized without legislation is the implied misstatement, it can be corrected by stating the truth; and a suitable acknowledgment of the source is all that the plaintiff can require." 248 U.S. at 248. Justice Brandeis, dissenting, thought that if there were to be such "an important extension of property rights and a corresponding curtailment of the free use of knowledge and of ideas" it would have better come from the legislature. "Courts are ill-equipped to make the investigations which should precede a determination of the limitations which should be set upon any property right in news...." 248 U.S. at 267.

See generally Douglas G. Baird, Common Law Intellectual Property and the Legacy of International News Service v. Associated Press, 50 U. Chi. L. Rev. 411 (1983).

2. *After I.N.S.* A 1994 survey and analysis of misappropriation doctrine after *I.N.S.* found that fourteen states have adopted the doctrine. "The earliest cases were in Missouri and Texas in the mid–1920's, just a few years after *I.N.S.*. Unquestionably, New York is the state that has most heartily embraced the doctrine. There may be as many misappropriation cases in New York as there are in all of the rest of the states together. New York cases vary from the famous *Metropolitan Opera* case, [Metropolitan Opera Assoc. v. Wagner–Nichols Recorder, 199 Misc. 786, 101 N.Y.S.2d 483 (Sup.Ct.1950), *aff'd*, 279 A.D. 632, 107 N.Y.S.2d 795 (1951).] to the fashion design cases, to the unauthorized public broadcasts of the World Series over leased telephone lines, and finally to the Madison Square Garden look-alike case. In no particular order, the other eleven states adopting the doctrine are Pennsylvania, California, Alaska, Colorado, Illinois, North Carolina, South Carolina, Wisconsin, New Jersey, Maryland and Delaware. In Alaska and Delaware, the only cases are federal cases, but the federal courts predicted that misappropriation would be adopted as state law." Edmund J. Sease, Misappropriation is Seventy–Five Years Old; Should We Bury It or Revive It?, 70 N.D. L. Rev. 781, 801–802 (1994)*.

Although some of misappropriation's critics feared that the doctrine would become a catch-all for rewarding otherwise unprotected investments of labor and capital, the doctrine has in fact stayed relatively close to its origins. According to Sease, "[t]he most successful misappropriation plaintiffs have been those in areas factually similar to *I.N.S.*. Thus, plaintiffs have a reasonable chance of success if the case involves rebroadcasting hot news items, appropriations of live performances, or during the 1970's, tape piracy. Unauthorized broadcasts of sporting events have also been routinely stopped on a misappropriation theory. Most recently, the doctrine has been applied in commercial data cases such as stock index cases." Id. at 804.

3. *The Restatement.* The Unfair Competition Restatement effectively withholds judge-made property rights in situations like those presented in Board of Trade v. Dow Jones by "rejecting the recognition of exclusive rights in intangible trade values, subject to a series of specified exceptions." Restatement of The Law, Third, Unfair Competition, Ch. 4, Introductory Note. The list of "specified exceptions" is narrow: trade secrets, the right of publicity, and conduct that "is actionable ... under federal or state statutes or international agreements, or is actionable as a breach of contract, or as an infringement of common law copyright as preserved under federal copyright law." *Id.* at § 38. According to Comment *b* to section 38, "[a]lthough courts have occasionally invoked the *INS* decision on an ad hoc basis to grant relief against other commercial appropriations,

---

* Copyright © 1994 North Dakota Law Review.

they have not articulated coherent principles for its application. It is clear that no general rule of law prohibits the appropriation of a competitor's ideas, innovations, or other intangible assets once they become publicly known. In addition, the federal patent and copyright statutes now preempt a considerable portion of the domain in which the common law tort might otherwise apply."

Is it good policy to limit the creation of new trade values to the legislative branch? Does misappropriation doctrine differ in kind or in degree from more traditional unfair competition doctrine, for which the Restatement continues to vest responsibility in the courts? If the difference is one of degree rather than kind, how can misappropriation effectively be cordoned off from the judiciary? See generally, Gary Myers, The Restatement's Rejection of the Misappropriation Tort: A Victory for the Public Domain, 47 S.C. L. Rev. 673 (1996).

4. *Competition.* Many courts require the existence of a competitive relationship for a misappropriation action to lie. In United States Golf Ass'n v. St. Andrews Sys., Data–Max, Inc., 749 F.2d 1028, 224 U.S.P.Q. 646 (3d Cir.1984), the court held that defendant's use of plaintiff U.S.G.A.'s handicapping formula in its computer program providing instant handicaps did not constitute misappropriation because plaintiff and defendant were not direct competitors: "The competition in this case is indirect. The U.S.G.A. is not in the business of selling handicaps to golfers, but is primarily interested in the promotion of the game of golf, and in its own position as the governing body of amateur golf."

Compare Standard & Poor's Corp. v. Commodity Exchange, Inc., 683 F.2d 704, 216 U.S.P.Q. 841 (2d Cir.1982), which involved facts similar to those in Board of Trade v. Dow Jones, and in which the court rested its decision for plaintiff in part on the fact that it had licensed its popular stock index to another commodities exchange and thus was effectively in competition with the defendant commodity exchange. Does the simple expedient of entering into a licensing arrangement break the "circular" reasoning that Justice Goldenhersh rejected in Board of Trade v. Dow Jones? If an existing license can be used to bootstrap a property right, should not the prospect of a licensing arrangement also support a property right? If neither a licensing arrangement nor the prospect of one will create the required competitive relationship, would the competition requirement be met if the plaintiff directly entered the market itself? What relevant difference is there between a firm's decision to enter a market itself and its decision to enter the market through a licensee?

Apart from the historical fact that misappropriation is rooted in unfair competition law, what reason is there for the competition requirement? Justice Goldenhersh may have touched on the reason in his reference to "the ability to license the product to prospective markets *which were not originally contemplated by the creator of the product.*" (Emphasis added.) Only if, at the outset of its investment, a firm contemplated reaping rewards from a particular market is it likely that the firm proportioned its investment to these prospective returns; after the event, the firm should receive a property right to secure these expectations.

B.   LIMITS OF PROTECTION

1.   PERSONAL INTERESTS: RIGHTS IN NAMES

David B. Findlay, Inc. v. Findlay

Court of Appeals of New York, 1966.
18 N.Y.2d 12, 271 N.Y.S.2d 652, 218 N.E.2d 531, 150 U.S.P.Q. 223, modified, 18 N.Y.2d 676, 273 N.Y.S.2d 422, 219 N.E.2d 872, cert. denied, 385 U.S. 930, 87 S.Ct. 289, 17 L.Ed.2d 212.

KEATING, J. When should a man's right to use his own name in his business be limited? This is the question before us.

The individual plaintiff David B. Findlay ("David") and the individual defendant Walstein C. Findlay ("Wally") are brothers. The Findlay art business was founded in 1870 by their grandfather in Kansas City. Their father continued and expanded the business with a Chicago branch managed by Wally and a New York branch established and managed by David on East 57th Street. In 1936 the Kansas City gallery was closed and in 1938, after a dispute, the brothers separated. By agreement David, as president of Findlay Galleries, Inc., and owner of nearly all of the stock of the original Missouri corporation, sold to Wally individually the Chicago gallery and allowed Wally to use the name "Findlay Galleries, Inc." in the conduct of his business in Chicago. Wally organized an Illinois corporation under the name "Findlay Galleries, Inc." in 1938 and has since operated his Chicago gallery. He also opened, in 1961, a Palm Beach, Florida, gallery.

David, since the separation, has operated his gallery on East 57th Street in Manhattan. For many years he has conducted his business on the second floor of 11–13 East 57th Street.

In October, 1963, Wally purchased the premises at 17 East 57th Street and informed David of his plans to open an art gallery. David objected to Wally's use of the name "Findlay" on 57th Street and by letter announced he would "resist any appropriation by you in New York of the name Findlay in connection with a gallery . . . any funds spent by you to establish a gallery at 17 East 57th Street under the name Findlay Galleries, Inc. (or any variation thereof using the name Findlay) are spent at your peril." David also, in self-defense and in an effort to survive, rented additional space at 15 East 57th Street so as to have a street level entrance.

David's objections and pleas seemed to have some effect on Wally. As renovation on the building was carried on from October, 1963 to September, 1964, a large sign proclaimed the coming opening of "W.C.F. Galleries, Inc." There was also a display and listing in the New York Telephone directory under the same name and similar advertisements in other publications. However, in September, 1964 the sign was suddenly changed to announce the imminent opening of "Wally Findlay Galleries" affiliated with "Findlay Galleries, Inc." David immediately sought an injunction.

Wally went ahead with his opening and erected a sidewalk canopy from the curb to the building displaying the name "Wally Findlay Galleries."

The trial court made very detailed findings and, based on them, enjoined defendant from using the names "Wally Findlay Galleries," "Findlay Galleries" and any other designation including the name "Findlay" in the conduct of an art gallery on East 57th Street. The Appellate Division has affirmed on the trial court's findings and we find evidence to sustain them.

The trial court concluded that if injunctive relief were not granted, plaintiff would continue to be damaged by confusion and diversion and would suffer great and irreparable loss in his business and in his name and reputation. In his quarter of a century on East 57th Street David has established a valuable good will and reputation as an art dealer. Through hard work, business ability and expenditure of large sums of money, David has reached the level where a significant portion of his business comes from people who have been referred to him by others and told to go to "Findlay's on 57th St."

The effect of Wally's new gallery, with its long canopy, can only be that those looking for "Findlay's on 57th St." will be easily confused and find their way into Wally's rather than David's gallery. Though Wally perhaps did not deliberately set out to exploit David's good will and reputation, the trial court found, and we agree, that such a result would follow if Wally were permitted to operate a gallery under the name "Wally Findlay Galleries" next door to David.

There were numerous instances of people telephoning or asking at David's for personnel of Wally's or for art work exhibited at Wally's. Many regular customers congratulated David on the opening of "his" new gallery next door. Moreover, advertisements frequently appeared on the same pages of the local press for "Findlay Galleries", "Findlay's", or "Wally Findlay Galleries" thus making it very difficult to tell whose advertisement it was. Even the art editors and reporters referred to Wally as "Findlay Galleries"—the name used for many years by David—or as "the new Findlay Gallery."

It is apparent that confusion has and must result from Wally's opening next to David. This is compounded by the fact that both brothers have for years specialized in French impressionist and post-impressionist painters. Therefore, quite naturally, both brothers have in the past dealt in the works of such famous deceased painters as Modigliani, Degas, Renoir, Gauguin, Bonnard, Braque, Monet and many others.

Although someone seeking a Renoir from David is unlikely to purchase a Degas from Wally, it is likely that with respect to some of the lesser-known impressionists such diversion might happen. More important, someone wishing to own a nude by Modigliani, a dancer by Degas or a portrait of a girl by Renoir would not necessarily have a particular painting in mind and would likely purchase any of these species, whether it be in Wally's or

David's. The items sold by the two brothers are not unique, nonsubstitutional works.

Moreover, art, particularly modern art, is sold only to those who see it. Works of art are sold to those who cross the threshold of the art gallery and the more people you get into your gallery, the more art you will sell. To this end David has worked hard to develop the name "Findlay's on 57th St." and bring in customers. Many people who have the finances to purchase art do not necessarily have the knowledge to distinguish between the works of all the various painters represented by galleries such as Wally's or David's. For this reason they rely on the reputation of the gallery. David has spent over 25 years in developing satisfied customers who will tell others to go to "Findlay's on 57th St." This good will brings in customers who look for a work of art that suits their fancy and if Wally were to continue to use the name Findlay, it is inevitable that some would walk into Wally's by mistake and would have their tastes satisfied there, to David's great harm.

The so-called "sacred right" theory that every man may employ his own name in his business is not unlimited. Moreover, fraud or deliberate intention to deceive or mislead the public are not necessary ingredients to a cause of action.

The present trend of the law is to enjoin the use even of a family name when such use tends or threatens to produce confusion in the public mind. Whether this confusion should be satisfied by misplaced phone calls or confusing advertisements alone we do not decide because there has been a finding that diversion, as well as confusion, will exist if Wally is not enjoined. Thus it is clear that the "confusion" with which we are dealing includes impairment of good will of a business.

In Meneely v. Meneely (62 N.Y. 427) this court noted that one can use his own name provided he does not resort to any artifice or contrivance for the purpose of producing the impression that the establishments are identical, or do anything calculated to mislead the public.

Thirty-five years later, we noted that, as a general principle of law, one's name is his property and he is entitled to its use. However, it was equally a principle of law that no man can sell his goods as those of another. "He may not through unfairness, artifice, misrepresentation or fraud injure the business of another or induce the public to believe his product is the product of that other." (World's Dispensary Medical Ass'n v. Pierce, 203 N.Y. 419, 424, 96 N.E. 738, 740.)

Ryan & Son v. Lancaster Homes (15 N.Y.2d 812, 257 N.Y.S.2d 934, 205 N.E.2d 859, aff'g 22 A.D.2d 186, 254 N.Y.S.2d 473) is distinguishable from the present case because there was lacking in *Ryan* the crucial finding that in the absence of relief plaintiff would be damaged by confusion and diversion. There was no real competition between the two businesses. Again, unlike the instant case where "Findlay's on 57th St." is synonymous in New York City with quality art galleries, "Homes by Ryan" had not become a trade name with a secondary meaning. The court reviewed the law and cited the rule in *Meneely*. "This rule has been qualified, as we have said, only to the extent that use of a family name will be restricted where such use tends or threatens to induce confusion in the public mind". (22 A.D.2d, p. 190, 254 N.Y.S.2d, p. 477.)

In the present case Wally knew that David had conducted his business and built a reputation under the names "Findlay Galleries" and "Findlay's on 57th St." and that many years of effort and expenses had gone into promoting the name of "Findlay" in the art business on 57th Street. He also knew that people would come into his gallery looking for "Findlay Galleries" and even instructed his employees on this matter before he opened. Nonetheless he opened his gallery next door to David dealing in substantially similar works and using the name Findlay. The bona fides of Wally's intentions do not change the applicable principles. The objective facts of this unfair competition and injury to plaintiff's business are determinative, not the defendant's subjective state of mind. Wally's conduct constituted unfair competition and an unfair trade practice, and it is most inequitable to permit Wally to profit from his brother's many years of effort in promoting the name of "Findlay" on 57th Street. Wally should use any name other than "Findlay" in the operation of his business next door to his brother.

In framing its injunction the trial court went no farther than was necessary to avoid the harm threatened. It prevented the use of the name Findlay but limited this to the particular area in which its use would cause confusion and diversion—East 57th Street. It resolved the conflict with as little injury as possible to Wally. The proof showed and the trial court found that many, if not most of the leading art galleries, are now located on Madison Avenue and in the area of the 60's, 70's and 80's in New York City. Wally could probably have found an appropriate place for his New York gallery other than at 17 East 57th Street and can now either find such another location or remain where he is under some name such as "W.C.F. Galleries."

The decision in this case is in accord with the directions of our court: "The defendant has the right to use his name. The plaintiff has the right to have the defendant use it in such a way as will not injure his business or mislead the public. Where there is such a conflict of rights, it is the duty of the court so to regulate the use of his name by the defendant that, due protection to the plaintiff being afforded, there will be as little injury to him as possible." (World's Dispensary Med. Ass'n v. Pierce, supra, 203 N.Y. p. 425, 96 N.E. p. 740.)

The order of the Appellate Division should be affirmed, with costs.

The opinion of BURKE, J., dissenting, is omitted.

N O T E S

1. In principle, unfair competition cases involving personal names are no different than cases involving other forms of commercial insignia. A plaintiff whose name is common and has no secondary meaning must show that defendant's use of the name is part of an active passing off scheme and that consumers have actually been confused. If plaintiff's name has attracted some secondary meaning, she need show only likelihood of confusion. And, if the plaintiff's name is particularly distinctive, and secondary meaning is particularly strong, courts will presume consumer deception and grant relief even absent proof that confusion is likely.

Courts sometimes intimate that personal name cases are different from other unfair competition cases: "A man's name is his own property, and he has the same right to its use and enjoyment as he has to that of any other species of property." This view was hardly more than dicta in the case that introduced it into the United States, Brown Chem. Co. v. Meyer, 139 U.S. 540, 544, 11 S.Ct. 625, 627, 35 L.Ed. 247 (1891). The name at issue, "Brown," was common—as indicated by the name of the opinion's author, Mr. Justice Brown. Since the name had captured scant secondary meaning, and no confusion or fraud had been proved, the decision permitting defendant's use of the name is easily rationalized in terms of general unfair competition doctrine. Compare Brown Sheet Iron & Steel Co. v. Brown Steel Tank Co., 198 Minn. 276, 269 N.W. 633 (1936), which recognized that free use of even a common name like Brown may be curtailed if, as to one user, it has gained secondary meaning.

Should the fact that the personal name used by the defendant is not her real name—or, in the case of a corporation, is not the name of a founder—bar its use, or should it only constitute some evidence of intent to palm off the goods or services as those of plaintiff whose name it is? Of plaintiff whose real name it also is not?

2. Many personal name cases are, like *Findlay,* precipitated by a family dispute. In Edison v. Thomas A. Edison, Jr., Chem. Co., 128 Fed. 957 (D.Del.1904), Thomas A. Edison filed a complaint that sounded as much in parental dismay as in unfair competition, seeking to restrain his son, Thomas A. Edison, Jr., from using his name in competing fields of invention:

> That your orator has a son named Thomas A. Edison, Jr., who is now about thirty years of age; that your orator's said son was employed by your orator in your orator's various interests for a short time; that since that time your orator's said son has had no regular occupation, but as your orator is informed and believes, partially supports himself by trading on his name and by selling the use of his name to various unprincipled persons, who use the said name for the purpose of defrauding the public; that your orator's said son while he was in your orator's employ made no practical inventions, and your orator is satisfied that he has made no invention since that time.

The court refused an injunction. Since defendant's advertisements referred to plaintiff only for the purpose of identifying its founder as his son, the court concluded that "There is nothing in any of them to confuse or confound, in the mind of any such [ordinarily intelligent and prudent] person, the complainant either with his son, Thomas A. Edison, Jr., or the defendant [corporation] with respect to the production and sale of the device." Id. at 961.

Should family cases, like *Findlay* and *Edison,* be decided on principles different from those governing nonfamily cases?

3. When a founder leaves the company that bears his name, can he, in competing with his former firm, publicize his own achievements? In Levitt Corp. v. Levitt, 593 F.2d 463, 201 U.S.P.Q. 513 (2d Cir.1979), the Second Circuit Court of Appeals concluded that cases of this sort should be treated differently from garden variety personal name cases. "Where, as here . . . the infringing party has previously sold his business, including use of his name and its goodwill to the plaintiff, sweeping injunctive relief is more tolerable." 593 F.2d at 468.

Defendant was the founder of Levitt & Sons, a major builder of residential communities best known for its "Levittown" tract developments in New York and Pennsylvania. After fifty years at the helm of Levitt & Sons, defendant merged the business into a wholly-owned subsidiary of ITT Corporation, the predecessor in interest to plaintiff. The new company succeeded to and continued to exploit Levitt & Sons' goodwill, trademarks and trade names, including "Levitt" and "Levittown." In November, 1975, as part of his arrangement with ITT and the successor owners of Levitt & Sons, defendant covenanted not to compete with Levitt & Sons until June, 1977. The agreement provided that, although defendant could enter the industry after that time, he did not "have any right to use the name 'Levitt' as a corporate title, trademark or trade name in the construction business. He did retain the right to use his own name publicly as a corporate officer or director of a business enterprise, but only to the extent that such use would not be likely to create confusion with the corporate title, trademarks, or trade names of Levitt & Sons, Inc." 593 F.2d at 466.

In February, 1978, after the covenant not to compete had expired, defendant issued a press release stating that plaintiff's acquisition of Levitt Corporation was "totally confusing the general public and the business community," and that the question being posed by all is "who and what is the real Levitt." The press release announced that Mr. Levitt would soon reveal plans to build "a new Levittown in the United States." Subsequently, defendant placed advertisements in the *Washington Post* and the *New York Times* for "Levittown Florida," and referring to "Levitt and Sons" and to "Levitt's Engineering and Planning Department." "Most significantly, William Levitt identified himself as the founder of the company that had built the Levittowns of New York, New Jersey, and elsewhere." 593 F.2d at 466.

Agreeing with the district court that defendant Levitt had infringed the trademarks of the Levitt Corporation, and that his use of his name in conjunction with the marks had caused substantial confusion between the two enterprises, the court of appeals affirmed the district court's order enjoining defendant from using the term "Levittown" in connection with his Florida project and requiring defendant not only to remove the "Levittown" name from all advertising, maps, streets, government application forms and other documents, but also, upon plaintiff's request, to issue corrective advertising explaining the lawsuit in order to restore the plaintiffs to the position they held before Mr. Levitt invaded the Florida market.

Since defendant Levitt's skill in planning, site selection and construction doubtless played an important role in the success of his former company, should he, at the least, have been allowed to identify himself with its past ventures? The court also affirmed a part of the district court decree that permanently enjoined Levitt from publicizing his prior connection with Levitt & Sons "to avoid the likelihood of confusion that would arise if the defendants should invoke the names of earlier Levitt projects in reciting the highlights of his career." 593 F.2d at 467. The circuit court concluded that "under these circumstances, a disclaimer of any *current* relationship between Mr. Levitt and the corporation will not protect the plaintiff's rights, for the effect of such a statement would be to inform the public that the achievements to which Levitt Corporation justly lays claim really are attributable to the efforts of someone else, now in business for himself." 593 F.2d at 470 n.12.

What does a company acquire when it buys goodwill? If defendant had given his original company a coined name, like "Strathmore," rather than his own name, would the court have allowed him to refer to his former association with the company by that name? Was the decision in *Levitt* properly sensitive to the expectations and interests of housing consumers?

2.   ECONOMIC INTERESTS: THE PLACE OF UNFAIR COMPETITION IN THE COMPETITIVE PLAN

Crescent Tool Co. v. Kilborn & Bishop Co.

Circuit Court of Appeals, Second Circuit, 1917.
247 Fed. 299.

LEARNED HAND, District Judge. The cases of so-called "nonfunctional" unfair competition, starting with the "coffee mill case," Enterprise Mfg. Co. v. Landers, Frary & Clark, 131 Fed. 240, 65 C.C.A. 587, are only instances of the doctrine of "secondary" meaning. All of them presuppose that the appearance of the article, like its descriptive title in true cases of "secondary" meaning, has become associated in the public mind with the first comer as manufacturer or source, and, if a second comer imitates the article exactly, that the public will believe his goods have come from the first, and will buy, in part, at least, because of that deception. Therefore it is apparent that it is an absolute condition to any relief whatever that the plaintiff in such cases show that the appearance of his wares has in fact come to mean that some particular person—the plaintiff may not be individually known—makes them, and that the public cares who does make them, and not merely for their appearance and structure. It will not be enough only to show how pleasing they are, because all the features of beauty or utility which commend them to the public are by hypothesis already in the public domain. The defendant has as much right to copy the "nonfunctional" features of the article as any others, so long as they have not become associated with the plaintiff as manufacturer or source. The critical question of fact at the outset always is whether the public is moved in any degree to buy the article because of its source and what are the features by which it distinguishes that source. Unless the plaintiff can answer this question he can take no step forward; no degree of imitation of details is actionable in its absence.

In the case at bar* it nowhere appears that before 1910, when the defendant began to make its wrenches, the general appearance of the plaintiff's wrench had come to indicate to the public any one maker as its source, or that the wrench had been sold in any part because of its source, as distinct from its utility or neat appearance. It is not enough to show that the wrench became popular under the name "Crescent"; the plaintiff must prove that before 1910 the public had already established the habit of buying it, not solely because they wanted that kind of wrench, but because they also wanted a Crescent, and thought all such wrenches were Crescents.

Upon the trial the plaintiff may, however, be able to establish this, and it is only fair to indicate broadly the considerations which will then

---

* "This is an appeal from a temporary injunction granted by the District Court for Connecticut on the 25th day of January, 1917, restraining the defendant pendente lite from manufacturing and selling its adjustable wrenches. The facts as set forth in the affidavits are substantially as follows:

"The plaintiff is a New York corporation, organized in 1907 for the purpose of manufacturing tools, and has since that time been engaged in the manufacture among other things of pliers and wrenches. In December, 1908, it put upon the market an adjustable wrench, and has widely advertised the same from that time to the present. The wrench, on account of its appearance and new and original shape, pleased the public, and its sales grew rapidly from year to year, so that it became known to the jobbing trade and retailers and consumers as the 'Crescent' type of wrench. Its main structural features were all old in detail. It was adjustable to bolts and nuts of different sizes somewhat after the manner of a monkey wrench, but it was nevertheless quite different mechanically from a monkey wrench. It had a straight handle of web and rib construction, spreading slightly from the neck to the end, with a hole in the end of the web by which it could be hung up. No adjustable wrench of precisely the same character had ever appeared upon the market. There had, however, been adjustable wrenches, some with straight handles,

some with web and rib curved handles, and there had been other tools with straight web and rib handles, somewhat broader at the end than at the neck. Plaintiff's name is plainly printed upon the web of the handle in raised letters.

"The defendant is a Connecticut corporation, organized in 1896 and engaged in the manufacture of wrenches and other hardware for some 18 years past. Some time in 1910 it began the manufacture of an adjustable wrench, which it called its 'K & B 22½ E adjustable.' This is substantially a direct facsimile of the plaintiff's wrench, with the exception that the defendant's name appears upon the web in place of the plaintiff's as follows: 'The Kilborn & Bishop Company, New Haven, Connecticut, U.S.A.,' in distinct raised letters. The defendant made no effort to imitate the boxes or packages of the plaintiff's wrench, nor did it use the word 'Crescent' in any way in its sale; but it did begin selling the goods in general competition with the plaintiff's wrenches until the order issued herein.

"There is evidence in the correspondence between the plaintiff and its customers that confusion has arisen between the plaintiff's wrenches and the defendant's, customers having supposed that the Kilborn & Bishop wrench was a Crescent, but there was no evidence that the defendant in any way facilitated this confusion." 247 F. 299–300.

determine the scope of his relief. In such cases neither side has an absolute right, because their mutual rights conflict. Thus the plaintiff has the right not to lose his customers through false representations that those are his wares which in fact are not, but he may not monopolize any design or pattern, however trifling. The defendant, on the other hand, may copy the plaintiff's goods slavishly down to the minutest detail; but he may not represent himself as the plaintiff in their sale. When the appearance of the goods has in fact come to represent a given person as their source, and that person is in fact the plaintiff, it is impossible to make these rights absolute; compromise is essential, exactly as it is with the right to use the common language in cases of "secondary" meaning. We can only say that the court must require such changes in appearance as will effectively distinguish the defendant's wares with the least expense to him; in no event may the plaintiff suppress the defendant's sale altogether. The proper meaning of the phrase "nonfunctional," is only this: That in such cases the injunction is usually confined to nonessential elements, since these are usually enough to distinguish the goods, and are the least burdensome for the defendant to change. Whether changes in them are in all conceivable cases the limit of the plaintiff's right is a matter not before us. If a case should arise in which no effective distinction was possible without change in functional elements, it would demand consideration; but the District Court may well find an escape here from that predicament. Certainly the precise extent and kind of relief must in the first instance be a matter for the discretion of that court.

Order reversed, and motion denied.

Sears, Roebuck & Co. v. Stiffel Co.

Supreme Court of the United States, 1964.
376 U.S. 225, 84 S.Ct. 784, 11 L.Ed.2d 661, 140 U.S.P.Q. 524.

Mr. Justice BLACK delivered the opinion of the Court.

The question in this case is whether a State's unfair competition law can, consistently with the federal patent laws, impose liability for or prohibit the copying of an article which is protected by neither a federal patent nor a copyright. The respondent, Stiffel Company, secured design and mechanical patents on a "pole lamp"—a vertical tube having lamp fixtures along the outside, the tube being made so that it will stand upright between the floor and ceiling of a room. Pole lamps proved a decided commercial success, and soon after Stiffel brought them on the market Sears, Roebuck & Company put on the market a substantially identical lamp, which it sold more cheaply, Sears' retail price being about the same as Stiffel's wholesale price. Stiffel then brought this action against Sears in the United States District Court for the Northern District of Illinois, claiming in its first count that by copying its design Sears had infringed Stiffel's patents and in its second count that by selling copies of Stiffel's lamp Sears had caused confusion in the trade as to the source of the lamps and had thereby engaged in unfair competition under Illinois law. There was evidence that identifying tags were not attached to the Sears lamps although labels appeared on the cartons in which they were delivered to customers, that customers had asked Stiffel whether its lamps differed from Sears', and that in two cases customers who had bought Stiffel lamps had complained to Stiffel on learning that Sears was selling substantially identical lamps at a much lower price.

The District Court, after holding the patents invalid for want of invention, went on to find as a fact that Sears' lamp was "a substantially exact copy" of Stiffel's and that the two lamps were so much alike, both in appearance and in functional details, "that confusion between them is likely, and some confusion has already occurred." On these findings the court held Sears guilty of unfair competition, enjoined Sears "from unfairly competing with [Stiffel] by selling or attempting to sell pole lamps identical to or confusingly similar to" Stiffel's lamp, and ordered an accounting to fix profits and damages resulting from Sears' "unfair competition."

The Court of Appeals affirmed. That court held that, to make out a case of unfair competition under Illinois law, there was no need to show that Sears had been "palming off" its lamps as Stiffel lamps; Stiffel had only to prove that there was a "likelihood of confusion as to the source of the products"—that the two articles were sufficiently identical that customers could not tell who had made a particular one. Impressed by the "remarkable sameness of appearance" of the lamps, the Court of Appeals upheld the trial court's findings of likelihood of confusion and some actual confusion, findings which the appellate court construed to mean confusion "as to the source of the lamps." The Court of Appeals thought this enough under Illinois law to sustain the trial court's holding of unfair competition, and thus held Sears liable under Illinois law for doing no more than copying and marketing an unpatented article. We granted certiorari to consider whether this use of a State's law of unfair competition is compatible with the federal patent law.

Before the Constitution was adopted, some States had granted patents either by special act or by general statute, but when the Constitution was adopted provision for a federal patent law was made one of the enumerated powers of Congress because, as Madison put it in The Federalist No. 43, the States "cannot separately make effectual provision" for either patents or copyrights. That constitutional provision is Art. I, § 8, cl. 8, which empowers Congress "To promote the Progress of Science and useful Arts, by securing for limited Times to Authors and Inventors the exclusive Right to their respective Writings and Discoveries." Pursuant to this constitutional authority, Congress in 1790 enacted the first federal patent and copyright law, and ever since that time has fixed the conditions upon which patents and copyright shall be granted. These laws, like other laws of the United States enacted pursuant to constitutional authority, are the supreme law of the land. When state law touches upon the area of these federal statutes, it is "familiar doctrine" that the federal policy "may not be set at naught, or its benefits denied" by the state law. Sola Elec. Co. v. Jefferson Elec. Co., 317 U.S. 173, 173, 176, 63 S.Ct. 172, 173, 87 L.Ed. 165 (1942). This is true, of course, even if the state law is enacted in the exercise of otherwise undoubted state power.

The grant of a patent is the grant of a statutory monopoly; indeed, the grant of patents in England was an explicit exception to the statute of James I prohibiting monopolies. Patents are not given as favors, as was the case of monopolies given by the Tudor monarchs, but are meant to encourage invention by rewarding the inventor with the right, limited to a term of years fixed by the patent, to exclude others from the use of his invention. During that period of time no one may make, use, or sell the patented product without the patentee's authority. But in rewarding useful invention, the "rights and welfare of the community must be fairly dealt with and effectually guarded." Kendall v. Winsor, 21 How. 322, 329, 16 L.Ed. 165 (1859). To that end the prerequisites to obtaining a patent are strictly observed, and when the patent has issued the limitations on its exercise are equally strictly enforced. To begin with, a genuine "invention" or "discovery" must be demonstrated "lest in the constant demand for new appliances the heavy hand of tribute be laid on each slight technological advance in an art." Cuno Engineering Corp. v. Automatic Devices Corp., 314 U.S. 84, 92, 62 S.Ct. 37, 41, 86 L.Ed. 58 (1941). Once the patent issues, it is strictly construed, it cannot be used to secure any monopoly beyond that contained in the patent, the patentee's control over the product when it leaves his hands is sharply limited, and the patent monopoly may not be used in disregard of the antitrust laws. Finally, and especially relevant here, when the patent expires the monopoly created by it expires, too, and the right to make the article—including the right to make it in precisely the shape it carried when patented—passes to the public.

Thus the patent system is one in which uniform federal standards are carefully used to promote invention while at the same time preserving free competition. Obviously a State could not, consistently with the Supremacy Clause of the Constitution, extend the life of a patent beyond its expiration date or give a patent on an article which lacked the level of invention required for federal patents. To do either would run counter to the policy of Congress of granting patents only to true inventions, and then only for a limited time. Just as a State cannot encroach upon the federal patent laws directly, it cannot, under some other law, such as that forbidding unfair competition, give protection of a kind that clashes with the objectives of the federal patent laws.

In the present case the "pole lamp" sold by Stiffel has been held not to be entitled to the protection of either a mechanical or a design patent. An unpatentable article, like an article on which the patent has expired, is in the public domain and may be made and sold by whoever chooses to do so. What Sears did was to copy Stiffel's design and to sell lamps almost identical to those sold by Stiffel. This it had every right to do under the federal patent laws. That Stiffel originated the pole lamp and made it popular is immaterial. "Sharing in the goodwill of an article unprotected by patent or trade-mark is the exercise of a right possessed by all—and in the free exercise of which the consuming public is deeply interested." Kellogg

Co. v. National Biscuit Co., 305 U.S., at 122, 59 S.Ct. at 115. To allow a State by use of its law of unfair competition to prevent the copying of an article which represents too slight an advance to be patented would be to permit the State to block off from the public something which federal law has said belongs to the public. The result would be that while federal law grants only 14 or 17 years' protection to genuine inventions, States could allow perpetual protection to articles too lacking in novelty to merit any patent at all under federal constitutional standards. This would be too great an encroachment on the federal patent system to be tolerated.

Sears has been held liable here for unfair competition because of a finding of likelihood of confusion based only on the fact that Sears' lamp was copied from Stiffel's unpatented lamp and that consequently the two looked exactly alike. Of course there could be "confusion" as to who had manufactured these nearly identical articles. But mere inability of the public to tell two identical articles apart is not enough to support an injunction against copying or an award of damages for copying that which the federal patent laws permit to be copied. Doubtless a State may, in appropriate circumstances, require that goods, whether patented or unpatented, be labeled or that other precautionary steps be taken to prevent customers from being misled as to the source, just as it may protect businesses in the use of their trademarks, labels, or distinctive dress in the packaging of goods so as to prevent others, by imitating such markings, from misleading purchasers as to the source of the goods. But because of the federal patent laws a State may not, when the article is unpatented and uncopyrighted, prohibit the copying of the article itself or award damages for such copying. The judgment below did both and in so doing gave Stiffel the equivalent of a patent monopoly on its unpatented lamp. That was error, and Sears is entitled to a judgment in its favor.

Reversed.

Compco Corp. v. Day–Brite Lighting, Inc.

Supreme Court of the United States, 1964.
376 U.S. 234, 84 S.Ct. 779, 11 L.Ed.2d 669, 140 U.S.P.Q. 531.

Mr. Justice BLACK delivered the opinion of the Court.

As in Sears, Roebuck & Co. v. Stiffel Co., ante, ... the question here is whether the use of a state unfair competition law to give relief against the copying of an unpatented industrial design conflicts with the federal patent laws. Both Compco and Day–Brite are manufacturers of fluorescent lighting fixtures of a kind widely used in offices and stores. Day–Brite in 1955 secured from the Patent Office a design patent on a reflector having cross-ribs claimed to give both strength and attractiveness to the fixture. Day–Brite also sought, but was refused, a mechanical patent on the same device. After Day–Brite had begun selling its fixture, Compco's predecessor began making and selling fixtures very similar to Day–Brite's. This action was then brought by Day–Brite. One count alleged that Compco had infringed Day–Brite's design patent; a second count charged that the public and the trade had come to associate this particular design with Day–Brite, that Compco had copied Day–Brite's distinctive design so as to confuse and deceive purchasers into thinking Compco's fixtures were actually Day–Brite's, and that by doing this Compco had unfairly competed with Day–Brite. The complaint prayed for both an accounting and an injunction.

The District Court held the design patent invalid; but as to the second count, while the court did not find that Compco had engaged in any deceptive or fraudulent practices, it did hold that Compco had been guilty of unfair competition under Illinois law. The court found that the overall appearance of Compco's fixture was "the same, to the eye of the ordinary observer, as the overall appearance" of Day–Brite's reflector, which embodied the design of the invalidated patent; that the appearance of Day–Brite's design had "the capacity to identify [Day–Brite] in the trade and does in fact so identify [it] to the trade"; that the concurrent sale of the two products was "likely to cause confusion in the trade"; and that "[a]ctual confusion has occurred." On these findings the court adjudged Compco guilty of unfair competition in the sale of its fixtures, ordered Compco to account to Day–Brite for damages, and enjoined Compco "from unfairly competing with plaintiff by the sale or attempted sale of reflectors identical to, or confusingly similar to" those made by Day–Brite. The Court of Appeals held there was substantial evidence in the record to support the District Court's finding of likely confusion and that this finding was sufficient to support a holding of unfair competition under Illinois law. Although the District Court had not made such a finding, the appellate court observed that "several choices of ribbing were apparently available to meet the functional needs of the product," yet Compco "chose precisely the same design used by the plaintiff and followed it so closely as to make confusion likely." 311 F.2d, at 30. A design which identifies its maker to the trade, the Court of Appeals held, is a "protectable" right under Illinois law, even though the design is unpatentable. We granted certiorari.

To support its findings of likelihood of confusion and actual confusion, the trial court was able to refer to only one circumstance in the record. A plant manager who had installed some of Compco's fixtures later asked Day–Brite to service the fixtures, thinking they had been made by Day–Brite. There was no testimony given by a purchaser or by anyone else that any customer had ever been misled, deceived, or "confused," that is, that anyone had ever bought a Compco fixture thinking it was a Day–Brite fixture. All the record shows, as to the one instance cited by the trial court, is that both Compco and Day–Brite fixtures had been installed in the same plant, that three years later some repairs were needed, and that the manager viewing the Compco fixtures—hung at least 15 feet above the floor and arranged end to end in a continuous line so that identifying marks were hidden-thought they were Day–Brite fixtures and asked Day–Brite to service them. Not only is this incident suggestive only of confusion *after* a purchase had been made, but also there is considerable evidence of the care taken by Compco to prevent customer confusion, including clearly labeling both the fixtures and the containers in which they were shipped and not selling through manufacturers' representatives who handled competing lines.

Notwithstanding the thinness of the evidence to support findings of likely and actual confusion among purchasers, we do not find it necessary in this case to determine whether there is "clear error" in these findings. They, like those in Sears, Roebuck & Co. v. Stiffel Co., supra, were based wholly on the fact that selling an article which is an exact copy of another unpatented article is likely to produce and did in this case produce confusion as to the source of the article. Even accepting the findings, we hold that the order for an accounting for damages and the injunction are in conflict with the federal patent laws. Today we have held in Sears, Roebuck & Co. v. Stiffel Co., supra, that when an article is unprotected by a patent or a copyright, state law may not forbid others to copy that article. To forbid copying would interfere with the federal policy, found in Art. I, § 8, cl. 8, of the Constitution and in the implementing federal statutes, of allowing free access to copy whatever the federal patent and copyright laws leave in the public domain. Here Day–Brite's fixture has been held not to be entitled to a design or mechanical patent. Under the federal patent laws it is, therefore, in the public domain and can be copied in every detail by whoever pleases. It is true that the trial court found that the configuration of Day–Brite's fixture identified Day–Brite to the trade because the arrangement of the ribbing had, like a trademark, acquired a "secondary meaning" by which that particular design was associated with Day–Brite. But if the design is not entitled to a design patent or other federal statutory protection, then it can be copied at will.

As we have said in Sears, while the federal patent laws prevent a State from prohibiting the copying and selling of unpatented articles, they do not stand in the way of state law, statutory or decisional, which requires those who make and sell copies to take precautions to identify their products as their own. A State of course has power to impose liability upon those who, knowing that the public is relying upon an original manufacturer's reputation for quality and integrity, deceive the public by palming off their copies as the original. That an article copied from an unpatented article could be made in some other way, that the design is "nonfunctional" and not essential to the use of either article, that the configuration of the article copied may have a "secondary meaning" which identifies the maker to the trade, or that there may be "confusion" among purchasers as to which article is which or as to who is the maker, may be relevant evidence in applying a State's law requiring such precautions as labeling; however, and regardless of the copier's motives, neither these facts nor any others can furnish a basis for imposing liability for or prohibiting the actual acts of copying and selling. And of course a State cannot hold a copier accountable in damages for failure to label or otherwise to identify his goods unless his failure is in violation of valid state statutory or decisional law requiring the copier to label or take other precautions to prevent confusion of customers as to the source of the goods.

Since the judgment below forbids the sale of a copy of an unpatented article and orders an accounting for damages for such copying, it cannot stand.

Reversed.

Mr. Justice HARLAN, concurring in the result.

In one respect I would give the States more leeway in unfair competition "copying" cases than the Court's opinions would allow. If copying is found, other than by an inference arising from the mere act of copying, to have been undertaken with the dominant purpose and effect of palming off one's goods as those of another or of confusing customers as to the source of such goods, I see no reason why the State may not impose reasonable restrictions on the future "copying" itself. Vindication of the paramount federal interest at stake does not require a State to tolerate such specifically oriented predatory business practices. Apart from this, I am in accord with the opinions of the Court, and concur in both judgments since neither case presents the point on which I find myself in disagreement.

N O T E S

1. *Sears–Compco.* How wide a preemptive swath did the Court intend in *Sears* and *Compco*? The decisions recognized that states might prohibit the imitation of trade insignia in order to prevent consumer deception as to source of goods. Would the Court require a showing of actual confusion before allowing an injunction against the competitor's use? Would likelihood of confusion suffice? What if the action was brought on a dilution or zone of expansion theory, and plaintiff could show no consumer confusion?

Is there any logic to the distinction between goods or articles on the one hand, and packages or marks on the other? Can you think of situations in which the trademark *is* the article? In National Football League Properties, Inc. v. Consumer Enterprises, Inc., 26 Ill.App.3d 814, 327 N.E.2d 242, 185 U.S.P.Q. 550 (1st Dist.1975), cert. denied, 423 U.S. 1018, 96 S.Ct. 454, 46 L.Ed.2d 390, 188 U.S.P.Q. 96 (1975), plaintiff, the exclusive licensing agent for the name and symbol of each club in the National Football League, obtained an injunction against defendant's unauthorized manufacture and sale of emblems duplicating club marks. Defendant unsuccessfully argued that it was "selling the emblem designs as merely decorative products," that the emblems were not "performing the trademark function of source identification," and that, under *Sears* and *Compco*, states cannot "prohibit the copying of unpatented and uncopyrighted" articles. 327 N.E.2d at 246. While the court could have rested its decision on *Sears'* exemption of trademarks, it chose instead to hold that a trademark could not be considered an "article" within the terms of *Sears* and *Compco*.

What force, if any, is left to *Sears* and *Compco* after the Court's decisions in *Aronson*, page 50, above, Kewanee v. Bicron, page 151, below, and Goldstein v. California, discussed at page 801? If these decisions reduced the sweep of *Sears* and *Compco,* did Bonito Boats v. Thunder Craft Boats, page 999, below, widen it?

One reason manufacturers have sought state unfair competition protection for product designs like those involved in *Sears* and *Compco* is that federal law does not offer full protection for industrial design. Protection of industrial design under copyright, patent and trademark law is considered in Part Five, below.

2. *Crescent Tool.* How would you have counselled plaintiff in *Crescent Tool* to market its wrench so that it would have been able to capture the goodwill that accrued to the wrench? Some courts equate functionality with strictly utilitarian aspects. Other courts treat functionality as encompassing any feature, including aesthetic appeal that affects consumer choice. See Zippo Mfg. Co. v. Rogers Imports, Inc., 216 F.Supp. 670, 137 U.S.P.Q. 413 (S.D.N.Y.1963). See also Inwood Laboratories, Inc. v. Ives Laboratories, Inc., 456 U.S. 844, 851 n. 10, 102 S.Ct. 2182, 2187 n. 10, 72 L.Ed.2d 606, 214 U.S.P.Q. 1 (1982) ("In general terms, a product feature is functional if it is essential to the use or purpose of the article or if it affects the cost or quality of the article.").

What, if anything, did *Sears* and *Compco* add to *Crescent?* The rule allowing simulation of an article's functional features, but not its distinctive nonfunctional features, accommodates state law to federal competitive interests. "If any portion of the goods or their packages are functional, then, in determining whether protection should be extended, the functional features are properly judged only by Federal patent law standards, such as novelty and nonobviousness, and not by a State's law of unfair competition. If protection is given to such functional aspects under a State's unfair competition law the State, in effect, would be granting a perpetual monopoly, whereas the protection available under the federal patent laws is only a limited monopoly. But where the feature, or more aptly design, is a mere arbitrary embellishment, imitation may be forbidden where the requisite showing of secondary meaning is made." Duo–Tint Bulb & Battery Co., Inc. v. Moline Supply Co., 46 Ill.App.3d 145, 151, 4 Ill.Dec. 685, 690, 360 N.E.2d 798 (3d Dist.1977).

Careful readers of *Sears* and *Compco* thought the Court had obliterated the functional-nonfunctional distinction by banning all state prohibitions of product simulation. See, for example, the essay by Ralph S. Brown, Jr., in Symposium, Product Simulation: A Right or a Wrong?, 64 Colum. L. Rev. 1178, 1220–1221 (1964). Reread the next-to-last paragraph in Justice Black's *Compco* opinion to see if you agree. The Eighth Circuit Court of Appeals has characterized this crucial passage as dictum. "The law of trademark and the issues of functionality and secondary meaning were not before the Court. The issue before the Court was whether state law could extend the effective term of patent protection granted by the federal statutes." Truck Equipment Serv. Co. v. Fruehauf Corp., 536 F.2d 1210, 1214, 191 U.S.P.Q. 79 (8th Cir.), cert. denied, 429 U.S. 861, 97 S.Ct. 164, 50 L.Ed.2d 139, 191 U.S.P.Q. 588 (1976).

3. *Preemption of Dilution Doctrine.* Some commentators predicted that when Congress amended the Trademark Act to add an antidilution provision, the amendments would also preempt state antidilution statutes. In fact, the Federal Trademark Dilution Act of 1995, Pub. Law 104–98, 109 Stat. 985, adding a new section 43(c) to the Trademark Act, did not override state antidilution provisions. Instead, it provided that ownership of a federally registered mark shall be a defense to an action brought "under the common law or a statute of a State ... that seeks to prevent dilution of the distinctiveness of a mark, label or form of advertisement." 15 U.S.C. § 1125(c)(3). According to the House Report on the Act, the provision offers "a further incentive for the federal registration of marks," while recognizing that "[u]nlike patent and copyright laws, federal trademark law coexists with state trademark law." H.R. Rep. 104–374 (1995). The federal antidilution provisions are discussed at page 299, below.

Should federal trademark law preempt state antidilution law? The injunction ordered by the district court in Mead v. Toyota, page 72 above, encompassed Lexus sales campaigns not only in New York, but across the United States. Asking whether it is "particularly unfair (or otherwise improper) to permit such extraterritorial regulation if the enjoined conduct is not prohibited in most of the country," Professor David S. Welkowitz has argued that "there are constitutional limitations on the power of a state to regulate activity in other states, and that injunctions like the one issued in *Mead* exceed those limits." David Welkowitz, Preemption, Extraterritoriality, and the Problem of State Antidilution Laws, 67 Tul. L. Rev. 1, 3–4 (1992). See also Paul Heald, Unfair Competition and Federal Law: Constitutional Restraints on the Scope of State Law, 54 U. Chi. L. Rev. 1411 (1987); Joseph P. Bauer, A Federal Law of Unfair Competition: What Should be the Reach of Section 43(a) of the Lanham Act?, 31 U.C.L.A. L. Rev. 671 (1984).

4. *Preemption of Misappropriation Doctrine.* Misappropriation doctrine, because it may confer property-like rights on unpatentable or uncopyrightable subject matter, is a natural candidate for constitutional preemption. Nonetheless, the doctrine has generally eluded preemption under the rule of *Sears* and *Compco*. Section 301 of the Copyright Act has proved to be more effective, at least in trimming misappropriation's more extended features. Under section 301, a state law will be preempted if three conditions are met: the protected work is fixed in a tangible medium of expression; the work comes within the subject matter of copyright as described in sections 102 and 103 of the Copyright Act; and the right granted is equivalent to one or more of the exclusive rights granted by section 106 of the Copyright Act.

In National Basketball Assoc. v. Motorola, Inc., 105 F.3d 841, 844–45, 853, 41 U.S.P.Q.2d 1585 (2d Cir.1997), the court of appeals reversed a district court decision that had enjoined Motorola from transmitting scores and other data about NBA games in progress through its SportsTrax pager; Motorola had obtained the data, without the NBA's permission, from correspondents who gathered them from television or radio broadcasts of the games. Relying on the legislative history to the 1976 Copyright Act for the proposition that a " 'hot-news' *INS*-like claim survives preemption," the court of appeals ruled that such claims should be limited to cases where: "(i) a plaintiff generates or gathers information at a cost; (ii) the information is time-sensitive; (iii) a defendant's use of the information constitutes free riding on the plaintiff's efforts; (iv) the defendant is in direct competition with a product or service offered by the plaintiffs; and (v) the ability of other parties to free-ride on the efforts of the plaintiff or others would so reduce the incentive to produce the product or service that its existence or quality would be substantially threatened. We conclude that SportsTrax does not meet that test." Specifically, while Motorola's conduct encompassed some of these elements, such as time-sensitivity, it did not encompass others, such as competitive effect. "With regard to the NBA's primary products—producing basketball games with live attendance and licensing copyrighted broadcasts of those games—there is no evidence that anyone regards SportsTrax or the AOL site as a substitute for attending NBA games or watching them on television."

Section 301 is discussed in detail beginning at page 793, below. See generally Howard B. Abrams, Copyright, Misappropriation, and Preemption: Constitutional and Statutory Limits of State Law Protection, 1983 Sup. Ct. Rev. 509.

5. *Preemption From Other Sources.* The Constitution's copyright-patent clause is not the only source of federal preemption of state law. Section 39(b) of the Lanham Act, 15 U.S.C.A. § 1121(b), prohibits states from requiring the alteration of a federally registered mark or requiring that "additional trademarks, service marks, trade names, or corporate names that may be associated with or incorporated into the registered mark be displayed in the mark in a manner differing from the display of such additional trademarks, service marks, trade names, or corporate names contemplated by the registered mark as exhibited in the certificate of registration issued by the United States Patent and Trademark Office." The provision, added in 1982, was specifically aimed at preventing state regulatory agencies from requiring a national real estate brokerage franchisor to display its mark along with the name of local franchisees in formats that departed from the format for which the franchisor had obtained federal registration. See J. Thomas McCarthy, Trademarks and Unfair Competition § 22.2 (3d ed. 1996).

Somewhat farther afield, the Washington Supreme Court has held that the exercise of federal regulatory authority over the names of national banks overrides state unfair competition law, so that a court could not prohibit a federally-regulated bank from using a name, approved by the Comptroller of the Currency, that was confusingly similar to a name earlier adopted by a savings and loan association in the state. Pioneer First Federal Savings & Loan Assoc. v. Pioneer Nat'l Bank, 98 Wn.2d 853, 659 P.2d 481 (1983).

III. Trade Secrets

A. Theory of Protection

Metallurgical Industries Inc. v. Fourtek, Inc.

United States Court of Appeals, Fifth Circuit 1986.
790 F.2d 1195, 229 U.S.P.Q. 945.

GEE, Circuit Judge:

Today's case requires us to review Texas law on the misappropriation of trade secrets. Having done so, we conclude that the district court misconceived the nature and elements of this cause of action, a misconception that led it to direct a verdict erroneously in favor of appellee Bielefeldt. We also conclude that the court abused its discretion in excluding certain evidence. Accordingly, we affirm in part, reverse in part, and remand the case for a new trial.

I. FACTS OF THE CASE

We commence with a brief description of the scientific process concerned. Tungsten carbide is a metallic compound of great value in certain industrial processes. Combined with the metal cobalt, it forms an extremely hard alloy known as "cemented tungsten carbide"[1] used in oil drills, tools for manufacturing metals, and wear-resistant coatings. Because of its great value, reclamation of carbide from scrap metals is feasible. For a long time, however, the alloy's extreme resistence to machining made reclamation difficult. In the late 1960's and early 1970's, a new solution—known as the zinc recovery process—was devised, a solution based on carbide's reaction with zinc at high temperatures. In the crucibles of a furnace, molten zinc will react with the cobalt in the carbide to cause swelling and cracking of the scrap metal. After this has occurred, the zinc is distilled from the crucible, leaving the scrap in a more brittle state. The carbide is then ground into a powder, usable in new products as an alternative to virgin carbide. This process is the generally recognized modern method of carbide reclamation.

Metallurgical Industries has been in the business of reclaiming carbide since 1967, using the more primitive "cold-stream process." In the mid-1970's, Metallurgical began to consider using the zinc recovery process. In that connection, it came to know appellee Irvin Bielefeldt, a representative of Therm–O–Vac Engineering & Manufacturing Company (Therm–O–Vac). Negotiations led to a contract authorizing Therm–O–Vac to design and construct two zinc recovery furnaces, the purchase order for the first being executed in July 1976.

---

1. Hereafter referred to simply as "carbide".

The furnace arrived in April 1977. Dissatisfied with its performance, Metallurgical modified it extensively. First, it inserted chill plates in one part of the furnace to create a better temperature differential for distilling the zinc. Second, Metallurgical replaced the one large crucible then in place with several smaller crucibles to prevent the zinc from dispersing in the furnace. Third, it replaced segmented heating elements which had caused electrical arcing with unitary graphite heating elements. Last, it installed a filter in the furnace's vacuum-pumps, which zinc particles had continually clogged. These efforts proved successful and the modified furnace soon began commercial operation.

In the market for a second furnace in mid–1978, Metallurgical provided to Consarc, another furnace manufacturer, all its hard-won information about zinc-recovery furnace design. Apparently allowed to watch the first furnace operate, Consarc employees learned of its modifications. Because Consarc proved unwilling or unable to build what Metallurgical wanted, however, the agreement fell through, and Metallurgical returned to Therm–O–Vac for its second furnace. A purchase order was signed in January 1979, and the furnace arrived that July. Further modifications again had to be made, but commercial production was allegedly achieved in January 1980.

In 1980, after Therm–O–Vac went bankrupt, Bielefeldt and three other former Therm–O–Vac employees—Norman Montesino, Gary Boehm, and Michael Sarvadi—formed Fourtek, Incorporated. Soon thereafter, Fourtek agreed to build a zinc recovery furnace for appellee Smith International, Incorporated (Smith). The furnace Fourtek provided incorporated the modifications Metallurgical had made in its furnaces; chilling systems, pump filters, multiple crucibles, and unitary heating elements. Smith has been unable to use this furnace commercially, however, because a current shortage of carbide scrap prevents its economically feasible operation.

Metallurgical nevertheless brought a diversity action against Smith, Bielefeldt, Montesino, Boehm, and Sarvadi in November 1981. In its complaint, Metallurgical charged the defendants with misappropriating its trade secrets. Other causes of action, not brought forward on appeal, were breach of contract, interference with business relations, conversion, and unfair competition. Trial began on June 4, 1984, and Metallurgical spent the next ten days presenting its case in chief. During this time, testimony indicated Metallurgical's frequent notices to Bielefeldt that the process was a secret and that the disclosures to him were made in confidence. Another witness recounted meetings in which the modifications were agreed to; Bielefeldt was allegedly unconvinced about the efficacy of these changes and contributed little to the discussion. Metallurgical also presented evidence that it had expended considerable time, effort, and money to modify the furnaces.

Such evidence apparently did not impress the trial court; at the close of Metallurgical's case, it granted the defendants' motions for directed verdicts. Ruling from the bench, the court provided an array of reasons for its order. The principal reason advanced was the court's conclusion that no trade secret is involved. At trial, Metallurgical acknowledged that the individual changes, by themselves, are not secrets; chill plates and pump filters, for example, are well-known. Metallurgical's position instead was that the process, taken as a whole, is a trade secret in the carbide business. The court, however, refused to recognize any protection Texas law provides to a modification process. It also concluded that the information Bielefeldt obtained from working with Metallurgical is too general to be legally protected. Finally, it ruled that "negative know-how"—the knowledge of what not to do—is unprotected. All these findings seem to have coalesced into a general conclusion by the court that this case involves no trade secret. The trial court went on to provide further rationales for its decision; it ruled that there was evidence of neither Bielefeldt's improper use nor disclosure of any secret, nor of Metallurgical's having been damaged by any improper misappropriation. Metallurgical appeals all these conclusions against Bielefeldt and Smith only. It also contends that the court erred in excluding certain evidence.

. . . Because the district court provided so many reasons for its order, we feel compelled to discuss the law of trade secrets in detail. Our discussion concentrates on Texas law, despite a clause in both purchase order agreements that their interpretation is to be made under New Jersey law. This stems from the nature of this case; as will be explained below, we are dealing with a cause of action sounding in tort, not one based on contract.

Individual attention to the various elements of this tort is necessary to provide an easily-understood analysis, but we can here briefly summarize the discussion. A plaintiff must certainly show that a "trade secret" is involved; the definition of this term is therefore crucial and must be based on several factors. If the trial court concludes that a trade secret exists, it then must determine whether the defendant committed any wrongdoing. One who breaches the confidence reposed in him by the holder of a trade secret and one who obtains the secret can be held accountable. No defendant may be liable, however, unless he has "disclosed" or "used" the secret improperly; again, defining these terms is required. These considerations are the sum and substance of the cause of action involved. After expounding the substantive law, we then turn to issues regarding the district court's evidentiary rulings and the relief available to Metallurgical.

III.   DEFINING A "TRADE SECRET"

We begin by reviewing the legal definition of a trade secret. Of course, to qualify as one, the subject matter involved must, in fact, be a secret; "[m]atters of general knowledge in an industry cannot be appropriated by one as his secret." Wissman v. Boucher, 150 Tex. 326, 240 S.W.2d 278, 280 (1951); Smith emphasizes the absence of any secret because the basic zinc recovery process has been publicized in the trade. Acknowledging the publicity of the zinc recovery process, however, we nevertheless conclude that Metallurgical's particular modification efforts can be as yet unknown to the industry. A general description of the zinc recovery process reveals nothing about the benefits unitary heating elements and vacuum pump filters can provide to that procedure. That the scientific principles involved are generally known does not necessarily refute Metallurgical's claim of trade secrets.

Metallurgical, furthermore, presented evidence to back up its claim. One of its main witnesses was Arnold Blum, a consultant very influential in the decisions to modify the furnaces. Blum testified as to his belief that Metallurgical's changes were unknown in the carbide reclamation industry. The evidence also shows Metallurgical's efforts to keep secret its modifications. Blum testified that he noted security measures taken to conceal the furnaces from all but authorized personnel. The furnaces were in areas hidden from public view, while signs warned all about restricted access. Company policy, moreover, required everyone authorized to see the furnace to sign a non-disclosure agreement. These measures constitute evidence probative of the existence of secrets. One's subjective belief of a secret's existence suggests that the secret exists. Security measures, after all, cost money; a manufacturer therefore presumably would not incur these costs if it believed its competitors already knew about the information involved. In University Computing Co. v. Lykes–Youngstown Corp., 504 F.2d 518, 535 (5th Cir.1974), we regarded subjective belief as a factor to consider in determining whether secrecy exists. Because evidence of security measures is relevant, that shown here helps us conclude that a reasonable jury could have found the existence of the requisite secrecy.

Smith argues, however, that Metallurgical's disclosure to other parties vitiated the secrecy required to obtain legal protection. As mentioned before, Metallurgical revealed its information to Consarc Corporation in 1978; it also disclosed information in 1980 to La Floridienne, its European licensee of carbide reclamation technology. Because both these disclosures occurred before Bielefeldt allegedly misappropriated the knowledge of modifications, others knew of the information when the Smith furnace was built. This being so, Smith argues, no trade secret in fact existed.

Although the law requires secrecy, it need not be absolute. Public revelation would, of course, dispel all secrecy, but the holder of a secret need not remain totally silent:

> He may, without losing his protection, communicate it to employees involved in its use. He may likewise communicate it to others pledged to secrecy.... Nevertheless, a substantial element of secrecy must exist, so that except by the use of improper means, there would be difficulty in acquiring the information.

Restatement of Torts, § 757 Comment b (1939). We conclude that a holder may divulge his information to a limited extent without destroying its status as a trade secret. To hold otherwise would greatly limit the holder's ability to profit from his secret. If disclosure to others is made to further the holder's economic interests, it should, in appropriate circumstances, be considered a limited disclosure that does not destroy the requisite secrecy. The only question is whether we are dealing with a limited disclosure here.

Prior caselaw provides no guidance on what constitutes limited disclosure. Metallurgical cites Hyde Corp. v. Huffines, 158 Tex. 566, 314 S.W.2d 763, *cert. denied* 358 U.S. 898, 79 S.Ct. 223, 3 L.Ed.2d 148 (1958), and Sikes v. McGraw Edison Co., 665 F.2d 731 (5th Cir.), *cert. denied* 458 U.S. 1108, 102 S.Ct. 3488, 73 L.Ed.2d 1369 (1982), in contending that subsequent disclosure of a trade secret does not free one from the constraint of a prior confidential disclosure. In both of these cases, however, publication of the trade secret by its holder *followed* an improper use by one in whom the holder had confided. This factual difference renders these cases inapposite.

Looking instead to the policy considerations involved, we glean two reasons why Metallurgical's disclosures to others are limited and therefore insufficient to extinguish the secrecy Metallurgical's other evidence has suggested. First, the disclosures were not public announcements; rather, Metallurgical divulged its information to only two businesses with whom it was dealing. This case thus differs from Luccous v. J.C. Kinley Co., 376 S.W.2d 336 (Tex.1964), in which the court concluded that the design of a device could not be a trade secret because it had been patented—and thus revealed to all the world—before any dealing between the parties. Second, the disclosures were made to further Metallurgical's economic interests. Disclosure to Consarc was made with the hope that Consarc could build the second furnace. A longstanding agreement gave La Floridienne the right, as a licensee, to the information in exchange for royalty payments. Metallurgical therefore revealed its discoveries as part of business transactions by which it expected to profit.

Metallurgical's case would have been stronger had it also presented evidence of confidential relationships with these two companies, but we are unwilling to regard this failure as conclusively disproving the limited nature of the disclosures. Smith correctly points out that Metallurgical bears the burden of showing the existence of confidential relationships. Contrary to Smith's assertion, however, confidentiality is not a requisite; it is only a factor to consider. Whether a disclosure is limited is an issue the resolution of which depends on weighing many facts. The inferences from those facts, construed favorably to Metallurgical, is that it wished only to profit from its secrets in its business dealings, not to reveal its secrets to the public. We therefore are unpersuaded by Smith's argument.

Existing law, however, emphasizes other requisites for legal recognition of a trade secret. In *Huffines*, 314 S.W.2d 763, a seminal case of trade secret law, Texas adopted the widely-recognized pronouncements of the American Law Institute's Restatement of the Law. The Texas Supreme Court quoted the Restatement's definition of a trade secret:

> A trade secret may consist of any formula, pattern, device, or compilation of information which is used in one's business, and which gives him an opportunity to obtain an advantage over competitors who do not know it. It may be a chemical compound, a process of manufacturing, treating or preserving materials, a pattern for a machine or other device or a list of customers.

Id. at 776, *quoting* Restatement of Torts, § 757 Comment b (1939). From this the criterion of value to the holder of the alleged secret arises, a criterion we have noted before. In *Zoecon Industries*, 713 F.2d at 1179, we concluded that a customer list was a trade secret in part because the list gave to its owner an advantage "over competitors who did not have this information."

Metallurgical met the burden of showing the value of its modifications. Lawrence Lorman, the company's vice president, testified that the zinc recovery process gave Metallurgical an advantage over its two competitors by aiding in the production of the highest quality reclaimed carbide powder. The quality of the powder, in fact, makes it an alternative to the more costly virgin carbide. Lorman testified that customers regarded Metallurgical's zinc reclaimed powder as a better product than that reclaimed by the coldstream process used by others. This evidence clearly indicates that the modifications that led to the commercial operation of the zinc recovery furnace provided a clear advantage over the competition.

Another requisite is the cost of developing the secret device or process. In *Huffines'* companion case, K & G Oil, Tool & Service Co. v. G & G Fishing Tool Service, 158 Tex. 594, 314 S.W.2d 782, 790 (1958), the court recognized the cost involved in developing the device in question; "[t]he record shows ... that much work and ingenuity have been applied to the development of a practical and successful device." No question exists that Metallurgical expended much time, effort, and money to make the necessary changes. It clearly has met the burden of demonstrating the effort involved in making a complex manufacturing process work.

That the cost of devising the secret and the value the secret provides are criteria in the legal formulation of a trade secret shows the equitable underpinnings of this area of the law. It seems only fair that one should be able to keep and enjoy the fruits of his labor. If a businessman has worked hard, has used his imagination, and has taken bold steps to gain an advantage over his competitors, he should be able to profit from his efforts. Because a commercial advantage can vanish once the competition learns of it, the law should protect the businessman's efforts to keep his achievements secret. As is discussed below, this is an area of law in which simple fairness still plays a large role.

We do not say, however, that all these factors need exist in every case. Because each case must turn on its own facts, no standard formula for weighing the factors can be devised. Secrecy is always required, of course, but beyond that there are no universal requirements. In a future case, for example, should the defendant's breach of confidence be particularly egregious, the injured party might still seek redress in court despite the possibility that the subject matter was discovered at little or no cost or that the object of secrecy is not of great value to him. The definition of "trade secret" will therefore be determined by weighing all equitable considerations. It is easy to recognize the possibility of a trade secret here, however, because Metallurgical presented evidence of all three factors discussed above.

Appellees posit two other reasons why Metallurgical's modification process cannot be defined as a trade secret. The first is premised on characterizing the process in question as the installation of various devices all well known to modern manufacturing. This being so, the argument runs, the process itself can be no secret, either. The technologies of chill plates, multiple crucibles, pump filters, and unitary graphite heating elements are all said to be public knowledge. This may well be so, but it does not prevent Metallurgical from seeking legal protection. Ventura Manufacturing Co. v. Locke, 454 S.W.2d 431 (Tex.Civ.App.1970), involved a process of finding and cleaning small yet valuable titanium scraps lost during the manufacturing of airplanes. Appellee Locke refined a previously unsuccessful process by implementing new procedures, none of which was innovative. The court nevertheless found that his efforts could constitute a trade secret:

> Obviously, the basic proposition involved in the cleaning of dirty parts by commercial detergents involves no trade secret. Also, the use of production line techniques as such must be considered as a matter of general knowledge. On the other hand, we cannot say that the details of the procedure followed in the cleaning of these fasteners are matters of general knowledge. To the contrary, the record demonstrates that such details as the types and amounts of chemicals to be used and the times and temperatures for cleaning the fasteners were developed by Ventura through extensive trial and error and at considerable expense.

Id. at 434. . . .

The second defense advances a supposed concept of "negative know how" in reliance on one sentence from Hurst v. Hughes Tool Co., 634 F.2d 895 (5th Cir.) *cert. denied* 454 U.S. 829, 102 S.Ct. 123, 70 L.Ed.2d 105 (1981). The court there ruled that Hughes Tool Company did not really use the information Hurst provided; "Hurst's information, while of some benefit, provided only negative, 'what not to do,' input to Hughes." Id. at 899. Both the district court and Smith interpret this to mean that negative know-how cannot constitute a trade secret. The sentence in *Hurst*, however, has nothing to do with whether the information was a trade secret. It is not found in the section of the opinion dealing with the existence of a trade secret; rather, we were determining whether Hughes Tool Company could be found to have used commercially any secrets Hurst conveyed.

Regardless of this misreading, the argument that negative know-how is involved here is unpersuasive. We do not understand how the changes that we have described can be seen as only showing what not to do. Metallurgical's evidence shows that it encountered many problems with the furnaces Therm–O–Vac delivered. Striving to solve these problems, Metallurgical took several steps to modify the furnaces. Installing unitary heating elements, chill plates, multiple crucibles, and pump filters are all "positive" steps resulting from conclusions on what *to do*. These changes allegedly turned unusable furnaces into ones fit for commercial operation. One may say, of course, that these actions result from realizations of what not to do; but so does every human process: the selection of one action at a given moment involves the rejection of every other conceivable one that might have been chosen. Using multiple crucibles, for example, stems from the conclusion that a single large crucible should not be used. This characterization, however, can always describe the invention or modification of a device. Knowing what not to do often leads automatically to knowing what to do. Although we decline to hold that this distinction will always be unavailing, in this case at least we regard the distinction between "positive" and "negative" knowledge to be unintelligible. Because this final claim of Smith is unpersuasive, we conclude that the evidence which was presented at trial could have led a reasonable jury to believe a trade secret existed.

IV. EXISTENCE OF A CONFIDENTIAL RELATIONSHIP

Deciding whether a confidential relationship existed between Metallurgical and Bielefeldt must naturally precede an inquiry into his possible breach of Metallurgical's confidence. Once again, we look to the Restatement of Torts as our starting point:

> One who discloses or uses another's trade secrets, without a privilege to do so, is liable to the other if ... (b) his disclosure or use constitutes a breach of confidence reposed in him by the other in disclosing the secret to him.
>
> * * *
>
> A breach of confidence under the rule stated in this Clause may also be a breach of contract which subjects the actor to liability.... But whether or not there is a breach of contract, the rule stated in this Section subjects the actor to liability if his disclosure or use of another's trade secret is a breach of the confidence reposed in him by the other in disclosing the secret to him.

Huffines, 314 S.W.2d at 769, *quoting* Restatement, § 757 and comment j. In *Huffines,* the Texas Court cited several cases to emphasize this message. Quoted at great length was Adolph Gottscho v. American Marking Corp., 18 N.J. 467, 114 A.2d 438 (1955). The *Gottscho* court stressed the blameworthy conduct of the defendant as the basis of this tort:

> [Defendants] now seek to appropriate these trade secrets to their own use and profit by a violation of their contractual agreements and a betrayal of the confidence reposed in them by plaintiff. This they may not do; such conduct is abhorrent to our conception of ordinary honesty.... Jackson learned the plaintiff's trade secrets in confidence and, in violation of his fiduciary obligations, he disclosed and used them for purposes other than his employer's benefit.... His conduct was grossly improper and gave rise to the plaintiff's cause of action, based on long-settled equitable principles and supported by the marked changes in the attitude of the law towards the need for commercial morality.

114 A.2d at 441–42. Our review of the evidence on the existence of a confidential relationship is hampered to some degree by the district court's

exclusion of several items of evidence. As we discuss below, the exclusions were improper; but regardless of the evidence excluded, the record contains testimony of Metallurgical's president, Ira Friedman, that he informed Bielefeldt of the confidentiality Metallurgical expected. Although these references are few, they would have sufficed to allow a reasonable jury to have believed that a confidential relationship existed between Metallurgical and Bielefeldt.

V.   OBTAINING SECRETS FROM ANOTHER

At this point we must devote separate attention to Smith, which stands in a different light from Bielefeldt. It had no significant dealings with Metallurgical and apparently was not heavily involved in the design of the furnace it purchased. The question therefore becomes whether Smith as purchaser, and thus as beneficiary of Bielefeldt's alleged misappropriation, can also be held liable for it.

The law imposes liability not only on those who wrongfully misappropriate trade secrets by breach of confidence but also, in certain situations, on others who might benefit from the breach:

> One who discloses or uses another's trade secret, without a privilege to do so, is liable to the other if . . . (c) he learned the secret from a third person with notice of the facts that it was a secret and that the third person's disclosure of it was otherwise a breach of his duty to the other. . . .

> * * *

> One has notice of facts under the rule stated in this Section when he knows of them or when he should know of them. . . . He should know of them if, from the information which he has, a reasonable man would infer the facts in question, or if, under the circumstances, a reasonable man would be put on inquiry and an inquiry pursued with reasonable intelligence and diligence would disclose the facts.

Restatement, § 757 & comment 1. Under this standard, we believe a reasonable jury could find that Smith should have inquired into the relationship between Bielefeldt and Metallurgical. Testimony shows that, during negotiations for the purchase of a furnace, Bielefeldt told Smith of his current involvement in then-pending litigation with Metallurgical regarding trade secrets in New Jersey. Smith learned that Metallurgical claimed ownership of the design and manufacturing processes of the zinc recovery furnace, a furnace which Smith wished Bielefeldt to build. Apparently satisfied by Bielefeldt's assertion of the meritlessness of Metallurgical's claims, Smith eventually gave him the go-ahead for construction of the furnace. There is no indication that it ever investigated the danger that Bielefeldt was wrongfully misappropriating the ideas of others. The evidence as it stood at the end of Metallurgical's presentation thus suggests that Smith knew of possible problems and did nothing but rely on Bielefeldt's dismissals. We think that this inattention to possible wrongdoing, unless refuted, amounts to a failure to reasonably inquire into the facts involved. Under § 757(c), Smith might therefore be held accountable, provided it used any trade secrets conveyed. This brings us to the next issue.

VI.   DISCLOSURE OR USE OF A TRADE SECRET

Wrongful misappropriation occurs if one "discloses or uses another's trade secret without a privilege to do so...." Restatement, § 757. The district court directed verdict for appellees in part because it saw no evidence of Bielefeldt's actual use or disclosure of Metallurgical's secrets. In reviewing this conclusion, we keep in mind the rule of *Boeing Co. v. Shipman* by scouring the record for reasonable inferences favorable to Metallurgical. One fact jumps out from this review: in their original form, the furnaces delivered to Metallurgical differed from those that Smith purchased. The former furnaces lacked the key features needed to achieve commercial operation, while the latter possessed those features—features that Metallurgical had devised by extensive and expensive trial and error. Bielefeldt himself testified that he did not look to public sources of information in designing the Smith furnace; he instead claimed that he relied on his memory. That his earlier efforts lacked the features at issue suggests that his "memories" may well have been of working with Metallurgical. This issue is therefore an inappropriate ground for a directed verdict.

Smith's liability can arise, however, only if it in turn used the secrets gained from Bielefeldt. "Use," as it turns out, is not so easily defined. Smith claims that it never used any secrets gained because its inability to procure substantial quantities of scrap carbide prevented commercial operation of the furnace Fourtek provided. *Lykes-Youngstown*, 504 F.2d 518, guides us in determining commercial use. We must first recognize the unfortunate blurring of analyses in that case. The *Lykes-Youngstown* court's discussion of commercial use was in the context of inquiring whether damages might be available. It is preferable, of course, to divorce these concepts. Commercial use is an element of the tort as enounced in § 757 of the Restatement; while the nature of the use may be relevant in determining the proper extent of damages, its existence must also be shown to establish wrongdoing in the first place. Despite this confusion, *Lykes-Youngstown* provides useful analysis.

Metallurgical looked to that case in arguing that the law provides a liberal definition of "commercial use." *Lykes-Youngstown* does indeed state a broad definition; "any misappropriation, followed by an exercise of control and dominion ... must constitute a commercial use...." 504 F.2d at 542. *Lykes-Youngstown* differs from our case, however, in one very important respect. It was a case in which "the trade secret itself was what was to be sold...." Id. at 540. The court there explicitly contrasted a case like ours, "where the trade secret is used to improve manufacturing, and subsequently manufactured items were sold at a profit...." *Id.* Although the court made this distinction in determining the proper method of computing damages, we think it also applies logically to developing a definition of "use." The discussion in *Lykes–Youngstown* following this distinction is therefore inapposite to our case, for which we instead employ the everyday meaning of the term. If Smith has not put the furnace into commercial operation to produce carbide powder it can then use, then no commercial use has occurred. Because Metallurgical failed to provide any evidence that Smith has so far benefitted from any misappropriation, directed verdict in Smith's favor was proper. Should it in future seek to profit from use or sale of the furnace, a new fact situation will be presented. . . .

VIII.   REMEDIES AND OTHER MATTERS

We now come to the issue of remedies available to Metallurgical. The district court apparently found crucial Smith's inability to operate its furnace profitably. Because there was no commercial use, it concluded that damages were unavailable. We have already concluded that Smith did not "use" the alleged secrets Bielefeldt provided; to say that this circumstance precludes all remedies goes too far, however. The court failed to distinguish consideration of the individual appellees; Smith is out of the picture, but Bielefeldt remains. Should he be found liable on retrial, the appropriate damages should be based on the tenets of *Lykes–Youngstown*. We there adopted the concept of the "reasonable royalty." This does not mean a simple percentage of actual profits; instead, the trier of fact, should it find Bielefeldt liable, must determine "the actual value of what has been appropriated." 504 F.2d at 537, *quoting* Vitro Corp. v. Hall Chemical Co., 292 F.2d 678, 683 (6th Cir.1961). We later expounded this concept:

> [T]he proper measure is to calculate what the parties would have agreed to as a fair price for licensing the defendant to put the trade secret to the use the defendants intended at the time the misappropriation took place.
>
> In calculating what a fair licensing price would have been had the parties agreed, the trier of fact should consider such factors as the resulting and foreseeable changes in the parties' competitive posture; the prices past purchasers or licensees may have paid; the total value of the secret to the plaintiff, including the plaintiff's development cost and the importance of the secret to the plaintiff's business; the nature and extent of the use the defendant intended for the secret, and finally whatever other unique factors in the particular case might have been affected by the parties' agreement, such as the ready availability of alternative process.

Id. at 540. Estimation of damages, however, should not be based on sheer speculation. If too few facts exist to permit the trier of fact to calculate proper damages, then a reasonable remedy in law is unavailable. In that instance, a permanent injunction is a proper remedy for the breach of a confidential relationship. In this case, moreover, an injunction against Bielefeldt in no way depends on whether Smith achieved commercial use. Should Metallurgical prove its point on retrial, therefore, it has a remedy available to right the wrong done it.

We emphasize the limited consequences of today's decision. In no way do we pass judgment on whether Bielefeldt committed any wrong; that task is for the trier of fact. We hold only that the opportunity for this determination to be made must be given. It may be that on retrial Bielefeldt can successfully show that his knowledge came from somewhere else or that the process of modification was no secret. . . .

The district court's order is AFFIRMED in part, REVERSED in part, and the cause is REMANDED.

NOTES

1. *The Sources of Trade Secret Law.* Every state in the United States today protects trade secrets. In some cases, such as *Fourtek*, the rules come from common law, as reflected in the Torts Restatement or the Unfair Competition Restatement; in other cases, the rules come from the Uniform Trade Secrets Act as enacted in the state.

In 1979, the Restatement of Torts, Second, dropped the first Restatement's provisions on trade secrets, along with several other provisions on interference with business relations. That same year, however, the National Conference of Commissioners on Uniform State Laws approved the Uniform Trade Secrets Act which, as amended in 1985 and enacted in one form or another in more than three-quarters of the states, follows the original Torts Restatement approach in many respects. Courts continue to rely on the Torts Restatement in applying their local version of the Uniform Act. The American Law Institute later had second—or third—thoughts on the subject, and the Restatement of the Law Third, Unfair Competition (1995) reintroduced trade secret provisions at sections 39–45.

Codification does not necessarily produce coherence. Observing that trade secret law "is based at its core on the breach of relationally specific duties," such as the duty of confidence arising from the employer-employee relationship, Professor Robert Bone has argued that "there is no such thing as a normatively autonomous body of trade secret law. Rather, trade secret law is merely a collection of other legal norms—contract, fraud, and the like—united only by the fact that they are used to protect secret information. Neither the fact that a trade secret is information nor the fact that it is secret provides a convincing reason to impose liability for a nonconsensual taking. Trade secret law in this sense is parasitic: it depends on a host theory for normative support." For example "in cases involving breach of contract, the reasons for enforcing contracts are the reasons—and the only persuasive reasons—for imposing trade secret liability." Robert G. Bone, A New Look at Trade Secret Law: Doctrine in Search of Justification, 86 Cal. L. Rev. 241, 244–45 (1998).

See also Vincent Chiappetta, Myth, Chameleon or Intellectual Property Olympian? A Normative Framework Supporting Trade Secret Law, 8 Geo. Mason L. Rev. 69 (1999); Marina Lao, Federalizing Trade Secrets Law in An Information Economy, 59 Ohio St. L.J. 1633 (1998).

2. *Subject Matter: Isolated Data and Negative Information.* Comment (b) to Restatement of Torts section 757 defines a trade secret as "a process or device for continuous use in the operation of the business," including information related to "the sale of goods or to other operations in the business, such as a code for determining discounts, rebates or other concessions in a price list or catalogue, or a list of specialized customers, or a method of bookkeeping or other office management." Comment (b) excludes protection for information that relates only to "single or ephemeral events in the conduct of the business, as, for example, the amount or other terms of a secret bid for a contract or the salary of certain employees, or the security investments made or contemplated, or the date fixed for the announcement of a new policy or for bringing out a new model or the like."*

Unlike the first Torts Restatement, the Uniform Trade Secrets Act protects isolated and ephemeral data such as the amount of a secret bid made by a firm or the salary of a key employee. The Uniform Act also extends protection to negative information—information about research paths or marketing programs that, after some experimentation, have proved unproductive or unprofitable and thus not worth pursuing further. Uniform Trade Secrets Act § 1 comment, 14 U.L.A. 439 (1990). The Unfair Competition Restatement follows the Uniform Act in both respects. Section 39, comments d, e.

So long as episodic or negative information meets such other requirements of trade secret law as secrecy, investment and competitive advantage, what reason is there not to protect it? Is there a valid argument that protecting negative information encourages wasteful behavior—investment in a research path that is already known (albeit by a competitor) to be fruitless? In a competitive setting, how can this expenditure be distinguished from the expense required to duplicate positive information?

3. *Secrecy.* Secrecy is the pivot on which trade secret protection turns. The Uniform Trade Secrets Act, and implicitly the Torts Restatement, require that, to be protected, the information in issue derive "independent economic value, actual or potential, from not being generally known to, and not being readily ascertainable by proper means by, other persons who can obtain economic value from its disclosure or use...." Uniform Trade Secrets Act § 1(4)(i) (1985). Restatement, Third of Unfair Competition § 39 Comment f, similarly absolves the trade secret defendant who took information directly from the plaintiff so long as he could have ascertained it from the public domain.

How heavy must the cloak of secrecy be for subject matter to qualify as a trade secret? The law does not require absolute secrecy; if information were completely secret no one other than its creator would know it and there would rarely be a need for the law to intervene. The test, rather, is one of reasonableness in the steps taken to contain the information in issue. The answer to the "question whether a plaintiff has taken 'all proper

---

* Copyright 1939 by the American Law Institute. Reprinted with the permission.

and reasonable steps' depends on the circumstances of each case considering the nature of the information sought to be protected as well *as the conduct of the parties.*" USM Corp. v. Marson Fastener Corp., 379 Mass. 90, 393 N.E.2d 895, 902, 204 U.S.P.Q. 233 (1979) (emphasis the court's).

The Massachusetts Supreme Court ruled in *Marson* that plaintiff's safeguards, though by no means foolproof, were adequate. Plaintiff, "USM required supervisory, technical, and research personnel, including the defendant Lahnston, to sign nondisclosure agreements." While these agreements did not itemize the information that USM considered secret, "such specificity is not required to put employees on notice that their work involves access to trade secrets and confidential information." Nor was it fatal "that the blueprints and parts drawings were not labeled 'confidential' or 'secret' or that USM had not expressly informed its employees that these parts drawings were considered secret by USM." Finally, although USM conducted escorted tours for employees' families and its distributors, the company's plant security precautions "were sufficient to exclude the general public from the production areas of USM's plants, thereby denying access to USM's factory equipment." 393 N.E.2d at 901.

The *Marson* court contrasted the facts before it with those it had faced several years earlier in J.T. Healy & Son, Inc. v. James A. Murphy & Son, Inc., 357 Mass. 728, 260 N.E.2d 723, 166 U.S.P.Q. 443 (1970): "Applying this standard, we denied trade secret protection in *Healy* because the plaintiff had made a conscious policy decision to do nothing to safeguard the confidentiality of its manufacturing processes. In *Healy*, the employees were never informed that any of the manufacturing processes were considered secret; employees were not required to sign nondisclosure agreements; the plant was not partitioned into sections; and employees engaged in other work could plainly see the two 'secret processes' in operation. The plaintiff in *Healy*, other than excluding the general public from the manufacturing plant, took no security precautions whatever." 393 N.E.2d at 902.

Although courts divide on whether a protectible trade secret must possess some degree of novelty, the division is probably nominal since novelty is a function of secrecy the evidence typically adduced to defeat novelty in jurisdictions that require it is widespread knowledge in the trade of the claimed or closely similar information—precisely the evidence used in all jurisdictions to disprove secrecy.

For an overview of the practical security measures that a firm can employ to protect its trade secrets, together with a program of legal protection, see Tom Arnold & David McGuire, Law and Practice of Corporate Information Security, 57 J.Pat.Off.Soc'y (pts. 1 & 2) 169, 237 (1975).

4. *Third Party Liability.* The Uniform Trade Secrets Act substantially follows the formula for third party liability prescribed in the first Restatement and applied by the *Fourtek* court. UTSA section 1(2) seeks to accommodate the interests of the good faith purchaser who becomes aware of the improper appropriation only after acquiring a business or assets, by defining actionable misappropriation to include an individual's disclosure or use of a trade secret knowing, or having reason to know that it was acquired by improper means or, before a material change of position, knowing or having "reason to know that it was a trade secret and that knowledge of it had been acquired by accident or mistake."

5. *Injunctions.* How long should a trade secret injunction run? Under the majority rule, a trade secret will be protected only so long as it remains secret, and the injunction will be dissolved once the protected information becomes generally known. Alternatively the court can pre-set the injunction's length by estimating the time that it would take a competitor to reverse engineer the product or process. To this period, Uniform Trade Secrets Act § 2(a) and most courts would add a "head start" period measured by the lead time over competitors that the defendant otherwise would have gained as a result of its improper appropriation. Shellmar Products Co. v. Allen–Qualley Co., 87 F.2d 104, 32 U.S.P.Q. 24 (7th Cir.1936) represents the minority rule. The court there issued a perpetual injunction permanently restraining the defendant from using the trade secret, even after secrecy was lost through the issuance of a patent. In some cases, courts will issue a perpetual injunction as a punitive measure to deter particularly egregious conduct. See Valco Cincinnati, Inc. v. N & D Machining Serv., 24 Ohio St.3d 41, 492 N.E.2d 814 (1986).

Under what circumstances, if any, should injunctive relief be withheld and monetary relief awarded instead? As originally approved, Uniform Trade Secrets Act § 2(b) provided, "If the court determines that it would be unreasonable to prohibit future use, an injunction may condition future use upon payment of a reasonable royalty for no longer than the period of time the use could have been prohibited." The 1985 amendments to the Act deleted the introductory clause, replaced it with the words "In exceptional circumstances," and defined "exceptional circumstances," as including, but "not limited to, a material and prejudicial change of position prior to acquiring knowledge or reason to know of misappropriation that renders a prohibitive injunction inequitable."

Is the shift from an "unreasonable" standard to a presumably more rigorous "exceptional circumstances" standard desirable? Outside the example given—"a material and prejudicial change of position"—what circumstances might qualify as "exceptional"? Section 44 of the Unfair Competition Restatement takes a more open-ended approach, making the "appropriateness and scope of injunctive relief depend upon a comparative appraisal of all the factors in the case," including eight listed factors. Courts in patent cases sometimes refuse injunctions on the basis of disproportionate harm to the infringer. Does this standard match the Uniform Act's "exceptional circumstances" standard?

6. *Monetary Awards.* Courts frequently measure monetary recovery for trade secret appropriations by the claimant's lost profits or the infringer's unlawfully gained profits. While the claimant is not entitled to a double recovery, he is "entitled to the profits he did not make but would have made had his secret not been unlawfully used, but not less than the monetary gain which the defendant reaped from his improper acts." Rudolf Callmann, Unfair Competition, Trademarks and Monopolies § 14.42 (4th ed. 1981). Once the plaintiffs demonstrate that the defendants have made profits from sales of products incorporating the misappropriated trade secrets, the burden shifts to the defendants to demonstrate the portion of their profits which is not attributable to the trade secrets. Jet Spray Cooler, Inc. v. Crampton, 377 Mass. 159, 174, 385 N.E.2d 1349, 1358–59 n. 14, 203 U.S.P.Q. 363 (1979). *Jet Spray* held that defendants had not sustained this burden, but allowed the corporate defendant to deduct from gross profits the bad debts it had incurred on sales of the infringing products and reasonable salaries and consultant fees it had paid to the individual defendants.

The original version of the Uniform Trade Secrets Act allowed a successful plaintiff to recover damages measured by "both the actual loss caused by misappropriation and the unjust enrichment caused by misappropriation that is not taken into account in computing actual loss." The 1985 amendments provided that "[d]amages can include both the actual loss caused by misappropriation and the unjust enrichment caused by misappropriation that is not taken into account in computing actual loss," and that "[i]n lieu of damages measured by any other methods, the damages caused by misappropriation may be measured by imposition of liability for a reasonable royalty for a misappropriator's unauthorized disclosure or use of a trade secret." Under both versions, if the misappropriation is "willful and malicious," the "court may award exemplary damages in an amount not exceeding twice any award" made under the damages and profits provisions, and reasonable attorney's fees. Reasonable attorney's fees may also be awarded if "a claim of misappropriation is made in bad faith" or "a motion to terminate an injunction is made or resisted in bad faith." Uniform Trade Secrets Act §§ 3, 4, 14 (1990).

Can a trade secret claimant recover the cost of security measures taken to rebuff defendant's forays? Observing that such damages "might well, under different circumstances be proper," the court of appeals in Telex Corp. v. International Business Machines Corp., 510 F.2d 894, 184 U.S.P.Q. 521 (10th Cir.1975), overturned the trial court's $3,000,000 award to IBM for "increased extraordinary security costs—additional guards, television cameras, sensors, locks, safes, computer-controlled access system and the like." The court of appeals failed to see "how the increased security costs were the proximate result of Telex's hiring of IBM employees. Telex was not climbing fences or breaking down doors in its appropriation of IBM trade secrets. Telex's methods were more subtle, involving the luring of IBM employees who brought with them the trade secrets in question." 510 F.2d at 933.

7. *Bibliographic Note.* The standard treatises on the law of trade secrets in the United States are Melvin F. Jager, Trade Secrets Law (1985) and Roger M. Milgrim, Trade Secrets (1992). Amédée E. Turner, The Law of Trade Secrets (1962), describes United States law in a chapter-by-chapter comparison with English law. On the economics of trade secret protection, see David D. Friedman, William M. Landes & Richard A. Posner, Some Economics of Trade Secret Law, 5 J. Econ. Persp. 61 (Winter 1991).

E. I. duPont deNemours & Co. v. Christopher

United States Court of Appeals, Fifth Circuit, 1970.
431 F.2d 1012, 166 U.S.P.Q. 421, cert. denied, 400 U.S. 1024, 91 S.Ct. 581, 27 L.Ed.2d 637, reh'g denied, 401 U.S. 967, 91 S.Ct. 968, 28 L.Ed.2d 250.

GOLDBERG, Circuit Judge:

This is a case of industrial espionage in which an airplane is the cloak and a camera the dagger. The defendants-appellants, Rolfe and Gary Christopher, are photographers in Beaumont, Texas. The Christophers were hired by an unknown third party to take aerial photographs of new construction at the Beaumont plant of E.I. DuPont deNemours & Company, Inc. Sixteen photographs of the DuPont facility were taken from the air on March 19, 1969, and these photographs were later developed and delivered to the third party.

DuPont employees apparently noticed the airplane on March 19 and immediately began an investigation to determine why the craft was circling over the plant. By that afternoon the investigation had disclosed that the craft was involved in a photographic expedition and that the Christophers were the photographers. DuPont contacted the Christophers that same afternoon and asked them to reveal the name of the person or corporation requesting the photographs. The Christophers refused to disclose this information, giving as their reason the client's desire to remain anonymous.

Having reached a dead end in the investigation, DuPont subsequently filed suit against the Christophers, alleging that the Christophers had wrongfully obtained photographs revealing DuPont's trade secrets which they then sold to the undisclosed third party. DuPont contended that it had developed a highly secret but unpatented process for producing methanol, a process which gave DuPont a competitive advantage over other producers. This process, DuPont alleged, was a trade secret developed after much expensive and time-consuming research, and a secret which the company had taken special precautions to safeguard. The area photographed by the Christophers was the plant designed to produce methanol by this secret process, and because the plant was still under construction parts of the process were exposed to view from directly above the construction area. Photographs of that area, DuPont alleged, would enable a skilled person to deduce the secret process for making methanol. DuPont thus contended that the Christophers had wrongfully appropriated DuPont trade secrets by taking the photographs and delivering them to the undisclosed third party. In its suit DuPont asked for damages to cover the loss it had already sustained as a result of the wrongful disclosure of the trade secret and sought temporary and permanent injunctions prohibiting any further circulation of the photographs already taken and prohibiting any additional photographing of the methanol plant.

The Christophers answered with motions to dismiss for lack of jurisdiction and failure to state a claim upon which relief could be granted. Depositions were taken during which the Christophers again refused to disclose the name of the person to whom they had delivered the photographs. DuPont then filed a motion to compel an answer to this question and all related questions.

On June 5, 1969, the trial court held a hearing on all pending motions and an additional motion by the Christophers for summary judgment. The court denied the Christophers' motions to dismiss for want of jurisdiction and failure to state a claim and also denied their motion for summary judgment. The court granted DuPont's motion to compel the Christophers to divulge the name of their client. Having made these rulings, the court then granted the Christophers' motion for an interlocutory appeal under 28 U.S.C.A. § 1292(b) to allow the Christophers to obtain immediate appellate review of the court's finding that DuPont had stated a claim upon which relief could be granted. Agreeing with the trial court's determination that DuPont had stated a valid claim, we affirm the decision of that court.

This is a case of first impression, for the Texas courts have not faced this precise factual issue, and sitting as a diversity court we must sensitize our *Erie* antennae to divine what the Texas courts would do if such a situation were presented to them. The only question involved in this interlocutory appeal is whether DuPont has asserted a claim upon which relief can be granted. The Christophers argued both at trial and before this court that they committed no "actionable wrong" in photographing the DuPont facility and passing these photographs on to their client because they conducted all of their activities in public airspace, violated no government aviation standard, did not breach any confidential relation, and did not engage in any fraudulent or illegal conduct. In short, the Christophers argue that for an appropriation of trade secrets to be wrongful there must be a trespass, other illegal conduct, or breach of a confidential relationship. We disagree.

It is true, as the Christophers assert, that the previous trade secret cases have contained one or more of these elements. However, we do not think that the Texas courts would limit the trade secret protection exclusively to these elements. On the contrary, in Hyde Corporation v. Huffines, 1958, 158 Tex. 566, 314 S.W.2d 763, the Texas Supreme Court specifically adopted the rule found in the Restatement of Torts which provides:

> One who discloses or uses another's trade secret, without a privilege to do so, is liable to the other if
>
> (a) he discovered the secret by improper means, or
>
> (b) his disclosure or use constitutes a breach of confidence reposed in him by the other in disclosing the secret to him . . . .

Restatement of Torts § 757 (1939).

Thus, although the previous cases have dealt with a breach of a confidential relationship, a trespass, or other illegal conduct, the rule is much broader than the cases heretofore encountered. Not limiting itself to specific wrongs, Texas adopted subsection (a) of the Restatement which recognizes a cause of action for the discovery of a trade secret by any "improper" means.

The defendants, however, read Furr's Inc. v. United Specialty Advertising Co., Tex.Civ.App.1960, 338 S.W.2d 762, writ ref'd n.r.e., as limiting the Texas rule to breach of a confidential relationship. The court in Furr's did make the statement that

> The use of someone else's idea is not automatically a violation of the law. It must be something that meets the requirements of a "trade secret" *and has been obtained through a breach of confidence* in order to entitle the injured party to damages and/or injunction. 338 S.W.2d at 766 (emphasis added).

We think, however, that the exclusive rule which defendants have extracted from this statement is unwarranted. In the first place, in Furr's the court specifically found that there was no trade secret involved because the entire advertising scheme claimed to be the trade secret had been completely divulged to the public. Secondly, the court found that the plaintiff in the course of selling the scheme to the defendant had voluntarily divulged the entire scheme. Thus the court was dealing only with a possible breach of confidence concerning a properly discovered secret; there was never a question of any impropriety in the discovery or any other improper conduct on the part of the defendant. The court merely held that under those circumstances the defendant had not acted improperly if no breach of confidence occurred. We do not read Furr's as limiting the trade secret protection to a breach of confidential relationship when the facts of the case do raise the issue of some other wrongful conduct on the part of one discovering the trade secrets of another. If breach of confidence were meant to encompass the entire panoply of commercial improprieties, subsection (a) of the Restatement would be either surplusage or persiflage, an interpretation abhorrent to the traditional precision of the Restatement. We therefore find meaning in subsection (a) and think that the Texas Supreme Court clearly indicated by its adoption that there is a cause of action for the discovery of a trade secret by any "improper means."

The question remaining, therefore, is whether aerial photography of plant construction is an improper means of obtaining another's trade secret. We conclude that it is and that the Texas courts would so hold. The Supreme Court of that state has declared that "the undoubted tendency of the law has been to recognize and enforce higher standards of commercial morality in the business world." Hyde Corporation v. Huffines, supra, 314 S.W.2d at 773. That court has quoted with approval articles indicating that the *proper* means of gaining possession of a competitor's secret process is "through inspection and analysis" of the product in order to create a duplicate. K & G Tool & Service Co. v. G & G Fishing Tool Service, 1958, 158 Tex. 594, 314 S.W.2d 782, 783, 788. Later another Texas court explained:

> The means by which the discovery is made may be obvious, and the experimentation leading from known factors to presently unknown results may be simple and lying in the public domain. But these facts do not destroy the value of the discovery and will not advantage a competitor who by unfair means obtains the knowledge *without paying*

the price expended by the discoverer. Brown v. Fowler, Tex.Civ.App. 1958, 316 S.W.2d 111, 114, writ ref'd n.r.e. (emphasis added).

We think, therefore, that the Texas rule is clear. One may use his competitor's secret process if he discovers the process by reverse engineering applied to the finished product; one may use a competitor's process if he discovers it by his own independent research; but one may not avoid these labors by taking the process from the discoverer without his permission at a time when he is taking reasonable precautions to maintain its secrecy. To obtain knowledge of a process without spending the time and money to discover it independently is *improper* unless the holder voluntarily discloses it or fails to take reasonable precautions to ensure its secrecy.

In the instant case the Christophers deliberately flew over the DuPont plant to get pictures of a process which DuPont had attempted to keep secret. The Christophers delivered their pictures to a third party who was certainly aware of the means by which they had been acquired and who may be planning to use the information contained therein to manufacture methanol by the DuPont process. The third party has a right to use this process only if he obtains this knowledge through his own research efforts, but thus far all information indicates that the third party has gained this knowledge solely by taking it from DuPont at a time when DuPont was making reasonable efforts to preserve its secrecy. In such a situation DuPont has a valid cause of action to prohibit the Christophers from improperly discovering its trade secret and to prohibit the undisclosed third party from using the improperly obtained information.

We note that this view is in perfect accord with the position taken by the authors of the Restatement. In commenting on improper means of discovery the savants of the Restatement said:

> f. *Improper means of discovery.* The discovery of another's trade secret by improper means subjects the actor to liability independently of the harm to the interest in the secret. Thus, if one uses physical force to take a secret formula from another's pocket, or breaks into another's office to steal the formula, his conduct is wrongful and subjects him to liability apart from the rule stated in this Section. Such conduct is also an improper means of procuring the secret under this rule. But means may be improper under this rule even though they do not cause any other harm than that to the interest in the trade secret. Examples of such means are fraudulent misrepresentations to induce disclosure, tapping of telephone wires, eavesdropping or other espionage. A complete catalogue of improper means is not possible. In general they are means which fall below the generally accepted standards of commercial morality and reasonable conduct. Restatement of Torts § 757, comment f at 10 (1939).

In taking this position we realize that industrial espionage of the sort here perpetrated has become a popular sport in some segments of our industrial community. However, our devotion to free wheeling industrial competition must not force us into accepting the law of the jungle as the standard of morality expected in our commercial relations. Our tolerance of the espionage game must cease when the protections required to prevent another's spying cost so much that the spirit of inventiveness is dampened. Commercial privacy must be protected from espionage which could not have been reasonably anticipated or prevented. We do not mean to imply, however, that everything not in plain view is within the protected vale, nor that all information obtained through every extra optical extension is forbidden. Indeed, for our industrial competition to remain healthy there must be breathing room for observing a competing industrialist. A competitor can and must shop his competition for pricing and examine his products for quality, components, and methods of manufacture. Perhaps ordinary fences and roofs must be built to shut out incursive eyes, but we need not require the discoverer of a trade secret to guard against the unanticipated, the undetectable, or the unpreventable methods of espionage now available.

In the instant case DuPont was in the midst of constructing a plant. Although after construction the finished plant would have protected much of the process from view, during the period of construction the trade secret was exposed to view from the air. To require DuPont to put a roof over the unfinished plant to guard its secret would impose an enormous expense to prevent nothing more than a school boy's trick. We introduce here no new or radical ethic since our ethos has never given moral sanction to piracy. The market place must not deviate far from our mores. We should not require a person or corporation to take unreasonable precautions to prevent another from doing that which he ought not do in the first place. Reasonable precautions against predatory eyes we may require, but an impenetrable fortress is an unreasonable requirement, and we are not disposed to burden industrial inventors with such a duty in order to protect the fruits of their efforts. "Improper" will always be a word of many nuances, determined by time, place, and circumstances. We therefore need not proclaim a catalogue of commercial improprieties. Clearly, however, one of its commandments does say "thou shall not appropriate a trade secret through deviousness under circumstances in which countervailing defenses are not reasonably available."

Having concluded that aerial photography, from whatever altitude, is an improper method of discovering the trade secrets exposed during construction of the DuPont plant, we need not worry about whether the flight pattern chosen by the Christophers violated any federal aviation regulations. Regardless of whether the flight was legal or illegal in that sense, the espionage was an improper means of discovering DuPont's trade secret.

The decision of the trial court is affirmed and the case remanded to that court for proceedings on the merits.

NOTES

1. *Reverse Engineering.* Individuals who have not violated a confidential relationship with the trade secret owner and who have not appropriated the secret improperly are free to replicate and use the secret subject matter. This freedom extends to "reverse engineering," a technique by which the product of a secret formula or process is analyzed, first to retrace the steps essential to its creation and then to recreate the formula or process itself.

The line between unlawful appropriation and lawful reverse engineering is not always clear. The question whether a defendant crossed the line will arise any time it used secondary information to obtain the secret information. Did the court draw the line correctly in *duPont?* Would the court have reached a different result if, instead of hiring a pilot to fly over DuPont's unfinished factory, the competitor had read classified advertisements in local newspapers and in trade journals to determine the kinds of employees DuPont was hiring, and had followed trucks making deliveries to the construction site to determine that nature of supplies DuPont was using?

Consider whether the court drew the line correctly in Chicago Lock Co. v. Fanberg, 676 F.2d 400, 216 U.S.P.Q. 289 (9th Cir.1982). Plaintiff there manufactured tubular locks, each with its own serial number, and maintained all of the serial numbers in secrecy. If a lock owner lost her key, she could either obtain a duplicate from the plaintiff or have a locksmith pick the lock and grind a duplicate key. Having once picked the lock, locksmiths often recorded the key code along with the serial number of the customer's lock in order to avoid having to pick the lock again. Defendant published a manual listing key codes and accompanying serial numbers for plaintiff's locks that it had received from locksmiths.

In plaintiff's suit for improper appropriation of its trade secret in the key codes, the court held that the defendant's conduct did not constitute "improper means" under Restatement section 757. Accepting for purposes of decision that the plaintiff had a trade secret in the serial numbers and accompanying key codes, the court observed that if the defendants had bought and examined the locks on their own, their reverse engineering and publication of the key codes would not have constituted an "improper means." Although the individual locksmiths may have been under a duty to their customers not to disclose their codes, neither the lock owners nor the locksmiths had any duty to the plaintiff. Defendants, "therefore, cannot be said to have procured the individual locksmiths to breach a duty of nondisclosure they owed to the [plaintiff] Company, for the locksmiths owed no such duty." 676 F.2d at 405.

2.   Restatement of Torts § 757, applied in *duPont*, outlawed only a trade secret's unauthorized disclosure or use. Would *duPont* have been an easier case if section 757 had also outlawed the unauthorized *acquisition* of a trade secret?

Both Uniform Trade Secrets Act § 1(2) and Unfair Competition Restatement § 40 proscribe the unprivileged acquisition, as well as the disclosure or use, of a trade secret. The Restatement observes: "A defendant's willingness to resort to improper means in order to acquire a trade secret is itself evidence of a substantial risk of subsequent use or disclosure. Subsection (a) of this Section follows the rule adopted in § 1(2)(i) of the Uniform Trade Secrets Act, which imposes liability for the acquisition of a trade secret by improper means. Thus, a person who obtains a trade secret through a wiretap or who induces or knowingly accepts a disclosure of the secret in breach of confidence is subject to liability. Subsequent use or disclosure of a trade secret that has been improperly acquired constitutes a further appropriation under the rule stated in Subsection (b)(2) of this Section. The relief available to the trade secret owner in such circumstances, however, may be more extensive than that available prior to any use or disclosure of the secret by the defendant." Restatement of the Law Third, Unfair Competition § 40 Comment b (1995).*

3.   *Litigation Hazards.* It is the wise trade secret claimant who does not rush into suit. "In such cases the greatest disadvantage of bringing suit is that plaintiff will have to disclose his trade secrets to defendant in the process of attempting to prove that defendant is using them. Although protective orders would be available to plaintiff to protect his disclosures in the course of litigation, they may not offer the degree of assurance plaintiff would like.

"A court, in entering a protective order, is faced with a seemingly unavoidable dilemma. If the order limits disclosure to the parties' counsel, it may well be impossible for the lawyers properly to prepare their cases, since they lack the technical background in the industry necessary to compare the processes involved. On the other hand, if a party's trade secrets are revealed to his opponent's technical staff, it may be virtually impossible to prevent their later use.

"Disclosures made in the course of litigation will have independent significance only in the event that plaintiff loses on his basic claim. In that event, plaintiff begins with one strike against him if he later tries to hold defendant liable for violation of the protective order. If defendant imposes a normal degree of industrial security, he may be able to use plaintiff's secrets without plaintiff ever becoming aware of it. Even assuming that plaintiff finds out about defendant's subsequent use, he will have difficulty proving that such use is due only to the disclosure under the protective order; a court, moreover, is less likely to foreclose defendant from use of a process because he may have learned it in the course of being unsuccessfully sued than if defendant's use is traceable to the wrongdoing of an ex-employee of plaintiff. In addition, defendant may, in the course of defending himself, discover a number of references in the literature or patents from which plaintiff's process can be put together, and it may be difficult to prove that the later use is necessarily due to plaintiff's disclosure rather than to defendant's search of sources in the public domain." Jerome Doyle & Allen S. Joslyn, The Role of Counsel in Litigation Involving Technologically Complex Trade Secrets, 6 B.C. Indus. & Com.L.Rev. 743, 744 (1965).**

Trade secrets may be exposed to discovery in contexts other than trade secret infringement cases. Products liability actions are one recurrent context. See, for example, Smith v. BIC Corp., 869 F.2d 194, 10 U.S.P.Q.2d 1052 (3d Cir.1989). Trade secret owners do not always succeed in obtaining protective orders in these contexts. See, for example, Farnum v. G.D. Searle & Co., 339 N.W.2d 384 (Iowa 1983).

4. *Criminal Liability.* The Economic Espionage Act of 1996, P.L. No. 104–294 (Oct. 11, 1996), added a new chapter 90 to Title 18 of the United States Code outlawing trade secret thefts committed "with intent to convert a trade secret, that is related to or included in a product that is produced for or placed in interstate or foreign commerce, to the economic benefit of anyone other than the owner thereof, and intending or knowing that the offence will injure any owner of that trade secret." Sanctions include a fine, imprisonment for not more than ten years, or both. 18 U.S.C. § 1832. Reverse engineering is exempt from liability. According to the bill's Senate managers, "[i]f a person can look at a product and, by using their own general skills and expertise, dissect the necessary attributes of the product, then that person should be free from any threat of prosecution." 142 Cong. Rec. No. 140 S122 12–13 (Oct. 2, 1996).

The Economic Espionage Act defines "trade secret" broadly: "all forms and types of financial, business, scientific, technical, economic, or engineering information, including patterns, plans, compilations, program devices, formulas, designs, prototypes, methods, techniques, processes, procedures, programs, or codes, whether tangible or intangible, and whether or how stored, compiled, or memorialized physically, electronically, graphically, photographically, or in writing if—(A) the owner thereof has taken reasonable measures to keep such information secret; and (B) the information derives independent economic value, actual or potential, from not being generally known to, and not being readily ascertainable through proper means by, the public." 18 U.S.C. § 1839(3).

See generally, Gerald J. Mossinghoff, J. Derek Mason & David A. Oblon, The Economic Espionage Act: A New Federal Regime of Trade Secret Protection, 79 J. Pat. & T. Off. Soc'y 191 (1997); James H.A. Pooley, Mark A. Lemley & Peter J. Toren, Understanding the Economic Espionage Act of 1996, 5 Tex. Intell. Prop. L.J. 177 (1997).

5. *Freedom of Information Act.* Local, state and federal administrative agencies routinely mark trade secrets for safe handling, often waiving their disclosure requirements or providing that they will maintain trade secrets submitted to them in confidence. At the same time, the Freedom of Information Act, 5 U.S.C.A. § 552 (1988), and counterpart state statutes subject trade secret submissions to the risk of exposure. Courts have not been entirely successful in striking a steady balance between the interests of submitters who want to keep their information secret and members of the public—including competitors—who desire access to the information.

The Freedom of Information Act provides at least two possible exemptions for trade secrets. Section 552(b)(4) specifically exempts "trade secrets and commercial or financial information obtained from a person and privileged or confidential" from disclosure. The United States Supreme Court has held that the exemption is permissive rather than mandatory, and that an agency could in its discretion disclose information that fell within section 552(b)(4)'s exemption. Chrysler Corp. v. Brown, 441 U.S. 281, 293, 99 S.Ct. 1705, 1713, 60 L.Ed.2d 208 (1979).

The second possible exemption for trade secrets is section 552(b)(3)'s exemption of matters that are specifically exempted from disclosure by another statute, "provided that such statute (A) requires that the matters be withheld from the public in such manner as to leave no discretion on the issue, or (B) establishes particular criteria for withholding or refers to particular types of matters to be withheld." This provision, taken together with the Trade Secrets Act, 18 U.S.C.A. § 1905 (1988), making it a crime for a federal official to disclose confidential information without authority of law, may provide an alternative basis for exempting trade secrets from disclosure under the Freedom of Information Act.

Before the *Chrysler* decision, many courts held that the Freedom of Information Act and the Trade Secrets Act gave submitters a private cause of action to enjoin an agency's proposed disclosure of their secret information in a so-called reverse FOIA suit. *Chrysler* held that neither statute created a private cause of action and that trade secret submitters must proceed instead under the Administrative Procedure Act's provision for judicial review of administration action. 441 U.S. at 316–18, 99 S.Ct. at 1725–26.

For an exhaustive analysis of the intersections between trade secret protection and the Freedom of Information Act, see Melvin F. Jager, Trade Secrets Law, ch. 12 (1988). See also Stephen S. Madsen, Protecting Confidential Business Information from Federal Agency Disclosure After Chrysler Corp. v. Brown, 80 Colum. L. Rev. 109 (1980).

6. *"Takings."* Does a federal statute that authorizes the administrative disclosure of trade secrets constitute a taking of property under the Fifth Amendment to the United States Constitution? In Ruckelshaus v. Monsanto Co., 467 U.S. 986, 104 S.Ct. 2862, 81 L.Ed.2d 815 (1984), the United States Supreme Court reviewed the constitutionality of several provisions of the Federal Insecticide, Fungicide, and Rodenticide Act (FIFRA) authorizing the Environmental Protection Agency to publicly disclose certain data submitted by applicants for pesticide registration. The Court held that plaintiff, Monsanto had a property right in data that it had submitted to the EPA "protected by the Takings Clause of the Fifth Amendment" to the extent that the data were protectible as a trade secret under the applicable state law. The Court further held that whether Monsanto's property had in fact been taken turned on whether, at the time Monsanto submitted its data to the government, the company had a "reasonable investment-backed expectation" that the information would be kept secret. The answer to this question in turn depended on the specific version of FIFRA that was in force at the time Monsanto submitted its data.

The Court held that in the case of submissions made after October 1, 1978, the effective date of the 1978 FIFRA amendments expanding the

EPA's right to disclose submitted information, "Monsanto could not have had a reasonable, investment-backed expectation that EPA would keep the data confidential beyond the limits prescribed in the amended statute itself. Monsanto was on notice of the manner in which EPA was authorized to use and disclose any data turned over to it by an applicant for registration." 467 U.S. at 1006, 104 S.Ct. at 2874. Similarly, no taking had occurred in connection with submissions made before October 22, 1972, the effective date of the 1972 FIFRA amendments, when FIFRA "was silent with respect to EPA's authorized use and disclosure of data submitted to it in connection with an application for registration;" during this period, too, there was "no basis for a reasonable investment-backed expectation that data submitted to EPA would remain confidential." 467 U.S. at 1009, 104 S.Ct. at 2876.

The Court held that the "situation may be different, however, with respect to data submitted by Monsanto to EPA during the period from October 22, 1972, through September 30, 1978. Under the statutory scheme then in effect, a submitter was given an opportunity to protect its trade secrets from disclosure by designating them as trade secrets at the time of submission. When Monsanto provided data to EPA during this period, it was with the understanding, embodied in FIFRA, that EPA was free to use any of the submitted data that were not trade secrets in considering the application of another, provided that EPA required the subsequent applicant to pay 'reasonable compensation' to the original submitter. But the statute also gave Monsanto explicit assurance that EPA was prohibited from disclosing publicly, or considering in connection with the application of another, any data submitted by an applicant if both the applicant and EPA determined the data to constitute trade secrets. Thus, with respect to trade secrets submitted under the statutory regime in force between the time of the adoption of the 1972 amendments and the adoption of the 1978 amendments, the Federal Government had explicitly guaranteed to Monsanto and other registration applicants an extensive measure of confidentiality and exclusive use. This explicit governmental guarantee formed the basis of a reasonable investment-backed expectation." 467 U.S. at 1010–11, 104 S.Ct. at 2877.

See Gregory Gelfand, "Taking" Informational Property Through Discovery, 66 Wash. U.L.Q. 703 (1988).

B. Limits of Protection

1. PERSONAL INTERESTS: RESTRAINTS ON POST–EMPLOYMENT COMPETITION

WEXLER v. GREENBERG, 399 Pa. 569, 160 A.2d 430, 434–35, 125 U.S.P.Q. 471 (1960). COHEN, J.: The burden the appellees must thus meet brings to the fore a problem of accommodating competing policies in our law: the right of a businessman to be protected against unfair competition stemming from the usurpation of his trade secrets and the right of an individual to the unhampered pursuit of the occupations and livelihoods for which he is best suited. There are cogent socio-economic arguments in favor of either position. Society as a whole greatly benefits from technological improvements. Without some means of post-employment protection to assure that valuable developments or improvements are exclusively those of the employer, the businessman could not afford to subsidize research or improve current methods. In addition, it must be recognized that modern economic growth and development has pushed the business venture beyond the size of the one-man firm, forcing the businessman to a much greater degree to entrust confidential business information relating to technological development to appropriate employees. While recognizing the utility in the dispersion of responsibilities in larger firms, the optimum amount of "entrusting" will not occur unless the risk of loss to the businessman through a breach of trust can be held to a minimum.

On the other hand, any form of post-employment restraint reduces the economic mobility of employees and limits their personal freedom to pursue a preferred course of livelihood. The employee's bargaining position is weakened because he is potentially shackled by the acquisition of alleged trade secrets; and thus, paradoxically, he is restrained, because of his increased expertise, from advancing further in the industry in which he is most productive. Moreover, as previously mentioned, society suffers because competition is diminished by slackening the dissemination of ideas, processes and methods.

Were we to measure the sentiment of the law by the weight of both English and American decisions in order to determine whether it favors protecting a businessman from certain forms of competition or protecting an individual in his unrestricted pursuit of a livelihood, the balance would heavily favor the latter. Indeed, even where the individual has to some extent assumed the risk of future restriction by express covenant, this Court will carefully scrutinize the covenant for reasonableness "in the light of the need of the employer for protection and the hardship of the restriction upon the employees." Morgan's Home Equipment Corp. v. Martucci, 1957, 390 Pa. 618, 631, 136 A.2d 838, 846. It follows that no less stringent an examination of the relationship should be necessary where the employer has *not* seen fit to protect himself by binding agreement.

PepsiCo, Inc. v. Redmond

United States Court of Appeals, Seventh Circuit, 1995.
54 F.3d 1262, 35 U.S.P.Q.2d 1010.

FLAUM, Circuit Judge.

Plaintiff PepsiCo, Inc., sought a preliminary injunction against defendants William Redmond and the Quaker Oats Company to prevent Redmond, a former PepsiCo employee, from divulging PepsiCo trade secrets and confidential information in his new job with Quaker and from assuming any duties with Quaker relating to beverage pricing, marketing, and distribution. The district court agreed with PepsiCo and granted the injunction. We now affirm that decision.

I.

The facts of this case lay against a backdrop of fierce beverage-industry competition between Quaker and PepsiCo, especially in "sports drinks"[1] and "new age drinks."[2] Quaker's sports drink, "Gatorade," is the dominant brand in its market niche. PepsiCo introduced its Gatorade rival, "All Sport," in March and April of 1994, but sales of All Sport lag far behind those of Gatorade. Quaker also has the lead in the new-age-drink category. Although PepsiCo has entered the market through joint ventures with the Thomas J. Lipton Company and Ocean Spray Cranberries, Inc., Quaker purchased Snapple Beverage Corp., a large new-age-drink maker, in late 1994. PepsiCo's products have about half of Snapple's market share. Both companies see 1995 as an important year for their products: PepsiCo has developed extensive plans to increase its market presence, while Quaker is trying to solidify its lead by integrating Gatorade and Snapple distribution. Meanwhile, PepsiCo and Quaker each face strong competition from Coca Cola Co., which has its own sports drink, "PowerAde," and which introduced its own Snapple-rival, "Fruitopia," in 1994, as well as from independent beverage producers.

William Redmond, Jr., worked for PepsiCo in its Pepsi–Cola North America division ("PCNA") from 1984 to 1994. Redmond became the General Manager of the Northern California Business Unit in June, 1993, and was promoted one year later to General Manager of the business unit covering all of California, a unit having annual revenues of more than 500 million dollars and representing twenty percent of PCNA's profit for all of the United States.

Redmond's relatively high-level position at PCNA gave him access to inside information and trade secrets. Redmond, like other PepsiCo management employees, had signed a confidentiality agreement with PepsiCo. That agreement stated in relevant part that he

> would not disclose at any time, to anyone other than officers or employees of [PepsiCo], or make use of, confidential information relating to the business of [PepsiCo] ... obtained while in the employ of [PepsiCo], which shall not be generally known or available to the public or recognized as standard practices.

Donald Uzzi, who had left PepsiCo in the beginning of 1994 to become the head of Quaker's Gatorade division, began courting Redmond for Quaker in May, 1994. Redmond met in Chicago with Quaker officers in August, 1994, and on October 20, 1994, Quaker, through Uzzi, offered Redmond the position of Vice President—On Premise Sales for Gatorade. Redmond did not then accept the offer but continued to negotiate for more

---

1. Sports drinks are also called "isotonics," implying that they contain the same salt concentration as human blood, and "electrolytes," implying that the substances contained in the drink have dissociated into ions.

2. "New age drink" is a catch-all category for non-carbonated soft drinks and includes such beverages as ready-to-drink tea products and fruit drinks. Sports drinks may also fall under the new-age-drink heading.

money. Throughout this time, Redmond kept his dealings with Quaker secret from his employers at PCNA.

On November 8, 1994, Uzzi extended Redmond a written offer for the position of Vice President—Field Operations for Gatorade and Redmond accepted. Later that same day, Redmond called William Bensyl, the Senior Vice President of Human Resources for PCNA, and told him that he had an offer from Quaker to become the Chief Operating Officer of the combined Gatorade and Snapple company but had not yet accepted it. Redmond also asked whether he should, in light of the offer, carry out his plans to make calls upon certain PCNA customers. Bensyl told Redmond to make the visits.

Redmond also misstated his situation to a number of his PCNA colleagues, including Craig Weatherup, PCNA's President and Chief Executive Officer, and Brenda Barnes, PCNA's Chief Operating Officer and Redmond's immediate superior. As with Bensyl, Redmond told them that he had been offered the position of Chief Operating Officer at Gatorade and that he was leaning "60/40" in favor of accepting the new position.

On November 10, 1994, Redmond met with Barnes and told her that he had decided to accept the Quaker offer and was resigning from PCNA. Barnes immediately took Redmond to Bensyl, who told Redmond that PepsiCo was considering legal action against him.

True to its word, PepsiCo filed this diversity suit on November 16, 1994, seeking a temporary restraining order to enjoin Redmond from assuming his duties at Quaker and to prevent him from disclosing trade secrets or confidential information to his new employer. The district court granted PepsiCo's request that same day but dissolved the order sua sponte two days later, after determining that PepsiCo had failed to meet its burden of establishing that it would suffer irreparable harm. The court found that PepsiCo's fears about Redmond were based upon a mistaken understanding of his new position at Quaker and that the likelihood that Redmond would improperly reveal any confidential information did not "rise above mere speculation."

From November 23, 1994, to December 1, 1994, the district court conducted a preliminary injunction hearing on the same matter. At the hearing, PepsiCo offered evidence of a number of trade secrets and confidential information it desired protected and to which Redmond was privy. First, it identified PCNA's "Strategic Plan," an annually revised document that contains PCNA's plans to compete, its financial goals, and its strategies for manufacturing, production, marketing, packaging, and distribution for the coming three years. Strategic Plans are developed by Weatherup and his staff with input from PCNA's general managers, including Redmond, and are considered highly confidential. The Strategic Plan derives much of its value from the fact that it is secret and competitors cannot anticipate PCNA's next moves. PCNA managers received the most recent Strategic Plan at a meeting in July, 1994, a meeting Redmond attended. PCNA also presented information at the meeting regarding its plans for

Lipton ready-to-drink teas and for All Sport for 1995 and beyond, including new flavors and package sizes.

Second, PepsiCo pointed to PCNA's Annual Operating Plan ("AOP") as a trade secret. The AOP is a national plan for a given year and guides PCNA's financial goals, marketing plans, promotional event calendars, growth expectations, and operational changes in that year. The AOP, which is implemented by PCNA unit General Managers, including Redmond, contains specific information regarding all PCNA initiatives for the forthcoming year. The AOP bears a label that reads "Private and Confidential— Do Not Reproduce" and is considered highly confidential by PCNA managers.

In particular, the AOP contains important and sensitive information about "pricing architecture"—how PCNA prices its products in the marketplace. Pricing architecture covers both a national pricing approach and specific price points for given areas. Pricing architecture also encompasses PCNA's objectives for All Sport and its new age drinks with reference to trade channels, package sizes and other characteristics of both the products and the customers at which the products are aimed. Additionally, PCNA's pricing architecture outlines PCNA's customer development agreements. These agreements between PCNA and retailers provide for the retailer's participation in certain merchandising activities for PCNA products. As with other information contained in the AOP, pricing architecture is highly confidential and would be extremely valuable to a competitor. Knowing PCNA's pricing architecture would allow a competitor to anticipate PCNA's pricing moves and underbid PCNA strategically whenever and wherever the competitor so desired. PepsiCo introduced evidence that Redmond had detailed knowledge of PCNA's pricing architecture and that he was aware of and had been involved in preparing PCNA's customer development agreements with PCNA's California and California-based national customers. Indeed, PepsiCo showed that Redmond, as the General Manager for California, would have been responsible for implementing the pricing architecture guidelines for his business unit.

PepsiCo also showed that Redmond had intimate knowledge of PCNA "attack plans" for specific markets. Pursuant to these plans, PCNA dedicates extra funds to supporting its brands against other brands in selected markets. To use a hypothetical example, PCNA might budget an additional $500,000 to spend in Chicago at a particular time to help All Sport close its market gap with Gatorade. Testimony and documents demonstrated Redmond's awareness of these plans and his participation in drafting some of them.

Finally, PepsiCo offered evidence of PCNA trade secrets regarding innovations in its selling and delivery systems. Under this plan, PCNA is testing a new delivery system that could give PCNA an advantage over its competitors in negotiations with retailers over shelf space and merchandising. Redmond has knowledge of this secret because PCNA, which has invested over a million dollars in developing the system during the past two years, is testing the pilot program in California.

Having shown Redmond's intimate knowledge of PCNA's plans for 1995, PepsiCo argued that Redmond would inevitably disclose that information to Quaker in his new position, at which he would have substantial input as to Gatorade and Snapple pricing, costs, margins, distribution systems, products, packaging and marketing, and could give Quaker an unfair advantage in its upcoming skirmishes with PepsiCo. Redmond and Quaker countered that Redmond's primary initial duties at Quaker as Vice President–Field Operations would be to integrate Gatorade and Snapple distribution and then to manage that distribution as well as the promotion, marketing and sales of these products. Redmond asserted that the integration would be conducted according to a pre-existing plan and that his special knowledge of PCNA strategies would be irrelevant. This irrelevance would derive not only from the fact that Redmond would be implementing pre-existing plans but also from the fact that PCNA and Quaker distribute their products in entirely different ways: PCNA's distribution system is vertically integrated (i.e., PCNA owns the system) and delivers its product directly to retailers, while Quaker ships its product to wholesalers and customer warehouses and relies on independent distributors. The defendants also pointed out that Redmond had signed a confidentiality agreement with Quaker preventing him from disclosing "any confidential information belonging to others," as well as the Quaker Code of Ethics, which prohibits employees from engaging in "illegal or improper acts to acquire a competitor's trade secrets." Redmond additionally promised at the hearing that should he be faced with a situation at Quaker that might involve the use or disclosure of PCNA information, he would seek advice from Quaker's in-house counsel and would refrain from making the decision.

PepsiCo responded to the defendants' representations by pointing out that the evidence did not show that Redmond would simply be implementing a business plan already in place. On the contrary, as of November, 1994, the plan to integrate Gatorade and Snapple distribution consisted of a single distributorship agreement and a two-page "contract terms summary." Such a basic plan would not lend itself to widespread application among the over 300 independent Snapple distributors. Since the integration process would likely face resistance from Snapple distributors and Quaker had no scheme to deal with this probability, Redmond, as the person in charge of the integration, would likely have a great deal of influence on the process. PepsiCo further argued that Snapple's 1995 marketing and promotion plans had not necessarily been completed prior to Redmond's joining Quaker, that Uzzi disagreed with portions of the Snapple plans, and that the plans were open to re-evaluation. Uzzi testified that the plan for integrating Gatorade and Snapple distribution is something that would happen in the future. Redmond would therefore likely have input in remaking these plans, and if he did, he would inevitably be making decisions with PCNA's strategic plans and 1995 AOP in mind. Moreover, PepsiCo continued, diverging testimony made it difficult to know exactly what Redmond would be doing at Quaker. Redmond described his job as "managing the entire sales effort of Gatorade at the field level, possibly including strategic planning," and at least at one point considered his job

to be equivalent to that of a Chief Operating Officer. Uzzi, on the other
hand, characterized Redmond's position as "primarily and initially to
restructure and integrate our—the distribution systems for Snapple and for
Gatorade, as per our distribution plan" and then to "execute marketing,
promotion and sales plans in the marketplace." Uzzi also denied having
given Redmond detailed information about any business plans, while Redmond described such a plan in depth in an affidavit and said that he
received the information from Uzzi. Thus, PepsiCo asserted, Redmond
would have a high position in the Gatorade hierarchy, and PCNA trade
secrets and confidential information would necessarily influence his decisions. Even if Redmond could somehow refrain from relying on this
information, as he promised he would, his actions in leaving PCNA, Uzzi's
actions in hiring Redmond, and the varying testimony regarding Redmond's new responsibilities, made Redmond's assurances to PepsiCo less
than comforting.

On December 15, 1994, the district court issued an order enjoining
Redmond from assuming his position at Quaker through May, 1995, and
permanently from using or disclosing any PCNA trade secrets or confidential information. The court entered its findings of fact and conclusions of
law on January 26, 1995, nunc pro tunc December 15, 1994. The court,
which completely adopted PepsiCo's position, found that Redmond's new
job posed a clear threat of misappropriation of trade secrets and confidential information that could be enjoined under Illinois statutory and common law. The court also emphasized Redmond's lack of forthrightness both
in his activities before accepting his job with Quaker and in his testimony
as factors leading the court to believe the threat of misappropriation was
real. This appeal followed.

II.

Both parties agree that the primary issue on appeal is whether the
district court correctly concluded that PepsiCo had a reasonable likelihood
of success on its various claims for trade secret misappropriation and
breach of a confidentiality agreement. We review the district court's legal
conclusions in issuing a preliminary injunction de novo and its factual
determinations and balancing of the equities for abuse of discretion.

A.

The Illinois Trade Secrets Act ("ITSA"), which governs the trade
secret issues in this case, provides that a court may enjoin the "actual or
threatened misappropriation" of a trade secret. A party seeking an injunction must therefore prove both the existence of a trade secret and the
misappropriation. The defendants' appeal focuses solely on misappropriation; although the defendants only reluctantly refer to PepsiCo's marketing
and distribution plans as trade secrets, they do not seriously contest that
this information falls under the ITSA.

The question of threatened or inevitable misappropriation in this case
lies at the heart of a basic tension in trade secret law. Trade secret law

serves to protect "standards of commercial morality" and "encourage invention and innovation" while maintaining "the public interest in having free and open competition in the manufacture and sale of unpatented goods." 2 Jager, [Trade Secrets Law] § IL.03 at IL–12. Yet that same law should not prevent workers from pursuing their livelihoods when they leave their current positions. It has been said that federal age discrimination law does not guarantee tenure for older employees. Similarly, trade secret law does not provide a reserve clause for solicitous employers.

This tension is particularly exacerbated when a plaintiff sues to prevent not the actual misappropriation of trade secrets but the mere threat that it will occur. While the ITSA plainly permits a court to enjoin the threat of misappropriation of trade secrets, there is little law in Illinois or in this circuit establishing what constitutes threatened or inevitable misappropriation. Indeed, there are only two cases in this circuit that address the issue: Teradyne, Inc. v. Clear Communications Corp., 707 F.Supp. 353 (N.D.Ill.1989), and AMP Inc. v. Fleischhacker, 823 F.2d 1199 (7th Cir. 1987).

In Teradyne, Teradyne alleged that a competitor, Clear Communications, had lured employees away from Teradyne and intended to employ them in the same field. In an insightful opinion, Judge Zagel observed that "[t]hreatened misappropriation can be enjoined under Illinois law" where there is a "high degree of probability of inevitable and immediate . . . use of . . . trade secrets." Teradyne, 707 F.Supp. at 356. Judge Zagel held, however, that Teradyne's complaint failed to state a claim because Teradyne did not allege "that defendants have in fact threatened to use Teradyne's secrets or that they will inevitably do so." Teradyne's claims would have passed Rule 12(b)(6) muster had they properly alleged inevitable disclosure, including a statement that Clear intended to use Teradyne's trade secrets or that the former Teradyne employees had disavowed their confidentiality agreements with Teradyne, or an allegation that Clear could not operate without Teradyne's secrets. However, [t]he defendants' claimed acts, working for Teradyne, knowing its business, leaving its business, hiring employees from Teradyne and entering the same field (though in a market not yet serviced by Teradyne) do not state a claim of threatened misappropriation. All that is alleged, at bottom, is that defendants could misuse plaintiff's secrets, and plaintiffs fear they will. This is not enough. It may be that little more is needed, but falling a little short is still falling short.

Id. at 357.

In AMP, we affirmed the denial of a preliminary injunction on the grounds that the plaintiff AMP had failed to show either the existence of any trade secrets or the likelihood that defendant Fleischhacker, a former AMP employee, would compromise those secrets or any other confidential business information. AMP, which produced electrical and electronic connection devices, argued that Fleishhacker's new position at AMP's competitor would inevitably lead him to compromise AMP's trade secrets regarding the manufacture of connectors. AMP, 823 F.2d at 1207. In rejecting that argument, we emphasized that the mere fact that a person assumed a similar position at a competitor does not, without more, make it "inevitable that he will use or disclose ... trade secret information" so as to "demonstrate irreparable injury." Id.

It should be noted that AMP, which we decided in 1987, predates the ITSA, which took effect in 1988. The ITSA abolishes any common law remedies or authority contrary to its own terms. The ITSA does not, however, represent a major deviation from the Illinois common law of unfair trade practices. The ITSA mostly codifies rather than modifies the common law doctrine that preceded it. Thus, we believe that AMP continues to reflect the proper standard under Illinois's current statutory scheme.

The ITSA, Teradyne, and AMP lead to the same conclusion: a plaintiff may prove a claim of trade secret misappropriation by demonstrating that defendant's new employment will inevitably lead him to rely on the plaintiff's trade secrets. The defendants are incorrect that Illinois law does not allow a court to enjoin the "inevitable" disclosure of trade secrets. Questions remain, however, as to what constitutes inevitable misappropriation and whether PepsiCo's submissions rise above those of the Teradyne and AMP plaintiffs and meet that standard. We hold that they do.

PepsiCo presented substantial evidence at the preliminary injunction hearing that Redmond possessed extensive and intimate knowledge about PCNA's strategic goals for 1995 in sports drinks and new age drinks. The district court concluded on the basis of that presentation that unless Redmond possessed an uncanny ability to compartmentalize information, he would necessarily be making decisions about Gatorade and Snapple by relying on his knowledge of PCNA trade secrets. It is not the "general skills and knowledge acquired during his tenure with" PepsiCo that PepsiCo seeks to keep from falling into Quaker's hands, but rather "the particularized plans or processes developed by [PCNA] and disclosed to him while the employer-employee relationship existed, which are unknown to others in the industry and which give the employer an advantage over his competitors." AMP, 823 F.2d at 1202. The Teradyne and AMP plaintiffs could do nothing more than assert that skilled employees were taking their skills elsewhere; PepsiCo has done much more.

Admittedly, PepsiCo has not brought a traditional trade secret case, in which a former employee has knowledge of a special manufacturing process or customer list and can give a competitor an unfair advantage by transferring the technology or customers to that competitor. PepsiCo has not contended that Quaker has stolen the All Sport formula or its list of distributors. Rather PepsiCo has asserted that Redmond cannot help but rely on PCNA trade secrets as he helps plot Gatorade and Snapple's new course, and that these secrets will enable Quaker to achieve a substantial advantage by knowing exactly how PCNA will price, distribute, and market its sports drinks and new age drinks and being able to respond strategically. This type of trade secret problem may arise less often, but it nevertheless falls within the realm of trade secret protection under the present circumstances.

Quaker and Redmond assert that they have not and do not intend to use whatever confidential information Redmond has by virtue of his former employment. They point out that Redmond has already signed an agreement with Quaker not to disclose any trade secrets or confidential information gleaned from his earlier employment. They also note with regard to distribution systems that even if Quaker wanted to steal information about PCNA's distribution plans, they would be completely useless in attempting to integrate the Gatorade and Snapple beverage lines.

The defendants' arguments fall somewhat short of the mark. Again, the danger of misappropriation in the present case is not that Quaker threatens to use PCNA's secrets to create distribution systems or co-opt PCNA's advertising and marketing ideas. Rather, PepsiCo believes that Quaker, unfairly armed with knowledge of PCNA's plans, will be able to anticipate its distribution, packaging, pricing, and marketing moves. Redmond and Quaker even concede that Redmond might be faced with a decision that could be influenced by certain confidential information that he obtained while at PepsiCo. In other words, PepsiCo finds itself in the position of a coach, one of whose players has left, playbook in hand, to join the opposing team before the big game. Quaker and Redmond's protestations that their distribution systems and plans are entirely different from PCNA's are thus not really responsive.

The district court also concluded from the evidence that Uzzi's actions in hiring Redmond and Redmond's actions in pursuing and accepting his new job demonstrated a lack of candor on their part and proof of their willingness to misuse PCNA trade secrets, findings Quaker and Redmond vigorously challenge. The court expressly found that:

Redmond's lack of forthrightness on some occasions, and out and out lies on others, in the period between the time he accepted the position with defendant Quaker and when he informed plaintiff that he had accepted that position leads the court to conclude that defendant Redmond could not be trusted to act with the necessary sensitivity and good faith under the circumstances in which the only practical verification that he was not using plaintiff's secrets would be defendant Redmond's word to that effect.

The facts of the case do not ineluctably dictate the district court's conclusion. Redmond's ambiguous behavior toward his PepsiCo superiors might have been nothing more than an attempt to gain leverage in employment negotiations. The discrepancy between Redmond's and Uzzi's comprehension of what Redmond's job would entail may well have been a simple misunderstanding. The court also pointed out that Quaker, through Uzzi, seemed to express an unnatural interest in hiring PCNA employees: all three of the people interviewed for the position Redmond ultimately accepted worked at PCNA. Uzzi may well have focused on recruiting PCNA employees because he knew they were good and not because of their confidential knowledge. Nonetheless, the district court, after listening to the witnesses, determined otherwise. That conclusion was not an abuse of discretion.

... Thus, when we couple the demonstrated inevitability that Redmond would rely on PCNA trade secrets in his new job at Quaker with the district court's reluctance to believe that Redmond would refrain from disclosing these secrets in his new position (or that Quaker would ensure Redmond did not disclose them), we conclude that the district court correctly decided that PepsiCo demonstrated a likelihood of success on its statutory claim of trade secret misappropriation.

C.

For the same reasons we concluded that the district court did not abuse its discretion in granting the preliminary injunction on the issue of trade secret misappropriation, we also agree with its decision on the likelihood of Redmond's breach of his confidentiality agreement should he begin working at Quaker. Because Redmond's position at Quaker would initially cause him to disclose trade secrets, it would necessarily force him to breach his agreement not to disclose confidential information acquired while employed in PCNA.

Quaker and Redmond do not assert that the confidentiality agreement is invalid; such agreements are enforceable when supported by adequate consideration. Rather, they argue that "inevitable" breaches of these contracts may not be enjoined. The case on which they rely, however, R.R. Donnelley & Sons Co. v. Fagan, 767 F.Supp. 1259 (S.D.N.Y.1991) (applying Illinois law), says nothing of the sort. The R.R. Donnelley court merely found that the plaintiffs had failed to prove the existence of any confidential information or any indication that the defendant would ever use it. Id. at 1267. The threat of misappropriation that drives our holding with regard to trade secrets dictates the same result here.

III.

Finally, Redmond and Quaker have contended in the alternative that the injunction issued against them is overbroad. They disagree in particular with the injunction's prohibition against Redmond's participation in the integration of the Snapple and Gatorade distribution systems. The defendants claim that whatever trade secret and confidential information Redmond has, that information is completely irrelevant to Quaker's integration task. They further argue that, because Redmond would only be implementing a plan already in place, the injunction is especially inappropriate. A district court ordinarily has wide latitude in fashioning injunctive relief, and we will restrict the breadth of an injunction only where the district court has abused its discretion. Nonetheless, a court abuses its discretion where the scope of injunctive relief "exceed[s] the extent of the plaintiff's protectible rights." International Kennel Club of Chicago, Inc. v. Mighty Star, Inc., 846 F.2d 1079, 1094 (7th Cir.1988).

While the defendants' arguments are not without some merit, the district court determined that the proposed integration would require Redmond to do more than execute a plan someone else had drafted. It also found that Redmond's knowledge of PCNA's trade secrets and confidential information would inevitably shape that integration and that Redmond could not be trusted to avoid that conflict of interest. If the injunction permanently enjoined Redmond from assuming these duties at Quaker, the defendants' argument would be stronger. However, the injunction against Redmond's immediate employment at Quaker extends no further than necessary and was well within the district court's discretion.

For the foregoing reasons, we affirm the district court's order enjoining Redmond from assuming his responsibilities at Quaker through May, 1995, and preventing him forever from disclosing PCNA trade secrets and confidential information.

AFFIRMED.

Reed, Roberts Associates, Inc. v. Strauman

Court of Appeals of New York, 1976.
40 N.Y.2d 303, 386 N.Y.S.2d 677, 353 N.E.2d 590.

WACHTLER, Judge.

These cross appeals involve the efficacy of an employment contract provision barring an employee from either directly or indirectly competing with, or soliciting clients of, his former employer. This restrictive covenant is not a proper subject for specific enforcement since the services of the employee were not unique or extraordinary and the employer failed to establish a studied copying of a customer list.

Reed, Roberts Associates, Inc., with over 6,000 customers being served through some 21 offices scattered throughout the nation and with gross sales of almost $4 million, is one of the top three companies in its field. The lion's share of its business involves supplying advice and guidance to employers with respect to their obligations under State unemployment laws. The object of this service is to minimize the tax liability and administrative expenses involved in complying with these laws. Other services performed by Reed, Roberts include consultation regarding workmen's compensation, disability benefits and pension plans. This action was commenced by Reed, Roberts to prevent a former employee from competing against them and soliciting their customers.

When John Strauman was hired by Reed, Roberts in November, 1962 he signed a restrictive covenant which read in pertinent part: "I do therefore consent that at no time shall I either directly or indirectly solicit any of your clients, and I do further agree that for a period of three years from the date of termination of my employment that I will not either directly or indirectly be engaged in, nor in any manner whatsoever become interested directly or indirectly, either as employee, owner, partner, agent, stockholder, director or officer of a corporation or otherwise, in any business of the type and character engaged in by your company within the geographical limits of the City of New York and the counties of Nassau, Suffolk and Westchester."

Strauman's first position as an employee of Reed, Roberts was technical man-auditor. Since he had four years' experience in the field by virtue of having previously worked for a major competitor, Strauman became a valuable employee and over the next 10 years received three important promotions rising to senior vice-president in charge of operations. Throughout his tenure with Reed, Roberts, Strauman was instrumental in devising most of the forms utilized by the company in rendering its service and in setting up its computer system. On becoming vice-president he was given increased responsibility with regard to internal affairs including the formulation of company policy. Importantly, however, he was not responsible for sales or obtaining new customers. The record indicates that while the business forms used by Reed, Roberts were unique to that service industry, they were not much different from those used by other companies.

After 11 years with Reed, Roberts, Strauman decided to strike off on his own and formed a company called Curator Associates, Inc. This company was in direct competition with his former employer and was even located in the same municipality. Although Reed, Roberts alleges that Curator has been soliciting its customers, Curator sustained losses of some $38,000 with gross sales of only $1,100 during its first year of operations. Nevertheless, fearful of competition from the former employee, Reed, Roberts commenced this action seeking to enforce the post-termination covenant not to compete signed by Strauman in 1962. Specifically Reed, Roberts seeks to enjoin Strauman and Curator from engaging in the business of unemployment tax control within the metropolitan area for a period of three years and to enjoin them from soliciting any of Reed, Roberts' customers permanently.

The trial court granted this relief in part. The court refused to prohibit defendants from engaging in a competitive enterprise finding that there were no trade secrets involved here and that although Strauman was a key employee his services were not so unique or extraordinary as to warrant restraining his attempt to compete with his former employer. Nevertheless the court believed that it would be unjust and unfair for Strauman to utilize his knowledge of Reed, Roberts' internal operations to solicit its clients and permanently enjoined defendants from doing so. The Appellate Division affirmed, without opinion. We believe the order of the Appellate Division should be modified to the extent of reversing so much thereof as grants a permanent injunction against the defendants.

Generally negative covenants restricting competition are enforceable only to the extent that they satisfy the overriding requirement of reasonableness. Yet the formulation of reasonableness may vary with the context and type of restriction imposed. For example, where a business is sold, anticompetition covenants will be enforceable, if reasonable in time, scope and extent. These covenants are designed to protect the goodwill integral to the business from usurpation by the former owner while at the same time allowing an owner to profit from the goodwill which he may have spent years creating. However, where an anticompetition covenant given by an employee to his employer is involved a stricter standard of reasonableness will be applied.

In this context a restrictive covenant will only be subject to specific enforcement to the extent that it is reasonable in time and area, necessary to protect the employer's legitimate interests, not harmful to the general public and not unreasonably burdensome to the employee. Undoubtedly judicial disfavor of these covenants is provoked by "powerful considerations of public policy which militate against sanctioning the loss of a man's livelihood" (Purchasing Assoc. v. Weitz, 13 N.Y.2d p. 272, 246 N.Y.S.2d p. 604, 196 N.E.2d p. 247). Indeed, our economy is premised on the competition engendered by the uninhibited flow of services, talent and ideas. Therefore, no restrictions should fetter an employee's right to apply to his own best advantage the skills and knowledge acquired by the overall experience of his previous employment. This includes those techniques which are but "skillful variations of general processes known to the particular trade" (Restatement, Agency 2d, § 396, Comment b).

Of course, the courts must also recognize the legitimate interest an employer has in safeguarding that which has made his business successful and to protect himself against deliberate surreptitious commercial piracy. Thus restrictive covenants will be enforceable to the extent necessary to prevent the disclosure or use of trade secrets or confidential customer information. In addition injunctive relief may be available where an employee's services are unique or extraordinary and the covenant is reasonable. This latter principle has been interpreted to reach agreements between members of the learned professions.

With these principles in mind we consider first the issue of solicitation of customers in the case at bar. The courts below found, and Reed, Roberts does not dispute, that there were no trade secrets involved here. The thrust of Reed, Roberts' argument is that by virtue of Strauman's position in charge of internal administration he was privy to sensitive and confidential customer information which he should not be permitted to convert to his own use. The law enunciated in Leo Silfen, Inc. v. Cream, 29 N.Y.2d 387, 328 N.Y.S.2d 423, 278 N.E.2d 636 is dispositive. There, as here, the plaintiff failed to sustain its allegation that the defendant had pirated the actual customer list. Rather Silfen argued that in light of the funds expended to compile the list it would be unfair to allow the defendant to solicit the clients of his former employer. We held that where the employee engaged in no wrongful conduct and the names and addresses of potential customers were readily discoverable through public sources, an injunction would not lie. Similarly here there was no finding that Strauman acted wrongfully by either pilfering or memorizing the customer list. More important, by Reed, Roberts' own admission every company with employees is a prospective customer and the solicitation of customers was usually done through the use of nationally known publications such as Dun and Bradstreet's Million Dollar Directory where even the name of the person to contact regarding these services is readily available. It strains credulity to characterize this type of information as confidential. Consequently, the trial court's determination that Strauman and Curator should be permanently enjoined from soliciting Reed, Roberts' customers as of the date of his termination was erroneous.

Apparently, the employer is more concerned about Strauman's knowledge of the intricacies of their business operation. However, absent any wrongdoing, we cannot agree that Strauman should be prohibited from utilizing his knowledge and talents in this area. A contrary holding would make those in charge of operations or specialists in certain aspects of an enterprise virtual hostages of their employers. Where the knowledge does not qualify for protection as a trade secret and there has been no conspiracy or breach of trust resulting in commercial piracy we see no reason to inhibit the employee's ability to realize his potential both professionally and financially by availing himself of opportunity. Therefore, despite Strauman's excellence or value to Reed, Roberts the trial court's finding that his services were not extraordinary or unique is controlling and properly resulted in a denial of the injunction against operating a competing business.

Accordingly, the order of the Appellate Division should be modified in accordance with this opinion.

NOTES

1. *Covenants Not to Compete and Trade Secrets Compared.* In their attempts to restrain departing employees from using or disclosing information developed in the course of employment, employers commonly take either or both of two precautions: (a) at the outset of employment, obtaining the employee's agreement not to engage in postemployment competition and (b) upon departure, seeking to enjoin the employee's disclosure or use of trade secrets imparted by the employer. Although the covenant not to compete might appear to be a broader, more effective precaution than trade secret protection, the two measures in fact have very similar effects.

Covenants Not to Compete. Courts construe covenants not to compete narrowly. Presumptively invalid, these covenants are generally enforced only upon proof that they are reasonably necessary to the integrity of the employer's business. The covenant must reasonably delimit the breadth of its subject matter and the period and geographic area in which the former employee cannot compete. Courts will roughly measure the reasonableness of a covenant's breadth by the scope of the employer's trade secrets along with some interstitial, otherwise unprotectible, technical information. In determining whether a covenant's duration is reasonable, courts often employ the same measure they use in determining how long a trade secret injunction may run—the time it would take a competitor to arrive independently at the former employer's protected methods.

Trade Secrets. The effects of a trade secret injunction against a departing employee will characteristically exceed the terms of the injunctive decree. Trade secrets commonly have value only in the industry in which the former employer is engaged, so that an injunction against their use is in effect an injunction against their use in competition. Since the departing employee carries a potential trade secret lawsuit with her, she may encounter difficulty getting a job with a competitor of her former employer—unless, of course, the competitor was responsible for luring her away in the first place.

There are at least two important differences between the scope of an enforceable covenant not to compete and the scope of protection that trade secret law would offer in the same circumstances. For purposes of sustaining a covenant not to compete, the employer need only show that the employee is in a position to use its trade secrets; to receive a trade secret injunction the employer usually has to prove that the employee is in fact using or about to use the trade secret. Further, in the trade secret action the employer bears the heavy burden of demonstrating that the particular information being used by the employee constitutes a trade secret and is not just part of the employee's general knowledge and skills.

To what extent does the *PepsiCo* decision, particularly its rule on inevitable disclosure, eliminate either or both of the differences between enforcement of trade secrets and enforcement of covenants not to compete?

2. *Covenants Not to Compete in California.* Unlike most states which, with limitations, enforce employee noncompetition covenants, California provides in section 16600 of its Business and Professions Code that, subject to exceptions related to the sale of a business, "every contract by which anyone is restrained from engaging in a lawful profession, trade or business of any kind is to that extent void." One writer has observed a connection between employee mobility and technological advance through the information that becomes available when employees are free to move between companies. He argues that the employee mobility fostered by section 16600, when contrasted with the relative immobility imposed in other states, enables a culture of job hopping that offers a possible explanation for the early economic vibrancy of Silicon Valley. Ronald J. Gilson, The Legal Infrastructure of High Technology Industrial Districts: Silicon Valley, Route 128, and Covenants Not to Compete, 74 N.Y.U. L. Rev. 575, 578 (1999).

In fact, California employees are not as unconstrained as the text of section 16600 might suggest. One reason is that California has adopted the Uniform Trade Secrets Act, Cal. Civ. Code §§ 3426–3426.11, so that courts in the state enforce trade secret liability against departing employees much as do courts in other states.

3. *Shop Rights.* As a general rule, absent an express contract between employer and employee allocating rights to inventions made by the employee in the course of his employment, all rights to the inventions belong to the employee. Two important exceptions virtually swallow this general rule. First, if the employee was specifically hired to engage in research and development, courts will imply an agreement that rights to his inventions belong to the employer. See Solomons v. United States, 137 U.S. 342, 346, 11 S.Ct. 88, 34 L.Ed. 667 (1890) ("If one is employed to devise or perfect an instrument, or a means for accomplishing a prescribed result, he cannot, after successfully accomplishing the work for which he was employed, plead title thereto as against his employer. That which he has been employed and paid to accomplish becomes, when accomplished, the property of his employer.'')

Second, if the employee was not hired specifically for research and development but made the invention during working hours, or with the use of his employer's equipment or materials, the employer obtains a "shop right," essentially an irrevocable, nonexclusive license to practice the invention. See, for example, United States v. Dubilier Condenser Corp., 289 U.S. 178, 188–89, 53 S.Ct. 554, 557–58, 77 L.Ed. 1114 (1933) ("Since the servant uses his master's time, facilities and materials to attain a concrete result, the latter is in equity entitled to use that which embodies his own property and to duplicate it as often as he may find occasion to employ similar appliances in his business. But the employer in such a case has no equity to demand a conveyance of the invention, which is the original conception of the employee alone, in which the employer had no part.").

Employee and employer can alter these common law allocations by contract. Statutes in several states limit the employer's contractual freedom to require an assignment of rights from its employees.

4. *Customer Lists.* In principle, an employer's customer list can qualify as a trade secret and a departing employee can be enjoined from using it in her new business. See Restatement of Torts § 757 comment b (1939); Restatement of the Law Third, Unfair Competition § 42, comment f (1995). In practice, former employers regularly fail in their efforts to protect customer lists, mainly because these lists frequently fall short of the standards imposed on trade secret subject matter.

American Red Cross v. Palm Beach Blood Bank, Inc., 143 F.3d 1407, 47 U.S.P.Q.2d 1139 (11th Cir.1998), vacating a preliminary injunction against defendant blood bank's use of plaintiff's lists of blood donors under the Florida version of the Uniform Trade Secrets Act, is typical. Defendant Palm Beach had hired a number of plaintiff's Miami employees for its Miami branch, and at least one of them had taken a list of Red Cross donors with her and used the list to contact these donors on behalf of Palm Beach. The court of appeals ruled that, on the incomplete record below, it would not be prudent to reach any conclusion respecting the list's protectibility. "Some of Red Cross's lists appear to have been posted on a computer bulletin board freely accessible to Red Cross's competitors, while many of Red Cross's donor groups have publicly revealed their sponsorship of Red Cross's blood drives. It may also be the case, as Palm Beach claims, that some former Red Cross employees have professional relationships with individual Red Cross donors, relationships which these workers may now rely upon without infringing any of Red Cross's rights." 143 F.3d at 1410–11.

Restatement of Agency, Second, § 396 (1958) takes a different approach to customer lists. After termination of an agency relationship, the agent has no duty not to compete with the principal, but does have a duty "not to use or to disclose to third persons, on his own account or on account of others, in competition with the principal or to his injury, trade secrets, written lists of names, or other similar confidential matters given to him only for the principal's use or acquired by the agent in violation of duty. The agent is entitled to use general information concerning the method of business of the principal and the names of the customers retained in his memory, if not acquired in violation of his duty as agent." What reason is there for the "memory rule" which prohibits the former employee from taking copies of customer lists with him, but allow him to use any customer information that he can remember? What is the status of information that the employee has deliberately committed to memory?

5. Why is there so little litigation over the use of trade secrets by departing employees? Against the vast number of defections that occur each year, the number of reported cases is very small. There is no evidence that this number would be significantly increased by the addition of settled cases. Compare the decision for a former employer in B.F. Goodrich Co. v. Wohlgemuth, 117 Ohio App. 493, 192 N.E.2d 99, 137 U.S.P.Q. 804 (1963), with its follow-up coverage, John Brooks, Annals of Business, The New Yorker, Jan. 11, 1964, at 37, suggesting that, litigation notwithstanding, the highly skilled employee in fact enjoys considerable freedom in competitive employ.

One reason for the dearth of litigation is doubtless the difficulty of proving that the employer's information qualifies as a trade secret, that the trade secret is hers, and that the departing employee is in fact using it. Even if the former employer had extracted a covenant against postemployment competition from all of her technical employees, she may be reluctant to take the risk that a court reviewing the covenant will hold it invalid. Litigation may also expose other information that the former employer wishes to keep secret, including information about the trade secrets that she may have pirated from her competitors.

6. *History.* Rules governing trade secrets and related postemployment restraints originated in commercial settings that differ in important respects from those that prevail today. The modern action for employee appropriation of trade secrets traces to Roman law's *actio servi corrupti.* Under the general action for corruption of a slave, the slave owner received double damages against a third person who maliciously enticed his slave to commit a wrong. Applied at the instance of a master against a business competitor, the *actio* compensated for the loss of business secrets divulged by the slave to the competitor at the latter's instigation. Damages included the diminution in the value of the slave and all other provable direct and indirect harm. See A. Arthur Schiller, Trade Secrets and the Roman Law: The *Actio Servi Corrupti*, 30 Colum. L. Rev. 837 (1930).

The fifteenth- and sixteenth-century cases, often cited as marking the common law's early distaste for postemployment restraints as departures from principles of economic freedom, should be viewed against the background of the craft guilds that were economically predominant at the time. Because the cases involved restraints imposed by masters upon apprentices to prolong their period of noncompetitive—and often wageless—service, it has been argued that the decisions striking down the restraints should be narrowly interpreted as endorsements of the guild customs which established a limited indenture period. "If the early cases represent, in fact, the courts' attempt to assist the guilds and legislative bodies in shoring up the crumbling values of the medieval economic system, they cannot fairly be described as indicative of an attitude of economic liberalism." Harlan M. Blake, Employee Agreements Not To Compete, 73 Harv. L. Rev. 625, 632 (1960).

2. ECONOMIC INTERESTS: THE PLACE OF TRADE SECRETS IN THE COMPETITIVE PLAN

Kewanee Oil Co. v. Bicron Corp.

Supreme Court of the United States, 1974.
416 U.S. 470, 94 S.Ct. 1879, 40 L.Ed.2d 315, 181 U.S.P.Q. 673.

Mr. Chief Justice BURGER delivered the opinion of the Court.

We granted certiorari to resolve a question on which there is a conflict in the courts of appeals: whether state trade secret protection is pre-empted by operation of the federal patent law. In the instant case the Court of Appeals for the Sixth Circuit held that there was preemption. The Courts of Appeals for the Second, Fourth, Fifth, and Ninth Circuits have reached the opposite conclusion.

I

Harshaw Chemical Co., an unincorporated division of petitioner, is a leading manufacturer of a type of synthetic crystal which is useful in the detection of ionizing radiation. In 1949 Harshaw commenced research into the growth of this type crystal and was able to produce one less than two inches in diameter. By 1966, as the result of expenditures in excess of $1 million, Harshaw was able to grow a 17-inch crystal, something no one else had done previously. Harshaw had developed many processes, procedures, and manufacturing techniques in the purification of raw materials and the growth and encapsulation of the crystals which enabled it to accomplish this feat. Some of these processes Harshaw considers to be trade secrets.

The individual respondents are former employees of Harshaw who formed or later joined respondent Bicron. While at Harshaw the individual respondents executed, as a condition of employment, at least one agreement each, requiring them not to disclose confidential information or trade secrets obtained as employees of Harshaw. Bicron was formed in August 1969 to compete with Harshaw in the production of the crystals and by April 1970, had grown a 17-inch crystal.

Petitioner brought this diversity action in United States District Court for the Northern District of Ohio seeking injunctive relief and damages for the misappropriation of trade secrets. The District Court, applying Ohio trade secret law, granted a permanent injunction against the disclosure or use by respondents of 20 of the 40 claimed trade secrets until such time as the trade secrets had been released to the public, had otherwise generally become available to the public, or had been obtained by respondents from sources having the legal right to convey the information.

The Court of Appeals for the Sixth Circuit held that the findings of fact by the District Court were not clearly erroneous, and that it was evident from the record that the individual respondents appropriated to the benefit of Bicron secret information on processes obtained while they were employees at Harshaw. Further, the Court of Appeals held that the District Court properly applied Ohio law relating to trade secrets. Nevertheless, the Court of Appeals reversed the District Court, finding Ohio's trade secret law to be in conflict with the patent laws of the United States. The Court of Appeals reasoned that Ohio could not grant monopoly protection to processes and manufacturing techniques that were appropriate subjects for consideration under 35 U.S.C.A. § 101 for a federal patent but which had been in commercial use for over one year and so were no longer eligible for patent protection under 35 U.S.C.A. § 102(b).

We hold that Ohio's law of trade secrets is not preempted by the patent laws of the United States, and, accordingly, we reverse.

II

Ohio has adopted the widely relied-upon definition of a trade secret found at Restatement of Torts § 757, comment *b* (1939). According to the Restatement,

> [a] trade secret may consist of any formula, pattern, device or compilation of information which is used in one's business, and which gives him an opportunity to obtain an advantage over competitors who do not know or use it. It may be a formula for a chemical compound, a process of manufacturing, treating or preserving materials, a pattern for a machine or other device, or a list of customers.

The subject of a trade secret must be secret, and must not be of public knowledge or of a general knowledge in the trade or business. This necessary element of secrecy is not lost, however, if the holder of the trade secret reveals the trade secret to another "in confidence, and under an implied obligation not to use or disclose it." Cincinnati Bell Foundry Co. v. Dodds, 10 Ohio Dec. Reprint 154, 156, 19 Weekly L.Bull. 84 (Super.Ct.1887). These others may include those of the holder's "employees to whom it is necessary to confide it, in order to apply it to the uses for which it is intended." National Tube Co. v. Eastern Tube Co., [3 Ohio C.C.R. (n.s.) 459, (1902)] 462. Often the recipient of confidential knowledge of the subject of a trade secret is a licensee of its holder.

The protection accorded the trade secret holder is against the disclosure or unauthorized use of the trade secret by those to whom the secret has been confided under the express or implied restriction of nondisclosure or nonuse. The law also protects the holder of a trade secret against disclosure or use when the knowledge is gained, not by the owner's volition, but by some "improper means," Restatement of Torts § 757(a), which may include theft, wiretapping, or even aerial reconnaissance. A trade secret law, however, does not offer protection against discovery by fair and honest means, such as by independent invention, accidental disclosure, or by so-called reverse engineering, that is by starting with the known product and working backward to divine the process which aided in its development or manufacture.

Novelty, in the patent law sense, is not required for a trade secret. "Quite clearly discovery is something less than invention." A.O. Smith Corp. v. Petroleum Iron Works Co., 73 F.2d 531, 538 (C.A.6 1934); modified to increase scope of injunction, 74 F.2d 934 (1935). However, some novelty will be required if merely because that which does not possess novelty is usually known; secrecy, in the context of trade secrets, thus implies at least minimal novelty.

The subject matter of a patent is limited to a "process, machine, manufacture, or composition of matter, or ... improvement thereof," 35 U.S.C.A. § 101, which fulfills the three conditions of novelty and utility as articulated and defined in 35 U.S.C.A. §§ 101 and 102, and nonobviousness, as set out in 35 U.S.C.A. § 103. If an invention meets the rigorous statutory tests for the issuance of a patent, the patent is granted, for a period of 17 years, giving what has been described as the "right of exclusion," R. Ellis, Patent Assignments and Licenses § 4, p.7 (2d ed. 1943). This protection goes not only to copying the subject matter, which is forbidden under the Copyright Act, but also to independent creation.

III

The first issue we deal with is whether the States are forbidden to act at all in the area of protection of the kinds of intellectual property which may make up the subject matter of trade secrets.

Article I, § 8, cl. 8, of the Constitution grants to the Congress the power

> [t]o promote the Progress of Science and useful Arts, by securing for limited Times to Authors and Inventors the exclusive Right to their respective Writings and Discoveries. . . .

In the 1972 Term, in Goldstein v. California, 412 U.S. 546, 93 S.Ct. 2303, 37 L.Ed.2d 163 (1973), we held that the cl. 8 grant of power to Congress was not exclusive and that, at least in the case of writings, the States were not prohibited from encouraging and protecting the efforts of those within their borders by appropriate legislation. The States could, therefore, protect against the unauthorized rerecording for sale of performances fixed on records or tapes, even though those performances qualified as "writings" in the constitutional sense and Congress was empowered to legislate regarding such performances and could pre-empt the area if it chose to do so. This determination was premised on the great diversity of interests in our Nation—the essentially nonuniform character of the appreciation of intellectual achievements in the various States. Evidence for this came from patents granted by the States in the 18th century.

Just as the States may exercise regulatory power over writings so may the States regulate with respect to discoveries. States may hold diverse viewpoints in protecting intellectual property relating to invention as they do in protecting the intellectual property relating to the subject matter of copyright. The only limitation on the States is that in regulating the area of patents and copyrights they do not conflict with the operation of the laws in this area passed by Congress, and it is to that more difficult question we now turn.

IV

The question of whether the trade secret law of Ohio is void under the Supremacy Clause involves a consideration of whether that law "stands as an obstacle to the accomplishment and execution of the full purposes and objectives of Congress." Hines v. Davidowitz, 312 U.S. 52, 67, 61 S.Ct. 399, 404, 85 L.Ed. 581 (1941). We stated in Sears, Roebuck & Co. v. Stiffel Co., 376 U.S. 225, 229, 84 S.Ct. 784, 11 L.Ed.2d 661 (1964), that when state law touches upon the area of federal statutes enacted pursuant to constitutional authority, "it is 'familiar doctrine' that the federal policy 'may not be set at naught, or its benefits denied' by the state law. Sola Elec. Co. v. Jefferson Elec. Co., 317 U.S. 173, 176, 63 S.Ct. 172, 173, 87 L.Ed. 165 (1942). This is true, of course, even if the state law is enacted in the exercise of otherwise undoubted state power."

The laws which the Court of Appeals in this case held to be in conflict with the Ohio law of trade secrets were the patent laws passed by the Congress in the unchallenged exercise of its clear power under Art. I, § 8, cl. 8, of the Constitution. The patent law does not explicitly endorse or forbid the operation of trade secret law. However, as we have noted, if the scheme of protection developed by Ohio respecting trade secrets "clashes with the objectives of the federal patent laws," Sears, Roebuck & Co. v. Stiffel Co., supra, 376 U.S., at 231, 84 S.Ct., at 789 then the state law must fall. To determine whether the Ohio law "clashes" with the federal law it is helpful to examine the objectives of both the patent and trade secret laws.

The stated objective of the Constitution in granting the power to Congress to legislate in the area of intellectual property is to "promote the Progress of Science and useful Arts." The patent laws promote this progress by offering a right of exclusion for a limited period as an incentive to inventors to risk the often enormous costs in terms of time, research, and development. The productive effort thereby fostered will have a positive effect on society through the introduction of new products and processes of manufacture into the economy, and the emanations by way of increased employment and better lives for our citizens. In return for the right of exclusion—this "reward for inventions," Universal Oil Co. v. Globe Co., 322 U.S. 471, 484, 64 S.Ct. 1110, 1116, 88 L.Ed. 1399 (1944)—the patent laws impose upon the inventor a requirement of disclosure. To insure adequate and full disclosure so that upon the expiration of the 17–

year period "the knowledge of the invention enures to the people, who are thus enabled without restriction to practice it and profit by its use," United States v. Dubilier Condenser Corp., 289 U.S. 178, 187, 53 S.Ct. 554, 77 L.Ed. 1114 (1933), the patent laws require that the patent application shall include a full and clear description of the invention and "of the manner and process of making and using it" so that any person skilled in the art may make and use the invention. 35 U.S.C.A. § 112. When a patent is granted and the information contained in it is circulated to the general public and those especially skilled in the trade, such additions to the general store of knowledge are of such importance to the public weal that the Federal Government is willing to pay the high price of 17 years of exclusive use for its disclosure, which disclosure, it is assumed, will stimulate ideas and the eventual development of further significant advances in the art. The Court has also articulated another policy of the patent law: that which is in the public domain cannot be removed therefrom by action of the States.

[F]ederal law requires that all ideas in general circulation be dedicated to the common good unless they are protected by a valid patent. Lear, Inc. v. Adkins, 395 U.S., at 668, 89 S.Ct., at 1910.

The maintenance of standards of commercial ethics and the encouragement of invention are the broadly stated policies behind trade secret law. "The necessity of good faith and honest, fair dealing, is the very life and spirit of the commercial world." National Tube Co. v. Eastern Tube Co., 3 Ohio Cir.Ct.R. (n.s.), at 462. In A.O. Smith Corp. v. Petroleum Iron Works Co., 73 F.2d, at 539, the Court emphasized that even though a discovery may not be patentable, that does not

destroy the value of the discovery to one who makes it, or advantage the competitor who by unfair means, or as the beneficiary of a broken faith, obtains the desired knowledge without himself paying the price in labor, money, or machines expended by the discoverer.

In Wexler v. Greenberg, 399 Pa. 569, 578–579, 160 A.2d 430, 434–435 (1960), the Pennsylvania Supreme Court noted the importance of trade secret protection to the subsidization of research and development and to increased economic efficiency within large companies through the dispersion of responsibilities for creative developments.

Having now in mind the objectives of both the patent and trade secret law, we turn to an examination of the interaction of these systems of protection of intellectual property—one established by the Congress and the other by a State—to determine whether and under what circumstances the latter might constitute "too great an encroachment on the federal patent system to be tolerated." Sears, Roebuck & Co. v. Stiffel Co., 376 U.S., at 232, 84 S.Ct., at 789.

As we noted earlier, trade secret law protects items which would not be proper subjects for consideration for patent protection under 35 U.S.C.A. § 101. As in the case of the recordings in Goldstein v. California, Congress, with respect to nonpatentable subject matter, "has drawn no balance; rather, it has left the area unattended, and no reason exists why the State should not be free to act." Goldstein v. California, supra, 412 U.S., at 570, 93 S.Ct., at 2316 (footnote omitted).

Since no patent is available for a discovery, however useful, novel, and nonobvious, unless it falls within one of the express categories of patentable subject matter of 35 U.S.C.A. § 101, the holder of such a discovery would have no reason to apply for a patent whether trade secret protection existed or not. Abolition of trade secret protection would, therefore, not result in increased disclosure to the public of discoveries in the area of nonpatentable subject matter. Also, it is hard to see how the public would be benefited by disclosure of customer lists or advertising campaigns; in fact, keeping such items secret encourages businesses to initiate new and individualized plans of operation, and constructive competition results. This, in turn, leads to a greater variety of business methods than would otherwise be the case if privately developed marketing and other data were passed illicitly among firms involved in the same enterprise.

Congress has spoken in the area of those discoveries which fall within one of the categories of patentable subject matter of 35 U.S.C.A. § 101 and which are, therefore, of a nature that would be subject to consideration for a patent. Processes, machines, manufactures, compositions of matter, and improvements thereof, which meet the tests of utility, novelty, and nonobviousness are entitled to be patented, but those which do not, are not. The question remains whether those items which are proper subjects for consideration for a patent may also have available the alternative protection accorded by trade secret law.

Certainly the patent policy of encouraging invention is not disturbed by the existence of another form of incentive to invention. In this respect the two systems are not and never would be in conflict. Similarly, the policy that matter once in the public domain must remain in the public domain is not incompatible with the existence of trade secret protection. By definition a trade secret has not been placed in the public domain.

The more difficult objective of the patent law to reconcile with trade secret law is that of disclosure, the *quid pro quo* of the right to exclude. We are helped in this stage of the analysis by Judge Henry Friendly's opinion in Painton & Co. v. Bourns, Inc., 442 F.2d 216 (C.A.2 1971). There the Court of Appeals thought it useful, in determining whether inventors will refrain because of the existence of trade secret law from applying for patents, thereby depriving the public from learning of the invention, to distinguish between three categories of trade secrets:

> (1) the trade secret believed by its owner to constitute a validly patentable invention; (2) the trade secret known to its owner not to be so patentable; and (3) the trade secret whose valid patentability is considered dubious. Id., at 224.

Trade secret protection in each of these categories would run against breaches of confidence—the employee and licensee situations—and theft and other forms of industrial espionage.

As to the trade secret known not to meet the standards of patentability, very little in the way of disclosure would be accomplished by abolishing trade secret protection. With trade secrets of nonpatentable subject matter, the patent alternative would not reasonably be available to the inventor. "There can be no public interest in stimulating developers of such [unpatentable] know-how to flood an overburdened Patent Office with applications [for] what they do not consider patentable." Ibid. The mere filing of applications doomed to be turned down by the Patent Office will bring forth no new public knowledge or enlightenment, since under federal statute and regulation patent applications and abandoned patent applications are held by the Patent Office in confidence and are not open to public inspection. 35 U.S.C.A. § 122; 37 C.F.R. § 1.14(b).

Even as the extension of trade secret protection to patentable subject matter that the owner knows will not meet the standards of patentability will not conflict with the patent policy of disclosure, it will have a decidedly beneficial effect on society. Trade secret law will encourage invention in areas where patent law does not reach, and will prompt the independent innovator to proceed with the discovery and exploitation of his invention. Competition is fostered and the public is not deprived of the use of valuable, if not quite patentable, invention.

Even if trade secret protection against the faithless employee were abolished, inventive and exploitive effort in the area of patentable subject matter that did not meet the standards of patentability would continue, although at a reduced level. Alternatively with the effort that remained, however, would come an increase in the amount of self-help that innovative companies would employ. Knowledge would be widely dispersed among the employees of those still active in research. Security precautions necessarily would be increased, and salaries and fringe benefits of those few officers or employees who had to know the whole of the secret invention would be fixed in an amount thought sufficient to assure their loyalty. Smaller companies would be placed at a distinct economic disadvantage, since the costs of this kind of self-help could be great, and the cost to the public of the use of this invention would be increased. The innovative entrepreneur with limited resources would tend to confine his research efforts to himself and those few he felt he could trust without the ultimate assurance of legal protection against breaches of confidence. As a result, organized scientific and technological research could become fragmented, and society, as a whole, would suffer.

Another problem that would arise if state trade secret protection were precluded is in the area of licensing others to exploit secret processes. The holder of a trade secret would not likely share his secret with a manufacturer who cannot be placed under binding legal obligation to pay a license fee or to protect the secret. The result would be to hoard rather than disseminate knowledge. Instead, then, of licensing others to use his invention and making the most efficient use of existing manufacturing and marketing structures within the industry, the trade secret holder would tend either to limit his utilization of the invention, thereby depriving the public of the maximum benefit of its use, or engage in the time-consuming and economically wasteful enterprise of constructing duplicative manufacturing and marketing mechanisms for the exploitation of the invention. The detrimental misallocation of resources and economic waste that would thus take place if trade secret protection were abolished with respect to employees or licensees cannot be justified by reference to any policy that the federal patent law seeks to advance.

Nothing in the patent law requires that States refrain from action to prevent industrial espionage. In addition to the increased costs for protection from burglary, wiretapping, bribery, and the other means used to misappropriate trade secrets, there is the inevitable cost to the basic decency of society when one firm steals from another. A most fundamental human right, that of privacy, is threatened when industrial espionage is condoned or is made profitable; the state interest in denying profit to such illegal ventures is unchallengeable.

The next category of patentable subject matter to deal with is the invention whose holder has a legitimate doubt as to its patentability. The risk of eventual patent invalidity by the courts and the costs associated with that risk may well impel some with a good-faith doubt as to patentability not to take the trouble to seek to obtain and defend patent protection for their discoveries, regardless of the existence of trade secret protection. Trade secret protection would assist those inventors in the more efficient exploitation of their discoveries and not conflict with the patent law. In most cases of genuine doubt as to patent validity the potential rewards of patent protection are so far superior to those accruing to holders of trade secrets, that the holders of such inventions will seek patent protection, ignoring the trade secret route. For those inventors "on the line" as to whether to seek patent protection, the abolition of trade secret protection might encourage some to apply for a patent who otherwise would not have done so. For some of those so encouraged, no patent will be granted and the result

> will have been an unnecessary postponement in the divulging of the trade secret to persons willing to pay for it. If [the patent does issue], it may well be invalid, yet many will prefer to pay a modest royalty than to contest it, even though *Lear* allows them to accept a license and pursue the contest without paying royalties while the fight goes on. The result in such a case would be unjustified royalty payments from many who would prefer not to pay them rather than agreed fees from one or a few who are entirely willing to do so. Painton & Co. v. Bourns, Inc., 442 F.2d, at 225.

The point is that those who might be encouraged to file for patents by the absence of trade secret law will include inventors possessing the chaff as well as the wheat. Some of the chaff—the nonpatentable discoveries—will be thrown out by the Patent Office, but in the meantime society will have been deprived of use of those discoveries through trade secret-protected licensing. Some of the chaff may not be thrown out. This Court has noted the difference between the standards used by the Patent Office and the courts to determine patentability. In Lear, Inc. v. Adkins, 395 U.S. 653, 89 S.Ct. 1902, 23 L.Ed.2d 610 (1969), the Court thought that an invalid patent was so serious a threat to the free use of ideas already in the public domain that the Court permitted licensees of the patent holder to challenge the validity of the patent. Better had the invalid patent never been issued. More of those patents would likely issue if trade secret law were abolished. Eliminating trade secret law for the doubtfully patentable invention is thus likely to have deleterious effects on society and patent policy which we cannot say are balanced out by the speculative gain which might result from the encouragement of some inventors with doubtfully patentable inventions which deserve patent protection to come forward and apply for patents. There is no conflict, then, between trade secret law and the patent law policy of disclosure, at least insofar as the first two categories of patentable subject matter are concerned.

The final category of patentable subject matter to deal with is the clearly patentable invention, i.e., that invention which the owner believes to meet the standards of patentability. It is here that the federal interest in disclosure is at its peak; these inventions, novel, useful and nonobvious, are " 'the things which are worth to the public the embarrassment of an exclusive patent.' " Graham v. John Deere Co., supra, at 9, 86 S.Ct., at 689 (quoting Thomas Jefferson). The interest of the public is that the bargain of 17 years of exclusive use in return for disclosure be accepted. If a State, through a system of protection, were to cause a substantial risk that holders of patentable inventions would not seek patents, but rather would rely on the state protection, we would be compelled to hold that such a system could not constitutionally continue to exist. In the case of trade secret law no reasonable risk of deterrence from patent application by those who can reasonably expect to be granted patents exists.

Trade secret law provides far weaker protection in many respects than the patent law. While trade secret law does not forbid the discovery of the trade secret by fair and honest means, e.g., independent creation or reverse engineering, patent law operates "against the world," forbidding any use of the invention for whatever purpose for a significant length of time. The holder of a trade secret also takes a substantial risk that the secret will be passed on to his competitors, by theft or by breach of a confidential relationship, in a manner not easily susceptible of discovery or proof. Where patent law acts as a barrier, trade secret law functions relatively as a sieve. The possibility that an inventor who believes his invention meets the standards of patentability will sit back, rely on trade secret law, and after one year of use forfeit any right to patent protection, 35 U.S.C.A. § 102(b), is remote indeed.

Nor does society face much risk that scientific or technological progress will be impeded by the rare inventor with a patentable invention who chooses trade secret protection over patent protection. The ripeness-of-time concept of invention, developed from the study of the many independent multiple discoveries in history, predicts that if a particular individual had not made a particular discovery others would have, and in probably a relatively short period of time. If something is to be discovered at all very likely it will be discovered by more than one person. Even were an inventor to keep his discovery completely to himself, something that neither the patent nor trade secret laws forbid, there is a high probability that it will be soon independently developed. If the invention, though still a trade secret, is put into public use, the competition is alerted to the existence of the inventor's solution to the problem and may be encouraged to make an extra effort to independently find the solution thus known to be possible. The inventor faces pressures not only from private industry, but from the skilled scientists who work in our universities and our other great publicly supported centers of learning and research.

We conclude that the extension of trade secret protection to clearly patentable inventions does not conflict with the patent policy of disclosure. Perhaps because trade secret law does not produce any positive effects in the area of clearly patentable inventions, as opposed to the beneficial effects resulting from trade secret protection in the areas of the doubtfully patentable and the clearly unpatentable inventions, it has been suggested that partial pre-emption may be appropriate, and that courts should refuse to apply trade secret protection to inventions which the holder should have patented, and which would have been, thereby, disclosed. However, since there is no real possibility that trade secret law will conflict with the federal policy favoring disclosure of clearly patentable inventions partial pre-emption is inappropriate. Partial pre-emption, furthermore, could well create serious problems for state courts in the administration of trade secret law. As a preliminary matter in trade secret actions, state courts would be obliged to distinguish between what a reasonable inventor would and would not correctly consider to be clearly patentable, with the holder of the trade secret arguing that the invention was not patentable and the misappropriator of the trade secret arguing its undoubted novelty, utility, and nonobviousness. Federal courts have a difficult enough time trying to determine whether an invention, narrowed by the patent application procedure and fixed in the specifications which describe the invention for which the patent has been granted, is patentable. Although state courts in some circumstances must join federal courts in judging whether an issued patent is valid, Lear, Inc. v. Adkins, supra, it would be undesirable to impose the almost impossible burden on state courts to determine the patentability—in fact and in the mind of a reasonable inventor—of a discovery which has not been patented and remains entirely uncircumscribed by expert analysis in the administrative process. Neither complete nor partial pre-emption of state trade secret law is justified.

Our conclusion that patent law does not pre-empt trade secret law is in accord with prior cases of this Court. Trade secret law and patent law have co-existed in this country for over one hundred years. Each has its particular role to play, and the operation of one does not take away from the need for the other. Trade secret law encourages the development and exploitation of those items of lesser or different invention than might be accorded protection under the patent laws, but which items still have an important part to play in the technological and scientific advancement of the Nation.

Trade secret law promotes the sharing of knowledge, and the efficient operation of industry; it permits the individual inventor to reap the rewards of his labor by contracting with a company large enough to develop and exploit it. Congress, by its silence over these many years, has seen the wisdom of allowing the States to enforce trade secret protection. Until Congress takes affirmative action to the contrary, States should be free to grant protection to trade secrets.

Since we hold that Ohio trade secret law is not pre-empted by the federal patent law, the judgment of the Court of Appeals for the Sixth Circuit is reversed, and the case is remanded to the Court of Appeals with directions to reinstate the judgment of the District Court.

It is so ordered.

Mr. Justice POWELL took no part in the decision of this case.

Mr. Justice MARSHALL, concurring in the result.

Unlike the Court, I do not believe that the possibility that an inventor with a patentable invention will rely on state trade secret law rather than apply for a patent is "remote indeed." State trade secret law provides substantial protection to the inventor who intends to use or sell the invention himself rather than license it to others, protection which in its unlimited duration is clearly superior to the 17–year monopoly afforded by the patent laws. I have no doubt that the existence of trade secret protection provides in some instances a substantial disincentive to entrance into the patent system, and thus deprives society of the benefits of public disclosure of the invention which it is the policy of the patent laws to encourage. This case may well be such an instance.

But my view of sound policy in this area does not dispose of this case. Rather, the question presented in this case is whether Congress, in enacting the patent laws, intended merely to offer inventors a limited monopoly in exchange for disclosure of their invention, or instead to exert pressure on inventors to enter into this exchange by withdrawing any alternative possibility of legal protection for their inventions. I am persuaded that the former is the case. State trade secret laws and the federal patent laws have co-existed for many, many years. During this time, Congress has repeatedly demonstrated its full awareness of the existence of the trade secret system, without any indication of disapproval. Indeed, Congress has in a number of instances given explicit federal protection to trade secret information provided to federal agencies. Because of this, I conclude that there is "neither such actual conflict between the two schemes of regulation that both cannot stand in the same area, nor evidence of a congressional design to pre-empt the field." Florida Lime Avocado Growers v. Paul, 373 U.S. 132, 141, 83 S.Ct. 1210, 1217, 10 L.Ed.2d 248 (1963). I therefore concur in the result reached by the majority of the Court.

Mr. Justice DOUGLAS, with whom Mr. Justice BRENNAN concurs, dissenting.

Today's decision is at war with the philosophy of Sears, Roebuck & Co. v. Stiffel Co., 376 U.S. 225, 84 S.Ct. 784, 11 L.Ed.2d 661, and Compco Corp.

v. Day–Brite Lighting, Inc., 376 U.S. 234, 84 S.Ct. 779, 11 L.Ed.2d 669. Those cases involved patents—one of a pole lamp and one of fluorescent lighting fixtures each of which was declared invalid. The lower courts held, however, that though the patents were invalid the sale of identical or confusingly similar products to the products of the patentees violated state unfair competition laws. We held that when an article is unprotected by a patent, state law may not forbid others to copy it, because every article not covered by a valid patent is in the public domain. Congress in the patent laws decided that where no patent existed, free competition should prevail; that where a patent is rightfully issued, the right to exclude others should obtain for no longer than 17 years, and that the States may not "under some other law, such as that forbidding unfair competition, give protection of a kind that clashes with the objectives of the federal patent laws," 376 U.S., at 231, 84 S.Ct., at 789.

The product involved in this suit, sodium iodide synthetic crystals, was a product that could be patented but was not. Harshaw the inventor apparently contributed greatly to the technology in that field by developing processes, procedures, and techniques that produced much larger crystals than any competitor. These processes, procedures, and techniques were also patentable; but no patent was sought. Rather Harshaw sought to protect its trade secrets by contracts with its employees. And the District Court found that, as a result of those secrecy precautions, "not sufficient disclosure occurred so as to place the claimed trade secrets in the public domain"; and those findings were sustained by the Court of Appeals.

The District Court issued a permanent injunction against respondents, ex-employees, restraining them from using the processes used by Harshaw. By a patent which would require full disclosure Harshaw could have obtained a 17–year monopoly against the world. By the District Court's injunction, which the Court approves and reinstates, Harshaw gets a permanent injunction running into perpetuity against respondents. In *Sears,* as in the present case, an injunction against the unfair competitor issued. We said: "To allow a State by use of its law of unfair competition to prevent the copying of an article which represents too slight an advance to be patented would be to permit the State to block off from the public something which federal law has said belongs to the public. The result would be that while federal law grants only 14 or 17 years' protection to genuine inventions, see 35 U.S.C.A. §§ 154, 173, States could allow perpetual protection to articles too lacking in novelty to merit any patent at all under federal constitutional standards. This would be too great an encroachment on the federal patent system to be tolerated." 376 U.S., at 231–232, 84 S.Ct., at 789.

The conflict with the patent laws is obvious. The decision of Congress to adopt a patent system was based on the idea that there will be much more innovation if discoveries are disclosed and patented than there will be when everyone works in secret. Society thus fosters a free exchange of technological information at the cost of a limited 17–year monopoly.

A trade secret, unlike a patent, has no property dimension. That was the view of the Court of Appeals, 478 F.2d 1074, 1081; and its decision is supported by what Mr. Justice Holmes said in Du Pont De Nemours Powder Co. v. Masland, 244 U.S. 100, 102, 37 S.Ct. 575, 576, 61 L.Ed. 1016:

> The word property as applied to trade-marks and trade secrets is an unanalyzed expression of certain secondary consequences of the primary fact that the law makes some rudimentary requirements of good faith. Whether the plaintiffs have any valuable secret or not the defendant knows the facts, whatever they are, through a special confidence that he accepted. The property may be denied but the confidence cannot be. Therefore the starting point for the present matter is not property or due process of law, but that the defendant stood in confidential relations with the plaintiffs, or one of them. These have given place to hostility, and the first thing to be made sure of is that the defendant shall not fraudulently abuse the trust reposed in him. It is the usual incident of confidential relations. If there is any disadvantage in the fact that he knew the plaintiffs' secrets he must take the burden with the good.

A suit to redress theft of a trade secret is grounded in tort damages for breach of a contract—a historic remedy. Damages for breach of a confidential relation are not pre-empted by this patent law, but an injunction against use is pre-empted because the patent law states the only monopoly over trade secrets that is enforceable by specific performance; and that monopoly exacts as a price full disclosure. A trade secret can be protected only by being kept secret. Damages for breach of a contract are one thing; an injunction barring disclosure does service for the protection accorded valid patents and is therefore pre-empted.

From the findings of fact of the lower courts, the process involved in this litigation was unique, such a great discovery as to make its patentability a virtual certainty. Yet the Court's opinion reflects a vigorous activist antipatent philosophy. My objection is not because it is activist. This is a problem that involves no neutral principle. The Constitution in Art. I, § 8, cl. 8, expresses the activist policy which Congress has enforced by statutes. It is that constitutional policy which we should enforce, not our individual notions of the public good.

I would affirm the judgment below.

NOTES

1. How extensively did *Kewanee* undermine *Sears* and *Compco,* pages 98, 101 above? Did *Kewanee* validate only trade secret causes of action that rest on contract or confidence grounds? Would the *Kewanee* Court have approved state law decisions like duPont v. Christopher, page 124, that rest trade secret protection on a property rationale? Or do *Sears* and *Compco* continue to control cases in this class?

This and other lines of inquiry are developed in Paul Goldstein, Kewanee Oil Co. v. Bicron Corp.: Notes on a Closing Circle, 1974 Sup. Ct. Rev. 81. For a different view, see Richard H. Stern, A Reexamination of State Trade Secret Law after Kewanee, 42 Geo. Wash. L. Rev. 927 (1974). See also Dan L. Burk, Protection of Trade Secrets in Outer Space Activity: A Study in Federal Preemption, 23 Seton Hall L. Rev. 560 (1993).

2. *Trade Secrets and Patents.* A trade secret holder has some freedom to choose which aspects of her discovery to lodge in a patent and which to withhold as a trade secret. She cannot, however, withhold facts that are necessary to the public's understanding of the patented subject matter. Van Products Co. v. General Welding & Fabricating Co., 419 Pa. 248, 213 A.2d 769, 147 U.S.P.Q. 221 (1965), indicates the extent to which a patentee can maintain the veil of secrecy. Plaintiff there had received a patent on an air drier apparatus and had retained as a trade secret the formula for the chemical desiccant that was crucial to its operation. "Of course, the idea and the practical functioning of such a deliquescent desiccant could not be a secret, in itself, since the product was advertised, described, and sold on the open market. Its remarkable characteristics, vaunted in sales literature, were the exact factor which made the Van drier desirable (i.e., it was a desiccant which did not require regeneration). Therefore, it was only the composition which was secret, and remained so. . . ." 419 Pa. at 268–69, 213 A.2d at 780.

3. In Warner–Lambert Pharmaceutical Co., Inc. v. John J. Reynolds, Inc., 178 F.Supp. 655, 123 U.S.P.Q. 431 (S.D.N.Y.1959), aff'd, 280 F.2d 197, 126 U.S.P.Q. 3 (2d Cir.1960), plaintiff unsuccessfully sought a declaratory judgment relieving it of royalty obligations for the manufacture of Listerine, the formula of which had been sold to plaintiff's predecessor by defendant's predecessor in 1881. The unpatented formula subsequently became public knowledge. Plaintiff argued that for this reason it should pay no tithe for what others were using free. Finding in the 1881, and subsequent, contracts no express or implied limitation on the royalty obligation, the court ruled that the plaintiff must abide by the royalty schedule so long as it used the formula.

What flaws, if any, can you find in the court's reasoning on the policy ground: "In the patent and copyright cases the parties are dealing with a fixed statutory term and the monopoly granted by that term. This monopoly, created by Congress, is designed to preserve exclusivity in the grantee during the statutory term and to release the patented or copyrighted material to the general public for general use thereafter. This is the public policy of the statutes in reference to which such contracts are made and it is against this background that the parties to patent and copyright license agreements contract. Here, however, there is no such public policy. The parties are free to contract with respect to a secret formula or trade secret in any manner which they determine for their own best interests. A secret formula or trade secret may remain secret indefinitely. It may be discovered by someone else almost immediately after the agreement is entered into. Whoever discovers it for himself by legitimate means is entitled to its use.

But that does not mean that one who acquires a secret formula or a trade secret through a valid and binding contract is then enabled to escape from an obligation to which he bound himself simply because the secret is discovered by a third party or by the general public." 178 F.Supp. 655.

Can *Warner–Lambert* be reconciled with cases like *Reed, Roberts,* page 144, above, that trim or void excessive covenants against post-employment competition? With decisions that confine trade secret injunctions to the time it would take to reverse engineer the trade secret in suit? What are *Kewanee's* implications for the continued vitality of *Warner–Lambert?* Note that the injunction approved in *Kewanee* was to last only "until such time as the trade secrets had been released to the public, had otherwise generally become available to the public or had been obtained by [defendants] from sources having the legal right to convey the information." Does *Aronson,* page 50, above, offer a complete vindication of *Warner–Lambert?*

Recall that *Kewanee* involved a trade secret appropriation, while *Aronson* and *Warner–Lambert* involved negotiated licenses. Should these different factual postures make a legal difference? Licensees can, between themselves, estimate the life and value of a secret and then settle on any mutually agreeable schedule for repaying its value—a continuing royalty, for example, or a lump sum representing the secret's continuing worth discounted to present value—and little reason exists for a court to intervene and rewrite the payment schedule. Where, however, a trade secret has been appropriated, and no voluntary bargain struck, courts need to approximate what the parties would have estimated as the secret's value; the natural starting point is for the court to estimate the secret's probable life, the same starting point as is used in fashioning trade secret injunctions.

Louis Altman, A *Quick Point* Regarding Perpetual Trade Secret Royalty Liability, 13 J. Marshall L. Rev. 127 (1979), offers some penetrating insights into these and connected issues.

4. *Trade Secrets in the Patent and Trademark Office.* The inventor who has doubts about the patentability of his invention faces a hard choice. To rely on trade secret law means that protection will be limited by the realities of reverse engineering, faithless employees and the difficulties of enforcement. To pursue a patent, however, entails not only the possibility of added expense without reward but, even if a patent issues, the risk that it may later be invalidated, by which point the secret information will have become public. The U.S. Patent Act partially reduces the difficulty of this choice by requiring the Patent and Trademark Office to hold all patent applications in confidence so that trade secret protection is maintained even after the application is filed. Rejection of the application will not destroy the invention's secrecy. 35 U.S.C. § 122.

The Court of Customs and Patent Appeals—the predecessor of the present Court of Appeals for the Federal Circuit—applied its rules of practice to maintain the secrecy on appeal of a patent application rejected by the Patent and Trademark Office. In Application of Sarkar, 575 F.2d 870, 197 U.S.P.Q. 788 (C.C.P.A.1978), the court, recognizing the public's interest in access to court records and proceedings, nonetheless ordered that the record be sealed, and that the proceedings be conducted *in camera*. "We are guided in our determination by the opinion of the Supreme Court in *Kewanee* ... that, wherever possible, trade secret law and patent law should be administered in such manner that the former will not deter an inventor from seeking the benefit of the latter, because the public is *most* benefited by the early disclosure of the invention in consideration of the patent grant." 575 F.2d at 872 (emphasis in original).

Although section 122 of the Patent Act has secured the secrecy of patent applications against requests made under the Freedom of Information Act, it has not proved to be a complete guard against public prying. See Irons & Sears v. Dann, 606 F.2d 1215, 202 U.S.P.Q. 798 (D.C.Cir.1979), cert. denied, 444 U.S. 1075, 100 S.Ct. 1021, 62 L.Ed.2d 757, 204 U.S.P.Q. 1060 (1980).

5. *Statutory Preemption.* Section 301 of the Copyright Act will preempt state trade secret law if three conditions are met: the subject matter of trade secret protection is fixed in a tangible medium of expression; the subject matter comes within the subject matter of copyright as defined by sections 102 and 103 of the Copyright Act; and the right granted by trade secret law is equivalent to one or more of the rights granted by section 106 of the Copyright Act. The first requirement, fixation in a tangible medium of expression, is easily applied; it will exempt from preemption state protection of a trade secret that has never been reduced to writing and has only been communicated orally by its owner. Section 301's second and third requirements—that the trade secret come within the subject matter of copyright and that the right granted be equivalent to copyright—are more problematic. They are considered beginning at page 793, below.

IV. RIGHT OF PUBLICITY

A. THEORY OF PROTECTION

Carson v. Here's Johnny Portable Toilets, Inc.

United States Court of Appeals, Sixth Circuit, 1983.
698 F.2d 831, 218 U.S.P.Q. 1.

BAILEY BROWN, Senior Circuit Judge.

This case involves claims of unfair competition and invasion of the right of privacy and the right of publicity arising from appellee's adoption of a phrase generally associated with a popular entertainer.

Appellant, John W. Carson (Carson), is the host and star of "The Tonight Show," a well-known television program broadcast five nights a week by the National Broadcasting Company. Carson also appears as an entertainer in night clubs and theaters around the country. From the time he began hosting "The Tonight Show" in 1962, he has been introduced on the show each night with the phrase "Here's Johnny." This method of introduction was first used for Carson in 1957 when he hosted a daily television program for the American Broadcasting Company. The phrase "Here's Johnny" is generally associated with Carson by a substantial segment of the television viewing public. In 1967, Carson first authorized use of this phrase by an outside business venture, permitting it to be used by a chain of restaurants called "Here's Johnny Restaurants."

Appellant Johnny Carson Apparel, Inc. (Apparel), formed in 1970, manufactures and markets men's clothing to retail stores. Carson, the president of Apparel and owner of 20% of its stock, has licensed Apparel to use his name and picture, which appear on virtually all of Apparel's products and promotional material. Apparel has also used, with Carson's consent, the phrase "Here's Johnny" on labels for clothing and in advertising campaigns. In 1977, Apparel granted a license to Marcy Laboratories to use "Here's Johnny" as the name of a line of men's toiletries. The phrase "Here's Johnny" has never been registered by appellants as a trademark or service mark.

Appellee, Here's Johnny Portable Toilets, Inc., is a Michigan corporation engaged in the business of renting and selling "Here's Johnny" portable toilets. Appellee's founder was aware at the time he formed the corporation that "Here's Johnny" was the introductory slogan for Carson on "The Tonight Show." He indicated that he coupled the phrase with a second one, "The World's Foremost Commodian," to make "a good play on a phrase."

Shortly after appellee went into business in 1976, appellants brought this action alleging unfair competition, trademark infringement under

167

federal and state law, and invasion of privacy and publicity rights. They sought damages and an injunction prohibiting appellee's further use of the phrase "Here's Johnny" as a corporate name or in connection with the sale or rental of its portable toilets.

After a bench trial, the district court issued a memorandum opinion and order which served as its findings of fact and conclusions of law. The court ordered the dismissal of the appellants' complaint. On the unfair competition claim, the court concluded that the appellants had failed to satisfy the "likelihood of confusion" test. On the right of privacy and right of publicity theories, the court held that these rights extend only to a "name or likeness," and "Here's Johnny" did not qualify.

I.

Appellants' first claim alleges unfair competition from appellee's business activities in violation of § 43(a) of the Lanham Act, 15 U.S.C. § 1125(a) (1976), and of Michigan common law. The district court correctly noted that the test for equitable relief under both § 43(a) and Michigan common law is the "likelihood of confusion" standard. Frisch's Restaurants, Inc. v. Elby's Big Boy of Steubenville, Inc., 670 F.2d 642 (6th Cir.), cert. denied, 459 U.S. 916, 103 S.Ct. 231, 74 L.Ed.2d 182 (1982).

In *Frisch's Restaurants* we approved the balancing of several factors in determining whether a likelihood of confusion exists among consumers of goods involved in a § 43(a) action. In that case we examined eight factors:

1. strength of the plaintiff's mark;

2. relatedness of the goods;

3. similarity of the marks;

4. evidence of actual confusion;

5. marketing channels used;

6. likely degree of purchaser care;

7. defendant's intent in selecting the mark;

8. likelihood of expansion of the product lines.

670 F.2d at 648. The district court applied a similar analysis. Under the two-step process adopted in *Frisch's Restaurants*, these eight foundational factors are factual and subject to a clearly erroneous standard of review, while the weighing of these findings on the ultimate issue of the likelihood of confusion is a question of law.

The district court first found that "Here's Johnny" was not such a strong mark that its use for other goods should be entirely foreclosed. Although the appellee had intended to capitalize on the phrase popularized by Carson, the court concluded that appellee had not intended to deceive the public into believing Carson was connected with the product. The court noted that there was little evidence of actual confusion and no evidence that appellee's use of the phrase had damaged appellants. For these reasons, the court determined that appellee's use of the phrase "Here's Johnny" did not present a likelihood of confusion, mistake, or deception.

Our review of the record indicates that none of the district court's findings is clearly erroneous. Moreover, on the basis of these findings, we agree with the district court that the appellants have failed to establish a likelihood of confusion. The general concept underlying the likelihood of confusion is that the public believe that "the mark's owner *sponsored or otherwise approved* the use of the trademark." Warner Bros., Inc. v. Gay Toys, Inc., 658 F.2d 76, 79 (2d Cir.1981) (emphasis added) (quoting Dallas Cowboys Cheerleaders, Inc. v. Pussycat Cinema, Ltd., 604 F.2d 200, 205 (2d Cir.1979)).

The facts as found by the district court do not implicate such likelihood of confusion, and we affirm the district court on this issue.

II.

The appellants also claim that the appellee's use of the phrase "Here's Johnny" violates the common law right of privacy and right of publicity.[1] The confusion in this area of the law requires a brief analysis of the relationship between these two rights.

In an influential article, Dean Prosser delineated four distinct types of the right of privacy: (1) intrusion upon one's seclusion or solitude, (2) public disclosure of embarrassing private facts, (3) publicity which places one in a false light, and (4) appropriation of one's name or likeness for the defendant's advantage. Prosser, *Privacy*, 48 Calif.L.Rev. 383, 389 (1960). This fourth type has become known as the "right of publicity." Henceforth we will refer to Prosser's last, or fourth, category as the "right of publicity."

Dean Prosser's analysis has been a source of some confusion in the law. His first three types of the right of privacy generally protect the right "to be let alone," while the right of publicity protects the celebrity's pecuniary interest in the commercial exploitation of his identity. Thus, the right of privacy and the right of publicity protect fundamentally different interests and must be analyzed separately.

We do not believe that Carson's claim that his right of privacy has been invaded is supported by the law or the facts. Apparently, the gist of this claim is that Carson is embarrassed by and considers it odious to be associated with the appellee's product. Clearly, the association does not appeal to Carson's sense of humor. But the facts here presented do not, it appears to us, amount to an invasion of any of the interests protected by the right of privacy. In any event, our disposition of the claim of an invasion of the right of publicity makes it unnecessary for us to accept or reject the claim of an invasion of the right of privacy.

---

1. Michigan law, which governs these claims, has not yet clearly addressed the right of publicity. But the general recognition of the right, see W. Prosser, Handbook of the Law of Torts § 117, at 805 (4th ed. 1971), suggests to us that the Michigan courts would adopt the right. Michigan has recognized a right of privacy.

The right of publicity has developed to protect the commercial interest of celebrities in their identities. The theory of the right is that a celebrity's identity can be valuable in the promotion of products, and the celebrity has an interest that may be protected from the unauthorized commercial exploitation of that identity. In Memphis Development Foundation v. Factors Etc., Inc., 616 F.2d 956 (6th Cir.), cert. denied, 449 U.S. 953, 101 S.Ct. 358, 66 L.Ed.2d 217 (1980), we stated: "The famous have an exclusive legal right during life to control and profit from the commercial use of their name and personality." Id. at 957.

The district court dismissed appellants' claim based on the right of publicity because appellee does not use Carson's name or likeness. It held that it "would not be prudent to allow recovery for a right of publicity claim which does not more specifically identify Johnny Carson." We believe that, on the contrary, the district court's conception of the right of publicity is too narrow. The right of publicity, as we have stated, is that a celebrity has a protected pecuniary interest in the commercial exploitation of his identity. If the celebrity's identity is commercially exploited, there has been an invasion of his right whether or not his "name or likeness" is used. Carson's identity may be exploited even if his name, John W. Carson, or his picture is not used.

In Motschenbacher v. R.J. Reynolds Tobacco Co., 498 F.2d 821 (9th Cir.1974), the court held that the unauthorized use of a picture of a distinctive race car of a well known professional race car driver, whose name or likeness were not used, violated his right of publicity. In this connection, the court said:

> We turn now to the question of "identifiability." Clearly, if the district court correctly determined as a matter of law that plaintiff is not identifiable in the commercial, then in no sense has plaintiff's identity been misappropriated nor his interest violated.

> Having viewed a film of the commercial, we agree with the district court that the "likeness" of plaintiff is itself unrecognizable; however, the court's further conclusion of law to the effect that the driver is not identifiable as plaintiff is erroneous in that it wholly fails to attribute proper significance to the distinctive decorations appearing on the car. As pointed out earlier, these markings were not only peculiar to the plaintiff's cars but they caused some persons to think the car in question was plaintiff's and to infer that the person driving the car was the plaintiff.

Id. at 826–827 (footnote omitted).

In Ali v. Playgirl, Inc., 447 F.Supp. 723 (S.D.N.Y.1978), Muhammad Ali, former heavyweight champion, sued Playgirl magazine under the New York "right of privacy" statute and also alleged a violation of his common law right of publicity. The magazine published a drawing of a nude, black male sitting on a stool in a corner of a boxing ring with hands taped and arms outstretched on the ropes. The district court concluded that Ali's right of publicity was invaded because the drawing sufficiently identified him in spite of the fact that the drawing was captioned "Mystery Man." The district court found that the identification of Ali was made certain because of an accompanying verse that identified the figure as "The Greatest." The district court took judicial notice of the fact that "Ali has regularly claimed that appellation for himself." Id. at 727.

In Hirsch v. S.C. Johnson & Son, Inc., 90 Wis.2d 379, 280 N.W.2d 129 (1979), the court held that use by defendant of the name "Crazylegs" on a shaving gel for women violated plaintiff's right of publicity. Plaintiff, Elroy Hirsch, a famous football player, had been known by this nickname. The court said:

> The fact that the name, "Crazylegs," used by Johnson, was a nickname rather than Hirsch's actual name does not preclude a cause of action. All that is required is that the name clearly identify the wronged person. In the instant case, it is not disputed at this juncture of the case that the nickname identified the plaintiff Hirsch. It is argued that there were others who were known by the same name. This, however, does not vitiate the existence of a cause of action. It may, however, if sufficient proof were adduced, affect the quantum of damages should the jury impose liability or it might preclude liability altogether. Prosser points out "that a stage or other fictitious name can be so identified with the plaintiff that he is entitled to protection against its use." 49 Cal.L.Rev., supra at 404. He writes that it would be absurd to say that Samuel L. Clemens would have a cause of action if that name had been used in advertising, but he would not have one for the use of "Mark Twain." If a fictitious name is used in a context which tends to indicate that the name is that of the plaintiff, the factual case for identity is strengthened.

280 N.W.2d at 137.

In this case, Earl Braxton, president and owner of Here's Johnny Portable Toilets, Inc., admitted that he knew that the phrase "Here's Johnny" had been used for years to introduce Carson. Moreover, in the opening statement in the district court, appellee's counsel stated:

> Now, we've stipulated in this case that the public tends to associate the words "Johnny Carson", the words "Here's Johnny" with plaintiff, John Carson and, Mr. Braxton, in his deposition, admitted that he knew that and probably absent that identification, he would not have chosen it.

That the "Here's Johnny" name was selected by Braxton because of its identification with Carson was the clear inference from Braxton's testimony irrespective of such admission in the opening statement.

We therefore conclude that, applying the correct legal standards, appellants are entitled to judgment. The proof showed without question that appellee had appropriated Carson's identity in connection with its corporate name and its product. . . .

The judgment of the district court is vacated and the case remanded for further proceedings consistent with this opinion.

CORNELIA G. KENNEDY, Circuit Judge, dissenting.

I respectfully dissent from that part of the majority's opinion which holds that appellee's use of the phrase "Here's Johnny" violates appellant Johnny Carson's common law right of publicity. While I agree that an individual's identity may be impermissibly exploited, I do not believe that the common law right of publicity may be extended beyond an individual's name, likeness, achievements, identifying characteristics or actual performances, to include phrases or other things which are merely associated with the individual, as is the phrase "Here's Johnny." The majority's extension of the right of publicity to include phrases or other things which are merely associated with the individual permits a popular entertainer or public figure, by associating himself or herself with a common phrase, to remove those words from the public domain.

The phrase "Here's Johnny" is merely associated with Johnny Carson, the host and star of "The Tonight Show" broadcast by the National Broadcasting Company. Since 1962, the opening format of "The Tonight Show," after the theme music is played, is to introduce Johnny Carson with the phrase "Here's Johnny." The words are spoken by an announcer, generally Ed McMahon, in a drawn out and distinctive manner. Immediately after the phrase "Here's Johnny" is spoken, Johnny Carson appears to begin the program. This method of introduction was first used by Johnny Carson in 1957 when he hosted a daily television show for the American Broadcasting Company. This case is not transformed into a "name" case simply because the diminutive form of John W. Carson's given name and the first name of his full stage name, Johnny Carson, appears in it. The first name is so common, in light of the millions of persons named John, Johnny or Jonathan that no doubt inhabit this world, that, alone, it is meaningless or ambiguous at best in identifying Johnny Carson, the celebrity. In addition, the phrase containing Johnny Carson's first stage name was certainly selected for its value as a double entendre. Appellee manufactures portable toilets. The value of the phrase to appellee's product is in the risqué meaning of "john" as a toilet or bathroom. For this reason, too, this is not a "name" case.

Appellee has stipulated that the phrase "Here's Johnny" is associated with Johnny Carson and that absent this association, he would not have chosen to use it for his product and corporation, Here's Johnny Portable Toilets, Inc. I do not consider it relevant that appellee intentionally chose to incorporate into the name of his corporation and product a phrase that is merely associated with Johnny Carson. What is not protected by law is not taken from public use. Research reveals no case in which the right of publicity has been extended to phrases or other things which are merely associated with an individual and are not part of his name, likeness, achievements, identifying characteristics or actual performances. Both the policies behind the right of publicity and countervailing interests and considerations indicate that such an extension should not be made.

I. Policies Behind Right of Publicity

The three primary policy considerations behind the right of publicity are succinctly stated in Hoffman, Limitations on the Right of Publicity, 28 Bull. Copr. Soc'y, 111, 116–22 (1980). First, "the right of publicity vindicates the economic interests of celebrities, enabling those whose achievements have imbued their identities with pecuniary value to profit from their fame." Id. 116. Second, the right of publicity fosters "the production of intellectual and creative works by providing the financial incentive for individuals to expend the time and resources necessary to produce them." Limitations on the Right of Publicity, supra, 118. Third, "[t]he right of publicity serves both individual and societal interests by preventing what our legal tradition regards as wrongful conduct: unjust enrichment and deceptive trade practices." Limitations on the Right of Publicity, supra, 118.

None of the above-mentioned policy arguments supports the extension of the right of publicity to phrases or other things which are merely associated with an individual. First, the majority is awarding Johnny Carson a windfall, rather than vindicating his economic interests, by protecting the phrase "Here's Johnny" which is merely associated with him. In *Zacchini,* the Supreme Court stated that a mechanism to vindicate an individual's economic rights is indicated where the appropriated thing is "the product of ... [the individual's] own talents and energy, the end result of much time, effort and expense." *Zacchini,* supra, 433 U.S. at 575, 97 S.Ct. at 2857. There is nothing in the record to suggest that "Here's Johnny" has any nexus to Johnny Carson other than being the introduction to his personal appearances. The phrase is not part of an identity that he created. In its content "Here's Johnny" is a very simple and common introduction. The content of the phrase neither originated with Johnny Carson nor is it confined to the world of entertainment. The phrase is not said by Johnny Carson, but said of him. Its association with him is derived, in large part, by the context in which it is said—generally by Ed McMahon in a drawn out and distinctive voice after the theme music to "The Tonight Show" is played, and immediately prior to Johnny Carson's own entrance. Appellee's use of the content "Here's Johnny," in light of its value as a double entendre, written on its product and corporate name, and therefore outside of the context in which it is associated with Johnny Carson, does little to rob Johnny Carson of something which is unique to him or a product of his own efforts.

The second policy goal of fostering the production of creative and intellectual works is not met by the majority's rule because in awarding publicity rights in a phrase neither created by him nor performed by him, economic reward and protection is divorced from personal incentive to produce on the part of the protected and benefited individual. Johnny Carson is simply reaping the rewards of the time, effort and work product of others.

Third, the majority's extension of the right of publicity to include the phrase "Here's Johnny" which is merely associated with Johnny Carson is not needed to provide alternatives to existing legal avenues for redressing wrongful conduct. The existence of a cause of action under section 43(a) of the Lanham Act, 15 U.S.C.A. § 1125(a) (1976) and Michigan common law does much to undercut the need for policing against unfair competition through an additional legal remedy such as the right of publicity. The majority has concluded, and I concur, that the District Court was warranted in finding that there was not a reasonable likelihood that members of the public would be confused by appellee's use of the "Here's Johnny" trademark on a product as dissimilar to those licensed by Johnny Carson as portable toilets. In this case, this eliminates the argument of wrongdoing. Moreover, the majority's extension of the right of publicity to phrases and other things merely associated with an individual is not conditioned upon wrongdoing and would apply with equal force in the case of an unknowing user. With respect to unjust enrichment, because a celebrity such as Johnny Carson is himself enriched by phrases and other things associated with him in which he has made no personal investment of time, money or effort, another user of such a phrase or thing may be enriched somewhat by such use, but this enrichment is not at Johnny Carson's expense. The policies behind the right of publicity are not furthered by the majority's holding in this case.

II. Countervailing Interests and Considerations

The right of publicity, whether tied to name, likeness, achievements, identifying characteristics or actual performances, etc. conflicts with the economic and expressive interests of others. Society's interests in free enterprise and free expression must be balanced against the interests of an individual seeking protection in the right of publicity where the right is being expanded beyond established limits. In addition, the right to publicity may be subject to federal preemption where it conflicts with the provisions of the Copyright Act of 1976.

A. Federal Policy: Monopolies

Protection under the right of publicity creates a common law monopoly that removes items, words and acts from the public domain. That federal policy favors free enterprise was recently reaffirmed by the Supreme Court in National Society of Professional Engineers v. United States, 435 U.S. 679, 98 S.Ct. 1355, 55 L.Ed.2d 637 (1978), in which the Supreme Court indicated that outside of the "rule of reason," only those anticompetitive restraints expressly authorized by Congress would be permitted to stand. Concern for the impact of adopting an overbroad approach to the right of publicity was also indicated in this Court's decision in Memphis Development Foundation v. Factors Etc., Inc., 616 F.2d 956 (6th Cir.), cert. denied, 449 U.S. 953, 101 S.Ct. 358, 66 L.Ed.2d 217 (1980). In *Memphis Development,* this Court held that the right of publicity does not survive a celebrity's death under Tennessee law. In so holding, this Court recognized that commercial and competitive interests are potentially compromised by an expansive approach to the right of publicity. This Court was concerned that an extension of the right of publicity to the exclusive control of the celebrity's heirs might compromise the efficiency, productivity and fairness of our economic system without enlarging the stock or quality of the goods, services, artistic creativity, information, invention or entertainment available and detract from the equal distribution of economic opportunity available in a free market system. *Memphis Development* recognized that the grant of a right of publicity is tantamount to the grant of a monopoly, in that case, for the life of the celebrity. The majority's grant to Johnny Carson of a publicity right in the phrase "Here's Johnny" takes this phrase away from the public domain, giving him a common law monopoly for it, without extracting from Johnny Carson a personal contribution for the public's benefit.

Protection under the right of publicity confers a monopoly on the protected individual that is potentially broader, offers fewer protections and potentially competes with federal statutory monopolies. As an essential part of three federal monopoly rights, copyright, trademark and patents, notice to the public is required in the form of filing with the appropriate governmental office and use of an appropriate mark. This apprises members of the public of the nature and extent of what is being removed from the public domain and subject to claims of infringement. The right of publicity provides limited notice to the public of the extent of the monopoly right to be asserted, if one is to be asserted at all. As the right of privacy is expanded beyond protections of name, likeness and actual performances, which provide relatively objective notice to the public of the extent of an individual's rights, to more subjective attributes such as achievements and identifying characteristics, the public's ability to be on notice of a common law monopoly right, if one is even asserted by a given famous individual, is severely diminished. Protecting phrases and other things merely associated with an individual provides virtually no notice to the public at all of what is claimed to be protected. By ensuring the invocation of the adjudicative process whenever the commercial use of a phrase or other associated thing is considered to have been wrongfully appropriated, the public is left to act at their peril. The result is a chilling effect on commercial innovation and opportunity.

Also unlike the federal statutory monopolies, this common law monopoly right offers no protections against the monopoly existing for an indefinite time or even in perpetuity.

B. Federal Policy: Free Expression and Use of Intellectual Property

The first amendment protects the freedom of speech, including commercial speech. U.S. Const. amend. I; Goldfarb v. Virginia State Bar, 421 U.S. 773, 95 S.Ct. 2004, 44 L.Ed.2d 572 reh'g denied, 423 U.S. 886, 96 S.Ct. 162, 46 L.Ed.2d 118 (1975). Strong federal policy permits the free use of intellectual property, words and ideas that are in general circulation and not protected by a valid copyright, patent or trademark. The federal copyright statute only protects original works that fix the author's particular expression of an idea or concept in a tangible form. State statutory or common law protection against activities violating rights that are not equivalent to those granted under copyright law or protection of subject matter which is not copyrightable, including works that are not fixed in any tangible form of expression, are not preempted. 17 U.S.C.A. § 301(b) (1977). Apart from the technical arguments regarding preemption, if federal law and policy does not protect phrases such as "Here's Johnny," which is certainly not an original combination of words, state law should not protect them either under a right of publicity for want of a sufficient interest justifying protection. See U.S. Const., art. I, § 8 (purpose of copyright and patent laws is to "promote the Progress of Science and the useful Arts"); *Zacchini, supra,* 433 U.S. at 575, 576–77, 97 S.Ct. at 2857, 2858 (purpose of right of publicity is to promote production of works that benefit the public that are product of individual's own talents and energy). In addition, because copyright does not restrain the use of a mere idea or concept but only protects particular tangible expressions of an idea or concept, it has been held not to run afoul of first amendment challenges. The protected tangible expressions are asserted to not run afoul of first amendment challenges because the notice requirements and limited duration of copyright protection balances the interest of individuals seeking protection under the copyright clause and the first amendment. Because the phrase "Here's Johnny" is more akin to an idea or concept of introducing an individual than an original protectable fixed expression of that idea and because the right of publicity in this instance is not complemented by saving notice or duration requirements, phrases such as "Here's Johnny" should not be entitled to protection under the right of publicity as a matter of policy and concern for the first amendment.

Apart from the possibility of outright federal preemption, public policy requires that the public's interest in free enterprise and free expression take precedence over any interest Johnny Carson may have in a phrase associated with his person.

III. Case Law

The common law right of publicity has been held to protect various aspects of an individual's identity from commercial exploitation: name, likeness, achievements, identifying characteristics, actual performances, and fictitious characters created by a performer. Research reveals no case which has extended the right of publicity to phrases and other things which are merely associated with an individual. . . .

Accordingly, neither policy nor case law supports the extension of the right of publicity to encompass phrases and other things merely associated with an individual as in this case. I would affirm the judgment of the District Court on this basis as well.

White v. Samsung Electronics America, Inc.

United States Court of Appeals, Ninth Circuit, 1992.
971 F.2d 1395, 23 U.S.P.Q.2d 1583, cert. denied, 508 U.S. 951, 113 S.Ct. 2443, 124 L.Ed.2d 660 (1993).

GOODWIN, Senior Circuit Judge:

This case involves a promotional "fame and fortune" dispute. In running a particular advertisement without Vanna White's permission, defendants Samsung Electronics America, Inc. (Samsung) and David Deutsch Associates, Inc. (Deutsch) attempted to capitalize on White's fame to enhance their fortune. White sued, alleging infringement of various intellectual property rights, but the district court granted summary judgment in favor of the defendants. We affirm in part, reverse in part, and remand.

Plaintiff Vanna White is the hostess of "Wheel of Fortune," one of the most popular game shows in television history. An estimated forty million people watch the program daily. Capitalizing on the fame which her participation in the show has bestowed on her, White markets her identity to various advertisers.

The dispute in this case arose out of a series of advertisements prepared for Samsung by Deutsch. The series ran in at least half a dozen publications with widespread, and in some cases national, circulation. Each of the advertisements in the series followed the same theme. Each depicted a current item from popular culture and a Samsung electronic product. Each was set in the twenty-first century and conveyed the message that the Samsung product would still be in use by that time. By hypothesizing outrageous future outcomes for the cultural items, the ads created humorous effects. For example, one lampooned current popular notions of an unhealthy diet by depicting a raw steak with the caption: "Revealed to be health food. 2010 A.D." Another depicted irreverent "news"-show host Morton Downey Jr. in front of an American flag with the caption: "Presidential candidate. 2008 A.D."

The advertisement which prompted the current dispute was for Samsung videocassette recorders (VCRs). The ad depicted a robot, dressed in a wig, gown, and jewelry which Deutsch consciously selected to resemble White's hair and dress. The robot was posed next to a game board which is instantly recognizable as the Wheel of Fortune game show set, in a stance for which White is famous. The caption of the ad read: "Longest-running game show. 2012 A.D." Defendants referred to the ad as the "Vanna White" ad. Unlike the other celebrities used in the campaign, White neither consented to the ads nor was she paid.

Following the circulation of the robot ad, White sued Samsung and Deutsch in federal district court under: (1) California Civil Code § 3344; (2) the California common law right of publicity; and (3) § 43(a) of the Lanham Act, 15 U.S.C. § 1125(a). The district court granted summary judgment against White on each of her claims. White now appeals.

I. Section 3344

White first argues that the district court erred in rejecting her claim under section 3344. Section 3344(a) provides, in pertinent part, that "[a]ny person who knowingly uses another's name, voice, signature, photograph, or likeness, in any manner, . . . for purposes of advertising or selling, . . .

without such person's prior consent ... shall be liable for any damages sustained by the person or persons injured as a result thereof."

White argues that the Samsung advertisement used her "likeness" in contravention of section 3344. In Midler v. Ford Motor Co., 849 F.2d 460 (9th Cir.1988), this court rejected Bette Midler's section 3344 claim concerning a Ford television commercial in which a Midler "sound-alike" sang a song which Midler had made famous. In rejecting Midler's claim, this court noted that "[t]he defendants did not use Midler's name or anything else whose use is prohibited by the statute. The voice they used was [another person's], not hers. The term 'likeness' refers to a visual image not a vocal imitation." *Id.* at 463.

In this case, Samsung and Deutsch used a robot with mechanical features, and not, for example, a manikin molded to White's precise features. Without deciding for all purposes when a caricature or impressionistic resemblance might become a "likeness," we agree with the district court that the robot at issue here was not White's "likeness" within the meaning of section 3344. Accordingly, we affirm the court's dismissal of White's section 3344 claim.

II.   Right of Publicity

White next argues that the district court erred in granting summary judgment to defendants on White's common law right of publicity claim. In *Eastwood v. Superior Court*, 149 Cal.App.3d 409, 198 Cal.Rptr. 342 (1983), the California court of appeal stated that the common law right of publicity cause of action "may be pleaded by alleging (1) the defendant's use of the plaintiff's identity; (2) the appropriation of plaintiff's name or likeness to defendant's advantage, commercially or otherwise; (3) lack of consent; and (4) resulting injury." *Id.* at 417. The district court dismissed White's claim for failure to satisfy Eastwood's second prong, reasoning that defendants had not appropriated White's "name or likeness" with their robot ad. We agree that the robot ad did not make use of White's name or likeness. However, the common law right of publicity is not so confined.

The *Eastwood* court did not hold that the right of publicity cause of action could be pleaded only by alleging an appropriation of name or likeness. *Eastwood* involved an unauthorized use of photographs of Clint Eastwood and of his name. Accordingly, the *Eastwood* court had no occasion to consider the extent beyond the use of name or likeness to which the right of publicity reaches. That court held only that the right of publicity cause of action "may be" pleaded by alleging, *inter alia*, appropriation of name or likeness, not that the action may be pleaded only in those terms.

The "name or likeness" formulation referred to in Eastwood originated not as an element of the right of publicity cause of action, but as a description of the types of cases in which the cause of action had been recognized. The source of this formulation is Prosser, *Privacy*, 48 Cal. L.Rev. 383, 401–07 (1960), one of the earliest and most enduring articulations of the common law right of publicity cause of action. In looking at the case law to that point, Prosser recognized that right of publicity cases involved one of two basic factual scenarios: name appropriation, and picture or other likeness appropriation.

Even though Prosser focused on appropriations of name or likeness in discussing the right of publicity, he noted that "[i]t is not impossible that there might be appropriation of the plaintiff's identity, as by impersonation, without the use of either his name or his likeness, and that this would be an invasion of his right of privacy." At the time Prosser wrote, he noted however, that "[n]o such case appears to have arisen."

Since Prosser's early formulation, the case law has borne out his insight that the right of publicity is not limited to the appropriation of name or likeness. In *Motschenbacher v. R.J. Reynolds Tobacco Co.*, 498 F.2d 821 (9th Cir.1974), the defendant had used a photograph of the plaintiff's race car in a television commercial. Although the plaintiff appeared driving the car in the photograph, his features were not visible. Even though the defendant had not appropriated the plaintiff's name or likeness, this court held that plaintiff's California right of publicity claim should reach the jury.

In *Midler*, this court held that, even though the defendants had not used Midler's name or likeness, Midler had stated a claim for violation of her California common law right of publicity because "the defendants ... for their own profit in selling their product did appropriate part of her identity" by using a Midler sound-alike.

In *Carson v. Here's Johnny Portable Toilets, Inc.*, 698 F.2d 831 (6th Cir.1983), the defendant had marketed portable toilets under the brand name "Here's Johnny"—Johnny Carson's signature "Tonight Show" introduction—without Carson's permission. The district court had dismissed Carson's Michigan common law right of publicity claim because the defendants had not used Carson's "name or likeness." In reversing the district court, the sixth circuit found "the district court's conception of the right of publicity ... too narrow" and held that the right was implicated because the defendant had appropriated Carson's identity by using, inter alia, the phrase "Here's Johnny."

These cases teach not only that the common law right of publicity reaches means of appropriation other than name or likeness, but that the specific means of appropriation are relevant only for determining whether the defendant has in fact appropriated the plaintiff's identity. The right of publicity does not require that appropriations of identity be accomplished through particular means to be actionable. It is noteworthy that the *Midler* and *Carson* defendants not only avoided using the plaintiff's name or likeness, but they also avoided appropriating the celebrity's voice, signature, and photograph. The photograph in *Motschenbacher* did include the plaintiff, but because the plaintiff was not visible the driver could have been an actor or dummy and the analysis in the case would have been the same.

Although the defendants in these cases avoided the most obvious means of appropriating the plaintiffs' identities, each of their actions directly implicated the commercial interests which the right of publicity is designed to protect.... It is not important *how* the defendant has appropriated the plaintiff's identity, but *whether* the defendant has done so. *Motschenbacher*, *Midler*, and *Carson* teach the impossibility of treating the right of publicity as guarding only against a laundry list of specific means of appropriating identity. A rule which says that the right of publicity can be infringed only through the use of nine different methods of appropriating identity merely challenges the clever advertising strategist to come up with the tenth.

Indeed, if we treated the means of appropriation as dispositive in our analysis of the right of publicity, we would not only weaken the right but effectively eviscerate it. The right would fail to protect those plaintiffs most in need of its protection. Advertisers use celebrities to promote their products. The more popular the celebrity, the greater the number of people who recognize her, and the greater the visibility for the product. The identities of the most popular celebrities are not only the most attractive for advertisers, but also the easiest to evoke without resorting to obvious means such as name, likeness, or voice.

Consider a hypothetical advertisement which depicts a mechanical robot with male features, an African–American complexion, and a bald head. The robot is wearing black hightop Air Jordan basketball sneakers, and a red basketball uniform with black trim, baggy shorts, and the number 23 (though not revealing "Bulls" or "Jordan" lettering). The ad depicts the robot dunking a basketball one-handed, stiff-armed, legs extended like open scissors, and tongue hanging out. Now envision that this ad is run on television during professional basketball games. Considered individually, the robot's physical attributes, its dress, and its stance tell us little. Taken together, they lead to the only conclusion that any sports viewer who has registered a discernible pulse in the past five years would reach: the ad is about Michael Jordan.

Viewed separately, the individual aspects of the advertisement in the present case say little. Viewed together, they leave little doubt about the celebrity the ad is meant to depict. The female-shaped robot is wearing a long gown, blond wig, and large jewelry. Vanna White dresses exactly like this at times, but so do many other women. The robot is in the process of turning a block letter on a game-board. Vanna White dresses like this while turning letters on a game-board but perhaps similarly attired Scrabble-playing women do this as well. The robot is standing on what looks to be the Wheel of Fortune game show set. Vanna White dresses like this, turns letters, and does this on the Wheel of Fortune game show. She is the only one. Indeed, defendants themselves referred to their ad as the "Vanna White" ad. We are not surprised.

Television and other media create marketable celebrity identity value. Considerable energy and ingenuity are expended by those who have achieved celebrity value to exploit it for profit. The law protects the celebrity's sole right to exploit this value whether the celebrity has achieved her fame out of rare ability, dumb luck, or a combination thereof. We decline Samsung and Deutch's invitation to permit the evisceration of the common law right of publicity through means as facile as those in this case. Because White has alleged facts showing that Samsung and Deutsch had appropriated her identity, the district court erred by rejecting, on summary judgment, White's common law right of publicity claim.

III. The Lanham Act

White's final argument is that the district court erred in denying her claim under § 43(a) of the Lanham Act, 15 U.S.C. § 1125(a). The version of section 43(a) applicable to this case provides, in pertinent part, that "[a]ny person who shall ... use, in connection with any goods or services ... any false description or representation ... shall be liable to a civil action ... by any person who believes that he is or is likely to be damaged by the use of any such false description or designation." 15 U.S.C. § 1125(a).

To prevail on her Lanham Act claim, White is required to show that in running the robot ad, Samsung and Deutsch created a likelihood of confusion over whether White was endorsing Samsung's VCRs.

This circuit recognizes several different multi-factor tests for determining whether a likelihood of confusion exists. None of these tests is correct to the exclusion of the others. Normally, in reviewing the district court's decision, this court will look to the particular test that the district court used. However, because the district court in this case apparently did not use any of the multi-factor tests in making its likelihood of confusion determination, and because this case involves an appeal from summary judgment and we review de novo the district court's determination, we will look for guidance to the 8–factor test enunciated in *AMF, Inc. v. Sleekcraft Boats*, 599 F.2d 341 (9th Cir.1979). According to *AMF*, factors relevant to a likelihood of confusion include:

> (1) strength of the plaintiff's mark;
>
> (2) relatedness of the goods;
>
> (3) similarity of the marks;
>
> (4) evidence of actual confusion;
>
> (5) marketing channels used;
>
> (6) likely degree of purchaser care;
>
> (7) defendant's intent in selecting the mark;
>
> (8) likelihood of expansion of the product lines.

We turn now to consider White's claim in light of each factor.

In cases involving confusion over endorsement by a celebrity plaintiff, "mark" means the celebrity's persona. The "strength" of the mark refers to the level of recognition the celebrity enjoys among members of society. If Vanna White is unknown to the segment of the public at whom Samsung's robot ad was directed, then that segment could not be confused as to whether she was endorsing Samsung VCRs. Conversely, if White is well-known, this would allow the possibility of a likelihood of confusion. For the purposes of the *Sleekcraft* test, White's "mark," or celebrity identity, is strong.

In cases concerning confusion over celebrity endorsement, the plaintiff's "goods" concern the reasons for or source of the plaintiff's fame. Because White's fame is based on her televised performances, her "goods" are closely related to Samsung's VCRs. Indeed, the ad itself reinforced the relationship by informing its readers that they would be taping the "longest-running game show" on Samsung's VCRs well into the future.

The third factor, "similarity of the marks," both supports and contradicts a finding of likelihood of confusion. On the one hand, all of the aspects of the robot ad identify White; on the other, the figure is quite clearly a robot, not a human. This ambiguity means that we must look to the other factors for resolution.

The fourth factor does not favor White's claim because she has presented no evidence of actual confusion.

Fifth, however, White has appeared in the same stance as the robot from the ad in numerous magazines, including the covers of some. Magazines were used as the marketing channels for the robot ad. This factor cuts toward a likelihood of confusion.

Sixth, consumers are not likely to be particularly careful in determining who endorses VCRs, making confusion as to their endorsement more likely.

Concerning the seventh factor, "defendant's intent," the district court found that, in running the robot ad, the defendants had intended a spoof of the "Wheel of Fortune." The relevant question is whether the defendants "intended to profit by confusing consumers" concerning the endorsement of Samsung VCRs. We do not disagree that defendants intended to spoof Vanna White and "Wheel of Fortune." That does not preclude, however, the possibility that defendants also intended to confuse consumers regarding endorsement. The robot ad was one of a series of ads run by defendants which followed the same theme. Another ad in the series depicted Morton Downey Jr. as a presidential candidate in the year 2008. Doubtless, defendants intended to spoof presidential elections and Mr. Downey through this ad. Consumers, however, would likely believe, and would be correct in so believing, that Mr. Downey was paid for his permission and was endorsing Samsung products. Looking at the series of advertisements as a whole, a jury could reasonably conclude that beneath the surface humor of the series lay an intent to persuade consumers that celebrity Vanna White, like celebrity Downey, was endorsing Samsung products.

Finally, the eighth factor, "likelihood of expansion of the product lines," does not appear apposite to a celebrity endorsement case such as this.

Application of the *Sleekcraft* factors to this case indicates that the district court erred in rejecting White's Lanham Act claim at the summary judgment stage. In so concluding, we emphasize two facts, however. First, construing the motion papers in White's favor, as we must, we hold only that White has raised a genuine issue of material fact concerning a likelihood of confusion as to her endorsement. Whether White's Lanham Act claim should succeed is a matter for the jury. Second, we stress that we reach this conclusion in light of the peculiar facts of this case. In particular, we note that the robot ad identifies White and was part of a series of ads in which other celebrities participated and were paid for their endorsement of Samsung's products.

Vanna White

Ms. C3PO?

IV. The Parody Defense

In defense, defendants cite a number of cases for the proposition that their robot ad constituted protected speech. The only cases they cite which are even remotely relevant to this case are *Hustler Magazine v. Falwell*, 485 U.S. 46, 108 S.Ct. 876, 99 L.Ed.2d 41 (1988) and *L.L. Bean, Inc. v. Drake Publishers, Inc.*, 811 F.2d 26 (1st Cir.1987). Those cases involved parodies of advertisements run for the purpose of poking fun at Jerry Falwell and L.L. Bean, respectively. This case involves a true advertisement run for the purpose of selling Samsung VCRs. The ad's spoof of Vanna White and Wheel of Fortune is subservient and only tangentially related to the ad's primary message: "buy Samsung VCRs." Defendants' parody arguments are better addressed to non-commercial parodies. The difference between a "parody" and a "knock-off" is the difference between fun and profit.

V.   Conclusion

In remanding this case, we hold only that White has pleaded claims which can go to the jury for its decision.

AFFIRMED IN PART, REVERSED IN PART, and REMANDED.

N O T E S

1.   In one form or another, the right of publicity has been adopted by common law, statute or both in about half the states. The right of publicity overlaps other bodies of tort and intellectual property law. If Johnny Carson had been able to show that defendant's use of the phrase, "Here's Johnny" placed the entertainer in a false light, he might have prevailed on a privacy theory. Had he been able to show that the phrase had acquired a secondary meaning, he might have prevailed on an unfair competition or trademark theory. Had the phrase been more expressively elaborated, it might have qualified for protection under a statutory or common law copyright theory.

What substantive distinction, if any, is there between the right of publicity and the cause of action for unfair competition as the two doctrines were defined and applied in White v. Samsung? When will an invasion of the right of publicity *not* create a likelihood of confusion over the plaintiff's endorsement of defendant's products? If Samsung had disclaimed sponsorship by White, would this have eliminated unfair competition as an issue?

The authoritative treatise on the right of publicity is J.Thomas McCarthy, The Rights of Publicity and Privacy (2d ed. 2000). See also, Oliver R. Goodenough, Go Fish: Evaluating the Restatements Formulation of the Law of Publicity, 47 S.C. L. Rev. 709 (1996). A right of publicity has been slower to develop outside the United States. See F. Jay Dougherty, Foreword: The Right of Publicity—Towards a Comparative and International Perspective, 18 Loy. L.A. Ent. L. J. 421 (1998).

For reflections on White v. Samsung, see Paul J. Heald, Filling Two Gaps in the Restatement (Third) of Unfair Competition: Mixed–Use Trademarks and the Problem with Vanna, 47 S.C. L. Rev. 783 (1996); David S. Welkowitz, Catching Smoke, Nailing JELL–O to a Wall: The Vanna White Case and the Limits of Celebrity Rights, 3 J. Intell. Prop. L. 67 (1995).

2.   Celebrity often provides its own abundant rewards in the form of fees and salaries, and it is the rare celebrity who would curb her activities if denied property rights in her persona. Does this suggest that unjust enrichment is the only true rationale for the right of publicity and that there is little room for the other economic rationales noted in Judge Kennedy's dissenting opinion? Even if celebrities do not need a property incentive to invest in developing their public personas, can the right of publicity be justified by the needs of their licensees? Would the operators of the "Here's Johnny" restaurant chain have been willing to invest in promoting that name without a licensed property right from the entertainer? Which better supports the right of publicity—the economic rationale for copyright, or the economic rationale for trademark?

Mark F. Grady, A Positive Economic Theory of the Right of Publicity, 1 U.C.L.A. Ent.L.Rev.97 (1994), argues that the most persuasive economic rationale for the right of publicity is that it is "needed to ensure that publicity assets are not wasted by a scramble to use them up as quickly as possible." *Id.* at 98. Professor Grady analogizes the problem of publicity values to the standard economic problem of the common pool: Absent property rights in a fish pond, anglers will quickly deplete the entire stock; subjecting the pond to property rights will enable the property holder to regulate the amount of fish taken daily, and will thus serve the socially desirable goal of orderly resource use.

As an example of the common pool problem in the right of publicity, Grady takes the case of Waits v. Frito–Lay, Inc., 978 F.2d 1093 (9th Cir.1992), cert. denied, 506 U.S. 1080, 113 S.Ct. 1047, 122 L.Ed.2d 355 (1993), in which raspy-voiced singer Tom Waits obtained relief against defendant's unauthorized use of a sound-alike to advertise its Doritos corn chips. "When Waits has a private property right over his singing style, he has the incentive and ability to regulate current uses so as to maximize the present value of the asset over the future. Indeed, he would become like a single owner of a fishery who for that reason would have an incentive effectively to manage the asset. Mindful of foregone values ten years from now, the private owner will limit uses today. By contrast, under the system of common ownership that would exist in the absence of a right of publicity, promoters and other publicists would draw down the value of the image too quickly, each in an effort to capture as much of it for herself as possible. Among other things, publicists would substitute too many low-valued uses (Doritos commercials) for uses that listeners value more (artistic uses)." *Id.* at 104.

Does the right of publicity also secure noneconomic values? Comment c to section 46 of the Restatement of the Law Third, Unfair Competition (1995), which embraces the right of publicity as part of unfair competition law, observes that, "[l]ike the right of privacy, the right of publicity protects an individual's interest in personal dignity and autonomy." See also Alice Haemmerli, Whose Who? The Case for a Kantian Right of Publicity, 49 Duke L.J. 383 (1999).

3. *Ownership.* The individual who receives the economic rewards of the right of publicity will not always be the one who invested in creating the protected persona. Judge Kennedy observed in a footnote to her *Carson* dissent that "Ed McMahon arguably has a competing publicity interest" in the "Here's Johnny" phrase "because it is said by him in a distinctive and drawn out manner as his introduction to entertainers who appear on 'The Tonight Show,' including Johnny Carson." 698 F.2d at 839 n. 5. Who should be entitled to publicity rights in the motion picture character, Count Dracula—the actor, Bela Lugosi, whose likeness as the Count was exploited by licensees, or the motion picture producer who helped shape, promote and give content to the Count's appearance? See Lugosi v. Universal Pictures, 25 Cal.3d 813, 160 Cal.Rptr. 323, 603 P.2d 425, 205 U.S.P.Q. 1090 (1979). Who should have been entitled to the value of the publicity rights in White v. Samsung?

Wendt v. Host International, Inc., 125 F.3d 806, 811, 44 U.S.P.Q.2d 1189 (9th Cir.1997), ruled that two actors in the *Cheers* television series could have a right of publicity claim against the use of animatronic robots based on their characters, Cliff and Norm, that defendant had licensed from the owner of the series. Defendant placed the robots in its airport bars, which were modeled on the set of the television show. Plaintiffs conceded that they owned no rights in the characters, but argued that it was their physical likeness, not the fictional characters, that gave the robots their value. The court agreed. "While it is true that appellants' fame arose in large part through their participation in *Cheers*, an actor or actress does not lose the right to control the commercial exploitation of his or her likeness by portraying a fictional character."

Judge Alex Kozinski dissented from the order rejecting the suggestion for rehearing *en banc*. "This case, unlike *White*, pits actor against copyright holder. The parties are fighting over the same bundle of intellectual property rights—the right to make dramatic representations of the characters Norm and Cliff. Host and Paramount assert their right under the Copyright Act to present the *Cheers* characters in airport bars; Wendt and Ratzenberger assert their right under California law to control the exploitation of their likenesses. But to millions of viewers, Wendt and Ratzenberger *are* Norm and Cliff; it's impossible to exploit the latter without also evoking thoughts about the former." In Kozinski's view, "[t]he Copyright Act makes it simple, at least insofar as the plaintiffs interfere with Paramount's right to exploit the *Cheers* characters.... The copyright to *Cheers* carries with it the right to make derivative works based on its characters. The presentation of the robots in the *Cheers* bars is a derivative work, just like a TV clip, promotion, photograph, poster, sequel or dramatic rendering of an episode. Thus, under federal law, Host has the unconditional right to present robots that resemble Norm and Cliff." 197 F.3d 1284, 1286.

Two rights may coexist in a portrait: the painter's or photographer's copyright in the manner in which she depicts the subject, and the subject's publicity right against commercial use of his image. Does the fact that the artist has a right under copyright to prevent others from copying the portrait imply that she is also free to use the subject's image for commercial purposes without his consent? Is it possible that the parties in *Wendt* were fighting not over "the same bundle of intellectual property rights," but two separate bundles?

4. *Right of Publicity in Voice.* The common law and statutory right of publicity traditionally encompass an individual's name and likeness. Some states protect other elements of an individual's persona. California's statute, for example, protects an individual's "name, voice, signature, photograph, or likeness" Cal.Civ.Code §§ 990(a), 3344(a) (West Supp.1989).

Nebraska's statute protects against commercial exploitation of "a natural person, name, picture, portrait, or personality." Neb.Rev.Stat. § 20–202 (1987).

Early decisions held that the right of publicity did not protect against imitations of a celebrity's voice, and that a plaintiff in these circumstances could recover only on an unfair competition theory. In Lahr v. Adell Chem. Co., 300 F.2d 256, 132 U.S.P.Q. 662 (1st Cir.1962), plaintiff Bert Lahr complained that "defendant Adell Chemical Company, in advertising its product 'Lestoil' on television, used as a commercial a cartoon film of a duck and, without the plaintiff's consent 'as the voice of the aforesaid duck, an actor who specialized in imitating the vocal sounds of the plaintiff.' " Reading New York's privacy statute literally, to cover only a "name, portrait or picture," the court concluded that plaintiff might instead recover on his unfair competition count. "Plaintiff's complaint is that defendant is 'stealing his thunder' in the direct sense; that defendant's commercial had greater value because his audience believed it was listening to him.... It could well be found that defendant's conduct saturated plaintiff's audience to the point of curtailing his market." 300 F.2d at 257–59.

Subsequently, a court held that the right of publicity extends to "sound-alikes." In Midler v. Ford Motor Co., 849 F.2d 460, 7 U.S.P.Q.2d 1398 (9th Cir.), cert. den., 503 U.S. 951 (1992), the defendant, rebuffed in its efforts to hire popular singer Bette Midler to perform in one of its commercials a song she had popularized, obtained the services of another singer, Ula Hedwig, whose performance of the song sounded like a Midler performance. The court ruled that Midler could recover on a common law, but not statutory, right of publicity theory. While holding that California's publicity statute, which protects against the unauthorized use of an individual's voice, did not help Midler—the "voice they used was Hedwig's, not hers"—the court concluded that "when a distinctive voice of a professional singer is widely known and is deliberately imitated in order to sell a product, the sellers have appropriated what is not theirs and have committed a tort in California." 849 F.2d at 463. Do you agree with the court that the defendant did not use the plaintiff's voice?

5. *Identifiability.* A defendant will violate the right to publicity only if it appropriates those elements that identify the plaintiff to the public. In one case a court held that a woodcarver named T.J. Hooker had no cause of action against the producer of a television series, "T.J. Hooker," featuring a fictional policeman, T.J. Hooker, as its star. The "facts and circumstances alleged by plaintiff provide no basis upon which it can be found that the name 'T.J. Hooker,' as used in the defendants' fictional television series, in any way refers to the real T.J. Hooker." T.J. Hooker v. Columbia Pictures Indus., 551 F.Supp. 1060, 1062 (N.D.Ill.1982). Similarly, the *Carson* court observed that the defendant would not have violated Carson's right of publicity if it had used plaintiff's name, "such as 'J. William Carson Portable Toilet' or the 'John William Carson Portable Toilet' or the 'J.W. Carson Portable Toilet.' The reason is that, though literally using appellant's 'name,' the appellee would not have appropriated Carson's identity as a celebrity." 698 F.2d at 837. Is there any element of Vanna White's persona that Samsung could have used without facing liability?

The identifiability requirement can raise thorny questions in cases involving celebrity "look-alikes." Will an individual's resemblance to a celebrity enable her to cash in on the value of the celebrity's identity or disable her from making any commercial use of her own identity? In Onassis v. Christian Dior–New York, Inc., 122 Misc.2d 603, 472 N.Y.S.2d 254 (Sup.Ct.1984), the court enjoined defendant's magazine advertisement portraying a model who bore a striking resemblance to the public figure, Jacqueline Kennedy Onassis. Allen v. National Video, Inc., 610 F.Supp. 612, 226 U.S.P.Q. 483 (S.D.N.Y.1985), involving a claim by Woody Allen against defendant's use of a "look-alike" in advertisements for its video rental chain, distinguished *Onassis:*

> When as in *Onassis,* the look-alike seems indistinguishable from the real person and the context of the advertisement clearly implies that he or she is the real celebrity, a court may hold as a matter of law that the look-alike's face is a "portrait or picture" of plaintiff. *Onassis* presented an unusual factual setting, in which the mixture of fantasy and reality suggested almost unavoidably the actual presence of the real-life celebrity. In order for the court to reach the same conclusion in the present case, it must conclude on the undisputed facts that the photograph in question similarly creates, as a matter of law, the illusion of Woody Allen's actual presence in the advertisement.

610 F.Supp. at 623–24.

6. *Infringement.* The fact that the defendant's unauthorized use identifies another's persona, does not necessarily imply that the use infringes that person's right of publicity. Dissenting from an order rejecting the suggestion for a rehearing en banc in White v. Samsung, 989 F.2d 1512, 26 U.S.P.Q.2d 1362 (9th Cir.1993), Judge Alex Kozinski started from the proposition that "[o]verprotecting intellectual property is as harmful as underprotecting it. Creativity is impossible without a rich public domain." Judge Kozinski concluded that "[t]he panel's opinion is a classic case of overprotection. Concerned about what it sees as a wrong done to Vanna White, the panel majority erects a property right of remarkable and dangerous breadth: Under the majority's opinion, it's now a tort for advertisers to *remind* the public of a celebrity. Not to use a celebrity's name, voice, signature or likeness; not to imply the celebrity endorses a product; but simply to evoke the celebrity's image in the public's mind. This Orwellian notion withdraws far more from the public domain than prudence and common sense allow." 989 F.2d at 1513–14.

Kozinski drew an analogy to the idea-expression distinction in copyright law. "I can't publish unauthorized copies of, say, *Presumed Innocent*; I can't make a movie out of it. But I'm perfectly free to write a book about an idealistic young prosecutor on trial for a crime he didn't commit. So what if I got the idea from *Presumed Innocent*? So what if it reminds readers of the original? Have I 'eviscerated' Scott Turow's intellectual property rights? Certainly not. All creators draw in part on the work of those who came before, referring to it, building on it, poking fun at it; we call this creativity, not piracy. . . . Consider how sweeping this new right is. What is it about the ad that makes people think of White? It's not the robot's wig, clothes or jewelry; there must be ten million blonde women (many of them quasi-famous) who wear dresses and jewelry like White's. It's that the robot is posed near the 'Wheel of Fortune' game board. Remove the game board from the ad, and no one would think of Vanna White. But once you include the game board, anybody standing beside it—a brunette woman, a man wearing women's clothes, a monkey in a wig and gown—would evoke White's image, precisely the way the robot did. It's the 'Wheel of Fortune' set, not the robot's face or dress or jewelry that evokes White's image. The panel is giving White an exclusive right not in what she looks like or who she is, but in what she does for a living." 989 F.2d at 1514–15.

7. *Remedies.* Statutes and common law offer coercive and monetary relief for violations of the right to publicity. Courts grant permanent injunctions freely on the premise that publicity interests are unique and that the computation of damages will be problematic. One court, applying the New York statute, held that once a plaintiff establishes a violation she "may have an absolute right to injunction, regardless of the relative damage to the parties." Onassis v. Christian Dior–New York, Inc., 122 Misc.2d 603, 607, 472 N.Y.S.2d 254, 258 (Sup.Ct.1984). Some statutes authorize courts to impound offending materials and, if the plaintiff prevails on the merits, to destroy or make other reasonable disposition of the offending materials and of articles used to produce the materials. See Tenn.Code Ann. § 47–25–1106(b), (c) (1988).

Courts measure damages for right of publicity violations by a reasonable royalty or market value. This is a floor, not a ceiling, to damages. In Waits v. Frito–Lay, Inc., 978 F.2d 1093, 1103 (9th Cir.1992), cert. den., 506 U.S. 1080, 113 S.Ct. 1047, 122 L.Ed.2d 355 (1993), awarding plaintiff $100,000 for the fair market value of his services, the court also approved an award of $200,000 for injury to his "peace, happiness and feelings," and $75,000 "for injury to his goodwill, professional standing and future publicity value."

Courts may also award any profits earned by the infringer from its unauthorized use of the plaintiff's persona. In many states a plaintiff can recover exemplary damages if he can show that the defendant acted knowingly. In the *Waits* case, for example, the court approved a $2 million punitive damage award against the defendants. 978 F.2d at 1104–06. Statutes in some states authorize the award of attorney's fees to prevailing plaintiffs, and in other states make attorney's fees awardable to any prevailing party, plaintiff or defendant. Compare Wis.Stat.Ann. § 895.50(1)(c) (West 1983) with Cal.Civ.Code §§ 990(a), 3344(a) (West Supp.1988).

B. Limits of Protection

Comedy III Productions, Inc. v. Gary Saderup, Inc.

Supreme Court of California, 2001.
25 Cal.4th 387, 106 Cal.Rptr.2d 126, 21 P.3d 797, 58 U.S.P.Q.2d 1823.

MOSK, J.

A California statute grants the *right of publicity* to specified successors in interest of deceased celebrities, prohibiting any other person from using a celebrity's name, voice, signature, photograph, or likeness for commercial purposes without the consent of such successors. The United States Constitution prohibits the states from abridging, among other fundamental rights, freedom of speech. (U.S. Const., 1st and 14th Amends.) In the case at bar we resolve a conflict between these two provisions. The Court of Appeal concluded that the lithographs and silkscreened T-shirts in question here received no First Amendment protection simply because they were reproductions rather than original works of art. As will appear, this was error: reproductions are equally entitled to First Amendment protection. We formulate instead what is essentially a balancing test between the First Amendment and the right of publicity based on whether the work in question adds significant creative elements so as to be transformed into something more than a mere celebrity likeness or imitation. Applying this test to the present case, we conclude that there are no such creative elements here and that the right of publicity prevails. On this basis, we will affirm the judgment of the Court of Appeal.

I. The Statute

In this state the right of publicity is both a statutory and a common law right. The statutory right originated in Civil Code section 3344 (hereafter section 3344), enacted in 1971, authorizing recovery of damages by any living person whose name, photograph, or likeness has been used for commercial purposes without his or her consent. Eight years later, in Lugosi v. Universal Pictures (1979) 25 Cal.3d 813, 160 Cal.Rptr. 323, 603 P.2d 425 (*Lugosi*), we also recognized a common law right of publicity, which the statute was said to complement. But because the common law right was derived from the law of privacy, we held in *Lugosi* that the cause of action did not survive the death of the person whose identity was exploited and was not descendible to his or her heirs or assignees.

In 1984 the Legislature enacted an additional measure on the subject, creating a second statutory right of publicity that *was* descendible to the heirs and assignees of deceased persons. (Stats.1984, ch. 1704, § 1, p. 6169.) The statute was evidently modeled on section 3344: many of the key provisions of the two statutory schemes were identical. The 1984 measure is the statute in issue in the case at bar. At the time of trial and while the appeal was pending before the Court of Appeal, the statute was numbered section 990 of the Civil Code.*

Section 990 declares broadly that "Any person who uses a deceased personality's name, voice, signature, photograph, or likeness, in any manner, on or in products, merchandise, or goods, or for purposes of advertising or selling, or soliciting purchases of, products, merchandise, goods, or services, without prior consent from the person or persons specified in subdivision (c), shall be liable for any damages sustained by the person or persons injured as a result thereof." The amount recoverable includes "any profits from the unauthorized use," as well as punitive damages, attorney fees, and costs.

The statute defines "deceased personality" as a person "whose name, voice, signature, photograph, or likeness has commercial value at the time of his or her death," whether or not the person actually used any of those features for commercial purposes while alive.

The statute further declares that "The rights recognized under this section are property rights" that are transferable before or after the personality dies, by contract or by trust or will. Consent to use the deceased personality's name, voice, photograph, etc., must be obtained from such a transferee or, if there is none, from certain described survivors of the personality. Any person claiming to be such a transferee or survivor must register the claim with the Secretary of State before recovering damages.

The right to require consent under the statute terminates if there is neither transferee nor survivor (§ 990, subd. (e)), or 50 years after the personality dies.[3]

The statute provides a number of exemptions from the requirement of consent to use. Thus a use "in connection with any news, public affairs, or sports broadcast or account, or any political campaign" does not require consent. Use in a "commercial medium" does not require consent solely because the material is commercially sponsored or contains paid advertising; "Rather it shall be a question of fact whether or not the use ... was so directly connected with" the sponsorship or advertising that it requires consent. Finally, subdivision (n) provides that "[a] play, book, magazine, newspaper, musical composition, film, radio or television program" (*id.,* subd. (n)(1)), work of "political or newsworthy value," "[s]ingle and original works of fine art" or "[a]n advertisement or commercial announcement" for the above works (*id.,* subd. (n)(4)) are all exempt from the provisions of the statute.

II. Facts

Plaintiff Comedy III Productions, Inc. (hereafter Comedy III), brought this action against defendants Gary Saderup and Gary Saderup, Inc.

---

* In 1999 the legislature renumbered the provision as Civil Code § 334.1. Stats 1999, ch. 998.

3. Under the new statute, this period has increased to 70 years. (Civ.Code, § 3344.1, subd. (g).)

(hereafter collectively Saderup), seeking damages and injunctive relief for violation of section 990 and related business torts. The parties waived the right to jury trial and the right to put on evidence, and submitted the case for decision on the following stipulated facts:

Comedy III is the registered owner of all rights to the former comedy act known as The Three Stooges, who are deceased personalities within the meaning of the statute.

Saderup is an artist with over 25 years' experience in making charcoal drawings of celebrities. These drawings are used to create lithographic and silkscreen masters, which in turn are used to produce multiple reproductions in the form, respectively, of lithographic prints and silkscreened images on T-shirts. Saderup creates the original drawings and is actively involved in the ensuing lithographic and silkscreening processes.

Without securing Comedy III's consent, Saderup sold lithographs and T-shirts bearing a likeness of The Three Stooges reproduced from a charcoal drawing he had made. These lithographs and T-shirts did not constitute an advertisement, endorsement, or sponsorship of any product.

Saderup's profits from the sale of unlicenced lithographs and T-shirts bearing a likeness of The Three Stooges was $75,000 and Comedy III's reasonable attorney fees were $150,000.

On these stipulated facts the court found for Comedy III and entered judgment against Saderup awarding damages of $75,000 and attorney fees of $150,000 plus costs. The court also issued a permanent injunction restraining Saderup from violating the statute by use of any likeness of The Three Stooges in lithographs, T-shirts, "or any other medium by which the [Saderup's] art work may be sold or marketed." The injunction further prohibited Saderup from "Creating, producing, reproducing, copying, distributing, selling or exhibiting any lithographs, prints, posters, t-shirts, buttons, or other goods, products or merchandise of any kind, bearing the photograph, image, face, symbols, trademarks, likeness, name, voice or signature of The Three Stooges or any of the individual members of The Three Stooges." The sole exception to this broad prohibition was Saderup's original charcoal drawing from which the reproductions at issue were made.

Saderup appealed. The Court of Appeal modified the judgment by striking the injunction. The court reasoned that Comedy III had not proved a likelihood of continued violation of the statute, and that the wording of the injunction was overbroad because it exceeded the terms of the statute and because it "could extend to matters and conduct protected by the First Amendment...."

The Court of Appeal affirmed the judgment as thus modified, however, upholding the award of damages, attorney fees, and costs. In so doing, it rejected Saderup's contentions that his conduct (1) did not violate the terms of the statute, and (2) in any event was protected by the constitutional guaranty of freedom of speech.

We granted review to address these two issues.

III. Discussion

A. *The Statutory Issue*

Saderup contends the statute applies only to uses of a deceased personality's name, voice, photograph, etc., for the purpose of advertising, selling, or soliciting the purchase of, products or services. He then stresses the stipulated fact (and subsequent finding) that the lithographs and T-shirts at issue in this case did not constitute an advertisement, endorsement, or sponsorship of any product. He concludes the statute therefore does not apply in the case at bar. As will appear, the major premise of his argument—his construction of the statute—is unpersuasive.

As noted above, the statute makes liable any person who, without consent, uses a deceased personality's name, voice, photograph, etc., "in any manner, *on or in products, merchandise, or goods, or* for purposes of advertising or selling, or soliciting purchases of, products, merchandise, goods, or services...." Saderup's construction reads the emphasized phrase out of the statute. Yet the Legislature deliberately inserted it, as the following sequence of events demonstrates. When first enacted in 1971, section 3344—the companion statute applying to living personalities—contained no such phrase: the statute simply made liable any person who uses another's identity "in any manner, for purposes of advertising products, merchandise, goods or services, or for purposes of solicitation of" such purchases. The Legislature inserted the phrase, "on or in products, merchandise, or goods, or," when it amended section 3344 in 1984. And in the very same legislation, the Legislature adopted section 990 and inserted the identical phrase in that statute as well.

We therefore give effect to the plain meaning of the statute: it makes liable any person who, without consent, uses a deceased personality's name, voice, photograph, etc., either (1) "on or in" a product, *or* (2) in "advertising or selling" a product. The two uses are not synonymous: in the apt example given by the Court of Appeal, there is an obvious difference between "placing a celebrity's name on a 'special edition' of a vehicle, and using that name in a commercial to endorse or tout the same or another vehicle."

Applying this construction of the statute to the facts at hand, we agree with the Court of Appeal that Saderup sold more than just the incorporeal likeness of The Three Stooges. Saderup's lithographic prints of The Three Stooges are themselves tangible personal property, consisting of paper and ink, made as products to be sold and displayed on walls like similar graphic art. Saderup's T-shirts are likewise tangible personal property, consisting of fabric and ink, made as products to be sold and worn on the body like similar garments. By producing and selling such lithographs and T-shirts, Saderup thus used the likeness of The Three Stooges "on ... products, merchandise, or goods" within the meaning of the statute....

B. *The Constitutional Issue*

Saderup next contends that enforcement of the judgment against him violates his right of free speech and expression under the First Amendment. He raises a difficult issue, which we address below.

The right of publicity is often invoked in the context of commercial speech when the appropriation of a celebrity likeness creates a false and misleading impression that the celebrity is endorsing a product. Because the First Amendment does not protect false and misleading commercial speech and because even nonmisleading commercial speech is generally subject to somewhat lesser First Amendment protection, the right of publicity may often trump the right of advertisers to make use of celebrity figures.

But the present case does not concern commercial speech. As the trial court found, Saderup's portraits of The Three Stooges are expressive works and not an advertisement for or endorsement of a product. Although his work was done for financial gain, "[t]he First Amendment is not limited to those who publish without charge.... [An expressive activity] does not lose its constitutional protection because it is undertaken for profit." (Guglielmi v. Spelling–Goldberg Productions (1979) 25 Cal.3d 860, 868, (conc. opn. of Bird, C.J.) (*Guglielmi*).)

The tension between the right of publicity and the First Amendment is highlighted by recalling the two distinct, commonly acknowledged purposes of the latter. First, " 'to preserve an uninhibited marketplace of ideas' and to repel efforts to limit the "uninhibited, robust and wide-open" debate on public issues.' " (*Guglielmi*, supra, 25 Cal.3d at p. 866, 160 Cal.Rptr. 352, 603 P.2d 454.) Second, to foster a "fundamental respect for individual development and self-realization. The right to self-expression is inherent in any political system which respects individual dignity. Each speaker must be free of government restraint regardless of the nature or manner of the views expressed unless there is a compelling reason to the contrary." (Ibid.)

The right of publicity has a potential for frustrating the fulfillment of both these purposes. Because celebrities take on public meaning, the appropriation of their likenesses may have important uses in uninhibited debate on public issues, particularly debates about culture and values. And because celebrities take on personal meanings to many individuals in the society, the creative appropriation of celebrity images can be an important avenue of individual expression. As one commentator has stated: "Entertainment and sports celebrities are the leading players in our Public Drama. We tell tales, both tall and cautionary, about them. We monitor their comings and goings, their missteps and heartbreaks. We copy their mannerisms, their styles, their modes of conversation and of consumption. Whether or not celebrities are 'the chief agents of moral change in the United States,' they certainly are widely used—far more than are institutionally anchored elites—to symbolize individual aspirations, group identities, and cultural values. Their images are thus important expressive and communicative resources: the peculiar, yet familiar idiom in which we conduct a fair portion of our cultural business and everyday conversation." (Madow, *Private Ownership of Public Image: Popular Culture and Publicity Rights* (1993) 81 Cal. L.Rev. 125, 128 (Madow)

As Madow further points out, the very importance of celebrities in society means that the right of publicity has the potential of censoring significant expression by suppressing alternative versions of celebrity images that are iconoclastic, irreverent, or otherwise attempt to redefine the celebrity's meaning. A majority of this court recognized as much in *Guglielmi*: "The right of publicity derived from public prominence does not confer a shield to ward off caricature, parody and satire. Rather, prominence invites creative comment." (*Guglielmi*, supra, 25 Cal.3d at p. 869.)

For similar reasons, speech about public figures is accorded heightened First Amendment protection in defamation law. As the United States Supreme Court held in Gertz v. Robert Welch, Inc. (1974) 418 U.S. 323, public figures may prevail in a libel action only if they prove that the defendant's defamatory statements were made with actual malice, i.e., actual knowledge of falsehood or reckless disregard for the truth, whereas private figures need prove only negligence. The rationale for such differential treatment is, first, that the public figure has greater access to the media and therefore greater opportunity to rebut defamatory statements, and second, that those who have become public figures have done so voluntarily and therefore "invite attention and comment." (Id. at pp. 344–345) Giving broad scope to the right of publicity has the potential of allowing a celebrity to accomplish through the vigorous exercise of that right the censorship of unflattering commentary that cannot be constitutionally accomplished through defamation actions.

Nor do Saderup's creations lose their constitutional protections because they are for purposes of entertaining rather than informing. As Chief Justice Bird stated in *Guglielmi*, invoking the dual purpose of the First Amendment: "Our courts have often observed that entertainment is entitled to the same constitutional protection as the exposition of ideas. That conclusion rests on two propositions. First, '[t]he line between informing and entertaining is too elusive for the protection of the basic right. Everyone is familiar with instances of propaganda through fiction. What is one man's amusement, teaches another doctrine.' " (*Guglielmi*, supra, 25 Cal.3d at p. 867) "Second, entertainment, as a mode of self-expression, is entitled to constitutional protection irrespective of its contribution to the marketplace of ideas. 'For expression is an integral part of the development of ideas, of mental exploration and of the affirmation of self. The power to realize his potentiality as a human being begins at this point and must extend at least this far if the whole nature of man is not to be thwarted.' " (Ibid.)

Nor does the fact that expression takes a form of nonverbal, visual representation remove it from the ambit of First Amendment protection. In Bery v. City of New York (2d Cir.1996) 97 F.3d 689, the court overturned an ordinance requiring visual artists—painters, printers, photographers, sculptors, etc.—to obtain licenses to sell their work in public places, but exempted the vendors of books, newspapers or other written matter. As the court stated: "Both the [district] court and the City demonstrate an unduly restricted view of the First Amendment and of visual art itself. Such myopic vision not only overlooks case law central to First Amendment jurisprudence but fundamentally misperceives the essence of visual communication and artistic expression. Visual art is as wide ranging in its depiction of ideas, concepts and emotions as any book, treatise, pamphlet or other writing, and is similarly entitled to full First Amendment protection.... One cannot look at Winslow Homer's paintings on the Civil War without seeing, in his depictions of the boredom and hardship of the individual soldier, expressions of anti-war sentiments, the idea that war is not heroic." (Id. at p. 695.)

Moreover, the United States Supreme Court has made it clear that a work of art is protected by the First Amendment even if it conveys no discernable message: "[A] narrow, succinctly articulable message is not a condition of constitutional protection, which if confined to expressions conveying a 'particularized message,' would never reach the unquestionably shielded painting of Jackson Pollock, music of Arnold Schoenberg, or Jabberwocky verse of Lewis Carroll." (Hurley v. Irish–American Gay, Lesbian and Bisexual Group of Boston, Inc. (1995) 515 U.S. 557.

Nor does the fact that Saderup's art appears in large part on a less conventional avenue of communications, T-shirts, result in reduced First Amendment protection. As Judge Posner stated in the case of a defendant who sold T-shirts advocating the legalization of marijuana, "its T-shirts ... are to [the seller] what the *New York Times* is to the Sulzbergers and the Ochs—the vehicle of her ideas and opinions." (Ayres v. City of Chicago (7th Cir.1997) 125 F.3d 1010, 1017.) First Amendment doctrine does not disfavor nontraditional media of expression.

But having recognized the high degree of First Amendment protection for noncommercial speech about celebrities, we need not conclude that all expression that trenches on the right of publicity receives such protection. The right of publicity, like copyright, protects a form of intellectual property that society deems to have some social utility. "Often considerable money, time and energy are needed to develop one's prominence in a particular field. Years of labor may be required before one's skill, reputation, notoriety or virtues are sufficiently developed to permit an economic return through some medium of commercial promotion. For some, the investment may eventually create considerable commercial value in one's identity." (*Lugosi*, supra, 25 Cal.3d at pp. 834–835, (dis. opn. of Bird, C. J.).)

The present case exemplifies this kind of creative labor. Moe and Jerome (Curly) Howard and Larry Fein fashioned personae collectively known as The Three Stooges, first in vaudeville and later in movie shorts, over a period extending from the 1920's to the 1940's. The three comic characters they created and whose names they shared—Larry, Moe, and Curly—possess a kind of mythic status in our culture. Their journey from ordinary vaudeville performers to the heights (or depths) of slapstick comic celebrity was long and arduous. Their brand of physical humor—the nimble, comically stylized violence, the "nyuk-nyuks" and "whoop-whoop-whoops," eye-pokes, slaps and head conks—created a distinct comedic trademark. Through their talent and labor, they joined the relatively small group of actors who constructed identifiable, recurrent comic personalities that they brought to the many parts they were scripted to play. . . .

Although surprisingly few courts have considered in any depth the means of reconciling the right of publicity and the First Amendment, we follow those that have in concluding that depictions of celebrities amounting to little more than the appropriation of the celebrity's economic value are not protected expression under the First Amendment. We begin with Zacchini v. Scripps-Howard Broadcasting Co. (1977) 433 U.S. 562, 576 (*Zacchini*), the only United States Supreme Court case to directly address the right of publicity. Zacchini, the performer of a human cannonball act, sued a television station that had videotaped and broadcast his entire performance without his consent. The court held the First Amendment did not protect the television station against a right of publicity claim under Ohio common law. In explaining why the enforcement of the right of publicity in this case would not violate the First Amendment, the court stated: " '[T]he rationale for [protecting the right of publicity] is the straightforward one of preventing unjust enrichment by the theft of good will. No social purpose is served by having the defendant get free some aspect of the plaintiff that would have market value and for which he would normally pay.' " (Id. at p. 576.) The court also rejected the notion that federal copyright or patent law preempted this type of state law protection of intellectual property: "[Copyright and patent] laws perhaps regard the 'reward to the owner [as] a secondary consideration,' but they were 'intended definitely to grant valuable, enforceable rights' in order to afford greater encouragement to the production of works of benefit to the public. The Constitution does not prevent Ohio from making a similar choice here in deciding to protect the entertainer's incentive in order to encourage the production of this type of work." (Id. at p. 577.)

To be sure, *Zacchini* was not an ordinary right of publicity case: the defendant television station had appropriated the plaintiff's entire act, a species of common law copyright violation. Nonetheless, two principles enunciated in *Zacchini* apply to this case: (1) state law may validly safeguard forms of intellectual property not covered under federal copyright and patent law as a means of protecting the fruits of a performing artist's labor; and (2) the state's interest in preventing the outright misappropriation of such intellectual property by others is not automatically trumped by the interest in free expression or dissemination of information; rather, as in the case of defamation, the state law interest and the interest in free expression must be balanced, according to the relative importance of the interests at stake. . . .

It is admittedly not a simple matter to develop a test that will unerringly distinguish between forms of artistic expression protected by the First Amendment and those that must give way to the right of publicity. Certainly, any such test must incorporate the principle that the right of publicity cannot, consistent with the First Amendment, be a right to control the celebrity's image by censoring disagreeable portrayals. Once the celebrity thrusts himself or herself forward into the limelight, the First

Amendment dictates that the right to comment on, parody, lampoon, and make other expressive uses of the celebrity image must be given broad scope. The necessary implication of this observation is that the right of publicity is essentially an economic right. What the right of publicity holder possesses is not a right of censorship, but a right to prevent others from misappropriating the economic value generated by the celebrity's fame through the merchandising of the "name, voice, signature, photograph, or likeness" of the celebrity.

Beyond this precept, how may courts distinguish between protected and unprotected expression? Some commentators have proposed importing the fair use defense from copyright law, which has the advantage of employing an established doctrine developed from a related area of the law. Others disagree, pointing to the murkiness of the fair use doctrine and arguing that the idea/expression dichotomy, rather than fair use, is the principal means of reconciling copyright protection and First Amendment rights.

We conclude that a wholesale importation of the fair use doctrine into right of publicity law would not be advisable. At least two of the factors employed in the fair use test, "the nature of the copyrighted work" and "the amount and substantiality of the portion used," seem particularly designed to be applied to the partial copying of works of authorship "fixed in [a] tangible medium of expression"; it is difficult to understand why these factors would be especially useful for determining whether the depiction of a celebrity likeness is protected by the First Amendment.

Nonetheless, the first fair use factor—"the purpose and character of the use"—does seem particularly pertinent to the task of reconciling the rights of free expression and publicity. As the Supreme Court has stated, the central purpose of the inquiry into this fair use factor "is to see, in Justice Story's words, whether the new work merely 'supersede[s] the objects' of the original creation, or instead adds something new, with a further purpose or different character, altering the first with new expression, meaning, or message; it asks, in other words, whether and to what extent the new work is 'transformative.' Although such transformative use is not absolutely necessary for a finding of fair use, the goal of copyright, to promote science and the arts, is generally furthered by the creation of transformative works." (Campbell v. Acuff–Rose Music, Inc. (1994) 510 U.S. 569, 579).

This inquiry into whether a work is "transformative" appears to us to be necessarily at the heart of any judicial attempt to square the right of publicity with the First Amendment. As the above quotation suggests, both the First Amendment and copyright law have a common goal of encouragement of free expression and creativity, the former by protecting such expression from government interference, the latter by protecting the creative fruits of intellectual and artistic labor. The right of publicity, at least theoretically, shares this goal with copyright law. When artistic expression takes the form of a literal depiction or imitation of a celebrity for commercial gain, directly trespassing on the right of publicity without adding significant expression beyond that trespass, the state law interest in protecting the fruits of artistic labor outweighs the expressive interests of the imitative artist.

On the other hand, when a work contains significant transformative elements, it is not only especially worthy of First Amendment protection, but it is also less likely to interfere with the economic interest protected by the right of publicity. As has been observed, works of parody or other distortions of the celebrity figure are not, from the celebrity fan's viewpoint, good substitutes for conventional depictions of the celebrity and therefore do not generally threaten markets for celebrity memorabilia that the right of publicity is designed to protect. Accordingly, First Amendment protection of such works outweighs whatever interest the state may have in enforcing the right of publicity. The right-of-publicity holder continues to enforce the right to monopolize the production of conventional, more or less fungible, images of the celebrity . . .

Another way of stating the inquiry is whether the celebrity likeness is one of the "raw materials" from which an original work is synthesized, or whether the depiction or imitation of the celebrity is the very sum and substance of the work in question. We ask, in other words, whether a product containing a celebrity's likeness is so transformed that it has become primarily the defendant's own expression rather than the celebrity's likeness. And when we use the word "expression," we mean expression of something other than the likeness of the celebrity.

We further emphasize that in determining whether the work is transformative, courts are not to be concerned with the quality of the artistic contribution—vulgar forms of expression fully qualify for First Amendment protection. On the other hand, a literal depiction of a celebrity, even if accomplished with great skill, may still be subject to a right of publicity challenge. The inquiry is in a sense more quantitative than qualitative, asking whether the literal and imitative or the creative elements predominate in the work.

Furthermore, in determining whether a work is sufficiently transformative, courts may find useful a subsidiary inquiry, particularly in close cases: does the marketability and economic value of the challenged work derive primarily from the fame of the celebrity depicted? If this question is answered in the negative, then there would generally be no actionable right of publicity. When the value of the work comes principally from some source other than the fame of the celebrity—from the creativity, skill, and reputation of the artist—it may be presumed that sufficient transformative elements are present to warrant First Amendment protection. If the question is answered in the affirmative, however, it does not necessarily follow that the work is without First Amendment protection—it may still be a transformative work.

In sum, when an artist is faced with a right of publicity challenge to his or her work, he or she may raise as affirmative defense that the work is protected by the First Amendment inasmuch as it contains significant transformative elements or that the value of the work does not derive primarily from the celebrity's fame.

Turning to the present case.... the inquiry is into whether Saderup's work is sufficiently transformative. Correctly anticipating this inquiry, he argues that all portraiture involves creative decisions, that therefore no portrait portrays a mere literal likeness, and that accordingly all portraiture, including reproductions, is protected by the First Amendment. We reject any such categorical position. Without denying that all portraiture involves the making of artistic choices, we find it equally undeniable, under the test formulated above, that when an artist's skill and talent is manifestly subordinated to the overall goal of creating a conventional portrait of a celebrity so as to commercially exploit his or her fame, then the artist's right of free expression is outweighed by the right of publicity. As is the case with fair use in the area of copyright law, an artist depicting a celebrity must contribute something more than a " 'merely trivial' " variation, [but must create] something recognizably " 'his own' " (L. Batlin & Son, Inc. v. Snyder (2d Cir.1976) 536 F.2d 486, 490), in order to qualify for legal protection.

On the other hand, we do not hold that all reproductions of celebrity portraits are unprotected by the First Amendment. The silkscreens of Andy Warhol, for example, have as their subjects the images of such celebrities as Marilyn Monroe, Elizabeth Taylor, and Elvis Presley. Through distortion and the careful manipulation of context, Warhol was able to convey a message that went beyond the commercial exploitation of celebrity images and became a form of ironic social comment on the dehumanization of celebrity itself. Such expression may well be entitled to First Amendment protection. Although the distinction between protected and unprotected expression will sometimes be subtle, it is no more so than other distinctions triers of fact are called on to make in First Amendment jurisprudence.

Turning to Saderup's work, we can discern no significant transformative or creative contribution. His undeniable skill is manifestly subordinated to the overall goal of creating literal, conventional depictions of The Three Stooges so as to exploit their fame. Indeed, were we to decide that Saderup's depictions were protected by the First Amendment, we cannot perceive how the right of publicity would remain a viable right other than in cases of falsified celebrity endorsements.

Moreover, the marketability and economic value of Saderup's work derives primarily from the fame of the celebrities depicted. While that fact alone does not necessarily mean the work receives no First Amendment protection, we can perceive no transformative elements in Saderup's works that would require such protection.

Saderup argues that it would be incongruous and unjust to protect parodies and other distortions of celebrity figures but not wholesome, reverential portraits of such celebrities. The test we articulate today, however, does not express a value judgment or preference for one type of depiction over another. Rather, it reflects a recognition that the Legislature has granted to the heirs and assigns of celebrities the property right to exploit the celebrities' images, and that certain forms of expressive activity protected by the First Amendment fall outside the boundaries of that right. Stated another way, we are concerned not with whether conventional celebrity images should be produced but with who produces them and, more pertinently, who appropriates the value from their production. Thus, under section 990, if Saderup wishes to continue to depict The Three Stooges as he has done, he may do so only with the consent of the right-of-publicity holder.

IV. Disposition

The judgment of the Court of Appeal is affirmed.

NOTES

1. As compared to other intellectual property doctrines, the right of publicity is a mere infant. Judicial decisions have only recently settled the elements of a *prima facie* case, and even on such fundamental questions as the right's descendibility the law in many states is silent. (Most but not all of the states that have addressed the question have made the right descendible.) It will be many years before the full range of limitations and defenses becomes fully articulated. Why wasn't the skill and effort that Saderup invested in creating his charcoal drawings sufficient to qualify them as a transformative use? Should a finding that drawings are copyrightable under the U.S. Copyright Act have any bearing on whether they are transformative? Would Saderup have done better to make his renderings less accurate in portraying the features and personality of his subjects? Would placing them in an unexpected, and perhaps satirical, setting be sufficient to qualify as a transformative use?

The *Comedy III Productions* court rested its limitation on the right of publicity not on the statutory text, but on the First Amendment. What freedom does this leave the California legislature in fine-tuning the right of publicity statutes to balance the perceived needs of celebrities and media users?

See generally Rosemary J. Coombe, Publicity Rights and Political Aspiration: Mass Culture, Gender Identity, and Democracy, 26 New Eng. L. Rev. 1221 (1992).

2. *Advertising or News?* Right of publicity statutes commonly prohibit unauthorized uses for purposes of trade or advertising but excuse uses made in connection with news and public affairs accounts. The New York Court of Appeals explored this distinction in Stephano v. News Group Publications, 64 N.Y.2d 174, 485 N.Y.S.2d 220, 474 N.E.2d 580 (1984), holding that it was not a trade or advertising purpose for defendant's magazine to publish a photograph of plaintiff modelling a jacket in a news feature about the jacket. Noting that the New York statute nowhere defines trade or advertising purposes, the court added that "courts have consistently held, from the time of its enactment, that these terms should not be construed to apply to publications concerning newsworthy events or matters of public interest."

In the *Stephano* court's view, the newsworthiness exception applies not only to reports of political happenings and social trends, but also to news stories and articles of consumer interest. Further, the "fact that the defendant may have included this item in its column solely or primarily to increase the circulation of its magazine and therefore its profits, as the Appellate Division suggested, does not mean that the defendant has used the plaintiff's picture for trade purposes within the meaning of the statute. Indeed, most publications seek to increase their circulation and also their profits. It is the content of the article and not the defendant's motive or primary motive to increase circulation which determines whether it is a newsworthy item, as opposed to a trade usage, under the Civil Rights Law." 64 N.Y.2d at 184–85, 485 N.Y.S.2d at 224–26.

3. *Merchandise or Entertainment?* Some states, California and New York among them, proscribe not only advertising uses of an individual's persona but, more generally, uses "on or in products, merchandise, or goods" or "for the purpose of trade." In speaking of "products, merchandise, or goods," these statutes presumably have novelty items such as T-shirts and coffee mugs in view; nonetheless, taken literally, information and entertainment products such as books and motion pictures are no less "products" and "goods" than are novelty items. Courts in these states generally treat information and entertainment products such as biographies and novels as coming within their publicity statute's literal compass, but excuse these uses on the ground that they are protected under the First Amendment's speech and press guarantees or under some state law counterpart to these guarantees.

In New York, for example, the reclusive billionaire Howard Hughes prevailed against the use of his name and likeness on a T-shirt and a board game, but not against the use of his identity in an unauthorized biography and in a fictional autobiography. *Compare* Rosemont Enters., Inc. v. Choppy Prods., Inc., 74 Misc.2d 1003, 347 N.Y.S.2d 83 (Sup.Ct.1972); Rosemont Enters., Inc. v. Urban Sys., Inc., 72 Misc.2d 788, 340 N.Y.S.2d 144 (N.Y.Sup.Ct.1973), *modified and aff'd*, 42 A.D.2d 544, 345 N.Y.S.2d 17 (N.Y.App.Div.1973) *with* Rosemont Enters., Inc. v. Random House, Inc., 58 Misc.2d 1, 294 N.Y.S.2d 122 (N.Y.Sup.Ct.1968), *aff'd*, 32 A.D.2d 892, 301 N.Y.S.2d 948 (N.Y.App.Div.1969); Rosemont Enters., Inc. v. McGraw–Hill Book Co., 85 Misc.2d 583, 380 N.Y.S.2d 839 (N.Y.Sup.Ct.1975).

According to the court in the board game case, "[i]n reality, defendants are not disseminating news. They are not educating the public as to the achievements of Howard Hughes. They are selling a commodity, a commercial product, an entertaining game of chance, the outcome of which is determined by maneuvering tokens on a game board by the throw of the dice. The use of plaintiff's name, biographic data etc. in this context is not legitimate to the public interest. It is merely the medium used to market a commodity familiar to us all in its various types and forms." 72 Misc.2d at 790, 340 N.Y.S.2d at 146.

Professor Thomas McCarthy, the leading commentator on the right of publicity, has astutely observed that "what is crucial" in these cases "is the medium not the message. The courts have routinely denied first amendment immunity from Right of Publicity liability when unpermitted use of identity is used even in 'messages' on T-shirts, dishes, ashtrays, drinking mugs, and the like. This result is usually reached on the basis that these are not the usual media for social or political messages." J.Thomas McCarthy, The Rights of Privacy and Publicity § 7.6 [A] (1996).

4.   *Preemption.* Section 301 of the 1976 Copyright Act will preempt a state right of publicity that meets all of three conditions: the subject matter of protection is fixed in a tangible medium of expression; the subject matter comes within the subject matter of copyright under sections 102 and 103 of the Copyright Act; and the state right is equivalent to one or more of the rights granted by section 106 of the Copyright Act.

The right of publicity will only rarely be preempted under section 301. Characteristically, the subject matter of the right of publicity will not be fixed in a tangible medium of expression; specifically, there is a distinction between the subject matter of the right of publicity—an individual's unfixed name or likeness—and the medium in which that persona is tangibly fixed—a photograph or other depiction of the individual's name or likeness. Second, names and likenesses will usually lie outside the subject matter of copyright because they are unprotectible "ideas" rather than protectible expressions. Third, the requirements of identifiability and commercial purpose will often distinguish the right of publicity from the rights extended by copyright.

See David E. Shipley, Three Strikes and They're Out at the Old Ball Game: Preemption of Performers' Rights of Publicity under the Copyright Act of 1976, 20 Ariz. St. L.J. 369 (1988).

PART THREE

Federal Law of Intellectual Property

NOTE: JURISDICTION AND COURTS

See Statute Supplement 28 U.S.C.A. §§ 1295, 1338, 1400.

A. FEDERAL AND STATE JURISDICTION

Section 1338 of the Judicial Code defines the jurisdiction of federal district courts over federal intellectual property actions and over certain state law claims connected to federal intellectual property actions. Section 1338(a) gives federal district courts original jurisdiction over "any civil action arising under any Act of Congress relating to patents, plant variety protection, copyrights and trade-marks." This jurisdiction "is exclusive of the courts of the states in patent, plant variety protection and copyright cases." District courts share their jurisdiction with state courts in trademark cases. Section 1338(b), which has been substantially augmented, if not displaced, by section 1367's provisions on supplemental jurisdiction, gives federal district courts pendent jurisdiction over certain related state actions.

1. *"Arising Under" Jurisdiction*

a. *When does an action arise under an act relating to copyrights, patents or trademarks?* In a much-cited passage that applies no less to the Patent and Trademark Acts than to the Copyright Act, Judge Henry Friendly wrote that "an action 'arises under' the Copyright Act if and only if the complaint is for a remedy expressly granted by the Act, e.g., a suit for infringement or for the statutory royalties for record reproduction, or asserts a claim requiring construction of the Act ... or, at the very least and perhaps more doubtfully, presents a case where a distinctive policy of the Act requires that federal principles control the disposition of the claim." T.B. Harms Co. v. Eliscu, 339 F.2d 823, 828, 144 U.S.P.Q. 46 (2d Cir.1964), cert. denied, 381 U.S. 915, 85 S.Ct. 1534, 14 L.Ed.2d 435, 145 U.S.P.Q. 743 (1965). Thirty-six years later, noting that this test has been adopted in all the circuits that have considered the question, the Second Circuit Court of Appeals reaffirmed the applicability of the *Harms* approach to claims of infringement arising from an alleged breach of contract. Bassett v. Mashantucket Pequot Tribe, 204 F.3d 343, 350, 53 U.S.P.Q.2d 1865 (2d Cir.2000).

Does an action to foreclose a copyright mortgage "arise under any act of Congress 'relating to patents, copyrights and trade-marks' simply because ... [17 U.S.C.A. § 28] provides that a copyright may be mortgaged?" Republic Pictures Corp. v. Security–First Nat'l Bank of Los Angeles, 197 F.2d 767, 769, 94 U.S.P.Q. 291 (9th Cir.1952), answered that it did not. Finding little help in the dictionary definition of "relate" and in the legislative history of section 28, Judge Goodrich considered the question from "a wider aspect": "It is not just because a right has its origin in federal law that a federal court has jurisdiction over matters which grow from that right. A large number of land titles in this country originate with a grant from the United States of America. Yet no one would now seriously claim that federal courts had authority to hear and decide litigation involving disputes among persons claiming the land because of the original grant by the United States." 197 F.2d at 769.

b.   *The Well–Pleaded Complaint.* In deciding whether an action arises under the Patent, Copyright or Trademark Acts, courts will honor the well-pleaded complaint. If the complaint alleges the elements required for an infringement action or makes a claim requiring construction of the federal statute, federal jurisdiction will lie under section 1338(a). If the complaint fails to allege any of these elements, federal jurisdiction will not lie. The fact that the defendant interposes a state law defense to a well-pleaded federal cause of action will not defeat federal jurisdiction. Nor will it defeat federal jurisdiction if, in an otherwise well-pleaded complaint, the copyright owner anticipates a state law defense; similarly, a complaint that discloses only state law grounds for recovery cannot bootstrap federal jurisdiction by anticipating possible defenses resting on federal law. Christianson v. Colt Industries Operating Corp., 486 U.S. 800, 108 S.Ct. 2166, 100 L.Ed.2d 811, 7 U.S.P.Q.2d 1109 (1988).

The well-pleaded complaint rule can enable the plaintiff to control the forum—federal or state—for its action. For example, a patent licensor whose licensee has broken their agreement, can "declare the license forfeited for breach of a condition subsequent and sue for infringement. If it is correct as to its right to declare such a forfeiture unilaterally (a question of state law) federal jurisdiction of the infringement suit exists. But where the licensor stands on the license agreement and seeks contract remedies, even an allegation of infringement will not create federal jurisdiction, for the existence of the license precludes the possibility of infringement." Milprint, Inc. v. Curwood, Inc., 562 F.2d 418, 420, 196 U.S.P.Q. 147 (7th Cir.1977).

2.   *Supplemental (Including Pendent) Jurisdiction*

Section 1338(b) of the Judicial Code tailors the general doctrine of pendent jurisdiction to the specific contours of intellectual property litigation, giving district courts original jurisdiction over "any civil action asserting a claim of unfair competition when joined with a substantial and related claim under the copyright, patent, plant variety protection or trademark laws." Section 1367, added to the Judicial Code by the Judicial Improvements Act of 1990, Pub. L. 101–650, 104 Stat. 5089, substantially supplements section 1338(b) by providing that, subject to exceptions, "in any civil action of which the district courts have original jurisdiction, the district courts shall have supplemental jurisdiction over all other claims that are so related to claims in the action within such original jurisdiction that they form part of the same case or controversy under Article III of the United States Constitution." 28 U.S.C. § 1367(a). Under section 1367(c), a district court may decline to exercise supplemental jurisdiction if "(1) the claim raises a novel or complex issue of State law, (2) the claim substantially predominates over the claim or claims over which the district court has original jurisdiction, (3) the district court has dismissed all claims over which it has original jurisdiction, or (4) in exceptional circumstances, there are other compelling reasons for declining jurisdiction."

Having taken pendent jurisdiction, what substantive law should a federal court apply in resolving the state claim? State law—the obvious answer since Erie v. Tompkins—is also the generally accepted answer. In an extensive footnote to his opinion for the court in Maternally Yours v. Your Maternity Shop, Inc., 234 F.2d 538, 540–41 n. 1, 110 U.S.P.Q. 462 (2d Cir.1956), Judge Waterman reasoned that "despite repeated statements implying the contrary, it is the *source* of the right sued upon, and not the ground on which federal jurisdiction over the case is founded, which determines the governing law.... Thus, the *Erie* doctrine applies, whatever the ground for federal jurisdiction, to any issue or claim which has its source in state law." (Emphasis the court's).

B. COURT OF APPEALS FOR THE FEDERAL CIRCUIT

The Federal Courts Improvement Act of 1982, P.L. 97–164, 96 Stat. 25 (April 2, 1982), created a thirteenth court of appeals, the United States Court of Appeals for the Federal Circuit (CAFC). The CAFC, an Article III court with twelve judges appointed by the President with the advice and consent of the Senate, merges the former Court of Customs and Patent Appeals and the Court of Claims. The court's initial membership consisted of the five sitting judges of the Court of Customs and Patent Appeals and the seven sitting judges of the Court of Claims. In its first decided case, the CAFC adopted the precedents of the Court of Customs and Patent Appeals and the Court of Claims as its own. South Corp. v. United States, 690 F.2d 1368, 1370, 215 U.S.P.Q. 657 (Fed.Cir.1982). Unlike the twelve other circuit courts, whose jurisdiction is defined by region, the CAFC's jurisdiction is defined by subject matter.

The Federal Courts Improvement Act gives the CAFC exclusive jurisdiction over appeals from district court decisions in patent and plant variety protection cases. 28 U.S.C.A. § 1295(a)(1). Courts have rigorously adhered to the grant of exclusivity. In Breed v. Hughes Aircraft Co., 253 F.3d 1173, 59 U.S.P.Q.2d 1146 (9th Cir.2001), the court applied the well-pleaded complaint rule to hold that the CAFC had exclusive jurisdiction to hear an appeal from a district court decision in a case involving thirteen contract and trade secret claims under California law and a single claim seeking correction of the named inventor under section 256 of the Patent Act.

The Federal Courts Improvement Act also vests in the CAFC the former jurisdiction of the Court of Customs and Patent Appeals over appeals from the Board of Patent Appeals and Interferences of the Patent and Trademark Office involving patent applications and interferences. 28 U.S.C.A. § 1295(a)(4)(A). Sections 1295(a)(4)(A) and 1295(a)(4)(C) contemplate two avenues for review of Board decisions. Under section 1295(a)(4)(A) a party can appeal a Board decision directly to the CAFC. Alternatively, a party can proceed by civil action against the Commissioner of Patents and Trademarks or against the adverse interference party in federal district court. See 35 U.S.C. §§ 145, 146. Section 1295(a)(4)(C) gives the CAFC exclusive jurisdiction over appeals from the district courts in these cases.

The principal reason Congress created the CAFC was to eliminate a persistent disparity in patent law standards among courts of appeals deciding patent cases coming to them from the district courts in their region. Today, district court decisions in patent infringement and declaratory judgment actions are the major source of patent issues coming before the CAFC. The CAFC also takes appeals from the United States Claims Court, some of whose decisions involve patent and copyright claims against the United States government; appeals from the International Trade Commission relating to unfair trade practices in the import trade, including patent infringement; and appeals from decisions of the Commissioner of Patents and Trademarks or the Trademark Trial and Appeal Board involving trademark registration applications and other proceedings.

On the CAFC, generally, see Robert L. Harmon, Patents and the Federal Circuit (2001).

I. TRADEMARK LAW

Merchants have used marks for centuries to indicate the ownership or source of goods. Archaeologists have unearthed Greek vases of the fifth and sixth centuries B.C. bearing the potter's mark. In the Middle Ages, merchants affixed distinctive marks to their goods before shipment to identify them in the event of shipwreck or piracy. Although such early practices may represent the beginnings of a tradition, these were essentially proprietary marks, intended to indicate ownership, and differed from modern trademarks intended to indicate the source of goods.

Guild practices requiring craftsmen to affix production marks to their goods lie closer to the source of modern trademarks. "Every craft, of course, either had its own ordinances concerning such marks or administered statutory or municipal regulations of a similar nature. All of these regulations, whatever their source, made use of the production mark compulsory. Their expressed purpose was to facilitate the tracing of 'false' or defective wares and the punishment of the offending craftsman. The compulsory production mark likewise assisted the gild authorities in preventing those outside the gild from selling their products within the area of the gild monopoly." Over time, in certain trades, these marks became "asset marks—that is to say they became valuable symbols of individual good-will." This was particularly so in the case of durable goods, and goods transported great distances, "especially in the clothing and cutlery trades." Frank I. Schechter, The Historical Foundations of the Law Relating to Trade–Marks 47 (1925).

Systematic legal protection of trademarks began to take shape in the early years of the nineteenth century as courts in England and the United States gradually evolved a distinct law of trademark infringement as a branch of the more general unfair competition doctrine of passing off. The first United States trademark statute, Act of July 8, 1870, ch. 230, 16 Stat. 198, created few substantive rights, providing instead for the registration of marks protected under common law. Congress amended the Act in 1876 to add criminal penalties for infringing or counterfeiting registered marks. Act of August 14, 1876, ch. 274, 19 Stat. 141. In 1879 the United States Supreme Court ruled that the Act of 1870, as amended, was unconstitutional. Trade–Mark Cases, 100 U.S. 82, 25 L.Ed. 550 (1879).

Justice Samuel Miller, writing for the Court in the Trade–Mark Cases, began by rejecting the argument that Article I, § 8, cl. 8, the copyright-patent clause, gave Congress the necessary authority. "The ordinary trademark has no necessary relation to invention or discovery. The trademark recognized by the common law is generally the growth of a considerable period of use, rather than a sudden invention. It is often the result of accident rather than design, and when under the act of Congress it is sought to establish it by registration, neither originality, invention, discovery, science, nor art is in any way essential to the right conferred by that act. If we should endeavor to classify it under the head of writings of authors, the objections are equally strong. . . . The writings which are to be protected are the *fruits of intellectual labor,* embodied in the form of books, prints, engravings and the like. The trade-mark may be, and generally is, the adoption of something already in existence as the distinctive symbol of the party using it." 100 U.S. at 94 (emphasis the Court's).

Justice Miller also rejected the argument that the Act could be rested on the commerce clause. When "Congress undertakes to enact a law, which can only be valid as a regulation of commerce, it is reasonable to expect to find on the face of the law, or from its essential nature, that it is a regulation of commerce with foreign nations, or among the several States, or with the Indian tribes. If not so limited, it is in excess of the power of Congress. If its main purpose be to establish a regulation applicable to all trade, to commerce at all points, especially if it be that it is designed to govern the commerce wholly between the citizens of the same State, it is obviously the exercise of a power not confided to Congress." Because the Act stated no such jurisdictional limits, the Court could not sustain it under the commerce power. 100 U.S. at 96–97.

Despite the care that Justice Miller took to narrow the Court's holding, and to signal to Congress that it could repair the constitutional flaw by expressly limiting the Act to objects covered by the commerce clause, it soon became evident that federal trademark protection had started off on the wrong foot. Until passage of the Lanham Act, nearly three-quarters of a century later, Congress and the courts took few steps toward an enlarged federal role. Congress' first response to the Court's decision, the Act of March 3, 1881, 21 Stat. 502, expressly conditioned federal registration on the mark's use in foreign commerce or in commerce with the Indian tribes. Registration of marks used in interstate commerce came only with passage of the comprehensive Act of Feb. 20, 1905, ch. 592, 33 Stat. 724. Influenced in part by the Trademark Cases, and in part by dicta in American Steel Foundries v. Robertson, 269 U.S. 372, 46 S.Ct. 160, 70 L.Ed. 317 (1926) and American Trading Co. v. Heacock Co., 285 U.S. 247, 52 S.Ct. 387, 76 L.Ed. 740, 12 U.S.P.Q. 453 (1932), courts as late as 1932 assumed that "Congress has been given no power to legislate on the substantive law of trademarks," and that congressional authority is limited to providing "a federally controlled place of registration and to deny registration therein, where confusion would likely result to the trade from the trademark use of such registered marks." A. Leschen & Sons Rope Co. v. American Steel and Wire Co., 55 F.2d 455, 459, 12 U.S.P.Q. 272 (C.C.P.A.1932).

The Lanham Act, signed into law on July 5, 1946, was the first major step toward substantive federal trademark legislation in the United States. The efforts at revision began in 1924, with the introduction of S. 2679. First spearheaded by Representative Albert Vestal, the revision effort was later taken over by Representative Fritz Lanham. Since 1946, the Lanham Act, which is the trademark statute now in force, has been amended several times. The 1962 "housekeeping" amendments, Act of October 9, 1962, P.L.

87–772, 76 Stat. 769, also contain some substance. See page 366, below. The 1975 amendments, Act of January 2, 1975, P.L. 93–600, § 3, 88 Stat.1955, provided, among other things, for the award of attorneys' fees in exceptional cases.

The Trademark Law Revision Act of 1988 materially altered the premises and provisions of the Lanham Act. Among other changes, the 1988 Act modifies trademark law's traditional use requirement; strengthens the evidentiary effect of a registration certificate; reduces the term of trademark registration; and widens the compass of federal unfair competition law under section 43(a), 15 U.S.C.A. § 1125(a). The 1988 Act traces to the work of the United States Trademark Association (now called the International Trademark Association) and its specially-chartered Trademark Review Commission. Although the Act differs in important respects from the Commission's recommendations, it reflects their impress. See United States Trademark Association Trademark Review Commission Report and Recommendations to USTA President and Board of Directors, 77 Trademark Rep. 375 (1987). For a detailed overview of the 1988 amendments, see Frank Z. Hellwig, The Trademark Law Revision Act of 1988: The 100th Congress Leaves Its Mark, 79 Trademark Rep. 287 (1989). The entire May–June, 1989 number of the Trademark Reporter is devoted to the 1988 amendments.

For a superb study of the evolution of trademark law from its earliest origins, see Frank I. Schechter, The Historical Foundations of the Law Relating to Trade–Marks (1925). See also John Burrell, Two Hundred Years of English Trademark Law and Beverly W. Pattishall, Two Hundred Years of American Trademark Law, in American Bar Association, Two Hundred Years of English and American Patent, Trademark and Copyright Law 35, 51 (1977); Sidney A. Diamond, The Historical Development of Trademarks, 65 Trademark Rep. 265 (1975); Daniel M. McClure, Trademarks and Unfair Competition: A Critical History of Legal Thought, 69 Trademark Rep. 305 (1979); Benjamin G. Paster, Trademarks—Their Early History, 59 Trademark Rep. 551 (1969).

General reference works on trademark law and practice include Rudolf Callmann, The Law of Unfair Competition, Trademarks, and Monopolies (L. Altman, 4th ed. 1981); Jerome Gilson, Trademark Protection and Practice (1974); J. Thomas McCarthy, McCarthy on Trademarks and Unfair Competition (4th ed. 1996).

The Trademark Reporter, published bimonthly by the International Trademark Association is an excellent source of articles on topics of current importance. One number of the Reporter, 87 Trademark Reporter No. 5 (1997), is devoted to trademark on the Internet and offers an excellent introduction to issues in the field.

A.   REQUIREMENTS FOR PROTECTION

1.   USE AND USE IN COMMERCE

See Statute Supplement 15 U.S.C.A. §§ 1051, 1055, 1057, 1060.

Until the Trademark Law Revision Act of 1988, which came into effect on November 16, 1989, trademark ownership and registration in the

United States turned on the mark's use in connection with goods or services in the marketplace. No ownership or rights attached to a mark until it was used in commerce. Use was also a condition precedent to an application to register the mark in the Patent and Trademark Office. Simply, a firm could not select a mark for a new but unmarketed product and reserve the mark until it was ready to market the product.

The Revision Act substantially loosened the use requirement by allowing trademark registration applications to be made upon a showing of a bona fide intention to use the mark. The change brings United States trademark law into line with the laws of most other countries. Some countries have long allowed registration based on the applicant's intent to use the mark; actual use in these countries is only a condition subsequent to the mark's continued validity. Other countries permit registration without a showing even of an intent to use the mark. See Paul Goldstein, International Intellectual Property Law: Cases and Materials 469 (2001).

The principal argument against a use requirement is that it requires a firm to invest sometimes substantial sums in marketing its goods or services before the firm has any assurance that the mark will meet the other conditions, such as distinctiveness, required for registration. The requirement also gave a distinct advantage to foreign applicants who, under Lanham Act § 44, 15 U.S.C.A. § 1126, did not have to allege use. One argument for retaining a use requirement is that it prevents firms from warehousing marks. Under this view, warehousing is bad because it prevents newcomers to the marketplace from using the warehoused marks, and confers no benefit on consumers, who have not begun to identify the warehoused mark with a source of goods or services. The use requirement also keeps deadwood off the trademark registers.

The Revision Act strikes a balance between these competing claims by introducing a new distinction into the Lanham Act's provisions on application, registration and use. The distinction is between trademark applications based on use of a mark and applications based only on an intent to use the mark.

Applications Based on Use. As amended, the Lanham Act generally treats applications based on use in the same way that it treated them before the 1988 amendments. Examiners in the Patent and Trademark Office will review the application for compliance with statutory formalities and determine whether registration of the mark is barred on any of the grounds specified in section 2 of the Lanham Act, 15 U.S.C.A. § 1052. If the mark qualifies for registration, the examiner will approve its publication in the Official Gazette for purposes of opposition. If no one successfully opposes the application, the Patent and Trademark Office will then register the mark.

Applications Based on Intent to Use. Under the 1988 amendments, the Patent and Trademark Office subjects intent to use applications to the same initial steps as applications based on use—comparison with possibly conflicting marks and publication for opposition. The difference lies in the steps that follow the opposition period. If no one successfully opposes the application, the Patent and Trademark Office will issue a "notice of allowance." Following the notice of allowance, it will register the mark if, within six months, the applicant files "a verified statement that the mark is in use in commerce. . . ." 15 U.S.C.A. § 1051(d)(1). Section 1051(d)(2) gives the intent to use applicant a second six-month waiting period as a matter of course and, "upon a showing of good cause," the Office may further extend the time for filing a statement of use for periods aggregating not more than 24 months. This three-year waiting period, when taken together with the twelve months or more that may elapse between the filing date and the date of allowance, effectively gives the intent to use applicant more than four years to reserve its mark.

What does an applicant gain by filing an intent to use application? Under section 1057(c), once the mark is registered on the Principal Register the filing of the application to register the mark "shall constitute constructive use of the mark, conferring a right of priority, nationwide in effect, on or in connection with the goods or services specified in the registration. . . . " The constructive use priority effectively gives the successful applicant the same rights it would have received had it actually used the mark throughout the United States on the date it filed its application—specifically the right to bar the mark's use by all later applicants or users. The priority does not, however, obtain against certain foreign applicants or against anyone who used the mark or applied for registration before the registrant's filing date.

The Trademark Review Commission, whose proposals formed the basis for the 1988 amendments, gives an example of the priority conferred by the intent to use provisions:

> P files an intent-to-use application on June 1, 1988 to register the mark BRAVO for cheese. D commences use of the mark BRAVO for yogurt November 1, 1988. P begins shipping BRAVO cheese in commercial quantities to its brokers and retail accounts in several states on February 1, 1989. In an injunction action by P against D, P prevails, provided: (a) P's application is allowed, (b) P files a declaration of use within six months after Notice of Allowance or during an extension thereof, (c) a principal register registration issues to P, and (d) P proves that the public in D's locale is likely to be confused by D's use of BRAVO on yogurt.

United States Trademark Association, Trademark Review Commission Report and Recommendations to USTA President and Board of Directors, 77 Trademark Rep. 398–99 (1987). D could in this case have protected itself by searching the Patent and Trademark Office records before adopting the Bravo mark for its yogurt.

Token Use. Even before passage of the intent to use provisions made it safe to invest in a mark prior to its use in trade, the Patent and Trademark Office offered a safety net by tolerating token uses—spare, contrived uses of a mark made for the single purpose of obtaining registration. See Blue

Bell, Inc. v. Farah Mfg. Co., below. The 1988 Revision Act abolished token use registrations across the board by defining "use in commerce" to mean "the bona fide use of a mark in the ordinary course of trade, and not made merely to reserve a right in a mark." 15 U.S.C.A. § 1127. In reporting the bill that became the Revision Act, Senator DeConcini stated that the amended definition of "use in commerce" was intended "to assure that the commercial sham of 'token use'—which becomes unnecessary under the intent-to-use application system we designed—would actually be eliminated. In doing so, however, Congress' intent that the revised definition still encompass genuine, but less traditional, trademark uses must be made clear. For example, such uses as clinical shipments of a new drug awaiting FDA approval, test marketing, or infrequent sales of large or expensive or seasonal products, reflect legitimate trademark uses in the normal course of trade and are not to be excluded by the House language." 134 Cong. Rec. 16,973 (Oct. 20, 1988).

For detailed discussions of the intent to use provisions, see Amy B. Cohen, Intent to Use: A Failed Experiment?, 35 U.S.F. L. Rev. 683 (2001); Henry W. Leeds, Intent to Use—Its Time Has Come, 79 Trademark Reporter 269 (1989).

Blue Bell, Inc. v. Farah Mfg. Co.

United States Court of Appeals, Fifth Circuit, 1975.
508 F.2d 1260, 185 U.S.P.Q. 1.

GEWIN, Circuit Judge.

In the spring and summer of 1973 two prominent manufacturers of men's clothing created identical trademarks for goods substantially identical in appearance. Though the record offers no indication of bad faith in the design and adoption of the labels, both Farah Manufacturing Company (Farah) and Blue Bell, Inc. (Blue Bell) devised the mark "Time Out" for new lines of men's slacks and shirts. Both parties market their goods on a national scale, so they agree that joint utilization of the same trademark would confuse the buying public. Thus, the only question presented for our review is which party established prior use of the mark in trade. A response to that seemingly innocuous inquiry, however, requires us to define the chameleonic term "use" as it has developed in trademark law.

After a full development of the facts in the district court both parties moved for summary judgment. The motion of Farah was granted and that of Blue Bell denied. It is not claimed that summary judgment procedure was inappropriate; the controversy presented relates to the application of the proper legal principles to undisputed facts. A permanent injunction was granted in favor of Farah but no damages were awarded, and Blue Bell was allowed to fill all orders for garments bearing the Time Out label received by it as of the close of business on December 5, 1973. For the reasons hereinafter stated we affirm.

Farah conceived of the Time Out mark on May 16, after screening several possible titles for its new stretch menswear. Two days later the firm adopted an hourglass logo and authorized an extensive advertising campaign bearing the new insignia. Farah presented its fall line of clothing, including Time Out slacks, to sales personnel on June 5. In the meantime, patent counsel had given clearance for use of the mark after scrutiny of current federal registrations then on file. One of Farah's top executives demonstrated samples of the Time Out garments to large customers in Washington, D.C. and New York, though labels were not attached to the slacks at that time. Tags containing the new design were completed June 27. With favorable evaluations of marketing potential from all sides, Farah sent one pair of slacks bearing the Time Out mark to each of its twelve regional sales managers on July 3. Sales personnel paid for the pants, and the garments became their property in case of loss.

Following the July 3 shipment, regional managers showed the goods to customers the following week. Farah received several orders and production began. Further shipments of sample garments were mailed to the rest of the sales force on July 11 and 14. Merchandising efforts were fully operative by the end of the month. The first shipments to customers, however, occurred in September.

Blue Bell, on the other hand, was concerned with creating an entire new division of men's clothing, as an avenue to reaching the "upstairs" market. Though initially to be housed at the Hicks–Ponder plant in El Paso, the new division would eventually enjoy separate headquarters. On June 18 Blue Bell management arrived at the name Time Out to identify both its new division and its new line of men's sportswear. Like Farah, it received clearance for use of the mark from counsel. Like Farah, it inaugurated an advertising campaign. Unlike Farah, however, Blue Bell did not ship a dozen marked articles of the new line to its sales personnel. Instead, Blue Bell authorized the manufacture of several hundred labels bearing the words Time Out and its logo shaped like a referee's hands forming a T. When the labels were completed on June 29, the head of the embryonic division flew them to El Paso. He instructed shipping personnel to affix the new Time Out labels to slacks that already bore the "Mr. Hicks" trademark. The new tags, of varying sizes and colors, were randomly attached to the left hip pocket button of slacks and the left hip pocket of jeans. Thus, although no change occurred in the design or manufacture of the pants, on July 5 several hundred pair left El Paso with two tags.

Blue Bell made intermittent shipments of the doubly-labeled slacks thereafter, though the out-of-state customers who received the goods had ordered clothing of the Mr. Hicks variety. Production of the new Time Out merchandise began in the latter part of August, and Blue Bell held a sales meeting to present its fall designs from September 4–6. Sales personnel solicited numerous orders, though shipments of the garments were not scheduled until October.

By the end of October Farah had received orders for 204,403 items of Time Out sportswear, representing a retail sales value of over $2,750,000.

Blue Bell had received orders for 154,200 garments valued at over $900,000. Both parties had commenced extensive advertising campaigns for their respective Time Out sportswear.

Soon after discovering the similarity of their marks, Blue Bell sued Farah for common law trademark infringement and unfair competition, seeking to enjoin use of the Time Out trademark on men's clothing. Farah counterclaimed for similar injunctive relief. The district court found that Farah's July 3 shipment and sale constituted a valid use in trade, while Blue Bell's July 5 shipment was a mere "token" use insufficient at law to create trademark rights. While we affirm the result reached by the trial court as to Farah's priority of use, the legal grounds upon which we base our decision are somewhat different from those undergirding the district court's judgment.

Federal jurisdiction is predicated upon diversity of citizenship, since neither party has registered the mark pursuant to the Lanham Act. Given the operative facts surrounding manufacture and shipment from El Paso, the parties agree the Texas law of trademarks controls. In 1967 the state legislature enacted a Trademark Statute.[5] Section 16.02 of the Act explains that a mark is "used" when it is affixed to the goods and "the goods are sold, displayed for sale, or otherwise publicly distributed." Thus the question whether Blue Bell or Farah established priority of trademark use depends upon interpretation of the cited provision. Unfortunately, there are no Texas cases construing § 16.02. This court must therefore determine what principles the highest state court would utilize in deciding such a question. In view of the statute's stated purpose to preserve common law rights, we conclude the Texas Supreme Court would apply the statutory provision in light of general principles of trademark law.

A trademark is a symbol (word, name, device or combination thereof) adopted and used by a merchant to identify his goods and distinguish them from articles produced by others. Ownership of a mark requires a combination of both appropriation and use in trade. Thus, neither conception of the mark, nor advertising alone establishes trademark rights at common law. Rather, ownership of a trademark accrues when goods bearing the mark are placed on the market.

The exclusive right to a trademark belongs to one who first uses it in connection with specified goods. Such use need not have gained wide public recognition, and even a single use in trade may sustain trademark rights if followed by continuous commercial utilization.

The initial question presented for review is whether Farah's sale and shipment of slacks to twelve regional managers constitutes a valid first use of the Time Out mark. Blue Bell claims the July 3 sale was merely an internal transaction insufficiently public to secure trademark ownership. After consideration of pertinent authorities, we agree.

5. Vernon's Tex.Code, Ann., Bus. & Comm. §§ 16.01–16.28 (1968).

Secret, undisclosed internal shipments are generally inadequate to support the denomination "use." Trademark claims based upon shipments from a producer's plant to its sales office, and vice versa, have often been disallowed. Though none of the cited cases dealt with *sales* to intra-corporate personnel, we perceive that fact to be a distinction without a difference. The sales were not made to customers, but served as an accounting device to charge the salesmen with their cost in case of loss. The fact that some sales managers actively solicited accounts bolsters the good faith of Farah's intended use, but does not meet our essential objection: that the "sales" were not made to the public.

The primary, perhaps singular purpose of a trademark is to provide a means for the consumer to separate or distinguish one manufacturer's goods from those of another. Personnel within a corporation can identify an item by style number or other unique code. A trademark aids the public in selecting particular goods. As stated by the First Circuit:

> But to hold that a sale or sales are the sine qua non of a use sufficient to amount to an appropriation would be to read an unwarranted limitation into the statute, for so construed registration would have to be denied to any manufacturer who adopted a mark to distinguish or identify his product, and perhaps applied it thereon for years, if he should in practice lease his goods rather than sell them, as many manufacturers of machinery do. It seems to us that although evidence of sales is highly persuasive, the question of use adequate to establish appropriation remains one to be decided on the facts of each case, and that evidence showing, first, adoption, and, second, *use in a way sufficiently public to identify or distinguish the marked goods in an appropriate segment of the public mind as those of the adopter of the mark,* is competent to establish ownership. . . .

New England Duplicating Co. v. Mendes, 190 F.2d 415, 418, 90 U.S.P.Q. 151, 153 (1st Cir.1951) (Emphasis added). Similarly, the Trademark Trial and Appeal Board has reasoned:

> To acquire trademark rights there has to be an "open" use, that is to say, a use has to be made to the relevant class of purchasers or prospective purchasers since a trademark is intended to identify goods and distinguish those goods from those manufactured or sold by others. There was no such "open" use, rather the use can be said to be an "internal" use, which cannot give rise to trademark rights.

Sterling Drug, Inc. v. Knoll A.G. Chemische Fabriken, supra at 631.

Farah nonetheless contends that a recent decision of the Board so undermines all prior cases relating to internal use that they should be ignored. In Standard Pressed Steel Co. v. Midwest Chrome Process Co., 183 U.S.P.Q. 758 (T.T.A.B.1974), the agency held that internal shipment of marked goods from a producer's manufacturing plant to its sales office constitutes a valid "use in commerce" for registration purposes.

An axiom of trademark law has been that the right to register a mark is conditioned upon its actual use in trade. Theoretically, then, common law use in trade should precede the use in commerce upon which Lanham Act registration is predicated. Arguably, since only a trademark owner can apply for registration, any activity adequate to create registrable rights must perforce also create trademark rights. A close examination of the Board's decision, however, dispels so mechanical a view. The tribunal took meticulous care to point out that its conclusion related solely to registration use rather than ownership use.

It has been recognized and especially so in the last few years that, in view of the expenditures involved in introducing a new product on the market generally and the attendant risk involved therein prior to the screening process involved in resorting to the federal registration system and in the absence of an "intent to use" statute, a token sale or a single shipment in commerce *may be sufficient to support an application to register a trademark* in the Patent Office notwithstanding that the evidence may not show what disposition was made of the product so shipped. That is, the fact that a sale or a shipment of goods bearing a trademark was *designed primarily to lay a foundation for the filing of an application for registration* does not, per se, invalidate any such application or subsequent registration issued thereon.

. . .

Inasmuch as it is our belief that a most liberal policy should be followed in a situation of this kind [*in which dispute as to priority of use and ownership of a mark is not involved*], applicant's initial shipment of fasteners, although an intra-company transaction in that it was to a company sales representative, was a bona fide shipment. . . .

Standard Pressed Steel Co. v. Midwest Chrome Process Co., supra at 764–65 (Emphasis added).

Priority of use and ownership of the Time Out mark are the only issues before this court. The language fashioned by the Board clearly indicates a desire to leave the common law of trademark ownership intact. The decision may demonstrate a reversal of the presumption that ownership rights precede registration rights, but it does not affect our analysis of common law use in trade. Farah had undertaken substantial preliminary steps toward marketing the Time Out garments, but it did not establish ownership of the mark by means of the July 3 shipment to its sales managers. The gist of trademark rights is actual use in trade. Though technically a "sale", the July 3 shipment was not "publicly distributed" within the purview of the Texas statute.

Blue Bell's July 5 shipment similarly failed to satisfy the prerequisites of a bona fide use in trade. Elementary tenets of trademark law require that labels or designs be affixed to the merchandise actually intended to bear the mark in commercial transactions. Furthermore, courts have recognized that the usefulness of a mark derives not only from its capacity to identify a certain manufacturer, but also from its ability to differentiate between different classes of goods produced by a single manufacturer. Here customers had ordered slacks of the Mr. Hicks species, and Mr. Hicks was the fanciful mark distinguishing these slacks from all others. Blue Bell intended to use the Time Out mark on an entirely new line of men's sportswear, unique in style and cut, though none of the garments had yet been produced.

While goods may be identified by more than one trademark, the use of each mark must be bona fide. Mere adoption of a mark without bona fide use, in an attempt to reserve it for the future, will not create trademark rights. In the instant case Blue Bell's attachment of a secondary label to an older line of goods manifests a bad faith attempt to reserve a mark. We cannot countenance such activities as a valid use in trade. Blue Bell therefore did not acquire trademark rights by virtue of its July 5 shipment.

We thus hold that neither Farah's July 3 shipment nor Blue Bell's July 5 shipment sufficed to create rights in the Time Out mark. Based on a desire to secure ownership of the mark and superiority over a competitor, both claims of alleged use were chronologically premature. Essentially, they took a time out to litigate their differences too early in the game. The question thus becomes whether we should continue to stop the clock for a remand or make a final call from the appellate bench. While a remand to the district court for further factual development would not be improper in these circumstances, we believe the interests of judicial economy and the parties' desire to terminate the litigation demand that we decide, if possible, which manufacturer first used the mark in trade.

Careful examination of the record discloses that Farah shipped its first order of Time Out clothing to customers in September of 1973. Blue Bell, approximately one month behind its competitor at other relevant stages of development, did not mail its Time Out garments until at least October. Though sales to customers are not the sine qua non of trademark use, they are determinative in the instant case. These sales constituted the first point at which the public had a chance to associate Time Out with a particular line of sportswear. Therefore, Farah established priority of trademark use; it is entitled to a decree permanently enjoining Blue Bell from utilization of the Time Out trademark on men's garments.

The judgment of the trial court is affirmed.

WarnerVision Entertainment, Inc. v. Empire of Carolina, Inc.

United States Court of Appeals, Second Circuit, 1996.
101 F.3d 259, 40 U.S.P.Q.2d 1855.

VAN GRAAFEILAND, Circuit Judge:

Empire of Carolina, Inc., Empire Industries, Inc. and Empire Manufacturing, Inc. (hereafter "Empire") and Thomas Lowe Ventures, Inc. d/b/a Playing Mantis (hereafter "TLV") appeal from orders of the United States District Court for the Southern District of New York (Baer, J.) preliminarily enjoining appellants from violating WarnerVision Entertainment Inc.'s trademark "REAL WHEELS," and denying Empire's cross-motion for injunctive relief. The appeal was argued on an emergency basis on May 31, 1996, and on June 12, 1996, we issued an order vacating the preliminary injunction with an opinion to follow. This is the opinion.

Appellants contend that the grant of preliminary relief in WarnerVision's favor should be reversed on any of several grounds. We limit our holding to one—the district court's misapplication of 15 U.S.C. § 1057(c), part of the intent-to-use ("ITU") provisions of the Lanham Act, to the facts of the instant case. This error constitutes an abuse of discretion.

Prior to 1988, an applicant for trademark registration had to have used the mark in commerce before making the application. Following the enactment of the ITU provisions in that year, a person could seek registration of a mark not already in commercial use by alleging a bona fide intent to use it. Registration may be granted only if, absent a grant of extension, the applicant files a statement of commercial use within six months of the date on which the Commissioner's notice of allowance pursuant to 15 U.S.C. § 1063(b) is issued. The ITU applicant is entitled to an extension of another six months, and may receive further extensions from the Commissioner for an additional twenty four months. If, but only if, the mark completes the registration process and is registered, the ITU applicant is granted a constructive use date retroactive to the ITU filing date. This retroactive dating of constructive use permits a more orderly development of the mark without the risk that priority will be lost. The issue we now address is whether the creator of a mark who files an ITU application pursuant to 15 U.S.C. § 1051(b) can be preliminarily enjoined from engaging in the commercial use required for full registration by 15 U.S.C. § 1051(d) on motion of the holder of a similar mark who commenced commercial use of its mark subsequent to the creator's ITU application but prior to the ITU applicant's commercial use. A brief statement of the pertinent facts follows.

On September 9, 1994, TLV sent the Patent and Trademark Office ("PTO") an ITU application for the mark "REAL WHEELS," stating an intent-to-use the mark in commerce on or in connection with "the following goods/services: wheels affiliated with 1/64th and 1/43rd scale toy vehicles." The application was filed on September 23, 1994. Around the same time, two other companies, apparently acting in innocence and good faith, decided that the "REAL WHEELS" mark would fit the products they were preparing to market. One of them, Buddy L, a North Carolina manufacturer that had been marketing toy replicas of vehicles for many years, selected the name for its 1995 line of vehicle replicas. The other, WarnerVision Entertainment Inc., found the name suitable for certain of its home videos which featured motorized vehicles. The videos and vehicles were shrink-wrapped together in a single package. Both companies ordered trademark searches for conflicts in the name, but, because TLV's application had not yet reached the PTO database, no conflict was found.

Both companies then filed for registration of their mark. However, because WarnerVision's application was filed on January 3, 1995, three days before Buddy L's, it was approved, and Buddy L's was rejected. Buddy L nonetheless continued with its marketing efforts and entered into negotiations with TLV for a possible license based on TLV's ITU application.

Unfortunately, Buddy L encountered financial problems, and on March 3, 1995, it filed for relief under Chapter 11 of the Bankruptcy Law as a debtor in possession. Thereafter, in an auction sale approved by the Bankruptcy Court, Buddy L sold substantially all of its assets to Empire. On October 20, 1995, Empire purchased from TLV all of TLV's title and interest in and to the REAL WHEELS product line, trademarks and good will associated therewith, including the September 23, 1994 ITU application. At the same time, Empire licensed TLV to use the REAL WHEELS mark for toy automobiles. On November 13, 1995, WarnerVision brought the instant action.

In granting the preliminary injunction at issue, the district court quoted the Supreme Court's admonition in *Connecticut Nat'l Bank v. Germain,* 503 U.S. 249, 253–54, 112 S.Ct. 1146, 1149–50, 117 L.Ed.2d 391 (1992), to the effect that when the words of a statute are unambiguous, judicial inquiry as to its meaning is complete. We do not quarrel with this statement as a general proposition; however, we question its application in the instant case. Section 1057(c) of Title 15, the statute at issue, provides that, "[c]ontingent on the registration of a mark ... the filing of the application to register such mark shall constitute constructive use of the mark, conferring a right of priority, nationwide in effect...." Empire is not claiming constructive use based on registration. Registration will not take place until after the section 1051(d) statement of use is filed and further examination is had of the application for registration. Empire contends that the district court erred in granting the preliminary injunction which bars it from completing the ITU process by filing a factually supported statement of use.

We agree. Empire does not contend that the filing of its ITU application empowered it to seek affirmative or offensive relief precluding WarnerVision's use of the REAL WHEELS mark. It seeks instead to assert the ITU filing as a defense to WarnerVision's efforts to prevent it from completing the ITU registration process. In substance, Empire requests that the normal principles of preliminary injunction law be applied in the instant case. This accords with the stated intent of Congress that the Lanham Act would be governed by equitable principles, which Congress described as "the core of U.S. trademark jurisprudence." *See* S.Rep. No. 515, 100th Cong., 2d Sess. 30 (1988), *reprinted in* 1988 U.S.C.C.A.N. 5577, 5592....

As the International Trademark Association ("ITA") correctly notes at page 9 of its amicus brief, if Empire's ITU application cannot be used to defend against WarnerVision's application for a preliminary injunction, Empire will effectively be prevented from undertaking the use required to obtain registration. In short, granting a preliminary injunction to Warner-Vision would prevent Empire from ever achieving use, registration and priority and would thus effectively and permanently terminate its rights as the holder of the ITU application. Quoting 2 *McCarthy on Trademarks and Unfair Competition* § 19.08[1][d] at 19–59 (3d ed. 1992), the ITA said "this result 'would encourage unscrupulous entrepreneurs to look in the record for new [intent-to-use] applications by large companies, rush in to make a few sales under the same mark and sue the large company, asking for a large settlement to permit the [intent-to-use] applicant to proceed on its plans for use of the mark.' " This vulnerability to pirates is precisely what the ITU enactments were designed to eliminate.

The Trademark Trial and Appeal Board believes that an ITU applicant should be able to defend against such piratical acts despite the fact that full registration has not yet been given. When the foregoing authorities were cited to the district court, the court correctly stated that it was not bound by them. However, the district court was bound not to construe and apply the ITU provisions in such a manner as to effectively convert a preliminary injunction based largely on disputed affidavits into a final adjudication on the merits.

The ITU provisions permit the holder of an ITU application to use the mark in commerce, obtain registration, and thereby secure priority retroactive to the date of filing of the ITU application. Of course, this right or privilege is not indefinite; it endures only for the time allotted by the statute. But as long as an ITU applicant's privilege has not expired, a court may not enjoin it from making the use necessary for registration on the grounds that another party has used the mark subsequent to the filing of the ITU application. To permit such an injunction would eviscerate the ITU provisions and defeat their very purpose.

This is not to say that a holder of a "live" ITU application may never be enjoined from using its mark. If another party can demonstrate that it used the mark before the holder filed its ITU application or that the filing was for some reason invalid, then it may be entitled to an injunction. WarnerVision says that it made analogous use of the REAL WHEELS mark before TLV filed its ITU application and also that the assignment to Empire of TLV's ITU application was invalid. But the district court did not pass on these contentions, and we will not consider them in the first instance.

The district court based its grant of preliminary relief on the proposition that "[t]he first party to adopt and use a mark in commerce obtains ownership rights," and held that "WarnerVision made prior use of the mark in commerce and is the senior user." 915 F.Supp. at 645. On the basis of the present record, that decision cannot stand. WarnerVision also contends that TLV's ITU application was not properly assigned to Empire because Empire did not succeed to a portion of TLV's business. Like the claims of analogous use, this contention raises fact issues which should not be addressed in the first instance by this Court. We vacate that portion of the district court's orders that grants WarnerVision preliminary injunctive relief and remand to the district court for further proceedings not inconsistent with this opinion.

We affirm the district court's denial of Empire's application for a preliminary injunction enjoining WarnerVision from using the REAL WHEELS mark for toys outside the video cassette market. Empire does not claim that it may use TLV's ITU application offensively to obtain this injunction, and we express no opinion on this subject. Empire says only that Buddy L, a company it acquired in a bankruptcy sale, made analogous use of the mark prior to WarnerVision's first use of the mark. On the record before us, we cannot say that the district court abused its discretion in denying a preliminary injunction on this ground.

NOTES

1. *Blue Bell's* discussion of *Standard Pressed Steel* highlights the two different use standards that courts employed before the Trademark Law Revision Act of 1988. For purposes of ownership and priority under state law, courts generally required substantial use in connection with goods or services in the marketplace and assigned ownership to the first firm that made such a use. By contrast, for purposes of federal registration, courts frequently held that a token, noncommercial use of the mark in commerce sufficed even though it was evident that the token use was made exclusively for the purpose of obtaining registration.

What is the effect of having two different standards of use—one for ownership and priority, the other for registration? If Blue Bell had made sufficient use of the mark to obtain registration, followed several months later by a *bona fide* commercial use establishing priority, what would it have gained from the earlier registration? How would Blue Bell have fared in an infringement action against Farah? Might Blue Bell have exposed itself to statutory liability by applying for early registration? Lanham Act § 38, 15 U.S.C.A. § 1120 provides that "[a]ny person who shall procure registration in the Patent and Trademark Office of a mark by false or fraudulent declaration or representation, oral or in writing, or by any false means, shall be liable in a civil action by any person injured thereby for any damages sustained in consequence thereof." See Blue Bell, Inc. v. Jaymar-Ruby, Inc., 497 F.2d 433, 182 U.S.P.Q. 65 (2d Cir.1974).

2. *Bona Fide Use.* What is a bona fide use sufficient to establish trademark ownership and priority? Anthony L. Fletcher has identified several factors that courts weigh in favor of finding a genuine commercial use. In order of importance they are: (1) quantity and continuity of sale ("the question, of course, is how much is enough? Perhaps the answer is that he who needs to ask the question has not enough."); (2) consumer purchases ("such sales would seem to be a *sine qua non* of real use"); (3) business of mark owner; (4) quality control; (5) a distinguishing mark ("Blue Bell's trouble was that it slapped Time Out labels at random on slacks known, listed, ordered and sold as Mr. Hicks slacks."); (6) intent; (7) profit or loss ("plainly, this consideration is little more than a makeweight; there are plenty of *bona fide* marks whose products are sold at a loss"); (8) advertising; and (9) test market. Anthony L. Fletcher, "Time Out," "Snob," "Wipe

Out," and "Chicken of the Sea": The Death Knell of "Token Use"?, 65 Trademark Rep. 336, 346–348 (1975).

Lucent Information Management, Inc. v. Lucent Technologies, Inc., 186 F.3d 311, 317, 51 U.S.P.Q.2d 1545 (3d Cir.1999), upheld a grant of summary judgment to defendant, the technology spinoff of industry giant AT & T, against the claim that plaintiff had used and acquired rights in the mark "Lucent" for its computer and management services before defendant filed an intent to use application for the same mark for telecommunications and computer-related goods. Equating use with market penetration "significant enough to pose the real likelihood of confusion among consumers in that area," the court ruled that a single sale for $323.50 and a small number of sales presentations did not establish prior use. Rejecting plaintiff's reliance on the *Blue Bell* dictum that "even a single use in trade may sustain trademark rights if followed by continuous commercial utilization," the court concluded that if "we look for 'continuous commercial utilization' beyond the first sale, as required under *Blue Bell*, we do not find that the continuous use—the further promotional efforts—[was] sufficiently public to identify or distinguish the marked goods in an appropriate segment of the public mind as those of the adopter of the mark." Judge Harold Ackerman dissented, finding sufficient evidence in the record to preclude summary judgment, including production of a company logo, letterhead and business cards, a letter announcing the new company to 25–50 potential clients, conclusion of distributorship agreements and sales presentations to three companies, all before the date on which defendant filed its intent to use application.

Should the standard for use applied to service marks, as in *Lucent*, be different from the standard applied to marks for goods, as in *Blue Bell*?

3. *Use in Commerce.* The Lanham Act defines commerce broadly, as "all commerce which may lawfully be regulated by Congress." 15 U.S.C.A. § 1127. Nonetheless, courts historically construed the term more narrowly than contemporary constitutional doctrine would allow. As late as 1957, the Court of Customs and Patent Appeals ruled that a Philadelphia restaurant could not obtain service mark registration for its name because it "failed to establish that the services for which registration is sought are rendered in commerce which may lawfully be regulated by Congress within the meaning of the Trademark Act of 1946." Application of Bookbinder's Restaurant, Inc., 240 F.2d 365, 368, 112 U.S.P.Q. 326, 328 (1957). The applicant argued to no avail that its customers traveled to the restaurant in interstate commerce.

Judicial and administrative attitudes began to change in the mid–1960's. In Application of Gastown, Inc., 326 F.2d 780, 140 U.S.P.Q. 216 (1964), the Court of Customs and Patent Appeals allowed registration of a service mark used by a filling station situated on an interstate highway. Although the applicant was situated in only one state, its services to interstate travelers were in commerce. The court ruled that use in commerce includes use in intrastate commerce that directly affects interstate commerce. The Court of Appeals for the Federal Circuit subsequently relied on *Gastown* to reject the argument that a service mark used by a single-location restaurant will qualify for registration only if the restaurant is located on an interstate highway, serves at least 50% of its meals to interstate travelers, or regularly advertises in out-of-state media. Larry Harmon Pictures Corp. v. Williams Restaurant Corp., 929 F.2d 662, 18 U.S.P.Q.2d 1292 (Fed.Cir.), cert. denied, 502 U.S. 823, 112 S.Ct. 85, 116 L.Ed.2d 58 (1991).

Gastown involved a service mark. Thirteen years elapsed before trademarks received similarly liberal treatment. In Application of Silenus Wines, Inc., 557 F.2d 806, 194 U.S.P.Q. 261 (1977), the Court of Customs and Patent Appeals held that applicant, a wine importer, could register a mark affixed to wine it imported from France and sold only in Massachusetts. Recognizing that the applicant's importation "is not itself a 'use in commerce'," the court drew on the *Gastown* rationale to conclude "that intrastate sale of goods by the party who caused those goods to move in regulatable commerce, directly affects that commerce and is itself regulatable. Clearly, intrastate sale of imported wines by the importer sufficiently affects commerce with foreign nations to qualify those intrastate sales for the Trademark Act definition of 'commerce'." 557 F.2d at 809.

For a thoughtful review of *Silenus* and its background, see Carol V. Calhoun, Use in Commerce After Silenus: What Does It Mean?, 70 Trademark Rep. 47 (1980).

4. *Foreign Registrations.* One purpose of the intent to use provisions introduced by the 1988 amendments to the Lanham Act was to level the playing field for domestic and foreign trademark applicants. Other countries, such as France, have allowed registration without use. By treaty, and under Lanham Act § 44, 15 U.S.C.A. § 1126, the United States is committed to honor these foreign registrations. As a result, first users in the United States can lose out to later users elsewhere.

SCM Corp. v. Langis Foods Ltd., 539 F.2d 196, 190 U.S.P.Q. 288 (D.C.Cir.1976), illustrates the problem. On March 28, 1969 defendant, a Canadian corporation, filed applications to register three trademarks in Canada. On May 15, 1969 defendant began to use these marks in Canada. On the same day—probably by coincidence—plaintiff's predecessor in interest, a United States corporation, began to use the identical mark in the United States. On June 18, 1969, plaintiff applied for registration in the United States. On September 19, 1969, defendant applied for registration in the United States, claiming priority on the basis of its Canadian applications. Registration issued to the defendant. Plaintiff petitioned for cancellation on the ground that it was the mark's first user in the United States. The Trademark Trial and Appeal Board ruled for the defendant. The District Court for the District of Columbia ruled for the plaintiff.

The Court of Appeals reversed. "Our holding in this case is that section 44(d) of the Trademark Act of 1946, which implements Article 4 of the Paris Union Treaty, accorded to appellant Langis a 'right to priority' for the six months following the filing of its Canadian application for registration, that is to say, from March 28, 1969 to September 27, 1969;

and that an intervening use in the United States during that period cannot invalidate Langis's right to registration in this country pursuant to an application filed on September 19, 1969." 539 F.2d at 201. The court left open the question whether the defendant would have prevailed if it had made no use of the mark anywhere prior to its United States application. In Crocker National Bank v. Canadian Imperial Bank of Commerce, 223 U.S.P.Q. 909 (1984), the Trademark Trial and Appeal Board ruled that foreign applicants can register without proof of use anywhere.

The 1988 amendments to the Lanham Act reduced the disparate treatment of domestic and foreign applicants in two ways. First, the amendments enable United States nationals to apply for registration on the basis of an intent to use their marks in trade. Second, under Lanham Act § 44(e), foreign applicants must state their bona fide intention to use their mark in commerce. 15 U.S.C.A. § 1126(d)(2). To be sure, section 44(e) provides that "use in commerce shall not be required prior to registration;" but the applicant must, as a practical matter use the mark within three years of its registration or face a presumption that it has abandoned the mark. See Lanham Act § 45, 15 U.S.C.A. § 1127 (definition of "abandoned.").

For a review of practice under Canada's intent to use provisions, see Daniel R. Bereskin, Intent–to–Use in Canada After Three Decades, 79 Trademark Rep. 379 (1989) ("Today, intent-to-use applications are very popular in Canada, accounting for more than half of all applications filed.").

5. *Affixation.* Trademark law has historically required that a trademark be affixed to the goods with which it is used in order to qualify for registration. Before the 1988 amendments, the Lanham Act required the mark to be "placed in any manner on the goods or their containers or the displays associated therewith or on the tags or labels affixed thereto." The 1988 amendments added: "or if the nature of the goods makes such placement impracticable, then on documents associated with the goods or their sale...." 15 U.S.C.A. § 1127 (definition of "use in commerce").

The affixation requirement traces to the early practice of attaching or embedding marks in the goods whose source they were intended to identify. The law developed around the assumption that marks could be effective only in connection with the goods to which they were affixed. But what of marks for services? Since trademark law made affixation to goods necessary to a mark's inception and continued validity, logic dictated that there could be no valid trademark if there were no goods to which the mark could be affixed. Since services characteristically involve no goods, it followed that service marks could not be protected as trademarks and could only be protected, if at all, under unfair competition law. Congress finally eluded this logic by ignoring it. The Lanham Act places service marks on a par with trademarks and treats use or display of the mark in the sale or advertising of services as the equivalent of affixation.

NOTE: TRADEMARK ABANDONMENT

There are two distinct tests for trademark abandonment. One treats trademark abandonment as the obverse of trademark use. Just as use of a mark in connection with goods or services is required to obtain substantive rights in the mark, so the mark's non-use in connection with goods or services can lead to the loss of rights. This abandonment test asks whether the mark's use has been discontinued with the intention not to resume use. The second test treats trademark abandonment as the obverse of distinctiveness and secondary meaning. Just as rights will attach to a mark only if the mark indicates the source of goods or services to consumers, so rights will be lost when the mark loses its capacity to indicate source. The two tests of trademark abandonment often overlap. For example, if a firm stops using a mark for a long period, the mark will probably lose its capacity to indicate source to consumers, and a court will hold the mark to have been abandoned both because of its nonuse and because of its incapacity to indicate source.

Abandonment Through Nonuse. Section 45 of the Lanham Act, 15 U.S.C.A. § 1127, provides that a mark shall be deemed to be abandoned "[w]hen its use has been discontinued with intent not to resume such use. Intent not to resume may be inferred from circumstances. Nonuse for 3 consecutive years shall be prima facie evidence of abandonment. 'Use' of a mark means the bona fide use of that mark made in the ordinary course of trade, and not made merely to reserve a right in a mark." The last sentence of this provision, added by the 1988 Trademark Law Revision Act amendments, means that token use of a mark will be insufficient to forestall a finding of abandonment.

Silverman v. CBS Inc., 870 F.2d 40 (2d Cir.1989), exemplifies the test for abandonment by non-use. Defendant there had acquired rights in the scripts and radio programs of the "Amos 'n' Andy Show" in 1948 and had subsequently broadcast the show, first on radio and then on television, through 1966 when it took the program off the air in response to complaints by civil rights organizations that the programs were demeaning to African–Americans. By the time the question of abandonment came before the district court, the "Amos 'n' Andy" marks had not been used for twenty-one years. The district court ruled that the marks had not been abandoned because CBS had offered a reasonable explanation for its decision to keep the program off the air and because the company claimed an intention to resume use at some indefinite point in the future.

The court of appeals reversed. The court rejected the district court's interpretation of the statutory phrase, "intent not to resume," to mean an intent never to resume use, and held instead that the phrase means "intent not to resume use within the reasonably foreseeable future." According to the court, "[a] proprietor who temporarily suspends use of a mark can rebut the presumption of abandonment by showing reasonable grounds for the suspension and plans to resume use in the reasonably foreseeable future when the conditions requiring suspension abate." In the court's view, "this standard is sufficient to protect against the forfeiture of marks by proprietors who are temporarily unable to continue using them, while it also prevents warehousing of marks, which impedes commerce and competition." 870 F.2d at 46–47.

The *Silverman* court distinguished two earlier decisions in which it had found no abandonment. "In Saratoga Vichy Spring Co. v. Lehman, [625 F.2d 1037 (2d Cir.1980)], we rejected a claim of abandonment based on seven years of non-use where the initial decision to cease use resulted from a decision of the state legislature and the state, which was the trademark owner, continuously sought to sell the mark along with the mineral water business to which it applied. Similarly, in Defiance Button Machine Co. v. C & C Metal Products Corp., 759 F.2d 1053 (2d Cir.), cert. denied, 474 U.S. 844, 106 S.Ct. 131, 88 L.Ed.2d 108 (1985), we rejected an abandonment claim where, during a brief period of non-use, the proprietor tried to sell the mark, its associated goodwill, and some other assets and, upon failing to find a buyer, became a subsidiary of a company in its original line of trade and prepared to resume its business. In both cases, the proprietor of the mark had an intention to exploit the mark in the reasonably foreseeable future by resuming its use or permitting its use by others." 870 F.2d at 47.

Abandonment Through Loss of Distinctiveness. Section 45 of the Lanham Act also defines abandonment to include the situation where "any course of conduct of the owner, including acts of omission as well as commission, causes the mark to become the generic name for the goods or services on or in connection with which it is used or otherwise to lose its significance as a mark...." For example, if the term, "Thermos," originally used to identify the source of a particular brand of vacuum bottle, comes in common parlance to describe the vacuum bottle itself, the mark will be held to have been abandoned under this provision. Other instances of abandonment through loss of capacity to indicate source include the trademark owner's licensing of the mark without adequate control over the quality of goods or services purveyed by the licensee; assignment of the mark without a contemporaneous transfer of the goodwill associated with the mark; and, possibly, the failure to sue infringers who are making confusingly similar uses of the mark.

Consequences of Abandonment. A finding of abandonment implies that the mark is in the public domain and that the mark's owner no longer has any rights in the mark. Does abandonment also imply that anyone is free to adopt the mark as her own? The answer turns on the rationale behind the finding of abandonment. If the trademark owner accompanies its cessation of use with a formal declaration of abandonment, any other firm can adopt the mark as its own. See Manhattan Industries, Inc. v. Sweater Bee by Banff, Ltd., 627 F.2d 628, 207 U.S.P.Q. 89 (2d Cir.1980). The question remains, however, whether the second comer *should* be allowed to use the mark since the mark will, for a time, identify the abandoning owner as the source of the second comer's goods or services, with consequent consumer confusion as to source. When the mark has been abandoned by non-use for three years or longer, or by uncontrolled licensing or assignment without associated goodwill, problems of consumer confusion are less likely to arise and the second comer has a better claim to making the mark its own. Where, however, the owner has abandoned the mark by allowing it to become generic, as in the *Thermos* case, no one firm should be entitled to make the mark its own since, by definition, the mark is incapable of indicating source.

2.   DISTINCTIVENESS AND RELATED STATUTORY STANDARDS

See Statute Supplement 15 U.S.C.A. § 1052.

Trademark law's distinctiveness requirement serves two related purposes. One is to ensure that a mark identifies a single source for goods or services, thus securing consumer expectations respecting source. Second, by denying protection to descriptive terms, the requirement ensures that competitors will be free to use these terms in describing their own goods or services. The distinctiveness requirement curbs the natural tendency of firms to select marks that not only have the capacity to indicate source but that also, through their descriptive aspect, may capture a greater market share for goods or services than would be obtained by indication of source alone.

Distinctiveness occupies a spectrum. At one end of the spectrum are generic or common descriptive terms that are generally used as the names or descriptions of the goods or services to which the trademark is applied. "Soap" or "Hand Soap" for a bar of soap are two examples. These terms cannot become trademarks under any circumstances. Next on the spectrum are merely descriptive terms that describe a characteristic or ingredient of an article or service. These terms can become valid trademarks by acquiring secondary meaning—the capacity to identify the goods with a single source. "100% Pure" as applied to soap is a possible example. A suggestive term only suggests an ingredient or characteristic of goods or services, and requires the consumer to use his imagination to determine the nature of the goods. "Ivory" as applied to soap is an example. Suggestive terms can be protected without proof of secondary meaning. Finally, there are arbitrary or fanciful terms that are so far removed from the quality of goods or services that they not only receive the same protection as suggestive marks, but are also invulnerable to attack as being merely descriptive rather than suggestive. "Camay Soap" is an example.

Geographic terms occupy a comparable spectrum of distinctiveness. Where the geographic term is synonymous with the quality of goods, courts will treat it as a generic or common descriptive term that is not entitled to protection. "Lackawanna" as applied to coal from the Lackawanna Valley is an example. See Delaware & Hudson Canal Co. v. Clark, 80 U.S. 311, 20 L.Ed. 581 (1871). If the geographic term does not describe the quality of the goods to which it is applied, courts may treat it as geographically descriptive—not because it describes a characteristic or ingredient of the goods, but because firms frequently use geographic names to describe the source of a good's manufacture. Like merely descriptive terms, courts will protect these geographic terms if they acquire secondary meaning. "Thus if a manufacturer located in Chicago were to display the name CHICAGO on his shirts, for example, it has been the law for over a century that he could prevent another's subsequent use only if he could establish 'secondary meaning' in the term." In re Nantucket, Inc., 677 F.2d 95, 102–103, 213 U.S.P.Q. 889 (C.C.P.A.1982) (Nies, J., concurring). Where the geographic term only suggests a quality of the goods with which it is used, or is entirely fanciful or arbitrary as applied to the goods, courts will protect it even absent proof of secondary meaning. Professor McCarthy gives as examples, "NORTH POLE for bananas; SALEM for cigarettes; ATLANTIC for magazines; ENGLISH LEATHER for men's after-shave lotion; or ARCTIC for ice cream." J.Thomas McCarthy, Trademarks and Unfair Competition § 14:3 (3d ed. 1996).

Section 2 of the Lanham Act, 15 U.S.C.A. § 1052, takes the common law formulations of distinctiveness as its touchstone for the registrability of marks, but also introduces other conditions as bars to registration on the Principal Register. In reading the cases and materials that follow, consider whether and to what extent these added conditions serve the same consumer or producer interests as the distinctiveness requirement.

a. *"Trademark by Which the Goods of the Applicant May Be Distinguished From the Goods of Others"*

King–Seeley Thermos Co. v. Aladdin Industries, Inc.

United States Court of Appeals, Second Circuit, 1963.
321 F.2d 577, 138 U.S.P.Q. 349.

LEONARD P. MOORE, Circuit Judge.

This action by [sic] brought by appellant King–Seeley Thermos Co. (King–Seeley) to enjoin the defendant, Aladdin Industries, Incorporated from threatened infringement of eight trademark registrations for the word "Thermos" owned by appellant. Defendant answered, acknowledging its intention to sell its vacuum-insulated containers as "thermos bottles," asserted that the term "thermos" or "thermos bottle" is a generic term in the English language, asked that plaintiff's registrations of its trademark "Thermos" be cancelled and that it be adjudicated that plaintiff have no trademark rights in the word "thermos" on its vacuum bottles. The trial court held that plaintiff's registrations were valid but that the word "thermos" had become "a generic descriptive word in the English language ... as a synonym for 'vacuum insulated' container." 207 F.Supp. 9.

The facts are set out at great length in the comprehensive and well-reasoned opinion of the district court and will not be detailed here. In that opinion, the court reviewed King–Seeley's corporate history and its use of the trademark "Thermos." He found that from 1907 to 1923, King–Seeley undertook advertising and educational campaigns that tended to make "thermos" a generic term descriptive of the product rather than of its origin. This consequence flowed from the corporation's attempt to popularize "Thermos bottle" as the name of that product without including any of the generic terms then used, such as "Thermos vacuum-insulated bottle." The court found that by 1923 the word "thermos" had acquired firm roots as a descriptive or generic word.

At about 1923, because of the suggestion in an opinion of a district court that "Thermos" might be a descriptive word, King–Seeley adopted the use of the word "vacuum" or "vacuum bottle" with the word "Thermos." Although "Thermos" was generally recognized in the trade as a trademark, the corporation did police the trade and notified those using "thermos" in a descriptive sense that it was a trademark. It failed, however, to take affirmative action to seek out generic uses by non-trade publications and protested only those which happened to come to its attention. Between 1923 and the early 1950's the generic use of "thermos" had grown to a marked extent in non-trade publications and by the end of this period there was wide-spread use by the unorganized public of "thermos" as a synonym for "vacuum insulated." The court concluded that King–Seeley had failed to use due diligence to rescue "Thermos" from becoming a descriptive or generic term.

Between 1954 and 1957, plaintiff showed awareness of the wide-spread generic use of "thermos" and of the need to educate the public to the word's trademark significance. It diversified its products to include those not directly related to containers designed to keep their contents hot or cold. It changed its name from the American Thermos Bottle Company to The American Thermos Products Company and intensified its policing activities of trade and non-trade publications. The court found, however, that the generic use of "thermos" had become so firmly impressed as a part of the everyday language of the American public that plaintiff's extraordinary efforts commencing in the mid–1950's came too late to keep "thermos" from falling into the public domain. The court also held that appellant's trademarks are valid and because there is an appreciable, though minority, segment of the consumer public which knows and recognizes plaintiff's trademarks, it imposed certain restrictions and limitations on the use of the word "thermos" by defendant.

We affirm the district court's decision that the major significance of the word "thermos" is generic. No useful purpose would be served by repeating here what is fully documented in the opinion of the court below.

Appellant's primary protest on appeal is directed at the district court's finding that

> The word "thermos" became a part of the public domain because of the plaintiff's wide dissemination of the word "thermos" used as a synonym for "vacuum-insulated" and as an adjectival-noun, "thermos", through its educational and advertising campaigns and because of the plaintiff's lack of reasonable diligence in asserting and protecting its trademark rights in the word "Thermos" among the members of the unorganized public, exclusive of those in the trade, from 1907 to the date of this action. 207 F.Supp. at 14.

We are not convinced that the trademark's loss of distinctiveness was the result of some failure on plaintiff's part. Substantial efforts to preserve the trademark significance of the word were made by plaintiff, especially with respect to members of the trade. However, there was little they could do to prevent the public from using "thermos" in a generic rather than a trademark sense. And whether the appropriation by the public was due to highly successful educational and advertising campaigns or to lack of diligence in policing or not is of no consequence; the fact is that the word "thermos" had entered the public domain beyond recall. Even as early as 1910 plaintiff itself asserted that "Thermos had become a household word."

Judge Anderson found that although a substantial majority of the public knows and used the word "thermos", only a small minority of the public knows that this word has trademark significance. He wrote at 207 F.Supp. at 21–22:

> The results of the survey [conducted at the behest of the defendant] were that about 75% of adults in the United States who were familiar with containers that keep the contents hot or cold, call such a container a "thermos"; about 12% of the adult American public know that "thermos" has a trade-mark significance, and about 11% use the term "vacuum bottle". This is generally corroborative of the court's conclusions drawn from the other evidence, except that such other evidence indicated that a somewhat larger minority than 12% was aware of the trade-mark meaning of "thermos"; and a somewhat larger minority than 11% used the descriptive term "vacuum" bottle or other container.

The record amply supports these findings.

Appellant argues that the court below misapplied the doctrine of the Aspirin and Cellophane cases. Its primary contention is that in those cases, there was no generic name, such as vacuum bottle, that was suitable for use by the general public. As a result, to protect the use of the only word that identified the product in the mind of the public would give the owners of the trademark an unfair competitive advantage. The rule of those cases, however, does not rest on this factor. Judge Learned Hand stated the sole issue in Aspirin to be: "What do the buyers understand by the word for whose use the parties are contending? If they understand by it only the kind of goods sold, then, I take it, it makes no difference whatever what efforts the plaintiff has made to get them to understand more." 272 F. at 509. Of course, it is obvious that the fact that there was no suitable descriptive word for either aspirin or cellophane made it difficult, if not impossible, for the original manufacturers to prevent their trademark from becoming generic. But the test is not what is available as an alternative to the public, but what the public's understanding is of the word that it uses. What has happened here is that the public had become accustomed to calling vacuum bottles by the word "thermos." If a buyer walked into a retail store asking for a thermos bottle, meaning any vacuum bottle and not specifically plaintiff's product, the fact that the appellation "vacuum bottle" was available to him is of no significance. The two terms had become synonymous; in fact, defendant's survey showed that the public was far more inclined to use the word "thermos" to describe a container that keeps its contents hot or cold than the phrase "vacuum bottle."

Appellant asserts that the courts in a number of cases have upheld the continued exclusive use of a dual functioning trademark, which both identifies the class of product as well as its source. As this court recently indicated:

> a mark is not generic merely because it has *some* significance to the public as an indication of the nature or class of an article.... In order to become generic the *principal* significance of the word must be its indication of the nature or class of an article, rather than an indication of its origin.

Feathercombs, Inc. v. Solo Products Corp., 306 F.2d 251, 256 (2 Cir.1962), cert. denied, 371 U.S. 910, 83 S.Ct. 253, 9 L.Ed.2d 170. But see Marks v. Polaroid Corp., supra, 129 F.Supp. at 270 ("a defendant alleging invalidity of a trademark for genericness must show that to the consuming public as a whole the word has lost all its trademark significance").

Since in this case, the primary significance to the public of the word "thermos" is its indication of the nature and class of an article rather than as an indication of its source, whatever duality of meaning the word still holds for a minority of the public is of little consequence except as a consideration in the framing of a decree. Since the great majority of those members of the public who use the word "thermos" are not aware of any trademark significance, there is not enough dual use to support King–Seeley's claims to monopoly of the word as a trademark.

No doubt, the Aspirin and Cellophane doctrine can be a harsh one for it places a penalty on the manufacturer who has made skillful use of advertising and has popularized his product. However, King–Seeley has enjoyed a commercial monopoly of the word "thermos" for over fifty years. During that period, despite its efforts to protect the trademark, the public has virtually expropriated it as its own. The word having become part of the public domain, it would be unfair to unduly restrict the right of a competitor of King–Seeley to use the word.

The court below, mindful of the fact that some members of the public and a substantial portion of the trade still recognize and use the word "thermos" as a trademark, framed an eminently fair decree designed to afford King–Seeley as much future protection as was possible. The decree provides that defendant must invariably precede the use of the word "thermos" by the possessive of the name "Aladdin"; that the defendant must confine its use of "thermos" to the lower-case "t"; and that it may never use the words "original" or "genuine" in describing its product. In addition, plaintiff is entitled to retain the exclusive right to all of its present forms of the trademark "Thermos" without change. These conditions provide a sound and proper balancing of the competitive disadvantage to defendants arising out of plaintiff's exclusive use of the word "thermos" and the risk that those who recognize "Thermos" as a trademark will be deceived.

Once a trademark, not always a trademark.

They were once proud trademarks, now they're just names. They failed to take precautions that would have helped them have a long and prosperous life.

We need your help to stay out of there. Whenever you use our name, please use it as a proper adjective in conjunction with our products and services: e.g., Xerox copiers or Xerox financial services. And never as a

verb: "to Xerox" in place of "to copy," or as a noun: "Xeroxes" in place of "copies."

With your help and a precaution or two on our part, it's "Once the Xerox trademark, always the Xerox trademark."

Team Xerox. We document the world.

The courts should be ever alert, as the district court said, "to eliminate confusion and the possibility of deceit." The purchasing public is entitled to know the source of the article it desires to purchase. It is not within our province to speculate whether the dire predictions made by appellant in forceful appellate argument will come to pass. Certain it is that the district court made every endeavor in its judgment to give as much protection to plaintiff as possible. The use by defendant of the now generic word "thermos" was substantially curtailed. Plaintiff's trademark "thermos" was protected in every style of printing except the lower case "thermos" and then the use of the word must be preceded by the possessive of defendant's name "Aladdin" or the possessive of "Aladdin" plus one of defendant's brand names. Any doubt about plaintiff's position in the field is removed by the prohibition against the use by defendant in labeling, advertising or publication of the words "genuine" or "original" in referring to the word "thermos". Furthermore, the district court has given both parties the opportunity to apply to it for such orders and directions as may be warranted in the light of changed circumstances and for the enforcement of compliance or for the punishment of violations. In our opinion the trial court has reached a most equitable solution which gives appropriate consideration to the law and the facts.

Affirmed.

NOTES

1. The *Thermos* court was premature in its optimism about the security to be afforded by the trial court decree. Although Judge Anderson's careful resolution no doubt gave "appropriate consideration to the law and the facts," it did not staunch the further erosion of plaintiff's mark. In 1968 the district court denied Aladdin's petition to modify the injunction, 289 F.Supp. 155, 159 U.S.P.Q. 604 (1968). On Aladdin's appeal, the court of appeals vacated the order of denial, 418 F.2d 31, 163 U.S.P.Q. 65 (2d Cir.1969).

Judge Anderson, who by now had ascended to the court of appeals, was designated to consider the petition on the remand to the district court. Recognizing that "it is unrealistic to assume that the situation has remained unchanged since 1962," and that "more than eight years of widespread use of the word 'thermos' as a generic term must, to a considerable degree, have brought home to the unorganized public, including the approximately 11% who in 1962 recognized and relied upon King–Seeley's trademarks, that there were both the trade name use and the generic use," he held that Aladdin was entitled to a modification of the decree, "which will, first, afford to it, in its advertising material, trade literature and press releases, the use of the word 'thermos' with an initial capital 'T' where such initial capitalization is required by the generally accepted and authoritatively approved rules of grammar, and second, eliminate the requirement that the use of lower case 'thermos,' in its advertising material, trade literature and press releases, be preceded by the possessive of 'Aladdin' or by the possessive of 'Aladdin' with one of Aladdin's brand names provided any such use makes clear that it emanates from Aladdin." 320 F.Supp. 1156, 1159, 166 U.S.P.Q. 381, 383 (D.Conn. 1970).

In Bayer Co. v. United Drug Co., 272 Fed. 505 (2d Cir.1921), Judge Learned Hand took a different approach to arresting the erosion of a mark that had generic connotations. Hand found that for physicians, manufacturing chemists, and probably retail druggists, the term "Aspirin" had always functioned as a trademark signifying the plaintiff, while for the general consuming public the term had become generic, describing acetylsalicylic acid. Hand entered a bifurcated decree enjoining defendant's use of the term in its sales to manufacturing chemists, physicians and retail druggists but permitting its unfettered use in direct sales to the general public. Given the typical ungainliness of names assigned on the basis of a product's chemical formula, could you, as counsel to a pharmaceutical concern, devise a program that would ensure your client full trademark protection in both markets, professional and nonprofessional, identified by Judge Hand?

2. It is a standard bromide of trademark law that a mark's distinctiveness turns on a showing "that the primary significance of the term in the minds of the consuming public is not the product but the producer." Kellogg Co. v. National Biscuit Co., 305 U.S. 111, 118, 59 S.Ct. 109, 113, 83 L.Ed. 73, 39 U.S.P.Q. 296 (1938). The test should be taken with a grain of salt. Few consumers know, or care to know, the name of the company that produced the cereal they had for breakfast. Doubtless, few even care to know that the same anonymous company that produced the last box of cereal also produced the one they are about to buy—so long as the quality of the product is the same.

At least one court read the standard distinctiveness test literally, and with disastrous results. In Anti–Monopoly, Inc. v. General Mills Fun Group, Inc., 684 F.2d 1316, 216 U.S.P.Q. 588 (9th Cir.1982), cert. denied, 459 U.S. 1227, 103 S.Ct. 1234, 75 L.Ed.2d 468 (1983), the court held that the word, "Monopoly" as applied to the popular board game had become generic because consumers associated the word with a product—the board game—rather than with its producer—Parker Brothers. A consumer survey introduced at trial had asked consumers to pick between two alternatives to describe their motivation in purchasing the Monopoly game: "Sixty-five percent chose: 'I want a "Monopoly" game primarily because I am interested in playing "Monopoly," I don't much care who makes it.' Thirty-two percent chose: 'I would like Parker Brothers' Monopoly" game primarily because I like Parker Brothers' products.'" In the court's view, the overwhelming choice of the first alternative indicated that the primary significance of the term to consumers was the product, not the producer. 684 F.2d, at 1324–26.

Congress moved quickly to reverse the *Anti–Monopoly* result. The Trademark Clarification Act of 1984, P.L. 98–620, § 102, 98 Stat. 3335 (1984), amended present section 14(3) of the Lanham Act, 15 U.S.C.A. § 1064(3), dealing with cancellation of registrations, to provide that "[t]he primary significance of the registered mark to the relevant public rather than purchaser motivation shall be the test for determining whether the registered mark has become the generic name of goods or services in connection with which it has been used." The Act also amended section 45's definition of "trademark" to read "[t]he term 'trademark' includes any word, name, symbol, or device or any combination thereof adopted and used by a manufacturer or merchant to identify and distinguish his goods, including a unique product, from those manufactured or sold by others and to indicate the source of the goods, even if that source is unknown." P.L. 98–620, § 103(1).

3. *Preventing Genericide.* What practical steps can a trademark owner take to prevent its mark from falling victim to genericide? What practical steps, in addition to those already undertaken, could King–Seeley have taken to protect its "Thermos" mark?

What legal steps can a trademark owner take to prevent its mark from becoming generic? Competitors' use of the mark on similar goods and services clearly falls within the ambit of trademark infringement. But what rights does the trademark owner have against individuals who use the term descriptively in conversation, dictionaries and television or radio broadcasts? In Selchow & Righter Co. v. McGraw–Hill Book Co., 580 F.2d 25, 198 U.S.P.Q. 577 (2d Cir.1978), plaintiff, registrant of the mark "Scrabble" for use in connection with games, scoring devices, score pads and accessories, obtained a preliminary injunction against defendant's distribution of "The Complete Scrabble Dictionary." The court of appeals agreed with the district court that, because publication of defendant's book "might render the 'SCRABBLE' trademark generic," plaintiff had sufficiently demonstrated the possibility of irreparable injury. 580 F.2d at 27. See Gary C. Robb, Trademark Misuse in Dictionaries: Inadequacy of Existing Legal Action and a Suggested Cure, 65 Marq. L. Rev. 179 (1981).

Compare Illinois High School Assoc. v. GTE Vantage, Inc., 99 F.3d 244, 40 U.S.P.Q.2d 1633 (7th Cir.1996), holding that plaintiff, which had since the 1940's used the trademark "March Madness" to identify its high school basketball tournament, but had failed to control media use of the phrase since the 1980's to designate the NCAA's Final Four championship, could not later stop use of "March Madness" by the NCAA or its licensees. Against plaintiff's argument that the term had not become generic, Chief Judge Richard Posner, wrote, "There is no magic in labels. Let 'March Madness' be called not a quasi-generic term, or a term on its way to becoming generic, but a dual-use term. Whatever you call it, it's a name that the public has affixed to something other than, as well as, the Illinois high school basketball tournament. A trademark owner is not allowed to withdraw from the public domain a name that the public is using to denote someone else's good or service, leaving that someone and his customers speechless. No case so holds, other than the cases involving generic names, but no case holds the contrary, either. It is an issue of first impression, and we think that for the sake of protecting effective communication it should be resolved against trademark protection, thus assimilating dual-use or multiple-use terms to generic terms." 99 F.3d at 247.

Do the antidilution provisions added to the Lanham Act in 1996, page 299 below, offer a legal basis for enjoining non-trademark uses of marks? According to Judge Posner, antidilution statutes "do protect the trademark owner from the erosion of the distinctiveness and prestige of a trademark caused by the sale of other goods or services under the same name (for example, the use of 'Tiffany & Co.' as the name of a hamburger stand, or simply a proliferation of borrowings that, while not degrading the original seller's mark, are so numerous as to deprive the mark of its distinctiveness and hence impact), even though there is no confusion of source. But the existence of a mark that designates a particular source is presupposed. When a trademark becomes generic, such as 'aspirin' or 'thermos,' and so loses trademark protection, because the public, perhaps egged on by the omnipresent media, decides to use the trademark to designate not the particular manufacturer's brand but the entire product comprising all the competing brands, the trademark is dead no matter how vigorously the holder has tried to prevent this usage." Id.

4. *Federal Trade Commission.* In May, 1978 the Federal Trade Commission filed a petition under Lanham Act § 14, 15 U.S.C.A. § 1064, seeking cancellation of the trademark, "Formica," on the ground that the term had become generic as applied to "laminated sheets of wood, fabric, or paper impregnated with synthetic resin and consolidated under heat and pressure, for use on table tops, furniture and wall panelling." Petition for Cancellation, F.T.C. v. Formica Corp., 200 U.S.P.Q. 182, 185 (T.T.A.B. May 31, 1978). The move produced a small furor among advertisers and the trademark bar. One result of the ensuing congressional inquiry was that Congress cut off funds for the F.T.C. suit. On June 13, 1980, the Trademark Trial and Appeal Board dismissed the action with prejudice. 209 U.S.P.Q. 255 (1980).

For a review and analysis of the *Formica* petition and the ensuing judicial and legislative developments, see John M. Fietkiewicz, Section 14 of the Lanham Act—FTC Authority to Challenge Generic Trademarks, 48 Fordham L. Rev. 437 (1980).

5. *Expired Patents.* Should a trademark used in connection with patented subject matter fall into the public domain upon expiration of the patent? In Kellogg Co. v. National Biscuit Co., 305 U.S. 111, 59 S.Ct. 109, 83 L.Ed. 73, 39 U.S.P.Q. 296 (1938), the Court ruled that it should: "Since during the life of the patent 'Shredded Wheat' was the general designation of the patented product, there passed to the public on the expiration of the patent, not only the right to make the article as it was made during the patent period, but also the right to apply thereto the name by which it had become known." 305 U.S. at 118.

Kellogg's logic might appear to imply that when the trademark *is* the patented subject matter—where, for example, a product's configuration is both a patentable invention and an indication of source—even greater reason exists for trademark protection to terminate upon the expiration of the patent. Nonetheless, in TrafFix Devices, Inc. v. Marketing Displays, Inc., 532 U.S. 23, 121 S.Ct. 1255, 149 L.Ed.2d 164, 58 U.S.P.Q.2d 1001 (2001), the Supreme Court observed that the existence of a patent is no more than evidence of the functionality that will bar trademark protection. "A utility patent is strong evidence that the features therein claimed are functional. If trade dress protection is sought for those features the strong evidence of functionality based on the previous patent adds great weight to the statutory presumption that features are deemed functional until proved otherwise by the party seeking trade dress protection. Where the expired patent claimed the features in question, one who seeks to establish trade dress protection must carry the heavy burden of showing that the feature is not functional, for instance by showing that it is merely an ornamental, incidental, or arbitrary aspect of the device." 121 S.Ct. at 1260.

6. *Bibliographic Note.* The question of generic marks has provoked a lively debate in the literature. See Ralph H. Folsom & Larry L. Teply, Trademarked Generic Words, 89 Yale L.J. 1323 (1980); Jerre B. Swann, The Economic Approach to Genericism: A Reply to Folsom and Teply, 70 Trademark Rep. 243 (1980); Jerre B. Swann & Vincent N. Palladino, Surveying "Genericness": A Critique of Folsom and Teply, 78 Trademark Rep. 179 (1988); Ralph H. Folsom & Larry L. Teply, A Reply to Swann and Palladino's Critique of Folsom and Teply's Model Survey, 78 Trademark Rep. 197 (1988); A. Samuel Oddi, Assessing "Genericness": Another View, 78 Trademark Rep. 560 (1988).

See also Itamar Simonson, An Empirical Investigation of the Meaning and Measurement of "Genericness," 84 Trademark Rep. 199 (1994); Lee B. Burgunder, An Economic Approach to Trademark Genericism, 23 Am. Bus. L.J. 391 (1985).

b. "Deceptive ... Matter"

In re Budge Manufacturing Co.

United States Court of Appeals, Federal Circuit, 1988.
857 F.2d 773, 8 U.S.P.Q.2d 1259.

NIES, Circuit Judge.

Budge Manufacturing Co., Inc., appeals from the final decision of the United States Trademark Trial and Appeal Board refusing registration of LOVEE LAMB for "automotive seat covers," application Serial No. 507,974 filed November 9, 1984. The basis for rejection is that the term LAMB is deceptive matter within the meaning of section 2(a) of the Lanham Act, 15 U.S.C. § 1052(a) (1982), as applied to Budge's goods which are made wholly from synthetic fibers. We affirm.

Opinion

Section 2(a) of the Lanham Act bars registration of a mark which: "Consists of or comprises ... deceptive ... matter...." As stated in Application of Automatic Radio Mfg. Co., 404 F.2d 1391, 1396, 160 U.S.P.Q. 233, 236 (CCPA 1969): "The proscription [of section 2(a)] is not against misdescriptive terms unless they are also deceptive." Thus, that a mark or part of a mark may be inapt or misdescriptive as applied to an applicant's goods does not make it "deceptive." Id. (AUTOMATIC RADIO not a deceptive mark for air conditioners, ignition systems, and antennas). Recognizing that premise, the Trademark Trial and Appeal Board has sought to articulate a standard by which "deceptive matter" under section 2(a) can be judged. In this case, the board applied the three-part test which was stated in In re Shapely, Inc., 231 U.S.P.Q. 72, 73 (TTAB 1986): (1) whether the term is misdescriptive as applied to the goods, (2) if so, whether anyone would be likely to believe the misrepresentation, and (3) whether the misrepresentation would materially affect a potential purchaser's decision to buy the goods.

Budge argues that the board was bound to follow the standard articulated in In re Simmons, Inc., 192 U.S.P.Q. 331 (TTAB 1976). Per Budge, *Simmons* sets forth a different standard in that it requires as a minimum that "the mark convey some information, upon which an intended customer may reasonably rely, concerning something about the character, quality, function, composition or use of the goods to induce the purchase thereof, but which information, in fact, is misleadingly false." Id. at 332.

The standard applied by the board for determining deceptive matter in section 2(a) cases has not been uniformly articulated in some material respects. For example, in at least one opinion an *intent* to mislead was required to establish section 2(a) deceptiveness. See Steinberg Bros., Inc. v. Middletown Rubber Corp., 137 U.S.P.Q. 319, 321 (TTAB 1963). However, while phrased differently, we discern no material difference between the standard set forth in *Shapely* and that in *Simmons*. Budge points to no substantive difference and, indeed, merely quarrels over the different result here from that in *Simmons*. Thus, we need not address the question of the extent to which panels of the board are required to follow prior decisions of other board panels.

What is more significant, in any event, is that this court is bound only by its own precedent, none of which Budge discusses. Although we will give deference in appropriate circumstances to a board's decision on a question of law, we are, of course, not bound by such rulings. Where the issue relates to deceptive misdescriptiveness within the meaning of 2(a), we are in general agreement with the standard set out by the board in *Shapely,* with the following amplification in part drawn from *Simmons:*

    (1) Is the term misdescriptive of the character, quality, function, composition or use of the goods?

    (2) If so, are prospective purchasers likely to believe that the misdescription actually describes the goods?

    (3) If so, is the misdescription likely to affect the decision to purchase?

In *ex parte* prosecution, the burden is initially on the Patent and Trademark Office (PTO) to put forth sufficient evidence that the mark for which registration is sought meets the above criteria of unregistrability. Mindful that the PTO has limited facilities for acquiring evidence—it cannot, for example, be expected to conduct a survey of the marketplace or obtain consumer affidavits—we conclude that the evidence of record here is sufficient to establish a *prima facie* case of deceptiveness. That evidence shows with respect to the three-pronged test:

    (1) Budge admits that its seat covers are not made from lamb or sheep products. Thus, the term LAMB is misdescriptive of its goods.

(2) Seat covers for various vehicles can be and are made from natural lambskin and sheepskin. Applicant itself makes automobile seat covers of natural sheepskin. Lambskin is defined, inter alia, as fine-grade sheepskin. See Webster's Third New International Dictionary 639 (unabr. 1976). The board's factual inference is reasonable that purchasers are likely to believe automobile seat covers denominated by the term LAMB or SHEEP are actually made from natural sheep or lamb skins.

(3) Evidence of record shows that natural sheepskin and lambskin is more expensive than simulated skins and that natural and synthetic skins have different characteristics. Thus, the misrepresentation is likely to affect the decision to purchase.

Faced with this *prima facie* case against registration, Budge had the burden to come forward with countering evidence to overcome the rejection. It wholly failed to do so.

Budge argues that its use of LAMB as part of its mark is not misdescriptive when considered in connection with the text in its advertising, which states that the cover is of "simulated sheepskin." Some, but not all, of Budge's specimen labels also have this text. This evidence is unpersuasive. In R. Neumann & Co. v. Overseas Shipments, Inc., 326 F.2d 786, 51 CCPA 946, 140 U.S.P.Q. 276 (1964), a similar argument was made that the mark DURAHYDE on shoes was not deceptive as an indication of leather because of tags affixed to the shoes proclaiming the legend "Outwears leather." In discounting the evidence, the court stated: "The legends constitute advertisement material separate and apart from any trademark significance." Id. at 790, 51 CCPA at 951, 140 U.S.P.Q. at 279. To the same effect is In re Bonide Chemical Co., 46 F.2d 705, 18 CCPA 909, 8 U.S.P.Q. 297 (1931). There the court held, with respect to a clarifying statement made in advertising circulars, which the applicant urged negated the deceptive nature of the mark, "This argument is beside the issue. It is the word of the mark, not the statement of an advertising circular which appellant seeks to register...." Id. at 708, 18 CCPA at 913, 8 U.S.P.Q. at 300.

Thus, we conclude that the board properly discounted Budge's advertising and labeling which indicate the actual fabric content. Misdescriptiveness of a term may be negated by its meaning in the context of the whole mark inasmuch as the combination is seen together and makes a unitary impression. A.F. Gallun & Sons Corp. v. Aristocrat Leather Prods., Inc., 135 U.S.P.Q. 459, 460 (TTAB 1962) (COPY CALF not misdescriptive, but rather suggests *imitation* of calf skin). The same is not true with respect to explanatory statements in advertising or on labels which purchasers may or may not note and which may or may not always be provided. The statutory provision bars registration of *a mark* comprising deceptive matter. Congress has said that the advantages of registration may not be extended to a mark which deceives the public. Thus, the mark standing alone must pass muster, for that is what the applicant seeks to register, not extraneous explanatory statements.

Budge next argues that no reasonable purchaser would expect to purchase lambskin automobile seat covers because none made of lambskin are on the market. Only sheepskin automobile seat covers are being made, per Budge. Not only was no evidence submitted on the point Budge seeks to make, only statements of Budge's attorney, but also the argument is without substance. The board properly equated sheepskin and lambskin based on the dictionary definition which indicates that the terms may be used interchangeably. In addition, while Budge would discount the evidence presented that bicycle and airline seat coverings are made of lambskin, we conclude that it does support the board's finding that there is nothing incongruous about automobile seat covers being made from lambskin. We also agree with the board's conclusion that any differences between sheepskin and lambskin would not be readily apparent to potential purchasers of automobile seat covers. The board's finding here that purchasers are likely to believe the misrepresentation is not clearly erroneous.

To overturn the board's finding that misdescribing synthetic fabric as "lamb" would affect a purchaser's decision to purchase the item, Budge merely reiterates its argument that its advertising negates the possibility of misdescriptiveness. We find that argument no more persuasive in this context than previously and, in any event, wholly unresponsive to this issue.

Finally, we note the evidence of Budge's extensive sales since 1974 under the mark. However, it is too well established for argument that a mark which includes deceptive matter is barred from registration and cannot acquire distinctiveness.

Conclusion

None of the facts found by the board have been shown to be clearly erroneous nor has the board erred as a matter of law. Accordingly, we affirm the board's decision that Budge's mark LOVEE LAMB for automobile seat covers made from synthetic fibers is deceptive within the meaning of 15 U.S.C. § 1052(a) and is, thus, barred from registration.

AFFIRMED.

The opinion of NICHOLS, Senior Circuit Judge, concurring, is omitted.

c. *Confusing Similarity to Prior Marks*

In re N.A.D., Inc.

United States Court of Appeals, Federal Circuit, 1985.
754 F.2d 996, 224 U.S.P.Q. 969.

RICH, Circuit Judge.

This appeal is from the February 29, 1984 decision of the United States Patent and Trademark Office (PTO) Trademark Trial and Appeal Board (board), 221 U.S.P.Q. 1115, affirming the PTO Trademark Attorney's refusal to register a trademark by reason of 15 U.S.C. § 1052(d), section 2(d) of the Trademark Act of 1946. We reverse.

The mark sought to be registered is NARKOMED. The goods named in the application are "anesthesia machines for use in surgery." Application to register was filed May 7, 1980, alleging first use April 3, 1972. The rejection is predicated on two prior registrations: (1) Reg. No. 982,657, April 23, 1974, or [sic] NARCO MEDICAL SERVICES for "rental and leasing of hospital and surgical equipment and consultation services relating to the operation of such equipment." This service mark registration issued to Air–Shields, Inc. and on April 26, 1978 was assigned to Narco Scientific Industries, Inc. (2) Reg. No. 1,036,695, March 30, 1976, of NARCO and design (see board opinion for illustration) for a long list of specialized medical equipment including, as most relevant here, "apparatus for administration of anesthesia." This registration issued to Narco Scientific Industries, Inc. which changed its name to Narco Scientific, Inc. The board opinion contains the full list of goods named in the registration.

The examining attorney and the board were both of the view that registration must be refused under § 2(d)[1] because, in their commonly held opinions, on which they had no doubts, "confusion between the applicant's mark and the cited registered marks is likely," to quote from the board's opinion. Applicant's arguments relying on differences in the marks, sophistication of purchasers of the equipment or services, and the high prices thereof were summarily dismissed as "not persuasive." As to registration (2), supra, there is no question that identical goods are named by both applicant and registrant. As to the services in registration (1), they are clearly closely related to applicant's goods, all being in the medical equipment field.

As this court and its predecessor, the Court of Customs and Patent Appeals, have often said, each likelihood-of-confusion trademark case must be determined on its own facts. Beside that, however, the salient feature of this case is an argument, which has several times been fully dealt with in earlier cases, based on agreements between appellant and the owner of the prior registrations relied on to support the rejection containing a consent to the use and registration of NARKOMED by appellant.

The agreements containing the consent to use and register came about as follows. Applicant-appellant, N.A.D., Inc., which also does business as North American Drager, is a Pennsylvania corporation the majority of the stock of which is owned by Draegerwerk AG, of Luebeck, Federal Republic of Germany. Draegerwerk AG brought cancellation proceedings to cancel the two reference registrations herein, now both owned by Narco Scientific, Inc. These cancellations were inter partes proceedings extending over

---

1. "No trademark by which the goods of the applicant may be distinguished from the goods of others shall be refused registration on the principal register on account of its nature unless it—

. . .

(d) Consists of or comprises a mark which so resembles a mark registered in the Patent and Trademark Office ... as to be likely, when applied to the goods of the applicant, to cause confusion, or to cause mistake, or to deceive...."

several years in which competitors in a relatively restricted field were involved, the disputes involving many marks other than NARKOMED. By written settlement agreements, Draegerwerk AG and N.A.D. undertook to abandon certain pending trademark registration applications and to discontinue the use of four different NARKO–marks, provision being made for a phasing-out period. Money changed hands. In the course of it all, the other party, Narco Scientific Inc., owner of the two references, expressly acknowledged N.A.D.'s right "to the use and registration of the trademark NARKOMED ... for use in the sale of hospital and medical equipment." The first agreement so providing was in November 1975 and the second one, reaffirming that provision, was in September 1979. While we are uninformed as to all the details of the disputes and negotiations, these competitors clearly thought out their commercial interests with care. We think it highly unlikely that they would have deliberately created a situation in which the sources of their respective products would be confused by their customers. As was said by our predecessor court in In re E.I. duPont de Nemours & Co., 476 F.2d 1357, 1362, 177 U.S.P.Q. 563, 568 (CCPA 1973), "It can be safely taken as fundamental that reputable businessmen-users of valuable trademarks have no interest in *causing* public confusion."

The Examining Attorney, while citing *DuPont* and saying that "great weight is to be accorded consent agreements," interpreted that case, erroneously, as allowing registration only "where the goods of the respective parties were disparate, and the markets and trade channels were different." She held that "Notwithstanding an agreement between the parties, the likelihood of confusion cannot be avoided." She concluded that "refusal of registration is appropriate notwithstanding the consent agreement." In affirming, the board refused to give any weight to the contractual consent to use and to register, saying:

> An *appropriate* consent agreement can tip the scales in favor of an applicant *if there is doubt* as to the likelihood of confusion. * * * In light of the *fact* that no doubt exists [in the board's mind] and the parties have failed to *specify how* customer confusion can be avoided, we do not find that the consent agreement is an appropriate basis upon which to base registration. [Emphasis ours.]

... Consents come in different forms and under circumstances in infinite variety. They are, however, but one factor to be taken into account with all of the other relevant circumstances bearing on the likelihood of confusion referred to in § 2(d). The board spent much of its opinion analyzing and dissecting the *marks* in arriving at its opinion that *they* are "confusingly similar," and then finding it "axiomatic that confusion is likely when confusingly similar marks are used to identify closely related goods and services." We have never found anything axiomatic about the application of § 2(d) to fact situations, especially when consent agreements are involved. All aspects of the fact situation must be appraised and the situation judged as a whole.

In the present case, we start with the marks. They are not identical, as the marks have been in some other cases such as *DuPont* [476 F.2d 1357

(CCPA 1973)], *United,* [508 F.2d 1341 (CCPA 1975)] and *Loew's* [197 U.S.P.Q. 183 (TTAB 1977)]. Appellant's mark is NARKOMED; the reference marks are NARCO and NARCO MEDICAL SERVICES. An alert purchaser could readily distinguish them. We turn next to the goods. With reference to NARCO, there is identity; with reference to NARCO MEDICAL SERVICES there is not. The most that can be said is that appellant's anesthesia machines and Narco Scientific's rental and leasing services are both in the medical field. A most important factor, in our view, is the specific nature of appellant's goods. The record shows the machines to be elaborate, sizeable, complex pieces of technical apparatus of the kind which would be purchased only in consultation with an anesthesiologist or someone with equivalent technical knowledge. In other words, only very sophisticated purchasers are here involved who would buy with great care and unquestionably know the source of the goods. There would be no likelihood of confusing source merely by reason of the similarity between NARCO and NARKOMED. Cf. In re General Electric Co., 304 F.2d 688, 134 U.S.P.Q. 190 (CCPA 1962) (VULCAN and VULKENE for commercial electrical wire held readily distinguishable). Another factor is the cost of appellant's apparatus. Though not of record, it would obviously be considerable—definitely not in the class of the cigarettes and smokers pipes involved in *Loew's.*

Taking all of the above facts into account, it is not at all surprising that the owner of the reference marks was willing to consent to the use and registration by N.A.D. Inc. of NARKOMED for "hospital and medical equipment." This consent, moreover, having been given by a competitor well acquainted with the realities of the business suffices to persuade us, when taken together with all of the other facts, that the board and the Examining Attorney were simply wrong in their opinions that there would be a likelihood of confusion, and we so hold. "A mere *assumption* that confusion is likely will rarely prevail against uncontroverted evidence from those on the firing line that it is not." *DuPont,* supra, 476 F.2d at 1363, 177 U.S.P.Q. at 568.

The decision of the board affirming the refusal to register is *reversed.*

REVERSED.

d.   *"Merely Descriptive or Deceptively Misdescriptive"*

Application of Sun Oil Co.

United States Court of Customs and Patent Appeals, 1970.
426 F.2d 401, 165 U.S.P.Q. 718.

ALMOND, Judge.

Sun Oil Company brings this appeal from the decision of the Trademark Trial and Appeal Board, affirming the examiner's refusal to allow appellant's application to register "Custom–Blended" for gasoline on the ground that the mark is merely descriptive of applicant's goods within the meaning of section 2(e)(1) of the Trademark Act of 1946 (15 U.S.C.A. § 1052(e)(1)) and because the evidence submitted has not clearly established a secondary meaning, denoting that the mark has become distinctive of appellant's goods, within section 2(f) of the Act (15 U.S.C.A. § 1052(f)).

The application seeking registration on the Principal Register alleges use since 1956. The mark is displayed on special pumps, called "blending pumps," at appellant's service stations. The application is designated a continuation of an earlier application filed July 13, 1961, in which registration on the Principal Register was sought for the same mark for gasoline and refused by the Trademark Trial and Appeal Board on the ground that the mark was merely a descriptive connotation to purchasers of applicant's goods.

In his Answer, the examiner predicated refusal of registration on the ground that Custom–Blended is merely descriptive of appellant's goods within the meaning of section 2(e)(1) because it is so highly descriptive of appellant's blended gasoline that it is incapable of becoming distinctive as claimed. It was the examiner's opinion that the term Custom–Blended merely informs purchasers that various grades of gasoline from appellant's blending pumps are custom blended for them; that the word "custom" is commonly used to indicate things made to order; that it has very little trademark significance when used in connection with blended gasoline; that appellant is not entitled to exclusive appropriation of this term, which so aptly describes custom-blended gasoline; and that the conclusion derived from surveys conducted by appellant is that purchasers who are acquainted with appellant's Blue Sunoco gasoline know that such gasoline is custom blended.

In affirming refusal of registration, the board stated that granted that the generic terms for appellant's blended gasolines are pump-blended and multiple-grade gasolines, there is no question that " 'Custom–Blended' has a merely descriptive significance in that it will immediately indicate to patrons of applicant's service stations that the various grades of gasoline dispensed thereat are custom blended to their needs and requirements;" that in view thereof and the decision on applicant's prior application, it was incumbent upon applicant to show that the facts and circumstances since that decision have changed in that " 'Custom–Blended' now serves as an indication of origin of applicant's gasoline to the general public;" that the case, therefore, turned upon the sufficiency of applicant's evidence in that regard; that "the only definite conclusion that can be drawn from the surveys is that purchasers who are acquainted with applicant's 'Sunoco' gasoline know that such gasoline is custom blended;" that this manifestly does not support applicant's assertion that Custom–Blended has acquired a secondary meaning as an indication of origin for gasoline, and that upon the record presented Custom–Blended does not possess anything "other than a descriptive significance to purchasers of gasoline."

We have given a synoptic analysis of the board's able, well-considered and exhaustive opinion without reiterating essential facts of record. These facts are detailed in their essence and relevancy and supportive of the board's conclusions so clearly and aptly enunciated in its decision. We, therefore, incorporate herein by reference the opinion of the board and affirm its refusal of registration. The decision of the Trademark Trial and Appeal Board is, accordingly, affirmed.

RICH, Acting Chief Judge, concurring.

I agree with the result reached by the majority which is supported by an opinion largely relying on and incorporating by reference the opinion of the board. While I do not disagree with anything said in the majority's opinion, I do not accord the survey evidence, by which it was attempted to show "secondary meaning," the significance apparently accorded it by the board. The examiner accorded it none. I do not agree with the board's statement that "This case turns upon the sufficiency of applicant's evidence" of "secondary meaning."

The examiner in this case was of the view, as the board reported, that Custom–Blended "is *so highly* descriptive of applicant's blended gasoline that it is *incapable* of becoming distinctive as claimed." (My emphasis.) If that is so, registration must be refused under 15 U.S.C.A. § 1052(e)(1) no matter what evidence of alleged "secondary meaning" is adduced; in other words, under the facts of this case the law proscribes the possibility of a de jure "secondary meaning," notwithstanding the existence of 15 U.S.C.A. § 1052(f) and a de facto "secondary meaning."

In my opinion, Custom–Blended is so highly descriptive that it cannot, under the law, be accorded trademark rights even though at some times, or to some people, or in some places, it has a de facto secondary meaning. My view was expressed by the examiner. I think that conclusively disposes of the matter. While I see no objection to pointing out to appellant that its evidence has not established "secondary meaning," I am unwilling to lead appellant or others to think that the fault was in the quantity or quality of its evidence rather than in the descriptiveness of the words sought to be registered. Appellant should not be encouraged to try again to prove "secondary meaning." The only particular in which I do not fully agree with the examiner is that he said the word "custom" in Custom–Blended "has very little trademark significance." I think it has none.

Appellant has argued that the descriptive term for its gasoline is "pump-blended." I do not question that that is a descriptive—or as appellant calls it "generic"—term; but a product may have more than one generically descriptive name. Because one merchandiser has latched onto one of the descriptive terms does not mean it can force its competitors to limit themselves to the use of the others, which appellant, it seems to me, is trying to do here. *All* of the generic names for a product belong in the public domain. The product itself, for example, is called gasoline in the United States but petrol in England. Clearly both of those names must remain free of proprietary claims, in either country. So it is, in my view, with respect to pump-blended and custom-blended. The examiner stated the factual basis for this view in pointing out that "custom," as in custom-built, custom-service, custom-cut, custom-made, custom-tailored, custom-work, etc., merely indicates that it is done according to the customer's desire. That is exactly how appellant's gasolines are pump-blended—to give the customer what he asks for. I can think of no descriptive term which is more apt.

FISHER, District Judge, dissenting.

Under the doctrine of "secondary meaning," a trademark, though originally descriptive of a type of product, is nonetheless entitled to registration if the mark has, by association with a business, come primarily to identify its user, rather than the product, to that part of the public interested in contracting with the trademark user. Whether a descriptive mark has acquired secondary meaning depends upon the particular facts of each case.

Briefly, it has been shown that appellant has used the mark in question for its gasoline exclusively and continuously over a period of some twelve years. There is evidence of extensive advertising of and sales of large volumes of gasoline under that mark during this period. Surveys of record suggest that in at least two areas where there are other marketers of multi-grade, pump-blended gasoline, the term Custom–Blended is associated in the public mind with this appellant in a preponderance which can only be accounted for by recognition of origin. There is no evidence which would imply that the mark is of such a descriptive nature that granting trade-mark rights therein to the user would deprive others of their right to normal use of the language.

In light of these facts, it is respectfully submitted that the decision of the Trademark Trial and Appeal Board should be reversed and registration granted on the basis that the mark Custom–Blended has acquired second-ary meaning within Section 2(f) of the Act (15 U.S.C.A. § 1052(f)).

e.   "Primarily Geographically Descriptive or Deceptively Misdescriptive"

In re Loew's Theatres, Inc.

United States Court of Appeals, Federal Circuit, 1985.
769 F.2d 764, 226 U.S.P.Q. 865.

NIES, Circuit Judge.

This appeal is from the decision of the Trademark Trial and Appeal Board sustaining a refusal to register the mark DURANGO for chewing tobacco. The board held that the subject mark was unregistrable under § 2(e)(2) of the Lanham Act (15 U.S.C. § 1052(e)(2)), which bars registra-tion of a mark which is "primarily geographically deceptively misdescrip-tive" of the goods to which it is applied. We affirm.

I.

Background

The subject of this appeal is Application Serial No. 341,663, filed on December 14, 1981, in the U.S. Patent and Trademark Office (PTO) by

Loew's Theatres, Inc., doing business through its Lorillard Division (hereinafter LTI) for the mark DURANGO for chewing tobacco, claiming use since on or before September 9, 1981. Registration was initially refused on the Principal Register on the grounds that the mark appeared to be either primarily geographically descriptive or deceptively misdescriptive of the goods and was, thus, barred from registration on the Principal Register pursuant to § 2(e) of the Lanham Act. In support of this rejection, the examiner relied on information in the Columbia Lippincott Gazetteer of the World, Columbia University Press (1952). The examiner concluded that because the reference disclosed that tobacco was a crop of the Durango, Mexico area, it would be reasonable for the purchasing public to expect chewing tobacco bearing the name DURANGO to have its origin in that area. He advised that additional evidence of registrability could be filed.

LTI sought to overcome this rejection by argument that: (1) LTI's existing Registration No. 923,094 for the mark DURANGOS for cigars on the Principal Register entitled it to registration of the subject mark, and (2) the evidence on which the examiner relied was insufficient to indicate that the purchasing public would make a goods/place association between tobacco and the Durango, Mexico area.

The examining attorney adhered to his rejection and buttressed the record with respect to the geographic significance of the name Durango by reference to the geographical names section of Webster's New Collegiate Dictionary, G. & C. Merriam Company, Springfield, Massachusetts (1979). In view of the substantial population of the state and city of Durango in Mexico, he concluded that Durango could not be deemed a "minor, obscure, or remote" geographic place name. Further, the examining attorney believed that the evidence of tobacco production in Durango established a *prima facie* case that there would be a goods/place association by the public, as required for a rejection under § 2(e), citing In re Nantucket, Inc., 677 F.2d 95, 213 U.S.P.Q. 889 (CCPA 1982). While acknowledging LTI's ownership of the registration for DURANGOS cigars, the examining attorney deemed such evidence insufficient to establish distinctiveness of the mark sought to be registered. He noted the continued absence of any evidence concerning the length and manner of LTI's use of the mark, the nature and extent of advertising, or any other efforts by LTI which would tend to establish that the mark had acquired distinctiveness and thereby entitle LTI to a registration in accordance with § 2(f) (15 U.S.C. § 1052(f)). Finally, he stated that, since LTI's goods did not come from the place named, the mark was being refused registration as primarily geographically deceptively misdescriptive.

Appellant did not controvert the statement concerning origin of the goods nor submit any additional evidence tending to establish secondary meaning in the mark sought to be registered. Instead, appeal was taken to the Trademark Trial and Appeal Board (board). In a thorough opinion reported at 223 U.S.P.Q. 513 (1984), adhered to on reconsideration, the board upheld the examining attorney's refusal of registration. This appeal, pursuant to 15 U.S.C. § 1071, followed.

II.

Issues

1. Did the PTO establish a *prima facie* case that the mark DURAN-GO is primarily geographically deceptively misdescriptive for chewing tobacco within the meaning of § 2(e)?

Since we conclude that a *prima facie* case was proved, the following issue must also be addressed.

2. Is registration, nevertheless, mandated by LTI's ownership of Registration No. 923,094 for the mark DURANGOS for cigars?

III.

Analysis

A.

Under § 2(e)(2) of the Lanham Act, a mark may not be registered on the Principal Register if the mark "when applied to the goods of the applicant is ... primarily geographically deceptively misdescriptive." This provision of the statute was extensively analyzed in the precedential decision In re Nantucket, Inc., 677 F.2d 95, 213 U.S.P.Q. 889 (CCPA 1982). That case concerned the registrability on the Principal Register of the mark NANTUCKET for shirts not originating in Nantucket, Massachusetts. The PTO had argued to the court in the *Nantucket* case that a *prima facie* case of unregistrability was shown simply by proof that the mark was the name of a geographic place known generally to the public. The court rejected this argument, holding that in order to make a valid rejection under § 2(e), the PTO not only had to establish that the mark was the name of a generally known geographic place, but also that the public would be likely to believe that the goods for which the mark is sought to be registered originate in that place. The latter requirement was held to follow from the statutory language that the descriptiveness or deceptive misdescriptiveness of the mark must be determined as "applied to the goods of the applicant." In this respect the statute reflects the common law principle that a geographic term, used in a fictitious, arbitrary, or fanciful manner, is protectable like any other nondescriptive term. Usage in such manner is not "primarily" as a geographic designation.

While the above cited precedent requires a goods/place association to support a refusal to register under § 2(e)(2), it does not follow that such association embraces only instances where the place is well-known or noted for the goods, a position which the *Nantucket* applicant, as well as LTI, have urged. The court, in *Nantucket,* did not adopt that position. Rather, our precedent continues to hold that to establish a "primarily geographically deceptively misdescriptive" bar, the PTO must show only a reasonable basis for concluding that the public is likely to believe the mark identifies the place from which the goods originate and that the goods do not come from there.[6]

6. In contrast, if the place is noted for the particular goods, a mark for such goods which do not originate there is likely to be deceptive under § 2(a) and not registrable under any circumstances.

B.

In support of its finding that more than a *de minimus* segment of the public would reasonably associate chewing tobacco with the city and/or state of Durango, Mexico, the PTO relies on the evidence of record which shows that tobacco is a crop produced and marketed in that area. This finding may only be overturned if clearly erroneous.

LTI attacks the sufficiency of the evidence of record on several grounds:

1. The Gazetteer relied upon by the PTO shows that Durango is also the name of towns in Colorado and in Spain. Therefore, per appellant, Durango would not be associated with Mexico's tobacco region of that name.

2. The PTO produced no evidence that the public would actually make the asserted association.

Contrary to LTI's position, we conclude that the PTO made a *prima facie* showing of a goods/place association between tobacco and the geographic name Durango. Durango (Mexico) is not an obscure place name to the Mexican population of this country nor to reasonably informed non-Mexicans. The cited Gazetteer shows tobacco to be one in a short list of principal crops of the region. No more can be expected from the PTO in the way of proof. The PTO does not have means to conduct a marketing survey as LTI would require. The practicalities of the limited resources available to the PTO are routinely taken into account in reviewing its administrative action. Accordingly, it was suggested in the *Nantucket* decision that precisely the type of evidence utilized here would establish a *prima facie* case by the PTO. 677 F.2d at 106, 213 U.S.P.Q. at 898 (Nies, J., concurring). The trademark examining attorney, in prosecuting the subject application, followed those suggestions which have been specifically endorsed by the board in this and other cases. We affirm that a *prima facie* case can be established by the type of evidence of record here where the question concerns the registrability of a geographic name.

Finally, it does not detract from the *prima facie* case made by the PTO that there are a few other uses of Durango as a geographic name, such as Durango, Colorado. The PTO's burden is simply to establish that there is a reasonable predicate for its conclusion that the public would be likely to make the particular goods/place association on which it relies. That there is more than one place bearing the name or that one place is better known than another is not dispositive. The issue is not the fame or exclusivity of the place name, but the likelihood that a particular place will be associated with particular goods. Thus, the mark DURANGO for skis might also be barred (without proof of secondary meaning) if it were shown that Durango, Colorado, is a ski resort.

We conclude that, on the record here, the findings underlying the *prima facie* case that DURANGO for tobacco falls within the proscription of § 2(e)(2) are not clearly erroneous.

C.

In rejecting the subject application, the trademark examining attorney followed a two-step examination process, first, determining whether the mark applied for came within the bar of § 2(e) and, second, evaluating whether the applicant had overcome it with evidence of distinctiveness in accordance with § 2(f).

LTI argues that, as the owner of an "incontestible" registration for virtually the identical mark for closely related goods, i.e., DURANGOS for cigars, registration of the subject mark is mandated. . . .

The basic flaw in LTI's analysis is that each application for registration of a mark for particular goods must be separately evaluated. Nothing in the statute provides a right *ipso facto* to register a mark for additional goods when items are added to a company's line or substituted for other goods covered by a registration. Nor do the PTO rules afford any greater rights. Under Rule 2.41(b), in appropriate cases, a prior registration on the Principal Register for the same mark "may" be accepted as "evidence" of distinctiveness, but the same rule reserves to the PTO discretion to require additional proof. The examining attorney and the board considered LTI's registration but were unpersuaded as to the sufficiency of this proof alone in view of the absence of any evidence concerning the extent of actual usage. LTI was unable or unwilling to supply *any* additional evidence to support a claim of distinctiveness.

The issue of acquired distinctiveness is a question of fact. We can not say that a requirement for some additional evidence was unduly burdensome or unreasonable or that the finding that distinctiveness was not established is clearly erroneous.

IV.

The trademark examining attorney acted entirely in accordance with the statute, the PTO rules, and precedent of this court in his refusal to register DURANGO for chewing tobacco on the record of this case. For the foregoing reasons, the decision of the Trademark Trial and Appeal Board upholding the rejection under § 2(e)(2) is *affirmed.*

AFFIRMED.

NOTES

1. *"Primarily Merely a Surname."* In addition to barring registration of marks that are merely descriptive or deceptively misdescriptive, primarily geographically descriptive or deceptively misdescriptive, or that as a whole are functional, Lanham Act § 2(e), 15 U.S.C.A. § 1052(e), bars the registration of marks that consist of "primarily merely a surname" absent proof of

secondary meaning. One reason for the bar is that a competitor having the same surname as an applicant should not be disabled from using her name in trade. Courts have generally relied on Assistant Commissioner Daphne Leeds's formulation of the "primarily merely a surname" test in Ex parte Rivera Watch Corp., 106 U.S.P.Q. 145, 149 (1955):

> A trademark is a trademark only if it is used in trade. When it is used in trade it must have some impact upon the purchasing public, and it is that impact or impression which should be evaluated in determining whether or not the primary significance of a word when applied to a product is a surname significance. If it is, *and it is only that,* then it is primarily merely a surname. "Reeves," "Higgins," and "Wayne" are thus primarily merely surnames. If the mark has well known meanings as a word in the language and the purchasing public, upon seeing it on the goods, may not attribute surname significance to it, it is not primarily merely a surname. "King", "Cotton," and "Boatman" fall in this category.

See generally, Charles Raymond Fowler, When are Surnames Registrable?, 70 Trademark Rep. 66 (1980).

2. *Secondary Meaning.* Except in the case of geographically deceptively misdescriptive marks and marks consisting of functional matter, which are entirely barred from registration, a mark that fails to qualify under Lanham Act section 2(e) may nonetheless be registered on the Principal Register if it "has become distinctive of the applicant's goods in commerce." Lanham Act § 2(f), 15 U.S.C.A. § 1052(f). Acquisition of secondary meaning is the fact to be proved, and any evidence is admissible if it tends to show that the mark signifies a single source to consumers. Applicants sometimes offer consumer survey evidence to prove that secondary meaning has attached to a term. Section 2(f) also provides that the Commissioner may accept proof of five years' "substantially exclusive and continuous" use of the mark by the applicant as prima facie evidence that the mark has become distinctive.

See generally, Vincent N. Palladino, Surveying Secondary Meaning, 84 Trademark Rep. 155 (1994). For an interesting, contextual approach to the treatment of secondary meaning marks, see Lewis Garner, A Display Theory of Trademarks, 25 Geo.Wash. L. Rev. 53 (1956).

3. *Concurrent Registration.* The Trademark Law Revision Act of 1988 amended the proviso of Lanham Act section 2(d), 15 U.S.C.A. § 1052(d), dealing with concurrent registrations by adding that "[u]se prior to the filing date of any pending application or a registration shall not be required when the owner of such application or registration consents to the grant of a concurrent registration to the applicant." According to the Senate report on the Act, the purpose of the amendment was "to modify existing language which prohibits institution of a concurrent use proceeding at the Patent and Trademark Office if the junior user initiated use of the mark after the filing date of the senior user's application or its registration, even if the parties enter into an agreement establishing their respective rights.

This provision is counterproductive because it often forces parties, who would otherwise be able to reach an amicable settlement, into litigation."

"As amended, the proviso will permit the Commissioner to institute a concurrent use proceeding if the owner of the earlier filed application or registration consents to the issuance of a concurrent use registration to the other party. In adopting this amendment, however, the committee does not intend to alter two important aspects of the law governing the issuance of concurrent use registrations: The Commissioner will still be required to determine that confusion or deception is not likely to result from issuance of the concurrent use registration and he will be able to impose conditions relating to the mode or place of use of the marks to prevent such confusion or deception." S.Rep. No. 100–515, 100th Cong., 2d Sess. 27 (1988).

See generally, David S. Welkowitz, The Problem of Concurrent Use of Trademarks: An Old/New Proposal, 28 U. Rich. L. Rev. 315 (1994).

4. *Suggestive Marks.* A firm that wants a mark to serve an advertising function by suggesting the qualities of its goods or services must chart a sometimes treacherous course between making the mark accurately suggestive—and thus descriptive—or inaccurately suggestive—and thus deceptively misdescriptive or deceptive.

Two Supreme Court cases provide common law guides to navigation between descriptive and deceptive marks. In Clinton E. Worden & Co. v. California Fig Syrup Co., 187 U.S. 516, 23 S.Ct. 161, 47 L.Ed. 282 (1903), the Court ruled that plaintiff, which marketed a laxative under the name, "Syrup of Figs" was not entitled to relief against defendant's use of the term, "Fig Syrup" for its laxative. "If this preparation is in fact a syrup of figs, the words are clearly descriptive, and not the proper subject of a trade mark." 187 U.S. at 533, 23 S.Ct. at 166. Since the plaintiff's compound in fact contained only minimal amounts of fig syrup, the Court concluded that use of the term tended to deceive consumers as to the nature of its product. By contrast, in The Coca–Cola Co. v. The Koke Co. of America, 254 U.S. 143, 41 S.Ct. 113, 65 L.Ed. 189 (1920), the Court ruled that, although plaintiff's product contained only trace amounts of coca leaf and cola nut derivative, "[w]e are dealing here with a popular drink not with a medicine. . . . Coca–Cola probably means to most persons the plaintiff's familiar product to be had everywhere rather than a compound of particular substances."*

5. *"Deceptive" and "Deceptively Misdescriptive" Marks.* The consequences of a mark's nonregistrability because it is "deceptive" under section 2(a) differ dramatically from the consequences of a mark's nonregistrability because it is "deceptively misdescriptive" under section 2(e). Deceptively

---

* "Before 1900 the beginning of the good will was more or less helped by the presence of cocaine, a drug that, like alcohol or caffeine or opium, may be described as a deadly poison or as a valuable item of the pharmacopoeia according to the rhetorical purposes in view. The amount seems to have been very small, but it may have been enough to begin a bad habit and after the Food and Drug Act of June 30, 1906, c. 3915, 34 Stat. 768, if not earlier, long before this suit was brought, it was eliminated from the plaintiff's compound." 254 U.S. at 145–146, 41 S.Ct. at 113–114.

misdescriptive marks can be registered upon proof of secondary meaning under section 2(f). Deceptive marks can never be registered. Despite this difference in consequence, the statute nowhere defines the distinction between "deceptive" and "deceptively misdescriptive." The scant legislative history suggests only that both disqualifications were intended to serve the same purpose. Hearings on H.R. 5461 before the Subcomm. on Trademarks of the House Comm. on Patents, 77th Cong. 1st Sess. 84–87 (1941).

In explicating the indicia of deceptive marks in *Budge Manufacturing,* Judge Nies also indicated the hallmarks of deceptively misdescriptive marks. Under *Budge,* a mark is deceptive if (1) it misdescribes the goods to which it is attached; (2) consumers are likely to believe that the misdescription accurately describes the goods; and (3) the misdescription is likely to be material to a consumer's decision to purchase the goods. If the mark has the first two characteristics, but not the third, it is only deceptively misdescriptive. See Gold Seal Co. v. Weeks, 129 F.Supp. 928, 105 U.S.P.Q. 407 (D.D.C.1955), aff'd, 230 F.2d 832, 108 U.S.P.Q. 400 (D.C.Cir.1956). This approach effectively distinguishes between untruths that injure consumers by distorting their purchase decisions and untruths that have no economic consequence.

Until passage of the North American Free Trade Agreement amendments to the Lanham Act, 107 Stat. 2057, P.L. 103–182 (Dec. 8, 1993), section 2(f) of the Act, 15 U.S.C.A. § 1052(f), treated "geographically deceptively misdescriptive marks" in the same way it treated deceptively misdescriptive marks, allowing their registration on the Principal Register upon proof that they had acquired the necessary secondary meaning. The NAFTA amendments effectively assimilated "geographically deceptively misdescriptive" marks under section 2(e) to "deceptive" marks under 2(a), and barred them from registration on the Principal and Supplemental Registers without regard to how distinctive they may have become. The amendment was prompted by NAFTA's requirement that member governments refuse registration to "geographically deceptively misdescriptive marks." S. Rep No. 189, 103d Cong. 1st Sess. 124 (1993).

6. *Scandalous or Disparaging Matter.* In Harjo v. Pro–Football, Inc., 50 U.S.P.Q.2d 1705 (T.T.A.B.1999), seven Native Americans, contending that the word "redskins" was "and is a pejorative, derogatory, denigrating, offensive, scandalous, contemptuous, disreputable, disparaging and racist designation for a Native American person," obtained cancellation of six trademarks of the Washington Redskins football team that contained the word. Although in cases involving allegedly prurient or otherwise scandalous marks the Board had often employed as its benchmark the perceptions of the general public, "[i]n determining whether or not a mark is disparaging, the perceptions of the general public are irrelevant. Rather, because the portion of Section 2(a) proscribing disparaging marks targets certain persons, institutions or beliefs, only the perceptions of those referred to, identified or implicated in some recognizable manner by the involved mark are relevant to this determination." 50 U.S.P.Q.2d at 1708, 1739. The Board declined to rule on the Redskins' argument that cancellation on the ground of "disparagement" would be unconstitutional under the First Amendment.

In In re McGinley, 660 F.2d 481, 211 U.S.P.Q. 668 (C.C.P.A.1981), where the Court of Customs and Patent Appeals affirmed rejection of an application to register a mark consisting of "a photograph of a nude man and woman kissing and embracing in a manner appearing to expose the male genitalia," the court discounted any First Amendment constraints with the observation that refusal to register a mark does not affect the right to use it. "No conduct is proscribed, and no tangible form of expression is suppressed." Further, in the court's view, "the term 'scandalous' is sufficiently precise to satisfy due process requirements." 660 F.2d at 484–85.

See generally, Theodore H. Davis, Jr., Registration of Scandalous, Immoral, and Disparaging Matter Under Section 2(a) of the Lanham Act: Can One Man's Vulgarity Be Another's Registered Trademark?, 83 Trademark Rep. 801 (1993); Stephen R. Baird, Moral Intervention in the Trademark Arena: Banning the Registration of Scandalous and Immoral Trademarks, 83 Trademark Rep. 661 (1993). See also Maury Audet, Native American Tribal Names as Monikers and Logos: Will These Registrations Withstand Cancellation Under Section 2(a) of the Lanham Act after Harjo v. Pro Football (Redskins), Inc., 29 AIPLA Q.J. 129 (2001).

3. STATUTORY SUBJECT MATTER

See Statute Supplement 15 U.S.C.A. §§ 1053, 1054, 1064(5), 1091–1096.

a. *Types of Marks*

(i.) TRADEMARKS AND SERVICE MARKS

In re Advertising & Marketing Development, Inc.

United States Court of Appeals, Federal Circuit, 1987.
821 F.2d 614, 2 U.S.P.Q.2d 2010.

EDWARD S. SMITH, Circuit Judge.

. . .

BACKGROUND

A. *Nature of the Case.*

A & M is in the business of providing sales promotion services by creating and licensing sales promotion campaigns. Sales promotion campaigns are used by various types of merchants, such as grocery stores, gas stations, banks, and automobile dealers, for the purpose of increasing customer traffic and sales.

A & M created the campaign known as THE NOW GENERATION or NOW GENERATION and licensed the campaign to banks for the purpose of advertising the banks' financial services, including NOW accounts, and to automobile dealers for the purpose of advertising automobiles. (A NOW account is a checking account that earns interest.) The license entitles the banks or automobile dealers to use THE NOW GENERATION as a mark for financial services or automobiles.

The NOW GENERATION licenses are individually tailored to include the right to use selected physical components from a total of 5 television commercials, 51 radio commercials, 30 newspaper advertisements, a musical theme, direct mail advertising materials, point of sale materials, and other materials. A & M provides services to its licensees including advice as to which components to select, how to use and benefit from the advertising, and how the campaign could assist in the merchandising of banking services or automobiles to the public.

A & M sought to register THE NOW GENERATION as a service mark for "PROMOTING THE SALE OF GOODS AND/OR SERVICES OF AU-TOMOBILE DEALERS, FINANCIAL INSTITUTIONS AND RETAILERS THROUGH THE DISTRIBUTION OF PRINTED PROMOTIONAL MA-TERIALS AND BY RENDERING MERCHANDISING AND SALES PRO-MOTION ADVICE" (hereinafter referred to as advertising or promotional services). The board affirmed the examiner's refusal to register the mark, finding that the mark had not been used for A & M's *promotional* services, but only for the banks' *financial* services. (In the board decision presently on appeal, the board focused on the bank licensees and not on the automobile dealer licensees.)

The board does not question that A & M provides promotional "services" as opposed to "goods." The board also does not suggest that there is any possibility of confusion or any difficulty in distinguishing between A & M's use of THE NOW GENERATION as a mark for promotional services to banks, on one hand, and the banks' use of the same mark for financial services to individuals, on the other. The question is whether, in fact, A & M has used THE NOW GENERATION as a mark for its promotional services. . . .

SERVICE MARK REGISTRATION FOR ADVERTISING OR PROMOTIONAL SERVICES

Section 3 of the Lanham Act provides for the registration of service marks. Section 45 of the Lanham Act defines "service mark" as "a mark used in the sale or advertising of services to identify and distinguish the services of one person, including a unique service, from the services of others and to indicate the source of the services, even if that source is unknown."

The Lanham Act, as amended, does not define "services," nor does the legislative history provide such a definition. However, our predecessor court stated that the term "services" was intended to have broad scope, reasoning that "no attempt was made to define 'services' simply because of the plethora of services that the human mind is capable of conceiving."[10]

The board has held that there is "no reason why a particular class of service" should be excluded from service mark registration, as long as the statutory requirements for registration are met.[11] Each application for registration of a mark must be separately evaluated with reference to the manner in which the mark has been used in the specimens of record.

In *In re Goodwill Advertising Co.*[14] and in *In re Universal Press Syndicate*,[15] the board has allowed registration of service marks for advertising or promotional services. In each case, the board found that the *advertising services* were sufficiently separate from the *subject* of the advertising, and that the mark had been used to identify the advertising services themselves.

However, in *Admark*[16] and in *In re Local Trademarks, Inc.*,[17] the board refused registration of service marks for advertising or promotional services. In each of the latter two cases, the board found that the marks had not been used to identify advertising services, but only to identify the *subject* of the advertising. In *Admark* and *Local Trademarks,* the board went beyond the issues presented in those cases to make statements which would appear to severely curtail the availability of service mark registration for advertising services.

At this point, it will be useful to discuss certain aspects of service marks as they relate to advertising services. The distinguishing characteristic of advertising services is that they are associated with the *subject* of the advertising, whether that subject is goods or services. However, service mark registration for advertising services must be based on use of the mark to identify the advertising services themselves.

A. *Advertising Services Must Be Sufficiently Separate from the Subject of the Advertising.*

In certain cases, the board has refused service mark registration when the advertising services are not "sufficiently separate" from the subject of the advertising.[18] Thus, in *In re Radio Corp. of America*,[19] the CCPA affirmed the board's decision refusing service mark registration of the slogan "The Music You Want When You Want It," where the slogan was used only to advertise the applicant's own goods, *i.e.*, records.

---

10. *American Int'l Reinsurance Co. v. Airco, Inc.*, 570 F.2d 941, 943, 197 USPQ 69, 71 (CCPA), *cert. denied*, 439 U.S. 866, 99 S.Ct. 190, 58 L.Ed.2d 175 (1978).

11. *In re Holiday Inns, Inc.*, 223 USPQ 149, 150 (TTAB 1984).

14. *In re Goodwill Advertising Co.*, 135 USPQ 331 (TTAB 1962).

15. *In re Universal Press Syndicate*, 229 USPQ 638 (TTAB 1986).

16. *Admark*, 214 USPQ 302.

17. *In re Local Trademarks, Inc.*, 220 USPQ 728 (TTAB 1983).

18. *See In re Landmark Communications, Inc.*, 204 USPQ 692, 695 (TTAB 1979).

19. *In re Radio Corp. of Am.*, 205 F.2d 180, 98 USPQ 157 (CCPA 1953).

On the other hand, as the board stated in *In re Heavenly Creations, Inc.*,[20] "the statute makes no distinction between services on the basis of primary, incidental or ancillary." In *Heavenly Creations*, the board allowed registration of a service mark for the promotion of wigs and hair pieces, where the promotion included demonstrations of hair pieces generally, such that the information and techniques conveyed would be usable with any type or brand of hair piece. The same mark had also been registered as a trademark for hair pieces. The board was "persuaded that applicant is rendering a service over and above that normally involved in promoting the sale of its goods."[21]

It may be helpful to think of a "service," defined in *In re Canadian Pacific, Ltd.*,[22] as "the performance of labor for the benefit of *another*." In the present case, A & M is in the business of providing advertising services for the benefit of another, *i.e.*, for the benefit of banks and automobile dealers. A & M's sale of advertising services to banks and automobile dealers is a wholly separate transaction from the banks' and automobile dealers' sale of financial services or automobiles to individuals. Here, the board correctly found that A & M's advertising services are sufficiently separate from the subject of the advertising, *i.e.*, financial services and automobiles.

B. *Mark Must Be Used To Identify Advertising Services, Not Merely To Identify Subject of the Advertising.*

It is not enough for the applicant to be a provider of services; the applicant also must have used the mark to identify the named services for which registration is sought. In *In re Universal Oil Products Co.*,[23] the CCPA affirmed the board's refusal to register PACOL and PENEX as marks for engineering services, even though the applicant was a provider of such services, because the marks had been used only to identify certain *processes* and not to identify the engineering services for which registration was sought. The CCPA stated that the applicant had failed to show a "direct association" between the mark and the services named in the application. The "direct association" test does not create an additional or more stringent requirement for registration; it is implicit in the statutory definition of "a mark used * * * to identify and distinguish the services of one person * * * from the services of others and to indicate the source of the services."[24]

In *Admark*, the board refused registration of "THE ROAD AUTHORITY" as a mark for advertising services, because the mark had been used

---

20. *In re Heavenly Creations, Inc.*, 168 USPQ 317, 318 (TTAB 1971).

21. *Id.*

22. *Canadian Pacific*, 754 F.2d at 994, 224 USPQ at 973 (citing WEBSTER'S COLLEGIATE DICTIONARY 909 (5th ed. 1948)).

23. *In re Universal Oil Prods. Co.*, 476 F.2d 653, 177 USPQ 456 (CCPA 1973).

24. 15 U.S.C. § 1127 (1982 & Supp. III 1985).

only to identify retail tire store services. The board went on to make the following sweeping statement:[25]

> [T]he mark or slogan that is the focus of an advertising campaign for a client's goods or services cannot be said to function as a service mark for the licensor's—applicant's—advertising agency services. . . .

In the present case, the examiner should not have relied on the statement made in *Admark* to refuse registration. However, on appeal to the board, the board correctly stated that A & M would be entitled to registration of THE NOW GENERATION as a mark for advertising services if A & M had actually used that mark to identify its advertising services. The board refused service mark registration based on its finding that A & M had *not* used THE NOW GENERATION as a mark for its advertising services.

WHETHER THE BOARD CLEARLY ERRED IN FINDING A & M DID NOT USE THE MARK FOR ADVERTISING SERVICES

Whether a mark has been used to identify a particular type of service is a question of fact reviewable under the clearly erroneous standard. This court reviews the board's findings for clear error based on the evidence of record, including the specimens of use of the mark and the affidavits of A & M's president and of the purchasers of A & M's services.

On this record, the board clearly erred in finding that A & M had not used THE NOW GENERATION as a mark for its promotional services. A & M (here, its predecessor in interest) submitted a letterhead specimen naming itself as the "creators, producers and *suppliers* of THE NOW GENERATION sales *promotion services* and specialized advertising campaigns *for* automobile dealers, financial institutions and retailers." (Emphasis supplied.) This letterhead was actually used in correspondence with financial institutions and automobile dealers regarding A & M's promotional services. It is difficult to imagine how A & M could have made a clearer use of the mark to identify its promotional services. However, if any doubt remained, on remand A & M submitted postcard and magazine advertising specimens to the same effect, as well as affidavits from purchasers of A & M's services stating that they considered THE NOW GENERATION to identify A & M's promotional services.

The board has equated the messenger with the message, as a result of which the messenger has been unjustly shot down. The board majority selectively focused only on those aspects of the evidence which showed the banks' use of THE NOW GENERATION to identify the banks' financial services. This analysis was unavailing, since the board conceded that there was no difficulty in distinguishing between the two different uses of the same mark, and that the mark would be registrable for promotional services if A & M showed that it had used the mark to identify such services.

25. *Admark,* 214 USPQ at 303.

CONCLUSION

Service mark registration is available for advertising or promotional services under the same standard as for other services, *i.e.,* the mark must have been "used in the sale or advertising of services to identify and distinguish the services of one person, including a unique service, from the services of others and to indicate the source of the services, even if that source is unknown." Cases involving advertising services may present factual considerations including whether the services are "sufficiently separate" from the subject of the advertising, and whether the mark has been used to identify the advertising services themselves.

Here, the board clearly erred in finding that A & M had not used THE NOW GENERATION to identify its promotional services; hence, the board's decision refusing registration is reversed.

REVERSED.

(ii.) CERTIFICATION MARKS AND COLLECTIVE MARKS

Midwest Plastic Fabricators, Inc. v. Underwriters Laboratories Inc.

United States Court of Appeals, Federal Circuit, 1990.
906 F.2d 1568, 15 U.S.P.Q.2d 1359.

MICHEL, Circuit Judge.

Midwest Plastic Fabricators, Inc. (Midwest) appeals the decision of the United States Patent and Trademark Office, Trademark Trial and Appeal Board (Board), denying Midwest's petition to cancel two certification mark registrations issued to Underwriters Laboratories Inc. (UL). Because the Board's findings that UL did not misuse and did control use of its certification marks are not clearly erroneous, we affirm.

BACKGROUND

UL, a corporation that promulgates and certifies compliance with safety standards for thousands of consumer and other products, is the owner and federal registrant of the two certification marks at issue in this appeal. Each registration states, in part, that the certification is used by persons authorized by UL to certify that representative samplings of the goods conform to the safety standards or requirements established by UL. A manufacturer that wishes to use the UL marks on its products to indicate compliance with UL safety standards must first submit samples to UL for testing and evaluation. Once those samples are determined to comply with UL standards, the products become eligible for listing with UL. Usually the manufacturer will enter into a listing and follow-up service agreement with UL.

This agreement provides, inter alia, that the manufacturer order UL marks through [UL] from an authorized printer; that no UL mark shall be used on products not in compliance with [UL's] requirements;

that the manufacturer agrees that it will ensure that the products bearing the UL mark are in compliance with [UL's] requirements; that a testing and inspection program will be maintained by the manufacturer to assure continued compliance . . .; that access to [UL's] inspectors shall be allowed together with providing adequate facilities for the conducting of product testing and that any tests which indicate noncompliance with [UL's] requirements shall result in the manufacturer's being required to either correct the problem or remove the UL mark from the noncomplying products.

[The] follow-up service agreement provides for a periodic inspection program whereby [UL's] inspectors will visit factories and plants in which listed products are produced. If an inspector finds a variation from [UL's] requirements, a variation notice is issued . . . [and] a manufacturer cannot ship products which are encompassed by the variation notice until the problem is resolved. The record shows that inspectors have discretion to allow products to be shipped with minor variations that do not affect the safety of the product. Inspectors are also authorized to remove the UL mark in appropriate situations.

[UL] exercises authority over use of the UL certification marks as described above by employing some 500 inspectors who work out of over 200 inspection centers throughout the United States. In 1987, [UL's] inspectors conducted approximately 438,000 inspections in approximately 38,900 factories and over 9 billion UL labels were issued covering approximately 12,500 different products.

Midwest, 12 U.S.P.Q. 2d at 1271.

Midwest is a manufacturer and seller of polyvinyl chloride (PVC) fittings and elbows for use with PVC conduit which encases electrical wiring. The company entered into a listing and follow-up service agreement with UL which provides, in part, that Midwest "agrees that his use of the Listing Mark constitutes *his declaration* that the products are Listed by [UL] and have been made in compliance with the requirements of [UL]." (Emphasis added).

Midwest now seeks reversal of the Board's denial of its petition to cancel UL's registrations on the same two bases it presented to the Board. First, Midwest alleged that UL permits use of the certification marks for purposes other than certification, in violation of 15 U.S.C. § 1064(e)(3) (1982). According to Midwest, UL's president testified that application of UL's mark represents not UL's, but merely the manufacturer's declaration that the products meet UL standards. Midwest argued that the failure of UL itself to certify that the products carrying the UL mark meet UL standards demonstrates that UL permits use of the marks for purposes other than certification.

As the second basis for cancellation, Midwest charged UL fails to control the use of its marks. Specifically, Midwest alleged: (1) certain PVC elbows carrying the UL marks failed impact tests performed by its expert, Professor Charles E. Rogers, of Case Western Reserve University; and (2) certain conduit pipe manufactured by a competitor of Midwest, National Pipe Company (National), carried counterfeit UL marks. If UL fails to control its marks, the registrations are subject to cancellation under 15 U.S.C. § 1064(e)(1) (1982). Alternatively, Midwest argued to the Board that as UL fails to control use of the marks on PVC conduit, the registrations should be cancelled at least as to such conduit. UL controverted these allegations and asserted that Midwest's cancellation petition was barred by the doctrine of licensee estoppel.

ISSUE

Whether either the Board's fact finding that UL does not use the marks other than for certification or that UL does control use of its marks is clearly erroneous.

OPINION

I.   *Use of the Marks for Purposes Other Than to Certify*

We have jurisdiction over this appeal under 28 U.S.C. § 1295(a)(4)(B) (1988).

Although our court has not previously addressed either the burden or the standard of proof in cancellation proceedings for certification mark registrations, we discern no reason to make them different than for trademark registration cancellations.

A certification mark registration may be cancelled if the mark is not used exclusively as a certification mark. For example, if a certification mark's owner also allowed the mark to be used as a trademark, there would be a basis for cancellation of the registration.

Midwest argues that UL's registrations must be cancelled because the UL certification marks are not UL's own declarations to consumers that the marked products comply with UL standards, but instead are the manufacturer's declarations. Midwest asserts the failure of UL itself to make that declaration is evidence that UL "permits the use of the certification mark for purposes other than to certify" and therefore the registrations must be cancelled.

There is an important difference, however, between the mark's use and the user. That others test products and apply UL's certification marks simply is not probative that the marks are used for other than certification. Certainly, on this record, there is no evidence that these certification marks are used, by anyone, as trademarks or service marks. Instead, Midwest merely complains about who applies the mark to the product. Midwest in effect argues that third party application of a certification mark constitutes per se misuse—use for a purpose other than certification. But Midwest offers no authority to support such a proposition.

The statute, however, plainly does not require that, as the registrant, UL itself must test the products and declare to the public that items carrying UL marks meet UL standards. It merely authorizes cancellation of a registration if the registrant allows use of the mark for purposes other than certification. In addition, the general practice, in accord with the statute, allows for a third party to apply the certification mark.

Thus, both registrations at issue here include a provision that the certification marks may be used by "persons authorized by [UL]" to indicate that "representative samplings" of the products conform to safety standards established by UL. The registrations clearly state what the marks do and do not represent to the public. The registrations certainly do not require UL to represent that UL itself tests the items.

UL agrees that UL marks, when applied by Midwest to Midwest's products, are Midwest's declaration of compliance with UL standards. The Board concluded that UL's use of the UL mark as a *manufacturer's* declaration that the marked product complies with UL standards is "a reasonable one designed to reflect the realities of the limitations involved in inspecting and certifying a large number of different products. We do not find that such a statement in any way constitutes a ground for cancelling the certification marks...." We cannot disagree.

We review findings of fact made by the Board to determine whether they are clearly erroneous. Midwest presented no evidence to the Board that UL allowed use of its marks for purposes other than to certify that representative samplings of a product comply with UL standards. The Board's finding that UL does not use the mark for purposes other than certification thus cannot be clearly erroneous. The Board therefore correctly decided that section 1064(e)(3)'s basis for cancelling UL's registrations has not been established.

II. *Failure to Control Use of the Marks*

Midwest also asserts UL does not control the use of the UL marks as required under 15 U.S.C. § 1064(e)(1), and cancellation is thus necessary. Section 1064(e)(1) provides for cancellation if the certification mark registrant "does not control, or is not able legitimately to exercise control over, the use of such mark."

The purpose of requiring a certification mark registrant to control use of its mark is the same as for a trademark registrant: to protect the public from being misled. In the case of a certification mark registrant, the risk of misleading the public may be even greater because a certification mark registration sets forth specific representations about the manufacture and characteristics of the goods to which the mark is applied.

As the purpose of the control requirement is to protect the public, the requirement places an affirmative obligation on the certification mark owner to monitor the activities of those who use the mark.

To obtain cancellation of the UL certification mark registrations, Midwest has the burden to demonstrate by a preponderance of the evidence that UL failed to exercise control over use of its marks. The statute, however, does not define "control" or otherwise indicate the degree of control that it requires. Clearly, the statutory requirement cannot mean absolute control, because it would be impracticable, if not impossible, to satisfy. The Board stated: "The specific degree of control necessary in determining whether or not a certification mark should be cancelled depends, of course, on the particular facts presented in each case." *Midwest,* 12 U.S.P.Q.2d at 1273.While interpretation of the statutory term "control" is a question of law which we review de novo, the Board explicated a rule of reasonableness which, because reasonableness cannot be gauged by some abstract standard, will vary depending on the particular facts. The "control" requirement of the statute means the mark owner must take reasonable steps, under all the circumstances of the case, to prevent the public from being misled.

This standard for demonstrating that a registrant has exercised control over the use of its marks is entirely consistent with the precedent of this court, which speaks in terms of "adequate control," *see Turian,* 581 F.2d at 261, 198 USPQ at 613, as well as "sufficient control," *see Stock Pot Restaurant,* 737 F.2d at 1578–79, 222 USPQ at 668. . . .

The Board found that UL has "a vast network of inspectors making hundreds of thousands of inspections of thousands of different products across the country" and that UL conducts comprehensive follow-up programs to ensure compliance with UL standards. *Midwest,* 12 USPQ2d at 1273. The Board also stated that UL demonstrated "considerable diligence in controlling the use of its marks; that while [the] inspection and follow-up procedures are not 100% accurate or foolproof, we know of no such requirement. . . ." *Id.* at 1275.

Midwest relies upon two types of evidence to challenge the Board finding on control. First, it relies on the results of impact tests performed on certain conduit and elbows carrying the UL mark. The Board found the tests were not "shown to be reliable and [are] entitled to very little, if any, probative value." We cannot overturn that finding as clearly erroneous because Midwest's testing of PVC conduit and elbows did not account for the age of the elbows tested or their exposure to sunlight, although it is undisputed that age and sunlight make PVC conduit brittle. Also, impact tests were performed on PVC elbows and Midwest concedes "that the [UL] standards for elbows do not require impact tests." The Board, therefore, appropriately discounted the impact tests.

The second type of evidence Midwest employs to demonstrate UL's failure to control use of its marks is the proven use of counterfeit UL marks on certain conduit manufactured by National, a competitor. The Board concluded that this limited counterfeiting problem was not sufficient to cancel UL's registrations and that UL exercised control over subsequent use of its marks by this company, based on findings about UL's responsiveness and the stringency of its corrective action. It included inspections being done solely by UL personnel and inspection of not just a "representative sampling," all that is required by the registrations, but of 100% of the conduit. *Id.* at 1274. These findings have not been shown to be clearly erroneous.

Because Midwest has not shown that the findings supporting the reasonableness of UL's control are clearly erroneous, we must sustain the

Board's determination that UL's control avoids cancellation of its registrations in these proceedings.

CONCLUSION

We hold Midwest has failed to prove either asserted basis for cancelling UL's registrations. We therefore need not, and do not, reach the remaining issues: Whether a certification mark registration may be partially cancelled for failure to control use of the mark on a single class of goods; and whether the doctrine of licensee estoppel bars Midwest's petition for cancellation. Finally, UL's request for sanctions under Rule 38 of the Federal Rules of Appellate Procedure on the ground of a frivolous appeal is denied. The decision of the Board denying cancellation is

AFFIRMED.

Frederick Breitenfeld, Collective Marks—Should They Be Abolished?

47 Trademark Rep. 1, 3–6, 9, 14–15 (1957).*

Assistant Commissioner of Patents Leeds said in 1947: "Certification marks are now in our law and some administrative difficulties may have to be overcome before the distinction between collective marks and certification marks is clearly defined."

The Trademark Act of 1946 has been in effect for over nine years, and it seems that there is still confusion surrounding these marks. The fact is that the indistinction got off to a good start long before the Lanham Act, when collective marks first appeared in the law in 1938, by amendment to the 1905 Act. In commenting upon these 1938 collective marks, Dr. Derenberg said in 1948: "Most of the marks registered as collective marks under the (1938) amendment would appear to come within the definition of a certification mark rather than a collective mark under the new Act."

The lack of any clear distinction between collective and certification marks was apparent even while the Lanham Act was still in the process of being enacted. In an early form in which the House passed the Act, collective marks and certification marks were defined together in a single definition; and the later separation of the definitions did little to distinguish the marks clearly. Confusion has continued and, in addition, the separate definitions have given rise to other perplexing questions. . . .

In her book, Mrs. Leeds distinguished between collective and certification marks with an illustration of the use of the name INDIAN RIVER for fruit. She pointed out that if the mark is used to indicate that the fruit comes from a certain region, it is a certification mark, whereas, if it is used by members of an association "to distinguish the fruit of the members, and not to certify regional origin, it is a 'collective mark'." This seems clear enough, but when organizations require that certain standards be met before membership is granted, or that members can be drawn only from a certain region, then membership itself may certify quality, regional origin, etc. In such cases it is clear that if Mrs. Leeds' criterion is used, the mark may be both a collective *and* a certification mark. . . .

To illustrate still more dramatically the lack of real distinction between the marks appearing on the two registers, the reader is invited to check his collective-certification mark I.Q. by indicating in the boxes on the left of the following list of marks, which, in his opinion, are certification marks, and which are collective marks.

Certifica- *tion*	*Collec-* *tive*	
1. ☐	☐	No. 568,413, granted to International Association of Clothing Designers, for Men's and Boys' clothing—namely, suits, overcoats, topcoats and sport coats; "The ... mark is used upon the goods to indicate that the clothing is designed by a member of the association."
2. ☐	☐	No. 589,240, granted to Douglas Fir Plywood Association, for Plywood; "The ... mark is used in connection with the goods to indicate that the plywood meets standards promulgated by the applicant."
3. ☐	☐	No. 567,487, granted to Prefinished Wallpanel Council, for Prefinished wall panels; "The ... mark is used upon the goods to indicate the quality and commercial standard of the goods and that the manufacturer of the goods is a member of the Prefinished Wallpanel Council."
4. ☐	☐	No. 577,817, granted to The Irish Linen Guild, for Irish linen piece goods; "The ... mark is used in connection with the goods to indicate membership in the association, source and origin, genuineness, and high quality of the goods."
5. ☐	☐	No. 529,630, granted to Paint Research Associates, Inc., for Ready-mixed paints, etc.; "The ... mark is used upon the goods to indicate the quality of same."
6. ☐	☐	No. 589,483, granted to The Missouri Farmers Association, Inc., for Vegetable seeds, lawn seeds and field crop seeds; "The ... mark is used in connection with the goods to indicate that they comply with certain requirements as to excellence and quality, which compliance with said requirements is maintained through inspection and supervi-

	Certifica-tion	*Collec-tive*	

sion by duly authorized representatives of the Missouri Farmers Association, Inc."

7. ☐ ☐   No. 515,204, granted to National Sanitary Supply Association, for Sanitary and janitor supplies—namely, cleaning compounds and cleaning chemicals; soaps; soap powders; liquid soaps; "The ... mark is used upon the goods to indicate the mode of manufacture and quality of such goods and to indicate membership in the association."

8. ☐ ☐   No. 569,909, granted to Brazil Nut Association, for Brazil nuts; "The ... mark is used in connection with the goods to indicate origin of the product sold."

9. ☐ ☐   No. 543,809, granted to The Journeymen Barbers, Hairdressers and Cosmetologists' International Union of America, for Cutting of hair, shampooing of hair, shaving, application of facial treatments; "... to indicate that all persons employed therein are members of the union."

10. ☐ ☐   No. 541,207, granted to Toy Manufacturers of the U.S.A., Inc., for Toys and playthings, etc.; "The ... mark is used in connection with the goods to indicate that the members using the mark are domestic U.S. manufacturers and distributors of toys and that the toys are American made."

If you studied the marks carefully and came to the conclusion that they are all certification marks except number 9, you are intelligent but mistaken. If you judged the even numbered registrations to be *collective* marks and the odd numbered registrations to be *certification* marks you were right; but the chances are that you peeked at this paragraph before making your choices.

It has been said that the essential difference between the two types of marks is that "collective marks indicate no more than mere association, while certification marks constitute a representation *with respect to the goods themselves* by someone other than the producer. The collective mark is a 'lodge button'; the certification mark is a 'guarantee'." ...

The difference between a mark which "identifies" the goods or services of members of an organization and one which "certifies" that the labor on the goods or services was performed by the members of the organization is not only difficult to ascertain, but a distinction that seems wholly unnecessary. The elimination of one of these classifications seems advisable, therefore, and it is suggested that it be stricken from the definition of a *collective* mark. This would leave, in the section defining collective marks, only the reference to membership marks. Obviously, "membership" has reference to a "collection" of persons, and the obfuscating term "collective" is therefore redundant and could be eliminated entirely. A new definition is suggested for marks to be included on the newly-established "Collective Membership Register" (a more suitable name for which might well be the shorter, easier term: "Membership Register"):

> The term "membership mark" means a mark used by the members of a cooperative, an association, or other collective group or organization to indicate membership in a union, an association or other organization.

This is believed to be a clean-cut statement of the membership "lodge-button" function of what is now known as a collective mark. It states what seems to have become Patent Office practice i.e., to classify *membership* registrations in one group (collective) and marks referring to *work done by members* in another (certification). . . .

The fourth ground for cancellation of a certification mark refers to the discriminate refusal of a registrant to certify the goods or services of a person who establishes standards or conditions that the mark certifies, but whom the registrant doesn't wish to take into camp. Of course this is a real shortcoming of certification marks, not suffered by collective marks. In fact, it was cited by Derenberg in 1949, as being one of the causes for the limited number of applications to register marks as certification marks. Dr. Derenberg contended, at that time, that because of this restriction

> . . . it would seem to be better business policy not to register such marks as certification marks, but wherever possible, as trademarks or service marks used by related companies.

As it happens, it appears that since then many registrants have registered such marks not only as trademarks or service marks but, in many instances, as collective marks.

However, is it sensible to maintain in existence a special register entitled "Collective Marks" merely to serve as a convenient alternative for those who own certification marks and are reluctant to register them as such? It would be preferable to amend the law to remove the cause of such reluctance; and if there is no legitimate need for collective marks they should be done away with.

NOTE

The Trademark Law Revision Act of 1988 amended the Lanham Act's definitional provisions, 15 U.S.C.A. § 1127, to expand the class whose use of a mark will qualify it as a trademark or service mark. Before the amendments, the definition of "trademark" contemplated use "by a manufacturer or merchant"; the definition now requires only use by "a person." The amended definition of "service mark" dropped the requirement of use "in the sale or advertising of services." These changes brought marks used by licensees, brokers and distributors within the definition of trademarks and service marks. The amendments also accommodated the Act's new intent to use provisions by encompassing both marks "used by a person" and marks "which a person has a bona fide intention to use in commerce...."

In addition to conforming the definitions of "certification mark" and "collective mark" to the new intent to use provisions, the 1988 amendments sharpened the distinction between the two types of marks by inserting the phrase, "in the case of certification marks," immediately after the word "except" in section 1054's provision that registered collective marks and certification marks "shall be entitled to the protection provided in this chapter in the case of trade-marks, except *in the case of certification marks* when used so as to represent falsely that the owner or user thereof makes or sells the goods or performs the services on or in connection with which such mark is used." According to the Senate Report on the Act, the change "clarifies the difference between collective and certification marks, the former of which, by definition, can be used to represent that their owners (that is, unions, associations or other organizations) make or sell the goods or perform the services on or in connection with which the mark is used." S.Rep. No. 100–515, p. 28 (1988).

b. Content

Qualitex Co. v. Jacobson Products Co., Inc.

Supreme Court of the United States, 1995.
514 U.S. 159, 115 S.Ct. 1300, 131 L.Ed.2d 248, 34 U.S.P.Q. 2d 1161.

JUSTICE BREYER delivered the opinion of the Court.

The question in this case is whether the Lanham Trademark Act of 1946 (Lanham Act), 15 U.S.C. §§ 1051–1127 (1988 ed. and Supp. V), permits the registration of a trademark that consists, purely and simply, of a color. We conclude that, sometimes, a color will meet ordinary legal trademark requirements. And, when it does so, no special legal rule prevents color alone from serving as a trademark.

I.

The case before us grows out of petitioner Qualitex Company's use (since the 1950's) of a special shade of green-gold color on the pads that it makes and sells to dry cleaning firms for use on dry cleaning presses. In 1989 respondent Jacobson Products (a Qualitex rival) began to sell its own press pads to dry cleaning firms; and it colored those pads a similar green-gold. In 1991 Qualitex registered the special green-gold color on press pads with the Patent and Trademark Office as a trademark. Registration No. 1,633,711 (Feb. 5, 1991). Qualitex subsequently added a trademark infringement count, 15 U.S.C. § 1114(1), to an unfair competition claim, § 1125(a), in a lawsuit it had already filed challenging Jacobson's use of the green-gold color.

Qualitex won the lawsuit in the District Court. But, the Court of Appeals for the Ninth Circuit set aside the judgment in Qualitex's favor on the trademark infringement claim because, in that Circuit's view, the Lanham Act does not permit Qualitex, or anyone else, to register "color alone" as a trademark.

The courts of appeals have differed as to whether or not the law recognizes the use of color alone as a trademark. We now hold that there is no rule absolutely barring the use of color alone, and we reverse the judgment of the Ninth Circuit.

II.

The Lanham Act gives a seller or producer the exclusive right to "register" a trademark and to prevent his or her competitors from using that trademark. Both the language of the Act and the basic underlying principles of trademark law would seem to include color within the universe of things that can qualify as a trademark. The language of the Lanham Act describes that universe in the broadest of terms. It says that trademarks "includ[e] any word, name, symbol or device, or any combination thereof." § 1127. Since human beings might use as a "symbol" or "device" almost anything at all that is capable of carrying meaning, this language, read literally, is not restrictive. The courts and the Patent and Trademark Office have authorized for use as a mark a particular shape (of a Coca–Cola bottle), a particular sound (of NBC's three chimes), and even a particular scent (of plumeria blossoms on sewing thread). If a shape, a sound, and a fragrance can act as symbols why, one might ask, can a color not do the same?

A color is also capable of satisfying the more important part of the statutory definition of a trademark, which requires that a person "us[e]" or "inten[d] to use" the mark

> "to identify and distinguish his or her goods, including a unique product, from those manufactured or sold by others and to indicate the source of the goods, even if that source is unknown." 15 U.S.C. § 1127.

True, a product's color is unlike "fanciful," "arbitrary," or "suggestive" words or designs, which almost *automatically* tell a customer that they refer to a brand. The imaginary word "Suntost," or the words "Suntost Marmalade," on a jar of orange jam immediately would signal a brand or a product "source"; the jam's orange color does not do so. But, over time, customers may come to treat a particular color on a product or its packaging (say, a color that in context seems unusual, such as pink on a firm's insulating material or red on the head of a large industrial bolt) as signifying a brand. And, if so, that color would have come to identify and distinguish the goods—*i.e.* "to indicate" their "source"—much in the way that descriptive words on a product (say, "Trim" on nail clippers or "Car–Freshener" on deodorizer) can come to indicate a product's origin. In this circumstance, trademark law says that the word (e.g., "Trim"), although not inherently distinctive, has developed "secondary meaning." Again, one might ask, if trademark law permits a descriptive word with secondary meaning to act as a mark, why would it not permit a color, under similar circumstances, to do the same?

We cannot find in the basic objectives of trademark law any obvious theoretical objection to the use of color alone as a trademark, where that color has attained "secondary meaning" and therefore identifies and distinguishes a particular brand (and thus indicates its "source"). In principle, trademark law, by preventing others from copying a source-identifying mark, "reduce[s] the customer's costs of shopping and making purchasing decisions," 1 J. McCarthy, McCarthy on Trademarks and Unfair Competition § 2.01[2], p. 2-3 (3d ed. 1994) (hereinafter McCarthy), for it quickly and easily assures a potential customer that *this* item—the item with this mark—is made by the same producer as other similarly marked items that he or she liked (or disliked) in the past. At the same time, the law helps assure a producer that it (and not an imitating competitor) will reap the financial, reputation-related rewards associated with a desirable product. The law thereby "encourage[s] the production of quality products," *ibid.*, and simultaneously discourages those who hope to sell inferior products by capitalizing on a consumer's inability quickly to evaluate the quality of an item offered for sale. It is the source-distinguishing ability of a mark—not its ontological status as color, shape, fragrance, word, or sign—that permits it to serve these basic purposes. And, for that reason, it is difficult to find, in basic trademark objectives, a reason to disqualify absolutely the use of a color as a mark.

Neither can we find a principled objection to the use of color as a mark in the important "functionality" doctrine of trademark law. The functionality doctrine prevents trademark law, which seeks to promote competition by protecting a firm's reputation, from instead inhibiting legitimate competition by allowing a producer to control a useful product feature. It is the province of patent law, not trademark law, to encourage invention by granting inventors a monopoly over new product designs or functions for a limited time, after which competitors are free to use the innovation. If a product's functional features could be used as trademarks, however, a monopoly over such features could be obtained without regard to whether they qualify as patents and could be extended forever (because trademarks may be renewed in perpetuity). Functionality doctrine therefore would require, to take an imaginary example, that even if customers have come to identify the special illumination-enhancing shape of a new patented light bulb with a particular manufacturer, the manufacturer may not use that shape as a trademark, for doing so, after the patent had expired, would impede competition—not by protecting the reputation of the original bulb maker, but by frustrating competitors' legitimate efforts to produce an equivalent illumination-enhancing bulb. This Court consequently has explained that, "[i]n general terms, a product feature is functional," and cannot serve as a trademark, "if it is essential to the use or purpose of the article or if it affects the cost or quality of the article," that is, if exclusive use of the feature would put competitors at a significant non-reputation-related disadvantage. *Inwood Laboratories, Inc.*, 456 U.S., at 850, n. 10, 102 S.Ct., at 2186, n. 10. Although sometimes color plays an important role (unrelated to source identification) in making a product more desirable, sometimes it does not. And, this latter fact—the fact that sometimes color is not essential to a product's use or purpose and does not affect cost or quality—indicates that the doctrine of "functionality" does not create an absolute bar to the use of color alone as a mark.

It would seem, then, that color alone, at least sometimes, can meet the basic legal requirements for use as a trademark. It can act as a symbol that distinguishes a firm's goods and identifies their source, without serving any other significant function. See U.S. Dept. of Commerce, Patent and Trademark Office, Trademark Manual of Examining Procedure § 1202.04(e), p. 1202–13 (2d ed. May, 1993) (hereinafter PTO Manual) (approving trademark registration of color alone where it "has become distinctive of the applicant's goods in commerce," provided that "there is [no] competitive need for colors to remain available in the industry" and the color is not "functional"); see also 1 McCarthy §§ 3.01[1], 7.26 ("requirements for qualification of a word or symbol as a trademark" are that it be (1) a "symbol," (2) "use[d] ... as a mark," (3) "to identify and distinguish the seller's goods from goods made or sold by others," but that it not be "functional"). Indeed, the District Court, in this case, entered findings (accepted by the Ninth Circuit) that show Qualitex's green-gold press pad color has met these requirements. The green-gold color acts as a symbol. Having developed secondary meaning (for customers identified the green-gold color as Qualitex's), it identifies the press pads' source. And, the green-gold color serves no other function. (Although it is important to use *some* color on press pads to avoid noticeable stains, the court found "no competitive need in the press pad industry for the green-gold color, since other colors are equally usable." 21 U.S.P.Q.2d, at 1460, 1991 WL 318798.) Accordingly, unless there is some special reason that convincingly militates against the use of color alone as a trademark, trademark law would protect Qualitex's use of the green-gold color on its press pads.

III.

Respondent Jacobson Products says that there are four special reasons why the law should forbid the use of color alone as a trademark. We shall explain, in turn, why we, ultimately, find them unpersuasive.

First, Jacobson says that, if the law permits the use of color as a trademark, it will produce uncertainty and unresolvable court disputes about what shades of a color a competitor may lawfully use. Because lighting (morning sun, twilight mist) will affect perceptions of protected color, competitors and courts will suffer from "shade confusion" as they try to decide whether use of a similar color on a similar product does, or does not, confuse customers and thereby infringe a trademark. Jacobson adds that the "shade confusion" problem is "more difficult" and "far different from" the "determination of the similarity of words or symbols."

We do not believe, however, that color, in this respect, is special. Courts traditionally decide quite difficult questions about whether two words or phrases or symbols are sufficiently similar, in context, to confuse buyers. They have had to compare, for example, such words as "Bonamine" and "Dramamine" (motion-sickness remedies); "Huggies" and "Dougies" (diapers); "Cheracol" and "Syrocol" (cough syrup); "Cyclone" and "Torna-do" (wire fences); and "Mattres" and "1–800–Mattres" (mattress franchi-sor telephone numbers). Legal standards exist to guide courts in making such comparisons. See, *e.g.*, 2 McCarthy § 15.08; 1 McCarthy §§ 11.24–11.25 ("[S]trong" marks, with greater secondary meaning, receive broader protection than "weak" marks). We do not see why courts could not apply those standards to a color, replicating, if necessary, lighting conditions under which a colored product is normally sold. Indeed, courts already have done so in cases where a trademark consists of a color plus a design, i.e., a colored symbol such as a gold stripe (around a sewer pipe), a yellow strand of wire rope, or a "brilliant yellow" band (on ampules).

Second, Jacobson argues, as have others, that colors are in limited supply. Jacobson claims that, if one of many competitors can appropriate a particular color for use as a trademark, and each competitor then tries to do the same, the supply of colors will soon be depleted. Put in its strongest form, this argument would concede that "[h]undreds of color pigments are manufactured and thousands of colors can be obtained by mixing." L. Cheskin, Colors: What They Can Do For You 47 (1947). But, it would add that, in the context of a particular product, only some colors are usable. By the time one discards colors that, say, for reasons of customer appeal, are not usable, and adds the shades that competitors cannot use lest they risk infringing a similar, registered shade, then one is left with only a handful of possible colors. And, under these circumstances, to permit one, or a few, producers to use colors as trademarks will "deplete" the supply of usable colors to the point where a competitor's inability to find a suitable color will put that competitor at a significant disadvantage.

This argument is unpersuasive, however, largely because it relies on an occasional problem to justify a blanket prohibition. When a color serves as a mark, normally alternative colors will likely be available for similar use by others. Moreover, if that is not so—if a "color depletion" or "color scarcity" problem does arise—the trademark doctrine of "functionality" normally would seem available to prevent the anticompetitive consequences that Jacobson's argument posits, thereby minimizing that argument's practical force.

The functionality doctrine, as we have said, forbids the use of a product's feature as a trademark where doing so will put a competitor at a significant disadvantage because the feature is "essential to the use or purpose of the article" or "affects [its] cost or quality." *Inwood Laborato-ries, Inc.*, 456 U.S., at 850, n. 10, 102 S.Ct., at 2186, n. 10. The functionality doctrine thus protects competitors against a disadvantage (unrelated to recognition or reputation) that trademark protection might otherwise im-pose, namely their inability reasonably to replicate important non-reputa-tion-related product features. For example, this Court has written that competitors might be free to copy the color of a medical pill where that color serves to identify the kind of medication (*e.g.*, a type of blood medicine) in addition to its source. See *id.*, at 853, 858, n. 20, 102 S.Ct., at 2188, 2190, n. 20. And, the federal courts have demonstrated that they can apply this doctrine in a careful and reasoned manner, with sensitivity to the effect on competition. Although we need not comment on the merits of specific cases, we note that lower courts have permitted competitors to copy the green color of farm machinery (because customers wanted their farm equipment to match) and have barred the use of black as a trademark on outboard boat motors (because black has the special functional attributes of decreasing the apparent size of the motor and ensuring compatibility with many different boat colors). The Restatement (Third) of Unfair Competition adds that, if a design's "aesthetic value" lies in its ability to "confe[r] a significant benefit that cannot practically be duplicated by the use of alternative designs," then the design is "functional." Restatement (Third) of Unfair Competition § 17, Comment *c*, pp. 175–176 (1995). The "ultimate test of aesthetic functionality," it explains, "is whether the recognition of trademark rights would significantly hinder competition." *Id.*, at 176.

The upshot is that, where a color serves a significant nontrademark function—whether to distinguish a heart pill from a digestive medicine or to satisfy the "noble instinct for giving the right touch of beauty to common and necessary things," G.K. Chesterton, Simplicity and Tolstoy 61 (1912)—courts will examine whether its use as a mark would permit one competitor (or a group) to interfere with legitimate (nontrademark-related) competition through actual or potential exclusive use of an important product ingredient. That examination should not discourage firms from creating aesthetically pleasing mark designs, for it is open to their competitors to do the same. But, ordinarily, it should prevent the anticompetitive consequences of Jacobson's hypothetical "color depletion" argument, when, and if, the circumstances of a particular case threaten "color depletion."

Third, Jacobson points to many older cases—including Supreme Court cases—in support of its position. In 1878, this Court described the common-law definition of trademark rather broadly to "consist of a name, symbol, figure, letter, form, or device, if adopted and used by a manufacturer or merchant in order to designate the goods he manufactures or sells to distinguish the same from those manufactured or sold by another." *McLean v. Fleming*, 96 U.S. 245, 254, 24 L.Ed. 828. Yet, in interpreting the Trademark Acts of 1881 and 1905, 21 Stat. 502, 33 Stat. 724, which retained that common-law definition, the Court questioned "[w]hether mere color can constitute a valid trade-mark," *A. Leschen & Sons Rope Co. v. Broderick & Bascom Rope Co.*, 201 U.S. 166, 171, 26 S.Ct. 425, 426, 50 L.Ed. 710 (1906), and suggested that the "product including the coloring matter is free to all who make it." *Coca-Cola Co. v. Koke Co. of America*, 254 U.S. 143, 147, 41 S.Ct. 113, 114, 65 L.Ed. 189 (1920). Even though these statements amounted to dicta, lower courts interpreted them as forbidding protection for color alone.

These Supreme Court cases, however, interpreted trademark law as it existed *before* 1946, when Congress enacted the Lanham Act. The Lanham Act significantly changed and liberalized the common law to "dispense with mere technical prohibitions," S.Rep. No. 1333, 79th Cong., 2d Sess., 3 (1946), most notably, by permitting trademark registration of descriptive words (say, "U–Build–It" model airplanes) where they had acquired "secondary meaning." The Lanham Act extended protection to descriptive marks by making clear that (with certain explicit exceptions not relevant here), "nothing ... shall prevent the registration of a mark used by the applicant which has become distinctive of the applicant's goods in commerce." 15 U.S.C. § 1052(f) (1988 ed., Supp. V). This language permits an ordinary word, normally used for a nontrademark purpose (*e.g.*, description), to act as a trademark where it has gained "secondary meaning." Its logic would appear to apply to color as well. Indeed, in 1985, the Federal Circuit considered the significance of the Lanham Act's changes as they related to color and held that trademark protection for color was consistent with the "jurisprudence under the Lanham Act developed in accordance with the statutory principle that if a mark is capable of being or becoming distinctive of [the] applicant's goods in commerce, then it is capable of serving as a trademark." Owens–Corning, 774 F.2d, at 1120.

In 1988 Congress amended the Lanham Act, revising portions of the definitional language, but left unchanged the language here relevant. It enacted these amendments against the following background: (1) the Federal Circuit had decided *Owens-Corning*; (2) the Patent and Trademark Office had adopted a clear policy (which it still maintains) permitting registration of color as a trademark, and (3) the Trademark Commission had written a report, which recommended that "the terms 'symbol, or device' ... not be deleted or narrowed to preclude registration of such things as a color, shape, smell, sound, or configuration which functions as a mark," The United States Trademark Association Trademark Review Commission Report and Recommendations to USTA President and Board of Directors, 77 T.M.Rep. 375, 421 (1987) (hereinafter Trademark Commission); see also 133 Cong.Rec. 32812 (1987) (statement of Sen. DeConcini) ("The bill I am introducing today is based on the Commission's report and recommendations"). This background strongly suggests that the language "any word, name, symbol, or device," had come to include color. And, when it amended the statute, Congress retained these terms. Indeed, the Senate Report accompanying the Lanham Act revision explicitly referred to this background understanding, in saying that the "revised definition intentionally retains ... the words 'symbol or device' so as not to preclude the registration of colors, shapes, sounds or configurations where they function as trademarks." S.Rep. No. 100–515, at 44 U.S.Code Cong. & Admin.News, 1988, p. 5607. (In addition, the statute retained language providing that "[n]o trademark by which the goods of the applicant may be distinguished from the goods of others shall be refused registration ... on account of its nature" (except for certain specified reasons not relevant here). 15 U.S.C. § 1052 (1988 ed., Supp. V)).

This history undercuts the authority of the precedent on which Jacobson relies. Much of the pre–1985 case law rested on statements in Supreme Court opinions that interpreted pre-Lanham Act trademark law and were not directly related to the holdings in those cases. Moreover, we believe the Federal Circuit was right in 1985 when it found that the 1946 Lanham Act embodied crucial legal changes that liberalized the law to permit the use of color alone as a trademark (under appropriate circumstances). At a minimum, the Lanham Act's changes left the courts free to reevaluate the preexisting legal precedent which had absolutely forbidden the use of color alone as a trademark. Finally, when Congress re-enacted the terms "word, name, symbol, or device" in 1988, it did so against a legal background in which those terms had come to include color, and its statutory revision embraced that understanding.

Fourth, Jacobson argues that there is no need to permit color alone to function as a trademark because a firm already may use color as part of a trademark, say, as a colored circle or colored letter or colored word, and may rely upon "trade dress" protection, under § 43(a) of the Lanham Act, if a competitor copies its color and thereby causes consumer confusion regarding the overall appearance of the competing products or their packaging, see 15 U.S.C. § 1125(a) (1988 ed., Supp. V). The first part of this argument begs the question. One can understand why a firm might find it difficult to place a usable symbol or word on a product (say, a large industrial bolt that customers normally see from a distance); and, in such instances, a firm might want to use color, pure and simple, instead of color as part of a design. Neither is the second portion of the argument convincing. Trademark law helps the holder of a mark in many ways that "trade dress" protection does not. See 15 U.S.C. § 1124 (ability to prevent importation of confusingly similar goods); § 1072 (constructive notice of ownership); § 1065 (incontestible status); § 1057(b) (prima facie evidence of validity and ownership). Thus, one can easily find reasons why the law might provide trademark protection in addition to trade dress protection.

IV.

Having determined that a color may sometimes meet the basic legal requirements for use as a trademark and that respondent Jacobson's arguments do not justify a special legal rule preventing color alone from serving as a trademark (and, in light of the District Court's here undisputed findings that Qualitex's use of the green-gold color on its press pads meets the basic trademark requirements), we conclude that the Ninth Circuit erred in barring Qualitex's use of color as a trademark. For these reasons, the judgment of the Ninth Circuit is

Reversed.

NOTES

1. *Fragrance.* If a product's color can be registered as a trademark, what about the product's fragrance? The Trademark Trial and Appeal Board evidently thought that distinctive fragrances are registrable when it approved registration for "a high-impact, fresh floral fragrance reminiscent of plumeria blossoms" as applied to embroidery yarn. In re Clarke, 17 U.S.P.Q. 2d 1238, 1240 (T.T.A.B.1990). According to the Board, it was satisfied that "[a]pplicant has demonstrated that customers, dealers and distributors of her scented yarns and threads have come to recognize applicant as the source of these goods." Should it make a difference whether the fragrance for which registration is sought distinguishes a separate product—yarn, for example—or is the very product itself, as would be the case with perfume or air freshener?

For an analysis of trademark registration for fragrances, see Bettina Elias, Do Scents Signify Source?—An Argument Against Trademark Protection for Fragrances, 82 Trademark Rep. 475 (1992).

2. *Location on Goods.* In Application of Kotzin, 47 C.C.P.A. 852, 276 F.2d 411, 125 U.S.P.Q. 347 (1960), the Court of Customs and Patent Appeals affirmed a refusal to register a mark consisting of "a woven rectangular tag distinctively located by being vertically disposed and having one longitudinal edge inserted beneath and permanently attached by a seam or pleat across the waistband of the trousers. . . ." Seeing no reason "why the mark sought to be registered could not be considered to be either a symbol or device or a combination thereof," the court nonetheless found that because the tag "is, as the specimen shows, more accurately described as a label, bearing a word trademark, descriptive indications of origin, and descriptions of the goods, we do not believe that the purchasing public would regard the described location of this label as an indication of the origin of the goods," and that the evidence of secondary meaning was, on the record, insufficient to support registration under Section 2(f).

Kotzin set the stage for a case in which the primary purpose of the specifically positioned tag was not to bear a word mark and in which the tag had attracted secondary meaning. The case was In re Levi Strauss & Co., 165 U.S.P.Q. 348 (T.T.A.B.1970), and the tag was the familiar rectangular bit of fabric affixed to applicant's garments at the hip pocket. Along with supporting letters, affidavits and results of reaction tests showing secondary meaning, "the advertisements illustrative of applicant's promotions of its goods show the garments displayed in such a fashion that the Tab is apparent to the reader and the Tab as so illustrated is without color and no mark or other indicia appears thereon, or if so, is illegible." To the examiner's argument "that applicant cannot obtain a registration (1) for a colorless tab or all tabs regardless of color (2) because of a particular location on its apparel," the Board answered that, (1) applicant had already obtained registration for red tabs, white tabs and black tabs similarly located and "purchasers do recognize that applicant's Tab, notwithstanding differences in color, indicates origin with applicant," and (2) "we do not see why a particular 'Tab' particularly located on particular goods cannot indicate origin."

In Levi Strauss & Co. v. Blue Bell, Inc., 632 F.2d 817, 208 U.S.P.Q. 713 (9th Cir.1980), the court held that defendant's use of a tab on the right rear pocket of its pants infringed plaintiff's registered mark. Subsequently, in Levi Strauss & Co. v. Blue Bell, Inc., 778 F.2d 1352, 228 U.S.P.Q. 346 (9th Cir.1985), the court held that the earlier decision did not collaterally estop the defendant from claiming that its placement of a tab on its shirts did not infringe plaintiff's registered mark. "The district court correctly recognized that secondary meaning inhered in the tab as applied to the pants market, but it did not err in finding no secondary meaning in the tab as applied to the shirt market. Because the tab is a location specific mark, the court could not properly have made findings concerning trademark rights in a pocket tab on garments generally." 778 F.2d at 1359.

3. *Families of Marks.* "If the owner of the trademark Servo seeks to prevent the registration of Servotorque, or Servospeed, for related products in the field of servomechanisms, is his position any stronger if he also owns Servoscope, Servosync, Servoflight, Servotherm, Servoflex and Servoboard? The Court of Customs and Patent Appeals said No. [Servo Corp. of America v. Servo–Tek Products Co., 289 F.2d 955, 129 U.S.P.Q. 352 (1961); Servo Corp. of America v. Kelsey–Hayes Co., 289 F.2d 957, 129 U.S.P.Q. 354 (1961).]

"Can the owner of the trademarks Clean–Master, Sweep–Master, Dust–Master, and Dirt–Master for carpet sweepers prevail in an opposition against Squeez–Master for sponge mops? The Trademark Trial and Appeal Board said No. [Bissell, Inc. v. Easy Day Mfg. Co., 130 U.S.P.Q. 485 (1958).]

"On the other hand, the owner of the trademarks Fritos, Chilitos, Fritatos, Ta–Tos, Chee–Tos, Corntos, and Tos successfully opposed the registration of Prontos. [The Frito Co. v. Buckeye Foods, Inc., 130 U.S.P.Q. 347 (T.T.A.B.1961).]

"Each of these cases involved the problem of a 'family of trademarks.' This is a term applied to a group of trademarks, owned by one company, in which the same syllable or syllables recur. Eastman Kodak Company, for example, owns not only the well-known trademarks Kodak, Kodachrome, and Kodacolor, but also Kodabromide, Kodacraft, Kodafix, Kodaflat, Kodagraph, Kodaguide, Kodaline, Kodamatic, and numerous others starting with the characteristic prefix Koda, thus creating a 'family' of Koda trademarks." Frederick Breitenfeld, When Is a "Family of Trademarks" Effective?, 52 Trademark Rep. 351 (1962).*

The Patent and Trademark Office has been reluctant to find rights in families of trademarks. The few cases in which it has sustained a family constellation reflect the view that the family should surround a strong mark; a sprinkling of related uses of the mark, such as in slogans or in the firm name, may help. As to the recommended number of progeny, the more the better. For example, in Dan River Mills, Inc. v. Danfra Ltd., 120 U.S.P.Q. 126 (T.T.A.B.1959), Dan River Mills successfully deployed its family of marks, used in connection with textiles, in opposing the proposed registration of "Danfra" for men's clothes. At the time, Dan River owned about 30 marks—"Dan Master," "Dantwill," "Danshrunk" and "Dantone" among them—and used the parent mark in such other settings as the slogan, "It's a Dan River Fabric."

4. *Slogans.* Slogan trademarks gained entry to the Principal Register only after considerable Patent Office resistance in the early years of the Lanham

Act. The ground commonly given for refusing registration was that the slogan constituted "an advertising feature used in connection with the actual trademarks used by applicant upon the goods." Ex Parte William Skinner & Sons, 82 U.S.P.Q. 315, 318 (Comm'r.1949).

The question of the registrability of slogans was eventually settled in the affirmative in American Enka Corp. v. Marzall, 92 U.S.P.Q. 111 (D.D.C.1952). The court there held that plaintiff's slogan, "The Fate of a Fabric Hangs by a Thread," was registrable. The court reasoned that "certain combinations of words, albeit that they are also slogans, may properly function as trademarks." That this last terse statement represents the sum of the court's reasoning on the matter may, in retrospect, not be surprising. Is it not self evident that a slogan is just "a combination" of "word[s]" within the terms of section 45? Or is this too simplistic a reading of section 45?

Because slogans are characteristically less concise than word or symbol marks, they inevitably invite the charge of descriptiveness—a charge frequently repelled on the ground that the slogan is only suggestive. In Lincoln Park Van Lines, 149 U.S.P.Q. 313 (1966), the Trademark Trial and Appeal Board reversed the examiner's refusal to register "From Maine's Cool Breeze to the Florida Keys" as a mark for applicant's moving and storage services conducted along the entire east coast. Alluding to applicant's assertion that "its mark is poetical or allegorical," the board concluded, "[t]rue the mark comprises bad poetry but nevertheless it is suggestive in connotation rather than descriptive." If the slogan is overly suggestive it may be attacked as puffery—an objection apparently drawn from a pre-Lanham Act case, Burmel Handkerchief Corp. v. Cluett, Peabody & Co., 127 F.2d 318, 53 U.S.P.Q. 369 (1942).

5. *Packages, Buildings, Industrial Design.* Color, location, names and slogans are clearly the stuff of which Principal Register marks are made— "any word, name symbol, or device or any combination thereof." The statutory case for registering packages and buildings is less clear. In Ex parte Minnesota Mining & Mfg. Co., 92 U.S.P.Q. 74 (1952), the Patent Office examiner-in-chief, affirming an examiner's refusal to register applicant's sleigh-shaped container for cellophane adhesive tape, noted that "the word 'device' appearing in the definition of a trademark cannot aid applicant. The word 'device,' which also appears in the older definitions, is not used as referring to a mechanical or structural device but is used in the sense of one of the definitions of the word: 'an artistic figure or design used as a heraldic bearing or as an emblem, badge, trademark, or the like,' rather than in one of the other meanings of the word." 92 U.S.P.Q. at 76.

Ex parte Haig & Haig Ltd., 118 U.S.P.Q. 229 (Comm'r 1958), marked the first faltering break from the position that packages are not registrable. Assistant Commissioner Leeds posed the issue obliquely: "The fundamental question, then, is not whether or not containers are registrable on the Principal Register, but it is whether or not what is presented" (applicant's well-known and distinctive pinch bottle for its Scotch whiskey) "is a trademark—a symbol or device—identifying applicant's goods and distinguishing them from those of others. This is really a question of fact and not of law...." Observing that "customers of today order applicant's whiskey as 'Pinch' and 'Pinch bottle,' " and that applicant had registered the word, "Pinch," Leeds concluded that because "there is no way of identifying or asking for such brand of product other than by describing the contour or conformation of the container ... the contour or conformation of the container may be a trademark—a symbol or device—which distinguishes the applicant's goods, and it may be registrable on the Principal Register." 118 U.S.P.Q. at 230–31.

The assistant commissioner's decision was a *tour de force* that necessarily turned on the unusual facts of the case. Taken literally, the decision offered little to encourage the use of package designs to designate source. It was, however, the spirit, not the holding, of *Haig & Haig* that prevailed. Two years later, the well-known Coca–Cola bottle configuration was registered on the Principal Register. See Julius R. Lunsford, Jr., The Protection of Packages and Containers, 56 Trademark Rep. 567 (1966). The registrability of packages on the Principal Register is today unquestioned. However, with the 1998 Trademark Law Treaty Implementation Act's amendment of Lanham Act § 2(e), 15 U.S.C.A. § 1052(e), to bar registration of marks that consist of "any matter that, as a whole, is functional," packages seem likely to undergo stricter scrutiny than in the past.

Since a container's design can be registered as a trademark if it indicates the source of the goods it contains, can the design of a structure be registered as a service mark if it indicates the source of the services it houses? The trend has been to allow the registration of buildings as marks so long as the applicant can overcome problems of distinctiveness and functionality. See generally, Anthony L. Fletcher, Buildings as Trademarks, 69 Trademark Rep. 229 (1979).

Industrial design—the configuration of a chair, for example, or a lamp—may also indicate source. The registrability of such designs is considered in Part Five, below, in the context of protection of industrial design generally.

6. *Product Depictions*. Can a two-dimensional depiction of a product be registered as a trademark for the product? In In re DC Comics, Inc., 689 F.2d 1042, 215 U.S.P.Q. 394 (C.C.P.A.1982), the Court of Customs and Patent Appeals held that it could. The Court reversed a decision of the Trademark Trial and Appeal Board which, asserting that the marks were descriptive, had denied registration for drawings of Superman, Batman and Joker for toy dolls resembling these fictional characters. Writing for the court, Judge Baldwin observed, "Whatever information a drawing of Superman or Batman or Joker might convey to the average prospective purchaser regarding a doll resembling one of the related fictional characters is wholly dependent on appellant's efforts to associate each character in the public's awareness with numerous attributes, including a single source of sponsorship. While a drawing of Superman on a box may tell a would-be buyer something about the actual appearance of a doll within, this information-conveying aspect of the drawing does not . . . conclusively eliminate its possible trademark role." 689 F.2d at 1044.

NOTE: THE SUPPLEMENTAL REGISTER

See Statute Supplement, 15 U.S.C.A. §§ 1091–1096.

The Supplemental Register embraces a wider range of subject matter than the Principal Register and is less insistent about the subject matter's distinctiveness. Lanham Act section 23, 15 U.S.C.A. § 1091, allows any "trade-mark, symbol, label, package, configuration of goods, name, word, slogan, phrase, surname, geographical name, numeral, device, any matter that, as a whole, is not functional, or any combination of the foregoing" to be registered on the Supplemental Register and requires only that the mark be "*capable* of distinguishing applicant's goods or services." (Emphasis added.) Section 27 of the Lanham Act, 15 U.S.C.A. § 1095, provides that a mark's registration on the Supplemental Register would not preclude registration on the Principal Register, and the 1988 amendments to the Lanham Act added, "[r]egistration of a mark on the supplemental register shall not constitute an admission that the mark has not acquired distinctiveness."

By design, the Supplemental Register encompasses virtually all subject matter that is protectible under state unfair competition law. The intention in creating the Register was to continue the register established by the Trademark Act of 1920 and to "provide a quick and simple registration to protect American traders abroad." Hearings on S. 4811 before Sen.Comm. on Patents, 69th Cong., 2d Sess. 13 (1927) (statement of Edward S. Rogers). "In many foreign countries, the only way one can get trademark protection is by registration. That is generally so in Latin America. Moreover, in order to get protection there—and protection depends on registration—a foreigner must produce a certificate of registration from his home land, and one purpose of the supplemental register is to provide protection in foreign countries." Hearings on H.R. 4744 Before the Subcomm. on Trademarks of the House Comm. on Patents, 76th Cong., 1st Sess. 127 (1939) (testimony of Edward S. Rogers).

As other countries drop the requirement that U.S. nationals seeking protection show that they have a U.S. registration, the importance of the Supplemental Register's original objective has declined. Yet, the Supplemental Register has continued domestic importance, offering an array of rights and remedies unavailable under state unfair competition law. Registration on the Supplemental Register ensures access to federal courts without a showing of diversity jurisdiction, amount in controversy or pendent jurisdiction. Marks on the Supplemental Register are subject neither to opposition nor to interferences; cancellation offers the only channel for attack.

Because the requirements for registration on the Supplemental Register are less exacting than those for registration on the Principal Register, it is no surprise that marks on the Supplemental Register enjoy a narrower range of rights. Among the benefits that do *not* attach to Supplemental Register registrations are the presumptions of validity, ownership and exclusive right to use that attach to registrations on the Principal Register, and constructive notice of the registrant's claim of ownership of the mark. Registrations on the Supplemental Register cannot be deposited with the Secretary of the Treasury or otherwise employed to bar the importation of goods bearing infringing marks. Supplemental Register applications do not qualify for intent to use status under 15 U.S.C.A. § 1051(b). Finally, the right to use the registered subject matter cannot become incontestable.

B.   ADMINISTRATIVE PROCEDURES

See Statute Supplement 15 U.S.C.A. §§ 1051, 1056–1059, 1062–1071, 1112–1113, 1123.

Before investing heavily in a mark, a prospective trademark owner will typically conduct a trademark search to determine, first, whether use of the mark will infringe the trademark rights of anyone else and, second, whether the mark will qualify for federal registration. The search, often performed by a professional search service, will be as wide and deep as the occasion warrants. At the least, the searcher will check the Patent and Trademark Office's application and registration files. If the company intends to mount a substantial merchandising program, it will probably also search application and registration files in each of the states as well as trade journals and telephone directories.

Even the most thorough search cannot ensure that the mark will be free of infringement claims or attacks on registration based on prior, undocumented uses. The National Broadcasting Company reportedly invested about $750,000 to develop an "N" logo, only to discover that eight months earlier the Nebraska Educational Television Network had begun using a virtually identical symbol which it had developed for less than $100. According to news reports, NBC gave the educational network $500,000 in new equipment and $25,000 cash in exchange for clear rights to the mark. Washington Post, Another Suit at NBC, Mar. 26, 1976, at B10, col. 1; Washington Post, At NBC, All's Well That N's Well, July 19, 1985, at B1, col. 1.

How extensive a search must a trademark user make in order to avoid the finding of bad faith that will trigger an increased damage award? In International Star Class Yacht Racing Association v. Tommy Hilfiger U.S.A. Inc., 80 F.3d 749, 38 U.S.P.Q.2d 1369 (2d Cir.1996), defendant adopted the words "Star Class" and a star symbol for its line of menswear after obtaining a search of registered federal trademarks that disclosed no such marks on the Principal Register. Plaintiff had already been using, but had not registered, the words and the star symbol in connection with Star Class boats and on hats, clothing and other paraphernalia sold to the public. Affirming the lower court's grant of an injunction against defendant's use of the unregistered mark, the Court of Appeals reversed and remanded on the question of damages because of defendant's possible bad faith in failing to follow its trademark counsel's suggestion to obtain a full trademark search, beyond the Principal Register. On remand, the district court again found insufficient evidence to indicate bad faith, taking judicial notice from an earlier decision that it was standard industry practice to confine defensive searches to the federal register, and to conduct more extensive searches only in connection with marks being considered for trademark registration. Again, the court of appeals reversed and remanded, this time faulting the lower court's reliance on judicial notice to demonstrate lack of bad faith. 146 F.3d 66 (2d Cir.1998).

See generally, Glenn A. Gundersen, Trademark Searching: A Practical and Strategic Guide to the Clearance of New Marks in the United States (1994).

A.   Examination

The first of the several administrative checkpoints confronting a Principal Register applicant is the trademark examiner's review of the application. The initial procedures will be the same whether the application is a use application under 15 U.S.C.A. § 1051(a) or an intent to use application under 15 U.S.C.A. § 1051(b). After reviewing the application for compliance with statutory formalities, the examiner will determine whether registration is barred on any of the grounds specified in section 2 of the Lanham Act, 15 U.S.C.A. § 1052. The examiner will search prior registrations and pending applications to determine whether the mark is confusingly similar to any other mark previously used and not abandoned. The examiner may consult trade periodicals to determine whether the mark has a descriptive connotation in the industry in which it is used.

If the examiner concludes that the mark qualifies for registration on the Principal Register, she will approve it for publication in the *Official Gazette*. If no one successfully files an opposition within thirty days of the mark's publication in the *Gazette,* a registration will issue in the case of a use application, and a notice of allowance will issue in the case of an intent to use application. 15 U.S.C.A. § 1063(b). If the examiner rejects the application, the applicant can amend the application to meet the examiner's objections or, if he disagrees with the examiner, can file a response rebutting the grounds for rejection. If these efforts fail and the mark is finally rejected, the applicant can appeal to the Trademark Trial and Appeal Board. 15 U.S.C.A. § 1070.

The *ex parte* proceeding before the trademark examiner is a relatively inexpensive way to screen trademark registration applications for the most obvious, easily discovered objections. For the comparatively few applications that require more extensive scrutiny, the system relies on *inter partes* actions between the applicant and potentially injured competitors to weed out marks that do not qualify for registration. The examiner's approval for publication in the *Official Gazette* sets the stage for the first three forms of *inter partes* proceedings—oppositions, concurrent use proceedings and interference proceedings.

B. *Inter Partes* Proceedings

1. *Oppositions.* Opposition proceedings, conducted by the Trademark Trial and Appeal Board under 15 U.S.C.A. § 1067, give competitors and other potentially injured parties the opportunity to object to registration of a mark. To be heard, the opposer must file its opposition within thirty days of the mark's publication in the *Official Gazette.* To prevail, the opposer must demonstrate that it is likely to be damaged by the mark's registration and that the mark is not entitled to registration under the terms of the Act. The opposer's claimed damage may be that the mark is a descriptive term and that its registration will jeopardize the opposer's freedom to use the term descriptively in its own business. The opposer may allege that the applicant's mark is confusingly similar to the opposer's mark. Having established standing through proof of prospective damage, the opposer can assert any of the available statutory grounds for denying registration—most typically, one or more of the section 2 bars.

2. *Concurrent Use Proceedings.* If the applicant's trademark search revealed an earlier, localized use of the same or a similar mark by someone else, the applicant could initiate a concurrent use proceeding to limit his registration to territories not yet occupied by the earlier user. Section 2(d) provides that the Commissioner may issue concurrent registrations upon determining that "confusion, mistake or deception is not likely to result from the continued use by more than one person of the same or similar marks under conditions and limitations as to the mode or place of use of the marks or the goods in connection with which such marks are used." A concurrent use application will first be reviewed *ex parte* by a trademark examiner. Rules of Practice in Trademark Cases, 37 C.F.R. § 2.99(a) (2001). After notice to the adverse parties named in the application, an *inter partes* proceeding before the Trademark Trial and Appeal Board may ensue. 15 U.S.C.A. § 1067.

3. *Interferences.* Lanham Act section 16, 15 U.S.C.A. § 1066, provides for interference proceedings to determine priority of use any time "application is made for the registration of a mark which so resembles a mark previously registered by another, or for the registration of which another has previously made application, as to be likely when used on or in connection with the goods or services of the applicant to cause confusion or mistake or to deceive." Since March 1, 1972, amendments to the Trademark Rules have substantially confined interference proceedings "to rare cases in which a party might be able to prove that he would suffer irrevocable harm if his only recourse was to file an opposition or a petition for cancellation." These amendments were expected "virtually to eliminate interferences in trademark cases." 36 Fed.Reg. 18002–03 (1971).

4. *Cancellation.* Many marks published for opposition in the *Official Gazette* will pass unnoticed by those most interested in opposing their registration. Fairness to competitors, and deference to the public's interest in freedom from confusion, require that interested parties be given some later opportunity to object to registration. But fairness to registrants and the public's interest in encouraging investment in trademarks, also re-

quires a secure foundation for the registrant's investment. Lanham Act § 14, 15 U.S.C.A. § 1064, balances these interests by authorizing cancellation of Principal Register registrations upon petition "by any person who believes that he is or will be damaged by the registration of a mark on the principal register...." Registrations may be cancelled within five years of the date of registration on any ground that would have barred registration initially. After five years, the grounds for cancellation become more limited. Like opposition and concurrent use proceedings, cancellation applications are heard by the Trademark Trial and Appeal Board under 15 U.S.C.A. § 1067.

C. Renewal

Even after the Trademark Law Revision Act of 1988, trademark rights mainly turn on use. The duration of trademark protection is consequently indeterminate, lasting as long as the trademark owner uses its mark commercially. To terminate the owner's exclusive rights at some fixed and arbitrary point, after which competitors could use the mark freely, would expose consumers to the very deception, confusion and mistake that the Trademark Act aims to prevent. Unlike the Patent and Copyright Acts, which impose fixed terms, the Lanham Act provides that certificates of registration shall remain in force for ten years, renewable indefinitely for successive ten year terms upon "payment of the prescribed fee and the filing of a written application." 15 U.S.C.A. §§ 1058, 1059. The ten-year term is the product of the 1988 amendments; the Lanham Act previously prescribed a twenty-year renewable term. Section 8, 15 U.S.C.A. § 1058, imposes one earlier checkpoint, six years after the mark's registration, that requires an affidavit listing the goods or services recited in the registration for which the mark is being used in commerce.

D. Appeals

The Trademark Trial and Appeal Board hears appeals from *ex parte* trademark examiner decisions refusing registration. The Board is also the initial forum for *inter partes* proceedings—oppositions, concurrent use, interferences and cancellations. The Commissioner of Patents and Trademarks hears appeals from trademark examiner decisions rejecting a registrant's section 8 affidavit, 15 U.S.C.A. § 1058, or application for renewal under section 1059. A trademark applicant or registrant who loses in an *ex parte* or *inter partes* proceeding before the Board, or before the Commissioner on a section 8 affidavit or registration renewal, may appeal to the Court of Appeals for the Federal Circuit under 15 U.S.C.A. § 1071(a) or seek *de novo* review through a civil action in a United States district court under 15 U.S.C.A. § 1071(b). Recourse from an adverse decision of the Court of Appeals for the Federal Circuit is to the United States Supreme Court under 28 U.S.C.A. § 1254. Recourse from an adverse district court decision is to the regional circuit court of appeals, under 15 U.S.C.A. § 1121, and then to the Supreme Court under 28 U.S.C.A. § 1254.

NOTE: INCONTESTABILITY AND IMMUNITY FROM CANCELLATION

The proponents of the Lanham Act's incontestability provisions had originally hoped for a strong, unified standard that would govern both cancellation proceedings and infringement actions. One early bill had provided that a mark's registration could not be cancelled or attacked in an infringement action after five years on the Principal Register. H.R. 9041, 75th Cong., 3d Sess., §§ 13, 14 (1938). The provisions that finally emerged from the push and tug of legislative compromise are far more limited and fragmented. They include the incontestability provisions of sections 15 and 33(b), 15 U.S.C.A. §§ 1065, 1115(b), and the cancellation provisions of section 14, 15 U.S.C.A. § 1064, which substantially parallel the incontestability provisions.

Sections 14, 15 and 33(b) rest on the premise that, to encourage investment in trademarks, time and use must be allowed to heal many original defects in a mark. Each section focuses its curative power on a different context. Section 14 applies when the registrant is defending its mark against a petition to cancel. Section 15, which establishes the registrant's incontestable right to use, applies when the registrant is defending an infringement action brought to enjoin it from using the mark. Section 33(b) applies when the registrant seeks to prevent someone else from using a confusingly similar mark. Several early cases rejected this last, offensive use of incontestability, but in 1985 the U.S. Supreme Court resolved any doubt about the offensive use of incontestability by holding that "the holder of a registered mark may rely on incontestability to enjoin infringement." Park 'N Fly, Inc. v. Dollar Park and Fly, Inc., 469 U.S. 189, 205, 105 S.Ct. 658, 83 L.Ed.2d 582, 224 U.S.P.Q. 327, 334 (1985).

Section 14. Although section 14 is sometimes called an incontestability provision, only sections 15 and 33(b) use the term expressly. Section 14 approximates incontestability by providing that, after five years on the Principal Register, a mark will generally be immune from attack in a cancellation proceeding. Among the grounds left open for attack after the five year period are functionality, fraudulent registration, abandonment, the mark's having become the "generic name for the goods or services, or a portion thereof, for which it is registered," and any of the grounds that would bar registration under section 2(a), (b) or (c). Thus, after five years, a registered mark cannot be cancelled simply because it lacks distinctiveness or is confusingly similar to other marks.

Section 15. Section 15 provides that a registrant's right to use its mark in commerce "shall be incontestable" if the mark has been used for five consecutive years after its registration and the registrant files an affidavit to that effect. Under section 15, a party can defeat incontestability on the same grounds that, under section 14, would require cancellation after five years' registration. Section 15 also provides that a registration will not become incontestable if use of the mark "infringes a valid right acquired under the law of any State or Territory by use of a mark or trade name continuing from a date prior to the date of registration" of the registered mark. Further, "no incontestable right shall be acquired in a mark which is the generic name for the goods or services or a portion thereof, for which it is registered."

Section 33(b). Section 33(a) of the Lanham Act provides that any registration of a mark on the Principal Register "shall be admissible in evidence and shall be prima facie evidence of the validity of the registered mark and of the registration of the mark, of the registrant's ownership of the mark, and of the registrant's exclusive right to use the registered mark in commerce...." 15 U.S.C.A. § 1115(a). Section 33(b) gives substantially greater evidential weight to incontestable marks by making them conclusive, rather than merely prima facie, evidence of validity, ownership and exclusive right to use. For example, in the *Park 'N Fly* case, the Supreme Court held that it is no defense to an action for infringement of an incontestable mark that the mark was merely descriptive under the terms of section 2(e), 15 U.S.C.A. 1052(e). Among other grounds, section 33(b) deprives the registration certificate of conclusive effect if the registration or incontestable right was obtained fraudulently or if the mark has been abandoned or used to violate federal antitrust laws, or is functional. 15 U.S.C.A. § 1115(b).

The 1988 amendments to the Lanham Act resolved a conflict among the circuits by adding as a defense to incontestability that "equitable principles, including laches, estoppel, and acquiescence, are applicable." § 33(b)(8). The 1988 amendments also removed any question whether a registrant can prevail in an infringement action on the basis of incontestability alone. As amended, section 33(b) provides that "conclusive evidence of the right to use the registered mark shall be subject to proof of infringement as defined in section 1114 of this title."

See generally Richard A. Wallen & Michael J. MacDermott, Federal Registration and Incontestability, 79 Trademark Rep. 373 (1989); Suman Naresh, Incontestability and Rights in Descriptive Trademarks, 53 U.Chi. L. Rev. 953 (1986).

C.   RIGHTS AND REMEDIES

1.   RIGHTS

See Statute Supplement 15 U.S.C.A. §§ 1057(b), 1060, 1065, 1072, 1114–1115, 1125(c).

a.   *Geographic Boundaries*

UNITED DRUG CO. v. THEODORE RECTANUS CO., 248 U.S. 90, 96–98, 100, 39 S.Ct. 48, 50, 63 L.Ed. 141 (1918). Mr. Justice PITNEY: The entire argument for the petitioner is summed up in the contention that whenever the first user of a trade-mark has been reasonably diligent in extending the territory of his trade, and as a result of such extension has in good faith come into competition with a later user of the same mark who in equal good faith has extended his trade locally before invasion of his field by the first user, so that finally it comes to pass that the rival traders are offering competitive merchandise in a common market under the same trade-mark, the later user should be enjoined at the suit of the prior adopter, even though the latter be the last to enter the competitive field and the former have already established a trade there. Its application to the case is based upon the hypothesis that the record shows that Mrs. Regis and her firm, during the entire period of limited and local trade in her medicine under the Rex mark, were making efforts to extend their trade so far as they were able to do with the means at their disposal. There is little in the record to support this hypothesis; but, waiving this, we will pass upon the principal contention.

... Undoubtedly, the general rule is that, as between conflicting claimants to the right to use the same mark, priority of appropriation determines the question. But the reason is that purchasers have come to understand the mark as indicating the origin of the wares, so that its use by a second producer amounts to an attempt to sell his goods as those of his competitor. The reason for the rule does not extend to a case where the same trade-mark happens to be employed simultaneously by two manufacturers in different markets separate and remote from each other, so that the mark means one thing in one market, an entirely different thing in another. It would be a perversion of the rule of priority to give it such an application in our broadly extended country that an innocent party who had in good faith employed a trade-mark in one State, and by the use of it had built up a trade there, being the first appropriator in that jurisdiction, might afterwards be prevented from using it, with consequent injury to his trade and good-will, at the instance of one who theretofore had employed the same mark but only in other and remote jurisdictions, upon the ground that its first employment happened to antedate that of the first-mentioned trader.

Dawn Donut Co. v. Hart's Food Stores, Inc.

United States Court of Appeals, Second Circuit, 1959.
267 F.2d 358, 121 U.S.P.Q. 430.

LUMBARD, Circuit Judge.

The principal question is whether the plaintiff, a wholesale distributor of doughnuts and other baked goods under its federally registered trade-marks "Dawn" and "Dawn Donut," is entitled under the provisions of the Lanham Trademark Act to enjoin the defendant from using the mark "Dawn" in connection with the retail sale of doughnuts and baked goods entirely within a six county area of New York State surrounding the city of Rochester. The primary difficulty arises from the fact that although plaintiff licenses purchasers of its mixes to use its trademarks in connection with the retail sales of food products made from the mixes, it has not licensed or otherwise exploited the mark at the retail level in defendant's market area for some thirty years.

We hold that because no likelihood of public confusion arises from the concurrent use of the mark in connection with retail sales of doughnuts and other baked goods in separate trading areas, and because there is no present likelihood that plaintiff will expand its retail use of the mark into defendant's market area, plaintiff is not now entitled to any relief under the Lanham Act, 15 U.S.C.A. § 1114. Accordingly, we affirm the district court's dismissal of plaintiff's complaint.

This is not to say that the defendant has acquired any permanent right to use the mark in its trading area. On the contrary, we hold that because of the effect of the constructive notice provision of the Lanham Act, should the plaintiff expand its retail activities into the six county area, upon a proper application and showing to the district court, it may enjoin defendant's use of the mark.

With respect to defendant's counterclaim to cancel plaintiff's registration on the ground that its method of licensing its trademarks violates the Lanham Act, a majority of the court holds that the district court's dismissal of defendant's counterclaim should be affirmed. They conclude that the district court's finding that the plaintiff exercised the degree of control over the nature and quality of the products sold by its licensees required by the Act was not clearly erroneous, particularly in view of the fact that the defendant had the burden of proving its claim for cancellation. I dissent from this conclusion because neither the finding of the trial judge nor the undisputed evidence in the record indicates the extent of supervision and control actually exercised by the plaintiff.

We are presented here with cross-appeals from a judgment entered by the District Court for the Western District of New York dismissing both plaintiff's complaint for infringement of its federally registered trademarks and defendant's counterclaim to cancel plaintiff's federal registrations.

Plaintiff, Dawn Donut Co., Inc., of Jackson, Michigan since June 1, 1922 has continuously used the trademark "Dawn" upon 25 to 100 pound bags of doughnut mix which it sells to bakers in various states, including New York, and since 1935 it has similarly marketed a line of sweet dough mixes for use in the baking of coffee cakes, cinnamon rolls and oven goods in general under that mark. In 1950 cake mixes were added to the company's line of products. Dawn's sales representatives call upon bakers to solicit orders for mixes and the orders obtained are filled by shipment to the purchaser either directly from plaintiff's Jackson, Michigan plant, where the mixes are manufactured, or from a local warehouse within the customer's state. For some years plaintiff maintained a warehouse in Jamestown, New York, from which shipments were made, but sometime prior to the commencement of this suit in 1954 it discontinued this warehouse and has since then shipped its mixes to its New York customers directly from Michigan.

Plaintiff furnishes certain buyers of its mixes, principally those who agree to become exclusive Dawn Donut Shops, with advertising and packaging material bearing the trademark "Dawn" and permits these bakers to sell goods made from the mixes to the consuming public under that trademark. These display materials are supplied either as a courtesy or at a moderate price apparently to stimulate and promote the sale of plaintiff's mixes.

The district court found that with the exception of one Dawn Donut Shop operated in the city of Rochester, New York during 1926–27, plaintiff's licensing of its mark in connection with the retail sale of doughnuts in the state of New York has been confined to areas not less than 60 miles from defendant's trading area. The court also found that for the past eighteen years plaintiff's present New York state representative has, without interruption, made regular calls upon bakers in the city of Rochester, N.Y., and in neighboring towns and cities, soliciting orders for plaintiff's mixes and that throughout this period orders have been filled and shipments made of plaintiff's mixes from Jackson, Michigan into the city of Rochester. But it does not appear that any of these purchasers of plaintiff's mixes employed the plaintiff's mark in connection with retail sales.

The defendant, Hart Food Stores, Inc., owns and operates a retail grocery chain within the New York counties of Monroe, Wayne, Livingston, Genesee, Ontario and Wyoming. The products of defendant's bakery, Starhart Bakeries, Inc., a New York corporation of which it is the sole stockholder, are distributed through these stores, thus confining the distribution of defendant's product to an area within a 45 mile radius of Rochester. Its advertising of doughnuts and other baked products over television and radio and in newspapers is also limited to this area. Defendant's bakery corporation was formed on April 13, 1951 and first used the imprint "Dawn" in packaging its products on August 30, 1951. The district court found that the defendant adopted the mark "Dawn" without any actual knowledge of plaintiff's use or federal registration of the mark, selecting it largely because of a slogan "Baked at midnight, delivered at Dawn" which was originated by defendant's president and used by defendant in its bakery operations from 1929 to 1935. Defendant's president testified, however, that no investigation was made prior to the adoption of the mark to see if anyone else was employing it. Plaintiff's marks were registered federally in 1927, and their registration was renewed in 1947. Therefore by virtue of the Lanham Act, 15 U.S.C.A. § 1072, the defendant had constructive notice of plaintiff's marks as of July 5, 1947, the effective date of the Act.

Defendant does not contest the similarity of the marks. Its principal contention is that because plaintiff has failed to exploit the mark "Dawn" for some thirty years at the retail level in the Rochester trading area, plaintiff should not be accorded the exclusive right to use the mark in this area. We reject this contention as inconsistent with the scope of protection afforded a federal registrant by the Lanham Act.

Prior to the passage of the Lanham Act courts generally held that the owner of a registered trademark could not sustain an action for infringement against another who, without knowledge of the registration, used the mark in a different trading area from that exploited by the registrant so that public confusion was unlikely. By being the first to adopt a mark in an area without knowledge of its prior registration, a junior user of a mark could gain the right to exploit the mark exclusively in that market.

But the Lanham Act, 15 U.S.C.A. § 1072, provides that registration of a trademark on the principal register is constructive notice of the registrant's claim of ownership. Thus, by eliminating the defense of good faith and lack of knowledge, § 1072 affords nationwide protection to registered marks, regardless of the areas in which the registrant actually uses the mark.

That such is the purpose of Congress is further evidenced by 15 U.S.C.A. § 1115(a) and (b) which make the certificate of registration evidence of the registrant's "exclusive right to use the mark in commerce." "Commerce" is defined in 15 U.S.C.A. § 1127 to include all the commerce which may lawfully be regulated by Congress. These two provisions of the Lanham Act make it plain that the fact that the defendant employed the mark "Dawn," without actual knowledge of plaintiff's registration, at the retail level in a limited geographical area of New York state before the plaintiff used the mark in that market, does not entitle it either to exclude the plaintiff from using the mark in that area or to use the mark concurrently once the plaintiff licenses the mark or otherwise exploits it in connection with retail sales in the area.

Plaintiff's failure to license its trademarks in defendant's trading area during the thirty odd years that have elapsed since it licensed them to a Rochester baker does not work an abandonment of the rights in that area. We hold that 15 U.S.C.A. § 1127, which provides for abandonment in certain cases of nonuse, applies only when the registrant fails to use his mark within the meaning of § 1127, anywhere in the nation. Since the Lanham Act affords a registrant nationwide protection, a contrary holding would create an insoluble problem of measuring the geographical extent of the abandonment. Even prior to the passage of the Lanham Act, when trademark protection flowed from state law and therefore depended on use within the state, no case, as far as we have been able to ascertain, held that a trademark owner abandoned his rights within only part of a state because of his failure to use the mark in that part of the state.

Accordingly, since plaintiff has used its trademark continuously at the retail level, it has not abandoned its federal registration rights even in defendant's trading area. . . .

Accordingly, we turn to the question of whether on this record plaintiff has made a sufficient showing to warrant the issuance of an injunction against the defendant's use of the mark "Dawn" in a trading area in which the plaintiff has for thirty years failed to employ its registered mark.

The Lanham Act, 15 U.S.C.A. § 1114, sets out the standard for awarding a registrant relief against the unauthorized use of his mark by another. It provides that the registrant may enjoin only that concurrent use which creates a likelihood of public confusion as to the origin of the products in connection with which the marks are used. Therefore if the use of the marks by the registrant and the unauthorized user are confined to two sufficiently distinct and geographically separate markets, with no likelihood that the registrant will expand his use into defendant's market, so that no public confusion is possible, then the registrant is not entitled to enjoin the junior user's use of the mark.

As long as plaintiff and defendant confine their use of the mark "Dawn" in connection with the retail sale of baked goods to their present separate trading areas it is clear that no public confusion is likely.

The district court took note of what it deemed common knowledge, that "retail purchasers of baked goods, because of the perishable nature of such goods, usually make such purchases reasonably close to their homes, say within about 25 miles, and retail purchases of such goods beyond that distance are for all practical considerations negligible." No objection is made to this finding and nothing appears in the record which contradicts it as applied to this case.

Moreover, we note that it took plaintiff three years to learn of defendant's use of the mark and bring this suit, even though the plaintiff was doing some wholesale business in the Rochester area. This is a strong indication that no confusion arose or is likely to arise either from concurrent use of the marks at the retail level in geographically separate trading areas or from its concurrent use at different market levels, viz. retail and wholesale in the same area.

The decisive question then is whether plaintiff's use of the mark "Dawn" at the retail level is likely to be confined to its current area of use or whether in the normal course of its business, it is likely to expand the retail use of the mark into defendant's trading area. If such expansion were probable, then the concurrent use of the marks would give rise to the conclusion that there was a likelihood of confusion.

The district court found that in view of the plaintiff's inactivity for about thirty years in exploiting its trademarks in defendant's trading area at the retail level either by advertising directed at retail purchasers or by retail sales through authorized licensed users, there was no reasonable expectation that plaintiff would extend its retail operations into defendant's trading area. There is ample evidence in the record to support this conclusion and we cannot say that it is clearly erroneous.

We note not only that plaintiff has failed to license its mark at the retail level in defendant's trading area for a substantial period of time, but also that the trend of plaintiff's business manifests a striking decrease in the number of licensees employing its mark at the retail level in New York state and throughout the country. In the 1922–1930 period plaintiff had 75 to 80 licensees across the country with 11 located in New York. At the time of the trial plaintiff listed only 16 active licensees not one of which was located in New York.

The normal likelihood that plaintiff's wholesale operations in the Rochester area would expand to the retail level is fully rebutted and overcome by the decisive fact that plaintiff has in fact not licensed or otherwise exploited its mark at retail in the area for some thirty years.

Accordingly, because plaintiff and defendant use the mark in connection with retail sales in distinct and separate markets and because there is no present prospect that plaintiff will expand its use of the mark at the retail level into defendant's trading area, we conclude that there is no likelihood of public confusion arising from the concurrent use of the marks and therefore the issuance of an injunction is not warranted. A fortiori plaintiff is not entitled to any accounting or damages. However, because of the effect we have attributed to the constructive notice provision of the Lanham Act, the plaintiff may later, upon a proper showing of an intent to use the mark at the retail level in defendant's market area, be entitled to enjoin defendant's use of the mark. . . .

We are all agreed that the Lanham Act places an affirmative duty upon a licensor of a registered trademark to take reasonable measures to detect and prevent misleading uses of his mark by his licensees or suffer cancellation of his federal registration. The Act, 15 U.S.C.A. § 1064, provides that a trademark registration may be cancelled because the trademark has been "abandoned." And "abandoned" is defined in 15 U.S.C.A. § 1127 to include any act or omission by the registrant which causes the trademark to lose its significance as an indication of origin.

Prior to the passage of the Lanham Act many courts took the position that the licensing of a trademark separately from the business in connection with which it had been used worked an abandonment. The theory of these cases was that:

> A trademark is intended to identify the goods of the owner and to safeguard his good will. The designation if employed by a person other than the one whose business it serves to identify would be misleading. Consequently a right to the use of a trademark or a trade name cannot be transferred in gross. American Broadcasting Co. v. Wahl Co., [121 F.2d 412, 413].

Other courts were somewhat more liberal and held that a trademark could be licensed separately from the business in connection with which it had been used provided that the licensor retained control over the quality of the goods produced by the licensee. But even in the duPont case the court was careful to point out that naked licensing, viz. the grant of licenses without the retention of control, was invalid. E.I. du Pont DSe Nemours & Co. v. Celanese Corporation of America, [35 C.C.P.A.1061, 167 F.2d 484, 489.]

The Lanham Act clearly carries forward the view of these latter cases that controlled licensing does not work an abandonment of the licensor's registration, while a system of naked licensing does. 15 U.S.C.A. § 1055 provides:

> Where a registered mark or a mark sought to be registered is or may be used legitimately by related companies, such use shall inure to the benefit of the registrant or applicant for registration, and such use shall not affect the validity of such mark or of its registration, provided such mark is not used in such manner as to deceive the public.

And 15 U.S.C.A. § 1127 defines "related company" to mean "any person who legitimately controls or is controlled by the registrant or applicant for registration in respect to the nature and quality of the goods or services in connection with which the mark is used."

Without the requirement of control, the right of a trademark owner to license his mark separately from the business in connection with which it has been used would create the danger that products bearing the same trademark might be of diverse qualities. If the licensor is not compelled to take some reasonable steps to prevent misuses of his trademark in the hands of others the public will be deprived of its most effective protection against misleading uses of a trademark. The public is hardly in a position to uncover deceptive uses of a trademark before they occur and will be at best slow to detect them after they happen. Thus, unless the licensor exercises supervision and control over the operations of its licensees the risk that the public will be unwittingly deceived will be increased and this is precisely what the Act is in part designed to prevent. Clearly the only effective way to protect the public where a trademark is used by licensees is to place on the licensor the affirmative duty of policing in a reasonable manner the activities of his licensees.

The critical question on these facts therefore is whether the plaintiff sufficiently policed and inspected its licensees' operations to guarantee the quality of the products they sold under its trademarks to the public. The trial court found that: "By reason of its contracts with its licensees, plaintiff exercised legitimate control over the nature and quality of the food products on which plaintiff's licensees used the trademark 'Dawn.' Plaintiff and its licensees are related companies within the meaning of Section 45 of the Trademark Act of 1946." It is the position of the majority of this court that the trial judge has the same leeway in determining what constitutes a reasonable degree of supervision and control over licensees under the facts and circumstances of the particular case as he has on other questions of fact; and particularly because it is the defendant who has the burden of proof on this issue they hold the lower court's finding not clearly erroneous.

[The following is the dissenting portion of Judge Lumbard's opinion.]

I dissent from the conclusion of the majority that the district court's findings are not clearly erroneous because (1) while it is true that the trial judge must be given some discretion in determining what constitutes reasonable supervision of licensees under the Lanham Act, it is also true that an appellate court ought not to accept the conclusions of the district court unless they are supported by findings of sufficient facts. It seems to me that the only findings of the district judge regarding supervision are in such general and conclusory terms as to be meaningless. In the absence of supporting findings or of undisputed evidence in the record indicating the kind of supervision and inspection the plaintiff actually made of its licensees, it is impossible for us to pass upon whether there was such supervision as to satisfy the statute. There was evidence before the district court in the matter of supervision, and more detailed findings thereon should have been made.

Plaintiff's licensees fall into two classes: (1) those bakers with whom it made written contracts providing that the baker purchase exclusively plaintiff's mixes and requiring him to adhere to plaintiff's directions in using the mixes; and (2) those bakers whom plaintiff permitted to sell at retail under the "Dawn" label doughnuts and other baked goods made from its mixes although there was no written agreement governing the quality of the foods sold under the Dawn mark.

The contracts that plaintiff did conclude, although they provided that the purchaser use the mix as directed and without adulteration, failed to provide for any system of inspection and control. Without such a system plaintiff could not know whether these bakers were adhering to its standards in using the mix or indeed whether they were selling only products made from Dawn mixes under the trademark "Dawn."

The absence, however, of an express contract right to inspect and supervise a licensee's operations does not mean that the plaintiff's method of licensing failed to comply with the requirements of the Lanham Act. Plaintiff may in fact have exercised control in spite of the absence of any express grant by licensees of the right to inspect and supervise.

The question then, with respect to both plaintiff's contract and non-contract licensees, is whether the plaintiff in fact exercised sufficient control.

Here the only evidence in the record relating to the actual supervision of licensees by plaintiff consists of the testimony of two of plaintiff's local sales representatives that they regularly visited their particular customers and the further testimony of one of them, Jesse Cohn, the plaintiff's New York representative, that "in many cases" he did have an opportunity to inspect and observe the operations of his customers. The record does not indicate whether plaintiff's other sales representatives made any similar efforts to observe the operations of licensees.

Moreover, Cohn's testimony fails to make clear the nature of the inspection he made or how often he made one. His testimony indicates that his opportunity to observe a licensee's operations was limited to "those cases where I am able to get into the shop" and even casts some doubt on whether he actually had sufficient technical knowledge in the use of plaintiff's mix to make an adequate inspection of a licensee's operations.

The fact that it was Cohn who failed to report the defendant's use of the mark "Dawn" to the plaintiff casts still further doubt about the extent of the supervision Cohn exercised over the operations of plaintiff's New York licensees.

Thus I do not believe that we can fairly determine on this record whether plaintiff subjected its licensees to periodic and thorough inspections by trained personnel or whether its policing consisted only of chance, cursory examinations of licensees' operations by technically untrained salesmen. The latter system of inspection hardly constitutes a sufficient program of supervision to satisfy the requirements of the Act.

Therefore it is appropriate to remand the counterclaim for more extensive findings on the relevant issues rather than hazard a determination on this incomplete and uncertain record. I would direct the district court to order the cancellation of plaintiff's registrations if it should find that the plaintiff did not adequately police the operations of its licensees.

But unless the district court finds some evidence of misuse of the mark by plaintiff in its sales of mixes to bakers at the wholesale level, the cancellation of plaintiff's registration should be limited to the use of the mark in connection with sale of the finished food products to the consuming public. Such a limited cancellation is within the power of the court. Section 1119 of 15 U.S.C.A. specifically provides that "In any action involving a registered mark the court may ... order cancellation of registrations in whole or in part, ..." Moreover, partial cancellation is consistent with § 1051(a)(1) of 15 U.S.C.A., governing the initial registration of trademarks which requires the applicant to specify "the goods in connection with which the mark is used and the manner in which the mark is used in connection with such goods...."

The district court's denial of an injunction restraining defendant's use of the mark "Dawn" on baked and fried goods and its dismissal of defendant's counterclaim are affirmed.

NOTES

1. There is probably no more intricate task in trademark law than coordinating the rights accruing to senior and junior users under common law and under section 22's constructive notice provisions. It is clear under the common law that, until a mark is registered, each user has rights in the territory it has occupied. But, to what extent will registration freeze the rights of one and expand the rights of the other? Say that *A* first used the mark, "Rex," in connection with its shampoo in 1951. It applied for registration on the Principal Register in 1954 and the registration issued in 1956. *A*'s distribution of the shampoo has at all times been restricted to three states, New York, New Jersey, and Connecticut. *B* first used the mark, "Rex," in connection with its shampoo in 1949 and applied for registration on the Principal Register in 1959. *B*'s distribution of its goods has at all times been restricted to three states, California, Oregon and Washington. Now, *B*'s 1959 application has become the basis for a concurrent use proceeding under section 2, 15 U.S.C.A. § 1052(d). What are the respective territorial rights of the parties?

In 1970, the Court of Customs and Patent Appeals definitively outlined the substantive rules governing concurrent use. Application of Beatrice Foods Co., 429 F.2d 466, 166 U.S.P.Q. 431 (C.C.P.A.1970). *Beatrice Foods* stated that, as a general rule in concurrent use proceedings between two applicants, the senior user is entitled to a registration covering the entire United States, less the area in which the junior user has established territorial rights. But, the court noted, territorial rights need not to be coextensive with territorial use. The court confirmed and elaborated the *Beatrice Foods* analysis in Weiner King, Inc. v. Weiner King Corp., 615 F.2d 512, 522–23 n. 6, 204 U.S.P.Q. 820 (C.C.P.A.1980): "While it is clear that appropriation of a mark with knowledge that it is being used by another is not in good faith, it does not follow that a later user who has adopted in good faith *must* forego any further expansion after learning of the prior user. We believe that, even under the common law, such an issue depends on such factors as natural area of expansion, the possibility of encroachment on the area of the other party, and other equitable considerations."

2. *Constructive Notice and Constructive Use.* The 1988 amendments to the Lanham Act complicated the allocation of territorial rights by introducing the concept of constructive use arising from the filing of an intent to use application. Constructive *notice* under section 22, 15 U.S.C.A. § 1072, has two consequences: it prevents a junior user who begins her use after the date of the senior user's registration from acquiring any right to use the mark; and it confines the rights of any senior, unregistered user to the territory that the user occupied at the time of the registration. Constructive *use* prevents a junior user from acquiring any right to use the mark after the filing date of an intent to use application; it does not, however, freeze the rights of any senior unregistered user.

3. *Injunctions.* Say that A first used the mark, "Rex," in connection with its shampoo in 1961, limiting its distribution at the time to east coast states. In 1968, A obtained registration for the mark on the Principal Register. In 1969, B first used the mark "Rex" in connection with its shampoo, limiting its trade to west coast states. A has not yet marketed its shampoo on the west coast. Should A be entitled to an injunction against B? Sterling Brewing, Inc. v. Cold Spring Brewing Corp., 100 F.Supp. 412, 90 U.S.P.Q. 242 (D.Mass.1951), the first case to apply section 22 to this fact situation, held that the injunction should issue at once even though "the plaintiff's zone of potential expansion of business cannot reasonably be expected to extend [into defendant's territory]." 100 F.Supp. 412, 415.

Which decision, *Dawn Donut* or *Sterling,* provides the better solution? As a practical matter, *Dawn Donut* converts the question whether the junior user should stop using the senior user's mark from a legal question to a business judgment. In arriving at its business decision, the junior user will, of course, speculate as to whether and when the senior user will enter. What other factors should it weigh? If the junior user decides to risk the senior user's entry into its market, and proceeds to invest heavily in the continued use and promotion of its mark, how will consumers be affected when the senior user enters the junior user's market and obtains an injunction against the junior user's continued use of the mark?

4. *Trademark Assignments and Licenses.* It is a hoary maxim that a trademark cannot be assigned in gross—that is, apart from the assignor's business, assets or goodwill. Section 10 of the Lanham Act, 15 U.S.C.A. § 1060, provides, "[a] registered mark or a mark for which application to register has been filed shall be assignable with the goodwill of the business in which the mark is used, or with that part of the goodwill of the business connected with the use of and symbolized by the mark." One consequence of an assignment in gross is that a court may hold the trademark to have been abandoned. A court may also hold that a mark has been abandoned if its owner licenses others to use the mark but fails to control the quality of goods or services that the licensees sell under the mark. As indicated by *Dawn Donut,* courts have been less than rigorous in requiring vigilant quality control programs.

The premise underlying the abandonment rules for both trademark assignments and licenses is that a mark symbolizes a particular level of quality to consumers and that transfers of the mark without the economic factors responsible for this quality may undermine consumer expectations. Do these rules make sense? What business reason will an assignee or licensee have to depart from the quality symbolized by the mark it is acquiring? What business reason does a trademark owner who does *not* assign or license its mark have to maintain the quality of its goods or services? For a sharp critique of rules in this area, see Kevin Parks, "Naked" is Not a Four–Letter Word: Debunking the Myth of the "Quality Control Requirement" in Trademark Licensing, 82 Trademark Rep. 531 (1992).

Some courts have substantially loosened the prohibition against assignments in gross. For example, in Sugar Busters L.L.C. v. Brennan, 177 F.3d 258, 50 U.S.P.Q.2d 1821 (5th Cir.1999), the court observed that a trademark could be transferred without any accompanying assets so long as the assignor's and assignee's businesses were sufficiently similar that customers would not be misled. Because, however, the assignor's business was a retail store for diabetics and the assignee's business was publishing a diet book, the court ruled that the transfer was invalid. Lawmakers have also had reservations about the rule against assignments in gross. An early version of the bill that eventually became the Lanham Act provided, "[a] registered trade-mark shall be assignable either with or without the goodwill of the business." H.R. 9041, 75th Cong., 3d Sess. (1938). Most countries today permit the assignment of trademarks without accompanying goodwill. 2 Stephen P. Ladas, Patents, Trademarks, and Related Rights: National and International Protection § 617 (1975).

b.   Product and Service Boundaries: Dilution

Ringling Bros.–Barnum & Bailey Combined Shows, Incorporated v. Utah Division of Travel Development

United States Court of Appeals, Fourth Circuit, 1999.
170 F.3d 449, 50 U.S.P.Q.2d 1065.

OPINION

PHILLIPS, Senior Circuit Judge:

This case requires us to interpret and apply the dauntingly elusive concept of trademark "dilution" as now embodied in the Federal Trademark Dilution Act of 1995 ("the Act"). The concept was invoked in this case by Ringling Bros.-Barnum & Bailey Combined Shows, Inc. ("Ringling") in a claim under the Act that Ringling's "famous" circus trademark slogan, THE GREATEST SHOW ON EARTH ("GREATEST SHOW mark"), had been diluted by the State of Utah's commercial use of its trademark slogan, THE GREATEST SNOW ON EARTH ("GREATEST SNOW mark"), as an advertisement of the state's winter sports attractions. The district court found that Ringling had not proved dilution under the Act and gave judgment for Utah. We affirm the judgment.

I

The relevant background facts as found by the district court are undisputed. From 1872 to the present, Ringling and its predecessors have offered their circus to the public as the "Greatest Show on Earth." In 1961, Ringling received federal trademark registration for its GREATEST SHOW mark for entertainment services in the nature of a circus.

Since its inception, Ringling has used its mark to advertise circus performances. The circus travels throughout the United States and presents approximately 1,000 shows annually to some 12 million people in 95 cities. More than 70 million people each year are exposed to the GREATEST SHOW mark in connection with the circus. Revenues derived from goods and services bearing or using the mark are substantial and exceeded $103 million for the fiscal year ending January, 1997.

Ringling advertises its circus using the GREATEST SHOW mark in print advertising, radio, television, videos, outdoor billboards, direct-mail pieces, press announcements, posters, program books, souvenirs, and joint promotions with other companies. In the fiscal year ending January 1997, expenditures on advertising using the mark totaled approximately $19 million. Through joint promotions with retailers, Ringling obtains significant additional exposure for its mark. Also, because of its renown, the GREATEST SHOW mark receives substantial free publicity.

Defendant Utah Division of Travel Development ("Utah") is an agency of the State of Utah. As early as 1962, Utah began using its GREATEST SNOW mark in connection with Utah tourism services. Utah has used its mark in magazine advertisements every year from 1962 to the present except 1963, 1977, and 1989. Utah has authorized the Utah Ski Association to use the GREATEST SNOW mark in connection with the Association's promotion of Utah tourism. Utah's primary use of its mark in Utah is its display on motor vehicle license plates. For each of the past fifteen years, Utah's budget for winter advertising, including advertising of the GREATEST SNOW mark, has ranged from $300,000 to $450,000.

In 1965, the Utah Attorney General opined that Utah's mark did not impair or violate Ringling's GREATEST SHOW mark. Utah registered its mark with the State of Utah in 1975 and renewed its registration in 1985 and 1995. In 1988, Utah applied to the United States Patent and Trademark Office to register its mark. Although Ringling opposed Utah's application, Utah was granted federal registration for its mark on January 21, 1997.

On June 6, 1996, Ringling commenced this action, seeking injunctive and monetary relief, on allegations that Utah's use of the GREATEST SNOW mark "diluted" Ringling's GREATEST SHOW mark in violation of the Act. Before trial, the district court granted Utah's motion to strike Ringling's demand for a jury trial, and after a bench trial, found for Utah.

This appeal by Ringling followed. Before us, Ringling challenges the district court's determination on the merits that Utah's mark did not dilute Ringling's mark in violation of the Act, and the court's denial of its demand for jury trial. We take these in turn.

II

The Federal Trademark Dilution Act, which became effective on January 16, 1996, amended Section 43 of the Lanham Act to provide a new cause of action for federal trademark "dilution." Under the Act, the owner of a "famous mark" is given protection "against another person's commercial use . . . of a mark or trade name, if such use begins after the mark has become famous and causes dilution of the distinctive quality of the mark." 15 U.S.C. § 1125(c)(1). A successful claimant may be given injunctive and, if a willful violation is proved, restitutionary, compensatory, and specific relief in the form of a destruction of offending articles.

The Act defines dilution as:

> the lessening of the capacity of a famous mark to identify and distinguish goods or services, regardless of the presence or absence of—
>
> (1) competition between the owner of the famous mark and other parties, or
>
> (2) likelihood of confusion, mistake, or deception.

Id. § 1127.

And, the Act's legislative history further indicates that Congress understood that "dilution" might result either from "uses that blur the distinctiveness of [a famous] mark or [that] tarnish or disparage it." *See* H.R.Rep. No. 104–374, at 2 (1995), U.S. Code Cong. & Admin. News at 1029, 1029. The parties here both accept this as a proper reflection of congressional intent respecting the meaning of "dilution," and further agree that only dilution by blurring is at issue in this case.

To prove its statutory dilution claim, Ringling's burden therefore was to prove (1) that its mark was a "famous" one; (2) that Utah adopted its mark after Ringling's had become famous; and (3) that Utah's mark diluted Ringling's by "blurring" it.

At trial, Ringling put on essentially undisputed evidence demonstrating that its mark had achieved "famous" status before Utah began use of its mark. This left as the dispositive issue whether Utah's mark had "diluted"

Ringling's by "blurring" it. On that issue, Ringling took the position that as a matter of statutory interpretation, "dilution" by "blurring" occurs whenever a junior mark is either identical to or sufficiently similar to the famous mark that persons viewing the two instinctively will make a "mental association" between the two. On this interpretation, viewers' knowledge of the goods or services represented by the two marks is irrelevant; all that counts is the identity or sufficient similarity of the marks as perceived by the viewer. Taking this as the legal meaning of "dilution by blurring," Ringling then contended that, though not identical, the similarity between Ringling's and Utah's marks was so strong and obvious that the required "mental association" of the two, hence the dilution by blurring of Ringling's senior mark, was evident as a matter of law, no other evidence being required to establish it. But, in a back-up position, Ringling presented evidence of a survey of hypothetical viewers designed to demonstrate empirically that the two marks did evoke in a properly representative sampling of viewers the mental association of the two that sufficed alone to prove a dilution violation.

In a comprehensive opinion, the district court rejected Ringling's critical legal contentions respecting the legal meaning of "dilution" as used in the Act and found its attempted factual proof of dilution by means of a viewer survey insufficient to establish a violation.

Specifically, the court rejected Ringling's contention that proof alone of an "instinctive mental association" of the two marks by viewers sufficed to prove "dilution." While recognizing that to prove dilution by blurring one must necessarily prove as a threshold element a mental association by viewers of the marks themselves, the court held that this alone did not suffice. Rather, the court held, dilution by blurring occurs only where consumers "mistakenly associate or confuse the marks and the goods or services they seek to identify and distinguish," and this association causes actual harm to the senior mark's capacity to "identify and distinguish." Applying this interpretation of "dilution" to Ringling's consumer survey evidence, the court found that the attempted proof by this means failed. And, finally, analyzing the evidence as a whole under a multi-factor balancing test proposed for the purpose in *Mead Data Central, Inc. v. Toyota Motor Sales, U.S.A., Inc.*, 875 F.2d 1026, 1035 (2d Cir.1989) (Sweet, J., concurring),* the court concluded that "dilution" had not been established on a balancing of those factors. *See id.* at 618–22.

On this appeal, Ringling challenges both the district court's interpretation of the statutory meaning of "dilution"; the court's rejection of its survey evidence as insufficient to prove "dilution"; and the court's rejection of its dilution claim under a *Mead Data* analysis. We take these in turn.

---

* Mead Data appears at page 72 above.
Judge Sweet's multi-factor balancing test is
summarized at note 1, page 78. Ed.

A.

Ringling's primary challenge is to the district court's interpretation of the statutory meaning of "dilution," hence of the elements of the "dilution" claim newly created by the Act. As in the district court, it contends for its contrary interpretation: that a famous mark is "diluted" whenever a junior mark is sufficiently similar that consumers viewing them "instinctively make a mental association" of the two. It therefore argues that the district court erred in interpreting the Act to require further proof that in making this "mental association" consumers "mistakenly associate or confuse the marks and the goods or services they seek to identify and distinguish." And, it further argues that the court erred in interpreting the Act to require proof of "actual dilution."

Reviewing *de novo* the statutory interpretation issue, we disagree with Ringling's proffered "mental-association-alone" interpretation. Though we do not agree in every particular with the district court's interpretation, we agree with its basic points that "dilution" under the federal Act consists of (1) a sufficient similarity of marks to evoke in consumers a mental association of the two that (2) causes (3) actual harm to the senior marks' economic value as a product-identifying and advertising agent.

That meaning surely does not leap fully and immediately from the statutory text. But, we believe it is the necessary meaning of the Act's critical provisions when read in light of the Act's legislative history. By that, we mean both the immediate but quite meager legislative record and, more critically, the broader background out of which the basic concept emerged and has evolved in state and federal trademark law. [The court's extensive analysis of the origins of dilution law is omitted.]

From this fifty-year course of judicial experience, several propositions can be ventured. The first is that a general agreement has emerged that "dilution" under the state statutes involves as an essential element some form of harm to the protected mark's selling power—its economic value— resulting otherwise than by consumer confusion from the junior mark's use. Because the statutes require proof only of a "likelihood" of dilution, however, the courts have not been required to work out either the exact nature of the end economic harm it contemplates nor how, if at all, it could be proved as accomplished economic fact. Instead, looking only to the likelihood of such a speculative future condition, the courts have either (1) assumed that its essential elements—mental association, causation, harm— could be found (or rejected) as fact by inference from a balancing of the "*Mead* factors," or (2) assumed that all those elements could be conclusively presumed—direct or inferential proof being impossible—simply from proof of the identity or near-identity of the two marks.

From all this, it is evident that the most significant feature of the state antidilution statutes has been their requirement that only a "likelihood of dilution" rather than actual dilution need be proved to entitle a claimant to the injunctive relief which they provide as the sole statutory remedy. This has enabled the courts to avoid hard definition of the economic harm to a senior mark's "selling power" that they generally agree is an essential element of statutory "dilution." And, even more critically, the necessary speculativeness of any inquiry into future states and conditions has led some courts to allow the essential elements of "likely" dilution to be inferred as fact from the *"Mead* factors," or, even more drastically, to be presumed from no more than the identity or sufficient similarity of the two marks.

We have explored the judicial experience with state antidilution statutes at this length because of the needed light it sheds upon the significance of key contrasting provisions of the federal Act. And, because of the light shed in turn by those provisions upon the specific interpretive issue we consider: whether, as Ringling essentially contends, "dilution" under the federal Act requires no more proof than sufficient similarity of junior mark to senior to evoke in consumers an "instinctive mental association" of the two.

Two key provisions of the federal Act, considered in relation to the state statutes and their interpretation bear directly upon that issue and provide its answer. Most critically, the federal Act proscribes and provides remedy only for actual, consummated dilution and not for the mere "likelihood of dilution" proscribed by the state statutes. And, by specifically defining dilution as "the lessening of the capacity of a famous mark to identify and distinguish goods or services," the federal Act makes plain what the state statutes arguably may not: that the end harm at which it is aimed is a mark's selling power, not its "distinctiveness" as such.

Accepting these two critical points, we therefore interpret the Act, in general agreement with the district court, as requiring for proof of "dilution" (1) a sufficient similarity between the junior and senior marks to evoke an "instinctive mental association" of the two by a relevant universe of consumers which (2) is the effective cause of (3) an actual lessening of the senior mark's selling power, expressed as "its capacity to identify and distinguish goods or services."

This concededly is a stringent interpretation of "dilution" under the federal Act. It confines the federal dilution claim to a more narrow scope than that generally now accorded by courts to state-law dilution claims. But, given the critical provisions that expressly differentiate the federal Act on key points from the state statutes, we must assume that this was exactly what was intended by Congress. It obviously is directly at odds with the mental-association-alone interpretation urged by Ringling, and Ringling challenges it in respects that require discussion.

Take first the property-right-in-gross interpretation. While Ringling does not press that interpretation in those exact terms, it is sufficiently implicit in its argument to require addressing. Doing so, we simply cannot believe that, as a general proposition, Congress could have intended, without making its intention to do so perfectly clear, to create property rights in gross, unlimited in time (via injunction), even in "famous" trademarks. Had that been the intention, it is one easily and simply expressed by merely proscribing use of any substantially replicating junior mark. And that surely is not what the Act says. However amorphously they may be expressed, and however difficult to prove in practice, the Act literally prescribes as elements of its dilution claim both specific harm to the senior mark's economic value in the form of a "lessening of [its] capacity ... to identify and distinguish goods and services," and a causal connection between that harm and the "commercial use" of a replicating junior mark. It will not bear a property-right-in-gross interpretation.

Neither can the Act be interpreted to require proof of actual economic harm and its effective cause but permit them to be judicially presumed from proof alone of the marks' sufficient similarity. As earlier noted, that process has been used by some courts in applying state antidilution statutes that require proof only of a "likelihood of dilution." Whatever may be the justification for using it in that setting, it could not properly be used under a statute requiring proof of actual harm already caused by use of a junior mark. Under basic evidentiary presumption principles, the probabilities are not high enough nor means of proof sufficiently lacking to allow such a presumption.

Take first causation. As the district court in this case rightly observed, "marks can lose their distinctiveness or power to identify goods and services for various reasons other than the use of a junior mark." 955 F.Supp. at 615. And, for that reason, the court opined that junior mark use could not be judicially presumed to be the cause of any actual economic harm to the senior mark that might be proved. We agree.

Nor, for similar reasons could actual harm itself be presumed. That economic harm inevitably will result from any replicating junior use is by no means that certain. It is not at all improbable that some junior uses will have no effect at all upon a senior mark's economic value, whether for lack of exposure, general consumer disinterest in both marks' products, or other reasons. Indeed, common sense suggests that an occasional replicating use might even enhance a senior mark's "magnetism"—by drawing renewed attention to it as a mark of unshakable eminence worthy of emulation by an unthreatening non-competitor. Imitation, that is, may occasionally operate in the marketplace as in social manners as the "sincerest form of flattery." In any event, there are enough reasons why replicating junior use of a mark might not cause any actual economic harm to a senior mark that it is not a proper subject for judicial presumption.

Nor can it be said (as perhaps it can with respect to proving mere "likelihood of dilution") that even if it is the fact that actual economic harm caused by replicating junior use has occurred, there is no way to prove those facts independently. Though proof of those elements of the elusive dilution concept may tax the skills of advocacy, that results more from their substantive uncertainty than from lack of available means of proof. As we will discuss, if they *do* exist, there are means of proving them by normal evidentiary processes. Impossibility or near-impossibility of proving them does not support their judicial presumption.

Perhaps recognizing the difficulty of interpreting the federal Act in either of these ways, both of which assume that some actual harm must be proved but say either that the harm is only to a famous mark's distinctiveness as such or that, if economic harm is required, it may be judicially presumed from similarity of marks, Ringling's principal argument seems to be that if the Act requires proof of any form of economic harm, it is only threatened harm, not actual consummated harm. In short, Ringling argues that though the Act does not literally proscribe mere "likelihood of dilution" in the manner of state antidilution statutes, that is its intended meaning. And, from that the argument implicitly runs that merely future harm could be much more easily proved (or judicially presumed?) than can the actual, consummated economic harm that the district court's interpretation requires be independently proved.

The literal parsing argument for mere threatened, future economic harm focuses on the word "capacity" in the Act's definition of "dilution" as the "lessening of the capacity of a famous mark to identify and distinguish goods or services." "Capacity," the argument runs, necessarily imports futurity; it means in this context the ability of a mark continuously over future time to "identify and distinguish," even if it has not yet suffered any lessening of that ability. We cannot accept that interpretation as a matter of the Act's plain meaning. We think it is belied both by the word's ordinary intrinsic meaning and by its use in context. One can surely speak expressly of "present capacity," or of "future capacity," or of a "former capacity," but unless it is so temporally modified or otherwise given its intended temporal meaning, the word is neutral in that respect. In context here, it is plain that the "capacity" spoken of is "former capacity." The verb of which it is the object is the clear indicator; the conduct proscribed is that which "lessens" capacity, not that which "will" or "may" lessen. There are other contextual indicators. The conduct proscribed is "another person's ... use," not merely threatened use; that "causes," not that "will" or "may" cause. Unlike the state antidilution statutes which provide only injunctive relief, reflecting their sole focus on prevention of future harm, the federal Act provides that where willful conduct is shown, both compensatory and restitutionary relief may be awarded—for necessarily consummated economic harm. Finally and most telling, there is the fact that in the face of the obvious centrality of "likelihood of dilution" provisions in the interpretation and application of state antidilution statutes for the fifty years of their existence, the federal Act does not so provide.

For all these reasons, we agree with the district court that to establish dilution of a famous mark under the federal Act requires proof that (1) a defendant has made use of a junior mark sufficiently similar to the famous mark to evoke in a relevant universe of consumers a mental association of the two that (2) has caused (3) actual economic harm to the famous mark's economic value by lessening its former selling power as an advertising agent for its goods or services.

B.

We turn now to Ringling's challenges to the district court's determination that on the evidence adduced, Ringling had not proved dilution under the federal Act. We review that determination, as one of mixed law and fact, under the clearly erroneous standard of Fed. R.Civ. P. 52(a).

As indicated, that evidence consisted of the general background facts summarized in Part I of this opinion and the results of a consumer survey introduced by Ringling. The district court of course assessed the evidence under its interpretation of the Act, and because we agree with that interpretation, we review its findings against that legal standard. And, because the court looked separately at the consumer survey evidence and the *"Mead"* factors in assessing the overall weight of the evidence, we proceed in the same way.

1.

It is important to remember that in keeping with its legal theory that it need prove only an "instinctive mental association" of the two marks, Ringling's survey was designed to develop only that fact. And, correspondingly, that in assessing the evidence under its quite different interpretation, the district court was looking for more: for actual harm to the senior mark's capacity to "identify and distinguish" resulting from any mental association of the marks evoked for consumers by the junior mark's use.

We begin our review of the district court's assessment of the survey evidence by summarizing the survey's methodology and results. The survey was conducted by interviewing individuals at seven shopping malls throughout the country, including one in Utah. At each location, randomly selected shoppers were presented with a card containing the fill-in-the-blank statement "THE GREATEST _____ ON EARTH" and were asked what word or words they would use to complete the phrase. If the shoppers completed the statement, they were asked with whom or what they associated the completed statement. And, they were asked further whether they could think of any other way to complete the statement, and with whom or what they associated the resulting statement.

The survey results showed that in Utah (1) 25% of the respondents completed the statement THE GREATEST _____ ON EARTH with only the word "show" and associated the completed statement with the Circus; (2) 24% completed the statement with only the word "snow" and associated the completed statement with Utah; and (3) 21% of respondents completed the statement with "show" and associated the result with the Circus and also completed the statement with "snow" and associated the completed statement with Utah. The survey further showed that outside of Utah (1) 41% of respondents completed the statement THE GREATEST _____ ON EARTH with only the word "show" and associated the completed statement with the Circus; (2) 0% completed the statement with only the word "snow" and associated the completed statement with Utah; and (3) fewer than 0.5% of respondents completed the statement with "show" and associated the result with the Circus and also completed the statement with "snow" and associated the completed statement with Utah.

The district court concluded that this evidence failed to show dilution under the Act. In the first place, the court found the survey results inadequate to prove that consumers even made the requisite threshold mental association of the marks. When faced with the fill-in-the-blank phrase, "The Greatest _____ on Earth," some consumers filled in the blank with both the words "show" and "snow." When asked with whom or what they associated the completed phrase "the Greatest Show on Earth," virtually every consumer—inside Utah and outside Utah—indicated in one way or other that they only associated Ringling's circus with that phrase. When asked with whom or what they associated the completed phrase, "The Greatest Snow on Earth," every single consumer—inside Utah and outside Utah—indicated that they only associated Utah with the completed phrase. Not one consumer indicated that he associated the phrase, "The Greatest Show on Earth" with the phrase, "The Greatest Snow on Earth." Summarizing these results, the district court concluded that they were "strong evidence of the absence of dilution, not the presence of it," 955 F.Supp. at 617, that is, that they tended to disprove rather than to prove the required threshold mental association of the marks.

And the court found the survey results even more lacking as proof that Utah's use of its mark had caused any "lessening" of the "capacity" of Ringling's trademark slogan to "identify and distinguish" its circus as the mark's subject. Specifically, the court pointed to survey results indicating that consumer familiarity with Ringling's mark was greater in Utah (46%), where Utah's mark was well-known, than in the rest of the country (41%), where Utah's mark was virtually unknown, and that virtually every viewer questioned associated Ringling's mark (as distinguished from the fill-in-the-blank slogan) with, and only with, the Ringling circus and not "with Utah, with wintersports, or with any activities that are attributable to Utah's use of [its mark]." *Id.* at 618.

We affirm as not clearly erroneous the district court's assessment that the consumer survey evidence does not support a finding of dilution under the federal Act. While we might have some concern with the implicit finding that this evidence does not even show the requisite threshold "mental association" of the two marks within the consumer market surveyed, we have no concern respecting the specific finding that the survey evidence does not show that use of Utah's junior mark had caused any actual harm to Ringling's mark in the form of a lessening of that mark's former capacity to identify and distinguish Ringling's circus as its subject. And that, of course, suffices to support the court's ultimate conclusion.

Ringling makes several challenges to this assessment of its survey evidence. We address only its principal contention: that the court's assessment was flawed by a legal misapprehension that the "mental association" of marks requisite to proof of dilution must go beyond mere association of the marks in isolation and involve some mistake or confusion as to the marks and their respective goods or services. This was indeed the court's position, and it of course traces to the court's correct interpretation of the Act which, at odds with Ringling's position, requires not just proof of visual similarity sufficient to evoke mental association of the marks, but actual harm resulting from that association to the senior mark's selling power.

While we might not have expressed the broader "mental association" requirement in exactly those terms, we think it accurately captured the proof requirements imposed by that court's legal interpretation, which we have affirmed as the correct one. What the district court was saying in effect was this. If you seek to rely for proof of dilution only upon evidence of the mental impressions evoked in consumers upon viewing the marks, then those impressions must go beyond mere recognition of a visual similarity of the two marks to allow a reasonable inference that the junior mark's use has caused actual harm to the senior mark's selling or advertising power.

That accurately reflects the interpretation of the Act that we have affirmed and confirms that the court's assessment of the survey evidence under that legal interpretation must be affirmed.

2.

We discuss only briefly the district court's alternative assessment of the evidence under the so-called "*Mead* factors." Recognizing that this judicial fact-finding process had been used by various courts as a device by which the "likelihood of dilution" might be inferred under state antidilution statutes from a set of relevant factors—similarity of marks, similarity of products, consumer sophistication, predatory intent, and renown of the two marks—the court, somewhat puzzlingly, undertook to apply it to this claim brought under the federal Act. Doing so on the basis of a run-through of the whole set and a final "balancing" of their separate indicators, the court concluded that neither did that evidence "demonstrate by a preponderance ... that Utah's mark lessens the capacity of [Ringling's mark] to identify and distinguish Ringling's circus." *Id.* at 622.

Ringling of course challenges the court's fact-finding by that process, suggesting that some of the factors are wholly inappropriate under the federal Act, and that if applied under that Act they require a different weighting than that accorded them by the district court. Utah of course defends the court's use of the device, but has to confess the inappropriateness of some of these factors developed under state antidilution statutes to cases under the federal Act.

We are persuaded, in agreement with other courts and commentators, and in probable agreement with some of the obvious discomfort of both parties in this case, that, by and large, the *Mead*-factor analysis simply is not appropriate for assessing a claim under the federal Act. As we have earlier noted, the process has obvious utility in making the long leaps of inference that can be used to find a mere "likelihood of dilution," but inferring actual harm and effective causation from such factors as "consumer sophistication," and "predatory intent" is a chancy process at best. Indeed, of the factors, only mark similarity and, possibly, degree of "renown" of the senior mark would appear to have trustworthy relevance under the federal Act.

In consequence, we conclude that though the district court's use of this process as a complementary fact-finding process was inappropriate, its use can be treated as one having no ultimate prejudicial effect upon Ringling as appellant.

3.

... The difficulties of proving actual dilution by practically available means is evident—as we have recognized, at length. It may have led a few federal courts early on simply to assume, without facing up to the interpretive difficulty of doing so, that the federal Act only requires proof of a "likelihood of dilution." Going this route permits proof of federal Act dilution by the long leaps of inference to, and judicial presumption of, future harm that have been considered allowable by some courts applying state antidilution statutes. And, it avoids the problems of proving actual, consummated harm effectively caused by junior mark use.

On the other hand, the perceived difficulties could lead to an interpretation that effectively requires proof of actual harm only to the mark's distinctiveness as such. This in fact is what the dilution-policy critic, Klieger, suggests must have been the intended meaning—though it was not the plain meaning—of the federal statute as enacted. *See* Klieger, *Trademark Dilution*, [58 U. Pitt. L. Rev.] at 840–41.

We think that proof of actual dilution cannot be considered impossible and therefore not possibly what Congress could have intended. Proof will be difficult, because actual, consummated dilutive harm and its cause are difficult concepts. But the concept is a substantively viable one, and the means of proof are available.

It surely must be possible in the marketing world that the replicating use of a "famous" mark causes it actually to lose to some extent the "selling power" deriving from its distinctiveness that it formerly had. And, without attempting to chart the exact shape and course of advocacy that might prove that occurrence, we think three general means are available. Most obviously, but most rarely, there might be proof of an actual loss of revenues, and proof of replicating use as cause by disproving other possible causes. Most obviously relevant, and readily available, is the skillfully constructed consumer survey designed not just to demonstrate "mental association" of the marks in isolation, but further consumer impressions from which actual harm and cause might rationally be inferred. Finally, relevant contextual factors such as the extent of the junior mark's exposure, the similarity of the marks, the firmness of the senior mark's hold, are of obvious relevance as indirect evidence that might complement other proof. . . .

AFFIRMED.

NOTES

1. In reaching its conclusion that section 43(c) imposes an actual dilution requirement, the *Ringling* court relied on Robert N. Klieger, Trademark Dilution: The Whittling Away of the Rational Basis for Trademark Protection, 58 U. Pitt. L. Rev. 789, 840 (1997), which the court described as "probably the most comprehensive recent commentary on the whole historical evolution of dilution law." 170 F.3d at 461 n. 6. According to Klieger, the requirement erects "an impenetrable barrier to any federal dilution action." Do you agree? How would you design a survey to meet the court's requirement for proof of actual dilution? See William G. Barber, How to Do a Trademark Dilution Survey (or Perhaps How Not to Do One), 89 Trademark Rep. 616 (1999).

Is the economic rationale for dilution closer to the rationale for copyright and patent law than it is to the rationale for trademark law? What counterpart, if any, is there in copyright and patent cases to *Ringling's* requirement of proof of harm in dilution cases? Is the burden that *Ringling* placed on dilution plaintiffs comparable to the burden a copyright or patent plaintiff would bear if a court required it to demonstrate that, without the prospect of victory, it would not have invested in the work or invention in suit?

2. *Ringling Brothers* has been followed by some courts outside the Fourth Circuit, but not by others. In Nabisco, Inc. v. PF Brands, Inc., 191 F.3d 208, 223–225, 51 U.S.P.Q.2d 1882 (2d Cir.1999), the Second Circuit Court of Appeals read *Ringling* as establishing either of two rules on proof of "actual dilution," and rejected both. "The narrower position would be that courts may not infer dilution from 'contextual factors (degree of mark and product similarity, etc.),' but must instead rely on evidence of 'actual loss of revenues' or the 'skillfully constructed consumer survey.' This strikes us as an arbitrary and unwarranted limitation on the methods of proof.... If the famous senior mark were being exploited with continually growing success, the senior user might never be able to show diminished revenues, no matter how obvious it was that the junior use diluted the distinctiveness of the senior. Even if diminished revenue could be shown, it would be extraordinarily speculative and difficult to prove that the loss was due to the dilution of the mark. And as to consumer surveys, they are expensive, time-consuming and not immune to manipulation. If a junior user began to market Buick aspirin or Schlitz shellac, we see no reason why the senior users could not rely on persuasive circumstantial evidence of dilution of the distinctiveness of their marks without being obligated to show lost revenue or engage in an expensive battle of surveys."

A second, "broader reading of the Fourth Circuit's 'actual, consummated' dilution element would require not only that dilution be proved by a showing of lost revenues or surveys but also that the junior be already established in the marketplace before the senior could seek an injunction.... Notwithstanding the use of the present tense in 'causes dilution,' it seems plausibly within Congress's meaning to understand the statute as intending to provide for an injunction to prevent the harm before it occurs. To read the statute as suggested by the *Ringling* opinion would subject the senior user to uncompensable injury. The statute could not be invoked until injury had occurred. And, because the statute provides only for an injunction and no damages (absent willfulness) such injury would never be compensated." 191 F.3d at 224.

3. *Fame and Distinctiveness.* The opening clause of section 43(c)(1) implies that the single requirement for protecting a mark against dilution is that it be "famous." Nonetheless, because a subsequent clause refers to "dilution of the distinctive quality of the mark," and because the provision's eight factors are aimed at determining whether a mark is "distinctive and famous," some confusion exists over the role of distinctiveness in dilution cases. One reason for the confusion may be that distinctiveness is a necessary, but not sufficient, condition to fame. When the "Kodak" mark first appeared, it was distinctive—as an arbitrary, inherently distinctive term—but not yet famous. Today the mark "Kodak" continues to be distinctive, because it identifies the source of products to consumers, but it is also famous because it is well known, and not only to consumers of Kodak photographic products.

Professor McCarthy has listed examples of some marks found to be famous and some found not to be famous:

Marks Held to be Famous

- BUDWEISER beer;
- CANDYLAND children's game;
- DON'T LEAVE HOME WITHOUT US slogan for traveler's checks and credit cards;
- fish-shaped GOLDFISH brand crackers;
- THE GREATEST SHOW ON EARTH slogan for a circus;
- HOTMAIL e-mail service;
- INTERMATIC electrical products;
- JEWS FOR JESUS religious organization;
- LEXINGTON investment advice services;
- NAILTIQUES fingernail care products;
- PANAVISION movie and TV cameras;
- POLO wearing apparel;
- PORSCHE autos;
- TOYS 'R US toy stores;
- WAWA chain of 500 convenience stores in five eastern states, in use for ninety years.

Marks Held Not to be Famous

- APPLESEED public advocacy group;
- AUTHORITY sporting goods retailer;
- BONGO wearing apparel;
- COLUMBIA healthcare services;
- KING OF THE MOUNTAIN SPORTS camouflage clothing;
- PETRO truck stop services;
- STAR MARKET chain of eight supermarkets only in Hawaii;
- STEALTH home and sporting goods;

- WEATHER GUARD vehicle tool boxes for contractors;
- WASHINGTON SPEAKERS BUREAU lecture agency;
- WE'LL TAKE GOOD CARE OF YOU slogan for retail drugstore chain.

4J. Thomas McCarthy, Trademarks and Unfair Competition § 24:92. 1–2 (4th ed. 1996).* How many of the famous marks did you know? How many, though distinctive, may not in fact be famous?

4. *Trade Dress.* Some of the earliest marks to be protected under the federal antidilution provisions were not word marks, such as "Budweiser" or "Porsche," but trade dress marks, such as bite-sized, cheese-flavored, goldfish-shaped crackers (Nabisco, Inc. v. PF Brands, Inc., 191 F.3d 208, 51 U.S.P.Q.2d 1882 (2d Cir.1999)). Consider whether protecting trade dress marks on a dilution theory runs afoul of policies behind the federal copyright and patent statutes which set their own qualitative standards for protection of three-dimensional designs and have tolerated trademark protection for such designs only because trademark law's traditional consumer confusion requirement effectively gives trademark a narrower scope than copyright or patent.

In I.P. Lund Trading v. Kohler Co., 163 F.3d 27, 50–51, 49 U.S.P.Q.2d 1225 (1st Cir.1998), defendants argued that the federal dilution provision would be unconstitutional if it were applied to protect plaintiff's faucet design because the protection would be unlimited in time and because "Congress's Commerce Clause power—the basis of Congress's regulation of trademarks and trade dress—cannot be used to trump the Patent Clause." Leaving resolution of the constitutional issue to "specific facts which present the issue with clarity," the court intimated that dilution protection for trade dress would survive constitutional attack, in part because "more than one form of intellectual property protection [such as design patent] may simultaneously protect particular product features," and in part because the plaintiff's obligation to demonstrate its design's nonfunctionality tends to ensure that dilution protection will not extend into the domain of utility patents; if the design in issue "or aspects of it are functional, then the only source of exclusive rights would be in a utility patent." 163 F.3d at 38, 48.

For a sharp critique of dilution protection for product configurations, see Paul Heald, *Sunbeam Products, Inc. v. The West Bend Co.*: Exposing the Malign Application of the Federal Dilution Statute to Product Configurations, 5 J. Intell. Prop. L. 415 (1998).

5. *Domain Names.* Traditional trademark doctrine offers limited relief to the owner of a registered trademark who discovers that someone else has registered his mark as a domain name. The economic harm to the trademark owner might be substantial—for example, depriving him of the opportunity to use the mark as his own domain name—but if the domain name registrant is using the mark solely as an address, and not to indicate the source of goods or services, no action for passing off will lie.

---

* Reprinted with permission.

Until passage of the Anticybersquatting Act and the institutional reform of domain name registration, both discussed at page 326, below, dilution doctrine offered the most effective relief against cybersquatting. In Panavision International v. Toeppen, 141 F.3d 1316, 46 U.S.P.Q.2d 1511 (9th Cir.1998), the Ninth Circuit Court of Appeals affirmed the grant of summary judgment to trademark owner Panavision against the owner of the domain names "Panavision.com" and "Panaflex.com" under both federal and state antidilution statutes. The court rejected defendant's argument that because a domain name is simply an address used to locate a web page, his use of plaintiff's trademarks did not constitute the "commercial use" required by the federal statute. The court observed that "Toeppen's 'business' is to register trademarks as domain names and then sell them to the rightful trademark owners. . . . So long as he held the Internet registrations, he curtailed Panavision's exploitation of the value of its trademarks on the Internet, a value which Toeppen then used when he attempted to sell the Panavision.com domain name to Panavision." 141 F.3d at 1325.

The court also concluded that Toeppen's domain name registration actionably diluted the marks. Noting that, "[t]o find dilution, a court need not rely on the traditional definition such as 'blurring' or 'tarnishment,'" the court observed that a "significant purpose of a domain name is to identify the entity that owns the web site"; "[u]sing a company's name or trademark as a domain name is also the easiest way to locate that company's web site"; and defendant's use "puts Panavision's name and reputation at his mercy." 141 F.3d at 1326–27. "On December 20, 1995, Panavision's counsel sent a letter from California to Toeppen in Illinois informing him that Panavision held a trademark in the name Panavision and telling him to stop using that trademark and the domain name Panavision.com. Toeppen responded by mail to Panavision in California, stating he had the right to use the name Panavision.com on the Internet as his domain name. Toeppen stated: If your attorney has advised you otherwise, he is trying to screw you. He wants to blaze new trails in the legal frontier at your expense. Why do you want to fund your attorney's purchase of a new boat (or whatever) when you can facilitate the acquisition of 'PanaVision.com' cheaply and simply instead? Toeppen then offered to 'settle the matter' if Panavision would pay him $13,000 in exchange for the domain name. Additionally, Toeppen stated that if Panavision agreed to his offer, he would not 'acquire any other Internet addresses which are alleged by Panavision Corporation to be its property.'" 141 F.3d at 1319.

D.   LIMITATIONS ON RIGHTS

New Kids on the Block v. News America Publishing, Inc.

United States Court of Appeals, Ninth Circuit, 1992.
971 F.2d 302, 23 U.S.P.Q.2d 1534.

KOZINSKI, Circuit Judge.

The individual plaintiffs perform professionally as The New Kids on the Block, reputedly one of today's hottest musical acts. This case requires us to weigh their rights in that name against the rights of others to use it in identifying the New Kids as the subjects of public opinion polls.

Background

No longer are entertainers limited to their craft in marketing themselves to the public. This is the age of the multi-media publicity blitzkrieg: Trading on their popularity, many entertainers hawk posters, T-shirts, badges, coffee mugs and the like—handsomely supplementing their incomes while boosting their public images. The New Kids are no exception; the record in this case indicates there are more than 500 products or services bearing the New Kids trademark. Among these are services taking advantage of a recent development in telecommunications: 900 area code numbers, where the caller is charged a fee, a portion of which is paid to the call recipient. Fans can call various New Kids 900 numbers to listen to the New Kids talk about themselves, to listen to other fans talk about the New Kids, or to leave messages for the New Kids and other fans.

The defendants, two newspapers of national circulation, conducted separate polls of their readers seeking an answer to a pressing question: Which one of the New Kids is the most popular? *USA Today*'s announcement contained a picture of the New Kids and asked, "Who's the best on the block?" The announcement listed a 900 number for voting, noted that "any USA Today profits from this phone line will go to charity," and closed with the following:

> New Kids on the Block are pop's hottest group. Which of the five is your fave? Or are they a turn off? ... Each call costs 50 cents. Results in Friday's Life section.

The Star's announcement, under a picture of the New Kids, went to the heart of the matter: "Now which kid is the sexiest?" The announcement, which appeared in the middle of a page containing a story on a New Kids concert, also stated:

> Which of the New Kids on the Block would you most like to move next door? STAR wants to know which cool New Kid is the hottest with our readers.

Readers were directed to a 900 number to register their votes; each call cost 95 cents per minute.

Fearing that the two newspapers were undermining their hegemony over their fans, the New Kids filed a shotgun complaint in federal court raising no fewer than ten claims: (1) common law trademark infringement; (2) Lanham Act false advertising; (3) Lanham Act false designation of origin; (4) Lanham Act unfair competition; (5) state trade name infringement; (6) state false advertising; (7) state unfair competition; (8) commercial misappropriation; (9) common-law misappropriation; and (10) intentional interference with prospective economic advantage. The two papers raised the First Amendment as a defense, on the theory that the polls were part and parcel of their "news-gathering activities." The district court granted summary judgment for defendants.

Discussion

While the district court granted summary judgment on First Amendment grounds, we are free to affirm on any ground fairly presented by the record. Indeed, where we are able to resolve the case on nonconstitutional grounds, we ordinarily must avoid reaching the constitutional issue. Therefore, we consider first whether the New Kids have stated viable claims on their various causes of action.

I

A. . . .

Throughout the development of trademark law, the purpose of trademarks remained constant and limited: Identification of the manufacturer or sponsor of a good or the provider of a service. And the wrong protected against was traditionally equally limited: Preventing producers from free-riding on their rivals' marks. Justice Story outlined the classic scenario a century and a half ago when he described a case of "unmitigated and designed infringement of the rights of the plaintiffs, for the purpose of defrauding the public and taking from the plaintiffs the fair earnings of their skill, labor and enterprise." *Taylor v. Carpenter,* 23 F.Cas. 742 (C.C.D.Mass.1844) at 744. The core protection of the Lanham Act remains faithful to this conception. Indeed, this area of the law is generally referred to as "unfair competition"—unfair because, by using a rival's mark, the infringer capitalizes on the investment of time, money and resources of his competitor; unfair also because, by doing so, he obtains the consumer's hard-earned dollar through something akin to fraud.

A trademark is a limited property right in a particular word, phrase or symbol. And although English is a language rich in imagery, we need not belabor the point that some words, phrases or symbols better convey their intended meanings than others. Indeed, the primary cost of recognizing property rights in trademarks is the removal of words from (or perhaps non-entrance into) our language. Thus, the holder of a trademark will be denied protection if it is (or becomes) generic, *i.e.,* if it does not relate exclusively to the trademark owner's product. This requirement allays fears that producers will deplete the stock of useful words by asserting exclusive rights in them. When a trademark comes to describe a class of goods rather than an individual product, the courts will hold as a matter of law that use of that mark does not imply sponsorship or endorsement of the product by the original holder.

A related problem arises when a trademark also describes a person, a place or an attribute of a product. If the trademark holder were allowed exclusive rights in such use, the language would be depleted in much the same way as if generic words were protectible. Thus trademark law recognizes a defense where the mark is used only "to describe the goods or services of [a] party, or their geographic origin." 15 U.S.C. § 1115(b)(4).

refer to the New Kids as an entity than it is to refer to the Chicago Bulls, Volkswagens or the Boston Marathon without using the trademark. Indeed, how could someone not conversant with the proper names of the individual New Kids talk about the group at all? While plaintiffs' trademark certainly deserves protection against copycats and those who falsely claim that the New Kids have endorsed or sponsored them, such protection does not extend to rendering newspaper articles, conversations, polls and comparative advertising impossible. The first nominative use requirement is therefore met.

Also met are the second and third requirements. Both *The Star* and *USA Today* reference the New Kids only to the extent necessary to identify them as the subject of the polls; they do not use the New Kids' distinctive logo or anything else that isn't needed to make the announcements intelligible to readers. Finally, nothing in the announcements suggests joint sponsorship or endorsement by the New Kids. The *USA Today* announcement implies quite the contrary by asking whether the New Kids might be "a turn off." *The Star*'s poll is more effusive but says nothing that expressly or by fair implication connotes endorsement or joint sponsorship on the part of the New Kids.

The New Kids argue that, even if the newspapers are entitled to a nominative fair use defense for the announcements, they are not entitled to it for the polls themselves, which were money-making enterprises separate and apart from the newspapers' reporting businesses. According to plaintiffs, defendants could have minimized the intrusion into their rights by using an 800 number or asking readers to call in on normal telephone lines which would not have resulted in a profit to the newspapers based on the conduct of the polls themselves.

The New Kids see this as a crucial difference, distinguishing this case from *Volkswagenwerk, WCBV–TV* and other nominative use cases. The New Kids' argument in support of this distinction is not entirely implausible: They point out that their fans, like everyone else, have limited resources. Thus a dollar spent calling the newspapers' 900 lines to express loyalty to the New Kids may well be a dollar not spent on New Kids products and services, including the New Kids' own 900 numbers. In short, plaintiffs argue that a nominative fair use defense is inapplicable where the use in question competes directly with that of the trademark holder.

We reject this argument. While the New Kids have a limited property right in their name, that right does not entitle them to control their fans' use of their own money. Where, as here, the use does not imply sponsorship or endorsement, the fact that it is carried on for profit and in competition with the trademark holder's business is beside the point. See, e.g., *Universal City Studios, Inc. v. Ideal Publishing Corp.*, 195 U.S.P.Q. 761 (S.D.N.Y. 1977) (magazine's use of TV program's trademark "Hardy Boys" in connection with photographs of show's stars not infringing). Voting for their favorite New Kid may be, as plaintiffs point out, a way for fans to articulate their loyalty to the group, and this may diminish the resources available for products and services they sponsor. But the trademark laws do not give the

New Kids the right to channel their fans' enthusiasm (and dollars) only into items licensed or authorized by them. See *International Order of Job's Daughters v. Lindeburg & Co.,* 633 F.2d 912 (9th Cir.1990) (no infringement where unauthorized jewelry maker produced rings and pins bearing fraternal organization's trademark). The New Kids could not use the trademark laws to prevent the publication of an unauthorized group biography or to censor all parodies or satires which use their name. We fail to see a material difference between these examples and the use here.

Summary judgment was proper as to the first seven causes of action because they all hinge on a theory of implied endorsement; there was none here as the uses in question were purely nominative.

II

The New Kids raise three additional claims that merit brief attention.

A.   The New Kids claim that *USA Today*'s and *The Star*'s use of their name amounted to both commercial and common law misappropriation under California law. Although there are subtle differences between these two causes of action, all that's material here is a key similarity between them: The papers have a complete defense to both claims if they used the New Kids name "in connection with any news, public affairs, or sports broadcast or account" which was true in all material respects. See Cal.Civ. Code § 3344(d).

In this case, *USA Today*'s and *The Star*'s use of the New Kids' name was "in connection with" news accounts: *The Star* ran concurrent articles on the New Kids along with its 900–number poll, while *USA Today* promised a subsequent story on the popularity of various members of the singing group. Both papers also have an established track record of polling their readers and then reporting the poll results as part of a later news story. The New Kids' misappropriation claims are barred by California Civil Code section 3344(d).

B.   The New Kids' remaining claim is for intentional interference with prospective economic advantage, but they ignore the maxim that all's fair in love, war and the free market. Plaintiffs' case rests on the assumption that the polls operated to siphon off the New Kids' fans or divert their resources away from "official" New Kids products. Even were we to accept this premise, no tort claim has been made out: "So long as the plaintiff's contractual relations are merely contemplated or potential, it is considered to be in the interest of the public that any competitor should be free to divert them to himself by all fair and reasonable means. . . . In short, it is no tort to beat a business rival to prospective customers." *A-Mark Coin Co. v. General Mills, Inc.,* 148 Cal.App.3d 312, 323, 195 Cal.Rptr. 859 (1983). Because we have already determined that the newspapers' use of the mark was "fair and reasonable," the New Kids do not have a tort claim based on the fact that they may have lost some business to a competitor.

Conclusion

The district court's judgment is AFFIRMED.

NOTES

1. How does the fair use test fashioned in *New Kids,* for cases where defendant uses plaintiff's trademark to refer to plaintiff's product, differ from traditional fair use defense which excuses defendant's descriptive reference to its own product? Does the *New Kids* test implicitly preempt state law doctrines, such as misappropriation or right of publicity, to the extent that they protect the same subject subject matter but without offering a comparable defense? Can the *New Kids* exemption be reconciled with the misappropriation rule followed in *Board of Trade* page 81 above? With the right of publicity rule followed in White v. Samsung, page 176, above? (Judge Alex Kozinski, the author of the *New Kids* opinion), dissented vigorously from the order rejecting the suggestion for a rehearing *en banc* in White v. Samsung. See page 187, above.

2. *Fair Use.* As indicated in *New Kids,* competitors are free to use the descriptive elements of a registered mark in a non-trademark sense. In Zatarains, Inc. v. Oak Grove Smokehouse, Inc., 698 F.2d 786, 217 U.S.P.Q. 988 (5th Cir.1983), the court held that defendants' use of the term "Fish Fry" on packages of its coating mix for fried foods was a noninfringing "fair use" of plaintiff's mark, "Fish–Fri," used in connection with a coating mix for fried foods. Upholding the lower court's finding that "Fish–Fri" is a descriptive term that had acquired secondary meaning, the court observed that "only that penumbra or fringe of secondary meaning is given legal protection. Zatarain's has no legal claim to an exclusive right in the original, descriptive sense of the term; therefore, Oak Grove and Visko's are still free to use the words 'fish fry' in their ordinary, descriptive sense, so long as such use will not tend to confuse customers as to the source of the goods." 698 F.2d at 796.

Is it a bar to the fair use defense that the plaintiff's mark is a design mark rather than a word mark? That it is suggestive rather than descriptive? Car–Freshner Corp. v. S.C. Johnson & Son, Inc., 70 F.3d 267, 36 U.S.P.Q.2d 1855 (2d Cir.1995), held that it was fair use for defendant to market, during the Christmas holiday season, a pine-tree-shaped plastic casing for air freshener where plaintiff had earlier adopted and marketed flat cardboard pine-tree-shaped air fresheners for automobiles. Even if plaintiff's use of the mark was not descriptive of *its* product, but only suggestive, "[w]hat matters is whether the *defendant* is using the protected word or image descriptively, and not as a mark.... Johnson's use of the pine-tree shape describes two aspects of its product. The pine tree refers to the pine scent of its air freshening agent. Furthermore, as a Christmas tree is traditionally a pine tree, the use of the pine-tree shape refers to the Christmas season, during which Johnson sells this item." 70 F.3d at 269–70.

3. *Collateral Use.* Can merchants refer to the goods they sell by the trademark of the manufacturer? The market for secondhand, repaired and reconstructed goods may complicate the question of collateral trademark use. In Prestonettes, Inc. v. Coty, 264 U.S. 359, 44 S.Ct. 350, 68 L.Ed. 731 (1924), Coty sought to "restrain alleged unlawful uses of the plaintiff's registered trademarks, 'Coty' and 'L'Origan' upon toilet powders and perfumes. The defendant purchases the genuine powder, subjects it to pressure, adds a binder to give it coherence and sells the compact in a metal case. It buys the genuine perfume in bottles and sells it in smaller bottles." The district court would have permitted a truthful allusion to Coty—a label on the compacts, for example, reading, "Prestonettes, Inc., not connected with Coty, states that the compact of face powder herein was independently compounded by it from Coty's—(giving the name) loose powder and its own binder. Loose powder—per cent, Binder—per cent," with "every word to be in letters of the same size, color, type and general distinctiveness."

The circuit court concluded that the district court's decree did not sufficiently protect Coty and absolutely enjoined any use of its marks: "to permit the plaintiff's name and trade-mark to be used on other than his original packages should be forbidden, as the value of his name and trade-mark would be endangered through the deterioration of his product due to the action of unauthorized and unsupervised persons in changing the perfumes from the receptacles in which they were originally placed into others which may be wholly unfit even though the perfumes remain unadulterated." 285 Fed. 501, 513 (2d Cir.1922).

The Supreme Court, in an opinion by Mr. Justice Holmes, reversed and ordered the district court decree reinstated. Since "[t]he plaintiff could not complain of its [defendant's] stating the nature of the component parts and the source from which they were derived if it did not use the trademark in doing so," the fact that its trademark was involved added nothing to plaintiff's rights. "When the mark is used in a way that does not deceive the public we see no such sanctity in the word as to prevent its being used to tell the truth. It is not taboo." As to the possible deterioration in the product's quality and consequent injury to the manufacturer's reputation, Justice Holmes concluded, "it might be a misfortune to the plaintiff, but the plaintiff would have no cause of action, as the defendant was exercising the rights of ownership and only telling the truth." 264 U.S. 359, 368, 44 S.Ct. 350, 351, 68 L.Ed. 731.

Twenty-three years later, in Champion Spark Plug Co. v. Sanders, 331 U.S. 125, 67 S.Ct. 1136, 91 L.Ed. 1386, 73 U.S.P.Q. 133 (1947), involving defendant's repair, reconditioning, and sale of spark plugs bearing the mark of their original manufacturer, the Court affirmed an order permitting collateral use of the plaintiff's mark so long as the plugs also bore the word "Repaired" or "Used." In dicta, however, the Court cautioned that "[c]ases may be imagined where the reconditioning or repair would be so extensive or basic that it would be a misnomer to call the article by its original name, even though the words 'used' or 'repaired' were added." Would it be such a case if defendant relabeled plaintiff's computer chip from a slower model to a faster, more costly model? See Intel Corp. v. Terabyte Int'l, Inc., 6 F.3d 614, 619, 28 U.S.P.Q. 2d 1182 (9th Cir.1993) ("Intel did not perform or authorize the chip modifications, and only the most formalistic of approaches could lead to a conclusion that Intel was the 'source' of those chips once they were relabeled. The relabeling was so basic that 'it would be a misnomer to call the article by its original name.' ").

4. *Metatags.* A site on the World Wide Web may include within its underlying code a "metatag" containing one or more trademarks which, when retrieved by a user's search engine, will bring the user to the site even though, once at the site, the user never sees the content of the metatag. For example, if a user interested in purchasing a camera instructs her search engine to identify all sites associated with the name "Nikon," the search engine will retrieve the addresses of sites that include "Nikon" in their metatags, even if the site itself has no content dealing with Nikon cameras. A seller of CD's may have included the Nikon name—and typically many other popular trademarks—to capture users who might otherwise be unaware of the site. In the more predatory case, a Nikon competitor would include the Nikon mark in its metatag in the hopes of bringing its own cameras to the attention of potential Nikon purchasers.

Do either of these uses constitute trademark infringement or dilution? Although the user has been taken on an unintended detour, will he be confused as to the source of goods? Does the practice lead to blurring or tarnishment under section 43(c)? Would the practice constitute an actionable misrepresentation under section 43(a)?

See generally, Maureen A. O'Rourke, Defining the Limits of Free–Riding in Cyberspace: Trademark Liability for Metatagging, 33 Gonz. L. Rev. 277 (1997–98); Stanley U. Paylago, Search Engine Manipulation: Creative Use of Metatags or Trademark Infringement?, 40 IDEA 451 (2000).

5. *Parody and Satire.* Will a parodic or satirical purpose excuse an otherwise infringing use of a trademark? In Reddy Communications, Inc. v. Environmental Action Foundation, 477 F.Supp. 936, 203 U.S.P.Q. 144 (D.D.C.1979), the court dismissed an infringement action brought by the owner of the service mark, "Reddy Kilowatt"—a cartoon figure licensed for advertising use by investor-owned public utilities—against defendant's use of caricatures of Reddy Kilowatt in newsletters and magazines criticizing the electric power industry. The gist of plaintiff's argument was that "by casting Reddy in a negative light as the 'villainous utility company' in its publications," defendant had "reduced Reddy's attractiveness to investor utilities as a public relations tool for promotion of the utility industry." Recognizing that the defendant had indeed imitated the "Reddy" mark, the court nonetheless concluded that "EAF's use of Reddy is merely incidental to the sale of its publications." "*[W]ithin the context of its publications,* ... EAF's caricatures are dissimilar from Reddy in connotation and overall impression ... the EAF publications are obtained by careful, sophisticated purchasers who will view the EAF caricatures not in isolation but in conjunction with the surrounding text; and ... the surrounding text and other identifying indicia adequately signal to the reader the critical use being made of Reddy by an opponent of the electric utility industry." 477 F.Supp. at 945–46, 948 (emphasis the court's).

APPENDIX A

SHOW CARD "A"   STUDY NO. 7881

APPENDIX B

SHOW CARD "B"   STUDY NO. 7881

Should the use of a trademark for a satiric purpose that has no connection to the trademark owner's business be treated less liberally than a trademark use for a parodic purpose as in *Reddy Communications*? In the latter case the use may be the only or most effective means for the defendant to make its statement, while in the former case there may be no compelling reason for defendant's selection of plaintiff's mark, rather than some other vehicle, for its satire. The distinction may explain the jaundiced view of satirical uses in the Eighth Circuit. See, e.g., Anheuser–Busch, Inc. v. Balducci Publications, 28 F.3d 769, 31 U.S.P.Q. 2d 1296 (8th Cir.1994) (reversing lower court decision that sanctioned humor magazine's "editorial" use of plaintiff's Michelob trademark—a mock advertisement on its back cover for the fictitious "Michelob Oily" with graphics including a can of "Michelob Dry" pouring oil into a fish's mouth and an oil-soaked depiction of plaintiff's trademark eagle); Mutual of Omaha Insurance Co. v. Novak, 836 F.2d 397, 5 U.S.P.Q.2d 1314 (8th Cir.1987) (permanent injunction granted against defendant's modified version of plaintiff's Indian head logo and use of the words "Mutant of Omaha" and "Nuclear Holocaust Insurance"), cert. denied, 488 U.S. 933, 109 S.Ct. 326, 102 L.Ed.2d 344 (1988).

Would it be preferable in these cases to treat satirical or parodic purpose not as a categorical defense but, rather, as one factor to be weighed in determining likelihood of consumer confusion? Hormel Foods Corp. v. Jim Henson Productions, Inc., 73 F.3d 497, 503, 37 U.S.P.Q.2d 1516 (2d Cir.1996), affirmed the trial court's ruling that defendant's use of a character named "Spa'am" in its Muppet movie and related merchandise did not infringe or dilute plaintiff's "SPAM" trademark for luncheon meat. "[T]he clarity of Henson's parodic intent, the widespread familiarity with Henson's Muppet parodies, and the strength of Hormel's mark, all weigh strongly against the likelihood of confusion as to source or sponsorship...." Courts have also weighed First Amendment interests in the "balance between the two competing considerations of allowing artistic expression and preventing consumer confusion." Cliffs Notes, Inc. v. Bantam Doubleday Dell Publishing Group, Inc., 886 F.2d 490, 494, 497, 12 U.S.P.Q.2d 1289 (2d Cir.1989) (*Spy Notes*, a parody which copied prominent trade dress features of *Cliffs Notes*, "raises only a slight risk of consumer confusion that is outweighed by the public interest in free expression, especially in a form of expression that must to some extent resemble the original.")

Compare a case noted by Professor Derenberg in which "the owner of the famous 4711' trademark for *eau de cologne* got an injunction in Cologne, Germany, against a manure collector who used his telephone number, 4711, painted in 20–inch high numerals across both sides of his horse-drawn fertilizer wagon." Walter Derenberg, The Problem of Trademark Dilution and the Anti-dilution Statutes, 44 Calif.L.Rev. 439, 448 n. 49 (1956).

6. *Dilution, Confusion and the Constitution.* If "New Kids on the Block" qualified as a famous mark under section 43(c) of the Lanham Act, would the group have prevailed against use of the mark by *U.S.A. Today* and *The Star*? According to the House Report on the Trademark Dilution Act of 1995, the legislation "adequately addresses legitimate First Amendment concerns" by exempting three categories of use from liability: "(A) Fair use of a famous mark by another person in comparative commercial advertising or promotion to identify the competing goods or services of the owner of the famous mark. (B) Noncommercial use of a mark. (C) All forms of news reporting and news commentary." See H.R.Rep.No. 374, 104th Cong. 1st Sess.4 (1995). Would the uses made by the newspapers come within any of these exceptions?

Compare San Francisco Arts & Athletics, Inc. v. United States Olympic Comm., 483 U.S. 522, 107 S.Ct. 2971, 97 L.Ed.2d 427, 3 U.S.P.Q.2d 1145

(1987), in which the United States Supreme Court held that section 110 of the Amateur Sports Act, 36 U.S.C.A. § 380, granted the United States Olympic Committee the exclusive right to prohibit certain commercial and promotional uses of the word, "Olympic," and of certain other Olympic symbols, apart from any showing that unauthorized use would confuse consumers. The defendant, which had used the term "Olympic" in promoting its "Gay Olympic Games," argued that, in eliminating the confusion requirement and withholding the normal statutory defenses, the Act violated the First Amendment. The Court rejected this argument and the argument that, because the term, "Olympic" had become generic, the First Amendment prohibited its statutory protection.

The Court observed: "Although the Lanham Act protects only against confusing uses, Congress' judgment respecting a certain word is not so limited. Congress reasonably could conclude that most commercial uses of the Olympic words and symbols are likely to be confusing. It also could determine that unauthorized uses, even if not confusing, nevertheless may harm the USOC by lessening the distinctiveness and thus the commercial value of the marks.... Even though this protection may exceed the traditional rights of a trademark owner in certain circumstances, the application of the Act to this commercial speech is not broader than necessary to protect the legitimate congressional interest and therefore does not violate the First Amendment." 483 U.S. at 539–540, 107 S.Ct. at 2982–2983.

Justice Brennan, joined by Justice Marshall, dissented. "Trademark protection has been carefully confined to the realm of commercial speech by two important limitations in the Lanham Act. First, the danger of substantial regulation of noncommercial speech is diminished by denying enforcement of a trademark against uses of words that are not likely to cause confusion, to cause mistake, or to deceive.... The fair use defense also prevents the award of a trademark from regulating a substantial amount of noncommercial speech. The Lanham Act allows 'the use of the name, term, or device ... which is descriptive of and used fairly and in good faith only to describe to users the goods or services of such party.' Again, a wide array of noncommercial speech may be characterized as merely descriptive of the goods or services of a party, and thus not intended to propose a commercial transaction. For example, the SFAA's description of its community services appears to be regulated by § 110, although the main purpose of such speech may be to educate the public about the social and political views of the SFAA. Congress' failure to incorporate this important defense in § 110(a)(4) confers an unprecedented right on the USOC." 483 U.S. at 564–565, 107 S.Ct. at 2995–2996.

NOTE: DOMAIN NAMES

Internet domain names, particularly names assigned to the popular top level .com domain, have presented a vexing challenge to trademark owners and to the trademark system, obliterating product, service and geographic boundaries that may have been carefully built up under trademark law over a lengthy period. A user who is interested in finding a nearby branch of Acme Hardware and goes to the acme.com address may find the Web page not of Acme Hardware, but of Acme Laboratories, even though both companies may have invested equally in attracting consumer goodwill to the Acme name and obtained equally strong trademark rights. The "Scrabble" mark is owned by Hasbro in the United States and Canada, but by Mattel in the rest of the world. The user who goes to scrabble.com will find that these two trademark owners have created a gateway site enabling the user to link to the site of the company that owns the mark in the user's part of the world. But, had the two trademark owners not reached this sensible solution, the first of them to register its domain name would have held global hegemony at the scrabble.com address. The problem, simply, is that while many trademark owners around the world can own rights in the same name, only one will typically maintain a particular name in a domain.

Institutional arrangements and judicial and legislative responses have at least initially focused on a far more tractable issue: Can a trademark owner obtain relief against a domain name registrant that has itself developed no business or goodwill under the mark, but has registered the mark simply to hold it hostage? It was the practice of Network Solutions, Inc., which had the first contract with the U.S. government to register domain names, to register names on a first come, first served basis. NSI policy provided limited relief to a trademark owner that objected to the registration of a domain name similar to its mark. For the trademark owner to prevail, its mark had to be registered; the domain name had to be identical to the mark; and the trademark owner's relief was generally limited to temporary suspension of the domain name registration.

Deficiencies in the domain name registration process (trademark conflicts were only one of several problems) prompted interested private groups, with support from the U.S. government and participation by the World Intellectual Property Organization, to form the non-profit Internet Corporation for Assigned Names and Numbers (ICANN) to assume responsibility for administering domain name systems. ICANN's intellectual property policy, adopted in October 1999, has as its central operational feature the Uniform Domain Name Dispute Resolution Policy, imposed by contract between an accredited domain name registrar and its customer, the domain name registrant. Under the Policy, disputes between registrants and trademark owners are heard in mandatory administrative proceedings conducted by ICANN-approved providers. Specifically, the Policy requires the registrant to submit to a proceeding upon a trademark owner's complaint that: the domain name is confusingly similar to its mark; that the registrant has no rights in the domain name; and that the domain name was registered and used in bad faith. A successful complainant may have the domain name cancelled or transferred to it.

Does the unauthorized use of a mark as a domain name constitute infringement? Early plaintiffs encountered hurdles in trademark law's traditional requirements of commercial use and competition. Later decisions substantially reduced these hurdles. In Panavision Int'l v. Toeppen, 141 F.3d 1316, 46 U.S.P.Q.2d 1511 (9th Cir.1998), the U.S. Court of Appeals for the Ninth Circuit ruled that the unauthorized domain name registration of plaintiff's "Panavision" and "Panaflex" marks violated the Federal Trademark Dilution Act, 15 U.S.C. § 1125(c), and rejected defendant's argument that its registration neither constituted the required "commercial use" of the Panavision marks nor diluted the capacity of the marks to identify goods or services.

The *Panavision* court recognized precedential support for the first, commercial use, argument, but nonetheless ruled that it was of no consequence that defendant had not attached the mark to goods. Also, a domain name is more than an address. "It marks the location of the site within cyberspace, much like a postal address in the real world, but it may also indicate to users some information as to the content of the site, and, in instances of well-known trade names or trademarks, may provide information as to the origin of the contents of the site.... Moreover, potential customers of Panavision will be discouraged if they cannot find its web page by typing in 'Panavision.com', but instead are forced to wade through hundreds of web sites. This dilutes the value of Panavision's trademark." 141 F.3d at 1327 n.8.

Deficiencies of traditional trademark law in protecting the interests of trademark owners against cybersquatters led Congress in 1999 to pass the Anticybersquatting Consumer Protection Act, Pub. L. No. 106–113, 113 Stat. 1501, adding a new subsection (d) to section 43 of the Lanham Act to bar the abusive use of marks and personal names in situations that traditional trademark law might not reach. The Act gives a mark owner rights against anyone who, with "a bad faith intent to profit from that mark," registers, traffics in or uses a domain name that is identical or confusingly similar to a distinctive mark, or that is "identical or confusingly similar to or dilutive of" a famous mark. The mark need not be registered to be protected, and protection is "without regard to the goods or services of the parties."

Section 43(d)(1)(B) lists several factors that a court may weigh in determining whether the defendant had the required bad faith, among them: the fact that defendant itself had trademark or other intellectual property rights in the domain name, or made prior use of the domain name in connection with the bona fide offering of goods or services; "the person's intent to divert consumers from the mark owner's online location to a site accessible under the domain name that could harm the goodwill represented by the mark, either for commercial gain or with the intent to tarnish or disparage the mark, by creating a likelihood of confusion as to the source, sponsorship, affiliation, or endorsement of the site"; and "the person's offer to transfer, sell or otherwise assign the domain name to the mark owner or any third party for financial gain without having used, or having an intent to use, the domain name in the bona fide offering of any goods or services, or the person's prior conduct indicating a pattern of such conduct." The amendments also prescribe remedies, including actual or statutory damages and costs, and forfeiture of the domain name or its cancellation or transfer to the owner of the mark.

Can a registrant who has lost his right to use a domain name under a UDRP proceeding bring an action in U.S. federal court under the Anticybersquatting Consumer Protection Act to bar the transfer of the domain name to the party that prevailed in the UDRP proceeding? Sallen v. Corinthians Licenciamentos Ltda., 273 F.3d 14, 26–27, 60 U.S.P.Q.2d 1941 (1st Cir.2001), held that such an action would lie. "First," the court observed, "the UDRP clearly contemplates judicial intervention and, in fact, that the judicial outcome will override the UDRP one." Further, "[u]nder § 1114(2)(D)(v), Congress has provided registrants such as Sallen with an affirmative cause of action to recover domain names lost in UDRP proceedings."

How would an action between Acme Hardware and Acme Laboratories be resolved under ICANN's Uniform Dispute Resolution Policy? Under the Anticybersquatting Consumer Protection Act? The problems raised by these conflicts promise to be most vexing in the international arena. See Graeme B. Dinwoodie, (National) Trademark Laws and the (Non–National) Domain Name System, 21 U. Pa. J. Int'l Econ. L. 495 (2000); Marshall Leaffer, Domain Names, Globalization, and Internet Governance, 6 Ind. J. Global Legal Stud. 139 (1998).

2. REMEDIES

See Statute Supplement 15 U.S.C.A. §§ 1111, 1114, 1116–1120, 1124.

Maltina Corp. v. Cawy Bottling Co.

United States Court of Appeals, Fifth Circuit, 1980.
613 F.2d 582, 205 U.S.P.Q. 489.

JOHNSON, Circuit Judge:

I. The Facts

Cawy Bottling Company (Cawy), defendant below, appeals from the judgment of the district court in favor of the plaintiffs Maltina Corporation and Julio Blanco–Herrera in their trademark infringement action. The district court enjoined Cawy from further infringement, awarded the plaintiffs $35,000 actual damages, and ordered the defendant to account for $55,050 of gross profit earned from the sale of infringing products.

Julio Blanco–Herrera fled to this country from Cuba in late 1960 after that country nationalized the company of which he was president and, along with his family, majority stockholder. Before that year, this company was one of the largest breweries and beverage distributors in Cuba. Among its products was malta, a dark, non-alcoholic carbonated beverage brewed similar to beer. The Cuban company distributed malta under the trademarks "Malta Cristal" and "Cristal" in Cuba and in the United States. The Cuban company had registered the marks both in Cuba and the United

States. When Blanco–Herrera arrived in the United States, he formed the Maltina Corporation and assigned the "Cristal" trademark to it. He attempted to produce and distribute "Cristal" in this country, but despite his efforts Maltina Corporation was never able to obtain sufficient financial backing to produce more than $356 worth of "Cristal".

Cawy Bottling, however, had an altogether different experience in producing malta. At the outset, it attempted to register the "Cristal" trademark so that it might be utilized in marketing the product. This attempt was rejected by the Patent Office because of plaintiffs' prior registration. After this attempted registration and with the knowledge of the plaintiffs' ownership of the trademark, Cawy began producing and distributing malta under the "Cristal" label in February 1968.

In 1970 the plaintiffs sued Cawy under 15 U.S.C.A. § 1117 for trademark infringement and unfair competition. They sought an injunction against further use of their mark, damages, and an accounting. The district court dismissed the suit on the ground that Cuba's confiscation of the assets of Blanco–Herrera's Cuban corporation made Blanco–Herrera's assignment of the "Cristal" mark to the Maltina Corporation invalid. This Court reversed, holding Cuba's confiscation decree did not extend to the "Cristal" mark registered by the United States Patent Office. On remand, the district court determined that the plaintiffs had a valid trademark. Cawy appealed, and we affirmed.

At trial on the merits, from which this appeal is taken, the district court determined that Cawy had infringed the plaintiffs' mark and assigned the case to a magistrate for determination of what recovery was appropriate under 15 U.S.C.A. Section 1117. Before holding a hearing the magistrate wrote a memorandum to the district court stating that he thought that the plaintiffs were entitled to an injunction but not to an accounting for defendant's profits.

After holding the hearing, however, the magistrate changed his recommendation. He noted that Cawy designed its "Cristal" label to resemble the label used by Maltina's predecessor in Cuba. He found that Cawy intended to exploit the reputation and good will of the "Cristal" mark and to deceive and mislead the Latin community into believing that the "Cristal" once sold in Cuba was now being sold in the United States. The magistrate further found that Cawy wilfully infringed the plaintiffs' mark and had been unjustly enriched to the detriment of plaintiffs' reputation and good will. He recommended that Cawy account to the plaintiffs for the profit it earned from the infringement, and he directed Cawy to report its sales of "Cristal" and associated costs to the plaintiffs for determination of its profits. The magistrate also found Cawy's infringement damaged the reputation and good will of the plaintiffs in the amount of $35,000. He recommended that Cawy compensate plaintiffs in that amount.

The district court, after a complete and independent review of the record, adopted the magistrate's recommendations as its order. As more fully discussed below, the district court eventually found Cawy liable to the plaintiffs for its gross profits from the sale of "Cristal", $55,050. The court entered judgment against Cawy for $55,050 gross profits plus $35,000 damages and enjoined Cawy from any further infringement of the plaintiffs' mark.

Cawy presents three arguments on appeal. First, it argues that an accounting was inappropriate. Second, that if an accounting was appropriate, the district court erred in awarding to the plaintiff Cawy's entire gross profits from the sales of "Cristal". Third, Cawy argues that the award of $35,000 actual damages cannot stand in the absence of any evidence to support it. We accept this final contention but reject the first two. Cawy does not complain on appeal of the district court's enjoining it from further infringement of the plaintiffs' mark.

II. Was an Accounting Appropriate?

Section 1117, 15 U.S.C.A. entitles a markholder to recover, subject to the principles of equity, the profits earned by a defendant from infringement of the mark. The courts have expressed two views of the circumstances in which an accounting is proper under 15 U.S.C.A. Section 1117. Some courts view the award of an accounting as simply a means of compensating a markholder for lost or diverted sales. Other courts view an accounting not as compensation for lost or diverted sales, but as redress for the defendant's unjust enrichment and as a deterrent to further infringement. See Maier Brewing Co. v. Fleischmann Distilling Corp., 390 F.2d 117, 121, 157 U.S.P.Q. 76, 78–79 (9th Cir.) cert. denied, 391 U.S. 966, 157 U.S.P.Q. 720 (1968). In this case, the plaintiffs never sold any appreciable amount of "Cristal" in the United States so they cannot claim that Cawy diverted any of their sales. Accordingly, we must decide whether diversion of sales is a prerequisite to an award of an accounting. We hold that it is not.

In *Maier Brewing* the Ninth Circuit awarded an accounting to a plaintiff who was not in direct competition with a defendant and who, accordingly, had not suffered any diversion of sales from the defendant's infringement. The court noted that the defendant had wilfully and deliberately infringed. It reasoned that awarding an accounting would further Congress' purpose in enacting 15 U.S.C.A. Section 1117 of making infringement unprofitable. This Court is in accord with this reasoning. The Fifth Circuit has not addressed the issue whether an accounting only compensates for diverted sales or whether an accounting serves the broader functions of remedying an infringer's unjust enrichment and deterring future infringement. A recent opinion by this Court, however, recognizes that a trademark is a protected property right. Boston Professional Hockey Association v. Dallas Cap and Emblem Manufacturing, Inc., 597 F.2d 71, 75, 202 U.S.P.Q. 536, 539 (5th Cir.1979). This recognition of a trademark as property is consistent with the view that an accounting is proper even if the defendant and plaintiff are not in direct competition, and the defendants' infringement has not diverted sales from the plaintiff. The Ninth Circuit in Maier Brewing noted that the infringer had used the markholder's property to make a profit and that an accounting would force the

infringer to disgorge its unjust enrichment. Here, the only valuable property Blanco–Herrera had when he arrived in this country was his right to the
"Cristal" mark. Cawy used this property, and an accounting is necessary to
partially remedy its unjust enrichment.

The district court relied, in part, on W.E. Bassett Co. v. Revlon, Inc.,
435 F.2d 656, 168 U.S.P.Q. 1 (2d Cir.1970), in ordering an accounting. That
case held that an accounting should be granted "if the defendant is
unjustly enriched, if the plaintiff sustained damages from the infringement,
or if an accounting is necessary to deter a willful infringer from doing so
again." Id. at 664, 168 U.S.P.Q. at 7. Revlon sold a cuticle trimmer
embossed with a "Cuti–Trim" mark "in the teeth of the Patent Office's
refusal to register" that mark. Id. at 662, 168 U.S.P.Q. at 5. This was
willful infringement that an accounting would deter in the future. In the
instant case, the district court found that Cawy's "infringement was willful
and that such infringement resulted in [Cawy] being unjustly enriched...." Cawy used the "Cristal" mark after the Patent Office refused
to register it. This clearly and explicitly supports the finding of willful
infringement. An injunction alone will not adequately deter future infringement. In short, we find the district court properly ordered Cawy to account
to the plaintiffs for the profits it earned from its willful infringement. This
accounting serves two purposes: remedying unjust enrichment and deterring future infringement.

III. Did the District Court Err in Requiring Cawy to Account for Its
     Entire Gross Profit From the Sale of "Cristal"?

The district court ordered Cawy to account to the plaintiffs for
$55,050, the entire gross profit (total revenue less cost of goods sold) from
the sale of "Cristal". The district court did not allow Cawy to deduct
overhead and other expenses. These expenses would have produced a net
loss from the sale of "Cristal" and, if allowed, would have enabled Cawy to
escape liability to the plaintiffs for its infringement.

Under 15 U.S.C.A. Section 1117, the plaintiff has the burden of
showing the amount of the defendant's sales of the infringing product. The
defendant has the burden of showing all elements of cost and other
deductions. In this case, the court ordered Cawy to report its total sales of
"Cristal" and associated costs to the plaintiffs. If the plaintiffs objected to
Cawy's estimate of its net profits from "Cristal", they were to file their
objection with the court. The record on appeal reflects that Cawy submitted
three exhibits showing its net loss on "Cristal" sales. These exhibits are set
out in the appendix. The plaintiffs filed their objections to Cawy's figures
with the court. They accepted Cawy's estimate of gross revenues from the
sale of "Cristal" and the cost of goods sold. Thus, they met the burden of
proving the amount of sales of the infringing product. The plaintiffs,
however, did not accept other deductions claimed by Cawy. Cawy claimed
deductions for *Expenses Specifically Identified with Malta Cristal*", as set
out in Exhibit 2. Plaintiffs objected to these claimed deductions because
Cawy did not show they were actually spent on "Cristal". Cawy also
claimed deductions for general overhead, apportioned to "Cristal" on the
basis of the ratio of "Cristal" sales to Cawy's total sales. Exhibit 3 displays

these claimed overhead deductions. The plaintiffs objected to the overhead deductions because the infringing product constituted only a small percentage of the defendant's business.

Cawy responded to the plaintiffs' objections by asserting that it did have "specific and detailed figures and corroborating sales slips, invoices and the like to support" its claims of expenses attributable to "Cristal". Cawy failed, however, to submit any of this corroboration to the district court.

The district court, after noting that Cawy had the burden of establishing deductions from gross profits, disallowed Cawy's claims of expenses specifically attributable to "Cristal" as set forth in Exhibit 2. The court stated that it could not determine whether the advertising, sales, commissions, legal fees, telephone, and other expenses claimed by Cawy related to "Cristal" sales or to the sales of other products. It then held that Cawy failed to sustain its burden of proof with respect to those claimed expenses. We cannot say that the district court erred in its holding. The record on appeal, like the record before the district court, simply affords no support for the contention that the claimed *"Expenses Specifically Identified with Malta Cristal"* actually related to "Cristal" sales. Furthermore, Cawy's claims of deductions of legal fees, as the district court noted, would not be allowable in any case. While we cannot tell whether these fees related to this suit, if they did, they would not be deductible.

The district court also disallowed Cawy's deductions of a proportionate part of its overhead expenses as set forth in Exhibit 3. Quoting from Societe Anonyme v. Western Distilling Co., 46 F. 921 (C.C.E.D.Mo.1891), the district court noted: "It appears that 'the unlawful venture increased the gross profits without swelling the gross expenses.' " It then held that Cawy failed to sustain its burden of showing the propriety of allowing deductions for overhead. Again, we must agree with the district court that Cawy failed to meet its burden of showing its expenses in the absence from the record on appeal of any evidence that Cawy's production of "Cristal" actually increased its overhead expenses. Furthermore, we note that a proportionate share of overhead is not deductible when the sales of an infringing product constitute only a small percentage of total sales. Here, on the average, infringing sales constituted just over 6% of total sales. Accordingly, we think it unlikely, especially in the absence of any evidence to the contrary, that Cawy's production of "Cristal" increased its overhead expenses.

The district court properly ordered Cawy to account for its entire gross profit from the sale of "Cristal". Cawy failed to meet its burden of showing that the overhead and other expenses that it claimed in Exhibits 2 and 3 actually related to the production of "Cristal".

IV. **Did the District Court Err in Awarding the Plaintiffs $35,000 as Actual Damages for Cawy's Infringement?**

The district court awarded the plaintiffs $35,000 as actual damages from Cawy's infringement. The record, however, is wholly devoid of support for this figure. Accordingly, we must reverse as to this element.

The plaintiffs have never been able to get sufficient financial backing to produce more than a very small amount of "Cristal" in the United States. That inability makes proof of actual damages from Cawy's infringement unlikely. In any event, the plaintiffs have had an opportunity to show their damages and have failed to do so. This Court concludes that plaintiffs should not have another opportunity to show their damages just as Cawy should not have another opportunity to prove its expenses.

In the ten years since the plaintiffs filed their original petition, this case has been before us three times. All litigation must end. We remand only for entry of judgment in accordance with this opinion.

Affirmed in part, reversed in part, and remanded for entry of judgment.

APPENDIX

DEFENDANT'S EXHIBIT 1
NET LOSS ON SALES OF MALTA CRISTAL

	1969	1970	1971	1972	1973	1974	1975	TOTAL
Revenues from sales of Malta Cristal	$40,032	$41,708	$83,861	$60,119	$31,099	$14,666	—	$271,482
Less cost of goods sold—Malta	31,883	34,059	67,285	46,438	25,209	11,558	—	216,432
GROSS PROFIT	8,149	7,646	16,576	13,681	5,890	3,108	—	55,050
Less expenses:								
per exhibit 2	8,165	6,479	10,175	17,870	17,007	9,353	500	69,549
per exhibit 3	6,683	4,250	7,859	6,448	3,199	1,762	—	30,201
TOTAL EXPENSES	14,848	10,729	18,034	24,318	20,206	11,115	500	99,750
NET LOSS( )	$(6,699)	$(3,083)	$(1,458)	$(10,637)	$(14,316)	$(8,007)	$(500)	$(44,700)

CAWY BOTTLING CO., INC.
(s) Vincent Cossio

DEFENDANT'S EXHIBIT 2
EXPENSES SPECIFICALLY IDENTIFIED WITH
MALTA CRISTAL

	1969	1970	1971	1972	1973	1974	1975	TOTAL
Advertising	$2,277	$1,723	$4,299	$13,080	$13,124	$6,510	—	$41,013
Sales commissions	3,137	3,172	5,505	4,116	1,732	752	—	18,414
Legal fees	2,130	1,500	200	483	1,988	709	—	7,010
Telephone and Telegraph	43	84	171	191	163	13	—	665
Other	578	—	—	—	—	1,369	500	2,447
	$8,165	$6,479	$10,175	$17,870	$17,007	$9,353	$500	$69,549

DEFENDANT'S EXHIBIT 3
EXPENSES RELATED TO MALTA CRISTAL
ALLOCATED BASED ON SALES RATIO

	1969	1970	1971	1972	1973	1974	1975	TOTAL
Malta Cristal cases sold	15,139	15,439	30,451	21,471	10,849	5,238	0	98,287
Total number of cases sold	176,458	228,000	276,424	288,500	296,590	314,485	0	1,580,457
Ratio of Malta's cases to total cases sold	8.58%	6.77%	10.91%	7.44%	3.66%	1.67%	—	6.22%

EXPENSES RELATED TO MALTA:

1. Repairs and maintenance	$ 1,323	$ 524	$ 762	$ 1,256	$ 663	$ 1,091		$ 5,619
2. Rent	6,864	6,864	7,938	—	—	—		21,666
3. Building depreciation	—	—	—	3,073	3,073	3,073		9,219
3. Interest—mostly building	—	—	—	11,958	14,408	13,758		40,124
4. Taxes other than payroll	4,932	8,065	5,645	12,456	11,964	10,791		53,853
5. Payroll taxes	7,718	6,282	8,582	6,624	6,859	6,787		42,852
6. Trucks' expenses	7,238	6,301	12,502	13,083	9,482	8,668		57,274
7. Utilities	1,620	—	509	—	—	—		2,129
5. Indirect labor	23,156	9,360	9,360	11,305	12,480	12,450		78,111
5. Officers salaries	17,500	13,000	13,000	13,000	31,750	—		101,250
8. Office expenses	403	665	—	1,046	767	1,503		4,384
9. Sales promotion	808	95	275	1,513	—	82		2,773
10. Insurance	3,536	5,031	6,967	6,566	8,722	8,265		39,087
11. Uniforms	916	926	1,119	1,129	1,180	1,483		6,753
11. Traveling	—	2,613	2,255	324	820	2,938		8,950
11. Accounting fees	165	970	800	1,485	—	2,875		6,295
11. Miscellaneous	1,714	2,088	2,320	1,843	3,980	—		11,945
TOTAL EXPENSES	77,893	62,784	72,034	86,661	87,398	105,514		492,281
MALTA TO TOTAL RATIO	8.58%	6.77%	10.91%	7.44%	3.66%	1.67%		
	$ 6,683	$ 4,250	$ 7,859	$ 6,448	$ 3,199	$ 1,762		$ 30,201

MINNESOTA PET BREEDERS, INC. v. SCHELL & KAMPETER, INC., 41 F.3d 1242, 1247–48, 33 U.S.P.Q.2d 1140 (8th Cir.1994). LOKEN, J: If a registered owner proves willful, deliberate infringement or deception, "an accounting of profits may be based upon 1) unjust enrichment, 2) damages, or 3) deterrence of a willful infringer." *Banff, Ltd. v. Colberts, Inc.*, 996 F.2d 33, 35 (2d Cir.), *cert. denied*, 510 U.S. 1010, 114 S.Ct. 599, 126 L.Ed.2d 564 (1993). However, § 35(a) of the Lanham Act does not permit the award of monetary relief as a penalty. Moreover, because the Act is grounded in equity and bars punitive remedies, "an accounting will be denied in a trademark infringement action where an injunction will satisfy the equities of the case." *Sweetarts v. Sunline, Inc.* 436 F.2d at 711–12, citing *Champion Spark Plug Co. v. Sanders*, 331 U.S. 125, 131, 67 S.Ct. 1136, 1139–40, 91 L.Ed. 1386 (1947), a pre-Lanham Act case often cited for the proposition that relief in a Lanham Act case should be limited to an injunction if that is sufficient to do equity.

Because an injunction is the preferred Lanham Act remedy, a court of equity may not even consider an award of profits in a geographic case of this kind until all injunction issues have been resolved. If the court grants an injunction limiting use of the infringing mark because plaintiff has shown likelihood of confusion in defendant's trade area, the court may then consider whether the equities require additional monetary relief for willful infringement.... But if the registered owner is not entitled to an injunction, the additional claim for an award of profits will almost inevitably be denied.

In this case, [plaintiff] MPB has dismissed its claim for injunctive relief, meaning that MPB has precluded entry of the Lanham Act's preferred remedy. There might be some situations in which a Lanham Act plaintiff would be entitled to monetary but not injunctive relief, for example, if the defendant's willful infringement has driven the trademark owner out of business. But in this case, in which there was *no* actual competition between the trademarked and the infringing products, it is most likely that MPB would be entitled to injunctive but not monetary relief, and virtually inconceivable that only monetary relief would be appropriate. In these unusual circumstances, although the district court should have deferred ruling on MPB's claim for profits until after trial of the injunction claim, MPB has deprived the court on remand of its ability to do equity, and therefore the judgment of the district court must be affirmed.

NOTES

1. Characterizing trademark rights as property rights may, as noted in *Maltina*, be "consistent with the view that an accounting is proper even if the defendant and plaintiff are not in direct competition.'' But does property status compel the accounting remedy? *Maltina* may obscure the real question—whether the trademark owner should be given profits earned in markets it has not yet entered. Will the answer to this question differ depending on whether the market not yet entered is a geographic market, as in *Maltina,* or a product or service market, as in dilution cases? Should the answer to the question be affected by the relative availability of injunctive relief? Reconsider the discussion of *Dawn Donut,* page 289, above.

2. *Monetary Relief.* Because the remedies of damages and profits are intertwined, and because each alone serves at least two functions, the array of monetary awards available to the successful trademark owner is far richer than might appear from the face of section 35 of the Lanham Act. Damages can be measured by

(1) loss of sales and profits caused by the infringer's use of the owner's mark; or

(2) consequent economic injury to the trademark owner's reputation and goodwill.

Profits earned by the infringer through its use of the mark can be treated

(1) as presumptively equivalent to the profits lost by the trademark owner and, thus, awarded on a compensatory basis; or

(2) under the approach taken in *Maltina,* as unjust enrichment.

Type (1) profit awards are the intended equivalent of type (1) damage awards, the difference lying in the critical shift of the burden of proof from owner to infringer. The assumption implicit in this shift, that the owner's sales have been diverted by the infringer's, is warranted only when the parties are in competition. Type (2) profit awards, because they rest on an unjust enrichment rationale, do not require competition between the parties. To bar double recovery, an award of type (1) profits will preclude an award of type (1) damages but will not preclude an award of type (2) damages. Is an award of type (1) damages inconsistent with an award of type (2) profits? Restatement, Restitution § 136, Comment a (1937), explores the general principles that underlie these distinctions.

Monetary awards generally are considered in James M. Koelemay, Jr., Monetary Relief for Trademark Infringement Under the Lanham Act, 72 Trademark Rep. 458 (1982). See also William G. Barber, Recovery of Profits Under the Lanham Act: Are the District Courts Doing Their Job?, 82 Trademark Rep. 141 (1992); Christopher P. Bussert & Theodore H. Davis, Jr., Calculating Profits Under Section 35 of the Lanham Act: A Practitioner's Guide, 82 Trademark Rep. 182 (1992).

3. *Marking.* Under section 29, 15 U.S.C.A. § 1111, the owner of a registered mark can recover damages and profits only if it can show that the infringer knew of the registration or that notice of the registration, such as the familiar ®, accompanied displays of the mark.

If the registrant intentionally employs a false or misleading notice, its unclean hands will bar injunctive relief. Is it false marking if the notice of registration is located under a composite mark, one part of which is registered and one part of which is not? Compare Straus v. Notaseme Hosiery Co., 240 U.S. 179, 36 S.Ct. 288, 60 L.Ed. 590 (1916), with Coca-Cola Co. v. Victor Syrup Corp., 42 C.C.P.A. 751, 218 F.2d 596, 104 U.S.P.Q. 275 (1954).

4.   *Attorney's Fees.* In Fleischmann Distilling Corp. v. Maier Brewing Co., 386 U.S. 714, 87 S.Ct. 1404, 18 L.Ed.2d 475, 153 U.S.P.Q. 432 (1967), the Supreme Court ruled that a prevailing trademark owner is not entitled to recover attorney's fees, even from a deliberate infringer. Justice Stewart dissented. "Until this case, every federal court that has faced the issue has upheld judicial power to award counsel fees in trademark infringement cases. In order to overrule that unbroken line of authority, I would have to be satisfied that Congress has made any such declaration."

Congress soon made its intentions clear. P.L. 93–600, 88 Stat. 1955 (1975), provides in part that "the court in exceptional cases may award reasonable attorney fees to the prevailing party." 15 U.S.C.A. § 1117. The rationale for the remedy was that "effective enforcement of trademark rights is left to the trademark owners and they should, in the interest of preventing purchaser confusion, be encouraged to enforce trademark rights." The revisors recognized that "section 35 of the present Trademark Act provides for awarding treble damages in appropriate circumstances in order to encourage the enforcement of trademark rights. The availability of treble damages, however, cannot be regarded as a substitute for the recovery of attorney fees. In suits brought primarily to obtain an injunction, attorney fees may be more important than treble damages. Frequently, in a flagrant infringement where the infringement action is brought promptly, the measurable damages are nominal." Sen.Rep. No. 93–1400, (93d Cong.2d Sess.).

5.   *Injunctive Relief.* Injunctions granted in unfair competition actions are typically shaped to meet the particular circumstances of the case. Trademark injunctions, by contrast, are characteristically granted absolutely or not at all, with scant attention given to the possibilities in between. The reason for the difference lies in trademark law's exclusive focus on marks and its disregard for contextual factors such as format, usage, typographic style and other overt elements of passing off. In appropriate circumstances, however, such as where the registered mark is weak, a court may only require the defendant to label its goods to disclaim an association with the plaintiff. See generally, Jacob Jacoby & George J. Szybillo, Why Disclaimers Fail, 84 Trademark Rep. 224 (1994); Theodore C. Max, Total Recall: A Primer on a Drastic Form of Equitable Relief, 84 Trademark Rep. 325 (1994).

6.   *Compulsory Licensing.* Congress and the courts sometimes compel copyright and patent owners to license their works in order to forestall or dissipate monopoly effects. Should trademarks be subjected to compulsory licensing in similar circumstances?

In Borden, Inc., 92 F.T.C. 669 (1976), a Federal Trade Commission administrative law judge found that Borden's trademark, "ReaLemon," used in connection with reconstituted lemon juice, was a significant barrier to the entry of new products, and ordered Borden to license the mark for ten years to any firm desiring to enter the reconstituted lemon juice market. Acknowledging that the Commission had never before ordered trademark licensing, the judge ruled that it "is not essentially different from a requirement of compulsory licensing of a patent." 92 F.T.C. 775.

The decision drew heavy fire. The United States Trademark Association filed an *amicus* brief with the F.T.C. arguing that compulsory licensing "could have an adverse impact upon the interests of the public in the use of trademarks and upon the integrity of trademarks." According to the Association, compulsory trademark licensing disserves the public interest because "it permits more than one business to use a single trademark on goods, causing the trademark to fail in its essential purpose and producing public injury by impairing consumers' freedom of choice, whether or not all goods sold under the trademark are of equal quality." The private value of the ReaLemon mark would be impaired to "the extent that its proprietor's right to the exclusive use thereof is abrogated for ten years. And, at the end of that term, it may be so diluted or sullied by the acts of competitor-licensees as to be worthless."

On November 7, 1978 the F.T.C. voted against ordering compulsory licensing of the ReaLemon mark. Recognizing that "an order requiring licensing or suspension of a trademark may be ordered as a means of dissipating illegally used or acquired monopoly power," a majority of the Commission was "mindful that the remedy is a severe one, and should be imposed only where less drastic means appear unlikely to suffice." In the judgment of the majority "an order that simply prohibits Borden from pricing to exclude or minimize new entry should be sufficient to dissipate its unlawfully maintained monopoly position, which is the only permissible object of relief in this case." 92 F.T.C. at 807–08. The case was eventually settled. Borden, Inc. v. Federal Trade Commission, 711 F.2d 758 (6th Cir.1983).

See generally William J. Keating, FTC Authority to Order Compulsory Trademark Licensing: Is "ReaLemon" Really Real Lemon?, 85 Dick.L.Rev. 191 (1981). On the economics of compulsory licensing for trademarks, see F. M. Scherer, The Posnerian Harvest: Separating Wheat from Chaff, 86 Yale L.J. 974, 998–1000 (1977).

7. *Counterfeiting Remedies.* Counterfeit goods—for example, fake Rolex watches sold on city street corners—pose special problems for trademark relief. Injunctive decrees have little effect and monetary awards promise scant recovery against offshore manufacturers and fly-by-night distributors. The real need of trademark owners is substantial deterrents.

The Trademark Counterfeiting Act of 1984, P.L. 98–473, 98 Stat. 2178, substantially bolstered the Lanham Act's provisions for civil relief and also introduced criminal sanctions against traffic in counterfeit goods or services. Amendments to the Lanham Act mandate awards of attorney's fees and treble damages against counterfeiters and authorize *ex parte* orders to seize counterfeit goods. See 15 U.S.C.A. §§ 1116(d), 1117(b). Section 1118 provides for destruction of infringing articles. Title 18 provides that individuals who intentionally traffic, or attempt to traffic, in goods or services and knowingly use a counterfeit mark on or in connection with the goods or services may be fined not more than $2,000 or imprisoned not more than 10 years, or both. For the same offense, companies may be fined not more than $5,000,000. 18 U.S.C.A. § 2320 (1989).

3. SECONDARY LIABILITY

Hard Rock Cafe Licensing Corp. v. Concession Services, Inc.

United States Court of Appeals, Seventh Circuit, 1992.
955 F.2d 1143, 21 U.S.P.Q.2d 1764.

CUDAHY, Circuit Judge.

The Hard Rock Café Licensing Corporation (Hard Rock) owns trademarks on several clothing items, including t-shirts and sweatshirts and apparently attempts to exploit its trademark monopoly to the full. In the summer of 1989, Hard Rock sent out specially trained private investigators to look for counterfeit Hard Rock Café merchandise. The investigators found Iqbal Parvez selling counterfeit Hard Rock t-shirts from stands in the Tri–State Swap–O–Rama and the Melrose Park Swap–O–Rama flea markets owned and operated by Concession Services Incorporated (CSI). The investigators also discovered that Harry's Sweat Shop (Harry's) was selling similar items. Hard Rock brought suit against Parvez, CSI, Harry's and others not relevant to this appeal under the Lanham Trademark Act, 15 U.S.C. § 1051 et seq. (1988). Most of the defendants settled, including Parvez, who paid Hard Rock some $30,000. CSI and Harry's went to trial.

After a bench trial, the district court found that both remaining defendants violated the Act and entered permanent injunctions forbidding Harry's to sell merchandise bearing Hard Rock's trademarks (whether counterfeit or genuine) and forbidding CSI to permit the sale of such merchandise at its flea markets. The court also awarded treble damages against Harry's. The court did not, however, award attorney's fees against either defendant.

All of the parties who participated in the trial appealed. CSI believes that it is not liable and that, in any event, entry of the injunction was inappropriate. Hard Rock wants attorney's fees from both defendants. Harry's appealed from the finding of liability and the entry of the injunction as well, but filed its appeal one day too late; its appeal has therefore been dismissed. Finding errors of law and a fatal ambiguity in the findings of fact, we vacate the judgment against CSI, vacate the denial of attorney's fees and remand for further proceedings.

I.

Most of the facts are undisputed. The following account draws from the district court's findings, the record on appeal and the submissions of the parties. Where there are disputes of fact we will note them and defer to the district court's resolution unless clearly erroneous.

A.   *The Parties and Their Practices*

1.   *Concession Services, Inc.*

In the summer of 1989, CSI owned and operated three "Swap–O–Rama" flea markets in the Chicago area: the Tri–State, in Alsip, Illinois; the Melrose Park, in Melrose Park, Illinois; and the Brighton Park, in Chicago itself. Although Parvez sold counterfeits at the Tri–State Swap–O–Rama and at Melrose Park, testimony at trial concentrated on the operations at the Tri–State. We too will refer mainly to the Tri–State Swap–O–Rama, although CSI's operations are apparently similar at all three flea markets.

CSI generates revenue from a flea market in four ways. First, it rents space to vendors for flat fees that vary by the day of the week and the location of the space. Second, CSI charges a reservation and storage fee to those vendors who want to reserve the same space on a month-to-month basis. Third, CSI charges shoppers a nominal 75 cents admission charge. Fourth, CSI runs concession stands inside the market. To promote its business, CSI advertises the markets, announcing "BARGAINS" to be had, but does not advertise the presence of any individual vendors or any particular goods. Supervision of the flea markets is minimal. CSI posts a sign at the Tri–State prohibiting vendors from selling "illegal goods." It also has "Rules For Sellers" which prohibit the sale of food or beverages, alcohol, weapons, fireworks, live animals, drugs and drug paraphernalia and subversive or un-American literature. Other than these limitations, vendors can, and do, sell almost any conceivable item. Two off-duty police officers provide security and crowd control (an arrangement that does not apply to the other markets). These officers also have some duty to ensure that the vendors obey the Sellers' Rules. The manager of the Tri–State, Albert Barelli, walks around the flea market about five times a day, looking for problems and violations of the rules. No one looks over the vendors' wares before they enter the market and set up their stalls, and any examination after that is cursory. Moreover, Barelli does not keep records of the names and addresses of the vendors. The only penalty for violating the Seller's Rules is expulsion from the market.

James Pierski, the vice president in charge of CSI's flea markets, testified that CSI has a policy of cooperating with any trademark owner that notifies CSI of possible infringing activity. But there is no evidence that this policy has ever been carried into effect. Before this case, there have been a few seizures of counterfeit goods at Swap–O–Rama flea markets. In no case was CSI informed of a pending seizure, involved in a seizure or notified as to the ultimate disposition of the seized goods. On the other hand, CSI did not investigate any of the seizures, though it knew they had occurred.

2.   *Harry's Sweat Shop*

Harry's is a small store in Darien, Illinois, owned and operated by Harry Spatero. The store sells athletic shoes, t-shirts, jackets with the names of professional sports teams and the like. Spatero testified that the store contains over 20,000 different items. When buying t-shirts, Harry's is somewhat indiscriminate. The store buys seconds, overruns and closeouts from a variety of sources. Harry's buys most of its t-shirts from Supply Brokers of Pennsylvania, a firm which specializes in buying up stocks from stores going out of business. Spatero testified that Supply Brokers sends him largely unidentified boxes of shirts which he may choose to return after looking them over. But Spatero testified that Harry's also bought shirts from people who came around in unmarked vans, offering shirts at a discount. The store kept no records of the sources of its inventory.

3.   *Hard Rock Licensing Corp.*

Hard Rock owns the rights to a variety of Hard Rock trademarks. The corporation grants licenses to use its trademarks to the limited partnerships that own and operate the various Hard Rock Café restaurants. These restaurants are the only authorized distributors of Hard Rock Café merchandise, but apparently this practice of exclusivity is neither publicized nor widely known. The shirts themselves are produced by Winterland Productions, which prints logos on blank, first quality t-shirts that it buys from Hanes, Fruit-of-the-Loom and Anvil. According to the manager of the Chicago Hard Rock Café, Scott Floersheimer, Winterland has an agreement with Hard Rock to retain all defective Hard Rock shirts. Thus, if Winterland performs as agreed, all legitimate Hard Rock shirts sold to the public are well-made and cleanly printed.

The Chicago Hard Rock Café has done very well from its business. Since 1986, it has sold over 500,000 t-shirts at an average gross profit of $10.12 per shirt.

B.   *The Investigation*

National Investigative Services Corporation (NISCOR) carried out the search for counterfeit merchandise on Hard Rock's behalf. Another firm, Trademark Facts, Inc., trained NISCOR's investigators to recognize counterfeit merchandise. Recognizing counterfeit Hard Rock goods was apparently easy. Any shirt not sold in a Hard Rock Café restaurant was, unless second-hand, counterfeit. Other than this, the investigators were instructed to check for the manufacturer of the t-shirt, a registration or trademark symbol, the quality of the printed design, the color of the design, the quality of the shirt stock and the price. But as to these latter factors (except for the price), Floersheimer testified that even he would have trouble distinguishing a good counterfeit from a legitimate t-shirt.

The investigators visited both the Melrose Park and the Tri–State Swap–O–Ramas and observed Iqbal Parvez (or his employees) offering more than a hundred Hard Rock t-shirts for sale. Cynthia Myers, the chief investigator on the project, testified that these shirts were obviously counterfeit. The shirts were poor quality stock, with cut labels and were being sold for $3 apiece (a legitimate Hard Rock shirt, we are told, goes for over $14). Harry's had four Hard Rock shirts for sale, sitting on a discount table for $3.99 each. The district court found that these too were of obviously low quality, with cut labels and cracked and worn designs. Nonetheless, both Parvez and Harry's were selling t-shirts made by approved manufacturers. Parvez was selling Hanes t-shirts, and Harry's was selling Fruit-of-the-Loom.

At no point before filing suit did Hard Rock warn Harry's or CSI (or Parvez, whose supplier Hard Rock was trying to track down) that the shirts were counterfeits.

C. *The District Court Proceedings*

Hard Rock brought suit against the defendants in September 1989, alleging violations of sections 32 and 43 of the Lanham Act. 15 U.S.C. §§ 1114 & 1125 (1988). Pending trial, the court entered temporary restraining orders and then preliminary injunctions against both CSI and Harry's. Harry's got rid of its remaining Hard Rock t-shirts, and CSI told any vendors selling Hard Rock merchandise in its flea markets to get rid of their stock as well. There have been no more violations.

After a bench trial, the district court entered permanent injunctions against both defendants and ordered Harry's to pay treble damages based on Hard Rock's lost profits on four t-shirts (in sum, $120). The court denied Hard Rock's request for attorney's fees.

The court's reasoning is crucial to the resolution of this appeal. Accordingly, we think it appropriate to quote from it at some length. The court concluded that both defendants were "guilty of willful blindness that counterfeit goods were being sold on [their] premises." Another sentence follows, however, which somewhat dilutes the impact of the preceding finding: "Neither defendant took reasonable steps to detect or prevent the sale of Hard Rock Café counterfeit T-shirts on its premise [sic]." This suggests mere negligence.

Willful blindness, the court said, "is a sufficient basis for a finding of violation of the Lanham Act. As to CSI's argument that it did not actually sell the offending goods, the court observed that CSI is not 'merely a landlord'; it also advertises and promotes the activity on its premises, sells admission tickets to buyers and supervises the premises. Under these circumstances it must also take reasonable precautions against the sale of counterfeit products."

II.

The Lanham Trademark Act protects consumers from deceptive claims about the nature and origin of products. 15 U.S.C. § 1114(1)(a) & (b) (use of mark violates Act if "likely to cause confusion, or to cause mistake, or to deceive"); 15 U.S.C. § 1125(a)(1) (false designation of origin violates Act if "likely to cause confusion, or to cause mistake, or to deceive"). But the Lanham Act also protects trademarks as a form of intellectual property. In this case, the Act protects Hard Rock's investment in a fashionable image and a reputation for selling high quality goods. See *Inwood Laboratories, Inc. v. Ives Laboratories, Inc.*, 456 U.S. 844, 854 n. 14, 102 S.Ct. 2182, 2188 n. 14, 72 L.Ed.2d 606 (1982) (citing S.Rep. No. 1333, 79th Cong., 2d Sess. 3 (1946)).

A. *Secondary Liability*

The most interesting issue in this case is CSI's liability for Parvez's sales. Hard Rock argues that CSI has incurred both contributory and vicarious liability for the counterfeits, and we take the theories of liability in that order.

It is well established that "if a manufacturer or distributor intentionally induces another to infringe a trademark, or if it continues to supply its product to one whom it knows or has reason to know is engaging in trademark infringement, the manufacturer or distributor is contributorily responsible for any harm done as a result of the deceit." Id. [*Inwood Laboratories*] at 854, 102 S.Ct. at 2188. Despite this apparently definitive statement, it is not clear how the doctrine applies to people who do not actually manufacture or distribute the good that is ultimately palmed off as made by someone else. A temporary help service, for example, might not be liable if it furnished Parvez the workers he employed to erect his stand, even if the help service knew that Parvez would sell counterfeit goods. Thus we must ask whether the operator of a flea market is more like the manufacturer of a mislabeled good or more like a temporary help service supplying the purveyor of goods. To answer questions of this sort, we have treated trademark infringement as a species of tort and have turned to the common law to guide our inquiry into the appropriate boundaries of liability.

CSI characterizes its relationship with Parvez as that of landlord and tenant. Hard Rock calls CSI a licensor, not a landlord. Either way, the Restatement of Torts tells us that CSI is responsible for the torts of those it permits on its premises "knowing or having reason to know that the other is acting or will act tortiously...." Restatement (Second) of Torts § 877(c) & cmt. d (1979). The common law, then, imposes the same duty on landlords and licensors that the Supreme Court has imposed on manufacturers and distributors. In the absence of any suggestion that a trademark violation should not be treated as a common law tort, we believe that the *Inwood Labs.* test for contributory liability applies. CSI may be liable for trademark violations by Parvez if it knew or had reason to know of them. But the factual findings must support that conclusion.

The district court found CSI to be willfully blind. Since we have held that willful blindness is equivalent to actual knowledge for purposes of the Lanham Act, this finding should be enough to hold CSI liable (unless clearly erroneous). But we very much doubt that the district court defined willful blindness as it should have. To be willfully blind, a person must suspect wrongdoing and deliberately fail to investigate. The district court, however, made little mention of CSI's state of mind and focused almost entirely on CSI's failure to take precautions against counterfeiting. In its conclusions of law, the court emphasized that CSI had a duty to take reasonable precautions. In short, it looks as if the district court found CSI to be negligent, not willfully blind.

This ambiguity in the court's findings would not matter if CSI could be liable for failing to take reasonable precautions. But CSI has no affirmative duty to take precautions against the sale of counterfeits. Although the "reason to know" part of the standard for contributory liability requires CSI (or its agents) to understand what a reasonably prudent person would understand, it does not impose any duty to seek out and prevent violations. We decline to extend the protection that Hard Rock finds in the common law to require CSI, and other landlords, to be more dutiful guardians of Hard Rock's commercial interests. Thus the district court's findings do not support the conclusion that CSI bears contributory liability for Parvez's transgressions.

Before moving on, we should emphasize that we have found only that the district court applied an incorrect standard. We have not found that the evidence cannot support the conclusion that CSI was in fact willfully blind. At the Tri–State, Barelli saw Parvez's shirts and had the opportunity to note that they had cut labels and were being sold cheap. Further, Barelli testified that he did not ask vendors whether their goods were counterfeit because they were sure to lie to him. One might infer from these facts that Barelli suspected that the shirts were counterfeits but chose not to investigate.

On the other hand, we do not wish to prejudge the matter. For it is undisputed that Hard Rock made no effort to broadcast the information that legitimate Hard Rock t-shirts could only be found in Hard Rock Cafes. Moreover, there does not seem to be any particular reason to believe that inexpensive t-shirts with cut labels are obviously counterfeit, no matter what logo they bear. The circumstantial evidence that Barelli suspected the shirts to be counterfeit is, at best, thin. On remand, the district court may choose to develop this issue more fully.

Perhaps recognizing that the district court's opinion is unclear, Hard Rock urges us to find CSI vicariously liable for Parvez's sales, regardless of its knowledge of the counterfeiting. Indeed, if we accept this theory, CSI is liable for Parvez's sales even if it was not negligent.

We have recognized that a joint tortfeasor may bear vicarious liability for trademark infringement by another. This theory of liability requires a finding that the defendant and the infringer have an apparent or actual partnership, have authority to bind one another in transactions with third parties or exercise joint ownership or control over the infringing product. The case before us does not fit into the joint tortfeasor model, and Hard Rock does not argue that it does.

Instead, Hard Rock wants us to apply the more expansive doctrine of vicarious liability applicable to copyright violations. Under the test developed by the Second Circuit, a defendant is vicariously liable for copyright infringement if it has "the right and ability to supervise the infringing activity and also has a direct financial interest in such activities." *Gershwin Publishing Corp. v. Columbia Artists Management, Inc.*, 443 F.2d 1159, 1162 (2d Cir.1971) (hereinafter CAMI). The purpose of the doctrine is to prevent an entity that profits from infringement from hiding behind undercapitalized "dummy" operations when the copyright owner eventually sues.

The parties have argued vigorously about the application of this doctrine to the facts. But we need not decide the question; for the Supreme Court tells us that secondary liability for trademark infringement should, in any event, be more narrowly drawn than secondary liability for copyright infringement. *Sony Corp. of America v. Universal City Studios, Inc.*, 464 U.S. 417, 439 n. 19, 104 S.Ct. 774, 787 n. 19, 78 L.Ed.2d 574 (1984) (citing "fundamental differences" between copyright and trademark law). If Hard Rock referred us to some principle of common law that supported its analogy to copyright, we would be more understanding of its claims. But it has not. Further, there is no hint that CSI is playing at the sort of obfuscation that inspired the Second Circuit to develop its more expansive form of vicarious copyright liability. Hard Rock must look to Congress to provide the level of protection it demands of CSI here.

In sum, we find that CSI may bear contributory liability for Parvez's unlawful sales, but we see no evidence on the record that would support a finding that CSI is vicariously liable. Accordingly, because the district court's findings fail to establish that CSI knew or had reason to know that Parvez was selling counterfeits, we must vacate the judgment against CSI and remand for further proceedings....

III.

For the foregoing reasons, we VACATE the finding of liability as to CSI, VACATE the denial of Hard Rock's request for attorney's fees against both defendants and REMAND for further proceedings consistent with this opinion.

NOTE

Historically, trademark law has aimed to economize legal recourse against deception respecting the source of goods and services. In a world without trademark law, consumers would have only an action for deceit, and manufacturers would have only an action for passing off, against retailers who engaged in deceptive practices. But retailers are numerous and their conduct is costly to monitor. It is the genius of trademarks to reach over the retailer's shoulder to create source identification for consumers, and to enable trademark owners to obtain complete relief by proceeding at comparatively low expense against a single offender, the manufacturer or distributor. As should be evident from *Hard Rock*, however, trademark law does not invariably economize on enforcement expense; distributors, like retailers, are sometimes too numerous to sue and too impecunious to satisfy judgments against them. Doctrines of contributory and vicarious liability seek to enhance trademark law's enforcement economies in this setting.

Together with Warner v. Eli Lilly, page 58, above, Inwood Laboratories, Inc. v. Ives Laboratories, Inc., 456 U.S. 844, 102 S.Ct. 2182, 72 L.Ed.2d 606, 214 U.S.P.Q. 1 (1982), is the seminal Supreme Court authority in the area. Following expiration of plaintiff's patent on the drug, Cyclospasmol, competing drug manufacturers had produced, and sold to pharmacists, a generic equivalent that copied the appearance of plaintiff's capsules. When pharmacists began repackaging and mislabelling the generic products as Cyclospasmol, plaintiff sued the generic drug manufacturers on the theory that their use of look-alike capsules, and distribution of catalogues comparing the prices of the generic drug with Cyclospasmol, induced pharmacists to substitute and mislabel the generic drug as Cyclospasmol.

The district court ruled for the defendant and the circuit court for the plaintiff. The Supreme Court reversed the circuit court decision on the ground that the court had failed to apply the Federal Rules' "clearly erroneous" standard in reviewing the district court decision. The Court's statement of the test for contributory trademark infringement, though *dicta*, has nonetheless been influential: "As the lower courts correctly discerned, liability for trademark infringement can extend beyond those who actually mislabel goods with the mark of another. Even if a manufacturer does not directly control others in the chain of distribution, it can be held responsible for their infringing activities under certain circumstances. Thus, if a manufacturer or distributor intentionally induces another to infringe a trademark, or if it continues to supply its product to one who it knows or has reason to know is engaging in trademark infringement, the manufacturer or distributor is contributorily responsible for any harm done as a result of the deceit." 456 U.S. at 853–854, 102 S.Ct. at 2188.

Justice White, joined by Justice Marshall, concurred in the reversal "because I believe the Court of Appeals has watered down to an impermissible extent the standard for finding a violation of § 32 of the Lanham Act, 15 U.S.C. § 1114," and because the Court's majority opinion acquiesced in this new standard. The test to which Justice White objected was that:

> By using capsules of identical color, size, and shape, together with a catalog describing their appearance and listing comparable prices of CYCLOSPASMOL and generic cyclandelate, appellees *could reasonably anticipate* that their generic drug product would by a substantial number of druggists be substituted illegally.... This amounted to a suggestion, at least by implication, that the druggists take advantage of the opportunity to engage in such misconduct. 638 F.2d at 543 (emphasis added).

In Justice White's view, "[t]he mere fact that a generic drug company can anticipate that some illegal substitution will occur to some unspecified extent and by some unknown pharmacists, should not by itself be a predicate for contributory liability." 456 U.S. at 859–860, 102 S.Ct. at 2191–92.

Congress recognized the importance of secondary liability to trademark owners when, in section 32(1) of the Lanham Act, 15 U.S.C.§ 1114(1), it imposed liability not only on those who, without the registrant's consent, use a registered mark in the sale of goods or services, but also on those, such as printers or newspaper publishers, who include the mark in labels, packaging or advertisements. Congress also recognized the need for more sensitively balanced liability in the latter class of cases, allowing only injunctive relief against innocent infringers; perhaps motivated by First Amendment concerns, it denied injunctive relief against innocent print or electronic publishers if the injunction would delay the timely publication of the infringing work. 15 U.S.C. § 1114(2).

Which is the appropriate standard to qualify secondary liability— willfulness or negligence? What would a proprietor of an electronic bulletin board have to do to avoid liability under either standard: Carefully monitor postings in an attempt to root out offending messages, or put his head in the sand and entirely decline to review posting content? If he chooses the first alternative, what are his legal risks if his monitoring efforts turn out to be less than completely successful? Comment a to section 7 of the Restatement of Torts Third, Unfair Competition (1995) observes: "In determining whether a person has directly and substantially assisted in making a misrepresentation, a relevant factor is whether the imposition of a remedy against that person is necessary to fully protect the interests of the complainant and the public."

E. INFRINGEMENT

See Statute Supplement 15 U.S.C.A. §§ 1114, 1121.

Pikle–Rite Co. v. Chicago Pickle Co.

United States Dist. Court, Northern Dist. Illinois, 1959.
171 F.Supp. 671, 121 U.S.P.Q. 128.

JULIUS J. HOFFMAN, District Judge.

This is an action for trade-mark infringement and unfair competition in which the plaintiff seeks an injunction, an accounting and treble damages.

The plaintiff is an Illinois corporation having its principal office and place of business in Pulaski, Wisconsin. The defendant is an Illinois corporation having its principal office and place of business in Chicago. In 1932, plaintiff's predecessor, John A. Wood, established the business of preparing and selling bottled pickles and related products. In 1942, this business was taken over by Pikle–Rite Company, an unincorporated business entity which was incorporated in 1948. Since 1932, plaintiff and its predecessors have owned and used the trade-mark "Polka" to designate different varieties of pickles which are sold primarily in self-service grocery stores in Illinois, Wisconsin, Iowa, Michigan, Minnesota, Indiana and Ohio. Since 1934, the name "Polka" has been registered as a trade-mark under the laws of Illinois. On August 7, 1956, plaintiff was granted a federal trade-mark registration on the name "Polka." As registered, the name is preceded and followed by a pair of musical notes. The name "Polka," as applied to pickle products, is fanciful, arbitrary, non-descriptive and non-generic, and is a valid trade-mark.

Representative labels under which plaintiff markets some of its "Polka"–brand pickle products are as follows:

Although the plaintiff prepares and bottles other vegetables, its "Polka"–brand pickle products are its principal items of business. The plaintiff has advertised its "Polka"–brand products through the media of television, radio, newspapers, window posters, shelf posters and gifts such as pencils, lazy susans and plastic aprons. However, the evidence discloses no comprehensive advertising expenditures.

For the period January 1953 through June 1957, the total amount of sales of "Polka"–brand products was $311,184.11. The yearly amount of sales of these products was as follows:

1953	$49,014.75
1954	45,230.58
1955	68,461.56
1956	100,037.32
1957	48,439.90
(through June)	

There is no evidence on the question whether the pickle business as a whole was substantially better in 1956 than it was in 1955. Nor is there any evidence on the question whether the plaintiff expanded its business or its advertising in 1956.

In December 1956, defendant began to distribute pickles in bottles which bore the brand-name "Pol–Pak." Defendant's label is as follows:

The defendant markets its products through self-service grocery stores. However, the evidence does not disclose whether the defendant utilizes this method exclusively or even primarily.

With reference to infringement, the basic issue in this case is whether the defendant's use of the name "Pol–Pak" on its products "... is likely to cause confusion or mistake or to deceive purchasers as to the source of origin of such goods." 15 U.S.C.A. § 1114(1)(a). For the reasons which follow, I am of the opinion that the defendant's brand-name "Pol–Pak" is confusingly similar to the plaintiff's trade-mark "Polka," and the plaintiff is entitled to injunctive relief. However, I am also of the opinion that the plaintiff is not entitled to an accounting and damages.

There is no dispute between the parties as to the law which is applicable to the instant case. In Northam Warren Corp. v. Universal

Cosmetic Co., 7 Cir., 1927, 18 F.2d 774, at page 775, the law of infringement was stated as follows:

> Whether there is an infringement of a trade-mark does not depend upon the use of identical words, nor on the question as to whether they are so similar that a person looking at one would be deceived into the belief that it was the other; but it is sufficient if one adopts a trade-name or a trade-mark so like another in form, spelling, or sound that one, *with a not very definite or clear recollection as to the real trade-mark, is likely to become confused or misled*.... (Emphasis added.)
>
> ...

In determining whether the likelihood of confusion exists, it should be noted that:

> The ascertainment of probability of confusion because of similarity of trade names presents a problem not solvable by a precise rule or measure. Rather is it a matter of varying human reactions to situations incapable of exact appraisement. We are to determine, as was the District Judge, the purchasing public's state of mind when confronted by somewhat similar trade names singly presented. Is the similarity of name or dress such as to delude the public or will the prospective buyer readily differentiate between the two names? We can only contemplate, speculate, and weigh the probabilities of deception arising from the similarities and conclude as our, and the District Judge's, reactions persuade us. Colburn v. Puritan Mills, 7 Cir., 1939, 108 F.2d 377, at page 378.

Although the question presented by the instant case cannot be solved by precise rule or measure, certain factors are relevant. Whether infringement exists is not to be determined solely by a side-by-side comparison of the names in question. Although it is proper to consider the names as a whole, the names should not be examined with a microscope to detect minute differences. To constitute infringement, it is not necessary that the defendant appropriate the whole of plaintiff's mark, and the imitation need only be slight if it attaches to the salient feature of plaintiff's mark. The court should also consider the form, spelling and sound of the marks in question; whether the products involved are the same or similar, whether the products are sold to the same prospective customers, and whether the conditions under which the products are purchased are the same or similar.

In the instant case, there is no evidence that any purchaser was, in fact, confused or misled by the defendant's use of the name of "Pol–Pak." However, it was not necessary for the plaintiff to prove actual confusion. The statutory test is likelihood of confusion.

I am of the opinion that the defendant's use of the name "Pol–Pak" gives rise to the likelihood of confusing similarity. The salient part of defendant's brand-name, i.e., "Pol," constitutes three-fifths of plaintiff's trade-mark. Common experience teaches that an individual will more readily remember the first part of a name than some other part. Further, to the extent that the defendant's pickles are sold in self-service grocery stores, the parties utilize the same or similar commercial channels, the prospective purchaser is the same, and the conditions under which the products are purchased are the same or similar. The names "Polka" and "Pol–Pak" are not more dissimilar than the names "Cutex" and "Cuticlean" which were held to be confusingly similar in Northam Warren Corp. v. Universal Cosmetic Co., 7 Cir., 1927, 18 F.2d 774. The Northam case also refutes defendant's contention that the name "Pol" is but an abbreviation for the descriptive word, "Polish," and is, therefore, not infringing. In the Northam case, the designation "Cuti" was an abbreviation for the descriptive or generic word, "cuticle," but the court held that "Cuticlean" infringed "Cutex."

The defendant contends that a side-by-side comparison of the *labels* in question discloses no confusing similarity. However, as noted above, infringement is not to be determined solely by such comparison. The reason for this rule is that the ultimate purchaser is seldom presented with the opportunity of making such comparison. Further, it is to be doubted that the labels, apart from the marks in question, should be considered. It has been asserted as a general rule that differences in labels should not be considered in determining whether defendant's brand-name infringes plaintiff's trade-mark. 1 Nims, Unfair Competition and Trade Marks, § 221k, p. 716 et seq. However, Nims cites, as a case contrary to the general rule, John Morrell & Co. v. Doyle, 7 Cir., 1938, 97 F.2d 232, certiorari denied 1938, 305 U.S. 643, 59 S.Ct. 146, 83 L.Ed. 415. In the Morrell case, the plaintiff sold dog food under the trade-mark "Red Heart" which comprised those words superimposed upon a red heart. The defendant sold dog and cat food under the brand-name "Strong Heart" which name was accompanied by the picture of a famous dog, Strongheart. In holding that the plaintiff's trade-mark was not infringed, the court considered and emphasized the picture of the dog, and the court expressly declined to consider the name "Strong Heart" in vacuo. In spite of this fact, I am of the opinion that the Morrell case does not derogate from the general rule. The rationale of that decision is that, with regard to the defendant's label,

> ... the characteristic feature, the thing which appeals to the eye and which, no doubt, makes the lasting impression upon a person's memory, is not Strongheart or Heart, but the picture of a dog. Assuming that persons who are interested in dog foods are dog fanciers, what could make such an appeal or create such a lasting impression as an imposing picture of a dog and especially if it be the picture of a dog of fame such as the record here indicates to be the case?

Thus, the court merely held that the essence of defendant's brand-name was a picture and not a name. In the instant case, the salient part of defendant's label is the brand-name "Pol–Pak"; the picture of a pickle is without significance. Further, to the extent that the representation of Polish dancers is a salient part of plaintiff's label, the representation reinforces the trade-mark "Polka." It does not derogate from the mark as the picture of the dog derogated from the brand-name "Strong Heart." In addition, it should be noted that the plaintiff has advertised the name "Polka" apart from the representation of Polish dancers.

Even in an economy in which diverse methods of advertising are employed, the spoken word is of great importance. A prospective purchaser may learn of plaintiff's "Polka"-brand products from her neighbor; she may hear radio advertisements; she may hear and see television advertisements and the memory of the spoken word may exist long after the memory of the image has faded. Further, the law does not presume that the prospective purchaser will have the opportunity to make a side-by-side comparison of different products and brand-names. As stated in Colburn v. Puritan Mills, 7 Cir., 1939, 108 F.2d 377, at page 378:

> We are to determine, as was the District Judge, the purchasing public's state of mind when confronted by somewhat similar trade names *singly presented*. (Emphasis added.)

Also, it must be borne in mind that we are dealing neither with an unusual product which requires discriminating purchase nor with a purchasing public which is discriminating. To the contrary, it has been asserted that the average purchaser undergoes, while in a super-market, an experience not unlike that of hypnosis. Packard, The Hidden Persuaders, pp. 91–2 (Cardinal Edition, 1958). Under such circumstances, it is not unduly harsh to restrain the defendant's use of the name "Pol–Pak." The defendant, in selecting a name for its product, could have drawn upon the entire range of its imagination. It chose not to do so and, instead, selected a name which is likely to confuse prospective purchasers of plaintiff's products. I conclude that the defendant's use of the name "Pol–Pak" should be enjoined.

Consideration will next be given to the territorial scope of the injunction. On this issue, a division of authority exists. In 87 C.J.S. Trade–Marks, etc. § 211d, p. 597, it is stated:

> The wrongful appropriation of plaintiff's trade-mark will be enjoined wherever it is used by him, including those places where he might do so in the course of normal business expansion. On the other hand, it has been held that injunctive relief should be limited to states in which plaintiff has established a market for the articles bearing his trade-mark. . . .

On the facts of the instant case, it is impossible to determine whether it may reasonably be anticipated that the plaintiff will expand its business. Accordingly, I am of the opinion that the injunction should be limited to those states in which plaintiff has established a market for its "Polka"-brand products.

The above discussion, although limited to the claim of trade-mark infringement, applies with equal vigor to plaintiff's claim of unfair competition, and as to both of these claims, I am of the opinion that plaintiff is entitled to no relief other than an injunction. In Square D Co. v. Sorenson, 7 Cir., 1955, 224 F.2d 61, at pages 65–66, it was stated:

Plaintiffs failed to prove fraud or a palming off by defendants of any article to persons who believed they were buying plaintiff's product. While the absence of fraud or palming off does not undermine a finding of unfair competition, the character of the conduct giving rise to the unfair competition is relevant to the remedy which should be afforded. An accounting will not be ordered merely because there has been an infringement. As under the trade mark act of 1905, under the present act an accounting has been denied where an injunction will satisfy the equities of the case.

In the instant case, the evidence is insufficient to warrant the conclusion that the defendant was guilty of fraud, palming off or intentional infringement, and I conclude that an injunction will satisfy the equities of the case. The defendant will bear the costs of this action. The plaintiff is directed to submit a judgment order in conformity with the views herein expressed on or before January 21, 1959.

McGregor–Doniger, Inc. v. Drizzle, Inc.

United States Court of Appeals, Second Circuit, 1979.
599 F.2d 1126, 202 U.S.P.Q. 81.

MESKILL, Circuit Judge.

McGregor–Doniger Inc. ("McGregor"), a New York corporation founded in 1921, is a manufacturer of apparel for both men and women. Since 1947 McGregor has sold golf jackets under the trademark Drizzler, and in 1965 the company registered this mark for use in connection with golf jackets. Although McGregor had in the past used the word Drizzler in connection with other types of apparel, by 1965 the company had ceased using the mark in connection with any goods other than golf jackets. McGregor owns a variety of other trademarks, such as Brolly Dolly and Bernhard Altmann, which have been used in connection with goods other than golf jackets. Drizzler jackets sell for about $25 to $50.

Drizzle Inc. ("Drizzle"), a New York corporation established in 1969, sells only women's coats. Drizzle's coats, which are manufactured for Drizzle by various contractors, have been sold under the unregistered trademark Drizzle since the founding of the company. It appears from the record that Drizzle has to date employed no other trademark. Drizzle coats range in price from about $100 to $900.

In 1974 McGregor's management first became aware of the Drizzle company and of its use of the Drizzle mark in connection with the sale of women's coats. In January of 1975 McGregor notified Drizzle that if use of the Drizzle trademark on Drizzle's goods continued, legal proceedings would be instituted. The warning went unheeded and in March of 1975 McGregor brought suit against Drizzle in the United States District Court for the Southern District of New York, alleging trademark infringement, 15 U.S.C.A. § 1114, false designation of origin, 15 U.S.C.A. § 1125(a), and, in a pendent claim, common law unfair competition. McGregor sought an injunction barring Drizzle's further use of Drizzle as a trademark, an accounting for profits, damages, and other relief.

After a two-day bench trial, Judge Morris E. Lasker dismissed McGregor's complaint. 446 F.Supp. 160, 199 U.S.P.Q. 466 (S.D.N.Y.1978). On appeal, McGregor challenges both the factual findings of the trial court and the trial court's interpretation of the legal significance of the facts found. Although the trial court's statement of the applicable principles needs modification, we conclude that reversal is not warranted.

Discussion

We are once again called upon to decide when a trademark owner will be protected against the use of its mark, or one very similar, on products other than those to which the owner has applied it. As we have observed before, the question "does not become easier of solution with the years." Polaroid Corp. v. Polarad Electronics Corp., 287 F.2d 492, 495, 128 U.S.P.Q. 411, 412–413 (2d Cir.), cert. denied, 368 U.S. 820, 82 S.Ct. 36, 7 L.Ed.2d 25, 131 U.S.P.Q. 499 (1961).

The crucial issue in these cases is "whether there is any likelihood that an appreciable number of ordinarily prudent purchasers are likely to be misled, or indeed simply confused, as to the source of the goods in question." Mushroom Makers, Inc. v. R.G. Barry Corp., 580 F.2d 44, 47, 199 U.S.P.Q. 65, 66–67 (2d Cir.1978), cert. denied, 439 U.S. 1116, 99 S.Ct. 1022, 59 L.Ed.2d 75, 200 U.S.P.Q. 832 (1979), 3 R. Callmann, The Law of Unfair Competition, Trademarks and Monopolies § 84, at 929 (3d ed. 1969) (hereinafter Callmann). In assessing the likelihood of such confusion we consider the factors laid out in the now classic Polaroid formula:

> Where the products are different, the prior owner's chance of success is a function of many variables: the strength of his mark, the degree of similarity between the two marks, the proximity of the products, the likelihood that the prior owner will bridge the gap, actual confusion, and the reciprocal of defendant's good faith in adopting its own mark, the quality of defendant's product, and the sophistication of the buyers. Even this extensive catalogue does not exhaust the possibilities— the court may have to take still other variables into account.

Polaroid Corp. v. Polarad Electronics Corp., supra, 287 F.2d at 495, 128 U.S.P.Q. at 412–413, citing Restatement of Torts §§ 729, 730, 731. The parties agree that Judge Lasker was correct in giving consideration to each of the factors mentioned in Polaroid before reaching a decision on the ultimate question of likelihood of confusion.

1.   Strength of the Mark

The most complex issue raised by McGregor concerns the trial court's attempt to gauge the strength of the Drizzler mark. Our prior opinions and those of the district courts of this Circuit have left litigants and judges uncertain as to the appropriate way to demonstrate and determine the strength of a mark. In the hope of providing some guidance to bench and bar, we set out in some detail our view of this issue.

The term "strength" as applied to trademarks refers to the distinctiveness of the mark, or more precisely, its tendency to identify the goods sold under the mark as emanating from a particular, although possibly anonymous, source. The Restatement of Torts uses the term "distinctiveness" in place of the term "strength." § 731(f) and Comment e at 602. The strength or distinctiveness of a mark determines both the ease with which it may be established as a valid trademark and the degree of protection it will be accorded.

In an effort to liberate this aspect of trademark law from the "welter of adjectives" which had tended to obscure its contours, we recently reviewed the four categories into which terms are classified for trademark purposes. Abercrombie & Fitch Co. v. Hunting World, Inc., 537 F.2d 4, 9, 189 U.S.P.Q. 759, 764 (2d Cir.1976). Arranged in ascending order of strength, these categories are: (1) generic, (2) descriptive, (3) suggestive, and (4) arbitrary or fanciful. A generic term can never become a valid trademark and cannot be registered. A descriptive term can be registered as a mark only if it has "become distinctive of the applicant's goods in commerce," 15 U.S.C.A. § 1052(f), that is, in the unfortunate parlance of the cases, only if it has acquired "secondary meaning." Suggestive marks, falling between the merely descriptive and the arbitrary or fanciful, are entitled to registration without proof of secondary meaning, as are fully arbitrary or fanciful terms. 537 F.2d at 9–11, 189 U.S.P.Q. at 764–765. The boundaries between these categories are not fixed.

> [A] term that is in one category for a particular product may be in quite a different one for another, because a term may shift from one category to another in light of differences in usage through time, because a term may have one meaning to one group of users and a different one to others, and because the same term may be put to different uses with respect to a single product.

Abercrombie & Fitch Co. v. Hunting World, Inc., supra, 537 F.2d at 9, 189 U.S.P.Q. at 764.

Thus, while these categories can be useful for analytical purposes, the strength of a mark depends ultimately on its distinctiveness, or its "origin-indicating" quality, in the eyes of the purchasing public. Two familiar examples suffice to illustrate this principle. A coined term, initially suggestive or even fanciful, can lose its full trademark status if it comes to signify to the public the generic name of an article rather than the source of a particular brand of that article. In contrast, a descriptive mark that is not distinctive on its face may acquire secondary meaning so as to identify the source of the goods and thus claim status as a valid mark deserving of registration and protection against infringement. In Judge Lasker's words, "strength may derive from the intrinsic quality of a mark or from its public history." 446 F.Supp. at 162, 199 U.S.P.Q. at 467.

The many cases announcing that a mark found to be suggestive, arbitrary or fanciful (i.e., more than merely descriptive) is entitled to protection without proof of secondary meaning are correct as far as they go, for any term that is more than descriptive can be established as a valid mark which others may not infringe. Where the products involved are competitive and the marks quite similar, for example, the senior user of a more-than-descriptive mark need not prove secondary meaning. And where the marks involved are virtually identical, even if the products are non-competitive, a senior user of a more-than-descriptive mark can carry its burden on the "strength of the mark" component of the Polaroid formula without proving secondary meaning. But these cases do not require us to hold that Judge Lasker erred in considering evidence of secondary meaning in determining whether McGregor is entitled to protection against the use, on non-competitive goods, of a mark similar to its own. The cases agree that it is appropriate to consider all factors bearing on the likelihood of confusion. We view evidence concerning the origin-indicating significance of a mark in the marketplace as relevant to and probative of the strength of a mark and hence useful in assessing the likelihood of confusion.

Consideration of evidence of secondary meaning will almost always work in favor of the senior user. Its mark, if registered, is presumptively distinctive. Proof of secondary meaning, acquired perhaps through successful advertising, can only enhance the strength of its mark and thus enlarge the scope of the protection to which it is entitled. On the other hand, the owner of a distinctive mark need not introduce evidence of secondary meaning in order to gain protection for its mark against the confusing similarity of others. Thus, for example, the relatively small size of a senior user's advertising budget or sales volume will not diminish the strength of its valid mark, and the scope of protection accorded to that mark will not be narrowed because of such evidence. Only if the junior user carries the burden of affirmatively demonstrating that a term is generic is the senior user stripped of protection.

McGregor claims that the district court erred in requiring proof of secondary meaning. We agree with McGregor's contention that the decision of the Patent and Trademark Office to register a mark without requiring proof of secondary meaning affords a rebuttable presumption that the mark is more than merely descriptive. The trial court did in fact find the term Drizzler more than merely descriptive, although apparently only barely over the "suggestive" line. As a suggestive term, the Drizzler mark would be entitled to protection, regardless of proof of secondary meaning, *if* McGregor could prove that confusion of origin was likely to result from the use of a similar mark on non-competing goods. To the extent the district court held proof of secondary meaning *necessary*, it was in error. However, it was *not* error for the court to consider evidence bearing on the strength of the mark in determining the likelihood of consumer confusion and thus the scope of protection to which the Drizzler mark was entitled. Trademark strength is "an amorphous concept with little shape or substance when divorced from the mark's commercial context," E.I. DuPont de Nemours & Co. v. Yoshida Internat'l, Inc., supra, 393 F.Supp. at 512, 185 U.S.P.Q. at 604–605. We see no advantage to be derived from barring judicial consideration of the realities that give content to the concept of trademark strength.

2. Similarity of the Marks

"To the degree that the determination of 'likelihood of confusion' rests upon a comparison of the marks themselves, the appellate court is in as good a position as the trial judge to decide the issue." Miss Universe, Inc. v. Patricelli, 408 F.2d 506, 509, 161 U.S.P.Q. 129, 130–131 (2d Cir.1969). There are two principles especially important to performing this task.

First, even close similarity between two marks is not dispositive of the issue of likelihood of confusion. "Similarity in and of itself is not the acid test. Whether the similarity is likely to provoke confusion is the crucial question." Callmann § 82.1(a), at 601–02 (footnote omitted). For this reason cases involving the alteration, addition or elimination of only a single letter from the old mark to the new reach divergent results. Second, in assessing the similarity of two marks, it is the effect upon prospective purchasers that is important. Restatement of Torts § 728, Comment b at 591.

The district court quite correctly took into consideration all the factors that could reasonably be expected to be perceived by and remembered by potential purchasers. "[T]he setting in which a designation is used affects its appearance and colors the impression conveyed by it." Id. § 729, Comment b at 593. Thus while observing that the typewritten and aural similarity of the two marks "approaches identity," the district judge noted that the contexts in which the respective marks are generally presented reduces the impact of this similarity. The court observed that the label in each Drizzler jacket prominently features the McGregor name, which is printed in striking plaid letters. In addition, although there was testimony that retail stores on occasion in independent advertisements omit the McGregor logo, the evidence showed that McGregor always emphasizes the company name in its own advertising of Drizzler jackets. The fact that a trademark is always used in conjunction with a company name may be considered by the trial court as bearing on the likelihood of confusion.

The law does not require that trademarks be carefully analyzed and dissected by the purchasing public. "[I]t is sufficient if the *impression* which the infringing product makes upon the consumer is such that he is likely to believe the product is from the same source as the one he knows under the trade-mark." Stix Products, Inc. v. United Merchants & Mfrs., Inc., 295 F.Supp. 479, 494, 160 U.S.P.Q. 777, 789–790 (S.D.N.Y.1968) (footnote omitted; emphasis added). The court below properly focused on the general impression conveyed by the two marks. If Drizzle had chosen consistently to present its mark in red plaid lettering or to advertise its coats as the McGregor Drizzle line, we would be compelled to conclude that the similarity between the Drizzler mark and the Drizzle mark, *as generally presented to the public,* had been heightened and that the likelihood of confusion had been enhanced. Conversely, the fact that only one mark generally appears in close conjunction with the red plaid McGregor name increases the likelihood that the public, even when viewing the marks individually, will not confuse the two. The likelihood of confusion is further reduced by Drizzle's use of its mark to identify itself as the producer of the products advertised by it rather than as the name of a particular jacket or line of jackets, in contrast to McGregor's practice.

The district court's reasoning is sound. The differing methods of presentation of the two marks were properly examined. We agree with Judge Lasker's appraisal that they reduce to some degree the potential for confusion inherent in the close similarity between the two marks.

3.   and 4.   Product Proximity and Quality of Defendant's Product

The district court concluded on the basis of differences in appearance, style, function, fashion appeal, advertising orientation, and price that the competitive distance between Drizzler jackets and Drizzle coats is "significant." This conclusion is too amply supported by the evidence to be characterized as clearly erroneous.

McGregor does not claim that Drizzler jackets and Drizzle coats are directly competitive. Customers shopping for an inexpensive golf jacket are not likely to become confused by the similarity of the marks and mistakenly purchase a fashionable and expensive woman's coat. Thus the degree of proximity between the two products is relevant here primarily insofar as it bears on the likelihood that customers may be confused as to the *source* of the products, rather than as to the products themselves, and the concern is not direct diversion of purchasers but indirect harm through loss of goodwill or tarnishment of reputation. It is evident that customers would be more likely to assume that Drizzler golf jackets and Drizzle golf jackets come from the same source than they would be likely to assume that Drizzler golf jackets and Drizzle steam shovels come from the same source. Drizzle coats for women fall between the two extremes. In locating the appropriate place for Drizzle coats on this continuum, the district court considered many of the factors that are generally viewed as relevant.

> The impression that noncompeting goods are from the same origin may be conveyed by such differing considerations as the physical attributes or essential characteristics of the goods, with specific reference to their form, composition, texture or quality, the service or function for which they are intended, the manner in which they are advertised, displayed or sold, the place where they are sold, or the class of customers for whom they are designed and to whom they are sold.

Callmann § 82.2(c), at 807.

Looking at these very factors, the district judge found:

> Beyond the fact that they might both be crudely classified as outerwear, the "Drizzler" and defendant's products have nothing in common. McGregor's garment is a relatively inexpensive, lightweight, waist-length jacket—a windbreaker.... As is apparent from advertisements for the jacket, it is intended for casual wear, particularly in connection with sports activities. Moreover, although the Drizzler can be worn by either men or women, sales are pitched primarily to the former.... Furthermore, a Drizzler is ordinarily sold in the men's

department of stores which carry both men's and women's garments....

Unlike McGregor's products, the coats manufactured by Drizzle are distinctly and exclusively tailored for women. They are generally full length raincoats and capes. Although it is true that Drizzle manufactures a style that might be called a jacket ... it is longer than the Drizzler and entirely different in appearance. Drizzle's garments are within the medium to high fashion range.... The price range of Drizzle's line, running from approximately $100 to $900 ... reflects the coats' position in the fashion hierarchy.

446 F.Supp. at 164, 199 U.S.P.Q. at 469.

In Blue Bell, Inc. v. Jaymar–Ruby, Inc., 497 F.2d 433, 182 U.S.P.Q. 65 (2d Cir.1974), we recognized that due to diversification in the garment business, men's apparel and women's apparel had in certain cases been regarded as sufficiently related to justify the denial of registration to similar marks. However, in Blue Bell we characterized the proximity between men's sportswear and women's sportswear as only "moderate" and held that the likelihood of confusion was reduced by the rather "detailed purchasing process" appropriate to the goods in question. 497 F.2d at 435–36, 182 U.S.P.Q. at 66–67. We know of no case holding that, as a matter of law, the competitive distance between men's apparel and women's apparel cannot be demonstrated to be significant on the basis of the many factors relevant to such a determination. The district court's finding on this issue, based on the proper indicia and supported by the evidence, should not be disturbed.

The high quality of Drizzle's coats is not contested by McGregor.

5. Bridging the Gap

In assessing the likelihood of confusion, the district court was required to consider the likelihood that Drizzler would "bridge the gap," that is, the likelihood that McGregor would enter the women's coat market under the Drizzler banner. McGregor presented no evidence that such a step was being considered. Clearly the absence of any present intention or plan indicates that such expansion is less, rather than more, probable. Also of probative value is the fact that McGregor has for many years marketed its women's apparel under names bearing no similarity to Drizzler—such as Brolly Dolly. On the other hand, the absence of a present intent to bridge the gap is not determinative. In a given case, sufficient likelihood of confusion may be established although likelihood of bridging the gap is not demonstrated. Because consumer confusion is the key, the assumptions of the typical consumer, whether or not they match reality, must be taken into account.

The district court's finding that it is unlikely that Drizzler will bridge the gap is not clearly erroneous. Nor does the evidence presented below regarding McGregor's own history of trademark use, as well as industry custom, compel the conclusion that, despite the improbability that McGregor will move into the women's coat market under the Drizzler trademark, consumers will assume otherwise.

6. Actual Confusion

McGregor's claim that the district court erred in considering the absence of proof of *actual* consumer confusion in assessing the *likelihood* of confusion is without merit. Actual confusion is one of several factors to be considered in making such a determination. Although we have recognized the difficulty of establishing confusion on the part of retail customers, the district judge quite properly noted that not a single instance of consumer confusion had actually been demonstrated. While a plaintiff need not prove actual confusion in order to prevail, "it is certainly proper for the trial judge to infer from the absence of actual confusion that there was also no likelihood of confusion." Affiliated Hosp. Prod., Inc. v. Merdel Game Mfg. Co., 513 F.2d 1183, 1188, 185 U.S.P.Q. 321, 324 (2d Cir.1975).

Finally, the district court was not required, as McGregor urges, to find actual *consumer* confusion on the basis of the testimony of one McGregor employee that she had been momentarily confused by a Drizzle advertisement. The weighing of evidence, particularly where credibility judgments must be made, is for the trial judge. His determination regarding actual confusion is not clearly erroneous.

7. Good Faith

McGregor contends that the district court improperly placed the burden of proof on the good faith issue on McGregor rather than on Drizzle. However, assuming without deciding that McGregor is correct in its view of the proper placement of the burden of proof, there is simply no indication in Judge Lasker's opinion that this burden was in fact placed on McGregor.

We recently held that adoption of the mark Mushroom for women's sportswear despite actual and constructive notice of another company's prior registration of the mark Mushrooms for women's shoes was not necessarily indicative of bad faith, because the presumption of an exclusive right to use a registered mark extends only so far as the goods or services noted in the registration certificate. Mushroom Makers, Inc. v. R.G. Barry Corp., supra, 580 F.2d at 48, 199 U.S.P.Q. at 67–68. Here, as in Mushroom Makers, the district court was entitled to consider and to credit the uncontradicted testimony of Drizzle's witnesses that the Drizzle mark was selected without knowledge of McGregor's prior use of the Drizzler mark. "Normally, the alleged infringer's intent is an issue for district court determination," Grotrian, Helfferich, Schulz, Etc. v. Steinway & Sons, supra, 523 F.2d at 1338 n. 14, 186 U.S.P.Q. at 441–442 n. 14, and findings as to such intent will be upset only if clearly erroneous.

8. Sophistication of Buyers

McGregor asserts that the trial court erroneously considered only the typical "sophisticated" purchaser of Drizzle's coats, to the exclusion of the casual or unsophisticated purchaser. We do not read the decision below in this manner.

The relevant cases not only authorize but instruct the trial courts, in making a determination as to likelihood of confusion, to consider the level of sophistication of the relevant purchasers. "The general impression of the ordinary purchaser, buying under the normally prevalent conditions of the market and giving the attention such purchasers usually give in buying that class of goods, is the touchstone." Callmann § 81.2, at 577. As we observed recently in Taylor Wine Co. v. Bully Hill Vineyards, Inc., 569 F.2d 731, 733, 196 U.S.P.Q. 593, 593–594 (2d Cir.1978), "every product has its own separate threshold for confusion of origin." The greater the value of an article the more careful the typical consumer can be expected to be; the average purchaser of an automobile will no doubt devote more attention to examining different products and determining their manufacturer or source than will the average purchaser of a ball of twine. The degree of reliance by consumers on labels and trademarks will also vary from product to product. It is easy to see that such differences in purchasing patterns affect the likelihood that confusion will result from the use of similar marks on noncompeting goods from different sources.

In some cases, of course, as where the products are identical and the marks are identical, the sophistication of buyers cannot be relied on to prevent confusion. For example, in Omega Importing Corp. v. Petri–Kine Camera Co., 451 F.2d 1190, 1195, 171 U.S.P.Q. 769, 772–773 (2d Cir.1971), we held that even though the ordinary purchaser would be expected to make "more than a casual inspection" before buying an expensive camera, such inspection would be of doubtful value because the cameras from each of two different sources were both labelled "Exakta." In the instant case, however, where both the products involved and the marks involved are distinguishable, the care exercised by typical consumers is likely to reduce confusion.

In Omega we noted that where a buyer market was composed of both discriminating and relatively unknowledgeable buyers, a court must consider the probability of confusion on the part of the latter as well as the former. However, it is also true that the crucial issue is confusion on the part of an "appreciable number" of consumers. Mushroom Makers, Inc. v. R.G. Barry Corp., supra, 580 F.2d at 47, 199 U.S.P.Q. at 66–67. At a certain point, confusion "will be too slight to bring the case above the rule of de minimis." Triumph Hosiery Mills v. Triumph Internat'l Corp., supra, 308 F.2d at 199, 135 U.S.P.Q. at 47–48. "The remote possibility of occasional confusion in those who observe less than ordinary care under the circumstances does not concern us." Modular Cinemas of America, Inc. v. Mini Cinemas Corp., supra, 348 F.Supp. at 582, 175 U.S.P.Q. at 358–359. " 'The purchasing public must be credited with at least a modicum of intelligence....' " Carnation Co. v. California Growers Wineries, 97 F.2d 80, 81, 37 U.S.P.Q. 735, 735–736 (C.C.P.A.1938).

McGregor offered no evidence establishing that any significant number of Drizzle purchasers are casual or unsophisticated. The district court was entitled to rely on the evidence indicating that the relevant purchasing group in fact tends to be sophisticated and knowledgeable about women's apparel. We cannot classify his findings in this regard as clearly erroneous.

Conclusion

In trademark infringement cases involving non-competing goods, it is rare that we are "overwhelmed by the sudden blinding light of the justness of one party's cause." King Research, Inc. v. Shulton, Inc., supra, 454 F.2d at 69, 172 U.S.P.Q. at 323. Most often our affirmances in such cases rest on the more modest conclusion that the trial judge was not wrong in reaching the result appealed from. It is on this basis that we affirm the district judge's decision. Judge Lasker applied the correct legal standard (likelihood of confusion) and the correct criteria (those enumerated in Polaroid) in reaching his result. Moreover, he quite properly regarded no single factor as determinative. Although the two marks at issue are concededly quite similar, the court below found that the Drizzler mark is only moderately strong, that the competitive distance between the products is significant, that there was no intention to bridge the gap, that no actual confusion has occurred, and that Drizzle adopted its mark in good faith. Thus the court's conclusion that likelihood of confusion had not been proved by McGregor is amply supported by its findings, none of which is clearly erroneous. And we do not believe that the error in analysis discussed in our opinion today compels reversal of the result reached by the district court.

Because McGregor has failed to establish a likelihood of confusion, the balance of interests of necessity tips in Drizzle's favor. Because the goods are concededly not competitive, McGregor's sales of Drizzler jackets cannot be expected to suffer. Where non-competitive goods are involved the trademark laws protect the senior user's interest in an untarnished reputation and his interest in being able to enter a related field at some future time. Because consumer confusion as to source is unlikely, McGregor's reputation cannot be expected to be harmed. Because of the improbability that McGregor will enter the women's coat field under the Drizzler name, its right to expand into other fields has not been unduly restricted. Thus we see no injury to McGregor resulting from denial of the relief requested. On the other hand, if forced to give up its mark Drizzle could be expected to be harmed by loss of the goodwill that has been associated with the Drizzle name since 1969.

As we noted in Chandon Champagne Corp. v. San Marino Wine Corp., 335 F.2d 531, 536, 142 U.S.P.Q. 239, 243 (2d Cir.1964):

Although this court was the leader in granting relief to a trademark owner when there had been and was no likelihood of actual diversion [i.e., in cases involving non-competitive products], we have likewise emphasized that, in such cases, "against these legitimate interests of the senior user are to be weighed the legitimate interests of the innocent second user" and that we must balance "the *conflicting interests* both parties have in the unimpaired continuation of their trade mark use." Avon Shoe Co. v. David Crystal, Inc. [supra, 279 F.2d at 613, 125 U.S.P.Q. at 612–613].

Following this approach, this Court has frequently supplemented its consideration of the Polaroid factors by balancing the conflicting interests of the parties involved. Particularly when viewed in light of a balancing of the interests involved, the decision below warrants affirmance.

INDIANAPOLIS COLTS, INC. v. METROPOLITAN BALTIMORE FOOTBALL CLUB LTD., 34 F.3d 410, 411, 414–416, 31 U.S.P.Q.2d 1811 (7th Cir.1994). POSNER, Chief Judge: The Indianapolis Colts and the National Football League, to which the Colts belong, brought suit for trademark infringement against the Canadian Football League's new team in Baltimore, which wants to call itself the "Baltimore CFL Colts." (Four of the Canadian Football League's teams are American.) The plaintiffs obtained a preliminary injunction against the new team's using the name "Colts," or "Baltimore Colts," or "Baltimore CFL Colts," in connection with the playing of professional football, the broadcast of football games, or the sale of merchandise to football fans and other buyers. The ground for the injunction was that consumers of "Baltimore CFL Colts" merchandise are likely to think, mistakenly, that the new Baltimore team is an NFL team related in some fashion to the Indianapolis Colts, formerly the Baltimore Colts. From the order granting the injunction the new team and its owners appeal to us under 28 U.S.C. § 1292(a)(1). Since the injunction was granted, the new team has played its first two games—without a name. . . .

Some people who might otherwise watch the Indianapolis Colts (or some other NFL team, for remember that the NFL, representing all the teams, is a coplaintiff) on television may watch the Baltimore CFL Colts instead, thinking they are the "real" Baltimore Colts, and the NFL will lose revenue. A few (doubtless very few) people who might otherwise buy tickets to an NFL game may buy tickets to a Baltimore CFL Colts game instead. Some people who might otherwise buy merchandise stamped with the name "Indianapolis Colts" or the name of some other NFL team may buy merchandise stamped "Baltimore CFL Colts," thinking it a kin of the NFL's Baltimore Colts in the glory days of Johnny Unitas rather than a newly formed team that plays Canadian football in a Canadian football league. It would be naive to suppose that no consideration of such possibilities occurred to the owners of the new Baltimore team when they were choosing a name, though there is no evidence that it was the dominant or even a major consideration.

Confusion thus is possible, and may even have been desired; but is it likely? There is great variance in consumer competence, and it would be undesirable to impoverish the lexicon of trade names merely to protect the most gullible fringe of the consuming public. The Lanham Act does not cast the net of protection so wide. The legal standard under the Act has been formulated variously, but the various formulations come down to whether it is likely that the challenged mark if permitted to be used by the defendant would cause the plaintiff to lose a substantial number of consumers. Pertinent to this determination is the similarity of the marks and of the parties' products, the knowledge of the average consumer of the product, the overlap in the parties' geographical markets, and the other factors that the cases consider. The aim is to strike a balance between, on the one hand, the interest of the seller of the new product, and of the consuming public, in an arresting, attractive, and informative name that will enable the new product to compete effectively against existing ones, and, on the other hand, the interest of existing sellers, and again of the consuming public, in consumers' being able to know exactly what they are buying without having to incur substantial costs of investigation or inquiry.

To help judges strike the balance, the parties to trademark disputes frequently as here hire professionals in marketing or applied statistics to conduct surveys of consumers. The battle of experts that ensues is frequently unedifying. Many experts are willing for a generous (and sometimes for a modest) fee to bend their science in the direction from which their fee is coming. The constraints that the market in consultant services for lawyers places on this sort of behavior are weak, as shown by the fact that both experts in this case were hired and, we have no doubt, generously remunerated even though both have been criticized in previous judicial opinions. The judicial constraints on tendentious expert testimony are inherently weak because judges (and even more so juries, though that is not an issue in a trademark case) lack training or experience in the relevant fields of expert knowledge. But that is the system we have. It might be improved by asking each party's hired expert to designate a third, a neutral expert who would be appointed by the court to conduct the necessary studies. The necessary authority exists, but was not exercised here.

Both parties presented studies. The defendants' was prepared by Michael Rappeport and is summarized in a perfunctory affidavit by Dr. Rappeport to which the district judge gave little weight. That was a kindness. The heart of Rappeport's study was a survey that consisted of three loaded questions asked in one Baltimore mall. Rappeport has been criticized before for his methodology, *Jaret Int'l, Inc. v. Promotion in Motion, Inc.*, 826 F.Supp. 69, 73–74 (E.D.N.Y.1993), and we hope that he will take these criticisms to heart in his next courtroom appearance.

The plaintiffs' study, conducted by Jacob Jacoby, was far more substantial and the district judge found it on the whole credible. The 28–page report with its numerous appendices has all the trappings of social scientific rigor. Interviewers showed several hundred consumers in 24 malls scattered around the country, shirts and hats licensed by the defendants for sale to consumers. The shirts and hats have "Baltimore CFL Colts" stamped on them. The consumers were asked whether they were football fans, whether they watched football games on television, and whether they ever bought merchandise with a team name on it. Then they were asked, with reference to the "Baltimore CFL Colts" merchandise that they were shown, such questions as whether they knew what sport the team played, what teams it played against, what league the team was in, and whether the team or league needed someone's permission to use this name, and if so whose. If, for example, the respondent answered that the team had to get permission from the Canadian Football League, the interviewer was directed to ask the respondent whether the Canadian Football League had in turn to get permission from someone. There were other questions, none however obviously loaded, and a whole other survey, the purpose of which was to control for "noise," in which another group of mallgoers was asked the identical questions about a hypothetical team unappetizingly named the "Baltimore Horses." The idea was by comparing the answers of the two groups to see whether the source of confusion was the name "Baltimore Colts" or just the name "Baltimore," in which event the injunction would do no good since no one suggests that the new Baltimore team should be forbidden to use "Baltimore" in its name, provided the name does not also include "Colts."

Rappeport threw darts at Jacoby's study. Some landed wide. We are especially perplexed by the argument that survey research belongs to sociology rather than psychology (we leave the reader to guess the respective disciplines to which our rival experts belong); the courtroom is a peculiar site for academic turf wars. We also do not think it was improper for Jacoby to inquire about confusion between "Baltimore CFL Colts" and "Baltimore Colts," even though the Indianapolis Colts have abandoned "Baltimore Colts." If consumers believe that the new Baltimore team is the old Baltimore Colts, and the Indianapolis Colts some sort of upstart (the Johnny Unitas position), they will be less likely to buy merchandise stamped "Indianapolis Colts." But Rappeport was right to complain that the choice of "Horses" for the comparison team loaded the dice and that some of Jacoby's questions were a bit slanted. That is only to say, however, that Jacoby's survey was not perfect, and this is not news. Trials would be very short if only perfect evidence were admissible.

Jacoby's survey of consumers' reactions to the "Baltimore CFL Colts" merchandise found rather astonishing levels of confusion not plausibly attributable to the presence of the name "Baltimore" alone, since "Baltimore Horses" engendered much less. (We don't like the name "Baltimore Horses," as we have said; but we doubt that a more attractive "Baltimore" name, the "Baltimore Leopards," for example, would have generated the level of confusion that "Baltimore CFL Colts" did. *National Football League v. Wichita Falls Sportswear, Inc., supra*, 532 F.Supp. at 660.) Among self-identified football fans, 64 percent thought that the "Baltimore CFL Colts" was either the old (NFL) Baltimore Colts or the Indianapolis Colts. But perhaps this result is not so astonishing. Although most American football fans have heard of Canadian football, many probably are unfamiliar with the acronym "CFL," and as we remarked earlier it is not a very conspicuous part of the team logo stamped on the merchandise. Among fans who watch football on television, 59 percent displayed the same confusion; and even among those who watch football on cable television, which attracts a more educated audience on average and actually carries CFL games, 58 percent were confused when shown the merchandise. Among the minority not confused about who the "Baltimore CFL

Colts" are, a substantial minority, ranging from 21 to 34 percent depending on the precise subsample, thought the team somehow sponsored or authorized by the Indianapolis Colts or the National Football League. It is unfortunate and perhaps a bit tricky that the subsample of consumers likely to buy merchandise with a team name on it was not limited to consumers likely to buy merchandise with a football team's name on it; the choice of the name "Baltimore Horses" for the comparison team was unfortunate; and no doubt there are other tricks of the survey researcher's black arts that we have missed. There is the more fundamental problem, one common to almost all consumer survey research, that people are more careful when they are laying out their money than when they are answering questions.

But with all this granted, we cannot say that the district judge committed a clear error (the standard, *Scandia Down Corp. v. Euroquilt, Inc.*, supra, 772 F.2d at 1427–28) in crediting the major findings of the Jacoby study and inferring from it and the other evidence in the record that the defendants' use of the name "Baltimore CFL Colts" whether for the team or on merchandise was likely to confuse a substantial number of consumers. . . .

NOTES

1. Despite frequent exhortations that marks should be viewed in their entirety, courts in infringement cases will usually first dissect the mark to separate its distinctive and protectible components from those that are nondistinctive. Against this background, the court will then evaluate plaintiff's and defendant's marks in their entirety to determine the likelihood of confusion.

Flintkote Co. v. Tizer, 158 F.Supp. 699, 701, 115 U.S.P.Q. 3, 4 (E.D.Pa.1957), aff'd, 266 F.2d 849, 121 U.S.P.Q. 284 (3d Cir.1959) is typical. "As to the alleged infringement of Tile–Tex by Tile–Tone, we start with the fact that the word 'tile' is wholly descriptive, could not by itself qualify as a trademark, and can be freely used by anyone. When it is used as one part of a trademark, the combination may be registrable, but when it comes to the question of infringement, while the entire mark must be considered as a whole, the descriptive word cannot constitute the dominant part of it. Whatever confusion may be caused by the fact that the same descriptive word appears in the two marks must be discounted. Conversely, infringement cannot be found if the nondescriptive parts of the two marks are distinctive enough to prevent confusion." Would a similarly careful dissection of the two marks in *Pikle–Rite* have led to a different result in that case? Might Chicago Pickle have availed itself of the fair use defense?

2. Trademark's common law design, transformed in many respects by the Lanham Act, was further altered by "housekeeping" amendments to the Act, P.L. 87–772, 76 Stat. 769, passed in 1962. One of these amendments went well beyond housekeeping to strike the last twelve words from section 32's prescription, "is likely to cause confusion, or to cause mistake, or

deceive *purchasers as to the source of origin of such goods or services.*"
(Emphasis added.) Some courts have relied on the new formulation to
support findings of infringement in cases where the only confusion is
among non-purchasers. For example, in Ferrari S.p.A. Esercizio Fabriche
Automobili E Corse v. Roberts, 944 F.2d 1235, 1244, 20 U.S.P.Q.2d 1001
(6th Cir.1991), *cert. denied*, 505 U.S. 1219, 112 S.Ct. 3028, 120 L.Ed.2d 899
(1992), the court upheld an injunction against defendant's sale of conversion kits for making lookalike Ferrari automobiles even though any confusion was not among kit purchasers, but rather among passersby who,
seeing a kit car on the street, might confuse it with an authentic Ferrari.
According to the court, "[t]he Lanham Act ... was intended to do more
than protect consumers at the point of sale."

3. *What Proportion of the Consuming Public Must Be Likely to Be Confused?* In the simpler, not distant past plaintiffs proved likelihood of
confusion by convincing the trier of fact that *it* would be likely to be
confused by the defendant's use of the plaintiff's mark. Since the parties
addressed only the fact-trier's perceptions, there was no need to quantify
the measure alluded to in *McGregor–Doniger*—whether "an appreciable
number of ordinarily prudent purchasers are likely to be misled, or indeed
simply confused, as to the source of goods in question." With the advent
and widespread use of consumer surveys, however, the numbers game has
become all-important.

Henri's Food Products Co. v. Kraft, Inc., 717 F.2d 352, 220 U.S.P.Q.
386 (7th Cir.1983), was a declaratory judgment action. The court of appeals
held that the district court had properly weighed survey evidence that only
7.6% of survey respondents had confused the source of plaintiff's "Yogowhip" salad dressing with defendant's "Miracle Whip" salad dressing against
a finding of infringement. "Kraft has pointed to no case in which a 7.6%
figure constituted likelihood of confusion." 717 F.2d at 358. Judge Coffey,
dissenting in part, objected that the relevant cases "are concerned with the
existence of *some* 'confusion' rather than a specific amount of confusion.
Indeed the underlying purpose of trademark law is to *prevent* confusion.
The survey evidence unquestionably proves that *some* 'confusion' exists in
the minds of consumers. This 'confusion' is sufficient to establish the
likelihood the public will be moved in some degree to purchase 'Yogowhip'
due to the misperception it is manufactured by Kraft." 717 F.2d at 365.

For the views on the survey evidence of one of the experts in the
Baltimore Colts case, see Michael Rappeport, The Role of the Survey
"Expert"—A Response to Judge Posner, 85 Trademark Rep. 211 (1995).

Techniques for the design and conduct of surveys are considered in
Lawrence E. Evans, Jr. & David M. Gunn, Trademark Surveys, 79 Trade-
mark Rep. 1 (1989). See also Itamar Simonson, The Effect of Survey
Method on Likelihood of Confusion Estimates: Conceptual Analysis and
Empirical Test, 83 Trademark Rep. 364 (1993).

4. *Similarity.* In the usual trademark infringement case, the registered
mark and the mark alleged to infringe will be in the same symbolic
format—word v. word or picture v. picture. The only question will be

whether the defendant's word or picture is sufficiently similar to the registered word or picture to support a finding of infringement.

Can a word mark infringe a picture mark? In Mobil Oil Corp. v. Pegasus Petroleum Corp., 818 F.2d 254, 2 U.S.P.Q.2d 1677 (2d Cir.1987), the court held that defendant's use of the term, "Pegasus" in connection with its oil trading activities infringed plaintiff's registered trademark of a flying horse—representing Pegasus, the winged horse of Greek mythology—in connection with its petroleum business. Agreeing "that words and their pictorial representations should not be equated as a matter of law," the court concluded that "a district court may make such a determination as a factual matter" and upheld the district court's determination "that the word 'Pegasus' evokes the symbol of the flying red horse and that the flying horse is associated in the mind with Mobil. In other words, the symbol of the flying horse and its name 'Pegasus' are synonymous." 818 F.2d at 257.

F.   FEDERAL UNFAIR COMPETITION LAW: LANHAM ACT § 43(a)

See Statute Supplement 15 U.S.C.A. § 1125.

Two Pesos, Inc. v. Taco Cabana, Inc.

Supreme Court of the United States, 1992.
505 U.S. 763, 112 S.Ct. 2753, 120 L.Ed.2d 615, 23 U.S.P.Q.2d 1081.

Justice WHITE delivered the opinion of the Court.

The issue in this case is whether the trade dress* of a restaurant may be protected under § 43(a) of the Trademark Act of 1946 (Lanham Act), 60 Stat. 441, 15 U.S.C. § 1125(a) (1982 ed.), based on a finding of inherent distinctiveness, without proof that the trade dress has secondary meaning.

I

Respondent Taco Cabana, Inc., operates a chain of fast-food restaurants in Texas. The restaurants serve Mexican food. The first Taco Cabana restaurant was opened in San Antonio in September 1978, and five more restaurants had been opened in San Antonio by 1985. Taco Cabana describes its Mexican trade dress as

---

* The District Court instructed the jury: " '[T]rade dress' is the total image of the business. Taco Cabana's trade dress may include the shape and general appearance of the exterior of the restaurant, the identifying sign, the interior kitchen floor plan, the decor, the menu, the equipment used to serve food, the servers' uniforms and other features reflecting on the total image of the restaurant." The Court of Appeals accepted this definition and quoted from Blue Bell Bio–Medical v. Cin–Bad, Inc., 864 F.2d 1253, 1256 (C.A.5 1989): "The 'trade dress' of a product is essentially its total image and overall appearance." See 932 F.2d 1113, 1118 (C.A.5 1991). It "involves the total image of a product and may include features such as size, shape, color or color combinations, texture, graphics, or even particular sales techniques." John H. Harland Co. v. Clarke Checks, Inc., 711 F.2d 966, 980 (C.A.11 1983). Restatement (Third) of Unfair Competition § 16, Comment a (Tent.Draft No. 2, Mar. 23, 1990).

"a festive eating atmosphere having interior dining and patio areas decorated with artifacts, bright colors, paintings and murals. The patio includes interior and exterior areas with the interior patio capable of being sealed off from the outside patio by overhead garage doors. The stepped exterior of the building is a festive and vivid color scheme using top border paint and neon stripes. Bright awnings and umbrellas continue the theme." 932 F.2d 1113, 1117 (C.A.5 1991).

In December 1985, a Two Pesos, Inc., restaurant was opened in Houston. Two Pesos adopted a motif very similar to the foregoing description of Taco Cabana's trade dress. Two Pesos restaurants expanded rapidly in Houston and other markets, but did not enter San Antonio. In 1986, Taco Cabana entered the Houston and Austin markets and expanded into other Texas cities, including Dallas and El Paso where Two Pesos was also doing business.

In 1987, Taco Cabana sued Two Pesos in the United States District Court for the Southern District of Texas for trade dress infringement under § 43(a) of the Lanham Act, 15 U.S.C. § 1125(a) (1982 ed.), and for theft of trade secrets under Texas common law. The case was tried to a jury, which was instructed to return its verdict in the form of answers to five questions propounded by the trial judge. The jury's answers were: Taco Cabana has a trade dress; taken as a whole, the trade dress is nonfunctional; the trade dress is inherently distinctive;[3] the trade dress has not acquired a secondary meaning[4] in the Texas market; and the alleged infringement creates a likelihood of confusion on the part of ordinary customers as to the source or association of the restaurant's goods or services. Because, as the jury was told, Taco Cabana's trade dress was protected if it either was inherently distinctive or had acquired a secondary meaning, judgment was entered awarding damages to Taco Cabana. In the course of calculating damages, the trial court held that Two Pesos had intentionally and deliberately infringed Taco Cabana's trade dress.

The Court of Appeals ruled that the instructions adequately stated the applicable law and that the evidence supported the jury's findings. In particular, the Court of Appeals rejected petitioner's argument that a finding of no secondary meaning contradicted a finding of inherent distinctiveness.

In so holding, the court below followed precedent in the Fifth Circuit. In Chevron Chemical Co. v. Voluntary Purchasing Groups, Inc., 659 F.2d 695, 702 (C.A.5 1981), the court noted that trademark law requires a

3. The instructions were that to be found inherently distinctive the trade dress must not be descriptive.

4. Secondary meaning is used generally to indicate that a mark or dress "has come through use to be uniquely associated with a specific source." Restatement (Third) of Unfair Competition § 13, Comment e (Tent. Draft No. 2, Mar. 23, 1990). "To establish secondary meaning, a manufacturer must show that, in the minds of the public, the primary significance of a product feature or term is to identify the source of the product rather than the product itself." Inwood Laboratories, Inc. v. Ives Laboratories, Inc., 456 U.S. 844, 851, n. 11, 102 S.Ct. 2182, 2187, n. 11, 72 L.Ed.2d 606 (1982).

demonstration of secondary meaning only when the claimed trademark is not sufficiently distinctive of itself to identify the producer; the court held that the same principles should apply to protection of trade dresses. The Court of Appeals noted that this approach conflicts with decisions of other courts, particularly the holding of the Court of Appeals for the Second Circuit in Vibrant Sales, Inc. v. New Body Boutique, Inc., 652 F.2d 299 (1981), cert. denied, 455 U.S. 909, 102 S.Ct. 1257, 71 L.Ed.2d 448 (1982), that § 43(a) protects unregistered trademarks or designs only where secondary meaning is shown. We granted certiorari to resolve the conflict among the Courts of Appeals on the question whether trade dress which is inherently distinctive is protectable under § 43(a) without a showing that it has acquired secondary meaning. We find that it is, and we therefore affirm.

II

The Lanham Act[7] was intended to make "actionable the deceptive and misleading use of marks" and "to protect persons engaged in . . . commerce against unfair competition." § 45, 15 U.S.C. § 1127. Section 43(a) "prohibits a broader range of practices than does § 32," which applies to registered marks, Inwood Laboratories, Inc. v. Ives Laboratories, Inc., 456 U.S. 844, 858, 102 S.Ct. 2182, 2190–2191, 72 L.Ed.2d 606 (1982), but it is common ground that § 43(a) protects qualifying unregistered trademarks and that the general principles qualifying a mark for registration under § 2 of the Lanham Act are for the most part applicable in determining whether an unregistered mark is entitled to protection under § 43(a).

A trademark is defined in 15 U.S.C. § 1127 as including "any word, name, symbol, or device or any combination thereof" used by any person "to identify and distinguish his or her goods, including a unique product, from those manufactured or sold by others and to indicate the source of the goods, even if that source is unknown." In order to be registered, a mark must be capable of distinguishing the applicant's goods from those of others. § 1052. Marks are often classified in categories of generally increasing distinctiveness; following the classic formulation set out by Judge Friendly, they may be (1) generic; (2) descriptive; (3) suggestive; (4) arbitrary; or (5) fanciful. See Abercrombie & Fitch Co. v. Hunting World, Inc., 537 F.2d 4, 9 (C.A.2 1976). The Court of Appeals followed this classification and petitioner accepts it. The latter three categories of marks, because their intrinsic nature serves to identify a particular source of a product, are deemed inherently distinctive and are entitled to protection. In contrast, generic marks—those that "refc[r] to the genus of which the particular product is a species," Park 'N Fly, Inc. v. Dollar Park and Fly, Inc., 469 U.S. 189, 194, 105 S.Ct. 658, 661, 83 L.Ed.2d 582 (1985), citing Abercrombie & Fitch, supra, at 9—are not registrable as trademarks.

---

7. The Lanham Act, including the provisions at issue here, has been substantially amended since the present suit was brought. See Trademark Law Revision Act of 1988, 102 Stat. 3946, 15 U.S.C. § 1121.

Marks which are merely descriptive of a product are not inherently distinctive. When used to describe a product, they do not inherently identify a particular source, and hence cannot be protected. However, descriptive marks may acquire the distinctiveness which will allow them to be protected under the Act. Section 2 of the Lanham Act provides that a descriptive mark that otherwise could not be registered under the Act may be registered if it "has become distinctive of the applicant's goods in commerce." § 2(e), (f), 15 U.S.C. § 1052(e), (f). This acquired distinctiveness is generally called "secondary meaning." The concept of secondary meaning has been applied to actions under § 43(a).

The general rule regarding distinctiveness is clear: an identifying mark is distinctive and capable of being protected if it *either* (1) is inherently distinctive *or* (2) has acquired distinctiveness through secondary meaning. Restatement (Third) of Unfair Competition, § 13, pp. 37–38, and Comment *a* (Tent.Draft No. 2, Mar. 23, 1990). It is also clear that eligibility for protection under § 43(a) depends on nonfunctionality. It is, of course, also undisputed that liability under § 43(a) requires proof of the likelihood of confusion.

The Court of Appeals determined that the District Court's instructions were consistent with the foregoing principles and that the evidence supported the jury's verdict. Both courts thus ruled that Taco Cabana's trade dress was not descriptive but rather inherently distinctive, and that it was not functional. None of these rulings is before us in this case, and for present purposes we assume, without deciding, that each of them is correct. In going on to affirm the judgment for respondent, the Court of Appeals, following its prior decision in *Chevron,* held that Taco Cabana's inherently distinctive trade dress was entitled to protection despite the lack of proof of secondary meaning. It is this issue that is before us for decision, and we agree with its resolution by the Court of Appeals. There is no persuasive reason to apply to trade dress a general requirement of secondary meaning which is at odds with the principles generally applicable to infringement suits under § 43(a). Petitioner devotes much of its briefing to arguing issues that are not before us, and we address only its arguments relevant to whether proof of secondary meaning is essential to qualify an inherently distinctive trade dress for protection under § 43(a).

Petitioner argues that the jury's finding that the trade dress has not acquired a secondary meaning shows conclusively that the trade dress is not inherently distinctive. The Court of Appeals' disposition of this issue was sound:

"Two Pesos' argument—that the jury finding of inherent distinctiveness contradicts its finding of no secondary meaning in the Texas market—ignores the law in this circuit. While the necessarily imperfect (and often prohibitively difficult) methods for assessing secondary meaning address the empirical question of current consumer association, the legal recognition of an inherently distinctive trademark or trade dress acknowledges the owner's legitimate proprietary interest in its unique and valuable informational device, regardless of whether substantial consumer association yet bestows the additional empirical protection of secondary meaning." 932 F.2d, at 1120, n. 7.

Although petitioner makes the above argument, it appears to concede elsewhere in its briefing that it is possible for a trade dress, even a restaurant trade dress, to be inherently distinctive and thus eligible for protection under § 43(a). Recognizing that a general requirement of secondary meaning imposes "an unfair prospect of theft [or] financial loss" on the developer of fanciful or arbitrary trade dress at the outset of its use, petitioner suggests that such trade dress should receive limited protection without proof of secondary meaning. Petitioner argues that such protection should be only temporary and subject to defeasance when over time the dress has failed to acquire a secondary meaning. This approach is also vulnerable for the reasons given by the Court of Appeals. If temporary protection is available from the earliest use of the trade dress, it must be because it is neither functional nor descriptive but an inherently distinctive dress that is capable of identifying a particular source of the product. Such a trade dress, or mark, is not subject to copying by concerns that have an equal opportunity to choose their own inherently distinctive trade dress. To terminate protection for failure to gain secondary meaning over some unspecified time could not be based on the failure of the dress to retain its fanciful, arbitrary, or suggestive nature, but on the failure of the user of the dress to be successful enough in the marketplace. This is not a valid basis to find a dress or mark ineligible for protection. The user of such a trade dress should be able to maintain what competitive position it has and continue to seek wider identification among potential customers.

This brings us to the line of decisions by the Court of Appeals for the Second Circuit that would find protection for trade dress unavailable absent proof of secondary meaning, a position that petitioner concedes would have to be modified if the temporary protection that it suggests is to be recognized. In Vibrant Sales, Inc. v. New Body Boutique, Inc., 652 F.2d 299 (1981), the plaintiff claimed protection under § 43(a) for a product whose features the defendant had allegedly copied. The Court of Appeals held that unregistered marks did not enjoy the "presumptive source association" enjoyed by registered marks and hence could not qualify for protection under § 43(a) without proof of secondary meaning. The court's rationale seemingly denied protection for unregistered but inherently distinctive marks of all kinds, whether the claimed mark used distinctive words or symbols or distinctive product design. The court thus did not accept the arguments that an unregistered mark was capable of identifying a source and that copying such a mark could be making any kind of a false statement or representation under § 43(a).

This holding is in considerable tension with the provisions of the Act. If a verbal or symbolic mark or the features of a product design may be registered under § 2, it necessarily is a mark "by which the goods of the applicant may be distinguished from the goods of others," 60 Stat. 428, and must be registered unless otherwise disqualified. Since § 2 requires secondary meaning only as a condition to registering descriptive marks, there are plainly marks that are registrable without showing secondary meaning. These same marks, even if not registered, remain inherently capable of distinguishing the goods of the users of these marks. Furthermore, the copier of such a mark may be seen as falsely claiming that his products may for some reason be thought of as originating from the plaintiff. . . .

It would be a different matter if there were textual basis in § 43(a) for treating inherently distinctive verbal or symbolic trademarks differently from inherently distinctive trade dress. But there is none. The section does not mention trademarks or trade dress, whether they be called generic, descriptive, suggestive, arbitrary, fanciful, or functional. Nor does the concept of secondary meaning appear in the text of § 43(a). Where secondary meaning does appear in the statute, 15 U.S.C. § 1052 (1982 ed.), it is a requirement that applies only to merely descriptive marks and not to inherently distinctive ones. We see no basis for requiring secondary meaning for inherently distinctive trade dress protection under § 43(a) but not for other distinctive words, symbols, or devices capable of identifying a producer's product.

Engrafting onto § 43(a) a requirement of secondary meaning for inherently distinctive trade dress also would undermine the purposes of the Lanham Act. Protection of trade dress, no less than of trademarks, serves the Act's purpose to "secure to the owner of the mark the goodwill of his business and to protect the ability of consumers to distinguish among competing producers. National protection of trademarks is desirable, Congress concluded, because trademarks foster competition and the maintenance of quality by securing to the producer the benefits of good reputation." *Park' N Fly,* 469 U.S., at 198, 105 S.Ct., at 663, citing S.Rep. No. 1333, 79th Cong., 2d Sess., 3–5 (1946) (citations omitted). By making more difficult the identification of a producer with its product, a secondary meaning requirement for a non-descriptive trade dress would hinder improving or maintaining the producer's competitive position.

Suggestions that under the Fifth Circuit's law, the initial user of any shape or design would cut off competition from products of like design and shape are not persuasive. Only nonfunctional, distinctive trade dress is protected under § 43(a). The Fifth Circuit holds that a design is legally functional, and thus unprotectable, if it is one of a limited number of equally efficient options available to competitors and free competition would be unduly hindered by according the design trademark protection. This serves to assure that competition will not be stifled by the exhaustion of a limited number of trade dresses.

On the other hand, adding a secondary meaning requirement could have anticompetitive effects, creating particular burdens on the start-up of small companies. It would present special difficulties for a business, such as respondent, that seeks to start a new product in a limited area and then expand into new markets. Denying protection for inherently distinctive nonfunctional trade dress until after secondary meaning has been established would allow a competitor, which has not adopted a distinctive trade dress of its own, to appropriate the originator's dress in other markets and to deter the originator from expanding into and competing in these areas.

As noted above, petitioner concedes that protecting an inherently distinctive trade dress from its inception may be critical to new entrants to the market and that withholding protection until secondary meaning has been established would be contrary to the goals of the Lanham Act. Petitioner specifically suggests, however, that the solution is to dispense with the requirement of secondary meaning for a reasonable, but brief period at the outset of the use of a trade dress. If § 43(a) does not require secondary meaning at the outset of a business' adoption of trade dress, there is no basis in the statute to support the suggestion that such a requirement comes into being after some unspecified time.

III

We agree with the Court of Appeals that proof of secondary meaning is not required to prevail on a claim under § 43(a) of the Lanham Act where the trade dress at issue is inherently distinctive, and accordingly the judgment of that court is affirmed.

It is so ordered.

Justice SCALIA, concurring.

I write separately to note my complete agreement with Justice THOMAS's explanation as to how the language of § 43(a) and its common-law derivation are broad enough to embrace inherently distinctive trade dress. Nevertheless, because I find that analysis to be complementary to (and not inconsistent with) the Court's opinion, I concur in the latter.

Justice STEVENS, concurring in the judgment.

As the Court notes in its opinion, the text of § 43(a) of the Lanham Act, 15 U.S.C. § 1125(a), "does not mention trademarks or trade dress." Nevertheless, the Court interprets this section as having created a federal cause of action for infringement of an unregistered trademark or trade dress and concludes that such a mark or dress should receive essentially the same protection as those that are registered. Although I agree with the Court's conclusion, I think it is important to recognize that the meaning of the text has been transformed by the federal courts over the past few decades. I agree with this transformation, even though it marks a departure from the original text, because it is consistent with the purposes of the statute and has recently been endorsed by Congress.

I

It is appropriate to begin with the relevant text of § 43(a). Section 43(a)[2] provides a federal remedy for using either "a false designation of

---

2. Section 43(a) replaced and extended the coverage of § 3 of the Trademark Act of 1920, Ch. 104, 41 Stat. 534, as amended. Section 3 was destined for oblivion largely because it referred only to false designation of origin, was limited to articles of merchandise, thus excluding services, and required a showing that the use of the false designation origin" or a "false description or representation" in connection with any goods or services. The full text of the section makes it clear that the word "origin" refers to the geographic location in which the goods originated, and in fact, the phrase "false designation of origin" was understood to be limited to false advertising of geographic origin. For example, the "false designation of origin" language contained in the statute makes it unlawful to represent that California oranges came from Florida, or vice versa.

For a number of years after the 1946 enactment of the Lanham Act, a "false description or representation," like "a false designation of origin," was construed narrowly. The phrase encompassed two kinds of wrongs: false advertising and the common-law tort of "passing off." False advertising meant representing that goods or services possessed characteristics that they did not actually have and passing off meant representing one's goods as those of another. Neither "secondary meaning" nor "inherent distinctiveness" had anything to do with false advertising, but proof of secondary meaning was an element of the common-law passing-off cause of action.

II

Over time, the Circuits have expanded the categories of "false designation of origin" and "false description or representation." One treatise identified the Court of Appeals for the Sixth Circuit as the first to broaden the meaning of "origin" to include "origin of source or manufacture" in addition to geographic origin. Another early case, described as unique among the Circuit cases because it was so "forward-looking," interpreted the "false description or representation" language to mean more than mere "palming off." L'Aiglon Apparel, Inc. v. Lana Lobell, Inc., 214 F.2d 649 (C.A.3 1954). The court explained: "We find nothing in the legislative history of the Lanham Act to justify the view that [§ 43(a)] is merely declarative of existing law.... It seems to us that Congress has defined a statutory civil wrong of false representation of goods in commerce and has given a broad class of suitors injured or likely to be injured by such wrong the right to relief in the federal courts." Id., at 651. Judge Clark, writing a concurrence in 1956, presciently observed: "Indeed, there is indication here and elsewhere that the bar has not yet realized the potential impact of this statutory provision [§ 43(a)]." Maternally Yours, Inc. v. Your Maternity Shop, Inc., 234 F.2d 538, 546 (CA2). Although some have criticized the expansion as unwise, it is now "a firmly embedded reality."[10] The United States Trademark Association Trademark Review Commission noted this transformation with approval: "Section 43(a) is an enigma, but a very popular one. Narrowly drawn and intended to reach false designations or representations as to the geographical origin of products, the section has been widely interpreted to create, in essence, a federal law of unfair

of origin occurred "willfully and with intent to deceive." Ibid. As a result, "[a]lmost no reported decision can be found in which relief was granted to either a United States or foreign party based on this newly created remedy." Derenberg, Federal Unfair Compe-

tition Law at the End of the First Decade of the Lanham Act: Prologue or Epilogue?, 32 N.Y.U.L.Rev. 1029, 1034 (1957).

10. 2 McCarthy § 27:3, p. 345.

competition.... It has definitely eliminated a gap in unfair competition law, and its vitality is showing no signs of age."[11]

Today, it is less significant whether the infringement falls under "false designation of origin" or "false description or representation" because in either case § 43(a) may be invoked. The federal courts are in agreement that § 43(a) creates a federal cause of action for trademark and trade dress infringement claims. They are also in agreement that the test for liability is likelihood of confusion: "[U]nder the Lanham Act [§ 43(a)], the ultimate test is whether the public is likely to be deceived or confused by the similarity of the marks.... Whether we call the violation infringement, unfair competition or false designation of origin, the test is identical—is there a 'likelihood of confusion?' " New West Corp. v. NYM Co. of California, Inc., 595 F.2d 1194, 1201 (C.A.9 1979) (footnote omitted). And the Circuits are in general agreement, with perhaps the exception of the Second Circuit, that secondary meaning need not be established once there is a finding of inherent distinctiveness in order to establish a trade dress violation under § 43(a).

III

Even though the lower courts' expansion of the categories contained in § 43(a) is unsupported by the text of the Act, I am persuaded that it is consistent with the general purposes of the Act. For example, Congressman Lanham, the bill's sponsor, stated: "The purpose of [the Act] is to protect legitimate business and the consumers of the country." 92 Cong.Rec. 7524 (1946). One way of accomplishing these dual goals was by creating uniform legal rights and remedies that were appropriate for a national economy. Although the protection of trademarks had once been "entirely a State matter," the result of such a piecemeal approach was that there were almost "as many different varieties of common law as there are States" so that a person's right to a trademark "in one State may differ widely from the rights which [that person] enjoys in another." H.R.Rep. No. 944, 76th Cong., 1st Sess., 4 (1939). The House Committee on Trademarks and Patents, recognizing that "trade is no longer local, but ... national," saw the need for "national legislation along national lines [to] secur[e] to the owners of trademarks in interstate commerce definite rights." Ibid.

Congress has revisited this statute from time to time, and has accepted the "judicial legislation" that has created this federal cause of action. Recently, for example, in the Trademark Law Revision Act of 1988, Pub.L. 100–667, 102 Stat. 3935, Congress codified the judicial interpretation of § 43(a), giving its imprimatur to a growing body of case law from the Circuits that had expanded the section beyond its original language.

Although Congress has not specifically addressed the question whether secondary meaning is required under § 43(a), the steps it has taken in this subsequent legislation suggest that secondary meaning is not required if

11. The United States Trademark Association Trademark Review Commission Report and Recommendations to USTA President and Board of Directors, 77 Trademark Rep. 375, 426 (1987).

inherent distinctiveness has been established. First, Congress broadened the language of § 43(a) to make explicit that the provision prohibits "any word, term, name, symbol, or device, or any combination thereof" that is "likely to cause confusion, or to cause mistake, or to deceive as to the affiliation, connection, or association of such person with another person, or as to the origin, sponsorship, or approval of his or her goods, services, or commercial activities by another person." 15 U.S.C. § 1125(a). That language makes clear that a confusingly similar trade dress is actionable under § 43(a), without necessary reference to "falsity." Second, Congress approved and confirmed the extensive judicial development under the provision, including its application to trade dress that the federal courts had come to apply. Third, the legislative history of the 1988 amendments reaffirms Congress' goals of protecting both businesses and consumers with the Lanham Act. And fourth, Congress explicitly extended to any violation of § 43(a) the basic Lanham Act remedial provisions whose text previously covered only registered trademarks. The aim of the amendments was to apply the same protections to unregistered marks as were already afforded to registered marks. These steps buttress the conclusion that § 43(a) is properly understood to provide protection in accordance with the standards for registration in § 2. These aspects of the 1988 legislation bolster the claim that an inherently distinctive trade dress may be protected under § 43(a) without proof of secondary meaning.

IV

In light of the general consensus among the Courts of Appeals that have actually addressed the question, and the steps on the part of Congress to codify that consensus, *stare decisis* concerns persuade me to join the Court's conclusion that secondary meaning is not required to establish a trade dress violation under § 43(a) once inherent distinctiveness has been established. Accordingly, I concur in the judgment, but not in the opinion of the Court.

Justice THOMAS, concurring in the judgment.

Both the Court and Justice STEVENS decide today that the principles that qualify a mark for registration under § 2 of the Lanham Act apply as well to determining whether an unregistered mark is entitled to protection under § 43(a). The Court terms that view "common ground," though it fails to explain why that might be so, and Justice STEVENS decides that the view among the Courts of Appeals is textually insupportable, but worthy nonetheless of adherence. I see no need in answering the question presented either to move back and forth among the different sections of the Lanham Act or to adopt what may or may not be a misconstruction of the statute for reasons akin to *stare decisis*. I would rely, instead, on the language of § 43(a).

Section 43(a) made actionable (before being amended) "any false description or representation, including words or other symbols tending falsely to describe or represent," when "use[d] in connection with any goods or services." 15 U.S.C. § 1125(a) (1982 ed.). This language codified, among other things, the related common-law torts of technical trademark infringement and passing off, which were causes of action for false descriptions or representations concerning a good's or service's source of production.

At common law, words or symbols that were arbitrary, fanciful, or suggestive (called "inherently distinctive" words or symbols, or "trademarks") were presumed to represent the source of a product, and the first user of a trademark could sue to protect it without having to show that the word or symbol represented the product's source in fact. That presumption did not attach to personal or geographic names or to words or symbols that only described a product (called "trade names"), and the user of a personal or geographic name or of a descriptive word or symbol could obtain relief only if he first showed that his trade name did in fact represent not just the product, but a producer (that the goods or service had developed "secondary meaning"). Trade dress, which consists not of words or symbols, but of a product's packaging (or "image," more broadly), seems at common law to have been thought incapable ever of being inherently distinctive, perhaps on the theory that the number of ways to package a product is finite. Thus, a user of trade dress would always have had to show secondary meaning in order to obtain protection.

Over time, judges have come to conclude that packages or images may be as arbitrary, fanciful, or suggestive as words or symbols, their numbers limited only by the human imagination. A particular trade dress, then, is now considered as fully capable as a particular trademark of serving as a "representation or designation" of source under § 43(a). As a result, the first user of an arbitrary package, like the first user of an arbitrary word, should be entitled to the presumption that his package represents him without having to show that it does so in fact. This rule follows, in my view, from the language of § 43(a), and this rule applies under that section without regard to the rules that apply under the sections of the Lanham Act that deal with registration.

Because the Court reaches the same conclusion for different reasons, I join its judgment.

NOTES

1. Has *Taco Cabana* effectively elevated section 43(a) subject matter to the level of federally-registered trademarks? The Lanham Act has historically exacted a price for the benefits conferred by registration on the Principal Register—*ex parte* examination; opposition, concurrent use, interference and cancellation proceedings; and the renewal requirement. Apart from the not insignificant benefits of constructive notice under section 1072, what incentive does a common law trademark owner have to pay this price after *Taco Cabana?*

The Supreme Court evidently agreed with the *Taco Cabana* trial court that "distinctive" is the opposite of "descriptive," and that any subject matter that is not descriptive is categorically distinctive. Is it relevant that trade dress will rarely "describe" the product or service being offered? A salad bar evoking a Mexican motif will not describe a Mexican restaurant in the sense that the word "enchilada" describes a tortilla rolled and filled with a seasoned mixture and enveloped in sauce. Does *Taco Cabana* open section 43(a)'s door to the protection of any nonfunctional trade dress, no matter how banal, without proof of secondary meaning? Would it have been better for the Court to have treated the term, "descriptive" as just a metaphor for a larger concept, "common," and required the plaintiff to prove that its trade dress rose above the ordinary?

Commentary on the nature, functions and appropriate limits of trade dress protection abounds. See generally Jeffrey M. Samuels, Trade Dress Protection: The Issue of Distinctiveness and Potential Conflicts, 27 N. Ky. L. Rev. 1041 (2000); Graeme B. Dinwoodie, The Death of Ontology: A Teleological Approach to Trademark Law, 84 Iowa L. Rev. 611 (1999); Tom W. Bell, Virtual Trade Dress: A Very Real Problem, 56 Md. L. Rev. 384 (1997); Glynn S. Lunney, Jr., The Trade Dress Emperor's New Clothes: Why Trade Dress Does not Belong on the Principal Register. 51 Hast. L. J. 1131 (2000).

2. *Trade Dress and Product Design.* In *Taco Cabana* the Supreme Court ruled that trade dress, such as product packaging, need not have acquired secondary meaning to be protected under section 43(a); if the dress is inherently distinctive, that will suffice. What if the object for which protection is sought is not the design of a package, but the design of the product itself? In Wal–Mart Stores, Inc. v. Samara Brothers, Inc., 529 U.S. 205, 120 S.Ct. 1339, 146 L.Ed.2d 182, 54 U.S.P.Q.2d 1065 (2000), the Court ruled that, unlike trade dress, product design cannot be inherently distinctive, so that the childrens' clothing designs in issue could be protected under section 43(a) only upon proof that they had acquired secondary meaning.

Referring to its *Qualitex* decision, page 270, above, in which it "held that a color could be protected a as a trademark, but only upon a showing of secondary meaning, "the *Wal–Mart* Court concluded that 'design, like color, is not inherently distinctive.' " In contrast to words and packaging, whose "predominant function remains source identification ... "[i]n the case of product design, as in the case of color, we think consumer predisposition to equate the feature with the source does not exist. Consumers are aware of the reality that, almost invariably, even the most unusual of product designs—such as a cocktail shaker shaped like a penguin—is intended not to identify the source, but to render the product itself more useful or more appealing." 529 U.S. at 206, 212–13.

What legal or esthetic principle separates a product design, such as a penguin-shaped cocktail shaker, from trade dress, such as a restaurant decor embodying a particular theme? Is it clear that the object protected in *Taco Cabana* was the package rather than the product? The Court acknowledged that "[t]here will indeed be some hard cases at the margin: a classic glass Coca–Cola bottle, for instance, may constitute packaging for those consumers who drink the Coke and then discard the bottle, but may constitute the product itself for those consumers who are bottle collectors, or part of the product itself for those consumers who buy Coke in the classic glass bottle, rather than a can, because they think it more stylish to drink from the former. We believe, however, that the frequency and the difficulty of having to distinguish between product design and product packaging will be much less than the frequency and the difficulty of having to decide when a product design is inherently distinctive. To the extent there are close cases, we believe that courts should err on the side of caution and classify ambiguous trade dress as product design, thereby requiring secondary meaning." 529 U.S. at 215.

As a practical matter, how much room does *Wal-Mart* leave for the protection of trade dress under section 43(a) without proof of secondary meaning?

See generally, David S. Welkowitz, Trade Dress and Patent—the Dilemma of Confusion, 30 Rutgers L.J. 289 (1999).

3. *Trade Dress and Functionality.* A 1999 amendment to section 43(a) added a new subsection (3) providing, "In a civil action for trade dress infringement under this Act for trade dress not registered on the principal register, the person who asserts trade dress protection has the burden of proving that the matter sought to be protected is not functional." Pub. L. No. 106–43 § 5. Should the fact that a feature of the trade dress is the subject of an expired utility patent affect the plaintiff's burden of proof on nonfunctionality?

In TrafFix Devices, Inc. v. Marketing Displays, Inc., 532 U.S. 23, 121 S.Ct. 1255, 149 L.Ed.2d 164, 58 U.S.P.Q.2d 1001 (2001), the Supreme Court observed a split among the circuits on "whether the existence of an expired utility patent forecloses the possibility of the patentee's claiming trade dress protection in the product's design," and ruled that a utility patent is strong, but not conclusive, evidence of functionality so that "[w]here the expired patent claimed the features in question, one who seeks to establish trade dress protection must carry the heavy burden of showing that the feature is not functional, for instance by showing that it is merely an ornamental, incidental, or arbitrary aspect of the device." 121 S.Ct. At 1259–60.

The Court ruled in *TrafFix* that because the formerly patented dual spring design was "the essential feature" of the plaintiff's trade dress for its temporary road signs, "MDI did not, and cannot, carry the burden of overcoming the strong evidentiary inference of functionality based on the disclosure of the dual-spring design in the expired patents." The Court also observed that the test of functionality applied by the circuit court below—"whether the particular product configuration is a competitive necessity"—was "incorrect as a comprehensive definition"; a feature is also functional

"when it is essential to the use or purpose of the device or when it affects the cost or quality of the device. The *Qualitex* decision did not purport to displace this traditional rule."

4. *Trade Dress and Copyright.* Hartford House, Ltd. v. Hallmark Cards, Inc., 846 F.2d 1268, 6 U.S.P.Q.2d 2038 (10th Cir.), cert. denied, 488 U.S. 908, 109 S.Ct. 260, 102 L.Ed.2d 248 (1988), holding that plaintiff was entitled to protection against defendant's imitation of its greeting cards, may be a high watermark for trade dress protection under section 43(a), and for trademark law's incursion into the realm of copyright. The protected trade dress embodied, among other elements, a two-fold card containing poetry on the first and third pages, a deckle edge on the right side of the first page, a rough-edge stripe of color on the outside of the deckle edge of the first page, hand-lettered calligraphy with the first letter of the words often enlarged, and an illustration that wrapped around the card and spread over three pages, including the back of the card. Against the defendant's claim that the protected features were functional, the court held that the district court's fact findings were not clearly erroneous: " '[a]n emotional non-occasion greeting card can be folded, colored, shaped, cut, edged, and designed in infinite ways and still function to send its message.' In light of the available alternatives, the district court further concluded that allowing Blue Mountain to exclude others from using its trade dress 'will not hinder competition nor will it interfere with the rights of others to compete.' Consequently, the district court found that the overall appearance, i.e., trade dress, of Blue Mountain's cards was nonfunctional. In the district court's words: 'Paper, verse and ink are functional features of a greeting card. The design and amalgamation of those features in a uniform fashion with other features, however, has produced the nonfunctional Blue Mountain "look".' " 846 F.2d at 1274.

Would section 43(a)(3) as applied by the *TrafFix* Court, note 3, above, have dictated a different result in *Hartford House*? Does *Hartford House* effectively give copyright-like protection unlimited on time? Section 43(a)'s expanded protection against trade dress imitation and product simulation came at a time when courts, under the preemptive compulsion of *Sears* and *Compco* and Copyright Act section 301 were trimming back state unfair competition law in the area. Because *Sears* and *Compco* were decided under the Constitution's Supremacy Clause, they do not control federal law unfair competition actions. Similarly, section 301(d) expressly excludes federal laws from the Copyright Act's preemptive thrust.

5. *Titles.* As a general rule, a work's title is uncopyrightable. However, a title may be protected against passing off under section 43(a) if it is distinctive or has acquired secondary meaning and if its unauthorized use will be likely to mislead consumers about the source of the work with which the title is used. A title that has been used in connection with only a single work will rarely obtain passing off protection against its unauthorized use on another work in the same medium; the reason usually given in this context is that because the title can do little more than describe the work itself, it will not generally point to the work's source. A plaintiff who has used a title in connection with only a single work will enjoy greater prospects for success in cases where the defendant uses the title in a *different* medium—for example, if the plaintiff publishes a novel under the title, *Gone with the Wind*, and the defendant markets a motion picture under the same title. The rationale in these cases is that the use of a work's title in a different medium does not describe the work but rather indicates the plaintiff as the source of the work in the different medium. See generally, 3 Paul Goldstein, Copyright § 15.14.1 (2d ed. 1996).

Courts, most notably in the Second Circuit, have subjected competitive use of titles to a particularly rigorous test for passing off. In Twin Peaks Prods., Inc. v. Publications Int'l, Ltd., 996 F.2d 1366, 1379, 27 U.S.P.Q.2d 1001 (2d Cir.1993), the court ruled that "[b]ecause of an author's significant First Amendment interest in choosing an appropriate title for his or her work, we have held that literary titles do not violate the Lanham Act 'unless the title has no artistic relevance to the underlying work whatsoever, or, if it has some artistic relevance, unless the title explicitly misleads as to the source or the content of the work,' " citing Rogers v. Grimaldi, 875 F.2d 994, 999, 10 U.S.P.Q.2d 1825 (2d Cir.1989).

6. *History.* As noted in Justice Stevens's concurring opinion in *Taco Cabana,* the phrase "false designation of origin" in section 43(a) was originally "understood to be limited to false advertising of geographic origin." For several years after its enactment, courts applied section 43(a) sparingly. Not until 1954 did a court authoritatively declare that section 43(a) created a more general federal cause of action against false advertising respecting product *quality.* L'Aiglon Apparel v. Lana Lobell, Inc., 214 F.2d 649, 102 U.S.P.Q. 94 (3d Cir.1954). The Lanham Act had been law for a decade before a federal circuit court suggested that section 43(a) also proscribed misrepresentation as to the *source* of products—common law trademark violations, in Joshua Meier Co. v. Albany Novelty Mfg. Co., 236 F.2d 144, 111 U.S.P.Q. 197 (2d Cir.1956), and common law passing off in Federal–Mogul–Bower Bearings, Inc. v. Azoff, 313 F.2d 405, 136 U.S.P.Q. 500 (6th Cir.1963). As noted in *Taco Cabana,* the 1988 amendments to the Lanham Act cemented liability for misrepresentation, common law trademark infringement, and passing off into the reworded text of section 43(a). The 1988 amendments also added product disparagement—misrepresentations about the goods or services of others—to section 43(a)'s formula.

7. *Defendant Misrepresents Quality of Its Own Goods or Services.* Common law courts were slow to extend unfair competition to encompass a producer's misrepresentations about the quality of its product or service, as distinguished from misrepresentations about its source. The leading case, American Washboard Co. v. Saginaw Mfg. Co., 103 F. 281 (6th Cir.1900), held that plaintiff, which manufactured genuine aluminum washboards, had no action for unfair competition against defendant which represented to consumers that its zinc washboards were made of aluminum. In Mosler Safe Co. v. Ely–Norris Safe Co., 273 U.S. 132, 47 S.Ct. 314, 71 L.Ed. 578 (1927), the Supreme Court suggested that an action might lie in such circumstances, but only if the plaintiff could show that it was the sole manufacturer of the genuine goods, so that any sales made by the deceitful competitor would necessarily divert sales from the manufacturer. The Unfair Competition Restatement generally follows this approach by making the likelihood of "commercial detriment" to the plaintiff an element of the cause of action for misrepresentation, and by defining "likely commercial detriment" to require "a reasonable basis for believing that the representation has caused or is likely to cause a diversion of trade from the other or harm to the other's reputation or good will." Restatement of the Law, Third, Unfair Competition §§ 2,3 (1995).

Section 43(a) of the Lanham Act, 15 U.S.C.A. § 1125(a), effectively reversed the rule of *American Washboard* as a matter of federal law. Early cases under this branch of section 43(a) involved defendants' blatant misrepresentations about the quality of their goods. See, for example, Crossbow, Inc. v. Dan–Dee Imports, Inc., 266 F.Supp. 335, 153 U.S.P.Q. 163 (S.D.N.Y.1967) (defendant liable for removing plaintiff's trademark and other identifying insignia from plaintiff's product, replacing them with its own, and using the mislabeled product as a demonstration model for its own inferior imitation); Mutation Mink Breeders Ass'n v. Lou Nierenberg Corp., 23 F.R.D. 155, 120 U.S.P.Q. 270 (S.D.N.Y.1959) (defendant enjoined from using the word "mink" on its "fake-fur" fabrics); Consumers Union of U.S., Inc. v. Theodore Hamm Brewing Co., 314 F.Supp. 697, 166 U.S.P.Q. 48 (D.C.Conn.1970) (defendant enjoined from misrepresenting the rating its product had received from the Consumers Union). More recent cases have employed section 43(a) to redress misrepresentations, most notably in connection with artists' contributions to sound recordings and motion pictures. See, e.g., Smith v. Montoro, 648 F.2d 602, 211 U.S.P.Q. 775 (9th Cir.1981) (film distributor's removal of actor's name from film credits and substitution of name of another actor constituted "express reverse passing off"—the mislabelling of plaintiff's product as defendant's); Lamothe v. Atlantic Recording Corp., 847 F.2d 1403, 7 U.S.P.Q.2d 1249 (9th Cir.1988) (omission of the names of co-authors from record albums and sheet music of co-authored compositions). Although puffery is not actionable, specific claims, such as an oil company's false claim that its product "outperforms any leading motor oil against viscosity breakdown," can be actionable. Castrol Inc. v. Pennzoil Co., 987 F.2d 939, 947, 25 U.S.P.Q.2d 1666 (3d Cir.1993).

8. *Defendant Misrepresents Quality of Plaintiff's Goods or Services.* Disparagement, because it misrepresents the quality of plaintiff's product, not defendant's, was originally not actionable under section 43(a) of the Lanham Act. See Bernard Food Industries v. Dietene Co., 415 F.2d 1279, 163 U.S.P.Q. 264 (7th Cir.1969), cert. denied, 397 U.S. 912, 90 S.Ct. 911, 25 L.Ed.2d 92, 164 U.S.P.Q. 481 (1970). If, however, defendant's criticism of plaintiff's product falsely implied that the defendant's product was better, an action could lie under traditional misrepresentation theory. See American Home Products Corp. v. Johnson & Johnson, 577 F.2d 160, 198 U.S.P.Q. 132 (2d Cir.1978). Several courts chafed under this limitation. Recognizing its obligation to follow *Dietene* as the law in its circuit, one district court observed that "it would seem that in comparison advertising, a false statement by the defendant about plaintiff's product would have the same detrimental effect as a false statement about defendant's product. I.e., it would tend to mislead the buying public concerning the relative merits and qualities of the products, thereby inducing the purchase of a possibly inferior product." Skil Corp. v. Rockwell Int'l Corp., 375 F.Supp. 777, 782 n. 10, 183 U.S.P.Q. 157 (N.D.Ill.1974).

The 1988 amendments to the Lanham Act made disparagement actionable under section 43(a). As amended, section 43(a) imposes liability on any person who uses a "false or misleading description of fact, or false or misleading representation of fact, which ... (2) in commercial advertising or promotion, misrepresents the nature, characteristics, qualities, or geographic origin of his or her *or another person's* goods, services, or commercial activities." (Emphasis added.) According to Senator DeConcini, Congress intended the requirement that the misrepresentation be made in "commercial advertising or promotion" to "eliminate any possibility that the section might be applied to political speech." 134 Cong.Rec. S 16,973 (daily ed. Oct. 20, 1988). In Congressman Kastenmeier's view, "consumer reporting, editorial comment, political advertising, and other constitutionally protected material is not covered by this provision." 134 Cong.Rec. H 10419 (daily ed. Oct. 19, 1988).

9. *Standing.* Read literally, section 43(a)'s prescription, "any person who believes that he or she is or is likely to be damaged" encompasses claims not only by competitors but by consumers as well. Nonetheless, courts have divided on whether consumers have standing to sue under section 43(a). In the leading case, Colligan v. Activities Club of New York, Ltd., 442 F.2d 686, 170 U.S.P.Q. 113 (2d Cir.1971), cert. denied, 404 U.S. 1004, 92 S.Ct. 559, 30 L.Ed.2d 557, 172 U.S.P.Q. 97, disappointed ski weekenders sought monetary and injunctive relief—the latter on behalf of "all high school students within the New York metropolitan area who are likely to be deceived and thereby injured by defendants' similarly deceptive practices in the future"—against defendant which, they alleged, had deceived and damaged them by "use of false descriptions and representations of the nature, sponsorship, and licensing of their interstate ski tour service." 442 F.2d at 687. The court of appeals affirmed the district court's dismissal of the complaint. "Congress' purpose in enacting section 43(a) was to create a special and limited unfair competition remedy, virtually without regard for the interests of consumers generally and almost certainly without any consideration of consumer rights of action in particular. The Act's purpose, as defined in § 45, is exclusively to protect the interests of a purely commercial class against unscrupulous commercial conduct." 442 F.2d at 692.

After some legislative to and fro, Congress, in passing the Trademark Law Revision Act of 1988, left the question of consumer standing unresolved. See Scott E. Thompson, Consumer Standing Under Section 43(a): More Legislative History, More Confusion, 79 Trademark Rep. 341 (1989). Courts have generally read the Act's legislative history to reflect an intention to preserve the status quo, and have denied standing to aggrieved consumers. See, e.g., Barrus v. Sylvania, 55 F.3d 468, 34 U.S.P.Q.2d 1859 (9th Cir.1995); Serbin v. Ziebart Int'l Corp., 11 F.3d 1163, 28 U.S.P.Q.2d 1881 (3d Cir.1993). See generally Richard A. DeSevo, Consumer Standing

Under Section 43(a)—An Issue Whose Time has Passed, 88 Trademark Rep. 1 (1998).

10. *Remedies.* The original language of Lanham Act section 35, 15 U.S.C.A. § 1117, literally limited recovery of profits, damages, costs and attorney fees to prevailing parties who had registered their marks in the Patent and Trademark Office. Nonetheless, courts generally granted profits, damages and, in some cases, attorney's fees to prevailing plaintiffs under section 43(a). Following the recommendations of the Trademark Review Commission, the 1988 amendments to the Lanham Act made damages, profits, attorney's fees, costs and destruction of infringing goods available to prevailing plaintiffs in actions under section 43(a).

11. Courts will not find in section 43(a) a salve for every conceivable competitive injury. In Societe Comptoir De L'Industrie Cotonniere Etablissements Boussac v. Alexander's Dept. Stores, 299 F.2d 33, 132 U.S.P.Q. 475 (2d Cir.1962), the Second Circuit Court of Appeals held that defendant should not be enjoined from truthfully advertising that its inexpensive dresses were copies of original Dior designs. "The Lanham Act does not prohibit a commercial rival's truthfully denominating his goods a copy of a design in the public domain, though he uses the name of the designer to do so." 299 F.2d 33, 36. Section 43(a) also gave the Girl Scouts of America no aid in its attempt to enjoin the distribution of a poster depicting "a smiling girl dressed in the well-known green uniform of the Junior Girl Scouts, with her hands clasped above her protruding, clearly pregnant abdomen. The caveat 'be prepared' appears next to her hands." With the terse observation that "plaintiff has failed utterly to establish the requisite element of customer confusion," the court dismissed the claim that defendant had violated section 43(a) by using plaintiff's marks and insignia to designate falsely the paternity of its poster. Girl Scouts of the United States of America v. Personality Posters Mfg. Co., 304 F.Supp. 1228, 1230–1231, 163 U.S.P.Q. 505 (S.D.N.Y.1969).

Alfred Dunhill, Ltd. v. Interstate Cigar Co., Inc., 364 F.Supp. 366, 177 U.S.P.Q. 346 (S.D.N.Y.1973), rev'd, 499 F.2d 232, 183 U.S.P.Q. 193 (2d Cir.1974), raised a more subtle question about section 43(a)'s scope. Does the language "affix, apply, or annex or use" cover acts of omission as well as commission? The lower court answered that it does, and enjoined defendant from distributing damaged tobacco, bearing plaintiff's trademark, purchased from plaintiff's agent at salvage prices. In the court's judgment, "sales of damaged tobacco in tins bearing trademarks associated with high quality tobacco without adequate warnings to customers that the goods are damaged, involve false representations of their quality." 364 F.Supp. 366, 372. The court of appeals reversed, holding that the district court's result "cannot be reached through an interpretation of the statutory language or legislative or judicial history of the Lanham Act." The court also noted that Dunhill's problem was in part of its own making. "If Dunhill had wished to distinguish the salvaged tobacco from that sold through its normal channels of distribution, it should have done so while the allegedly damaged tobacco was still under its control and before it was released into the salvage markets. From the beginning Dunhill was in the best position to effect the relabeling." 499 F.2d 232, 237–238.

II. PATENT LAW

The first known system for awarding patents for inventions in the useful arts dates to Venice in the mid-fifteenth century. The Venetian system, codified into a general patent statute in 1474, sought to spur the introduction of new technologies and industries by awarding patentees the exclusive right to practice their art for a specified period, generally ranging from ten to fifty years. Some patents issued to technologies that had been imported into Venice from other regions and that had been invented by someone other than the individual seeking the patent. Other patented inventions originated with the patentee. Bruce Bugbee writes of a 1460 patent "issued to one Jacobus 'in reward of his pertinent thoughts and labors' as the 'first inventor and builder' of a water-raising mechanism. Evidently a true patent of invention, it carried a term of protection measured by the life of the grantee. Each imitator constructing such a device in Venetian territory without the 'express license' of Jacobus was to be fined 1,000 gold ducats and the infringing machines were to be 'thoroughly destroyed.'" Bruce Bugbee, Genesis of American Patent and Copyright Law 21 (1967).

Early English patent practice followed the Venetian model, awarding durationally limited monopolies to importers of already established crafts and industries as well as to originators of new devices. The system was generally ratified by the Statute of Monopolies, 21 Jac. 1 c. 3 (1624), the seminal document in the history of English patent law. The Statute, which prohibited monopolies "for the sole buying, selling, making, working, or using of anything within this Realm," was enacted in response to the Crown's overly generous grants of monopolies to court favorites to manufacture such common items as vinegar and starch. The Statute did, however, allow the Crown to grant patents for fourteen years or less "to the true and first inventor or inventors" for "the sole working or making of any manner of new manufactures within this realm" provided "they be not contrary to the law nor mischievous to the state, by raising prices of commodities at home, or hurt of trade, or generally inconvenient."

The American colonies and, after the Revolution, the state legislatures, generally followed England's *ad hoc* system, awarding patents through private acts passed in response to individual petitions. The first federal patent law, Act of April 10, 1790, ch. 7, 1 Stat. 109–110, was a general, rather than a private act, authorizing patents for "any useful art, manufacture, engine, machine, or device, or any improvement therein not before known or used." Upon a showing that the claimed invention was "sufficiently useful and important," a patent board composed of the Secretary of State, the Secretary of War and the Attorney General was to grant a patent for a term of up to fourteen years. The burden of examining patent applications soon proved too heavy for these busy civil servants, and a new patent law, Act of February 21, 1793, ch. 11, 1 Stat. 318, substituted the simple act of registration for the previous examination system. The new act also eliminated the requirement that the invention be "sufficiently useful and important." The Act of July 4, 1836, ch. 357, 5 Stat. 117, reinstated the examination system and the inventiveness requirement and also fixed the patent term at fourteen years with a seven year renewal period.

To the chagrin of many observers today, the 1836 Act continues to provide the basic structure and principles of United States patent law. The Act's last major revision, in the Act of July 19, 1952, 66 Stat. 792, left the basic system virtually unchanged. Congress has, in the years since, significantly amended several features of the 1952 Act.

The Court of Appeals for the Federal Circuit, created by the Federal Courts Improvement Act of 1982, has significantly changed contemporary patent law and practice. Congress created the CAFC to eliminate a persistent disparity in patent law standards among courts of appeals deciding cases coming to them from the district courts in their region. The Act withdrew the patent jurisdiction of the twelve regional courts of appeals and vested exclusive jurisdiction over these appeals in the CAFC. The CAFC has not only eliminated intramural conflict and forum shopping; it has also buttressed the patent grant itself, giving new force to the statutory presumption of validity, easing the standards of patentability and strengthening the procedural and remedial relief available to patent owners.

Bruce Bugbee, Genesis of American Patent and Copyright Law (1967) chronicles the history of United States patent law from its early European roots. For a detailed study of the first decades of the U.S. patent system, see Edward C. Walterscheid, To Promote the Progress of Useful Arts: American Patent Law and Administration, 1798–1836 (1998). Summary reviews of the English and American history appear in a special number of the Journal of the Patent Office Society celebrating the centennial of the 1836 Act, 18 J.P.O.S. No. 7 (1936), and in American Bar Association, Two–Hundred Years of English and American Patent, Trademark and Copyright Law, 3, 21 (1976).

Donald S. Chisum, Chisum on Patents (1978); Robert L. Harmon, Patents and the Federal Circuit (5th ed. 2001), Ernest Bainbridge Lipscomb III, Walker on Patents (1991) and Peter D. Rosenberg, Patent Law Fundamentals (2d ed. 1980), are useful treatises. John W. Schlicher, Patent Law: Legal and Economic Principles (1992) is a clear and comprehensive exposition of the United States patent system and its underlying economics. The American Intellectual Property Law Association Quarterly Journal and the Journal of the Patent and Trademark Office Society regularly publish topical papers.

INTRODUCTORY NOTE: PATENT CLAIMS

Section 112 of the Patent Act requires a patent application to include a "specification" describing the invention and "the manner and process of making and using it"; the specification should "conclude with one or more claims particularly pointing out and distinctly claiming the subject matter which the applicant regards as his invention." Put simply, the specification is the windup, and the claim is the pitch.

More than a century ago, Professor William Robinson of Yale defined the purpose of the patent claim in terms that still ring true today: "It is the office of the Claim to define the limits of that exclusive use which is secured to the inventor by the patent, and thus to draw the line between those arts or instruments that are open to the public, and those whose employment by it is forbidden until the patent has expired.... Hence the statutes require not only that the inventor shall fully *describe* his invention in the specification, so that any person skilled in the art can practice it, but also that he shall particularly point out and distinctly *claim* the part, improvement, or combination which he claims as his invention or discovery." 2 William Robinson, The Law of Patents for Useful Inventions § 504 (1890).

It is natural to think of a patented invention in terms of its physical embodiment—to think, for example, of Alexander Graham Bell's 1876 patent on telephony by visualizing an old-fashioned telephone. In fact, the reach of a patent—the scope of the legal monopoly it confers—is defined by the terms and limitations set forth in that abstract formulation called the "claim." Thus, for telephony:

> 5.   The method of, and apparatus for, transmitting vocal or other sounds telegraphically, as herein described, by causing electrical undulations, similar in form to the vibrations of the air accompanying the said vocal or other sounds, substantially as set forth.

Any unauthorized embodiment of that claim, whether it looked like Bell's telephone or not, would have infringed the Bell patent.

Like a metes and bounds description in a deed to real property, a patent's claim or claims establishes the boundary of the property owner's exclusive rights; unlike real property descriptions, however, patent claims raise questions in virtually every corner of the law:

> *Statutory subject matter.* Claims are sometimes drafted to encompass unpatentable subject matter—for example, a claim to a computer program that is defined by an unpatentable algorithm. Such claims will be rejected by the Patent and Trademark Office or, if allowed, declared invalid in court. See pages 894–931, below.

> *Standards.* A claim will be unpatentable if it replicates—"reads on"—information that is already known—"prior art." Claims that are not "nonobvious" in light of the prior art are also unpatentable. In some cases, a claim may be narrowed to avoid the prior art. See pages 407, 434, below.

> *Prosecution practice.* The inevitable tug of war between a patent applicant and the patent examiner who is assigned to her case will usually center on the proper scope of the claims ultimately to be allowed. The applicant will, within reason, press for the broadest possible claims, and the patent examiner for the narrowest. See page 485, below.

> *Infringement.* Patent infringement lawsuits often boil down to a dispute over whether the alleged infringer's product or process comes

within the literal scope of the owner's patent claims and, if it does not, whether the court should nonetheless interpret the claims to encompass the allegedly infringing subject matter. See page 542, below.

Public policy. In drawing the line that divides exclusive rights from the public domain, a patent claim should implement the constitutional balance between incentive to invent and freedom to imitate, a balance intended to stimulate the optimal level of innovation as reflected in Congress' constitutional power "to promote the Progress of Useful Arts, by securing ... to Inventors the exclusive Right to their ... Discoveries...." In this sense, every decision rendered on the scope of a claim, whether made in the Patent and Trademark Office or in the courts, implicates central issues of public policy.

As you read the cases in this chapter, consider how, if at all, the drafting of the claim or claims in issue affected the result reached. Would narrower claims have avoided a finding of anticipation or obviousness? Would broader claims have avoided a finding of noninfringement, or would they have resulted in a finding of anticipation or obviousness?

A. REQUIREMENTS FOR PROTECTION

1. STATUTORY SUBJECT MATTER

See Statute Supplement 35 U.S.C.A. §§ 100, 101.

Utility patents, the usual grist of the patent law mill, may be granted for "any new and useful process, machine, manufacture, or composition of matter, or any new and useful improvement thereof...." 35 U.S.C.A. § 101. A *process* will claim a series of steps aimed at achieving a particular result; as defined by section 100(a), the term "means process, art or method, and includes a new use of a known process, machine, manufacture, composition of matter or material." The other three classes of subject matter claims—machine, manufacture, or composition or matter—are called *product* claims. Claims for machines and manufactures are also called *apparatus* claims, and the rough difference between them is that machines have moving parts. Unlike machines and manufactures, which are mechanical or structural, compositions are typically chemical compounds.

The Patent Act also authorizes patents for plants and patents for designs. Plant patents are discussed at page 406, note 5, below. Design patents are considered in connection with legal protection for industrial design generally, beginning at page 940, below. Patent protection for computer programs is considered in connection with legal protection for computer programs generally, beginning at page 803, below.

Diamond v. Chakrabarty

Supreme Court of the United States, 1980.
447 U.S. 303, 100 S.Ct. 2204, 65 L.Ed.2d 144, 206 U.S.P.Q. 193.

Mr. Chief Justice BURGER delivered the opinion of the Court.

We granted certiorari to determine whether a live, human-made microorganism is patentable subject matter under 35 U.S.C.A. § 101.

I.

In 1972, respondent Chakrabarty, a microbiologist, filed a patent application, assigned to the General Electric Company. The application asserted 36 claims related to Chakrabarty's invention of "a bacterium from the genus *Pseudomonas* containing therein at least two stable energy-generating plasmids, each of said plasmids providing a separate hydrocarbon degradative pathway."[1] This human-made, genetically engineered bacterium is capable of breaking down multiple components of crude oil. Because of this property, which is possessed by no naturally occurring bacteria, Chakrabarty's invention is believed to have significant value for the treatment of oil spills.[2]

Chakrabarty's patent claims were of three types: first, process claims for the method of producing the bacteria; second, claims for an inoculum comprised of a carrier material floating on water, such as straw, and the new bacteria; and third, claims to the bacteria themselves. The patent examiner allowed the claims falling into the first two categories, but rejected claims for the bacteria. His decision rested on two grounds: (1) that micro-organisms are "products of nature," and (2) that as living things they are not patentable subject matter under 35 U.S.C.A. § 101.

Chakrabarty appealed the rejection of these claims to the Patent Office Board of Appeals, and the Board affirmed the Examiner on the second ground.[3] Relying on the legislative history of the 1930 Plant Patent Act, in which Congress extended patent protection to certain asexually reproduced plants, the Board concluded that § 101 was not intended to cover living things such as these laboratory created microorganisms.

The Court of Customs and Patent Appeals, by a divided vote, reversed on the authority of its prior decision in *In re Bergy*, 563 F.2d 1031, 195 U.S.P.Q. 344 (1977), which held that "the fact that microorganisms ... are alive ... [is] without legal significance" for purposes of the patent law.

---

1. Plasmids are hereditary units physically separate from the chromosomes of the cell. In prior research, Chakrabarty and an associate discovered that plasmids control the oil degradation abilities of certain bacteria. In particular, the two researchers discovered plasmids capable of degrading camphor and octane, two components of crude oil. In the work represented by the patent application at issue here, Chakrabarty discovered a process by which four different plasmids, capable of degrading four different oil components, could be transferred to and maintained stably in a single Pseudomonas bacteria, which itself has no capacity for degrading oil.

2. At present, biological control of oil spills requires the use of a mixture of natu-

rally occurring bacteria, each capable of degrading one component of the oil complex. In this way, oil is decomposed into simpler substances which can serve as food for aquatic life. However, for various reasons, only a portion of any such mixed culture survives to attack the oil spill. By breaking down multiple components of oil, Chakrabarty's micro-organism promises more efficient and rapid oil-spill control.

3. The Board concluded that the new bacteria were not "products of nature," because Pseudomonas bacteria containing two or more different energy-generating plasmids are not naturally occurring.

Subsequently, we granted the Government's petition for certiorari in Bergy, vacated the judgment, and remanded the case "for further consideration in light of *Parker v. Flook*, 437 U.S. 584." The Court of Customs and Patent Appeals then vacated its judgment in *Chakrabarty* and consolidated the case with *Bergy* for reconsideration. After re-examining both cases in the light of our holding in Flook, that court, with one dissent, reaffirmed its earlier judgments.

The Government again sought certiorari, and we granted the writ as to both *Bergy* and *Chakrabarty*. Since then, *Bergy* has been dismissed as moot, leaving only *Chakrabarty* for decision.

II.

The Constitution grants Congress broad power to legislate to "promote the Progress of Science and the useful Arts, by securing for limited times to authors and inventors the exclusive right to their respective writings and discoveries." Art. I, § 8. The patent laws promote this progress by offering inventors exclusive rights for a limited period as an incentive for their inventiveness and research efforts. The authority of Congress is exercised in the hope that "[t]he productive effort thereby fostered will have a positive effect on society through the introduction of new products and processes of manufacture into the economy, and the emanations by way of increased employment and better lives for our citizens." *Kewanee [Oil Co. v. Bicron Corp.* 416 U.S.] supra, at 480.

The question before us in this case is a narrow one of statutory interpretation requiring us to construe 35 U.S.C.A. § 101, which provides:

> Whoever invents or discovers any new and useful process, machine, manufacture, or composition of matter, or any new and useful improvement thereof, may obtain a patent therefor, subject to the conditions and requirements of this title.

Specifically, we must determine whether respondent's micro-organism constitutes a "manufacture" or "composition of matter" within the meaning of the statute.

III.

In cases of statutory construction we begin, of course, with the language of the statute. And "unless otherwise defined, words will be interpreted as taking their ordinary, contemporary, common meaning." *Perrin v. United States*, 444 U.S. 37, (1979). We have also cautioned that courts "should not read into the patent laws limitations and conditions which the legislature has not expressed." *United States v. Dubilier Condenser Corp.*, 289 U.S. 178, 199, 53 S.Ct. 554, 561, 77 L.Ed. 1114, 17 U.S.P.Q. 154, 162 (1933).

Guided by these canons of construction, this Court has read the term "manufacture" in § 101 in accordance with its dictionary definition to mean "the production of articles for use from raw materials prepared by giving to these materials new forms, qualities, properties, or combinations whether by hand labor or by machinery." *American Fruit Growers, Inc. v. Brogdex Co.*, 283 U.S. 1, 11, (1931). Similarly, "composition of matter" has been construed consistent with its common usage to include "all compositions of two or more substances and ... all composite articles, whether they be the results of chemical union, or of mechanical mixture, or whether they be gases, fluids, powders, or solids." *Shell Dev. Co. v. Watson*, 149 F.Supp. 279, 280 (D.C.1957). In choosing such expansive terms as "manufacture" and "composition of matter," modified by the comprehensive "any," Congress plainly contemplated that the patent laws would be given wide scope.

The relevant legislative history also supports a broad construction. The Patent Act of 1793, authored by Thomas Jefferson, defined statutory subject matter as "any new and useful art, machine, manufacture, or composition of matter, or any new or useful improvement [thereof]." Act of Feb. 21, 1793, ch. 11, § 1, 1 Stat. 318. The Act embodied Jefferson's philosophy that "ingenuity should receive a liberal encouragement." V Writings of Thomas Jefferson, at 75–76. Subsequent patent statutes in 1836, 1870 and 1874 employed this same broad language. In 1952, when the patent laws were recodified, Congress replaced the word "art" with "process," but otherwise left Jefferson's language intact. The Committee Reports accompanying the 1952 act inform us that Congress intended statutory subject matter to "include anything under the sun that is made by man." S.Rep.No.1979, 82d Cong., 2d Sess., 5 (1952); H.R.Rep. No.1923, 82d Cong., 2d Sess., 6 (1952).

This is not to suggest that § 101 has no limits or that it embraces every discovery. The laws of nature, physical phenomena, and abstract ideas have been held not patentable. Thus, a new mineral discovered in the earth or a new plant found in the wild is not patentable subject matter. Likewise, Einstein could not patent his celebrated law that $E = mc^2$; nor could Newton have patented the law of gravity. Such discoveries are "manifestations of ... nature, free to all men and reserved exclusively to none." *Funk* [*Seed Co. v. Kalo* Co., 333 U.S.] supra, at 130, 76 U.S.P.Q. at 281.

Judged in this light, respondent's micro-organism plainly qualifies as patentable subject matter. His claim is not to a hitherto unknown natural phenomenon, but to a nonnaturally occurring manufacture or composition of matter—a product of human ingenuity "having a distinctive name, character [and] use." *Hartranft v. Wiegmann*, 121 U.S. 609, 615 (1887). The point is underscored dramatically by comparison of the invention here with that in Funk. There, the patentee had discovered that there existed in nature certain species of root-nodule bacteria which did not exert a mutually inhibitive effect on each other. He used that discovery to produce a mixed culture capable of inoculating the seeds of leguminous plants. Concluding that the patentee had discovered "only some of the handiwork of nature," the Court ruled the product nonpatentable:

> Each of the species of root-nodule bacteria contained in the package infects the same group of leguminous plants which it always infected. No species acquires a different use. The combination of the six species

produces no new bacteria, no change in the six bacteria, and no enlargement of the range of their utility. Each species has the same effect it always had. The bacteria perform in their natural way. Their use in combination does not improve in any way their natural functioning. They serve the same ends nature originally provided and act quite independently of any effort by the patentee. 333 U.S., at 127.

Here, by contrast, the patentee has produced a new bacterium with markedly different characteristics from any found in nature and one having the potential for significant utility. His discovery is not nature's handiwork, but his own; accordingly it is patentable subject matter under § 101.

IV.

Two contrary arguments are advanced, neither of which we find persuasive.

A.

The Government's first argument rests on the enactment of the 1930 Plant Patent Act, which afforded patent protection to certain asexually reproduced plants, and the 1970 Plant Variety Protection Act, which authorized patents for certain sexually reproduced plants but excluded bacteria from its protection. In the Government's view, the passage of these Acts evidences congressional understanding that the terms "manufacture" or "composition of matter" do not include living things; if they did, the Government argues, neither Act would have been necessary.

We reject this argument. Prior to 1930, two factors were thought to remove plants from patent protection. The first was the belief that plants, even those artificially bred, were products of nature for purposes of the patent law. This position appears to have derived from the decision of the Patent Office in *Ex parte Latimer*, 1889 C.D. 123, in which a patent claim for fiber found in the needle of the Pinus australis was rejected. The Commissioner reasoned that a contrary result would permit "patents [to] be obtained upon the trees of the forests and the plants of the earth, which of course would be unreasonable and impossible." Id., at 126. The Latimer case, it seems, came to "set[ ] forth the general stand taken in these matters" that plants were natural products not subject to patent protection. H. Thorne, Relation of Patent Law to Natural Products, 6 J.Pat.Off. Soc. 23, 24 (1923). The second obstacle to patent protection for plants was the fact that plants were thought not amenable to the "written description" requirement of the patent law. Because new plants may differ from old only in color or perfume, differentiation by written description was often impossible....

Congress thus recognized that the relevant distinction was not between living and inanimate things, but between products of nature, whether living or not, and human-made inventions. Here respondent's microorganism is the result of human ingenuity and research. Hence, the passage of the Plant Patent Act affords the Government no support.

Nor does the passage of the 1970 Plant Variety Protection Act support the Government's position. As the Government acknowledges, sexually reproduced plants were not included under the 1930 Act because new varieties could not be reproduced true-to-type through seedlings. By 1970, however, it was generally recognized that true-to-type reproduction was possible and that plant patent protection was therefore appropriate. The 1970 Act extended that protection. There is nothing in its language or history to suggest that it was enacted because § 101 did not include living things. . . .

B.

The Government's second argument is that micro-organisms cannot qualify as patentable subject matter until Congress expressly authorizes such protection. Its position rests on the fact that genetic technology was unforeseen when Congress enacted § 101. From this it is argued that resolution of the patentability of inventions such as respondent's should be left to Congress. The legislative process, the Government argues, is best equipped to weigh the competing economic, social, and scientific considerations involved, and to determine whether living organisms produced by genetic engineering should receive patent protection. In support of this position, the Government relies on our recent holding in *Parker v. Flook*, 437 U.S. 584 (1978), and the statement that the judiciary "must proceed cautiously when ... asked to extend patent rights into areas wholly unforeseen by Congress." Id., at 596.

It is, of course, correct that Congress, not the courts, must define the limits of patentability; but it is equally true that once Congress has spoken it is "the province and duty of the judicial department to say what the law is." *Marbury v. Madison*, 1 Cranch 137, 177 (1803). Congress has performed its constitutional role in defining patentable subject matter in § 101; we perform ours in construing the language Congress has employed. In so doing, our obligation is to take statutes as we find them, guided, if ambiguity appears, by the legislative history and statutory purpose. Here, we perceive no ambiguity. The subject matter provisions of the patent law have been cast in broad terms to fulfill the constitutional and statutory goal of promoting "the Progress of Science and the useful Arts" with all that means for the social and economic benefits envisioned by Jefferson. Broad general language is not necessarily ambiguous when congressional objectives require broad terms. . . .

To buttress its argument, the Government, with the support of amicus, points to grave risks that may be generated by research endeavors such as respondent's. The briefs present a gruesome parade of horribles. Scientists, among them Nobel laureates, are quoted suggesting that genetic research may pose a serious threat to the human race, or, at the very least, that the dangers are far too substantial to permit such research to proceed apace at this time. We are told that genetic research and related technological developments may spread pollution and disease, that it may result in a loss of genetic diversity, and that its practice may tend to depreciate the value of human life. These arguments are forcefully, even passionately presented; they remind us that, at times, human ingenuity seems unable to control fully the forces it creates—that, with Hamlet, it is sometimes better "to bear those ills we have than fly to others that we know not of."

It is argued that this Court should weigh these potential hazards in considering whether respondent's invention is patentable subject matter under § 101. We disagree. The grant or denial of patents on microorganisms is not likely to put an end to genetic research or to its attendant risks. The large amount of research that has already occurred when no researcher had sure knowledge that patent protection would be available suggests that legislative or judicial fiat as to patentability will not deter the scientific mind from probing into the unknown any more than Canute could command the tides. Whether respondent's claims are patentable may determine whether research efforts are accelerated by the hope of reward or slowed by want of incentives, but that is all.

What is more important is that we are without competence to entertain these arguments—either to brush them aside as fantasies generated by fear of the unknown, or to act on them. The choice we are urged to make is a matter of high policy for resolution within the legislative process after the kind of investigation, examination, and study that legislative bodies can provide and courts cannot. That process involves the balancing of competing values and interests, which in our democratic system is the business of elected representatives. Whatever their validity, the contentions now pressed on us should be addressed to the political branches of the government, the Congress and the Executive, and not to the courts.

We have emphasized in the recent past that "[o]ur individual appraisal of the wisdom or unwisdom of a particular [legislative] course ... is to be put aside in the process of interpreting a statute." *TVA v. Hill*, 437 U.S. 153, 194 (1978). Our task, rather, is the narrow one of determining what Congress meant by the words it used in the statute; once that is done our powers are exhausted. Congress is free to amend § 101 so as to exclude from patent protection organisms produced by genetic engineering. Compare 42 U.S.C.A. § 2181, exempting from patent protection inventions "useful solely in the utilization of special nuclear material or atomic energy in an atomic weapon." Or it may choose to craft a statute specifically designed for such living things. But, until Congress takes such action, this Court must construe the language of § 101 as it is. The language of that section fairly embraces respondent's invention.

Accordingly, the judgment of the Court of Customs and Patent Appeals is affirmed.

Affirmed.

[The opinion of BRENNAN, J., dissenting, is omitted.]

State Street Bank & Trust Co. v. Signature Financial Group, Inc.

United States Court of Appeals, Federal Circuit, 1998.
149 F.3d 1368, 47 U.S.P.Q.2d 1596, *cert. denied*, 525 U.S. 1093, 119 S.Ct. 851, 142 L.Ed.2d 704.

RICH, Circuit Judge.

Signature Financial Group, Inc. (Signature) appeals from the decision of the United States District Court for the District of Massachusetts granting a motion for summary judgment in favor of State Street Bank & Trust Co. (State Street), finding U.S. Patent No. 5,193,056 (the '056 patent) invalid on the ground that the claimed subject matter is not encompassed by 35 U.S.C. § 101 (1994). We reverse and remand because we conclude that the patent claims are directed to statutory subject matter.

BACKGROUND

Signature is the assignee of the '056 patent which is entitled "Data Processing System for Hub and Spoke Financial Services Configuration." The '056 patent issued to Signature on 9 March 1993, naming R. Todd Boes as the inventor. The '056 patent is generally directed to a data processing system (the system) for implementing an investment structure which was developed for use in Signature's business as an administrator and accounting agent for mutual funds. In essence, the system, identified by the proprietary name Hub and Spoke (R), facilitates a structure whereby mutual funds (Spokes) pool their assets in an investment portfolio (Hub) organized as a partnership. This investment configuration provides the administrator of a mutual fund with the advantageous combination of economies of scale in administering investments coupled with the tax advantages of a partnership.

State Street and Signature are both in the business of acting as custodians and accounting agents for multi-tiered partnership fund financial services. State Street negotiated with Signature for a license to use its patented data processing system described and claimed in the '056 patent. When negotiations broke down, State Street brought a declaratory judgment action asserting invalidity, unenforceability, and noninfringement in Massachusetts district court, and then filed a motion for partial summary judgment of patent invalidity for failure to claim statutory subject matter under § 101. The motion was granted and this appeal followed.

DISCUSSION

On appeal, we are not bound to give deference to the district court's grant of summary judgment, but must make an independent determination that the standards for summary judgment have been met. Summary judgment is properly granted where there are no genuine issues of material fact and the moving party is entitled to judgment as a matter of law. The substantive issue at hand, whether the '056 patent is invalid for failure to claim statutory subject matter under § 101, is a matter of both claim construction and statutory construction. "[W]e review claim construction *de novo* including any allegedly fact-based questions relating to claim construction." *Cybor Corp. v. FAS Techs.*, 138 F.3d 1448, 1451, 46 USPQ2d 1169, 1174 (Fed.Cir.1998) (*in banc*). We also review statutory construction *de novo*. We hold that declaratory judgment plaintiff State Street was not entitled to the grant of summary judgment of invalidity of the '056 patent under § 101 as a matter of law, because the patent claims are directed to statutory subject matter.

The following facts pertinent to the statutory subject matter issue are either undisputed or represent the version alleged by the nonmovant. The patented invention relates generally to a system that allows an administrator to monitor and record the financial information flow and make all calculations necessary for maintaining a partner fund financial services configuration. As previously mentioned, a partner fund financial services configuration essentially allows several mutual funds, or "Spokes," to pool their investment funds into a single portfolio, or "Hub," allowing for consolidation of, inter alia, the costs of administering the fund combined with the tax advantages of a partnership. In particular, this system provides means for a daily allocation of assets for two or more Spokes that are invested in the same Hub. The system determines the percentage share that each Spoke maintains in the Hub, while taking into consideration daily changes both in the value of the Hub's investment securities and in the concomitant amount of each Spoke's assets.

In determining daily changes, the system also allows for the allocation among the Spokes of the Hub's daily income, expenses, and net realized and unrealized gain or loss, calculating each day's total investments based on the concept of a book capital account. This enables the determination of a true asset value of each Spoke and accurate calculation of allocation ratios between or among the Spokes. The system additionally tracks all the relevant data determined on a daily basis for the Hub and each Spoke, so that aggregate year end income, expenses, and capital gain or loss can be determined for accounting and for tax purposes for the Hub and, as a result, for each publicly traded Spoke.

It is essential that these calculations are quickly and accurately performed. In large part this is required because each Spoke sells shares to the public and the price of those shares is substantially based on the Spoke's percentage interest in the portfolio. In some instances, a mutual fund administrator is required to calculate the value of the shares to the nearest penny within as little as an hour and a half after the market closes. Given the complexity of the calculations, a computer or equivalent device is a virtual necessity to perform the task.

The '056 patent application was filed 11 March 1991. It initially contained six "machine" claims, which incorporated means-plus-function clauses, and six method claims. According to Signature, during prosecution the examiner contemplated a § 101 rejection for failure to claim statutory subject matter. However, upon cancellation of the six method claims, the examiner issued a notice of allowance for the remaining present six claims on appeal. Only claim 1 is an independent claim.

The district court began its analysis by construing the claims to be directed to a process, with each "means" clause merely representing a step in that process. However, "machine" claims having "means" clauses may only be reasonably viewed as process claims if there is no supporting structure in the written description that corresponds to the claimed "means" elements. This is not the case now before us.

When independent claim 1 is properly construed in accordance with § 112, ¶ 6, it is directed to a machine, as demonstrated below, where representative claim 1 is set forth, the subject matter in brackets stating the structure the written description discloses as corresponding to the respective "means" recited in the claims.

1.   A data processing system for managing a financial services configuration of a portfolio established as a partnership, each partner being one of a plurality of funds, comprising:

(a) computer processor means [a personal computer including a CPU] for processing data;

(b) storage means [a data disk] for storing data on a storage medium;

(c) first means [an arithmetic logic circuit configured to prepare the data disk to magnetically store selected data] for initializing the storage medium;

(d) second means [an arithmetic logic circuit configured to retrieve information from a specific file, calculate incremental increases or decreases based on specific input, allocate the results on a percentage basis, and store the output in a separate file] for processing data regarding assets in the portfolio and each of the funds from a previous day and data regarding increases or decreases in each of the funds, [sic, funds'] assets and for allocating the percentage share that each fund holds in the portfolio;

(e) third means [an arithmetic logic circuit configured to retrieve information from a specific file, calculate incremental increases and decreases based on specific input, allocate the results on a percentage basis and store the output in a separate file] for processing data regarding daily incremental income, expenses, and net realized gain or loss for the portfolio and for allocating such data among each fund;

(f) fourth means [an arithmetic logic circuit configured to retrieve information from a specific file, calculate incremental increases and decreases based on specific input, allocate the results on a percentage basis and store the output in a separate file] for processing data regarding daily net unrealized gain or loss for the portfolio and for allocating such data among each fund; and

(g) fifth means [an arithmetic logic circuit configured to retrieve information from specific files, calculate that information on an aggregate basis and store the output in a separate file] for processing data regarding aggregate year-end income, expenses, and capital gain or loss for the portfolio and each of the funds.

Each claim component, recited as a "means" plus its function, is to be read, of course, pursuant to § 112, ¶ 6, as inclusive of the "equivalents" of the structures disclosed in the written description portion of the specification. Thus, claim 1, properly construed, claims a machine, namely, a data processing system for managing a financial services configuration of a portfolio established as a partnership, which machine is made up of, at the very least, the specific structures disclosed in the written description and corresponding to the means-plus-function elements (a)-(g) recited in the claim. A "machine" is proper statutory subject matter under § 101. We note that, for the purposes of a § 101 analysis, it is of little relevance whether claim 1 is directed to a "machine" or a "process," as long as it falls within at least one of the four enumerated categories of patentable subject matter, "machine" and "process" being such categories.

This does not end our analysis, however, because the court concluded that the claimed subject matter fell into one of two alternative judicially-created exceptions to statutory subject matter. The court refers to the first exception as the "mathematical algorithm" exception and the second exception as the "business method" exception. Section 101 reads:

> Whoever invents or discovers any new and useful process, machine, manufacture, or composition of matter, or any new and useful improvement thereof, may obtain a patent therefor, subject to the conditions and requirements of this title.

The plain and unambiguous meaning of § 101 is that any invention falling within one of the four stated categories of statutory subject matter may be patented, provided it meets the other requirements for patentability set forth in Title 35, i.e., those found in §§ 102, 103, and 112, ¶ 2.

The repetitive use of the expansive term "any" in § 101 shows Congress's intent not to place any restrictions on the subject matter for which a patent may be obtained beyond those specifically recited in § 101. Indeed, the Supreme Court has acknowledged that Congress intended § 101 to extend to "anything under the sun that is made by man." *Diamond v. Chakrabarty,* 447 U.S. 303, 309, 100 S.Ct. 2204, 65 L.Ed.2d 144 (1980); *see also Diamond v. Diehr,* 450 U.S. 175, 182, 101 S.Ct. 1048, 67 L.Ed.2d 155 (1981). Thus, it is improper to read limitations into § 101 on the subject matter that may be patented where the legislative history indicates that Congress clearly did not intend such limitations.

The "Mathematical Algorithm" Exception

The Supreme Court has identified three categories of subject matter that are unpatentable, namely "laws of nature, natural phenomena, and abstract ideas." *Diehr,* 450 U.S. at 185, 101 S.Ct. 1048. Of particular relevance to this case, the Court has held that mathematical algorithms are not patentable subject matter to the extent that they are merely abstract ideas. In *Diehr,* the Court explained that certain types of mathematical subject matter, standing alone, represent nothing more than abstract ideas until reduced to some type of practical application, i.e., "a useful, concrete and tangible result." *Alappat,* 33 F.3d at 1544, 31 USPQ2d at 1557.

Unpatentable mathematical algorithms are identifiable by showing they are merely abstract ideas constituting disembodied concepts or truths that are not "useful." From a practical standpoint, this means that to be patentable an algorithm must be applied in a "useful" way. In *Alappat,* we held that data, transformed by a machine through a series of mathematical calculations to produce a smooth waveform display on a rasterizer monitor, constituted a practical application of an abstract idea (a mathematical algorithm, formula, or calculation), because it produced "a useful, concrete and tangible result"—the smooth waveform.

Similarly, in *Arrhythmia Research Technology Inc. v. Corazonix Corp.,* 958 F.2d 1053, 22 USPQ2d 1033 (Fed.Cir.1992), we held that the transformation of electrocardiograph signals from a patient's heartbeat by a machine through a series of mathematical calculations constituted a practical application of an abstract idea (a mathematical algorithm, formula, or calculation), because it corresponded to a useful, concrete or tangible thing—the condition of a patient's heart.

Today, we hold that the transformation of data, representing discrete dollar amounts, by a machine through a series of mathematical calculations into a final share price, constitutes a practical application of a mathematical algorithm, formula, or calculation, because it produces "a useful, concrete and tangible result"—a final share price momentarily fixed for recording and reporting purposes and even accepted and relied upon by regulatory authorities and in subsequent trades.

The district court erred by applying the Freeman–Walter–Abele test to determine whether the claimed subject matter was an unpatentable abstract idea. The Freeman–Walter–Abele test was designed by the Court of Customs and Patent Appeals, and subsequently adopted by this court, to extract and identify unpatentable mathematical algorithms in the aftermath of *Benson* and *Flook. See In re Freeman,* 573 F.2d 1237, 197 USPQ 464 (CCPA 1978) as modified by *In re Walter,* 618 F.2d 758, 205 USPQ 397 (CCPA 1980). The test has been thus articulated:

> First, the claim is analyzed to determine whether a mathematical algorithm is directly or indirectly recited. Next, if a mathematical algorithm is found, the claim as a whole is further analyzed to determine whether the algorithm is "applied in any manner to physical elements or process steps," and, if it is, it "passes muster under § 101."

In re Pardo, 684 F.2d 912, 915, 214 USPQ 673, 675–76 (CCPA 1982) (citing *In re Abele,* 684 F.2d 902, 214 .U.S.P.Q. 682 (CCPA 1982)).

After *Diehr* and *Chakrabarty,* the Freeman–Walter–Abele test has little, if any, applicability to determining the presence of statutory subject matter. As we pointed out in *Alappat,* 33 F.3d at 1543, 31 USPQ2d at 1557, application of the test could be misleading, because a process, machine, manufacture, or composition of matter employing a law of nature, natural phenomenon, or abstract idea is patentable subject matter even though a law of nature, natural phenomenon, or abstract idea would not, by itself, be entitled to such protection. The test determines the presence of, for example, an algorithm. Under *Benson,* this may have been a sufficient indicium of nonstatutory subject matter. However, after *Diehr* and *Alappat,* the mere fact that a claimed invention involves inputting numbers, calculating numbers, outputting numbers, and storing numbers, in and of itself, would not render it nonstatutory subject matter, unless, of course, its operation does not produce a "useful, concrete and tangible result." *Alappat,* 33 F.3d at 1544, 31 USPQ2d at 1557. After all, as we have repeatedly stated,

> every step-by-step process, be it electronic or chemical or mechanical, involves an algorithm in the broad sense of the term. Since § 101 expressly includes processes as a category of inventions which may be patented and § 100(b) further defines the word "process" as meaning "process, art or method, and includes a new use of a known process, machine, manufacture, composition of matter, or material," it follows that it is no ground for holding a claim is directed to nonstatutory subject matter to say it includes or is directed to an algorithm. This is why the proscription against patenting has been limited to *mathematical* algorithms. . . .

The question of whether a claim encompasses statutory subject matter should not focus on *which* of the four categories of subject matter a claim is directed to—process, machine, manufacture, or composition of matter—but rather on the essential characteristics of the subject matter, in particular, its practical utility. Section 101 specifies that statutory subject matter must also satisfy the other "conditions and requirements" of Title 35, including novelty, nonobviousness, and adequacy of disclosure and notice. For purpose of our analysis, as noted above, claim 1 is directed to a machine programmed with the Hub and Spoke software and admittedly produces a "useful, concrete, and tangible result." *Alappat,* 33 F.3d at 1544, 31 USPQ2d at 1557. This renders it statutory subject matter, even if the useful result is expressed in numbers, such as price, profit, percentage, cost, or loss.

The Business Method Exception

As an alternative ground for invalidating the '056 patent under § 101, the court relied on the judicially-created, so-called "business method" exception to statutory subject matter. We take this opportunity to lay this ill-conceived exception to rest. Since its inception, the "business method" exception has merely represented the application of some general, but no longer applicable legal principle, perhaps arising out of the "requirement for invention"—which was eliminated by § 103. Since the 1952 Patent Act, business methods have been, and should have been, subject to the same legal requirements for patentability as applied to any other process or method.

The business method exception has never been invoked by this court, or the CCPA, to deem an invention unpatentable. Application of this particular exception has always been preceded by a ruling based on some clearer concept of Title 35 or, more commonly, application of the abstract idea exception based on finding a mathematical algorithm. Illustrative is the CCPA's analysis in *In re Howard,* 55 C.C.P.A. 1121, 394 F.2d 869, 157 USPQ 615 (CCPA 1968), wherein the court affirmed the Board of Appeals' rejection of the claims for lack of novelty and found it unnecessary to reach the Board's section 101 ground that a method of doing business is "inherently unpatentable." *Id.* at 872, 55 C.C.P.A. 1121, 394 F.2d 869, 157 USPQ at 617.

Similarly, *In re Schrader,* 22 F.3d 290, 30 USPQ2d 1455 (Fed.Cir. 1994), while making reference to the business method exception, turned on the fact that the claims implicitly recited an abstract idea in the form of a mathematical algorithm and there was no "transformation or conversion of subject matter representative of or constituting physical activity or objects." 22 F.3d at 294, 30 USPQ2d at 1459 (emphasis omitted).

State Street argues that we acknowledged the validity of the business method exception in *Alappat* when we discussed *Maucorps* and *Meyer:*

> *Maucorps* dealt with a business methodology for deciding how salesmen should best handle respective customers and *Meyer* involved a "system" for aiding a neurologist in diagnosing patients. Clearly, neither of the alleged "inventions" in those cases falls within any § 101 category.

Alappat, 33 F.3d at 1541, 31 USPQ2d at 1555. However, closer scrutiny of these cases reveals that the claimed inventions in both *Maucorps* and *Meyer* were rejected as abstract ideas under the mathematical algorithm exception, not the business method exception.

Even the case frequently cited as establishing the business method exception to statutory subject matter, *Hotel Security Checking Co. v. Lorraine Co.,* 160 F. 467 (2d Cir.1908), did not rely on the exception to strike the patent. In that case, the patent was found invalid for lack of novelty and "invention," not because it was improper subject matter for a patent. The court stated "the fundamental principle of the system is as old as the art of bookkeeping, i.e., charging the goods of the employer to the agent who takes them." *Id.* at 469. "If at the time of [the patent] application, there had been no system of bookkeeping of any kind in restaurants, we would be confronted with the question whether a new and useful system of cash registering and account checking is such an art as is patentable under the statute." *Id.* at 472.

This case is no exception. The district court announced the precepts of the business method exception as set forth in several treatises, but noted as its primary reason for finding the patent invalid under the business method exception as follows:

> If Signature's invention were patentable, any financial institution desirous of implementing a multi-tiered funding complex modelled (sic) on a Hub and Spoke configuration would be required to seek Signature's permission before embarking on such a project. *This is so because the '056 Patent is claimed [sic] sufficiently broadly to foreclose virtually any computer-implemented accounting method necessary to manage this type of financial structure.*

927 F.Supp. 502, 516, 38 USPQ2d 1530, 1542 (emphasis added). Whether the patent's claims are too broad to be patentable is not to be judged under § 101, but rather under §§ 102, 103 and 112. Assuming the above state-

ment to be correct, it has nothing to do with whether what is claimed is statutory subject matter.

In view of this background, it comes as no surprise that in the most recent edition of the Manual of Patent Examining Procedures (MPEP) (1996), a paragraph of § 706.03(a) was deleted. In past editions it read:

> Though seemingly within the category of process or method, a method of doing business can be rejected as not being within the statutory classes.

MPEP § 706.03(a) (1994). This acknowledgment is buttressed by the U.S. Patent and Trademark 1996 Examination Guidelines for Computer Related Inventions which now read:

> Office personnel have had difficulty in properly treating claims directed to methods of doing business. Claims should not be categorized as methods of doing business. Instead such claims should be treated like any other process claims.

Examination Guidelines, 61 Fed.Reg. 7478, 7479 (1996). We agree that this is precisely the manner in which this type of claim should be treated. Whether the claims are directed to subject matter within § 101 should not turn on whether the claimed subject matter does "business" instead of something else.

CONCLUSION

The appealed decision is reversed and the case is remanded to the district court for further proceedings consistent with this opinion.

REVERSED and *REMANDED*.

NOTES

1. *What Should Patent Law Protect?* Patent law withholds protection for different reasons. Of the three categories identified in *Chakrabarty*—"laws of nature, physical phenomena, and abstract ideas"—the last is unprotectible because abstract ideas are essential tools of invention that should be freely available to all; the second, such as a new plant found in the wild, is unprotectible because physical phenomena are the product of discovery rather than invention; and the first, such as the law of gravity, is unprotectible for both reasons. Patents may also be withheld under the so-called "mental steps" and "printed matter" doctrines if the invention contemplates the exercise of human judgment, which is variable, rather than technological steps, which are not.

None of these exceptions is absolute, for in most cases claims can be drafted to avoid the standard objections to patentability. Mental steps and printed matter, if claimed in the context of a programmed digital computer, will be patentable so long as they meet the patent statute's other standards. As indicated in *State Street Bank*, mathematical algorithms, although "not patentable subject matter to the extent that they are merely abstract ideas," can be patented to the extent that they correspond "to a useful, concrete or tangible result." The law of gravity is itself not patentable, but the countless inventions that embody it certainly are.

Is it necessarily true that, as technological building blocks, natural principles are too important to be subjected to private control? What dangers, if any, would in fact attend private control of basic principles? What effect, if any, does the absence of patent protection have on private incentives to invest in the research required to discover and apply important and far-reaching principles? Can firm size, industry structure and public subsidies safely be relied on to produce the needed level and direction of investment in basic research?

If patents are withheld from "a new mineral discovered in the earth or a new plant found in the wild," will firms underinvest in the search for such minerals and plants? If society would benefit from a newly discovered mineral or plant—and suffer correspondingly if the mineral or plant were not discovered—-can society be said to be worse off if a patent for a limited term were granted as an inducement to these discoveries? Is it correct to assume that existing minerals and plants will at some point be discovered even without the promise of a patent, but that a new bacterium, not existing in nature, would not have been created unless it could be patented?

See generally Michael D. Davis, The Patenting of Products of Nature, 21 Rutgers Comp. & Tech. L. J. 293 (1995).

2. *Patenting Animals.* The evolution of life forms as patentable subject matter since *Chakrabarty* was rapid and increasingly controversial. In 1987 the Board of Patent Appeals and Interferences held that certain man-made, non-naturally occurring polyploid oysters were patentable subject matter. In re Allen, 2 U.S.P.Q.2d 1425 (1987). Four days later the Commissioner of Patents and Trademarks announced the Office's intention to treat "nonnaturally occurring non-human multicellular organisms, including animals, [as] patentable subject matter." The Patent and Trademark Office later agreed to an eight-month moratorium on animal patents at the request of Robert Kastenmeier, Chairman of the House Subcommittee on Courts, Civil Liberties and the Administration of Justice. 36 Pat., Trademark & Copyr.J. 272 (1988). On April 12, 1988, after the voluntary moratorium had expired, the Patent and Trademark Office issued its first animal patent. The patent was for a mouse, developed by researchers at Harvard University, that had been genetically altered to facilitate cancer research, U.S. Patent No. 4,736,866.

Moral and economic arguments have dominated the debate over animal patents. In the view of the General Secretary of the National Council of Churches, "[t]he gift of life from God, in all its forms and species, should not be regarded solely as if it were a chemical product, subject to genetic alteration and patentable for economic benefit." The National Farmers Union said "it favors a moratorium on patenting animals until the impact on the farm animal gene pool can be assessed and royalty obligations understood. The Humane Society of America worries that animals will suffer as a result of human genes being spliced into their genetic code for experimental and possibly for commercial purposes." Crawford, Religious Groups Join Animal Patent Battle, 237 Science 480 (1987).

See generally, Geri J. Yonover, What Hath (Not) *Chakrabarty* Wrought: From the "Mouse That Roared" to "Hello Dolly" and Beyond, 32 Val. U. L. Rev. 349 (1998), Thomas Traian Moga, Transgenic Animals as Intellectual Property (or the Patented Mouse that Roared), 76 J. Pat. & Trademark Off. Soc'y 511 (1994); Reid G. Adler, Controlling the Applications of Biotechnology: A Critical Analysis of the Proposed Moratorium on Animal Patenting, 1 Harv. J. Law & Tech. 1 (1988).

3. *Medical Procedures.* If medical devices and pharmaceuticals are patentable as machines and compositions of matter, are medical procedures, such as a technique for eye surgery, protectible as patentable processes? Although the Patent Office at one time rejected patents for medical and surgical procedures on the ground that they affect human behavior or depend on human judgment for their execution, closely drafted claims can nonetheless bring such procedures within the patent realm.

Whatever their success in the Patent Office, patents for medical procedures have not won widespread acceptance in the medical profession. Responding to a case in which one eye surgeon sued another for infringement of his patent on a cataract surgery technique, Pallin v. Singer, 36 U.S.P.Q. 2d 1050 (D.Vt.1995), the American Medical Association succeeded in obtaining an amendment to the Patent Act which, although implicitly accepting the patentability of medical procedures, generally eliminates any infringement remedies against "a medical practitioner's performance of a medical activity." 35 U.S.C. § 287 (c). The provision does, however, allow remedies against infringing machines, manufactures, compositions of matter or uses of compositions of matter.

See generally, Todd Martin, Patentability of Methods of Medical Treatment: A Comparative Study, 82 J. Pat. & Trademark Off. Soc'y 381 (2000).

4. *"New Use" Patents.* The 1952 amendments to the Patent Act replaced the term "art" with "process" and defined "process" to mean "process, art or method, and includes a new use of a known process, machine, manufacture, composition of matter, or material." 35 U.S.C.A. § 101(b). The definition confirmed a line of decisions that had allowed the grant of process patents for new uses of old products, such as the use of the old and well-known compound, DDT, in insects sprays. Ex parte Muller, 81 U.S.P.Q. 261 (Pat.Off.Bd.App.1947). The new definition also dispelled the lingering question left by a much earlier decision, Morton v. New York Eye Infirmary, 17 F.Cas. 879 (C.C.S.D.N.Y.1862) (No. 9865), which held that plaintiffs, who had discovered the anesthetic qualities of the old compound, ether, were not entitled to a patent on the process of using ether as an anesthetic in surgery.

The claimed invention in a "new use" patent will often combine an old process and an old product to produce a new result. Does this suggest that "new use" applicants will face higher hurdles under patent law's nonobviousness standard than applicants whose subject matter involves entirely new processes or products? As a practical matter, what range of protection will a patented "new use" receive? Since the patent owner will typically have no rights in the old product, it can bring a direct infringement action only against those who use the old product according to the method described in the patent. How much success is the patent owner likely to enjoy in bringing a contributory infringement action against the manufacturer of the old product that is used to infringe the process patent?

5. *Plant Patents.* A bare handful of judicial decisions have defined the scope and thrust of the Plant Patent Act, 35 U.S.C.A. §§ 161–164, discussed in *Chakrabarty*. Legislative history has been particularly influential. In answering the question, "what is meant by 'invented or discovered' and by 'new variety of plant' in the statute," The Board of Appeals in Ex parte Foster, 90 U.S.P.Q. 16 (1951), turned to the legislative history to determine whether "these words mean that the plant must be new in fact in the sense that the plant did not exist before," or whether "they include what is old and has existed before but what has been merely newly found." "The bill which resulted in the Act was Senate Bill 4015 introduced March 24, 1930, by Senator Townsend, superseding a previous bill, S. 3530 February 11, 1930. This bill defined the added class of patentable subject matter in the words in italics in the following quotation from the bill: 'Any person ... *who has invented or discovered and asexually reproduced (1) any distinct and new variety of plant or (2) any distinct and newly found variety of plant, other than a tuberpropagated plant, ... may ...* obtain a patent therefore.' Two classes of plants were thus specified in the bill, one, distinct and new varieties of plants, and two, distinct and newly found varieties of plants, and a clear distinction made between new plants and newly found plants."

"The Senate Committee on Patents reported the bill favorably, with amendments, Senate Report No. 315, 71st Congress, April 3, 1930. One of the amendments consisted in striking out from the bill the words 'or (2) any distinct and newly found variety of plant,' thus eliminating newly found plants from the scope of the bill. In explanation of this amendment the Senate Committee Report (page 1) states that it 'eliminates from the scope of the bill patents for varieties of plants which exist in an uncultivated or wild state, but are newly found by plant explorers or others.' " 90 U.S.P.Q. at 17–18.

For a richly detailed account of the origins of plant patents in the U.S., see Cary Fowler, The Plant Patent Act of 1930: A Sociological History of Its Creation, 82 J. Patent & Trademark Off. Soc'y 621 (2000).

6. *Plant Variety Protection Act.* The plant patent provisions authorize protection only for asexually reproduced plant varieties. The Plant Variety Protection Act, enacted December 24, 1970, Pub.L. No. 91–577, 84 Stat. 1542, and amended on December 22, 1980, Pub.L. No. 96–574, 94 Stat. 3350, offers protection for new varieties of plants that reproduce sexually, through seeds. A certificate of plant variety protection will issue if the applicant's variety meets the statutory requirements of distinctness, uniformity and stability, and passes several novelty and other statutory bars comparable to those imposed by section 102 of the Patent Act. 7 U.S.C. § 2402. Protection lasts for a period of twenty years from the date the certificate is issued. 7 U.S.C. § 2483(b). The Act is administered by the Plant Variety Protection Office in the United States Department of Agriculture.

Among the reasons given for enacting the Plant Variety Protection Act was that "it will allow our Government Agricultural experiment stations to increase their efforts on needed basic research." Also, according to the House Report, "the new law will definitely stimulate plant breeding. Experience in England provides a good case history. Prior to the enactment of its Plant Varieties and Seeds Act 1964, little plant breeding was done in England by private companies, and not much was done by government agencies. Since the new law came into effect, there has been a great upsurge of plant breeding, and a once moribund seed industry is now showing signs of great new vitality." H.R.Rep. No. 91–1605, 91st Cong., 2d Sess. (1970).

As the dissenters in *Chakrabarty* perhaps foresaw, the majority opinion may have reduced the attractions of plant variety protection since utility patents offer seed developers greater protection than do plant variety protection certificates. Observing that the PTO "has issued some 1,800 utility patents for plants, plant parts and seeds pursuant to 35 U.S.C. § 101," the Supreme Court subsequently ruled that neither the Plant Patent Act nor the Plant Variety Protection Act "forecloses utility patent coverage for plants." J.E.M. AG Supply, Inc. v. Pioneer Hi–Bred International, Inc., 534 U.S. 124, 122 Ct. 593, 151 L.Ed.2d 508, 60 U.S.P.Q2d 1865 (2001).

7. *Foreign Practice: Utility Models and Petty Patents.* Some worthwhile inventions will fail to meet a patent statute's high inventive standard or will lack the market value to justify the lengthy patent examination process. Rather than leave these modest inventions to the uncertainties of unfair competition protection—or to the public domain—many countries, but not the United States, supplement utility patents with "petty patents" or "utility models" that require only registration, not examination, provide a significantly shorter term of protection and, though imposing the traditional novelty requirement, do not impose a patent law standard of nonobviousness or inventiveness. Britain, which introduced the concept of the utility model in 1843, Act. 6 & 7 Vict. ch. 65, dropped the system forty years later, and is one of the few European countries without utility model legislation.

2. STATUTORY STANDARDS

See Statute Supplement 35 U.S.C.A. §§ 101–105, 111, 112, 116–120, 256.

a. Section 102: Novelty and the Statutory Bars

Application of Borst

United States Court of Customs and Patent Appeals, 1965.
52 C.C.P.A. 1398, 345 F.2d 851, 145 U.S.P.Q. 554, cert. denied, 382 U.S. 973, 86 S.Ct. 537, 15 L.Ed.2d 465, 148 U.S.P.Q. 771.

SMITH, Judge.

The invention for which appellant seeks a patent comprises means for safely and effectively controlling a relatively large neutron output by varying a small and easily controlled neutron input source....

Appellant asserts that the claimed invention affords a revolutionary approach to the safety problem in the nuclear reactor art. As the amplifier is said to be inherently safe from divergent nuclear chain reaction, the intricate systems needed to monitor and control the operation of conventional neutron amplifiers to prevent an explosion are unnecessary.

The single reference relied upon by the Patent Office in rejecting the appealed claims is an Atomic Energy Commission document entitled "KAPL–M–RWS–1, A Stable Fission Pile with High Speed Control." The document is in the form of an unpublished memorandum authored by one Samsel, and will hereinafter be referred to as "Samsel." Samsel is dated February 14, 1947 and was classified as a secret document by the Commission until March 9, 1957, when it was declassified. In essence, Samsel sets forth and discusses the problems present in the control of a nuclear reactor, the concept of use of successive fuel stages to effect such control, and a description of the arrangement, composition and relative proportions of materials required to obtain the sought-for results. Samsel is prefaced by a statement that it was made to record an idea, and it nowhere indicates that the idea had been tested in an operating reactor.

The Patent Office does not invoke Samsel as a publication (which it apparently was not, at any pertinent date). Rather, the contention is that Samsel constitutes evidence of prior knowledge within the meaning of 35 U.S.C.A. § 102(a).

While there seems to be some disagreement on the part of the solicitor, we think the most reasonable interpretation of the examiner's rejection, and one which is concurred in by the board and by appellant, is that claims 27, 30, 31 and 32 are fully met by Samsel and thus the subject matter defined therein is unpatentable because it was known by another in this country prior to appellant's invention thereof. As to claims 28, 29 and 33, even though not fully met by Samsel, they are said to be obvious within the meaning of 35 U.S.C.A. § 103 in view of the prior knowledge evidenced by Samsel.

Our own independent consideration of Samsel has convinced us that it contains adequate enabling disclosure of the invention of claims 27 and 30–32, and appellant does not appear to contend otherwise. Rather, appellant contends that Samsel is not available as evidence of prior knowledge under sections 102(a) and 103. Appellant also argues that, even if Samsel is available, the subject matter of claims 28, 29 and 33 is not obvious in view thereof. We agree with this characterization of the essential issues presented on this appeal, and will treat them in the order stated above.

In the case of In re Schlittler, 234 F.2d 882, 43 C.C.P.A. 986, this court was presented with the following situation: A manuscript containing an anticipatory disclosure of the appellants' claimed invention had been submitted to The Journal of the American Chemical Society and was later published. The date to which the appellants' application was entitled for purposes of constructive reduction to practice was earlier than the publication date of the Journal article, and therefore the Patent Office did not contend that the "printed publication" portion of section 102(a) was applicable. However, the manuscript bore a notation that it had been received by the publisher on a date prior to the effective filing date of the appellants' application. On the basis of this notation the Patent Office argued that the article constituted sufficient evidence of prior knowledge under section 102(a).

After an exhaustive review of the authorities, and of the legislative history of the Patent Act of 1952, this court rejected the contention of the Patent Office, and concluded that such a document was not proper evidence of prior knowledge. In reversing, the court stated (234 F.2d at 886, 433 C.C.P.A. at 992):

> In our opinion, one of the essential elements of the word "known" as used in 35 U.S.C.A. § 102(a) is knowledge of an invention which has been completed by reduction to practice, actual or constructive, and is not satisfied by disclosure of a conception only.

And therefore, since the Journal article, "at best, could be evidence of nothing more than conception and disclosure of the invention," the

> ... placing of the Nystrom article in the hands of the publishers did not constitute either prima facie or conclusive evidence of knowledge or use by others in this country of the invention disclosed by the article, within the meaning of Title 35, § 102(a) of the United States Code, since the knowledge was of a conception only and not of a reduction to practice.

Another aspect of the court's discussion in Schlittler involved the well-established principle that "prior knowledge of a patented invention would not invalidate a claim of the patent unless such knowledge was available to the public." After reaffirming that principle, the court went on to state:

> Obviously, in view of the above authorities, the mere placing of a manuscript in the hands of a publisher does not necessarily make it available to the public within the meaning of said authorities.

However, the court did not go on to determine whether the Journal article was in fact available to the public, since such determination was deemed unnecessary for disposition of the case, under the court's theory.

We shall consider first the public availability aspect of the Schlittler case. Although that portion of the Schlittler opinion is clearly dictum, we think it just as clearly represents the settled law. The knowledge contemplated by section 102(a) must be accessible to the public.

In the instant case, Samsel was clearly not publicly available during the period it was under secrecy classification by the Atomic Energy Commission. We note that the date of declassification, however, was prior to appellant's filing date, and it is perhaps arguable that Samsel became accessible to the public upon declassification. But we do not find it necessary to decide that difficult question, for there is a statutory provision which is, we think, dispositive of the question of publicity. Section 155 of the Atomic Energy Act of 1954 (42 U.S.C.A. § 2185) provides:

> In connection with applications for patents covered by this sub-chapter, the fact that the invention or discovery was known or used before shall be a bar to the patenting of such invention or discovery even though such prior knowledge or use was under secrecy within the atomic energy program of the United States.

We think the meaning and intent of this provision is so clear as to admit of no dispute: With respect to subject matter covered by the patent provisions of the Atomic Energy Act, prior knowledge or use under section 102(a) *need not* be accessible to the public. Therefore, Samsel is available as evidence of prior knowledge insofar as the requirement for publicity is concerned.

The remaining consideration regarding the status of Samsel as evidence of prior knowledge directly calls into question the correctness of the unequivocal holding in Schlittler that the knowledge must be of a reduction to practice, either actual or constructive. After much deliberation, we have concluded that such a requirement is illogical and anomalous, and to the extent Schlittler is inconsistent with the decision in this case, it is hereby expressly overruled.

The mere fact that a disclosure is contained in a patent or application and thus "constructively" reduced to practice, or that it is found in a printed publication, does not make the disclosure itself any more meaningful to those skilled in the art (and thus, ultimately, to the public). Rather, the criterion should be whether the disclosure is *sufficient to enable one skilled in the art to reduce the disclosed invention to practice.* In other words, the disclosure must be such as will give possession of the invention to the person of ordinary skill. Even the act of publication or the fiction of constructive reduction to practice will not suffice if the disclosure does not meet this standard.

Where, as is true of Samsel, the disclosure constituting evidence of prior knowledge contains, in the words of the Board of Appeals, "a description of the invention fully commensurate with the present patent application," we hold that the disclosure need not be of an invention reduced to practice, either actually or constructively. We therefore affirm the rejection of claims 27, 30, 31 and 32. . . . Modified.

Pfaff v. Wells Electronics, Inc.

Supreme Court of the United States, 1998.
525 U.S. 55, 119 S.Ct. 304, 142 L.Ed.2d 261, 48 U.S.P.Q.2d 1641.

Justice STEVENS delivered the opinion of the Court.

Section 102(b) of the Patent Act of 1952 provides that no person is entitled to patent an "invention" that has been "on sale" more than one year before filing a patent application. We granted certiorari to determine whether the commercial marketing of a newly invented product may mark the beginning of the 1–year period even though the invention has not yet been reduced to practice.[2]

I

On April 19, 1982, petitioner, Wayne Pfaff, filed an application for a patent on a computer chip socket. Therefore, April 19, 1981, constitutes the critical date for purposes of the on-sale bar of 35 U.S.C. § 102(b); if the 1–year period began to run before that date, Pfaff lost his right to patent his invention.

Pfaff commenced work on the socket in November 1980, when representatives of Texas Instruments asked him to develop a new device for mounting and removing semiconductor chip carriers. In response to this request, he prepared detailed engineering drawings that described the design, the dimensions, and the materials to be used in making the socket. Pfaff sent those drawings to a manufacturer in February or March 1981.

Prior to March 17, 1981, Pfaff showed a sketch of his concept to representatives of Texas Instruments. On April 8, 1981, they provided Pfaff with a written confirmation of a previously placed oral purchase order for 30,100 of his new sockets for a total price of $91,155. In accord with his normal practice, Pfaff did not make and test a prototype of the new device before offering to sell it in commercial quantities.[3]

The manufacturer took several months to develop the customized tooling necessary to produce the device, and Pfaff did not fill the order until July 1981. The evidence therefore indicates that Pfaff first reduced his invention to practice in the summer of 1981. The socket achieved substantial commercial success before Patent No. 4,491,377 (the '377 patent) issued to Pfaff on January 1, 1985.

After the patent issued, petitioner brought an infringement action against respondent, Wells Electronics, Inc., the manufacturer of a competing socket. Wells prevailed on the basis of a finding of no infringement. When respondent began to market a modified device, petitioner brought

---

2. "A process is reduced to practice when it is successfully performed. A machine is reduced to practice when it is assembled adjusted and used. A manufacture is reduced to practice when it is completely manufactured. A composition of matter is reduced to practice when it is completely composed." *Corona Cord Tire Co. v. Dovan Chemical Corp.,* 276 U.S. 358, 383, 48 S.Ct. 380, 72 L.Ed. 610 (1928).

3. At his deposition, respondent's counsel engaged in the following colloquy with Pfaff:

"Q. Now, at this time [late 1980 or early 1981] did we [sic] have any prototypes devel-

oped or anything of that nature, working embodiment?

"A. No.

"Q. It was in a drawing. Is that correct?

"A. Strictly in a drawing. Went from the drawing to the hard tooling. That's the way I do my business.

"Q. 'Boom-boom'?

"A. You got it.

"Q. You are satisfied, obviously, when you come up with some drawings that it is going to go—'it works'?

"A. I know what I'm doing, yes, most of the time.".

this suit, alleging that the modifications infringed six of the claims in the '377 patent.

After a full evidentiary hearing before a Special Master, the District Court held that two of those claims (1 and 6) were invalid because they had been anticipated in the prior art. Nevertheless, the court concluded that four other claims (7, 10, 11, and 19) were valid and three (7, 10, and 11) were infringed by various models of respondent's sockets. Adopting the Special Master's findings, the District Court rejected respondent's § 102(b) defense because Pfaff had filed the application for the '377 patent less than a year after reducing the invention to practice.

The Court of Appeals reversed, finding all six claims invalid. Four of the claims (1, 6, 7, and 10) described the socket that Pfaff had sold to Texas Instruments prior to April 8, 1981. Because that device had been offered for sale on a commercial basis more than one year before the patent application was filed on April 19, 1982, the court concluded that those claims were invalid under § 102(b). That conclusion rested on the court's view that as long as the invention was "substantially complete at the time of sale," the 1–year period began to run, even though the invention had not yet been reduced to practice. The other two claims (11 and 19) described a feature that had not been included in Pfaff's initial design, but the Court of Appeals concluded as a matter of law that the additional feature was not itself patentable because it was an obvious addition to the prior art. Given the court's § 102(b) holding, the prior art included Pfaff's first four claims.

Because other courts have held or assumed that an invention cannot be "on sale" within the meaning of § 102(b) unless and until it has been reduced to practice, and because the text of § 102(b) makes no reference to "substantial completion" of an invention, we granted certiorari.

II

The primary meaning of the word "invention" in the Patent Act unquestionably refers to the inventor's conception rather than to a physical embodiment of that idea. The statute does not contain any express requirement that an invention must be reduced to practice before it can be patented. Neither the statutory definition of the term in § 100 nor the basic conditions for obtaining a patent set forth in § 101 make any mention of "reduction to practice." The statute's only specific reference to that term is found in § 102(g), which sets forth the standard for resolving priority contests between two competing claimants to a patent. That subsection provides:

> In determining priority of invention there shall be considered not only the respective dates of conception and reduction to practice of the invention, but also the reasonable diligence of one who was first to conceive and last to reduce to practice, from a time prior to conception by the other.

Thus, assuming diligence on the part of the applicant, it is normally the first inventor to conceive, rather than the first to reduce to practice, who establishes the right to the patent.

It is well settled that an invention may be patented before it is reduced to practice. In 1888, this Court upheld a patent issued to Alexander Graham Bell even though he had filed his application before constructing a working telephone. Chief Justice Waite's reasoning in that case merits quoting at length:

It is quite true that when Bell applied for his patent he had never actually transmitted telegraphically spoken words so that they could be distinctly heard and understood at the receiving end of his line, but in his specification he did describe accurately and with admirable clearness his process, that is to say, the exact electrical condition that must be created to accomplish his purpose, and he also described, with sufficient precision to enable one of ordinary skill in such matters to make it, a form of apparatus which, if used in the way pointed out, would produce the required effect, receive the words, and carry them to and deliver them at the appointed place. The particular instrument which he had, and which he used in his experiments, did not, under the circumstances in which it was tried, reproduce the words spoken, so that they could be clearly understood, but the proof is abundant and of the most convincing character, that other instruments, carefully constructed and made exactly in accordance with the specification, without any additions whatever, have operated and will operate successfully. A good mechanic of proper skill in matters of the kind can take the patent and, by following the specification strictly, can, without more, construct an apparatus which, when used in the way pointed out, will do all that it is claimed the method or process will do. . . .

The law does not require that a discoverer or inventor, in order to get a patent for a process, must have succeeded in bringing his art to the highest degree of perfection. It is enough if he describes his method with sufficient clearness and precision to enable those skilled in the matter to understand what the process is, and if he points out some practicable way of putting it into operation. *The Telephone Cases,* 126 U.S. 1, 535–536, 8 S.Ct. 778, 31 L.Ed. 863 (1888).

When we apply the reasoning of *The Telephone Cases* to the facts of the case before us today, it is evident that Pfaff could have obtained a patent on his novel socket when he accepted the purchase order from Texas Instruments for 30,100 units. At that time he provided the manufacturer with a description and drawings that had "sufficient clearness and precision to enable those skilled in the matter" to produce the device. The parties agree that the sockets manufactured to fill that order embody Pfaff's conception as set forth in claims 1, 6, 7, and 10 of the '377 patent. We can find no basis in the text of § 102(b) or in the facts of this case for concluding that Pfaff's invention was not "on sale" within the meaning of the statute until after it had been reduced to practice.

III

Pfaff nevertheless argues that longstanding precedent, buttressed by the strong interest in providing inventors with a clear standard identifying the onset of the 1–year period, justifies a special interpretation of the word "invention" as used in § 102(b). We are persuaded that this nontextual argument should be rejected.

As we have often explained, most recently in *Bonito Boats, Inc. v. Thunder Craft Boats, Inc.,* 489 U.S. 141, 151, 109 S.Ct. 971, 103 L.Ed.2d 118 (1989), the patent system represents a carefully crafted bargain that encourages both the creation and the public disclosure of new and useful advances in technology, in return for an exclusive monopoly for a limited period of time. The balance between the interest in motivating innovation and enlightenment by rewarding invention with patent protection on the one hand, and the interest in avoiding monopolies that unnecessarily stifle competition on the other, has been a feature of the federal patent laws since their inception. As this Court explained in 1871:

> Letters patent are not to be regarded as monopolies ... but as public franchises granted to the inventors of new and useful improvements for the purpose of securing to them, as such inventors, for the limited term therein mentioned, the exclusive right and liberty to make and use and vend to others to be used their own inventions, as tending to promote the progress of science and the useful arts, and as matter of compensation to the inventors for their labor, toil, and expense in making the inventions, and reducing the same to practice for the public benefit, as contemplated by the Constitution and sanctioned by the laws of Congress. *Seymour v. Osborne,* 11 Wall. 516, 533–534.

Consistent with these ends, § 102 of the Patent Act serves as a limiting provision, both excluding ideas that are in the public domain from patent protection and confining the duration of the monopoly to the statutory term.

We originally held that an inventor loses his right to a patent if he puts his invention into public use before filing a patent application. "His voluntary act or acquiescence in the public sale and use is an abandonment of his right" *Pennock v. Dialogue,* 2 Pet. 1, 24, 7 L.Ed. 327 (1829) (Story, J.). A similar reluctance to allow an inventor to remove existing knowledge from public use undergirds the on-sale bar.

Nevertheless, an inventor who seeks to perfect his discovery may conduct extensive testing without losing his right to obtain a patent for his invention—even if such testing occurs in the public eye. The law has long recognized the distinction between inventions put to experimental use and products sold commercially. In 1878, we explained why patentability may turn on an inventor's use of his product.

"It is sometimes said that an inventor acquires an undue advantage over the public by delaying to take out a patent, inasmuch as he thereby preserves the monopoly to himself for a longer period than is allowed by the policy of the law; but this cannot be said with justice when the delay is occasioned by a *bona fide* effort to bring his invention to perfection, or to ascertain whether it will answer the purpose intended. His monopoly only continues for the allotted period, in any event; and it is the interest of the public, as well as himself, that the invention should be perfect and properly tested, before a patent is granted for it. Any attempt to use it for a profit, and not by way of experiment, for a longer period than two years before the application, would deprive the inventor of his right to a patent." Elizabeth v. American Nicholson Pavement Co., *97 U.S. 126, 137, 24 L.Ed. 1000 (1877).*

The patent laws therefore seek both to protect the public's right to retain knowledge already in the public domain and the inventor's right to control whether and when he may patent his invention. The Patent Act of 1836, 5 Stat. 117, was the first statute that expressly included an on-sale bar to the issuance of a patent. Like the earlier holding in *Pennock,* that provision precluded patentability if the invention had been placed on sale at any time before the patent application was filed. In 1839, Congress ameliorated that requirement by enacting a 2–year grace period in which the inventor could file an application.

In *Andrews v. Hovey,* 123 U.S. 267, 274, 8 S.Ct. 101, 31 L.Ed. 160 (1887), we noted that the purpose of that amendment was "to fix a period of limitation which should be certain"; it required the inventor to make sure that a patent application was filed "within two years from the completion of his invention," *ibid.* In 1939, Congress reduced the grace period from two years to one year.

Petitioner correctly argues that these provisions identify an interest in providing inventors with a definite standard for determining when a patent application must be filed. A rule that makes the timeliness of an application depend on the date when an invention is "substantially complete" seriously undermines the interest in certainty. Moreover, such a rule finds no support in the text of the statute. Thus, petitioner's argument calls into question the standard applied by the Court of Appeals, but it does not persuade us that it is necessary to engraft a reduction to practice element into the meaning of the term "invention" as used in § 102(b).

The word "invention" must refer to a concept that is complete, rather than merely one that is "substantially complete." It is true that reduction to practice ordinarily provides the best evidence that an invention is complete. But just because reduction to practice is sufficient evidence of completion, it does not follow that proof of reduction to practice is necessary in every case. Indeed, both the facts of the *Telephone Cases* and the facts of this case demonstrate that one can prove that an invention is complete and ready for patenting before it has actually been reduced to practice.

We conclude, therefore, that the on-sale bar applies when two conditions are satisfied before the critical date. First, the product must be the subject of a commercial offer for sale. An inventor can both understand and control the timing of the first commercial marketing of his invention. The experimental use doctrine, for example, has not generated concerns about indefiniteness, and we perceive no reason why unmanageable uncertainty should attend a rule that measures the application of the on-sale bar of § 102(b) against the date when an invention that is ready for patenting is first marketed commercially. In this case the acceptance of the purchase order prior to April 8, 1981, makes it clear that such an offer had been made, and there is no question that the sale was commercial rather than experimental in character.

Second, the invention must be ready for patenting. That condition may be satisfied in at least two ways: by proof of reduction to practice before the critical date; or by proof that prior to the critical date the inventor had prepared drawings or other descriptions of the invention that were sufficiently specific to enable a person skilled in the art to practice the invention. In this case the second condition of the on-sale bar is satisfied because the drawings Pfaff sent to the manufacturer before the critical date fully disclosed the invention.

The evidence in this case thus fulfills the two essential conditions of the on-sale bar. As succinctly stated by Learned Hand:

> [I]t is a condition upon an inventor's right to a patent that he shall not exploit his discovery competitively after it is ready for patenting; he must content himself with either secrecy, or legal monopoly. *Metallizing Engineering Co. v. Kenyon Bearing & Auto Parts Co.,* 153 F.2d 516, 520 (C.A.2 1946).

The judgment of the Court of Appeals finds support not only in the text of the statute but also in the basic policies underlying the statutory scheme, including § 102(b). When Pfaff accepted the purchase order for his new sockets prior to April 8, 1981, his invention was ready for patenting. The fact that the manufacturer was able to produce the socket using his detailed drawings and specifications demonstrates this fact. Furthermore, those sockets contained all the elements of the invention claimed in the '377 patent. Therefore, Pfaff's '377 patent is invalid because the invention had been on sale for more than one year in this country before he filed his patent application. Accordingly, the judgment of the Court of Appeals is affirmed.

It is so ordered.

TP Laboratories, Inc. v. Professional Positioners, Inc.

United States Court of Appeals, Federal Circuit, 1984.
724 F.2d 965, 220 U.S.P.Q. 577, cert.den., 469 U.S. 826, 105 S.Ct. 108, 83 L.Ed.2d 51.

NIES, Circuit Judge. These appeals are from the October 27, 1982 judgment of the United States District Court for the Eastern District of Wisconsin (Warren, J.) dismissing a charge of infringement of a patent for an orthodontic appliance. Sitting without a jury, the court held U.S. Patent No. 3,178,820 ('820), owned by TP Laboratories, Inc. (TP), invalid under 35 U.S.C. § 102(b), on the ground that a public use occurred more than one year prior to the filing date of the application for the subject patent.

TP appeals the holding of invalidity. TP admits that the inventor used the dental appliance on three orthodontal patients during the critical period but asserts that such use was non-barring experimental use. On this issue we agree with appellant and reverse. However, since the issue of whether the accused devices are infringements, as well as other issues, were not decided, it is necessary to remand....

I.

Appellant-plaintiff, TP Laboratories, Inc., makes and sells orthodontic supplies and appliances to the dental profession. TP Laboratories is a separate business from the professional practice of the Kesling and Rocke Orthodontic Group (K & R), a group of four orthodontists, Doctors Harold D. Kesling, Robert A. Rocke, Peter C. Kesling and David L. Kesling, but the firms are closely connected. The record before us shows that Dr. Harold Kesling, now deceased, (Kesling), who is the inventor named in the patent in suit, was an officer and one of the owners of TP Laboratories. Dr. Peter Kesling is president. The two businesses share a small building and employ the same office manager.

Kesling conceived and made the first prototype of the invention of the patent in suit in 1956. It was not, however, until February 19, 1962, that Kesling filed a patent application on his invention for which the '820 patent was granted on April 20, 1965. On November 1, 1965, the patent was assigned to TP Laboratories.

The subject matter of the '820 patent is a molded tooth positioning appliance which is to be worn several hours a day by a person undergoing orthodontal treatment. The general type of device is not new. The improvement by Kesling lies in placing wires in the device which fit in the embrasure area between the teeth and keep the appliance in position without the necessity of the patient exerting constant jaw pressure. The wires are referred to as "seating devices," "seating springs," "precision seating springs," "springs," or "metal adjuncts." Because of the shape, as seen below, the invention is also referred to as a tooth positioner with "C's":

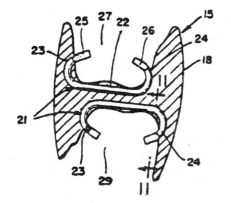

This figure is a transverse section view illustrating one form of positioning means or clip employed for obtaining proper positioning of the dental appliance in a person's mouth.

The use of tooth positioners with C's in the treatment of three K & R patients during the period 1958–61 led to the issues under 35 U.S.C. § 102(b). It is undisputed that these three devices fell within the language of the '820 claims and no modification of design was made a consequence of these uses. The evidence which established these uses was found in the patient records of K & R and the underlying facts are not in dispute. Appellant characterizes these uses as secret and/or experimental; appellees urge that they are, as found by the district court, public uses within the meaning of the statute.

The first use of the claimed invention on a patient occurred on August 25, 1958. Orthodontal treatment of this patient (Furst) spanned the time period between February 1958 and April 1964. Use of the device terminated after approximately two months. During discovery, the device itself was produced, having been retained by K & R in the patient's model box. This patient's mandibular model from the model box was inscribed "experimental wires." Over the six year period of treatment, this patient was also fitted with other devices, retainers as well as positioners not embraced by the '820 claims.

Another patient (Rumely–Brady) who had begun treatment in August 1958 was supplied with a tooth positioner equipped with C's on November 10, 1959. Entry on the record card of this patient indicates "results fair" on December 18, 1959; "results better" on February 5, 1960, and "results good" on August 1, 1960. Nevertheless, use of the device was discontinued on January 16, 1961, in favor of retainers, because certain spacing irregularities were not being corrected. The same positioner with C's was again prescribed on May 5, 1961, and was used in conjunction with various other devices until at least March 1962. The patient missed a later scheduled appointment which is the last entry on her card.

A positioner with C's was prescribed for a third patient (Spiers–Elliott) on November 1, 1960. Its use apparently was discontinued about three months later, a different device being mailed to the patient on February 2, 1961. During the treatment of this patient, which spanned the period of time between January 21, 1960, and November 24, 1961, three different positioners were prescribed, only one of which was embraced by the '820 claims.

The initial use in each of the above cases occurred prior to the critical date of February 19, 1961. During the years 1958–60, K & R placed 606 tooth positioners, of which only the three described above were within the claims of '820. In 1961, after the critical date, 28 tooth positioners with C's were prescribed by K & R out of a total of 151.

The above devices were made for the K & R patients by TP, including C's handmade by Kesling. There is no evidence that K & R charged patients specifically for any positioner. With two of the three patients, K & R followed its regular practice of setting on a fixed total fee for professional services, which included necessary appliances. One patient (Furst), whose father was a dentist, received free treatment as a professional courtesy.

Sales of the patented device to other orthodontists began in 1966, that is, only after TP's acquisition of the patent. Appellees, Huge and Allessee, had no knowledge of the invention even though employed at TP prior to 1961.

The district court did not rule on whether appellees' allegedly infringing devices came within the scope of the claims of the '820 patent and we know only that infringement is charged since 1972.

II.

A.

The patent statute provides in pertinent part in 35 U.S.C. § 102:

A person shall be entitled to a patent unless—

* * *

(b) the invention was ... in public use ... in this country, more than one year prior to the date of the application for patent in the United States.

Decisions under this provision and comparable provisions in earlier statutes are marked by confusion and inconsistency.

"The general purpose behind all the [§ 102(b)] bars is to require inventors to assert with due diligence their right to a patent through the prompt filing ... of a patent application." 2 D. Chisum, *Patents* § 601 (1981 & Supp.1983).

More specifically, courts have discerned a number of factors which must be weighed in applying the statutory bar of § 102(b). Operating against the inventor are the policies of 1) protecting the public in its use of the invention where such use began prior to the filing of the application, 2) encouraging prompt disclosure of new and useful information, 3) discouraging attempts to extend the length of the period of protection by not allowing the inventor to reap the benefits for more than one year prior to the filing of the application. In contrast to these considerations, the public interest is also deemed to be served by allowing an inventor time to perfect his invention, by public testing, if desired, and prepare a patent application.

The district court's consideration of the issue of public use proceeded according to the following two-step analysis:

Consequently, the first step in analyzing PRO's 35 U.S.C. § 102(b) assertion is to determine whether a public use occurred.

If a public use is found, then the Court must ascertain whether the use was not a public use under the statute because it was experimental.

As to the first step, the district court reasoned:

The evidence in this case clearly establishes use by at least three patients more than one year prior to the application date. Furthermore, these users were "under no limitation, restriction or obligation of secrecy to the inventor." *Randolph v. Allis–Chalmers Manufacturing Co.*, 264 F.2d [533] at 535 [120 U.S.P.Q. at 513]. Certainly there is no evidence to the contrary and there is testimony to support such a finding.... Consequently, the Court can only conclude that the patients were under no obligations of secrecy or for that matter any restrictions.

TP argues that these items were in secret because even the patients were not aware of the "testing." This is not significant. The plain fact is that the claimed invention was not kept secret. It was open to public observation without restriction which is sufficient to constitute "public use." Furthermore, Dr. Furst was aware that the precision seating springs were a new device.... In addition, several of Mrs. Spiers Elliott's associates saw the device. Consequently, the feigned secrecy relied upon by TP accords it no aid in claiming that the "use" was not "public."

On the second issue as perceived by the district court, the court placed a heavy burden of proof on the patent owner to prove that the inventor's use had been experimental and expressly found that TP did not carry that "burden." In the words of the court:

The inventor bears a heavy burden of showing that the public use was bona fide experimentation.

* * *

The experimental exception is unavailable to plaintiff TP for two reasons. First, the evidence presented does not establish that the patentee was conducting a bona fide experiment. On the contrary, the record shows that the uses were random and poorly monitored. The only records kept by Dr. H. Kesling were the patient records. Dr. H. Kesling, the inventor, did not always evaluate how well the precision seating springs worked when the patients visited the clinic. Other doctors often made evaluations of performance. Furthermore, while the issue of experimentation is in effect a matter of the inventor's intent, in the present case the evidence indicates that his intent was not experimentation. In experimenting on a prior "invention," Dr. H. Kesling kept accurate records of the results of his experiments. In the present case, the records are scanty at best.

It is important to note that the burden was on the plaintiff TP to show that use was a genuine experiment. Accurate records of the results of an experiment are certainly an indicia that the use was a bona fide experiment. In contrast the dearth of such records indicate that the use was not an experiment. The experimental use exception "is to be guarded close." *Atlas Chemical Industries, Inc. v. Moraine Products,* [509 F.2d 1,4] 184 U.S.P.Q. 281, 283 (6th Cir.1974). TP has simply failed to prove that the inventor, Dr. H. Kesling, was conducting a bona fide experiment.

Assuming, however, that the use was experimental, the delay in filing the patent application was unreasonable. The first use of the invention was in August of 1958. By April of 1959, Dr. H. Kelsing knew that the precision seating springs operated as designated.... Nevertheless, Dr.

H. Kelsing waited until February 19, 1962 to file his patent application. Significantly, the claimed invention disclosed in figure 7 of the patent in suit is substantially the same as the precision seating spring disclosed in the positioner ... supplied to Nancy Furst in August of 1958.

* * *

The delay here was unreasonable because the device proved satisfactory immediately. At least as early as 1960 Dr. Kesling learned the invention was workable. At that point his time began to run under 35 U.S.C. § 102(b). Even if he had made minor improvements over the period, all this Court needs [sic] find is that the application was filed more than one year after the basic invention was disclosed within the meaning of section 102(b). This court is of the opinion that when an experiment tolls section 102(b), the one-year period of limitations commences to run when the invention disclosed proves workable.

We disagree with this analysis and the shift in the burden of proof which led the district court to an erroneous result.

B.

It is not public knowledge of his invention that precludes the inventor from obtaining a patent for it, but a public use or sale of it.

The above quotation is from *City of Elizabeth v. American Nicholson Pavement Co.*, 97 U.S. 126, 136, 24 L.Ed. 1000 (1877), which is the starting place for analysis of any case involving experimental use. There, a toll road, built according to the invention of the patent in suit, was in daily use for a period of 6 years before the inventor filed for a patent. In upholding the validity of the patent, the Supreme Court spoke with clarity but through the years the guidelines set forth therein have been obfuscated. Returning to the original, we quote the following passages which are particularly pertinent to our analysis here:

That the use of the pavement in question was public in one sense cannot be disputed. But can it be said that the invention was in public use? The use of an invention by the inventor himself, or of any other person under his direction, by way of experiment, and in order to bring the invention to perfection, has never been regarded as such a use.

Now, the nature of a street pavement is such that it cannot be experimented upon satisfactorily except on a highway, which is always public.

When the subject of invention is a machine, it may be tested and tried in a building, either with or without closed doors. In either case, such use is not a public use, within the meaning of the statute, so long as the inventor is engaged, in good faith, in testing its operation. He may see cause to alter it and improve it, or not. His experiments will reveal the fact whether any and what alterations may be necessary. If durability is one of the qualities to be attained, a long period, perhaps years, may be necessary to enable the inventor to discover whether his purpose is accomplished. And though, during all that period, he may not find that any changes are necessary, yet he may be justly said to be using his machine only by way of experiment; and no one would say that such a use, pursued with a *bona fide* intent of testing the qualities of the machine, would be a public use, within the meaning of the statute. So long as he does not voluntarily allow others to make it and use it, and so long as it is not on sale for general use, he keeps the invention under his own control and does not lose his title to a patent.

It would not be necessary, in such a case, that the machine should be put up and used only in the inventor's own shop or premises. He may have it put up and used in the premises of another, and the use may inure to the benefit of the owner of the establishment. Still, if used under the surveillance of the inventor, and for the purpose of enabling him to test the machine, and ascertain whether it will answer the purpose intended, and make such alterations and improvements as experience demonstrates to be necessary, it will still be a mere experimental use, and not a public use, within the meaning of the statute.

Whilst the supposed machine is in such experimental use, the public may be incidentally deriving a benefit from it. If it is be a grist-mill, or a carding-machine, customers from the surrounding country may enjoy the use of it by having their grain made into flour, or their wool into rolls, and still it will not be in public use, within the meaning of the law.

But if the inventor allows his machine to be used by other persons generally, either with or without compensation, or if it is, with his consent, put on sale for such use, then it will be in public use and on public sale, within the meaning of the law.

97 U.S. at 134–35.

In the decision on appeal, the trial court looked for proof of an exception to the public use bar. However, in *Elizabeth*, the Supreme Court did not refer to "experimental use" as an "exception" to the bar otherwise created by a public use. More precisely, the Court reasoned that, if a use is experimental, even though not secret, "public use" is negated. This difference between "exception" and "negation" is not merely semantic. Under the precedent of this court, the statutory presumption of validity provided in 35 U.S.C. § 282 places the burden of proof upon the party attacking the validity of the patent, and that burden of persuasion does not shift at any time to the patent owner. It is constant and remains throughout the suit on the challenger. As stated in *Richdel, Inc. v. Sunspool Corp.*, 714 F.2d 1573, 1579, 219 U.S.P.Q. 8, 11–12 (Fed.Cir.1983):

35 U.S.C. 282 *permanently* places the burden of proving facts necessary to a conclusion of invalidity on the party asserting such invalidity.

Under this analysis, it is incorrect to impose on the patent owner, as the trial court in this case did, the burden of proving that a "public use" was "experimental." These are not two separable issues. It is incorrect to ask: "Was it public use?" and then, "Was it experimental?" Rather, the court is faced with a single issue: Was it public use under § 102(b)?

Thus, the court should have looked at all of the evidence put forth by both parties and should have decided whether the entirety of the evidence led to the conclusion that there had been "public use." This does not mean, of course, that the challenger has the burden of proving that the use is not experimental. Nor docs it mean that the patent owner is relieved of explanation. It means that if a *prima facie* case is made of public use, the patent owner must be able to point to or must come forward with convincing evidence to counter that showing. The length of the test period is merely a piece of evidence to add to the evidentiary scale. The same is true with respect to whether payment is made for the device, whether a user agreed to use secretly, whether records were kept of progress, whether persons other than the inventor conducted the asserted experiments, how many tests were conducted, how long the testing period was in relationship to tests of other similar devices. In other words, a decision on whether there has been a "public use" can only be made upon consideration of the entire surrounding circumstances.

While various objective indicia may be considered in determining whether the use is experimental, the expression by an inventor of his subjective intent to experiment, particularly after institution of litigation, is generally of minimal value.

C.

Applying the principles set forth above to this case, that non-secret uses of the device were made prior to the critical date is not in itself dispositive of the issue of whether activity barring a patent under 35 U.S.C. § 102(b) occurred. The fact that the device was not hidden from view may make the use not secret but non-secret use is not *ipso facto* "public use" activity. *City of Elizabeth v. American Nicholson Pavement Co.*, 97 U.S. at 136. Nor, it must be added, is all secret use *ipso facto* not "public use" within the meaning of the statute, if the inventor is making commercial use of the invention under circumstances which preserve its secrecy.

Turning to the instant case, we note first that disclosure of the seating device to patients could not be avoided in any testing. In some circumstances, no doubt it would be significant that no pledge of confidentiality was obtained from the user. In the circumstances of use by orthodontal patients, we attach no importance to the fact that the doctor did not ask a patient to swear to secrecy. As in *City of Elizabeth*, testing of the device had to be public to some extent and it is beyond reasonable probability that a patient would show the device to others who would understand the function of the C's or would want to duplicate the device. One is all that is needed and, if lost or broken, the patient would expect it to be replaced by the treating dentist.

In any event, a pledge of confidentiality is indicative of the inventor's continued control which here is established inherently by the dentist-patient relationship of the parties. Nothing in the inventor's use of the device on his patients (or the transfer to them) is inconsistent with experimentation. Similarly, the routine checking of patients by one of the other K & R orthodontists does not indicate the inventor's lack of control or abandonment to the public.

Secondly, the finding is clearly erroneous that the invention "proved satisfactory immediately," or "by April of 1959." In this connection, it is noted that the '820 patent itself describes a utility of the patented device for correcting orthodontal irregularities as "urging teeth into preselected positions." The patient records discussed above indicate that treatment to correct such orthodontal irregularities can range from two to six years. Moreover, while results appeared to be good within six months use by one patient, the variable of patient cooperation cannot be checked by one patient alone. Use on three patients is not an obviously excessive number. In other words, the test for success of the improvement was not whether it could be used at all, but whether it could be said to work better on patients than a positioner without C's. Again, as in *City of Elizabeth*, the test of necessity had to run for a considerable time and on several patients before the inventor could know whether "it was what he claimed it to be" and would "answer the purpose intended."

A factor in favor of the patentee is that during this critical time the inventor had readily available all of the facilities of TP to commercially exploit the device. Yet, no positioners with C's were offered to competing orthodontists despite the fact this was one facet of the inventor's total business activity. Further, the inventor made no extra charge for fitting the three patients with the improved positioners although that in itself is not critical. The facts here indicate the inventor was testing the device, not the market. No commercial exploitation having been made to even a small degree prior to filing the patent application, the underlying policy of prohibiting an extension of the term is clearly not offended in this respect.

Indeed, none of the policies which underlie the public use bar and which, in effect, define it have been shown to be violated. At most, the record shows that the uses were not secret, but when the evidence as to the facts of use by the inventor is considered as a whole, we conclude that appellees failed to prove that the inventor made a public use of the subject invention within the meaning of 35 U.S.C. § 102(b). The patent may not be held invalid on this ground. . . .

Summary

The decision of the district court holding U.S. Patent No. 3,178,820 invalid is reversed. The decision of the court awarding costs and fees under Rule 37(d) is *affirmed*. The cross-appeal is *dismissed*. The case is *remanded* to the district court for proceedings consistent herewith.

REVERSED–IN–PART; AFFIRMED–IN–PART; REMANDED CROSS–APPEAL; DISMISSED.

PAULIK v. RIZKALLA, 760 F.2d 1270, 1272–1275, 226 U.S.P.Q. 224 (Fed.Cir.1985). NEWMAN, J.: United States patent law embraces the principle that the patent right is granted to the first inventor rather than the first to file a patent application. The law does not inquire as to the fits and starts by which an invention is made. The historic jurisprudence from which 35 U.S.C. § 102(g) flowed reminds us that "the mere lapse of time" will not prevent the inventor from receiving a patent. Mason v. Hepburn, 13 App.D.C. 86, 91, 1898 C.D. 510, 513 (1898). The sole exception to this principle resides in section 102(g) and the exigencies of the priority contest.

There is no impediment in the law to holding that a long period of inactivity need not be a fatal forfeiture, if the first inventor resumes work on the invention before the second inventor enters the field. We deem this result to be a fairer implementation of national patent policy, while in full accord with the letter and spirit of section 102(g).

The Board misapplied the rule that the first inventor does not have to show activity following reduction to practice to mean that the first inventor will not be allowed to show such activity. Such a showing may serve either of two purposes: to rebut an inference of abandonment, suppression, or concealment; or as evidence of renewed activity with respect to the invention. Otherwise, if an inventor were to set an invention aside for "too long" and later resume work and diligently develop and seek to patent it, according to the Board he would always be worse off than if he never did the early work, even as against a much later entrant.

Such a restrictive rule would merely add to the burden of those charged with the nation's technological growth. Invention is not a neat process. The value of early work may not be recognized or, for many reasons, it may not become practically useful, until months or years later. Following the Board's decision, any "too long" delay would constitute a forfeiture fatal in a priority contest, even if terminated by extensive and productive work done long before the newcomer entered the field.

We do not suggest that the first inventor should be entitled to rely for priority purposes on his early reduction to practice if the intervening inactivity lasts "too long," as that principle has evolved in a century of judicial analysis. Precedent did not deal with the facts at bar. There is no authority that would estop Paulik from relying on his resumed activities in order to pre-date Rizkalla's earliest date. We hold that such resumed activity must be considered as evidence of priority of invention. Should Paulik demonstrate that he had renewed activity on the invention and that he proceeded diligently to filing his patent application, starting before the earliest date to which Rizkalla is entitled—all in accordance with established principles of interference practice—we hold that Paulik is not prejudiced by the fact that he had reduced the invention to practice some years earlier. . . .

This appeal presents a question not previously treated by this court or, indeed, in the historical jurisprudence on suppression or concealment. We take this opportunity to clarify an apparent misperception of certain opinions of our predecessor court which the Board has cited in support of its holding.

There is over a hundred years of judicial precedent on the issue of suppression or concealment due to prolonged delay in filing. From the earliest decisions, a distinction has been drawn between deliberate suppression or concealment of an invention, and the legal inference of suppression or concealment based on "too long" a delay in filing the patent application. Both types of situations were considered by the courts before the 1952 Patent Act, and both are encompassed in 35 U.S.C. § 102(g). The result is consistent over this entire period—loss of the first inventor's priority as against an intervening second inventor—and has consistently been based on equitable principles and public policy as applied to the facts of each case. . . .

The decisions applying section 102(g) balanced the law and policy favoring the first person to make an invention, against equitable considerations when more than one person had made the same invention: in each case where the court deprived the de facto first inventor of the right to the patent, the second inventor had entered the field during a period of either inactivity or deliberate concealment by the first inventor. Often the first inventor had been spurred to file a patent application by news of the second inventor's activities. Although "spurring" is not necessary to a finding of suppression or concealment, the courts' frequent references to spurring indicate their concern with this equitable factor. . . .

NOTES

1. Should a single, unitary measure govern the determination of when an invention has been completed? Should one measure be used to determine novelty under section 102(a) and another to apply the statutory bars under section 102(b)? Should one measure be employed for purposes of the on sale bar, as in *Pfaff*, and another for the public use bar, as in *TP Laboratories*? Should a different measure be employed in determining interference priorities under section 102(g)?

2. The path through section 102 is tortuous and strewn with snares. The basic principle, that patents should not protect subject matter that fails to increase society's store of technological information, offers a rough-and-ready guide through the thicket: If the subject matter sought to be patented is disclosed by any other source, a patent will be denied because it serves no socially useful purpose.

Section 102's complexity lies not in its deviation from this principle, but in its use of several distinctions to enforce the principle. Consider, for example, the distinctions that underlie this synthesis of section 102: An inventor cannot obtain a patent for his subject matter if it has been known or used in this country by others before he invented it, or if it has been patented or described in a printed publication in this or a foreign country more than one year before he applied for a patent, or if it has been in public use or on sale in this country for more than one year before the date of his patent application.

3. *The Novelty Requirement and the Statutory Bars.* Section 102 distinguishes between the acts of an applicant seeking patent protection and the acts of others. A comparison of subsections (a) and (b) reveals a difference not only in operative point of time, but also in the range of persons whose conduct is relevant. Knowledge or use under subsection (a) must be "by others," while public use or sale in (b) is not so limited. Simply, under section 102(b) the incautious inventor may discover that he has barred his own claim. Although this bar looks like the novelty bar, its motive is different. "It is well settled that the policy consideration behind the 'public use' rule is to stimulate a seasonable disclosure of new inventions within the framework of the patent laws." Atlas v. Eastern Air Lines, Inc., 311 F.2d 156, 136 U.S.P.Q. 4 (1st Cir.1962). An analogous motive underlies subsections (d), (e) and, in part, subsection (g).

4. There is some overlap between the terms that subsections 102(a) and (b) employ to itemize and distinguish among the various anticipating sources—"known," "used," "patented," "described in a printed publication," "public use" and "sale." For example, although a patent can anticipate even if it is not printed, a patent once printed also constitutes a printed publication. When, as in many countries, an invention's complete specification is published before the patent is granted, it is the printed publication rather than the patent that poses the earlier bar. Since for a sale to anticipate under section 102(b) it can be neither secret nor conditional, some "knowledge" or "use" of the invention will be implicit in the transaction.

Two requirements are common to all these sources of prior art. First, the anticipating source must place the claimed subject matter within public reach. Second, the source must disclose the subject matter for which patent protection is sought with sufficient clarity to instruct those skilled in the relevant art to recreate it—a requirement explicated in *Borst*.

Several of section 102's distinctions are rehearsed in section 102(g). For example, the term, "abandoned" holds the same consequence for the prior inventor under section 102(g) as it does for the applicant inventor under section 102(c). Unlike its companion subsections, however, section 102(g) does double service. It forms the basis for determining which of two or more applicants claiming priority for the same invention is to receive a patent. The role of these determinations, rendered in the first instance in the Patent and Trademark Office in the course of interference proceedings, is noted at page 431, below.

5. *Anticipation.* Section 102 bars a patent only if the prior art is identical to—"anticipates"—the invention for which a patent is sought. The identity requirement distinguishes section 102 from section 103, where prior art—though nonidentical—may make an invention obvious and unpatentable. Unlike section 103, section 102 requires a single prior art reference to disclose every element of the invention for which the patent is sought. The Court of Appeals for the Federal Circuit observed in Structural Rubber Products Co. v. Park Rubber Co., 749 F.2d 707, 715–716, 223 U.S.P.Q. 1264, 1270–71 (1984) that "[w]hile the teaching in the prior reference need not be *ipsissimis verbis,* nevertheless, there must be a teaching with respect to the entirety of the claimed invention."

Can a product or process that was produced accidentally or unwittingly anticipate a later, advertent and conscious invention of the same subject matter? In Tilghman v. Proctor, 102 U.S. 707, 26 L.Ed. 279 (1880), the United States Supreme Court held that an earlier, accidental formation of fat acid would not defeat a patent on a process for separating fats into fat acids and glycerine: "We do not regard the accidental formation of fat acid in Perkins's steam cylinder from the tallow introduced to lubricate the piston (if the scum which rose on the water issuing from the ejection pipe was fat acid) as of any consequence in this inquiry. What the process was by which it was generated or formed was never fully understood. Those engaged in the art of making candles, or in any other art in which fat acids are desirable, certainly never derived the least hint from this accidental phenomenon in regard to any practicable process for manufacturing such acids." 102 U.S. at 711.

6. *Printed Publication.* What is a "printed publication"? In a long and thoughtful essay, Gerald Rose concludes that the law on the subject is "a muddled mess." Rose samples some holdings on what is and is not a printed publication:

"(a) a handwritten manuscript in a public library is *not.*

(b) a single typewritten thesis in a college library *is.*

(c) a scientific paper delivered orally to an audience is *not.*

(d) a scientific paper submitted for refereeing before publication *is.*

(e) an article in a Russian library was *not.*

(f) an instruction sheet distributed on one island in Japan *is.*

(g) a microfilm in the Library of Congress *is* or *is not,* depending on whether it is properly indexed.

(h) a trade circular that is thrown away *is.*"

Gerald Rose, Do You Have a "Printed Publication?" If Not, Do You Have Evidence of Prior "Knowledge or Use?" 61 J.Pat. Off. Soc'y 643, 644 (1979).

The golden thread running through the cases is that the term, "printed publication," embodies section 102's general requirement that prior art be publicly accessible; the fact that a reference is both printed and published is strong evidence of its public availability. Under this standard, when, if at all, did publication occur under the following facts: On April 30, 1959, a printer delivered a report disclosing the claimed subject matter to *J,* a research laboratory's technical editor. On May 5, 1959, *J* mailed these copies to individuals on a distribution list. *J,* testifies "that if counsel had come to his office on April 30, and requested a copy of the report, he would 'very likely' have been given one." Both parties concede that if the report was published more than one year before May 3, 1960, the patent would be invalid under section 102(b). See University of Illinois Foundation v.

Blonder–Tongue Laboratories, Inc., 422 F.2d 769, 164 U.S.P.Q. 545 (7th Cir.1970), vacated, 402 U.S. 313, 91 S.Ct. 1434, 28 L.Ed.2d 788, 169 U.S.P.Q. 513. Would the invention have been "known" under section 102(a)?

7. Was section 102(b) applied too strictly in Egbert v. Lippmann, 104 U.S. 333, 26 L.Ed. 755 (1881)? Defendant, charged with infringement, argued that the inventor had publicly used the subject matter in suit—corset springs—more than two years (the grace period then in effect) before he filed his patent application. Evidently, eleven years before filing, the inventor had presented his fiancee with a pair of the corset springs. During this period she was the only person to use them and, by their nature, they were not exposed to public view.

The Court, concerned that the inventor had "slept on his rights for eleven years," decided that the facts supported a finding of public use. To be public, the Court declared, a use need not be of more than one device, nor by more than one person. The decisive fact was that the inventor had given the device to his fiancee without at the same time restricting its use. Justice Miller indulged some refreshing realism in his dissent: "It may well be imagined that a prohibition to the party so permitted against exposing her use of the steel spring to public observation would have been supposed to be a piece of irony." 104 U.S. at 339.

8. *Anticipating Events that Occur Abroad.* Section 102 distinguishes between anticipating events that occur in the United States and those that occur abroad. Two questions frequently arise in determining whether a foreign patent or printed publication anticipates: Does the foreign document, regardless of its characterization under local law, in fact constitute a patent or a printed publication? If so, to what extent does the patent or publication disclose the subject matter in question?

Carter Products Inc. v. Colgate–Palmolive Co., 130 F.Supp. 557, 104 U.S.P.Q. 314 (D.Md.1955), aff'd, 230 F.2d 855, 108 U.S.P.Q. 383 (4th Cir.1956), raised and answered both questions. Defendant claimed that, over a year before the patent in suit was applied for, an Argentine patent had been granted on identical subject matter. The Argentine patent, defendant argued, also constituted a printed publication so that section 102(b) barred a patent on not one, but two grounds.

Reasoning from the undisputed premise "that what was publicly known or used in the foreign country is not a bar to a United States patent unless such was either patented or described in a printed publication in the foreign country," the court rejected both contentions. First, "since the Argentine patent is a typewritten document, it could not qualify as printed." Second, the court found it "necessary to determine what was in fact 'patented' by the Argentine patent." Resting its conclusion upon the testimony of two experts in Argentine law and upon a statement in the patent itself, the court ruled that the scope of the patent was limited to its claim, which in no way taught the subject matter in question: "the three composition examples set forth in the Argentine patent, upon which defendants rely ... bear no relationship to the claimed subject matter of the

Argentine patent, and also are unrelated to anything else in the patent specification." The court was alternatively disposed to ignore Argentine law entirely and impose the United States domestic rule of patent construction: "That nothing is to be treated as patented except what is actually claimed therein is well settled under our decisions." 130 F.Supp. at 566.

Can foreign acts establish a date of invention? Until passage of the Uruguay Round Agreements Act, Pub. L. No. 103–465, 108 Stat. 4809 (1994), a patent applicant could not establish a date of invention by reference to activities that occurred outside the United States. The Act, signed into law on December 8, 1994, amended section 104 of the Patent Act to provide that activities in any member country of the World Trade Organization—created by the GATT Uruguay Round—can be used to prove date of invention. The amendment implements Article 27(1) of the Agreement on Trade–Related Aspects of Intellectual Property Rights (TRIPs), which requires that patents be available in all WTO member countries "without discrimination as to the place of invention." See generally, Stephen M. Bodenheimer, Jr., Edward J. Kessler & Guy R. Gosnell, The Effect of the Interference Rule Revisions Enacted in Response to NAFTA and GATT, 36 IDEA 19 (1995).

9.   *Experimental Use.* As explicated by *TP Laboratories*, experimental use of an invention does not constitute public use or sale for purposes of section 102(b). Courts exclude time devoted to the invention's development and refinement from section 102's prior use period. The experimental use exception is narrow. Courts exclude the time taken for tests of an invention's utility and practical value, but include the time taken by tests of the invention's marketability and commercial value.

In re Smith, 714 F.2d 1127, 218 U.S.P.Q. 976 (Fed.Cir.1983), illustrates the distinction between experimentation and marketing tests. The applicant in *Smith* had invented a vacuumable carpet and room deodorizer. The applicant's assignee had given seventy-six St. Louis consumers two different prototypes of the composition to use in their homes for two weeks without legal restriction. The court rejected the applicant's assertion that the testing activities constituted an "integral part of their research and development process" and emphasized the importance of objective evidence of experimentation—evidence, for example, that the inventor inspected the invention regularly, that the inventor retained control over the invention, and that "the commercial exploitation was merely incidental to the primary purpose of experimentation." 714 F.2d at 1135.

> Contrary to appellants' contention that the St. Louis test was needed to obtain scientific data on their invention's operation and usefulness, such data could have been easily obtained in their own facilities. The operability and other properties of the claimed invention could have been verified without the assistance of "typical housewives" (consumers). Instead, there was a more dominant purpose behind the St. Louis test, *viz.* to determine whether potential consumers would buy the product and how much they would pay for it—commercial exploitation.

Further, "the procedures used by the appellants suggest that the test was designed primarily to determine how well the product would sell, not to isolate systematically technical problems which remained in the product. Appellants did not control the actual testing of the composition. For example, the testing of the composition in the instant case was not conducted in the presence of appellants. Nor were restrictions placed on the consumers as to the use of the product." 714 F.2d at 1135–36.

10. *Conception and Reduction to Practice.* To qualify for protection, patent subject matter must have been "conceived" and "reduced to practice." The distinction between conception and reduction to practice is central to section 102's operation. Section 102(g) employs the distinction to determine priority of invention as between competing inventors. It assigns priority not to the first inventor who completed the invention—conceived and reduced it to practice—but rather to the first who conceived it. Reduction to practice comes into play only in the requirement that priority may be defeated if the first inventor to conceive was not reasonably diligent in reducing his conception to practice. The distinction is also implicit in subsections 102(a) and (b). For subject matter to anticipate or to act as a statutory bar it must have been reduced to practice or, in *Pfaff's* formulation, the invention must be "complete." Knowledge or use of a conception alone will not suffice.

The measure of conception is straightforward. As formulated in Burroughs Wellcome Co. v. Barr Laboratories, Inc., 40 F.3d 1223, 1228, 32 U.S.P.Q.2d 1915 (Fed.Cir.1994), "the test for conception is whether the inventor had an idea that was definite and permanent enough that one skilled in the art could understand the invention; the inventor must prove his conception by corroborating evidence, preferably by showing a contemporaneous disclosure. An idea is definite and permanent when the inventor has a specific, settled idea, a particular solution to the problem at hand, not just a general goal or research plan he hopes to pursue. The conception analysis necessary turns on the inventor's ability to describe his invention with particularity. Until he can do so, he cannot prove possession of the complete mental picture of the invention."

Reduction to practice, which requires that the conception be embodied in readily utilizable form, has received three different formulations. The first, original formula identifies reduction with that moment at which the invention is first made to work in the environment in which it is to be used rather than in some experimental setting. Under this rule, a voting machine intended for use in public elections is not reduced to practice by its use in the election of a corporate board of directors. Ocumpaugh v. Norton, 25 App.D.C. 90 (D.C.Cir.1905).

The Telephone Cases, 126 U.S. 1, 8 S.Ct. 778, 31 L.Ed. 863 (1888), followed in *Pfaff*, established the first broad exception to the orthodox formula. The Court there decided that it was inconsequential that, at the time the patent in dispute issued to him, Bell had not reduced his device to actual practice, nor even demonstrated that it could transmit intelligible sounds. Actual reduction was unnecessary, the Court held, since Bell had in the specification of his patent application described the device with sufficient accuracy to instruct a worker ordinarily skilled in the art to construct a manifestly operative device. The Court viewed reduction to practice as a function of two statutory objectives—that patented subject matter be operative, and that it be placed in a form capable of teaching the public how to recreate it. The first objective could be met under the statutory test of utility, for which proof of operativeness short of reduction will suffice. The second could be met by the detailed and precise disclosure required for the patent application. From this the Court concluded that the filing of a patent application should operate as a constructive reduction to practice of the underlying invention.

Borst, decided almost a century later, invoked the same statutory objectives to derive the third formulation of reduction to practice.

See generally, Janice Mueller, Conception, Testing, Reduction to Practice: When Is It Really on Sale? 80 J. Patent & Trademark Off. Soc'y 305 (1998); Timothy Holbrook, The More Things Change The More They Stay the Same: Implications of *Pfaff v. Wells Electronics, Inc.* and the Quest for Predictability in the On–Sale Bar, 15 Berkeley Tech. L.J. 933 (2000).

11. *First-to-Invent v. First-to-File.* Section 102's foundation stone is the principle that a patent belongs to the first person who invented the claimed subject matter and not to the first person who filed a patent application for it. This principle, which dates to the 1836 Patent Act, predicates that the patent system should reward the first, true inventor rather than a later inventor who wins the race to the Patent and Trademark Office.

The only remarkable feature of the first-to-invent principle is its uniqueness. Apart from the Philippines, the United States is the only country in the world to follow a first-to-invent system. All other countries with patent laws have a first-to-file system. Systematic efforts to introduce a first-to-file rule in the United States date to the 1966 Report of the President's Commission on the Patent System, To Promote the Progress of Useful Arts in an Age of Exploding Technology.

Among the arguments in favor of a first-to-file system are: it will eliminate costly interference proceedings in which, as a general rule, the first party to file will prevail in any event; patent practice in the United States already approximates a first-to-file system since inventors file promptly in order to obtain priority under the first-to-file systems of other countries; and a first-to-file system would eliminate the uncertainty associated with the determination of who in fact first invented the subject matter in issue.

Among the arguments against a first-to-file system are: most interference proceedings are settled and, in those that are not, the first party to invent prevails in a substantial number of cases; early filing to obtain priority in other countries has been true only of large multinational corporations with international interests; and a first-to-invent system protects against theft of patents by later "inventors" who devote their resources not to invention but to early filing.

Practical politics—specifically international politics—may prove to be more important than reasoned argument in resolving the first-to-file debate. A draft treaty on the harmonization of patent laws, prepared under the auspices of the World Intellectual Property Organization, would have required all adhering countries to maintain a first-to-file system. The United States at one time indicated a willingness to adhere to the proposed treaty, but on conditions; one condition was that the treaty provide for a grace period like the one currently provided under the United States Patent Act, allowing an inventor to publish her invention before filing a patent application.

On the pros and cons of a first-to-file system, see Donald R. Dunner, First to File: Should Our Interference System Be Abolished?, 68 J. Pat. & Trademark Off. Soc'y 561 (1986); Mark T. Banner & John J. McDonnell, First-to-File, Mandatory Reexamination, and Mandatory "Exceptional Circumstance": Ideas for Better? Or Worse?, 69 J. Pat. & Trademark Off. Soc'y 595 (1987).

12. *Prior User Rights*. Research leading to patentable invention will often be highly competitive, with only one competitor ultimately receiving a patent. Many countries have adopted a prior user right to meliorate the losses incurred by losers in the patent race. For example, section 79 of the Japanese Patent Law provides that if *B* independently makes, and undertakes to exploit, an invention before *A* files an application for a patent on the same invention, *B* will be entitled to a compulsory nonexclusive license to continue to exploit the invention once the patent issues to *A*.

In 1999, Congress added a highly limited prior user right to the U.S. Patent Act, providing in section 273(b)(1) that, in the case of business method patents, an alleged infringer has a defense to an infringement action if, acting in good faith, it actually reduced the invention to practice at least one year before the patent's filing date, and commercially used the invention before the filing date. Unlike foreign prior user rights, this right is formulated as an absolute defense rather than as a compulsory license.

13. *Publish or Perish?* Section 102 contemplates that researchers will carefully time the publication of their results so that they do not run afoul of the provision's patentability bars. Professor Gideon Parchomovsky has suggested that in some competitive settings a firm that believes its competitor will complete a similar invention first may want to strategically publish its own results in order to defeat the novelty or nonobviousness—and consequently the patentability—of the competitor's invention. "The ability to adversely affect the patentability of rivals' inventions through publication explains the otherwise peculiar practice of commercial firms that routinely publish research results in scientific and technological journals. While firms engaging in research and development ('R & D') ultimately wish to obtain patent protection, their research results often fall short of supporting a patent application. In many cases research does lead to improvements over the prior art, but those improvements are insufficient to satisfy the nonobviousness standard. Although minor improvements over the prior art cannot secure a patent grant, they are by no means valueless.

The publication of such results alters the chances of rival firms reaching the patent mark and is, thus, of value to the publishing firm." Gideon Parchomovsky, Publish or Perish, 98 Mich. L. Rev. 926, 929 (2000).

For a response to Parchomovsky's argument, see Rebecca S. Eisenberg, The Promise and Perils of Strategic Publication to Create Prior Art: A Response to Professor Parchomovsky, 98 Mich. L. Rev. 2358 (2000).

b.   Section 103: Nonobviousness

Graham v. John Deere Co.

Supreme Court of the United States, 1966.
383 U.S. 1, 86 S.Ct. 684, 15 L.Ed.2d 545, 148 U.S.P.Q. 459.

Mr. Justice CLARK delivered the opinion of the Court.

After a lapse of 15 years, the Court again focuses its attention on the patentability of inventions under the standard of Art. I, § 8, cl. 8, of the Constitution and under the conditions prescribed by the laws of the United States. Since our last expression on patent validity, Great A. & P. Tea Co. v. Supermarket Equip. Corp., 340 U.S. 147, 71 S.Ct. 127, 95 L.Ed. 162 (1950), the Congress has for the first time expressly added a third statutory dimension to the two requirements of novelty and utility that had been the sole statutory test since the Patent Act of 1793. This is the test of obviousness, i.e., whether "the subject matter sought to be patented and the prior art are such that the subject matter as a whole would have been obvious at the time the invention was made to a person having ordinary skill in the art to which said subject matter pertains. Patentability shall not be negatived by the manner in which the invention was made." § 103 of the Patent Act of 1952, 35 U.S.C.A. § 103.

The questions, involved in each of the companion cases before us, are what effect the 1952 Act had upon traditional statutory and judicial tests of patentability and what definitive tests are now required. We have concluded that the 1952 Act was intended to codify judicial precedents embracing the principle long ago announced by this Court in Hotchkiss v. Greenwood, 52 U.S. (11 How.) 248, 13 L.Ed. 683 (1850), and that, while the clear language of § 103 places emphasis on an inquiry into obviousness, the general level of innovation necessary to sustain patentability remains the same. . . .

II.

At the outset it must be remembered that the federal patent power stems from a specific constitutional provision which authorizes the Congress "To promote the Progress of . . . useful Arts, by securing for limited Times to . . . Inventors the exclusive Right to their . . . Discoveries." Art. I, § 8, cl. 8. The clause is both a grant of power and a limitation. This qualified authority, unlike the power often exercised in the sixteenth and seventeenth centuries by the English Crown, is limited to the promotion of advances in the "useful arts." It was written against the backdrop of the practices—eventually curtailed by the Statute of Monopolies—of the Crown in granting monopolies to court favorites in goods or businesses which had long before been enjoyed by the public. The Congress in the exercise of the patent power may not overreach the restraints imposed by the stated constitutional purpose. Nor may it enlarge the patent monopoly without regard to the innovation, advancement or social benefit gained thereby. Moreover, Congress may not authorize the issuance of patents whose effects are to remove existent knowledge from the public domain, or to restrict free access to materials already available. Innovation, advancement, and things which add to the sum of useful knowledge are inherent requisites in a patent system which by constitutional command must "promote the Progress of . . . useful Arts." This is the *standard* expressed in the Constitution and it may not be ignored. And it is in this light that patent validity "requires reference to a standard written into the Constitution." A. & P. Tea Co. v. Supermarket Corp., supra, at 154 (concurring opinion).

Within the limits of the constitutional grant, the Congress may, of course, implement the stated purpose of the Framers by selecting the policy which in its judgment best effectuates the constitutional aim. This is but a corollary to the grant to Congress of any Article I power. Within the scope established by the Constitution, Congress may set out conditions and tests for patentability. It is the duty of the Commissioner of Patents and of the courts in the administration of the patent system to give effect to the constitutional standard by appropriate application, in each case, of the statutory scheme of the Congress. . . .

III.

The difficulty of formulating conditions for patentability was heightened by the generality of the constitutional grant and the statutes implementing it, together with the underlying policy of the patent system that "the things which are worth to the public the embarrassment of an exclusive patent," as [Thomas] Jefferson put it, must outweigh the restrictive effect of the limited patent monopoly. The inherent problem was to develop some means of weeding out those inventions which would not be disclosed or devised but for the inducement of a patent.

This Court formulated a general condition of patentability in 1851 in Hotchkiss v. Greenwood, 11 How. 248. The patent involved a mere substitution of materials—porcelain or clay for wood or metal in doorknobs—and the Court condemned it, holding:

> [U]nless more ingenuity and skill . . . were required . . . than were possessed by an ordinary mechanic acquainted with the business, there was an absence of that degree of skill and ingenuity which constitute essential elements of every invention. In other words, the improvement is the work of the skillful mechanic, not that of the inventor. At p. 267.

Hotchkiss, by positing the condition that a patentable invention evidence more ingenuity and skill than that possessed by an ordinary mechanic acquainted with the business, merely distinguished between new and useful innovations that were capable of sustaining a patent and those that were not. The Hotchkiss test laid the cornerstone of the judicial evolution suggested by Jefferson and left to the courts by Congress. The language in the case, and in those which followed, gave birth to "invention" as a word of legal art signifying patentable inventions. Yet, as this Court has observed, "[t]he truth is the word ['invention'] cannot be defined in such manner as to afford any substantial aid in determining whether a particular device involves an exercise of the inventive faculty or not." McClain v. Ortmayer, 141 U.S. 419, 427, 12 S.Ct. 76, 78, 35 L.Ed. 800 (1891); A. & P. Tea Co. v. Supermarket Corp., supra, at 151. Its use as a label brought about a large variety of opinions as to its meaning both in the Patent Office, in the courts, and at the bar. The Hotchkiss formulation, however, lies not in any label, but in its functional approach to questions of patentability. In practice, Hotchkiss has required a comparison between the subject matter of the patent, or patent application, and the background skill of the calling. It has been from this comparison that patentability was in each case determined.

IV.

The 1952 Patent Act

The Act sets out the conditions of patentability in three sections. An analysis of the structure of these three sections indicates that patentability is dependent upon three explicit conditions: novelty and utility as articulated and defined in § 101 and § 102, and nonobviousness, the new statutory formulation, as set out in § 103. The first two sections, which trace closely the 1874 codification, express the "new and useful" tests which have always existed in the statutory scheme and, for our purposes here, need no clarification. The pivotal section around which the present controversy centers is § 103. It provides:

> § 103.   *Conditions for patentability; non-obvious subject matter*
>
> A patent may not be obtained though the invention is not identically disclosed or described as set forth in section 102 of this title, if the differences between the subject matter sought to be patented and the prior art are such that the subject matter as a whole would have been obvious at the time the invention was made to a person having ordinary skill in the art to which said subject matter pertains. Patentability shall not be negatived by the manner in which the invention was made.

The section is cast in relatively unambiguous terms. Patentability is to depend, in addition to novelty and utility, upon the "non-obvious" nature of the "subject matter sought to be patented" to a person having ordinary skill in the pertinent art.

The first sentence of this section is strongly reminiscent of the language in Hotchkiss. Both formulations place emphasis on the pertinent art existing at the time the invention was made and both are implicitly tied to advances in that art. The major distinction is that Congress has emphasized "nonobviousness" as the operative test of the section, rather than the less definite "invention" language of Hotchkiss that Congress thought had led to "a large variety" of expressions in decisions and writings....

It is undisputed that this section was, for the first time, a statutory expression of an additional requirement for patentability, originally expressed in Hotchkiss. It also seems apparent that Congress intended by the last sentence of § 103 to abolish the test it believed this Court announced in the controversial phrase "flash of creative genius," used in Cuno Corp. v. Automatic Devices Corp., 314 U.S. 84, 62 S.Ct. 37, 86 L.Ed. 58 (1941)....

V.

Approached in this light, the § 103 additional condition, when followed realistically, will permit a more practical test of patentability. The emphasis on nonobviousness is one of inquiry, not quality, and, as such, comports with the constitutional strictures.

While the ultimate question of patent validity is one of law, the § 103 condition, which is but one of three conditions, each of which must be satisfied, lends itself to several basic factual inquiries. Under § 103, the scope and content of the prior art are to be determined; differences between the prior art and the claims at issue are to be ascertained; and the level of ordinary skill in the pertinent art resolved. Against this background, the obviousness or nonobviousness of the subject matter is determined. Such secondary considerations as commercial success, long felt but unsolved needs, failure of others, etc., might be utilized to give light to the circumstances surrounding the origin of the subject matter sought to be patented. As indicia of obviousness or nonobviousness, these inquiries may have relevancy....

We now turn to the application of the conditions found necessary for patentability to the cases involved here:

A.   The Patent in Issue in No. 11, Graham v. John Deere Co.

This patent, No. 2,627,798 (hereinafter called the '798 patent) relates to a spring clamp which permits plow shanks to be pushed upward when they hit obstructions in the soil, and then springs the shanks back into normal position when the obstruction is passed over. The device, which we show diagrammatically in the accompanying sketches (Appendix, Fig. 1), is fixed to the plow frame as a unit. The mechanism around which the controversy centers is basically a hinge. The top half of it, known as the upper plate (marked 1 in the sketches), is a heavy metal piece clamped to the plow frame (2) and is stationary relative to the plow frame. The lower half of the hinge, known as the hinge plate (3), is connected to the rear of the upper plate by a hinge pin (4) and rotates downward with respect to it. The shank (5), which is bolted to the forward end of the hinge plate (at 6), runs beneath the plate and parallel to it for about nine inches, passes through a stirrup (7), and then continues backward for several feet curving down toward the ground. The chisel (8), which does the actual plowing, is attached to the rear end of the shank. As the plow frame is pulled forward, the chisel rips through the soil, thereby plowing it. In the normal position, the hinge plate and the shank are kept tight against the upper plate by a spring (9), which is atop the upper plate. A rod (10) runs through the center of the spring, extending down through holes in both plates and the shank. Its upper end is bolted to the top of the spring while its lower end is hooked against the underside of the shank.

When the chisel hits a rock or other obstruction in the soil, the obstruction forces the chisel and the rear portion of the shank to move upward. The shank is pivoted (at 11) against the rear of the hinge plate and pries open the hinge against the closing tendency of the spring. (See sketch labeled "Open Position," Appendix, Fig. 1.) This closing tendency is caused by the fact that, as the hinge is opened, the connecting rod is pulled downward and the spring is compressed. When the obstruction is passed over, the upward force on the chisel disappears and the spring pulls the shank and hinge plate back into their original position. The lower, rear portion of the hinge plate is constructed in the form of a stirrup (7) which brackets the shank, passing around and beneath it. The shank fits loosely into the stirrup (permitting a slight up and down play). The stirrup is designed to prevent the shank from recoiling away from the hinge plate, and thus prevents excessive strain on the shank near its bolted connection. The stirrup also girds the shank, preventing it from fish-tailing from side to side.

In practical use, a number of spring-hinge-shank combinations are clamped to a plow frame, forming a set of ground-working chisels capable of withstanding the shock of rocks and other obstructions in the soil without breaking the shanks.

Background of the Patent

Chisel plows, as they are called, were developed for plowing in areas where the ground is relatively free from rocks or stones. Originally, the shanks were rigidly attached to the plow frames. When such plows were used in the rocky, glacial soils of some of the Northern States, they were found to have serious defects. As the chisels hit buried rocks, a vibratory motion was set up and tremendous forces were transmitted to the shank near its connection to the frame. The shanks would break. Graham, one of the petitioners, sought to meet that problem, and in 1950 obtained a patent, U.S. No. 2,493,811 (hereinafter '811), on a spring clamp which solved some of the difficulties. Graham and his companies manufactured and sold the '811 clamps. In 1950, Graham modified the '811 structure and filed for a patent. That patent, the one in issue, was granted in 1953. This suit against competing plow manufacturers resulted from charges by petitioners that several of respondents' devices infringed the '798 patent.

The Prior Art

Five prior patents indicating the state of the art were cited by the Patent Office in the prosecution of the '798 application. Four of these patents, 10 other United States patents and two prior-use spring-clamp arrangements not of record in the '798 file wrapper were relied upon by respondents as revealing the prior art. The District Court and the Court of Appeals found that the prior art "as a whole in one form or another contains all of the mechanical elements of the '798 Patent." One of the prior-use clamp devices not before the Patent Examiner—Glencoe—was found to have "all of the elements."

We confine our discussion to the prior patent of Graham, '811, and to the Glencoe clamp device, both among the references asserted by respondents. The Graham '811 and '798 patent devices are similar in all elements, save two: (1) the stirrup and the bolted connection of the shank to the hinge plate do not appear in '811; and (2) the position of the shank is reversed, being placed in patent '811 above the hinge plate, sandwiched between it and the upper plate. The shank is held in place by the spring rod which is hooked against the bottom of the hinge plate passing through a slot in the shank. Other differences are of no consequence to our examination. In practice the '811 patent arrangement permitted the shank to wobble or fish-tail because it was not rigidly fixed to the hinge plate; moreover, as the hinge plate was below the shank, the latter caused wear on the upper plate, a member difficult to repair or replace.

Graham's '798 patent application contained 12 claims. All were rejected as not distinguished from the Graham '811 patent. The inverted position of the shank was specifically rejected as was the bolting of the shank to the hinge plate. The Patent Office examiner found these to be "matters of design well within the expected skill of the art and devoid of invention." Graham withdrew the original claims and substituted the two new ones which are substantially those in issue here. His contention was that wear was reduced in patent '798 between the shank and the heel or rear of the upper plate. He also emphasized several new features, the relevant one here being that the bolt used to connect the hinge plate and shank maintained the upper face of the shank in continuing and constant contact with the underface of the hinge plate.

Graham did not urge before the Patent Office the greater "flexing" qualities of the '798 patent arrangement which he so heavily relied on in the courts. The sole element in patent '798 which petitioners argue before us is the interchanging of the shank and hinge plate and the consequences flowing from this arrangement. The contention is that this arrangement—which petitioners claim is not disclosed in the prior art—permits the shank to flex under stress for its *entire* length. As we have sketched (see sketch, "Graham '798 Patent" in Appendix, Fig. 2), when the chisel hits an obstruction the resultant force (A) pushes the rear of the shank upward and the shank pivots against the rear of the hinge plate at (C). The natural tendency is for that portion of the shank between the pivot point and the bolted connection (i.e., between C and D) to bow downward and away from the hinge plate. The maximum distance (B) that the shank moves away from the plate is slight—for emphasis, greatly exaggerated in the sketches. This is so because of the strength of the shank and the short—nine inches or so—length of that portion of the shank between (C) and (D). On the contrary, in patent '811 (see sketch, "Graham '811 Patent" in Appendix,

Fig. 2), the pivot point is the upper plate at point (c); and while the tendency for the shank to bow between points (c) and (d) is the same as in '798, the shank is restricted because of the underlying hinge plate and cannot flex as freely. In practical effect, the shank flexes only between points (a) and (c), and not along the entire length of the shank, as in '798. Petitioners say that this difference in flex, though small, effectively absorbs the tremendous forces of the shock of obstructions whereas prior art arrangements failed.

The Obviousness of the Differences

We cannot agree with petitioners. We assume that the prior art does not disclose such an arrangement as petitioners claim in patent '798. Still we do not believe that the argument on which petitioners' contention is bottomed supports the validity of the patent. The tendency of the shank to flex is the same in all cases. If free-flexing, as petitioners now argue, is the crucial difference above the prior art, then it appears evident that the desired result would be obtainable by not boxing the shank within the confines of the hinge. The only other effective place available in the arrangement was to attach it below the hinge plate and run it through a stirrup or bracket that would not disturb its flexing qualities. Certainly a person having ordinary skill in the prior art, given the fact that the flex in the shank could be utilized more effectively if allowed to run the entire length of the shank, would immediately see that the thing to do was what Graham did, i.e., invert the shank and the hinge plate.

Petitioners' argument basing validity on the free-flex theory raised for the first time on appeal is reminiscent of Lincoln Engineering Co. v. Stewart–Warner Corp., 303 U.S. 545, 58 S.Ct. 662, 82 L.Ed. 1008 (1938), where the Court called such an effort "an afterthought. No such function . . . is hinted at in the specifications of the patent. If this were so vital an element in the functioning of the apparatus it is strange that all mention of it was omitted." At p. 550. No "flexing" argument was raised in the Patent Office. Indeed, the trial judge specifically found that "flexing is not a claim of the patent in suit . . ." and would not permit interrogation as to flexing in the accused devices. Moreover, the clear testimony of petitioners' experts shows that the flexing advantages flowing from the '798 arrangement are not, in fact, a significant feature in the patent.

We find no nonobvious facets in the '798 arrangement. The wear and repair claims were sufficient to overcome the patent examiner's original conclusions as to the validity of the patent. However, some of the prior art, notably Glencoe, was not before him. There the hinge plate is below the shank but, as the courts below found, all of the elements in the '798 patent are present in the Glencoe structure. Furthermore, even though the position of the shank and hinge plate appears reversed in Glencoe, the mechanical operation is identical. The shank there pivots about the underside of the stirrup, which in Glencoe is *above* the shank. In other words, the stirrup in Glencoe serves exactly the same function as the heel of the hinge plate in '798. The mere shifting of the wear point to the heel of the '798 hinge plate from the stirrup of Glencoe—itself a part of the hinge plate—presents no operative mechanical distinctions, much less nonobvious differences.

The judgment of the Court of Appeals in No. 11 is affirmed.

Appendix to Opinion of the Court

Figure 1.—GRAHAM '798 PATENT

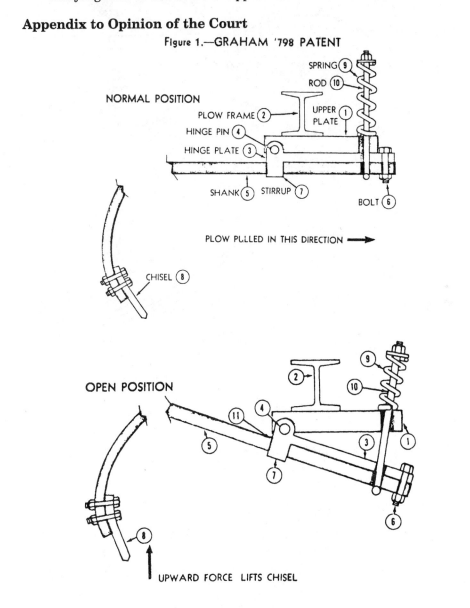

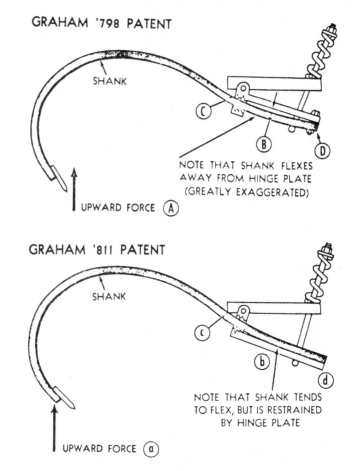

Figure 2.—FLEX COMPARISON

GRAHAM '798 PATENT

SHANK

NOTE THAT SHANK FLEXES
AWAY FROM HINGE PLATE
(GREATLY EXAGGERATED)

UPWARD FORCE (A)

GRAHAM '811 PATENT

SHANK

NOTE THAT SHANK TENDS
TO FLEX, BUT IS RESTRAINED
BY HINGE PLATE

UPWARD FORCE (a)

Stratoflex, Inc. v. Aeroquip Corp.

United States Court of Appeals, Federal Circuit, 1983.
713 F.2d 1530, 218 U.S.P.Q. 871.

MARKEY, Chief Judge.

Appeal from a judgment of the District Court for the Eastern District
of Michigan, 561 F.Supp. 618, declaring Claims 1, 3, 4, 6, and 7 of U.S.
Patent No. 3,473,087 to Winton Slade ('087 patent) invalid and not infringed. We affirm.

When Stratoflex filed suit seeking a declaration of invalidity and non-
infringement of the '087 patent, Aeroquip, as assignee, counterclaimed for
infringement of claims 1, 3, 4, 6, and 7. After a non-jury trial, Judge Boyle
declared those claims invalid and found them not infringed. Though Stratoflex filed for a declaratory judgment that the patent was invalid, trial,
judgment, and the briefs on appeal dealt only with claims 1, 3, 4, 6, and 7.

Accordingly, we make no holding respecting validity of claims 2, 5, and 8–19.

I. Background

A. The Technology

Stratoflex and Aeroquip manufacture electrically conductive polytetrafluoroethylene tubing used in the aircraft and missile industry to convey pressurized fuel, lubricants, and other fluids. The parties refer to polytetrafluoroethylene also as "Teflon," a registered trademark of the E.I. Dupont de Nemours Company.

PTFE has replaced organic and synthetic rubbers and plastic in fuel hoses because it has a number of superior characteristics. Though pure PTFE is dielectric (non-conductive), it can be made with fillers to make it conductive, though the "filled" tubing is more susceptible to leakage when voids form between the PTFE and filler particles.

B. The Invention

The Slade invention relates to a composite PTFE tubing, formed of an inner layer of electrically conductive PTFE having particles such as carbon black uniformly distributed in it and an outer layer of essentially pure nonconductive PTFE. Claims 1 and 7 are representative:

> 1. A tubular extrudate formed of attached concentric tubular extrusions, the inner tubular extrusion comprising associated particles of unsintered tetrafluoroethylene polymer and pulverulent, inert, electrically conductive particles, and the outer tubular extrusion comprising associated particles of unsintered tetrafluoroethylene polymer.

> 7. A tube of polytetrafluoroethylene and the like for conducting fluids under pressure and including means for discharge of internal static electricity to the ends of the tube and grounding the same from the tube interior at said ends in order to maintain the polytetrafluoroethylene tubing performance characteristics, said tubing having an integral polytetrafluoroethylene wall structure with an interior liner portion of a substantially annular conformation from end to end and having a uniform dispersion of electrically conductive particles embedded therein, the major portion of said tubing wall completely surrounding said liner portion exteriorly and being relatively nonconductive in character, said surrounding portion together with said liner containing fluid under pressures uniformly within said tubing.

Claims 3, 4, and 6 are similar to claim 1, but specify various percentages of ingredients.

The particles in the inner layer of the claimed tubing dissipate electrostatic charges built up on the inner surface of the tubing, conducting them lengthwise of the tubing to grounded metal fittings at the ends of a hose assembly of which the tubing is part, to prevent arcing or discharging through the tubing wall to the surrounding metal braid. Arcing causes "pin holes" through which fuel can leak. The outer layer is coextruded or bonded around the inner layer to contain any fuel leaking through the inner layer. The composite tubing has excellent conductivity, while retaining the desirable characteristics of PTFE tubing.

C.   Events Leading to the '087 Patent

Pure PTFE tubing had been used successfully in aircraft engines since at least 1956. In 1959, with the introduction of hydrocarbon jet fuels, leaks were noticed. Aeroquip assigned two staff engineers, Abbey and Upham, to determine the cause. They found the problem to be the arcing of electrostatic charges through the wall of the pure dielectric PTFE tubing to create "pin holes" as described above.

Abbey and Upham found the "pin hole" phenomenon exhibited by all three types of PTFE (White—Titeflex; Pink/Red—Aeroquip; Black—Goodrich) used in aircraft engines. The black tubing appeared superior because the carbon black it contained gave it an intermittent conductivity. The carbon black took the form of discontinuous strings and arcing across the spaces between string ends conveyed charges to the ends of the tubing. Electrical erosion of the strings, however, widened the spaces, destroying conductivity and leading to the "pin hole" phenomenon. Abbey and Upham concluded that susceptibility of PTFE tubing to "pin holing" was proportional to its conductivity, and that carbon black increased the conductivity of PTFE tubing.

In early 1960, having determined the cause of leaking, Aeroquip approached Raybestos–Manhattan (Raybestos), a PTFE hose manufacturer, for a solution. Aeroquip later purchased the hose section of Raybestos, obtaining the Slade patent by mesne assignment.

Raybestos assigned the project to the inventor, Winton Slade, who prepared several samples of conductive PTFE tubing (powdered lead, copper, chemically etched, and carbon black) and sent them for testing to Aeroquip in the summer of 1960. In the Fall, Aeroquip ordered a small production quantity of carbon black tubing. That tubing was not a composite and the carbon black was not uniformly distributed in it.

Slade conceived of the composite tube of the invention as early as August 5, 1960 and reduced it to practice in November of 1961. He filed a patent application on May 22, 1962, with claims directed to the composite tubing and also to various processes for making it.

During prosecution, Slade's assignee Raybestos sought and was denied declaration of an interference with a patent application assigned to Titeflex. The Titeflex application issued as U.S. Patent 3,166,688 ('688 patent). Raybestos then was granted an interference with claims 1 and 2 of the '688 patent. An agreement provided that the loser of the interference would receive a royalty free license. Slade was awarded priority and Titeflex was licensed.

When the examiner imposed a restriction requirement on the Slade application, Slade elected to prosecute the product claims, and filed the process claims in a co-pending application which issued as U.S. Patent No.

3,658,976. Slade's original application issued with its product claims as the '087 patent on October 1, 1969.

D. Stratoflex Actions

From 1962 to 1970, Stratoflex purchased PTFE tubing containing carbon black from B.F. Goodrich. When Goodrich ceased production, Stratoflex purchased conductive PTFE tubing made by Titeflex under its license. Stratoflex then began manufacturing and selling its own "124" and "127" composite tubing having an inner layer with conductive carbon black uniformly dispersed throughout, and an outer layer that is essentially nonconductive, though that outer layer includes a small amount of carbon black to color the tubing and to aid extrusion.

On December 8, 1978, Aeroquip charged that Stratoflex's unauthorized manufacture and sale of "124" and "127" tubing infringed its rights under the '087 patent.

E. Trial and Opinion

Trial was held on December 15, 16, 18, 19 and 22, 1980. Stratoflex alleged that the '087 patent was invalid as anticipated under 35 U.S.C. § 102, as having been in public use or on sale, 35 U.S.C. § 102(b); for obviousness, 35 U.S.C. § 103; or because the claims were indefinite, 35 U.S.C. § 112. Judge Boyle decided the validity issue on 35 U.S.C. § 103, and the appeal concerns only that Section.

On August 16, 1982, Judge Boyle issued judgment and an accompanying opinion. In that opinion, Judge Boyle indicated: that the presumption of validity is weakened when the challenger introduces pertinent prior art not considered by the examiner; that Aeroquip was therefore not entitled to the presumption's full benefit; that the relevant prior art included rubber hose; that one of ordinary skill in the art had a degree in chemical engineering or its equivalent and substantial experience in the extrusion art; that the prior art taught addition of conductive carbon black to tubing to dissipate electrostatic charges on its inner surface; that composite tubing incorporating various materials in each layer to yield superior products was known; that addition of carbon black to PTFE to induce conductivity was known; that the only differences between the claims and the prior art were use of PTFE in concentric tubes and the "salt and pepper" method of forming the inner tube layer; that secondary considerations were not to be considered because the claimed inventions were clearly obvious and "those matters without invention will not make patentability;" that those matters should be considered only in a close case where they could "tip the balance in favor of patentability;" that it was unnecessary to determine whether synergism was a separate requirement for validity "since either standard justifies a conclusion that the combination of these elements simply lacks 'the unique essence of authentic contribution' to the (PTFE) art which is the heart of invention;" that Stratoflex did not infringe claims 1, 3, 4, 6 or 7 because the only non-obvious difference between the claims and the prior art was the "salt and pepper" process for making the tubing layer and Stratoflex did not use that process.

Issues

Whether Judge Boyle erred in: (1) declaring claims 1, 3, 4, 6, and 7 invalid; (2) finding non-infringement.

II. VALIDITY

(A) Presumption of Validity

... (B) Obviousness

The declaration that claims 1, 3, 4, 6, and 7 of the '087 patent are invalid was based on a conclusion that the inventions set forth in those claims would have been obvious under 35 U.S.C. § 103, in the light of facts found in the course of following the guidelines set forth in Graham v. John Deere Co., 383 U.S. 1, 17, 86 S.Ct. 684, 693, 15 L.Ed.2d 545 (1966).

Aeroquip contends that error occurred in findings on the scope and content of the prior art, level of ordinary skill, and differences between the prior art and the claimed invention, and in the legal conclusion of obviousness based on those findings.

Judge Boyle said, "[T]he question of obviousness is a mixed question of fact and law requiring factual findings," citing the then-applicable view expressed by the Court of Appeals for the Sixth Circuit. In this court, the obviousness determination is "a legal conclusion based on factual evidence." Stevenson v. International Trade Commission, 612 F.2d 546, 67 CCPA 109, 204 U.S.P.Q. 276 (CCPA 1979). The difference does not affect the outcome on this appeal, because it did not in this case lead to error in either the findings or conclusion.

Under Rule 52(a), Federal Rules of Civil Procedure, our review of the findings undergirding the conclusion on obviousness is limited to a determination of whether they were clearly erroneous in light of the entire record.

Scope and Content of the Prior Art

Aeroquip contends that the scope of the relevant prior art excludes rubber hose because PTFE is a unique material, possessing properties that differ significantly from rubber, and that, because the claims are limited to PTFE, the rubber hose art could at most be peripherally relevant as background information.

The scope of the prior art has been defined as that "reasonably pertinent to the particular problem with which the inventor was involved." In re Wood, 599 F.2d 1032, 1036, 202 U.S.P.Q. 171, 174 (Cust. & Pat.App. 1979). The problem confronting Slade was preventing electrostatic buildup in PTFE tubing caused by hydrocarbon fuel flow while precluding leakage of fuel. None of the unique properties of PTFE would change the nature of that problem. Nor would anything of record indicate that one skilled in the art would not include the rubber hose art in his search for a solution to that problem.

Indeed, Slade himself referred to a standard textbook on conductive carbon black in rubber when he began his search for a solution. Judge Boyle correctly found Slade's act an acknowledgement by the problem solver of what he considered relevant prior art.

The examiner cited two prior art references in the rubber hose art, one disclosing the problem of electrostatic buildup caused by fuel flow. The Abbey–Upham report, though concerned with PTFE, included a conductivity comparison with carbon black filled rubber hose, and its bibliography listed several articles on electrostatic buildup in rubber. The record reflects that PTFE and rubber are used by the same hose manufacturers to make hoses and that the same and similar problems have been experienced with both. There is no basis for finding that a solution found for a problem experienced with one material would not be looked to when facing a problem with the other. The finding that the rubber hose art is relevant and thus within the scope of the art was not clearly erroneous.

The content of the prior art included the Abbey–Upham Report and several patents relating to conductive and composite rubber hose and to PTFE tubing.

The Abbey–Upham Report, as above indicated, discloses the cause of PTFE tubing "pin holes" as the arcing of electrostatic charges laterally through the non-conductive PTFE tubing wall to the surrounding metal braid, that carbon black increases conductivity of PTFE, and that susceptibility of PTFE tubing to "pinholing" is directly proportional to its conductivity. Judge Boyle correctly found the report to have disclosed the basic concepts underlying the claimed invention, but not that of forming PTFE tubing as a composite having a conductive inner layer and a nonconductive outer layer.

United States Patent No. 2,341,360 ('360 patent) teaches composite tubing having carbon black in one layer to make it electrically conductive for dissipation of static electricity.

U.S. Patent No. 2,632,205 ('205 patent) teaches a rubber or plastic composite tubing for conveying fluids and having powdered metal or other conductive materials embedded along the inner wall to conduct electric charges lengthwise of the tubing.

U.S. Patent No. 3,070,132 teaches extrusion of carbon black mixed with plastic to form a continuous conductive stripe in a normally dielectric tubing to prevent accumulation of electrostatic charges. It teaches that electrostatic discharge causes leaks through the wall of the tubing and explosions when inflammable materials are conveyed. It mentions rubber tubing.

U.S. Patent No. 2,108,759 discloses an "antistatic" fuel nozzle. It teaches dissipation of electrostatic charges caused by hydrocarbon fuel flow, before those charges can arc, by employing conductive materials like synthetic rubber in an inner layer of the nozzle.

U.S. Patent No. 2,781,288 ('288 patent) teaches a composite rubber hose with each layer arranged to take advantage of its particular properties. It suggests carbon black as a filler, but not as a conductor.

U.S. Patent No. 2,645,249 ('249 patent) and U.S. Patent No. 2,501,690 ('690 patent) teach composite tubing with each layer containing different fillers to impart varying characteristics to the inner and outer layers.

U.S. Patent No. 2,863,174, U.S. Patent No. 2,685,707, and U.S. Patent No. 2,752,637 disclose the use of carbon black as an extrusion aid in forming PTFE.

U.S. Patent No. 2,945,265 ('265 patent) teaches co-extrusion of PTFE with different fillers, carbon black being used as a coloring agent.

Aeroquip's attack on the content-of-the-prior-art findings is limited to its argument that rubber hose should be excluded. That argument having been found wanting, the findings on the content of the prior art cannot be viewed as clearly erroneous.

Consideration of the scope and content of the prior art tilts the scales of decision toward a conclusion of obviousness. Thus the Abbey–Upham report teaches use of carbon black to increase conductivity of PTFE tubing to reduce the chance of electrostatic buildup on the tubing wall. It would appear to have been obvious to one skilled in the art to place the conductive material in the wall where the electrostatic buildup occurs (here the inner wall subjected to electrostatic buildup by fuel flow) as suggested by the '360 and '205 patents. It would appear to have been obvious from the '288, '249, and '690 patents to form a composite tubing with layers arranged to take advantage of their physical and chemical properties. On this record, consideration of the prior art as a whole, and in the absence of evidence that any special problem in following its teachings was created by the unique properties of PTFE, it would appear to have been obvious to place a conductive PTFE layer inside an essentially non-conductive outer PTFE layer to prevent fuel seepage associated with the conductive layer.

Differences Between the Claimed Invention and the Prior Art

Though claim 7 differs substantially from the others, claims 1, 3, 4, 6, and 7 have not been argued separately. They therefore stand or fall together.

Aeroquip concedes that pure PTFE had been known to be dielectric, that carbon black was known to be conductive, and that PTFE had been made into tubing containing at least a small amount of carbon black. It alleges that the prior art does not show the composite tubing set forth in the claims, specifically a composite PTFE tubing with its inner layer formed of uniformly distributed carbon black and PTFE, to provide conductivity sufficient to dissipate electrostatic buildup, and an outer layer of relatively pure PTFE that prevents fuel leakage. It is true that no single reference shows all elements of the claims, but the holding here is one of invalidity for obviousness, not for anticipation. The question, therefore, is whether the inventions set forth in claims 1, 3, 4, 6 and 7, each as a whole, would have been obvious to one of ordinary skill in the art when they were made, in view of the teachings of the prior art as a whole.

Though findings on the "differences" from the prior art are suggested by *Graham v. John Deere*, supra, the question under 35 U.S.C. § 103 is not whether the differences themselves would have been obvious. Consideration of differences, like each of the findings set forth in *Graham*, is but an aid in reaching the ultimate determination of whether the claimed invention *as a whole* would have been obvious.

Judge Boyle found that the differences between the claimed invention and the prior art were use of PTFE in concentric tubes and the "salt and pepper" process of forming the inner layer. The first difference would indicate a mere change of material. The second difference is, of course, irrelevant as stated, the claimed inventions having nothing to do with the process of making the inner layer. The finding may have been meant to indicate that the second difference lay in the structural *result* of the "salt and pepper" process, namely a uniform dispersion of carbon black particles in the inner layer (a limitation appearing only in claim 7).

With respect to use of a different material, the problem (leakage) and the cause ("pin holes" from electrostatic charges) were known with respect to that material (PTFE). A solution for the electrostatic charge problems, i.e., dissipation of charges lengthwise of the tubing, was known. Nothing in the first difference found would indicate that it would have been nonobvious to transfer that solution from tubing formed of other materials to tubing formed of PTFE. As above indicated, no special problem needed to be or was overcome in substituting a different material (PTFE) for the materials (rubber and plastics) of the prior art.

Similarly, with respect to uniform dispersion of conductive particles, it was known that spaces between carbon black areas in tubing permit arcing. Nothing of record establishes that use of uniform dispersion to limit or eliminate such spaces would not have been obvious. The same is true respecting use of a nonconductive outer layer to contain leakage from the inner conductive layer.

Aeroquip challenges the finding that the Abbey–Upham report does not teach away from use of carbon black in PTFE tubing, citing this language in the report: "The possibility of establishing continuous longitudinal strings of carbon particles during extrusion, especially in view of the relatively small percentage of carbon black used in Teflon hose seemed remote." It appears between two others in a segment having a thrust quite opposite from that suggested by Aeroquip:

> An explanation of this intermittent conductive behavior required some further investigation. The possibility of establishing continuous longitudinal strings of carbon particles during extrusion, especially in view of the relatively small percentage of carbon black used in Teflon hose seemed remote. If, however, the carbon particle strings were discontinuous, and the individual particles were distributed at varying dis-

tances from each other, the intermittent conduction observed in the carbon black filled tubes could be easily understood.

Investigators Abbey and Upham were speculating on the cause of intermittent conductivity in a PTFE tube containing carbon black. They rejected as "remote" the possibility that in *extruding* the tubing the carbon formed continuous strings because there was a small percentage of carbon present. That sentence dealt with a process of making the tubing. As subsequently proven in the report, a better explanation was the presence of discontinuous strings in the tubing under investigation.

In the sentence following that cited to us by Aeroquip, the Abbey–Upham report describes uneven spacing between carbon black particles as a possible cause of intermittent conductivity. Far from "teaching away," therefore, the report may be viewed as pointing in the direction of uniform dispersion of such particles, as set forth in claim 7, to produce less intermittent conductivity.

The findings that the differences here were use of a different material and uniform dispersion of carbon black particles were not clearly erroneous. Those differences do not tilt the scales toward a conclusion of nonobviousness of the invention as a whole in light of all prior art teachings summarized above.

Level of Ordinary Skill

The district court found the level of ordinary skill to be that of a chemical engineer or equivalent, having substantial experience in the extrusion arts. Aeroquip says that was too high, suggesting that of an engineer or technician in the PTFE art, as described by its expert, Townsend Beaman. The suggestion is but another effort to limit the prior art to PTFE tubing and avoid inclusion of the art of making fuel hoses of other materials.

The level of ordinary skill may be determined from several factors. Slade had the level of skill set by the district court. Stratoflex witness Linger was a mechanical engineer with years of experience in the rubber and PTFE hose art. Mr. Beaman was patent counsel for Aeroquip. Judge Boyle correctly viewed Beaman as an observer of, not a worker in, the relevant art.

The statute, 35 U.S.C. § 103, requires that a claim be declared invalid only when the invention set forth in that claim can be said to have been obvious "to one of *ordinary* skill in the art." (emphasis added) As an aid in determining obviousness, that requirement precludes consideration of whether the invention would have been obvious (as a whole and just before it was made) to the rare genius in the art, or to a judge or other layman after learning all about the invention.

Aeroquip has not shown the finding on the level of ordinary skill in the art to have been erroneous here.

Secondary Considerations

It is jurisprudentially inappropriate to disregard any relevant evidence on any issue in any case, patent cases included. Thus evidence rising out of the so-called "secondary considerations" must always when present be considered en route to a determination of obviousness. Indeed, evidence of secondary considerations may often be the most probative and cogent evidence in the record. It may often establish that an invention appearing to have been obvious in light of the prior art was not. It is to be considered as part of all the evidence, not just when the decisionmaker remains in doubt after reviewing the art.

Judge Boyle made findings on secondary considerations, but said she did not include them in her analysis because she believed the claimed inventions were plainly obvious and "those matters without invention will not make patentability" and should be considered only in a close case. That was error. . . .

The evidence and findings on secondary considerations being present in the record, the interests of judicial economy dictate its consideration and evaluation on this appeal. The result being unchanged, a remand for reconsideration of the evidence would in this case constitute a waste of resources for the courts and the parties.

A nexus is required between the merits of the claimed invention and the evidence offered, if that evidence is to be given substantial weight enroute to conclusion on the obviousness issue.

Aeroquip says commercial success is shown because: the "entire industry" makes the tubing claimed in the '087 patent; only Stratoflex is not licensed under the '087 patent; Curtiss–Wright retrofitted 10,000 engines with conductive tubing; and military specifications for conductive tubing are met only by tubing claimed in the '087 patent. We are not persuaded.

Recognition and acceptance of the patent by competitors who take licenses under it to avail themselves of the merits of the invention is evidence of nonobviousness. Here, however, Aeroquip does not delineate the make-up of the "entire industry." The record reflects only two manufacturers, Titeflex and Resistoflex, in addition to the parties. Titeflex has a royalty-free license, resulting from the interference settling agreement described above. Resistoflex has a license that includes several other patents and the right to use the trademark "HI–PAC" for complete hose assemblies. Aeroquip has shown neither a nexus between the merits of the invention and the licenses of record, nor that those licenses arose out of recognition and acceptance of the patent.

No evidence of record establishes that tubing covered by the claims of the '087 patent was used in the Curtiss–Wright retrofit. It cannot therefore be given weight in respect of commercial success.

The military specifications were promulgated after the claimed invention was known. Thus the invention did not meet a longfelt but unfilled need expressed in the specifications. Moreover, the record does not support Aeroquip's assertion that the specifications can be met only by tubing covered by the claims of the '087 patent. The nexus required to establish commercial success is therefore not present with respect to the military specifications.

Nor is there evidence that others skilled in the art tried and failed to find a solution for the problem. Aeroquip cites Abbey and Upham, but their effort was limited to investigation of the problem and its cause, and was not directed to its solution.

Upon full consideration of the evidence respecting the secondary considerations in this case, and of Aeroquip's arguments, we are persuaded that nonobviousness is not established by that evidence. Judge Boyle's error in refusing to include that evidence in her analysis was therefore in this case harmless.

"Synergism" and "Combination Patents"

Judge Boyle said "synergism" is "a symbolic reminder of what constitutes nonobviousness when a combination patent is at issue," and that under "either standard (*Graham* analysis or synergism) the combination ... simply lacks the unique essence of authentic contribution to the Teflon art which is the heart of invention."

A requirement for "synergism" or a "synergistic effect" is nowhere found in the statute, 35 U.S.C. When present, for example in a chemical case, synergism may point toward nonobviousness, but its absence has no place in evaluating the evidence on obviousness. The more objective findings suggested in *Graham*, supra, are drawn from the language of the statute and are fully adequate guides for evaluating the evidence relating to compliance with 35 U.S.C. § 103. Judge Boyle treated synergism as an alternative consideration. Hence the error of its analytical inclusion is harmless in view of Judge Boyle's employment of the Graham aids.

The reference to a "combination patent" is equally without support in the statute. There is no warrant for judicial classification of patents, whether into "combination" patents and some other unnamed and undefined class or otherwise. Nor is there warrant for differing treatment or consideration of patents based on a judicially devised label. Reference to "combination" patents is, moreover, meaningless. Virtually all patents are "combination patents," if by that label one intends to describe patents having claims to inventions formed of a combination of elements. It is difficult to visualize, at least in the mechanical-structural arts, a "non-combination" invention, i.e., an invention consisting of a *single* element. Such inventions, if they exist, are rare indeed. Again, however, Judge Boyle's inclusion in her analysis of a reference to the '087 patent as a "combination" patent was harmless in view of her application of *Graham* guidelines.

Similarly, Judge Boyle's reference to "the heart of invention" was here a harmless fall-back to the fruitless search for an inherently amorphous concept that was rendered unnecessary by the statute, 35 U.S.C. The

Graham analysis here applied properly looked to *patentability*, not to "invention."

Conclusion

The judgment declaring claims 1, 3, 4, 6, and 7 invalid is affirmed.

IN RE DEUEL, 51 F.3d 1552, 1557–1559, 34 U.S.P.Q.2d 1210 (Fed.Cir. 1995): On appeal, Deuel challenges the Board's determination that the applied references establish a *prima facie* case of obviousness. In response, the PTO maintains that the claimed invention would have been *prima facie* obvious over the combined teachings of Bohlen and Maniatis. Thus, the appeal raises the important question whether the combination of a prior art reference teaching a method of gene cloning, together with a reference disclosing a partial amino acid sequence of a protein, may render DNA and cDNA molecules encoding the protein *prima facie* obvious under § 103.

Deuel argues that the PTO failed to follow the proper legal standard in determining that the claimed cDNA molecules would have been *prima facie* obvious despite the lack of structurally similar compounds in the prior art. Deuel argues that the PTO has not cited a reference teaching cDNA molecules, but instead has improperly rejected the claims based on the alleged obviousness of a method of making the molecules. We agree.

Because Deuel claims new chemical entities in structural terms, a *prima facie* case of unpatentability requires that the teachings of the prior art suggest *the claimed compounds* to a person of ordinary skill in the art. Normally a *prima facie* case of obviousness is based upon structural similarity, *i.e.,* an established structural relationship between a prior art compound and the claimed compound. Structural relationships may provide the requisite motivation or suggestion to modify known compounds to obtain new compounds. For example, a prior art compound may suggest its homologs because homologs often have similar properties and therefore chemists of ordinary skill would ordinarily contemplate making them to try to obtain compounds with improved properties. Similarly, a known compound may suggest its analogs or isomers, either geometric isomers (cis v. trans) or position isomers (*e.g.,* ortho v. para).

In all of these cases, however, the prior art teaches a specific, structurally-definable compound and the question becomes whether the prior art would have suggested making the specific molecular modifications necessary to achieve the claimed invention.

Here, the prior art does not disclose any relevant cDNA molecules, let alone close relatives of the specific, structurally-defined cDNA molecules of claims 5 and 7 that might render them obvious. Maniatis suggests an allegedly obvious process for trying to isolate cDNA molecules, but that, as we will indicate below, does not fill the gap regarding the subject matter of claims 5 and 7. Further, while the general idea of the claimed molecules, their function, and their general chemical nature may have been obvious from Bohlen's teachings, and the knowledge that some gene existed may have been clear, the precise cDNA molecules of claims 5 and 7 would not have been obvious over the Bohlen reference because Bohlen teaches proteins, not the claimed or closely related cDNA molecules. The redundancy of the genetic code precluded contemplation of or focus on the specific cDNA molecules of claims 5 and 7. Thus, one could not have conceived the subject matter of claims 5 and 7 based on the teachings in the cited prior art because, until the claimed molecules were actually isolated and purified, it would have been highly unlikely for one of ordinary skill in the art to contemplate what was ultimately obtained. What cannot be contemplated or conceived cannot be obvious.

The PTO's theory that one might have been motivated to try to do what Deuel in fact accomplished amounts to speculation and an impermissible hindsight reconstruction of the claimed invention. It also ignores the fact that claims 5 and 7 are limited to specific compounds, and any motivation that existed was a general one, to try to obtain a gene that was yet undefined and may have constituted many forms. A general motivation to search for some gene that exists does not necessarily make obvious a specifically-defined gene that is subsequently obtained as a result of that search. More is needed and it is not found here.

The genetic code relationship between proteins and nucleic acids does not overcome the deficiencies of the cited references. A prior art disclosure of the amino acid sequence of a protein does not necessarily render particular DNA molecules encoding the protein obvious because the redundancy of the genetic code permits one to hypothesize an enormous number of DNA sequences coding for the protein. No particular one of these DNAs can be obvious unless there is something in the prior art to lead to the particular DNA and indicate that it should be prepared.... A different result might pertain, however, if there were prior art, *e.g.,* a protein of sufficiently small size and simplicity, so that lacking redundancy, each possible DNA would be obvious over the protein. That is not the case here.

The PTO's focus on known methods for potentially isolating the claimed DNA molecules is also misplaced because the claims at issue define compounds, not methods. *See* In re Bell, 991 F.2d 781, 785, 26 USPQ2d 1529, 1532 (Fed.Cir.1993). In Bell, the PTO asserted a rejection based upon the combination of a primary reference disclosing a protein (*and its complete amino acid sequence*) with a secondary reference describing a general method of gene cloning. We reversed the rejection, holding in part that "[t]he PTO's focus on Bell's method is misplaced. Bell does not claim a method. Bell claims compositions, and the issue is the obviousness of the claimed compositions, not of the method by which they are made." Id.

We today reaffirm the principle, stated in Bell, that the existence of a general method of isolating cDNA or DNA molecules is essentially irrelevant to the question whether the specific molecules themselves would have been obvious, in the absence of other prior art that suggests the claimed DNAs. A prior art disclosure of a process *reciting a particular compound* or obvious variant thereof as a product of the process is, of course, another matter, raising issues of anticipation under 35 U.S.C. § 102 as well as obviousness under § 103. Moreover, where there is prior art that suggests a claimed compound, the existence, or lack thereof, of an enabling process for making that compound is surely a factor in any patentability determination. There must, however, still be prior art that suggests the claimed compound in order for a *prima facie* case of obviousness to be made out; as we have already indicated, that prior art was lacking here with respect to claims 5 and 7.

NOTES

1. *Section 103, Forum Shopping and the CAFC.* In the decades before Congress created the Court of Appeals for the Federal Circuit, the regional circuits divided over how, and how high, to set patent law's standard of invention. By choosing the right circuit for suit, the adroit forum shopper could save a patent that might fall in other circuits. An agile infringer, seeking a declaratory judgment of invalidity, could pick a less hospitable circuit. Supreme Court decisions abetted the disarray by continually rephrasing the standard of invention:

> Back in the late "twenties you can see the courts were holding from 35% to 40% of all the litigated patents valid and infringed. Following this period, the trend is downward, and in 1937 and 1938 came the TNEC hearings which had a definitely anti-patent flavor. In 1941 the *Cuno* case was decided, with its 'flash of genius' test, and in the following year, 1942, only 10% of the litigated patents were upheld. Then things tended to improve a little bit up to the point where *Graver v. Linde* case [sic] was decided.... [T]hat was the only case in which either Mr. Justice Douglas or Mr. Justice Black ever voted to uphold a patent. Right after that the curve climbs back almost to 30%, but the gain was short-lived. In the following year came the *A & P* case and *Crest v. Trager* (the infant feeding device). The curve then drops back down to 7%, the lowest point at any time during the thirty year period. The new Patent Act was passed in 1952, and presumably as a result the curve has shot up, wavering at first, but in 1956 it reached 33%, and in 1957 through September 9th, 30%, which seems to me quite encouraging."

Discussion following presentation of a paper by Thomas Cooch, The Standard of Invention in the Courts, in Dynamics of the Patent System 34, 56 (William B. Ball, ed. 1960). By taking over the jurisdiction of the regional courts of appeals in patent cases, the CAFC has eliminated intramural conflicts involving section 103's nonobviousness test. The CAFC has also put its own gloss on the nonobviousness standard. As is evident from *Stratoflex*, the court has enhanced the role played by secondary tests of invention, such as commercial success, and has rejected the rigorous nonobviousness test earlier applied to so-called combination patents.

According to one empirical study, "despite the creation of the Federal Circuit, choice of forum continues to play a critical role in the outcome of patent litigation. The data indicate that patent cases are not dispersed evenly throughout the ninety-four judicial districts nor dispersed according to the relative size of the court's civil docket generally, but rather consolidated in a few select jurisdictions. This suggests that patent holders are actively selecting particular forums. The empirical results substantiate procedural and substantive differences in district court adjudication of patent cases. The differing procedures for resolving patent cases and differing potential outcomes create an environment in which forum shopping has a major impact on litigation." Kimberly A. Moore, Forum Shopping in Patent Cases: Does Geographic Choice Affect Innovation?, 79 N.C. L. Rev. 889, 892 (2001).

2. *Secondary Tests of Nonobviousness.* In *Deere*, the Supreme Court prescribed three inquiries into nonobviousness: "the scope and content of the prior art are to be determined; differences between the prior art and the claims at issue are to be ascertained; and the level of ordinary skill in the pertinent art resolved." The Court added, "[s]uch secondary considerations as commercial success, long felt but unsolved needs, failure of others, etc., might be utilized to give light to the circumstances surrounding the origin of the subject matter sought to be patented. As indicia of obviousness or nonobviousness, these inquiries may have relevancy." 383 U.S. at 17–18, 86 S.Ct. at 693–94.

The Court of Appeals for the Federal Circuit has set secondary considerations alongside the three factual inquiries prescribed in *Deere*. Uniroyal, Inc. v. Rudkin–Wiley Corp., 837 F.2d 1044, 5 U.S.P.Q.2d 1434 (Fed.Cir.), cert. denied, 488 U.S. 825, 109 S.Ct. 75, 102 L.Ed.2d 51 (1988). Where earlier courts admitted secondary proofs only if the patent owner could directly connect them to the patented invention, *Stratoflex* allowed these proofs as a matter of course. Further, where earlier courts required a direct connection between commercial success and nonobviousness, the CAFC requires only a "nexus." Windsurfing Int'l, Inc. v. AMF, Inc., 782 F.2d 995, 228 U.S.P.Q. 562 (Fed.Cir.), cert. denied, 477 U.S. 905, 106 S.Ct. 3275, 91 L.Ed.2d 565 (1986).

Commercial success is the most frequently employed subtest of nonobviousness. The subtest predicates that commercial success is a competitive goal, and that if the successful invention had been obvious to competitors they would have developed it first. Professor Edmund Kitch has traced the chain of inferences that underlies this subtest: "First, that the commercial success is due to the innovation. Second, that if an improvement has in fact become commercially successful, it is likely that this potential commercial success was perceived before its development. Third, the potential commercial success having been perceived, it is likely that efforts were made to develop the improvement. Fourth, the efforts having been made by men of skill in the art, they failed because the patentee was the first to reduce his development to practice." Edmund Kitch, Graham v. John Deere Co.: New Standards for Patents, 1966 Sup.Ct.Rev. 293, 332.

Courts also admit proof of industry acquiescence in patentability and long-felt demand for the invention as evidence of nonobviousness. The theory behind commercial acquiescence is that when competitors, who have the greatest interest in attacking a patent, take a license or try to invent around the patent, it is evidence that they consider the patent claims to be valid. The theory behind long-felt demand is that firms characteristically seek to correct defects that increase production costs or decrease product quality; if a corrective method or apparatus had been obvious to workers ordinarily skilled in the industry, they would have adopted it earlier. Other subtests of nonobviousness include the failure of others to make the invention, research and development in directions diverging from the patentee's results, and the accused infringer's admission of nonobviousness.

Courts recognize that facts other than nonobviousness sometimes explain commercial success, industry acquiescence or satisfaction of long felt demand. A patent owner must show that commercial success stems from the quality of the invention and not from such extrinsic factors as market position and advertising efforts. Pentec, Inc. v. Graphic Controls Corp., 776 F.2d 309, 227 U.S.P.Q. 766 (Fed.Cir.1985). Proof of long felt demand may be undercut by proof that the invention was made possible only by a recent advance in the art. Allen v. Standard Crankshaft and Hydraulic Co., 323 F.2d 29, 139 U.S.P.Q. 20 (4th Cir.1963). Proof of industry acquiescence may collapse before the fact that "[t]o take a license, calling for small royalty payments, frequently involves less expense than prolonged litigation...." Kleinman v. Kobler, 230 F.2d 913, 914, 108 U.S.P.Q. 301 (2d Cir.1956), cert. denied, 352 U.S. 830, 77 S.Ct. 44, 1 L.Ed.2d 51.

See generally, Robert W. Harris, The Emerging Primacy of "Secondary Considerations" as Validity Ammunition: Has the Federal Circuit Gone Too Far?, 71 J. Pat. & Trademark Off. Soc'y 185, 191–192 (1989).

3. *"Person Having Ordinary Skill in the Art...."* Section 103 views nonobviousness from the perspective of a person having ordinary skill in the art to which the subject matter in issue pertains. Essentially this person is the counterpart of tort law's "reasonable person." The Court of Appeals for the Federal Circuit elaborated the standard in Standard Oil Co. v. American Cyanamid Co., 774 F.2d 448, 454, 227 U.S.P.Q. 293 (Fed.Cir. 1985): "The issue of obviousness is determined entirely with reference to a *hypothetical* 'person having ordinary skill in the art.' It is only that hypothetical person who is presumed to be aware of all the pertinent prior art. The actual inventor's skill is irrelevant to the inquiry, and this is for a very important reason. The statutory emphasis is on a person of *ordinary* skill. Inventors, as a class, according to the concepts underlying the Constitution and the statutes that have created the patent system, possess something—call it what you will—which sets them apart from the workers of *ordinary* skill, and one should not go about determining obviousness under § 103 by inquiring into what *patentees* (i.e., inventors) would have known or would likely have done, faced with the revelations of references." (Emphasis the court's).

4. *Expert Testimony.* Courts, and the Patent and Trademark Office, often rely on expert testimony in determining the scope of prior art and the level of skill of a person ordinarily skilled in the art. A court unconvinced by either party's witnesses may appoint an independent expert. There is good reason for courts to rely on expert testimony when the relevant art is technical and complex. Is there even greater reason to defer to expertise in cases involving easily comprehensible subject matter, where the tendency is to equate an invention's apparent simplicity with its obviousness?

5. *Is Nonobviousness a Question of Law or Fact?* The answer to this question has consequence both at the trial and appellate levels. At the trial level, the answer will control the allocation of responsibility between judge and jury. On appeal, it will control the scope of review and the applicability of the "clearly erroneous" standard of Federal Rules of Civil Procedure, Rule 52(a).

Deere established the principle that "the ultimate question of patent validity is one of law...." 383 U.S. at 17, 86 S.Ct. at 693. In Dennison Mfg. Co. v. Panduit Corp., 475 U.S. 809, 106 S.Ct. 1578, 89 L.Ed.2d 817 (1986), the Supreme Court remanded to the CAFC for consideration of the "complex issue of the degree to which the obviousness determination is one of fact." The CAFC responded:

> A § 103 determination involves fact and law. There may be these facts: what a prior art patent as a whole discloses; what it in fact disclosed to workers in the art; what differences exist between the entire prior art, or a whole prior art structure, and the whole claimed invention; what the differences enabled the claimed subject matter as a whole to achieve; that others for years sought and failed to arrive at the claimed invention; that one of those others copied it; that the invention met on its merits with outstanding commercial success.

> With the involved facts determined, the decisionmaker confronts a ghost, i.e., "a person having ordinary skill in the art," not unlike the "reasonable man" and other ghosts in the law. To reach a proper conclusion under § 103, the decisionmaker must step backward in time and into the shoes worn by that "person" when the invention was unknown and just before it was made. In light of *all* the evidence, the decisionmaker must then determine whether the patent challenger has convincingly established that the claimed invention as a whole would have been obvious at *that* time to *that* person. The answer to that question partakes more of the nature of law than of fact, for it is an ultimate conclusion based on a foundation formed of all the probative facts. If itself a fact, it would be part of its own foundation.

Panduit Corp. v. Dennison Mfg. Co., 810 F.2d 1561, 1566, 1 U.S.P.Q.2d 1593 (Fed.Cir.), cert. denied, 481 U.S. 1052, 107 S.Ct. 2187, 95 L.Ed.2d 843 (1987) (emphasis the court's).

6. *The Nonobviousness Standard in the Patent and Trademark Office.* The Supreme Court in *Deere* criticized the Patent Office for applying a more liberal invention standard than the one announced by the Court. Was the criticism correct? A patent, before it is judicially declared invalid, can give its owner an unwarranted monopoly. However, few issued patents will ever enjoy commercial success, much less give their owner a market advantage. Can you think of a system that is more efficient than one that has the Patent and Trademark Office make a comparatively quick pass at investigating prior art and that postpones closer, more costly, inquiry to infringement actions involving the relatively few patents that turn out to have commercial significance? See Mark A. Lemley, Rational Ignorance at the Patent Office, 95 Nw. U. L. Rev. 1495 (2001).

Difference in standards may also stem from the different proofs available to the Patent and Trademark Office and to the courts. Patent and Trademark Office proceedings usually measure nonobviousness directly. The examiner compares the claimed subject matter with the prior art to determine whether the subject matter would have been obvious to a worker ordinarily skilled in the art. Evidence of other considerations, such as commercial success, will often be unavailable. By the time the patent reaches the courts in the context of an infringement or declaratory judgment action, evidence bearing on commercial success and the other secondary considerations is more likely to have materialized, and failure to meet these subtests may lead a court to invalidate the patent.

Does the invalidation of patents coming into the courts suggest that the two tribunals are effectively serving different functions—the Patent and Trademark Office to grant patents on the basis of *ex parte* prior art appraisals, and the courts to weed out subject matter that more highly-focussed factfindings and subsequently-occurring events prove to have been obvious?

7. *"Combination" Patents.* In rejecting "synergism" as a requirement of invention, and the notion of a separate category for "combination patents," the *Stratoflex* court confronted substantial Supreme Court authority. The Court had historically held mechanical inventions that combined old elements—"combination" patents—to a more stringent standard than other inventions. For example, in Sakraida v. Ag Pro, Inc., 425 U.S. 273, 96 S.Ct. 1532, 47 L.Ed.2d 784, 189 U.S.P.Q. 449 (1976), reh'g denied, 426 U.S. 955, 96 S.Ct. 3182, 49 L.Ed.2d 1194 (1976), the Court ruled that the trial court had correctly invalidated a patent for a water flush system combining several old elements into a mechanism for removing cow manure from dairy barn floors: "the combination of these old elements to produce an abrupt release of water directly on the barn floor from storage tanks or pools" cannot "properly be characterized as synergistic, that is, 'result[ing] in an effect greater than the sum of the several effects taken separately.' Anderson's–Black Rock v. Pavement Salvage Co., 396 U.S. 57, 61, 90 S.Ct. 305, 308, 24 L.Ed.2d 258 (1969). Rather, this patent simply arranges old elements with each performing the same function it had been known to perform, although perhaps producing a more striking result than in previous combinations. Such combinations are not patentable under standards appropriate for a combination patent." 425 U.S. at 282, 96 S.Ct. at 1537.

8. *The Economics of Nonobviousness.* Professor Robert Merges has argued that Federal Circuit decisions encouraging the use of the secondary considerations to prove nonobviousness have effectively reduced the level of invention required by section 103. "By relying on this objective evidence of patentability, as the Federal Circuit calls it, the court threatens to transform patents into rewards for such nontechnical achievements as superior distribution systems, marketing decisions, and service networks. In so doing, it has begun to undermine the patent system's traditional emphasis on rewarding invention." Robert Merges, Commercial Success and Patent Standards: Economic Perspectives on Innovation, 76 Cal.L.Rev. 803, 806 (1988). Do you agree?

To what extent should economic analysis inform the nonobviousness standard? Judge Richard Posner, concurring and dissenting in Roberts v. Sears, Roebuck & Co., 723 F.2d 1324, 1344, 221 U.S.P.Q. 504 (7th Cir. 1983), acknowledged "that many lawyers and judges find the language of economics repulsive. Yet the policies that have given shape to the patent statute are quintessentially economic, and the language of economics is therefore the natural language in which to articulate the test for obviousness." 723 F.2d at 1347. In Posner's view, the statutory term, " 'obvious' ... identifies the cases in which patent protection is not necessary to induce invention and would therefore visit the costs of monopoly on the consuming public with no offsetting gains." Consequently, "if a court thinks an invention for which a patent is being sought would have been made as soon or almost as soon as it was made even if there were no patent laws, then it must pronounce the invention obvious and the patent invalid." 723 F.2d at 1346.

Is it pertinent that, according to a study of patent validity decisions by district courts and the Federal Circuit between 1989–1996, obviousness was the ground for the greatest percentage of invalidity findings—-42%? See John R. Allison & Mark A. Lemley, Empirical Evidence on the Validity of Litigated Patents, 26 AIPLA Q.J. 185 (1998).

c.   Sections 102 and 103 in Concert: What Is Prior Art?

Hazeltine Research, Inc. v. Brenner

Supreme Court of the United States, 1965.
382 U.S. 252, 86 S.Ct. 335, 15 L.Ed.2d 304, 147 U.S.P.Q. 429.

Mr. Justice BLACK delivered the opinion of the Court.

The sole question presented here is whether an application for patent pending in the Patent Office at the time a second application is filed constitutes part of the "prior art" as that term is used in 35 U.S.C.A. § 103, which reads in part:

> A patent may not be obtained ... if the differences between the subject matter sought to be patented and the prior art are such that the subject matter as a whole would have been obvious at the time the invention was made to a person having ordinary skill in the art....

The question arose in this way. On December 23, 1957, petitioner Robert Regis filed an application for a patent on a new and useful improvement on a microwave switch. On June 24, 1959, the Patent Examiner denied Regis' application on the ground that the invention was not one which was new or unobvious in light of the prior art and thus did not meet the standards set forth in § 103. The Examiner said that the invention was unpatentable because of the joint effect of the disclosures made by patents previously issued, one to Carlson (No. 2,491,644) and one to Wallace (No. 2,822,526). The Carlson patent had been issued on December 20, 1949, over eight years prior to Regis' application, and that patent is admittedly a part of the prior art insofar as Regis' invention is concerned. The Wallace patent, however, was pending in the Patent Office when the Regis application was filed. The Wallace application had been pending since March 24, 1954, nearly three years and nine months before Regis filed his application and the Wallace patent was issued on February 4, 1958, 43 days after Regis filed his application.[1]

After the Patent Examiner refused to issue the patent, Regis appealed to the Patent Office Board of Appeals on the ground that the Wallace patent could not be properly considered a part of the prior art because it had been a "co-pending patent" and its disclosures were secret and not known to the public. The Board of Appeals rejected this argument and affirmed the decision of the Patent Examiner. Regis and Hazeltine, which had an interest as assignee, then instituted the present action in the District Court pursuant to 35 U.S.C.A. § 145 to compel the Commissioner to issue the patent. The District Court agreed with the Patent Office that the co-pending Wallace application was a part of the prior art and directed that the complaint be dismissed. On appeal the Court of Appeals affirmed per curiam. We granted certiorari to decide the question of whether a co-pending application is included in the prior art, as that term is used in 35 U.S.C.A. § 103.

Petitioners' primary contention is that the term "prior art," as used in § 103, really means only art previously publicly known. In support of this position they refer to a statement in the legislative history which indicates that prior art means "what was known before as described in section 102."[2] They contend that the use of the word "known" indicates that Congress intended prior art to include only inventions or discoveries which were already publicly known at the time an invention was made.

If petitioners are correct in their interpretation of "prior art," then the Wallace invention, which was not publicly known at the time the Regis application was filed, would not be prior art with regard to Regis' invention. This is true because at the time Regis filed his application the Wallace invention, although pending in the Patent Office, had never been made public and the Patent Office was forbidden by statute from disclosing to the

1. It is not disputed that Regis' alleged invention, as well as his application, was made after Wallace's application was filed. There is, therefore, no question of priority of invention before us.

2. H.R.Rep. No. 1923, 82d Cong., 2d Sess., p. 7 (1952).

public, except in special circumstances, anything contained in the application.

The Commissioner, relying chiefly on Alexander Milburn Co. v. Davis–Bournonville Co., 270 U.S. 390, 46 S.Ct. 324, 70 L.Ed. 651, contends that when a patent is issued, the disclosures contained in the patent become a part of the prior art as of the time the application was filed, not, as petitioners contend, at the time the patent is issued. In that case a patent was held invalid because, at the time it was applied for, there was already pending an application which completely and adequately described the invention. In holding that the issuance of a patent based on the first application barred the valid issuance of a patent based on the second application, Mr. Justice Holmes, speaking for the Court, said, "The delays of the patent office ought not to cut down the effect of what has been done. . . . [The first applicant] had taken steps that would make it public as soon as the Patent Office did its work, although, of course, amendments might be required of him before the end could be reached. We see no reason in the words or policy of the law for allowing [the second applicant] to profit by the delay. . . ." At p. 401, 46 S.Ct. at p. 325.

In its revision of the patent laws in 1952, Congress showed its approval of the holding in *Milburn* by adopting 35 U.S.C.A. § 102(e) which provides that a person shall be entitled to a patent unless "(e) the invention was described in a patent granted on an application for patent by another filed in the United States before the invention thereof by the applicant for patent." Petitioners suggest, however, that the question in this case is not answered by mere reference to § 102(e), because in *Milburn,* which gave rise to that section, the co-pending applications described the same identical invention. But here the Regis invention is not precisely the same as that contained in the Wallace patent, but is only made obvious by the Wallace patent in light of the Carlson patent. We agree with the Commissioner that this distinction is without significance here. While we think petitioners' argument with regard to § 102(e) is interesting, it provides no reason to depart from the plain holding and reasoning in the *Milburn* case. The basic reasoning upon which the Court decided the *Milburn* case applies equally well here. When Wallace filed his application, he had done what he could to add his disclosures to the prior art. The rest was up to the Patent Office. Had the Patent Office acted faster, had it issued Wallace's patent two months earlier, there would have been no question here. As Justice Holmes said in *Milburn,* "The delays of the patent office ought not to cut down the effect of what has been done." P. 401, 46 S.Ct. at p. 325.

To adopt the result contended for by petitioners would create an area where patents are awarded for unpatentable advances in the art. We see no reason to read into § 103 a restricted definition of "prior art" which would lower standards of patentability to such an extent that there might exist two patents where the Congress has plainly directed that there should be only one.

Affirmed.

APPLICATION OF FOSTER, 343 F.2d 980, 987–990, 145 U.S.P.Q. 166 (C.C.P.A.1965), cert. denied, 383 U.S. 966, 86 S.Ct. 1270, 16 L.Ed.2d 307, 149 U.S.P.Q. 906 (1966). ALMOND, J.: Sections 101, 102 and 103, generally speaking, deal with two different matters: (1) the factors to be considered in determining whether a patentable invention has been *made,* i.e., novelty, utility, unobviousness, and the categories of patentable subject matter; and (2) "loss of right to patent" as stated in the heading of section 102, even though an otherwise patentable invention has been made. On the subject of loss of right, appellant's brief contains a helpful review of the development of the statutory law since 1793. It says:

> In 1897 the patent laws were amended to make the ... two-year bar period apply to all public uses, publications and patents *regardless of the source* from which they emanated. The change was a consequence, primarily, of greatly improved communications within the country which had rendered inventors easily able to acquire knowledge of the public acts of others within their own fields. It was reasoned that any inventor who *delayed in filing* a patent application for more than two years after a public disclosure of the invention would obtain *an undeserved reward in derogation of the rights of the public* if he were granted a patent.

> In 1939, in recognition of further improvements in communications, Congress reduced the two-year bar period to one year....

> That 1939 Act was carried over unchanged in the 1952 recodification of the patent laws as 35 U.S.C.A. § 102(b)....

> Manifestly, Section 102(b) from its earliest beginnings has been and was intended to be directed toward the encouragement of *diligence* in the filing of patent applications and the protection of the public from monopolies on subject matter which had already been fully disclosed to it.

These statements are in accord with our understanding of the history and purposes of section 102(b). It presents a sort of statute of limitations, formerly two years, now one year, within which an inventor, even though he has made a patentable invention, must act on penalty of loss of his right to patent. What starts the period running is clearly the availability of the invention *to the public* through the categories of disclosure enumerated in 102(b), which include "a printed publication" anywhere describing the invention. There appears to be no dispute about the operation of this statute in "complete anticipation" situations but *the contention seems to be that 102(b) has no applicability where the invention is not completely disclosed in a single patent or publication,* that is to say where the rejection involves the addition to the disclosure of the reference of the ordinary skill of the art or the disclosure of another reference which indicates what those of ordinary skill in the art are presumed to know, *and to have known for more than a year before the application was filed.* Upon a complete reexamination of this matter we are convinced that the contention is contrary to the policy consideration which motivated the enactment by Congress of a statutory bar. On logic and principle we think this contention is unsound, and we also believe it is contrary to the patent law as it has actually existed since at least 1898.

First, as to principle, since the purpose of the statute has always been to require filing of the application within the prescribed period after the time the public came into possession of the invention, we cannot see that it makes any difference *how* it came into such possession, whether by a public use, a sale, a single patent or publication, or by combinations of one or more of the foregoing. In considering this principle *we assume,* of course, that by these means *the invention has become obvious* to that segment of the "public" having ordinary skill in the art. Once this has happened, the purpose of the law is to give the inventor only a year within which to file and this would seem to be liberal treatment. Whenever an applicant undertakes, under Rule 131,[8] to swear back of a reference having an effective date more than a year before his filing date, he is automatically conceding that he made his invention more than a year before he filed. If the reference contains enough disclosure to make his invention obvious, the principle of the statute would seem to require denial of a patent to him. The same is true where a combination of two publications or patents makes the invention obvious and they both have dates more than a year before the filing date.

As to dealing with the express language of 102(b), for example, "described in a printed publication," technically, we see no reason to so read the words of the statute as to preclude the use of more than one reference; nor do we find in the context anything to show that "a printed publication" cannot include two or more printed publications. We do not have two publications here, but we did in Palmquist [319 F.2d 547, 138 U.S.P.Q. 234 (1963)] and it is a common situation.

As to what the law has been, more particularly what it was prior to 1953, when the new patent act and its section 103 became effective, there is a paucity of direct precedents on the precise problem. We think there is a reason for this. Under the old law (R.S. § 4886, where 102(b) finds its origin) patents were refused or invalidated on references dated more than a year before the filing date because the invention was anticipated or, if they

8. *"131. Affidavit of prior invention to overcome cited patent or publication.* (a) When any claim of an application is rejected on reference to a domestic patent which substantially shows or describes but does not claim the rejected invention, or on reference to a foreign patent or to a printed publication, and the applicant shall make oath to facts showing a completion of the invention in this country before the filing date of the application on which the domestic patent issued, or before the date of the foreign patent, or before the date of the printed publication, then the patent or publication cited shall not bar the grant of a patent to the applicant, *unless the date of such patent or printed publication be more than one year prior to the date on which the application was filed in this country."* [Emphasis ours.]

The italicized clause at the end of the foregoing paragraph or its equivalent has been present in the rule and its predecessor Rule 75 since January 1, 1898, when the rule was amended to include:

... unless the date of such patent or printed publication is more than two years prior to the date on which application was filed in this country.

[Opinion of court, 343 F.2d 980, 987 n. 8.]

were not, then *because there was no "invention,"* the latter rejection being based either on (a) a single nonanticipatory reference plus the skill of the art *or (b) on a plurality of references.* There was no need to seek out the precise statutory basis because it was R.S. § 4886 in any event, read in the light of the Supreme Court's interpretation of the law that there must always be "invention." This issue was determined on the disclosures of the references relied on and if they had dates more than one year before the filing date, it was assumed they could be relied on to establish a "statutory bar." There was an express prohibition in Rule 131 and in its predecessor Rule 75 against antedating a reference having a date more than a year prior to the filing date and there was no basis on which to contest it....

It would seem that the practical operation of the prior law was that references having effective dates more than a year before applicant's filing date were always considered to be effective as references, regardless of the applicant's date of invention, and that rejections were then predicated thereon for "lack of invention" without making the distinction which we now seem to see as implicit in sections 102 and 103, "anticipation" or no novelty situations under 102 and "obviousness" situations under 103. But on further reflection, we now feel bound to point out that of equal importance is the question of *loss of right* predicated on a one-year *time-bar* which, it seems clear to us, has never been limited to "anticipation" situations, involving only a single reference, but has included as well "no invention" (now "obviousness") situations. It follows that where the time-bar is involved, *the actual date of invention becomes irrelevant* and that it is not in accordance with either the letter or the principle of the law, or its past interpretation over a very long period, to permit an applicant to dispose of a reference having a date more than one year prior to his filing date by proving his actual date of invention.

Such a result was permitted by our decision in Palmquist and to the extent that it permitted a reference, having a publication date more than one year prior to the United States filing date to which the applicant was entitled, to be disposed of by proof of a date of invention earlier than the date of the reference, that decision is hereby overruled.

We wish to make it clear that this ruling is predicated on our construction of section 102(b) and has no effect on the statements in Palmquist respecting the determination of obviousness under section 103 when a statutory time-bar is not involved. The existence of unobviousness under that section, as a necessary prerequisite to patentability, we reiterate, must be determined as of "the time the invention was made" without utilizing after-acquired knowledge.

NOTES

1. *Is Section 102(g) Subject Matter Prior Art?* Just as *Hazeltine* included section 102(e) subject matter in prior art for purposes of section 103, and *Foster* included section 102(b) subject matter, *In re Bass*, 474 F.2d 1276, 1277, 1285, 177 U.S.P.Q. 178 (C.C.P.A.1973), invoked the principle that "what is prior art for one purpose is prior art for all purposes" to hold that "§ 102(g) makes available as 'prior art,' within the meaning of § 103, the prior invention of another who has not abandoned, suppressed or concealed it."

Bass created a perhaps unforeseen problem for the activities of corporate research teams: Since the knowledge of each employee working on a common research project would become prior art for purposes of inventions by her fellow employees, each would be denied a patent under section 103. To solve this problem, the Patent Law Amendments Act of 1984 added a sentence to section 103: "Subject matter developed by another person, which qualifies as prior art only under subsection (f) or (g) of section 102 of this title, shall not preclude patentability under this section where the subject matter and the claimed invention were, at the time the invention was made, owned by the same person or subject to an obligation of assignment to the same person." Pub.L. No. 98–622, § 103, 98 Stat. 3383. The purpose of the amendment was to change existing case law, including *In re Bass* "and its progeny," and to provide "material benefit to university and corporate research laboratories where the free exchange of ideas and concepts may have been hampered by the current state of the law with respect to what constitutes 'prior art.' " Remarks of Robert W. Kastenmeier, 129 Cong.Rec. E5777, E5778 (daily ed. Nov. 18, 1983, part II).

2. *Is Section 102(f) Subject Matter Prior Art?* In OddzOn Products, Inc. v. Just Toys, Inc., 122 F.3d 1396, 43 U.S.P.Q.2d 1641 (Fed.Cir.1997), the court ruled that, "although there is a basis to suggest that § 102(f) should not be considered as a prior art provision, we hold that a fair reading of § 103, as amended in 1984, leads to the conclusion that § 102(f) is a prior art provision for purposes of § 103." The court distinguished section 102(f), which "is a derivation provision, which provides that one may not obtain a patent on that which is obtained from someone else whose possession of the subject matter is inherently 'prior,' " from subsections (a), (b), (e) and (g), which are clearly prior art provisions:

> They relate to knowledge manifested by acts that are essentially public. Subsections (a) and (b) relate to public knowledge or use, or prior patents and printed publications; subsection (e) relates to prior filed applications for patents of others which have become public by grant; and subsection (g) relates to prior inventions of others that are either public or will likely become public in the sense that they have not been abandoned, suppressed, or concealed. Subsections (c) and (d) are loss-of-right provisions. Section 102(c) precludes the obtaining of a patent by inventors who have abandoned their invention. Section 102(d) causes an inventor to lose the right to a patent by delaying a filing of a patent application too long after having filed a corresponding patent application in a foreign country. Subsections (c) and (d) are therefore not prior art provisions.

122 F.3d at 1401–02.

Observing that "the patent laws have not generally recognized as prior art that which is not accessible to the public" and, further, that "as between an earlier inventor who has not given the public the benefit of the invention, *e.g.*, because the invention has been abandoned without public disclosure, suppressed or concealed, and a subsequent inventor who obtains a patent, the policy of the law is for the subsequent inventor to prevail," the court nonetheless determined that the result was dictated by the 1984 amendments to section 103 which included section 102(f) as well as section 102(g) within its scope:

> The statutory language provides a clear statement that subject matter that qualifies as prior art under subsection (f) or (g) cannot be combined with other prior art to render a claimed invention obvious and hence unpatentable when the relevant prior art is commonly owned with the claimed invention at the time the invention was made. While the statute does not expressly state in so many words that § 102(f) creates a type of prior art for purposes of § 103, nonetheless that conclusion is inescapable; the language that states that § 102(f) subject matter is not prior art under limited circumstances clearly implies that it is prior art otherwise. That is what Congress wrote into law in 1984 and that is the way we must read the statute.

122 F.3d at 1403.

3. *Should Section 102 Subject Matter Constitute Prior Art?* Judge Arthur Smith, who wrote for a unanimous court in *Palmquist,* dissented in *Foster* which overruled it. In Judge Smith's view, neither section 102 nor section 103 expressly addressed the issue raised by *Foster* and *Palmquist,* and the court reached too far to repair the legislative oversight. According to Smith, "the majority decision amounts to an interpretation of section 102(b) as though it contained the following italicized words:"

> A person shall be entitled to a patent unless— ... (b) the invention was patented or described in a printed publication in this or a foreign country *or* in public use or on sale in this country or *unless the invention became obvious* more than one year prior to the date of the application for patent in the United States....

Further, "the majority must also intend to rewrite section 103 so that the phrase 'at the time the invention was made' now is to be limited by a proviso which reduces this time to a period of one year prior to the filing of the application." 343 F.2d at 980, 996–997.

In Judge Smith's view, the majority decision also contradicted sound patent policy. "In overruling *Palmquist,* the majority gives lip service to the truism that 'section 103 per se has nothing whatever to do' with the issue of loss of right to patent, but then proceeds to decide the case as one of obviousness using Binder [the defeating reference] as *prior art* under section 103, which it most emphatically is not, since it *did not exist* 'at the time the invention was made.' ... Today's decision destroys any meaningful differences that may have existed in the past between sections 102(a) and (b) and section 103.... Most disturbing of all is the fact that from this day forward obviousness under section 103 will be tested, *not as of the time the invention was made,* but *as of one year prior to the filing date of the application."* 343 F.2d at 980, 998–999 (emphasis in original).

To what extent does Judge Smith's critique of *Foster* apply to the subsequent extensions of section 102 subject matter into section 103 prior art?

d. *Utility*

LOWELL v. LEWIS, 15 Fed.Cas. 1018 (No. 8568) (C.C.D.Mass.1817). STORY, Circuit Justice (charging jury): The present action is brought by the plaintiff for a supposed infringement of a patent-right, granted, in 1813, to Mr. Jacob Perkins (from whom the plaintiff claims by assignment) for a new and useful improvement in the construction of pumps. The defendant asserts, in the first place, that the invention is neither new nor useful; and, in the next place, that the pumps used by him are not of the same construction as those of Mr. Perkins, but are of a new invention of a Mr. Baker, under whom the defendant claims by assignment. . . .

To entitle the plaintiff to a verdict, he must establish, that his machine is a new and useful invention; and of these facts his patent is to be considered merely prima facie evidence of a very slight nature. He must, in the first place, establish it to be a useful invention; for the law will not allow the plaintiff to recover, if the invention be of a mischievous or injurious tendency. The defendant, however, has asserted a much more broad and sweeping doctrine; and one, which I feel myself called upon to negative in the most explicit manner. He contends that it is necessary for the plaintiff to prove that his invention is of general utility; so that in fact, for the ordinary purposes of life, it must supersede the pumps in common use. In short, that it must be, for the public, a better pump than the common pump; and that unless the plaintiff can establish this position, the law will not give him the benefit of a patent, even though in some peculiar cases his invention might be applied with advantage. I do not so understand the law. The patent act (Act Feb. 21, 1793, c. 11 [1 Stat. 31])uses the phrase "useful invention" mere incidentally; it occurs only in the first section, and there it seems merely descriptive of the subject matter of the application, or of the conviction of the applicant. The language is, "when any person or persons shall allege, that he or they have invented any new and useful art, machine," & c., he or they may, on pursuing the directions of the act, obtain a patent. Neither the oath required by the second section, nor the special matter of defence allowed to be given in evidence by the sixth section of the act, contains any such qualification or reference to general utility, to establish the validity of the patent. Nor is it alluded to in the tenth section as a cause, for which the patent may be vacated. To be sure, all the matters of defence or of objection to the patent are not enumerated in these sections. But if such an one as that now contended for had been intended, it is scarcely possible to account for its omission. In my judgement the argument is utterly without foundation. All that the law requires is, that the invention should not be frivolous or injurious to the well-being, good policy, or sound morals of society. The word "useful," therefore, is incorporated into the act in contradistinction to mischievous or immoral. For instance, a new invention to poison people, or to promote debauchery, or to facilitate private assassination, is not a patentable invention. But if the invention steers wide of these objections, whether it be more or less useful is a circumstance very material to the interests of the patentee, but of no importance to the public. If it be not extensively useful, it will silently sink into contempt and disregard. There is no pretence, that Mr. Perkins' pump is a mischievous invention; and if it has been used injuriously to the patentee by the defendant, it certainly does not lie in his mouth to contest its general utility. Indeed the defendant asserts, that Baker's pump is useful in a very eminent degree, and, if it be substantially the same as Perkins', there is an end of the objection; if it be not substantially the same, then the plaintiff must fail in his action. So that, in either view, the abstract question seems hardly of any importance in this cause.

Brenner v. Manson

Supreme Court of the United States, 1966.
383 U.S. 519, 86 S.Ct. 1033, 16 L.Ed.2d 69, 148 U.S.P.Q. 689.

Mr. Justice FORTAS delivered the opinion of the Court.

. . . Our starting point is the proposition, neither disputed nor disputable, that one may patent only that which is "useful." In Graham v. John Deere Co., 383 U.S. 1, at 5–10, 86 S.Ct. 684, at 687–690, 148 U.S.P.Q. 459, we have reviewed the history of the requisites of patentability, and it need not be repeated here. Suffice it to say that the concept of utility has maintained a central place in all of our patent legislation, beginning with the first patent law in 1790 and culminating in the present law's provision that

> Whoever invents or discovers any new and useful process, machine, manufacture, or composition of matter, or any new and useful improvement thereof, may obtain a patent therefor, subject to the conditions and requirements of this title.

As is so often the case, however, a simple, everyday word can be pregnant with ambiguity when applied to the facts of life. That this is so is demonstrated by the present conflict between the Patent Office and the C.C.P.A. over how the test is to be applied to a chemical process which yields an already known product whose utility—other than as a possible object of scientific inquiry—has not yet been evidenced. It was not long ago that agency and court seemed of one mind on the question. In Application of Bremner, 182 F.2d 216, 217, 37 C.C.P.A. (Pat.) 1032, 1034, 86 U.S.P.Q. 74, 75, the court affirmed rejection by the Patent Office of both process and product claims. It noted that "no use for the products claimed to be developed by the processes had been shown in the specification." It held that "It was never intended that a patent be granted upon a product, or a process producing a product, unless such product be useful." Nor was this new doctrine in the court.

The Patent Office has remained steadfast in this view. The C.C.P.A. however, has moved sharply away from Bremner. The trend began in Application of Nelson, 280 F.2d 172, 47 C.C.P.A. (Pat.) 1031, 126 U.S.P.Q. 242. There, the court reversed the Patent Office's rejection of a claim on a process yielding chemical intermediates "useful to chemists doing research on steroids," despite the absence of evidence that any of the steroids thus ultimately produced were themselves "useful." The trend has accelerated, culminating in the present case where the court held it sufficient that a process produces the result intended and is not "detrimental to the public interest." 333 F.2d, at 238, 52 C.C.P.A., at 745, 142 U.S.P.Q. at 38.

It is not remarkable that differences arise as to how the test of usefulness is to be applied to chemical processes. Even if we knew precisely what Congress meant in 1790 when it devised the "new and useful" phraseology and in subsequent re-enactments of the test, we should have difficulty in applying it in the context of contemporary chemistry where research is as comprehensive as man's grasp and where little or nothing is wholly beyond the pale of "utility"—if that word is given its broadest reach.

Respondent does not—at least, in the first instance—rest upon the extreme proposition, advanced by the court below, that a novel chemical process is patentable so long as it yields the intended product and so long as the product is not itself "detrimental." Nor does he commit the outcome of his claim to the slightly more conventional proposition that any process is "useful" within the meaning of § 101 if it produces a compound whose potential usefulness is under investigation by serious scientific researchers, although he urges this position too as an alternative basis for affirming the decision of the C.C.P.A. Rather, he begins with the much more orthodox argument that his process has a specific utility which would entitle him to a declaration of interference even under the Patent Office's reading of § 101. The claim is that the supporting affidavits filed pursuant to Rule 204(b), by reference to Ringold's 1956 article, reveal that an adjacent homologue of the steroid yielded by his process has been demonstrated to have tumor-inhibiting effects in mice, and that this discloses the requisite utility. We do not accept any of these theories as an adequate basis for overriding the determination of the Patent Office that the "utility" requirement has not been met.

Even on the assumption that the process would be patentable were respondent to show that the steroid produced had a tumor-inhibiting effect in mice, we would not overrule the Patent Office finding that respondent has not made such a showing. The Patent Office held that, despite the reference to the adjacent homologue, respondent's papers did not disclose a sufficient likelihood that the steroid yielded by his process would have similar tumor-inhibiting characteristics. Indeed, respondent himself recognized that the presumption that adjacent homologues have the same utility has been challenged in the steroid field because of "a greater known unpredictability of compounds in that field." In these circumstances and in this technical area, we would not overturn the finding of the Primary

Examiner, affirmed by the Board of Appeals and not challenged by the C.C.P.A.

The second and third points of respondent's argument present issues of much importance. Is a chemical process "useful" within the meaning of § 101 either (1) because it works—i.e., produces the intended product? or (2) because the compound yielded belongs to a class of compounds now the subject of serious scientific investigation? These contentions present the basic problem for our adjudication. Since we find no specific assistance in the legislative materials underlying § 101, we are remitted to an analysis of the problem in light of the general intent of Congress, the purposes of the patent system, and the implications of a decision one way or the other.

In support of his plea that we attenuate the requirement of "utility," respondent relies upon Justice Story's well-known statement that a "useful" invention is one "which may be applied to a beneficial use in society, in contradistinction to an invention injurious to the morals, health, or good order of society, or frivolous and insignificant"—and upon the assertion that to do so would encourage inventors of new processes to publicize the event for the benefit of the entire scientific community, thus widening the search for uses and increasing the fund of scientific knowledge. Justice Story's language sheds little light on our subject. Narrowly read, it does no more than compel us to decide whether the invention in question is "frivolous and insignificant"—a query no easier of application than the one built into the statute. Read more broadly, so as to allow the patenting of any invention not positively harmful to society, it places such a special meaning on the word "useful" that we cannot accept it in the absence of evidence that Congress so intended. There are, after all, many things in this world which may not be considered "useful" but which, nevertheless, are totally without a capacity for harm.

It is true, of course, that one of the purposes of the patent system is to encourage dissemination of information concerning discoveries and inventions. And it may be that inability to patent a process to some extent discourages disclosure and leads to greater secrecy than would otherwise be the case. The inventor of the process, or the corporate organization by which he is employed, has some incentive to keep the invention secret while uses for the product are searched out. However, in light of the highly developed art of drafting patent claims so that they disclose as little useful information as possible—while broadening the scope of the claim as widely as possible—the argument based upon the virtue of disclosure must be warily evaluated. Moreover, the pressure for secrecy is easily exaggerated, for if the inventor of a process cannot himself ascertain a "use" for that which his process yields, he has every incentive to make his invention known to those able to do so. Finally, how likely is disclosure of a patented process to spur research by others into the uses to which the product may be put? To the extent that the patentee has power to enforce his patent, there is little incentive for others to undertake a search for uses.

Whatever weight is attached to the value of encouraging disclosure and of inhibiting secrecy, we believe a more compelling consideration is that a process patent in the chemical field, which has not been developed and pointed to the degree of specific utility, creates a monopoly of knowledge which should be granted only if clearly commanded by the statute. Until the process claim has been reduced to production of a product shown to be useful, the metes and bounds of that monopoly are not capable of precise delineation. It may engross a vast, unknown, and perhaps unknowable area. Such a patent may confer power to block off whole areas of scientific development, without compensating benefit to the public. The basic quid pro quo contemplated by the Constitution and the Congress for granting a patent monopoly is the benefit derived by the public from an invention with substantial utility. Unless and until a process is refined and developed to this point—where specific benefit exists in currently available form—there is insufficient justification for permitting an applicant to engross what may prove to be a broad field.

These arguments for and against the patentability of a process which either has no known use or is useful only in the sense that it may be an object of scientific research would apply equally to the patenting of the product produced by the process. Respondent appears to concede that with respect to a product, as opposed to a process, Congress has struck the balance on the side of nonpatentability unless "utility" is shown. Indeed, the decisions of the C.C.P.A. are in accord with the view that a product may not be patented absent a showing of utility greater than any adduced in the present case. We find absolutely no warrant for the proposition that although Congress intended that no patent be granted on a chemical compound whose sole "utility" consists of its potential role as an object of use-testing, a different set of rules was meant to apply to the process which yielded the unpatentable product. That proposition seems to us little more than an attempt to evade the impact of the rules which concededly govern patentability of the product itself.

This is not to say that we mean to disparage the importance of contributions to the fund of scientific information short of the invention of something "useful," or that we are blind to the prospect that what now seems without "use" may tomorrow command the grateful attention of the public. But a patent is not a hunting license. It is not a reward for the search, but compensation for its successful conclusion. "[A] patent system must be related to the world of commerce rather than to the realm of philosophy.... "

The judgment of the C.C.P.A. is reversed.

Mr. Justice DOUGLAS, while acquiescing in Part I of the Court's opinion, dissents on the merits of the controversy for substantially the reasons stated by Mr. Justice HARLAN.

Mr. Justice HARLAN, concurring in part and dissenting in part.

While I join the Court's opinion on the issue of certiorari jurisdiction, I cannot agree with its resolution of the important question of patentability.

Respondent has contended that a workable chemical process, which is both new and sufficiently nonobvious to satisfy the patent statute, is by its existence alone a contribution to chemistry and "useful" as the statute employs that term. Certainly this reading of "useful" in the statute is within the scope of the constitutional grant, which states only that "[t]o promote the Progress of Science and useful Arts," the exclusive right to "Writings and Discoveries" may be secured for limited times to those who produce them. Art. I, § 8. Yet the patent statute is somewhat differently worded and is on its face open both to respondent's construction and to the contrary reading given it by the Court. In the absence of legislative history on this issue, we are thrown back on policy and practice. Because I believe that the Court's policy arguments are not convincing and that past practice favors the respondent, I would reject the narrow definition of "useful" and uphold the judgment of the Court of Customs and Patent Appeals (hereafter C.C.P.A.).

The Court's opinion sets out about half a dozen reasons in support of its interpretation. Several of these arguments seem to me to have almost no force. For instance, it is suggested that "[u]ntil the process claim has been reduced to production of a product shown to be useful, the metes and bounds of that monopoly are not capable of precise delineation" and "[i]t may engross a vast, unknown, and perhaps unknowable area." I fail to see the relevance of these assertions; process claims are not disallowed because the products they produce may be of "vast" importance nor, in any event, does advance knowledge of a specific product use provide much safeguard on this score or fix "metes and bounds" precisely since a hundred more uses may be found after a patent is granted and greatly enhance its value.

The further argument that an established product use is part of "[t]he basic quid pro quo" for the patent or is the requisite "successful conclusion" of the inventor's search appears to beg the very question whether the process is "useful" simply because it facilitates further research into possible product uses. The same infirmity seems to inhere in the Court's argument that chemical products lacking immediate utility cannot be distinguished for present purposes from the processes which create them, that respondent appears to concede and the C.C.P.A. holds that the products are nonpatentable, and that therefore the processes are nonpatentable. Assuming that the two classes cannot be distinguished, a point not adequately considered in the briefs, and assuming further that the C.C.P.A. has firmly held such products nonpatentable this permits us to conclude only that the C.C.P.A. is wrong either as to the products or as to the processes and affords no basis for deciding whether both or neither should be patentable absent a specific product use.

More to the point, I think, are the Court's remaining, prudential arguments against patentability: namely that disclosure induced by allowing a patent is partly undercut by patent-application drafting techniques, that disclosure may occur without granting a patent, and that a patent will discourage others from inventing uses for the product. How far opaque drafting may lessen the public benefits resulting from the issuance of a patent is not shown by any evidence in this case but, more important, the argument operates against all patents and gives no reason for singling out the class involved here. The thought that these inventions may be more likely than most to be disclosed even if patents are not allowed may have more force; but while empirical study of the industry might reveal that chemical researchers would behave in this fashion, the abstractly logical choice for them seems to me to maintain secrecy until a product use can be discovered. As to discouraging the search by others for product uses, there is no doubt this risk exists but the price paid for any patent is that research on other uses or improvements may be hampered because the original patentee will reap much of the reward. From the standpoint of the public interest the Constitution seems to have resolved that choice in favor of patentability.

What I find most troubling about the result reached by the Court is the impact it may have on chemical research. Chemistry is a highly interrelated field and a tangible benefit for society may be the outcome of a number of different discoveries, one discovery building upon the next. To encourage one chemist or research facility to invent and disseminate new processes and products may be vital to progress, although the product or process be without "utility" as the Court defines the term, because that discovery permits someone else to take a further but perhaps less difficult step leading to a commercially useful item. In my view, our awareness in this age of the importance of achieving and publicizing basic research should lead this Court to resolve uncertainties in its favor and uphold the respondent's position in this case.

This position is strengthened, I think, by what appears to have been the practice of the Patent Office during most of this century. While available proof is not conclusive, the commentators seem to be in agreement that until Application of Bremner, 182 F.2d 216, 37 C.C.P.A. (Pat.) 1032, 86 U.S.P.Q. 74, in 1950, chemical patent applications were commonly granted although no resulting end use was stated or the statement was in extremely broad terms. Taking this to be true, Bremner represented a deviation from established practice which the C.C.P.A. has now sought to remedy in part only to find that the Patent Office does not want to return to the beaten track. If usefulness was typically regarded as inherent during a long and prolific period of chemical research and development in this country, surely this is added reason why the Court's result should not be adopted until Congress expressly mandates it, presumably on the basis of empirical data which this Court does not possess.

Fully recognizing that there is ample room for disagreement on this problem when, as here, it is reviewed in the abstract, I believe the decision below should be affirmed.

NOTES

1. *Utility and Morality.* Justice Story's observation in Lowell v. Lewis that mischievous or immoral inventions are not patentable has received more attention than his point that "useful" under the Patent Act is an essentially nominal requirement best mediated by the marketplace. In Juicy Whip,

Inc. v. Orange Bang, Inc., 185 F.3d 1364, 51 U.S.P.Q.2d 1700 (Fed.Cir. 1999), the Court of Appeals for the Federal Circuit decisively rejected the rule that an invention's deceptive intentions will bar patentability, and overturned a district court decision that an invention lacked the requisite utility "because its purpose was to increase sales by deception, *i.e.*, through imitation of another product."

The patent in issue was for a "Post–Mix Beverage Dispenser With an Associated Simulated Display of Beverage" that was designed to make purchasers believe that it was a pre-mix beverage dispenser. ("A 'post-mix' beverage dispenser stores beverage syrup concentrate and water in separate locations until the beverage is ready to be dispensed. The syrup and water are mixed together immediately before the beverage is dispensed, which is usually after the consumer requests the beverage. In contrast, in a 'pre-mix' beverage dispenser, the syrup concentrate and water are pre-mixed and the beverage is stored in a display reservoir bowl until it is ready to be dispensed. The display bowl is said to stimulate impulse buying by providing the consumer with a visual beverage display.")

Declining to follow two Second Circuit decisions from the early twentieth century, one holding unpatentable a device for altering tobacco leaves to make them appear to be of superior quality, the other doing much the same with an imitation seamed stocking, the court ruled that "[t]he fact that one product can be altered to make it look like another is in itself a specific benefit sufficient to satisfy the statutory requirement of utility." In the court's view, "[t]he requirement of 'utility' in patent law is not a directive to the Patent and Trademark Office or the courts to serve as arbiters of deceptive trade practices. Other agencies, such as the Federal Trade Commission and the Food and Drug Administration, are assigned the task of protecting consumers from fraud and deception in the sale of food products." 185 F.3d at 1367–68.

2. *Operability.* "Operability" in the patent lexicon is different from "utility." Operability's function is to assist in determinations of actual reduction to practice. Recall from the earlier discussion of novelty that invention consists of conception and reduction to practice, and that reduction to practice is demonstrated either actually, through completion of a working model of the invention, or constructively, through the filing of a patent application. Operability is the hallmark of actual reduction to practice.

Even if an invention is inoperative as disclosed, it will be considered operative if it can be made to operate by procedures that would naturally occur to a worker ordinarily skilled in the relevant art. Also, an invention is considered operative if it substantially achieves its avowed purpose. Excluded from the benefits of both these rules is the invention that, unless it is perfect, is no good at all. In McKenzie v. Cummings, 24 App.D.C. 137 (D.C.Cir.1904), the court ruled that a vote-registering machine that failed to properly register one of every hundred votes cast was inoperative. Distinguishing Coffee v. Guerrant, 3 App.D.C. 497 (D.C.Cir.1894), in which the operability of a tobacco-stemming device with 70% efficiency was sustained, the court held that, "[i]n order to be operative at all, absolute accuracy is here required."

Although an invention's operability may be saved under either of these two meliorative rules, some positive evidence of operability may be required. Proof of commercial success, typically associated with section 103's nonobviousness requisite, is frequently adduced. If the invention obviously contradicts established physical laws, as in the case of a perpetual motion machine, or if absolute accuracy is critical, the Director of the PTO may avail himself or herself of the authority provided by section 114 of the Patent Act to require the applicant to furnish a working model of the subject matter.

3.   *Pharmaceuticals.* In a footnote, *Manson* raised but did not decide the question of the proper utility test to be applied to pharmaceuticals. 383 U.S. 519, 531 n. 17, 86 S.Ct. 1033, 1040, 16 L.Ed.2d 69. One line of decisions, dating from the early 1900's, engrafted on the general utility requisite a specific requirement that a drug's fitness for human use be convincingly proved. Proof of successful tests on laboratory animals was considered insufficient to establish utility. "While the granting of a patent does not legally constitute a certificate that the medicine to which it relates is a good medicine and will cure the disease or successfully make the test which it was intended to do, nevertheless, the granting of such a patent gives a kind of official imprimatur to the medicine in question on which as a moral matter some members of the public are likely to rely." Isenstead v. Watson, 157 F.Supp. 7, 115 U.S.P.Q. 408 (D.D.C.1957).

The modern trend, inaugurated by In re Krimmel, 292 F.2d 948, 130 U.S.P.Q. 215 (C.C.P.A.1961), has been to liberalize the utility test for pharmaceuticals. The applicant in *Krimmel* sought a patent for an eye medicine that he had successfully tested on rabbits. The examiner, affirmed by the Board of Appeals, ruled that absent a showing of successful tests on humans, utility had not been proved. The Court of Customs and Patent Appeals reversed, holding that applicant had proved some usefulness for his medicine—to cure eye disease in rabbits—and that this was sufficient to meet the statutory test. The court took another liberalizing step the following year when, in Application of Hartop, 311 F.2d 249, 135 U.S.P.Q. 419 (C.C.P.A.1962), it held that although the applicant had specifically asserted that his medicine had utility for humans, but had only demonstrated its safety and effectiveness on animals, "appellants' claimed solutions have been shown to be useful within the meaning of 35 U.S.C.A. § 101.... We think that a sufficient probability of safety in human therapy has been demonstrated in the case at bar to set aside the requirements of 35 U.S.C.A. § 101 that appellants' invention be useful."

In re Anthony, 414 F.2d 1383, 162 U.S.P.Q. 594 (C.C.P.A.1969), expanded on the rationale underlying *Krimmel* and *Hartop:* "Congress has given the responsibility to the FDA, not to the Patent Office, to determine in the first instance whether drugs are sufficiently safe for use that they can be introduced in the commercial market, under the conditions prescribed, recommended, or suggested in the proposed labeling thereof...."

The court emphasized that although 21 U.S.C.A. § 372(d) authorized the Secretary of Health, Education and Welfare to furnish the Commissioner of Patents with FDA data respecting drugs for which a patent was sought, this information had only persuasive, and not binding, effect on the issue of utility.

See generally, Antoinette F. Konski, The Utility Rejection in Biotechnology and Pharmaceutical Prosecution Practice, 76 J. Pat. & Trademark Off. Soc'y 821 (1994); Christopher A. Michaels, Biotechnology and the Requirement for Utility in Patent Law, 76 J. Pat. & Trademark Off. Soc'y 247 (1994).

4. *PTO Utility Guidelines.* On January 5, 2001, the PTO issued guidelines to be used by patent examiners when inquiring into the utility of a claimed invention. Although the guidelines will apply by their terms to all areas of technology, earlier drafts had specifically responded to concerns raised by pharmaceutical and biotechnology companies. As a consequence, the guidelines reflect a particular concern for application of the utility requirement to biotechnology-related inventions.

Under the Guidelines, "an inventor's discovery of a gene can be the basis for a patent on the genetic composition isolated from its natural state and processed through purifying steps that separate the gene from other molecules naturally associated with it. If a patent application discloses only nucleic acid molecular structure for a newly discovered gene, and no utility for the claimed isolated gene, the claimed invention is not patentable. But when the inventor also discloses how to use the purified gene isolated from its natural state, the application satisfies the 'utility' requirement.... Like other chemical compounds, DNA molecules are eligible for patents when isolated from their natural state and purified or when synthesized in a laboratory from chemical starting materials." 66 Fed. Reg. 1093.

The Guidelines rejected a proposed premise, "that the disclosure of a DNA sequence has inherent value and that possible uses for the DNA appear endless, even if no single use has been worked out," and instead followed Brenner v. Manson by "requiring the disclosure of at least one specific, substantial, and credible utility." 66 Fed. Reg. 1094, 1098.

e. *Inventorship*

For a valid patent to issue, the claimed invention must have originated with the applicant or applicants. See 35 U.S.C.A. § 102(f). The inventor may of course draw his ideas from other sources and may arrange for others to assemble his invention, all without losing his claim of originality. But, for the patent to be valid, the named inventor or inventors must themselves have conceived the specific invention claimed. In Hess v. Advanced Cardiovascular Systems, Inc., 106 F.3d 976, 981, 41 U.S.P.Q.2d 1782 (Fed.Cir.1997), the court declined to overturn the district court finding that an employee of a materials supplier was, in his consultations with the inventors, "doing nothing more than explaining to the inventors what the then state of the art was and supplying a product to them for use in their invention"; that "most, if not all, of his discussion with them were [sic] telling them what was available in the marketplace by way of product, and telling them how the product worked"; and that "what Mr. Hess was doing was showing them available product, telling them its properties, telling them how it could be used, and how it might be used." "The principles Mr. Hess explained to them were well known and found in textbooks. Mr. Hess did no more than a skilled salesman would do in explaining how his employer's product could be used to meet a customer's requirements. The extensive research and development work that produced the catheter was done by Drs. Simpson and Robert." Consequently, the district court was correct to conclude "that whatever contribution Mr. Hess made to Drs. Simpson and Robert did not constitute conception and therefore did not make Mr. Hess a co-inventor of the catheter claimed in the '071 patent."

The requirement that the patent application accurately identify the inventor or inventors becomes particularly problematic in modern research and development departments where joint, rather than individual, invention is the rule. An invention may be the product of many hands and minds, from the research director, who first suggested and guided the idea, to product engineers and technicians who executed it. And what of the patent attorney who, in advising on prior art, may have suggested important, patentable alterations in the invention? Because some products and processes are developed over long periods, workers may have left or joined the research team at all stages of development. These and other realities of large scale research and development create a substantial risk that the patent application will be underinclusive, omitting some inventors, or overinclusive, naming some noninventors.

Judicial decisions offer only the broadest guidelines for determining when a contributor to an invention will be considered a co-inventor. Worden v. Fisher, 11 Fed. 505, (C.C.E.D.Mich.1882) made what has become the classic statement of criteria for joint inventorship:

> To constitute two persons joint inventors it is not necessary that exactly the same idea should have occurred to each at the same time, and that they should work out together the embodiment of this idea in a perfected machine. Such a coincidence of ideas would scarcely ever occur to two persons at the same time. If an idea is suggested to one, and he even goes so far as to construct a machine embodying this idea, but it is not a completed and working machine, and another person takes hold of it, and by their joint labors, one suggesting one thing and the other another, a perfect machine is made, a joint patent may properly issue to them. If, upon the other hand, one person invents a distinct part of a machine, and another person invents another distinct and independent part of the same machine, then each should obtain a patent for his own invention.

After reviewing *Worden* and many later decisions, John Tresansky arrived at the following restatement: "Joint inventorship exists where parties working in a cooperative effort to solve a problem make a mental contribution to the final conception of the solution. All of the parties need not have participated in each contribution nor need the contribution of each party have occurred simultaneously while working proximately with the others.

The contributions of each need not be equal either qualitatively or quantitatively. The contributors need not personally have performed the actual reduction to practice of the inventive concept." John Tresansky, Joint Inventorship, 7 APLA Q.J. 96, 108–109 (1979).

The Patent Law Amendments Act of 1984 amended section 116 to provide: "Inventors may apply for a patent jointly even though (1) they did not physically work together or at the same time, (2) each did not make the same type or amount of contribution, or (3) each did not make a contribution to the subject matter of every claim of the patent." Pub.L. No. 98–622, § 104(a), 98 Stat. 3384–85.

The hazards of misjoinder and nonjoinder are significantly reduced by the fact that courts are generally slow to invalidate patents on these essentially technical grounds and, further, attach a presumption of correctness to the patentee's identification of inventors. See, e.g., General Motors Corp. v. Toyota Motor Co., 667 F.2d 504, 212 U.S.P.Q. 659 (6th Cir.1981), cert. denied, 456 U.S. 937, 102 S.Ct. 1994, 72 L.Ed.2d 457, 215 U.S.P.Q. 95 (1982). Sections 116 and 256 respectively create procedures for correcting the identification of inventors in applications and in patents. The provisions require a showing that the misjoinder or nonjoinder was the result of a mistake made without intent to deceive.

What if the patent fails to name *any* of the true inventors? The Act contains no provisions comparable to sections 116 or 256 for correcting the misidentification of an invention's sole inventor—from *A* named as the inventor, to *B* who was in fact the inventor. In a much-discussed decision, the District of Columbia Court of Appeals read section 116 broadly and relied on section 251's reissue provisions to allow correction of a wrongly named sole inventor in a pending application and in an issued patent. A.F. Stoddard & Co., Ltd. v. Dann, 564 F.2d 556, 195 U.S.P.Q. 97 (D.C.Cir. 1977). "Congress having provided [in section 116] for the correction of innocent error in stating the inventive entity when the application is filed, whether that entity be singular or plural, we see no rational reason to discriminate against the correction of the same innocent error involving sole inventors and their assignees, or to impute that intent to Congress." 564 F.2d 556, 566. See Paul T. Meiklejohn, Misjoinder, Non–Joinder and Whatever—Stoddard v. Dann, 60 J. Pat. Off. Soc'y 487 (1978); John L. Welch, Stoddard v. Dann—Fundamental Principles from A to C, 61 J. Pat. Off. Soc'y 185 (1979).

See generally, David W. Carstens, Joint Inventorship Under 35 U.S.C. § 116, 73 J. Pat. & Trademark Off. Soc'y 616 (1991).

f. Enabling Disclosure

W.L. Gore & Associates v. Garlock, Inc.

United States Court of Appeals, Federal Circuit, 1983.
721 F.2d 1540, 220 U.S.P.Q. 303, cert. denied, 469 U.S. 851, 105 S.Ct. 172, 83 L.Ed.2d 107 (1984).

MARKEY, Chief Judge.

Appeal from a judgment of the District Court for the Northern District of Ohio holding U.S. Patents 3,953,566 ('566) and 4,187,390 ('390) invalid.

We affirm in part, reverse in part, and remand for a determination of the infringement issue.

Background

Tape of unsintered polytetrafluorethylene (PTFE) (known by the trademark TEFLON of E.I. du Pont de Nemours, Inc.) had been stretched in small increments. W.L. Gore & Associates, Inc. (Gore), assignee of the patents in suit, experienced a tape breakage problem in the operation of its "401" tape stretching machine. Dr. Robert Gore, Vice President of Gore, developed the invention disclosed and claimed in the '566 and '390 patents in the course of his effort to solve that problem. The 401 machine was disclosed and claimed in Gore's U.S. Patent 3,664,915 ('915) and was the invention of Wilbert L. Gore, Dr. Gore's father. PTFE tape had been sold as thread seal tape, i.e., tape used to keep pipe joints from leaking. The '915 patent, the application for which was filed on October 3, 1969, makes no reference to stretch rate, at 10% per second or otherwise, or to matrix tensile strength in excess of 7,300 psi.

Dr. Gore experimented with heating and stretching of highly crystalline PTFE rods. Despite slow, careful stretching, the rods broke when stretched a relatively small amount. Conventional wisdom in the art taught that breakage could be avoided only by slowing the stretch rate or by decreasing the crystallinity. In late October, 1969, Dr. Gore discovered, contrary to that teaching, that stretching the rods as fast as possible enabled him to stretch them to more than ten times their original length with no breakage. Further, though the rod was thus greatly lengthened, its diameter remained virtually unchanged throughout its length. The rapid stretching also transformed the hard, shiny rods into rods of a soft, flexible material.

Gore developed several PTFE products by rapidly stretching highly crystalline PTFE, including: (1) porous film for filters and laminates; (2) fabric laminates of PTFE film bonded to fabric to produce a remarkable material having the contradictory properties of impermeability to liquid water and permeability to water vapor, the material being used to make "breathable" rainwear and filters; (3) porous yarn for weaving or braiding into other products, like space suits and pump packing; (4) tubes used as replacements for human arteries and veins; and (5) insulation for high performance electric cables.

On May 21, 1970, Gore filed the patent application that resulted in the patents in suit. The '566 patent has 24 claims directed to processes for stretching highly crystalline, unsintered, PTFE. The processes, *inter alia*, include the steps of stretching PTFE at a rate above 10% per second and at a temperature between about 35°C and the crystalline melt point of PTFE. The '390 patent has 77 claims directed to various products obtained by processes of the '566 patent. . . .

(c) § 112 and the '566 and '390 patents

The patents in suit resulted from a single application and thus have substantially identical specifications. The holding of invalidity on the basis of § 112 is common to both patents.

The district court found that the patents did not disclose sufficient information to enable a person of ordinary skill in the art to make and use the invention, as required by § 112, first paragraph, and that certain claim language was indefinite, presumably in light of § 112, second paragraph, because: (1) there was no definition in the specification of "stretch rate", different formulae for computing stretch rate having been developed and presented at trial; (2) there was no way taught in the specification to calculate the minimum rate of stretch above 35°C; (3) the phrase "matrix tensile strength" is indefinite; and (4) the phrase "specific gravity of the solid polymer" is indefinite.

The findings rest on a misinterpretation of § 112, its function and purpose. The district court considered whether certain terms would have been enabling to the public and looked to formula developments and publications occurring well after Dr. Gore's filing date in reaching its conclusions under § 112. Patents, however, are written to enable those skilled in the art to practice the invention, not the public, and § 112 speaks as of the application filing date, not as of the time of trial. There was no evidence and no finding that those skilled in the art would have found the specification non-enabling or the claim language indefinite on May 21, 1970, when the application which resulted in issuance of Dr. Gore's patents was filed. Indeed, the expert quoted by the district court and whose testimony was primarily relied upon respecting formulae, was still in school at that time.

There is uncontradicted evidence in the record that at the time the application was filed "stretch rate" meant to those skilled in the art the percent of stretch divided by the time of stretching, and that the latter was measurable, for example, with a stopwatch. Concern for the absence from the specification of a formula for calculating stretch rate is therefore misplaced, and the post-filing date development of varying formulae, including Dr. Gore's later addition of a formula in his corresponding Japanese patent, is irrelevant.

Section 112 requires that the inventor set forth the best mode of practicing the invention known to him at the time the application was filed. Calculating stretch rate at that time was accomplished by actually measuring the time required to stretch the PTFE material. That was the only mode then used by the inventor, and it worked. The record establishes that calculation by that mode would have been employed by those of ordinary skill in the art at the time the application was filed. As indicated, Dr. Gore's disclosure must be examined for § 112 compliance in light of knowledge extant in the art on his application filing date.

The district court, though discussing enablement, spoke also of indefiniteness of "stretch rate", a matter having to do with § 112, second paragraph, and relevant in assessment of infringement. The use of "stretching ... at a rate exceeding about 10% per second" in the claims is not indefinite. Infringement is clearly assessable through use of a stop-watch. No witness said that could not be done. As above indicated, subsequently developed and therefore irrelevant formulae cannot be used to render non-enabling or indefinite that which was enabling and definite at the time the application was filed.

Similarly, absence from the specification of a method for calculating the minimum rate of stretch above 35°C does not render the specification non-enabling. The specification discloses that "[t]he lower limit of expansion rates interact with temperature in a roughly logarithmic fashion, being much higher at higher temperatures." Calculation of minimum stretch rate above 35°C is nowhere in the claims, and it is the *claimed* invention for which enablement is required. The claims require stretching at a rate greater than 10% per second at temperatures between 35°C and the crystalline melt point of unsintered PTFE. That the minimum rate of stretch may increase with temperature does not render non-enabling Dr. Gore's specification, particularly in the absence of convincing evidence that those skilled in the art would have found it non-enabling at the time the application was filed.

The district court invalidated both patents for indefiniteness because of its view that some "trial and error" would be needed to determine the "lower limits" of stretch rate above 10% per second at various temperatures above 35°C. That was error. Assuming some experimentation were needed, a patent is not invalid because of a need for experimentation. A patent is invalid only when those skilled in the art are required to engage in *undue* experimentation to practice the invention. There was no evidence and the court made no finding that undue experimentation was required.

Moreover, the finding here rested on confusion of the role of the specification with that of the claims. The court found that the specification's failure to state the lower limit of stretch rate (albeit above 10% per second) at each degree of temperature above 35°C (a requirement for at least hundreds of entries in the specification) did not "distinguish processes performed above the 'lower limit' from those performed below the 'lower limit' ". The claims of the '390 patent say nothing of processes and lower limits. Distinguishing what infringes from what doesn't is the role of the claims, not of the specification. It is clear that the specification is enabling and that the claims of both patents are precise within the requirements of the law.

The finding that "matrix tensile strength" is indefinite, like the other findings under § 112, appears to rest on a confusion concerning the roles of the claims and the specification. While finding "matrix tensile strength" in the claims indefinite, the district court at the same time recognized that the specification itself disclosed how to compute matrix tensile strength, in stating "to compute matrix tensile strength of a porous specimen, one divides the maximum force required to break the sample by the cross sectional area of the porous sample, and then multiplies this quantity by the ratio of the specific gravity of the solid polymer divided by the specific gravity of the porous specimen." Further, the specification provided the actual matrix tensile strength in several examples. It is well settled that a patent applicant may be his own lexicographer. In light of the disclosure of its calculation in the specification, we cannot agree that "matrix tensile strength" is either indefinite or non-enabling.

Nor does absence from the specification of a definition for "specific gravity of the solid polymer", a part of the computation of matrix tensile strength, render that computation indefinite. It is undisputed that in the many examples in the application the specific gravity values used for unsintered and sintered PTFE were 2.3 and 2.2, respectively. There was no testimony that those values were not known to persons of ordinary skill in the art or could not be calculated or measured. There is simply no support for the conclusion that "specific gravity of the solid polymer" is indefinite or that absence of its definition renders the specification non-enabling.

We conclude that Garlock has failed to prove that at the time the application was filed, the specification was not enabling or that the claims were indefinite within the meaning of § 112....

Decision

The holdings of invalidity of claim 1 of the '566 patent under § 102(a) and of claim 17 of the '566 patent under § 103, the determination that Gore did not commit fraud on the PTO, and the denial of attorney fees, are affirmed; the holdings that all claims of the '566 patent are invalid under § 102(b), that claims 3 and 19 of the '566 patent are invalid under § 103, and that all claims of the '566 patent are invalid under § 112, are reversed. The holdings that claims 1, 9, 12, 14, 18, 35, 36, 43, 67, and 77 of the '390 patent are invalid under §§ 102 and 103, and that all claims of the '390 patent are invalid under § 112, are reversed. The case is remanded for determination of the infringement issue.

AFFIRMED IN PART, REVERSED IN PART, AND REMANDED.

[The opinion of Davis, J., concurring in part and dissenting in part, is omitted.]

NOTE

Section 112's requirement of an enabling disclosure dates to the first United States patent law, Act of Apr. 10, 1790, ch. 7, § 2, 1 Stat. 109. The requirement reflects the bargain struck by the patent system generally: society grants exclusive property rights in an invention in return for disclosure of information sufficient to enable practice of the invention upon the patent's expiration.

The enablement requirement is distinct from the "best mode" requirement that also appears in section 112. The enablement requirement is objective; the best mode requirement is subjective. Where the enablement requirement calls for an objective description of the invention and the method for making or using it, the best mode requirement requires the inventor only to disclose what she contemplates as the best mode for carrying out the invention. Best mode does not mean an objectively optimal mode, nor even a better mode that may be contemplated by someone else. For a patent to be denied or invalidated for failure to disclose the best mode, it must be shown that the inventor concealed a better mode than the one disclosed. See generally, Kenneth R. Adamo, What's Better, What's Best—The Best Mode Requirement in U.S. Patent Practice, 73 J. Pat. & Trademark Off. Soc'y 811 (1991).

Paragraph 6 of section 112, providing that "[a]n element in a claim for a combination may be expressed as a means or step for performing a specified function without the recital of structure, material, or acts in support thereof," was added by Congress to overturn a Supreme Court decision, Halliburton Oil Well Cementing Co. v. Walker, 329 U.S. 1, 12–13, 67 S.Ct. 6, 91 L.Ed. 3, 71 U.S.P.Q. 175 (1946), which held that a claim drafted in terms of means plus function was invalid. As characterized in one commentary, Paragraph 6 "allows inventors to define their creation by its function, but limits what is covered by the claims to the specific device described in the patent specification and its structural equivalents. Thus, a patentee should have no need to worry that an infringer changing a nail to a screw in what is otherwise identical to what has been claimed will take a device outside the literal scope of the claims. Instead, if 'means for fastening' is used in the claims, a nail is described in the specification, and a screw is the 'structural equivalent' of a nail, the claim will literally cover both the nail and the screw." William F. Lee & Eugene M. Paige, Means Plus and Step Plus Function Claims: Do We Only Know Them When We See Them? 80 J. Pat. & Trademark Off. Soc'y 251–252 (1998).

B.   ADMINISTRATIVE PROCEDURES

See Statute Supplement 35 U.S.C.A. §§ 1–13, 21–26, 32–33, 41–42, 111–122, 131–135, 141–146, 151–157, 251–256.

An empirical study by John R. Allison and Mark A. Lemley, Who's Patenting What? An Empirical Exploration of Patent Prosecution, 53 Vand. L. Rev. 2099, 2100–02 (2000), analyzed a random sample of one thousand utility patents issued between 1996 and 1998 and, among other findings, determined that: mechanical patents, not "high-tech" patents, represented the largest single category of invention; more than half the patents originated in the U.S. and more than 97% came from only twelve countries; the average time for prosecution of a patent was 2.77 years; and chemical, pharmaceutical and biotechnology patents took more time to prosecute than other patents.

This section narrates the application, prosecution and grant to Baxter I. Scoggin, Jr., of a mechanical patent, Patent No. 2,870,943 for a pump-type liquid sprayer with hold-down cap. The section also introduces the litigation, culminating in Calmar, Inc. v. Cook Chem. Co., 383 U.S. 1, 26, 86 S.Ct. 684, 698, 15 L.Ed.2d 545, 148 U.S.P.Q. 459 (1966), that subsequently enmeshed the Scoggin patent.

1. APPLICATION

Once a preliminary search of the art has been completed, and a decision reached to file a patent application, the application is assembled for submission to the United States Patent and Trademark Office. Typically, the application consists of a signed oath or declaration, power of attorney, an executed assignment if one has been made, filing fee, receipt postcard, transmittal letter, an information disclosure statement, and the claims, specification and drawings.

a. *Claims*

"Having thus described the invention what is claimed as new and desired to be secured by Letters Patent is:

"1. In a closure assembly for an open-top container having a perforated cap over said open top thereof mounting a spray unit including a barrel provided with a tubular extension passing coaxially upwardly through the perforation in said cap, a plunger reciprocally carried by the barrel and normally extending therebeyond and a spray head on the upper end of the plunger above said extension, the combination with said spray unit of an annular retainer telescoped over and secured to the extension above said cap and provided with external, circumferentially disposed screw threads and an annular, continuous segment at the upper part of the retainer above said screw threads, and a cup-shaped hold-down member housing the head and holding the plunger depressed at substantially the innermost path of travel thereof within the barrel, said member being provided with internal screw threads complementally engaging said screw threads on the retainer and having an internal, circumferentially extending, continuous shoulder disposed to engage said segment around the entire periphery thereof and thereby present a liquid-tight seal located between the spray head and said threads on the retainer and said member respectively, said shoulder being spaced from the lower annular peripheral edge of the member a distance at least slightly less than the distance from that portion of said segment normally engaged by said shoulder, to the proximal upper surface of the cap whereby said lower edge of the member is maintained out of contacting relationship with the cap when the member is on the retainer in a position with said shoulder in tight sealing engagement with the segment.

"2. A closure assembly as set forth in claim 1 wherein one of the normally interengaged surfaces of the shoulder and segment respectively is substantially conical to present an inclined annular face coaxial with the member and said retainer and of sufficient diameter at the largest end thereof to cause the seal effected between the shoulder and said segment to become tighter as the shoulder slides on said segment during shifting of the member toward the cap.

"3. A closure assembly as set forth in claim 2 wherein said retainer is provided with a continuous, annular rib integral with the normally upper edge thereof and defining said segment, said rib having an outwardly facing, inclined surface presenting said conical face of greatest external diameter at the zone of juncture of the rib with the retainer, said member having a pair of inner, coaxial, longitudinally spaced, cylindrical surfaces, the innermost cylindrical surface having a smaller diameter than the outermost cylindrical surface and presenting said shoulder therebetween lying in a plane perpendicular to the axes of said cylindrical surfaces, the diameter of said innermost cylindrical surface of the member being intermediate the diameters of opposed external end margins of said rib.

"4. A closure assembly as set forth in claim 3 wherein the member and retainer are constructed of materials having different coefficients of hardness whereby one of the interengaged faces of the rib and said shoulder respectively is deformed as the member is shifted toward the cap to thereby produce a more effective seal therebetween."

———

Like a legal description of real property, each claim of a patent describes the boundaries of the patent owner's exclusive rights. Note, for example, that in claim 1, which is presented as a one-sentence paragraph, each of the comma-separated clauses following the words, "the combination with said spray unit of" cooperatively defines an essential structural element of the invention—a "retainer." By use of more specific language and additional structural elements, each of the four claims successively narrows the invention's boundaries. Thus if, because of its breadth, claim 1 is declared invalid as anticipated by the prior art, claim 2 may succeed by reason of its narrower construction. Note that claim 1 is complete in itself and, for this reason, is characterized as an "independent claim." Claims 2–4, on the other hand, are written in "dependent" form, with claim 2 including the elements of claim 1, claim 3 including the elements of claims 1 and 2, and claim 4 including the elements of claims 1, 2, and 3.

b. Specification

The language of the specification is the dictionary, or exegesis, for the claims. Both drawings and specification must support the claims. The format followed in the Scoggin specification was: title; statement of the field of invention [col. 1, lines 15–18]; background description of the prior art, setting forth the problem to be solved [col. 1, lines 19–35]; series of objects to which the claims should respond [col. 1, lines 36–57]; brief description of the drawings [col. 1, lines 58–72]; and, using reference numerals for the correspondingly labelled drawing elements, a detailed description of a preferred embodiment of the invention's construction and operation. Under the practice preferred by the Patent and Trademark Office, the format employs subheadings to identify these sections:

2,870,943

PUMP-TYPE LIQUID SPRAYER HAVING HOLD-DOWN CAP

Baxter I. Scoggin, Jr., Kansas City, Mo., assignor, by mesne assignments, to Cook Chemical Company, Kansas City, Mo., a corporation of Missouri

Application March 4, 1957, Serial No. 643,711

4 Claims. (Cl 222–182)

This invention relates to improvements in structures for dispensing liquids wherein is provided a spray-type hand pump mounted within a container for the liquid through use of the closure cap of such container.

It is common practice, as exemplified for example by Patent No. 2,362,080, issued November 7, 1944, to dispense various types of liquids such as insecticides, through use of a finger-manipulated spray pump normally sold as a component part of the container itself. The pump includes a vertically reciprocable plunger extending upwardly beyond the top of the cap within which the pump is mounted and provided with a spray head or nozzle structure capable of emitting a fine mist-like spray when the plunger is depressed by engagement with a finger-receiving saddle forming a part of the spray head.

Difficulties have been experienced in the field by virtue of the inherent nature of such structure since accidental actuation of the plunger causes dispensing of the fluid and oftentimes the material is used in part by store employees prior to sale because of the ready accessibility to the pump itself.

It is the most important object of the present invention, therefore, to provide structure for rendering the pump inoperable during shipment and while in storage, as well as on the shelves of the retail dealer.

Another important object of the present invention is to provide structure capable of carrying out the functions above set forth which is also adapted to enclose the head of the plunger and thereby protect the same, as well as handlers of the merchandise by virtue of the fact that the said plunger is completely enclosed and held at the innermost end of its reciprocable path of travel.

A further object of the instant invention is to provide a hold-down cap that may be quickly and easily applied and removed by virtue of a releasable attachment to a part of the entire unit such as by use of screw-threaded interengagement therewith.

A further object of this invention is to provide improvements of the aforementioned character that advantageously employs a part of the unit which has a secondary function of attaching the barrel of the spray pump to the closure cap of the container.

Other objects include important details of construction to be made clear or become apparent as the following specification progresses, reference being had to the accompanying drawing, wherein:

Figure 1 is a fragmentary, elevational view of a liquid container showing a pump-type sprayer as a part thereof and including the novel hold-down cap of the instant invention, parts being in section for clearness.

Figure 2 is a fragmentary, vertical, cross-sectional view through the container and its cap showing the pump assembly in its operable position with the hold-down cap removed; and

Figure 3 is an exploded perspective view showing the hold-down cap and certain parts of the sprayer with which the same is operably associated.

Pump-type sprayer 10 for liquid container 12 is attached to cap 14 for retention thereby when cap 14 is removed from threaded neck 16 of container 12, and if desired, there may be provided sufficient clearance between cup-shaped retainer 18 and annular outturned flange 20 to permit rotation of cap 14 relative to sprayer 10.

Both cap or closure 14 and retainer 18 are received by a cylindrical extension 22 of frusto-conical barrel 24, forming a part of the sprayer 10, extension 22 being integral with flange 20 at the innermost edge of the latter. Flange 20 is integral with barrel 24 near the larger, uppermost edge of the latter and is held against the under side of gasket 38 in the cap 14 when the sprayer 10 is operably associated with container 12.

Retainer 18 is provided with a central opening 25 which receives tubular plunger 26 and has a cavity 27 that accommodates the enlarged extension 22 as is clear in Fig. 2. Retainer 18 is fitted tightly over the extension 22 and maintains the retainer in place with flange 20 against gasket 38 as above set forth.

Reduced end 28 of barrel 24 receives a tube 30 that extends to the bottom of container 12, it being understood that the sprayer 10 is internally constructed in a suitable manner as, for example, in accordance with teachings of the aforementioned patent to pump liquid from the container 12 into the tube 30 and thence through nozzle 32 forming a part of a spray head 34 secured to the uppermost end of plunger 26. The enlarged head 34 is normally depressed by one finger as the operator grasps the container 12 as is well understood in this art.

Cap 14 has a clearance opening therein, as best shown in Fig. 2, for the extension 22 of barrel 24 and when the cap 14 is in screw-threaded engagement with neck 16, the gasket 38 which surrounds barrel 24, is clamped tightly between flange 20 and the under side of the top of cap 14.

A hold-down member broadly designated by the numeral 40, is provided to hold the plunger 26 at the lowermost end of its path of travel within the barrel 24 in the manner illustrated by Fig. 1, it being understood as by reference to said patent, that a spring (not shown) within the barrel 24, yieldably biases the plunger 26 upwardly to the position shown in Fig. 2. The hold-down member 40 is preferably in the nature of a hollow cap so that the same not only encloses or houses the upper end of plunger 26, i. e. spray head 34, but releasably attaches to the retainer 18 and also houses the latter.

A cylindrical bore 42 within the hold-down cap 40 receives the head 34 as seen in Fig. 1, and enlargement of the bore 42 adjacent the lowermost open end of the cap 40 is provided with internal screw threads 44 that mesh with external screw threads 46 on the retainer 18, thereby releasably attaching the cap 40 to the retainer 18.

An enlarged, annular boss 48 on the cap 40 is provided with a ribbed, outermost surface to facilitate mounting and removal of the cap 40 relative to retainer 18. A downwardly-facing shoulder 50 within the cap 40 engages the upper surface of retainer 18, thereby preventing engagement between cap 40 and closure 14 to prevent forcing of the retainer 18 from its tight press-fit engagement with extension 22. As illustrated, the screw threads 46 on the retainer 18 are in the nature of a pair of substantially semi-circular, spirally arranged sections 52 and 54, permitting molding of the retainer 18 with its screw threads 46 as a single unitary part.

In addition to the seal provided between shoulder 50 and the top surface of retainer 18, there is established an additional annular seal between annular rib 56 and the annular surface of cap 40 immediately adjacent to shoulder 50. This seal is clearly illustrated in Figure 1. The cross-sectional contour of rib 56 is as shown in Fig. 2 to present an upwardly and inwardly inclined annular face which snugly fits against the "corner," or line of juncture between shoulder 50 and the adjacent annular inner face of cap 40.

The interfitting surfaces between extension 22 and retainer 18 are as illustrated in Fig. 2. There is an annular notch formed in extension 22 at the outer extremity thereof and this notch 58 receives a similarly formed, continuous annular projection 60 formed integrally with retainer 18 and at a point where elements 58 and 60 will interlock when the parts are in assembled condition.

Thus, any accidental leakage or seepage from container 12 through the parts after they are assembled is obviated.

The material from which retainer 18 is produced is soft enough to be slightly compressed when shoulder 50 and the corner adjacent thereto, rides along the upwardly and inwardly inclined outer face of rib 56 when cap 40 is moved to position.

c. Drawings

Jan. 27, 1959   B. I. SCOGGIN, JR   **2,870,943**

PUMP-TYPE LIQUID SPRAYER HAVING HOLD-DOWN CAP

Filed March 4, 1957

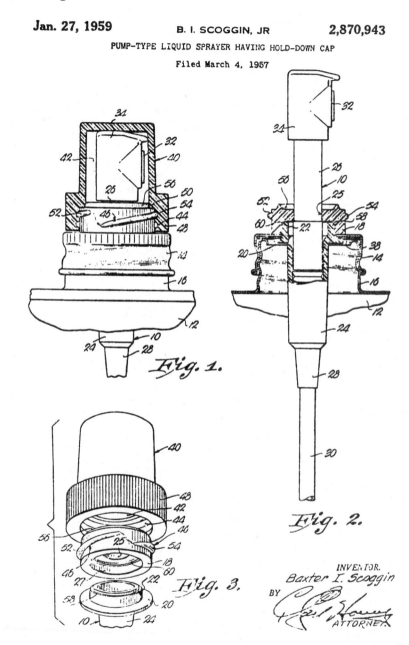

Fig. 1.

Fig. 2.

Fig. 3.

INVENTOR.
Baxter I. Scoggin

BY

ATTORNEY.

2. PROSECUTION

The claims, specification and drawings set out above are taken not from Scoggin's original application, filed March 4, 1957, but from a strikingly different document—the patent that finally issued. The Patent Office positions and the argument and negotiation that produced the differences—a small change in the specification and a complete revision of the claims—are typical of patent prosecutions generally.

a. *First Office Action.* Scoggin received the first Office Action on November 5, 1957. In this action, the examiner pointed out a minor discrepancy between the specification and drawings and rejected claims 1–11; apparently inadvertently, he overlooked claims 12–15. The examiner gave two grounds for rejecting claims 1–11: they were (1) vague and indefinite; and (2) "substantially met by Lohse"—Patent No. 2,119,884 issued to F.W. Lohse, June 7, 1938.

Scoggin's first amendment, filed April 30, 1958, corrected the specification, cancelled claims 1–15, added new claims 16 and 17, and attempted to demonstrate that the new claims were distinguishable over Lohse. The new claims and the arguments in support of their allowability stressed a leakproof sealing feature of the hold-down cap, a feature not defined in the original claims and only peripherally alluded to in the specification.

b. *Second Office Action.* The examiner initiated this action on October 1, 1958, widening his prior art references to include two patents, Slade and Nilson, covering threaded container caps without a spray head. Specifically, the examiner rejected claims 16 and 17 as unpatentable over a combination of prior art—Lohse in view of either Slade or Nilson. Scoggin responded with a second amendment cancelling claims 16 and 17 and adding narrower new claims, 18–24; he also offered detailed arguments to distinguish the new claims from the cited art.

Subsequently, Scoggin's attorney and the examiner met for a personal interview in the course of which the examiner cited two new patents in combination with Lohse—Darley and Mellon.

At the interview, attorney and examiner finally agreed on the claim limitations necessary to define the invention over the new combination of prior art. Shortly afterward, Scoggin submitted a third, supplementary amendment cancelling claims 18–24 and adding new claims, 25–28. Apart from being more definite in three areas, claim 25 was similar to claim 18 and claims 26–28 were identical to claims 19–21. Claims 22–24 were dropped.

c. *Notice of Allowance.* The notice, dated November 20, 1958, allowed claims 25–28, which became claims 1–4 of the issued patent. Upon payment of the requisite fee, Patent No. 2,870,943 issued January 27, 1959. The application's pending period, slightly under two years, was shorter than usual.

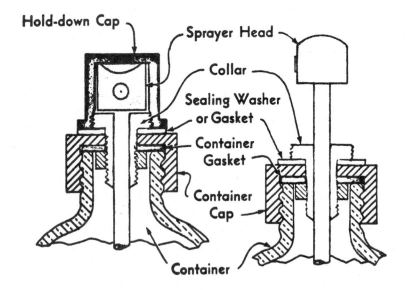

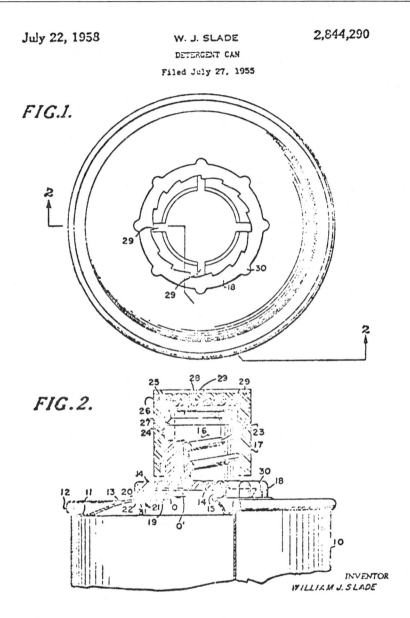

July 22, 1958   W. J. SLADE   2,844,290

DETERGENT CAN

Filed July 27, 1955

FIG.1.

FIG.2.

INVENTOR
WILLIAM J. SLADE

BY *Cushman, Darby & Cushman*
ATTORNEYS

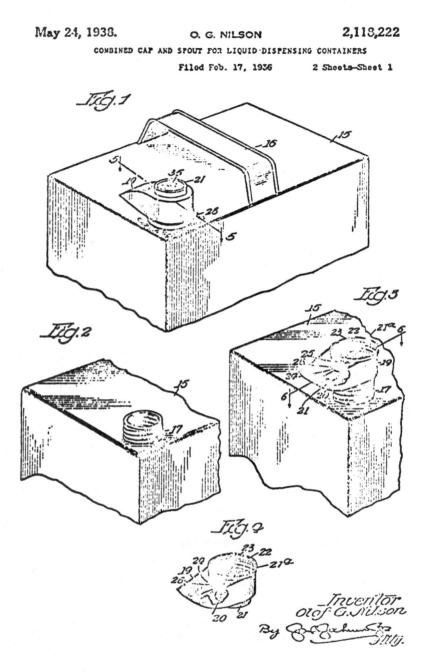

May 24, 1938.   O. G. NILSON   2,118,222

COMBINED CAP AND SPOUT FOR LIQUID-DISPENSING CONTAINERS

Filed Feb. 17, 1936   2 Sheets-Sheet 1

Fig.1

Fig.2

Fig.3

Fig.4

Inventor
Olof G. Nilson

By

Atty.

May 24, 1938.   O. G. NILSON   2,118,222

COMBINED CAP AND SPOUT FOR LIQUID DISPENSING CONTAINERS

Filed Feb. 17, 1936   2 Sheets-Sheet 2

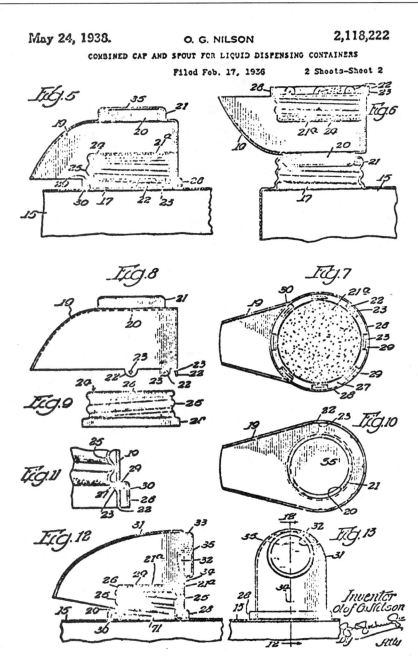

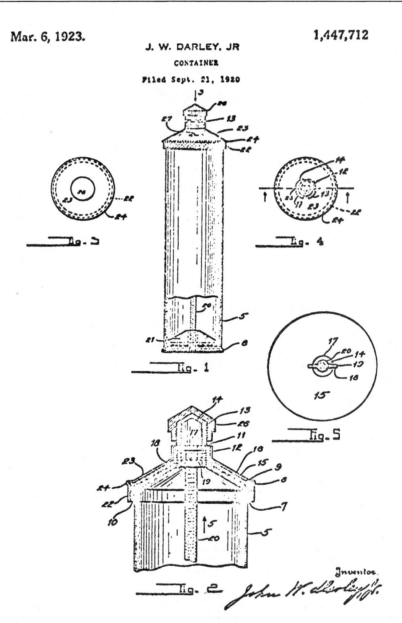

Mar. 6, 1923.

1,447,712

J. W. DARLEY, JR

CONTAINER

Filed Sept. 21, 1920

Fig. 3

Fig. 4

Fig. 1

Fig. 5

Fig. 2

Inventor

John W. Darley Jr.

FIG. 5. MELLON PATENT 2,586,687
(Prior art 1952)

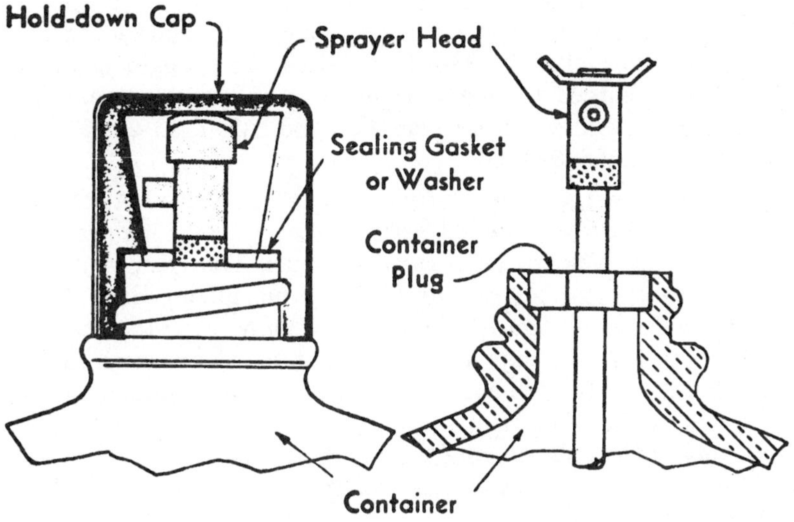

Hold-down Cap

Sprayer Head

Sealing Gasket
or Washer

Container
Plug

Container

3. JUDICIAL REVIEW

"By 1956 Scoggin had perfected the shipper-sprayer in suit and a patent was granted in 1959 to Cook Chemical as his assignee. In the interim Cook Chemical began to use Scoggin's device and also marketed it to the trade. The device was well received and soon became widely used. In the meanwhile, Calmar employed two engineers, Corsette and Cooprider, to perfect a shipper-sprayer and by 1958 it began to market its SS–40, a device very much similar to Scoggin's. When the Scoggin patent issued, Cook Chemical charged Calmar's SS–40 with infringement and this suit followed." Calmar, Inc. v. Cook Chem. Co., 383 U.S. 1, 28–29, 86 S.Ct. 684, 699, 700, 15 L.Ed.2d 545 (1966).

Upon being charged with infringement, Calmar, on April 27, 1959, instituted a declaratory judgment action against Cook Chemical in Cook's home district, the Western District of Missouri. The complaint asked the court to declare Scoggin's patent invalid and not infringed by Calmar. On October 5, 1960, the Colgate–Palmolive Company, a customer of Calmar, and user-seller of the Calmar device, brought a similar action in the same court. In its answers to both complaints, Cook admitted jurisdiction and the existence of a justiciable controversy, and counterclaimed for a declaration of the validity of the patent and a finding that it was infringed by Calmar's device. The actions were consolidated for trial on the issues of validity and infringement only.

The court's judgment, rendered July 31, 1963, decreed that (1) Cook was owner of the patent; (2) claims 1 and 2 were valid; (3) Calmar had infringed claims 1 and 2 by manufacture and sale, and Colgate had infringed claims 1 and 2 by use and sale; (4) plaintiffs' request for relief was dismissed; (5) plaintiffs were permanently enjoined from making, using or selling the accused device; (6) defendant was entitled to damages and an accounting and (7) defendant could move for an accounting and attorney's fees under 35 U.S.C.A. § 285.

Calmar and Colgate appealed to the Court of Appeals for the Eighth Circuit, which affirmed the judgment below, holding claims 1 and 2 valid and infringed. On certiorari to the court of appeals, the Supreme Court considered the *Calmar* and *Colgate* cases along with Graham v. John Deere Co., page 434, above, and rendered its decision on February 21, 1966.

Calmar, Inc. v. Cook Chem. Co.

Supreme Court of the United States, 1966.
383 U.S. 1, 86 S.Ct. 684, 15 L.Ed.2d 545, 148 U.S.P.Q. 459.

CLARK, J.

The Opinions of the District Court and the Court of Appeals.

At the outset it is well to point up that the parties have always disagreed as to the scope and definition of the invention claimed in the patent in suit. Cook Chemical contends that the invention encompasses a unique combination of admittedly old elements and that patentability is found in the result produced. Its expert testified that the invention was "the first commercially successful, inexpensive integrated shipping closure pump unit which permitted automated assembly with a container of household insecticide or similar liquids to produce a practical, ready-to-use package which could be shipped without external leakage and which was so organized that the pump unit with its hold-down cap could be itself assembled and sealed and then later assembled and sealed on the container without breaking the first seal." Cook Chemical stresses the long-felt need in the industry for such a device; the inability of others to produce it; and its commercial success—all of which, contends Cook, evidences the nonobvious nature of the device at the time it was developed. On the other hand, Calmar says that the differences between Scoggin's shipper-sprayer and the prior art relate only to the design of the overcap and that the differences are so inconsequential that the device as a whole would have been obvious at the time of its invention to a person having ordinary skill in the art.

Both courts accepted Cook Chemical's contentions. While the exact basis of the District Court's holding is uncertain, the court did find the subject matter of the patent new, useful and nonobvious. It concluded that Scoggin "had produced a sealed and protected sprayer unit which the manufacturer need only screw onto the top of its container in much the same fashion as a simple metal cap." 220 F.Supp., at 418. Its decision seems to be bottomed on the finding that the Scoggin sprayer solved the long-standing problem that had confronted the industry. The Court of Appeals also found validity in the "novel 'marriage' of the sprayer with the insecticide container" which took years in discovery and in "the immediate commercial success" which it enjoyed. While finding that the individual elements of the invention were "not novel per se" the court found "nothing in the prior art suggesting Scoggin's unique combination of these old features ... as would solve the ... problems which for years beset the insecticide industry." It concluded that "the ... [device] meets the exacting standard required for a combination of old elements to rise to the level of patentable invention by fulfilling the long-felt need with an economical, efficient, utilitarian apparatus which achieved novel results and immediate commercial success." 336 F.2d, at 114.

The Prior Art

Only two of the five prior art patents cited by the Patent Office Examiner in the prosecution of Scoggin's application are necessary to our discussion, i.e., Lohse U.S. Patent No. 2,119,884 (1938) and Mellon U.S. Patent No. 2,586,687 (1952). Others are cited by Calmar that were not before the Examiner, but of these our purposes require discussion of only the Livingstone U.S. Patent No. 2,715,480 (1953). Simplified drawings of each of these patents are reproduced in the Appendix, Figs. 4–6, for comparison and description.

The Lohse patent is a shipper-sprayer designed to perform the same function as Scoggin's device. The differences, recognized by the District Court, are found in the overcap seal which in Lohse is formed by the skirt of the overcap engaging a washer or gasket which rests upon the upper surface of the container cap. The court emphasized that in Lohse "[t]here are no seals above the threads and below the sprayer head." 220 F.Supp., at 419.

The Mellon patent (Fig. 5), however, discloses the idea of effecting a seal above the threads of the overcap. Mellon's device, likewise a shipper-sprayer, differs from Scoggin's in that its overcap screws directly on the container, and a gasket, rather than a rib, is used to effect the seal.

Finally, Livingstone shows a seal above the threads accomplished without the use of a gasket or washer. Although Livingstone's arrangement was designed to cover and protect pouring spouts, his sealing feature is strikingly similar to Scoggin's. Livingstone uses a tongue and groove technique in which the tongue, located on the upper surface of the collar, fits into a groove on the inside of the overcap. Scoggin employed the rib and shoulder seal in the identical position and with less efficiency because the Livingstone technique is inherently a more stable structure, forming an interlock that withstands distortion of the overcap when subjected to rough handling. Indeed, Cook Chemical has now incorporated the Livingstone closure into its own shipper-sprayers as had Calmar in its SS–40.

The Invalidity of the Patent

Let us first return to the fundamental disagreement between the parties. Cook Chemical, as we noted at the outset, urges that the invention must be viewed as the overall combination, or—putting it in the language of the statute—that we must consider the subject matter sought to be patented taken as a whole. With this position, taken in the abstract, there is, of course, no quibble. But the history of the prosecution of the Scoggin application in the Patent Office reveals a substantial divergence in respondent's present position.

As originally submitted, the Scoggin application contained 15 claims which in very broad terms claimed the entire combination of spray pump and overcap. No mention of, or claim for, the sealing features was made. All 15 claims were rejected by the Examiner because (1) the applicant was vague and indefinite as to what the invention was, and (2) the claims were met by Lohse. Scoggin canceled these claims and submitted new ones. Upon a further series of rejections and new submissions, the Patent Office Examiner, after an office interview, at last relented. It is crystal clear that after the first rejection, Scoggin relied entirely upon the sealing arrangement as the exclusive patentable difference in his combination. It is likewise clear that it was on that feature that the Examiner allowed the claims. In fact, in a letter accompanying the final submission of claims, Scoggin, through his attorney, stated that "agreement was reached between the Honorable Examiner and applicant's attorney relative to *limitations* which must be in the claims in order to define novelty over the previously applied disclosure of Lohse when considered in view of the newly cited patents of Mellon and Darley, Jr." (Italics added.)

Moreover, those limitations were specifically spelled out as (1) the use of a rib seal and (2) an overcap whose lower edge did not contact the container cap. Mellon was distinguished, as was the Darley patent on the basis that although it disclosed a hold-down cap with a seal located above the threads, it did not disclose a rib seal disposed in such position as to cause the lower peripheral edge of the overcap "to be maintained out of contacting relationship with [the container] cap ... when ... [the overcap] was screwed [on] tightly...." Scoggin maintained that the "obvious modification" of Lohse in view of Mellon would be merely to place the Lohse gasket above the threads with the lower edge of the overcap remaining in tight contact with the container cap or neck of the container itself. In other words, the Scoggin invention was limited to the use of a rib—rather than a washer or gasket—and the existence of a slight space between the overcap and the container cap.

It is, of course, well settled that an invention is construed not only in the light of the claims, but also with reference to the file wrapper or prosecution history in the Patent Office. Claims as allowed must be read and interpreted with reference to rejected ones and to the state of the prior art; and claims that have been narrowed in order to obtain the issuance of a patent by distinguishing the prior art cannot be sustained to cover that which was previously by limitation eliminated from the patent.

Here, the patentee obtained his patent only by accepting the limitations imposed by the Examiner. The claims were carefully drafted to reflect these limitations and Cook Chemical is not now free to assert a broader view of Scoggin's invention. The subject matter as a whole reduces, then, to the distinguishing features clearly incorporated into the claims. We now turn to those features.

As to the space between the skirt of the overcap and the container cap, the District Court found:

> Certainly without a space so described, there could be no inner seal within the cap, but such a space is not new or novel, but it is necessary to the formation of the seal within the hold-down cap.

> *To me this language is descriptive of an element of the patent but not a part of the invention.* It is too simple, really, to require much discussion. In this device the hold-down cap was intended to perform two functions—to hold down the sprayer head and to form a solid tight seal between the shoulder and the collar below. In assembling the element it is necessary to provide this space in order to form the seal. 220 F.Supp. at 420. (Italics added.)

The court correctly viewed the significance of that feature. We are at a loss to explain the Examiner's allowance on the basis of such a distinction. Scoggin was able to convince the Examiner that Mellon's cap contacted the bottle neck while his did not. Although the drawings included in the Mellon application show that the cap might touch the neck of the bottle when fully screwed down, there is nothing—absolutely nothing—which indicates that the cap was designed at any time to *engage* the bottle neck. It is palpably evident that Mellon embodies a seal formed by a gasket compressed between the cap and the bottle neck. It follows that the cap in Mellon will not seal if it does not bear down on the gasket and this would be impractical, if not impossible, under the construction urged by Scoggin before the Examiner. Moreover, the space so strongly asserted by Cook Chemical appears quite plainly on the Livingstone device, a reference not cited by the Examiner.

The substitution of a rib built into a collar likewise presents no patentable difference above the prior art. It was fully disclosed and dedicated to the public in the Livingstone patent. Cook Chemical argues, however, that Livingstone is not in the *pertinent* prior art because it relates to liquid containers having pouring spouts rather than pump sprayers. Apart from the fact that respondent made no such objection to similar references cited by the Examiner, so restricted a view of the applicable prior art is not justified. The problems confronting Scoggin and the insecticide industry were not insecticide problems; they were mechanical closure problems. Closure devices in such a closely related art as pouring spouts for liquid containers are at the very least pertinent references.

Cook Chemical insists, however, that the development of a workable shipper-sprayer eluded Calmar, who had long and unsuccessfully sought to solve the problem. And, further, that the long-felt need in the industry for a device such as Scoggin's together with its wide commercial success supports its patentability. These legal inferences or subtests do focus attention on economic and motivational rather than technical issues and are, therefore, more susceptible of judicial treatment than are the highly technical facts often present in patent litigation. Such inquiries may lend a helping hand to the judiciary which, as Mr. Justice Frankfurter observed, is most ill-fitted to discharge the technological duties cast upon it by patent legislation. Marconi Wireless Co. v. United States, 320 U.S. 1, 60, 63 S.Ct. 1393, 87 L.Ed. 1731 (1943). They may also serve to "guard against slipping into use of hindsight," Monroe Auto Equipment Co. v. Heckethorn Mfg. & Supply Co., 332 F.2d 406, 412 (1964), and to resist the temptation to read into the prior art the teachings of the invention in issue.

However, these factors do not, in the circumstances of this case, tip the scales of patentability. The Scoggin invention, as limited by the Patent Office and accepted by Scoggin, rests upon exceedingly small and quite nontechnical mechanical differences in a device which was old in the art. At the latest, those differences were rendered apparent in 1953 by the appearance of the Livingstone patent, and unsuccessful attempts to reach a solution to the problems confronting Scoggin made before that time became wholly irrelevant. It is also irrelevant that no one apparently chose to avail himself of knowledge stored in the Patent Office and readily available by the simple expedient of conducting a patent search—a prudent and nowadays common preliminary to well organized research. To us, the limited claims of the Scoggin patent are clearly evident from the prior art as it stood at the time of the invention.

We conclude that the claims in issue in the Scoggin patent must fall as not meeting the test of § 103, since the differences between them and the pertinent prior art would have been obvious to a person reasonably skilled in that art.

The judgment of the Court of Appeals in No. 11 is affirmed. The judgment of the Court of Appeals in Nos. 37 and 43 is reversed and the cases remanded to the District Court for disposition not inconsistent with this opinion.

It is so ordered.

NOTES

1. *Review of PTO Decisions as a Question of Administrative Law.* Should courts reviewing decisions of the U.S. Patent and Trademark Office employ the standards generally applied to decisions of administrative agencies under the Administrative Procedure Act, 5 U.S.C. § 706 (1994)? Despite decades of lower court decisions applying a "clearly erroneous" standard to PTO factfindings, the U.S. Supreme Court held in Dickinson v. Zurko, 527 U.S. 150, 119 S.Ct. 1816, 144 L.Ed.2d 143, 50 U.S.P.Q.2d 1930 (1999), that the APA's somewhat less stringent standards, such as "arbitrary," "capricious" and "abuse of discretion," should be applied to PTO decisions.

For arguments for and against subjecting judicial review of PTO decisions to APA and related standards, see Orin S. Kerr, Rethinking Patent Law in the Administrative State, 42 Wm. & Mary L. Rev. 127 (2000); Craig Allen Nard, Deference, Defiance, and the Useful Arts, 56 Ohio St. L.J. 1415, 1450–67 (1995) William Woodward, A Reconsideration of the Patent System as a Problem of Administrative Law, 55 Harv. L. Rev. 950 (1942).

2. *Publication of Patent Applications.* Section 122(a) of the Patent Act reflects the longstanding American tradition of keeping the contents of patent applications in confidence until a patent issues. In 1999, following the recommendation of the 1992 Advisory Commission on Patent Law Reform that the United States adopt the publication approach widely employed abroad, Congress amended section 122 to establish a default rule that patent applications will be published after eighteen months "from the earliest filing date for which a benefit is sought under this title." An applicant may request earlier publication or may request that there be no publication at all; in the latter case, the applicant must certify that no foreign application has been, or will be, filed for the invention under terms requiring publication eighteen months after filing. To give the applicant an incentive to elect eighteen-month, or earlier, publication, section 154(d) provides that a patentee may recover a reasonable royalty for infringements occurring after publication if the infringer actually knew of the publication and if the patent claims ultimately granted are "substantially identical" to the claims published.

3. *Reissue and Reexamination.* Two avenues exist for modifying issued patents. Section 251 of the Patent Act provides for patent reissue: "Whenever any patent is, through error without any deceptive intention, deemed wholly or partly inoperative or invalid, by reason of a defective specification or drawing, or by reason of the patentee claiming more or less than he had a right to claim in the patent, the Director shall, on the surrender of such patent and the payment of the fee required by law, reissue the patent for the invention disclosed in the original patent, and in accordance with a new and amended application, for the unexpired part of the term of the original patent. No new matter shall be introduced into the application for reissue."

Chapter 30 of the Patent Act, added by Pub.L. No. 96–517, 94 Stat. 3015 (1980), provides that "[a]ny person at any time may file a request for reexamination by the Office of any claim of a patent on the basis of any prior art...." 35 U.S.C.A. § 302. On signing Public Law 96–517, President Jimmy Carter observed:

> The patent reexamination procedures established by this legislation constitute the most significant improvement in our patent laws in more than a century. Under these procedures, during the life of an issued patent any interested person—for example, a patent owner, a potential licensee, or a competitor—may obtain a prompt and relatively inexpensive reevaluation of its validity by the Patent and Trademark Office. Patent reexamination will make it possible to focus extra attention on the most commercially significant patents. This legislation will improve the reliability of reexamined patents, thereby reducing the costs and uncertainties of testing patent validity in the courts. The provisions of this legislation will result in less cost to the public for patent reexamination.

Public Papers of Presidents of the United States, Jimmy Carter 2803 (Dec. 12, 1980).

By allowing competitors, as well as patent owners, to obtain reexamination of a patent, Congress in passing the 1980 amendments intended to provide a route less costly less costly than litigation to challenging a patient's validity. Because, however, the procedure was essentially *ex parte*—once it initiated the proceeding, the challenger could not participate further—the procedure was used only sparingly by those with the greatest interest in testing a patent's validity. To overcome this deficiency, Congress amended the Patent Act in 1999 to add new sections 311–318, designated "Optional *Inter Partes* Reexamination Procedures," to complement the *ex parte* reexamination procedures of sections 302–307. The new procedures entitle third parties such as competitors to participate in the PTO proceedings and to appeal the PTO decision on the reexamination. See Michael L. Goldman & Alice Y. Choi, The New Optional *Inter Partes* Reexamination Procedure and Its Strategic Use, 28 AIPLA QJ 307 (2000).

What interests would be served by a system that postponed *all* examination of claimed subject matter to a point sometime after a patent issues? Outside the United States, many countries provide for deferred patent examination for periods ranging from months to years. Section 48*ter* of the

Japanese Patent Act gives the applicant three years from filing of a patent application to request examination. Also, a large number of countries winnow out invalid patents through an opposition procedure under which any interested party can oppose the grant of a patent within a period that is usually measured in months from the application's passage to acceptance by the examiner. One popular technique for weeding out patents that have enjoyed limited commercial success is to impose periodic levies—variously called renewal fees, maintenance fees or annuities; in addition to clearing out undesired monopolies, the fees help to subvent patent office operations. See generally J.W. Baxter, *et al.* 2 World Patent Law and Practice chapters 3, 7, 14 (2nd ed. 1973).

4. *Statutory Invention Registrations.* The Patent Law Amendments of 1984, Pub.L. No. 98–622, 98 Stat. 3383, introduced statutory invention registrations into the patent system, effectively enabling inventors to obtain defensive patent protection. "Under current law, there is no simple, practical method by which an inventor can protect his ability to exploit the invention without obtaining a patent. The new procedure created by section 102 [35 U.S.C.A. § 157] would confer on an inventor the same rights that a patent provides to prevent others from patenting the invention. However, it would not permit the holder to exclude others from making, using or selling the invention.... Due to the fact that a SIR does not grant an exclusive right to an inventor, it would not be necessary to subject a SIR to the lengthy examination process required for the granting of a patent. Such an examination would only be necessary if the SIR was subjected to an interference proceeding to determine priority of invention. In all other instances, the Patent and Trademark Office would only review the application for adherence to formal printing and payment requirements and to ensure that the requirements of 35 U.S.C. § 112 were satisfied." Statement of Rep. Robert Kastenmeier, 130 Cong.Rec.H.10526 (daily ed. Oct. 1, 1984).

NOTE: FRAUD AND INEQUITABLE CONDUCT IN THE PATENT AND TRADEMARK OFFICE

A patent is a contract between the patentee and society: society gives the patentee a durationally limited property right in return for the patentee's enabling disclosure of her invention. With rights come responsibilities. In her "contract negotiations" with the Patent and Trademark Office, the patent applicant has a duty not to use fraudulent misrepresentations to induce the patent grant. This duty dates to the first patent act, Act of Apr. 10, 1790, ch. 7, § 5, 1 Stat. 109, 111, which gave private parties standing to seek repeal of a patent "obtained surreptitiously by, or upon false suggestion...." Today, fraud or inequitable conduct may lead the Patent and Trademark Office to strike a patent application from its files or prompt the government to cancel the patent. Antitrust liability may also ensue. Probably most important, fraud or inequitable conduct in the Patent and Trademark Office may give an accused infringer the defense that the patent is invalid or unenforceable. See D. Chisum, Patents § 19.03[6] (1989).

Patent fraud or inequitable conduct characteristically involves nondisclosure of pertinent information such as relevant prior art. In FMC Corp. v. Manitowoc Co., 835 F.2d 1411, 5 U.S.P.Q.2d 1112 (Fed.Cir.1987), Chief Judge Howard Markey described the "clear and convincing proof" that a party must offer to support a claim of inequitable nondisclosure: "(1) prior art or information that is material; (2) knowledge chargeable to applicant of that prior art or information and of its materiality; and (3) failure of the applicant to disclose the art or information resulting from an intent to mislead the PTO. That proof may be rebutted by a showing that: (a) the prior art or information was not material (e.g., because it is less pertinent than or merely cumulative with prior art or information cited to or by the PTO); (b) if the prior art or information was material, a showing that applicant did not know of that art or information; (c) if applicant did know of that art or information, a showing that applicant did not know of its materiality; (d) a showing that applicant's failure to disclose art or information did not result from an intent to mislead the PTO." 835 F.2d at 1415.

Kingsdown Medical Consultants, Ltd. v. Hollister Inc., 863 F.2d 867, 9 U.S.P.Q.2d 1384 (Fed.Cir.1988), cert. denied, 490 U.S. 1067, 109 S.Ct. 2068, 104 L.Ed.2d 633 (1989), clarified the role of gross negligence in proof of intent to mislead the Patent and Trademark Office. Recognizing that "[s]ome of our opinions have suggested that a finding of gross negligence compels a finding of an intent to deceive" and that "[o]thers have indicated that gross negligence alone does not mandate a finding of intent to deceive," the court, en banc, adopted "the view that a finding that particular conduct amounts to 'gross negligence' does not of itself justify an inference of intent to deceive; the involved conduct, viewed in light of all the evidence, including evidence indicative of good faith, must indicate sufficient culpability to require a finding of intent to deceive." 863 F.2d at 876.

Judicial decisions on fraud and inequitable conduct have been unpredictable. One reason is that the standards are so fact-specific; another is that courts often weigh the two relevant elements—intent and materiality—together, sometimes allowing strong proof of materiality to offset a weak showing of intent. The elements themselves have fluctuated widely. The intent requirement has wavered between objective and subjective measures, and materiality has fluctuated between a "but for" test and an "influence" test—whether it is likely that a reasonable examiner would have considered the information withheld to be important to the decision to grant a patent.

Although, in an absolute sense, fraud and inequitable conduct are bad, making them a defense in patent infringement actions can be costly. Professor Donald Chisum has observed that the defense injects "an element of moral turpitude into an area of law where it is especially important that attention be focused on the technical and economic facts."Donald Chisum, Patent Law and the Presumption of Moral Regularity: A Critical Review of Recent Federal Circuit Decisions on Inequitable Conduct and Willful Infringement, 69 J.Pat. & Trademark Off.Soc'y 27, 28 (1987). An overly sensitive standard for fraud and inequitable conduct will lead applicants and their attorneys to search for and disclose information that offers no independent benefit to them or society; an uncertain standard will only magnify these expenditures.

See generally, Symposium, Evolution and Future of New Rule 56 and the Duty of Candor, 20 AIPLA Q. J 136 (1992); Charles M. McMahon, Intent to Commit Fraud on the USPTO: Is Mere Negligence Once Again Inequitable? 27 A.I.P.L. A.O.J.49 (1999).

C. RIGHTS AND REMEDIES

See Statute Supplement 35 U.S.C.A. §§ 154, 261–262, 271–273, 281–296.

1. RIGHTS

Paper Converting Machine Co. v. Magna–Graphics Corp.

United States Court of Appeals, Federal Circuit, 1984.
745 F.2d 11, 223 U.S.P.Q. 591.

NICHOLS, Senior Circuit Judge.

This appeal is from a judgment of the United States District Court for the Eastern District of Wisconsin (Reynolds, C.J.) entered on December 1, 1983, and awarding plaintiff Paper Converting Machine Company (Paper Converting) $893,064 as compensation for defendant Magna–Graphics Corporation's (Magna–Graphics) willful infringement of United States Patent No. Re. 28,353. We *affirm-in-part and vacate-in-part.*

I

Although the technology involved here is complex, the end product is one familiar to most Americans. The patented invention relates to a machine used to manufacture rolls of densely wound ("hard-wound") industrial toilet tissue and paper toweling. The machine, commonly known as an automatic rewinder, unwinds a paper web continuously under high tension at speeds up to 2,000 feet per minute from a large-diameter paper roll—known as the parent roll or bedroll—and simultaneously rewinds it onto paperboard cores to form individual consumer products.

Before the advent of automatic rewinders, toilet tissue and paper towel producers used "stop-start" rewinders. With these machines, the entire rewinding operation had to cease after a retail-sized "log" was finished so that a worker could place a new mandrel (the shaft for carrying the paperboard core) in the path of the paper web. In an effort to increase production, automatic rewinders were introduced in the early 1950's. These machines automatically moved a new mandrel into the path of the paper web while the machine was still winding the paper web onto another mandrel, and could operate at a steady pace at speeds up to about 1,200 feet per minute.

In 1962, Nystrand, Bradley, and Spencer invented the first successful "sequential" automatic rewinder, a machine which not only overcame previous speed limitations, but also could handle two-ply tissue. This rewinder simultaneously cut the paper web and impaled it on pins against the parent roll. Then, after a new mandrel was automatically moved into place, a "pusher" would move the paper web away from the parent roll and against a glue-covered paperboard core to begin winding a new paper log.

On April 20, 1965, United States Patent No. 3,179,348 (the '348 patent) issued, giving to Paper Converting (to whom rights in the invention had been assigned) patent protection for machines incorporating the sequential rewinding approach. On September 1, 1972, Paper Converting applied to have the claims of the '348 patent narrowed by reissue, and on March 4, 1975, United States Patent No. Re. 28,353 (the '353 patent) issued on this application. The '353 patent, like the original '348 patent on which it is based, received an expiration date of April 20, 1982. Claim 1 of the '353 patent defines the improvement in the web-winding apparatus as an improvement comprising:

> (C) means for transversely severing said web to provide a free leading edge on said web for approaching a mandrel on which said web is to be wound in said path, and

> (D) pin means extensibly mounted on said roll for maintaining a web portion spaced from said edge in contact with said roll, and pusher means extensibly mounted on said roll to urge said maintained web portion against an adjacent mandrel.

Paper Converting achieved widespread commercial success with its patented automatic rewinder. Although there are not many domestic producers of toilet tissue and paper toweling, Paper Converting has sold more than 500 machines embodying the invention.

In 1979, Paper Converting brought the present action against Magna–Graphics for infringement of the '353 patent. After a trial concerning only issues of liability, the district court held the '353 patent valid and found it willfully infringed. It awarded treble damages, finding that Magna–Graphics had acted without the advice of counsel as to the change it made in its machines to avoid infringement. The Seventh Circuit affirmed. The parties commendably raise no issues here which the Seventh Circuit has already decided as to Magna–Graphics' liability.

When the district court held the accounting for damages (after the Seventh Circuit had affirmed it on the liability portion of the case), it found that Magna–Graphics had made two sales of infringing rewinders and associated equipment: one to the Fort Howard Paper Company (Fort Howard) under circumstances to be described, and one to the Scott Paper Company (Scott). The court awarded to Paper Converting $112,163 for Magna–Graphics' sale to Scott, and $145,583 for Magna–Graphics' sale to Fort Howard. The court then trebled these damages, and added $119,826 as prejudgment interest on the untrebled award. This appeal is from the judgment awarding damages....

III

A

Magna–Graphics first argues that it should bear no liability whatsoever for its manufacture, sale, or delivery of the Fort Howard rewinder because that machine was never *completed* during the life of the '353 patent. We disagree.

In early 1980 Fort Howard became interested in purchasing a new high-speed rewinder line. Both Paper Converting and Magna–Graphics offered bids. Because Magna–Graphics offered to provide an entire rewinder line for about 10 percent less than did Paper Converting, it won the contract. Delivery would have been before the '353 patent expired. Magna–Graphics began to build the contracted for machinery, but before it completed the rewinder, on February 26, 1981, the federal district court in Wisconsin determined that a similar Magna–Graphics' rewinder built for and sold to Scott infringed the '353 patent. The court enjoined Magna–Graphics from any future infringing activity.

Because at the time of the federal injunction the rewinder intended for Fort Howard was only 80 percent complete, Magna–Graphics sought a legal way to fulfill its contract with Fort Howard rather than abandon its machine. First, Magna–Graphics tried to change the construction of the rewinder so as to avoid infringement. It submitted to Paper Converting's counsel three drawings illustrating three proposed changes, and asked for an opinion as to whether the changes would avoid infringement. Paper Converting's counsel replied, however, that until a fully built and operating machine could be viewed, no opinion could be given. Magna–Graphics, believing such a course of action unfeasible because of the large risks in designing, engineering, and building a machine without knowing whether it would be considered an infringement, instead negotiated with Fort Howard to delay the final assembly and delivery of an otherwise infringing rewinder until after the '353 patent expired in April 1982.

Magna–Graphics thereafter continued to construct the Fort Howard machine, all the while staying in close consultation with its counsel. After finishing substantially all of the machine, Magna–Graphics tested it to ensure that its moving parts would function as intended at a rate of 1,600 feet of paper per minute. Although Magna–Graphics normally *fully* tested machines at its plant before shipment, to avoid infringement in this instance, Magna–Graphics ran its tests in two stages over a period of several weeks in July and August of 1981.

To understand Magna–Graphics' testing procedure, it is necessary to understand the automatic transfer operation of the patented machine. First, from within a 72-inch long "cutoff" roll, a 72-inch blade ejects to sever the continuous web of paper which is wound around the bedroll. Then, pins attached to the bedroll hold the severed edge of the web while pushers, also attached to the bedroll, transfer the edge of the web towards the mandrel (the roll on which the paperboard core is mounted).

In the first stage of its test, Magna–Graphics checked the bedroll to determine whether the pushers actuated properly. It installed on the bedroll two pusher pads instead of the thirty pads normally used in an operating machine. It greased the pads and operated the bedroll to determine whether the pads, when unlatched, would contact the core on the mandrel. (Magna–Graphics greased the pads so as to provide a visual indication that they had touched the core.) During this stage of tests, no cutoff blades or pins were installed.

In the second stage of the test, Magna–Graphics checked the cutoff roll to determine whether the cutting blade actuated as intended. It tested the knife actuating mechanism by installing into the cutoff roll a short 4–inch section of cutter blade rather than the 72–inch blade normally used. After taping a 4–inch wide piece of paper to the outer surface of the cutoff roll, Magna–Graphics operated the cutoff roll to determine whether the latch mechanism would eject the blade to cut the paper. During *this* phase of the testing, no pins or pusher pads were installed. At no time during the tests were the pins, pushers, and blade installed and operated together.

To further its scheme to avoid patent infringement, Magna–Graphics negotiated special shipment and assembly details with Fort Howard. Under the advice of counsel, Fort Howard and Magna–Graphics agreed that the rewinder's cutoff and transfer mechanism would not be finally assembled until April 22, 1982, two days after the expiration of the '353 patent. With this agreement in hand, Magna–Graphics shipped the basic rewinder machine to Fort Howard on September 17, 1981, and separately shipped the cutoff roll and bedroll on October 23, 1981. The rewinder machine was not assembled or installed at the Fort Howard plant until April 26, 1982.

B

With this case we are once again confronted with a situation which tests the temporal limits of the American patent grant. See Roche Products, Inc. v. Bolar Pharmaceutical Co., 733 F.2d 858, 221 U.S.P.Q. 937 (Fed.Cir.1984). We must decide here the extent to which a competitor of a patentee can *manufacture* and test during the life of a patent a machine intended solely for post-patent use. Magna–Graphics asserts that no law prohibits it from soliciting orders for, *substantially* manufacturing, testing, or even delivering machinery which, if *completely* assembled during the patent term, would infringe. We notice, but Magna–Graphics adds that it is totally irrelevant, that Paper Converting has lost, during the term of its patent, a contract for the patented machine which it would have received but for the competitor's acts.

Clearly, any federal right which Paper Converting has to suppress Magna–Graphics' patent-term activities, or to receive damages for those activities, must be derived from its patent grant, and thus from the patent statutes. "Care should be taken not to extend by judicial construction the rights and privileges which it was the purpose of Congress to bestow."

Bauer v. O'Donnell, 229 U.S. 1, 10, 33 S.Ct. 616, 617, 57 L.Ed. 1041 (1913). The Supreme Court, in Brown v. Duchesne, 60 U.S. (19 How.) 183, 195, 15 L.Ed. 595 (1856), stated that:

> [T]he right of property which a patentee has in his invention, and his right to its exclusive use, is derived altogether from these statutory provisions; * * * an inventor has no right of property in his invention, upon which he can maintain a suit, unless he obtains a patent for it, according to the acts of Congress; and * * * his rights are to be regulated and measured by these laws, and cannot go beyond them.

The disjunctive language of the patent grant gives a patentee the "right to exclude others from making, using or selling" a patented invention during the 17 years of the patent's existence. 35 U.S.C. § 154. Congress has never deemed it necessary to define any of this triad of excludable activities, however, leaving instead the meaning of "make," "use," and "sell" for judicial interpretation. Nevertheless, by the terms of the patent grant, *no* activity other than the unauthorized making, using, or selling of the claimed invention can constitute direct infringement of a patent, *no matter* how great the adverse impact of that activity on the economic value of a patent. Judge Learned Hand stated, in Van Kannell Revolving Door Co. v. Revolving Door & Fixture Co., 293 F. 261, 262 (S.D.N.Y.1920), that irrespective of where the equities may lie:

> [A] patent confers an exclusive right upon the patentee, limited in those terms. He may prevent any one from making, selling, or using a structure embodying the invention, but the monopoly goes no further than that. It restrains every one from the conduct so described, and it does not restrain him from anything else. If, therefore, any one says to a possible customer of a patentee, "I will make the article myself; don't buy of the patentee," while he may be doing the patentee a wrong, and while equity will forbid his carrying out his promise, the promise itself is not part of the conduct which the patent forbids; it is not a "subtraction" from the monopoly. If it injures the plaintiff, though never performed, perhaps it is a wrong, like a slander upon his title, but certainly it is not an infringement of the patent.

Here, the dispositive issue is whether Magna–Graphics engaged in the making, use, or sale of something which the law recognizes as embodying an invention protected by a patent. Magna–Graphics relies on Deepsouth Packing Co. v. Laitram Corp., 406 U.S. 518, 92 S.Ct. 1700, 32 L.Ed.2d 273, 173 U.S.P.Q. 769 (1972). That case dealt with a "combination patent" covering machinery for shrimp deveining. The only active issue was whether certain export sales were properly prohibited in the district court's injunction and whether damages should include compensation for past infringement by these exports. The infringer had put in effect a practice of selling the machines disassembled for export, but with the subassemblies so far advanced, and with such instructions, that the foreign consignee could put them together on receipt in operable condition with an hour's work. The Supreme Court's five to four holding that these exports did not infringe was interwoven of three strands of thought: (1) that the patent laws must be construed strictly because they create a "monopoly" in the patentee; (2) that a "combination patent" is not infringed until its elements are brought together into an "operable assembly;" and (3) that an attempt to enforce the patent against a machine assembled abroad was an attempt to give it extraterritorial application and to invade improperly the sovereignty of the country where the final assembly and the intended use occurred.

Magna–Graphics' effort to apply *Deepsouth* as precedential runs into the obvious difficulty that the element of extraterritoriality is absent here, yet it obviously was of paramount importance to the *Deepsouth* Court. We must be cautious in extending five to four decisions by analogy. The analysis of *where* infringement occurs is applicable, Magna–Graphics says, to determining *when* an infringement occurs, whether before or after a patent expires. We have not found any case that has so held, and are not cited to any. It does not at all necessarily follow, for the *Deepsouth* analysis is made to avert a result, extraterritoriality, that would not occur whatever analysis was made in the instant case.

Although in *Deepsouth* the Court at times used broad language in reaching its decision, it is clear that *Deepsouth* was intended to be narrowly construed as applicable only to the issue of the extraterritorial effect of the American patent law. The Court so implied not only in *Deepsouth* ("[A]t stake here is the right of American companies to compete with an American patent holder *in foreign markets. Our patent system makes no claim to extraterritorial effect, * * *"* 406 U.S. at 531, 92 S.Ct. at 1708, 173 U.S.P.Q. at 774 (emphasis added)), but in a subsequent decision as well ("The question under consideration [in *Deepsouth*] was whether a patent is infringed when unpatented elements are assembled into the combination *outside the United States."* Dawson Chemical Co. v. Rohm & Haas Co., 448 U.S. 176, 216, 100 S.Ct. 2601, 2623, 65 L.Ed.2d 696, 206 U.S.P.Q. 385, 405 (1980) (emphasis added).). Moreover, in Decca Limited v. United States, 544 F.2d 1070 (Ct.Cl.1976), the Court of Claims considered the worldwide system of electronic navigation aids called "Omega," which employs as a means of fixing the locations of ships and planes "master" and "slave" transmission stations, and receivers making computer printouts on board the ships and planes to be guided. The government relied on *Deepsouth* to establish that the involved patent, if enforced against it, would be given an extraterritorial application. The Court of Claims held that the application was not extraterritorial and therefore *Deepsouth* was not implicated. The Court of Claims viewed *Deepsouth* as simply and wholly a decision against extraterritorial application of United States patent laws.

While there is thus a horror of giving extraterritorial effect to United States patent protection, there is no corresponding horror of a valid United States patent giving economic benefits not cut off entirely on patent expiration. Thus, we hold that the expansive language used in *Deepsouth* is not controlling in the present case. The facts in *Deepsouth* are *not* the facts here. Because no other precedent controls our decision here, however, we nevertheless look to *Deepsouth* and elsewhere for guidance on the issue of whether what Magna–Graphics did is an infringement of the '353 patent. . . .

Whether Magna–Graphics' rewinder infringed the '353 patent is a question of fact which the Federal Rules leave to the district court to decide. The question is not always so simply decided as the dissent makes it out to be. In particular, where it is necessary to decide whether a complex mechanical contraption infringes a claim in a patent, the district court is often faced with a difficult chore. To require that in all situations the district court must decide a complicated factual issue within the narrow confines of a simple bright-line test makes the district judge's function nothing more than that of a master assigned to set out simple facts.

The dissent's argument is based on the utopian belief that a copier "should be able to look to the patent claims and know whether his [or her] activity infringes or not." Although this may be a desirable goal for the patent laws, it is *not* the law as it exists. In particular, the doctrine of equivalents has been judicially created to ensure that a patentee can receive full protection for his or her patented ideas by making it difficult for a copier to maneuver around a patent's claims. In view of this doctrine, a copier rarely knows whether his product "infringes" a patent or not until a district court passes on the issue. We see no difference in putting a copier into the same position here.

It is undisputed that Magna–Graphics intended to finesse Paper Converting out of the sale of a machine on which Paper Converting held a valid patent during the life of that patent. Given the amount of testing performed here, coupled with the sale and delivery during the patent-term of a "completed" machine (completed by being ready for assembly and with no useful noninfringing purpose), we are not persuaded that the district court committed clear error in finding that the Magna–Graphics' machine infringed the '353 patent.

To reach a contrary result would emasculate the congressional intent to prevent the making of a patented item during the patent's full term of 17 years. If without fear of liability a competitor can assemble a patented item past the point of testing, the last year of the patent becomes worthless whenever it deals with a long lead-time article. Nothing would prohibit the unscrupulous competitor from aggressively marketing its own product and constructing it to all but the final screws and bolts, as Magna–Graphics did here. We rejected any reduction to the patent-term in *Roche;* we cannot allow the inconsistency in the patent law which would exist if we permitted it here. Magna–Graphics built and tested a patented machine, albeit in a less than preferred fashion. Because an "operable assembly" of components was tested, this case is distinguishable from Interdent Corp. v. United States, 531 F.2d 547, 552 (Ct.Cl.1976) (omission of a claimed element from the patented combination avoids infringement) and Decca Ltd. v. United States, 640 F.2d 1156, 1168, 209 U.S.P.Q. 52, 61 (Ct.Cl.1980) (infringement does not occur until the combination has been constructed and available for use). Where, as here, significant, unpatented assemblies of elements are tested during the patent term, enabling the infringer to deliver the patented combination in parts to the buyer, without testing the entire combination together as was the infringer's usual practice, testing the assemblies can be held to be in essence testing the patented combination and, hence, infringement.

That the machine was not operated in its optimum mode is inconsequential: imperfect practice of an invention does not avoid infringement. We affirm the district court's finding that "[d]uring the testing of the Fort Howard machine in July and August 1981, Magna–Graphics completed an operable assembly of the infringing rewinder."

V . . .

The judgment of the district court awarding damages and prejudgment interest for Paper Converting's lost profits on two automatic rewinder lines is affirmed. The trebling of damages on the Fort Howard machine is vacated, and remanded for a determination of willfulness. Each party is to bear its own costs of this appeal.

Affirmed in Part and Vacated in Part.

NIES, Circuit Judge, dissenting-in-part.

I dissent from the majority's holding that Magna–Graphics' activities in connection with the Fort Howard machine constitute direct infringement of any claim of Paper Converting's patent. The majority's conclusion necessitates giving a meaning to "patented invention" contrary to the definition set forth by the Supreme Court in Deepsouth Packing Co. v. Laitram Corp., 406 U.S. 518, 92 S.Ct. 1700, 32 L.Ed.2d 273, 173 U.S.P.Q. 769 (1972).

The analysis must begin with the statutory language of 35 U.S.C. § 271(a):

> Except as otherwise provided in this title, whoever without authority makes, uses or sells any *patented invention,* within the United States during the term of the patent therefor, infringes the patent. [Emphasis added.]

The majority holds that *incomplete assembly* of the patented invention is making, *testing of subassemblies* is using, and *a sale of an unassembled machine* is selling the *patented invention* within the meaning of the above section. The majority reasons that a contrary result would emasculate the congressional intent to prevent the making of a patented item during the patent's full term of 17 years. It could be said with equal validity that, given the lead time necessary to make the invention here, the majority effectively extends the patentee's right of exclusivity beyond the statutory 17 years.

I do not see in *Deepsouth* that the Supreme Court's only concern was the extraterritorial operation of our patent laws. The activities of Deepsouth under attack were all performed in the United States and were found not to result in direct or contributory infringement of the patent. That the activities of final assembly occurred abroad merely precluded a holding that

Deepsouth's activities constituted contributory infringement. Contributory infringement cannot arise without a direct infringement. The situation in *Deepsouth* is exactly comparable to the one at hand. That the activities of final assembly occurred after the patent expired precludes holding Magna–Graphics to be a contributory infringer, there being no direct infringement by another to which the charge can be appended.

Thus, we are back to the dispositive direct infringement issue in *Deepsouth,* which is the same as the issue here. What is the meaning of "patented invention" in 35 U.S.C. § 271(a)? The alleged infringer, in each case, made and sold something, but was it the "patented invention"? . . .

It is not surprising that Magna–Graphics' counsel read *Deepsouth* as permitting the course of conduct condemned here. The majority opinion is no less than a reversal of *Deepsouth.* Regardless of the reasonableness of the alternative interpretation of § 271(a) given by the majority, we are bound by the Supreme Court's decision. No greater prerogative to modify it accrues to us from a 5–4 vote than from a unanimous decision. Change must be left to Congress, or the Court itself. In *Deepsouth* the extension of patent protection which had been urged was viewed as a matter for a legislative directive:

> In sum: the case and statutory law resolves this case against the respondent. When so many courts have so often held what appears so evident—a combination patent can be infringed only by combination—we are not prepared to break the mold and begin anew. And were the matter not so resolved, we would still insist on a clear congressional indication of intent to extend the patent privilege before we could recognize the monopoly here claimed. Such an indication is lacking.

406 U.S. at 532, 92 S.Ct. at 1708, 173 U.S.P.Q. at 774.

Such indication is still lacking. We cannot assume that the present Court would find reason to depart from *Deepsouth* in the face of congressional inaction over the twelve years since the decision was handed down.

Indeed, the *Deepsouth* decision is not without redeeming virtue. This is one of the few areas of patent law where a bright line can be, and has been, drawn. That consideration in itself has merit. A competitor should be able to look to the patent claims and know whether his activity infringes or not. Here, the majority provides no guidance to industry or the district courts. One cannot tell from the opinion whether testing and sales activity must also accompany substantial assembly, as it appears to hold, or whether simply substantially making the device preparatory to selling after the patent expires would be sufficient. Given the disjunctive language of the statute, no basis appears for "summing up" partial making with the testing of partial assemblies and with sales made by the alleged infringer. Those activities do not, in some nebulous way, supply the missing physical elements of the "patented invention."

The determinative factor in *Deepsouth* was that the alleged infringer had never made, used or sold the "patented invention." Its activities fell short of direct infringement because the court rejected the view that direct infringement required anything less than "the operable assembly of the whole and not the manufacture of its parts." In this case as well, no operable assembly of the whole was ever made by Magna–Graphics. If the patented invention was not made, *a fortiori,* it could not have been used or sold. Thus, there is no direct infringement.

As a final matter, a decision of non-infringement here would not create an "inconsistency" with the decision in Roche Products, Inc. v. Bolar Pharmaceutical Co., 733 F.2d 858, 221 U.S.P.Q. 937 (Fed.Cir.1984). In *Roche,* the patented invention had been made, albeit not by the alleged infringer, Bolar. The only issue was whether Bolar's testing of the patented invention for FDA purposes was "use" within § 271(a). The *Roche* decision lends no support to the proposition that testing of components of a patented invention constitutes infringement.

I would, accordingly, reverse.

Wilbur–Ellis Co. v. Kuther

Supreme Court of the United States, 1964.
377 U.S. 422, 84 S.Ct. 1561, 12 L.Ed.2d 419, 141 U.S.P.Q. 703.

Mr. Justice DOUGLAS delivered the opinion of the Court.

Respondent is the owner of a combination patent covering a fish-canning machine. A number of machines covered by the patent were manufactured and sold under his authorization. Among them were the four machines in suit, petitioner Wilbur–Ellis Company being the second-hand purchaser. Respondent received out of the original purchase price a royalty of $1,500 per machine. As originally constructed each of these machines packed fish into "1–pound" cans: 3 inches in diameter and 4⅟₁₆ inches high. Three of the machines when acquired by Wilbur–Ellis were corroded, rusted, and inoperative; and all required cleaning and sandblasting to make them usable. Wilbur–Ellis retained petitioner Leuschner to put the machines in condition so they would operate and to resize six of the 35 elements that made up the patented combination. The resizing was for the purpose of enabling the machines to pack fish into "5–ounce" cans: 2⅛ inches in diameter and 3½ inches long. One of the six elements was so corroded that it could be rendered operable only by grinding it down to a size suitable for use with the smaller "5–ounce" can.

This suit for infringement followed; and both the District Court and the Court of Appeals, held for respondent. The case is here on certiorari.

We put to one side the case where the discovery or invention resided in or embraced either the size or locational characteristics of the replaced elements of a combination patent or the size of the commodity on which the machine operated. The claims of the patent before us do not reach that far. We also put to one side the case where replacement was made of a patented component of a combination patent. We deal here with a patent that covered only a combination of unpatented components.

The question in terms of patent law precedents is whether what was done to these machines, the original manufacture and sale of which had been licensed by the patentee, amounted to "repair," in which event there was no infringement, or "reconstruction," in which event there was. The idea of "reconstruction" in this context has the special connotation of those acts which would impinge on the patentee's right *"to exclude others from making,"* 35 U.S.C.A. § 154, the article. As stated in Wilson v. Simpson, 9 How. 109, 123, 13 L.Ed. 66, "... when the material of the combination ceases to exist, in whatever way that may occur, the right to renew it depends upon the right to make the invention. If the right to make does not exist, there is no right to rebuild the combination." On the other hand, "When the wearing or injury is partial, then repair is restoration, and not reconstruction." Ibid. Replacing worn-out cutting knives in a planing machine was held to be "repair," not "reconstruction," in Wilson v. Simpson, supra. Our latest case was Aro Mfg. Co. v. Convertible Top Replacement Co., 365 U.S. 336, 81 S.Ct. 599, 5 L.Ed.2d 592, which a majority of the Court construe as holding that it was not infringement to replace the worn-out fabric of a patented convertible automobile top, whose original manufacture and sale had been licensed by the patentee. See No. 75, Aro Mfg. Co. v. Convertible Top Replacement Co., 377 U.S. 476, 84 S.Ct. 1526, decided this day....

Whatever view may be taken of the holding in the first Aro case, the majority believe that it governs the present one. These four machines were not spent; they had years of usefulness remaining though they needed cleaning and repair. Had they been renovated and put to use on the "1-pound" cans, there could be no question but that they were "repaired," not "reconstructed," within the meaning of the cases. When six of the 35 elements of the combination patent were resized or relocated, no invasion of the patent resulted, for as we have said the size of cans serviced by the machine was no part of the invention; nor were characteristics of size, location, shape and construction of the six elements in question patented. Petitioners in adapting the old machines to a related use were doing more than repair in the customary sense; but what they did was kin to repair for it bore on the useful capacity of the old combination, on which the royalty had been paid. We could not call it "reconstruction" without saying that the patentee's right "to exclude others from making" the patented machine, 35 U.S.C.A. § 154, had been infringed. Yet adaptation for use of the machine on a "5-ounce" can is within the patent rights purchased, since size was not an invention.

The adaptation made in the six nonpatented elements improved the usefulness of these machines. That does not, however, make the adaptation "reconstruction" within the meaning of the cases. We are asked in substance to treat the case as if petitioners had a license for use of the machines on "1-pound" cans only. But the sales here were outright, without restriction. Adams v. Burke, 17 Wall. 453, 456, 21 L.Ed. 700, therefore controls:

... when the patentee, or the person having his rights, sells a machine or instrument whose sole value is in its use, he receives the consideration for its use and he parts with the right to restrict that use.

Reversed.

Mr. Justice HARLAN would affirm the judgment substantially for the reasons given in the majority opinion in the Court of Appeals.

NOTES

1. At the time the United States Supreme Court decided Deepsouth Packing v. Laitram, discussed in *Magna–Graphics,* it had set a singularly high standard of invention for "combination" patents. By contrast, the Court of Appeals for the Federal Circuit, which decided *Magna–Graphics,* believed that "[v]irtually *all* patents are combination patents" and had rejected a special standard of invention for these inventions. See Stratoflex v. Aeroquip, page 442, above. Is there a connection between the Supreme Court's patentability standard for combinations and its infringement standard for combination patents? Between the CAFC's undifferentiated standards for patentability and infringement?

2. *Repair or Reconstruction?* Aro Mfg. Co., Inc. v. Convertible Top Replacement Co., 365 U.S. 336, 81 S.Ct. 599, 5 L.Ed.2d 592, 128 U.S.P.Q. 354 (1961), mentioned in *Wilbur–Ellis,* held that replacement of the fabric in a convertible automobile top constituted repair, rather than reconstruction, of the entire top assembly so that the unauthorized manufacture and sale of replacement fabrics did not directly or contributorily infringe the combination patent covering the top assembly. Writing for the Court, Justice Whittaker stated the question for decision to be "whether the owner of a combination patent, comprised entirely of unpatented elements, has a patent monopoly on the manufacture, sale or use of the several unpatented components of the patented combination." By framing the issue in terms of the distinction between unpatented and patented components, rather than between repair and reconstruction, Justice Whittaker anticipated the decision in the case; replacement of any part of a combination, no matter how significant, can never be reconstruction. "The decisions of this Court require the conclusion that reconstruction of a patented entity, comprised of unpatented elements, is limited to such a true reconstruction of the entity as to 'in fact make a new article' ... after the entity, viewed as a whole, has become spent."

Justice Brennan, concurring, and Justice Harlan, dissenting, disagreed with Justice Whittaker's test. According to Justice Harlan, "none of the past cases in this Court or in the lower federal courts remotely suggests that 'reconstruction' can be found only in a situation where the patented combination has been rebuilt de novo from the ground up." Because the two lower courts "adverted to all the relevant standards," Justice Harlan thought it best to defer to their decisions.

Justice Brennan perceived "circumstances in which the replacement of a singly unpatented component of a patented combination short of a second creation of the patent entity may constitute 'reconstruction.'" Brennan interpreted the precedents to require that the determination in any case "be based upon the consideration of a number of factors.... Appropriately to be considered are the life of the part replaced in relation to the useful life of the whole combination, the importance of the replaced element to the inventive concept, the cost of the component relative to the cost of the combination, the common sense understanding and intention of the patent owner and the buyer of the combination as to its perishable components, whether the purchased component replaces a worn-out part or is bought for some other purpose, and other pertinent factors." Although the district and circuit courts below had considered such factors, Justice Brennan concurred in the reversal because, under his own analysis, the replacement of tops constituted repair.

3. *Experimental Use.* In two cases decided on circuit in 1813, Justice Joseph Story carved out an experimental use exception from patent infringement. Whittemore v. Cutter, 29 F.Cas. 1120 (C.C.D.Mass.1813) (No. 17,600); Sawin v. Guild, 21 F.Cas. 554 (C.C.D.Mass.1813) (No. 12,391). Accused infringers have asserted the experimental use exception in relatively few cases since, and courts have applied the exception sparingly.

One writer has concluded that "[i]n order to qualify for the experimental use exception to patent infringement, the infringing activity must fall within one of two classes of activities introduced by Justice Story in *Sawin:* (1) ascertain the verity and exactness of the specification, and (2) philosophical experiment. If the infringing activity falls within one of these categories, then it must be determined if the experimentor infringed the patent for profit.... The cases support the position that the experimental use exception applies to testing a patented invention for adaptation to the experimenter's business provided that the experimental use does not result in a 'use for profit.' As determined in the cases involving private parties, 'use for profit' means to make or attempt to make a monetary profit while infringing the patented invention." Ronald D. Hantman, Experimental Use as an Exception to Patent Infringement, 67 J. Pat. & Trademark Off. Soc'y 617, 644 (1985).

Roche Products, Inc. v. Bolar Pharmaceutical Co., 733 F.2d 858, 221 U.S.P.Q. 937 (Fed.Cir.), cert. denied, 469 U.S. 856, 105 S.Ct. 183, 83 L.Ed.2d 117 (1984), held that, because defendant's testing and investigation of a patented drug to obtain Food and Drug Administration approval was done "solely for business reasons," it did not qualify for the experimental use exception. Congress overturned *Bolar* by adding section 271(e)(1) to the Patent Act:

> It shall not be an act of infringement to make, use, or sell a patented invention (other than a new animal drug or veterinary biological product (as those terms are used in the Federal Food, Drug, and Cosmetic Act and the Act of March 4, 1913) which is primarily manufactured using recombinant DNA, recombinant RNA, hybridoma

technology, or other processes involving site specific genetic manipulation techniques) solely for uses reasonably related to the development and submission of information under a Federal law which regulates the manufacture, use, or sale of drugs or veterinary biological products.

The United States Supreme Court has read this provision to encompass medical devices as well as pharmaceuticals. Eli Lilly & Co. v. Medtronic, Inc., 496 U.S. 661, 110 S.Ct. 2683, 110 L.Ed.2d 605, 15 U.S.P.Q.2d 1121 (1990).

Would it be appropriate to engraft onto patent law a more wide-ranging defense, patterned after copyright's fair use defense, to "allow courts to weigh defined factors that assess both the social benefit and market harm to the patentee of allowing an infringement to continue"? See Maureen O'Rourke, Toward a Doctrine of Fair Use in Patent Law, 100 Colum. L. Rev. 1177, 1180 (2000).

4. *Liability in the United States for Acts Abroad.* Deepsouth Packing v. Laitram, discussed in *Magna–Graphics,* illustrates one strategy that competitors have used to circumvent United States patent law—shipping domestically manufactured components of a patented invention for final assembly abroad. Another strategy has been to make a product abroad through a process patented in the United States and then to import the finished—unpatented—product into the United States. Amendments to the United States Patent Act in 1984 and 1988, respectively, substantially curtailed both strategies.

Section 271(f), added by the Patent Law Amendments Act of 1984, Pub.L. No. 98–622, § 101(a) 98 Stat. 3383, plugged the *Deepsouth* loophole by providing in part that "[w]hoever without authority supplies or causes to be supplied in or from the United States all or a substantial portion of the components of a patented invention, where such components are uncombined in whole or in part, in such manner as to actively induce the combination of such components outside of the United States in a manner that would infringe the patent if such combination occurred within the United States, shall be liable as an infringer."

Section 271(g) of the Patent Act, added by the Omnibus Trade and Competitiveness Act of 1988, Pub.L. No. 100–418, § 9003, 102 Stat. 1563–1564, enlarges the scope of patent rights by providing in part: "[w]hoever without authority imports into the United States or sells or uses within the United States a product which is made by a process patented in the United States shall be liable as an infringer, if the importation, sale, or use of the product occurs during the term of such process patent." Section 295 buttresses the new right by creating a presumption that a product was made by a patented process where the court finds "(1) that a substantial likelihood exists that the product was made by the patented process, and (2) that the plaintiff has made a reasonable effort to determine the process actually used in the production of the product and was unable to so determine...."

Section 271(a) and related provisions of the Patent Act historically conferred three exclusive rights on patent owners: the rights to make, use, and sell the patented invention. As indicated in *Laitram*, these rights encompass only conduct occurring in the United States. To conform the Patent Act to the requirements of Article 28(1) of the TRIPs Agreement, Congress in 1994 added the rights to "offer to sell" and to "import into the United States." Pub. L. No. 103–465 §§ 532(a)(1), 533(a)(1)–(4), 108 Stat. 4809 (Dec. 8, 1994). What limits does *Laitram's* territoriality principle place on this new right? Will an offer telephoned into the United States from abroad be actionable? An advertisement from abroad for patented goods or services? See generally, Edwin D. Garlepp, An Analysis of the Patentee's New Exclusive Right to "Offer to Sell," 81 J. Pat. & Trademark Off. Soc'y 315 (1999).

5. *Inducement to Infringe.* Section 271(b) imposes liability on anyone who actively induces direct infringement. Among the acts that may be proscribed are: distribution of brochures advertising the sale of infringing equipment or instructing in the use of a patented process, purchase of articles made by an infringing process, indemnification of an infringer, and encouragement of a licensee to breach its patent license agreement.

Consider the advantages that section 271(b) may give patent owners in the following situations:

The direct infringer is judgment proof and the contributory infringer is solvent; the direct infringer's liability is limited by its corporate form and certain corporate officers can be treated as contributory infringers.

Acts of contributory, but not direct, infringement have occurred in the district most convenient for suit under the patent venue statute.

A contributory infringer, but not a direct infringer, exhibits the animus necessary to recovery of treble or otherwise increased damages.

Charles E. Miller, Some Views on the Law of Patent Infringement by Inducement, 53 J. Pat. Off. Soc'y 86, 139 (1971), is a comprehensive survey of the subject. See also, Erwin J. Basinski, Some Comments on Contributory and Induced Patent Infringement: Implications for Software Developers, 81 J. Pat. & Trademark Off. Soc'y 777 (1999).

6. *Contributory Infringement and Patent Misuse.* A patent owner will sometimes condition a customer's use of its patented product—a refrigerator for example—on the customer's purchase from the patent owner of an unpatented product—dry ice—used with the patented product. If the customer instead purchases its dry ice from a third party, this would breach the agreement with the patent owner, giving it an action for patent infringement against the customer; the third party supplier, who facilitated the infringement, would presumably be liable for contributory infringement. Nonetheless, courts have long recognized that for the patent owner to use the threat of a contributory infringement action to monopolize the market for an unpatented product may constitute patent misuse because it gives the patent owner greater market power than its patent warrants.

Section 271(c) of the Patent Act employs the concept of "staple" article to draw the line between contributory infringement and patent misuse:

> Whoever sells a component of a patented machine, manufacture, combination or composition, or a material or apparatus for use in practicing a patented process, constituting a material part of the invention, knowing the same to be especially made or especially adapted for use in an infringement of such patent, and not a staple article or commodity of commerce suitable for substantial noninfringing use, shall be liable as a contributory infringer.

Section 271(d) provides: "No patent owner otherwise entitled to relief for infringement or contributory infringement of a patent shall be denied relief or deemed guilty of misuse or illegal extension of the patent right by reason of his having done one or more of the following: (1) derived revenue from acts which if performed by another without his consent would constitute contributory infringement of the patent...."

What of nonstaple articles? In Dawson Chem. Co. v. Rohm & Haas Co., 448 U.S. 176, 100 S.Ct. 2601, 65 L.Ed.2d 696, 206 U.S.P.Q. 385 (1980), Rohm & Haas owned a patent on a process for applying an unpatented herbicide, propanil. Rohm & Haas impliedly licensed farmers who purchased the herbicide from it to practice the patented process but refused to give defendants, chemical manufacturers, a license to practice the patented process so that they could sell the herbicide to farmers. The defendants conceded that propanil was a nonstaple article and that their manufacture and sale of the herbicide, including instructions for its use, contributorily infringed the process patent. However, they argued that plaintiff's practices constituted patent misuse.

The United States Supreme Court held that the plaintiff's conduct did not constitute patent misuse:

> In our view, the provisions of § 271(d) effectively confer upon the patentee, as a lawful adjunct of his patent rights, a limited power to exclude others from competition in nonstaple goods. A patentee may sell a nonstaple article himself while enjoining others from marketing that same good without his authorization. By doing so, he is able to eliminate competitors and thereby to control the market for that product. Moreover, his power to demand royalties from others for the privilege of selling the nonstaple item itself implies that the patentee may control the market for the nonstaple good; otherwise, his "right" to sell licenses for the marketing of the nonstaple good would be meaningless, since no one would be willing to pay him for a superfluous authorization.
>
> Rohm & Haas' conduct is not dissimilar in either nature or effect from the conduct that is thus clearly embraced within § 271(d). It sells propanil; it authorizes others to use propanil; and it sues contributory infringers. These are all protected activities. Rohm & Haas does *not* license others to sell propanil, but nothing on the face of the statute requires it to do so. To be sure, the sum effect of Rohm & Haas' action

is to suppress competition in the market for an unpatented commodity. But as we have observed, in this its conduct is no different from that which the statute expressly protects.

448 U.S. at 201–02, 100 S.Ct. at 2615–16. The Court read section 271's legislative history to support the conclusion that "Congress granted to patent holders a statutory right to control nonstaple goods that are capable only of infringing use in a patented invention, and that are essential to that invention's advance over prior art." 448 U.S. at 213, 100 S.Ct. at 2622.

Justice White, joined by Justices Brennan, Marshall and Stevens, dissented. According to Justice White, the Supreme Court had for decades "denied relief from contributory infringement to patent holders who attempt to extend their patent monopolies to unpatented materials used in connection with patented inventions. The Court now refuses to apply this 'patent misuse' principle in the very area in which such attempts to restrain competition are most likely to be successful." 448 U.S. at 223, 100 S.Ct. at 2627. In White's view, the Court misread section 271(d). "The plain language of section 271(d) indicates that respondent's conduct is not immunized from application of the patent misuse doctrine.... Section 271(d) does not define conduct that constitutes patent misuse; rather it simply outlines certain conduct that is not patent misuse." 448 U.S. at 232–34, 100 S.Ct. at 2631–33.

Courts have divided on whether conduct that does not rise to the level of an antitrust violation can constitute patent misuse. Compare USM Corp. v. SPS Technologies, Inc., 694 F.2d 505, 512, 216 U.S.P.Q. 959 (7th Cir.1982) ("... apart from the conventional applications of the doctrine we have found no cases where standards different from those of antitrust law were actually applied to yield different results.") with Senza–Gel Corp. v. Seiffhart, 803 F.2d 661, 668, 231 U.S.P.Q. 363 (Fed.Cir.1986) ("... [an] act may constitute patent misuse without rising to the level of an antitrust violation.") In 1988 the Senate passed a bill that would have provided that it is not misuse for a patent owner to engage in "licensing practices, actions or inactions relating to his or her patent, unless such practices or actions or inactions, in view of the circumstances in which such practices or actions or inactions are employed, violate the antitrust laws." S.Rep. No. 100–492, 100th Cong., 2d Sess. 17–18 (Aug. 25, 1988). A subsequent compromise with the House resulted in Pub.L. No. 100–703, 102 Stat. 4674 (1988), adding subsections (4) and (5) to section 271(d).

See generally, A. Samuel Oddi, Contributory Infringement/Patent Misuse: Metaphysics and Metamorphoses, 44 U. Pitt. L. Rev. 73 (1982): Joel R. Bennett, Patent Misuse: Must an Alleged Infringer Prove an Antitrust Violation?, 17 AIPLA Q.J. 1 (1989).

7. In Brulotte v. Thys Co., 379 U.S. 29, 85 S.Ct. 176, 13 L.Ed.2d 99, 143 U.S.P.Q. 264 (1964), defendants, hop farmers, had bought from plaintiff, patent owner, hop picking machines that incorporated several of plaintiff's patented devices. Under the purchase agreement, the buyers were to pay royalties based upon the quantities of crops harvested over a seventeen-year period. The contract period exceeded the life of all of the patents.

Alleging patent misuse, defendants refused to pay royalties accruing both before and after expiration of the patents' statutory term.

The Supreme Court, in an opinion by Justice Douglas, ruled that defendants could not be held for royalties accruing after the expiration of the last of the patents. The problem with the seventeen-year license, Douglas wrote, was that it extended the patent monopoly beyond the point that the Constitution's "limited times" provision required to be free from monopoly restraint. Reasoning that, if contractual devices of this sort were tolerated, "the free market visualized for the post-expiration period would be subject to monopoly influences that have no proper place there," the Court struck down the contract rule applied by the state courts as "unlawful *per se*." 379 U.S. 29, 32–33, 85 S.Ct. 176, 179–80, 13 L.Ed.2d 99.

If they had anticipated the result in *Brulotte*, the parties to the agreement would presumably have negotiated a shorter license term—and a higher royalty rate—in order to achieve the same economic result that a seventeen-year license term would have achieved. Does this suggest that the Court's decision was misguided? Did the Court's 1979 decision in Aronson v. Quick Point, page 50 above, implicitly overrule *Brulotte?*

8. *Licensee Estoppel.* Can a patent licensee defend an action for nonpayment of royalties by asserting that the licensed patent is invalid? Courts have long held that licensees are privileged to stop paying royalties if a third party proves that the patent is invalid. But, where the licensee itself sought to challenge validity, the doctrine of licensee estoppel traditionally barred the defense. Automatic Radio Mfg. Co. v. Hazeltine Research, Inc., 339 U.S. 827, 70 S.Ct. 894, 94 L.Ed. 1312, 85 U.S.P.Q. 378 (1950). In Adkins v. Lear, Inc., 67 Cal.2d 882, 891, 64 Cal.Rptr. 545, 435 P.2d 321, 156 U.S.P.Q. 258 (1967), the California Supreme Court recognized that "one of the oldest doctrines in the field of patent law establishes that so long as a licensee is operating under a license agreement he is estopped to deny the validity of his licensor's patent in a suit for royalties under the agreement. The theory underlying this doctrine is that a licensee should not be permitted to enjoy the benefit afforded by the agreement while simultaneously urging that the patent which forms the basis of the agreement is void."

The Supreme Court granted *certiorari* in Lear v. Adkins to "reconsider the validity of the *Hazeltine* rule in the light of our recent decisions emphasizing the strong federal policy favoring free competition in ideas which do not merit patent protection, Sears, Roebuck v. Stiffel Co., 376 U.S. 225, 84 S.Ct. 784, 11 L.Ed.2d 661 (1964); Compco Corp. v. Day–Brite Lighting, Inc., 376 U.S. 234, 84 S.Ct. 779, 11 L.Ed.2d 669 (1964)." 395 U.S. 653, 89 S.Ct. 1902, 23 L.Ed.2d 610, 162 U.S.P.Q. 1 (1969). The first part of Justice Harlan's opinion for the Court traced *Hazeltine's* "clouded history" to conclude that "the uncertain status of licensee estoppel in the case law is a product of judicial efforts to accommodate the competing demands of the common law of contracts and the federal law of patents. On the one hand, the law of contracts forbids a purchaser to repudiate his promises simply because he later becomes dissatisfied with the bargain he has made. On the other hand, federal law requires that all ideas in general circulation be dedicated to the common good unless they are protected by a valid patent. When faced with this basic conflict in policy, both this Court and courts throughout the land have naturally sought to develop an intermediate position which somehow would remain responsive to the radically different concerns of the two different worlds of contract and patent. The result has been a failure. Rather than creative compromise, there has been a chaos of conflicting case law, proceeding on inconsistent premises." 395 U.S. at 668, 89 S.Ct. at 1910.

It was the practical marketplace effects of licensee estoppel that convinced the Court to overrule *Hazeltine*. "A patent, in the last analysis, simply represents a legal conclusion reached by the Patent Office. Moreover, the legal conclusion is predicated on factors as to which reasonable men can differ widely. Yet the Patent Office is often obliged to reach its decision in an ex parte proceeding, without the aid of the arguments which could be advanced by parties interested in proving patent invalidity. Consequently, it does not seem to us to be unfair to require a patentee to defend the Patent Office's judgment when his licensee places the question in issue, especially since the licensor's case is buttressed by the presumption of validity which attaches to his patent. Thus, although licensee estoppel may be consistent with the letter of contractual doctrine, we cannot say that it is compelled by the spirit of contract law, which seeks to balance the claims of promisor and promisee in accord with the requirements of good faith.

"Surely the equities of the licensor do not weigh very heavily when they are balanced against the important public interest in permitting full and free competition in the use of ideas which are in reality a part of the public domain. Licensees may often be the only individuals with enough economic incentive to challenge the patentability of an inventor's discovery. If they are muzzled, the public may continually be required to pay tribute to would-be monopolists without need or justification. We think it plain that the technical requirements of contract doctrine must give way before the demands of the public interest in the typical situation involving the negotiation of a license after a patent has issued." 395 U.S. at 670–671, 89 S.Ct. at 1911.

Can a patent assignor, later sued by its assignee for patent infringement, defend on the ground that the patent is invalid? The doctrine of assignor estoppel has not suffered the fate of licensee estoppel. In Diamond Scientific Co. v. Ambico, Inc., 848 F.2d 1220, 6 U.S.P.Q.2d 2028 (Fed.Cir.), cert. dismissed, 487 U.S. 1265, 109 S.Ct. 28, 101 L.Ed.2d 978 (1988), the Court of Appeals for the Federal Circuit held that the doctrine estopped an inventor from challenging the validity of a patent that he had earlier assigned to his former employer. "We are, of course, not unmindful of the general public policy disfavoring the repression of competition by the enforcement of worthless patents. Yet despite the public policy encouraging people to challenge potentially invalid patents, there are still circumstances in which the equities of the contractual relationships between the parties should deprive one party (as well as others in privity with it) of the right to bring that challenge." 848 F.2d at 1225. See William G. Schuurman, Eric B. Meyertons & Amber L. Hatfield, Assignor Estoppel: Infringement, Inequitable Conduct, and Privity in Light of Diamond Scientific and Shamrock Technologies, 72 J. Pat. & Trademark Off. Soc'y 723 (1990).

9. *Suppression of Patents.* There is no stronger belief in patent folklore than that patentees will sometimes use the patent grant to suppress their inventions for reasons that are mercenary at best, evil at worst. Justice William Douglas invoked this suspicion in his dissenting opinion in Special Equipment Co. v. Coe, 324 U.S. 370, 380, 65 S.Ct. 741, 746, 89 L.Ed. 1006, 64 U.S.P.Q. 525 (1945):

> It is difficult to see how that use [suppression] of patents can be reconciled with the purpose of the Constitution "to promote the Progress of Science and the useful Arts." Can the suppression of patents which arrests the progress of technology be said to promote that progress? It is likewise difficult to see how suppression of patents can be reconciled with the provision of the statute which authorizes a grant of the "exclusive right to make, use, and vend the invention or discovery." Rev.Stat. § 4884, 35 U.S.C.A. § 40. How may the words "to make, use, and vend" be read to mean "not to make, not to use, and not to vend"? Take the case of an invention or discovery which unlocks the doors of science and reveals the secrets of a dread disease. Is it possible that a patentee could be permitted to suppress that invention for seventeen years (the term of the letters patent) and withhold from humanity the benefits of the cure? But there is no difference in principle between that case and any case where a patent is suppressed because of some immediate advantage to the patentee.

324 U.S. at 383, 65 S.Ct. at 747.

What motive would a patent owner have to patent but not market its invention? How likely is it that the owner of a patent on an invention that "unlocks the doors of science and reveals the secrets of a dread disease" will "withhold from humanity the benefits of the cure" rather than cash in on the value of the discovery?

Many countries remedy patent suppression through compulsory licensing. These systems generally provide that if a patent owner fails to exploit an invention within a specified period, anyone may, upon payment of a predetermined reasonable royalty, take a license under the patent. One observer has noted that there are very few applications for these compulsory licenses. This "does not mean, however, that the system has no effect, but rather that the prospective licensee and patentee usually try to reach an agreement directly rather than through official channels, with the patentee of course realizing that compulsory licensing is available if agreement is not reached." S. Delvalle Goldsmith, Patent Protection for United States Inventions in the Principal European Countries—Existing Systems, 6 B.C.Comm. & Indus.L.Rev. 533, 535 (1965).

10. *Patent Term.* The first patent statute, Act of April 10, 1790, ch. 7, 1 Stat. 109, prescribed a fourteen-year term, following the term used in the

English Statute of Monopolies of 1623, 21 Jac. 1, ch. 3. The English term had been based on the seven-year apprenticeship period universally practiced by the mid-sixteenth century and on the theory that an invention should come into general use only after the artisan-inventor had the opportunity to instruct two consecutive sets of apprentices in the subject matter. The Act of July 4, 1836, ch. 357, 5 Stat. 117, supplemented the fourteen-year term with a seven-year renewal period. In 1861, a Senate attempt to repeal this renewal period, and a House effort to retain it, resulted in a compromise: the Conference Committee roughly split the difference and reported out a provision changing the term to seventeen years and dropping the renewal period.

Well over one hundred years later, as part of the Uruguay Round Agreements Act, Pub. L. No. 103–465, 108 Stat. 4809 (1994), Congress altered the patent term from seventeen years counted from the date of issue, to a "term beginning on the date on which the patent issues and ending twenty years from the date on which the application for the patent was filed in the United States." The amendment conforms the Patent Act to the requirement of Article 33 of the TRIPs Agreement that WTO member countries protect patents for no less than twenty years from the date the patent application was filed. The new term represents a floor, not a ceiling, to protection.

Section 154 of the Patent Act, as amended, allows extensions to compensate for specified delays in the Patent and Trademark Office. Section 156, added in 1984 and amended in 1988, extends the patent term for certain human and animal drugs and other federally regulated products to compensate for the time lost in federal regulatory review of the drugs. See generally two articles by Alan D. Lourie, Patent Term Restoration, 66 J. Pat. Off. Soc'y 526 (1984); A Review of Recent Patent Term Extension Data, 71 J. Pat. & Trademark Off. Soc'y 171 (1989).

How desirable is a single patent term, applied uniformly to all types of subject matter? Custom-tailored terms, varying in length from three to twenty years, were common under early colonial patent practice. Consider one economist's view of the present system: "[A] moment's consideration suggests that patents of uniform duration unduly reward some inventions and inadequately compensate others. Surely, all inventions cannot be exploited in exactly the same length of time nor can the monetary profitability, if any, of patent monopolies of uniform length be equated to the social contribution of the inventions covered." C. Michael White, Why a Seventeen Year Patent?, 38 J. Pat. Off. Soc'y 839, 842 (1956).

2. REMEDIES

Rite–Hite Corp. v. Kelley Company, Inc.

United States Court of Appeals, Federal Circuit, 1995.
56 F.3d 1538, 35 U.S.P.Q.2d 1065, cert. denied, 516 U.S. 867, 116 S.Ct. 184, 133 L.Ed.2d 122 (1995).

LOURIE, Circuit Judge.

Kelley Company appeals from a decision of the United States District Court for the Eastern District of Wisconsin, awarding damages for the infringement of U.S. Patent 4,373,847, owned by Rite–Hite Corporation. The district court determined, *inter alia*, that Rite–Hite was entitled to lost profits for lost sales of its devices that were in direct competition with the infringing devices, but which themselves were not covered by the patent in suit. The appeal has been taken *in banc* to determine whether such damages are legally compensable under 35 U.S.C. § 284. We affirm in part, vacate in part, and remand.

BACKGROUND

On March 22, 1983, Rite–Hite sued Kelley, alleging that Kelley's "Truk Stop" vehicle restraint infringed Rite–Hite's U.S. Patent 4,373,847 ("the '847 patent"). The '847 patent, issued February 15, 1983, is directed to a device for securing a vehicle to a loading dock to prevent the vehicle from separating from the dock during loading or unloading. Any such separation would create a gap between the vehicle and dock and create a danger for a forklift operator.

Rite–Hite distributed all its products through its wholly-owned and operated sales organizations and through independent sales organizations (ISOs). During the period of infringement, the Rite–Hite sales organizations accounted for approximately 30 percent of the retail dollar sales of Rite–Hite products, and the ISOs accounted for the remaining 70 percent. Rite–Hite sued for its lost profits at the wholesale level and for the lost retail profits of its own sales organizations. Shortly after this action was filed, several ISOs moved to intervene, contending that they were "exclusive licensees" of the '847 patent by virtue of "Sales Representative Agreements" and "Dok–Lok Supplement" agreements between themselves and Rite–Hite. The court determined that the ISOs were exclusive licensees and accordingly, on August 31, 1984, permitted them to intervene. The ISOs sued for their lost retail profits.

The district court bifurcated the liability and damage phases of the trial and, on March 5, 1986, held the '847 patent to be not invalid and to be infringed by the manufacture, use, and sale of Kelley's Truk Stop device. The court enjoined further infringement. The judgment of liability was affirmed by this court.

On remand, the damage issues were tried to the court. Rite–Hite sought damages calculated as lost profits for two types of vehicle restraints that it made and sold: the "Manual Dok–Lok" model 55 (MDL–55), which incorporated the invention covered by the '847 patent, and the "Automatic Dok–Lok" model 100 (ADL–100), which was not covered by the patent in suit. The ADL–100 was the first vehicle restraint Rite–Hite put on the market and it was covered by one or more patents other than the patent in suit. The Kelley Truk Stop restraint was designed to compete primarily with Rite–Hite's ADL–100. Both employed an electric motor and functioned automatically, and each sold for $1,000–$1,500 at the wholesale level, in contrast to the MDL–55, which sold for one-third to one-half the price of the motorized devices. Rite–Hite does not assert that Kelley's Truk Stop restraint infringed the patents covering the ADL–100.

Of the 3,825 infringing Truk Stop devices sold by Kelley, the district court found that, "but for" Kelley's infringement, Rite–Hite would have made 80 more sales of its MDL–55; 3,243 more sales of its ADL–100; and 1,692 more sales of dock levelers, a bridging platform sold with the restraints and used to bridge the edges of a vehicle and dock. The court awarded Rite–Hite as a manufacturer the wholesale profits that it lost on lost sales of the ADL–100 restraints, MDL–55 restraints, and restraint-leveler packages. It also awarded to Rite–Hite as a retailer and to the ISOs reasonable royalty damages on lost ADL–100, MDL–55, and restraint-leveler sales caused by Kelley's infringing sales. Finally, prejudgment interest, calculated without compounding, was awarded. Kelley's infringement was found to be not willful.

On appeal, Kelley contends that the district court erred as a matter of law in its determination of damages. Kelley does not contest the award of damages for lost sales of the MDL–55 restraints; however, Kelley argues that (1) the patent statute does not provide for damages based on Rite–Hite's lost profits on ADL–100 restraints because the ADL–100s are not covered by the patent in suit; (2) lost profits on unpatented dock levelers are not attributable to demand for the '847 invention and, therefore, are not recoverable losses; (3) the ISOs have no standing to sue for patent infringement damages; and (4) the court erred in calculating a reasonable royalty based as a percentage of ADL–100 and dock leveler profits. Rite–Hite and the ISOs challenge the district court's refusal to award lost retail profits and its award of prejudgment interest at a simple, rather than a compound, rate.

We affirm the damage award with respect to Rite–Hite's lost profits as a manufacturer on its ADL–100 restraint sales, affirm the court's computation of a reasonable royalty rate, vacate the damage award based on the dock levelers, and vacate the damage award with respect to the ISOs because they lack standing. We remand for dismissal of the ISOs' claims and for a redetermination of damages consistent with this opinion. The issues raised by Rite–Hite are unpersuasive.

DISCUSSION

Because the technology, the '847 patent, and the history of the parties and their litigation are fully described in the opinions of the district court and that of the earlier panel of our court that affirmed the liability judgment, we will discuss the facts only to the extent necessary to discuss the issues raised in this appeal.

In order to prevail on appeal on an issue of damages, an appellant must convince us that the determination was based on an erroneous conclusion of law, clearly erroneous factual findings, or a clear error of judgment amounting to an abuse of discretion.

A.

Kelley's Appeal

I.   Lost Profits on the ADL–100 Restraints

The district court's decision to award lost profits damages pursuant to 35 U.S.C. § 284 turned primarily upon the quality of Rite–Hite's proof of actual lost profits. The court found that, "but for" Kelley's infringing Truk Stop competition, Rite–Hite would have sold 3,243 additional ADL–100 restraints and 80 additional MDL–55 restraints. The court reasoned that awarding lost profits fulfilled the patent statute's goal of affording complete compensation for infringement and compensated Rite–Hite for the ADL–100 sales that Kelley "anticipated taking from Rite–Hite when it marketed the Truk Stop against the ADL–100." The court stated, "[t]he rule applied here therefore does not extend Rite–Hite's patent rights excessively, because Kelley could reasonably have foreseen that its infringement of the '847 patent would make it liable for lost ADL–100 sales in addition to lost MDL–55 sales." The court further reasoned that its decision would avoid what it referred to as the "whip-saw" problem, whereby an infringer could avoid paying lost profits damages altogether by developing a device using a first patented technology to compete with a device that uses a second patented technology and developing a device using the second patented technology to compete with a device that uses the first patented technology.

Kelley maintains that Rite–Hite's lost sales of the ADL–100 restraints do not constitute an injury that is legally compensable by means of lost profits. It has uniformly been the law, Kelley argues, that to recover damages in the form of lost profits a patentee must prove that, "but for" the infringement, it would have sold a product covered by the patent in suit to the customers who bought from the infringer. Under the circumstances of this case, in Kelley's view, the patent statute provides only for damages calculated as a reasonable royalty. Rite–Hite, on the other hand, argues that the only restriction on an award of actual lost profits damages for patent infringement is proof of causation-in-fact. A patentee, in its view, is entitled to all the profits it would have made on any of its products "but for" the infringement. Each party argues that a judgment in favor of the other would frustrate the purposes of the patent statute. Whether the lost profits at issue are legally compensable is a question of law, which we review *de novo*.

Our analysis of this question necessarily begins with the patent statute. Implementing the constitutional power under Article I, section 8, to secure to inventors the exclusive right to their discoveries, Congress has provided in 35 U.S.C. § 284 as follows:

> Upon finding for the claimant the court shall award the claimant damages adequate to compensate for the infringement, but in no event less than a reasonable royalty for the use made of the invention by the infringer, together with interest and costs as fixed by the court.

35 U.S.C. § 284 (1988). The statute thus mandates that a claimant receive damages "adequate" to compensate for infringement. Section 284 further instructs that a damage award shall be "in no event less than a reasonable royalty"; the purpose of this alternative is not to direct the form of compensation, but to set a floor below which damage awards may not fall. Thus, the language of the statute is expansive rather than limiting. It affirmatively states that damages must be adequate, while providing only a lower limit and no other limitation.

The Supreme Court spoke to the question of patent damages in *General Motors*, stating that, in enacting § 284, Congress sought to "ensure that the patent owner would in fact receive full compensation for 'any damages' [the patentee] suffered as a result of the infringement." *General Motors*, 461 U.S. at 654, 103 S.Ct. at 2062. Thus, while the statutory text states tersely that the patentee receive "adequate" damages, the Supreme Court has interpreted this to mean that "adequate" damages should approximate those damages that will *fully compensate* the patentee for infringement. Further, the Court has cautioned against imposing limitations on patent infringement damages, stating: "When Congress wished to limit an element of recovery in a patent infringement action, it said so explicitly." *General Motors*, 461 U.S. at 653, 103 S.Ct. at 2061 (refusing to impose limitation on court's authority to award interest).

In *Aro Mfg. Co. v. Convertible Top Replacement Co.*, 377 U.S. 476, 84 S.Ct. 1526, 12 L.Ed.2d 457, 141 U.S.P.Q. 681 (1964), the Court discussed the statutory standard for measuring patent infringement damages, explaining:

> The question to be asked in determining damages is "how much had the Patent Holder and Licensee suffered by the infringement. And that question [is] primarily: had the Infringer not infringed, what would the Patentee Holder–Licensee have made?"

377 U.S. at 507, 84 S.Ct. at 1542, 141 U.S.P.Q. at 694 (plurality opinion) (citations omitted). This surely states a "but for" test. In accordance with the Court's guidance, we have held that the general rule for determining actual damages to a patentee that is itself producing the patented item is to determine the sales and profits lost to the patentee because of the infringement. To recover lost profits damages, the patentee must show a reasonable probability that, "but for" the infringement, it would have made the sales that were made by the infringer.

Panduit Corp. v. Stahlin Bros. Fibre Works, Inc., 575 F.2d 1152, 197 U.S.P.Q. 726 (6th Cir.1978), articulated a four-factor test that has since been accepted as a useful, but non-exclusive, way for a patentee to prove entitlement to lost profits damages. The *Panduit* test requires that a patentee establish: (1) demand for the patented product; (2) absence of acceptable non-infringing substitutes; (3) manufacturing and marketing capability to exploit the demand; and (4) the amount of the profit it would have made. *Panduit*, 575 F.2d at 1156, 197 U.S.P.Q. at 730. A showing under Panduit permits a court to reasonably infer that the lost profits claimed were in fact caused by the infringing sales, thus establishing a patentee's *prima facie* case with respect to "but for" causation. A patentee need not negate every possibility that the purchaser might not have purchased a product other than its own, absent the infringement. The patentee need only show that there was a reasonable probability that the sales would have been made "but for" the infringement. When the patentee establishes the reasonableness of this inference, e.g., by satisfying the *Panduit* test, it has sustained the burden of proving entitlement to lost profits due to the infringing sales. *Id.* at 1141, 17 U.S.P.Q.2d at 1832. The burden then shifts to the infringer to show that the inference is unreasonable for some or all of the lost sales.

Applying *Panduit*, the district court found that Rite–Hite had established "but for" causation. In the court's view, this was sufficient to prove entitlement to lost profits damages on the ADL–100. Kelley does not challenge that Rite–Hite meets the *Panduit* test and therefore has proven "but for" causation; rather, Kelley argues that damages for the ADL–100, even if in fact caused by the infringement, are not legally compensable because the ADL–100 is not covered by the patent in suit.

Preliminarily, we wish to affirm that the "test" for compensability of damages under § 284 is not solely a "but for" test in the sense that an infringer must compensate a patentee for any and all damages that proceed from the act of patent infringement. Notwithstanding the broad language of § 284, judicial relief cannot redress every conceivable harm that can be traced to an alleged wrongdoing. For example, remote consequences, such as a heart attack of the inventor or loss in value of shares of common stock of a patentee corporation caused indirectly by infringement are not compensable. Thus, along with establishing that a particular injury suffered by a patentee is a "but for" consequence of infringement, there may also be a background question whether the asserted injury is of the type for which the patentee may be compensated.

Judicial limitations on damages, either for certain classes of plaintiffs or for certain types of injuries have been imposed in terms of "proximate cause" or "foreseeability." Such labels have been judicial tools used to limit legal responsibility for the consequences of one's conduct that are too remote to justify compensation. The general principles expressed in the common law tell us that the question of legal compensability is one "to be determined on the facts of each case upon mixed considerations of logic, common sense, justice, policy and precedent." *See 1 Street, Foundations of Legal Liability* 110 (1906) (quoted in W. Page Keeton *et al.*, *Prosser & Keeton on the Law of Torts* § 42, at 279 (5th ed. 1984)).

We believe that under § 284 of the patent statute, the balance between full compensation, which is the meaning that the Supreme Court has attributed to the statute, and the reasonable limits of liability encompassed by general principles of law can best be viewed in terms of reasonable, objective foreseeability. If a particular injury was or should have been reasonably foreseeable by an infringing competitor in the relevant market, broadly defined, that injury is generally compensable absent a persuasive reason to the contrary. Here, the court determined that Rite–Hite's lost sales of the ADL–100, a product that directly competed with the infringing product, were reasonably foreseeable. We agree with that conclusion. Being responsible for lost sales of a competitive product is surely foreseeable; such losses constitute the full compensation set forth by Congress, as interpreted by the Supreme Court, while staying well within the traditional meaning of proximate cause. Such lost sales should therefore clearly be compensable.

Recovery for lost sales of a device not covered by the patent in suit is not of course expressly provided for by the patent statute. Express language is not required, however. Statutes speak in general terms rather than specifically expressing every detail. Under the patent statute, damages should be awarded "where necessary to afford the plaintiff full compensation for the infringement." *General Motors*, 461 U.S. at 654, 103 S.Ct. at 2062. Thus, to refuse to award reasonably foreseeable damages necessary to make Rite–Hite whole would be inconsistent with the meaning of § 284.

Kelley asserts that to allow recovery for the ADL–100 would contravene the policy reason for which patents are granted: "[T]o promote the progress of . . . the useful arts." U.S. Const., art. I, § 8, cl. 8. Because an inventor is only entitled to exclusivity to the extent he or she has invented and disclosed a novel, nonobvious, and useful device, Kelley argues, a patent may never be used to restrict competition in the sale of products not covered by the patent in suit. In support, Kelley cites antitrust case law condemning the use of a patent as a means to obtain a "monopoly" on unpatented material. *See, e.g., Ethyl Gasoline Corp. v. United States*, 309 U.S. 436, 459, 60 S.Ct. 618, 626, 84 L.Ed. 852 (1940) ("The patent monopoly of one invention may no more be enlarged for the exploitation of a monopoly of another than for the exploitation of an unpatented article, or for the exploitation or promotion of a business not embraced within the patent."); *Leitch Mfg. Co. v. Barber Co.*, 302 U.S. 458, 463, 58 S.Ct. 288, 291, 82 L.Ed. 371 (1938) ("[E]very use of a patent as a means of obtaining a limited monopoly on unpatented material is prohibited . . . whatever the nature of the device by which the owner of the patent seeks to effect unauthorized extension of the monopoly.").

These cases are inapposite to the issue raised here. The present case does not involve expanding the limits of the patent grant in violation of the antitrust laws; it simply asks, once infringement of a valid patent is found, what compensable injuries result from that infringement, *i.e.*, how may the patentee be made whole. Rite–Hite is not attempting to exclude its competitors from making, using, or selling a product not within the scope of its patent. The Truk Stop restraint was found to infringe the '847 patent, and Rite–Hite is simply seeking adequate compensation for that infringement; this is not an antitrust issue. Allowing compensation for such damage will "promote the Progress of . . . the useful Arts" by providing a stimulus to the development of new products and industries.

Kelley further asserts that, as a policy matter, inventors should be encouraged by the law to practice their inventions. This is not a meaningful or persuasive argument, at least in this context. A patent is granted in exchange for a patentee's disclosure of an invention, not for the patentee's use of the invention. There is no requirement in this country that a patentee make, use, or sell its patented invention. If a patentee's failure to practice a patented invention frustrates an important public need for the invention, a court need not enjoin infringement of the patent. *See* 35 U.S.C. § 283 (1988) (courts may grant injunctions in accordance with the principles of equity). Accordingly, courts have in rare instances exercised their discretion to deny injunctive relief in order to protect the public interest. *See, e.g., Hybritech, Inc. v. Abbott Lab.*, 4 U.S.P.Q.2d 1001, 1987 WL 123997 (C.D.Cal.1987) (public interest required that injunction not stop supply of medical test kits that the patentee itself was not marketing), *aff'd*, 849 F.2d 1446, 7 U.S.P.Q.2d 1191 (Fed.Cir.1988); *Vitamin Technologists, Inc. v. Wisconsin Alumni Research Found.*, 64 U.S.P.Q. 285 (9th Cir.1945) (public interest warranted refusal of injunction on irradiation of oleomargarine); *City of Milwaukee v. Activated Sludge, Inc.*, 21 U.S.P.Q. 69 (7th Cir.1934) (injunction refused against city operation of sewage disposal plant because of public health danger). Whether a patentee sells its patented invention is not crucial in determining lost profits damages. Normally, if the patentee is not selling a product, by definition there can be no lost profits. However, in this case, Rite–Hite did sell its own patented products, the MDL–55 and the ADL–100 restraints.

Kelley next argues that to award lost profits damages on Rite–Hite's ADL–100s would be contrary to precedent. Citing *Panduit*, Kelley argues that case law regarding lost profits uniformly requires that "the intrinsic value of the patent in suit is the only proper basis for a lost profits award." Kelley argues that each prong of the *Panduit* test focuses on the patented invention; thus, Kelley asserts, Rite–Hite cannot obtain damages consisting of lost profits on a product that is not the patented invention.

Generally, the *Panduit* test has been applied when a patentee is seeking lost profits for a device covered by the patent in suit. However, *Panduit* is not the *sine qua non* for proving "but for" causation. If there are other ways to show that the infringement in fact caused the patentee's lost profits, there is no reason why another test should not be acceptable. Moreover, other fact situations may require different means of evaluation, and failure to meet the *Panduit* test does not *ipso facto* disqualify a loss from being compensable.

In any event, the only *Panduit* factor that arguably was not met in the present fact situation is the second one, absence of acceptable non-infringing substitutes. Establishment of this factor tends to prove that the patentee would not have lost the sales to a non-infringing third party rather than to the infringer. That, however, goes only to the question of proof. Here, the only substitute for the patented device was the ADL–100, another of the patentee's devices. Such a substitute was not an "acceptable, non-infringing substitute" within the meaning of *Panduit* because, being patented by Rite–Hite, it was not available to customers except from Rite–Hite. Rite–Hite therefore would not have lost the sales to a third party. The second *Panduit* factor thus has been met. If, on the other hand, the ADL–100 had not been patented and was found to be an acceptable substitute, that would have been a different story, and Rite–Hite would have had to prove that its customers would not have obtained the ADL–100 from a third party in order to prove the second factor of *Panduit*.

Kelley's conclusion that the lost sales must be of the patented invention thus is not supported. Kelley's concern that lost profits must relate to the "intrinsic value of the patent" is subsumed in the "but for" analysis; if the patent infringement had nothing to do with the lost sales, "but for" causation would not have been proven. However, "but for" causation is conceded here. The motive, or motivation, for the infringement is irrelevant if it is proved that the infringement in fact caused the loss. We see no basis for Kelley's conclusion that the lost sales must be of products covered by the infringed patent.

Kelley has thus not provided, nor do we find, any justification in the statute, precedent, policy, or logic to limit the compensability of lost sales of a patentee's device that directly competes with the infringing device if it is proven that those lost sales were caused in fact by the infringement. Such lost sales are reasonably foreseeable and the award of damages is necessary to provide adequate compensation for infringement under 35 U.S.C. § 284. Thus, Rite–Hite's ADL–100 lost sales are legally compensable and we affirm the award of lost profits on the 3,283 sales lost to Rite–Hite's wholesale business in ADL–100 restraints.

II.   Damages on the Dock Levelers

Based on the "entire market value rule," the district court awarded lost profits on 1,692 dock levelers that it found Rite–Hite would have sold with the ADL–100 and MDL–55 restraints. Kelley argues that this award must be set aside because Rite–Hite failed to establish that the dock levelers were eligible to be included in the damage computation under the entire market value rule. We agree.

When a patentee seeks damages on unpatented components sold with a patented apparatus, courts have applied a formulation known as the "entire market value rule" to determine whether such components should be included in the damage computation, whether for reasonable royalty purposes, or for lost profits purposes. Early cases invoking the entire market value rule required that for a patentee owning an "improvement patent" to recover damages calculated on sales of a larger machine incorporating that improvement, the patentee was required to show that the entire value of the whole machine, as a marketable article, was "properly and legally attributable" to the patented feature. Subsequently, our predecessor court held that damages for component parts used with a patented apparatus were recoverable under the entire market value rule if the patented apparatus "was of such paramount importance that it substantially created the value of the component parts." *Marconi Wireless Telegraph Co. v. United States*, 53 U.S.P.Q. 246, 250 (Ct.Cl.1942), aff'd in part and vacated in part, 320 U.S. 1, 63 S.Ct. 1393, 87 L.Ed. 1731 (1943). We have held that the entire market value rule permits recovery of damages based on the value of a patentee's entire apparatus containing several features when the patent-related feature is the "basis for customer demand." *State Indus.*,

883 F.2d at 1580, 12 U.S.P.Q.2d at 1031; *TWM Mfg. Co. v. Dura Corp.*, 789 F.2d 895, 900–01, 229 U.S.P.Q. 525, 528 (Fed.Cir.), *cert. denied*, 479 U.S. 852, 107 S.Ct. 183, 93 L.Ed.2d 117 (1986).

The entire market value rule has typically been applied to include in the compensation base unpatented components of a device when the unpatented and patented components are physically part of the same machine. The rule has been extended to allow inclusion of physically separate unpatented components normally sold with the patented components. However, in such cases, the unpatented and patented components together were considered to be components of a single assembly or parts of a complete machine, or they together constituted a functional unit.

In *Paper Converting*, [745 F.2d at 23, 223 U.S.P.Q. at 599–600], this court articulated the entire market value rule in terms of the objectively reasonable probability that a patentee would have made the relevant sales. Furthermore, we may have appeared to expand the rule when we emphasized the financial and marketing dependence of the unpatented component on the patented component. In *Paper Converting*, however, the rule was applied to allow recovery of profits on the unpatented components only because all the components together were considered to be parts of a single assembly. The references to "financial and marketing dependence" and "reasonable probability" were made in the context of the facts of the case and did not separate the rule from its traditional moorings.

Specifically, recovery was sought for the lost profits on sales of an entire machine for the high speed manufacture of paper rolls comprising several physically separate components, only one of which incorporated the invention. The machine was comprised of the patented "rewinder" component and several auxiliary components, including an "unwind stand" that supported a large roll of supply paper to the rewinder, a "core loader" that supplied paperboard cores to the rewinder, an "embosser" that embossed the paper and provided a special textured surface, and a "tail sealer" that sealed the paper's trailing end to the finished roll. Although we noted that the auxiliary components had "separate usage" in that they each separately performed a part of an entire rewinding operation, the components together constituted one functional unit, including the patented component, to produce rolls of paper. The auxiliary components derived their market value from the patented rewinder because they had no useful purpose independent of the patented rewinder.

Similarly, our subsequent cases have applied the entire market value rule only in situations in which the patented and unpatented components were analogous to a single functioning unit.

Thus, the facts of past cases clearly imply a limitation on damages, when recovery is sought on sales of unpatented components sold with patented components, to the effect that the unpatented components must function together with the patented component in some manner so as to produce a desired end product or result. All the components together must be analogous to components of a single assembly or be parts of a complete machine, or they must constitute a functional unit. Our precedent has not extended liability to include items that have essentially no functional relationship to the patented invention and that may have been sold with an infringing device only as a matter of convenience or business advantage. We are not persuaded that we should extend that liability. Damages on such items would constitute more than what is "adequate to compensate for the infringement."

The facts of this case do not meet this requirement. The dock levelers operated to bridge the gap between a loading dock and a truck. The patented vehicle restraint operated to secure the rear of the truck to the loading dock. Although the two devices may have been used together, they did not function together to achieve one result and each could effectively have been used independently of each other. The parties had established positions in marketing dock levelers long prior to developing the vehicle restraints. Rite–Hite and Kelley were pioneers in that industry and for many years were primary competitors. Although following Rite–Hite's introduction of its restraints onto the market, customers frequently solicited package bids for the simultaneous installation of restraints and dock levelers, they did so because such bids facilitated contracting and construction scheduling, and because both Rite–Hite and Kelley encouraged this linkage by offering combination discounts. The dock levelers were thus sold by Kelley with the restraints only for marketing reasons, not because they essentially functioned together. We distinguish our conclusion to permit damages based on lost sales of the unpatented (not covered by the patent in suit) ADL–100 devices, but not on lost sales of the unpatented dock levelers, by emphasizing that the Kelley Truk Stops were devices competitive with the ADL–100s, whereas the dock levelers were merely items sold together with the restraints for convenience and business advantage. It is a clear purpose of the patent law to redress competitive damages resulting from infringement of the patent, but there is no basis for extending that recovery to include damages for items that are neither competitive with nor function with the patented invention. Promotion of the useful arts, see U.S. Const., art. I, § 8, cl. 8, requires one, but not the other. These facts do not establish the functional relationship necessary to justify recovery under the entire market value rule. Therefore, the district court erred as a matter of law in including them within the compensation base. Accordingly, we vacate the court's award of damages based on the dock leveler sales....

IV. Computation of Reasonable Royalty

The district court found that Rite–Hite as a manufacturer was entitled to an award of a reasonable royalty on 502 infringing restraint or restraint-leveler sales for which it had not proved that it contacted the Kelley customer prior to the infringing Kelley sale. The court awarded a royalty equal to approximately fifty percent of Rite–Hite's estimated lost profits per unit sold to retailers. Further, the court found that Rite–Hite as a retailer was entitled to a reasonable royalty amounting to approximately one-third its estimated lost distribution income per infringing sale. Kelley challenges the amount of the royalty as grossly excessive and legally in error.

A patentee is entitled to no less than a reasonable royalty on an infringer's sales for which the patentee has not established entitlement to lost profits. The royalty may be based upon an established royalty, if there is one, or if not, upon the supposed result of hypothetical negotiations between the plaintiff and defendant.[13] The hypothetical negotiation requires the court to envision the terms of a licensing agreement reached as the result of a supposed meeting between the patentee and the infringer at the time infringement began. "One challenging only the court's finding as to amount of damages awarded under the 'reasonable royalty' provision of § 284, therefore, must show that the award is, in view of all the evidence, either so outrageously high or so outrageously low as to be insupportable as an estimation of a reasonably royalty." *Lindemann Maschinenfabrik GmbH v. American Hoist & Derrick Co.*, 895 F.2d 1403, 1406, 13 U.S.P.Q.2d 1871, 1874 (Fed.Cir.1990).

The district court here conducted the hypothetical negotiation analysis. It determined that Rite–Hite would have been willing to grant a competitor a license to use the '847 invention only if it received a royalty of no less than one-half of the per unit profits that it was foregoing. In so determining, the court considered that the '847 patent was a "pioneer" patent with manifest commercial success; that Rite–Hite had consistently followed a policy of exploiting its own patents, rather than licensing to competitors; and that Rite–Hite would have had to forego a large profit by granting a license to Kelley because Kelley was a strong competitor and Rite–Hite anticipated being able to sell a large number of restraints and related products. It was thus not unreasonable for the district court to find that an unwilling patentee would only license for one-half its expected lost profits and that such an amount was a reasonable royalty. The fact that the award was not based on the infringer's profits did not make it an unreasonable award. Furthermore, the fact that the award was based on and was a significant portion of the patentee's profits also does not make the award unreasonable. The language of the statute requires "damages adequate to compensate," which does not include a royalty that a patentee who does not wish to license its patent would find unreasonable. Moreover, what an infringer would prefer to pay is not the test for damages.

We conclude that the district court made no legal error and was not clearly erroneous in determining the reasonable royalty rate. Accordingly, we affirm the trial court's calculation of a reasonable royalty rate. Howev-

---

13. The hypothetical negotiation is often referred to as a "willing licensor/willing licensee" negotiation. However, this is an inaccurate, and even absurd, characterization when, as here, the patentee does not wish to grant a license. *See Hanson v. Alpine Valley Ski Area, Inc.*, 718 F.2d 1075, 1081, 219 U.S.P.Q. 679, 684 (Fed.Cir.1983) (The willing licensee/licensor concept is "employed by the court as a means of arriving at reasonable compensation and its validity does not depend on the actual willingness of the parties to the lawsuit to engage in such negotiations[; t]here is, of course, no actual willingness on either side."); *TWM Mfg. Co. v. Dura Corp.*, 789 F.2d 895, 900, 229 U.S.P.Q. 525, 528 (Fed.Cir.) ("The willing licensee/licensor approach must be flexibly applied as a 'device in the aid of justice.'") (citation omitted), cert. denied, 479 U.S. 852, 107 S.Ct. 183, 93 L.Ed.2d 117 (1986).

er, because we vacate the court's decision to include dock levelers in the royalty base, we remand for a redetermination of damages based only on the sale of the infringing restraints and not on the restraint-leveler packages.

B.

Rite–Hite's Cross Appeal

Rite–Hite and the ISOs sought damages based on lost profits at the retail level for ADL–100 and MDL–55 restraints and dock levelers. The district court denied the award on the basis that both Rite–Hite and the ISOs failed to meet their evidentiary burden of proving lost profits. Rite–Hite has not persuaded us that the court's decision was erroneous. As for the ISOs, this issue is mooted by the above rulings.

Rite–Hite also argues that the district court erred in awarding interest at a simple rather than a compound rate because, as a matter of law, prejudgment interest must be compounded. We disagree. It has been recognized that "an award of compound rather than simple interest assures that the patent owner is fully compensated." *Fromson v. Western Litho Plate & Supply Co.*, 13 U.S.P.Q.2d 1856, 1862, 1989 WL 149268 (E.D.Mo. 1989), aff'd mem., 909 F.2d 1495 (Fed.Cir.1990). However, the determination whether to award simple or compound interest is a matter largely within the discretion of the district court. Rite–Hite has not persuaded us that the court abused its discretion in awarding interest at a simple rate.

CONCLUSION

On Kelley's appeal, we affirm the district court's decision that Rite–Hite is entitled to an award of lost profit damages based on its lost business in ADL–100 restraints. We affirm the court's determination of the reasonable royalty rate. We vacate the awards to the ISOs and vacate the damage award based on the dock levelers. We remand for the court to dismiss the ISOs as plaintiffs and recalculate damages to Rite–Hite. On Rite–Hite's cross-appeal, we affirm.

COSTS

Each party will bear its own costs of this appeal. AFFIRMED–IN–PART, VACATED–IN–PART, and REMANDED.

NOTES

1. Judge Nies, joined by Judges Archer, Smith and Mayer, dissented in part from the *Rite–Hite* majority opinion on the ground that its approach to damages was too generous; Judge Newman, joined by Judge Rader, concurred in part and dissented in part on the ground that the majority's approach was too stinting.

Judge Nies objected to the majority's use of damages "as a tool to expand the property rights granted by a patent": "To constitute legal injury for which lost profits may be awarded, the infringer must interfere with the patentee's property right to an exclusive market in goods embodying the invention of the patent in suit. The patentee's property rights do not extend to its market in other goods unprotected by the litigated patent. Rite–Hite was compensated for the lost profits for 80 sales associated with the MDL–55, the only product it sells embodying the '847 invention. That is the totality of any possible entitlement to lost profits." 56 F.3d at 1556.

Judge Nies also disagreed "that the calculations of a reasonable royalty may be based on a percentage of Rite–Hite's lost profits. Under 35 U.S.C. § 284, a reasonable royalty must be attributed to Kelley's 'use of the invention.' A royalty must be based on the value of the patented hook, not on other features in the infringing device, *e.g.*, the motors, which form no part of the patented invention used by Kelley." *Id.*

Judge Newman concurred in the majority's formulation of damages for lost sales of the ADL–100, but rejected its approach to "lost sales of collateral items, the so-called 'convoyed' sales. Such remedy is now eliminated entirely unless the convoyed item is 'functionally' inseparable from the patented item. The court thus propounds a legally ambivalent and economically unsound policy, authorizing damages for the lost sales of the ADL–100 but not those dock levelers that were required to be bid and sold as a package with the MDL–55 and the ADL–100." 56 F.3d at 1578.

2. *Permanent Injunctions.* Courts will grant a prevailing patent owner an injunction for the remainder of the patent's life almost as a matter of course; they will, however, withhold injunctive relief on such traditional equitable grounds as laches, estoppel or disproportionate harm to the public interest. Courts will—though less frequently—deny injunctive relief where the disproportionate harm is only to the infringer; the infringer may, for example, have innocently and substantially invested in the equipment necessary to manufacture the patented subject matter. See Electric Smelting & Aluminum Co. v. Carborundum Co., 189 Fed. 710 (C.C.W.D.Pa.1900), rev'd on other grounds, 203 Fed. 976 (3d Cir.1913), cert. denied, 231 U.S. 754, 34 S.Ct. 323, 58 L.Ed. 467 (1913).

3. *Preliminary Injunctions.* For many years, courts in patent cases dispensed preliminary relief sparingly. Apart from requiring the patent owner to show that it would be irreparably harmed unless it received a preliminary injunction, courts required the patent owner to establish title, validity and infringement to an extent variously described as "beyond question" or "without reasonable doubt." One reason for these rigorous standards was judicial skepticism about the validity of patents issued *ex parte* in the Patent and Trademark Office. Another reason was the fear that "[t]he granting of temporary injunctive relief on the basis of incomplete facts may often settle the ultimate issues immediately and cause irreparable injury to the enjoined party. If a temporary injunction is unwarranted, a few years will probably elapse before final determination that the injunction was improvidently granted. By this time, the alleged infringer's loss of competitive advantage over the patentee may be incapable of repair by money damages." Note, Injunctive Relief in Patent Infringement Suits, 112 U.Pa. L.Rev. 1025 (1964).

The Court of Appeals for the Federal Circuit has loosened the require-ments for preliminary relief in patent cases. "The burden upon the movant should be no different in a patent case than for other kinds of intellectual property, where, generally, only a 'clear showing' is required. Requiring a 'final adjudication,' 'full trial,' or proof 'beyond question' would support the issuance of a permanent injunction and nothing would remain to establish the liability of the accused infringer. That is not the situation before us. We are dealing with a provisional remedy which provides equitable *preliminary* relief. Thus, when a patentee 'clearly shows' that his patent is valid and infringed, a court may, after a balance of all of the competing equities, preliminarily enjoin another from violating the rights secured by the patent." Atlas Powder Co. v. Ireco Chemicals, 773 F.2d 1230, 1233, 227 U.S.P.Q. 289 (Fed.Cir.1985).

See generally, John Mills, The Developing Standard for Irreparable Harm in Preliminary Injunctions to Prevent Infringement, 81 J. Patent & Trademark Off. Soc'y. 51 (1999).

4. *Damages.* Before 1946, when Congress amended the Patent Act's damages provision to substantially its present form, a successful patent claimant could choose between the amount of damages she suffered and the amount of profits earned by the infringer. To discover which was greater, the patent owner could request judicial determination of both amounts. The high cost of determining an infringer's profits eventually led Congress to drop infringer's profits as an alternative measure of recovery. However, evidence of an infringer's profits continues to be relevant in computing the patent owner's damages—either as a factor in determining a reasonable royalty or as a surrogate for the patent owner's lost profits. See Kori Corp. v. Wilco Marsh Buggies & Draglines, Inc., 761 F.2d 649, 225 U.S.P.Q. 985 (Fed.Cir.), cert. denied, 474 U.S. 902, 106 S.Ct. 230, 88 L.Ed.2d 229 (1985).

Courts originally awarded a reasonable royalty out of reluctance to award only nominal damages in cases where the successful claimant could prove neither actual damages nor infringer's profits. Congress introduced the reasonable royalty measure into the statute in 1922. Under the present act, a reasonable royalty represents the floor of recovery. Courts will sometimes assess a reasonable royalty for those aspects of an infringement that are not compensated by other damage measures. For example, in Broadview Chem. Corp. v. Loctite Corp., 311 F.Supp. 447, 164 U.S.P.Q. 419 (D.Conn.1970), the court applied the lost profit measure to sales in the United States—where defendant was the plaintiff's sole competitor—but applied the reasonable royalty measure to the more competitive foreign market.

See generally, John W. Schlicher, Measuring Patent Damages by the Market Value of Inventions—The *Grain Processing, Rite–Hite*, and *Aro* Rules, 82 J. Pat. & Trademark Off. Soc'y 503 (2000); Roger D. Blair & Thomas F. Cotter, An Economic Analysis of Damages Rules in Intellectual Property Law, 39 Wm. & Mary L. Rev. 1585 (1998). For a helpful statistical comparison of different forms of monetary awards reported between 1982–

1992, see Ronald B. Coolley, Overview and Statistical Study of the Law on Patent Damages, 75 J. Pat. & Trademark Off. Soc'y 515 (1993).

5. *Increased Damages; Attorney Fees.* Section 284 of the Patent Act authorizes courts to treble patent infringement damages. Section 285 authorizes courts, "in exceptional cases," to award reasonable attorney fees to the prevailing party.

Willful infringement is the principal ground for giving prevailing patent owners increased damages and attorney fees. In determining whether an infringer's conduct was willful, the Court of Appeals for the Federal Circuit has given particular weight to whether the infringer had obtained a lawyer's opinion before undertaking its manufacture, use or sale of the patented invention. See, e.g., Underwater Devices, Inc. v. Morrison–Knudsen Co., 717 F.2d 1380, 1389, 219 U.S.P.Q. 569 (Fed.Cir.1983) ("Where . . . a potential infringer has actual notice of another's patent rights, he has an affirmative duty to exercise due care to determine whether or not he is infringing. Such an affirmative duty includes, *inter alia,* the duty to seek and obtain competent legal advice from counsel *before* the initiation of any possible infringing activity.")

Congress intended attorney fee awards to deter not only willful infringers but vexatious patent owners as well. A prevailing defendant may, for example, recover attorney fees where the patent owner litigated in bad faith or engaged in fraud or other inequitable conduct in the Patent and Trademark Office. See Rohm & Haas Co. v. Crystal Chem. Co., 736 F.2d 688, 222 U.S.P.Q. 97 (Fed.Cir.), cert. denied, 469 U.S. 851, 105 S.Ct. 172, 83 L.Ed.2d 107 (1984). Proof that a defeated opponent acted unconscionably is not always a sufficient basis for recovery, and not every successful party is a "prevailing" party. In one case, a court set aside an award of $500,000 attorney's fees to claimant, Union Carbide, on the ground that it was not the prevailing party. "After years of litigation it prevailed only on four claims, under the doctrine of equivalents, out of a total of twenty-nine claims. It lost all process claims. It can hardly be said that Union Carbide was the prevailing party and Lincoln the losing party." Union Carbide Corp. v. Graver Tank & Mfg. Co., 345 F.2d 409, 145 U.S.P.Q. 240, 242 (7th Cir.1965).

6. *Marking.* Section 287 of the Patent Act conditions recovery of damages on notice to the infringer of the subsisting patent. Notice is typically given by the mark, "Patent" or "Pat.," along with the patent number, placed on articles manufactured or sold under the patent. In the absence of marking, the patent owner can give the requisite notice directly—orally or in writing—and, at the latest, by filing an infringement action.

Section 292 of the Patent Act proscribes counterfeit marking and false marking. The purpose of the counterfeit marking provision is to protect the public against deception about the source of goods. The purpose of the false marking provisions is to keep the marketplace free of unwarranted monopoly effects. Section 292's predecessors provided exclusively for a *qui tam* action. The section now makes false and counterfeit marking an ordinary federal criminal offense and retains the *qui tam* action as a supplementary sanction. Informer-plaintiffs are rarely disinterested. In Brose v. Sears, Roebuck & Co., 455 F.2d 763, 172 U.S.P.Q. 454 (5th Cir.1972), an appeal from dismissal of a *qui tam* action, the court observed that, "[a]s is true in nearly all of the relatively few *qui tam* informer actions brought in the past one and a quarter century this one is used as a weapon in the arsenal of patent litigation...."

7. *The Costs of Time: Laches and Equitable Estoppel.* A patent owner facing several infringers may want to sue them all promptly, but limited resources for litigation may require it to postpone suit against some of the smaller infringers. An alternative strategy is to stage the lawsuits, suing the less resourceful defendants first in the hope of creating favorable precedents for later suits against the more resourceful defendants. For their part, possible infringers may desire prompt resolution of their potential liability; until the question is definitively resolved, they are at risk of substantial monetary recovery and of injunctive relief that could wipe out their capital investment.

The doctrines of laches and equitable estoppel aim to mediate between these competing realities. In an important *in banc* decision, A.C. Aukerman Co. v. R.L. Chaides Construction Co., 960 F.2d 1020, 22 U.S.P.Q.2d 1321 (Fed.Cir.1992), the Court of Appeals for the Federal Circuit laid down the applicable rules.

With respect to laches, the court held:

1. Laches is cognizable under 35 U.S.C. § 282 (1988) as an equitable defense to a claim for patent infringement.

2. Where the defense of laches is established, the patentee's claim for damages prior to suit may be barred.

3. Two elements underlie the defense of laches: (a) the patentee's delay in bringing suit was unreasonable and inexcusable, and (b) the alleged infringer suffered material prejudice attributable to the delay. The district court should consider these factors and all of the evidence and other circumstances to determine whether equity should intercede to bar pre-filing damages.

4. A presumption of laches arises where a patentee delays bringing suit for more than six years after the date the patentee knew or should have known of the alleged infringer's activity.

5. A presumption has the effect of shifting the burden of going forward with evidence, not the burden of persuasion.

With respect to equitable estoppel, the court held:

1. Equitable estoppel is cognizable under 35 U.S.C. § 282 as an equitable defense to a claim for patent infringement.

2. Where an alleged infringer establishes the defense of equitable estoppel, the patentee's claim may be entirely barred.

3. Three elements must be established to bar a patentee's suit by reason of equitable estoppel:

a. The patentee, through misleading conduct, leads the alleged infringer to reasonably infer that the patentee does not intend to enforce its patent against the alleged infringer. Conduct may include specific statements, action, inaction, or silence where there was an obligation to speak.

b. The alleged infringer relies on that conduct.

c. Due to its reliance, the alleged infringer will be materially prejudiced if the patentee is allowed to proceed with its claim.

4. No presumption is applicable to the defense of equitable estoppel.

960 F.2d at 1028.

D. INFRINGEMENT

Floyd H. Crews, Patent Claims and Infringement

Dynamics of the Patent System 128, 133 (William B. Ball ed, 1960).*

In the subject of patent claims and infringement we all know that what you do is take the copy of the patent and the copy of the accused device and you read the claims and if the claims read, there is infringement, and if the claims do not read there is not infringement. There is a little more to it than that. The little more I think, reminds me somewhat of the law of evidence. You take a course in evidence in law school and you spend the first five minutes learning the rules of evidence and the next two years trying to learn the exceptions to the hearsay rule. And it is really the exceptions to the rule of simply reading the claims on the device that we are concerned with in considering the question of patent claims and infringement. . . .

So in any and every question of infringement, the prior art makes a difference and must be looked at. What difference it makes depends upon the difference between the patent, the prior art and the patent, the difference between the patent and the accused structure and the difference between the prior art and the accused structure. All must be considered and it is impossible to have any sound opinion on the question of whether or not a claim of a patent is infringed, in my opinion, unless all are considered. Of course, what that means as a practical matter, is that since you never know all the prior art, you never know when another patent will turn up; it may be a little closer than anything you know of; you can do the best you can with what you have, but like so many questions of patent law, we have to advise our clients that it is a field of uncertainty. It depends so much on subjective analysis and subjective appraisal, that you cannot advise with great confidence that any patent is valid or invalid or is infringed or is not infringed.

EIBEL PROCESS CO. v. MINNESOTA & ONTARIO PAPER CO., 261 U.S. 45, 43 S.Ct. 322, 67 L.Ed. 523 (1923). TAFT, C.J.: In administering the patent law the court first looks into the art to find what the real merit of the alleged discovery or invention is and whether it has advanced the art substantially. If it has done so, then the court is liberal in its construction of the patent to secure to the inventor the reward he deserves. If what he has done works only a slight step forward and that which he says is a discovery is on the border line between mere mechanical change and real invention, then his patent, if sustained, will be given a narrow scope and infringement will be found only in approximate copies of the new device. It is this differing attitude of the courts toward genuine discoveries and slight improvements that reconciles the sometimes apparently conflicting instances of construing specifications and the finding of equivalents in alleged infringements. In the case before us, for the reasons we have already reviewed, we think that Eibel made a very useful discovery which has substantially advanced the art. His was not a pioneer patent, creating a new art; but a patent which is only an improvement on an old machine may be very meritorious and entitled to liberal treatment. Indeed, when one notes the crude working of machines of famous pioneer inventions and discoveries, and compares them with the modern machines and processes exemplifying the principle of the pioneer discovery, one hesitates in the division of credit between the original inventor and the improvers; and certainly finds no reason to withhold from the really meritorious improver, the application of the rule *"ut res magis valeat quam pereat,"* which has been sustained in so many cases in this Court.

Graver Tank & Mfg. Co. v. Linde Air Products Co.

Supreme Court of the United States, 1950.
339 U.S. 605, 70 S.Ct. 854, 94 L.Ed. 1097, 85 U.S.P.Q. 328.

Mr. Justice JACKSON delivered the opinion of the Court.

Linde Air Products Co., owner of the Jones patent for an electric welding process and for fluxes to be used therewith, brought an action for infringement against Lincoln and the two Graver companies. The trial court held four flux claims valid and infringed and certain other flux claims and all process claims invalid. 75 U.S.P.Q. 231. The Court of Appeals affirmed findings of validity and infringement as to the four flux claims but reversed the trial court and held valid the process claims and the remaining contested flux claims. 167 F.2d 531. We granted certiorari, 335 U.S. 810, 69 S.Ct. 50, 93 L.Ed. 366, and reversed the judgment of the Court of Appeals insofar as it reversed that of the trial court, and reinstated the District Court decree. 336 U.S. 271, 69 S.Ct. 535, 93 L.Ed. 672. Rehearing was granted, limited to the question of infringement of the four valid flux claims and to the applicability of the doctrine of equivalents to findings of fact in this case.

At the outset it should be noted that the single issue before us is whether the trial court's holding that the four flux claims have been infringed will be sustained. Any issue as to the validity of these claims was unanimously determined by the previous decision in this Court and attack on their validity cannot be renewed now by reason of limitation on grant of rehearing. The disclosure, the claims, and the prior art have been adequately described in our former opinion and in the opinions of the courts below.

In determining whether an accused device or composition infringes a valid patent, resort must be had in the first instance to the words of the claim. If accused matter falls clearly within the claim, infringement is made out and that is the end of it.

But courts have also recognized that to permit imitation of a patented invention which does not copy every literal detail would be to convert the protection of the patent grant into a hollow and useless thing. Such a limitation would leave room for—indeed encourage—the unscrupulous copyist to make unimportant and insubstantial changes and substitutions in the patent which, though adding nothing, would be enough to take the copied matter outside the claim, and hence outside the reach of law. One who seeks to pirate an invention, like one who seeks to pirate a copyrighted book or play, may be expected to introduce minor variations to conceal and shelter the piracy. Outright and forthright duplication is a dull and very rare type of infringement. To prohibit no other would place the inventor at the mercy of verbalism and would be subordinating substance to form. It would deprive him of the benefit of his invention and would foster concealment rather than disclosure of inventions, which is one of the primary purposes of the patent system.

The doctrine of equivalents evolved in response to this experience. The essence of the doctrine is that one may not practice a fraud on a patent. Originating almost a century ago in the case of Winans v. Denmead, 15 How. 330, it has been consistently applied by this Court and the lower federal courts, and continues today ready and available for utilization when the proper circumstances for its application arise. "To temper unsparing logic and prevent an infringer from stealing the benefit of an invention" a patentee may invoke this doctrine to proceed against the producer of a device "if it performs substantially the same function in substantially the same way to obtain the same result." Sanitary Refrigerator Co. v. Winters, 280 U.S. 30, 42, 50 S.Ct. 9, 13, 74 L.Ed. 147. The theory on which it is founded is that "if two devices do the same work in substantially the same way, and accomplish substantially the same result, they are the same, even though they differ in name, form, or shape." Machine Co. v. Murphy, 97 U.S. 120, 125, 24 L.Ed. 935. The doctrine operates not only in favor of the patentee of a pioneer or primary invention, but also for the patentee of a secondary invention consisting of a combination of old ingredients which produce new and useful results, although the area of equivalence may vary under the circumstances. The wholesome realism of this doctrine is not always applied in favor of a patentee but is sometimes used against him. Thus, where a device is so far changed in principle from a patented article that it performs the same or a similar function in a substantially different way, but nevertheless falls within the literal words of the claim, the doctrine of equivalents may be used to restrict the claim and defeat the patentee's action for infringement. In its early development, the doctrine was usually applied in cases involving devices where there was equivalence in mechanical components. Subsequently, however, the same principles were also applied to compositions, where there was equivalence between chemical ingredients. Today the doctrine is applied to mechanical or chemical equivalents in compositions or devices.

What constitutes equivalency must be determined against the context of the patent, the prior art, and the particular circumstances of the case. Equivalence, in the patent law, is not the prisoner of a formula and is not an absolute to be considered in a vacuum. It does not require complete identity for every purpose and in every respect. In determining equivalents, things equal to the same thing may not be equal to each other and, by the same token, things for most purposes different may sometimes be equivalents. Consideration must be given to the purpose for which an ingredient is used in a patent, the qualities it has when combined with the other ingredients, and the function which it is intended to perform. An important factor is whether persons reasonably skilled in the art would have known of the interchangeability of an ingredient not contained in the patent with one that was.

A finding of equivalence is a determination of fact. Proof can be made in any form: through testimony of experts or others versed in the technology; by documents, including texts and treatises; and, of course, by the disclosures of the prior art. Like any other issue of fact, final determination requires a balancing of credibility, persuasiveness and weight of evidence. It is to be decided by the trial court and that court's decision, under general principles of appellate review, should not be disturbed unless clearly erroneous. Particularly is this so in a field where so much depends upon familiarity with specific scientific problems and principles not usually contained in the general storehouse of knowledge and experience.

In the case before us, we have two electric welding compositions or fluxes: the patented composition, Unionmelt Grade 20, and the accused composition, Lincolnweld 660. The patent under which Unionmelt is made claims essentially a combination of alkaline earth metal silicate and calcium fluoride; Unionmelt actually contains, however, silicates of calcium and magnesium, two alkaline earth metal silicates. Lincolnweld's composition is similar to Unionmelt's, except that it substitutes silicates of calcium and manganese—the latter not an alkaline earth metal—for silicates of calcium and magnesium. In all other respects, the two compositions are alike. The mechanical methods in which these compositions are employed are similar. They are identical in operation and produce the same kind and quality of weld.

The question which thus emerges is whether the substitution of the manganese which is not an alkaline earth metal for the magnesium which is, under the circumstances of this case, and in view of the technology and the prior art, is a change of such substance as to make the doctrine of equivalents inapplicable; or conversely, whether under the circumstances the change was so insubstantial that the trial court's invocation of the doctrine of equivalents was justified.

Without attempting to be all-inclusive, we note the following evidence in the record: Chemists familiar with the two fluxes testified that manganese and magnesium were similar in many of their reactions. There is testimony by a metallurgist that alkaline earth metals are often found in manganese ores in their natural state and that they serve the same purpose in the fluxes, and a chemist testified that "in the sense of the patent" manganese could be included as an alkaline earth metal. Much of this testimony was corroborated by reference to recognized texts on inorganic chemistry. Particularly important, in addition, were the disclosures of the prior art, also contained in the record. The Miller patent, No. 1,754,566, which preceded the patent in suit, taught the use of manganese silicate in welding fluxes. Manganese was similarly disclosed in the Armor patent, No. 1,467,825, which also described a welding composition. And the record contains no evidence of any kind to show that Lincolnweld was developed as the result of independent research or experiments.

It is not for this Court to even essay an independent evaluation of this evidence. This is the function of the trial court. And, as we have heretofore observed, "To no type of case is this . . . more appropriately applicable than to the one before us, where the evidence is largely the testimony of experts as to which a trial court may be enlightened by scientific demonstrations. This trial occupied some three weeks, during which, as the record shows, the trial judge visited laboratories with counsel and experts to observe actual demonstrations of welding as taught by the patent and of the welding accused of infringing it, and of various stages of the prior art. He viewed motion pictures of various welding operations and tests and heard many experts and other witnesses." 336 U.S. 271, 274–275, 69 S.Ct. 535, 537, 93 L.Ed. 672.

The trial judge found on the evidence before him that the Lincolnweld flux and the composition of the patent in suit are substantially identical in operation and in result. He found also that Lincolnweld is in all respects equivalent to Unionmelt for welding purposes. And he concluded that "for all practical purposes, manganese silicate can be efficiently and effectually substituted for calcium and magnesium silicates as the major constituent of the welding composition." These conclusions are adequately supported by the record; certainly they are not clearly erroneous.

It is difficult to conceive of a case more appropriate for application of the doctrine of equivalents. The disclosures of the prior art made clear that manganese silicate was a useful ingredient in welding compositions. Specialists familiar with the problems of welding compositions understood that manganese was equivalent to and could be substituted for magnesium in the composition of the patented flux and their observations were confirmed by the literature of chemistry. Without some explanation or indication that Lincolnweld was developed by independent research, the trial court could properly infer that the accused flux is the result of imitation rather than experimentation or invention. Though infringement was not literal, the changes which avoid literal infringement are colorable only. We conclude that the trial court's judgment of infringement respecting the four flux claims was proper, and we adhere to our prior decision on this aspect of the case.

Affirmed.

Mr. Justice BLACK, with whom Mr. Justice DOUGLAS concurs, dissenting.

I heartily agree with the Court that "fraud" is bad, "piracy" is evil, and "stealing" is reprehensible. But in this case, where petitioners are not charged with any such malevolence, these lofty principles do not justify the Court's sterilization of Acts of Congress and prior decisions, none of which are even mentioned in today's opinion.

The only patent claims involved here describe respondent's product as a flux "containing a major proportion of alkaline earth metal silicate." The trial court found that petitioners used a flux "composed principally of manganese silicate." Finding also that "manganese is not an alkaline earth metal," the trial court admitted that petitioners' flux did not "literally infringe" respondent's patent. Nevertheless it invoked the judicial "doctrine of equivalents" to broaden the claim for "alkaline earth metals" so as to embrace "manganese." On the ground that "the fact that manganese is a proper substitute ... is fully disclosed in the specification" of respondent's patent, it concluded that "no determination need be made whether it is a known chemical fact *outside* the teachings of the patent that manganese is an equivalent...." Since today's affirmance unquestioningly follows the findings of the trial court, this Court necessarily relies on what the specifications revealed. In so doing, it violates a direct mandate of Congress without even discussing that mandate.

R.S. § 4888, as amended, 35 U.S.C.A. § 33, provides that an applicant "shall particularly point out and distinctly claim the part, improvement, or combination which he claims as his invention or discovery." We have held in this very case that this statute precludes invoking the specifications to alter a claim free from ambiguous language, since "it is the claim which measures the grant to the patentee." Graver Mfg. Co. v. Linde Co., 336 U.S. 271, 277, 69 S.Ct. 535, 538, 93 L.Ed. 672. What is not specifically claimed is dedicated to the public. For the function of claims under R.S. § 4888, as we have frequently reiterated, is to exclude from the patent monopoly field all that is not specifically claimed, whatever may appear in the specifications. Today the Court tacitly rejects those cases. It departs from the underlying principle which, as the Court pointed out in White v. Dunbar, 119 U.S. 47, 51, 7 S.Ct. 72, 74, 30 L.Ed. 303, forbids treating a patent claim "like a nose of wax which may be turned and twisted in any direction, by merely referring to the specification, so as to make it include something more than, or something different from what its words express.... The claim is a statutory requirement, prescribed for the very purpose of making the patentee define precisely what his invention is; and it is unjust to the public, as well as an evasion of the law, to construe it in a manner different from the plain import of its terms." Giving this patentee the benefit of a grant that it did not precisely claim is no less "unjust to the public" and no less an evasion of R.S. § 4888 merely because done in the name of the "doctrine of equivalents."

In seeking to justify its emasculation of R.S. § 4888 by parading potential hardships which literal enforcement might conceivably impose on patentees who had for some reason failed to claim complete protection for their discoveries, the Court fails even to mention the program for alleviation of such hardships which Congress itself has provided. 35 U.S.C.A. § 64 authorizes reissue of patents where a patent is "wholly or partly inoperative" due to certain errors arising from "inadvertence, accident, or mistake" of the patentee. And while the section does not expressly permit a patentee to expand his claim, this Court has reluctantly interpreted it to justify doing so. Miller v. Bridgeport Brass Co., 104 U.S. 350, 353–354, 26 L.Ed. 783. That interpretation, however, was accompanied by a warning that "Reissues for the enlargement of claims should be the exception and not the rule." Id. at 355. And Congress was careful to hedge the privilege of reissue by exacting conditions. It also entrusted the Patent Office, not the courts, with initial authority to determine whether expansion of a claim was justified, and barred suits for retroactive infringement based on such expansion. Like the Court's opinion, this congressional plan adequately protects patentees from "fraud," "piracy," and "stealing." Unlike the Court's opinion, it also protects businessmen from retroactive infringement suits and judicial expansion of a monopoly sphere beyond that which a patent expressly authorizes. The plan is just, fair, and reasonable. In effect it is nullified by this decision undercutting what the Court has heretofore recognized as wise safeguards. One need not be a prophet to suggest that today's rhapsody on the virtue of the "doctrine of equivalents" will, in direct contravention of the Miller case, supra, make enlargement of patent claims the "rule" rather than the "exception."

Whatever the merits of the "doctrine of equivalents" where differences between the claims of a patent and the allegedly infringing product are de minimis, colorable only, and without substance, that doctrine should have no application to the facts of this case. For the differences between respondent's welding substance and petitioners' claimed flux were not nearly so slight. The claims relied upon here did not involve any mechanical structure or process where invention lay in the construction or method rather than in the materials used. Rather they were based wholly on using particular materials for a particular purpose. Respondent's assignors experimented with several metallic silicates, including that of manganese. According to the specifications (if these are to be considered) they concluded that while several were "more or less efficacious in our process, we prefer to use silicates of the alkaline earth metals." Several of their claims which this Court found too broad to be valid encompassed manganese silicate; the only claims found valid did not. Yet today the Court disregards that crucial deficiency, holding those claims infringed by a composition of which 88.49% by weight is manganese silicate.

In view of the intense study and experimentation of respondent's assignors with manganese silicate, it would be frivolous to contend that failure specifically to include that substance in a precise claim was unintentional. Nor does respondent attempt to give that or any other explanation for its omission. But the similar use of manganese in prior expired patents, referred to in the Court's opinion, raises far more than a suspicion that its elimination from the valid claims stemmed from fear that its inclusion by name might result in denial or subsequent invalidation of respondent's patent.

Under these circumstances I think petitioners had a right to act on the belief that this Court would follow the plain mandates of Congress that a patent's precise claims mark its monopoly boundaries, and that expansion of those claims to include manganese could be obtained only in a statutory reissue proceeding. The Court's ruling today sets the stage for more patent "fraud" and "piracy" against business than could be expected from faithful observance of the congressionally enacted plan to protect business against judicial expansion of precise patent claims. Hereafter a manufacturer cannot rely on what the language of a patent claims. He must be able, at the peril of heavy infringement damages, to forecast how far a court relatively unversed in a particular technological field will expand the claim's language after considering the testimony of technical experts in that field. To burden business enterprise on the assumption that men possess such a prescience bodes ill for the kind of competitive economy that is our professed goal.

The way specific problems are approached naturally has much to do with the decisions reached. A host of prior cases, to some of which I have referred, have treated the 17–year monopoly authorized by valid patents as a narrow exception to our competitive enterprise system. For that reason, they have emphasized the importance of leaving business men free to utilize all knowledge not preempted by the precise language of a patent claim. E.g., Sontag Stores Co. v. Nut Co., 310 U.S. 281, and cases there cited. In the Sontag case Mr. Justice McReynolds, speaking for a unanimous Court, said in part: "In the case under consideration the patentee might have included in the application for the original patent, claims broad enough to embrace petitioner's accused machine, but did not. This 'gave the public to understand' that whatever was not claimed 'did not come within his patent and might rightfully be made by anyone.' " Id. at 293.

The Court's contrary approach today causes it to retreat from this sound principle. The damages retroactively assessed against petitioners for what was authorized until today are but the initial installment on the cost of that retreat.

Mr. Justice DOUGLAS, dissenting.

The Court applies the doctrine of equivalents in a way which subverts the constitutional and statutory scheme for the grant and use of patents.

The claims of the patent are limited to a flux "containing a major proportion of alkaline earth metal silicate." Manganese silicate, the flux which is held to infringe, is not an alkaline earth metal silicate. It was disclosed in the application and then excluded from the claims. It therefore became public property. It was, to be sure, mentioned in the specifications. But the measure of the grant is to be found in the claims, not in the specifications. The specifications can be used to limit but never to expand the claim.

The Court now allows the doctrine of equivalents to erase those time-honored rules. Moreover, a doctrine which is said to protect against practicing "a fraud on a patent" is used to extend a patent to a composition which could not be patented. For manganese silicate had been covered by prior patents, now expired. Thus we end with a strange anomaly: a monopoly is obtained on an unpatented and unpatentable article.

Warner–Jenkinson Company, Inc. v. Hilton Davis Chemical Co.

Supreme Court of the United States, 1997.
520 U.S. 17, 117 S.Ct. 1040, 137 L.Ed.2d 146, 41 U.S.P.Q.2d 1865.

Justice THOMAS delivered the opinion of the Court.

Nearly 50 years ago, this Court in *Graver Tank & Mfg. Co. v. Linde Air Products Co.,* 339 U.S. 605, 70 S.Ct. 854, 94 L.Ed. 1097 (1950), set out the modern contours of what is known in patent law as the "doctrine of equivalents." Under this doctrine, a product or process that does not literally infringe upon the express terms of a patent claim may nonetheless be found to infringe if there is "equivalence" between the elements of the accused product or process and the claimed elements of the patented invention. Petitioner, which was found to have infringed upon respondent's patent under the doctrine of equivalents, invites us to speak the death of that doctrine. We decline that invitation. The significant disagreement within the Court of Appeals for the Federal Circuit concerning the application of *Graver Tank* suggests, however, that the doctrine is not free from confusion. We therefore will endeavor to clarify the proper scope of the doctrine.

I

The essential facts of this case are few. Petitioner Warner–Jenkinson Co. and respondent Hilton Davis Chemical Co. manufacture dyes. Impurities in those dyes must be removed. Hilton Davis holds United States Patent No. 4,560,746 ('746 patent), which discloses an improved purification process involving "ultrafiltration." The '746 process filters impure dye through a porous membrane at certain pressures and pH levels,[1] resulting in a high purity dye product.

---

1. The pH, or power (exponent) of Hydrogen, of a solution is a measure of its acidity or alkalinity. A pH of 7.0 is neutral; a pH below 7.0 is acidic; and a pH above 7.0 is alkaline. Although measurement of pH is on a logarithmic scale, with each whole number difference representing a ten-fold difference in acidity, the practical significance of any

The '746 patent issued in 1985. As relevant to this case, the patent claims as its invention an improvement in the ultrafiltration process as follows:

> In a process for the purification of a dye ... the improvement which comprises: subjecting an aqueous solution ... to ultrafiltration through a membrane having a nominal pore diameter of 5–15 Angstroms under a hydrostatic pressure of approximately 200 to 400 p.s.i.g., *at a pH from approximately 6.0 to 9.0,* to thereby cause separation of said impurities from said dye....

The inventors added the phrase "at a pH from approximately 6.0 to 9.0" during patent prosecution. At a minimum, this phrase was added to distinguish a previous patent (the "Booth" patent) that disclosed an ultrafiltration process operating at a pH above 9.0. The parties disagree as to why the low-end pH limit of 6.0 was included as part of the claim.[2]

In 1986, Warner–Jenkinson developed an ultrafiltration process that operated with membrane pore diameters assumed to be 5–15 Angstroms, at pressures of 200 to nearly 500 p.s.i.g., and at a pH of 5.0. Warner–Jenkinson did not learn of the '746 patent until after it had begun commercial use of its ultrafiltration process. Hilton Davis eventually learned of Warner–Jenkinson's use of ultrafiltration and, in 1991, sued Warner–Jenkinson for patent infringement.

As trial approached, Hilton Davis conceded that there was no literal infringement, and relied solely on the doctrine of equivalents. Over Warner–Jenkinson's objection that the doctrine of equivalents was an equitable doctrine to be applied by the court, the issue of equivalence was included among those sent to the jury. The jury found that the '746 patent was not invalid and that Warner–Jenkinson infringed upon the patent under the doctrine of equivalents. The jury also found, however, that Warner–Jenkinson had not intentionally infringed, and therefore awarded only 20% of the damages sought by Hilton Davis. The District Court denied Warner–Jenkinson's post-trial motions, and entered a permanent injunction prohibiting Warner–Jenkinson from practicing ultrafiltration below 500 p.s.i.g. and below 9.01 pH. A fractured en banc Court of Appeals for the Federal Circuit affirmed. 62 F.3d 1512 (C.A.Fed.1995).

The majority below held that the doctrine of equivalents continues to exist and that its touchstone is whether substantial differences exist between the accused process and the patented process. The court also held

---

such difference will often depend on the context. Pure water, for example, has a neutral pH of 7.0, whereas carbonated water has an acidic pH of 3.0, and concentrated hydrochloric acid has a pH approaching 0.0. On the other end of the scale, milk of magnesia has a pH of 10.0, whereas household ammonia has a pH of 11.9.

2. Petitioner contends that the lower limit was added because below a pH of 6.0 the patented process created "foaming" problems in the plant and because the process was not shown to work below that pH level. Respondent counters that the process was successfully tested to pH levels as low as 2.2 with no effect on the process because of foaming, but offers no particular explanation as to why the lower level of 6.0 pH was selected.

that the question of equivalence is for the jury to decide and that the jury in this case had substantial evidence from which it could conclude that the Warner–Jenkinson process was not substantially different from the ultrafiltration process disclosed in the '746 patent.

There were three separate dissents, commanding a total of 5 of 12 judges. Four of the five dissenting judges viewed the doctrine of equivalents as allowing an improper expansion of claim scope, contrary to this Court's numerous holdings that it is the claim that defines the invention and gives notice to the public of the limits of the patent monopoly. The fifth dissenter, the late Judge Nies, was able to reconcile the prohibition against enlarging the scope of claims and the doctrine of equivalents by applying the doctrine to each element of a claim, rather than to the accused product or process "overall." As she explained it, "[t]he 'scope' is not enlarged if courts do not go beyond the substitution of equivalent elements." Id., at 1574. All of the dissenters, however, would have found that a much narrowed doctrine of equivalents may be applied in whole or in part by the court.

We granted certiorari and now reverse and remand.

II

In *Graver Tank* we considered the application of the doctrine of equivalents to an accused chemical composition for use in welding that differed from the patented welding material by the substitution of one chemical element. The substituted element did not fall within the literal terms of the patent claim, but the Court nonetheless found that the "question which thus emerges is whether the substitution [of one element for the other] . . . is a change of such substance as to make the doctrine of equivalents inapplicable; or conversely, whether under the circumstances the change was so insubstantial that the trial court's invocation of the doctrine of equivalents was justified." 339 U.S. at 610. The Court also described some of the considerations that go into applying the doctrine of equivalents:

> What constitutes equivalency must be determined against the context of the patent, the prior art, and the particular circumstances of the case. Equivalence, in the patent law, is not the prisoner of a formula and is not an absolute to be considered in a vacuum. It does not require complete identity for every purpose and in every respect. In determining equivalents, things equal to the same thing may not be equal to each other and, by the same token, things for most purposes different may sometimes be equivalents. Consideration must be given to the purpose for which an ingredient is used in a patent, the qualities it has when combined with the other ingredients, and the function which it is intended to perform. An important factor is whether persons reasonably skilled in the art would have known of the interchangeability of an ingredient not contained in the patent with one that was. *Id.*, at 609.

Considering those factors, the Court viewed the difference between the chemical element claimed in the patent and the substitute element to be "colorable only," and concluded that the trial court's judgment of infringement under the doctrine of equivalents was proper.

A

Petitioner's primary argument in this Court is that the doctrine of equivalents, as set out in *Graver Tank* in 1950, did not survive the 1952 revision of the Patent Act, 35 U.S.C. § 100 *et seq.*, because it is inconsistent with several aspects of that Act. In particular, petitioner argues: (1) the doctrine of equivalents is inconsistent with the statutory requirement that a patentee specifically "claim" the invention covered by a patent, 35 U.S.C. § 112; (2) the doctrine circumvents the patent reissue process—designed to correct mistakes in drafting or the like—and avoids the express limitations on that process, 35 U.S.C. §§ 251–252; (3) the doctrine is inconsistent with the primacy of the Patent and Trademark Office (PTO) in setting the scope of a patent through the patent prosecution process; and (4) the doctrine was implicitly rejected as a general matter by Congress' specific and limited inclusion of the doctrine in one section regarding "means" claiming, 35 U.S.C. § 112, ¶ 6. All but one of these arguments were made in *Graver Tank* in the context of the 1870 Patent Act, and failed to command a majority.

The 1952 Patent Act is not materially different from the 1870 Act with regard to claiming, reissue, and the role of the PTO. Such minor differences as exist between those provisions in the 1870 and the 1952 Acts have no bearing on the result reached in *Graver Tank,* and thus provide no basis for our overruling it. In the context of infringement, we have already held that pre–1952 precedent survived the passage of the 1952 Act.

Petitioner's fourth argument for an implied congressional negation of the doctrine of equivalents turns on the reference to "equivalents" in the "means" claiming provision of the 1952 Act. Section 112, ¶ 6, a provision not contained in the 1870 Act, states:

> An element in a claim for a combination may be expressed as a means or step for performing a specified function without the recital of structure, material, or acts in support thereof, and such claim shall be construed to cover the corresponding structure, material, or acts described in the specification *and equivalents thereof.*

Thus, under this new provision, an applicant can describe an element of his invention by the result accomplished or the function served, rather than describing the item or element to be used (*e.g.,* "a means of connecting Part A to Part B," rather than "a two-penny nail"). Congress enacted § 112, ¶ 6 in response to *Halliburton Oil Well Cementing Co. v. Walker,* which rejected claims that "do not describe the invention but use 'conveniently functional language at the exact point of novelty,'" 329 U.S. 1, 8, 67 S.Ct. 6, 9–10, 91 L.Ed. 3 (1946). Section 112, ¶ 6 now expressly allows so-called "means" claims, with the proviso that application of the broad literal language of such claims must be limited to only those means that are "equivalent" to the actual means shown in the patent specification. This is an application of the doctrine of equivalents in a restrictive role, narrowing the application of broad literal claim elements. We recognized this type of role for the doctrine of equivalents in *Graver Tank* itself. The added provision, however, is silent on the doctrine of equivalents as applied where there is no literal infringement.

Because § 112, ¶ 6 was enacted as a targeted cure to a specific problem, and because the reference in that provision to "equivalents" appears to be no more than a prophylactic against potential side effects of that cure, such limited congressional action should not be overread for negative implications. Congress in 1952 could easily have responded to *Graver Tank* as it did to the *Halliburton* decision. But it did not. Absent something more compelling than the dubious negative inference offered by petitioner, the lengthy history of the doctrine of equivalents strongly supports adherence to our refusal in *Graver Tank* to find that the Patent Act conflicts with that doctrine. Congress can legislate the doctrine of equivalents out of existence any time it chooses. The various policy arguments now made by both sides are thus best addressed to Congress, not this Court.

B

We do, however, share the concern of the dissenters below that the doctrine of equivalents, as it has come to be applied since *Graver Tank*, has taken on a life of its own, unbounded by the patent claims. There can be no denying that the doctrine of equivalents, when applied broadly, conflicts with the definitional and public-notice functions of the statutory claiming requirement. Judge Nies identified one means of avoiding this conflict:

> [A] distinction can be drawn that is not too esoteric between substitution of an equivalent for a component *in* an invention and enlarging the metes and bounds of the invention *beyond* what is claimed.

> Where a claim to an invention is expressed as a combination of elements, as here, "equivalents" in the sobriquet "Doctrine of Equivalents" refers to the equivalency of an *element* or *part* of the invention with one that is substituted in the accused product or process.

> This view that the accused device or process must be more than "equivalent" *overall* reconciles the Supreme Court's position on infringement by equivalents with its concurrent statements that "the courts have no right to enlarge a patent beyond the scope of its claims as allowed by the Patent Office." The "scope" is not enlarged if courts do not go beyond the substitution of equivalent elements. 62 F.3d, at 1573–1574 (Nies, J., dissenting).

We concur with this apt reconciliation of our two lines of precedent. Each element contained in a patent claim is deemed material to defining the scope of the patented invention, and thus the doctrine of equivalents must be applied to individual elements of the claim, not to the invention as a whole. It is important to ensure that the application of the doctrine, even as to an individual element, is not allowed such broad play as to effectively eliminate that element in its entirety. So long as the doctrine of equivalents does not encroach beyond the limits just described, or beyond related limits to be discussed *infra,* we are confident that the doctrine will not vitiate the central functions of the patent claims themselves.

III

Understandably reluctant to assume this Court would overrule *Graver Tank,* petitioner has offered alternative arguments in favor of a more restricted doctrine of equivalents than it feels was applied in this case. We address each in turn.

A

Petitioner first argues that *Graver Tank* never purported to supersede a well-established limit on non-literal infringement, known variously as "prosecution history estoppel" and "file wrapper estoppel." According to petitioner, any surrender of subject matter during patent prosecution, regardless of the reason for such surrender, precludes recapturing any part of that subject matter, even if it is equivalent to the matter expressly claimed. Because, during patent prosecution, respondent limited the pH element of its claim to pH levels between 6.0 and 9.0, petitioner would have those limits form bright lines beyond which no equivalents may be claimed. Any inquiry into the reasons for a surrender, petitioner claims, would undermine the public's right to clear notice of the scope of the patent as embodied in the patent file.

We can readily agree with petitioner that *Graver Tank* did not dispose of prosecution history estoppel as a legal limitation on the doctrine of equivalents. But petitioner reaches too far in arguing that the reason for an amendment during patent prosecution is irrelevant to any subsequent estoppel. In each of our cases cited by petitioner and by the dissent below, prosecution history estoppel was tied to amendments made to avoid the prior art, or otherwise to address a specific concern—such as obviousness—that arguably would have rendered the claimed subject matter unpatentable. Thus, in *Exhibit Supply Co. v. Ace Patents Corp.,* Chief Justice Stone distinguished inclusion of a limiting phrase in an original patent claim from the "very different" situation in which "the applicant, in order to meet objections in the Patent Office, *based on references to the prior art,* adopted the phrase as a substitute for the broader one" previously used. 315 U.S. 126, 136, 62 S.Ct. 513, 518, 86 L.Ed. 736 (1942) (emphasis added). Similarly, in *Keystone Driller Co. v. Northwest Engineering Corp.,* 294 U.S. 42, 55 S.Ct. 262, 79 L.Ed. 747 (1935), estoppel was applied where the initial claims were "rejected on the prior art," *id.,* at 48, n. 6, 55 S.Ct., at 265, n. 6, and where the allegedly infringing equivalent element was outside of the revised claims and within the prior art that formed the basis for the rejection of the earlier claims, *id.,* at 48, 55 S.Ct., at 264–265.

It is telling that in each case this Court probed the reasoning behind the Patent Office's insistence upon a change in the claims. In each instance, a change was demanded because the claim as otherwise written was viewed as not describing a patentable invention at all—typically because what it described was encompassed within the prior art. But, as the United States informs us, there are a variety of other reasons why the PTO may request a change in claim language. And if the PTO has been requesting changes in claim language without the intent to limit equivalents or, indeed, with the expectation that language it required would in many cases allow for a range of equivalents, we should be extremely reluctant to upset the basic assumptions of the PTO without substantial reason for doing so. Our prior cases have consistently applied prosecution history estoppel only where claims have been amended for a limited set of reasons, and we see no substantial cause for requiring a more rigid rule invoking an estoppel regardless of the reasons for a change.

In this case, the patent examiner objected to the patent claim due to a perceived overlap with the Booth patent, which revealed an ultrafiltration process operating at a pH above 9.0. In response to this objection, the phrase "at a pH from approximately 6.0 to 9.0" was added to the claim. While it is undisputed that the upper limit of 9.0 was added in order to distinguish the Booth patent, the reason for adding the lower limit of 6.0 is unclear. The lower limit certainly did not serve to distinguish the Booth patent, which said nothing about pH levels below 6.0. Thus, while a lower limit of 6.0, by its mere inclusion, became a material *element* of the claim, that did not necessarily preclude the application of the doctrine of equivalents as to that element. Where the reason for the change was not related to avoiding the prior art, the change may introduce a new element, but it does not necessarily preclude infringement by equivalents of that element.

We are left with the problem, however, of what to do in a case like the one at bar, where the record seems not to reveal the reason for including the lower pH limit of 6.0. In our view, holding that certain reasons for a claim amendment may avoid the application of prosecution history estoppel is not tantamount to holding that the *absence* of a reason for an amendment may similarly avoid such an estoppel. Mindful that claims do indeed serve both a definitional and a notice function, we think the better rule is to place the burden on the patent-holder to establish the reason for an amendment required during patent prosecution. The court then would decide whether that reason is sufficient to overcome prosecution history estoppel as a bar to application of the doctrine of equivalents to the element added by that amendment. Where no explanation is established, however, the court should presume that the PTO had a substantial reason related to patentability for including the limiting element added by amendment. In those circumstances, prosecution history estoppel would bar the application of the doctrine equivalents as to that element. The presumption we have described, one subject to rebuttal if an appropriate reason for a required amendment is established, gives proper deference to the role of claims in defining an invention and providing public notice, and to the primacy of the PTO in ensuring that the claims allowed cover only subject matter that is properly patentable in a proffered patent application. Applied in this fashion, prosecution history estoppel places reasonable limits on the doctrine of equivalents, and further insulates the doctrine from any feared conflict with the Patent Act.

Because respondent has not proffered in this Court a reason for the addition of a lower pH limit, it is impossible to tell whether the reason for that addition could properly avoid an estoppel. Whether a reason in fact exists, but simply was not adequately developed, we cannot say. On remand, the Federal Circuit can consider whether reasons for that portion of the amendment were offered or not and whether further opportunity to establish such reasons would be proper.

B

Petitioner next argues that even if *Graver Tank* remains good law, the case held only that the absence of substantial differences was a *necessary* element for infringement under the doctrine of equivalents, not that it was *sufficient* for such a result. Relying on *Graver Tank*'s references to the problem of an "unscrupulous copyist" and "piracy," 339 U.S., at 607, petitioner would require judicial exploration of the equities of a case before allowing application of the doctrine of equivalents. To be sure, *Graver Tank* refers to the prevention of copying and piracy when describing the benefits of the doctrine of equivalents. That the doctrine produces such benefits, however, does not mean that its application is limited only to cases where those particular benefits are obtained.

Elsewhere in *Graver Tank* the doctrine is described in more neutral terms. And the history of the doctrine as relied upon by *Graver Tank* reflects a basis for the doctrine not so limited as petitioner would have it. In *Winans v. Denmead,* 15 How. 330, 343, 14 L.Ed. 717 (1854), we described the doctrine of equivalents as growing out of a legally implied term in each patent claim that "the claim extends to the thing patented, however its form or proportions may be varied." Under that view, application of the doctrine of equivalents involves determining whether a particular accused product or process infringes upon the patent claim, where the claim takes the form—half express, half implied—of "X and its equivalents."

Union Paper-Bag Machine Co. v. Murphy, 97 U.S. 120, 125, 24 L.Ed. 935 (1878), on which *Graver Tank* also relied, offers a similarly intent-neutral view of the doctrine of equivalents:

[T]he substantial equivalent of a thing, in the sense of the patent law, is the same as the thing itself; so that if two devices do the same work in substantially the same way, and accomplish substantially the same result, they are the same, even though they differ in name, form, or shape.

If the essential predicate of the doctrine of equivalents is the notion of identity between a patented invention and its equivalent, there is no basis for treating an infringing equivalent any differently than a device that infringes the express terms of the patent. Application of the doctrine of equivalents, therefore, is akin to determining literal infringement, and neither requires proof of intent.

Petitioner also points to *Graver Tank*'s seeming reliance on the absence of independent experimentation by the alleged infringer as supporting an equitable defense to the doctrine of equivalents. The Federal Circuit explained this factor by suggesting that an alleged infringer's behavior, be it copying, designing around a patent, or independent experimentation, indirectly reflects the substantiality of the differences between the patented invention and the accused device or process. According to the Federal Circuit, a person aiming to copy or aiming to avoid a patent is imagined to be at least marginally skilled at copying or avoidance, and thus intentional copying raises an inference—rebuttable by proof of independent development—of having only insubstantial differences, and intentionally designing around a patent claim raises an inference of substantial differences. This explanation leaves much to be desired. At a minimum, one wonders how ever to distinguish between the intentional copyist making minor changes to lower the risk of legal action, and the incremental innovator designing around the claims, yet seeking to capture as much as is permissible of the patented advance.

But another explanation is available that does not require a divergence from generally objective principles of patent infringement. In both instances in *Graver Tank* where we referred to independent research or experiments, we were discussing the known interchangeability between the chemical compound claimed in the patent and the compound substituted by the alleged infringer. The need for independent experimentation thus could reflect knowledge—or lack thereof—of interchangeability possessed by one presumably skilled in the art. The known interchangeability of substitutes for an element of a patent is one of the express objective factors noted by *Graver Tank* as bearing upon whether the accused device is substantially the same as the patented invention. Independent experimentation by the alleged infringer would not always reflect upon the objective question whether a person skilled in the art would have known of the interchangeability between two elements, but in many cases it would likely be probative of such knowledge.

Although *Graver Tank* certainly leaves room for petitioner's suggested inclusion of intent-based elements in the doctrine of equivalents, we do not read it as requiring them. The better view, and the one consistent with *Graver Tank*'s predecessors and the objective approach to infringement, is that intent plays no role in the application of the doctrine of equivalents.

C

Finally, petitioner proposes that in order to minimize conflict with the notice function of patent claims, the doctrine of equivalents should be limited to equivalents that are disclosed within the patent itself. A milder version of this argument, which found favor with the dissenters below, is that the doctrine should be limited to equivalents that were known at the time the patent was issued, and should not extend to after-arising equivalents.

As we have noted, *supra,* with regard to the objective nature of the doctrine, a skilled practitioner's knowledge of the interchangeability between claimed and accused elements is not relevant for its own sake, but rather for what it tells the fact-finder about the similarities or differences between those elements. Much as the perspective of the hypothetical "reasonable person" gives content to concepts such as "negligent" behavior, the perspective of a skilled practitioner provides content to, and limits on, the concept of "equivalence." Insofar as the question under the doctrine of equivalents is whether an accused element is equivalent to a claimed element, the proper time for evaluating equivalency—and thus knowledge of interchangeability between elements—is at the time of infringement, not at the time the patent was issued. And rejecting the milder version of petitioner's argument necessarily rejects the more severe proposition that equivalents must not only be known, but must also be actually disclosed in the patent in order for such equivalents to infringe upon the patent.

IV

The various opinions below, respondents, and *amici* devote considerable attention to whether application of the doctrine of equivalents is a task for the judge or for the jury. However, despite petitioner's argument below that the doctrine should be applied by the judge, in this Court petitioner makes only passing reference to this issue.

Petitioner's comments go more to the alleged inconsistency between the doctrine of equivalents and the claiming requirement than to the role of the jury in applying the doctrine as properly understood. Because resolution of whether, or how much of, the application of the doctrine of equivalents can be resolved by the court is not necessary for us to answer the question presented, we decline to take it up. The Federal Circuit held that it was for the jury to decide whether the accused process was equivalent to the claimed process. There was ample support in our prior cases for that holding. Nothing in our recent *Markman* decision necessitates a different result than that reached by the Federal Circuit. Indeed, *Markman* cites with considerable favor, when discussing the role of judge and jury, the seminal *Winans* decision. 517 U.S., at 384–385. Whether, if the issue were squarely presented to us, we would reach a different conclusion than did the Federal Circuit is not a question we need decide today.

V

All that remains is to address the debate regarding the linguistic framework under which "equivalence" is determined. Both the parties and the Federal Circuit spend considerable time arguing whether the so-called "triple identity" test—focusing on the *function* served by a particular claim element, the *way* that element serves that function, and the *result* thus obtained by that element—is a suitable method for determining equivalence, or whether an "insubstantial differences" approach is better. There seems to be substantial agreement that, while the triple identity test may be suitable for analyzing mechanical devices, it often provides a poor framework for analyzing other products or processes. On the other hand, the insubstantial differences test offers little additional guidance as to what might render any given difference "insubstantial."

In our view, the particular linguistic framework used is less important than whether the test is probative of the essential inquiry: Does the accused product or process contain elements identical or equivalent to each claimed element of the patented invention? Different linguistic frameworks may be more suitable to different cases, depending on their particular facts. A focus on individual elements and a special vigilance against allowing the concept of equivalence to eliminate completely any such elements should reduce considerably the imprecision of whatever language is used. An analysis of the role played by each element in the context of the specific patent claim will thus inform the inquiry as to whether a substitute element matches the function, way, and result of the claimed element, or whether the substitute element plays a role substantially different from the claimed element. With these limiting principles as a backdrop, we see no purpose in going further and micro-managing the Federal Circuit's particular word-choice for analyzing equivalence. We expect that the Federal Circuit will refine the formulation of the test for equivalence in the orderly course of case-by-case determinations, and we leave such refinement to that court's sound judgment in this area of its special expertise.

VI

Today we adhere to the doctrine of equivalents. The determination of equivalence should be applied as an objective inquiry on an element-by-element basis. Prosecution history estoppel continues to be available as a defense to infringement, but if the patent-holder demonstrates that an amendment required during prosecution had a purpose unrelated to patentability, a court must consider that purpose in order to decide whether an estoppel is precluded. Where the patentholder is unable to establish such a purpose, a court should presume that the purpose behind the required amendment is such that prosecution history estoppel would apply. Because the Court of Appeals for the Federal Circuit did not consider all of the requirements as described by us today, particularly as related to prosecution history estoppel and the preservation of some meaning for each element in a claim, we reverse and remand for further proceedings consistent with this opinion.

It is so ordered.

Justice GINSBURG, with whom Justice KENNEDY joins, concurring.

I join the opinion of the Court and write separately to add a cautionary note on the rebuttable presumption the Court announces regarding prosecution history estoppel. I address in particular the application of the presumption in this case and others in which patent prosecution has already been completed. The new presumption, if applied woodenly, might in some instances unfairly discount the expectations of a patentee who had no notice at the time of patent prosecution that such a presumption would apply. Such a patentee would have had little incentive to insist that the reasons for all modifications be memorialized in the file wrapper as they were made. Years after the fact, the patentee may find it difficult to establish an evidentiary basis that would overcome the new presumption. The Court's opinion is sensitive to this problem, noting that "the PTO may have relied upon a flexible rule of estoppel when deciding whether to ask for a change" during patent prosecution.

Because respondent has not presented to this Court any explanation for the addition of the lower pH limit, I concur in the decision to remand the matter to the Federal Circuit. On remand, that court can determine—bearing in mind the prior absence of clear rules of the game—whether suitable reasons for including the lower pH limit were earlier offered or, if not, whether they can now be established.

Festo Corporation v. Shoketsu Kinzoku Kogyo Kabushiki Co., Ltd.

[See Appendix at page 1009].

Floyd H. Crews, Patent Claims and Infringement
Dynamics of the Patent System 128, 139–140 (William B. Ball Ed.1960).*

In other words, if you go to the Patent Office and are required to restrict your claim by the prior art, and you come out with a narrower claim than when you went in and then you try to interpret it to be infringed by a device you are accusing, you cannot, of course, give it in the court the interpretation that you had to read out of it in order to get it allowed by the Patent Office. But suppose the Patent Office does not make you amend your claim. Then when the prior art is shown under this decision, the District Court, or the courts, will do exactly what the Patent Office would have done if this particular prior art had been cited during the prosecution. Since the Patent Office would not have allowed the claim, the courts said, we will hold that the claim cannot be read on the accused device, and it is not infringed. In other words, you have a doctrine of file wrapper estoppel, but does the doctrine of file wrapper estoppel mean anything? What difference does it make whether your claim is limited by the Patent Office by reason of the prior art that is cited there, when if you get into the courts and the same prior art is cited against you, the court says this claim must be held to be limited in exactly the same manner in which we think it would have been limited if this art had been cited in the Patent Office. The doctrine of file wrapper estoppel does not seem to have

---

* Copyright 1960 by Villanova University.

any significance when looked at in that light. And yet in actual practice, the doctrine is a doctrine of tremendous importance. If you have two alleged infringing devices in one case, you have limited your claims in the Patent Office in order to assert a limitation and you are now trying to read it out. Your chances of success in court are practically nil. However, if you do not have that limitation and that art was not cited by the Patent Office, your chances of success in court are, in my opinion, very much greater.

NOTES

1. *Role of Judge and Jury in Infringement Cases.* It has long been clear that the jury's role in patent infringement cases includes the determination whether the allegedly infringing device or process falls within the patent's claims. But, until the Supreme Court's decision in Markman v. Westview Instruments, Inc., 517 U.S. 370, 116 S.Ct. 1384, 134 L.Ed.2d 577 (1996), it was unsettled whether, as Justice Souter phrased the issue in his opinion for the Court, "the interpretation of a so-called patent claim, the portion of the patent document that defines the scope of the patentee's rights, is as a matter of law reserved entirely for the court, or subject to a Seventh Amendment guarantee that a jury will determine the meaning of any disputed term of art about which expert testimony is offered." 517 U.S. at 372, 116 S.Ct. at 1387.

The Court held that "the construction of a patent, including terms of art within its claim, is exclusively within the province of the court." 517 U.S. at 372, 116 S.Ct. at 1387. The Court rested its decision in part on historical materials, which only ambiguously reflected the judge-jury allocation in patent cases at the time the Seventh Amendment was adopted; on subsequent judicial decisions; on "functional considerations"—"judges, not juries, are the better suited to find the acquired meaning of patent terms"—and, finally, on "the importance of uniformity in the treatment of a given patent as an independent reason to allocate all issues of construction to the court."

In A Theory of Claims Interpretation, 14 Harv. J.L. & Tech 1, 4–6 (2000), Professor Craig Allen Nard has divided the Federal Circuit's approach to claim interpretation into two schools. One is "hypertextualism"—"the predominant interpretative theory"—which "stresses textual fidelity and internal textual coherence, but eschews extrinsic evidence as an interpretive tool, portraying its use 'as rarely, if ever,' proper. Although hypertextualism posits that expert testimony may be used if the intrinsic record is ambiguous, a hypertextualist judge rarely finds ambiguity." The other school of interpretation is "pragmatic textualism," which "is gradually asserting itself," and "emphasizes the relevance of extrinsic context and industry custom, of which patent law's 'person having ordinary skill in the art' ... is representative.... Because the meaning of a word cannot be 'divorced from the circumstances in which it is used,' a pragmatic textualism approach would consider extrinsic evidence *without* a threshold determination of intrinsic ambiguity."

Markman hearings aimed at early judicial construction of patent claims have become a regular feature of patent litigation, often accelerating dispute resolution by limiting discovery and setting the stage for summary judgment or settlement. Soon after the Supreme Court's decision, several district courts promulgated local rules intended to encourage early and efficient *Markman* hearings. See, for example, N.D. Calif., Civil L. R. 16–10, 16–11.

2. *Do Juries Decide Patent Cases Differently Than Judges*? The results of a study of the 1209 patent cases that were resolved by the factfinder between 1983–1999 (533 jury trials, 676 bench trials) suggest "at first blush," that "complaints about jury bias and incompetency are unfounded." According to the study's author, Professor Kimberly A. Moore, "[j]udges and juries decide some issues differently. For example, juries are significantly more likely to find patents valid, infringed, and willfully infringed than judges. The differences, however, are not as profound or pervasive as one might expect. Judges and juries find patents enforceable with similar frequency. Additionally, juries seem as 'accurate' in their decisionmaking as judges are, as measured by appellate affirmance rate."

However, Professor Moore found that, "despite similar affirmance rates for judge and jury trials, there is some ground for concern with jury resolution of patent cases. To a greater degree than judges, juries tend to decide whole suits rather than delineate individual issues, even when separate issues are presented to them via special verdict forms or interrogatories. This finding suggests that judges are subtler at managing the complex nature of patent cases and the technical distinctions between patents and products." Further, "who filed the suit is a significant predictor of win rate in jury trials. Juries are significantly pro-patentee in suits for infringement (68% patentee win rate); but when a possible infringer initiates a declaratory judgment action, the patentee only has a 38% win rate. If the same were true of judges, then one could attribute the difference in win rate to the strength of the cases—namely, that alleged infringers only bring declaratory judgment suits when they have strong cases. But patentee win rates are substantially uniform in bench trials, regardless of who initiated the suit." Kimberly A. Moore, Judges, Juries, and Patent Cases—An Empirical Peek Inside the Black Box, 99 Mich. L. Rev. 365, 367–68 (2000).

3. *Doctrine of Equivalents: History*. At least at the time of its origin in Winans v. Denmead, 15 How. 330, 56 U.S. 330, 14 L.Ed. 717 (1853), elastic application of the doctrine of equivalents was clearly proper: "The doctrine of equivalents is an inheritance from that period during which the patent statutes required the patent claim merely to 'specify and point out' the invention protected. At that time, claims were usually of the 'as shown and described' variety, importing into the claim the text of the specification and the drawing. 'Interpretation' of patent claims was then the rule; the courts were called upon to determine the actual extent of the invention, and it is obvious that the doctrine of equivalents was then continually necessary as a routine rule of the patent law. Today, patent applicants are required to 'particularly point out and distinctly claim' their inventions and patent claims are now recognized as definitions of the scope of the patent—word fences which exclude the public from the patented invention but also leave open that public domain which the patent may not protect. So long as a claim of a modern patent is not ambiguous, that claim is certainly the measure of the patentee's monopoly under all normal situations, and it now appears futile to contend that the claim may be expanded by the doctrine of equivalents or any other doctrine every time that the claim fails to encompass that which is used by a potential infringer." Note, The Doctrine of Equivalents Revalued, 19 Geo.Wash.L.Rev. 491–492 (1951).

One conclusion to be drawn from this historical analysis is that, under present practice, the doctrine of equivalents should be available only in cases of ambiguous claims and, then, only as an interpretive tool. Aside from whether the application in *Graver* was historically correct, it was probably excessive in terms of the range of equivalents commonly applied. Can you reconcile *Graver's* expansionist views with the antimonopoly bias of the court's contemporaneous decisions on the standard of patentability?

For an extensive (novella-length) account of the Graver v. Linde litigation, and the suggestion that "the courts, moved by the passions that drove the case and particularly by the perceived justice of Linde's cause, misapplied the doctrine [of equivalents], inadvertently causing the Linde patent to cover the prior art," see Paul M. Janicke, Heat of Passion: What Really Happened in *Graver Tank*, 24 AIPLA. Q.J. 1, 6 (1996).

4. The general tests of infringement announced in *Graver* represent only part of the picture. Specific tests, oriented to the particular type of subject matter in suit, also play a role. Because patent claims for compositions of matter can be distinctly characterized in terms of the ingredients' nature and proportions, infringement consists of replication of the ingredients in substantially the same proportions. For a process patent, it is the series of steps comprising the process that is central; replication of every step in substantially the same operative order constitutes infringement. In the case of a machine or device, it is substantial similarity in the means, mode and results of operation that infringes.

5. *"Reverse Doctrine of Equivalents."* *Graver* observed that the doctrine of equivalents "is not always applied in favor of a patentee but is sometimes used against him. Thus, where a device is so far changed in principle from a patented article that it performs the same or a similar function in a substantially different way, but nevertheless falls within the literal words of the claim, the doctrine of equivalents may be used to restrict the claim and defeat the patentee's action for infringement." 339 U.S. at 608–09, 70 S.Ct. at 856–57.

In Mead Digital Systems, Inc. v. A.B. Dick Co., 723 F.2d 455, 221 U.S.P.Q. 1035 (6th Cir.1983), the court applied the doctrine of equivalents as a "two-edged sword" and held that an ink jet printer designed to print letters did not infringe a patent on a printer designed to record waveforms of electrical signals. In the court's view, the accused printer "is a more sophisticated device, embodying inventive insights not part of the Sweet patent." Although the accused device relied on Sweet's "fundamental concept of ink jet charging and deflection," the device incorporated other concepts as well, including "the coordination of multiple jets, interception for creating an apparent discontinuity in the image, and a charging and deflection system whereby the final picture is not characteristic of the charging signals." 723 F.2d at 464.

The court rejected *Graver's* assertion that "[i]f accused matter falls clearly within the claim, infringement is made out and that is the end of it." According to the court, "[t]his so-called doctrine of 'literal infringement' continues to live in the cases despite repeated pronouncements that infringement is not a mere matter of words.... Courts, however unfortunately, continue to pay lip service to the doctrine of literal infringement as though it were the rule in *Shelley's Case*. Perhaps we are embarrassed to expose the 'wholesale realism' which controls many infringement cases, and we choose instead to present the facade of precision and certainty which attends the doctrine of literal infringement." 723 F.2d at 462.

6. *Prosecution History Estoppel.* Three possible rationales underlie the doctrine of prosecution history estoppel—earlier called "file wrapper estoppel"—discussed in *Warner-Jenkinson.* One is a common law estoppel theory. Because competitors may circumvent in reliance on the recorded prosecution history in the Patent and Trademark Office, the patent owner should be estopped from reclaiming later what it gave up earlier. The difference from common law estoppel is that an accused infringer does not have to prove reliance to invoke the estoppel. Second is an abandonment rationale: the patent applicant abandoned for all time the scope of claims that it gave up in the Patent and Trademark Office. Third is an exhaustion of administrative remedies rationale. "If an inventor adopts a narrow definition in the Patent and Trademark Office in order to obtain a patent and then relies upon a broader definition in an infringement suit, he *pro tanto* circumvents the administrative procedures and expertise of the Office." Donald S. Chisum, 5A Chisum on Patents § 18.05[1] (1978).

The fact that prosecution history estoppel is not a true common law estoppel may have procedural consequence. In General Instrument Corp. v. Hughes Aircraft Co., 399 F.2d 373, 158 U.S.P.Q. 498 (1st Cir.1968), the patent owner prevailed in the district court on a finding that the accused composition fell within its claims under the doctrine of equivalents. On appeal, the defendant asserted the doctrine of file wrapper estoppel for the first time. Agreeing that file wrapper estoppel applied, the court of appeals reversed. "Were this doctrine only that of 'estoppel' and nothing more, we would be inclined to treat this as a defense which, not having been asserted below, is deemed waived. But this doctrine is more. 'It is a rule of patent construction consistently observed that a claim in a patent as allowed must be read and interpreted with reference to claims that have been cancelled or rejected, and the claims allowed cannot by construction be read to cover what was thus eliminated from the patent.' Schriber–Schroth v. Cleveland Trust Co., 311 U.S. 211, 220–221, 61 S.Ct. 235, 239–40, 85 L.Ed. 132, 47 U.S.P.Q. 345, 348–349 (1940)." 399 F.2d at 385.

7. Subsequent developments in the protracted *Graver* litigation illustrate the close relationship between the doctrine of equivalents and prosecution history estoppel. Union Carbide & Carbon Corp. v. Graver Tank & Mfg. Co., Inc., 196 F.2d 103, 93 U.S.P.Q. 137 (7th Cir.1952), involved review of a judgment holding Graver in contempt for marketing a new flux series in violation of the injunction that had issued under the Supreme Court's mandate in the principal case. Union Carbide—Linde's parent—had argued in the contempt proceeding that Graver's new series, no less than its old, infringed flux claims, 18, 20, 22, 23. Specifically, it charged that the fraction of silicates in Graver's compositions—between 24% and 41% by plaintiff's count—was substantially equivalent to the "major proportion of silicates" protected by plaintiff's patent claims.

The court of appeals ruled that, by its concessions in the Patent Office, plaintiff was estopped from maintaining that a fraction of less than 50% is equivalent to a "major proportion." "We suspect, however, that plaintiff's failure previously to advance its present definition of 'a major proportion' was due to the realization that such a concession would place in serious question the validity of the claims." In argument to the examiner, plaintiff had distinguished an anticipating reference on the ground that it contained only a "minor proportion of silicates"—between 20% and 33%. Reversing the judgment below, the court of appeals noted: "The question arises, however, as to the validity of its [the doctrine of equivalents'] application where the doctrine of estoppel is properly invoked. While we find no case where this question has been discussed, we think it obvious that there are instances where both doctrines cannot be given effect because of their inconsistency." 196 F.2d at 108.

8. *Collateral Estoppel.* Can a patent owner who has once suffered a finding of invalidity relitigate the patent's validity in another action against another infringer? Until 1971, the answer was that, under the mutuality of estoppel doctrine, he could. That year, the Supreme Court decided Blonder–Tongue Laboratories, Inc. v. University of Illinois Foundation, 402 U.S. 313, 91 S.Ct. 1434, 28 L.Ed.2d 788, 169 U.S.P.Q. 513, overturning Triplett v. Lowell, 297 U.S. 638, 56 S.Ct. 645, 80 L.Ed. 949, 29 U.S.P.Q. 1 (1936) "to the extent it forecloses a plea of estoppel by one facing a charge of infringement of a patent that has once been declared invalid." 402 U.S. 313, 350, 91 S.Ct. 1434, 1453, 1454, 28 L.Ed.2d 788.

The Court's decision drew in part on the contemporary erosion of the mutuality of estoppel doctrine in other fields. Also, in the Court's opinion, the doctrine's cost—to plaintiffs, defendants and courts facing recurrent litigation over the same issue—far outweighed its benefits. "Some courts have frankly stated that patent litigation can present issues so complex that legal minds, without appropriate grounding in science and technology, may have difficulty in reaching decision.... Assuming a patent case so difficult as to provoke a frank admission of judicial uncertainty, one might ask what reason there is to expect that a second District Judge or Court of Appeals would be able to decide the issue more accurately." Finally, "when these judicial developments are considered in the light of our consistent view—last presented in Lear, Inc. v. Adkins—that the holder of a patent should not be insulated from the assertion of defenses and thus allowed to exact royalties for the use of an idea that is not in fact patentable or that is beyond the scope of the patent monopoly granted, it is apparent that the uncritical acceptance of the principle of mutuality of estoppel expressed in Triplett v. Lowell is today out of place." 402 U.S. 313, 349–350, 91 S.Ct. 1434, 1453, 1454, 28 L.Ed.2d 788.

The Court ruled that an alleged infringer's plea of estoppel would not entirely bar the patent owner from a second hearing. "Rather the patentee-plaintiff must be permitted to demonstrate, if he can, that he did not have a 'fair opportunity procedurally, substantively and evidentially to pursue his claim the first time.' " The Court gave some examples of the facts to be found in determining whether the patent owner had enjoyed a fair opportunity: "If the issue is nonobviousness, appropriate inquiries would be whether the first validity determination purported to employ the standards announced in Graham v. John Deere Co., whether the opinions filed by the District Court and the reviewing court, if any, indicate that the prior case was one of those relatively rare instances where the courts wholly failed to grasp the technical subject matter and issues in suit; and whether without fault of his own, the patentee was deprived of crucial evidence or witnesses in the first litigation."

Will an initial determination of a patent's *validity* bar nonparticipants in the litigation from subsequently asserting the patent's invalidity? Or is comity the only constraint? See Boutell v. Volk, 449 F.2d 673, 171 U.S.P.Q. 668 (10th Cir.1971); Columbia Broadcasting System, Inc. v. Zenith Radio Corp., 391 F.Supp. 780, 185 U.S.P.Q. 662 (N.D.Ill.1975). ("A prior finding of validity should be given as much weight as possible consistent with the dictates of due process. Without violating due process, a court can require a defendant to prove that a factual or legal error occurred in the previous adjudication of validity or that the previous litigation was incomplete in some material aspect.") 391 F.Supp. 386. See John Kidwell, Comity, Patent Validity and The Search for Symmetry: Son of Blonder–Tongue, 57 J.Pat. Off.Soc'y 473 (1975).

III. COPYRIGHT LAW

Copyright law began in England with the printing press. Within a decade after William Caxton founded his press at Westminster in 1476, the Crown sought to control the new art through royal grants of patents for printing. In 1557 control was largely transferred to the printers themselves with the formation of the Stationers' Company to prosecute printers who published seditious matter or who infringed others' licensed works. Through a series of Star Chamber decrees, royal proclamations and legislation, censorship and the regulation of piracy became inseparable. As Benjamin Kaplan observed, "copyright has the look of being gradually secreted in the interstices of the censorship." B. Kaplan, An Unhurried View of Copyright 4 (1967). As censorship declined at the end of the seventeenth century, the Stationers petitioned Parliament for aid. The response was the Statute of Anne, 8 Ann., c. 19 (1709), the first English copyright act, which established a copyright term of 14 years from the date of publication, renewable once, and provided for fines and forfeiture of infringing copies. The Stationers' role under the statute was limited to registering titles and accepting deposits of copyrighted works.

The American colonies adopted the English copyright system. On May 2, 1783, the Continental Congress passed a resolution urging "the several States ... to secure to the authors or publishers of any new books ... the copy right of such books...." See U.S. Copyright Office, Copyright Enactments, Bull. No. 3, p. 1 (1973). Like the state legislation, the first federal copyright law, Act of May 31, 1790, was modeled on the Statute of Anne. As new economic interests and technologies pressed for recognition, Congress added to the Act's original subject matter. The last comprehensive revision, Pub.L. No. 94–553, was signed into law on October 19, 1976 and came into effect for most purposes on January 1, 1978. Twenty year later, the Digital Millennium Copyright Act, P.L. No. 105–304 (October 28, 1998), sought to adjust the copyright statute to the new realities of Internet technology and commerce by providing for technological protection measures, electronic rights management and safe harbors for online service providers.

Until the 1976 Act, protection of unpublished works was almost entirely the province of state common law. Common law copyright was potentially perpetual, beginning at the moment of the work's creation and ending only upon the work's publication with the authority of the copyright owner. (The doctrine was the exclusive source of protection for unpublished maps, books, charts and even letters, including the private, unpublished correspondence of George Washington. See Folsom v. Marsh, 9 Fed.Cas. 342 (C.C.D.Mass.1841).) Upon publication, common law protection ceased and the work came under federal copyright protection—*if* the statutorily-required copyright notice appeared on all publicly distributed copies. If the required copyright notice did not appear, the work fell into the public domain. The 1976 Copyright Act changed all this by eliminating common law copyright for most purposes and making federal copyright attach not from the moment of a work's publication, but from the moment of its first fixation in tangible form. The 1976 Act did not, however, entirely eliminate common law copyright. Because the Act extends federal protection only to works that are fixed in a "tangible medium of expression," it leaves to state common law the protection of unfixed works such as choreography that has never been filmed or notated, extemporaneous speeches or conversations, live broadcasts and improvised musical compositions.

After more than a century outside the oldest and most important international copyright convention, the United States adhered to the Berne Convention for the Protection of Literary and Artistic Works, effective March 1, 1989. The Berne Convention Implementation Act of 1988, Pub.L. No. 100–568, 102 Stat. 2853 (Oct. 31, 1988), conformed United States law to the Convention's requirements. The Act's most dramatic feature was to eliminate the requirement that copyright notice be affixed to publicly-distributed copies and phonorecords as a condition of copyright protection; after the Act's effective date, copyright notice is optional rather than mandatory.

Paul Goldstein, Copyright's Highway: From Gutenberg to the Celestial Jukebox (1995), traces copyright law's encounters with new technologies from the printing press to the present. On the early history of copyright, see L. Ray Patterson, Copyright in Historical Perspective (1968); Bruce W. Bugbee, Genesis of American Patent and Copyright Law (1967). The efforts leading to passage of the 1976 Act stimulated some good writing on copyright law and policy. Thirty-five studies initiated by the Copyright Office, and reprinted in Studies on Copyright (Arthur Fisher Memorial Ed. 1963), examine a variety of topics within the reform context. H.R. Rep. No. 94–1476, 94th Cong., 2d Sess. (1976) and House Conf. Rep. No. 94–1733, 94th Cong., 2d Sess. (1976), are the authoritative legislative sources interpreting the 1976 Act.

Multivolume reference works include: Paul Goldstein, Copyright (2d ed. 1996); Melville Nimmer & David Nimmer, Nimmer on Copyright (1995); William Patry, Copyright Law and Practice (1994). Marshall Leaffer, Understanding Copyright Law (1989) is an excellent student text. The Journal of the Copyright Society of the U.S.A. regularly publishes articles on copyright law.

A. REQUIREMENTS FOR PROTECTION

1. FORMALITIES

See Statute Supplement 17 U.S.C.A. §§ 104A, 401–412, 601, 701–709.

a. *Notice*

Until March 1, 1989, the effective date of the Berne Implementation Act, successive United States copyright acts required copyright notice to appear on publicly distributed copies of a work as a condition to the work's protection. As a rule, if the required notice did not appear, the work fell into the public domain.

Over the course of the twentieth century, Congress and the courts gradually relaxed the notice requirement. The 1909 Copyright Act liberalized the requirement imposed by predecessor acts, and judicial decisions under the 1909 Act loosened it still more. The 1976 Act further eased the notice requirement, principally by loosening the earlier rules on form, content and position, and by carving out more generous excuses for errors or omissions. Finally, the Berne Implementation Act entirely eliminated the notice requirement in order to bring United States copyright law into compliance with the Berne Convention for the Protection of Literary and Artistic Works, to which the United States adhered, effective March 1, 1989.

Although copyright notice as a condition to protection has now disappeared from the Copyright Act, it will continue to be important in copyright litigation for many years to come. The reason is that the Berne amendments operate prospectively, eliminating the notice requirement only for copies or phonorecords disseminated after the amendments' effective date. Any work that was published before the amendments' effective date without the then-required notice fell into the public domain unless the error or omission was excused by the terms of the statute.

March 1, 1989 is not the only relevant date for determining the applicability of the notice requirement. The determination whether a work has fallen into the public domain for failure to comply with the notice formality also requires an archeological dig into whether the work was published before or after the effective date of the 1976 Act, January 1, 1978. If the copies or phonorecords were publicly distributed on or after January 1, 1978, but before the effective date of the Berne amendments, the 1976 Act's notice rules will govern. If the work was published before January 1, 1978, the 1909 Act's rules will govern. As a result, a work published before January 1, 1978 without the notice required by the 1909 Act will be in the public domain today unless the terms of the 1909 Act excused the error or omission; it will make no difference that the notice would have met the 1976 Act's less stringent requirements or that the 1976 Act would have excused the error or omission.

Hasbro Bradley, Inc. v. Sparkle Toys, Inc.

United States Court of Appeals, Second Circuit, 1985.
780 F.2d 189, 228 U.S.P.Q. 423.

FRIENDLY, Circuit Judge:

The companies involved in this copyright case in the District Court for the Southern District of New York are Takara Co., Ltd. ("Takara"), a Japanese company that designed the toys here in question; plaintiff Hasbro Bradley, Inc. ("Hasbro"), a large American toy manufacturer and seller that acquired Takara's rights to United States copyrights for the toys; and

defendant Sparkle Toys, Inc. ("Sparkle"), a smaller American toy manufacturer and seller that copied the toys in Asia from models manufactured by
Takara which did not carry the copyright notice required by § 401 of the
Copyright Act of 1976 (the "Act"), 17 U.S.C. § 101 et seq., and by Article
III(1) of the Revised Universal Copyright Convention (U.C.C.), 25 U.S.T.
1341 (1971), to which the United States and Japan are parties. The appeal,
by Sparkle, is from an order of Judge Broderick entered April 29, 1985,
granting Hasbro a preliminary injunction prohibiting Sparkle from "distributing, selling, marketing, promoting, advertising, imitating or exploiting, in this country, its toys, formerly denoted 'Trans Robot,' which are in
violation of plaintiff's registered copyrights in the sculptural embodiments
of its 'Topspin' and 'Twin Twist' toys."

"Topspin" and "Twin Twist" (the "toys") are part of Hasbro's "The
Transformers" series of changeable robotic action figures. The sculptural
expressions of the toys are original designs of Takara, which manufactures
"The Transformers" for Hasbro. Takara authored the designs in the
summer of 1983 and by the end of November had completed molds for
manufacturing the toys. These molds did not contain a copyright notice.
Takara avers that the omission was due to the facts that Japanese law does
not recognize copyright in toy products and that Takara was unaware that
American law does recognize copyright in such works but requires notice,
even on copies of the work distributed outside the United States, for
copyright protection to be claimed inside the United States. Production of
the unmarked toys began in December 1983 and ended in February 1984.
Between January and March, approximately 213,000 of the unmarked toys
were sold; thereafter, sales were minor and were made only to remove
inventory. Whether the unmarked toys were sold only in Asia or some of
them were sold as well in the United States is in dispute.

Hasbro was shown the toys by Takara in June 1984 and decided to
adopt them into "The Transformers" series. In the course of modifying the
toys to meet Hasbro's specifications, Takara designed new molds that
contained a copyright notice; at the same time, it added a copyright notice
to its old molds. Takara avers that after August 1984 no toys using molds
that did not contain a copyright notice were manufactured for sale anywhere in the world. Hasbro has widely distributed the toys in the United
States, beginning in January 1985. Sparkle does not dispute that all of the
toys sold in this country by Hasbro have born copyright notice.

Sometime in June 1984, Takara orally granted Hasbro the exclusive
right to import and sell the toys in the United States and assigned to
Hasbro the United States copyrights in the designs of the toys, including
the right to apply for copyright registration. A written confirmation of
assignment was executed as of November 12, 1984. Hasbro applied to
register copyrights in the United States in both sculptural expressions of
each toy on November 29, 1984, listing Takara as the "author" and itself
as the "copyright claimant" by virtue of the assignment from Takara.
Certificates of registration were granted effective December 3, 1984.

Discussion

The settled law of this circuit is that a preliminary injunction may be granted only upon a showing of "(a) irreparable harm and (b) either (1) likelihood of success on the merits or (2) sufficiently serious questions going to the merits to make them a fair ground for litigation and a balance of hardships tipping decidedly toward the party requesting the preliminary relief." Jackson Dairy, Inc. v. H.P. Hood & Sons, 596 F.2d 70, 72 (2 Cir.1979). Irreparable harm may ordinarily be presumed from copyright infringement. A prima facie case of copyright infringement consists of proof that the plaintiff owns a valid copyright and the defendant has engaged in unauthorized copying. Novelty Textile Mills, Inc. v. Joan Fabrics Corp., 558 F.2d 1090, 1092 (2 Cir.1977); 3 Nimmer on Copyright § 13.01 (1985) [hereafter *Nimmer*]. Since Sparkle admits to unauthorized copying, the only issue before us in reviewing the grant of the preliminary injunction is whether Hasbro's copyrights for the toys are valid. Under § 410(c) of the Act, Hasbro's certificates of copyright registration are prima facie evidence that the copyrights are valid, shifting to Sparkle the burden of proving the contrary. Sparkle attempts to meet this burden with various lines of argument, all stemming from the fact that the toys were initially sold by Takara without copyright notice. We hold that the efforts fail on the facts of this case, although we reject some of the arguments made by Hasbro in seeking to counter them.

Sparkle's most basic position is that sale of the unmarked toys by Takara in Japan injected the designs into the public domain. If the designs were truly in the public domain, Hasbro could have enjoyed no copyrights in the toys, and Sparkle's copying would have been permissible. Sparkle's argument, however, ignores the scheme for the protection of copyrightable works set up by the Act and the U.C.C. If the toys, though not initially qualifying for copyright protection, subsequently did, Sparkle's position loses its glow.

There is no dispute that the toys here at issue were originally designed by Takara in June 1983. Although the toys enjoyed no copyright protection under Japanese law,[3] they fell within the class of "pictorial, graphic, and sculptural works" covered by § 102(a)(5) of the Act. Since the toys were authored by a Japanese national and first "published" (i.e. sold) in Japan, they enjoyed copyright protection under United States law from the moment they were created by virtue of both § 104(b) of the Act and Article II(1) of the U.C.C.

As previously stated, there is also no dispute that before the assignment of Takara's copyrights to Hasbro approximately 213,000 of the toys were sold, mostly in Japan, without copyright notice. This omission of notice from toys sold by Takara or with its authority outside the United States violated § 401(a) of the Act, which requires:

---

3. See 4 Z. Kitagawa, Doing Business in Japan § 8.02[5][c] (1985) ("[M]odels devised for the purpose of mass-producing practical goods are subject to the Design Act rather than the Copyright Act.").

Whenever a work protected under this title is published in the United States *or elsewhere* by authority of the copyright owner, a notice of copyright as provided by this section shall be placed on all publicly distributed copies from which the work can be visually perceived, either directly or with the aid of a machine or device. (Emphasis added.)

This does not mean, however, that the Takara designs were immediately thrust into the public domain. The Act explicitly provides in § 405(a) that the omission of notice from copies of a protected work may be excused or cured under certain circumstances, in which case the copyright is valid from the moment the work was created, just as if no omission had occurred. The House Report accompanying the Act stated with respect to § 405(a) that "[u]nder the general scheme of the bill, statutory copyright protection is secured automatically when a work is created, and is not lost when the work is published, even if the copyright notice is omitted entirely." H.Rep. No. 1476, 94th Cong., 2d Sess. 147 [hereafter *House Report*], *reprinted in* 1976 U.S.Code Cong. & Ad.News 5659, 5763. In the opinion of the committee that authored the report, the excuse and cure provisions of § 405(a) represented "a major change in the theoretical framework of American copyright law." Id. at 146, *reprinted in* 1976 U.S.Code Cong. & Ad.News at 5762.[6]

It is not contended that the omission of notice from the toys could have been excused under either subsections (1) or (3) of § 405(a); rather, reliance is placed on subsection (2). In effect, § 405(a)(2) allows a person who publishes a copyrightable work without notice to hold a kind of incipient copyright in the work for five years thereafter: if the omission is cured in that time through registration and the exercise of "a reasonable effort ... to add notice to all copies ... that are distributed to the public in the United States after the omission has been discovered," the copyright is perfected and valid retroactively for the entire period after cure; if the omission is not cured in that time, the incipient copyright never achieves enforceability. The *quid pro quo* in the Act for persons who have been misled by the omission of copyright notice before the cure is the more liberal provision of § 405(b), as compared with § 21 of the 1909 Act, regarding innocent infringers, of which more hereafter.

There is no dispute that Takara had not cured the omission of notice from the toys under § 405(a)(2) before assigning to Hasbro in June 1984 "the entire right, title and interest to any copyrights on the DESIGNS for the United States of America." Takara's copyrights thus were merely incipient—though subject to cure—at the time of the assignment. It is axiomatic that an assignee of a copyright can take no more than his

---

6. Section 21 of the Copyright Act of 1909, Pub.L. No. 60–349, 35 Stat. 1075 (codified as amended at 17 U.S.C. (1976)), had relieved against failure to affix the notice of copyright required by § 10 only where the copyright proprietor had sought to comply with the notice provisions and the omission from a particular copy or copies was by accident or a mistake. Even in such cases damages could not be recovered against an innocent infringer who had been misled by the omission of the notice.

assignor has to give. See Bong v. Alfred S. Campbell Art Co., 214 U.S. 236, 245–47, 29 S.Ct. 628, 629–30, 53 L.Ed. 979 (1909) (if a foreign author is ineligible to claim copyright under United States law, his assignee may claim no greater rights, even if the assignee would otherwise be eligible to claim copyright in the United States were he the author).

In view of this, we reject Hasbro's argument that the omission of notice by Takara is irrelevant in assessing the validity of Hasbro's copyrights. Hasbro relies on the language of § 401(a), see supra, pointing out that this requires notice only with respect to works published "by authority of the copyright owner." According to Hasbro, since it—not Takara—is the copyright owner in the United States, and since all of the toys sold by its authority in the United States and elsewhere have displayed proper copyright notice, it cannot be in violation of the notice requirement. The fallacy with this argument is that it starts by assuming the very point here in dispute: that Hasbro is the owner of valid copyrights in the United States. Our discussion of *Bong* shows that Hasbro's copyrights initially had only such validity as Takara's. For purposes of determining the validity in the United States of Takara's copyrights at the time of assignment, Takara is the relevant "copyright owner" under § 401(a). As shown above, Takara's violation of the notice requirement left Hasbro with only an incipient copyright, subject to cure.

The issue thus becomes whether Hasbro has cured Takara's omission of notice under § 405(a)(2). There is no question that Hasbro, as Takara's assignee, is permitted to effect cure through its own efforts. The "copyright claimant" entitled under the Act to register a copyright in the United States may be either the author of the work or his assignee, and any registration is of the work *per se* and redounds to the benefit of the assignor as well as the assignee. Not disputing this, Sparkle argues that Hasbro cannot effect cure under § 405(a)(2) because Takara's omission of notice was deliberate.

On its face, § 405(a)(2) is not restricted to unintentional omissions. Its language permits cure if registration is made "within five years after *the publication without notice*"—not, as Sparkle would read it, "the [unintentional] publication without notice." The difference between the broad language of § 405(a) and the more limited language of § 21 of the 1909 Act, see supra note 6, shows that Congress no longer wished to deal only with omissions of notice due to accident or mistake. Moreover, the legislative history of the 1976 Act affords ample demonstration that Congress intended to bring deliberate omissions within the ambit of § 405(a)(2). The House Report comments with respect to § 405(a) that "[u]nder the proposed law a work published without any copyright notice will still be subject to statutory protection for at least 5 years, whether the omission was partial or total, *unintentional or deliberate*." *House Report,* supra, at 147 (emphasis added), *reprinted in* 1976 U.S.Code Cong. & Ad.News at 5763. Professor Nimmer adds:

> In explaining the same statutory text [§ 405], the Register of Copyrights stated: "... it was urged that, to make the validity of a

copyright turn on the question of whether the omission of notice was 'deliberate' or 'unintentional' would involve impossible problems of proof and would result in uncertainty and injustice. After considering these arguments we concluded that questions involving the subjective state of mind of one or more persons and their ignorance or knowledge of the law should be avoided if at all possible ... we decided that the bill should drop any distinction between 'deliberate' and 'inadvertent' or 'unintentional' omission and, subject to certain conditions, should preserve the copyright in all cases." Reg.Supp.Rep., p. 105.

2 *Nimmer,* supra, § 7.13[B][3], at 7–96 n. 43.

Against this, Sparkle relies on Judge Sand's opinion in Beacon Looms, Inc. v. S. Lichtenberg & Co., 552 F.Supp. 1305 (S.D.N.Y.1982), and on Professor Nimmer's approval of the reasoning of that opinion, see 2 *Nimmer,* supra, § 7.13[B][3].

The result in *Beacon Looms* depended almost entirely on the language in § 405(a)(2) that reasonable efforts to affix notice need begin only "after the omission has been discovered." Judge Sand reasoned that since "one cannot 'discover' an omission that has been deliberate," 552 F.Supp. at 1310, to permit the cure of deliberate omissions would do violence to the unambiguous "plain meaning" of the statute. See contra O'Neill Developments, Inc. v. Galen Kilburn, Inc., 524 F.Supp. 710 (N.D.Ga.1981) (deliberate omissions curable under § 405(a)(2); reasonable efforts requirement applies to "copies published after 'discovery' of the fact that the existence of a copyright has become an issue."). In view of this supposedly plain meaning, Judge Sand felt compelled to ignore the legislative history outlined above.

With due respect, we cannot agree with *Beacon Looms*. The operative language of the statute in this context comes at the beginning of § 405(a), covers all three methods of cure, and is not restricted in any way. The language relied on by Judge Sand, which comes at the end of § 405(a)(2), is relevant only with respect to unmarked copies that have been publicly distributed in the United States. More important, the premise of the argument—namely, that a deliberate omission cannot be "discovered"—is unsound. As discussed above, an assignee or licensee may effect cure under § 405(a)(2) on behalf of itself and its assignor or licensor. In such a situation—the very one presented in this case—no violence is done to the statutory language by saying that the omission, though deliberate on the part of the assignor or licensor, was "discovered" by the person later attempting to cure it. Similarly, a deliberate omission at a lower level of a corporate hierarchy might well be "discovered," in realistic terms, by someone at a higher level. Instances like these at least indicate that the "discovered" language does not reveal a plain intent to exclude all deliberate omissions.

The meaning that § 405(a)(2) does not apply to intentional omissions thus seems to us anything but "plain." At most, the "discovered" language introduces an ambiguity. It thus becomes appropriate to look at the legislative history, and this demonstrates that intentional as well as unintentional omissions were intended to be made curable. While there may be some difficulties in determining what constitutes "a reasonable effort to add notice to all copies ... that are distributed to the public in the United States after the omission has been discovered" in cases where the omission was intentional and the person attempting to cure is the same person who omitted notice, as argued in *Beacon Looms,* 552 F.Supp. at 1310–11, and 2 *Nimmer,* supra, § 7.13B3, at 7–96, these difficulties are by no means insuperable and constitute no sufficient reason for disregarding the declared legislative intent. We therefore conclude that the omission of notice from the toys, even if deliberate on Takara's part, was subject to cure under § 405(a)(2), and we pass on to the question whether Hasbro in fact effectuated cure.

Apart from Sparkle's contention that Hasbro committed fraud on the Copyright Office, see infra, there is no dispute that Hasbro validly registered its copyrights in the Takara designs within five years of publication of the unmarked toys, thus satisfying one of the two requirements for cure under § 405(a)(2). Sparkle admits also that Hasbro has affixed notice to all of the toys since sold under its authority in the United States and elsewhere. It argues, however, that Hasbro did not make "a reasonable effort" to affix notice to toys from the unmarked batch initially produced by Takara and thus failed to satisfy the second requirement of § 405(a)(2). Hasbro asserts that this was unnecessary: that its obligations under § 405(a)(2) are limited to unmarked toys distributed to the public in the United States by its own authority as the "copyright owner" and, insofar as we have previously concluded that this phrase includes Takara, to unmarked toys so distributed by Takara before the assignment.

We are not prepared to endorse this. The introductory words to § 405(a) indeed speak of copies "publicly distributed by authority of the copyright owner." However, as we have held above, the sales of unmarked toys by Takara in Japan before the assignment of the copyright fall within this phrase. In the absence of any prohibition on resale of these toys in the United States, the purchasers were free to sell them here. To be sure, the requirement of § 405(a)(2) to add notice is limited to copies "that are distributed to the public in the United States," but it seems significant that Congress did not here repeat the words "by authority of the copyright owner."

We are content, however, to leave undecided the question whether Hasbro would be obligated under § 405(a)(2) to make a reasonable effort to affix notice even with respect to unmarked toys distributed in the United States by persons other than itself or Takara. At this juncture, Sparkle has yet to produce credible evidence that any of the unmarked toys have been publicly distributed in the United States *at all,* let alone evidence of who distributed them. Whether any unmarked toys were introduced into the United States and, if so, who introduced them and what efforts to mark them would be reasonable are questions that can be resolved at trial when Hasbro seeks a permanent injunction.

Sparkle further alleges that Hasbro failed to advise the Copyright Office of the prior sales of the unmarked toys by Takara when applying for registration and argues that this constituted fraud on the Copyright Office, thereby invalidating Hasbro's copyrights. But Sparkle did not respond in brief or at argument to Hasbro's contention, which is supported by the record, that the Copyright Office was informed of the sales of the unmarked toys when registration was made. Sparkle likewise has not shown that Hasbro was even obligated under the Act to give the Copyright Office this information. The legislative history of § 405(a) suggests that no such obligation exists: "[S]ince the reasons for the omission have no bearing on the validity of copyright [under § 405(a)(2)], there would be no need for the [registration] application to refer to them." *House Report,* supra, at 147, *reprinted in* 1976 U.S.Code Cong. & Ad.News at 5763. Finally, this point was not raised in the district court, and we see no reason to permit Sparkle to raise it here for the first time.

Turning finally to Sparkle's claim that it should have been recognized as an innocent infringer under § 405(b), we think the record did not contain sufficient information for the district judge to have decided this issue, and he properly declined to do so. However, it should be promptly dealt with, either on an application by Hasbro for a permanent injunction or on one by Sparkle for a declaration of its rights.

Affirmed.

NOTES

1. *Berne Amendments.* Doubtless the most dramatic feature of the Berne amendments to the 1976 Copyright Act was to make the affixation of copyright notice optional rather than mandatory. Copyright owners nonetheless still have good reason to affix copyright notice to copies or phonorecords of their works. Affixation of notice may affect the copyright owner's monetary recovery for infringement. New subsections 401(d) and 402(d) provide as a general rule that if notice appears on the published copy or phonorecord to which the infringer had access, a court shall give no weight to a defense that innocent infringement mitigates actual or statutory damages. Also, apart from its legal consequence, a copyright notice serves as a "No Trespassing" sign that may effectively warn off otherwise unsuspecting infringers.

2. *Pre-Berne Notice Requirements.* As noted in the introduction to this section, a work's publication before March 1, 1989 without copyright notice in the required form and position could place the work in the public domain. The 1909 Copyright Act was more stringent in its requirements than the pre-Berne 1976 Act. For example, section 20 of the 1909 Act required notice on books and other printed publications to appear on the "title page or the page immediately following"; mislocation forfeited copyright. Some courts were relentless in their insistence on *punctilio*. In Booth v. Haggard, 184 F.2d 470, 87 U.S.P.Q. 141 (8th Cir.1950), the court concluded that the cover of plaintiff's book, bearing the phrase "1948–1949,

Kossuth County, Iowa TAM Service," was the book's title page and not page 3, which contained a full page of printed text bearing, at the top, the words "The 1948–1949 rural TAM for Kossuth County, Iowa." The notice, "Copyright 1948, R.C. Booth Enterprises, Harlan, Iowa," appeared at the bottom of page 3. The court held that plaintiff's notice was deficient because it did not appear on the title page or the page immediately following.

3. *Pre-Berne Excuses from Notice Requirements.* The 1909 Copyright Act excused faulty or omitted copyright notices on narrow grounds. Section 21 of the Act provided that "[w]here the copyright proprietor has sought to comply with the provisions of this title with respect to notice, the omission by accident or mistake of the prescribed notice from a particular copy or copies" would not invalidate the copyright. In National Comics Publications v. Fawcett Publications, 191 F.2d 594, 90 U.S.P.Q. 274 (2d Cir.1951), Judge Learned Hand suggested that a work would not lose copyright if the notice was omitted in violation of an agreement that conditioned the licensee's publication of the work on proper affixation of notice, an excuse roughly approximated in section 405(a) of the 1976 Act which excuses omissions of notice "in violation of an express requirement in writing" that the copies or phonorecords "bear the prescribed notice."

Section 405(a)(2), explicated in *Hasbro*, allows a five-year *locus poenitentiae* for publication without notice if the work is registered in the interim and a reasonable effort is made to place notice on copies publicly distributed in the United States after discovery of the omission. What constitutes "reasonable effort"? Where 900,000 copies of a work had been distributed without notice, it was not a "reasonable effort" for the copyright owner to send distributors 50,000 notice labels and offer to send additional labels if needed. Beacon Looms, Inc. v. S. Lichtenberg & Co., 552 F.Supp. 1305, 220 U.S.P.Q. 960 (S.D.N.Y.1982).

4. *Restoration of Copyright.* Foreign copyright owners, whose own countries did not impose affixation of notice as a condition to copyright protection, sometimes fell victim to the rule explored in *Hasbro* that publication without notice forfeited a United States copyright. In the case of qualifying foreign works, copyrights that had been lost for this or other formal reasons were restored in the 1990's by two trade-inspired measures, the North American Free Trade Agreement Implementation Act, Pub.L. No. 103–182, 107 Stat. 2057 (1993), and the Uruguay Round Agreements Act, Pub.L. No. 103–465, tit. 5, § 514, 108 Stat. 4809, 4976 (1994).

The NAFTA amendments took a first, small step by introducing a new section 104A into the 1976 Act enabling motion picture copyright owners to cure the omission of copyright notice from films first fixed or published in Canada or Mexico. A year later, the Uruguay Round amendments entirely rewrote section 104A to restore copyright in works coming from member countries of the Berne Union and the World Trade Organization. The Uruguay Round amendments restored copyright in all forms of works, not just motion pictures, and cured not only omissions of copyright notice but noncompliance with other formalities as well—failure to renew a copyright, for example, or to comply with domestic manufacturing requirements.

Restoration of copyright can come as an unpleasant surprise to the author or publisher who has created an unlicensed derivative work, such as a translation or motion picture screenplay, on the assumption—correct at the time—that the underlying work was in the public domain. Section 104A(d)(3) attempts to reconcile protection for restored works with investments made in reliance on their earlier public domain status by allowing a "reliance party" to "continue to exploit that [derivative] work for the duration of the restored copyright if the reliance party pays to the owner of the restored copyright reasonable compensation for conduct which would be subject to a remedy for infringement but for the provisions of this paragraph."

NOTE: PUBLICATION IN COPYRIGHT LAW

Publication has played an important role in U.S. copyright law from the first Copyright Act, Act of May 31, 1790, to the present. The definition and consequences of publication have changed over time.

1909 Act. Under the 1909 Copyright Act, publication marked the dividing line between state and federal copyright protection: As a rule, state common law copyright protected a work until its publication and federal statutory copyright protected the work from the moment of publication through the expiration of a fixed statutory term. If the work was published without the notice required by the 1909 Act, it fell into the public domain. As a rule, publication occurred under the 1909 Act when the copyright owner distributed copies of her work to the general public. The distribution, if not to the general public, could still constitute publication and divest common law copyright if the copyright owner imposed no express or implied restrictions on further distribution or copying. However, the distribution of copies to a limited class of persons and for a limited purpose did not divest common law copyright under the 1909 Act. Dissemination through means other than the distribution of copies—for example, the display of a painting in a public gallery—did not constitute publication under the 1909 Act.

Was it publication of the motion picture industry's famous Oscar statuette to award 158 of them between 1929 and 1941 without the required copyright notice? In Academy of Motion Picture Arts and Sciences v. Creative House Promotions, Inc., 728 F.Supp. 1442, 1447, 13 U.S.P.Q.2d 1435 (C.D.Cal.1989), a district court held that, because notice was omitted, the Oscar had fallen into the public domain. Although the mere public display of the statuette did not publish it, and although the Oscar was awarded "only to a select group of persons," the district court ruled that the Academy's purpose in distributing the statuette was not sufficiently limited to circumvent divestitive publication: "[F]rom the very beginning, the Academy has annually presented the Oscar not only to the recipients, but to promote the film industry." The Court of Appeals for the Ninth

Circuit reversed. "From 1929 until the end of the Oscar's common law copyright protection in 1941"—after which all of the statuettes bore the required copyright notice—"the Academy distributed personalized Oscar statuettes to a select group of distinguished artists. The Academy did not sell or directly profit from the award, nor did it encourage its further distribution." Academy of Motion Picture Arts and Sciences v. Creative House Promotions, Inc., 944 F.2d 1446, 1454, 19 U.S.P.Q.2d 1491, 1497 (9th Cir.1991).

1976 Act. The 1976 Copyright Act removed publication as the dividing line between state and federal protection. Protection under the 1976 Act begins not with a work's publication but, rather, with its first fixation in a tangible medium of expression. Publication nonetheless retains considerable importance under the 1976 Act. If a work was published without copyright notice before the effective date of the Berne amendments, March 1, 1989, and if one of the Act's curative provisions did not save the copyright, the work fell into the public domain. Also, although the 1976 Act measures the statutory term of copyright for most purposes by the life of the author plus seventy years, it measures the term of protection for anonymous and pseudonymous works and works made for hire by ninety-five years from the year of the work's first publication or 120 years from its creation, whichever expires first. Section 101 of the 1976 Act defines publication in terms that borrow extensively from judicial decisions under the 1909 Act. Publication is "the distribution of copies or phonorecords of a work to the public by sale or other transfer of ownership, or by rental, lease, or lending. The offering to distribute copies or phonorecords to a group of persons for purposes of further distribution, public performance, or public display, constitutes publication. A public performance or display of a work does not of itself constitute publication."

b. Registration and Deposit

Benjamin Kaplan, The Registration of Copyright

Study No. 17, Subcommittee on Patents, Trademarks, and Copyrights, Senate Committee on the Judiciary, 86th Cong., 2d Sess. 35–36, 41 (Comm.Print 1960).

1. Record Material

The chief record material flowing into the Copyright Office in consequence of the various provisions of the act consists of applications for original registration and works (or substitutes) deposited therewith; applications for renewal of copyright; assignments and related documents; notices of use and notices of intention to use. The records of the Copyright Office are built fundamentally upon this submitted material. Library of Congress collections are fed from the deposited copies. . . .

3. Examination of Applications and Deposits

When applications are received in the Copyright Office, the Examining Division scrutinizes them together with the accompanying deposited copies.

The check is for compliance with law, but the examiner does not and cannot investigate at large; he generally confines himself to the application and the deposited copies; occasionally, when put on inquiry by this internal examination, he may go elsewhere to relevant records of the Copyright Office. He is certainly not expected to check whether the work duplicates a previously copyrighted work or a work in the public domain. He checks for adequacy of the notice of copyright; agreement in dates, names, etc., between the application and the deposited copies; propriety of the "class" in which copyright is claimed; evident copyrightability of the work, and some other matters. The various forms of letters sent to claimants calling attention to errors spotted by the examiners, and usually soliciting corrections by the claimants, are revealing of the kind of examination that is conducted, as is section 202.2 of the Copyright Office regulations, listing common defects in the notice.

The Register has stated that an examiner is expected to deal with about 40 registrations per day. With respect to perhaps 15 percent of the applications correspondence with the claimant becomes necessary. As to rejections, the Register's annual report for fiscal 1957 says:

> Approximately 3 percent of the applications filed during the fiscal year were rejected.... Most rejections were in connection with published works lacking notice of copyright, uncopyrightable items, and works other than books, periodicals, or musical compositions, although many renewal applications had to be rejected because of untimely filing (p. 2).

Reasons are given for rejections and claimants are permitted to present arguments in writing and orally. There is no formally established procedure by which a claimant or other interested party can secure review of a decision within the Copyright Office; but apparently informal "appeal" lies to the Chief or Assistant Chief of the Examining Division, with final resort to the Register. The policy of the Office, as we have seen, is to be liberal in registering claims.

Assignments and related instruments appearing on their face to relate to copyrights and to be properly executed are not checked but are immediately recorded. Renewal applications are checked and in ordinary cases will not be registered unless original registration has been accomplished.

When a claimant files his application and makes deposit he is in effect submitting himself to an official determination of whether he has complied with the law. The check carried out by the Examining Division is a means of enforcing both formal and substantive requirements including provisions or standards governing notice, copyrightability, manufacturing, import, etc. As a practical matter this check is perhaps the chief official instrument of law enforcement. Were it not for administrative surveillance "at the source," a considerable number of works belonging in the public domain would circulate with notice of copyright inhibiting access to the works. In many cases the check serves to advise or warn claimants about legal requirements with which they are then quite willing to comply. The fact that applications are officially examined puts a certain pressure on claim-

FEE CHANGES
Fees are effective through June 30, 2002. After that date, check the Copyright Office Website at www.loc.gov/copyright or call (202) 707-3000 for current fee information.

FORM TX
For a Nondramatic Literary Work
UNITED STATES COPYRIGHT OFFICE

REGISTRATION NUMBER

_____

TX _____ TXU

EFFECTIVE DATE OF REGISTRATION

_____
Month   Day   Year

DO NOT WRITE ABOVE THIS LINE. IF YOU NEED MORE SPACE, USE A SEPARATE CONTINUATION SHEET.

1

TITLE OF THIS WORK ▼

PREVIOUS OR ALTERNATIVE TITLES ▼

PUBLICATION AS A CONTRIBUTION If this work was published as a contribution to a periodical, serial, or collection, give information about the collective work in which the contribution appeared.   Title of Collective Work ▼

If published in a periodical or serial give: Volume ▼   Number ▼   Issue Date ▼   On Pages ▼

2 a

NAME OF AUTHOR ▼

DATES OF BIRTH AND DEATH
Year Born ▼   Year Died ▼

Was this contribution to the work a "work made for hire"?
☐ Yes
☐ No

AUTHOR'S NATIONALITY OR DOMICILE
Name of Country
OR { Citizen of ▶ _____
Domiciled in ▶ _____

WAS THIS AUTHOR'S CONTRIBUTION TO THE WORK
Anonymous?   ☐ Yes ☐ No
Pseudonymous? ☐ Yes ☐ No
If the answer to either of these questions is "Yes," see detailed instructions.

NATURE OF AUTHORSHIP Briefly describe nature of material created by this author in which copyright is claimed. ▼

NOTE

Under the law, the "author" of a "work made for hire" is generally the employer, not the employee (see instructions). For any part of this work that was "made for hire" check "Yes" in the space provided, give the employer (or other person for whom the work was prepared) as "Author" of that part, and leave the space for dates of birth and death blank.

b

NAME OF AUTHOR ▼

DATES OF BIRTH AND DEATH
Year Born ▼   Year Died ▼

Was this contribution to the work a "work made for hire"?
☐ Yes
☐ No

AUTHOR'S NATIONALITY OR DOMICILE
Name of Country
OR { Citizen of ▶ _____
Domiciled in ▶ _____

WAS THIS AUTHOR'S CONTRIBUTION TO THE WORK
Anonymous?   ☐ Yes ☐ No
Pseudonymous? ☐ Yes ☐ No
If the answer to either of these questions is "Yes," see detailed instructions.

NATURE OF AUTHORSHIP Briefly describe nature of material created by this author in which copyright is claimed. ▼

c

NAME OF AUTHOR ▼

DATES OF BIRTH AND DEATH
Year Born ▼   Year Died ▼

Was this contribution to the work a "work made for hire"?
☐ Yes
☐ No

AUTHOR'S NATIONALITY OR DOMICILE
Name of Country
OR { Citizen of ▶ _____
Domiciled in ▶ _____

WAS THIS AUTHOR'S CONTRIBUTION TO THE WORK
Anonymous?   ☐ Yes ☐ No
Pseudonymous? ☐ Yes ☐ No
If the answer to either of these questions is "Yes," see detailed instructions.

NATURE OF AUTHORSHIP Briefly describe nature of material created by this author in which copyright is claimed. ▼

3 a

YEAR IN WHICH CREATION OF THIS WORK WAS COMPLETED   This information must be given in all cases.
◀ Year

b DATE AND NATION OF FIRST PUBLICATION OF THIS PARTICULAR WORK
Complete this information ONLY if this work has been published.
Month ▶ _____ Day ▶ _____ Year ▶ _____
◀ Nation

4

See instructions before completing this space.

COPYRIGHT CLAIMANT(S) Name and address must be given even if the claimant is the same as the author given in space 2. ▼

TRANSFER If the claimant(s) named here in space 4 is (are) different from the author(s) named in space 2, give a brief statement of how the claimant(s) obtained ownership of the copyright. ▼

DO NOT WRITE HERE OFFICE USE ONLY

APPLICATION RECEIVED

ONE DEPOSIT RECEIVED

TWO DEPOSITS RECEIVED

FUNDS RECEIVED

MORE ON BACK ▶   • Complete all applicable spaces (numbers 5-9) on the reverse side of this page.
• See detailed instructions.   • Sign the form at line 8.

DO NOT WRITE HERE
Page 1 of _____ pages

EXAMINED BY	FORM TX
CHECKED BY	
☐ CORRESPONDENCE Yes	FOR COPYRIGHT OFFICE USE ONLY

DO NOT WRITE ABOVE THIS LINE. IF YOU NEED MORE SPACE, USE A SEPARATE CONTINUATION SHEET.

PREVIOUS REGISTRATION Has registration for this work, or for an earlier version of this work, already been made in the Copyright Office?

☐ Yes ☐ No If your answer is "Yes," why is another registration being sought? (Check appropriate box.) ▼

a. ☐ This is the first published edition of a work previously registered in unpublished form.

b. ☐ This is the first application submitted by this author as copyright claimant.

c. ☐ This is a changed version of the work, as shown by space 6 on this application.

If your answer is "Yes," give: **Previous Registration Number** ▶   **Year of Registration** ▶

5

DERIVATIVE WORK OR COMPILATION

Preexisting Material Identify any preexisting work or works that this work is based on or incorporates. ▼

a

6

Material Added to This Work Give a brief, general statement of the material that has been added to this work and in which copyright is claimed. ▼

b

See instructions before completing this space.

DEPOSIT ACCOUNT If the registration fee is to be charged to a Deposit Account established in the Copyright Office, give name and number of Account.
Name ▼   **Account Number** ▼

a

7

CORRESPONDENCE Give name and address to which correspondence about this application should be sent.   Name/Address/Apt/City/State/ZIP ▼

b

Area code and daytime telephone number ▶   Fax number ▶

Email ▶

CERTIFICATION* I, the undersigned, hereby certify that I am the

Check only one ▶
☐ author
☐ other copyright claimant
☐ owner of exclusive right(s)
☐ authorized agent of _____
Name of author or other copyright claimant, or owner of exclusive right(s) ▲

of the work identified in this application and that the statements made by me in this application are correct to the best of my knowledge.

8

Typed or printed name and date ▼ If this application gives a date of publication in space 3, do not sign and submit it before that date.

_____ Date ▶ _____

Handwritten signature (X) ▼

X _

Certificate will be mailed in window envelope to this address:	Name ▼	YOU MUST • Complete all necessary spaces • Sign your application in space 8
	Number/Street/Apt ▼	SEND ALL 3 ELEMENTS IN THE SAME PACKAGE: 1. Application form 2. Nonrefundable filing fee in check or money order payable to Register of Copyrights 3. Deposit material
	City/State/ZIP ▼	MAIL TO: Library of Congress Copyright Office 101 Independence Avenue, S.E. Washington, D.C. 20559-6000

As of July 1, 1999, the filing fee for Form TX is $30.

9

*17 U.S.C. § 506(e): Any person who knowingly makes a false representation of a material fact in the application for copyright registration provided for by section 409, or in any written statement filed in connection with the application, shall be fined not more than $2,500.

June 1999—200,000
WEB REV: June 1999   ⬤ PRINTED ON RECYCLED PAPER   ☆U.S. GOVERNMENT PRINTING OFFICE: 1999-454-879/49

ants to examine and attempt to comply with the law before attempting registration.

Administrative examination of claims to copyright is however far from complete. It is necessarily limited in the great majority of cases to a check of obvious points arising on the claimants' ex parte submissions. Invalid claims may slip by; and when they do, they carry a kind of official imprimatur which may itself operate unjustly in creating a preserve that is practically effective although legally unjustified.

The Copyright Office policy of registering doubtful claims can be objected to on the ground that it fosters "monopolies" which are in last analysis illegal. On the other side, objection has been voiced to any administrative decisions of invalidity. As these decisions are not conclusive on the courts, it has been argued that the Office should abandon the whole effort to examine claims and register all claims as such, so that the contentions of interested parties regarding particular works will be disclosed of record, giving users and others a better basis for deciding how they should act.

ORIGINAL APPALACHIAN ARTWORKS, INC. v. THE TOY LOFT, INC., 684 F.2d 821, 215 U.S.P.Q. 745 (11th Cir.1982), KRAVITCH, J.: Lawson's third defense is that Roberts is guilty of fraud and unclean hands in failing to supply certain relevant information on the copyright application. Specifically, Lawson cites Roberts' failure to list Ms. Morehead as a co-author and his failure to complete item six on the copyright application headed "Compilation or Derivative Work" as the fraudulent omissions which make OAA's copyright unenforceable.

In Russ Berrie & Co., Inc. v. Jerry Elsner Co., 482 F.Supp. 980, 205 U.S.P.Q. 320 (S.D.N.Y.1980), the court found that the copyright holder had intentionally failed to inform the copyright office that his copyrighted stuffed gorilla was based on a pre-existing Japanese gorilla, and held that "the knowing failure to advise the copyright office of facts which might have occasioned a rejection of the application constitutes reason for holding the copyright invalid." Id. at 988. Similar situations occurred in Vogue Ring Creations, Inc. v. Hardman, 410 F.Supp. 609, 190 U.S.P.Q. 329 (D.R.I.1976) (unexplained omission of pre-existing work coupled with other misleading conduct made copyright unenforceable); and Ross Products, Inc. v. New York Merchandise Co., 242 F.Supp. 878, 146 U.S.P.Q. 107 (S.D.N.Y. 1965) (failure to indicate prior publication of work in Japan raised issue of whether omission was purposeful thus invalidating copyright).

While these cases establish that omissions or misrepresentations in a copyright application can render the registration invalid, a common element among them has been intentional or purposeful concealment of relevant information. Where this element of "scienter" is lacking, courts generally have upheld the copyright.

The evidence in this case fails to show the scienter element necessary for Lawson to assert his claim successfully. Roberts explained that his omission of Morehead as a co-author was due to Morehead's leaving the doll operation in February 1978 and indicating she wanted nothing further to do with the company. Given that Roberts freely admitted he and Morehead had collaborated on the dolls, and that several newspaper and magazine articles during 1977 indicated that the dolls were the joint product of Roberts and Morehead, we find it impossible to ascribe to this omission an intent to mislead. As to item 6, the pre-existing works, the undisputed evidence showed that Roberts and Allen completed this item initially in some detail, even indicating that the dolls were derived in part from viewing other artists' soft-sculpture work. Although item 6 was left blank in the application that finally was filed with the copyright office, the sole reason for this omission was that after speaking to copyright office personnel, Roberts and Allen thought that the information was unnecessary. Accordingly, we reject Lawson's assertion that OAA's copyright is unenforceable due to fraud on the Copyright Office.

NOTES

1. *Reasons to Register.* Registration is not a condition of copyright protection, and a copyright owner may obtain registration for her work at any time during the copyright term. The 1976 Copyright Act offers several incentives to prompt registration. As indicated in the *Hasbro* case, page 570, above, section 405(a)(2) allows registration to cure errors or omissions in copyright notice only if "registration for the work has been made before or is made within five years after the publication without notice." Section 410(c) limits the automatic prima facie effect of registration certificates to registrations made "before or within five years after first publication of the work." As a general rule, section 412 provides that no award of statutory damages or attorney's fees can be made for "(1) any infringement of copyright in an unpublished work commenced before the effective date of its registration; or (2) any infringement of copyright commenced after first publication of the work and before the effective date of its registration, unless such registration is made within three months after the first publication of the work."

2. *Registration as a Condition to Suit.* Before the effective date of the Berne Implementation Act, March 1, 1989, section 411(a) of the 1976 Act generally required copyright owners to obtain registration in order to file a copyright infringement action. As amended, section 411(a) retains this requirement for works originating in the United States, but eliminates the requirement for works originating in countries that are party to one or more of several copyright treaties, principally the Berne Convention. The amendments' exemption for works originating in Berne member countries was a compromise between the Senate bill—which viewed registration as a formal condition to protection proscribed by the Berne Convention—and the House bill—which did not view registration as a condition to protection, and would have retained the requirement for both domestic and foreign works. See Joint Explanatory Statement on House–Senate Compromise Incorporated in Senate Amendment to H.R. 4262, 134 Cong.Rec. H10095 (daily ed. Oct. 12, 1988).

Under the 1909 Copyright Act, a copyright owner could not bring an infringement action until registration of its claim to copyright had been completed. If the Register refused registration, an infringement suit had to await the copyright owner's success in a direct action against the Register. Vacheron & Constantin–Le Coultre Watches, Inc. v. Benrus Watch Co., 260 F.2d 637, 119 U.S.P.Q. 189 (2d Cir.1958). Section 411(a) of the 1976 Act reversed the *Vacheron* rule and allows the applicant to institute an infringement action if the "deposit, application and fee required for registration have been delivered to the Copyright Office in proper form and registration has been refused." The copyright owner must give notice of the action and a copy of the complaint to the Register, who is allowed to intervene.

Copyright owners, particularly in fast-paced industries like newspaper and magazine publishing, sometimes need an injunction within days of publication and cannot abide the delay that registration entails. Does section 411(a) enable them to bring an infringement action without registration? Compare sections 410(d) and 411(b).

3. *Classification.* Application Form TX, reproduced above, covers nondramatic literary works such as fiction, nonfiction, poetry, directories, catalogs, advertising copy and periodicals. The Register of Copyrights has prescribed four other classes of works for purposes of copyright registration. Class PA covers works "prepared for the purpose of being performed directly before an audience or indirectly by means of a device or process," including musical works, dramatic works, choreographic works, and motion pictures and other audiovisual works. Class VA encompasses pictorial, graphic and sculptural works such as photographs, maps, advertisements, and works of fine, graphic and applied arts. Class SR covers "all published and unpublished sound recordings fixed on and after February 15, 1972," and Class SE covers "serials," such as periodicals and newspapers. 37 C.F.R. § 202.3(b) (1995).

4. *Deposit.* Deposit of copies or phonorecords of a copyrighted work in the Copyright Office, though not a condition to copyright protection, is nonetheless mandatory. Failure to deposit copies or phonorecords within three months after receiving a written demand for deposit from the Register of Copyrights will expose the person obligated to make the deposit to fines and charges. 1976 Act § 407(d). Section 407's purpose is to supply the Library of Congress with copies and phonorecords for its collections.

5. *"Secure Tests."* The Copyright Office's "secure test" regulations attempt to reconcile the registration and deposit provisions with interests in closeting some copyrighted information—such as questions repeatedly used in standardized tests—from public view. "In the case of tests, and answer material for tests, published separately from other literary works, the deposit of one complete copy will suffice in lieu of two copies. In the case of any secure test the Copyright Office will return the deposit to the applicant promptly after examination: Provided, That sufficient portions, description, or the like are retained so as to constitute a sufficient archival record of the deposit." 37 C.F.R. 202.20(c)(2)(vi) (2001). The Regulations define "secure test" in part as "a nonmarketed test administered under supervision at specified centers on specific dates, all copies of which are accounted for and either destroyed or returned to restricted locked storage following each administration." 37 C.F.R. § 202.20(b)(4) (2001).

In National Conference of Bar Examiners v. Multistate Legal Studies, Inc., 692 F.2d 478, 216 U.S.P.Q. 279 (7th Cir.1982), cert. denied, 464 U.S. 814, 104 S.Ct. 69, 78 L.Ed.2d 83 (1983), the copyright owner of the multistate portion of state bar examinations sued a bar review program for reconstructing and reproducing questions from its exam. The defendant answered that the secure test regulations, under which the plaintiff had obtained its copyright registration, exceeded the Register's statutory authority and that, if the statute authorized the regulation, it violated the Constitution's copyright clause, art. 1, § 8, cl. 8.

The court rejected both arguments. Against the argument that section 704(d) requires the Library of Congress to retain the entire deposit of an unpublished work during the copyright term, and that section 408(b) requires a deposit to include "in the case of unpublished works, one complete copy or phonorecord," the court cited section 408(c)(1)'s provision that "[t]he Register of Copyrights is authorized to specify by regulation the administrative classes into which works are to be placed for purposes of deposit and registration, and the nature of the copies or phonorecords to be deposited in the various classes specified. The regulations may require or permit, for particular classes, the deposit of identifying material instead of copies or phonorecords, the deposit of only one copy or phonorecord where two would normally be required, or a single registration for a group of related works." 692 F.2d at 483.

The court also rejected defendant's argument "that the regulation serves to conceal the deposited material from public view and thus defeats the purpose of copyright registration as mandated by art. I, § 8 cl. 8, of the United States Constitution. . . ." Against the claim that "actual copies are necessary to provide a public record that delineates the scope of the copyright monopoly," the court concluded that "the statutory scheme of the Copyright Act demonstrates that the deposit provisions are not for the purposes of disclosure." 692 F.2d at 484–86.

2. STATUTORY SUBJECT MATTER

See Statute Supplement 17 U.S.C.A. §§ 101–105.

Copyright Law Revision, H.R. Rep. No. 94–1476

94th Cong., 2d Sess. 51–58 (1976).

Section 102. General Subject Matter of Copyright

"Original Works of Authorship"

The two fundamental criteria of copyright protection—originality and fixation in tangible form—are restated in the first sentence of this cornerstone provision. The phrase "original works of authorship," which is purposely left undefined, is intended to incorporate without change the standard of originality established by the courts under the present copyright statute. This standard does not include requirements of novelty, ingenuity, or esthetic merit, and there is no intention to enlarge the standard of copyright protection to require them.

In using the phrase "original works of authorship," rather than "all the writings of an author" now in section 4 of the statute, the committee's purpose is to avoid exhausting the constitutional power of Congress to legislate in this field, and to eliminate the uncertainties arising from the latter phrase. Since the present statutory language is substantially the same as the empowering language of the Constitution, a recurring question has been whether the statutory and the constitutional provisions are coextensive. If so, the courts would be faced with the alternative of holding copyrightable something that Congress clearly did not intend to protect, or of holding constitutionally incapable of copyright something that Congress might one day want to protect. To avoid these equally undesirable results, the courts have indicated that "all the writings of an author" under the present statute is narrower in scope than the "writings" of "authors" referred to in the Constitution. The bill avoids this dilemma by using a different phrase—"original works of authorship"—in characterizing the general subject matter of statutory copyright protection.

The history of copyright law has been one of gradual expansion in the types of works accorded protection, and the subject matter affected by this expansion has fallen into two general categories. In the first, scientific discoveries and technological developments have made possible new forms of creative expression that never existed before. In some of these cases the new expressive forms—electronic music, filmstrips, and computer programs, for example—could be regarded as an extension of copyrightable subject matter Congress had already intended to protect, and were thus considered copyrightable from the outset without the need of new legislation. In other cases, such as photographs, sound recordings, and motion pictures, statutory enactment was deemed necessary to give them full recognition as copyrightable works.

Authors are continually finding new ways of expressing themselves, but it is impossible to foresee the forms that these new expressive methods will take. The bill does not intend either to freeze the scope of copyrightable subject matter at the present stage of communications technology or to allow unlimited expansion into areas completely outside the present congressional intent. Section 102 implies neither that that subject matter is unlimited nor that new forms of expression within that general area of subject matter would necessarily be unprotected.

The historic expansion of copyright has also applied to forms of expression which, although in existence for generations or centuries, have only gradually come to be recognized as creative and worthy of protection. The first copyright statute in this country, enacted in 1790, designated only "maps, charts, and books"; major forms of expression such as music, drama, and works of art achieved specific statutory recognition only in later enactments. Although the coverage of the present statute is very broad, and would be broadened further by the explicit recognition of all forms of choreography, there are unquestionably other areas of existing subject matter that this bill does not propose to protect but that future Congresses may want to.

Fixation in Tangible Form. . . .

Under the first sentence of the definition of "fixed" in section 101, a work would be considered "fixed in a tangible medium of expression" if there has been an authorized embodiment in a copy or phonorecord and if that embodiment "is sufficiently permanent or stable" to permit the work "to be perceived, reproduced, or otherwise communicated for a period of more than transitory duration." The second sentence makes clear that, in the case of "a work consisting of sounds, images, or both, that are being transmitted," the work is regarded as "fixed" if a fixation is being made at the same time as the transmission.

Under this definition "copies" and "phonorecords" together will comprise all of the material objects in which copyrightable works are capable of being fixed. The definitions of these terms in section 101, together with their usage in section 102 and throughout the bill, reflect a fundamental distinction between the "original work" which is the product of "authorship" and the multitude of material objects in which it can be embodied. Thus, in the sense of the bill, a "book" is not a work of authorship, but is a particular kind of "copy." Instead, the author may write a "literary work," which in turn can be embodied in a wide range of "copies" and "phonorecords," including books, periodicals, computer punch cards, microfilm, tape recordings, and so forth. It is possible to have an "original work of authorship" without having a "copy" or "phonorecord" embodying it, and it is also possible to have a "copy" or "phonorecord" embodying something that does not qualify as an "original work of authorship." The two essential elements—original work and tangible object—must merge through fixation in order to produce subject matter copyrightable under the statute.

Categories of Copyrightable Works

The second sentence of section 102 lists seven broad categories which the concept of "works of authorship" is said to "include." The use of the word "include," as defined in section 101, makes clear that the listing is "illustrative and not limitative," and that the seven categories do not necessarily exhaust the scope of "original works of authorship" that the bill is intended to protect. Rather, the list sets out the general area of copyrightable subject matter, but with sufficient flexibility to free the courts from rigid or outmoded concepts of the scope of particular categories. The items are also overlapping in the sense that a work falling within one class may encompass works coming within some or all of the other categories. In the aggregate, the list covers all classes of works now specified in section 5 of title 17; in addition, it specifically enumerates "pantomimes and choreographic works".

Of the seven items listed, four are defined in section 101. The three undefined categories—"musical works," "dramatic works," and "pantomimes and choreographic works"—have fairly settled meanings. There is no need, for example, to specify the copyrightability of electronic or concrete music in the statute since the form of a work would no longer be of any importance, nor is it necessary to specify that "choreographic works" do not include social dance steps and simple routines.

The four items defined in section 101 are "literary works," "pictorial, graphic, and sculptural works," "motion pictures and audiovisual works," and "sound recordings." In each of these cases, definitions are needed not only because the meaning of the term itself is unsettled but also because the distinction between "work" and "material object" requires clarification. The term "literary works" does not connote any criterion of literary merit or qualitative value: it includes catalogs, directories, and similar factual reference, or instructional works and compilations of data. It also includes computer data bases, and computer programs to the extent that they incorporate authorship in the programmer's expression of original ideas, as distinguished from the ideas themselves.

Correspondingly, the definition of "pictorial, graphic, and sculptural works" carries with it no implied criterion of artistic taste, aesthetic value, or intrinsic quality. The term is intended to comprise not only "works of art" in the traditional sense but also works of graphic art and illustration, art reproductions, plans and drawings, photographs and reproductions of them, maps, charts, globes, and other cartographic works, works of these kinds intended for use in advertising and commerce, and works of "applied art." There is no intention whatever to narrow the scope of the subject matter now characterized in section 5(k) as "prints or labels used for articles of merchandise." However, since this terminology suggests the material object in which a work is embodied rather than the work itself, the bill does not mention this category separately. . . .

Enactment of Public Law 92–140 in 1971 marked the first recognition in American copyright law of sound recordings as copyrightable works. As defined in section 101, copyrightable "sound recordings" are original works of authorship comprising an aggregate of musical, spoken, or other sounds that have been fixed in tangible form. The copyrightable work comprises the aggregation of sounds and not the tangible medium of fixation. Thus, "sound recordings" as copyrightable subject matter are distinguished from "phonorecords," the latter being physical objects in which sounds are fixed. They are also distinguished from any copyrighted literary, dramatic, or musical works that may be reproduced on a "phonorecord."

As a class of subject matter, sound recordings are clearly within the scope of the "writings of an author" capable of protection under the Constitution, and the extension of limited statutory protection to them was too long delayed. Aside from cases in which sounds are fixed by some purely mechanical means without originality of any kind, the copyright protection that would prevent the reproduction and distribution of unauthorized phonorecords of sound recordings is clearly justified.

The copyrightable elements in a sound recording will usually, though not always, involve "authorship" both on the part of the performers whose performance is captured and on the part of the record producer responsible for setting up the recording session, capturing and electronically processing the sounds, and compiling and editing them to make the final sound recording. There may, however, be cases where the record producer's contribution is so minimal that the performance is the only copyrightable element in the work, and there may be cases (for example, recordings of birdcalls, sounds of racing cars, et cetera) where only the record producer's contribution is copyrightable.

Sound tracks of motion pictures, long a nebulous area in American copyright law, are specifically included in the definition of "motion pictures," and excluded in the definition of "sound recordings." To be a "motion picture," as defined, requires three elements: (1) a series of images, (2) the capability of showing the images in certain successive order, and (3) an impression of motion when the images are thus shown. Coupled with the basic requirements of original authorship and fixation in tangible form, this definition encompasses a wide range of cinematographic works embodied in films, tapes, video disks, and other media. However, it would not include: (1) unauthorized fixations of live performances or telecasts, (2) live telecasts that are not fixed simultaneously with their transmission, or (3) filmstrips and slide sets which, although consisting of a series of images intended to be shown in succession, are not capable of conveying an impression of motion.

On the other hand, the bill equates audiovisual materials such as filmstrips, slide sets, and sets of transparencies with "motion pictures" rather than with "pictorial, graphic, and sculptural works." Their sequential showing is closer to a "performance" than to a "display," and the definition of "audiovisual works," which applies also to "motion pictures," embraces works consisting of a series of related images that are by their nature, intended for showing by means of projectors or other devices.

Baker v. Selden

Supreme Court of the United States, 1879.
101 U.S. (11 Otto) 99, 25 L.Ed. 841.

Mr. Justice BRADLEY delivered the opinion of the court.

Charles Selden, the testator of the complainant in this case, in the year 1859 took the requisite steps for obtaining the copyright of a book, entitled "Selden's Condensed Ledger, or Bookkeeping Simplified," the object of which was to exhibit and explain a peculiar system of book-keeping. In 1860 and 1861, he took the copyright of several other books, containing additions to and improvements upon the said system. The bill of complaint was filed against the defendant, Baker, for an alleged infringement of these copyrights. The latter, in his answer, denied that Selden was the author or designer of the books, and denied the infringement charged, and contends on the argument that the matter alleged to be infringed is not a lawful subject of copyright.

The parties went into proofs, and the various books of the complainant, as well as those sold and used by the defendant, were exhibited before the examiner, and witnesses were examined on both sides. A decree was rendered for the complainant, and the defendant appealed.

The book or series of books of which the complainant claims the copyright consists of an introductory essay explaining the system of book-keeping referred to, to which are annexed certain forms or blanks, consisting of ruled lines, and headings, illustrating the system and showing how it is to be used and carried out in practice. This system effects the same results as book-keeping by double entry; but, by a peculiar arrangement of columns and headings, presents the entire operation, of a day, a week, or a month, on a single page, or on two pages facing each other, in an account-book. The defendant uses a similar plan so far as results are concerned; but makes a different arrangement of the columns, and uses different headings. If the complainant's testator had the exclusive right to the use of the system explained in his book, it would be difficult to contend that the defendant does not infringe it, notwithstanding the difference in his form of arrangement; but if it be assumed that the system is open to the public use, it seems to be equally difficult to contend that the books made and sold by the defendant are a violation of the copyright of the complainant's book considered merely as a book explanatory of the system. Where the truths of a science or the methods of an art are the common property of the whole world, any author has the right to express the one, or explain and use the other, in his own way. As an author, Selden explained the system in a particular way. It may be conceded that Baker makes and uses account-books arranged on substantially the same system; but the proof fails to show that he has violated the copyright of Selden's book, regarding the latter merely as an explanatory work; or that he has infringed Selden's right in any way, unless the latter became entitled to an exclusive right in the system.

The evidence of the complainant is principally directed to the object of showing that Baker uses the same system as that which is explained and illustrated in Selden's books. It becomes important, therefore, to determine whether, in obtaining the copyright of his books, he secured the exclusive right to the use of the system or method of book-keeping which the said books are intended to illustrate and explain. It is contended that he has secured such exclusive right, because no one can use the system without using substantially the same ruled lines and headings which he has appended to his books in illustration of it. In other words, it is contended that the ruled lines and headings, given to illustrate the system, are a part of the book, and, as such, are secured by the copyright; and that no one can make or use similar ruled lines and headings, or ruled lines and headings made and arranged on substantially the same system, without violating the copyright. And this is really the question to be decided in this case. Stated in another form, the question is, whether the exclusive property in a system of book-keeping can be claimed, under the law of copyright, by means of a book in which that system is explained? The complainant's bill, and the case made under it, are based on the hypothesis that it can be.

It cannot be pretended, and indeed it is not seriously urged, that the ruled lines of the complainant's account-book can be claimed under any special class of objects, other than books, named in the law of copyright existing in 1859. The law then in force was that of 1831, and specified only books, maps, charts, musical compositions, prints, and engravings. An account-book, consisting of ruled lines and blank columns, cannot be called by any of these names unless by that of a book.

There is no doubt that a work on the subject of book-keeping, though only explanatory of well-known systems, may be the subject of a copyright; but, then, it is claimed only as a book. Such a book may be explanatory either of old systems, or of an entirely new system; and, considered as a book, as the work of an author, conveying information on the subject of book-keeping, and containing detailed explanations of the art, it may be a very valuable acquisition to the practical knowledge of the community. But there is a clear distinction between the book, as such, and the art which it is intended to illustrate. The mere statement of the proposition is so evident, that it requires hardly any argument to support it. The same distinction may be predicated of every other art as well as that of book-keeping. A treatise on the composition and use of medicines, be they old or new; on the construction and use of ploughs, or watches, or churns; or on the mixture and application of colors for painting or dyeing; or on the mode of drawing lines to produce the effect of perspective,—would be the subject of copyright; but no one would contend that the copyright of the treatise would give the exclusive right to the art or manufacture described therein. The copyright of the book, if not pirated from other works, would be valid without regard to the novelty, or want of novelty, of its subject-matter. The novelty of the art or thing described or explained has nothing to do with the validity of the copyright. To give to the author of the book an exclusive property in the art described therein, when no examination of its novelty has ever been officially made, would be a surprise and a fraud upon the public. That is the province of letters-patent, not of copyright. The claim to an invention or discovery of an art or manufacture must be subjected to the examination of the Patent Office before an exclusive right therein can be obtained; and it can only be secured by a patent from the government.

The difference between the two things, letters-patent and copyright, may be illustrated by reference to the subjects just enumerated. Take the case of medicines. Certain mixtures are found to be of great value in the healing art. If the discoverer writes and publishes a book on the subject (as regular physicians generally do), he gains no exclusive right to the manufacture and sale of the medicine; he gives that to the public. If he desires to acquire such exclusive right, he must obtain a patent for the mixture as a new art, manufacture, or composition of matter. He may copyright his book, if he pleases; but that only secures to him the exclusive right of printing and publishing his book. So of all other inventions or discoveries.

The copyright of a book on perspective, no matter how many drawings and illustrations it may contain, gives no exclusive right to the modes of drawing described, though they may never have been known or used before. By publishing the book, without getting a patent for the art, the latter is given to the public. The fact that the art described in the book by illustrations of lines and figures which are reproduced in practice in the application of the art, makes no difference. Those illustrations are the mere language employed by the author to convey his ideas more clearly. Had he used words of description instead of diagrams (which merely stand in the place of words), there could not be the slightest doubt that others, applying the art to practical use, might lawfully draw the lines and diagrams which were in the author's mind, and which he thus described by words in his book.

The copyright of a work on mathematical science cannot give to the author an exclusive right to the methods of operation which he propounds, or to the diagrams which he employs to explain them, so as to prevent an engineer from using them whenever occasion requires. The very object of publishing a book on science or the useful arts is to communicate to the world the useful knowledge which it contains. But this object would be frustrated if the knowledge could not be used without incurring the guilt of piracy of the book. And where the art it teaches cannot be used without employing the methods and diagrams used to illustrate the book, or such as are similar to them, such methods and diagrams are to be considered as necessary incidents to the art, and given therewith to the public; not given for the purpose of publication in other works explanatory of the art, but for the purpose of practical application.

Of course, these observations are not intended to apply to ornamental designs, or pictorial illustrations addressed to the taste. Of these it may be said, that their form is their essence, and their object, the production of pleasure in their contemplation. This is their final end. They are as much the product of genius and the result of composition, as are the lines of the poet or the historian's periods. On the other hand, the teachings of science and the rules and methods of useful art have their final end in application and use; and this application and use are what the public derive from the publication of a book which teaches them. But as embodied and taught in a literary composition or book, their essence consists only in their statement. This alone is what is secured by the copyright. The use by another of the same methods of statement, whether in words or illustrations, in a book published for teaching the art, would undoubtedly be an infringement of the copyright.

Recurring to the case before us, we observe that Charles Selden, by his books, explained and described a peculiar system of book-keeping, and illustrated his method by means of ruled lines and blank columns, with proper headings on a page, or on successive pages. Now, whilst no one has a right to print or publish his book, or any material part thereof, as a book intended to convey instruction in the art, any person may practice and use the art itself which he has described and illustrated therein. The use of the art is a totally different thing from a publication of the book explaining it. The copyright of a book on book-keeping cannot secure the exclusive right to make, sell, and use account-books prepared upon the plan set forth in such book. Whether the art might or might not have been patented, is a question which is not before us. It was not patented, and is open and free to the use of the public. And, of course, in using the art, the ruled lines and headings of accounts must necessarily be used as incident to it.

The plausibility of the claim put forward by the complainant in this case arises from a confusion of ideas produced by the peculiar nature of the art described in the books which have been made the subject of copyright. In describing the art, the illustrations and diagrams employed happen to correspond more closely than usual with the actual work performed by the operator who uses the art. Those illustrations and diagrams consist of ruled lines and headings of accounts; and it is similar ruled lines and headings of accounts which, in the application of the art, the book-keeper makes with his pen, or the stationer with his press; whilst in most other cases the diagrams and illustrations can only be represented in concrete forms of wood, metal, stone, or some other physical embodiment. But the principle is the same in all. The description of the art in a book, though entitled to the benefit of copyright, lays no foundation for an exclusive claim to the art itself. The object of the one is explanation; the object of the other is use. The former may be secured by copyright. The latter can only be secured, if it can be secured at all, by letters-patent. . . .

The conclusion to which we have come is, that blank account-books are not the subject of copyright; and that the mere copyright of Selden's book did not confer upon him the exclusive right to make and use account-books, ruled and arranged as designated by him and described and illustrated in said book.

The decree of the Circuit Court must be reversed, and the cause remanded with instructions to dismiss the complainant's bill; and it is so ordered.

NOTES

1. Copyright in computer programs is considered beginning at page 803, below. Copyright in industrial design is considered beginning at page 955, below.

2. *The Idea–Expression Distinction.* Section 102(b) of the 1976 Copyright Act enshrines the longstanding rule of Baker v. Selden: "In no case does copyright protection for an original work of authorship extend to any idea, procedure, process, system, method of operation, concept, principle, or discovery, regardless of the form in which it is described, explained, illustrated, or embodied in such work."

Baker v. Selden recognized the need for a legal distinction between functional works, such as treatises on bookkeeping, and fanciful works, such as "ornamental designs, or pictorial illustrations addressed to the taste. Of these it may be said, that their form is their essence, and their object, the production of pleasure is their contemplation." The distinction explains why functional and factual works characteristically receive a narrower scope of protection than do fanciful works. It also demonstrates that the term, "idea" is not to be taken literally, but rather should be viewed as a metaphor for a work's unprotected elements—method of operation in the case of functional works; basic elements of plot, theme and character in literary works; or line, color and perspective in works of visual art.

See generally Amy B. Cohen, Copyright Law and the Myth of Objectivity: The Idea–Expression Dichotomy and the Inevitability of Artistic Value Judgments, 66 Ind. L. J. 175 (1990); Edward Samuels, The Idea–Expression Dichotomy in Copyright Law, 56 Tenn. L. Rev. 321 (1989)

3. *Merger.* Under the "merger" doctrine, courts will withhold protection from an otherwise copyrightable expression if the idea embodied in the expression can effectively be expressed in only one or a limited number of ways. In Herbert Rosenthal Jewelry Corp. v. Kalpakian, 446 F.2d 738, 170 U.S.P.Q. 557 (9th Cir.1971), the seminal case on merger doctrine, the court held that the plaintiff's jewelled pin in the shape of a bee was not copyrightable because a jewelled bee pin was "an 'idea' that defendants were free to copy" and "the 'idea' and its 'expression' appear to be indistinguishable." In the court's view, when "the 'idea' and its 'expression' are thus inseparable, copying the 'expression' will not be barred, since protecting the 'expression' in such circumstances would confer a monopoly of the 'idea' upon the copyright owner free of the conditions and limitations imposed by the patent law." 446 F.2d at 742.

What if, at the time the author created the work, there were no practical limits on the number of ways she could express the work's underlying idea, and the limitations only arose later? For example, an arrangement such as the commonly used QWERTY keyboard, which was arbitrarily chosen at the time it was devised, may over time become a *de facto* standard that others must employ if their typewriters and computers are to be able to compete with the products of the first person to use this keyboard. Some courts have ruled against merger so long as alternative expressive possibilities existed at the time the *copyrighted work* was created; other courts have ruled that it is the range of expressive choice that exists at the time the *competing work* was created that controls, so that, in the QWERTY example, there would be merger. Compare Apple Computer, Inc. v. Franklin Computer Corp., 714 F.2d 1240, 1253, 219 U.S.P.Q. 113 (3d Cir.1983), *cert. dismissed*, 464 U.S. 1033, 104 S.Ct. 690, 79 L.Ed.2d 158 (1984), with Apple Computer, Inc. v. Microsoft Corp., 799 F.Supp. 1006, 1025, 24 U.S.P.Q.2d 1081 (N.D.Cal.1992), *aff'd*, 35 F.3d 1435, 32 U.S.P.Q.2d 1086 (9th Cir.1994), *cert. den.*, 513 U.S. 1184, 115 S.Ct. 1176, 130 L.Ed.2d 1129 (1995).

What practical difficulties attend a rule that merger occurs any time an otherwise copyrightable expression becomes a *de facto* standard? How will a court determine whether a particular form of expression has in fact become a standard? Would such a rule, under which expression that is protectible one day becomes unprotectible the next, undermine business planning? Consider whether these problems differ significantly from those that courts—and businesses—face in the context of trademark "genericide" under which an originally distinctive mark, such as "Aspirin" or "Thermos," will enjoy trademark protection in its early years but will lose this protection over time as it becomes the product's descriptive, generic designation that competitors must be free to use if they are to be able to enter the product market. See page 230, above.

4. *Scènes à Faire.* Where merger doctrine applies mainly to factual and functional works, the closely related doctrine of *scènes à faire* applies principally to fictional works, and withholds protection from elements in these works, such as incidents or character attributes, that are preordained by the work's unprotectible ideas, such as basic plot or character types. The doctrine was first expressly applied in a copyright infringement action involving similar church sequences in plaintiff's novel and defendant's motion picture: "[O]ther small details . . . such as the playing of the piano, the prayer, the hunger motive . . . are inherent in the situation itself. They are what the French call '*scènes à faire.*' Once having placed two persons in a church during a big storm, it was inevitable that incidents like these and others which are, necessarily, associated with such a situation should force themselves upon the writer in developing the theme." Cain v. Universal Pictures Co., 47 F.Supp. 1013, 1017 (S.D.Cal.1942).

See generally, Leslie Kurtz, Copyright: The Scenes a Faire Doctrine, 41 Fla. L. Rev. 79 (1993).

5. *Characters.* Copyrightable characters may emerge from literary works, dramatic works, pictorial works and audiovisual works. To be protected, fictional characters must possess the same degree of original expression required of other copyright subject matter. Learned Hand stated the test for copyright in characters in Nichols v. Universal Pictures Corp., 45 F.2d 119, 121 (2d Cir.1930):

> If Twelfth Night were copyrighted, it is quite possible that a second comer might so closely imitate Sir Toby Belch or Malvolio as to infringe, but it would not be enough that for one of his characters he cast a riotous knight who kept wassail to the discomfort of the household, or a vain and foppish steward who became amorous of his mistress. These would be no more than Shakespeare's "ideas" in the play, as little capable of monopoly as Einstein's Doctrine of Relativity, or Darwin's theory of the Origin of Species. It follows that the less developed the characters, the less they can be copyrighted; that is the penalty an author must bear for marking them too indistinctly.

Unlike literary characters, which must be verbally delineated to a fairly high degree, protectible graphic characters can be sketched with a few strokes of the pen. As one court observed in a case involving Mickey

Mouse and other Disney characters, while "it is difficult to delineate distinctively a literary character," if "the author can add a visual image, however, the difficulty is reduced. Put another way, while many literary characters may embody little more than an unprotected idea, a comic book character, which has physical as well as conceptual qualities, is more likely to contain some unique elements of expression." Walt Disney Productions v. Air Pirates, 581 F.2d 751, 755, 199 U.S.P.Q. 769 (9th Cir.1978).

What doctrines other than copyright offer shelter to characters? For one possibility under trademark law, see Frederick Warne & Co. v. Book Sales, Inc., 481 F.Supp. 1191, 1196, 205 U.S.P.Q. 444 (S.D.N.Y.1979) ("The fact that a copyrightable character or design has fallen into the public domain should not preclude protection under the trademark laws so long as it is shown to have acquired independent trademark significance, identifying in some way the source or sponsorship of the goods.")

See generally Leslie A. Kurtz, The Independent Legal Lives of Fictional Characters, 1986 Wis. L. Rev. 429. On the legal questions raised by the digital re-animation of deceased performers, see Joseph Beard, Casting Call at Forest Lawn: The Digital Resurrection of Deceased Entertainers—A 21st Century Challenge for Intellectual Property Law, 41 J. Copyright Soc'y U.S.A. 19 (1993).

6. *Architecture.* The Architectural Works Copyright Protection Act, signed into law in 1990, amended section 102(a) to add "architectural works" as a new class of copyright subject matter, and amended section 101 to add a definition of "architectural work": "the design of a building as embodied in any tangible medium of expression, including a building, architectural plans, or drawings. The work includes the overall form as well as the arrangement and composition of spaces and elements in the design, but does not include individual standard features."

What is a "building"? According to the House Report on the Architectural Works Act, the term encompasses "habitable structures such as houses and office buildings. It also covers structures that are used, but not inhabited, by human beings, such as churches, pergolas, gazebos, and garden pavilions." The term presumably excludes structures not intended for human occupancy, such as bridges, highway cloverleaves and dams. H.R.Rep. No. 735, 101st Cong., 2d Sess. 20 (1990).

7. *Unlawful Content.* Should copyright be withheld if a work is seditious, libelous, fraudulent or obscene? Courts early declined to protect such works on the ground that protection would contravene the constitutional purpose "to promote the progress of ... science." See, e.g., Martinetti v. Maguire, 16 F.Cas. 920 (C.C.Cal.1867) (No. 9173) (obscenity); Stone & McCarrick v. Dugan Piano Co., 220 Fed. 837, 842–43 (5th Cir.1915) (deceptive advertising).

Mitchell Bros. Film Group v. Cinema Adult Theater, 604 F.2d 852, 203 U.S.P.Q. 1041 (5th Cir.1979), cert. denied, 445 U.S. 917, 100 S.Ct. 1277, 63 L.Ed.2d 601 (1980), marks a turning point for decision in the area. In an action brought by the copyright owners of the motion picture, "Behind the

Green Door," the district court had accepted the defense that because the movie was obscene the plaintiffs were barred from relief under the unclean hands doctrine. The court of appeals reversed. In an extensive and closely-reasoned opinion, the court held that neither the Copyright Act nor the Constitution's copyright clause required protection to be withheld because of obscene content.

The court of appeals looked first at the Copyright Act and found nothing to suggest a congressional intent to withhold copyright from obscene subject matter. Indeed, "the history of content-based restrictions on copyrights, trademarks and patents suggests that the absence of such limitations in the Copyright Act of 1909 is the result of an intentional policy choice and not simply an omission." 604 F.2d at 854. The court noted that, on the few occasions Congress introduced content-based restrictions into the Copyright Act, it later removed them and that, by contrast, Congress placed express content restrictions in the Trademark and Patent Acts. The court was particularly concerned that to deny copyright "to works adjudged obscene by the standards of one era would frequently result in lack of copyright protection (and thus lack of financial incentive to create) for works that later generations might consider to be not only non-obscene but even of great literary merit." Among the works "held in high regard today," but "adjudged obscene in previous eras" were Edmund Wilson's Memoirs of Hecate County, Henry Miller's Tropic of Cancer and Tropic of Capricorn, Erskine Caldwell's God's Little Acre, D.H. Lawrence's Lady Chatterley's Lover and Theodore Dreiser's An American Tragedy. 604 F.2d at 857.

To the argument that copyright protection for obscene works would violate the constitutional limit on Congress's copyright power "to promote the progress of science and useful arts," the court answered that, while Congress could indeed "require that each copyrighted work be shown to promote the useful arts (as it has with patents,) it need not do so." Instead, Congress could put "promotion of science and useful arts" in a larger frame, and "conclude that the best way to promote creativity is not to impose any governmental restrictions on the subject matter of copyrightable works." 604 F.2d at 860.

Mitchell relied in part on Belcher v. Tarbox, 486 F.2d 1087, 180 U.S.P.Q. 1 (9th Cir.1973), which had declined to withhold copyright protection from allegedly fraudulent subject matter. "There is nothing in the Copyright Act to suggest that the courts are to pass upon the truth or falsity, the soundness or unsoundness, of the views embodied in a copyrighted work. The gravity and immensity of the problems, theological, philosophical, economic and scientific, that would confront a court if this view were adopted are staggering to contemplate. It is surely not a task lightly to be assumed, and we decline the invitation to assume it." 486 F.2d at 1088.

8. *U.S. Government Works.* Section 105 of the 1976 Copyright Act provides that "[c]opyright protection under this title is not available for any work of the United States Government, but the United States Government is not precluded from receiving and holding copyrights transferred to it by assignment, bequest, or otherwise." Section 101 defines a "work of the United States Government" as "a work prepared by an officer or employee of the United States Government as part of that person's official duties."

When is a work by a government employee prepared as part of her "official duties?" According to the House Report on the 1976 Act, "a Government official or employee would not be prevented from securing copyright in a work written at that person's own volition and outside his or her duties, even though the subject matter involves the Government work or professional field of the official or employee." H.R.Rep. No. 1476, 94th Cong., 2d Sess. 58 (1976). Under this test, presidential testimony would constitute a United States government work while the President's reflections on events during his tenure, written after he left office, would not. See Harper & Row Publishers, Inc. v. Nation Enters., 723 F.2d 195, 220 U.S.P.Q. 321 (2d Cir.1983), rev'd on other grounds, 471 U.S. 539, 105 S.Ct. 2218, 85 L.Ed.2d 588 (1985).

9. The Copyright Office has listed several examples of "works not subject to copyright" for which it will not issue certificates of registration:

(a) Words and short phrases such as names, titles, and slogans; familiar symbols or designs; mere variations of typographic ornamentation, lettering or coloring; mere listing of ingredients or contents;

(b) Ideas, plans, methods, systems, or devices, as distinguished from the particular manner in which they are expressed or described in a writing;

(c) Blank forms, such as time cards, graph paper, account books, diaries, bank checks, scorecards, address books, report forms, order forms and the like, which are designed for recording information and do not in themselves convey information;

(d) Works consisting entirely of information that is common property containing no original authorship, such as, for example: Standard calendars, height and weight charts, tape measures and rulers, schedules of sporting events, and lists or tables taken from public documents or other common sources.

(e) Typeface as typeface.

37 C.F.R. § 202.1 (2001). Why should the fact that a work is designed for recording information, and does not in itself "convey information," disqualify it from copyright protection? If the copyright registration application reproduced at page 582, above were not a U.S. Government work, would it qualify for copyright protection?

10. *Neighboring Rights.* In protecting all forms of original works, the U.S. Copyright Act embraces a wider range of subject matter than do the copyright laws of many other countries, particularly those following the continental "author's right" tradition. Performances, sound recordings and broadcasts that in the United States would be protected by copyright, will in these countries be protected under the rubric of neighboring rights on the premise that they are not works of authorship at all, but mere "productions" entitled to a lower level of protection than traditional literary and artistic works.

See generally, Paul Goldstein, International Copyright: Principles, Law and Practice § 2.2 (2001).

3. ORIGINALITY

SHELDON v. METRO–GOLDWYN PICTURES CORP., 81 F.2d 49, 28 U.S.P.Q. 330 (2d Cir.1936), cert. denied, 298 U.S. 669, 56 S.Ct. 835, 80 L.Ed. 1392 (1936), L. HAND, J.: We are to remember that it makes no difference how far the play was anticipated by works in the public demesne which the plaintiffs did not use. The defendants appear not to recognize this, for they have filled the record with earlier instances of the same dramatic incidents and devices, as though, like a patent, a copyrighted work must be not only original, but new. That is not however the law as is obvious in the case of maps or compendia, where later works will necessarily be anticipated. At times, in discussing how much of the substance of a play the copyright protects, courts have indeed used language which seems to give countenance to the notion that, if a plot were old, it could not be copyrighted. But we understand by this no more than that in its broader outline a plot is never copyrightable, for it is plain beyond peradventure that anticipation as such cannot invalidate a copyright. Borrowed the work must indeed not be, for a plagiarist is not himself pro tanto an "author"; but if by some magic a man who had never known it were to compose anew Keats's Ode on a Grecian Urn, he would be an "author," and, if he copyrighted it, others might not copy that poem, though they might of course copy Keats's. But though a copyright is for this reason less vulnerable than a patent, the owner's protection is more limited, for just as he is no less an "author" because others have preceded him, so another who follows him, is not a tort-feasor unless he pirates his work. If the copyrighted work is therefore original, the public demesne is important only on the issue of infringement; that is, so far as it may break the force of the inference to be drawn from likenesses between the work and the putative piracy. If the defendant has had access to other material which would have served him as well, his disclaimer becomes more plausible.

Bleistein v. Donaldson Lithographing Co.

Supreme Court of the United States, 1903.
188 U.S. 239, 23 S.Ct. 298, 47 L.Ed. 460.

Mr. Justice HOLMES delivered the opinion of the court.

This case comes here from the United States Circuit Court of Appeals for the Sixth Circuit by writ of error. It is an action brought by the plaintiffs in error to recover the penalties prescribed for infringements of copyrights. The alleged infringements consisted in the copying in reduced form of three chromolithographs prepared by employees of the plaintiffs for advertisements of a circus owned by one Wallace. Each of the three contained a portrait of Wallace in the corner and lettering bearing some slight relation to the scheme of decoration, indicating the subject of the design and the fact that the reality was to be seen at the circus. One of the designs was of an ordinary ballet, one of a number of men and women, described as the Stirk family, performing on bicycles, and one of groups of men and women whitened to represent statues. The Circuit Court directed a verdict for the defendant on the ground that the chromolithographs were not within the protection of the copyright law, and this ruling was sustained by the Circuit Court of Appeals. Courier Lithographing Co. v. Donaldson Lithographing Co., 104 Fed.Rep. 993.

There was evidence warranting the inference that the designs belonged to the plaintiffs, they having been produced by persons employed and paid by the plaintiffs in their establishment to make those very things. It fairly might be found also that the copyrights were taken out in the proper names. One of them was taken out in the name of the Courier Company and the other two in the names of the Courier Lithographing Company. The former was the name of an unincorporated joint stock association formed under the laws of New York, Laws of 1894, c. 235, and made up of the plaintiffs, the other a trade variant on that name.

Finally, there was evidence that the pictures were copyrighted before publication. There may be a question whether the use by the defendant for Wallace was not lawful within the terms of the contract with Wallace, or a more general one as to what rights the plaintiffs reserved. But we cannot pass upon these questions as matter of law; they will be for the jury when the case is tried again, and therefore we come at once to the ground of decision in the courts below. That ground was not found in any variance between pleading and proof, such as was put forward in argument, but in the nature and purpose of the designs.

We shall do no more than mention the suggestion that painting and engraving unless for a mechanical end are not among the useful arts, the progress of which Congress is empowered by the Constitution to promote. The Constitution does not limit the useful to that which satisfies immediate bodily needs. It is obvious also that the plaintiffs' case is not affected by the fact, if it be one, that the pictures represent actual groups—visible things. They seem from the testimony to have been composed from hints or description, not from sight of a performance. But even if they had been drawn from the life, that fact would not deprive them of protection. The opposite proposition would mean that a portrait by Velasquez or Whistler was common property because others might try their hand on the same face. Others are free to copy the original. They are not free to copy the copy. The copy is the personal reaction of an individual upon nature. Personality always contains something unique. It expresses its singularity even in handwriting, and a very modest grade of art has in it something irreducible, which is one man's alone. That something he may copyright unless there is a restriction in the words of the act.

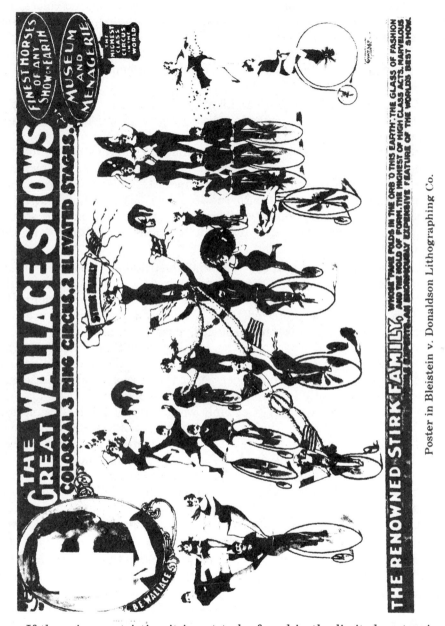

Poster in Bleistein v. Donaldson Lithographing Co.

If there is a restriction it is not to be found in the limited pretensions of these particular works. The least pretentious picture has more originality in it than directories and the like, which may be copyrighted. The amount of training required for humbler efforts than those before us is well indicated by Ruskin. "If any young person, after being taught what is, in polite circles, called 'drawing,' will try to copy the commonest piece of real *work*,—suppose a lithograph on the title page of a new opera air, or a woodcut in the cheapest illustrated newspaper of the day—they will find themselves entirely beaten." Elements of Drawing, 1st ed. 3. There is no reason to doubt that these prints in their *ensemble* and in all their details, in their design and particular combinations of figures, lines and colors, are the original work of the plaintiffs' designer. If it be necessary, there is express testimony to that effect. It would be pressing the defendant's right to the verge, if not beyond, to leave the question of originality to the jury upon the evidence in this case, as was done in Hegeman v. Springer, 110 Fed.Rep. 374.

We assume that the construction of Rev.Stat. § 4952, allowing a copyright to the "author, inventor, designer, or proprietor ... of any engraving, cut, print ... [or] chromo" is affected by the act of 1874, c. 301, § 3, 18 Stat. 78, 79. That section provides that "in the construction of this act the words 'engraving,' 'cut' and 'print' shall be applied only to pictorial illustrations or works connected with the fine arts." We see no reason for taking the words "connected with the fine arts" as qualifying anything except the word "works," but it would not change our decision if we should assume further that they also qualified "pictorial illustrations," as the defendant contends.

These chromolithographs are "pictorial illustrations." The word "illustrations" does not mean that they must illustrate the text of a book, and that the etchings of Rembrandt or Steinla's engraving of the Madonna di San Sisto could not be protected today if any man were able to produce them. Again, the act however construed, does not mean that ordinary posters are not good enough to be considered within its scope. The antithesis to "illustrations or works connected with the fine arts" is not works of little merit or of humble degree, or illustrations addressed to the less educated classes; it is "prints or labels designed to be used for any other articles of manufacture." Certainly works are not the less connected with the fine arts because their pictorial quality attracts the crowd and therefore gives them a real use—if use means to increase trade and to help to make money. A picture is none the less a picture and none the less a subject of copyright that it is used for an advertisement. And if pictures may be used to advertise soap, or the theatre, or monthly magazines, as they are, they may be used to advertise a circus. Of course, the ballet is as legitimate a subject for illustration as any other. A rule cannot be laid down that would excommunicate the paintings of Degas.

Finally, the special adaptation of these pictures to the advertisement of the Wallace shows does not prevent a copyright. That may be a circumstance for the jury to consider in determining the extent of Mr. Wallace's rights, but it is not a bar. Moreover, on the evidence, such prints are used by less pretentious exhibitions when those for whom they were prepared have given them up.

It would be a dangerous undertaking for persons trained only to the law to constitute themselves final judges of the worth of pictorial illustrations, outside of the narrowest and most obvious limits. At the one extreme some works of genius would be sure to miss appreciation. Their very novelty would make them repulsive until the public had learned the new language in which their author spoke. It may be more than doubted, for instance, whether the etchings of Goya or the paintings of Manet would have been sure of protection when seen for the first time. At the other end, copyright would be denied to pictures which appealed to a public less educated than the judge. Yet if they command the interest of any public, they have a commercial value—it would be bold to say that they have not an aesthetic and educational value—and the taste of any public is not to be treated with contempt. It is an ultimate fact for the moment, whatever may be our hopes for a change. That these pictures had their worth and their success is sufficiently shown by the desire to reproduce them without regard to the plaintiffs' rights. We are of opinion that there was evidence that the plaintiffs have rights entitled to the protection of the law.

The judgment of the Circuit Court of Appeals is reversed; the judgment of the Circuit Court is also reversed and the cause remanded to that court with directions to set aside the verdict and grant a new trial.

Mr. Justice HARLAN, with whom concurred Mr. Justice McKENNA, dissenting.

Judges Lurton, Day and Severens, of the Circuit Court of Appeals, concurred in affirming the judgment of the District Court. Their views were thus expressed in an opinion delivered by Judge Lurton: "What we hold is this: That if a chromo, lithograph, or other print, engraving, or picture has no other use than that of a mere advertisement, and no value aside from this function, it would not be promotive of the useful arts, within the meaning of the constitutional provision, to protect the 'author' in the exclusive use thereof, and the copyright statute should not be construed as including such a publication, if any other construction is admissible. If a mere label simply designating or describing an article to which it is attached, and which has no value separated from the article, does not come within the constitutional clause upon the subject of copyright, it must follow that a pictorial illustration designed and useful only as an advertisement, and having no intrinsic value other than its function as an advertisement, must be equally without the obvious meaning of the Constitution. It must have some connection with the fine arts to give it intrinsic value, and that it shall have is the meaning which we attach to the act of June 18, 1874, amending the provisions of the copyright law. We are unable to discover anything useful or meritorious in the design copyrighted by the plaintiffs in error other than as an advertisement of acts to be done or exhibited to the public in Wallace's show. No evidence, aside from the deductions which are to be drawn from the prints themselves, was offered to show that these designs had any original artistic qualities. The jury could not reasonably have found merit or value aside from the purely business object of advertising a show, and the instruction to find for the defendant was not error. Many other points have been urged as justifying the result reached in the court below. We find it unnecessary to express any opinion upon them, in view of the conclusion already announced. The judgment must be affirmed." Courier Lithographing Co. v. Donaldson Lithographing Co., 104 Fed.Rep. 993, 996.

I entirely concur in these views, and therefore dissent from the opinion and judgment of this court. The clause of the Constitution giving Congress power to promote the progress of science and useful arts, by securing for limited terms to authors and inventors the exclusive right to their respective works and discoveries, does not, as I think, embrace a mere advertisement of a circus.

Mr. Justice McKENNA authorizes me to say that he also dissents.

Feist Publications, Inc. v. Rural Telephone Service Co.

Supreme Court of the United States, 1991.
499 U.S. 340, 111 S.Ct. 1282, 113 L.Ed.2d 358, 18 U.S.P.Q.2d 1275.

Justice O'CONNOR delivered the opinion of the Court.

This case requires us to clarify the extent of copyright protection available to telephone directory white pages.

I.

Rural Telephone Service Company is a certified public utility that provides telephone service to several communities in northwest Kansas. It is subject to a state regulation that requires all telephone companies operating in Kansas to issue annually an updated telephone directory. Accordingly, as a condition of its monopoly franchise, Rural publishes a typical telephone directory, consisting of white pages and yellow pages. The white pages list in alphabetical order the names of Rural's subscribers, together with their towns and telephone numbers. The yellow pages list Rural's business subscribers alphabetically by category and feature classified advertisements of various sizes. Rural distributes its directory free of charge to its subscribers, but earns revenue by selling yellow pages advertisements.

Feist Publications, Inc., is a publishing company that specializes in area-wide telephone directories. Unlike a typical directory, which covers only a particular calling area, Feist's area-wide directories cover a much larger geographical range, reducing the need to call directory assistance or consult multiple directories. The Feist directory that is the subject of this litigation covers 11 different telephone service areas in 15 counties and contains 46,878 white pages listings—compared to Rural's approximately 7,700 listings. Like Rural's directory, Feist's is distributed free of charge and includes both white pages and yellow pages. Feist and Rural compete vigorously for yellow pages advertising.

As the sole provider of telephone service in its service area, Rural obtains subscriber information quite easily. Persons desiring telephone service must apply to Rural and provide their names and addresses; Rural then assigns them a telephone number. Feist is not a telephone company, let alone one with monopoly status, and therefore lacks independent access to any subscriber information. To obtain white pages listings for its area-wide directory, Feist approached each of the 11 telephone companies operating in northwest Kansas and offered to pay for the right to use its white pages listings.

Of the 11 telephone companies, only Rural refused to license its listings to Feist. Rural's refusal created a problem for Feist, as omitting these listings would have left a gaping hole in its area-wide directory, rendering it less attractive to potential yellow pages advertisers. In a decision subsequent to that which we review here, the District Court determined that this was precisely the reason Rural refused to license its listings. The refusal was motivated by an unlawful purpose "to extend its monopoly in telephone service to a monopoly in yellow pages advertising." Rural Telephone Service Co. v. Feist Publications, Inc., 737 F.Supp. 610, 622 (D.Kan.1990).

Unable to license Rural's white pages listings, Feist used them without Rural's consent. Feist began by removing several thousand listings that fell outside the geographic range of its area-wide directory, then hired personnel to investigate the 4,935 that remained. These employees verified the data reported by Rural and sought to obtain additional information. As a result, a typical Feist listing includes the individual's street address; most of Rural's listings do not. Notwithstanding these additions, however, 1,309 of the 46,878 listings in Feist's 1983 directory were identical to listings in Rural's 1982–1983 white pages. Four of these were fictitious listings that Rural had inserted into its directory to detect copying.

Rural sued for copyright infringement in the District Court for the District of Kansas taking the position that Feist, in compiling its own directory, could not use the information contained in Rural's white pages. Rural asserted that Feist's employees were obliged to travel door-to-door or conduct a telephone survey to discover the same information for themselves. Feist responded that such efforts were economically impractical and, in any event, unnecessary because the information copied was beyond the scope of copyright protection. The District Court granted summary judgment to Rural, explaining that "[c]ourts have consistently held that telephone directories are copyrightable" and citing a string of lower court decisions. In an unpublished opinion, the Court of Appeals for the Tenth Circuit affirmed "for substantially the reasons given by the district court." We granted certiorari, to determine whether the copyright in Rural's directory protects the names, towns, and telephone numbers copied by Feist.

II.

A

This case concerns the interaction of two well-established propositions. The first is that facts are not copyrightable; the other, that compilations of facts generally are. Each of these propositions possesses an impeccable pedigree. That there can be no valid copyright in facts is universally understood. The most fundamental axiom of copyright law is that "[n]o author may copyright his ideas or the facts he narrates." Harper & Row, Publishers, Inc. v. Nation Enterprises, 471 U.S. 539, 556, 105 S.Ct. 2218, 2228, 85 L.Ed.2d 588 (1985). Rural wisely concedes this point, noting in its brief that "[f]acts and discoveries, of course, are not themselves subject to copyright protection." At the same time, however, it is beyond dispute that compilations of facts are within the subject matter of copyright. Compilations were expressly mentioned in the Copyright Act of 1909, and again in the Copyright Act of 1976.

There is an undeniable tension between these two propositions. Many compilations consist of nothing but raw data—*i.e.,* wholly factual information not accompanied by any original written expression. On what basis may one claim a copyright in such a work? Common sense tells us that 100 uncopyrightable facts do not magically change their status when gathered together in one place. Yet copyright law seems to contemplate that compilations that consist exclusively of facts are potentially within its scope.

The key to resolving the tension lies in understanding why facts are not copyrightable. The *sine qua non* of copyright is originality. To qualify for copyright protection, a work must be original to the author. Original, as the term is used in copyright, means only that the work was independently created by the author (as opposed to copied from other works), and that it possesses at least some minimal degree of creativity. To be sure, the requisite level of creativity is extremely low; even a slight amount will suffice. . . .

Originality is a constitutional requirement. The source of Congress' power to enact copyright laws is Article I, § 8, cl. 8, of the Constitution, which authorizes Congress to "secur[e] for limited Times to Authors . . . the exclusive Right to their respective Writings." In two decisions from the late 19th Century—The Trade–Mark Cases, 100 U.S. 82, 25 L.Ed. 550 (1879); and Burrow–Giles Lithographic Co. v. Sarony, 111 U.S. 53, 4 S.Ct. 279, 28 L.Ed. 349 (1884)—this Court defined the crucial terms "authors" and "writings." In so doing, the Court made it unmistakably clear that these terms presuppose a degree of originality.

In *The Trade–Mark Cases,* the Court addressed the constitutional scope of "writings." For a particular work to be classified "under the head of writings of authors," the Court determined, "originality is required." 100 U.S., at 94. The Court explained that originality requires independent creation plus a modicum of creativity: "[W]hile the word *writings* may be liberally construed, as it has been, to include original designs for engraving, prints, & c., it is only such as are *original,* and are founded in the creative powers of the mind. The writings which are to be protected are *the fruits of intellectual labor,* embodied in the form of books, prints, engravings, and the like." *Ibid.* (emphasis in original).

In *Burrow–Giles,* the Court distilled the same requirement from the Constitution's use of the word "authors." The Court defined "author," in a constitutional sense, to mean "he to whom anything owes its origin; originator; maker." 111 U.S., at 58, 4 S.Ct., at 281 (internal quotations omitted). As in *The Trade–Mark Cases,* the Court emphasized the creative component of originality. It described copyright as being limited to "original intellectual conceptions of the author," ibid., and stressed the importance of requiring an author who accuses another of infringement to prove "the existence of those facts of originality, of intellectual production, of thought, and conception." Id., 111 U.S., at 59–60.

The originality requirement articulated in *The Trade–Mark Cases* and *Burrow–Giles* remains the touchstone of copyright protection today. It is the very "premise of copyright law." Miller v. Universal City Studios, Inc., 650 F.2d 1365, 1368 (C.A.5 1981). Leading scholars agree on this point. As one pair of commentators succinctly puts it: "the originality requirement is *constitutionally mandated* for all works." Patterson & Joyce, Monopolizing the Law: The Scope of Copyright Protection for Law Reports and Statutory Compilations, 36 UCLA L.Rev. 719, 763, n. 155 (1989) (emphasis in original) (hereinafter Patterson & Joyce).

It is this bedrock principle of copyright that mandates the law's seemingly disparate treatment of facts and factual compilations. "No one may claim originality as to facts." M. Nimmer & D. Nimmer Copyright § 2.11[A], p. 2–157. This is because facts do not owe their origin to an act of authorship. The distinction is one between creation and discovery: the first person to find and report a particular fact has not created the fact; he or she has merely discovered its existence. To borrow from *Burrow–Giles,* one who discovers a fact is not its "maker" or "originator." 111 U.S., at 58, 4 S.Ct. at 281.... The same is true of all facts—scientific, historical, biographical, and news of the day. "[T]hey may not be copyrighted and are part of the public domain available to every person." *Miller,* supra, at 1369.

Factual compilations, on the other hand, may possess the requisite originality. The compilation author typically chooses which facts to include, in what order to place them, and how to arrange the collected data so that they may be used effectively by readers. These choices as to selection and arrangement, so long as they are made independently by the compiler and entail a minimal degree of creativity, are sufficiently original that Congress may protect such compilations through the copyright laws. Thus, even a directory that contains absolutely no protectible written expression, only facts, meets the constitutional minimum for copyright protection if it features an original selection or arrangement.

This protection is subject to an important limitation. The mere fact that a work is copyrighted does not mean that every element of the work may be protected. Originality remains the *sine qua non* of copyright; accordingly, copyright protection may extend only to those components of a work that are original to the author. Thus, if the compilation author clothes facts with an original collocation of words, he or she may be able to claim a copyright in this written expression. Others may copy the underlying facts from the publication, but not the precise words used to present them. In *Harper & Row,* for example, we explained that President Ford could not prevent others from copying bare historical facts from his autobiography, but that he could prevent others from copying his "subjective descriptions and portraits of public figures." Id., at 563. Where the compilation author adds no written expression but rather lets the facts speak for themselves, the expressive element is more elusive. The only conceivable expression is the manner in which the compiler has selected and arranged the facts. Thus, if the selection and arrangement are original, these elements of the work are eligible for copyright protection. No matter how original the format, however, the facts themselves do not become original through association.

This inevitably means that the copyright in a factual compilation is thin. Notwithstanding a valid copyright, a subsequent compiler remains free to use the facts contained in another's publication to aid in preparing a competing work, so long as the competing work does not feature the same selection and arrangement. As one commentator explains it: "[N]o matter how much original authorship the work displays, the facts and ideas it exposes are free for the taking.... [T]he very same facts and ideas may be divorced from the context imposed by the author, and restated or reshuffled by second comers, even if the author was the first to discover the facts or to propose the ideas." Ginsburg, Creation and Commercial Value: Copyright Protection of Works of Information, 90 Colum.L.Rev. 1865, 1868 (1990).

It may seem unfair that much of the fruit of the compiler's labor may be used by others without compensation. As Justice Brennan has correctly observed, however, this is not "some unforeseen byproduct of a statutory scheme." *Harper & Row,* 471 U.S., at 589, 105 S.Ct., at 2245 (dissenting opinion). It is, rather, "the essence of copyright," ibid., and a constitutional requirement. The primary objective of copyright is not to reward the labor of authors, but "[t]o promote the Progress of Science and useful Arts." Art. I, § 8, cl. 8. To this end, copyright assures authors the right to their original expression, but encourages others to build freely upon the ideas and information conveyed by a work. This principle, known as the idea/expression or fact/expression dichotomy, applies to all works of authorship. As applied to a factual compilation, assuming the absence of original written expression, only the compiler's selection and arrangement may be protected; the raw facts may be copied at will. This result is neither unfair nor unfortunate. It is the means by which copyright advances the progress of science and art....

This, then, resolves the doctrinal tension: Copyright treats facts and factual compilations in a wholly consistent manner. Facts, whether alone or as part of a compilation, are not original and therefore may not be copyrighted. A factual compilation is eligible for copyright if it features an original selection or arrangement of facts, but the copyright is limited to the particular selection or arrangement. In no event may copyright extend to the facts themselves.

B

As we have explained, originality is a constitutionally mandated prerequisite for copyright protection. The Court's decisions announcing this rule predate the Copyright Act of 1909, but ambiguous language in the 1909 Act caused some lower courts temporarily to lose sight of this requirement.

The 1909 Act embodied the originality requirement, but not as clearly as it might have....

... [S]ome courts misunderstood the statute. See, e.g., Leon v. Pacific Telephone & Telegraph Co., 91 F.2d 484 (C.A.9 1937); Jeweler's Circular Publishing Co. v. Keystone Publishing Co., 281 F. 83 (C.A.2 1922)....

Making matters worse, these courts developed a new theory to justify the protection of factual compilations. Known alternatively as "sweat of the brow" or "industrious collection," the underlying notion was that copyright was a reward for the hard work that went into compiling facts. The classic formulation of the doctrine appeared in *Jeweler's Circular Publishing Co.,* 281 F., at 88:

"The right to copyright a book upon which one has expended labor in its preparation does not depend upon whether the materials which he has collected consist or not of matters which are publici juris, or whether such materials show literary skill *or originality,* either in thought or in language, or anything more than industrious collection. The man who goes through the streets of a town and puts down the names of each of the inhabitants, with their occupations and their street number, acquires material of which he is the author" (emphasis added).

The "sweat of the brow" doctrine had numerous flaws, the most glaring being that it extended copyright protection in a compilation beyond selection and arrangement—the compiler's original contributions—to the facts themselves. Under the doctrine, the only defense to infringement was independent creation. A subsequent compiler was "not entitled to take one word of information previously published," but rather had to "independently wor[k] out the matter for himself, so as to arrive at the same result from the same common sources of information." Id., at 88–89 (internal quotations omitted). "Sweat of the brow" courts thereby eschewed the most fundamental axiom of copyright law—that no one may copyright facts or ideas....

C

. . .

The definition of "compilation" is found in § 101 of the 1976 Act. It defines a "compilation" in the copyright sense as "a work formed by the collection and assembly of preexisting materials or of data *that* are selected, coordinated, or arranged *in such a way that* the resulting work as a whole constitutes an original work of authorship" (emphasis added).

The purpose of the statutory definition is to emphasize that collections of facts are not copyrightable *per se.* It conveys this message through its tripartite structure, as emphasized above by the italics. The statute identifies three distinct elements and requires each to be met for a work to qualify as a copyrightable compilation: (1) the collection and assembly of pre-existing material, facts, or data; (2) the selection, coordination, or arrangement of those materials; and (3) the creation, by virtue of the particular selection, coordination, or arrangement, of an "original" work of authorship....

The key to the statutory definition is the second requirement. It instructs courts that, in determining whether a fact-based work is an original work of authorship, they should focus on the manner in which the collected facts have been selected, coordinated, and arranged. This is a straight-forward application of the originality requirement. Facts are never original, so the compilation author can claim originality, if at all, only in the way the facts are presented. To that end, the statute dictates that the principal focus should be on whether the selection, coordination, and arrangement are sufficiently original to merit protection. . . .

As discussed earlier, however, the originality requirement is not particularly stringent. A compiler may settle upon a selection or arrangement that others have used; novelty is not required. Originality requires only that the author make the selection or arrangement independently (i.e., without copying that selection or arrangement from another work), and that it display some minimal level of creativity. Presumably, the vast majority of compilations will pass this test, but not all will. There remains a narrow category of works in which the creative spark is utterly lacking or so trivial as to be virtually nonexistent. See generally Bleistein v. Donaldson Lithographing Co., 188 U.S. 239, 251, 23 S.Ct. 298, 300, 47 L.Ed. 460 (1903) (referring to "the narrowest and most obvious limits"). Such works are incapable of sustaining a valid copyright.

Even if a work qualifies as a copyrightable compilation, it receives only limited protection. This is the point of § 103 of the Act. Section 103 explains that "[t]he subject matter of copyright . . . includes compilations," § 103(a), but that copyright protects only the author's original contributions—not the facts or information conveyed:

> "The copyright in a compilation . . . extends only to the material contributed by the author of such work, as distinguished from the preexisting material employed in the work, and does not imply any exclusive right in the preexisting material." § 103(b).

As § 103 makes clear, copyright is not a tool by which a compilation author may keep others from using the facts or data he or she has collected. "The most important point here is one that is commonly misunderstood today: copyright . . . has no effect one way or the other on the copyright or public domain status of the preexisting material." H.R.Rep., at 57; S.Rep., at 55. The 1909 Act did not require, as "sweat of the brow" courts mistakenly assumed, that each subsequent compiler must start from scratch and is precluded from relying on research undertaken by another. Rather, the facts contained in existing works may be freely copied because copyright protects only the elements that owe their origin to the compiler— the selection, coordination, and arrangement of facts.

In summary, the 1976 revisions to the Copyright Act leave no doubt that originality, not "sweat of the brow," is the touchstone of copyright protection in directories and other fact-based works. Nor is there any doubt that the same was true under the 1909 Act. The 1976 revisions were a direct response to the Copyright Office's concern that many lower courts had misconstrued this basic principle, and Congress emphasized repeatedly that the purpose of the revisions was to clarify, not change, existing law. The revisions explain with painstaking clarity that copyright requires originality, § 102(a); that facts are never original, § 102(b); that the copyright in a compilation does not extend to the facts it contains, § 103(b); and that a compilation is copyrightable only to the extent that it features an original selection, coordination, or arrangement, § 101. . . .

III.

There is no doubt that Feist took from the white pages of Rural's directory a substantial amount of factual information. At a minimum, Feist copied the names, towns, and telephone numbers of 1,309 of Rural's subscribers. Not all copying, however, is copyright infringement. To establish infringement, two elements must be proven: (1) ownership of a valid copyright, and (2) copying of constituent elements of the work that are original. The first element is not at issue here; Feist appears to concede that Rural's directory, considered as a whole, is subject to a valid copyright because it contains some foreword text, as well as original material in its yellow pages advertisements.

The question is whether Rural has proved the second element. In other words, did Feist, by taking 1,309 names, towns, and telephone numbers from Rural's white pages, copy anything that was "original" to Rural? Certainly, the raw data does not satisfy the originality requirement. Rural may have been the first to discover and report the names, towns, and telephone numbers of its subscribers, but this data does not " 'ow[e] its origin' " to Rural. *Burrow–Giles,* 111 U.S., at 58. Rather, these bits of information are uncopyrightable facts; they existed before Rural reported them and would have continued to exist if Rural had never published a telephone directory. The originality requirement "rule[s] out protecting . . . names, addresses, and telephone numbers of which the plaintiff by no stretch of the imagination could be called the author." Patterson & Joyce 776.

Rural essentially concedes the point by referring to the names, towns, and telephone numbers as "preexisting material." Section 103(b) states explicitly that the copyright in a compilation does not extend to "the preexisting material employed in the work."

The question that remains is whether Rural selected, coordinated, or arranged these uncopyrightable facts in an original way. As mentioned, originality is not a stringent standard; it does not require that facts be presented in an innovative or surprising way. It is equally true, however, that the selection and arrangement of facts cannot be so mechanical or routine as to require no creativity whatsoever. The standard of originality is low, but it does exist. As this Court has explained, the Constitution mandates some minimal degree of creativity, see *The Trade–Mark Cases,* 100 U.S., at 94; and an author who claims infringement must prove "the existence of . . . intellectual production, of thought, and conception." *Burrow–Giles, supra,* 111 U.S., at 59–60.

The selection, coordination, and arrangement of Rural's white pages do not satisfy the minimum constitutional standards for copyright protection. As mentioned at the outset, Rural's white pages are entirely typical. Persons desiring telephone service in Rural's service area fill out an application and Rural issues them a telephone number. In preparing its white pages, Rural simply takes the data provided by its subscribers and lists it alphabetically by surname. The end product is a garden-variety white pages directory, devoid of even the slightest trace of creativity.

Rural's selection of listings could not be more obvious: it publishes the most basic information—name, town, and telephone number—about each person who applies to it for telephone service. This is "selection" of a sort, but it lacks the modicum of creativity necessary to transform mere selection into copyrightable expression. Rural expended sufficient effort to make the white pages directory useful, but insufficient creativity to make it original.

We note in passing that the selection featured in Rural's white pages may also fail the originality requirement for another reason. Feist points out that Rural did not truly "select" to publish the names and telephone numbers of its subscribers; rather, it was required to do so by the Kansas Corporation Commission as part of its monopoly franchise. See 737 F.Supp., at 612. Accordingly, one could plausibly conclude that this selection was dictated by state law, not by Rural.

Nor can Rural claim originality in its coordination and arrangement of facts. The white pages do nothing more than list Rural's subscribers in alphabetical order. This arrangement may, technically speaking, owe its origin to Rural; no one disputes that Rural undertook the task of alphabetizing the names itself. But there is nothing remotely creative about arranging names alphabetically in a white pages directory. It is an age-old practice, firmly rooted in tradition and so commonplace that it has come to be expected as a matter of course. It is not only unoriginal, it is practically inevitable. This time-honored tradition does not possess the minimal creative spark required by the Copyright Act and the Constitution.

We conclude that the names, towns, and telephone numbers copied by Feist were not original to Rural and therefore were not protected by the copyright in Rural's combined white and yellow pages directory. As a constitutional matter, copyright protects only those constituent elements of a work that possess more than a *de minimis* quantum of creativity. Rural's white pages, limited to basic subscriber information and arranged alphabetically, fall short of the mark. As a statutory matter, 17 U.S.C. § 101 does not afford protection from copying to a collection of facts that are selected, coordinated, and arranged in a way that utterly lacks originality. Given that some works must fail, we cannot imagine a more likely candidate. Indeed, were we to hold that Rural's white pages pass muster, it is hard to believe that any collection of facts could fail.

Because Rural's white pages lack the requisite originality, Feist's use of the listings cannot constitute infringement. This decision should not be construed as demeaning Rural's efforts in compiling its directory, but rather as making clear that copyright rewards originality, not effort. As this Court noted more than a century ago, " 'great praise may be due to the plaintiffs for their industry and enterprise in publishing this paper, yet the law does not contemplate their being rewarded in this way.' " Baker v. Selden, 101 U.S., at 105.

The judgment of the Court of Appeals is

Reversed.

Justice BLACKMUN concurs in the judgment.

NOTES

1. It is some measure of the originality test Learned Hand propounded in *Sheldon* that, in a long career deciding copyright cases, he never once found that a work was insufficiently original to qualify for copyright protection.* What are the "narrowest and most obvious limits," referred to in *Bleistein,* within which courts may judge a work's artistic worth?

Feist departed from precedent in two striking respects. First was the Court's observation, repeated no fewer than thirteen times, that originality is a constitutional requirement. The scant record of the Framers' deliberations on the Constitution's patent-copyright clause reflects no intention to make originality a condition of Congress' copyright power, and the two nineteenth-century decisions cited by the Court—the *Trade–Mark Cases* and Burrow–Giles v. Sarony—at most only hint that originality has a constitutional dimension. Nonetheless, *Feist* implies that if Congress decides to protect such nonoriginal works as alphabetized telephone listings, it must do so under some power other than the copyright power—presumably the commerce power. Second, *Feist's* assertion that originality imports "creativity" also lacks general precedential support. Lower courts have equated originality with "creativity" only in cases involving photographs and art reproductions, presumably because a photographer or copyist will typically not contribute original content in the form of visual elements that are absent from the object photographed or the work reproduced.

For an analysis of different legal approaches to originality, see Russ VerSteeg, Rethinking Originality, 34 Wm. & Mary L. Rev. 801 (1993).

2. *Directories*. In BellSouth Advertising & Publishing Corp. v. Donnelley Information Publishing, Inc., 999 F.2d 1436, 28 U.S.P.Q. 2d 1001 (11th Cir.1993), cert. den., 510 U.S. 1101, 114 S.Ct. 943, 127 L.Ed.2d 232, telephone directory yellow pages fared little better under *Feist's* originality standard than did telephone directory white pages. Vacating the earlier opinion of a three-judge panel, and reversing the judgment of the district court, the Eleventh Circuit Court of Appeals ruled that plaintiff's business yellow pages lacked the level of original selection, arrangement or coordination required of compilation copyrights. The court could not find the

---

*I am grateful to Professor Douglas Baird of the University of Chicago Law School for this observation, made in his un- published study, *The Copyright Decisions of Learned Hand.*

requisite degree of selection in Bellsouth's choice of the geographic scope and closing date for its directory; "any collection of facts fixed in any tangible medium of expression will by necessity have a closing date and, where applicable, a geographic limit selected by the compiler." Nor could it find original selection in the techniques used to screen and attract subscribers: "The protection of copyright must inhere in a creatively original *selection* of facts to be reported and not in the creative means used to discover those facts." 999 F.2d at 1441.

The court also ruled that Bellsouth's alphabetized list of business categories was insufficiently original as arrangement or coordination. "Because this is the one way to construct a useful business directory, the arrangement has merged with the idea of a business directory, and thus is uncopyrightable." 999 F.2d at 1442. Further, many of Bellsouth's headings "result from certain standard industry practices, such as the recommendations of the National Yellow Pages Sales Association, with regard to the selection and phrasing of headings in business directories. Finally, as established by the testimony of BAPCO's representatives, the ultimate appearance of a particular subscriber under a certain heading is determined by the subscriber's willingness to purchase those listings in the BAPCO directory." While Bellsouth "may select the headings that are *offered* to the subscriber, it is the *subscriber* who *selects* from those alternatives the headings under which the subscriber will appear in the copyrighted directory." 999 F.2d at 1444.

3. *Research.* In Miller v. Universal Studios, Inc., 650 F.2d 1365, 212 U.S.P.Q. 345 (5th Cir.1981), the court reversed a jury verdict for plaintiff, which had claimed that defendant's made-for-television movie infringed its copyright in a book depicting a kidnapping because "the case was presented and argued to the jury on a false premise: that the labor of research by an author is protected by copyright." Was the court correct to conclude that "[t]here is no rational basis for distinguishing between facts and the research involved in obtaining facts?" Fact works will often be protected as compilations—works "formed by the collection and assembling of preexisting materials or of data that are selected, coordinated, or arranged in such a way that the resulting work as a whole constitutes an original work of authorship." 17 U.S.C.A. § 101. Why should copyright law treat the research involved in obtaining facts less generously than the selection, coordination or arrangement of facts? At bottom, is research anything more than selection—identifying the few facts that are relevant from the mass of irrelevant data?

Courts, even after *Feist*, will sometimes assimilate research into protectible "selection." CCC Information Services, Inc. v. Maclean Hunter Market Reports, Inc., 44 F.3d 61, 33 U.S.P.Q.2d 1183 (2d Cir.1994), cert. den., 516 U.S. 817, 116 S.Ct. 72, 133 L.Ed.2d 32 (1995), characterized a district court decision that a book's projection of values for used cars failed to meet *Feist's* originality standard as "simply mistaken in its conclusion that the *Red Book* valuations were, like the telephone numbers in *Feist*, pre-existing facts that had merely been discovered by the *Red Book* editors." In the circuit court's view, the "valuations were neither reports of historical prices nor mechanical derivations of historical prices or other data. Rather, they represented predictions by the *Red Book* editors of future prices estimated to cover specified geographic regions ... based not only on a multitude of data sources, but also on professional judgment and expertise." 44 F.3d at 67.

Will real property title data that a title insurance company extracts from its title plant, and selects and organizes in preparing a title commitment, qualify for copyright under this standard? See Mid America Title Co. v. Kirk, 59 F.3d 719, 722, 35 U.S.P.Q. 2d 1502 (7th Cir.1995) ("... [W]e conclude that the selection process used to prepare Mid America's Title Commitment No. 125266 fails to meet this [*Feist's*] minimal level of creativity. Selecting which facts to include in this compilation of data was not a matter of discretion based on Mid America's personal judgment or taste, but instead it was a matter of convention and strict industry standards.").

4. *Maps.* Maps have long raised thorny issues for copyright protection. Amsterdam v. Triangle Publications, Inc., 189 F.2d 104, 89 U.S.P.Q. 468 (3d Cir.1951), typifies some of the doctrinal problems. Plaintiff contended that defendant's county map infringed the copyright in its map consisting of information compiled at the expense of "considerable time and effort," and obtained almost exclusively "from maps already in existence, although none of this information had been published previously on any one map." Acknowledging defendant's concession that it had copied, the court of appeals ruled that plaintiff's map was insufficiently original to qualify for copyright protection. First, "[t]he location of county lines, township lines and municipal lines is information within the public domain, and is not copyrightable." Second, "the presentation of information available to everybody, such as is found on maps, is protected only when the publisher of the map in question obtains originally some of that information by the sweat of his own brow.... He, or his agents, must first do some original work, get more than an infinitesimal amount of original information." 189 F.2d at 106.

United States v. Hamilton, 583 F.2d 448, 200 U.S.P.Q. 14 (9th Cir. 1978), is the leading case to reject *Amsterdam*'s direct observation rule. *Hamilton* upheld copyright in a map that, though based on a state highway department map, also contained elements compiled from other maps and information that had not previously appeared in map form. "[T]he elements of authorship embodied in a map consist not only of the depiction of a previously undiscovered landmark or the correction or improvement of scale or placement, but also in selection, design, and synthesis." The court observed that "[e]xpression in cartography is not so different from other artistic forms seeking to touch upon external realities that unique rules are needed to judge whether the authorship is original." Consequently, "elements of compilation which amount to more than a matter of trivial selection may, either alone or when taken into consideration with direct observation, support a finding that a map is sufficiently original to merit copyright protection." 583 F.2d at 451–52.

Does *Hamilton's* requirement of more than trivial selection meet the *Feist* standard? Does "direct observation," also weighed in *Hamilton*, count for anything in the *Feist* calculus?

5. *Case Reports.* The leading decision on case reports, Callaghan v. Myers, 128 U.S. 617, 9 S.Ct. 177, 32 L.Ed. 547 (1888), held that copyright extends not only to a report's "title-page, table of cases, head-notes, statements of facts, arguments of counsel, and index," but also to "the order of arrangement of the cases, the division of the reports into volumes, the numbering and paging of the volumes, the table of cases cited in the opinions, (where such table is made,) and the subdivision of the index into appropriate, condensed titles, involving the distribution of the subjects of the various head-notes, and cross-references, where such exist." 128 U.S. at 649, 9 S.Ct. at 185.

In West Publishing Co. v. Mead Data Central, Inc., 799 F.2d 1219, 230 U.S.P.Q. 801 (8th Cir.1986), cert. denied, 479 U.S. 1070, 107 S.Ct. 962, 93 L.Ed.2d 1010 (1987), the Eighth Circuit Court of Appeals upheld the lower court's grant of preliminary relief to West on the ground that the legal publisher's arrangement of cases in its case reports was protectible as the "result of considerable labor, talent, and judgment." The court held that the pagination of West's reports, which reflected this arrangement, was also copyrightable, and that the insertion of plaintiff's page numbers in defendant's computer-based legal research system—so-called "star pagination"—would infringe plaintiff's copyright.

Is West v. Mead good law after *Feist*? Matthew Bender & Co., Inc. v. West Publishing Co., 158 F.3d 693, 708, 48 U.S.P.Q.2d 1545 (2d Cir.1998), *cert. denied*, 526 U.S. 1154, 119 S.Ct. 2039, 143 L.Ed.2d 1048 (1999), similarly involved West's claim to copyright in pagination that reflected its arrangement of cases. The Second Circuit Court of Appeals observed that the Eighth Circuit's opinion "adduces no authority for protecting pagination as a 'reflection' of arrangement, and does not explain how the insertion of star pagination creates a 'copy' featuring an arrangement of cases substantially similar to West's—rather than a dissimilar arrangement that simply references the location of text in West's case reporters and incidentally simplifies the task of someone who wants to reproduce West's arrangement of cases." Further, in the court's view, the Eighth Circuit decision "rests upon the now defunct 'sweat of the brow' doctrine"; thus "the Eighth Circuit in *West Publishing Co.* erroneously protected West's industrious collection rather than it original creation. Because *Feist* undermines the reasoning of *West Publishing Co.*, we decline to follow it."

6. *Reproductions.* Consider the result that the *Sheldon, Bleistein* and *Feist* tests would produce in the following case. Plaintiff, who executed a scaled-down reproduction of Rodin's "Hand of God" that is identical to the Rodin piece in all respects other than size and configuration of base, seeks to enjoin defendant from producing and distributing exact copies of the reproduction. Defendant answers that, because plaintiff admittedly copied the public domain Rodin work, the reproduction necessarily fails the originality test. In Alva Studios, Inc. v. Winninger, 177 F.Supp. 265, 267, 123 U.S.P.Q. 487 (S.D.N.Y.1959), the court held plaintiff's reproduction to be original in light of the "great skill and originality" required to "produce a scale reduction of a great work with exactitude." Are "skill and originality" to be equated with creativity or with sweat of the brow?

Compare L. Batlin & Son, Inc. v. Snyder, 536 F.2d 486, 189 U.S.P.Q. 753 (2d Cir.1976), cert. denied, 429 U.S. 857, 97 S.Ct. 156, 50 L.Ed.2d 135, 191 U.S.P.Q. 588, in which the court held a plastic model of an antique cast iron "Uncle Sam" bank to be unoriginal. The plastic model differed from the prototype in size and details. Among other differences, "the carpetbag shape of the plastic bank is smooth, the iron bank is rough; the metal bank bag is fatter at its base; the eagle on the front of the platform in the metal bank is holding arrows in his talons while in the plastic bank he clutches leaves." 536 F.2d at 489. In the court's judgment, the "complexity and exactitude ... involved [in Alva v. Winninger] distinguishes that case amply from the one at bar." 536 F.2d at 491–492. From this, the court turned the proof of differences between the plastic model and the cast iron prototype *against* the copyright claimant: "[t]hus concededly the plastic version is not, and was scarcely meticulously produced to be, an exactly faithful reproduction." 536 F.2d 486, 492.

Are the results in *Alva* and *Batlin* just the opposite of what they should be? The copyright claimant in *Alva* presumably invested more painstaking effort than the copyright claimant in *Batlin*. Is the purpose of copyright to induce investment in the production of works that exactly copy public domain works, or production of works that embody expressive differences?

7.   *"Novelty" and "Originality."* Novelty has a limited use in determinations of originality. In Alfred Bell & Co. v. Catalda Fine Arts, 191 F.2d 99, 104–05, 90 U.S.P.Q. 153 (2d Cir.1951), the court upheld the originality of plaintiff's mezzotint engravings of paintings by old masters on the ground that "[t]here is evidence that they were not intended to and did not, imitate the paintings they reproduced. But even if their substantial departures from the paintings were inadvertent, the copyrights would be valid. A copyist's bad eyesight or defective musculature, or a shock caused by a clap of thunder, may yield sufficiently distinguishable variations. Having hit upon such a variation unintentionally, the 'author' may adopt it as his and copyright it." In cases like this, in which copying is either admitted or, as in Hand's Keats example, is irrebuttably self-evident, the court looks for new matter, for some variation from previous works, not to break the inference of copying, for copying is assumed, but rather to find some copyrightable—uncopied—component in claimant's work. Do these novel additions meet *Feist's* minimal standard for creativity?

Should novelty enjoy even this limited role? Copyright law possesses none of the search mechanisms for determining novelty that have developed around patent law's novelty and nonobviousness requirements. The few recorded and largely vain efforts at introducing prior art on the issue of copyright novelty only underscore copyright law's incapacity to measure novelty systematically. The fact was apparently lost on Justice Douglas who, dissenting from the Court's denial of certiorari in Lee v. Runge, 404 U.S. 887, 890–91, 92 S.Ct. 197, 30 L.Ed.2d 169, 171 U.S.P.Q. 322 (1971), suggested that the lower court had erred in holding that "[t]he standard of 'novelty' urged by appellants is applicable to patents, but not copyrights. The copyright standard is one of 'originality' ... Runge v. Lee, 441 F.2d 579, 169 U.S.P.Q. 388 (9th Cir.1971)." Giving a constitutional dimension to patent law's novelty requirement, Douglas argued that "no reason can be offered why we should depart from the plain import of this grant of congressional power and apply more lenient constitutional standards to copyrights than to patents.... To create a monopoly under the copyright power which would not be available under the patent power would be to betray the common birthright of all men at the altar of hollow formalisms."

B. OWNERSHIP

See Statute Supplement 17 U.S.C.A. §§ 201–202.

1. WORKS FOR HIRE AND JOINT WORKS

Copyright Law Revision, H.R. Rep. No. 1476

94th Cong., 2d Sess. 120–121 (1976).

Section 201.   Ownership of Copyright

Initial Ownership

Two basic and well-established principles of copyright law are restated in section 201(a): that the source of copyright ownership is the author of the work, and that, in the case of a "joint work," the coauthors of the work are likewise coowners of the copyright. Under the definition of section 101, a work is "joint" if the authors collaborated with each other, or if each of the authors prepared his or her contribution with the knowledge and intention that it would be merged with the contributions of other authors as "inseparable or interdependent parts of a unitary whole." The touch-stone here is the intention, at the time the writing is done, that the parts be absorbed or combined into an integrated unit, although the parts themselves may be either "inseparable" (as the case of a novel or painting) or "interdependent" (as in the case of a motion picture, opera, or the words and music of a song). The definition of "joint work" is to be contrasted with the definition of "collective work," also in section 101, in which the elements of merger and unity are lacking; there the key elements are assemblage or gathering of "separate and independent works ... into a collective whole."

The definition of "joint works" has prompted some concern lest it be construed as converting the authors of previously written works, such as plays, novels, and music, into coauthors of a motion picture in which their work is incorporated. It is true that a motion picture would normally be a joint rather than a collective work with respect to those authors who actually work on the film, although their usual status as employees for hire would keep the question of coownership from coming up. On the other hand, although a novelist, playwright, or songwriter may write a work with the hope or expectation that it will be used in a motion picture, this is clearly a case of separate or independent authorship rather than one where the basic intention behind the writing of the work was for motion picture use. In this case, the motion picture is a derivative work within the definition of that term, and section 103 makes plain that copyright in a derivative work is independent of, and does not enlarge the scope of rights in, any pre-existing material incorporated in it. There is thus no need to spell this conclusion out in the definition of "joint work."

There is also no need for a specific statutory provision concerning the rights and duties of the coowners of a work; court-made law on this point is left undisturbed. Under the bill, as under the present law, coowners of a copyright would be treated generally as tenants in common, with each coowner having an independent right to use or license the use of a work, subject to a duty of accounting to the other coowners for any profits.

Works Made for Hire

Section 201(b) of the bill adopts one of the basic principles of the present law: that in the case of works made for hire the employer is considered the author of the work, and is regarded as the initial owner of copyright unless there has been an agreement otherwise. The subsection also requires that any agreement under which the employee is to own rights be in writing and signed by the parties.

The work-made-for-hire provisions of this bill represent a carefully balanced compromise, and as such they do not incorporate the amendments proposed by screenwriters and composers for motion pictures. Their proposal was for the recognition of something similar to the "shop right" doctrine of patent law: with some exceptions, the employer would acquire the right to use the employee's work to the extent needed for purposes of his regular business, but the employee would retain all other rights as long as he or she refrained from the authorizing of competing uses. However, while this change might theoretically improve the bargaining position of screenwriters and others as a group, the practical benefits that individual authors would receive are highly conjectural. The presumption that initial ownership rights vest in the employer for hire is well established in American copyright law, and to exchange that for the uncertainties of the shop right doctrine would not only be of dubious value to employers and employees alike, but might also reopen a number of other issues.

The status of works prepared on special order or commission was a major issue in the development of the definition of "works made for hire" in section 101, which has undergone extensive revision during the legislative process. The basic problem is how to draw a statutory line between those works written on special order or commission that should be considered as "works made for hire," and those that should not. The definition now provided by the bill represents a compromise which, in effect, spells out those specific categories of commissioned works that can be considered "works made for hire" under certain circumstances.

Community for Creative Non–Violence v. Reid

Supreme Court of the United States, 1989.
490 U.S. 730, 109 S.Ct. 2166, 104 L.Ed.2d 811, 10 U.S.P.Q.2d 1985.

Justice MARSHALL delivered the opinion of the Court.

In this case, an artist and the organization that hired him to produce a sculpture contest the ownership of the copyright in that work. To resolve this dispute, we must construe the "work made for hire" provisions of the Copyright Act of 1976 (Act or 1976 Act), 17 U.S.C. §§ 101 and 201(b), and in particular, the provision in § 101, which defines as a "work made for hire" a "work prepared by an employee within the scope of his or her employment" (hereinafter § 101(1)).

I.

Petitioners are the Community for Creative Non–Violence (CCNV), a nonprofit unincorporated association dedicated to eliminating homelessness in America, and Mitch Snyder, a member and trustee of CCNV. In the fall of 1985, CCNV decided to participate in the annual Christmastime Pageant of Peace in Washington, D.C., by sponsoring a display to dramatize the plight of the homeless. As the District Court recounted:

> Snyder and fellow CCNV members conceived the idea for the nature of the display: a sculpture of a modern Nativity scene in which, in lieu of the traditional Holy Family, the two adult figures and the infant would appear as contemporary homeless people huddled on a streetside steam grate. The family was to be black (most of the homeless in Washington being black); the figures were to be life-sized, and the steam grate would be positioned atop a platform "pedestal," or base, within which special-effects equipment would be enclosed to emit simulated "steam" through the grid to swirl about the figures. They also settled upon a title for the work—"Third World America"—and a legend for the pedestal: "and still there is no room at the inn." 652 F.Supp. 1453, 1454 (D.D.C.1987).

Snyder made inquiries to locate an artist to produce the sculpture. He was referred to respondent James Earl Reid, a Baltimore, Maryland, sculptor. In the course of two telephone calls, Reid agreed to sculpt the three human figures. CCNV agreed to make the steam grate and pedestal for the statue. Reid proposed that the work be cast in bronze, at a total cost of approximately $100,000 and taking six to eight months to complete. Snyder rejected that proposal because CCNV did not have sufficient funds, and because the statue had to be completed by December 12 to be included in the pageant. Reid then suggested, and Snyder agreed, that the sculpture would be made of a material known as "Design Cast 62," a synthetic substance that could meet CCNV's monetary and time constraints, could be tinted to resemble bronze, and could withstand the elements. The parties agreed that the project would cost no more than $15,000, not including Reid's services, which he offered to donate. The parties did not sign a written agreement. Neither party mentioned copyright.

After Reid received an advance of $3,000, he made several sketches of figures in various poses. At Snyder's request, Reid sent CCNV a sketch of a proposed sculpture showing the family in a creche-like setting: the mother seated, cradling a baby in her lap; the father standing behind her, bending over her shoulder to touch the baby's foot. Reid testified that Snyder asked for the sketch to use in raising funds for the sculpture. Snyder testified that it was also for his approval. Reid sought a black family to serve as a model for the sculpture. Upon Snyder's suggestion, Reid visited a family living at CCNV's Washington shelter but decided that only their newly born child was a suitable model. While Reid was in Washington, Snyder took him to see homeless people living on the streets. Snyder pointed out that they tended to recline on steam grates, rather than sit or stand, in order to warm their bodies. From that time on, Reid's sketches contained only reclining figures.

Throughout November and the first two weeks of December 1985, Reid worked exclusively on the statue, assisted at various times by a dozen different people who were paid with funds provided in installments by CCNV. On a number of occasions, CCNV members visited Reid to check on his progress and to coordinate CCNV's construction of the base. CCNV rejected Reid's proposal to use suitcases or shopping bags to hold the family's personal belongings, insisting instead on a shopping cart. Reid and CCNV members did not discuss copyright ownership on any of these visits.

On December 24, 1985, 12 days after the agreed upon date, Reid delivered the completed statue to Washington. There it was joined to the steam grate and pedestal prepared by CCNV and placed on display near the site of the pageant. Snyder paid Reid the final installment of the $15,000. The statue remained on display for a month. In late January 1986, CCNV members returned it to Reid's studio in Baltimore for minor repairs. Several weeks later, Snyder began making plans to take the statue on a tour of several cities to raise money for the homeless. Reid objected, contending that the Design Cast 62 material was not strong enough to withstand the ambitious itinerary. He urged CCNV to cast the statue in bronze at a cost of $35,000, or to create a master mold at a cost of $5,000. Snyder declined to spend more of CCNV's money on the project.

In March 1986, Snyder asked Reid to return the sculpture. Reid refused. He then filed a certificate of copyright registration for "Third World America" in his name and announced plans to take the sculpture on a more modest tour than the one CCNV had proposed. Snyder, acting in his capacity as CCNV's trustee, immediately filed a competing certificate of copyright registration.

Snyder and CCNV then commenced this action against Reid and his photographer, Ronald Purtee, seeking return of the sculpture and a determination of copyright ownership. The District Court granted a preliminary injunction, ordering the sculpture's return. After a 2–day bench trial, the District Court declared that "Third World America" was a "work made for hire" under § 101 of the Copyright Act and that Snyder, as trustee for CCNV, was the exclusive owner of the copyright in the sculpture. The court reasoned that Reid had been an "employee" of CCNV within the meaning of § 101(1) because CCNV was the motivating force in the statue's production. Snyder and other CCNV members, the court explained, "conceived the idea of a contemporary Nativity scene to contrast with the national celebration of the season," and "directed enough of [Reid's] effort to assure that, in the end, he had produced what they, not he, wanted." Id., at 1456.

The Court of Appeals for the District of Columbia reversed and remanded, holding that Reid owned the copyright because "Third World America" was not a work for hire. Adopting what it termed the "literal interpretation" of the Act as articulated by the Fifth Circuit in Easter Seal Society for Crippled Children and Adults of Louisiana, Inc. v. Playboy Enterprises, 815 F.2d 323, 329 (1987), cert. denied, 485 U.S. 981, 108 S.Ct. 1280, 99 L.Ed.2d 491 (1988), the court read § 101 as creating "a simple dichotomy in fact between employees and independent contractors." 270 U.S.App.D.C., at 33, 846 F.2d, at 1492. Because, under agency law, Reid was an independent contractor, the court concluded that the work was not "prepared by an employee" under § 101(1). Id., at 35, 846 F.2d, at 1494. Nor was the sculpture a "work made for hire" under the second subsection of § 101 (hereinafter § 101(2)): sculpture is not one of the nine categories of works enumerated in that subsection, and the parties had not agreed in writing that the sculpture would be a work for hire. The court suggested that the sculpture nevertheless may have been jointly authored by CCNV and Reid, and remanded for a determination whether the sculpture is indeed a joint work under the Act.

We granted certiorari to resolve a conflict among the Courts of Appeals over the proper construction of the "work made for hire" provisions of the Act. We now affirm.

II.

A

The Copyright Act of 1976 provides that copyright ownership "vests initially in the author or authors of the work." 17 U.S.C. § 201(a). As a general rule, the author is the party who actually creates the work, that is, the person who translates an idea into a fixed, tangible expression entitled to copyright protection. The Act carves out an important exception, however, for "works made for hire." If the work is for hire, "the employer or other person for whom the work was prepared is considered the author" and owns the copyright, unless there is a written agreement to the contrary. § 201(b). Classifying a work as "made for hire" determines not only the initial ownership of its copyright, but also the copyright's duration, § 302(c), and the owners' renewal rights, § 304(a), termination rights, § 203(a), and right to import certain goods bearing the copyright, § 601(b)(1). The contours of the work for hire doctrine therefore carry profound significance for freelance creators—including artists, writers, photographers, designers, composers, and computer programmers—and for the publishing, advertising, music, and other industries which commission their works.[4]

Section 101 of the 1976 Act provides that a work is "for hire" under two sets of circumstances:

(1) a work prepared by an employee within the scope of his or her employment; or

(2) a work specially ordered or commissioned for use as a contribution to a collective work, as a part of a motion picture or other audiovisual work, as a translation, as a supplementary work, as a compilation, as an instructional text, as a test, as answer material for a test, or as an atlas, if the parties expressly agree in a written instrument signed by them that the work shall be considered a work made for hire.

The petitioners do not claim that the statue satisfies the terms of § 101(2). Quite clearly, it does not. Sculpture does not fit within any of the nine categories of "specially ordered or commissioned" works enumerated in that subsection, and no written agreement between the parties establishes "Third World America" as a work for hire.

The dispositive inquiry in this case therefore is whether "Third World America" is "a work prepared by an employee within the scope of his or her employment" under § 101(1). The Act does not define these terms. In the absence of such guidance, four interpretations have emerged. The first holds that a work is prepared by an employee whenever the hiring party retains the right to control the product. See Peregrine v. Lauren Corp., 601 F.Supp. 828, 829 (D.Colo.1985); Clarkstown v. Reeder, 566 F.Supp. 137, 142 (S.D.N.Y.1983). Petitioners take this view. A second, and closely related, view is that a work is prepared by an employee under § 101(1) when the hiring party has actually wielded control with respect to the creation of a particular work. This approach was formulated by the Court of Appeals for the Second Circuit, Aldon Accessories Ltd. v. Spiegel, Inc., 738 F.2d 548, cert. denied, 469 U.S. 982, 105 S.Ct. 387, 83 L.Ed.2d 321 (1984), and adopted by the Fourth Circuit, Brunswick Beacon, Inc. v. Schock–Hopchas Publishing Co., 810 F.2d 410 (1987), the Seventh Circuit, Evans Newton, Inc. v. Chicago Systems Software, 793 F.2d 889, cert. denied, 479 U.S. 949, 107 S.Ct. 434, 93 L.Ed.2d 383 (1986), and, at times, by petitioners. A third view is that the term "employee" within § 101(1) carries its common law agency law meaning. This view was endorsed by the Fifth Circuit in Easter Seal Society for Crippled Children and Adults of Louisiana, Inc. v. Playboy Enterprises, 815 F.2d 323 (1987), and by the

---

4. As of 1955, approximately 40 percent of all copyright registrations were for works for hire, according to a Copyright Office study. See Varmer, Works Made for Hire and On Commission, in Studies Prepared for the Subcommittee on Patents, Trademarks, and Copyrights of the Senate Committee on the Judiciary, Study No. 13, 86th Cong., 2d Sess. 139, n. 49 (Comm.Print, 1960) (hereinafter Varmer, Works Made for Hire). The Copyright Office does not keep more recent statistics on the number of work for hire registrations.

Court of Appeals below. Finally, respondent and numerous amici curiae contend that the term "employee" only refers to "formal, salaried" employees. The Court of Appeals for the Ninth Circuit recently adopted this view. See Dumas v. Gommerman, 865 F.2d 1093 (1989).

The starting point for our interpretation of a statute is always its language. The Act nowhere defines the terms "employee" or "scope of employment." It is, however, well established that "[w]here Congress uses terms that have accumulated settled meaning under . . . the common law, a court must infer, unless the statute otherwise dictates, that Congress means to incorporate the established meaning of these terms." NLRB v. Amax Coal Co., 453 U.S. 322, 329, 101 S.Ct. 2789, 2794, 69 L.Ed.2d 672 (1981). In the past, when Congress has used the term "employee" without defining it, we have concluded that Congress intended to describe the conventional master-servant relationship as understood by common law agency doctrine. Nothing in the text of the work for hire provisions indicates that Congress used the words "employee" and "employment" to describe anything other than " 'the conventional relation of employer and employeé.' " On the contrary, Congress' intent to incorporate the agency law definition is suggested by § 101(1)'s use of the term, "scope of employment," a widely used term of art in agency law. See Restatement (Second) of Agency § 228 (1958) (hereinafter Restatement).

In past cases of statutory interpretation, when we have concluded that Congress intended terms such as "employee," "employer," and "scope of employment" to be understood in light of agency law, we have relied on the general common law of agency, rather than on the law of any particular State, to give meaning to these terms. This practice reflects the fact that "federal statutes are generally intended to have uniform nationwide application." Mississippi Band of Choctaw Indians v. Holyfield, 109 S.Ct. 1597, 1605, 104 L.Ed.2d 29 (1989). Establishment of a federal rule of agency, rather than reliance on state agency law, is particularly appropriate here given the Act's express objective of creating national uniform copyright law by broadly pre-empting state statutory and common-law copyright regulation. We thus agree with the Court of Appeals that the term "employee" should be understood in light of the general common law of agency.

In contrast, neither test proposed by petitioners is consistent with the text of the Act. The exclusive focus of the right to control the product test on the relationship between the hiring party and the product clashes with the language of § 101(1), which focuses on the relationship between the hired and hiring parties. The right to control the product test also would distort the meaning of the ensuing subsection, § 101(2). Section 101 plainly creates two distinct ways in which a work can be deemed for hire: one for works prepared by employees, the other for those specially ordered or commissioned works which fall within one of the nine enumerated categories and are the subject of a written agreement. The right to control the product test ignores this dichotomy by transforming into a work for hire under § 101(1) any "specially ordered or commissioned" work that is subject to the supervision and control of the hiring party. Because a party who hires a "specially ordered or commissioned" work by definition has a right to specify the characteristics of the product desired, at the time the commission is accepted, and frequently until it is completed, the right to control the product test would mean that many works that could satisfy § 101(2) would already have been deemed works for hire under § 101(1). Petitioners' interpretation is particularly hard to square with § 101(2)'s enumeration of the nine specific categories of specially ordered or commissioned works eligible to be works for hire, e.g., "a contribution to a collective work," "a part of a motion picture," and "answer material for a test." The unifying feature of these works is that they are usually prepared at the instance, direction, and risk of a publisher or producer. By their very nature, therefore, these types of works would be works by an employee under petitioners' right to control the product test.

The actual control test, articulated by the Second Circuit in *Aldon Accessories,* fares only marginally better when measured against the language and structure of § 101. Under this test, independent contractors who are so controlled and supervised in the creation of a particular work are deemed "employees" under § 101(1). Thus work for hire status under § 101(1) depends on a hiring party's *actual* control, rather than *right* to control, of the product. Under the actual control test, a work for hire could arise under § 101(2), but not under § 101(1), where a party commissions, but does not actually control, a product which falls into one of the nine enumerated categories. Nonetheless, we agree with the Fifth Circuit Court of Appeals that "[t]here is simply no way to milk the 'actual control' test of *Aldon Accessories* from the language of the statute." *Easter Seal Society,* 815 F.2d, at 334. Section 101 clearly delineates between works prepared by an employee and commissioned works. Sound though other distinctions might be as a matter of copyright policy, there is no statutory support for an additional dichotomy between commissioned works that are actually controlled and supervised by the hiring party and those that are not.

We therefore conclude that the language and structure of § 101 of the Act do not support either the right to control the product or the actual control approaches.[8] The structure of § 101 indicates that a work for hire can arise through one of two mutually exclusive means, one for employees and one for independent contractors, and ordinary canons of statutory

---

8. We also reject the suggestion of respondent and *amici* that the § 101(1) term "employee" refers only to formal, salaried employees. While there is some support for such a definition in the legislative history, the language of § 101(1) cannot support it. The Act does not say "formal" or "salaried" employee, but simply "employee." Moreover, the respondent and those *amici* who endorse a formal, salaried employee test do not agree upon the content of this test. Compare, e.g., Brief for Respondent 37 (hired party who is on payroll is an employee within § 101(1)) with Tr. of Oral Arg. 31 (hired party who receives a salary or commissions regularly is an employee within § 101(1)); and Brief for Volunteer Lawyers for the Arts Inc. *et al.* as *Amici Curiae* 4 (hired party who receives a salary *and* is treated as an employee for Social Security and tax purposes is an employee within § 101(1)). Even the one Court of Appeals to adopt what it termed a formal, salaried employee test in fact embraced an approach incorporating numerous factors drawn from the agency law definition of employee which we endorse. See *Dumas,* 865 F.2d, at 1104.

interpretation indicate that the classification of a particular hired party should be made with reference to agency law. . . .

Finally, petitioners' construction of the work for hire provisions would impede Congress' paramount goal in revising the 1976 Act of enhancing predictability and certainty of copyright ownership. In a "copyright marketplace," the parties negotiate with an expectation that one of them will own the copyright in the completed work. With that expectation, the parties at the outset can settle on relevant contractual terms, such as the price for the work and the ownership of reproduction rights.

To the extent that petitioners endorse an actual control test, CCNV's construction of the work for hire provisions prevents such planning. Because that test turns on whether the hiring party has closely monitored the production process, the parties would not know until late in the process, if not until the work is completed, whether a work will ultimately fall within § 101(1). Under petitioners' approach, therefore, parties would have to predict in advance whether the hiring party will sufficiently control a given work to make it the author. "If they guess incorrectly, their reliance on 'work for hire' or an assignment may give them a copyright interest that they did not bargain for." *Easter Seal Society,* 815 F.2d, at 333. This understanding of the work for hire provisions clearly thwarts Congress' goal of ensuring predictability through advance planning. Moreover, petitioners' interpretation "leaves the door open for hiring parties, who have failed to get a full assignment of copyright rights from independent contractors falling outside the subdivision (2) guidelines, to unilaterally obtain work-made-for-hire rights years after the work has been completed as long as they directed or supervised the work, a standard that is hard not to meet when one is a hiring party." Hamilton, Commissioned Works as Works Made for Hire Under the 1976 Copyright Act: Misinterpretation and Injustice, 135 U.Pa.L.Rev. 1281, 1304 (1987).

In sum, we must reject petitioners' argument. Transforming a commissioned work into a work by an employee on the basis of the hiring party's right to control, or actual control of, the work is inconsistent with the language, structure, and legislative history of the work for hire provisions. To determine whether a work is for hire under the Act, a court first should ascertain, using principles of general common law of agency, whether the work was prepared by an employee or an independent contractor. After making this determination, the court can apply the appropriate subsection of § 101.

B

We turn, finally, to an application of § 101 to Reid's production of "Third World America." In determining whether a hired party is an employee under the general common law of agency, we consider the hiring party's right to control the manner and means by which the product is accomplished. Among the other factors relevant to this inquiry are the skill required; the source of the instrumentalities and tools; the location of the work; the duration of the relationship between the parties; whether the hiring party has the right to assign additional projects to the hired party; the extent of the hired party's discretion over when and how long to work;

the method of payment; the hired party's role in hiring and paying assistants; whether the work is part of the regular business of the hiring party; whether the hiring party is in business; the provision of employee benefits; and the tax treatment of the hired party. See Restatement § 220(2) (setting forth a nonexhaustive list of factors relevant to determining whether a hired party is an employee). No one of these factors is determinative.

Examining the circumstances of this case in light of these factors, we agree with the Court of Appeals that Reid was not an employee of CCNV but an independent contractor. True, CCNV members directed enough of Reid's work to ensure that he produced a sculpture that met their specifications. But the extent of control the hiring party exercises over the details of the product is not dispositive. Indeed, all the other circumstances weigh heavily against finding an employment relationship. Reid is a sculptor, a skilled occupation. Reid supplied his own tools. He worked in his own studio in Baltimore, making daily supervision of his activities from Washington practicably impossible. Reid was retained for less than two months, a relatively short period of time. During and after this time, CCNV had no right to assign additional projects to Reid. Apart from the deadline for completing the sculpture, Reid had absolute freedom to decide when and how long to work. CCNV paid Reid $15,000, a sum dependent on "completion of a specific job, a method by which independent contractors are often compensated." Holt v. Winpisinger, 258 U.S.App.D.C. 343, 351, 811 F.2d 1532, 1540 (1987). Reid had total discretion in hiring and paying assistants. "Creating sculptures was hardly 'regular business' for CCNV." 270 U.S.App.D.C., at 35, n. 11, 846 F.2d, at 1494, n. 11. Indeed, CCNV is not a business at all. Finally, CCNV did not pay payroll or social security taxes, provide any employee benefits, or contribute to unemployment insurance or workers' compensation funds.

Because Reid was an independent contractor, whether "Third World America" is a work for hire depends on whether it satisfies the terms of § 101(2). This petitioners concede it cannot do. Thus, CCNV is not the author of "Third World America" by virtue of the work for hire provisions of the Act. However, as the Court of Appeals made clear, CCNV nevertheless may be a joint author of the sculpture if, on remand, the District Court so determines that CCNV and Reid prepared the work "with the intention that their contributions be merged into inseparable or interdependent parts of a unitary whole." 17 U.S.C. § 101. In that case, CCNV and Reid would be co-owners of the copyright in the work. See § 201(a).

For the aforestated reasons, we affirm the judgment of the Court of Appeals for the District of Columbia.

It is so ordered.

Erickson v. Trinity Theatre, Inc.

United States Court of Appeals, Seventh Circuit, 1994.
13 F.3d 1061, 29 U.S.P.Q.2d 1347.

RIPPLE, Circuit Judge.

The plaintiff Karen Erickson brought this action seeking a preliminary and permanent injunction to prevent the defendant Trinity Theatre d/b/a/

Trinity Square Ensemble ("Trinity") from performing three plays and using two videotapes to which she owned the copyrights. The magistrate judge recommended enjoining the performance of the plays but not the use of the videotapes. Both parties filed objections. The district court sustained Ms. Erickson's objections to the portions of the recommendation addressing the videotapes but denied Trinity's objections to the portion of the recommendation addressing performance of the plays. Accordingly, the district court enjoined Trinity from using either the plays or the videotapes. Trinity now appeals. We now affirm.

I

BACKGROUND

A. *Facts*

Ms. Erickson was one of the founders of a theatre company in Evanston, Illinois, that ultimately became known as Trinity Theatre. Between 1981 and January 1991, Ms. Erickson served Trinity in various capacities: as playwright, artistic director, actress, play director, business manager, and member of the board of directors. This suit revolves around Ms. Erickson's role as playwright.

At issue here are the rights to three plays: *Much Ado About Shakespeare* ("*Much Ado*"); *The Theatre Time Machine* ("*Time Machine*"); and *Prairie Voices: Tales from Illinois* ("*Prairie Voices*"). *Much Ado* is a compilation of scenes and sonnets from William Shakespeare and other writers of his time. Ms. Erickson revised this work from an earlier script entitled *Sounds and Sweet Aires*. Michael Osborne, a Trinity actor, testified that Ms. Erickson compiled *Much Ado* in 1988 and that many decisions about what was to be included were made during rehearsals. Osborne identified two portions of the copyrighted script that resulted from his suggestions: a passage to *Macbeth* and the introduction to the play. The editing of the text, Osborne continued, was accomplished largely by consensus; however, when a consensus could not be had, Ms. Erickson made the final decisions. Osborne further testified that he understood at the time that the play was being created for Trinity and not for Ms. Erickson. Ms. Erickson does not dispute the process described by Osborne, but characterizes it differently. She perceived the process only as actors making suggestions for her script.

Time Machine is a play of five scenes based on a public domain Native American folk tale. Each scene depicts dramatic styles from different historical periods. Ms. Erickson received a copyright registration for *Time Machine* on September 12, 1988. She described the development of the play as beginning in 1977 when she was in school. At that time, she wrote the Greek-style drama scene. Later, while teaching high school drama, she wrote the second scene based on *commedia dell'arte*. She also began work on the melodrama and improvisational scenes of the play at that time. Ms. Erickson started producing the play independently of Trinity in 1984 with two other actors, Paddy Lynn and Will Clinger. Ms. Erickson claimed that she worked to develop the scenes alone; however, the evidence shows that the actors were involved in the development of the melodrama and improvisational scenes. The improvisational process, as described by Ms. Lynn, is a form of theatre in which there is no script. Rather, actors work with an idea and a loose structure to create a play. Ms. Lynn described the development of the improvisational scene in *Time Machine* as a collaborative effort. However, she conceded that Ms. Erickson took all of the notes from rehearsals and compiled them into the script; furthermore, nothing was included in the script without Ms. Erickson's approval. Initially, Ms. Erickson attributed the script to both herself and to Ms. Lynn. Ms. Lynn also received royalties for performances of the play. Ms. Erickson denied that she ever intended to include Ms. Lynn as joint author. She conceded that Ms. Lynn was credited on publicity materials as an author but denied that she approved such credit. The later change in attribution, Ms. Erickson claims, merely corrected the initial error.

In 1990, Ms. Erickson developed *Prairie Voices*, a play based on tales from Illinois history. She had the idea to develop the play as a Trinity production. Her original intent was to launch a collaborative effort in which each of the actors would contribute a story to the play. However, none of the actors initiated writing a script and the play, as it resulted, was based entirely on tales provided by Ms. Erickson. As with *Time Machine*, Ms. Erickson worked with the actors in the improvisational format. Although testifying that she alone wrote the play, Ms. Erickson admitted that the actors provided ideas for the dialogue. Another actor, Ruth Ann Weyna, testified that the writing of the play was a creative process involving a number of actors. However, she conceded that Ms. Erickson controlled what eventually was put in the script.

In 1987, Trinity began paying Ms. Erickson royalties for its performances of her plays. On July 5, 1988, Ms. Erickson entered into a two-year licensing agreement with Trinity that designated her as a "playwright" entitling her to royalties for performances of two of her plays, *Much Ado* and *Time Machine*. Trinity stipulated that it also paid Erickson royalties for its performances of *Prairie Voices*, although that play was not expressly covered by the licensing agreement. Trinity continued to pay Ms. Erickson royalties after the expiration of the licensing agreement. Trinity discontinued making royalty payments on November 15, 1990.

Ms. Erickson was also subject to an actors' agreement with Trinity. In July 1988, Ms. Erickson signed the agreement which stated: "The actor expressly agrees that Trinity reserves the rights to any recording, audio, video or both of the Production...." The contract covered the tour which was forecast to run through June 30, 1989.

Ms. Erickson left Trinity Theatre in January 1991. Shortly thereafter, she applied for and was issued copyright registration for *Much Ado* and *Prairie Voices*. Concurrently, she received registration for the video productions of *Time Machine*, taped in October 1989, and *Prairie Voices*, taped in November 1990. She had previously obtained a copyright certificate for

Time Machine on September 12, 1988. On January 21, 1991, Ms. Erickson's attorneys wrote Trinity a letter demanding that the theatre discontinue performing the plaintiff's plays. Trinity refused to comply with the request.

On April 3, 1991, Ms. Erickson filed a seventeen-count complaint against Trinity Theatre, members of Trinity's management, and individual Trinity actors seeking injunctive and legal relief in which she alleged copyright infringement, unfair competition, and other related tortious activity. In October 1992, Ms. Erickson filed a motion for a preliminary injunction to prevent the defendant from producing or performing five plays for which Ms. Erickson claimed exclusive copyright ownership, from displaying videotapes, photographs, and brochures regarding these plays, and from reproducing any materials from a copyrighted work entitled "Drama/Learning Process." After a partial settlement agreement, the parties stipulated that the district court did not need to resolve the plaintiff's request for injunctive relief as to two of the five plays. As a result, the only plays at issue for purposes of the plaintiff's motion for preliminary injunction were *Time Machine*, *Much Ado*, and *Prairie Voices*, as well as videotapes of *Time Machine* and *Prairie Voices*.

II

ANALYSIS

B. *Joint Work*

We now turn to the issue of whether any of the material in question is a "joint work." In a joint work, the joint authors hold undivided interests in a work, despite any differences in each author's contribution. Each author as co-owner has the right to use or to license the use of the work, subject to an accounting to the other co-owners for any profits. Thus, even a person whose contribution is relatively minor, if accorded joint authorship status, enjoys a significant benefit.

In determining whether any of the works at issue in this case may be classified as a "joint work," our starting point must be the language of the statute. Section 101 of the Copyright Act defines a "joint work" as

> a work prepared by two or more authors with the intention that their contributions be merged into inseparable or interdependent parts of a unitary whole.

17 U.S.C. § 101.

1.

Neither the Act nor its legislative history defines "inseparable" or "interdependent." The legislative history states that examples of inseparable parts are the joint contributions of two authors to a single novel or the contributions of two painters to a single work; an example of interdependent parts are the lyrics and music for a song. Apart from these examples, the reports do little to clarify the criteria for determining joint authorship. Indeed, they increase the ambiguity. The committee reports state:

> [A] work is "joint" if the authors collaborated with each other, *or* if *each* of the authors prepared his or her contribution with the knowledge and *intention* that it would be merged with the contributions of other authors as "inseparable or interdependent parts of a unitary whole." The touchstone here is *the intention, at the time the writing is done*, that the parts be absorbed or combined into an integrated unit. . . .

House Report at 120; Senate Report at 103, U.S.Code Cong. & Admin.News 1976, pp. 5736 (emphasis added). The statute clearly requires a focus on the intention to collaborate. However, the disjunctive first sentence in the legislative reports, set out directly above, seemingly contradicts that statutory language by focusing on collaboration and not mentioning intent to create a joint work.

This ambiguity presents analytical problems in cases such as this one, in which the parties have collaborated in some sense but dispute whether there was a mutual intent to create a joint work. In resolving this ambiguity, we believe that it is important to note, at the outset, that the statute itself requires that there be an intent to create a joint work. Therefore, reliance on collaboration alone, as Trinity suggests, would be incompatible with the clear statutory mandate. On this point, we find ourselves in agreement with the analysis of Judge Newman writing for the Second Circuit in *Childress* [*v. Taylor*]. He pointed out that a disjunctive standard based solely on the legislative history would not square with the plain meaning of the statute:

> This passage appears to state two alternative criteria—one focusing on the act of collaboration and the other on the parties' intent. However, it is hard to imagine activity that would constitute meaningful "collaboration" unaccompanied by the requisite intent on the part of both participants that their contributions be merged into a unitary whole, and the case law has read the statutory language literally so that the intent requirement applies to all works of joint authorship.

Childress, 945 F.2d at 505–06. Like the Second Circuit in *Childress*, we believe that the statutory language clearly requires that each author intend that their respective contributions be merged into a unitary whole. Focusing solely upon the fact of contemporaneous input by several parties does not satisfy the statutory requirement that the parties intend to merge their contributions into a unified work. In addition, the "collaboration alone" standard would frustrate the goal of the Act "[t]o promote the Progress of Science and the useful Arts." U.S. Const. art. I, § 8, cl. 8. Seldom would an author subject his work to pre-registration peer review if this were the applicable test. Those seeking copyrights would not seek further refinement that colleagues may offer if they risked losing their sole authorship. Thus, we cannot accept Trinity's proposed "collaboration alone" test as compatible with the language and purpose of the Act.

2.

Even if two or more persons collaborate with the intent to create a unitary work, the product will be considered a "joint work" only if the collaborators can be considered "authors." Courts have applied two tests to evaluate the contributions of authors claiming joint authorship status: Professor Nimmer's de minimis test and Professor Goldstein's copyrightable subject matter ("copyrightability") test. The de minimis and copyrightability tests differ in one fundamental respect. The de minimis test requires that only the combined product of joint efforts must be copyrightable. By contrast, Professor Goldstein's copyrightability test requires that each author's contribution be copyrightable. We evaluate each of these tests in turn.

In undertaking this task, we focus on how well the test promotes the primary objective of the Act. This objective is not to reward an author for her labors, but "[t]o promote the Progress of Science and useful Arts." U.S. Const. art. I, § 8, cl. 8; *see also Feist Publications, Inc. v. Rural Tel. Serv. Co., Inc.*, 499 U.S. 340, 350, 111 S.Ct. 1282, 1290, 113 L.Ed.2d 358 (1991). This objective is accomplished by "assur[ing] authors the right to their original expression," but also by "encourag[ing] others to build freely upon the ideas and information conveyed by a work." *Feist Publications*, 499 U.S. at 349–50, 111 S.Ct. at 1290 (citing *Harper & Row, Publishers, Inc. v. Nation Enters.*, 471 U.S. 539, 556–57, 105 S.Ct. 2218, 2228–29, 85 L.Ed.2d 588 (1985)). It is in light of this goal that § 102(b) exempts ideas from protection under the Copyright Act.

In addition to promoting the Act's primary objective, we must consider how well the test will further goals of administrative and judicial efficiency. In this inquiry, we must adopt a standard that is sufficiently clear to enable parties to predict whether their contributions to a work will receive copyright protection. A standard satisfying these aims will allow contributors to avoid post-contribution disputes concerning authorship, and to protect themselves by contract if it appears that they would not enjoy protections of the Act itself.

a. Professor Nimmer's de minimis standard

Professor Nimmer, the late scholar on copyright, took the position that all that should be required to achieve joint author status is more than a de minimis contribution by each author. "De minimis" requires that "more than a word or line must be added by one who claims to be a joint author." *Nimmer* § 6.07, at 6–21. Professor Nimmer distinguishes his de minimis standard from the standard for copyrightability. As an example, Professor Nimmer asserts that if two authors collaborate, with one contributing only uncopyrightable plot ideas and another incorporating those ideas into a completed literary expression, the two authors should be regarded as joint authors of the resulting work.

This position has not found support in the courts. The lack of support in all likelihood stems from one of several weaknesses in Professor Nimmer's approach. First, Professor Nimmer's test is not consistent with one of the Act's premises: ideas and concepts standing alone should not receive protection. Because the creative process necessarily involves the development of existing concepts into new forms, any restriction on the free exchange of ideas stifles creativity to some extent. Restrictions on an author's use of existing ideas in a work, such as the threat that accepting suggestions from another party might jeopardize the author's sole entitlement to a copyright, would hinder creativity. Second, contribution of an idea is an exceedingly ambiguous concept. Professor Nimmer provides little guidance to courts or parties regarding when a contribution rises to the level of joint authorship except to state that the contribution must be "more than a word or a line." *Nimmer*, § 6.07, at 6–20.

Professor Nimmer's approach is of little pragmatic use in resolving actual cases. Rarely will minor contributors have the presumption to claim authorship status. In such easy cases, the parties' intent as to authorship status likely will be apparent without resort to any formal test evaluating the parties' respective contributions to discern intent. In the more complex situations, such as the case before us, in which the improvisational process undoubtedly yielded valuable insights to the primary author, the test gives no guidance on how we are to assess the respective contributions of the parties to distinguish the author from the critic or advisor. For these reasons, we, as the majority of the other courts, cannot accept Professor Nimmer's test as an adequate judicial tool to ascertain joint authorship.

b.   Professor Goldstein's copyrightability test

The copyrightable subject matter test was formulated by Professor Paul Goldstein and has been adopted, in some form, by a majority of courts that have considered the issue. According to Professor Goldstein, "[a] collaborative contribution will not produce a joint work, and a contributor will not obtain a co-ownership interest, unless the contribution represents original expression that could stand on its own as the subject matter of copyright." Paul Goldstein, *Copyright: Principles, Law, and Practice* § 4.2.1.2, at 379 (1989). Furthermore, the parties must have intended to be joint authors at the time the work was created. Professor Goldstein and the courts adopting his test justify this position by noting that § 101's and § 302(b)'s use of the word "authors" suggests that each collaborator's contribution must be a copyrightable "work of authorship" within the meaning of § 102(a).

We agree that the language of the Act supports the adoption of a copyrightability requirement. Section 101 of the Act defines a "joint work" as a "work prepared by two or more *authors*" (emphasis added). To qualify as an author, one must supply more than mere direction or ideas. An author is "the party who actually creates the work, that is, the person who translates an idea into a fixed, tangible expression entitled to copyright protection." *Community for Creative Non–Violence v. Reid*, 490 U.S. 730, 737, 109 S.Ct. 2166, 2171, 104 L.Ed.2d 811 (1989). As to the requirement of fixation, § 101 states:

> A work is "fixed" in a tangible medium of expression when its embodiment in a copy or phonorecord, by or under the authority of the author, is sufficiently permanent or stable to permit it to be perceived,

reproduced, or otherwise communicated for a period of more than transitory duration.

17 U.S.C. § 101.

The copyrightable subject matter test does not suffer from the same infirmities as Professor Nimmer's de minimis test. The copyrightability test advances creativity in science and art by allowing for the unhindered exchange of ideas, and protects authorship rights in a consistent and predictable manner. It excludes contributions such as ideas which are not protected under the Copyright Act. This test also enables parties to predict whether their contributions to a work will entitle them to copyright protection as a joint author. Compared to the uncertain exercise of divining whether a contribution is more than de minimis, reliance on the copyrightability of an author's proposed contribution yields relatively certain answers. The copyrightability standard allows contributors to avoid post-contribution disputes concerning authorship, and to protect themselves by contract if it appears that they would not enjoy the benefits accorded to authors of joint works under the Act.

We agree with the *Childress* court's observation that the copyrightability test "strikes an appropriate balance in the domains of both copyright and contract law." 945 F.2d at 507. Section 201(b) of the Act allows any person to contract with another to create a work and endow the employer with authorship status under the Act. A contributor of uncopyrightable ideas may also protect her rights to compensation under the Act by contract. Section 201(d) of the Act provides in part that any of the exclusive ownership rights comprised in a copyright may be transferred from the person who satisfied the requirements for obtaining the copyright to one who contracts for such rights. Thus, anyone who contributes to the creation of a work, either as patron, employer, or contributor of ideas, has the opportunity to share in the profits produced by the work through an appropriate contractual arrangement.

C. *Application*

We now address Trinity's claims of joint authorship under the copyrightability test. As stated above, Trinity must clear two hurdles in order to establish that the plays at issue are joint works. First, it must show the parties intended to be joint authors at the time the work was created. Second, Trinity must show that its contributions to the works were independently copyrightable.

It is clear that, with regard to at least two works, *Much Ado* and *Prairie Voices*, Trinity cannot clear the first hurdle. *Much Ado* is based on a work that Ms. Erickson had largely completed before Trinity actors improvised based on Ms. Erickson's creation. The fact that one actor, Michael Osborne, suggested that Ms. Erickson include a passage from *Macbeth* and an introduction to the play does not make him a joint author. He conceded that whether his contributions were included and where they went into the compilation were entirely Ms. Erickson's decisions. Furthermore, neither Ms. Erickson nor Trinity considered any of the actors to be co-authors with her in *Much Ado*, as is evidenced by the licensing agreement. Similarly with *Prairie Voices*, Ms. Erickson provided the stories on which the play was based, and she decided which of the actors' suggestions were incorporated into the script. The actors did not consider themselves to be joint authors with Ms. Erickson, and there is no evidence that Ms. Erickson considered the actors as co-authors of the script. Because Trinity cannot establish the requisite intent for *Much Ado* or *Prairie Voices*, the actors cannot be considered joint authors for the purposes of copyright protection.

Time Machine, as both the magistrate judge and the district court noted, is more problematic. Paddy Lynn testified that at least two scenes from *Time Machine* were developed through a collaborative process. Ms. Lynn considered the created dialogue to be hers as well as Ms. Erickson's. Furthermore, there is evidence that Ms. Erickson, too, intended at the time to create a joint work because she initially attributed the script to both Ms. Lynn and herself. Consequently, Trinity has produced some evidence that there was the requisite intent for joint authorship with regard to *Time Machine*. In *Childress*, the Second Circuit specifically acknowledged that " 'billing' or 'credit' " may be evidence of intent to create a joint work. Here there is evidence that Ms. Lynn was credited with authorship of *Time Machine*.

In order for the plays to be joint works under the Act, Trinity also must show that actors' contributions to Ms. Erickson's work could have been independently copyrighted. Trinity cannot establish this requirement for any of the above works. The actors, on the whole, could not identify specific contributions that they had made to Ms. Erickson's works. Even when Michael Osborne was able to do so, the contributions that he identified were not independently copyrightable. Ideas, refinements, and suggestions, standing alone, are not the subjects of copyrights. Consequently, Trinity cannot establish the two necessary elements of the copyrightability test and its claims must fail. Trinity cannot establish joint authorship to the plays at issue. As a result, Trinity cannot overcome the presumption in favor of the validity of Ms. Erickson's copyrights. Consequently, Ms. Erickson is very likely to succeed on the merits of her claims for copyright infringement.

Conclusion

For the foregoing reasons, the judgment of the district court is affirmed.

AFFIRMED.

NOTES

1. *Works for Hire.* Is *Reid* likely to promote "Congress' paramount goal in revising the 1976 Act of enhancing predictability and certainty of copyright ownership?" Does the Agency Restatement's "nonexhaustive" list of common law factors—relied upon by the *Reid* Court—offer greater predictability than the supervision and control test previously employed in work for hire cases? Note that "control" is an essential element of the Restatement's definition of "servant": "A servant is a person employed to perform services in the affairs of another and who with respect to the physical conduct in the performance of the services is subject to the other's control or right to control." Restatement (Second) of Agency § 220(1) (1957). See generally, Robert Kreiss, Scope of Employment and Being an Employee Under Work–Made-for-Hire Provisions of the Copyright Law: Applying the Common Law Agency Tests, 40 U. Kan. L. Rev. 119 (1991).

A copyright owner can always transfer ownership expressly through a written instrument. As a practical matter, is *Reid* likely to have any effect on prospective allocations of ownership? What justification is there to give special treatment to works that fall into one or more of the nine categories listed in the second clause of section 101's definition of "work made for hire"? The most obvious explanation—that work for hire treatment avoids the transaction costs of transferring copyright by contract—is undercut by the facts that not all of the works in these nine categories present unusually high contracting costs and that such costs will be present in any event because of the requirement that the parties "expressly agree in a written instrument signed by them that the work shall be considered a work made for hire." Consider, when you read the description of the 1976 Act's provisions on termination of transfers, page 648 below, whether a better explanation can be found in the fact that works for hire are exempt from the termination of transfers provisions.

2. *Joint Works.* In the case of an interview, will the interviewer and interviewee be joint authors? What of an author and the editor who revises his manuscript? In both cases, the two contributors presumably intended their contributions to merge into a unitary whole. Is it nonetheless relevant that, at least in the case of the author and his editor, they probably did not intend their shared effort to result in the legal status of joint authorship? Childress v. Taylor, 945 F.2d 500, 20 U.S.P.Q.2d 1191 (2d Cir.1991), cited in the *Erickson* case, held that for a joint work to exist there must be an "intent of both participants in the venture to regard themselves as authors." Under this test, an editor who revises an author's draft manuscript would not be a coauthor even though her revisions rose to the level of copyrightable expression: "Both intend their contributions to be merged into inseparable parts of a unitary whole, yet very few editors and even fewer writers would expect the editor to be accorded the status of joint author, enjoying an undivided half interest in the copyright in the published work." 945 F.2d at 507.

If an editor and author each contribute copyrightable expression to a work, but their collaborative efforts do not produce a joint work, how will ownership of the copyright(s) in the work be held? What effect is *Childress* likely to have on certainty in copyright transactions? Outside of a small handful of categories such as the editor-writer relationship, and particularly after the passage of time, it will often be hard for a court to determine what legal result the parties subjectively intended, and for potential licensees to determine which contributors it must negotiate with for rights in a work. Under the *Childress* rule, with whom would you negotiate for the right to reprint a ghost-written autobiography?

See generally, Laura Lape, A Narrow View of Creative Cooperation: The Current State of Joint Work Doctrine, 61 Alb. L. Rev. 43 (1997).

3. *Applicable Law.* Does the 1909 Copyright Act or the 1976 Copyright Act govern determinations of ownership? Some works that would be considered to have been made for hire under the 1909 Act would not be considered to have been made for hire under the 1976 Act. Some works that would be considered joint works under the 1909 Act would not be considered joint works under the 1976 Act. The 1909 Act's ownership rules govern works created—and legal relationships formed—before the effective date of the 1976 Act, and the 1976 Act governs works and relationships created since. See Roth v. Pritikin, 710 F.2d 934, 937–39, 219 U.S.P.Q. 204 (2d Cir.), cert. denied, 464 U.S. 961, 104 S.Ct. 394, 78 L.Ed.2d 337, 220 U.S.P.Q. 385 (1983), aff'd in part, rev'd in part on remand, 787 F.2d 54, 229 U.S.P.Q. 388 (2d Cir.1986).

2. TRANSFER AND TERM

See Statute Supplement 17 U.S.C.A. § 201–205, 302–305.

New York Times Company, Inc. v. Tasini

Supreme Court of the United States, 2001.
533 U.S. 483, 121 S.Ct. 2381, 150 L.Ed.2d 500, 59 U.S.P.Q.2d 1001.

Justice GINSBURG delivered the opinion of the Court.

This copyright case concerns the rights of freelance authors and a presumptive privilege of their publishers. The litigation was initiated by six freelance authors and relates to articles they contributed to three print periodicals (two newspapers and one magazine). Under agreements with the periodicals' publishers, but without the freelancers' consent, two computer database companies placed copies of the freelancers' articles—along with all other articles from the periodicals in which the freelancers' work appeared—into three databases. Whether written by a freelancer or staff member, each article is presented to, and retrievable by, the user in isolation, clear of the context the original print publication presented.

The freelance authors' complaint alleged that their copyrights had been infringed by the inclusion of their articles in the databases. The publishers, in response, relied on the privilege of reproduction and distribution accorded them by § 201(c) of the Copyright Act, which provides:

"Copyright in each separate contribution to a collective work is distinct from copyright in the collective work as a whole, and vests initially in the author of the contribution. In the absence of an express transfer of the copyright or of any rights under it, the owner of copyright in the collective work is presumed to have acquired only the privilege of reproducing and distributing the contribution as part of that particular collective work, any revision of that collective work, and any later collective work in the same series." 17 U.S.C. § 201(c).

Specifically, the publishers maintained that, as copyright owners of collective works, *i.e.,* the original print publications, they had merely exercised "the privilege" § 201(c) accords them to "reproduc[e] and distribut[e]" the author's discretely copyrighted contribution.

In agreement with the Second Circuit, we hold that § 201(c) does not authorize the copying at issue here. The publishers are not sheltered by § 201(c), we conclude, because the databases reproduce and distribute articles standing alone and not in context, not "as part of that particular collective work" to which the author contributed, "as part of . . . any revision" thereof, or "as part of . . . any later collective work in the same series." Both the print publishers and the electronic publishers, we rule, have infringed the copyrights of the freelance authors.

I

A

Respondents Jonathan Tasini, Mary Kay Blakely, Barbara Garson, Margot Mifflin, Sonia Jaffe Robbins, and David S. Whitford are authors (Authors). Between 1990 and 1993, they wrote the 21 articles (Articles) on which this dispute centers. Tasini, Mifflin, and Blakely contributed 12 Articles to The New York Times, the daily newspaper published by petitioner The New York Times Company (Times). Tasini, Garson, Robbins, and Whitford wrote eight Articles for Newsday, another New York daily paper, published by petitioner Newsday, Inc. (Newsday). Whitford also contributed one Article to Sports Illustrated, a weekly magazine published by petitioner Time, Inc. (Time). The Authors registered copyrights in each of the Articles. The Times, Newsday, and Time (Print Publishers) registered collective work copyrights in each periodical edition in which an Article originally appeared. The Print Publishers engaged the Authors as independent contractors (freelancers) under contracts that in no instance secured consent from an Author to placement of an Article in an electronic database.

At the time the Articles were published, all three Print Publishers had agreements with petitioner LEXIS/NEXIS (formerly Mead DataCentral Corp.), owner and operator of NEXIS, a computerized database that stores information in a text-only format. NEXIS contains articles from hundreds of journals (newspapers and periodicals) spanning many years. The Print Publishers have licensed to LEXIS/NEXIS the text of articles appearing in the three periodicals. The licenses authorize LEXIS/NEXIS to copy and sell any portion of those texts.

Pursuant to the licensing agreements, the Print Publishers regularly provide LEXIS/NEXIS with a batch of all the articles published in each periodical edition. The Print Publisher codes each article to facilitate computerized retrieval, then transmits it in a separate file. After further coding, LEXIS/NEXIS places the article in the central discs of its database.

Subscribers to NEXIS, accessing the system through a computer, may search for articles by author, subject, date, publication, headline, key term, words in text, or other criteria. Responding to a search command, NEXIS scans the database and informs the user of the number of articles meeting the user's search criteria. The user then may view, print, or download each of the articles yielded by the search. The display of each article includes the print publication (*e.g.*, The New York Times), date (September 23, 1990), section (Magazine), initial page number (26), headline or title ("Remembering Jane"), and author (Mary Kay Blakely). Each article appears as a separate, isolated "story"—without any visible link to the other stories originally published in the same newspaper or magazine edition. NEXIS does not contain pictures or advertisements, and it does not reproduce the original print publication's formatting features such as headline size, page placement (*e.g.*, above or below the fold for newspapers), or location of continuation pages.

The Times (but not Newsday or Time) also has licensing agreements with petitioner University Microfilms International (UMI). The agreements authorize reproduction of Times materials on two CD–ROM products, the New York Times OnDisc (N.Y.TO) and General Periodicals OnDisc (GPO).

Like NEXIS, NYTO is a text-only system. Unlike NEXIS, NYTO, as its name suggests, contains only the Times. Pursuant to a three-way agreement, LEXIS/NEXIS provides UMI with computer files containing each article as transmitted by the Times to LEXIS/NEXIS. Like LEXIS/NEXIS, UMI marks each article with special codes. UMI also provides an index of all the articles in NYTO. Articles appear in NYTO in essentially the same way they appear in NEXIS, *i.e.*, with identifying information (author, title, etc.), but without original formatting or accompanying images.

GPO contains articles from approximately 200 publications or sections of publications. Unlike NEXIS and NYTO, GPO is an image-based, rather than a text-based, system. The Times has licensed GPO to provide a facsimile of the Times' Sunday Book Review and Magazine. UMI "burns" images of each page of these sections onto CD–ROMs. The CD–ROMs show each article exactly as it appeared on printed pages, complete with photographs, captions, advertisements, and other surrounding materials. UMI provides an index and abstracts of all the articles in GPO.

Articles are accessed through NYTO and GPO much as they are accessed through NEXIS. The user enters a search query using similar criteria (*e.g.*, author, headline, date). The computer program searches available indexes and abstracts, and retrieves a list of results matching the query. The user then may view each article within the search result, and may print the article or download it to a disc. The display of each article provides no links to articles appearing on other pages of the original print publications.

B

On December 16, 1993, the Authors filed this civil action in the United States District Court for the Southern District of New York. The Authors alleged that their copyrights were infringed when, as permitted and facilitated by the Print Publishers, LEXIS/NEXIS and UMI (Electronic Publishers) placed the Articles in the NEXIS, NYTO, and GPO databases (Databases). The Authors sought declaratory and injunctive relief, and damages. In response to the Authors' complaint, the Print and Electronic Publishers raised the reproduction and distribution privilege accorded collective work copyright owners by 17 U.S.C. § 201(c). After discovery, both sides moved for summary judgment.

The District Court granted summary judgment for the Publishers, holding that § 201(c) shielded the Database reproductions. The privilege conferred by § 201(c) is transferable, the court first concluded, and therefore could be conveyed from the original Print Publishers to the Electronic Publishers. Next, the court determined, the Databases reproduced and distributed the Authors' works, in § 201(c)'s words, "as part of ... [a] revision of that collective work" to which the Authors had first contributed. To qualify as "revisions," according to the court, works need only "preserve some significant original aspect of [collective works]—whether an original selection or an original arrangement." This criterion was met, in the District Court's view, because the Databases preserved the Print Publishers' "selection of articles" by copying all of the articles originally assembled in the periodicals' daily or weekly issues. The Databases "highlight[ed]" the connection between the articles and the print periodicals, the court observed, by showing for each article not only the author and periodical, but also the print publication's particular issue and page numbers. ("[T]he electronic technologies not only copy the publisher defendants' complete original 'selection' of articles, they tag those articles in such a way that the publisher defendants' original selection remains evident online.").

The Authors appealed, and the Second Circuit reversed. The Court of Appeals granted summary judgment for the Authors on the ground that the Databases were not among the collective works covered by § 201(c), and specifically, were not "revisions" of the periodicals in which the Articles first appeared. Just as § 201(c) does not "permit a Publisher to sell a hard copy of an Author's article directly to the public even if the Publisher also offered for individual sale all of the other articles from the particular edition," the court reasoned, so § 201(c) does not allow a Publisher to "achieve the same goal indirectly" through computer databases. In the Second Circuit's view, the Databases effectively achieved this result by providing multitudes of "individually retrievable" articles. As stated by the Court of Appeals, the Databases might fairly be described as containing "new antholog[ies] of innumerable" editions or publications, but they do not qualify as "revisions" of particular editions of periodicals in the Databases. Having concluded that § 201(c) "does not permit the Publishers," acting without the author's consent, "to license individually copyrighted works for inclusion in the electronic databases," the court did not reach the question whether the § 201(c) privilege is transferable.

We granted certiorari to determine whether the copying of the Authors' Articles in the Databases is privileged by 17 U.S.C. § 201(c). Like the Court of Appeals, we conclude that the § 201(c) privilege does not override the Authors' copyrights, for the Databases do not reproduce and distribute the Articles as part of a collective work privileged by § 201(c). Accordingly, and again like the Court of Appeals, we find it unnecessary to determine whether the privilege is transferable.

II

Under the Copyright Act, as amended in 1976, "[c]opyright protection subsists . . . in original works of authorship fixed in any tangible medium of expression . . . from which they can be perceived, reproduced, or otherwise communicated." 17 U.S.C. § 102(a). When, as in this case, a freelance author has contributed an article to a "collective work" such as a newspaper or magazine, see § 101 (defining "collective work"), the statute recognizes two distinct copyrighted works: "Copyright in *each separate contribution to a collective work* is distinct from copyright in *the collective work as a whole* . . . ." § 201(c) (emphasis added). Copyright in the separate contribution "vests initially in the author of the contribution" (here, the freelancer). *Ibid.* Copyright in the collective work vests in the collective author (here, the newspaper or magazine publisher) and extends only to the creative material contributed by that author, not to "the preexisting material employed in the work," § 103(b).

Prior to the 1976 revision, as the courts below recognized, authors risked losing their rights when they placed an article in a collective work. Pre–1976 copyright law recognized a freelance author's copyright in a published article only when the article was printed with a copyright notice in the author's name. When publishers, exercising their superior bargaining power over authors, declined to print notices in each contributor's name, the author's copyright was put in jeopardy. The author did not have the option to assign only the right of publication in the periodical; such a partial assignment was blocked by the doctrine of copyright "indivisibility." Thus, when a copyright notice appeared only in the publisher's name, the author's work would fall into the public domain, unless the author's copyright, in its entirety, had passed to the publisher. Such complete transfer might be accomplished by a contract, perhaps one with a provision, not easily enforced, for later retransfer of rights back to the author. Or, absent a specific contract, a court might find that an author had tacitly transferred the entire copyright to a publisher, in turn deemed to hold the copyright in "trust" for the author's benefit.

In the 1976 revision, Congress acted to "clarify and improve [this] confused and frequently unfair legal situation with respect to rights in contributions." H.R.Rep. No. 94–1476, p. 122 (1976), (hereinafter H.R. Rep.). The 1976 Act rejected the doctrine of indivisibility, recasting the copyright as a bundle of discrete "exclusive rights," 17 U.S.C. § 106 each of which "may be transferred . . . and owned separately," § 201(d)(2). Congress also provided, in § 404(a), that "a single notice applicable to the collective work as a whole is sufficient" to protect the rights of freelance contributors. And in § 201(c), Congress codified the discrete domains of "[c]opyright in each separate contribution to a collective work" and "copyright in the collective work as a whole." Together, § 404(a) and § 201(c) "preserve the author's copyright in a contribution even if the contribution does not bear a separate notice in the author's name, and without requiring any unqualified transfer of rights to the owner of the collective work." H.R. Rep. 122.

Section 201(c) both describes and circumscribes the "privilege" a publisher acquires regarding an author's contribution to a collective work:

> "In the absence of an express transfer of the copyright or of any rights under it, the owner of copyright in the collective work is presumed to have acquired *only* the privilege of reproducing and distributing the contribution as part of that particular collective work, any revision of that collective work, and any later collective work in the same series." (Emphasis added.)

A newspaper or magazine publisher is thus privileged to reproduce or distribute an article contributed by a freelance author, absent a contract otherwise providing, only "as part of" any (or all) of three categories of collective works: (a) "that collective work" to which the author contributed her work, (b) "any revision of that collective work," or (c) "any later collective work in the same series." In accord with Congress' prescription, a "publishing company could reprint a contribution from one issue in a later issue of its magazine, and could reprint an article from a 1980 edition of an encyclopedia in a 1990 revision of it; the publisher could not revise the contribution itself or include it in a new anthology or an entirely different magazine or other collective work." H.R. Rep. 122–123.

Essentially, § 201(c) adjusts a publisher's copyright in its collective work to accommodate a freelancer's copyright in her contribution. If there is demand for a freelance article standing alone or in a new collection, the Copyright Act allows the freelancer to benefit from that demand; after authorizing initial publication, the freelancer may also sell the article to others. It would scarcely "preserve the author's copyright in a contribution" as contemplated by Congress, H.R. Rep. 122, if a newspaper or magazine publisher were permitted to reproduce or distribute copies of the author's contribution in isolation or within new collective works.

III

In the instant case, the Authors wrote several Articles and gave the Print Publishers permission to publish the Articles in certain newspapers and magazines. It is undisputed that the Authors hold copyrights and, therefore, exclusive rights in the Articles. It is clear, moreover, that the Print and Electronic Publishers have exercised at least some rights that § 106 initially assigns exclusively to the Authors: LEXIS/NEXIS' central discs and UMI's CD–ROMs "reproduce ... copies" of the Articles, § 106(1); UMI, by selling those CD–ROMs, and LEXIS/NEXIS, by selling copies of the Articles through the NEXIS Database, "distribute copies" of the Articles "to the public by sale," § 106(3); and the Print Publishers, through contracts licensing the production of copies in the Databases, "authorize" reproduction and distribution of the Articles, § 106.[8]

Against the Authors' charge of infringement, the Publishers do not here contend the Authors entered into an agreement authorizing reproduction of the Articles in the Databases. Nor do they assert that the copies in the Databases represent "fair use" of the Authors' Articles. Instead, the Publishers rest entirely on the privilege described in § 201(c). Each discrete edition of the periodicals in which the Articles appeared is a "collective work," the Publishers agree. They contend, however, that reproduction and distribution of each Article by the Databases lie within the "privilege of reproducing and distributing the [Articles] as part of . . . [a] revision of that collective work," § 201(c). The Publishers' encompassing construction of the § 201(c) privilege is unacceptable, we conclude, for it would diminish the Authors' exclusive rights in the Articles.

In determining whether the Articles have been reproduced and distributed "as part of" a "revision" of the collective works in issue, we focus on the Articles as presented to, and perceptible by, the user of the Databases. In this case, the three Databases present articles to users clear of the context provided either by the original periodical editions or by any revision of those editions. The Databases first prompt users to search the universe of their contents: thousands or millions of files containing individual articles from thousands of collective works (*i.e.*, editions), either in one series (the Times, in NYTO) or in scores of series (the sundry titles in NEXIS and GPO). When the user conducts a search, each article appears as a separate item within the search result. In NEXIS and NYTO, an article appears to a user without the graphics, formatting, or other articles with which the article was initially published. In GPO, the article appears with the other materials published on the same page or pages, but without any material published on other pages of the original periodical. In either circumstance, we cannot see how the Database perceptibly reproduces and distributes the article "as part of" either the original edition or a "revision" of that edition.

One might view the articles as parts of a new compendium—namely, the entirety of works in the Database. In that compendium, each edition of each periodical represents only a minuscule fraction of the ever-expanding Database. The Database no more constitutes a "revision" of each constituent edition than a 400–page novel quoting a sonnet in passing would represent a "revision" of that poem. "Revision" denotes a new "version," and a version is, in this setting, a "distinct form of something regarded by its creators or others as one work." Webster's Third New International

---

8. Satisfied that the Publishers exercised rights § 106 initially assigns exclusively to the Author, we need resolve no more on that score. Thus, we do not reach an issue the Register of Copyrights has argued vigorously. The Register maintains that the Databases publicly "display" the Articles, § 106(5); because § 201(c) does not privilege "display," the Register urges, the § 201(c) privilege does not shield the Databases.

Dictionary 1944, 2545 (1976). The massive whole of the Database is not recognizable as a new version of its every small part.

Alternatively, one could view the Articles in the Databases "as part of" no larger work at all, but simply as individual articles presented individually. That each article bears marks of its origin in a particular periodical (less vivid marks in NEXIS and NYTO, more vivid marks in GPO) suggests the article was *previously* part of that periodical. But the markings do not mean the article is *currently* reproduced or distributed as part of the periodical. The Databases' reproduction and distribution of individual Articles—simply *as individual Articles*—would invade the core of the Authors' exclusive rights under § 106.

The Publishers press an analogy between the Databases, on the one hand, and microfilm and microfiche, on the other. We find the analogy wanting. Microforms typically contain continuous photographic reproductions of a periodical in the medium of miniaturized film. Accordingly, articles appear on the microforms, writ very small, in precisely the position in which the articles appeared in the newspaper. The Times, for example, printed the beginning of Blakely's "Remembering Jane" Article on page 26 of the Magazine in the September 23, 1990, edition; the microfilm version of the Times reproduces that same Article on film in the very same position, within a film reproduction of the entire Magazine, in turn within a reproduction of the entire September 23, 1990, edition. True, the microfilm roll contains multiple editions, and the microfilm user can adjust the machine lens to focus only on the Article, to the exclusion of surrounding material. Nonetheless, the user first encounters the Article in context. In the Databases, by contrast, the Articles appear disconnected from their original context. In NEXIS and NYTO, the user sees the "Jane" Article apart even from the remainder of page 26. In GPO, the user sees the Article within the context of page 26, but clear of the context of page 25 or page 27, the rest of the Magazine, or the remainder of the day's newspaper. In short, unlike microforms, the Databases do not perceptibly reproduce articles as part of the collective work to which the author contributed or as part of any "revision" thereof.

Invoking the concept of "media neutrality," the Publishers urge that the "transfer of a work between media" does not "alte[r] the character of" that work for copyright purposes. But unlike the conversion of newsprint to microfilm, the transfer of articles to the Databases does not represent a mere conversion of intact periodicals (or revisions of periodicals) from one medium to another. The Databases offer users individual articles, not intact periodicals. In this case, media neutrality should protect the Authors' rights in the individual Articles to the extent those Articles are now presented individually, outside the collective work context, within the Databases' new media.

For the purpose at hand—determining whether the Authors' copyrights have been infringed—an analogy to an imaginary library may be instructive. Rather than maintaining intact editions of periodicals, the library would contain separate copies of each article. Perhaps these copies would exactly reproduce the periodical pages from which the articles derive (if the model is GPO); perhaps the copies would contain only typescript characters, but still indicate the original periodical's name and date, as well as the article's headline and page number (if the model is NEXIS or NYTO). The library would store the folders containing the articles in a file room, indexed based on diverse criteria, and containing articles from vast numbers of editions. In response to patron requests, an inhumanly speedy librarian would search the room and provide copies of the articles matching patron-specified criteria.

Viewing this strange library, one could not, consistent with ordinary English usage, characterize the articles "as part of" a "revision" of the editions in which the articles first appeared. In substance, however, the Databases differ from the file room only to the extent they aggregate articles in electronic packages (the LEXIS/NEXIS central discs or UMI CD-ROMs), while the file room stores articles in spatially separate files. The crucial fact is that the Databases, like the hypothetical library, store and retrieve articles separately within a vast domain of diverse texts. Such a storage and retrieval system effectively overrides the Authors' exclusive right to control the individual reproduction and distribution of each Article, 17 U.S.C. §§ 106(1), (3).

The Publishers claim the protection of § 201(c) because users can manipulate the Databases to generate search results consisting entirely of articles from a particular periodical edition. By this logic, § 201(c) would cover the hypothetical library if, in response to a request, that library's expert staff assembled all of the articles from a particular periodical edition. However, the fact that a third party can manipulate a database to produce a noninfringing document does not mean the database is not infringing. Under § 201(c), the question is not whether a user can generate a revision of a collective work from a database, but whether the database itself perceptibly presents the author's contribution as part of a revision of the collective work. That result is not accomplished by these Databases.

The Publishers finally invoke *Sony Corp. of America v. Universal City Studios, Inc.*, 464 U.S. 417, 104 S.Ct. 774, 78 L.Ed.2d 574 (1984). That decision, however, does not genuinely aid their argument. *Sony* held that the "sale of copying equipment" does not constitute contributory infringement if the equipment is "capable of substantial noninfringing uses." *Id.*, at 442, 104 S.Ct. 774. The Publishers suggest that their Databases could be liable only under a theory of contributory infringement, based on end-user conduct, which the Authors did not plead. The Electronic Publishers, however, are not merely selling "equipment"; they are selling copies of the Articles. And, as we have explained, it is the copies themselves, without any manipulation by users, that fall outside the scope of the § 201(c) privilege.

IV

The Publishers warn that a ruling for the Authors will have "devastating" consequences. The Databases, the Publishers note, provide easy access to complete newspaper texts going back decades. A ruling for the Authors, the Publishers suggest, will punch gaping holes in the electronic record of history. The Publishers' concerns are echoed by several historians, see Brief for Ken Burns et al. as *Amici Curiae*, but discounted by several other historians, see Brief for Ellen Schrecker et al. as *Amici Curiae;* Brief for Authors' Guild, Jacques Barzun et al. as *Amici Curiae.*

Notwithstanding the dire predictions from some quarters, it hardly follows from today's decision that an injunction against the inclusion of these Articles in the Databases (much less all freelance articles in any databases) must issue. See 17 U.S.C. § 502(a) (court "may" enjoin infringement); *Campbell v. Acuff–Rose Music, Inc.,* 510 U.S. 569, 578, n. 10, 114 S.Ct. 1164, 127 L.Ed.2d 500 (1994) (goals of copyright law are "not always best served by automatically granting injunctive relief"). The parties (Authors and Publishers) may enter into an agreement allowing continued electronic reproduction of the Authors' works; they, and if necessary the courts and Congress, may draw on numerous models for distributing copyrighted works and remunerating authors for their distribution. In any event, speculation about future harms is no basis for this Court to shrink authorial rights Congress established in § 201(c). Agreeing with the Court of Appeals that the Publishers are liable for infringement, we leave remedial issues open for initial airing and decision in the District Court.

* * *

We conclude that the Electronic Publishers infringed the Authors' copyrights by reproducing and distributing the Articles in a manner not authorized by the Authors and not privileged by § 201(c). We further conclude that the Print Publishers infringed the Authors' copyrights by authorizing the Electronic Publishers to place the Articles in the Databases and by aiding the Electronic Publishers in that endeavor. We therefore affirm the judgment of the Court of Appeals.

It is so ordered.

Copyright Law Revision, H.R. Rep. No. 1476

94th Cong., 2d Sess. 122–129 (1976).

Section 203. Termination of Transfers and Licenses

The Problem in General

The provisions of section 203 are based on the premise that the reversionary provisions of the present section on copyright renewal (17 U.S.C.A. § 24) should be eliminated, and that the proposed law should substitute for them a provision safeguarding authors against unremunerative transfers. A provision of this sort is needed because of the unequal bargaining position of authors, resulting in part from the impossibility of determining a work's value until it has been exploited. Section 203 reflects a practical compromise that will further the objectives of the copyright law while recognizing the problems and legitimate needs of all interests involved.

Scope of the Provision

Instead of being automatic, as is theoretically the case under the present renewal provision, the termination of a transfer or license under section 203 would require the serving of an advance notice within specified time limits and under specified conditions. However, although affirmative action is needed to effect a termination, the right to take this action cannot be waived in advance or contracted away. Under section 203(a) the right of termination would apply only to transfers and licenses executed after the effective date of the new statute, and would have no retroactive effect.

The right of termination would be confined to inter vivos transfers or licenses executed by the author, and would not apply to transfers by the author's successors in interest or to the author's own bequests. The scope of the right would extend not only to any "transfer of copyright ownership," as defined in section 101, but also to nonexclusive licenses. The right of termination would not apply to "works made for hire," which is one of the principal reasons the definition of that term assumed importance in the development of the bill. . . .

When a Grant Can Be Terminated

Section 203 draws a distinction between the date when a termination becomes effective and the earlier date when the advance notice of termination is served. With respect to the ultimate effective date, section 203(a)(3) provides, as a general rule, that a grant may be terminated during the 5 years following the expiration of a period of 35 years from the execution of the grant. As an exception to this basic 35–year rule, the bill also provides that "if the grant covers the right of publication of the work, the period begins at the end of 35 years from the date of publication of the work under the grant or at the end of 40 years from the date of execution of the grant, whichever term ends earlier." This alternative method of computation is intended to cover cases where years elapse between the signing of a publication contract and the eventual publication of the work.

The effective date of termination, which must be stated in the advance notice, is required to fall within the 5 years following the end of the applicable 35–or 40–year period, but the advance notice itself must be served earlier. Under section 203(a)(4)(A), the notice must be served "not less than two or more than ten years" before the effective date stated in it.

As an example of how these time-limit requirements would operate in practice, we suggest two typical contract situations:

Case 1: Contract for theatrical production signed on September 2, 1987. Termination of grant can be made to take effect between September 2, 2022 (35 years from execution) and September 1, 2027 (end of 5 year termination period). Assuming that the author decides to terminate on September 1, 2022 (the earliest possible date) the advance notice must be filed between September 1, 2012 and September 1, 2020.

Case 2: Contract for book publication executed on April 10, 1980; book finally published on August 23, 1987. Since contract covers the right of publication, the 5–year termination period would begin on April 10, 2020 (40 years from execution) rather than April 10, 2015 (35 years from execution) or August 23, 2022 (35 years from publication). Assuming that the author decides to make the termination effective on January 1, 2024, the advance notice would have to be served between January 1, 2014, and January 1, 2022.

Effect of Termination

Section 203(b) makes clear that, unless effectively terminated within the applicable 5–year period, all rights covered by an existing grant will continue unchanged, and that rights under other Federal, State, or foreign laws are unaffected. However, assuming that a copyright transfer or license is terminated under section 203, who are bound by the termination and how are they affected?

Under the bill, termination means that ownership of the rights covered by the terminated grant reverts to everyone who owns termination interests on the date the notice of termination was served, whether they joined in signing the notice or not. In other words, if a person could have signed the notice, that person is bound by the action of the majority who did; the termination of the grant will be effective as to that person, and a proportionate share of the reverted rights automatically vests in that person. Ownership is divided proportionately on the same per stirpes basis as that provided for the right to effect termination under section 203(a) and, since the reverted rights vest on the date notice is served, the heirs of a dead beneficiary would inherit his or her share.

Under clause (3) of subsection (b), majority action is required to make a further grant of reverted rights. A problem here, of course, is that years may have passed between the time the reverted rights vested and the time the new owners want to make a further transfer; people may have died and children may have been born in the interim. To deal with this problem, the bill looks back to the date of vesting; out of the group in whom rights vested on that date, it requires the further transfer or license to be signed by "the same number and proportion of the owners" (though not necessarily the same individuals) as were then required to terminate the grant under subsection (a). If some of those in whom the rights originally vested have died, their "legal representatives, legatees, or heirs at law" may represent them for this purpose and, as in the case of the termination itself, any one of the minority who does not join in the further grant is nevertheless bound by it.

An important limitation on the rights of a copyright owner under a terminated grant is specified in section 203(b)(1). This clause provides that, notwithstanding a termination, a derivative work prepared earlier may "continue to be utilized" under the conditions of the terminated grant; the clause adds, however, that this privilege is not broad enough to permit the preparation of other derivative works. In other words, a film made from a play could continue to be licensed for performance after the motion picture contract had been terminated but any remake rights covered by the contract would be cut off. For this purpose, a motion picture would be considered as a "derivative work" with respect to every "preexisting work" incorporated in it, whether the preexisting work was created independently or was prepared expressly for the motion picture.

Section 203 would not prevent the parties to a transfer or license from voluntarily agreeing at any time to terminate an existing grant and negotiating a new one, thereby causing another 35–year period to start running. However, the bill seeks to avoid the situation that has arisen under the present renewal provision, in which third parties have bought up contingent future interests as a form of speculation. Section 203(b)(4) would make a further grant of rights that revert under a terminated grant valid "only if it is made after the effective date of the termination." An exception, in the nature of a right of "first refusal," would permit the original grantee or a successor of such grantee to negotiate a new agreement with the persons effecting the termination at any time after the notice of termination has been served.

NOTES

1. Justice John Paul Stevens, joined by Justice Stephen Breyer, dissented in *Tasini*. In Stevens's view, it would have been more consistent with the 1976's Act redrawing of the lines of ownership and control respecting contributions to collective works to have held for the print and electronic publishers: "neither the publication of the collective works by the Print Publishers, nor their transfer to the Electronic Databases had any impact on the legal status of the copyrights of the respondents' individual contributions"; moreover, the publishers had neither modified the contributions nor "published them in a 'new anthology or an *entirely different magazine or other collective work*.' H.R. Rep. 122–123 (emphasis in original)." 533 U.S. 483, 121 S.Ct. 2381, 2396, 150 L.Ed.2d 500.

According to Stevens, within the terms prescribed by section 201(c),"neither the conversion of the Print Publishers' collective works from printed to electronic form, nor the transmission of those electronic versions of the collective works to the Electronic Databases, nor even the actions of the Electronic Databases once they receive those electronic versions does anything to deprive those electronic versions of their status as mere 'revisions[s]' of the original collective works." Agreeing with the majority that "the crucial inquiry is whether the article appears within the 'context' of the original collective work," Stevens asserted that "this question simply raises the further issue of precisely how much 'context' is enough." Unlike the majority, Stevens viewed the relevant context as a single edition of the newspaper: "I see no compelling reason why a collection of files corresponding to a single edition of the New York Times, standing alone, cannot constitute a 'revision' of that day's New York Times." 121 S.Ct. at 2397.

Acknowledging that, once a version of an issue of the *Times* is surrounded by additional content, it can be conceptualized as existing as part of an even larger collective work (*e.g.*, the entire NEXIS database), Stevens observed that the "question then becomes whether this ability to conceive of a revision of a collective work as existing within a larger 'collective work' changes the status of the original revision. Section 201(c)'s requirement that the article be published only as 'part of ... any revision of *that collective work*' does not compel any particular answer to that question. A microfilm of the New York Times for October 31, 2000, does not cease to be a revision of that individual collective work simply because it is stored on the same role of film as other editions of the Times or on a library shelf containing hundreds of other microfilm periodicals. Nor does § 201(c) compel the counterintuitive conclusion that the microfilm version of the Times would cease to be a revision simply because its publishers might choose to sell it on rolls of film that contained a year's editions of both the New York Times *and* the Herald–Tribune." 121 S.Ct. at 2400 (emphasis in original).

Finally, Justice Stevens contended, the majority decision unnecessarily subverted copyright's fundamental goal of benefiting the public "in favor of a narrow focus on 'authorial rights'. Although the desire to protect such rights is certainly a laudable sentiment, copyright law demands that 'private motivation must ultimately serve the cause of promoting *broad public availability* of literature, music, and other arts.' Twentieth Century Music Corp. v. Aiken, 422 U.S. 151, 156, 95 S.Ct. 2040, 45 L.Ed.2d 84 (1975) (emphasis added). The majority discounts the effect its decision will have on the availability of comprehensive digital databases, but I am not as confident. As petitioners' *amici* have persuasively argued, the difficulties of locating individual freelance authors and the potential of exposure to statutory damages may well have the effect of forcing electronic archives to purge freelance pieces from their databases." 121 S.Ct. at 2401.

2. *Copyright Term.* One of the 1976 Act's main innovations was to alter the duration of copyright from a term measured by 28 years from the date of publication, with a renewal period of 28 years, to a term measured by the life of the author plus 50 years. The term is the minimum required by the Berne Convention for the Protection of Literary and Artistic Works, and the change brought United States law into line with the copyright terms of most other nations. A 1993 E.C. Directive requiring the extension of copyright throughout the European Union to a term measured by the author's life plus 70 years set the stage in the United States for the Sonny Bono Copyright Term Extension Act, P.L. No. 105–298 Tit. I (Oct. 27, 1998), extending the term of subsisting and future copyrights by twenty years. For example, section 302(a)'s general term of copyright for works created on or after January 1, 1978 now provides "the copyright endures for a term consisting of the life of the author and 70 years after the author's death."

(a) *If the copyright term is measured by the "life of the author," how is the term measured when a work has more than one author?* Section 302(b) provides that where two or more authors prepare a joint work, the copyright will last for a term measured by the life of the last surviving author plus 70 years. The rule obviously requires careful attention to the Act's definition of "joint work."

(b) *How is the term measured for anonymous or pseudonymous works, or works made for hire, whose author is not known or, as a corporation, enjoys an indeterminate life?* Section 302(c)'s response to these situations is to approximate an author's life plus 70 years with a term of 95 years from the year of a work's first publication or 120 years from the year of its creation, whichever expires first. If, before the end of this term, the identity of the anonymous or pseudonymous author is revealed in Copyright Office records, the copyright will last for the standard life plus 70 term.

(c) *How, as a practical matter, will prospective users be able to determine the life and death facts that will tell them whether a work is in or out of copyright?* Section 302(d) gives the copyright owner, or anyone having an interest in the copyright, the opportunity to record in the Copyright Office a statement of the date of the author's death, or a statement that the author is still living. Why should the owner record? Section 302(e) provides that if, after 95 years from first publication or 120 years from a work's creation, whichever expires first, a prospective user obtains a certified report from the Copyright Office that its records disclose nothing to indicate that the author of the work is living or died less than 70 years before, the prospective user becomes entitled to the benefit of a presumption that the author has been dead for at least 70 years. Good faith reliance on the report constitutes a complete defense to any action for infringement.

(d) *What of works created and copyrighted before the Act's effective date, January 1, 1978?* Section 304 divides its treatment of these works between those that were in their first copyright term on January 1, 1978 and those that were in their renewal term, or registered for renewal, before January 1, 1978. For copyrights in their first term on January 1, 1978, section 304(a) retains the previous 28–year copyright term, allows renewal, but extends the renewal term from the previous 28–year term to 67 years. Effectively, this creates a total term of 95 years from publication, establishing parity between works protected under the old Act and works created after January 1, 1978 and protected under the new Act as amended.

Section 304(b) creates parity for works still in their renewal term on the Term Extension Act's effective date by automatically extending the renewal term to 95 years from the date copyright was originally secured. Of course, for the extension to apply, the renewal term must have subsisted on the Term Extension Act's effective date, October 27, 1998, since a copyright that expired before that date will remain in the public domain.

(e) *What of works created, but not under statutory copyright, before January 1, 1978?* Congress recognized that there may be many unpublished works that have been in existence for a long time—centuries even— and whose authors are long since dead. It provided in section 303 that these works are to enjoy the same term as works created after January 1, 1978, but added that copyright in this class of works will in any event not expire before December 31, 2002, thus assuring at least 25 years of protection. As an inducement to publication, section 303 also provides that if the work is published on or before December 31, 2002, the term will be extended through December 31, 2047.

3. *Was Congress Right to Extend the Copyright Term?* Proposals to extend the 1976 Act's original term of protection by twenty years date to two bills introduced in Congress in 1995. The bills' proponents argued that increased human longevity and the European Union's adoption of a life plus seventy year term required the change; opponents argued that, applied prospectively, copyright term extension would have little if any effect on incentives to produce copyrighted works, and applied retrospectively it would have no incentive effect at all.

The reasoning of those who opposed term extension rested mainly on the phenomenon of discounting to present value. Specifically, since a dollar to be received seventy years hence has a present value of pennies at most, a distant, twenty-year stream of income will not appreciably affect present incentives to create new literary and artistic works. Did the opponents leave anything important out of their equation? Should the discount to present value address not only *private benefits*, but also *social costs—* specifically the social cost of the public's diminished future access to works that will stay out of the public domain twenty years longer than under the existing law? If extending copyright by twenty years may yield only a few pennies in the way of present incentives to authors, consider whether, once the equally distant social costs are discounted to present value, they too look like small change.

Might the opponents of term extension have better focused on its impact on transaction costs? The longer a copyright's term lasts, the more dispersed its owners are likely to become, and the more difficult it will be for a prospective licensee to identify the copyright owner from whom she must obtain the license or assignment that will enable her to exploit the work. The increased cost of seeking out a new generation of owners many years after the work was first published, and the increased risk that the needed clearance has not been obtained from every owner, may hamper the exploitation of copyrighted works in the extended term. Can you devise a title clearance mechanism that is capable of reducing these transaction costs without upsetting the expectations of copyright owners?

On copyright term extension generally, see Tyler T. Ochoa, Patent and Copyright Term Extension and the Constitution: A Historical Perspective, 49 J. Copyr. Soc'y USA 19 (2001).

4. *Copyright Renewal.* The 1909 Act's renewal provisions, which were among the more problematic features of the Act, promise to create problems for many years to come, for section 304(a) perpetuates the renewal scheme for works in their first copyright term before January 1, 1978. The House Report explains: "A great many of the present expectancies in these cases are the subject of existing contracts, and it would be unfair and immensely confusing to cut off or alter these interests." H.R.Rep. No. 94–1476, 94th Cong. 2d Sess. at 139 (1976).

Fred Fisher Music Co. v. M. Witmark & Sons, 318 U.S. 643, 647, 63 S.Ct. 773, 87 L.Ed. 1055, 57 U.S.P.Q. 50 (1943), a seminal decision under the 1909 Act, presented the question, "Does the Copyright Act nullify an agreement by an author, made during the original copyright term, to assign his renewal?" Writing for the Court, Justice Felix Frankfurter rested a negative answer upon an extensive review of the pre–1909 legislation, which did not restrict assignability, and the legislative history of the 1909 Act, which indicated an intent to continue the earlier position. Although freely assignable, the author's interest in the renewal term was contingent and would vest in him or his assignee only if the author was alive at the time prescribed for renewal. If the author was not alive, rights to the renewal term vested in the "widow, widower, or children of the author" or, if they were not alive, in the other individuals designated by section 24 of the 1909 Act, free of any earlier transfer made by the author.

The rule that an author's renewal interest is contingent, and will vest in her transferee only if the author is alive at the time prescribed for vesting, can create problems if the author dies before the renewal term vests. In Rohauer v. Killiam Shows, Inc., 551 F.2d 484, 192 U.S.P.Q. 545 (2d Cir.), cert. denied, 431 U.S. 949, 97 S.Ct. 2666, 53 L.Ed.2d 266 (1977), a licensee had produced a derivative work, relying on a license—for both the initial and renewal terms—obtained from a grantor who had died before the renewal term vested; the court held that the licensee could nonetheless continue exploiting the derivative work during the renewal term. But, in Abend v. MCA, Inc., 863 F.2d 1465, 9 U.S.P.Q.2d 1337 (9th Cir.1988), involving the motion picture, *Rear Window*, based on a short story by Cornell Woolrich the Ninth Circuit Court of Appeals held that, in comparable circumstances, an initial term licensee could not continue exploiting the work during the renewal term without the consent of the renewal term copyright owner. The Supreme Court resolved the conflict between the circuits by affirming the Ninth Circuit decision, holding in Stewart v. Abend, 495 U.S. 207, 110 S.Ct. 1750, 109 L.Ed.2d 184, 14 U.S.P.Q.2d 1614 (1990), that "if the author dies before the renewal period, then the assignee may continue to use the original work only if the author's successor transfers the renewal rights to the assignee." 495 U.S. at 221, 110 S.Ct. at 1760.

5. *Registration as a Requirement for Renewal.* The 1976 Copyright Act, like the 1909 Act, required as a condition of renewal that the author—or, if deceased, her statutory successor—apply for renewal registration during the last year of the initial copyright term. Many works have fallen into the public domain after expiration of the initial twenty-eight year term because the copyright owner failed to make timely application for a renewal registration. (Frank Capra's "It's a Wonderful Life" is a notable example.) In 1992, to bring the Copyright Act into line with the Berne Convention's proscription against formalities as a condition to copyright protection, Congress amended section 304(a) to eliminate the registration renewal formality, effectively making renewal automatic. By their terms, the amendments "apply only to those copyrights secured between January 1, 1964 and December 31, 1977. Copyright secured before January 1, 1964 shall be governed by the provisions of section 304(a) of title 17, United States Code, as in effect before the effective date of this section." Pub.L. 102–307, 106 Stat. 264 (1992).

The 1992 amendments retain some incentives to timely registration, one of which is to preserve a copyright owner's rights against derivative works—rights that the Supreme Court confirmed in *Stewart v. Abend,* note 4, above. New section 304(a)(4)(A) provides: "If an application to register a claim to the renewed and extended term of copyright in a work is not made within 1 year before the expiration of the original term of copyright in a work, or if the claim pursuant to such application is not registered, then a derivative work prepared under authority of a grant of a transfer or license of the copyright that is made before the expiration of the original term of copyright may continue to be used under the terms of the grant during the renewed and extended term of copyright without infringing the copyright, except that such use does not extend to the preparation during such renewed and extended term of other derivative works based upon the copyrighted work covered by such grant."

6. *Termination of Transfers and Derivative Works.* As noted in the House Report's discussion of termination of transfers, page 648, above, a derivative work prepared under the terms of a grant may "continue to be utilized" under the conditions of the terminated grant, but this privilege does not encompass the preparation of new derivative works. Does motion picture studio *A,* that wants to make a sequel employing the same characters and title as the original derivative work, enjoy any leverage in its negotiations with terminating party, *B*? Can *A* effectively prevent *B* from assigning the terminated rights to another motion picture company by asserting trademark or unfair competition rights in the characters or title? Works made for hire are categorically exempt from terminations of transfer, and motion picture companies commonly avoid termination of transfers by structuring their arrangements with creative contributors as works for hire. What if the film is based on a story outline proposed by the contributor before she becomes an employee? See Michael H. Davis, The Screenwriter's Indestructible Right to Terminate Her Assignment of Copyright: Once a Story is "Pitched," A Studio Can Never Obtain All Copyrights in the Story, 18 Cardozo Arts & Ent. L.J. 93 (2000).

An author will often assign his copyright to an intermediary—typically a publisher—and the intermediary will then license derivative rights to one or more third parties. If the author later terminates his grant to the intermediary, must the third-party licensee—who can continue to use the derivative work under section 203(b)(1)—pay its royalties to the intermediary or to the author? In Mills Music, Inc. v. Snyder, 469 U.S. 153, 105 S.Ct. 638, 83 L.Ed.2d 556, 224 U.S.P.Q. 313 (1985), reh'g denied, 470 U.S. 1065, 105 S.Ct. 1782, 84 L.Ed.2d 841 (1985), the United States Supreme Court held that, in these circumstances, the intermediary, not the author, is entitled to the royalties paid by the licensee for continued use of the derivative work. Although the case involved section 304(c) rather than section 203, the Court left no doubt that it intended its decision to govern terminations of transfers under section 203 as well as under section 304(c). 469 U.S. at 159 n. 17, 105 S.Ct. at 643 n. 17. See generally, Howard B. Abrams, Who's Sorry Now? Termination Rights and the Derivative Works Exception, 62 U.Det.L.Rev. 181 (1985).

C. RIGHTS AND REMEDIES

1. RIGHTS

See Statute Supplement 17 U.S.C.A. §§ 106–122, 512, 602–603, 801–803, 1201–1205.

a. *The Statutory Rights*

Copyright Law Revision, H.R. Rep. No. 94–1476

94th Cong., 2d Sess. 61–65 (1976).

Section 106. Exclusive Rights in Copyrighted Works

General Scope of Copyright

The five fundamental rights that the bill gives to copyright owners— the exclusive rights of reproduction, adaptation, publication, performance, and display—are stated generally in section 106. These exclusive rights, which comprise the so-called "bundle of rights" that is a copyright, are cumulative and may overlap in some cases. Each of the five enumerated rights may be subdivided indefinitely and, as discussed below in connection with section 201, each subdivision of an exclusive right may be owned and enforced separately.

The approach of the bill is to set forth the copyright owner's exclusive rights in broad terms in section 106, and then to provide various limitations, qualifications, or exemptions in the 12 sections that follow. Thus, everything in section 106 is made "subject to sections 107 through 118,"* and must be read in conjunction with those provisions.

The exclusive rights accorded to a copyright owner under section 106 are "to do and to authorize" any of the activities specified in the five numbered clauses. Use of the phrase "to authorize" is intended to avoid any questions as to the liability of contributory infringers. For example, a person who lawfully acquires an authorized copy of a motion picture would be an infringer if he or she engages in the business of renting it to others for purposes of unauthorized public performance.

Rights of Reproduction, Adaptation, and Publication

The first three clauses of section 106, which cover all rights under a copyright except those of performance and display, extend to every kind of copyrighted work. The exclusive rights encompassed by these clauses, though closely related, are independent; they can generally be character-

---

* Presently sections 107–122 [Ed.].

ized as rights of copying, recording, adaptation, and publishing. A single act of infringement may violate all of these rights at once, as where a publisher reproduces, adapts, and sells copies of a person's copyrighted work as part of a publishing venture. Infringement takes place when any one of the rights is violated: where, for example, a printer reproduces copies without selling them or a retailer sells copies without having anything to do with their reproduction. The references to "copies or phonorecords," although in the plural, are intended here and throughout the bill to include the singular (1 U.S.C.A. § 1).

Reproduction.—Read together with the relevant definitions in section 101, the right "to reproduce the copyrighted work in copies or phonorecords" means the right to produce a material object in which the work is duplicated, transcribed, imitated, or simulated in a fixed form from which it can be "perceived, reproduced, or otherwise communicated, either directly or with the aid of a machine or device." As under the present law, a copyrighted work would be infringed by reproducing it in whole or in any substantial part, and by duplicating it exactly or by imitation or simulation. Wide departures or variations from the copyrighted work would still be an infringement as long as the author's "expression" rather than merely the author's "ideas" are taken. An exception to this general principle, applicable to the reproduction of copyrighted sound recordings, is specified in section 114.

"Reproduction" under clause (1) of section 106 is to be distinguished from "display" under clause (5). For a work to be "reproduced," its fixation in tangible form must be "sufficiently permanent or stable to permit it to be perceived, reproduced, or otherwise communicated for a period of more than transitory duration." Thus, the showing of images on a screen or tube would not be a violation of clause (1), although it might come within the scope of clause (5).

Preparation of Derivative Works.—The exclusive right to prepare derivative works, specified separately in clause (2) of section 106, overlaps the exclusive right of reproduction to some extent. It is broader than that right, however, in the sense that reproduction requires fixation in copies or phonorecords, whereas the preparation of a derivative work, such as a ballet, pantomime, or improvised performance, may be an infringement even though nothing is ever fixed in tangible form.

To be an infringement the "derivative work" must be "based upon the copyrighted work," and the definition in section 101 refers to "a translation, musical arrangement, dramatization, fictionalization, motion picture version, sound recording, art reproduction, abridgment, condensation, or any other form in which a work may be recast, transformed, or adapted." Thus, to constitute a violation of section 106(2), the infringing work must incorporate a portion of the copyrighted work in some form; for example, a detailed commentary on a work or a programmatic musical composition inspired by a novel would not normally constitute infringements under this clause. . . .

Public Distribution.—Clause (3) of section 106 establishes the exclusive right of publication: The right "to distribute copies or phonorecords of the copyrighted work to the public by sale or other transfer of ownership, or by rental, lease, or lending." Under this provision the copyright owner would have the right to control the first public distribution of an authorized copy or phonorecord of his work, whether by sale, gift, loan, or some rental or lease arrangement. Likewise, any unauthorized public distribution of copies or phonorecords that were unlawfully made would be an infringement. As section 109 makes clear, however, the copyright owner's rights under section 106(3) cease with respect to a particular copy or phonorecord once he has parted with ownership of it.

Rights of Public Performance and Display

Performing Rights and the "For Profit" Limitation.—The right of public performance under section 106(4) extends to "literary, musical, dramatic, and choreographic works, pantomimes, and motion pictures and other audiovisual works ..." and, unlike the equivalent provisions now in effect, is not limited by any "for profit" requirement. The approach of the bill, as in many foreign laws, is first to state the public performance right in broad terms, and then to provide specific exemptions for educational and other nonprofit uses.

This approach is more reasonable than the outright exemption of the 1909 statute. The line between commercial and "nonprofit" organizations is increasingly difficult to draw. Many "non-profit" organizations are highly subsidized and capable of paying royalties, and the widespread public exploitation of copyrighted works by public broadcasters and other noncommercial organizations is likely to grow. In addition to these trends, it is worth noting that performances and displays are continuing to supplant markets for printed copies and that in the future a broad "not for profit" exemption could not only hurt authors but could dry up their incentive to write.

The exclusive right of public performance is expanded to include not only motion pictures, including works recorded on film, video tape, and video disks, but also audiovisual works such as filmstrips and sets of slides. This provision of section 106(4), which is consistent with the assimilation of motion pictures to audiovisual works throughout the bill, is also related to amendments of the definitions of "display" and "perform" discussed below. The important issue of performing rights in sound recordings is discussed in connection with section 114.

Right of Public Display.—Clause (5) of section 106 represents the first explicit statutory recognition in American copyright law of an exclusive right to show a copyrighted work, or an image of it, to the public. The existence or extent of this right under the present statute is uncertain and subject to challenge. The bill would give the owners of copyright in "literary, musical, dramatic, and choreographic works, pantomimes, and pictorial, graphic, or sculptural works," including the individual images of a motion picture or other audiovisual work, the exclusive right "to display the copyrighted work publicly."

Definitions

Under the definitions of "perform," "display," "publicly," and "transmit" in section 101, the concepts of public performance and public display cover not only the initial rendition or showing, but also any further act by which that rendition or showing is transmitted or communicated to the public. Thus, for example: a singer is performing when he or she sings a song; a broadcasting network is performing when it transmits his or her performance (whether simultaneously or from records); a local broadcaster is performing when it transmits the network broadcast; a cable television system is performing when it retransmits the broadcast to its subscribers; and any individual is performing whenever he or she plays a phonorecord embodying the performance or communicates the performance by turning on a receiving set. Although any act by which the initial performance or display is transmitted, repeated, or made to recur would itself be a "performance" or "display" under the bill, it would not be actionable as an infringement unless it were done "publicly," as defined in section 101. Certain other performances and displays, in addition to those that are "private," are exempted or given qualified copyright control under sections 107 through 118.

To "perform" a work, under the definition in section 101, includes reading a literary work aloud, singing or playing music, dancing a ballet or other choreographic work, and acting out a dramatic work or pantomime. A performance may be accomplished "either directly or by means of any device or process," including all kinds of equipment for reproducing or amplifying sounds or visual images, any sort of transmitting apparatus, any type of electronic retrieval system, and any other techniques and systems not yet in use or even invented.

The definition of "perform" in relation to "a motion picture or other audio visual work" is "to show its images in any sequence or to make the sounds accompanying it audible." The showing of portions of a motion picture, filmstrip, or slide set must therefore be sequential to constitute a "performance" rather than a "display," but no particular order need be maintained. The purely aural performance of a motion picture sound track, or of the sound portions of an audiovisual work, would constitute a performance of the "motion picture or other audiovisual work"; but, where some of the sounds have been reproduced separately on phonorecords, a performance from the phonorecord would not constitute performance of the motion picture or audiovisual work.

The corresponding definition of "display" covers any showing of a "copy" of the work, "either directly or by means of a film, slide, television image, or any other device or process." Since "copies" are defined as including the material object "in which the work is first fixed," the right of public display applies to original works of art as well as to reproductions of them. With respect to motion pictures and other audiovisual works, it is a "display" (rather than a "performance") to show their "individual images nonsequentially." In addition to the direct showings of a copy of a work, "display" would include the projection of an image on a screen or other surface by any method, the transmission of an image by electronic or other means, and the showing of an image on a cathode ray tube, or similar viewing apparatus connected with any sort of information storage and retrieval system.

Under clause (1) of the definition of "publicly" in section 101, a performance or display is "public" if it takes place "at a place open to the public or at any place where a substantial number of persons outside of a normal circle of a family and its social acquaintances is gathered." One of the principal purposes of the definition was to make clear that, contrary to the decision in Metro–Goldwyn–Mayer Distributing Corp. v. Wyatt, 21 C.O.Bull. 203 (D.Md.1932), performances in "semipublic" places such as clubs, lodges, factories, summer camps, and schools are "public performances" subject to copyright control. The term "a family" in this context would include an individual living alone, so that a gathering confined to the individual's social acquaintances would normally be regarded as private. Routine meetings of businesses and governmental personnel would be excluded because they do not represent the gathering of a "substantial number of persons."

Clause (2) of the definition of "publicly" in section 101 makes clear that the concepts of public performance and public display include not only performances and displays that occur initially in a public place, but also acts that transmit or otherwise communicate a performance or display of the work to the public by means of any device or process. The definition of "transmit"—to communicate a performance or display "by any device or process whereby images or sound are received beyond the place from which they are sent"—is broad enough to include all conceivable forms and combinations of wired or wireless communications media, including but by no means limited to radio and television broadcasting as we know them. Each and every method by which the images or sounds comprising a performance or display are picked up and conveyed is a "transmission," and if the transmission reaches the public in any form, the case comes within the scope of clauses (4) or (5) of section 106.

Under the bill, as under the present law, a performance made available by transmission to the public at large is "public" even though the recipients are not gathered in a single place, and even if there is no proof that any of the potential recipients was operating his receiving apparatus at the time of the transmission. The same principles apply whenever the potential recipients of the transmission represent a limited segment of the public, such as the occupants of hotel rooms or the subscribers of a cable television service. Clause (2) of the definition of "publicly" is applicable "whether the members of the public capable of receiving the performance or display receive it in the same place or in separate places and at the same time or at different times."

Mirage Editions, Inc. v. Albuquerque A.R.T. Co.

United States Court of Appeals, Ninth Circuit, 1988.
856 F.2d 1341, 8 U.S.P.Q.2d 1171, cert. denied, 489 U.S. 1018, 109 S.Ct. 1135, 103 L.Ed.2d 196 (1989).

BRUNETTI, Circuit Judge:

Albuquerque A.R.T. (appellant or A.R.T.) appeals the district court's granting of summary judgment in favor of appellees Mirage, Dumas, and Van Der Marck (Mirage). The district court, in granting summary judgment, found that appellant had infringed Mirage's copyright and issued an order enjoining appellant from further infringing Mirage's copyright.

Patrick Nagel was an artist whose works appeared in many media including lithographs, posters, serigraphs, and as graphic art in many magazines, most notably Playboy. Nagel died in 1984. His widow Jennifer Dumas owns the copyrights to the Nagel art works which Nagel owned at the time of his death. Mirage is the exclusive publisher of Nagel's works and also owns the copyrights to many of those works. Dumas and Mirage own all of the copyrights to Nagel's works. No one else holds a copyright in any Nagel work. Appellee Alfred Van Der Marck Editions, Inc. is the licensee of Dumas and Mirage and the publisher of the commemorative book entitled *NAGEL: The Art of Patrick Nagel* ("the book"), which is a compilation of selected copyrighted individual art works and personal commentaries.

Since 1984, the primary business of appellant has consisted of: 1) purchasing artwork prints or books including good quality artwork page prints therein; 2) gluing each individual print or page print onto a rectangular sheet of black plastic material exposing a narrow black margin around the print; 3) gluing the black sheet with print onto a major surface of a rectangular white ceramic tile; 4) applying a transparent plastic film over the print, black sheet and ceramic tile surface; and 5) offering the tile with artwork mounted thereon for sale in the retail market.

It is undisputed, in this action, that appellant did the above process with the Nagel book. The appellant removed selected pages from the book, mounted them individually onto ceramic tiles and sold the tiles at retail.

Mirage, Dumas and Van Der Marck brought an action alleging infringement of registered copyrights in the artwork of Nagel and in the book. Mirage also alleged trademark infringement and unfair competition under the Lanham Act, 15 U.S.C. § 1051 et seq. and the state law of unfair competition, Cal.Bus. & Prof.Code §§ 17200 et seq.

Appellant moved for summary judgment on the Lanham Act and Copyright Act causes of action. The district court granted summary judgment as to the Lanham Act cause of action but denied summary judgment on the copyright cause of action. Mirage then moved for summary judgment on the copyright claim which was granted. The court also enjoined appellants from removing individual art images from the book, mounting each individual image onto a separate tile and advertising for sale and/or selling the tiles with the images mounted thereon.

The Copyright Act of 1976, 17 U.S.C. § 101 et seq., confers upon the copyright holder exclusive rights to make several uses of his copyright. Among those rights are: (1) the right to reproduce the copyrighted work in copies, 17 U.S.C. § 106(1); (2) the right to prepare derivative works based upon the copyrighted work, 17 U.S.C. § 106(2); (3) the right to distribute copies of the copyrighted work to the public by sale or other transfer of ownership, or by rental, lease or lending, 17 U.S.C. § 106(3); and (4) in the case of literary, pictorial, graphic and sculptural works, including individual images, the right to display the copyrighted work publicly.

The district court concluded appellant infringed the copyrights in the individual images through its tile-preparing process and also concluded that the resulting products comprised derivative works.

Appellant contends that there has been no copyright infringement because (1) its tiles are not derivative works, and (2) the "first sale" doctrine precludes a finding of infringement.

The Copyright Act of 1976, 17 U.S.C. § 101 defines a derivative work as:

> [A] work based upon one or more preexisting works such as a translation, musical arrangement, dramatization, fictionalization, motion picture version, sound recording, art reproduction, abridgment, condensation or *any other form in which a work may be recast, transformed, or adapted.* A work consisting of editorial revisions, annotations, elaborations, or other modifications which, as a whole, represent an original work of authorship is a "derivative work."

(Emphasis added).

The protection of derivative rights extends beyond mere protection against unauthorized copying to include the right to make other versions of, perform, or exhibit the work. . . .

What appellant has clearly done here is to make another version of Nagel's art works, and that amounts to preparation of a derivative work. By borrowing and mounting the preexisting, copyrighted individual art images without the consent of the copyright proprietors—Mirage and Dumas as to the art works and Van Der Marck as to the book—appellant has prepared a derivative work and infringed the subject copyrights.

Appellant's contention that since it has not engaged in "art reproduction" and therefore its tiles are not derivative works is not fully dispositive of this issue. Appellant has ignored the disjunctive phrase "or any other form in which a work may be recast, transformed or adapted." The legislative history of the Copyright Act of 1976 indicates that Congress intended that for a violation of the right to prepare derivative works to occur "the infringing work must incorporate a portion of the copyrighted work in *some form.*" 1976 U.S.Code Cong. & Admin.News 5659, 5675. (emphasis added). The language "recast, transformed or adapted" seems to encompass other alternatives besides simple art reproduction. By removing the individual images from the book and placing them on the tiles, perhaps the appellant has not accomplished reproduction. We conclude, though, that appellant has certainly recast or transformed the individual images by incorporating them into its tile-preparing process.

The "first sale" doctrine, which appellant also relies on in its contention that no copyright infringement has occurred, appears at 17 U.S.C. § 109(a). That section provides:

> Notwithstanding the provisions of Section 106(3), the owner of a particular copy or phonorecord lawfully made under this title, or any person authorized by such owner, is entitled, without the authority of the copyright owner, to sell or otherwise dispose of the possession of that copy or phonorecord.

In United States v. Wise, 550 F.2d 1180 (9th Cir.1977), which concerned a criminal prosecution under the pre–1976 Copyright Act, this court held that:

> [T]he "first sale" doctrine provides that where a copyright owner parts with title to a particular copy of his copyrighted work, he divests himself of his exclusive right to vend that particular copy. While the proprietor's other copyright rights (reprinting, copying, etc.) remain unimpaired, the exclusive right to vend the transferred copy rests with the vendee, who is not restricted by statute from further transfers of that copy.

550 F.2d at 1187.

We recognize that, under the "first sale" doctrine as enunciated at 17 U.S.C. § 109(a) and as discussed in *Wise,* appellant can purchase a copy of the Nagel book and subsequently alienate its ownership in that book. However, the right to transfer applies only to the particular copy of the book which appellant has purchased and nothing else. The mere sale of the book to the appellant without a specific transfer by the copyright holder of its exclusive right to prepare derivative works, does not transfer that right to appellant. The derivative works right, remains unimpaired and with the copyright proprietors—Mirage, Dumas and Van Der Marck. As we have previously concluded that appellant's tile-preparing process results in derivative works and as the exclusive right to prepare derivative works belongs to the copyright holder, the "first sale" doctrine does not bar the appellees' copyright infringement claims.

We AFFIRM.

Lee v. A.R.T. Company

United States Court of Appeals, Seventh Circuit, 1997.
125 F.3d 580, 44 U.S.P.Q.2d 1153.

EASTERBROOK, Circuit Judge.

Annie Lee creates works of art, which she sells through her firm Annie Lee & Friends. Deck the Walls, a chain of outlets for modestly priced art, is among the buyers of her works, which have been registered with the Register of Copyrights. One Deck the Walls store sold some of Lee's notecards and small lithographs to A.R.T. Company, which mounted the works on ceramic tiles (covering the art with transparent epoxy resin in the process) and resold the tiles. Lee contends that these tiles are derivative works, which under 17 U.S.C. § 106(2) may not be prepared without the permission of the copyright proprietor. She seeks both monetary and injunctive relief. Her position has the support of two cases holding that A.R.T.'s business violates the copyright laws. Munoz v. Albuquerque A.R.T. Co., 38 F.3d 1218 (9th Cir.1994), affirming without published opinion, 829 F.Supp. 309 (D.Alaska 1993); Mirage Editions, Inc. v. Albuquerque A.R.T. Co., 856 F.2d 1341 (9th Cir.1988). Mirage Editions, the only full appellate discussion, dealt with pages cut from books and mounted on tiles; the court of appeals' brief order in Munoz concludes that the reasoning of Mirage Editions is equally applicable to works of art that were sold loose. Our district court disagreed with these decisions and entered summary judgment for the defendant.

Now one might suppose that this is an open and shut case under the doctrine of first sale, codified at 17 U.S.C. § 109(a). A.R.T. bought the work legitimately, mounted it on a tile, and resold what it had purchased. Because the artist could capture the value of her art's contribution to the finished product as part of the price for the original transaction, the economic rationale for protecting an adaptation as "derivative" is absent. An alteration that includes (or consumes) a complete copy of the original lacks economic significance. One work changes hands multiple times, exactly what § 109(a) permits, so it may lack legal significance too. But § 106(2) creates a separate exclusive right, to "prepare derivative works", and Lee believes that affixing the art to the tile is "preparation," so that A.R.T. would have violated § 106(2) even if it had dumped the finished tiles into the Marianas Trench. For the sake of argument we assume that this is so and ask whether card-on-a-tile is a "derivative work" in the first place.

"Derivative work" is a defined term:

A "derivative work" is a work based upon one or more preexisting works, such as a translation, musical arrangement, dramatization, fictionalization, motion picture version, sound recording, art reproduction, abridgment, condensation, or any other form in which a work may be recast, transformed, or adapted. A work consisting of editorial revisions, annotations, elaborations, or other modifications which, as a whole, represent an original work of authorship, is a "derivative work".

17 U.S.C. § 101. The district court concluded that A.R.T.'s mounting of Lee's works on tile is not an "original work of authorship" because it is no different in form or function from displaying a painting in a frame or placing a medallion in a velvet case. No one believes that a museum violates § 106(2) every time it changes the frame of a painting that is still under copyright, although the choice of frame or glazing affects the impression the art conveys, and many artists specify frames (or pedestals for sculptures) in detail. Munoz and Mirage Editions acknowledge that framing and other traditional means of mounting and displaying art do not

infringe authors' exclusive right to make derivative works. Nonetheless, the ninth circuit held, what A.R.T. does creates a derivative work because the epoxy resin bonds the art to the tile. Our district judge thought this a distinction without a difference, and we agree. If changing the way in which a work of art will be displayed creates a derivative work, and if Lee is right about what "prepared" means, then the derivative work is "prepared" when the art is mounted; what happens later is not relevant, because the violation of the § 106(2) right has already occurred. If the framing process does not create a derivative work, then mounting art on a tile, which serves as a flush frame, does not create a derivative work. What is more, the ninth circuit erred in assuming that normal means of mounting and displaying art are easily reversible. A painting is placed in a wooden "stretcher" as part of the framing process; this leads to some punctures (commonly tacks or staples), may entail trimming the edges of the canvas, and may affect the surface of the painting as well. Works by Jackson Pollock are notoriously hard to mount without damage, given the thickness of their paint. As a prelude to framing, photographs, prints, and posters may be mounted on stiff boards using wax sheets, but sometimes glue or another more durable substance is employed to create the bond.

Lee wages a vigorous attack on the district court's conclusion that A.R.T.'s mounting process cannot create a derivative work because the change to the work "as a whole" is not sufficiently original to support a copyright. Cases such as Gracen v. The Bradford Exchange, Inc., 698 F.2d 300 (7th Cir.1983), show that neither A.R.T. nor Lee herself could have obtained a copyright in the card-on-a-tile, thereby not only extending the period of protection for the images but also eliminating competition in one medium of display. After the ninth circuit held that its mounting process created derivative works, A.R.T. tried to obtain a copyright in one of its products; the Register of Copyrights sensibly informed A.R.T. that the card-on-a-tile could not be copyrighted independently of the note card itself. But Lee says that this is irrelevant—that a change in a work's appearance may infringe the exclusive right under § 106(2) even if the alteration is too trivial to support an independent copyright. Pointing to the word "original" in the second sentence of the statutory definition, the district judge held that "originality" is essential to a derivative work. This understanding has the support of both cases and respected commentators. E.g., L. Batlin & Son, Inc. v. Snyder, 536 F.2d 486 (2d Cir.1976); Melville B. Nimmer & David Nimmer, 1 *Nimmer on Copyrights* § 3.03 (1997). Pointing to the fact that the first sentence in the statutory definition omits any reference to originality, Lee insists that a work may be derivative despite the mechanical nature of the transformation. This view, too, has the support of both cases and respected commentators. E.g., Lone Ranger Television, Inc. v. Program Radio Corp., 740 F.2d 718, 722 (9th Cir.1984); Paul Goldstein, *Copyright: Principles, Law and Practice* § 5.3.1 (2d ed.1996) (suggesting that a transformation is covered by § 106(2) whenever it creates a "new work for a different market").

Fortunately, it is not necessary for us to choose sides. Assume for the moment that the first sentence recognizes a set of non-original derivative works. To prevail, then, Lee must show that A.R.T. altered her works in one of the ways mentioned in the first sentence. The tile is not an "art reproduction"; A.R.T. purchased and mounted Lee's original works. That leaves the residual clause: "any other form in which a work may be recast, transformed, or adapted." None of these words fits what A.R.T. did. Lee's works were not "recast" or "adapted". "Transformed" comes closer and gives the ninth circuit some purchase for its view that the permanence of the bond between art and base matters. Yet the copyrighted note cards and lithographs were not "transformed" in the slightest. The art was bonded to a slab of ceramic, but it was not changed in the process. It still depicts exactly what it depicted when it left Lee's studio. If mounting works a "transformation," then changing a painting's frame or a photograph's mat equally produces a derivative work. Indeed, if Lee is right about the meaning of the definition's first sentence, then *any* alteration of a work, however slight, requires the author's permission. We asked at oral argument what would happen if a purchaser jotted a note on one of the note cards, or used it as a coaster for a drink, or cut it in half, or if a collector applied his seal (as is common in Japan); Lee's counsel replied that such changes prepare derivative works, but that as a practical matter artists would not file suit. A definition of derivative work that makes criminals out of art collectors and tourists is jarring despite Lee's gracious offer not to commence civil litigation.

If Lee (and the ninth circuit) are right about what counts as a derivative work, then the United States has established through the back door an extraordinarily broad version of authors' moral rights, under which artists may block any modification of their works of which they disapprove. No European version of *droit moral* goes this far. Until recently it was accepted wisdom that the United States did not enforce any claim of moral rights; even bowdlerization of a work was permitted unless the modifications produced a new work so different that it infringed the exclusive right under § 106(2). The Visual Artists Rights Act of 1990, Pub.L. 101–650, 104 Stat. 5089, 5123–33, moves federal law in the direction of moral rights, but the cornerstone of the new statute, 17 U.S.C. § 106A, does not assist Lee. Section 106A(a)(3)(A) gives an artist the right to "prevent any intentional distortion, mutilation, or other modification of that work which would be prejudicial to his or her honor or reputation". At oral argument Lee's lawyer disclaimed any contention that the sale of her works on tile has damaged her honor or reputation. What is more, § 106A applies only to a "work of visual art", a new term defined in § 101 to mean either a unique work or part of a limited edition (200 copies or fewer) that has been "signed and consecutively numbered by the author". Lee's note cards and lithographs are not works of visual art under this definition, so she could not invoke § 106A even if A.R.T.'s use of her works to produce kitsch had damaged her reputation. It would not be sound to use § 106(2) to provide artists with exclusive rights deliberately omitted from the Visual Artists Rights Act. We therefore decline to follow Munoz and Mirage Editions.

Columbia Pictures Industries, Inc. v. Redd Horne, Inc.

United States Court of Appeals, Third Circuit, 1984.
749 F.2d 154, 224 U.S.P.Q. 641.

RE, Chief Judge.

In this copyright infringement case, defendants appeal from an order of the United States District Court for the Western District of Pennsylvania which granted the plaintiffs' motion for summary judgment, and enjoined defendants from exhibiting plaintiffs' copyrighted motion pictures. The defendants, Redd Horne, Inc., Maxwell's Video Showcase, Ltd., Glenn W. Zeny and Robert Zeny, also appeal from the dismissal of their antitrust counterclaims, and from an award of damages against them in the amount of $44,750.00.

Defendant-appellants raise three questions on this appeal: (1) whether the activities of the defendant Maxwell's Video Showcase, Ltd. (Maxwell's) constitute an infringement of plaintiffs' copyright protections which would entitle the plaintiffs to injunctive relief and damages; (2) if so, whether the activities of the other defendants, Robert Zeny, the president and sole shareholder of Maxwell's, Redd Horne, Inc., Maxwell's advertising and public relations firm, and Glenn W. Zeny, the president of Redd Horne, Inc., and Robert Zeny's brother, are sufficient to hold each of them liable as co-infringers with Maxwell's; and (3) whether the antitrust counterclaims of the defendants were properly dismissed by the district court. Since we agree with the district court, we affirm.

The Facts

Maxwell's Video Showcase, Ltd., operates two stores in Erie, Pennsylvania. At these two facilities, Maxwell's sells and rents video cassette recorders and prerecorded video cassettes, and sells blank video cassette cartridges. These activities are not the subject of the plaintiffs' complaint. The copyright infringement issue in this case arises from defendants' *exhibition* of video cassettes of the plaintiffs' films, or what defendants euphemistically refer to as their "showcasing" or "in-store rental" concept.

Each store contains a small showroom area in the front of the store, and a "showcase" or exhibition area in the rear. The front showroom contains video equipment and materials for sale or rent, as well as dispensing machines for popcorn and carbonated beverages. Movie posters are also displayed in this front area. In the rear "showcase" area, patrons may view any of an assortment of video cassettes in small, private booths with space for two to four people. There are a total of eighty-five booths in the two stores. Each booth or room is approximately four feet by six feet and is carpeted on the floor and walls. In the front there is a nineteen inch color television and an upholstered bench in the back.

The procedure followed by a patron wishing to utilize one of the viewing booths or rooms is the same at both facilities. The customer selects a film from a catalogue which contains the titles of available films. The fee charged by Maxwell's depends on the number of people in the viewing room, and the time of day. The price is $5.00 for one or two people before 6 p.m., and $6.00 for two people after 6 p.m. There is at all times a $1.00 surcharge for the third and fourth person. The fee also entitles patrons to help themselves to popcorn and soft drinks before entering their assigned rooms. Closing the door of the viewing room activates a signal in the counter area at the front of the store. An employee of Maxwell's then places the cassette of the motion picture chosen by the viewer into one of the video cassette machines in the front of the store and the picture is transmitted to the patron's viewing room. The viewer may adjust the light in the room, as well as the volume, brightness, and color levels on the television set.

Access to each room is limited to the individuals who rent it as a group. Although no restriction is placed on the composition of a group, strangers are not grouped in order to fill a particular room to capacity. Maxwell's is open to any member of the public who wishes to utilize its facilities or services.

Maxwell's advertises on Erie radio stations and on the theatre pages of the local newspapers. Typically, each advertisement features one or more motion pictures, and emphasizes Maxwell's selection of films, low prices, and free refreshments. The advertisements do not state that these motion pictures are video cassette copies. At the entrance to the two Maxwell's facilities, there are also advertisements for individual films, which resemble movie posters.

Infringement of Plaintiffs' Copyright

It may be stated at the outset that this is not a case of unauthorized taping or video cassette piracy. The defendants obtained the video cassette copies of plaintiffs' copyrighted motion pictures by purchasing them from either the plaintiffs or their authorized distributors. The sale or rental of these cassettes to individuals for home viewing is also not an issue. Plaintiffs do not contend that in-home use infringes their copyright.

The plaintiffs' complaint is based on their contention that the exhibition or showing of the video cassettes in the private booths on defendants' premises constitutes an unauthorized public performance in violation of plaintiffs' exclusive rights under the federal copyright laws.

It is acknowledged that it is the role of the Congress, not the courts, to formulate new principles of copyright law when the legislature has determined that technological innovations have made them necessary. See, e.g., Sony Corp. v. Universal City Studios, Inc., 464 U.S. 417, 104 S.Ct. 774, 783, 78 L.Ed.2d 574 (1984); Teleprompter Corp. v. CBS, 415 U.S. 394, 414, 94 S.Ct. 1129, 1141, 39 L.Ed.2d 415 (1974). In the words of Justice Stevens, "Congress has the constitutional authority and the institutional ability to accommodate fully the varied permutations of competing interests that are inevitably implicated by such new technology." Sony Corp., supra, 104 S.Ct. at 783. A defendant, however, is not immune from liability for copyright infringement simply because the technologies are of recent origin or are being applied to innovative uses. Although this case involves a novel application of relatively recent technological developments, it can nonetheless be readily analyzed and resolved within the existing statutory framework.

Section 106 of the Copyright Act confers upon the copyright holder certain exclusive rights. This section provides:

Subject to sections 107 through 118, the owner of copyright under this title has the exclusive rights to do and to authorize any of the following:

(1) to reproduce the copyrighted work in copies or phonorecords;

(2) to prepare derivative works based upon the copyrighted work;

(3) to distribute copies or phonorecords of the copyrighted work to the public by sale or other transfer of ownership, or by rental, lease, or lending;

(4) in the case of literary, musical, dramatic, and choreographic works, pantomimes, and *motion pictures and other audiovisual works, to perform the copyrighted work publicly;* and

(5) in the case of literary, musical, dramatic, and choreographic works, pantomimes, and pictorial, graphic, or sculptural works, including the individual images of a motion picture or other audiovisual work, to display the copyrighted work publicly.

17 U.S.C. § 106 (1982) (emphasis supplied).

It is undisputed that the defendants were licensed to exercise the right of distribution. A copyright owner, however, may dispose of a copy of his work while retaining all underlying copyrights which are not expressly or impliedly disposed of with that copy. Thus, it is clear that the plaintiffs have retained their interest in the other four enumerated rights. Since the rights granted by section 106 are separate and distinct, and are severable from one another, the grant of one does not waive any of the other exclusive rights. Thus, plaintiffs' sales of video cassette copies of their copyrighted motion pictures did not result in a waiver of any of the other exclusive rights enumerated in section 106, such as the exclusive right to perform their motion pictures publicly. In essence, therefore, the fundamental question is whether the defendants' activities constitute a public performance of the plaintiffs' motion pictures. We agree with the conclusion of the district court that these activities constitute a public performance, and are an infringement.

"To perform a work means . . . in the case of a motion picture or other audiovisual work, to show its images in any sequence or to make the sounds accompanying it audible." 17 U.S.C. § 101 (1982). Clearly, playing a video cassette results in a sequential showing of a motion picture's images and in making the sounds accompanying it audible. Thus, Maxwell's activities constitute a performance under section 101.

The remaining question is whether these performances are public. Section 101 also states that to perform a work "publicly" means "[t]o perform . . . it at a place open to the public or at any place where a substantial number of persons outside of a normal circle of a family and its social acquaintances is gathered." The statute is written in the disjunctive, and thus two categories of places can satisfy the definition of "to perform a work publicly." The first category is self-evident; it is "a place open to the public." The second category, commonly referred to as a semi-public place, is determined by the size and composition of the audience.

The legislative history indicates that this second category was added to expand the concept of public performance by including those places that, although not open to the public at large, are accessible to a significant number of people. Clearly, if a place is public, the size and composition of the audience are irrelevant. However, if the place is not public, the size and composition of the audience will be determinative.

We find it unnecessary to examine the second part of the statutory definition because we agree with the district court's conclusion that Maxwell's was open to the public. On the composition of the audience, the district court noted that "the showcasing operation is not distinguishable in any significant manner from the exhibition of films at a conventional movie theater." 568 F.Supp. at 500. Any member of the public can view a motion picture by paying the appropriate fee. The services provided by Maxwell's are essentially the same as a movie theatre, with the additional feature of privacy. The relevant "place" within the meaning of section 101 is each of Maxwell's two stores, not each individual booth within each store. Simply because the cassettes can be viewed in private does not mitigate the essential fact that Maxwell's is unquestionably open to the public.

The conclusion that Maxwell's activities constitute public performances is fully supported by subsection (2) of the statutory definition of public performance:

> (2) to transmit or otherwise communicate a performance ... of the work to a place specified by clause (1) or to the public, by means of any device or process, whether the members of the public capable of receiving the performance ... receive it in the same place or in separate places and at the same time or at different times.

17 U.S.C. § 101 (1982). As explained in the House Report which accompanies the Copyright Revision Act of 1976, "a performance made available by transmission to the public at large is 'public' even though the recipients are not gathered in a single place.... The same principles apply whenever the potential recipients of the transmission represent a limited segment of the public, such as the occupants of hotel rooms...." *House Report,* supra, at 64–65, U.S.Code Cong. & Admin.News, p. 5678. Thus, the transmission of a performance to members of the public, even in private settings such as hotel rooms or Maxwell's viewing rooms, constitutes a public performance. As the statutory language and legislative history clearly indicate, the fact that members of the public view the performance at different times does not alter this legal consequence....

Although Maxwell's has only one copy of each film, it shows each copy repeatedly to different members of the public. This constitutes a public performance.

The First Sale Doctrine

The defendants also contend that their activities are protected by the first sale doctrine. The first sale doctrine is codified in section 109(a) of Title 17. This section provides:

> Notwithstanding the provisions of section 106(3), the owner of a particular copy or phonorecord lawfully made under this title, or any person authorized by such owner, is entitled, without the authority of the copyright owner, to sell or otherwise dispose of the possession of that copy or phonorecord.

17 U.S.C. § 109(a) (1982). Section 109(a) is an extension of the principle that ownership of the material object is distinct from ownership of the copyright in this material. See 17 U.S.C. § 202 (1982). The first sale doctrine prevents the copyright owner from controlling the future transfer of a particular copy once its material ownership has been transferred. The transfer of the video cassettes to the defendants, however, did not result in the forfeiture or waiver of all of the exclusive rights found in section 106. The copyright owner's exclusive right "to perform the copyrighted work publicly" has not been affected; only its distribution right as to the transferred copy has been circumscribed.

In essence, the defendants' "first sale" argument is merely another aspect of their argument that their activities are not public performances. For the defendants' argument to succeed, we would have to adopt their characterization of the "showcasing" transaction or activity as an "in-store rental." The facts do not permit such a finding or conclusion. The record clearly demonstrates that showcasing a video cassette at Maxwell's is a significantly different transaction than leasing a tape for home use. Maxwell's never disposed of the tapes in its showcasing operations, nor did the tapes ever leave the store. At all times, Maxwell's maintained physical dominion and control over the tapes. Its employees actually played the cassettes on its machines. The charges or fees received for viewing the cassettes at Maxwell's facilities are analytically indistinguishable from admission fees paid by patrons to gain admission to any public theater. Plainly, in their showcasing operation, the appellants do not sell, rent, or otherwise dispose of the video cassette. On the facts presented, Maxwell's "showcasing" operation is a public performance, which, as a matter of law, constitutes a copyright infringement.

Liability of Co–Defendants

Defendant-appellants, Robert Zeny, Glenn W. Zeny, and Redd Horne, Inc., challenge that part of the district court's order which holds them liable as co-infringers. We agree with the district court and affirm.

It is well settled that "one who, with knowledge of the infringing activity, induces, causes or materially contributes to the infringing activity of another, may be held liable as a 'contributory' infringer." Gershwin Publishing Corp. v. Columbia Artists Management, Inc., 443 F.2d 1159, 1162 (2d Cir.1971). An officer or director of a corporation who knowingly participates in the infringement can be held personally liable, jointly and severally, with the corporate defendant.

Robert Zeny is the president and the sole shareholder of Maxwell's Video Showcase, Ltd. He knowingly initiated and participated in the infringing activity, and ignored repeated requests from the plaintiffs that he cease and desist the activity. He too, therefore, is clearly liable as a co-infringer.

Glenn W. Zeny, Robert's brother, is not a stockholder or officer, nor does he have a direct financial interest in Maxwell's Video Showcase, Ltd. Glenn W. Zeny, however, conducted negotiations and wrote letters, on Redd Horne, Inc., stationery, on behalf of Maxwell's and its predecessor corporation. Some of these letters on Redd Horne, Inc., stationery, refer to "our company" and "our concept" without mentioning Maxwell's. The impression conveyed by the letters is that Glenn Zeny and Redd Horne, Inc., are principals in the venture. Glenn W. Zeny, like his brother, participated knowingly and significantly in the infringing activity and ignored the plaintiffs' persistent requests that the activity cease.

Redd Horne, Inc., conducted all of the advertising and promotional work for Maxwell's. It also provided financial, accounting, and administrative services for Maxwell's. All of these services, and the advertising services in particular, contributed and, indeed, were essential to the copyright infringement. In addition, Glenn W. Zeny's knowledge of, and substantial participation in, the infringing activities may be imputed to his employer, Redd Horne, Inc. Thus, we hold that the substantial, knowing participation of Glenn W. Zeny and Redd Horne, Inc., was more than sufficient to hold them liable as co-infringers. . . .

Conclusion

In view of the foregoing, it is the holding of this Court that the defendants' activities constituted an unauthorized, and, therefore, an unlawful public performance of the plaintiffs' copyrighted motion pictures. We also conclude that the activities of each named defendant were sufficient to hold each jointly and severally liable for the copyright infringement. In addition, we hold that the defendants' counterclaims were properly dismissed.

The judgment of the district court, therefore, will be affirmed.

NOTES

1. *Derivative Works and Underlying Works.* Derivative works and the works on which they are based will often have different terms of protection. A motion picture, for example, may be a work for hire protected for 95 years from its first distribution, while copyright in the novel on which it is based will endure for 70 years after the death of the author. Once copyright in the motion picture expires, can anyone freely copy, distribute and perform it if the underlying novel is still under copyright? If not, what does it mean to say that a derivative work is in the public domain?

In Russell v. Price, 612 F.2d 1123, 1128 205 U.S.P.Q. 206 (9th Cir.1979), *cert. denied,* 446 U.S. 952, 100 S.Ct. 2919, 64 L.Ed.2d 809 (1980), the copyright owners of George Bernard Shaw's stage play, *Pygmalion,* sued the distributors of the motion picture, *Pygmalion* which had been produced under license from Shaw. Copyright in the play, renewed in 1941, was still in force at the time of suit; copyright in the motion picture had terminated in 1966 for failure to renew. Against defendant's argument that, because the film copyright had expired the film was in the public domain and so could be freely copied and distributed, the court held that "although the derivative work may enter the public domain, the matter contained therein which derives from a work still covered by statutory copyright is not dedicated to the public. The established doctrine prevents unauthorized copying or other infringing use of the underlying work or any part of that work contained in the derivative product so long as the underlying work itself remains copyrighted. Therefore, since exhibition of the film 'Pygmalion' necessarily involves exhibition of parts of Shaw's play, which is still copyrighted, plaintiffs here may prevent defendants from renting the film for exhibition without their authorization."

On derivative rights generally, see Amy B. Cohen, When Does a Work Infringe the Derivative Works Right of a Copyright Owner?, 17 Cardozo Arts & Ent. L.J. 623 (1999).

2. After *Redd Horne,* does it constitute public performance for a hotel to rent videodiscs of copyrighted motion pictures to guests for viewing on videodisc players in their individual rooms? Columbia Pictures Industries, Inc. v. Professional Real Estate Investors, Inc., 866 F.2d 278, 281, 9 U.S.P.Q.2d 1653 (9th Cir.1989), held that it does not. The court rejected plaintiffs' argument that, because defendant's hotel rooms can be rented by members of the public, they are "open to the public" within the terms of section 101; "[w]hile the hotel may indeed be 'open to the public,' a guest's hotel room, once rented, is not." The court also rejected plaintiffs' argument that the effect of defendant's activities was to "otherwise communicate" the motion pictures to the public within the terms of section 101's "transmit or otherwise communicate" clause.

Will the current statutory formulation of public performance encompass future "on-demand" communication technologies? On Command Video Corp. v. Columbia Pictures Industries, 777 F.Supp. 787, 21 U.S.P.Q. 2d 1545 (N.D.Cal.1991), a declaratory judgment action brought by a potential infringer, involved a wired motion picture performance system that connected hotel guest rooms to a centrally located console containing motion picture videocassettes, enabling guests to view a movie anytime they wished, rather than according to a schedule predetermined by the hotel or programmer; once a guest selected a particular video, that selection became unavailable to other guests in the hotel, and could be seen only in the room of the guest who selected it.

The court held that this system would infringe the motion picture company's public performance right, and rejected the argument that, because the system would transmit performances from each videocassette to only one room at a time, none of its transmissions would be "to the public." The court observed that hotel guests watching a motion picture in their rooms are "members of" " 'the public' ... because the relationship between the transmitter of the performance, On Command, and the audience, hotel guests, is a commercial, 'public' one regardless of where the viewing takes place." 777 F.Supp. at 790.

The court also found legislative history indicating Congress' intention, when adding the phrase "at the same time or at different times" to the definition of public performance, to "cover precisely the sort of single-viewer system developed by plaintiff." According to a 1967 House Report, "[t]he same principles [that a transmission is 'to the public'] apply whenever the potential recipients of the transmission represent a limited segment of the public, such as the occupants of hotel rooms ...; they are also applicable where the transmission is capable of reaching different recipients at different times, as in the case of sounds or images stored in an information system and capable of being performed or displayed at the initiative of individual members of the public." 777 F.Supp. at 790 (quoting H.R.Rep.No.83, 90th Cong., 1st Sess. 29 (1967)).

3. *Rights in Sound Recordings.* Until 1972, the United States Copyright Act gave no rights at all to sound recordings. Protection, when it finally came, was closely circumscribed. Under sections 106 and 114(a) of the 1976 Act, rights in sound recordings include the reproduction right, the right to prepare derivative works and the distribution right, but not the performance right or the display right. Section 114(b) further confines the reproduction and derivative rights in sound recordings to exact replication or dubbing; imitations are exempted.

Section 114(d) required the Register of Copyrights to file a report on the desirability of performance rights in sound recordings. The Register's report, submitted to Congress on January 3, 1978, and supplemented on March 13, 1978, recommended that "section 114 be amended to provide performance rights, subject to compulsory licensing, in copyrighted sound recordings, and that the benefits of this right be extended both to performers (including employees for hire) and to record producers as joint authors of sound recordings." In part, the Register rested her recommendation on the view that the "lack of copyright protection for performers since the commercial development of records has had a drastic and destructive effect on both the performing and the recording arts." Performance Rights in Sound Recordings 43 Fed.Reg. 12765–66 (1978).

The Register's report failed to persuade a Congress that, some have said, was beholden to members of the National Association of Broadcasters, a trade group that has historically opposed a performance right in sound recordings. Record companies did, however, achieve a breakthrough with passage of the Digital Performance Right in Sound Recordings Act of 1995, Pub.L. No. 104–39, 109 Stat. 336, which added a new subsection (6) to section 106's catalogue of exclusive rights, granting the right "in the case of sound recordings, to perform the copyrighted work publicly by means of a digital audio transmission" as defined in new section 114(j). The labyrinthine amendments subject the narrowly defined right to exemptions, compulsory licenses and limitations on voluntarily licenses.

4. *The Display Right.* The 1976 Copyright Act created a new statutory right—section 106(5)'s right, "in the case of literary, musical, dramatic, and choreographic works, pantomimes, and pictorial, graphic, or sculptural works, including the individual images of a motion picture or other audiovisual work, to display the copyrighted work publicly." Can an artist who has sold a painting prevent the buyer from displaying it publicly? Section 109(c) of the 1976 Act gives the expected answer.

Congress's addition of a display right in the 1976 Act responded to a concern over "the enormous potential importance of showing, rather than distributing, copies as a means of disseminating an author's work. . . . It is not inconceivable that, in certain areas at least, 'exhibition' may take over from 'reproduction' of 'copies' as the means of presenting authors' works to the public, and we are now convinced that a basic right of public exhibition should be expressly recognized in the statute." House Comm. on the Judiciary, 89th Cong., 1st Sess., Copyright Law Revision Part 6: Supplementary Report of the Register of Copyrights on the General Revision of the U.S. Copyright Law: 1965 Revision Bill 20 (Comm.Print 1965).

In the first extended analysis of the public display right, Professor Anthony Reese has observed that "[c]hanging technology is now presenting precisely the problem that the display right was designed to solve, but courts and lawyers continue to neglect the right. The controversial doctrine of 'RAM copies'—the notion that accessing a work on a computer infringes the reproduction right because it requires temporary storage in the computer's random-access memory (RAM)—is a strained and problematic attempt to solve the problems of computer technology with the familiar reproduction right instead of the unfamiliar display right. But it turns out that Congress intended the display right for exactly this purpose. In a remarkable act of foresight, Congress and the Copyright Office in the 1960s predicted the development of computer or other electronic networks that would be capable of displaying a copyrighted work at a distance without making a new copy. Congress designed the public display right to address this anticipated technology, and it built into the right a sensible balance between the interests of copyright owners and those of users of copyrighted works." R. Anthony Reese, The Public Display Right: The Copyright Act's Neglected Solution to the Controversy Over RAM "Copies," 2001 U. Ill. L. Rev. 83, 84.

5. *The Distribution Right and the First Sale Doctrine.* Section 106(3) of the Copyright Act grants the exclusive right to distribute "copies or phonorecords of the copyrighted work to the public by sale or other transfer of ownership, or by rental, lease, or lending." The most important limitation on the distribution right is the first sale doctrine embodied in section 109(a): "the owner of a particular copy or phonorecord lawfully made under this title, or any person authorized by such owner, is entitled, without the authority of the copyright owner, to sell or otherwise dispose of the possession of that copy or phonorecord." This limitation is in turn limited by section 109(b)'s provisions respecting rental of phonorecords and computer programs.

Phonorecords. Section 109(b), as added by the Record Rental Amendment of 1984, Pub.L. No. 98–450, 98 Stat. 1727, created a narrow exception to the first sale doctrine by providing that an owner of a phonorecord may not rent, lease or lend the phonorecord without the copyright owner's permission. The House Report explains:

> At present, according to industry estimates, there are approximately 200 commercial record rental establishments in the United States. Testimony before this Committee's Subcommittee had indicated that these establishments rent phonorecords for 24 to 72 hours for fees of $.99 to $2.50 per disc. Frequently, blank audio cassette tapes are sold in the same establishment. One such establishment advertised, "Never, ever buy another record."
>
> The direct link between the commercial rental of a phonorecord and the making of a copy of a record without the permission of or compensation to the copyright owners is the economic and policy concern behind this legislation. The Subcommittee has found that the nexus of commercial record rental and duplication may directly and adversely affect the ability of copyright holders to exercise their reproduction and distribution rights under the Copyright Act.

H.R.Rep. No. 987, 98th Cong., 2d Sess. 2 (1984).

Computer Programs. In 1990 Congress amended section 109(b) to bar anyone who possesses a copy of a computer program from renting the copy for purposes of direct or indirect commercial advantage without the copyright owner's consent. The amendment parallels the phonorecord provisions in both method and purpose—to forestall the emergence of a rental marketplace that would encourage unauthorized home copying of computer programs.

Public Lending Right. Should authors have a right to remuneration when their works are borrowed from public libraries? These free uses will sometimes cut into revenue-producing markets, and the notion of compensating authors has won legislative support in a small number of countries, mostly in Europe, but not in the United States. The British public lending right, introduced in 1982, entitles qualifying authors to a payment of funds provided by the government and proportioned to the number of times their books are borrowed from public libraries. See generally Silke von Lewinski, Public Lending Right: A General and Comparative Survey of the Existing Systems in Law and Practice, 154 R.I.D.A. 3 (1992).

6. *Exemptions and Statutory Licenses.* Sections 108–122 of the 1976 Act carve out exemptions and compulsory or "statutory" licenses narrowly tailored to the economic and political exigencies of particular applications of copyright. The purpose of some of the exemptions is to enable uses of copyrighted works in situations where transaction costs characteristically exceed the value of the use and would consequently stand in the way of a negotiated license. Some examples are section 108's exemption for library photocopying, section 110(5)'s exemption for performances on homestyle equipment and section 117's exemption for copying of computer programs for specified exigent uses. Other exemptions, such as section 110(3)'s exemption of certain performances in the course of religious services and section 110(6)'s exemption of certain performances in the course of annual agricultural or horticultural fairs, more likely respond to political pressures from user organizations.

The Act's provisions for statutory licenses, which effectively substitute regulated prices for negotiated license fees, similarly seek to resolve problems of transaction costs and issues of distributional preference. Sections 111 and 119 respectively subject cable and satellite retransmissions of copyrighted programming to a statutory license in prescribed circumstances; section 118 does the same for certain uses by public broadcasters, and section 115, the so-called mechanical license, provides that once phonorecords of a nondramatic musical work have been distributed to the public with permission of the copyright owner, anyone may make and distribute his own recording of the work (commonly called a "cover") upon payment of a prescribed fee and compliance with specified conditions. Section 115(c)(3), added in 1995, extends the mechanical compulsory license to include "the right of the compulsory licensee to distribute or authorize the distribution of a phonorecord of a nondramatic musical work by means of a digital transmission which constitutes a digital phonorecord delivery."

The 1976 Copyright Act established a five-member Copyright Royalty Tribunal as an independent agency in the legislative branch to periodically adjust the statutorily prescribed royalty rates under the four compulsory licenses that the Act created for cable retransmissions, mechanical reproduction of musical compositions, jukebox performances and public broadcasting, and directed the Tribunal "to distribute royalty fees deposited with the Register of Copyrights under sections 111, 116, and 119(b), and to determine, in cases where controversy exists, the distribution of such fees." 1976 Copyright Act § 801(b)(3). Almost from the Copyright Royalty Tribunal's beginning, it was evident that Congress had created a full-time agency to perform a part-time job. The Copyright Royalty Tribunal Reform Act of 1993, 103 Pub.L. No. 103–198, 107 Stat. 2304 (1993), eliminated the Tribunal and replaced it with *ad hoc* copyright arbitration royalty panels to be appointed and convened by the Librarian of Congress on the recommendation of the Register of Copyrights. (Can you guess why Congress chose to call the new institution "Copyright Arbitration Royalty Panels" rather than the more accurately descriptive "Copyright Royalty Arbitration Panels"?)

b. Secondary Liability

Fonovisa, Inc. v. Cherry Auction, Inc.

United States Court of Appeals, Ninth Circuit, 1996.
76 F.3d 259, 37 U.S.P.Q.2d 1590.

SCHROEDER, Circuit Judge:

This is a copyright and trademark enforcement action against the operators of a swap meet, sometimes called a flea market, where third-party vendors routinely sell counterfeit recordings that infringe on the plaintiff's copyrights and trademarks. The district court dismissed on the pleadings, holding that the plaintiffs, as a matter of law, could not maintain any cause of action against the swap meet for sales by vendors who leased its premises. The district court's decision is published. *Fonovisa Inc. v. Cherry Auction, Inc.*, 847 F.Supp. 1492 (E.D.Cal.1994). We reverse.

Background

The plaintiff and appellant is Fonovisa, Inc., a California corporation that owns copyrights and trademarks to Latin/Hispanic music recordings. Fonovisa filed this action in district court against defendant-appellee, Cherry Auction, Inc., and its individual operators (collectively "Cherry Auction"). For purposes of this appeal, it is undisputed that Cherry Auction operates a swap meet in Fresno, California, similar to many other swap meets in this country where customers come to purchase various merchandise from individual vendors. The vendors pay a daily rental fee to the swap meet operators in exchange for booth space. Cherry Auction supplies parking, conducts advertising and retains the right to exclude any vendor for any reason, at any time, and thus can exclude vendors for patent [sic] and trademark infringement. In addition, Cherry Auction receives an entrance fee from each customer who attends the swap meet.

There is also no dispute for purposes of this appeal that Cherry Auction and its operators were aware that vendors in their swap meet were selling counterfeit recordings in violation of Fonovisa's trademarks and copyrights. Indeed, it is alleged that in 1991, the Fresno County Sheriff's Department raided the Cherry Auction swap meet and seized more than 38,000 counterfeit recordings. The following year, after finding that vendors at the Cherry Auction swap meet were still selling counterfeit recordings, the Sheriff sent a letter notifying Cherry Auction of the on-going sales of infringing materials, and reminding Cherry Auction that they had agreed to provide the Sheriff with identifying information from each vendor. In addition, in 1993, Fonovisa itself sent an investigator to the Cherry Auction site and observed sales of counterfeit recordings.

Fonovisa filed its original complaint in the district court on February 25, 1993, and on March 22, 1994, the district court granted defendants' motion to dismiss pursuant to Federal Rule of Civil Procedure 12(b)(6). In this appeal, Fonovisa does not challenge the district court's dismissal of its claim for direct copyright infringement, but does appeal the dismissal of its claims for contributory copyright infringement, vicarious copyright infringement and contributory trademark infringement.

The copyright claims are brought pursuant to 17 U.S.C. §§ 101 *et seq.* Although the Copyright Act does not expressly impose liability on anyone other than direct infringers, courts have long recognized that in certain circumstances, vicarious or contributory liability will be imposed.

Similar principles have also been applied in the trademark field. The Seventh Circuit, for example, has upheld the imposition of liability for contributory trademark infringement against the owners of a flea market similar to the swap meet operated by Cherry Auction. *Hard Rock Cafe Licensing Corp. v. Concession Services, Inc.*, 955 F.2d 1143 (7th Cir.1992). The district court in this case, however, expressly rejected the Seventh Circuit's reasoning on the contributory trademark infringement claim. Contributory and vicarious copyright infringement, however, were not addressed in *Hard Rock Cafe*, making this the first case to reach a federal appeals court raising issues of contributory and vicarious copyright infringement in the context of swap meet or flea market operations.

We analyze each of the plaintiff's claims in turn.

Vicarious Copyright Infringement

The concept of vicarious copyright liability was developed in the Second Circuit as an outgrowth of the agency principles of respondeat superior. The landmark case on vicarious liability for sales of counterfeit recordings is *Shapiro, Bernstein and Co. v. H.L. Green Co.*, 316 F.2d 304 (2d Cir.1963). In *Shapiro,* the court was faced with a copyright infringement suit against the owner of a chain of department stores where a concessionaire was selling counterfeit recordings. Noting that the normal agency rule of respondeat superior imposes liability on an employer for copyright infringements by an employee, the court endeavored to fashion a principle for enforcing copyrights against a defendant whose economic interests were intertwined with the direct infringer's, but who did not actually employ the direct infringer.

The *Shapiro* court looked at the two lines of cases it perceived as most clearly relevant. In one line of cases, the landlord-tenant cases, the courts had held that a landlord who lacked knowledge of the infringing acts of its tenant and who exercised no control over the leased premises was not liable for infringing sales by its tenant. In the other line of cases, the so-called "dance hall cases," the operator of an entertainment venue was held liable for infringing performances when the operator (1) could control the premises and (2) obtained a direct financial benefit from the audience, who paid to enjoy the infringing performance.

From those two lines of cases, the *Shapiro* court determined that the relationship between the store owner and the concessionaire in the case before it was closer to the dance-hall model than to the landlord-tenant model. It imposed liability even though the defendant was unaware of the infringement. *Shapiro* deemed the imposition of vicarious liability neither unduly harsh nor unfair because the store proprietor had the power to cease the conduct of the concessionaire, and because the proprietor derived an obvious and direct financial benefit from the infringement. The test was more clearly articulated in a later Second Circuit case as follows: "even in the absence of an employer-employee relationship one may be vicariously liable if he has the right and ability to supervise the infringing activity and also has a direct financial interest in such activities." *Gershwin Publishing*

Corp. v. Columbia Artists Management, Inc., 443 F.2d 1159, 1162 (2d Cir.1971). The most recent and comprehensive discussion of the evolution of the doctrine of vicarious liability for copyright infringement is contained in Judge Keeton's opinion in *Polygram Intern. Pub., Inc. v. Nevada/TIG, Inc.*, 855 F.Supp. 1314 (D.Mass.1994).

The district court in this case agreed with defendant Cherry Auction that Fonovisa did not, as a matter of law, meet either the control or the financial benefit prong of the vicarious copyright infringement test articulated in *Gershwin, supra*. Rather, the district court concluded that based on the pleadings, "Cherry Auction neither supervised nor profited from the vendors' sales." 847 F.Supp. at 1496. In the district court's view, with respect to both control and financial benefit, Cherry Auction was in the same position as an absentee landlord who has surrendered its exclusive right of occupancy in its leased property to its tenants.

This analogy to absentee landlord is not in accord with the facts as alleged in the district court and which we, for purposes of appeal, must accept. The allegations below were that vendors occupied small booths within premises that Cherry Auction controlled and patrolled. According to the complaint, Cherry Auction had the right to terminate vendors for any reason whatsoever and through that right had the ability to control the activities of vendors on the premises. In addition, Cherry Auction promoted the swap meet and controlled the access of customers to the swap meet area. In terms of control, the allegations before us are strikingly similar to those in *Shapiro* and *Gershwin*.

In *Shapiro*, for example, the court focused on the formal licensing agreement between defendant department store and the direct infringer-concessionaire. There, the concessionaire selling the bootleg recordings had a licensing agreement with the department store (H.L. Green Company) that required the concessionaire and its employees to "abide by, observe and obey all regulations promulgated from time to time by the H.L. Green Company," and H.L. Green Company had the "unreviewable discretion" to discharge the concessionaires' employees. In practice, H.L. Green Company was not actively involved in the sale of records and the concessionaire controlled and supervised the individual employees. Nevertheless, H.L. Green's ability to police its concessionaire—which parallels Cherry Auction's ability to police its vendors under Cherry Auction's similarly broad contract with its vendors—was sufficient to satisfy the control requirement.

In *Gershwin*, the defendant lacked the formal, contractual ability to control the direct infringer. Nevertheless, because of defendant's "pervasive participation in the formation and direction" of the direct infringers, including promoting them (i.e. creating an audience for them), the court found that defendants were in a position to police the direct infringers and held that the control element was satisfied. As the promoter and organizer of the swap meet, Cherry Auction wields the same level of control over the direct infringers as did the *Gershwin* defendant.

The district court's dismissal of the vicarious liability claim in this case was therefore not justified on the ground that the complaint failed to allege sufficient control.

We next consider the issue of financial benefit. The plaintiff's allegations encompass many substantive benefits to Cherry Auction from the infringing sales. These include the payment of a daily rental fee by each of the infringing vendors; a direct payment to Cherry Auction by each customer in the form of an admission fee, and incidental payments for parking, food and other services by customers seeking to purchase infringing recordings.

Cherry Auction nevertheless contends that these benefits cannot satisfy the financial benefit prong of vicarious liability because a commission, directly tied to the sale of particular infringing items, is required. They ask that we restrict the financial benefit prong to the precise facts presented in *Shapiro*, where defendant H.L. Green Company received a 10 or 12 per cent commission from the direct infringers' gross receipts. Cherry Auction points to the low daily rental fee paid by each vendor, discounting all other financial benefits flowing to the swap meet, and asks that we hold that the swap meet is materially similar to a mere landlord. The facts alleged by Fonovisa, however, reflect that the defendants reap substantial financial benefits from admission fees, concession stand sales and parking fees, all of which flow directly from customers who want to buy the counterfeit recordings at bargain basement prices. The plaintiff has sufficiently alleged direct financial benefit.

Our conclusion is fortified by the continuing line of cases, starting with the dance hall cases, imposing vicarious liability on the operator of a business where infringing performances enhance the attractiveness of the venue to potential customers. In *Polygram*, for example, direct infringers were participants in a trade show who used infringing music to communicate with attendees and to cultivate interest in their wares. 855 F.Supp. at 1332. The court held that the trade show participants "derived a significant financial benefit from the attention" that attendees paid to the infringing music. *Id.*; *See also Famous Music Corp. v. Bay State Harness Horse Racing and Breeding Ass'n*, 554 F.2d 1213, 1214 (1st Cir.1977) (race track owner vicariously liable for band that entertained patrons who were not "absorbed in watching the races"); *Shapiro*, 316 F.2d at 307 (dance hall cases hold proprietor liable where infringing "activities provide the proprietor with a source of customers and enhanced income"). In this case, the sale of pirated recordings at the Cherry Auction swap meet is a "draw" for customers, as was the performance of pirated music in the dance hall cases and their progeny.

Plaintiffs have stated a claim for vicarious copyright infringement.

Contributory Copyright Infringement

Contributory infringement originates in tort law and stems from the notion that one who directly contributes to another's infringement should be held accountable. Contributory infringement has been described as an outgrowth of enterprise liability, and imposes liability where one person knowingly contributes to the infringing conduct of another. The classic statement of the doctrine is in *Gershwin*, 443 F.2d 1159, 1162: "[O]ne who, with knowledge of the infringing activity, induces, causes or materially contributes to the infringing conduct of another, may be held liable as a 'contributory' infringer."

There is no question that plaintiff adequately alleged the element of knowledge in this case. The disputed issue is whether plaintiff adequately alleged that Cherry Auction materially contributed to the infringing activity. We have little difficulty in holding that the allegations in this case are sufficient to show material contribution to the infringing activity. Indeed, it would be difficult for the infringing activity to take place in the massive quantities alleged without the support services provided by the swap meet. These services include, *inter alia*, the provision of space, utilities, parking, advertising, plumbing, and customers.

Here again Cherry Auction asks us to ignore all aspects of the enterprise described by the plaintiffs, to concentrate solely on the rental of space, and to hold that the swap meet provides nothing more. Yet Cherry Auction actively strives to provide the environment and the market for counterfeit recording sales to thrive. Its participation in the sales cannot be termed "passive," as Cherry Auction would prefer.

The district court apparently took the view that contribution to infringement should be limited to circumstances in which the defendant "expressly promoted or encouraged the sale of counterfeit products, or in some manner protected the identity of the infringers." 847 F.Supp. 1492, 1496. Given the allegations that the local sheriff lawfully requested that Cherry Auction gather and share basic, identifying information about its vendors, and that Cherry Auction failed to comply, the defendant appears to qualify within the last portion of the district court's own standard that posits liability for protecting infringers' identities. Moreover, we agree with the Third Circuit's analysis in *Columbia Pictures Industries, Inc. v. Aveco, Inc.*, 800 F.2d 59 (3d Cir.1986) that providing the site and facilities for known infringing activity is sufficient to establish contributory liability.

Contributory Trademark Infringement

Just as liability for copyright infringement can extend beyond those who actually manufacture or sell infringing materials, our law recognizes liability for conduct that assists others in direct trademark infringement. In *Inwood Laboratories*, 456 U.S. 844, 102 S.Ct. 2182, the Court said that contributory trademark liability is applicable if defendant (1) intentionally induces another to infringe on a trademark or (2) continues to supply a product knowing that the recipient is using the product to engage in trademark infringement. *Inwood* at 854–55, 102 S.Ct. at 2188–89. As Cherry Auction points out, the *Inwood* case involved a manufacturer-distributor, and the *Inwood* standard has generally been applied in such cases. The Court in *Inwood*, however, laid down no limiting principle that would require defendant to be a manufacturer or distributor.

The defendant in *Inwood* distributed drugs to a pharmacist, knowing that the pharmacist was mislabeling the drugs with a protected trademark rather than a generic label. In this case, plaintiffs correctly point out that while Cherry Auction is not alleged to be supplying the recordings themselves, it is supplying the necessary marketplace for their sale in substantial quantities.

In *Hard Rock Cafe*, 955 F.2d 1143, the Seventh Circuit applied the *Inwood* test for contributory trademark liability to the operator of a flea market. In that case, there was no proof that the flea market had actual knowledge of the sale by vendors of counterfeit Hard Rock Cafe trademark merchandise, but the court held that contributory liability could be imposed if the swap meet was "willfully blind" to the ongoing violations. *Hard Rock Cafe*, 955 F.2d at 1149. It observed that while trademark infringement liability is more narrowly circumscribed than copyright infringement, the courts nevertheless recognize that a company "is responsible for the torts of those it permits on its premises 'knowing or having reason to know that the other is acting or will act tortiously. . . .' " *Id. quoting* Restatement (Second) of Torts § 877(c) & cmt. d (1979).

Hard Rock Cafe's application of the *Inwood* test is sound; a swap meet can not disregard its vendors' blatant trademark infringements with impunity. Thus, Fonovisa has also stated a claim for contributory trademark infringement.

The judgment of the district court is REVERSED and the case is REMANDED FOR FURTHER PROCEEDINGS.

QUESTIONS

As new technologies emerge for disseminating copyrighted works, the occasions for direct infringement increase. The usual pattern of new information and communications technologies is to divert accountability from centralized institutions such as publishers and television networks to widely dispersed users. In a world in which everyone with access to a home videotape or DVD player is his own movie exhibitor and everyone with access to a computer is her own record distributor, copyright owners are concerned that substantial portions of copyright value will migrate away from centralized, easily policed uses.

Are doctrines of contributory infringement and vicarious liability effective in enabling copyright owners to capture the value of dispersed uses without incurring the enforcement costs of pursuing dispersed users? In allocating secondary liability fairly and efficiently? Would the "landlord-tenant" line of cases alluded to in *Fonovisa* exempt a shopping center landlord whose lease with a copyright-infringing tenant called for a percentage rental and subjected the tenant to negative covenants controlling its use of the premises? Would the "dance hall" line of cases impose liability on an arena operator who received only a flat fee from a musical group and who exerted no control over the group's play list? Should responsibility for controlling infringing conduct—which contracting parties are free to allocate as between themselves—ever be allowed to determine secondary liability?

Sony Corp. of America v. Universal City Studios, Inc., the U.S. Supreme Court's seminal decision on secondary liability in the context of emerging copyright technologies, appears at page 717, below.

c. *Fair Use*

Harper & Row Publishers, Inc. v. Nation Enterprises

Supreme Court of the United States, 1985.
471 U.S. 539, 105 S.Ct. 2218, 85 L.Ed.2d 588.

Justice O'CONNOR delivered the opinion of the Court.

This case requires us to consider to what extent the "fair use" provision of the Copyright Revision Act of 1976, 17 U.S.C. § 107 (hereinafter the Copyright Act), sanctions the unauthorized use of quotations from a public figure's unpublished manuscript. In March 1979, an undisclosed source provided The Nation magazine with the unpublished manuscript of "A Time to Heal: The Autobiography of Gerald R. Ford." Working directly from the purloined manuscript, an editor of The Nation produced a short piece entitled "The Ford Memoirs—Behind the Nixon Pardon." The piece was timed to "scoop" an article scheduled shortly to appear in Time magazine. Time had agreed to purchase the exclusive right to print prepublication excerpts from the copyright holders, Harper & Row Publishers, Inc. (hereinafter Harper & Row) and Reader's Digest Association, Inc. (hereinafter Reader's Digest). As a result of The Nation article, Time canceled its agreement. Petitioners brought a successful copyright action against The Nation. On appeal, the Second Circuit reversed the lower court's finding of infringement, holding that The Nation's act was sanctioned as a "fair use" of the copyrighted material. We granted certiorari and we now reverse.

I.

In February 1977, shortly after leaving the White House, former President Gerald R. Ford contracted with petitioners Harper & Row and The Reader's Digest, to publish his as yet unwritten memoirs. The memoirs were to contain "significant hitherto unpublished material" concerning the Watergate crisis, Mr. Ford's pardon of former President Nixon and "Mr. Ford's reflections on this period of history, and the morality and personalities involved." In addition to the right to publish the Ford memoirs in book form, the agreement gave petitioners the exclusive right to license prepublication excerpts, known in the trade as "first serial rights." Two years later, as the memoirs were nearing completion, petitioners negotiated a prepublication licensing agreement with Time, a weekly news magazine. Time agreed to pay $25,000, $12,500 in advance and an additional $12,500 at publication, in exchange for the right to excerpt 7,500 words from Mr. Ford's account of the Nixon pardon. The issue featuring the excerpts was timed to appear approximately one week before shipment of the full length book version to bookstores. Exclusivity was an important consideration; Harper & Row instituted procedures designed to maintain the confidentiality of the manuscript, and Time retained the right to renegotiate the second payment should the material appear in print prior to its release of the excerpts.

Two to three weeks before the Time article's scheduled release, an unidentified person secretly brought a copy of the Ford manuscript to Victor Navasky, editor of The Nation, a political commentary magazine. Mr. Navasky knew that his possession of the manuscript was not authorized and that the manuscript must be returned quickly to his "source" to avoid discovery. He hastily put together what he believed was "a real hot news story" composed of quotes, paraphrases and facts drawn exclusively from the manuscript. Mr. Navasky attempted no independent commentary, research or criticism, in part because of the need for speed if he was to "make news" by "publish[ing] in advance of publication of the Ford book." The 2,250 word article, reprinted in the Appendix to this opinion, appeared on April 3, 1979. As a result of The Nation's article, Time canceled its piece and refused to pay the remaining $12,500.

Petitioners brought suit in the District Court for the Southern District of New York, alleging conversion, tortious interference with contract and violations of the Copyright Act. After a 6–day bench trial, the District Judge found that "A Time to Heal" was protected by copyright at the time of The Nation publication and that respondents' use of the copyrighted material constituted an infringement under the Copyright Act, § 106(1), (2), and (3), protecting respectively the right to reproduce the work, the right to license preparation of derivative works, and the right of first distribution of the copyrighted work to the public. The District Court rejected respondents' argument that The Nation's piece was a "fair use" sanctioned by § 107 of the Act. Though billed as "hot news," the article contained no new facts. The magazine had "published its article for profit," taking "the heart" of "a soon-to-be-published" work. This unauthorized use "caused the *Time* agreement to be aborted and thus diminished the value of the copyright." 557 F.Supp., at 1072. Although certain elements of the Ford memoir, such as historical facts and memoranda, were not *per se* copyrightable the District Court held that it was "the totality of these facts and memoranda collected together with Ford's reflections that made them of value to The Nation, [and] this ... totality ... is protected by the copyright laws." Id., at 1072–1073. The court awarded actual damages of $12,500.

A divided panel of the Court of Appeals for the Second Circuit reversed. The majority recognized that Mr. Ford's verbatim "reflections" were original "expression" protected by copyright. But it held that the District Court had erred in assuming the "coupling [of these reflections] with uncopyrightable fact transformed that information into a copyrighted 'totality.' " 723 F.2d 195, 205 (2d Cir.1983). The majority noted that copyright attaches to expression, not facts or ideas. It concluded that, to avoid granting a copyright monopoly over the facts underlying history and news, " 'expression' [in such works must be confined] to its barest elements—the ordering and choice of the words themselves." Id., at 204. Thus similarities between the original and the challenged work traceable to the copying or paraphrasing of uncopyrightable material, such as historical facts, memoranda and other public documents, and quoted remarks of third parties, must be disregarded in evaluating whether the second author's use was fair or infringing.

> When the uncopyrighted material is stripped away, the article in *The Nation* contains, at most, approximately 300 words that are copyrighted. These remaining paragraphs and scattered phrases are all verbatim quotations from the memoirs which had not appeared previously in other publications. They include a short segment of Ford's conversations with Henry Kissinger and several other individuals. Ford's impressionistic depictions of Nixon, ill with phlebitis after the resignation and pardon, and of Nixon's character, constitute the major portion of this material. It is these parts of the magazine piece on which [the court] must focus in [its] examination of the question whether there was a "fair use" of copyrighted matter. Id., at 206.

Examining the four factors enumerated in § 107, the majority found the purpose of the article was "news reporting," the original work was essentially factual in nature, the 300 words appropriated were insubstantial in relation to the 2,250 word piece, and the impact on the market for the original was minimal as "the evidence [did] not support a finding that it was the very limited use of expression *per se* which led to Time's decision not to print the excerpt." The Nation's borrowing of verbatim quotations merely "len[t] authenticity to this politically significant material ... complementing the reporting of the facts." 723 F.2d, at 208. The Court of Appeals was especially influenced by the "politically significant" nature of the subject matter and its conviction that it is not "the purpose of the Copyright Act to impede that harvest of knowledge so necessary to a democratic state" or "chill the activities of the press by forbidding a circumscribed use of copyrighted words." Id., at 197, 209.

II.

We agree with the Court of Appeals that copyright is intended to increase and not to impede the harvest of knowledge. But we believe the Second Circuit gave insufficient deference to the scheme established by the Copyright Act for fostering the original works that provide the seed and substance of this harvest. The rights conferred by copyright are designed to assure contributors to the store of knowledge a fair return for their labors.

Article I, § 8, of the Constitution provides that:

> The Congress shall have Power ... to Promote the Progress of Science and useful Arts, by securing for limited Times to Authors and Inventors the exclusive Right to their respective Writings and Discoveries.

As we noted last Term, "[this] limited grant is a means by which an important public purpose may be achieved. It is intended to motivate the creative activity of authors and inventors by the provision of a special reward, and to allow the public access to the products of their genius after the limited period of exclusive control has expired." Sony Corp. v. Universal City Studios, Inc., 464 U.S. 417, 429 (1984). "The monopoly created by copyright thus rewards the individual author in order to benefit the public." Id., at 477 (dissenting opinion). This principle applies equally to works of fiction and nonfiction. The book at issue here, for example, was two years in the making, and began with a contract giving the author's copyright to the publishers in exchange for their services in producing and marketing the work. In preparing the book, Mr. Ford drafted essays and word portraits of public figures and participated in hundreds of taped interviews that were later distilled to chronicle his personal viewpoint. It is evident that the monopoly granted by copyright actively served its intended purpose of inducing the creation of new material of potential historical value.

Section 106 of the Copyright Act confers a bundle of exclusive rights to the owner of the copyright. Under the Copyright Act, these rights—to publish, copy, and distribute the author's work—vest in the author of an original work from the time of its creation. In practice, the author commonly sells his rights to publishers who offer royalties in exchange for their services in producing and marketing the author's work. The copyright owner's rights, however, are subject to certain statutory exceptions. Among these is § 107 which codifies the traditional privilege of other authors to make "fair use" of an earlier writer's work. In addition, no author may copyright facts or ideas. The copyright is limited to those aspects of the work—termed "expression"—that display the stamp of the author's originality.

Creation of a nonfiction work, even a compilation of pure fact, entails originality.... The copyright holders of "A Time to Heal" complied with the relevant statutory notice and registration procedures. Thus there is no dispute that the unpublished manuscript of "A Time to Heal," as a whole, was protected by § 106 from unauthorized reproduction. Nor do respondents dispute that verbatim copying of excerpts of the manuscript's original form of expression would constitute infringement unless excused as fair use. Yet copyright does not prevent subsequent users from copying from a prior author's work those constituent elements that are not original—for example, quotations borrowed under the rubric of fair use from other copyrighted works, facts, or materials in the public domain—as long as such use does not unfairly appropriate the author's original contributions. Perhaps the controversy between the lower courts in this case over copyrightability is more aptly styled a dispute over whether The Nation's appropriation of unoriginal and uncopyrightable elements encroached on the originality embodied in the work as a whole. Especially in the realm of factual narrative, the law is currently unsettled regarding the ways in which uncopyrightable elements combine with the author's original contributions to form protected expression....

We need not reach these issues, however, as The Nation has admitted to lifting verbatim quotes of the author's original language totalling between 300 and 400 words and constituting some 13% of The Nation article. In using generous verbatim excerpts of Mr. Ford's unpublished manuscript to lend authenticity to its account of the forthcoming memoirs, The Nation effectively arrogated to itself the right of first publication, an important marketable subsidiary right. For the reasons set forth below, we find that this use of the copyrighted manuscript, even stripped to the verbatim quotes conceded by the Nation to be copyrightable expression, was not a fair use within the meaning of the Copyright Act.

III.

A

Fair use was traditionally defined as "a privilege in others than the owner of the copyright to use the copyrighted material in a reasonable manner without his consent." H. Ball, Law of Copyright and Literary Property 260 (1944) (hereinafter Ball). The statutory formulation of the defense of fair use in the Copyright Act of 1976 reflects the intent of Congress to codify the common-law doctrine. Section 107 requires a case-by-case determination whether a particular use is fair, and the statute notes four nonexclusive factors to be considered. This approach was "intended to restate the [pre-existing] judicial doctrine of fair use, not to change, narrow, or enlarge it in any way." H.R.Rep. No. 94–1476, p. 66 (1976) (hereinafter House Report).

"[T]he author's consent to a reasonable use of his copyrighted works ha[d] always been implied by the courts as a necessary incident of the constitutional policy of promoting the progress of science and the useful arts, since a prohibition of such use would inhibit subsequent writers from attempting to improve upon prior works and thus ... frustrate the very ends sought to be attained." Ball 260. Professor Latman, in a study of the doctrine of fair use commissioned by Congress for the revision effort, see Sony Corp. v. Universal City Studios, Inc., 464 U.S., at 462–463, n. 9 (dissenting opinion), summarized prior law as turning on the "importance of the material copied or performed from the point of view of the reasonable copyright owner. In other words, would the reasonable copyright owner have consented to the use?"

As early as 1841, Justice Story, gave judicial recognition to the doctrine in a case that concerned the letters of another former President, George Washington.

> [A] reviewer may fairly cite largely from the original work, if his design be really and truly to use the passages for the purposes of fair and reasonable criticism. On the other hand, it is as clear, that if he thus cites the most important parts of the work, with a view, not to criticize, but to supersede the use of the original work, and substitute the review for it, such a use will be deemed in law a piracy. Folsom v. Marsh, 9 F.Cas. 342, 344–345 (No. 4,901) (CC Mass.).

As Justice Story's hypothetical illustrates, the fair use doctrine has always precluded a use that "supersede[s] the use of the original." Ibid. Accord S.Rep. No. 94–473, p. 65 (1975) (hereinafter Senate Report).

Perhaps because the fair use doctrine was predicated on the author's implied consent to "reasonable and customary" use when he released his work for public consumption, fair use traditionally was not recognized as a defense to charges of copying from an author's as yet unpublished works. Under common-law copyright, "the property of the author ... in his intellectual creation [was] absolute until he voluntarily part[ed] with the same." American Tobacco Co. v. Werckmeister, 207 U.S. 284, 299 (1907). This absolute rule, however, was tempered in practice by the equitable nature of the fair use doctrine. In a given case, factors such as implied consent through *de facto* publication or performance or dissemination of a work may tip the balance of equities in favor of prepublication use. But it has never been seriously disputed that "the fact that the plaintiff's work is unpublished ... is a factor tending to negate the defense of fair use." Ibid. Publication of an author's expression before he has authorized its dissemination seriously infringes the author's right to decide when and whether it will be made public, a factor not present in fair use of published works. Respondents contend, however, that Congress, in including first publication among the rights enumerated in § 106, which are expressly subject to fair use under § 107, intended that fair use would apply *in pari materia* to published and unpublished works. The Copyright Revision Act does not support this proposition.

The Copyright Act represents the culmination of a major legislative reexamination of copyright doctrine. Among its other innovations, it eliminated publication "as a dividing line between common law and statutory protection," House Report, at 129, extending statutory protection to all works from the time of their creation. It also recognized for the first time a distinct statutory right of first publication, which had previously been an element of the common-law protections afforded unpublished works. The Report of the House Committee on the Judiciary confirms that "Clause (3) of section 106, establishes the exclusive right of publication.... Under this provision the copyright owner would have the right to control the first public distribution of an authorized copy ... of his work." Id., at 62.

Though the right of first publication, like the other rights enumerated in § 106, is expressly made subject to the fair use provision of § 107, fair use analysis must always be tailored to the individual case. The nature of the interest at stake is highly relevant to whether a given use is fair. From the beginning, those entrusted with the task of revision recognized the "overbalancing reasons to preserve the common law protection of undisseminated works until the author or his successor chooses to disclose them." Copyright Law Revision, Report of the Register of Copyrights on the General Revision of the U.S. Copyright Law, 87th Cong., 1st Sess., 41 (Comm. Print 1961). The right of first publication implicates a threshold decision by the author whether and in what form to release his work. First publication is inherently different from other § 106 rights in that only one person can be the first publisher; as the contract with Time illustrates, the commercial value of the right lies primarily in exclusivity. Because the potential damage to the author from judicially enforced "sharing" of the first publication right with unauthorized users of his manuscript is substantial, the balance of equities in evaluating such a claim of fair use inevitably shifts.

The Senate Report confirms that Congress intended the unpublished nature of the work to figure prominently in fair use analysis. In discussing fair use of photocopied materials in the classroom the Committee Report states:

> A key, though not necessarily determinative, factor in fair use is whether or not the work is available to the potential user. If the work is "out of print" and unavailable for purchase through normal channels, the user may have more justification for reproducing it.... The applicability of the fair use doctrine to unpublished works is narrowly limited since, although the work is unavailable, this is the result of a deliberate choice on the part of the copyright owner. Under ordinary circumstances, the copyright owner's "right of first publication" would outweigh any needs of reproduction for classroom purposes. Senate Report, at 64.

Although the Committee selected photocopying of classroom materials to illustrate fair use, it emphasized that "the same general standards of fair use are applicable to all kinds of uses of copyrighted material." Id., at 65. We find unconvincing respondent's contention that the absence of the quoted passage from the House Report indicates an intent to abandon the traditional distinction between fair use of published and unpublished works. It appears instead that the fair use discussion of photocopying of classroom materials was omitted from the final report because educators and publishers in the interim had negotiated a set of guidelines that rendered the discussion obsolete. House Report, at 67. The House Report nevertheless incorporates the discussion by reference, citing to the Senate Report and stating that "The Committee has reviewed this discussion, and considers it still has value as an analysis of various aspects of the [fair use] problem." Ibid.

Even if the legislative history were entirely silent, we would be bound to conclude from Congress' characterization of § 107 as a "restatement" that its effect was to preserve existing law concerning fair use of unpublished works as of other types of protected works and not to "change, narrow, or enlarge it." Id., at 66. We conclude that the unpublished nature of a work is "[a] key, though not necessarily determinative, factor" tending to negate a defense of fair use. Senate Report, at 64.

We also find unpersuasive respondents' argument that fair use may be made of a soon-to-be-published manuscript on the ground that the author has demonstrated he has no interest in nonpublication. This argument assumes that the unpublished nature of copyrighted material is only relevant to letters or other confidential writings not intended for dissemination. It is true that common-law copyright was often enlisted in the service of personal privacy. In its commercial guise, however, an author's right to choose when he will publish is no less deserving of protection. The period encompassing the work's initiation, its preparation, and its grooming for public dissemination is a crucial one for any literary endeavor. The Copyright Act, which accords the copyright owner the "right to control the first public distribution" of his work, House Report, at 62, echoes the common law's concern that the author or copyright owner retain control throughout this critical stage. The obvious benefit to author and public alike of assuring authors the leisure to develop their ideas free from fear of expropriation outweighs any short term "news value" to be gained from premature publication of the author's expression. The author's control of first public distribution implicates not only his personal interest in creative control but his property interest in exploitation of prepublication rights, which are valuable in themselves and serve as a valuable adjunct to publicity and marketing. Under ordinary circumstances, the author's right to control the first public appearance of his undisseminated expression will outweigh a claim of fair use....

IV.

Fair use is a mixed question of law and fact. Where the District Court has found facts sufficient to evaluate each of the statutory factors, an appellate court "need not remand for further factfinding ... [but] may conclude as a matter of law that [the challenged use] do[es] not qualify as a fair use of the copyrighted work." Id., at 1495. Thus whether The Nation article constitutes fair use under § 107 must be reviewed in light of the principles discussed above. The factors enumerated in the section are not meant to be exclusive: "[S]ince the doctrine is an equitable rule of reason, no generally applicable definition is possible, and each case raising the question must be decided on its own facts." House Report, at 65. The four factors identified by Congress as especially relevant in determining whether the use was fair are: (1) the purpose and character of the use; (2) the nature of the copyrighted work; (3) the substantiality of the portion used in relation to the copyrighted work as a whole; (4) the effect on the potential market for or value of the copyrighted work. We address each one separately.

Purpose of the Use. The Second Circuit correctly identified news reporting as the general purpose of The Nation's use. News reporting is one of the examples enumerated in § 107 to "give some idea of the sort of activities the courts might regard as fair use under the circumstances." Senate Report, at 61. This listing was not intended to be exhaustive, see id.; § 101 (definition of "including" and "such as"), or to single out any particular use as presumptively a "fair" use. The drafters resisted pressures from special interest groups to create presumptive categories of fair use, but structured the provision as an affirmative defense requiring a case by case analysis. "[W]hether a use referred to in the first sentence of section 107 is a fair use in a particular case will depend upon the application of the determinative factors, including those mentioned in the second sentence." Senate Report, at 62. The fact that an article arguably is "news" and therefore a productive use is simply one factor in a fair use analysis.

We agree with the Second Circuit that the trial court erred in fixing on whether the information contained in the memoir was actually new to the public. As Judge Meskill wisely noted, "[c]ourts should be chary of deciding what is and what is not news." 723 F.2d, at 215 (Meskill, J., dissenting). "The issue is not what constitutes 'news,' but whether a claim of newsreporting is a valid fair use defense to an infringement of *copyrightable expression*." Patry [The Fair Use Privilege in Copyright Law (1985)] 119. The Nation has every right to seek to be the first to publish information. But The Nation went beyond simply reporting uncopyrightable information and actively sought to exploit the headline value of its infringement, making a "news event" out of its unauthorized first publication of a noted figure's copyrighted expression.

The fact that a publication was commercial as opposed to non-profit is a separate factor that tends to weigh against a finding of fair use. "[E]very commercial use of copyrighted material is presumptively an unfair exploitation of the monopoly privilege that belongs to the owner of the copyright." Sony Corp. v. Universal City Studios, Inc., 464 U.S., at 451. In arguing that the purpose of news reporting is not purely commercial, The Nation misses the point entirely. The crux of the profit/nonprofit distinction is not whether the sole motive of the use is monetary gain but whether the user stands to profit from exploitation of the copyrighted material without paying the customary price.

In evaluating character and purpose we cannot ignore The Nation's stated purpose of scooping the forthcoming hardcover and Time abstracts. The Nation's use had not merely the incidental effect but the *intended purpose* of supplanting the copyright holder's commercially valuable right of first publication. Also relevant to the "character" of the use is "the propriety of the defendant's conduct." "Fair use presupposes 'good faith' and 'fair dealing.'" Time Inc. v. Bernard Geis Associates, 293 F.Supp. 130, 146 (S.D.N.Y.1968), quoting Schulman, Fair Use and the Revision of the Copyright Act, 53 Iowa L.Rev. 832 (1968). The trial court found that The Nation knowingly exploited a purloined manuscript. Unlike the typical claim of fair use, The Nation cannot offer up even the fiction of consent as justification. Like its competitor newsweekly, it was free to bid for the right of abstracting excerpts from "A Time to Heal." Fair use "distinguishes between 'a true scholar and a chiseler who infringes a work for personal profit.'" Wainwright Securities Inc. v. Wall Street Transcript Corp., 558 F.2d, at 94, quoting from Hearings on Bills for the General Revision of the Copyright Law before the House Committee on the Judiciary, 89th Cong., 1st Sess., ser. 8, pt. 3, p. 1706 (1966) (Statement of John Schulman).

Nature of the Copyrighted Work. Second, the Act directs attention to the nature of the copyrighted work. "A Time to Heal" may be characterized as an unpublished historical narrative or autobiography. The law generally recognizes a greater need to disseminate factual works than works of fiction or fantasy.

> [E]ven within the field of fact works, there are gradations as to the relative proportion of fact and fancy. One may move from sparsely embellished maps and directories to elegantly written biography. The extent to which one must permit expressive language to be copied, in order to assure dissemination of the underlying facts, will thus vary from case to case. Id., at 563.

Some of the briefer quotes from the memoir are arguably necessary adequately to convey the facts; for example, Mr. Ford's characterization of the White House tapes as the "smoking gun" is perhaps so integral to the idea expressed as to be inseparable from it. But The Nation did not stop at isolated phrases and instead excerpted subjective descriptions and portraits of public figures whose power lies in the author's individualized expression. Such use, focusing on the most expressive elements of the work, exceeds that necessary to disseminate the facts.

The fact that a work is unpublished is a critical element of its "nature." Our prior discussion establishes that the scope of fair use is narrower with respect to unpublished works. While even substantial quotations might qualify as fair use in a review of a published work or a news account of a speech that had been delivered to the public or disseminated to the press, the author's right to control the first public appearance of his expression weighs against such use of the work before its release. The right of first publication encompasses not only the choice whether to publish at all, but also the choices when, where and in what form first to publish a work.

In the case of Mr. Ford's manuscript, the copyright holder's interest in confidentiality is irrefutable; the copyrightholders had entered into a contractual undertaking to "keep the manuscript confidential" and required that all those to whom the manuscript was shown also "sign an agreement to keep the manuscript confidential." While the copyrightholders' contract with Time required Time to submit its proposed article seven days before publication, The Nation's clandestine publication afforded no such opportunity for creative or quality control. It was hastily patched together and contained "a number of inaccuracies." A use that so clearly infringes the copyright holder's interests in confidentiality and creative control is difficult to characterize as "fair."

Amount and Substantiality of the Portion Used. Next, the Act directs us to examine the amount and substantiality of the portion used in relation to the copyrighted work as a whole. In absolute terms, the words actually quoted were an insubstantial portion of "A Time to Heal." The district court, however, found that "[T]he Nation took what was essentially the heart of the book." 557 F.Supp., at 1072. We believe the Court of Appeals erred in overruling the district judge's evaluation of the qualitative nature of the taking. A Time editor described the chapters on the pardon as "the most interesting and moving parts of the entire manuscript." The portions actually quoted were selected by Mr. Navasky as among the most powerful passages in those chapters. He testified that he used verbatim excerpts because simply reciting the information could not adequately convey the "absolute certainty with which [Ford] expressed himself," or show that "this comes from President Ford," or carry the "definitive quality" of the original. In short, he quoted these passages precisely because they qualitatively embodied Ford's distinctive expression.

As the statutory language indicates, a taking may not be excused merely because it is insubstantial with respect to the *infringing* work. As Judge Learned Hand cogently remarked, "[N]o plagiarist can excuse the wrong by showing how much of his work he did not pirate." Sheldon v. Metro–Goldwyn Pictures Corp., 81 F.2d 49, 56 (CA2), cert. denied, 298 U.S. 669 (1936). Conversely, the fact that a substantial portion of the infringing work was copied verbatim is evidence of the qualitative value of the copied material, both to the originator and to the plagiarist who seeks to profit from marketing someone else's copyrighted expression.

Stripped to the verbatim quotes,[8] the direct takings from the unpublished manuscript constitute at least 13% of the infringing article. The Nation article is structured around the quoted excerpts which serve as its dramatic focal points. In view of the expressive value of the excerpts and their key role in the infringing work, we cannot agree with the Second Circuit that the "magazine took a meager, indeed an infinitesimal amount of Ford's original language." 723 F.2d, at 209.

Effect on the Market. Finally, the Act focuses on "the effect of the use upon the potential market for or value of the copyrighted work." This last factor is undoubtedly the single most important element of fair use. "Fair use, when properly applied, is limited to copying by others which does not materially impair the marketability of the work which is copied." 1 Nimmer § 1.10[D], at 1–87. The trial court found not merely a potential but an actual effect on the market. Time's cancellation of its projected serialization and its refusal to pay the $12,500 were the direct effect of the infringement. The Court of Appeals rejected this fact finding as clearly erroneous, noting that the record did not establish a causal relation between Time's nonperformance and respondents' unauthorized publication of Mr. Ford's *expression* as opposed to the facts taken from the memoirs. We disagree. Rarely will a case of copyright infringement present such clear cut evidence of actual damage. Petitioners assured Time that there would be no other authorized publication of *any* portion of the unpublished manuscript prior to April 23, 1979. *Any* publication of material from chapters 1 and 3 would permit Time to renegotiate its final payment. Time cited The Nation's article, which contained verbatim quotes from the

---

8. The Court of Appeals found that only "approximately 300 words" were copyrightable but did not specify which words. The court's discussion, however, indicates it excluded from consideration those portions of The Nation's piece that, although copied verbatim from Ford's manuscript, were quotes attributed by Ford to third persons and quotations from government documents. At oral argument, counsel for The Nation did not dispute that verbatim quotes and very close paraphrase could constitute infringement. Thus the Appendix identifies as potentially infringing only verbatim quotes or very close paraphrase and excludes from consideration government documents and words attributed to third persons. The Appendix is not intended to endorse any particular rule of copyrightability but is intended merely as an aid to facilitate our discussion.

unpublished manuscript, as a reason for its nonperformance. With respect to apportionment of profits flowing from a copyright infringement, this Court has held that an infringer who commingles infringing and noninfringing elements "must abide the consequences, unless he can make a separation of the profits so as to assure to the injured party all that justly belongs to him." Sheldon v. Metro–Goldwyn Pictures Corp., 309 U.S. 390, 406 (1940). Cf. 17 U.S.C. § 504(b) (the infringer is required to prove elements of profits attributable to other than the infringed work). Similarly, once a copyright holder establishes with reasonable probability the existence of a causal connection between the infringement and a loss of revenue, the burden properly shifts to the infringer to show that this damage would have occurred had there been no taking of copyrighted expression. Petitioners established a prima facie case of actual damage that respondent failed to rebut. The trial court properly awarded actual damages and accounting of profits.

More important, to negate fair use one need only show that if the challenged use "should become widespread, it would adversely affect the *potential* market for the copyrighted work." Sony Corp. v. Universal City Studios, Inc., 464 U.S., at 451 (emphasis added); id., at 484, and n. 36 (collecting cases) (dissenting opinion). This inquiry must take account not only of harm to the original but also of harm to the market for derivative works. "If the defendant's work adversely affects the value of any of the rights in the copyrighted work (in this case the adaptation [and serialization] right) the use is not fair." 3 Nimmer § 13.05[B], at 13–77—13–78 (footnote omitted).

It is undisputed that the factual material in the balance of The Nation's article, besides the verbatim quotes at issue here, was drawn exclusively from the chapters on the pardon. The excerpts were employed as featured episodes in a story about the Nixon pardon—precisely the use petitioners had licensed to Time. The borrowing of these verbatim quotes from the unpublished manuscript lent The Nation's piece a special air of authenticity—as Navasky expressed it, the reader would know it was Ford speaking and not The Nation. Thus it directly competed for a share of the market for prepublication excerpts. The Senate Report states:

> With certain special exceptions ... a use that supplants any part of the normal market for a copyrighted work would ordinarily be considered an infringement. Senate Report, at 65.

Placed in a broader perspective, a fair use doctrine that permits extensive prepublication quotations from an unreleased manuscript without the copyright owner's consent poses substantial potential for damage to the marketability of first serialization rights in general. "Isolated instances of minor infringements, when multiplied many times, become in the aggregate a major inroad on copyright that must be prevented." Ibid.

V.

The Court of Appeals erred in concluding that The Nation's use of the copyrighted material was excused by the public's interest in the subject matter. It erred, as well, in overlooking the unpublished nature of the work and the resulting impact on the potential market for first serial rights of permitting unauthorized prepublication excerpts under the rubric of fair use. Finally, in finding the taking "infinitesimal," the Court of Appeals accorded too little weight to the qualitative importance of the quoted passages of original expression. In sum, the traditional doctrine of fair use, as embodied in the Copyright Act, does not sanction the use made by The Nation of these copyrighted materials. Any copyright infringer may claim to benefit the public by increasing public access to the copyrighted work. But Congress has not designed, and we see no warrant for judicially imposing, a "compulsory license" permitting unfettered access to the unpublished copyrighted expression of public figures.

The Nation conceded that its verbatim copying of some 300 words of direct quotation from the Ford manuscript would constitute an infringement unless excused as a fair use. Because we find that The Nation's use of these verbatim excerpts from the unpublished manuscript was not a fair use, the judgment of the Court of Appeals is reversed and remanded for further proceedings consistent with this opinion.

It is so ordered.

[The Appendix and the opinion of Justice Brennan, with whom Justices White and Marshall joined, dissenting, are omitted.]

Campbell v. Acuff–Rose Music, Inc.

Supreme Court of the United States, 1994.
510 U.S. 569, 114 S.Ct. 1164, 127 L.Ed.2d 500, 29 U.S.P.Q.2d 1961.

Justice SOUTER delivered the opinion of the Court.

We are called upon to decide whether 2 Live Crew's commercial parody of Roy Orbison's song, "Oh, Pretty Woman," may be a fair use within the meaning of the Copyright Act of 1976, 17 U.S.C. § 107 (1988 ed. and Supp. IV). Although the District Court granted summary judgment for 2 Live Crew, the Court of Appeals reversed, holding the defense of fair use barred by the song's commercial character and excessive borrowing. Because we hold that a parody's commercial character is only one element to be weighed in a fair use enquiry, and that insufficient consideration was given to the nature of parody in weighing the degree of copying, we reverse and remand.

I

In 1964, Roy Orbison and William Dees wrote a rock ballad called "Oh, Pretty Woman" and assigned their rights in it to respondent Acuff–Rose Music, Inc. Acuff–Rose registered the song for copyright protection.

Petitioners Luther R. Campbell, Christopher Wongwon, Mark Ross, and David Hobbs, are collectively known as 2 Live Crew, a popular rap music group. In 1989, Campbell wrote a song entitled "Pretty Woman," which he later described in an affidavit as intended, "through comical lyrics, to satirize the original work...." On July 5, 1989, 2 Live Crew's manager informed Acuff–Rose that 2 Live Crew had written a parody of "Oh, Pretty Woman," that they would afford all credit for ownership and authorship of the original song to Acuff–Rose, Dees, and Orbison, and that they were willing to pay a fee for the use they wished to make of it. Enclosed with the letter were a copy of the lyrics and a recording of 2 Live Crew's song. Acuff–Rose's agent refused permission, stating that "I am aware of the success enjoyed by 'The 2 Live Crews', but I must inform you that we cannot permit the use of a parody of 'Oh, Pretty Woman.'" Nonetheless, in June or July 1989, 2 Live Crew released records, cassette tapes, and compact discs of "Pretty Woman" in a collection of songs entitled "As Clean As They Wanna Be." The albums and compact discs identify the authors of "Pretty Woman" as Orbison and Dees and its publisher as Acuff–Rose.

Almost a year later, after nearly a quarter of a million copies of the recording had been sold, Acuff–Rose sued 2 Live Crew and its record company, Luke Skyywalker Records, for copyright infringement. The District Court granted summary judgment for 2 Live Crew, reasoning that the commercial purpose of 2 Live Crew's song was no bar to fair use; that 2 Live Crew's version was a parody, which "quickly degenerates into a play on words, substituting predictable lyrics with shocking ones" to show "how bland and banal the Orbison song" is; that 2 Live Crew had taken no more than was necessary to "conjure up" the original in order to parody it; and that it was "extremely unlikely that 2 Live Crew's song could adversely affect the market for the original." 754 F.Supp. 1150, 1154–1155, 1157–1158 (M.D.Tenn.1991). The District Court weighed these factors and held that 2 Live Crew's song made fair use of Orbison's original.

The Court of Appeals for the Sixth Circuit reversed and remanded. Although it assumed for the purpose of its opinion that 2 Live Crew's song was a parody of the Orbison original, the Court of Appeals thought the District Court had put too little emphasis on the fact that "every commercial use ... is presumptively ... unfair," *Sony Corp. of America v. Universal City Studios, Inc.*, 464 U.S. 417, 451, 104 S.Ct. 774, 792, 78 L.Ed.2d 574 (1984), and it held that "the admittedly commercial nature" of the parody "requires the conclusion" that the first of four factors relevant under the statute weighs against a finding of fair use. 972 F.2d, at 1435, 1437. Next, the Court of Appeals determined that, by "taking the heart of the original and making it the heart of a new work," 2 Live Crew had, qualitatively, taken too much. Finally, after noting that the effect on the potential market for the original (and the market for derivative works) is "undoubtedly the single most important element of fair use," *Harper & Row, Publishers, Inc. v. Nation Enterprises*, 471 U.S. 539, 566, 105 S.Ct. 2218, 2233, 85 L.Ed.2d 588 (1985), the Court of Appeals faulted the District Court for "refus[ing] to indulge the presumption" that "harm for purposes of the fair use analysis has been established by the presumption attaching to commercial uses." 972 F.2d, at 1438–1439. In sum, the court concluded that its "blatantly commercial purpose ... prevents this parody from being a fair use." *Id.*, at 1439.

We granted certiorari to determine whether 2 Live Crew's commercial parody could be a fair use.

II

It is uncontested here that 2 Live Crew's song would be an infringement of Acuff–Rose's rights in "Oh, Pretty Woman," under the Copyright Act of 1976, 17 U.S.C. § 106 (1988 ed. and Supp. IV), but for a finding of fair use through parody. From the infancy of copyright protection, some opportunity for fair use of copyrighted materials has been thought necessary to fulfill copyright's very purpose, "[t]o promote the Progress of Science and useful Arts...." U.S. Const., Art. I, § 8, cl. 8. For as Justice Story explained, "[i]n truth, in literature, in science and in art, there are, and can be, few, if any, things, which in an abstract sense, are strictly new and original throughout. Every book in literature, science and art, borrows, and must necessarily borrow, and use much which was well known and used before." *Emerson v. Davies*, 8 F.Cas. 615, 619 (No. 4,436) (CCD Mass.1845). Similarly, Lord Ellenborough expressed the inherent tension in the need simultaneously to protect copyrighted material and to allow others to build upon it when he wrote, "while I shall think myself bound to secure every man in the enjoyment of his copy-right, one must not put manacles upon science." *Carey v. Kearsley*, 4 Esp. 168, 170, 170 Eng.Rep. 679, 681 (K.B.1803). In copyright cases brought under the Statute of Anne of 1710, English courts held that in some instances "fair abridgements" would not infringe an author's rights, and although the First Congress enacted our initial copyright statute, Act of May 31, 1790, 1 Stat. 124, without any explicit reference to "fair use," as it later came to be known, the doctrine was recognized by the American courts nonetheless.

In *Folsom v. Marsh*, Justice Story distilled the essence of law and methodology from the earlier cases: "look to the nature and objects of the selections made, the quantity and value of the materials used, and the degree in which the use may prejudice the sale, or diminish the profits, or supersede the objects, of the original work." 9 F.Cas. 342, 348 (No. 4,901) (CCD Mass.1841). Thus expressed, fair use remained exclusively judge-made doctrine until the passage of the 1976 Copyright Act, in which Story's summary is discernible:

"§ 107. Limitations on exclusive rights: Fair use

"Notwithstanding the provisions of sections 106 and 106A, the fair use of a copyrighted work, including such use by reproduction in copies or phonorecords or by any other means specified by that section, for purposes such as criticism, comment, news reporting, teaching (including multiple copies for classroom use), scholarship, or research, is not an infringement of copyright. In determining whether the use made of a work in any particular case is a fair use the factors to be considered shall include—

"(1) the purpose and character of the use, including whether such use is of a commercial nature or is for nonprofit educational purposes;

"(2) the nature of the copyrighted work;

"(3) the amount and substantiality of the portion used in relation to the copyrighted work as a whole; and

"(4) the effect of the use upon the potential market for or value of the copyrighted work.

"The fact that a work is unpublished shall not itself bar a finding of fair use if such finding is made upon consideration of all the above factors." 17 U.S.C. § 107 (1988 ed. and Supp. IV).

Congress meant § 107 "to restate the present judicial doctrine of fair use, not to change, narrow, or enlarge it in any way" and intended that courts continue the common law tradition of fair use adjudication. The fair use doctrine thus "permits [and requires] courts to avoid rigid application of the copyright statute when, on occasion, it would stifle the very creativity which that law is designed to foster." *Stewart v. Abend*, 495 U.S. 207, 236, 110 S.Ct. 1750, 1767, 109 L.Ed.2d 184 (1990)

The task is not to be simplified with bright-line rules, for the statute, like the doctrine it recognizes, calls for case-by-case analysis. The text employs the terms "including" and "such as" in the preamble paragraph to indicate the "illustrative and not limitative" function of the examples given, which thus provide only general guidance about the sorts of copying that courts and Congress most commonly had found to be fair uses. Nor may the four statutory factors be treated in isolation, one from another. All are to be explored, and the results weighed together, in light of the purposes of copyright.

A

The first factor in a fair use enquiry is "the purpose and character of the use, including whether such use is of a commercial nature or is for nonprofit educational purposes." § 107(1). This factor draws on Justice Story's formulation, "the nature and objects of the selections made." *Folsom v. Marsh*, 9 F.Cas., at 348. The enquiry here may be guided by the examples given in the preamble to § 107, looking to whether the use is for criticism, or comment, or news reporting, and the like, see § 107. The central purpose of this investigation is to see, in Justice Story's words, whether the new work merely "supersede[s] the objects" of the original creation, or instead adds something new, with a further purpose or different character, altering the first with new expression, meaning, or message; it asks, in other words, whether and to what extent the new work is "transformative." Although such transformative use is not absolutely necessary for a finding of fair use, the goal of copyright, to promote science and the arts, is generally furthered by the creation of transformative works. Such works thus lie at the heart of the fair use doctrine's guarantee of breathing space within the confines of copyright, and the more transformative the new work, the less will be the significance of other factors, like commercialism, that may weigh against a finding of fair use.

This Court has only once before even considered whether parody may be fair use, and that time issued no opinion because of the Court's equal division. *Benny v. Loew's Inc.*, 239 F.2d 532 (C.A.9 1956), aff'd sub nom. *Columbia Broadcasting System, Inc. v. Loew's Inc.*, 356 U.S. 43, 78 S.Ct. 667, 2 L.Ed.2d 583 (1958). Suffice it to say now that parody has an obvious claim to transformative value, as Acuff–Rose itself does not deny. Like less ostensibly humorous forms of criticism, it can provide social benefit, by shedding light on an earlier work, and, in the process, creating a new one. We thus line up with the courts that have held that parody, like other comment or criticism, may claim fair use under § 107.

The germ of parody lies in the definition of the Greek *parodeia*, quoted in Judge Nelson's Court of Appeals dissent, as "a song sung alongside another." 972 F.2d, at 1440, quoting 7 Encyclopedia Britannica 768 (15th ed. 1975). Modern dictionaries accordingly describe a parody as a "literary or artistic work that imitates the characteristic style of an author or a work for comic effect or ridicule," or as a "composition in prose or verse in which the characteristic turns of thought and phrase in an author or class of authors are imitated in such a way as to make them appear ridiculous." For the purposes of copyright law, the nub of the definitions, and the heart of any parodist's claim to quote from existing material, is the use of some elements of a prior author's composition to create a new one that, at least in part, comments on that author's works. If, on the contrary, the commentary has no critical bearing on the substance or style of the original composition, which the alleged infringer merely uses to get attention or to avoid the drudgery in working up something fresh, the claim to fairness in borrowing from another's work diminishes accordingly (if it does not vanish), and other factors, like the extent of its commerciality, loom larger. Parody needs to mimic an original to make its point, and so has some claim to use the creation of its victim's (or collective victims') imagination, whereas satire can stand on its own two feet and so requires justification for the very act of borrowing.

The fact that parody can claim legitimacy for some appropriation does not, of course, tell either parodist or judge much about where to draw the line. Like a book review quoting the copyrighted material criticized, parody may or may not be fair use, and petitioner's suggestion that any parodic use is presumptively fair has no more justification in law or fact than the equally hopeful claim that any use for news reporting should be presumed fair, see *Harper & Row*, 471 U.S., at 561, 105 S.Ct., at 2230. The Act has no hint of an evidentiary preference for parodists over their victims, and no workable presumption for parody could take account of the fact that parody often shades into satire when society is lampooned through its creative artifacts, or that a work may contain both parodic and non-parodic elements. Accordingly, parody, like any other use, has to work its way through the relevant factors, and be judged case by case, in light of the ends of the copyright law.

Here, the District Court held, and the Court of Appeals assumed, that 2 Live Crew's "Pretty Woman" contains parody, commenting on and criticizing the original work, whatever it may have to say about society at large. As the District Court remarked, the words of 2 Live Crew's song copy the original's first line, but then "quickly degenerat[e] into a play on words, substituting predictable lyrics with shocking ones ... [that] derisively demonstrat[e] how bland and banal the Orbison song seems to them." 754 F.Supp., at 1155. Judge Nelson, dissenting below, came to the same conclusion, that the 2 Live Crew song "was clearly intended to ridicule the white-bread original" and "reminds us that sexual congress with nameless streetwalkers is not necessarily the stuff of romance and is not necessarily without its consequences. The singers (there are several) have the same thing on their minds as did the lonely man with the nasal voice, but here there is no hint of wine and roses." 972 F.2d, at 1442. Although the majority below had difficulty discerning any criticism of the original in 2 Live Crew's song, it assumed for purposes of its opinion that there was some.

We have less difficulty in finding that critical element in 2 Live Crew's song than the Court of Appeals did, although having found it we will not take the further step of evaluating its quality. The threshold question when fair use is raised in defense of parody is whether a parodic character may reasonably be perceived. Whether, going beyond that, parody is in good taste or bad does not and should not matter to fair use. As Justice Holmes explained, "[i]t would be a dangerous undertaking for persons trained only to the law to constitute themselves final judges of the worth of [a work], outside of the narrowest and most obvious limits. At the one extreme some works of genius would be sure to miss appreciation. Their very novelty would make them repulsive until the public had learned the new language in which their author spoke." *Bleistein v. Donaldson Lithographing Co.,* 188 U.S. 239, 251, 23 S.Ct. 298, 300, 47 L.Ed. 460 (1903) (circus posters have copyright protection).

While we might not assign a high rank to the parodic element here, we think it fair to say that 2 Live Crew's song reasonably could be perceived as commenting on the original or criticizing it, to some degree. 2 Live Crew juxtaposes the romantic musings of a man whose fantasy comes true, with degrading taunts, a bawdy demand for sex, and a sigh of relief from paternal responsibility. The later words can be taken as a comment on the naivete of the original of an earlier day, as a rejection of its sentiment that ignores the ugliness of street life and the debasement that it signifies. It is this joinder of reference and ridicule that marks off the author's choice of parody from the other types of comment and criticism that traditionally have had a claim to fair use protection as transformative works.

The Court of Appeals, however, immediately cut short the enquiry into 2 Live Crew's fair use claim by confining its treatment of the first factor essentially to one relevant fact, the commercial nature of the use. The court then inflated the significance of this fact by applying a presumption ostensibly culled from Sony, that "every commercial use of copyrighted material is presumptively ... unfair...." *Sony,* 464 U.S., at 451, 104 S.Ct., at 792. In giving virtually dispositive weight to the commercial nature of the parody, the Court of Appeals erred.

The language of the statute makes clear that the commercial or nonprofit educational purpose of a work is only one element of the first factor enquiry into its purpose and character. Section 107(1) uses the term "including" to begin the dependent clause referring to commercial use, and the main clause speaks of a broader investigation into "purpose and character." As we explained in *Harper & Row*, Congress resisted attempts to narrow the ambit of this traditional enquiry by adopting categories of presumptively fair use, and it urged courts to preserve the breadth of their traditionally ample view of the universe of relevant evidence. 471 U.S., at 561, 105 S.Ct. at 2230. Accordingly, the mere fact that a use is educational and not for profit does not insulate it from a finding of infringement, any more than the commercial character of a use bars a finding of fairness. If, indeed, commerciality carried presumptive force against a finding of fairness, the presumption would swallow nearly all of the illustrative uses listed in the preamble paragraph of § 107, including news reporting, comment, criticism, teaching, scholarship, and research, since these activities "are generally conducted for profit in this country." *Harper & Row*, *supra*, at 592, 105 S.Ct., at 2246 (Brennan, J., dissenting). Congress could not have intended such a rule, which certainly is not inferable from the common-law cases, arising as they did from the world of letters in which Samuel Johnson could pronounce that "[n]o man but a blockhead ever wrote, except for money." 3 Boswell's Life of Johnson 19 (G. Hill ed. 1934).

Sony itself called for no hard evidentiary presumption. There, we emphasized the need for a "sensitive balancing of interests," 464 U.S., at 455, n. 40, 104 S.Ct., at 795, n. 40, noted that Congress had "eschewed a rigid, bright-line approach to fair use," *id.*, at 449, n. 31, 104 S.Ct., at 792, n. 31, and stated that the commercial or nonprofit educational character of a work is "not conclusive," id., at 448–449, 104 S.Ct., at 792, but rather a fact to be "weighed along with other[s] in fair use decisions." *Id.*, at 449, n. 32, 104 S.Ct. at 792, n. 32, (quoting House Report, p. 66) U.S.Code Cong. & Admin.News 1976, pp. 5659, 5679. The Court of Appeals's elevation of one sentence from *Sony* to a *per se* rule thus runs as much counter to Sony itself as to the long common-law tradition of fair use adjudication. Rather, as we explained in *Harper & Row*, *Sony* stands for the proposition that the "fact that a publication was commercial as opposed to nonprofit is a separate factor that tends to weigh against a finding of fair use." 471 U.S., at 562, 105 S.Ct., at 2231. But that is all, and the fact that even the force of that tendency will vary with the context is a further reason against elevating commerciality to hard presumptive significance. The use, for example, of a copyrighted work to advertise a product, even in a parody, will be entitled to less indulgence under the first factor of the fair use enquiry, than the sale of a parody for its own sake, let alone one performed a single time by students in school.

B

The second statutory factor, "the nature of the copyrighted work," § 107(2), draws on Justice Story's expression, the "value of the materials used." *Folsom v. Marsh*, 9 F.Cas., at 348. This factor calls for recognition that some works are closer to the core of intended copyright protection than others, with the consequence that fair use is more difficult to establish when the former works are copied. We agree with both the District Court and the Court of Appeals that the Orbison original's creative expression for public dissemination falls within the core of the copyright's protective purposes. This fact, however, is not much help in this case, or ever likely to help much in separating the fair use sheep from the infringing goats in a parody case, since parodies almost invariably copy publicly known, expressive works.

C

The third factor asks whether "the amount and substantiality of the portion used in relation to the copyrighted work as a whole," § 107(3) (or, in Justice Story's words, "the quantity and value of the materials used," *Folsom v. Marsh, supra*, at 348) are reasonable in relation to the purpose of the copying. Here, attention turns to the persuasiveness of a parodist's justification for the particular copying done, and the enquiry will harken back to the first of the statutory factors, for, as in prior cases, we recognize that the extent of permissible copying varies with the purpose and character of the use. The facts bearing on this factor will also tend to address the fourth, by revealing the degree to which the parody may serve as a market substitute for the original or potentially licensed derivatives.

The District Court considered the song's parodic purpose in finding that 2 Live Crew had not helped themselves overmuch. The Court of Appeals disagreed, stating that "[w]hile it may not be inappropriate to find that no more was taken than necessary, the copying was qualitatively substantial.... We conclude that taking the heart of the original and making it the heart of a new work was to purloin a substantial portion of the essence of the original." 972 F.2d, at 1438.

The Court of Appeals is of course correct that this factor calls for thought not only about the quantity of the materials used, but about their quality and importance, too. In *Harper & Row*, for example, the Nation had taken only some 300 words out of President Ford's memoirs, but we signalled the significance of the quotations in finding them to amount to "the heart of the book," the part most likely to be newsworthy and important in licensing serialization. We also agree with the Court of Appeals that whether "a substantial portion of the infringing work was copied verbatim" from the copyrighted work is a relevant question, for it may reveal a dearth of transformative character or purpose under the first factor, or a greater likelihood of market harm under the fourth; a work composed primarily of an original, particularly its heart, with little added or changed, is more likely to be a merely superseding use, fulfilling demand for the original.

Where we part company with the court below is in applying these guides to parody, and in particular to parody in the song before us. Parody presents a difficult case. Parody's humor, or in any event its comment, necessarily springs from recognizable allusion to its object through distorted imitation. Its art lies in the tension between a known original and its parodic twin. When parody takes aim at a particular original work, the parody must be able to "conjure up" at least enough of that original to make the object of its critical wit recognizable. What makes for this recognition is quotation of the original's most distinctive or memorable features, which the parodist can be sure the audience will know. Once enough has been taken to assure identification, how much more is reasonable will depend, say, on the extent to which the song's overriding purpose and character is to parody the original or, in contrast, the likelihood that the parody may serve as a market substitute for the original. But using some characteristic features cannot be avoided.

We think the Court of Appeals was insufficiently appreciative of parody's need for the recognizable sight or sound when it ruled 2 Live Crew's use unreasonable as a matter of law. It is true, of course, that 2 Live Crew copied the characteristic opening bass riff (or musical phrase) of the original, and true that the words of the first line copy the Orbison lyrics. But if quotation of the opening riff and the first line may be said to go to the "heart" of the original, the heart is also what most readily conjures up the song for parody, and it is the heart at which parody takes aim. Copying does not become excessive in relation to parodic purpose merely because the portion taken was the original's heart. If 2 Live Crew had copied a significantly less memorable part of the original, it is difficult to see how its parodic character would have come through.

This is not, of course, to say that anyone who calls himself a parodist can skim the cream and get away scot free. In parody, as in news reporting, see *Harper & Row*, *supra*, context is everything, and the question of fairness asks what else the parodist did besides go to the heart of the original. It is significant that 2 Live Crew not only copied the first line of the original, but thereafter departed markedly from the Orbison lyrics for its own ends. 2 Live Crew not only copied the bass riff and repeated it, but also produced otherwise distinctive sounds, interposing "scraper" noise, overlaying the music with solos in different keys, and altering the drum beat. This is not a case, then, where "a substantial portion" of the parody itself is composed of a "verbatim" copying of the original. It is not, that is, a case where the parody is so insubstantial, as compared to the copying, that the third factor must be resolved as a matter of law against the parodists.

Suffice it to say here that, as to the lyrics, we think the Court of Appeals correctly suggested that "no more was taken than necessary," 972 F.2d, at 1438, but just for that reason, we fail to see how the copying can be excessive in relation to its parodic purpose, even if the portion taken is the original's "heart." As to the music, we express no opinion whether repetition of the bass riff is excessive copying, and we remand to permit evaluation of the amount taken, in light of the song's parodic purpose and character, its transformative elements, and considerations of the potential for market substitution sketched more fully below.

D

The fourth fair use factor is "the effect of the use upon the potential market for or value of the copyrighted work." § 107(4). It requires courts to consider not only the extent of market harm caused by the particular actions of the alleged infringer, but also "whether unrestricted and widespread conduct of the sort engaged in by the defendant ... would result in a substantially adverse impact on the potential market" for the original. The enquiry "must take account not only of harm to the original but also of harm to the market for derivative works." *Harper & Row, supra,* 471 U.S. at 568, 105 S.Ct., at 2234.

Since fair use is an affirmative defense, its proponent would have difficulty carrying the burden of demonstrating fair use without favorable evidence about relevant markets. In moving for summary judgment, 2 Live Crew left themselves at just such a disadvantage when they failed to address the effect on the market for rap derivatives, and confined themselves to uncontroverted submissions that there was no likely effect on the market for the original. They did not, however, thereby subject themselves to the evidentiary presumption applied by the Court of Appeals. In assessing the likelihood of significant market harm, the Court of Appeals quoted from language in *Sony* that " '[i]f the intended use is for commercial gain, that likelihood may be presumed. But if it is for a noncommercial purpose, the likelihood must be demonstrated.' " 972 F.2d, at 1438, quoting Sony, 464 U.S., at 451, 104 S.Ct., at 104 S.Ct., at 793. The court reasoned that because "the use of the copyrighted work is wholly commercial, ... we presume a likelihood of future harm to Acuff–Rose exists." 972 F.2d, at 1438. In so doing, the court resolved the fourth factor against 2 Live Crew, just as it had the first, by applying a presumption about the effect of commercial use, a presumption which as applied here we hold to be error.

No "presumption" or inference of market harm that might find support in *Sony* is applicable to a case involving something beyond mere duplication for commercial purposes. *Sony's* discussion of a presumption contrasts a context of verbatim copying of the original in its entirety for commercial purposes, with the non-commercial context of *Sony* itself (home copying of television programming). In the former circumstances, what Sony said simply makes common sense: when a commercial use amounts to mere duplication of the entirety of an original, it clearly "supersede[s] the objects," *Folsom v. Marsh,* 9 F.Cas., at 348, of the original and serves as a market replacement for it, making it likely that cognizable market harm to the original will occur. But when, on the contrary, the second use is transformative, market substitution is at least less certain, and market harm may not be so readily inferred. Indeed, as to parody pure and simple, it is more likely that the new work will not affect the market for the original in a way cognizable under this factor, that is, by acting as a substitute for it ("supersed[ing] [its] objects"). This is so because the parody and the original usually serve different market functions.

We do not, of course, suggest that a parody may not harm the market at all, but when a lethal parody, like a scathing theater review, kills demand for the original, it does not produce a harm cognizable under the Copyright Act. Because "parody may quite legitimately aim at garroting the original, destroying it commercially as well as artistically," B. Kaplan, An Unhurried View of Copyright 69 (1967), the role of the courts is to distinguish between "[b]iting criticism [that merely] suppresses demand [and] copyright infringement[, which] usurps it." *Fisher v. Dees*, 794 F.2d, at 438.

This distinction between potentially remediable displacement and unremediable disparagement is reflected in the rule that there is no protectable derivative market for criticism. The market for potential derivative uses includes only those that creators of original works would in general develop or license others to develop. Yet the unlikelihood that creators of imaginative works will license critical reviews or lampoons of their own productions removes such uses from the very notion of a potential licensing market. "People ask ... for criticism, but they only want praise." S. Maugham, Of Human Bondage 241 (Penguin ed. 1992). Thus, to the extent that the opinion below may be read to have considered harm to the market for parodies of "Oh, Pretty Woman," see 972 F.2d, at 1439, the court erred.

In explaining why the law recognizes no derivative market for critical works, including parody, we have, of course, been speaking of the later work as if it had nothing but a critical aspect (i.e., "parody pure and simple"). But the later work may have a more complex character, with effects not only in the arena of criticism but also in protectable markets for derivative works, too. In that sort of case, the law looks beyond the criticism to the other elements of the work, as it does here. 2 Live Crew's song comprises not only parody but also rap music, and the derivative market for rap music is a proper focus of enquiry. Evidence of substantial harm to it would weigh against a finding of fair use, because the licensing of derivatives is an important economic incentive to the creation of originals. Of course, the only harm to derivatives that need concern us, as discussed above, is the harm of market substitution. The fact that a parody may impair the market for derivative uses by the very effectiveness of its critical commentary is no more relevant under copyright than the like threat to the original market.

Although 2 Live Crew submitted uncontroverted affidavits on the question of market harm to the original, neither they, nor Acuff–Rose, introduced evidence or affidavits addressing the likely effect of 2 Live Crew's parodic rap song on the market for a non-parody, rap version of "Oh, Pretty Woman." And while Acuff–Rose would have us find evidence of a rap market in the very facts that 2 Live Crew recorded a rap parody of "Oh, Pretty Woman" and another rap group sought a license to record a rap derivative, there was no evidence that a potential rap market was harmed in any way by 2 Live Crew's parody, rap version. The fact that 2 Live Crew's parody sold as part of a collection of rap songs says very little about the parody's effect on a market for a rap version of the original, either of the music alone or of the music with its lyrics. The District Court essentially passed on this issue, observing that Acuff–Rose is free to record "whatever version of the original it desires," 754 F.Supp. at 1158; the Court of Appeals went the other way by erroneous presumption. Contrary to each treatment, it is impossible to deal with the fourth factor except by recognizing that a silent record on an important factor bearing on fair use disentitled the proponent of the defense, 2 Live Crew, to summary judgment. The evidentiary hole will doubtless be plugged on remand.

III

It was error for the Court of Appeals to conclude that the commercial nature of 2 Live Crew's parody of "Oh, Pretty Woman" rendered it presumptively unfair. No such evidentiary presumption is available to address either the first factor, the character and purpose of the use, or the fourth, market harm, in determining whether a transformative use, such as parody, is a fair one. The court also erred in holding that 2 Live Crew had necessarily copied excessively from the Orbison original, considering the parodic purpose of the use. We therefore reverse the judgment of the Court of Appeals and remand for further proceedings consistent with this opinion.

It is so ordered.

APPENDIX A

"Oh, Pretty Woman" by Roy Orbison and William Dees

Pretty Woman, walking down the street,

Pretty Woman, the kind I like to meet,

Pretty Woman, I don't believe you, you're not the truth,

No one could look as good as you

Mercy

Pretty Woman, won't you pardon me,

Pretty Woman, I couldn't help but see,

Pretty Woman, that you look lovely as can be

Are you lonely just like me?

Pretty Woman, stop a while,

Pretty Woman, talk a while,

Pretty Woman give your smile to me

Pretty woman, yeah, yeah, yeah

Pretty Woman, look my way,

Pretty Woman, say you'll stay with me

'Cause I need you, I'll treat you right

Come to me baby, Be mine tonight

Pretty Woman, don't walk on by,

Pretty Woman, don't make me cry,

Pretty Woman, don't walk away,

Hey, O.K.

If that's the way it must be, O.K.

I guess I'll go on home, it's late

There'll be tomorrow night, but wait!

What do I see

Is she walking back to me?

Yeah, she's walking back to me!

Oh, Pretty Woman.

APPENDIX B

"Pretty Woman" as Recorded by 2 Live Crew

Pretty woman walkin' down the street

Pretty woman girl you look so sweet

Pretty woman you bring me down to that knee

Pretty woman you make me wanna beg please

Oh, pretty woman

Big hairy woman you need to shave that stuff

Big hairy woman you know I bet it's tough

Big hairy woman all that hair it ain't legit

'Cause you look like 'Cousin It'

Big hairy woman

Bald headed woman girl your hair won't grow

Bald headed woman you got a teeny weeny afro

Bald headed woman you know your hair could look nice

Bald headed woman first you got to roll it with rice

Bald headed woman here, let me get this hunk of biz for ya

Ya know what I'm saying you look better than rice a roni

Oh bald headed woman

Big hairy woman come on in

And don't forget your bald headed friend

Hey pretty woman let the boys

Jump in

Two timin' woman girl you know you ain't right

Two timin' woman you's out with my boy last night

Two timin' woman that takes a load off my mind

Two timin' woman now I know the baby ain't mine

Oh, two timin' woman

Oh pretty woman

[The opinion of Justice KENNEDY, concurring, is omitted.]

NOTES

1. *"... purpose and character of the use...."* Justice Souter's opinion for the Court in *Acuff–Rose* substantially altered fair use doctrine by centering inquiry under the first factor on whether and to what extent the defendant's work is "transformative." Observing that a "transformative use is not absolutely necessary for a finding of fair use," Justice Souter added that promotion of science and the arts is generally furthered by the creation of transformative works, which "lie at the heart of the fair use doctrine's guarantee of breathing space within the confines of copyright." Consequently, in Souter's view, "the more transformative the new work, the less will be the significance of other factors, like commercialism, that may weigh against a finding of fair use." Does this new factor so dominate fair use analysis that uses that have in the past been treated as fair, would today be held to infringe? Would home videotaping of television programs for purposes of "time-shifting"—held to be a fair use in Sony v. Universal, page 717, below—, be considered fair under *Acuff–Rose*? What of photocopying of materials for class handouts?

Did Justice Souter's opinion adequately reconcile a work's transformation as an occasion for fair use under section 107, with transformation as the predicate for infringement under section 106(2)'s exclusive right to prepare derivative works? In Suntrust Bank v. Houghton Mifflin Co., 268 F.3d 1257,1267, 60 U.S.P.Q.2d 1225 (11th Cir.2001), the court relied extensively on the transformative use doctrine to excuse as fair *The Wind Done Gone*, a claimed parody of *Gone With the Wind* which, according to the court "appropriates numerous characters, settings, and plot twists" from *Gone With the Wind*: "TWDG copies, often in wholesale fashion, the descriptions and histories of these fictional characters and places from GWTW, as well as their relationships and interactions with one another. TWDG appropriates or otherwise explicitly references many aspects of GWTW's plot as well, such as the scenes in which Scarlett kills a Union soldier and the scene in which Rhett stays in the room with his dead daughter Bonnie, burning candles. After carefully comparing the two works, we agree with the district court that, particularly in its first half, TWDG is largely an encapsulation of GWTW that exploits its copyrighted characters, story lines, and settings as the palette for the new story."

If, as observed by the court, defendant's work was "a specific criticism of and rejoinder to the depiction of slavery and the relationships between blacks and whites in GWTW," was this a sufficient transformation to include it in, or remove it from, the domain of derivative works?

See generally Diane Leenheer Zimmerman, The More Things Change the Less They Seem "Transformed": Some Reflections on Fair Use, 46 J. Copyright Soc'y U.S.A. 251 (1998).

2. "*... nature of the copyrighted work....*" Two questions about the nature of the copyrighted work recur in fair use cases: Is the work fictional or factual? Is it published or unpublished? One difficulty in the *Nation* case was that, as a factual, historical work, Ford's memoirs invited free use; but, as an unpublished work, they rejected it. In the view of the dissenters, "[t]he quotation of 300 words from the manuscript infringed no privacy interest of Mr. Ford. This author intended the words in the manuscript to be a public statement about his Presidency.... What the Court depicts as the copyright owner's 'confidentiality' interest is not a privacy interest at all. Rather, it is no more than an economic interest in capturing the full value of initial release of information to the public, and is properly analyzed as such. Lacking too is any suggestion that *The Nation's* use interfered with the copyright owner's interest in editorial control of the manuscript. The Nation made use of the Ford quotes on the eve of official publication." 471 U.S. at 597–98, 105 S.Ct. at 2249–50.

Compare Salinger v. Random House, Inc., 811 F.2d 90, 1 U.S.P.Q.2d 1673 (2d Cir.), cert. denied, 484 U.S. 890, 108 S.Ct. 213, 98 L.Ed.2d 177 (1987), directing a preliminary injunction against defendant's publication of a biography of the reclusive writer, J.D. Salinger, that drew in part on several of Salinger's unpublished letters. The court relied on the special protection that the *Nation* Court gave to unpublished works. "[T]he tenor of the Court's entire discussion of unpublished works conveys the idea that such works normally enjoy complete protection against copying any protected expression." 811 F.2d at 97.

In 1992, Congress responded to concerns that Second Circuit decisions, including *Salinger*, had effectively immunized unpublished works from fair use by adding a last sentence to section 107: "The fact that a work is unpublished shall not itself bar a finding of fair use if such finding is made upon consideration of all the above factors." 102 Pub. L. No. 102–492, 106 Stat. 3145 (1992).

3. "*... amount and substantiality of the portion used in relation to the copyrighted work as a whole....*" Courts have used quantitative measures in weighing section 107's third factor, holding that it is not fair use to copy four notes and two words out of 100 musical measures and 45–words, or 2.5 minutes out of a 28–minute film. See Elsmere Music, Inc. v. National Broadcasting Co., 482 F.Supp. 741, 206 U.S.P.Q. 913 (S.D.N.Y.1980), aff'd per curiam, 623 F.2d 252, 207 U.S.P.Q. 277 (2d Cir.); Iowa State Univ. Research Found., Inc. v. American Broadcasting Cos., 621 F.2d 57, 207 U.S.P.Q. 97 (2d Cir.1980). Courts have also employed qualitative measures, weighing this factor against fair use where the portions taken were particularly important to the copyrighted work as a whole. See Meredith Corp. v. Harper & Row, Publishers, Inc., 378 F.Supp. 686, 182 U.S.P.Q. 609 (S.D.N.Y.1974), aff'd, 500 F.2d 1221, 182 U.S.P.Q. 577 (2d Cir.).

The weight given to the third factor will vary with the context of the use. Justice Brennan, dissenting in the *Nation* case, observed that "[h]ad these quotations been used in the context of a critical book review of the Ford work, there is little question that such a use would be fair use within the meaning of § 107 of the Act. The amount and substantiality of the use—in both quantitative and qualitative terms—would have certainly been appropriate to the purpose of such a use. It is difficult to see how the use of these quoted words in a news report is less appropriate. The Court acknowledges as much: '[E]ven substantial quotations might qualify as a fair use in a review of a published work or a news account of a speech that had been delivered to the public.' With respect to the motivation for the pardon and the insights into the psyche of the fallen President, for example, Mr. Ford's reflections and perceptions are so laden with emotion and deeply personal value judgments that full understanding is immeasurably enhanced by reproducing a limited portion of Mr. Ford's own words. The importance of the work, after all, lies not only in revelation of previously unknown fact but also in revelation of the thoughts, ideas, motivations, and fears of two Presidents at a critical moment in our national history. Thus, while the question is not easily resolved, it is difficult to say that the use of the six quotations was gratuitous in relation to the news reporting purpose." 471 U.S. at 601, 105 S.Ct. at 2252.

4. *"... effect of the use upon the potential market for or value of the copyrighted work."* Courts find it comparatively easy to apply section 107's fourth factor when plaintiff and defendant occupy the same market—sale of journal subscriptions, for example—but encounter difficulty when the copyright owner has neither made nor licensed the type of use made by the defendant—for example, photocopying journal articles.

Williams & Wilkins Co. v. United States, 487 F.2d 1345, 180 U.S.P.Q. 49 (Ct.Cl.1973), aff'd by an equally divided Court, 420 U.S. 376, 95 S.Ct. 1344, 43 L.Ed.2d 264, 184 U.S.P.Q. 705 (1975), is typical. The Court of Claims held there that it was fair use for the defendant to photocopy articles from plaintiff's medical journals for distribution to medical researchers. In the court's view, plaintiff had not shown "that it is being or will be harmed substantially" by defendants' practices. "It is wrong to measure the detriment to plaintiff by loss of presumed royalty income—a standard which necessarily assumes that plaintiff had a right to issue licenses. That would be true, of course, only if it were first decided that the defendant's practices did not constitute 'fair use.' In determining whether the company has been sufficiently hurt to cause these practices to become 'unfair,' one cannot assume at the start the merit of the plaintiff's position...." 487 F.2d at 1357 n. 19.

Although courts following the *Williams & Wilkins* approach can be criticized for giving insufficient weight to the fourth factor's use of the word "potential," consider the *reductio ad absurdum* of the alternative approach under which *all* markets, no matter how far removed from the original, are considered potential markets for the copyrighted work and *any* use made by a defendant will invade such a market. Did *Acuff-Rose* offer a practical middle ground by drawing a line between the market for works that merely copy the original and the market for those that transform them, and "supersede the object of the original"?

5. *Parody and Satire.* Should courts in fair use cases draw a line between *parody*, in which the defendant reproduces elements in plaintiff's work for the purpose of lampooning the work, and *satire*, in which the defendant uses plaintiff's work as a vehicle for commenting on some individual or institution and not on the work itself? Justice Souter evidently thought so when he observed in *Acuff-Rose*, that "[p]arody needs to mimic an original to make its point, and so has some claim to use the creation of its victim's (or collective victims') imagination, whereas satire can stand on its own two feet and so requires justification for the very act of borrowing." 510 U.S. at 580–81, 114 S.Ct. at 1172.

Should satire even come within the general scope of the fair use defense? While a copyright owner might understandably be unwilling to license a parody of his work, what reason might he have not to license use of his work as a vehicle for social comment? Even if the copyright owner refuses to license the proposed satirical use at an acceptable price, is there any good reason to give the satirist a free ride on the plaintiff's work? There will rarely be a shortage of other works, including public domain works, that, with some ingenuity can be made to serve as an equally effective vehicle for satire.

See Tyler Ochoa, Dr. Seuss, the Juice and Fair Use: How the Grinch Silenced a Parody, 45 J. Copyright Soc'y U.S.A. 546 (1998).

6. *Classroom Photocopying.* From the time that section 107 was first proposed, debate centered on the status of classroom copying, particularly photocopying, of copyrighted works. According to the House Report, the House Committee resisted educators' proposals for "a specific exemption freeing certain reproductions of copyrighted works for educational and scholarly purposes from copyright control." The Committee did, however, recognize "a need for greater certainty and protection for teachers." One step toward meeting this need was section 504(c), "to provide innocent teachers and other nonprofit users of copyrighted material with broad insulation against unwarranted liability for infringement." H.R.Rep. No. 94–1476, 66–67.

As another step in the direction of certainty, the House Committee encouraged education and trade groups to agree on joint guidelines for permissible classroom uses. The effort bore fruit. On March 19, 1976 educator groups, the Authors League, and the Association of American Publishers reached an Agreement on Guidelines for Classroom Copying in Not–For–Profit Educational Institutions with Respect to Books and Periodicals. The Guidelines cover unlicensed copying in the form both of single copies made by teachers for their own use, and multiple copies made for classroom use. Under the Guidelines a teacher may, for research or teaching purposes, make a single copy of a chapter from a book, an article from a periodical or newspaper, a short story, essay or poem, or a chart, graph, diagram, drawing, cartoon or picture. The Guidelines impose more rigorous and detailed standards of "brevity," "spontaneity" and "cumulative effect" for multiple copies for classroom use. H.R.Rep. No. 94–1476, 68–70.

The House Committee accepted these, and counterpart Guidelines for educational uses of music, as "a reasonable interpretation of the minimum standards of fair use. Teachers will know that copying within the Guidelines is fair use." H.R.Rep. No. 94–1476, 72. The House and Senate Conferees also accepted the Guidelines "as part of their understanding of fair use." House Conf.Rep. No. 94–1733, 94th Cong.2d Sess. 72 (1976). Six years later, the House Committee on the Judiciary endorsed negotiated guidelines for classroom videotaping of audiovisual works. The guidelines apply only to nonprofit educational institutions' off-air recording of programs "transmitted by television stations for reception by the general public without charge." See H.R.Rep. No. 495, 97th Cong., 2d Sess. 8–9 (1982).

Publishers have enjoyed greater success in the battle against unauthorized educational photocopying outside the schoolroom. In Basic Books, Inc. v. Kinko's Graphics Corp., 758 F.Supp. 1522, 18 U.S.P.Q.2d 1437 (S.D.N.Y. 1991), several publishers won an injunction, attorneys fees, costs, and $510,000 statutory damages against a photocopy service that compiled excerpts from their books into course readers for sale to college students.

See generally, Ann Bartow, Educational Fair Use in Copyright: Reclaiming the Right to Photocopy Freely, 60 U. Pitt. L. Rev. 149 (1998).

7. *Fair Use and the Problem of Transaction Costs.* In a pathbreaking article, Fair Use as Market Failure: A Structural and Economic Analysis of the *Betamax* Case and its Predecessors, 82 Colum. L. Rev. 1600 (1982), Professor Wendy Gordon concluded that "[a]n economic and structural analysis of the fair use doctrine and its place in the copyright scheme reveals that fair use is ordinarily granted when the market cannot be relied upon to allow socially desirable access to, and use of, copyrighted works." *Id.* at 1657. Specifically, "[w]here (1) defendant could not appropriately purchase the desired use through the market; (2) transferring control over the use to defendant would serve the public interest; and (3) the copyright owner's incentives would not be substantially impaired by allowing the user to proceed, courts have in the past considered, and should in the future consider, defendant's use 'fair'." *Id.* at 1601.

If transaction costs are a hurdle to freely negotiated copyright licenses, should courts in fair use cases consider the availability of institutional mechanisms that can reduce transaction costs to acceptable levels? See American Geophysical Union v. Texaco, Inc., 60 F.3d 913, 35 U.S.P.Q. 2d 1513 (2d Cir.1994), where, in deciding that defendant's reproduction of single copies from plaintiff's journals, even for research purposes, was not fair use, the court weighed the effect of the licensing activities of the Copyright Clearance Center in reducing transaction costs. Should a court ever consider the prospective effect that a decision denying fair use might have on the parties' mutual willingness to invest in institutional or technological arrangements capable of reducing transaction costs to acceptable levels?

Automated payment and rights management systems promise significantly to reduce the cost of negotiating permissions to use copyrighted works. If transaction costs drop to a level at which uses presently excused as fair—copying an article for a course paper, for example—can be licensed instantly at low cost or no cost, should this be a ground for denying a fair use defense to the user? Or does fair use serve other values? See Lydia Pallas Loren, Redefining the Market Failure Approach to Fair Use in an Era of Copyright Permission Systems, 5 J. Intell. Prop. L. 1 (1997); Tom W. Bell, Fair Use vs. Fared Use: The Impact of Automated Rights Management on Copyright's Fair Use Doctrine, 76 N.C. L. Rev. 557 (1998).

Sony Corporation of America v. Universal City Studios, Inc., the U.S. Supreme Court's seminal decision on fair use in the context of emerging technologies appears at page 717, below.

8. *Fair Use and the First Amendment.* What connections, if any, are there between the fair use defense and the First Amendment's speech and press guarantees? Although defendants in several cases starting in the 1970's raised free speech defenses to copyright infringement actions, the sweeping analysis in Justice O'Connor's opinion for the *Nation* Court may have ended any debate over the First Amendment's substantive role in copyright cases: "In our haste to disseminate news, it should not be forgotten that the Framers intended copyright itself to be the engine of free expression. By establishing a marketable right to the use of one's expression, copyright supplies the economic incentive to create and disseminate ideas.... In view of the First Amendment protections already embodied in the Copyright Act's distinction between copyrightable expression and uncopyrightable facts and ideas, and the latitude for scholarship and comment traditionally afforded by fair use, we see no warrant for expanding the doctrine of fair use to create what amounts to a public figure exception to copyright. Whether verbatim copying from a public figure's manuscript in a given case is or is not fair must be judged according to the traditional equities of fair use." 471 U.S. at 558, 560, 105 S.Ct. at 2230.

Free speech concerns may constrain the availability of preliminary injunctive relief. In Suntrust Bank v. Houghton Mifflin Co., 252 F.3d 1165, 58 U.S.P.Q.2d 1800 (11th Cir.2001), the court vacated a district court order preliminarily enjoining defendant from distributing its claimed parody of *Gone With the Wind* on the grounds that it was an unconstitutional prior restraint. See generally Andrew Beckerman–Rodau, Prior Restraints and Intellectual Property: The Clash Between Intellectual Property and the First Amendment from an Economic Perspective, 12 Fordham Int. Prop. Media & Ent. L. J. 1 (2001); Mark A. Lemley & Eugene Volokh, Freedom of Speech and Injunctions in Intellectual Property Cases, 48 Duke L.J. 147 (1998).

9. *De Minimis Uses.* The urban landscape is filled with copyrighted images, the air with copyrighted sounds. Does a photographer infringe copyright when the background of a snapshot reveals a copyrighted billboard poster? Does a television station infringe copyright when its videotape of a Labor Day parade reproduces a snatch of copyrighted music?

The case law on *de minimis* uses is sparse. One court held that it was not actionable to copy thirty characters from fifty pages of computer source code. Vault Corp. v. Quaid Software Ltd., 847 F.2d 255, 267–268, 7 U.S.P.Q.2d 1281 (5th Cir.1988). The Court of Appeals for the Second Circuit ruled that it was *de minimis* for a film to copy plaintiff's photographs where the photographs appeared "fleetingly" and were "obscured, severely out of focus, and virtually unidentifiable," Sandoval v. New Line Cinema Corp., 147 F.3d 215, 218, 47 U.S.P.Q.2d 1215 (2d. Cir.1998), but that it was not *de minimis* for a television program to display a poster of an artistic work as part of a set decoration where virtually all or part of the poster appeared in nine segments lasting between 1.86 and 4.16 seconds, for an aggregate of 26.75 seconds. Ringgold v. Black Entertainment Television, Inc., 126 F.3d 70, 74, 44 U.S.P.Q.2d 1001 (2d Cir.1997).

Should courts draw a line between situations where the defendant had no direct control over the environment in which the copyrighted work appeared—a street scene, for example—and one where it did have control—a movie set?

d. Exclusive Rights and New Technologies

The legislative and judicial history of copyright law in the United States is in substantial part the history of copyright's encounter with new technologies. Barbara Ringer, a former Register of Copyrights, traced a recurrent theme in the political evolution of copyright law under the 1909 Copyright Act. According to Ringer, the process begins with the exploitation of a new technological development expanding the use of copyrighted works. Next comes the question whether the new use infringes copyright, the discovery that "the 1909 Copyright Statute and the cases interpreting it contain no answers, only analogies," and then a lawsuit for copyright infringement. Because the allegedly infringing activities have become widespread, and because the 1909 Act is considered inapposite, courts "reluctantly hold against the copyright owner and urgently call upon Congress to do its duty and reform an archaic and unjust statute." Caught between the traditionally protected interests of creators and the pressures exerted by representatives of the newly emergent user industries, Congress is politically compelled to compromise. "Now, and even more in the future, the compromises seem likely to consist of compulsory licensing." Barbara Ringer, Copyright and the Future of Authorship, 101 Libr. J. 229, 231 (1976).

The 1909 Act embodied the first copyright compulsory license, section 1(e)'s provision for the new technologies of piano rolls and phonograph records, enacted in response to the Supreme Court's decision in White–Smith v. Apollo, 209 U.S. 1, 28 S.Ct. 319, 52 L.Ed. 655 (1908), holding that pianola rolls that reproduced copyrighted musical works were not infringing copies of the works. Section 115 of the 1976 Copyright Act carried forward section 1(e)'s compulsory license and was itself subsequently amended to bring digital transmissions constituting digital phonorecord deliveries within the compulsory license. Following two Supreme Court decisions holding that cable television systems were not liable for retransmitting television signals, section 111 of the 1976 Act subjected the cable industry to a mixed regime of absolute liability, compulsory licensing and outright exemptions. Subsequently, section 119 of the Act brought satellite transmissions under a comparable regime.

Private uses of copyrighted works have presented a persisting challenge to copyright law, and courts have applied the fair use doctrine to mediate the intersection of copyright and such new technologies as photocopying (Williams & Wilkins Co. v. United States, note 4, page 712, above), home videotaping (Sony v. Universal, page 717 below) and music file sharing on the Internet (A & M Records v. Napster, note 4, page 733, below). Courts have also shaped doctrines of secondary liability—contributory and vicarious copyright infringement—to impose copyright liability on the providers of equipment and services that enable direct copyright infringement without at the same time burdening noninfringing activities. Sony v. Universal, page 717, below, is an example. Safe harbor provisions, added to the 1976 Act by Title II of the Digital Millennium Copyright Act to adjust the needs of Internet intermediaries to those of copyright owners, are described in note 3, page 732 below.

Non-legal mechanisms have also played a substantial role in adjusting copyright to new technologies. The music collecting societies, discussed at page 735, below, have made it possible to collect revenues from broadcasts and other dispersed uses of copyrighted works and to distribute them to composers, authors and publishers. The Copyright Clearance Center has sought to achieve the same economies for copyright owners of literary works. More recently, technical measures to encrypt copyrighted works have won legislative support in the form of DMCA provisions outlawing disencryption and traffic in the technologies of disencryption. The provisions are discussed at pages 734 and 873, below.

Perhaps because music—in the form both of musical works and sound recordings—has been the first economically valuable object of Internet activity, the development of legislation and institutional arrangements in the field has been particularly intense and complex. For helpful guides through the regulatory maze, see R. Anthony Reese, Copyright and Internet Music Transmissions: Existing Law, Major Controversies, Possible Solutions, 55 U. Miami L. Rev. 237 (2001); Eric D. Leach, Everything You Always Wanted to Know About Digital Performance Rights But Were Afraid to Ask, 48 J. Copyright Soc'y U.S.A. 191 (2000).

Sony Corporation of America v. Universal City Studios, Inc.

Supreme Court of the United States, 1984.
464 U.S. 417, 104 S.Ct. 774, 78 L.Ed.2d 574, 220 U.S.P.Q. 665.

Justice STEVENS delivered the opinion of the Court.

Petitioners manufacture and sell home video tape recorders. Respondents own the copyrights on some of the television programs that are broadcast on the public airwaves. Some members of the general public use video tape recorders sold by petitioners to record some of these broadcasts, as well as a large number of other broadcasts. The question presented is whether the sale of petitioners' copying equipment to the general public violates any of the rights conferred upon respondents by the Copyright Act.

Respondents commenced this copyright infringement action against petitioners in the United States District Court for the Central District of California in 1976. Respondents alleged that some individuals had used Betamax video tape recorders (VTR's) to record some of respondents' copyrighted works which had been exhibited on commercially sponsored television and contended that these individuals had thereby infringed respondents' copyrights. Respondents further maintained that petitioners were liable for the copyright infringement allegedly committed by Betamax consumers because of petitioners' marketing of the Betamax VTR's. Respondents sought no relief against any Betamax consumer. Instead, they sought money damages and an equitable accounting of profits from petitioners, as well as an injunction against the manufacture and marketing of Betamax VTR's.

After a lengthy trial, the District Court denied respondents all the relief they sought and entered judgment for petitioners. The United States Court of Appeals for the Ninth Circuit reversed the District Court's judgment on respondent's copyright claim, holding petitioners liable for contributory infringement and ordering the District Court to fashion appropriate relief. We granted certiorari; since we had not completed our study of the case last Term, we ordered reargument, We now reverse.

An explanation of our rejection of respondents' unprecedented attempt to impose copyright liability upon the distributors of copying equipment requires a quite detailed recitation of the findings of the District Court. In summary, those findings reveal that the average member of the public uses a VTR principally to record a program he cannot view as it is being televised and then to watch it once at a later time. This practice, known as "time-shifting," enlarges the television viewing audience. For that reason, a significant amount of television programming may be used in this manner without objection from the owners of the copyrights on the programs. For the same reason, even the two respondents in this case, who do assert objections to time-shifting in this litigation, were unable to prove that the practice has impaired the commercial value of their copyrights or has created any likelihood of future harm. Given these findings, there is no basis in the Copyright Act upon which respondents can hold petitioners liable for distributing VTR's to the general public. The Court of Appeals' holding that respondents are entitled to enjoin the distribution of VTR's, to collect royalties on the sale of such equipment, or to obtain other relief, if affirmed, would enlarge the scope of respondents' statutory monopolies to encompass control over an article of commerce that is not the subject of copyright protection. Such an expansion of the copyright privilege is beyond the limits of the grants authorized by Congress.

I

The two respondents in this action, Universal Studios, Inc. and Walt Disney Productions, produce and hold the copyrights on a substantial number of motion pictures and other audiovisual works. In the current marketplace, they can exploit their rights in these works in a number of ways: by authorizing theatrical exhibitions, by licensing limited showings on cable and network television, by selling syndication rights for repeated airings on local television stations, and by marketing programs on prerecorded videotapes or videodiscs. Some works are suitable for exploitation through all of these avenues, while the market for other works is more limited.

Petitioner Sony manufactures millions of Betamax video tape recorders and markets these devices through numerous retail establishments, some of which are also petitioners in this action. Sony's Betamax VTR is a mechanism consisting of three basic components: (1) a tuner, which receives electromagnetic signals transmitted over the television band of the public airwaves and separates them into audio and visual signals; (2) a recorder, which records such signals on a magnetic tape; and (3) an adapter, which converts the audio and visual signals on the tape into a composite signal that can be received by a television set.

Several capabilities of the machine are noteworthy. The separate tuner in the Betamax enables it to record a broadcast off one station while the television set is tuned to another channel, permitting the viewer, for example, to watch two simultaneous news broadcasts by watching one "live" and recording the other for later viewing. Tapes may be reused, and programs that have been recorded may be erased either before or after viewing. A timer in the Betamax can be used to activate and deactivate the equipment at predetermined times, enabling an intended viewer to record programs that are transmitted when he or she is not at home. Thus a person may watch a program at home in the evening even though it was broadcast while the viewer was at work during the afternoon. The Betamax is also equipped with a pause button and a fast-forward control. The pause button, when depressed, deactivates the recorder until it is released, thus enabling a viewer to omit a commercial advertisement from the recording, provided, of course, that the viewer is present when the program is recorded. The fast forward control enables the viewer of a previously recorded program to run the tape rapidly when a segment he or she does not desire to see is being played back on the television screen.

The respondents and Sony both conducted surveys of the way the Betamax machine was used by several hundred owners during a sample period in 1978. Although there were some differences in the surveys, they both showed that the primary use of the machine for most owners was "time-shifting,"—the practice of recording a program to view it once at a later time, and thereafter erasing it. Time-shifting enables viewers to see programs they otherwise would miss because they are not at home, are occupied with other tasks, or are viewing a program on another station at the time of a broadcast that they desire to watch. Both surveys also showed, however, that a substantial number of interviewees had accumulated libraries of tapes. Sony's survey indicated that over 80% of the interviewees watched at least as much regular television as they had before owning a Betamax. Respondents offered no evidence of decreased television viewing by Betamax owners.

Sony introduced considerable evidence describing television programs that could be copied without objection from any copyright holder, with special emphasis on sports, religious, and educational programming. For example, their survey indicated that 7.3% of all Betamax use is to record sports events, and representatives of professional baseball, football, basketball, and hockey testified that they had no objection to the recording of their televised events for home use.

Respondents offered opinion evidence concerning the future impact of the unrestricted sale of VTR's on the commercial value of their copyrights. The District Court found, however, that they had failed to prove any likelihood of future harm from the use of VTR's for time-shifting....

II

Article I, Sec. 8, of the Constitution provides:

The Congress shall have Power ... to Promote the Progress of Science and useful Arts, by securing for limited Times to Authors and Inventors the exclusive Right to their respective Writings and Discoveries.

The monopoly privileges that Congress may authorize are neither unlimited nor primarily designed to provide a special private benefit. Rather, the limited grant is a means by which an important public purpose may be achieved. It is intended to motivate the creative activity of authors and inventors by the provision of a special reward, and to allow the public access to the products of their genius after the limited period of exclusive control has expired.

The copyright law, like the patent statute, makes reward to the owner a secondary consideration. In *Fox Film Corp. v. Doyal,* 286 U.S. 123, 127 [52 S.Ct. 546, 547, 76 L.Ed. 1010], Chief Justice Hughes spoke as follows respecting the copyright monopoly granted by Congress, "The sole interest of the United States and the primary object in conferring the monopoly lie in the general benefits derived by the public from the labors of authors." It is said that reward to the author or artist serves to induce release to the public of the products of his creative genius. *United States v. Paramount Pictures,* 334 U.S. 131, 158, 68 S.Ct. 915, 929, 92 L.Ed. 1260.

As the text of the Constitution makes plain, it is Congress that has been assigned the task of defining the scope of the limited monopoly that should be granted to authors or to inventors in order to give the public appropriate access to their work product. Because this task involves a difficult balance between the interests of authors and inventors in the control and exploitation of their writings and discoveries on the one hand, and society's competing interest in the free flow of ideas, information, and commerce on the other hand, our patent and copyright statutes have been amended repeatedly.

From its beginning, the law of copyright has developed in response to significant changes in technology. Indeed, it was the invention of a new form of copying equipment—the printing press—that gave rise to the original need for copyright protection. Repeatedly, as new developments have occurred in this country, it has been the Congress that has fashioned the new rules that new technology made necessary. Thus, long before the enactment of the Copyright Act of 1909, it was settled that the protection given to copyrights is wholly statutory. The remedies for infringement "are only those prescribed by Congress." *Thompson v. Hubbard,* 131 U.S. 123, 151, 9 S.Ct. 710, 720, 33 L.Ed. 76 (1889).

The judiciary's reluctance to expand the protections afforded by the copyright without explicit legislative guidance is a recurring theme. Sound policy, as well as history, supports our consistent deference to Congress when major technological innovations alter the market for copyrighted materials. Congress has the constitutional authority and the institutional ability to accommodate fully the varied permutations of competing interests that are inevitably implicated by such new technology.

In a case like this, in which Congress has not plainly marked our course, we must be circumspect in construing the scope of rights created by a legislative enactment which never contemplated such a calculus of interests. In doing so, we are guided by Justice Stewart's exposition of the correct approach to ambiguities in the law of copyright:

> The limited scope of the copyright holder's statutory monopoly, like the limited copyright duration required by the Constitution, reflects a balance of competing claims upon the public interest: Creative work is to be encouraged and rewarded, but private motivation must ultimately serve the cause of promoting broad public availability of literature, music, and the other arts. The immediate effect of our copyright law is to secure a fair return for an 'author's' creative labor. But the ultimate aim is, by this incentive, to stimulate artistic creativity for the general public good. "The sole interest of the United States and the primary object in conferring the monopoly,' this Court has said, 'lie in the general benefits derived by the public from the labors of authors.' " *Fox Film Corp. v. Doyal,* 286 U.S. 123, 127 [52 S.Ct. 546, 547, 76 L.Ed. 1010]. When technological change has rendered its literal terms ambiguous, the Copyright Act must be construed in light of this basic purpose. *Twentieth Century Music Corp. v. Aiken,* 422 U.S. 151, 156, (1975), 95 S.Ct. 2040, 2043, 45 L.Ed.2d 84.

Copyright protection "subsists ... in original works of authorship fixed in any tangible medium of expression." 17 U.S.C. § 102(a). This protection has never accorded the copyright owner complete control over all possible uses of his work. Rather, the Copyright Act grants the copyright holder "exclusive" rights to use and to authorize the use of his work in five qualified ways, including reproduction of the copyrighted work in copies. All reproductions of the work, however, are not within the exclusive domain of the copyright owner; some are in the public domain. Any individual may reproduce a copyrighted work for a "fair use;" the copyright owner does not possess the exclusive right to such a use.

"Anyone who violates any of the exclusive rights of the copyright owner," that is, anyone who trespasses into his exclusive domain by using or authorizing the use of the copyrighted work in one of the five ways set forth in the statute, "is an infringer of the copyright." § 501(a). Conversely, anyone who is authorized by the copyright owner to use the copyrighted work in a way specified in the statute or who makes a fair use of the work is not an infringer of the copyright with respect to such use.

The Copyright Act provides the owner of a copyright with a potent arsenal of remedies against an infringer of his work, including an injunction to restrain the infringer from violating his rights, the impoundment and destruction of all reproductions of his work made in violation of his rights, a recovery of his actual damages and any additional profits realized by the infringer or a recovery of statutory damages, and attorneys fees.

The two respondents in this case do not seek relief against the Betamax users who have allegedly infringed their copyrights. Moreover, this is not a class action on behalf of all copyright owners who license their works for television broadcast, and respondents have no right to invoke whatever rights other copyright holders may have to bring infringement actions based on Betamax copying of their works. As was made clear by their own evidence, the copying of the respondents' programs represents a small portion of the total use of VTR's. It is, however, the taping of respondents' own copyrighted programs that provides them with standing to charge Sony with contributory infringement. To prevail, they have the burden of proving that users of the Betamax have infringed their copyrights and that Sony should be held responsible for that infringement.

III

The Copyright Act does not expressly render anyone liable for infringement committed by another. In contrast, the Patent Act expressly brands anyone who "actively induces infringement of a patent" as an infringer, 35 U.S.C. § 271(b), and further imposes liability on certain individuals labeled "contributory" infringers, § 271(c). The absence of such express language in the copyright statute does not preclude the imposition of liability for copyright infringements on certain parties who have not themselves engaged in the infringing activity. For vicarious liability is imposed in virtually all areas of the law, and the concept of contributory infringement is merely a species of the broader problem of identifying the circumstances in which it is just to hold one individual accountable for the actions of another.

Such circumstances were plainly present in Kalem Co. v. Harper Brothers, 222 U.S. 55, 32 S.Ct. 20, 56 L.Ed. 92 (1911), the copyright decision of this Court on which respondents place their principal reliance. In *Kalem,* the Court held that the producer of an unauthorized film dramatization of the copyrighted book *Ben Hur* was liable for his sale of the motion picture to jobbers, who in turn arranged for the commercial exhibition of the film. Justice Holmes, writing for the Court, explained:

> The defendant not only expected but invoked by advertisement the use of its films for dramatic reproduction of the story. That was the most conspicuous purpose for which they could be used, and the one for which especially they were made. If the defendant did not contribute to the infringement it is impossible to do so except by taking part in the final act. It is liable on principles recognized in every part of the law. Id., at 63–63.

The use for which the item sold in *Kalem* had been "especially" made was, of course, to display the performance that had already been recorded upon it. The producer had personally appropriated the copyright owner's protected work and, as the owner of the tangible medium of expression upon which the protected work was recorded, authorized that use by his sale of the film to jobbers. But that use of the film was not his to authorize: the copyright owner possessed the exclusive right to authorize public performances of his work. Further, the producer personally advertised the unauthorized public performances, dispelling any possible doubt as to the use of the film which he had authorized.

Respondents argue that *Kalem* stands for the proposition that supplying the "means" to accomplish an infringing activity and encouraging that activity through advertisement are sufficient to establish liability for copyright infringement. This argument rests on a gross generalization that cannot withstand scrutiny. The producer in *Kalem* did not merely provide the "means" to accomplish an infringing activity; the producer supplied the work itself, albeit in a new medium of expression. Petitioners in the instant case do not supply Betamax consumers with respondents' works; respondents do. Petitioners supply a piece of equipment that is generally capable of copying the entire range of programs that may be televised: those that are uncopyrighted, those that are copyrighted but may be copied without objection from the copyright holder, and those that the copyright holder would prefer not to have copied. The Betamax can be used to make authorized or unauthorized uses of copyrighted works, but the range of its potential use is much broader than the particular infringing use of the film *Ben Hur* involved in *Kalem*. *Kalem* does not support respondents' novel theory of liability.

Justice Holmes stated that the producer had "contributed" to the infringement of the copyright, and the label "contributory infringement" has been applied in a number of lower court copyright cases involving an ongoing relationship between the direct infringer and the contributory infringer at the time the infringing conduct occurred. In such cases, as in other situations in which the imposition of vicarious liability is manifestly just, the "contributory" infringer was in a position to control the use of copyrighted works by others and had authorized the use without permission from the copyright owner. This case, however, plainly does not fall in that category. The only contact between Sony and the users of the Betamax that is disclosed by this record occurred at the moment of sale. The District

Court expressly found that "no employee of Sony, Sonam or DDBI had either direct involvement with the allegedly infringing activity or direct contact with purchasers of Betamax who recorded copyrighted works off-the-air." And it further found that "there was no evidence that any of the copies made by Griffiths or the other individual witnesses in this suit were influenced or encouraged by [Sony's] advertisements."

If vicarious liability is to be imposed on petitioners in this case, it must rest on the fact that they have sold equipment with constructive knowledge of the fact that their customers may use that equipment to make unauthorized copies of copyrighted material. There is no precedent in the law of copyright for the imposition of vicarious liability on such a theory. The closest analogy is provided by the patent law cases to which it is appropriate to refer because of the historic kinship between patent law and copyright law.

In the Patent Code both the concept of infringement and the concept of contributory infringement are expressly defined by statute. The prohibition against contributory infringement is confined to the knowing sale of a component especially made for use in connection with a particular patent. There is no suggestion in the statute that one patentee may object to the sale of a product that might be used in connection with other patents. Moreover, the Act expressly provides that the sale of a "staple article or commodity of commerce suitable for substantial noninfringing use" is not contributory infringement. 35 U.S.C. § 271(c).

When a charge of contributory infringement is predicated entirely on the sale of an article of commerce that is used by the purchaser to infringe a patent, the public interest in access to that article of commerce is necessarily implicated. A finding of contributory infringement does not, of course, remove the article from the market altogether; it does, however, give the patentee effective control over the sale of that item. Indeed, a finding of contributory infringement is normally the functional equivalent of holding that the disputed article is within the monopoly granted to the patentee.

For that reason, in contributory infringement cases arising under the patent laws the Court has always recognized the critical importance of not allowing the patentee to extend his monopoly beyond the limits of his specific grant. These cases deny the patentee any right to control the distribution of unpatented articles unless they are "unsuited for any commercial noninfringing use." *Dawson Chemical Co. v. Rohm & Hass Co.,* 448 U.S. 176, 198, 100 S.Ct. 2601, 2614, 65 L.Ed.2d 696 (1980). Unless a commodity "has no use except through practice of the patented method," *ibid,* the patentee has no right to claim that its distribution constitutes contributory infringement. "To form the basis for contributory infringement the item must almost be uniquely suited as a component of the patented invention." P. Rosenberg, Patent Law Fundamentals § 17.02[2] (1982). "[A] sale of an article which though adapted to an infringing use is also adapted to other and lawful uses, is not enough to make the seller a contributory infringer. Such a rule would block the wheels of commerce."

Henry v. A.B. Dick Co., 224 U.S. 1, 48, 32 S.Ct. 364, 379, 56 L.Ed. 645 (1912), overruled on other grounds, *Motion Picture Patents Co. v. Universal Film Mfg. Co.,* 243 U.S. 502, 517, 37 S.Ct. 416, 421, 61 L.Ed. 871 (1917).

We recognize there are substantial differences between the patent and copyright laws. But in both areas the contributory infringement doctrine is grounded on the recognition that adequate protection of a monopoly may require the courts to look beyond actual duplication of a device or publication to the products or activities that make such duplication possible. The staple article of commerce doctrine must strike a balance between a copyright holder's legitimate demand for effective—not merely symbolic—protection of the statutory monopoly, and the rights of others freely to engage in substantially unrelated areas of commerce. Accordingly, the sale of copying equipment, like the sale of other articles of commerce, does not constitute contributory infringement if the product is widely used for legitimate, unobjectionable purposes. Indeed, it need merely be capable of substantial noninfringing uses.

IV

The question is thus whether the Betamax is capable of commercially significant noninfringing uses. In order to resolve that question, we need not explore *all* the different potential uses of the machine and determine whether or not they would constitute infringement. Rather, we need only consider whether on the basis of the facts as found by the district court a significant number of them would be non-infringing. Moreover, in order to resolve this case we need not give precise content to the question of how much use is commercially significant. For one potential use of the Betamax plainly satisfies this standard, however it is understood: private, noncommercial time-shifting in the home. It does so both (A) because respondents have no right to prevent other copyright holders from authorizing it for their programs, and (B) because the District Court's factual findings reveal that even the unauthorized home time-shifting of respondents' programs is legitimate fair use.

A. *Authorized Time–Shifting*

Each of the respondents owns a large inventory of valuable copyrights, but in the total spectrum of television programming their combined market share is small. The exact percentage is not specified, but it is well below 10%. If they were to prevail, the outcome of this litigation would have a significant impact on both the producers and the viewers of the remaining 90% of the programming in the Nation. No doubt, many other producers share respondents' concern about the possible consequences of unrestricted copying. Nevertheless the findings of the District Court make it clear that time-shifting may enlarge the total viewing audience and that many producers are willing to allow private time-shifting to continue, at least for an experimental time period.

The District Court found:

Even if it were deemed that home-use recording of copyrighted material constituted infringement, the Betamax could still legally be used to record noncopyrighted material or material whose owners consented to the copying. An injunction would deprive the public of the ability to use the Betamax for this noninfringing off-the-air recording.

Defendants introduced considerable testimony at trial about the potential for such copying of sports, religious, educational and other programming. This included testimony from representatives of the Offices of the Commissioners of the National Football, Basketball, Baseball and Hockey Leagues and Associations, the Executive Director of National Religious Broadcasters and various educational communications agencies. Plaintiffs attack the weight of the testimony offered and also contend that an injunction is warranted because infringing uses outweigh noninfringing uses.

Whatever the future percentage of legal versus illegal home-use recording might be, an injunction which seeks to deprive the public of the very tool or article of commerce capable of some noninfringing use would be an extremely harsh remedy, as well as one unprecedented in copyright law.

Although the District Court made these statements in the context of considering the propriety of injunctive relief, the statements constitute a finding that the evidence concerning "sports, religious, educational, and other programming" was sufficient to establish a significant quantity of broadcasting whose copying is now authorized, and a significant potential for future authorized copying. That finding is amply supported by the record. In addition to the religious and sports officials identified explicitly by the District Court, two items in the record deserve specific mention.

First is the testimony of John Kenaston, the station manager of Channel 58, an educational station in Los Angeles affiliated with the Public Broadcasting Service. He explained and authenticated the station's published guide to its programs. For each program, the guide tells whether unlimited home taping is authorized, home taping is authorized subject to certain restrictions (such as erasure within seven days), or home taping is not authorized at all. The Spring 1978 edition of the guide described 107 programs. Sixty-two of those programs or 58% authorize some home taping. Twenty-one of them or almost 20% authorize unrestricted home taping.

Second is the testimony of Fred Rogers, president of the corporation that produces and owns the copyright on *Mr. Rogers' Neighborhood*. The program is carried by more public television stations than any other program. Its audience numbers over 3,000,000 families a day. He testified that he had absolutely no objection to home taping for noncommercial use and expressed the opinion that it is a real service to families to be able to record children's programs and to show them at appropriate times.

If there are millions of owners of VTR's who make copies of televised sports events, religious broadcasts, and educational programs such as

Mister Rogers' Neighborhood, and if the proprietors of those programs welcome the practice, the business of supplying the equipment that makes such copying feasible should not be stifled simply because the equipment is used by some individuals to make unauthorized reproductions of respondents' works. The respondents do not represent a class composed of all copyright holders. Yet a finding of contributory infringement would inevitably frustrate the interests of broadcasters in reaching the portion of their audience that is available only through time-shifting.

Of course, the fact that other copyright holders may welcome the practice of time-shifting does not mean that respondents should be deemed to have granted a license to copy their programs. Third party conduct would be wholly irrelevant in an action for direct infringement of respondents' copyrights. But in an action for *contributory* infringement against the seller of copying equipment, the copyright holder may not prevail unless the relief that he seeks affects only his programs, or unless he speaks for virtually all copyright holders with an interest in the outcome. In this case, the record makes it perfectly clear that there are many important producers of national and local television programs who find nothing objectionable about the enlargement in the size of the television audience that results from the practice of time-shifting for private home use. The seller of the equipment that expands those producers' audiences cannot be a contributory infringer if, as is true in this case, it has had no direct involvement with any infringing activity.

B. *Unauthorized Time–Shifting*

Even unauthorized uses of a copyrighted work are not necessarily infringing. An unlicenced use of the copyright is not an infringement unless it conflicts with one of the specific exclusive rights conferred by the copyright statute. Moreover, the definition of exclusive rights in § 106 of the present Act is prefaced by the words "subject to sections 107 through 118." Those sections describe a variety of uses of copyrighted material that "are not infringements of copyright notwithstanding the provisions of § 106." The most pertinent in this case is § 107, the legislative endorsement of the doctrine of "fair use."

That section identifies various factors that enable a Court to apply an "equitable rule of reason" analysis to particular claims of infringement. Although not conclusive, the first factor requires that "the commercial or nonprofit character of an activity" be weighed in any fair use decision. If the Betamax were used to make copies for a commercial or profit-making purpose, such use would presumptively be unfair. The contrary presumption is appropriate here, however, because the District Court's findings plainly establish that time-shifting for private home use must be characterized as a noncommercial, nonprofit activity. Moreover, when one considers the nature of a televised copyrighted audiovisual work, and that timeshifting merely enables a viewer to see such a work which he had been invited to witness in its entirety free of charge, the fact that the entire work is reproduced, see *id.*, at § 107(3), does not have its ordinary effect of militating against a finding of fair use.

This is not, however, the end of the inquiry because Congress has also directed us to consider "the effect of the use upon the potential market for or value of the copyrighted work." *Id.*, at § 107(4). The purpose of copyright is to create incentives for creative effort. Even copying for noncommercial purposes may impair the copyright holder's ability to obtain the rewards that Congress intended him to have. But a use that has no demonstrable effect upon the potential market for, or the value of, the copyrighted work need not be prohibited in order to protect the author's incentive to create. The prohibition of such noncommercial uses would merely inhibit access to ideas without any countervailing benefit.

Thus, although every commercial use of copyrighted material is presumptively an unfair exploitation of the monopoly privilege that belongs to the owner of the copyright, noncommercial uses are a different matter. A challenge to a noncommercial use of a copyrighted work requires proof either that the particular use is harmful, or that if it should become widespread, it would adversely affect the potential market for the copyrighted work. Actual present harm need not be shown; such a requirement would leave the copyright holder with no defense against predictable damage. Nor is it necessary to show with certainty that future harm will result. What is necessary is a showing by a preponderance of the evidence that *some* meaningful likelihood of future harm exists. If the intended use is for commercial gain, that likelihood may be presumed. But if it is for a noncommercial purpose, the likelihood must be demonstrated.

In this case, respondents failed to carry their burden with regard to home time-shifting. The District Court described respondents' evidence as follows:

> Plaintiffs' experts admitted at several points in the trial that the time-shifting without librarying would result in "not a great deal of harm." Plaintiffs' greatest concern about time-shifting is with "a point of important philosophy that transcends even commercial judgment."They fear that with any Betamax usage, 'invisible boundaries' are passed: "the copyright owner has lost control over his program."

Later in its opinion, the District Court observed:

> Most of plaintiffs' predictions of harm hinge on speculation about audience viewing patterns and ratings, a measurement system which Sidney Sheinberg, MCA's president, calls a "black art" because of the significant level of imprecision involved in the calculations.

There was no need for the District Court to say much about past harm. "Plaintiffs have admitted that no actual harm to their copyrights has occurred to date."

On the question of potential future harm from time-shifting, the District Court offered a more detailed analysis of the evidence. It rejected respondents' "fear that persons 'watching' the original telecast of a program will not be measured in the live audience and the ratings and revenues will decrease," by observing that current measurement technology allows the Betamax audience to be reflected. It rejected respondents' prediction "that live television or movie audiences will decrease as more people watch Betamax tapes as an alternative," with the observation that "[t]here is no factual basis for [the underlying] assumption." It rejected respondents' "fear that time-shifting will reduce audiences for telecast reruns," and concluded instead that "given current market practices, this should aid plaintiffs rather than harm them." And it declared that respondents' suggestion "that theater or film rental exhibition of a program will suffer because of time-shift recording of that program" "lacks merit."

After completing that review, the District Court restated its overall conclusion several times, in several different ways. "Harm from time-shifting is speculative and, at best, minimal." "The audience benefits from the time-shifting capability have already been discussed. It is not implausible that benefits could also accrue to plaintiffs, broadcasters, and advertisers, as the Betamax makes it possible for more persons to view their broadcasts." "No likelihood of harm was shown at trial, and plaintiffs admitted that there had been no actual harm to date." "Testimony at trial suggested that Betamax may require adjustments in marketing strategy, but it did not establish even a likelihood of harm." "Television production by plaintiffs today is more profitable than it has ever been, and, in five weeks of trial, there was no concrete evidence to suggest that the Betamax will change the studios' financial picture."

The District Court's conclusions are buttressed by the fact that to the extent time-shifting expands public access to freely broadcast television programs, it yields societal benefits. Earlier this year, in *Community Television of Southern California v. Gottfried,* 459 U.S. 498, 508, n. 12 (1983), we acknowledged the public interest in making television broadcasting more available. Concededly, that interest is not unlimited. But it supports an interpretation of the concept of "fair use" that requires the copyright holder to demonstrate some likelihood of harm before he may condemn a private act of time-shifting as a violation of federal law.

When these factors are all weighed in the "equitable rule of reason" balance, we must conclude that this record amply supports the District Court's conclusion that home time-shifting is fair use. In light of the findings of the District Court regarding the state of the empirical data, it is clear that the Court of Appeals erred in holding that the statute as presently written bars such conduct.

In summary, the record and findings of the District Court lead us to two conclusions. First, Sony demonstrated a significant likelihood that substantial numbers of copyright holders who license their works for broadcast on free television would not object to having their broadcasts time-shifted by private viewers. And second, respondents failed to demonstrate that time-shifting would cause any likelihood of nonminimal harm to the potential market for, or the value of, their copyrighted works. The Betamax is, therefore, capable of substantial noninfringing uses. Sony's sale of such equipment to the general public does not constitute contributory infringement of respondent's copyrights.

V

The direction of Art. I is that *Congress* shall have the power to promote the progress of science and the useful arts. When, as here, the Constitution is permissive, the sign of how far Congress has chosen to go can come only from Congress. *Deepsouth Packing Co. v. Laitram Corp.*, 406 U.S. 518, 530, 92 S.Ct. 1700, 1707, 32 L.Ed.2d 273 (1972).

One may search the Copyright Act in vain for any sign that the elected representatives of the millions of people who watch television every day have made it unlawful to copy a program for later viewing at home, or have enacted a flat prohibition against the sale of machines that make such copying possible.

It may well be that Congress will take a fresh look at this new technology, just as it so often has examined other innovations in the past. But it is not our job to apply laws that have not yet been written. Applying the copyright statute, as it now reads, to the facts as they have been developed in this case, the judgment of the Court of Appeals must be reversed.

It is so ordered.

[The opinion of Justice Blackmun, joined by Justices Marshall, Powell and Rehnquist, dissenting, is omitted.]

NOTES

1. Justice Blackmun's lengthy dissenting opinion in Sony v. Universal reads more like a majority opinion—probably because at one point it was. Justice Thurgood Marshall's Court papers, opened to the public a decade after the decision, reveal that a majority of Justices initially lined up with Blackmun's position and that Blackmun had been assigned to write the majority opinion. Six days after oral argument, Justice Stevens, who had planned to write the dissenting opinion, wrote to Blackmun suggesting that he and his adherents reconsider whether the statute excepted private copies from liability. Subsequently, Justice Brennan, who had initially voted with the majority, proposed a subtle but crucial shift in the test for contributory infringement, to have it ask not whether the VCR's "primary use" was to infringe, but rather whether the equipment had a "substantial noninfringing use," in which case there would be no liability. Justice White agreed with Brennan's reformulation of the test for contributory infringement, and at the same time, Justice O'Connor was moving toward reversal because "I have considerable difficulty in rejecting the District Court's view that the respondents suffered no harm, actual or potential, as a result of Sony's use."

Although it was clear by the end of the Term that a new majority position had emerged, time was too short for the preparation of a new opinion. The Court put the case down for reargument the next year and the final tally, as announced in the Court's January 17, 1984 decision was Brennan, Burger, O'Connor, Stevens, and White to reverse the Ninth Circuit; Blackmun, Marshall, Powell, and Rehnquist to affirm. Justice Stevens's opinion for the majority resembled the Brennan and O'Connor memos of the previous term more than it did his original dissent. The opinion made no mention of a statutory exemption for private copying.

The history of the Court's decision is recounted in Jonathan Band & Andrew J. McLaughlin, The Marshall Papers: A Peek Behind the Scenes at the Making of Sony v. Universal, 17 Colum.—VLA J.L. & Arts 427 (1993); Paul Goldstein, Copyright's Highway: From Gutenberg to the Celestial Jukebox 149–156 (1994).

2. *Secondary Liability: Case Law.* The ease and economy with which copyrighted texts, images and sounds can be uploaded and downloaded on digital information networks, and the potential loss of paying customers to an information freeway, have led copyright owners to argue for the imposition of secondary liability on network service providers. Service providers have responded that the volume and pace of message transmission make it impossible for them to monitor copyright infringements as they would need to do if they were subject to copyright liability.

In Religious Technology Center v. Netcom On–Line Communication Services, Inc., 907 F.Supp. 1361, 37 U.S.P.Q.2d 1545 (N.D.Cal.1995), which presented "an issue of first impression regarding intellectual property rights in cyberspace," and has since been widely followed, the court considered whether Netcom, a major Internet access provider, should be subjected to copyright liability for facilitating the alleged direct infringements of plaintiff's works by an individual who subscribed to a computer bulletin board that Netcom connected to the Internet. Plaintiff, which conceded that Netcom did not itself originate any of the infringements, argued that "it nonetheless should be liable for infringement, either directly, contributorily, or vicariously." 907 F.Supp. at 1365, 1367.

The court ruled first that Netcom was not "directly liable for the copies that are made and stored on its computer. Where the infringing subscriber is clearly directly liable for the same act, it does not make sense to adopt a rule that could lead to the liability of countless parties whose role in the infringement is nothing more than setting up and operating a system that is necessary for the functioning of the Internet. Such a result is unnecessary as there is already a party directly liable for causing the copies to be made." 907 F.Supp. at 1372.

Against Netcom's argument, based on the landlord-tenant line of cases, that it lacked the knowledge required for a finding of contributory infringement because it did not know of the planned direct infringements before they were made, the court ruled that, unlike a landlord, defendant retained some control over the use of its system, so that the relevant "time frame" was when it made its services available to the direct infringer. "Thus, it is fair, assuming Netcom is able to take simple measures to prevent further damage to plaintiffs' copyrighted works, to hold Netcom liable for contributory infringement where Netcom has knowledge of [alleged direct infringer] Erlich's infringing postings yet continues to aid in the accomplishment of Erlich's purpose of publicly distributing the postings." 907 F.Supp. at 1375.

For purposes of vicarious liability, the court treated Netcom's "prohibition of copyright infringement and its requirement that its subscribers indemnify it for any damage to third parties" as evidence of its right and ability to control the infringing activity. However, the court found the required direct financial benefit missing: "Netcom receives a fixed fee. There is no evidence that infringement by Erlich, or any other user of Netcom's services, in any way enhances the value of Netcom's services to subscribers or attracts new subscribers." 907 F.Supp. at 1377. The court relied in part for this conclusion on the district court decision in *Fonovisa*. Would it have reached the opposite result after the reversal in that case, page 678 above?

See generally Alfred C. Yen, Internet Service Provider Liability for Subscriber Copyright Infringement, Enterprise Liability, and the First Amendment, 88 Geo. L.J. 1833 (2000).

Should network providers receive any more generous treatment than book and record store owners who are subject to strict liability for public distribution of infringing copies or phonorecords? Than photofinishers who process millions of copyrighted photographs each day and are also strictly liable? See, e.g., Olan Mills, Inc. v. Linn Photo Co., 23 F.3d 1345, 30 U.S.P.Q.2d 1798 (8th Cir.1994). Would imposition of liability on service providers simply lead to blanket licensing arrangements of the sort already administered for musical compositions by ASCAP and BMI, page 735, below? Frank Music Corp. v. CompuServe, Inc., No. 93 Civ. 8153 (S.D.N.Y., JFK), a 1993 copyright class action brought by music publishers against industry giant CompuServe, whose MIDI/Music forum allegedly enabled subscribers to upload and download copyrighted compositions without permission, ended with a settlement agreement calling for a lump sum payment for past infringements and, for the future, a blanket license from the licensing arm of the National Music Publisher's Association. 51 Pat., Trademark & Copyright J. (B.N.A.) 48 (Nov. 9, 1995).

3. *Secondary Liability: Legislation.* Title II of the Digital Millennium Copyright Act, P.L. No. 105–304 (Oct. 28, 1998), adds a new section 512 to the 1976 Copyright Act, giving Internet service providers safe harbors from direct or secondary copyright liability when they offer transmission or routing services, information location tools or system caching or storage. The amendments generally define "service provider" as "a provider of online services or network access, or the operator of facilities therefor," and the safe harbors supplement any other defenses a service provider may enjoy.

Each safe harbor prescribes its own conditions. In addition, an on-line service provider must implement and inform its users of a policy for terminating service to repeat infringers, and must accommodate standard technical measures, such as digital watermarks, used by copyright owners to identify and protect their works. Some of the safe harbors will be available only if the OSP complies with prescribed notice and take down procedures enabling copyright owners to notify an OSP that their copyrights are being infringed by material on the OSP's system.

In addition to insulating qualified OSPs from liability for monetary relief, section 512 limits the availability of injunctive relief. OSPs engaged only in transmission and routing are generally immune from both monetary and injunctive relief. In other cases—storage and information systems, system caching—an OSP can be enjoined from providing access to infringing material and ordered to terminate the accounts of subscribers who engage in infringing conduct.

4. *Napster.* No new technology has presented a greater perceived threat to copyright owners than the sharing of copyrighted works stored in easily transmitted and reproduced digital formats such as MP3. One example, described by the court in A & M Records, Inc. v. Napster, Inc., 239 F.3d 1004,1011, 57 U.S.P.Q.2d 1729 (9th Cir.2001), is the Napster system that enabled its users to "(1) make MP3 music files stored on individual computer hard drives available for copying by other Napster users; (2) search for MP3 music files stored on other users' computers; and (3) transfer exact copies of the contents of other users' MP3 files from one computer to another via the Internet."

The court of appeals affirmed the district court's ruling that Napster was contributorily and vicariously liable for direct infringements by its subscribers. The system was contributorily liable because it had notice, both actual and constructive, of the direct infringement, and materially contributed to the infringing conduct. It was vicariously liable because it retained the right to control user access to the system; the fact that the availability of copyrighted works served as a "draw" for customers, satisfied the requirement of financial benefit. 239 F.3d 1004.

Against Napster's argument that its subscribers' use of the system was fair use, the court ruled that the copies being made were neither transformative nor noncommercial (copies "were made to save the expense of purchasing authorized copies"); the copied works were creative, and thus close to the core purpose of copyright protection; entire works were copied; and the system had a "deleterious effect on the present and future digital download market." 239 F.3d 1015–1017.

The appellate court did, however, reject the district court's categorical conclusion that section 512(d)'s safe harbor for information location tools is unavailable to contributory infringers. The court also held that the preliminary relief ordered by the district court was "overbroad because it places on Napster the entire burden of ensuring that no 'copying, downloading, uploading, transmitting, or distributing' of plaintiffs' works occur on the system. As stated, we place the burden on plaintiffs to provide notice to Napster of copyrighted works and files containing such works available on the Napster system before Napster has the duty to disable access to the offending content. Napster, however, also bears the burden of policing the system within the limits of the system. Here, we recognize that this is not an exact science in that the files are user named. In crafting the injunction on remand, the district court should recognize that Napster's system does not currently appear to allow Napster access to users' MP3 files." 239 F.3d at1027.

5. *Criminal Liability.* The Copyright Act has long imposed criminal liability on anyone who willfully infringes a copyright for purposes of financial gain. By 1997, however, it was evident that the great bulk of copyright uses on the Internet lacked financial gain as a motive, a perception spurred by United States v. LaMacchia, 871 F.Supp. 535, 33 U.S.P.Q.2d 1978 (D.Mass. 1994), a failed wire fraud prosecution, where, for lack of the required financial motive, the government had been unable to charge defendant, an MIT student, with criminal copyright infringement for facilitating the uploading and downloading of copyrighted software on an electronic bulletin board. The No Electronic Theft Act, Pub. L. No. 105–147, 111 Stat. 267, 268, enacted that year, introduced a new formulation of "financial gain" into section 101 of the 1976 Act: "The term 'financial gain' includes receipt, or expectation of receipt, of anything of value, including the receipt of other copyrighted works." According to the House Report, this language will enable "authorities to prosecute someone like La Macchia who steals or helps others to steal copyrighted works but who otherwise does not profit financially from the theft." H.R. Rep. No. 105–339, 105th Cong., 1st Sess. at 7 (1997).

See generally Lydia Pallas Loren, Digitization, Commodification, Criminalization: The Evolution of Criminal Copyright Infringement and the Importance of the Willfulness Requirement, 77 Wash. U. L. Q. 835 (1999).

6. *Encryption and Liability for Circumvention.* Some copyright owners have turned to encryption of content to augment copyright protection for their works. This self-help tactic has much in common with the industrial strategy of erecting walls of secrecy around technical know-how, with the difference that where trade secret law broadly permits reverse engineering, copyright owners have obtained federal anti-circumvention legislation barring all but a small number of inroads into their encrypted content.

Section 1201, added to Title 17 of the U.S. Code (but not as part of the Copyright Act) by the Digital Millennium Copyright Act, P.L. No. 105–304 (Oct. 28, 1998), regulates the circumvention of technological measures that prevent either unauthorized access, or the unauthorized exercise of rights, to a copyrighted work, either directly or through the manufacture, distribution or traffic in circumvention devices. To be subject to liability, an offending device must have circumvention as its primary purpose, must have only a limited commercial purpose other than circumvention, or must be marketed for use in circumvention. Several exceptions to liability aim to approximate traditional copyright exemptions and defenses. Section 1201(f), for example, carves out a reverse engineering exception that allows software developers to identify and copy elements of a computer program essential to interoperability.

What reason is there to superimpose regulatory solutions on a copyright law that has historically relied on crisply-formulated rights and privately-negotiated transactions to put literary and artistic works to their highest and best use? Do these regulatory structures improperly distort incentives to create and to use copyrighted works? Section 1202 of Title 17, also added by the Digital Millennium Copyright Act, aims to support market transactions by fostering the dissemination of ownership and licensing information about copyrighted works. Is section 1201 susceptible to attack under the free speech guarantee of the First Amendment? See Universal v. Corley page 873 below.

See generally Glynn Lunney, Jr., The Death of Copyright: Digital Technology, Private Copying, and the Digital Millennium Copyright Act, 87 Va. L. Rev. 813 (2001).

7. *Private Copies Abroad.* Unlike U.S. copyright law, which does not categorically immunize private copies, copyright legislation in other countries expressly exempts small numbers of copies made for research or other private purposes. For example, section 29(1) of the Copyright, Designs & Patents Act in Britain exempts "[f]air dealing with a literary, dramatic, musical or artistic work for the purposes of research or private study," and Article 30 of the Japanese Copyright Act permits copying within a family or similarly limited circle, so long as it does not employ publicly available photocopiers. Article 53 of the German Copyright Act exempts single copies made for specified private or personal uses and Article 54 establishes a compulsory license for photocopying on a larger scale, imposing a levy on manufacturers of photocopying equipment and on the educational and research institutions and copy shops that operate the equipment. In France, Articles L. 121–10 through L. 121–12 of the Intellectual Property Code contemplate photocopying licenses administered by reprographic collecting societies.

NOTE: COLLECTING SOCIETIES

Institutions will often be more effective than legal rules in reducing the transaction costs of obtaining payment for dispersed copyright uses. Copyright collecting societies first appeared in Europe in 1851 and have since flourished around the world, but have made more limited inroads in the United States where traditions of individual bargaining continue to have a strong influence.

Musical Performance Rights. In 1914, responding to the decline of sheet music sales and the rise of new media for public performance, Victor Herbert led several composers, authors and music publishers to form ASCAP. They organized ASCAP as a nonprofit association to pool the nondramatic ("small") performance rights in members' musical compositions for licensing to anyone who wished to make a nondramatic public performance for profit. Under this arrangement, ASCAP would give a blanket license to perform its repertory, and the royalties collected would be distributed among association members according to a schedule that accounted for the general character and standing of their works and for the number of times each work was performed. In calendar year 2000, ASCAP distributed $480.3 million to its 129,748 writer, publisher and associate members. Radio and television networks and stations are ASCAP's major licensees; restaurants, night clubs and hotels also purchase licenses.

ASCAP's success invited competition—and antitrust regulation. Competition came from broadcasters, who formed Broadcast Music, Inc. (BMI) in 1939. BMI has proved to be a worthy rival. Together with ASCAP, it controls the small performance rights to virtually all domestic copyrighted musical compositions. A consent decree entered in March, 1941 terminating Justice Department charges filed earlier that year, significantly resolved ASCAP's antitrust exposure. The 1941 decree was amended in 1950 and 1960 to relax the society's membership requirements, adjust voting rights, put revenue distributions on a more objective basis and impose reasonable royalties when ASCAP and an applicant are unable to reach agreement. The consent decree was again revised in 2000; among the changes, Internet companies obtained the same licensing rights as broadcasters and ASCAP was required to make a list of its repertory available online so that users unwilling to take a blanket license can steer clear of the society's repertory. BMI is also governed by an antitrust consent decree. In Broadcast Music, Inc. v. Columbia Broadcasting System, Inc., 441 U.S. 1, 24, 99 S.Ct. 1551, 60 L.Ed.2d 1, 201 U.S.P.Q. 497 (1979), the Supreme Court reversed a court of appeals ruling that the ASCAP and BMI blanket licenses constituted *per se* price fixing under the antitrust laws, and held that they should instead "be subjected to a more discriminating examination under the rule of reason."

On the operations of ASCAP, BMI and SESAC—a much smaller collecting society—see Sidney Shemel & M. William Krasilovsky, This Business of Music 182–201 (5th ed. 1985).

Literary Reproduction Rights. The Senate Report on the bill that eventually became the 1976 Copyright Act recommended the development of workable clearance procedures for library photocopying. S.Rep. No. 94–473, 94th Cong., 1st Sess. at 70–71 (1975). On January 1, 1978—the day the 1976 Act came into effect—the Copyright Clearance Center began operations. Organized by publishers, the CCC facilitates the collection of photocopying fees from users and the distribution of fees to member publishers.

The CCC has employed two collecting mechanisms. Under the Transactional Reporting System, the first page of each work registered with the CCC will indicate a copying permission fee and instructions for remitting the fee to the CCC for each copy made; the CCC then distributes the fees collected for each work to the member who owns the copyright in the work. Under its Annual Authorization Service, the CCC audits a user's photocopying activity and uses this audit to derive a statistical model indicating the frequency with which the user photocopies works of particular publishers; this model becomes the basis for determining the user's annual license fee and each individual publisher's entitlement.

For an institutional and comparative overview of copyright collecting societies, see Stanley M. Besen & Sheila Nataraj Kirby, Compensating Creators of Intellectual Property: Collectives that Collect (1989). The operations of collecting societies around the world are profiled in David Sinacore–Guinn, International Guide to Collective Administrative Organizations (1993).

2.   REMEDIES

See Statute Supplement 17 U.S.C.A. §§ 412, 502–513.

Copyright Law Revision, H.R. Rep. No. 1476

94th Cong., 2d Sess. 160–164 (1976).

Section 502.   Injunctions

Section 502(a) reasserts the discretionary power of courts to grant injunctions and restraining orders, whether "preliminary," "temporary," "interlocutory," "permanent," or "final," to prevent or stop infringements of copyright. This power is made subject to the provisions of section 1498 of title 28, dealing with infringement actions against the United States. The latter reference in section 502(a) makes it clear that the bill would not permit the granting of an injunction against an infringement for which the Federal Government is liable under section 1498.

Under subsection (b), which is the counterpart of provisions in sections 112 and 113 of the present statute, a copyright owner who has obtained an injunction in one State will be able to enforce it against a defendant located anywhere else in the United States.

Section 503.   Impounding and Disposition of Infringing Articles

The two subsections of section 503 deal respectively with the courts' power to impound allegedly infringing articles during the time an action is pending, and to order the destruction or other disposition of articles found to be infringing. In both cases the articles affected include "all copies or phonorecords" which are claimed or found "to have been made or used in violation of the copyright owner's exclusive rights," and also "all plates, molds, matrices, masters, tapes, film negatives, or other articles by means of which such copies of phonorecords may be reproduced." The alternative phrase "made or used" in both subsections enables a court to deal as it sees fit with articles which, though reproduced and acquired lawfully, have been used for infringing purposes such as rentals, performances, and displays.

Articles may be impounded under subsection (a) "at any time while an action under this title is pending," thus permitting seizures of articles alleged to be infringing as soon as suit has been filed and without waiting for an injunction. The same subsection empowers the court to order impounding "on such terms as it may deem reasonable." The present Supreme Court rules with respect to seizure and impounding were issued even though there is no specific provision authorizing them in the copyright statute, and there appears no need for including a special provision on the point in the bill.

Under section 101(d) of the present statute, articles found to be infringing may be ordered to be delivered up for destruction. Section 503(b) of the bill would make this provision more flexible by giving the court discretion to order "destruction or other reasonable disposition" of the articles found to be infringing. Thus, as part of its final judgment or decree, the court could order the infringing articles sold, delivered to the plaintiff, or disposed of in some other way that would avoid needless waste and best serve the ends of justice.

Section 504.   Damages and Profits

In General

A cornerstone of the remedies sections and of the bill as a whole is section 504, the provision dealing with recovery of actual damages, profits, and statutory damages. The two basic aims of this section are reciprocal and correlative: (1) to give the courts specific unambiguous directions concerning monetary awards, thus avoiding the confusion and uncertainty that have marked the present law on the subject, and, at the same time, (2) to provide the courts with reasonable latitude to adjust recovery to the circumstances of the case, thus avoiding some of the artificial or overly technical awards resulting from the language of the existing statute.

Subsection (a) lays the groundwork for the more detailed provisions of the section by establishing the liability of a copyright infringer for either "the copyright owner's actual damages and any additional profits of the infringer," or statutory damages. Recovery of actual damages and profits under section 504(b) or of statutory damages under section 504(c) is alternative and for the copyright owner to elect; as under the present law, the plaintiff in an infringement suit is not obliged to submit proof of damages and profits and may choose to rely on the provision for minimum statutory damages. However, there is nothing in section 504 to prevent a court from taking account of evidence concerning actual damages and profits in making an award of statutory damages within the range set out in subsection (c).

Actual Damages and Profits

In allowing the plaintiff to recover "the actual damages suffered by him or her as a result of the infringement," plus any of the infringer's profits "that are attributable to the infringement and are not taken into account in computing the actual damages," section 504(b) recognizes the different purposes served by awards of damages and profits. Damages are awarded to compensate the copyright owner for losses from the infringement, and profits are awarded to prevent the infringer from unfairly benefiting from a wrongful act. Where the defendant's profits are nothing more than a measure of the damages suffered by the copyright owner, it would be inappropriate to award damages and profits cumulatively, since in effect they amount to the same thing. However, in cases where the copyright owner has suffered damages not reflected in the infringer's profits, or where there have been profits attributable to the copyrighted work but not used as a measure of damages, subsection (b) authorizes the award of both.

The language of the subsection makes clear that only those profits "attributable to the infringement" are recoverable; where some of the defendant's profits result from the infringement and other profits are caused by different factors, it will be necessary for the court to make an apportionment. However, the burden of proof is on the defendant in these cases; in establishing profits the plaintiff need prove only "the infringer's gross revenue," and the defendant must prove not only "his or her deductible expenses" but also "the element of profit attributable to factors other than the copyrighted work."

Statutory Damages

Subsection (c) of section 504 makes clear that the plaintiff's election to recover statutory damages may take place at any time during the trial before the court has rendered its final judgment. The remainder of clause (1) of the subsection represents a statement of the general rates applicable to awards of statutory damages.[1] Its principal provisions may be summarized as follows:

1. As a general rule, where the plaintiff elects to recover statutory damages, the court is obliged to award between $250 and $10,000. It can exercise discretion in awarding an amount within that range but, unless one of the exceptions provided by clause (2) is applicable, it cannot make an award of less than $250 or of more than $10,000 if the copyright owner has chosen recovery under section 504(c).

2. Although, as explained below, an award of minimum statutory damages may be multiplied if separate works and separately liable infringers are involved in the suit, a single award in the $250 to $10,000 range is to be made "for all infringements involved in the action." A single infringer of a single work is liable for a single amount between $250 and $10,000, no matter how many acts of infringement are involved in the action and regardless of whether the acts were separate, isolated, or occurred in a related series.

3. Where the suit involves infringement of more than one separate and independent work, minimum statutory damages for each work must be awarded. For example, if one defendant has infringed three copyrighted works, the copyright owner is entitled to statutory damages of at least $750 and may be awarded up to $30,000. Subsection (c)(1) makes clear, however, that, although they are regarded as independent works for other purposes, "all the parts of a compilation or derivative work constitute one work" for this purpose. Moreover, although the minimum and maximum amounts are to be multiplied where multiple "works" are involved in the suit, the same is not true with respect to multiple copyrights, multiple owners, multiple exclusive

---

1. Under section 504(c)(1), the present standard range of statutory damages is "not less than $750 or more than $30,000 as the court considers just."

rights, or multiple registrations. This point is especially important since, under a scheme of divisible copyright, it is possible to have the rights of a number of owners of separate "copyrights" in a single "work" infringed by one act of a defendant.

4. Where the infringements of one work were committed by a single infringer acting individually, a single award of statutory damages would be made. Similarly, where the work was infringed by two or more joint tort feasors, the bill would make them jointly and severally liable for an amount in the $250 to $10,000 range. However, where separate infringements for which two or more defendants are not jointly liable are joined in the same action, separate awards of statutory damages would be appropriate.

Clause (2) of section 504(c) provides for exceptional cases in which the maximum award of statutory damages could be raised from $10,000 to $50,000, and in which the minimum recovery could be reduced from $250 to $100.[2]

Stevens Linen Associates v. Mastercraft Corp.

United States Court of Appeals, Second Circuit, 1981.
656 F.2d 11, 210 U.S.P.Q. 865.

LUMBARD, Circuit Judge:

Plaintiff Stevens Linen Co. appeals from that part of an order entered in the Southern District of New York, Motley, J., denying plaintiff compensatory damages resulting from the copyright infringement of plaintiff's upholstery fabric entitled "Chestertown." The district court held that defendant's fabrics "Rio Grande" and "Grand Canyon" infringed plaintiff's copyright for its Chestertown fabric, granted a permanent injunction barring future sales of the infringing fabrics, and awarded plaintiff reasonable attorney's fees. The district court denied an award of compensatory damages, however, because it believed any damages suffered by plaintiff to be too speculative to be determined. We now modify the order and remand it for computation of damages.

I.

Stevens Linen Co. and defendant Mastercraft Corp. are direct competitors in the manufacture and marketing of woven upholstery fabrics. In the summer of 1976, a Stevens Linen employee created a new fabric design, known as Chestertown. The fabric was first shown publicly in July of 1976 and first sold in September of that year. A copyright registration was then obtained. Stevens Linen displayed the fabric in North Carolina at a national furniture market called the "High Point Market." After attending

---

2. Under section 504(c)(2), the current maximum award in the case of willful infringement is $150,000 and the current minimum award for innocent infringement is $200.

that market, a Mastercraft designer created the two infringing fabrics: Rio Grande and Grand Canyon.

Stevens commenced this suit on April 19, 1979, alleging that Master-craft's two fabrics infringed Steven's copyright for the Chestertown fabric. The district court found the Mastercraft fabrics to be substantially similar in appearance to Steven's copyrighted fabric and therefore entered an order of preliminary injunction, temporarily enjoining the sale of the infringing fabrics, on February 15, 1980. The order was affirmed by this court in an unpublished ruling on April 21, 1980.

A non-jury trial of the merits ensued. At trial, the parties again contested the issue of infringement. In addition, Stevens presented evidence to support several possible theories as to its damages from infringement. First, Mastercraft admitted having sold 253,867 yards of its Rio Grande and Grand Canyon fabrics. Therefore, Stevens claimed that it suffered damages of lost profits on the entire amount of Mastercraft's sales, since it could have sold this amount of Chestertown had there been no infringement. Stevens offered testimony that it had excess production capacity during the time of Mastercraft's sales.

Second, Stevens offered evidence that twenty-two of its Chestertown customers had also purchased Mastercraft's Rio Grande and Grand Canyon fabrics. These twenty-two customers purchased a total of 95,422⅝ yards of Mastercraft's two fabrics. Thus, Stevens argued that it was damaged at the minimum in the amount of lost profits on these sales. Stevens also placed into evidence the 14,234⅛ yards of sales by Mastercraft of its two fabrics to purchasers to whom Stevens had distributed samples of its Chestertown fabrics, and the 97,258 yards of Mastercraft sales to customers who had been solicited to purchase Chestertown.

Third, Stevens offered testimony by its Vice President and Director of Design as to Steven's original projections for Chestertown sales. Based upon the fact that Chestertown had tripled in sales from 1977 to 1978, Stevens had projected that sales would again triple in 1979 (to about 270,000 yards), would increase by about 12% in 1980, would begin tapering off in 1981, and would have a total sales life of about ten years. Stevens also introduced evidence of Chestertown's actual performance: in 1979, the year in which Mastercraft's fabrics were first sold in competition with Chestertown, sales increased only 4%, instead of the tripling projected, and in the first six months of 1980, sales of Chestertown declined by 64%.

Finally, Stevens compared the sales of Chestertown with its overall sales during the times in question. During 1978, before Mastercraft began sales of its two fabrics, Chestertown's sales had increased by 216%, while Stevens's overall sales increased by 37% and its sales not including Chestertown increased 30%. In 1979, when Mastercraft began its sales of Rio Grande and Grand Canyon, and when sales of Chestertown increased only 4%, Stevens's overall sales increased 28%, and sales without including Chestertown increased 30%. In the six months ending July 31, 1980, when Chestertown sales declined 64%, overall sales declined only 16% and sales not including Chestertown declined only 12%.

Stevens also introduced into evidence certain Mastercraft invoices for sales of Rio Grande and Grand Canyon. Twenty-four of the invoices, totalling 4,329⅜ yards with a total sales price of $15,362.91, carried dates subsequent to entry of the preliminary injunction. Stevens argued that it should be awarded that sum in addition to any compensatory damages for losses of sales prior to the granting of the preliminary injunction.

With respect to damages, Mastercraft pointed out that Stevens's Chestertown fabric was priced at $5.40 per yard, while Mastercraft's fabrics sold for approximately $3.50 per yard. Mastercraft's President testified that, because of the difference in price, he did not believe Stevens would have obtained all of Mastercraft's sales in the period in question. He also pointed to the existence of similar, cheaper fabrics on the market. Finally, Mastercraft offered evidence suggesting that the dates on the invoices in question did not reflect dates of shipping, but merely dates of billing.

The district court held that the two Mastercraft fabrics infringed Stevens's copyright for its Chestertown fabric. As for damages, the court noted that the applicable statute, 17 U.S.C. § 504 (1976 & Supp. III 1979), provides for an award of either the copyright owner's damages plus the infringer's profits or, at the election of the copyright owner, specified statutory damages, and that Stevens had elected to pursue actual damages and any of the infringer's profits. The court found that Mastercraft had indeed lost money on its infringing fabrics, and therefore no profits could be awarded. As to actual damages to Stevens, although finding that "it is reasonable to assume that the infringement affected plaintiff's sales," the court refused to award any compensatory damages, finding them too speculative.

The court specifically rejected the theory that Stevens would have sold additional amounts of its Chestertown fabric in the total amounts of the infringing fabrics sold by Mastercraft. It also rejected the theory that Stevens would have sold additional amounts of Chestertown to those of its customers who purchased both Chestertown and Mastercraft's fabrics. Finally, it dismissed the projections testified to by a Stevens employee as even more speculative than the other theories of lost sales. The court made no mention of either the comparison to sales of Stevens's other fabrics or the evidence as to post-injunction sales of Mastercraft's fabrics. The court did award Stevens its attorney's fees.

II.

We believe the district court erred in failing to award Stevens compensatory damages. In establishing lost sales due to sales of an infringing product, courts must necessarily engage in some degree of speculation. Although, as Mastercraft argues on appeal, there is a distinction between proof of causation—meaning proof that defendant's acts caused any harm to plaintiff at all—and proof of the amount of damage, in this case the district court found that Stevens's copyright had been infringed and that this infringement necessarily caused some loss of sales by Stevens. Therefore the only issue was the extent of that damage.

Given the difference in price between the infringed and infringing products, the district court was correct in refusing to grant to Stevens damages based upon the assumption that it would have sold the entire amount of fabric sold by Mastercraft. Moreover, it was also proper for the district court to reject the projections of Chestertown sales offered by Stevens's Vice President and Director of Design. While under other circumstances, such testimony might support an award of damages, here the testimony was completely devoid of documentary support, and the witness furnished the court with no basis for the projections and hence no basis on which the court could evaluate the validity of the projections.

Nevertheless, the district court should have awarded damages measured either (1) by lost profits which Stevens would have realized from sales to customers who bought both Stevens and Mastercraft fabrics, or (2) by lost profits based upon the difference between sales of Chestertown and the average sales of all of Stevens's other fabrics, whichever sum proves to be larger. As to the first theory, admittedly we cannot be certain that all of the purchases of these twenty-two customers would have been made from Stevens rather than Mastercraft had no infringing products been offered. Nevertheless, we can reasonably believe that these customers of Stevens had a demand for this type of fabric and were shifting their purchasing to the cheaper infringing fabrics and away from Chestertown. Although Stevens might not have made every one of Mastercraft's sales, we believe that once Stevens established that it had been damaged, and that its customers purchased both the infringed and the infringing products, the burden shifted to the infringer, Mastercraft, to prove that the customers of Chestertown to whom it sold would not have acquired from Stevens alone all of the yardage they purchased had there been no infringement.

Regarding the second plausible theory, we believe that, at the least, Stevens should be able to recover lost profits based upon the difference between its actual sales of Chestertown during the period in which it was forced to compete with the infringing fabrics and Stevens's average sales figures for its remaining fabric products. This approach was recently taken in a copyright infringement suit involving competing sales of infringing record albums. See Big Seven Music Corp. v. Lennon, 554 F.2d 504 (2d Cir.1977) (comparing sales of infringed album with sales of contemporary albums by same performer). We believe it more appropriate to compare sales of Chestertown to Stevens's sales for all of its fabrics *not including* Chestertown, since the Chestertown figures were clearly affected by competition with the infringing items, and since the object of the damages inquiry is to determine what sales probably would have been made without the infringement. Therefore, under this theory, the district court could award Stevens lost profits based upon the difference between the 4% increase in Chestertown sales in 1979 and the 30% sales increase in Stevens's other fabric lines, and the difference between the 64% decline in Chestertown sales in the first six months of 1980 and the 12% decline in Stevens's other products during that period.

Thus we must remand to the district court to determine the amount of damages. Under the first of the two foregoing measures, damages would be awarded in the amount of Stevens's lost profits for additional sales of Chestertown to those of its customers who also purchased the infringing fabrics, less profits on sales which Mastercraft proves that Stevens would not have made. The measure under the alternative theory would be lost profits based upon the difference between Chestertown sales in the period in question and Stevens's average sales of its other fabric products. Having calculated damages according to these two alternative measures, the court should award to Stevens whatever sum proves to be greater.

Finally, upon remand, the court should consider an additional award of damages based upon the Mastercraft invoices introduced by Stevens which bear dates subsequent to the entry of the injunction. Mastercraft argues on appeal that Stevens did not ask the district court to award these damages, but the trial record clearly refutes this position. Stevens entered these invoices into evidence and asked questions of Mastercraft employees concerning them. Mastercraft obviously saw the potentially damaging nature of these invoices for it responded by eliciting testimony suggesting that the dates on the invoices were billing dates rather than dates of delivery. The district court, however, made no findings as to these sales. With respect to any sales referred to in these invoices which Mastercraft cannot establish as having been made prior to the preliminary injunction, the total amount of the revenues received by Mastercraft from these sales should be awarded to Stevens.

Order modified and remanded for further proceedings consistent with this opinion.

Cream Records, Inc. v. Jos. Schlitz Brewing Co.

United States Court of Appeals, Ninth Circuit, 1985.
754 F.2d 826, 225 U.S.P.Q. 896.

PER CURIAM:

Appellant Cream sued appellees alleging that music in a TV commercial prepared by Benton and Bowles to advertise Schlitz beer infringed appellant's copyright on a popular rhythm and blues composition, "The Theme from Shaft."

The jury found infringement. By agreement of the parties the issue of damages was submitted to the court which awarded Cream a total of $17,000. Cream appealed.

DAMAGES

Schlitz applied to Cream for a one-year license to use the Shaft theme music in its commercial. Cream quoted a fee of $100,000. (Cream conceded at trial, and the district court found, that the market value of such a license was $80,000.) After Schlitz failed to take a license, another manufacturer approached Cream for a license but withdrew when the Schlitz commercial was aired. There was testimony that use of a well-known popular song in a commercial destroys its value to other advertisers for that purpose.

The district court awarded Cream $12,000 in damages for loss of the license fee. The court reasoned that the value of a license for use of the entire song for a year was $80,000, that only a small portion of the song was actually used in the Schlitz commercial, and the reasonable value of a license for use of that portion was 15% of the value of a license to use the entire song.

The only evidence before the court was that unauthorized use of the Shaft theme music in Schlitz's commercial ended Cream's opportunity to license the music for this purpose. There was no evidence that Schlitz sought, or Cream was willing to grant, a license for use of less than the entire copyrighted work, that a license limited to the portion used in the commercial would have had less value, or that use limited to this portion would have had a less devastating effect upon Cream's opportunity to license to another. Since defendants' unauthorized use destroyed the value of the copyrighted work for this purpose, plaintiff was entitled to recover that value as damages.

PROFITS

17 U.S.C. § 504(b) (1982) provides that, in addition to actual damages suffered as a result of the infringement, the copyright owner is entitled to recover "any profits of the infringer that are attributable to the infringement and are not taken into account in computing the actual damages." The statute also defines and allocates the burden of proof, providing, "[i]n establishing the infringer's profits, the copyright owner is required to present proof only of the infringer's gross revenue, and the infringer is required to prove his or her deductible expenses and the elements of profit attributable to factors other than the copyrighted work."

Schlitz. Cream offered proof that Schlitz's profit on malt liquor for the period during which the infringing commercial was broadcast was $4.876 million. Cream sought to recover $66,800 as the portion of Schlitz's profit attributable to the infringement, arguing that the expenditure for the infringing commercial constituted 13.7% of Schlitz's advertising budget for the year, the infringing music was responsible for 10% of the commercial's advertising power, and, therefore, 1.37% of the profit on malt liquor were attributable to the infringement.

The district court concluded that the infringement "was minimal," consisting principally of a ten-note ostinato, and that the infringing material did not add substantially to the value of the commercial. The court also concluded, however, that the commercial was successful, that "it sold some beer," and "that the music had a portion of that." The court continued, "So I have to find some profit of the defendants which is allocable to the infringement, but, as I say, I think it's minuscule. I have interpolated as best I can. They made a profit of $5 million. One-tenth of 1 percent is $5,000, so I will add that...."

Cream argues that since it established Schlitz's total profits from the sale of malt liquor, the burden was placed on Schlitz to prove any portion of the profits not attributable to the infringement, and since the defendants put on no evidence, Cream was entitled to recover the part of Schlitz's profits it sought. The court's lesser award, Cream argues, was wholly arbitrary, and supported by no evidence in the record.

Defendants respond that Cream failed to establish that any part of the profits from the sale of malt liquor were attributable to the commercial, much less to its infringing portion, and was therefore entitled to no share of the profits at all. One of the court's formal findings, prepared by defendants, might be read as stating that no causal connection had been shown between the infringement and defendants' profits. It is clear from the court's statements, including those quoted above, however, that the court concluded from the jury's verdict and from the evidence that some of the profits from malt liquor sales were in fact attributable to the use of plaintiff's copyrighted music in the commercial. The court determined the share of the profits attributable to the infringing material as best it could and awarded Cream ⅒oth of 1% of those profits. Defendants have not cross-appealed the judgment, and may not challenge the determination of causation upon which it rests.

We also reject Cream's contention. Although the statute imposes upon the infringer the burden of showing "the elements of profit attributable to factors other than the copyrighted work," 17 U.S.C. § 504(b), nonetheless where it is clear, as it is in this case, that not all of the profits are attributable to the infringing material, the copyright owner is not entitled to recover all of those profits merely because the infringer fails to establish with certainty the portion attributable to the non-infringing elements. "In cases such as this where an infringer's profits are not entirely due to the infringement, and the evidence suggests some division which may rationally be used as a springboard it is the duty of the court to make some apportionment." Orgel v. Clark Boardman Co., 301 F.2d 119, 121 (2d Cir.1962). As Learned Hand said in Sheldon v. Metro–Goldwyn Pictures Corp., 106 F.2d 45, 51 (2d Cir.1939), aff'd, 309 U.S. 390, 60 S.Ct. 681, 84 L.Ed. 825 (1940):

> But we are resolved to avoid the one certainly unjust course of giving the plaintiffs everything, because the defendants cannot with certainty compute their own share. In cases where plaintiffs fail to prove their damages exactly, we often make the best estimate we can, even though it is really no more than a guess and under the guise of resolving all doubts against the defendants we will not deny the one fact that stands undoubted.

By claiming only 1.37% of Schlitz's malt liquor profits, Cream recognizes the impropriety of awarding Cream all of Schlitz's profits on a record that reflects beyond argument that most of these profits were attributable to elements other than the infringement. As to the amount of profits attributable to the infringing material, "what is required is ... only a reasonable approximation," Sheldon v. Metro–Goldwyn Pictures Corp., 309

U.S. at 408, 60 S.Ct. at 688 and Cream's calculation is in the end no less speculative than that of the court. The disparity between the amount sought by Cream and the amount awarded by the court appears to rest not so much upon a difference in methods of calculation as upon a disagreement as to the extent to which the commercial infringed upon the copyright and the importance of the copyrighted material to the effectiveness of the commercial. These were determinations for the district court to make.

The parties agreed that the issue of damages and profits would be tried to the court. The jury's verdict did not expressly determine the degree to which the commercial infringed upon Cream's copyright. The court's factual findings, though perhaps unfavorable to Cream, do not conflict with the general verdict.

Benton. Cream claimed all of Benton's profit from the TV commercial; the district court awarded none at all. In announcing its judgment the court initially overlooked the claim against Benton. When alerted to the omission the court said, "I will somehow incorporate that into the profit that I awarded with respect to the company. I can't conceive of an award of more than the amount I gave. You can find Benton and Bowles' profit in there by reducing the amount of profit of the beer company."

Obviously it would be improper to assume the profits of the advertising company would be subsumed in the profits of the firm hiring it, if that was the court's intention. Indeed, the profits of the advertising firm were necessarily excluded from the award against the hiring company, since, under § 504(b), Schlitz must be allowed to deduct the monies paid to the advertising firm in calculating its profits.

To avoid unjust enrichment of Benton as a result of its unlawful use of Cream's copyrighted music, the district court must assess a separate award of damages against Benton by making a reasonable approximation of the portion of Benton's profits due to the use of the infringing music.

Plaintiff is awarded costs on appeal including reasonable attorney's fees in an amount to be determined by the district court.

Reversed and remanded for proceedings not inconsistent with this opinion.

NOTES

1. In a handful of short, bold strokes, section 504 of the 1976 Act resolved several questions that had vexed the 1909 Act's provisions for monetary awards. One question, whether the 1909 Act intended awards for damages and profits to be cumulative or alternative, had sharply divided the two major copyright circuits. Compare Thomas Wilson & Co. v. Irving J. Dorfman Co., 433 F.2d 409, 167 U.S.P.Q. 417 (2d Cir.1970), cert. denied, 401 U.S. 977, 91 S.Ct. 1200, 28 L.Ed.2d 326, 169 U.S.P.Q. 65 (1971) (cumulative) with Sid & Marty Krofft Television Productions, Inc. v. McDonald's Corp., 562 F.2d 1157, 196 U.S.P.Q. 97 (9th Cir.1977) (alternative). Section 504(b) strikes a balance between the Second Circuit's deterrent approach and the Ninth Circuit's compensatory approach by allowing the copyright owner to recover actual damages and any of the infringer's profits "not taken into account in computing the damages." Thus if, as one element of damages, the copyright owner recovers the profits it would have made on sales lost to the infringer, it can only recover the infringer's profits to the extent that they exceed the owner's lost profits.

Section 504(c), allowing the copyright owner to elect statutory damages, resolves earlier questions about the circumstances in which statutory damage awards were discretionary and the circumstances in which they were mandatory.

2. *Damages.* There are two basic measures of copyright damages. Where the infringer directly competes with the copyright owner, courts commonly use a lost sales measure of damages on the theory that defendant's sales displaced plaintiff's. If the infringer does not directly compete with the copyright owner, courts will typically measure damages by a reasonable royalty or market value. Courts will use the reasonable royalty measure where the copyright owner has previously given licenses; the license fees charged become the "reasonable royalty." If there are no preexisting licenses, courts will measure damages by market value—"what a willing buyer would have been reasonably required to pay to a willing seller for plaintiff['s] work." Sid & Marty Krofft Television Prods., Inc. v. McDonald's Corp., 562 F.2d 1157, 1174, 196 U.S.P.Q. 97 (9th Cir.1977).

3. *Profits.* Sheldon v. Metro–Goldwyn Pictures Corp., 309 U.S. 390, 60 S.Ct. 681, 84 L.Ed. 825, 44 U.S.P.Q. 607 (1940), presaged section 504(b)'s provision for apportioning defendant's profits between those allocable to use of the copyrighted work and those allocable to other elements in the infringing work. The defendant in *Sheldon* had copied plaintiff's play, *Dishonored Lady,* in producing its motion picture, *Letty Lynton.* Defendant had also obtained a license to use another copyrighted work as the basis for its production and had made a substantial investment in producing and promoting the motion picture. Recognizing that a large part of defendant's profits traced to these expenditures, and to the reputation and effort of the movie stars involved, the Court affirmed the lower court's decree apportioning plaintiff's recovery to twenty percent of the profits earned by the motion picture—"only that part of the profits found to be attributable to the use of the copyrighted material as distinguished from what the infringer himself has supplied...." 309 U.S. at 396, 60 S.Ct. at 682.

Awards of indirect profits, as in the *Cream* case, are particularly appropriate where the infringing use generates no profits of its own, as is typically the case with advertising. Consider the abuses that might result in these cases from section 504(b)'s allocation of the burden of proof to the infringer: "If General Motors were to steal your copyright and put it in a sales brochure, you could not just put a copy of General Motors' corporate income tax return in the record and rest your case for an award of infringer's profits." Taylor v. Meirick, 712 F.2d 1112, 1122, 219 U.S.P.Q. 420 (7th Cir.1983).

4. *Attorney's Fees.* Most courts will award attorney's fees where the losing party—plaintiff or defendant—acted in bad faith. As a rule, a defendant acts in bad faith if it proceeds without any reasonable defense or refuses a reasonable settlement offer, while a plaintiff acts in bad faith if its "real motive" is "to vex and harass the defendant" or if its "claim is so lacking in merit as to present no arguable question of law or genuine issue of fact." Cloth v. Hyman, 146 F.Supp. 185, 193, 112 U.S.P.Q. 254 (S.D.N.Y.1956).

Until the United States Supreme Court's decision in Fogerty v. Fantasy, Inc., 510 U.S. 517, 114 S.Ct. 1023, 127 L.Ed.2d 455, 29 U.S.P.Q.2d 1881 (1994), the circuits divided on whether the discretionary factors for awarding attorney's fees should be applied symmetrically. Some circuits applied a "double standard" under which a prevailing defendant, to recover, had to demonstrate that the plaintiff acted in bad faith, while a prevailing plaintiff could recover attorney's fees apart from any showing of the defendant's bad faith. Other circuits took an "evenhanded approach," allowing an award of attorney's fees to the prevailing party—plaintiff or defendant—absent any showing of bad faith by either.

The *Fogerty* Court unanimously ruled that, in exercising their discretion to award attorney's fees to prevailing plaintiffs or defendants, courts should take an "even-handed" approach that treats both sides equally. Observing that "[t]he legislative history of § 505 provides no support for treating prevailing plaintiffs and defendants differently with respect to the recovery of attorney's fees," the Court concluded that the policies underlying the 1976 Act also offered no support for a double standard. "Because copyright law ultimately serves the purpose of enriching the general public through access to creative works, it is peculiarly important that the boundaries of copyright law be demarcated as clearly as possible. To that end, defendants who seek to advance a variety of meritorious copyright defenses should be encouraged to litigate them to the same extent that plaintiffs are encouraged to litigate meritorious claims of infringement." 510 U.S. at 527.

5. *Temporary (Preliminary) Injunctions.* Generally, a copyright owner can obtain a temporary injunction upon making a prima facie case of its copyright's validity and infringement. Demonstration of irreparable harm, though helpful, is usually not necessary. What considerations weigh for and against such liberality in giving threshold relief? Is it a matter for concern that the injunction is directed against conduct that in other contexts might be protected under the First Amendment's free speech and press guarantees and rules against prior restraint? If the underlying concern is that the eventual monetary award, coupled with a permanent injunction, will not make the copyright owner whole, would it be better to increase the statutory damage schedule or, possibly, introduce treble damages?

Should the tests for preliminary relief be more closely attuned to the equities and hardships of particular copyright industries? Compare, for example, the situation of fabric designers, whose designs go out of fashion quickly and are even more quickly appropriated by competitors, with the situation of the writer who claims that her story or script outline is being appropriated by defendant motion picture producer in the course of a multimillion dollar production. What are the relative costs of delay to the parties in these two situations? Does it matter that, while the ultimate award of defendant's profits will be apportioned to the benefits gained from use of plaintiff's work, a preliminary injunction will not cut nearly so fine and will effectively halt *all* of defendant's production activities?

6. *Final (Permanent) Injunctions.* On principle, if an infringing work takes only part of a copyrighted work a court will frame its injunction to require only that the infringing matter be deleted. But in cases involving derivative works such as translations and motion pictures, where the infringing and noninfringing material are inextricably intertwined, courts will enjoin dissemination of the entire infringing work, even though this will prevent the defendant from exploiting its independent contribution.

In cases where the infringing and noninfringing elements cannot be separated, and where the copyrighted elements form only a small part of the defendant's work, would it be preferable to withhold injunctive relief and award only damages or profits? The United States Supreme Court took this approach in Dun v. Lumbermen's Credit Ass'n, 209 U.S. 20, 28 S.Ct. 335, 52 L.Ed. 663 (1908). Noting that the defendant had copied only a small amount of copyrighted material from plaintiff's work, the Court affirmed the lower court's ruling that "the proportion is so insignificant compared with the injury from stopping appellees' use of their enormous volume of independently acquired information, that an injunction would be unconscionable. In such cases, the copyright owner should be remitted to his remedy at law." Specifically, "we think the discretion of the court was wisely exercised in refusing an injunction and remitting the appellants to a court of law to recover such damage as they might there prove that they had sustained." 209 U.S. at 23–24, 28 S.Ct. at 337.

Justice Blackmun, dissenting in Sony Corp. v. Universal City Studios, 464 U.S. 417, 104 S.Ct. 774, 78 L.Ed.2d 574 (1984), concurred in the lower court's "suggestion that an award of damages, or continuing royalties, or even some form of limited injunction, may well be an appropriate means of balancing the equities in this case." 464 U.S. at 499, 104 S.Ct. at 817. See Guido Calabresi & A.Douglas Melamed, Property Rules, Liability Rules, and Inalienability: One View of the Cathedral, 85 Harv. L. Rev. 1089 (1972).

D.   Infringement

See Statute Supplement 17 U.S.C.A. § 501.

ARNSTEIN v. PORTER, 154 F.2d 464, 68 U.S.P.Q. 288 (2d Cir.1946). FRANK, J.: The principal question on this appeal is whether the lower court, under Rule 56, properly deprived plaintiff of a trial of his copyright infringement action. The answer depends on whether "there is the slightest doubt as to the facts."

In applying that standard here, it is important to avoid confusing two separate elements essential to a plaintiff's case in such a suit: (a) that defendant copied from plaintiff's copyrighted work and (b) that the copying (assuming it to be proved) went so far as to constitute improper appropriation.

As to the first—copying—the evidence may consist (a) of defendant's admission that he copied or (b) of circumstantial evidence—usually evidence of access—from which the trier of the facts may reasonably infer copying. Of course, if there are no similarities, no amount of evidence of access will suffice to prove copying. If there is evidence of access and similarities exist, then the trier of the facts must determine whether the similarities are sufficient to prove copying. On this issue, analysis ("dissection") is relevant, and the testimony of experts may be received to aid the trier of the facts. If evidence of access is absent, the similarities must be so striking as to preclude the possibility that plaintiff and defendant independently arrived at the same result.

If copying is established, then only does there arise the second issue, that of illicit copying (unlawful appropriation). On that issue ... the test is the response of the ordinary lay hearer; accordingly, on that issue, "dissection" and expert testimony are irrelevant.

In some cases, the similarities between the plaintiff's and defendant's work are so extensive and striking as, without more, both to justify an inference of copying and to prove improper appropriation. But such double-purpose evidence is not required; that is, if copying is otherwise shown, proof of improper appropriation need not consist of similarities which, standing alone, would support an inference of copying.

2 PAUL GOLDSTEIN, COPYRIGHT § 7.1 (2d ed. 1996)[1]

Section 501(a) of the 1976 Copyright Act states the rule on copyright infringement with deceptive simplicity: "Anyone who violates any of the exclusive rights of the copyright owner as provided by sections 106 through 118, or who imports copies or phonorecords into the United States in violation of section 602, is an infringer of the copyright." The legal reality is more complex. To prevail in an action for copyright infringement, a plaintiff must prove that it owns the right or rights in issue and that the defendant's conduct infringes one or more of these rights. To prove infringement, the plaintiff must show (1) that the defendant copied from plaintiff's work and (2) that, taken together, the elements copied amount to an improper appropriation. To prove copying, the plaintiff must show directly or by inference that the defendant mechanically copied plaintiff's work, such as by photocopying it, or that the defendant had plaintiff's work in mind when he composed the allegedly infringing work. To prove improper appropriation, the plaintiff must show (a) that at least some of the elements the defendant copied constitute protected subject matter, and (b) that audiences for the two works will find these elements in the defendant's work to be similar to elements in the plaintiff's work.

§ 7.1.1 The Role of Similarity in Proof of Infringement

Infringement turns strictly on proof of copying and improper appropriation. The fact that the defendant's work is similar, even substantially

---

1. Copyright © 1996 Paul Goldstein.

similar, to the plaintiff's work does not necessarily mean that it infringes the plaintiff's copyright. Although similarity does not necessarily imply infringement, it may play one or more important roles in proving infringement. Striking similarities between the plaintiff's and defendant's works may support an inference of copying on the theory that two works would be unlikely to share such similarities unless one had copied from the other. Similarities can also support a finding that either or both tests of improper appropriation have been met: similarities between the expressive elements of the plaintiff's and defendant's works may indicate that the defendant appropriated the plaintiff's protected expression, satisfying the first test of improper appropriation; the fact that audiences perceive substantial similarities between the two works may satisfy the second test of improper appropriation.

In some cases, the plaintiff's and defendant's works will be so close that their similarity will support both an inference of copying and a finding of improper appropriation. Examples of such similarities are defendant's 300–page novel tracking plaintiff's 300–page novel word for word; defendant's highly detailed mural tracing plaintiff's mural, line for line and color for color; and defendant's popular song mimicking the plaintiff's not only note for note, but also in rhythm, harmony and tone. It will be the rare and naive defendant who, in the face of such similarities, asserts that he has not infringed; if the plaintiff produced his work before the defendant produced his, such complete identity between the two works will leave little room for doubt that the defendant copied from the plaintiff. Such extensive similarities will also dictate a finding of improper appropriation. Complete identity in expressive details implies that, if plaintiff's work has any protected content, defendant has borrowed it and that, if plaintiff's work has any audience, defendant has taken it.

Plaintiffs may also rely on similarities to prove infringement when two works, though similar, are not identical. In some of these cases, though, similarities that are sufficient to show copying may not be sufficient to show improper appropriation. For example, the fact that the defendant's 300–page novel contains a few terse lines of dialogue that also appear in plaintiff's novel may indicate that defendant copied from plaintiff; but if these are the only points of similarity, the amount taken may be too small to constitute improper appropriation. In other cases, similarities between two works may indicate appropriation but not copying. For example, plaintiff's and defendant's novels may share enough elements of plot, incident, character and background to suggest appropriation, but have none of the telltale surface details that betray copying. If in this situation the plaintiff can adduce other evidence to prove that the defendant copied— defendant's admission that he copied, for example, or testimony of an eyewitness who saw the defendant copy—the plaintiff will likely prevail in an infringement action.

NOTES

1. *Copying: Common Errors.* The presence of common errors in plaintiff's and defendant's works provides virtually irrefutable proof that the defendant copied from the plaintiff. As with striking similarities generally, coincidence can rarely explain why defendant's map, like plaintiff's, contains sixteen misspellings and locates a river on the wrong side of a main highway, or why defendant's doll has the same misplaced right thumbnail as does plaintiff's. Defendant's only excuse in these cases may be that the error appeared in a common source from which both the plaintiff and defendant copied.

A study of fifty-two cases involving common errors revealed that in at least eight cases the plaintiff had inserted the error to trap unwary copyists; seven of these cases involved directories and one involved a catalogue. In American Travel & Hotel Directory Co. v. Gehring Publishing Co., 4 F.2d 415 (S.D.N.Y.1925), for example, the plaintiff listed several nonexistent hotels in its hotel directory. The study's author observed, "My sympathies, however, are with the weary traveler who late at night tries to locate one of the trap hotels." John A. Taylor, Common Errors as Evidence of Copying, 22 Bull. Copyright Soc'y 444, 448 (1975).

2. *Expert Testimony.* Courts today generally admit expert testimony on the question of copying. Just as surface similarities may lead a lay factfinder to conclude that the defendant copied from plaintiff's work, so dissimilarities may lead to the opposite conclusion. The expert eye or ear can discern more subtle, structural clues. Courts also allow experts to dissect the competing works to identify the protectible elements they have in common. However, courts generally reject expert testimony on the question of audience reaction.

3. *Strict Liability.* Although a plaintiff must, to prevail, prove that the defendant copied her work, she need not prove that the copying was intentional. One who copies an overheard tune or another's copy of a copyrighted work is liable even if he had no knowledge that the work was covered by copyright. The reason for the rule, given in De Acosta v. Brown, 146 F.2d 408, 412, 63 U.S.P.Q. 311 (2d Cir.1944), cert. denied, 325 U.S. 862, 65 S.Ct. 1197, 89 L.Ed. 1983 (1945), is that "the protection accorded literary property would be of little value if it did not go against third persons, or if, it might be added, insulation from payment of damages could be secured by a publisher by merely refraining from making inquiry." Learned Hand dissented in *De Acosta.* "If my brothers are right, a publisher must be prepared to respond in damages to any author who can prove that the publisher has incorporated, however innocently, and at whatever remove, any part of the author's work. If that possibility were to hover over all publication, it would, I believe, be a not negligible depressant upon the dissemination of knowledge." 146 F.2d at 413.

1. LITERATURE

Nichols v. Universal Pictures Corp.
United States Circuit Court of Appeals, Second Circuit, 1930.
45 F.2d 119, 7 U.S.P.Q. 84.

L. HAND, Circuit Judge.

The plaintiff is the author of a play, "Abie's Irish Rose," which it may be assumed was properly copyrighted under section five, subdivision (d), of the Copyright Act, 17 U.S.C.A. § 5(d). The defendant produced publicly a motion picture play, "The Cohens and The Kellys," which the plaintiff alleges was taken from it. As we think the defendant's play too unlike the plaintiff's to be an infringement, we may assume, arguendo, that in some details the defendant used the plaintiff's play, as will subsequently appear, though we do not so decide. It therefore becomes necessary to give an outline of the two plays.

"Abie's Irish Rose" presents a Jewish family living in prosperous circumstances in New York. The father, a widower, is in business as a merchant, in which his son and only child helps him. The boy has philandered with young women, who to his father's great disgust have always been Gentiles, for he is obsessed with a passion that his daughter-in-law shall be an orthodox Jewess. When the play opens the son, who has been courting a young Irish Catholic girl, has already married her secretly before a Protestant minister, and is concerned to soften the blow for his father, by securing a favorable impression of his bride, while concealing her faith and race. To accomplish this he introduces her to his father at his home as a Jewess, and lets it appear that he is interested in her, though he conceals the marriage. The girl somewhat reluctantly falls in with the plan; the father takes the bait, becomes infatuated with the girl, concludes that they must marry, and assumes that of course they will, if he so decides. He calls in a rabbi, and prepares for the wedding according to the Jewish rite.

Meanwhile the girl's father, also a widower, who lives in California, and is as intense in his own religious antagonism as the Jew, has been called to New York, supposing that his daughter is to marry an Irishman and a Catholic. Accompanied by a priest, he arrives at the house at the moment when the marriage is being celebrated, but too late to prevent it, and the two fathers, each infuriated by the proposed union of his child to a heretic, fall into unseemly and grotesque antics. The priest and the rabbi become friendly, exchange trite sentiments about religion, and agree that the match is good. Apparently out of abundant caution, the priest celebrates the marriage for a third time, while the girl's father is inveigled away. The second act closes with each father, still outraged, seeking to find some way by which the union, thus trebly insured, may be dissolved.

The last act takes place about a year later, the young couple having meanwhile been abjured by each father, and left to their own resources. They have had twins, a boy and a girl, but their fathers know no more than that a child has been born. At Christmas each, led by his craving to see his grandchild, goes separately to the young folks' home, where they encounter each other, each laden with gifts, one for a boy, the other for a girl. After some slapstick comedy, depending upon the insistence of each that he is right about the sex of the grandchild, they become reconciled when they learn the truth, and that each child is to bear the given name of a grandparent. The curtain falls as the fathers are exchanging amenities, and the Jew giving evidence of an abatement in the strictness of his orthodoxy.

"The Cohens and The Kellys" presents two families, Jewish and Irish, living side by side in the poorer quarters of New York in a state of perpetual enmity. The wives in both cases are still living, and share in the mutual animosity, as do two small sons, and even the respective dogs. The Jews have a daughter, the Irish a son; the Jewish father is in the clothing business; the Irishman is a policeman. The children are in love with each other, and secretly marry, apparently after the play opens. The Jew, being in great financial straits, learns from a lawyer that he has fallen heir to a large fortune from a great-aunt, and moves into a great house, fitted luxuriously. Here he and his family live in vulgar ostentation, and here the Irish boy seeks out his Jewish bride, and is chased away by the angry father. The Jew then abuses the Irishman over the telephone, and both become hysterically excited. The extremity of his feelings makes the Jew sick, so that he must go to Florida for a rest, just before which the daughter discloses her marriage to her mother.

On his return the Jew finds that his daughter has borne a child; at first he suspects the lawyer, but eventually learns the truth and is overcome with anger at such a low alliance. Meanwhile, the Irish family who have been forbidden to see the grandchild, go to the Jew's house, and after a violent scene between the two fathers in which the Jew disowns his daughter, who decides to go back with her husband, the Irishman takes her back with her baby to his own poor lodgings. The lawyer, who had hoped to marry the Jew's daughter, seeing his plan foiled, tells the Jew that his fortune really belongs to the Irishman, who was also related to the dead woman, but offers to conceal his knowledge, if the Jew will share the loot. This the Jew repudiates, and, leaving the astonished lawyer, walks through the rain to his enemy's house to surrender the property. He arrives in great dejection, tells the truth, and abjectly turns to leave. A reconciliation ensues, the Irishman agreeing to share with him equally. The Jew shows some interest in his grandchild, though this is at most a minor motive in the reconciliation, and the curtain falls while the two are in their cups, the Jew insisting that in the firm name for the business, which they are to carry on jointly, his name shall stand first.

It is of course essential to any protection of literary property, whether at common-law or under the statute, that the right cannot be limited literally to the text, else a plagiarist would escape by immaterial variations. That has never been the law, but, as soon as literal appropriation ceases to be the test, the whole matter is necessarily at large, so that, as was recently well said by a distinguished judge, the decisions cannot help much in a new case. Fendler v. Morosco, 253 N.Y. 281, 292, 171 N.E. 56. When plays are concerned, the plagiarist may excise a separate scene, or he may appropriate part of the dialogue. Then the question is whether the part so taken is "substantial," and therefore not a "fair use" of the copyrighted work; it is the same question as arises in the case of any other copyrighted work. But when the plagiarist does not take out a block in situ, but an abstract of the whole, decision is more troublesome. Upon any work, and especially upon a play, a great number of patterns of increasing generality will fit equally well, as more and more of the incident is left out. The last may perhaps be no more than the most general statement of what the play is about, and at times might consist only of its title; but there is a point in this series of abstractions where they are no longer protected, since otherwise the playwright could prevent the use of his "ideas," to which, apart from their expression, his property is never extended. Nobody has ever been able to fix that boundary, and nobody ever can. In some cases the question has been treated as though it were analogous to lifting a portion out of the copyrighted work, but the analogy is not a good one, because, though the skeleton is a part of the body, it pervades and supports the whole. In such cases we are rather concerned with the line between expression and what is expressed. As respects plays, the controversy chiefly centers upon the characters and sequence of incident, these being the substance.

We did not in Dymow v. Bolton, 11 F. (2d) 690, hold that a plagiarist was never liable for stealing a plot; that would have been flatly against our rulings in Dam v. Kirk La Shelle Co., 175 F. 902, 41 L.R.A.(N.S.) 1002, 20 Am.Ann.Cas. 1173, and Stodart v. Mutual Film Co., 249 F. 513, affirming my decision in (D.C.) 249 F. 507; neither of which we meant to overrule. We found the plot of the second play was too different to infringe, because the most detailed pattern, common to both, eliminated so much from each that its content went into the public domain; and for this reason we said, "this mere subsection of a plot was not susceptible of copyright." But we do not doubt that two plays may correspond in plot closely enough for infringement. How far that correspondence must go is another matter. Nor need we hold that the same may not be true as to the characters, quite independently of the "plot" proper, though, as far as we know, such a case has never arisen. If Twelfth Night were copyrighted, it is quite possible that a second comer might so closely imitate Sir Toby Belch or Malvolio as to infringe, but it would not be enough that for one of his characters he cast a riotous knight who kept wassail to the discomfort of the household, or a vain and foppish steward who became amorous of his mistress. These would be no more than Shakespeare's "ideas" in the play, as little capable of monopoly as Einstein's Doctrine of Relativity, or Darwin's theory of the Origin of Species. It follows that the less developed the characters, the less they can be copyrighted; that is the penalty an author must bear for marking them too indistinctly.

In the two plays at bar we think both as to incident and character, the defendant took no more—assuming that it took anything at all—than the law allowed. The stories are quite different. One is of a religious zealot who insists upon his child's marrying no one outside his faith; opposed by another who is in this respect just like him, and is his foil. Their difference in race is merely an obbligato to the main theme, religion. They sink their differences through grandparental pride and affection. In the other, zealotry is wholly absent; religion does not even appear. It is true that the parents are hostile to each other in part because they differ in race; but the marriage of their son to a Jew does not apparently offend the Irish family at all, and it exacerbates the existing animosity of the Jew, principally because he has become rich, when he learns it. They are reconciled through the honesty of the Jew and the generosity of the Irishman; the grandchild has nothing whatever to do with it. The only matter common to the two is a quarrel between a Jewish and an Irish father, the marriage of their children, the birth of grandchildren and a reconciliation.

If the defendant took so much from the plaintiff, it may well have been because her amazing success seemed to prove that this was a subject of enduring popularity. Even so, granting that the plaintiff's play was wholly original, and assuming that novelty is not essential to a copyright, there is no monopoly in such a background. Though the plaintiff discovered the vein, she could not keep it to herself; so defined, the theme was too generalized an abstraction from what she wrote. It was only a part of her "ideas."

Nor does she fare better as to her characters. It is indeed scarcely credible that she should not have been aware of those stock figures, the low comedy Jew and Irishman. The defendant has not taken from her more than their prototypes have contained for many decades. If so, obviously so to generalize her copyright, would allow her to cover what was not original with her. But we need not hold this as matter of fact, much as we might be justified. Even though we take it that she devised her figures out of her brain de novo, still the defendant was within its rights.

There are but four characters common to both plays, the lovers and the fathers. The lovers are so faintly indicated as to be no more than stage properties. They are loving and fertile; that is really all that can be said of them, and anyone else is quite within his rights if he puts loving and fertile lovers in a play of his own, wherever he gets the cue. The plaintiff's Jew is quite unlike the defendant's. His obsession is his religion, on which depends such racial animosity as he has. He is affectionate, warm and patriarchal. None of these fit the defendant's Jew, who shows affection for his daughter only once, and who has none but the most superficial interest in his grandchild. He is tricky, ostentatious and vulgar, only by misfortune redeemed into honesty. Both are grotesque, extravagant and quarrelsome; both are fond of display; but these common qualities make up only a small part of their simple pictures, no more than any one might lift if he chose. The Irish fathers are even more unlike; the plaintiff's a mere symbol for religious fanaticism and patriarchal pride, scarcely a character at all. Neither quality appears in the defendant's, for while he goes to get his grandchild, it is rather out of a truculent determination not to be forbidden, than from pride in his progeny. For the rest he is only a grotesque hobbledehoy, used for low comedy of the most conventional sort, which any one might borrow, if he chanced not to know the exemplar.

The defendant argues that the case is controlled by my decision in Fisher v. Dillingham (D.C.) 298 F. 145. Neither my brothers nor I wish to throw doubt upon the doctrine of that case, but it is not applicable here. We assume that the plaintiff's play is altogether original, even to an extent that in fact it is hard to believe. We assume further that, so far as it has been anticipated by earlier plays of which she knew nothing, that fact is immaterial. Still, as we have already said, her copyright did not cover everything that might be drawn from her play; its content went to some extent into the public domain. We have to decide how much, and while we are as aware as any one that the line, wherever it is drawn, will seem arbitrary, that is no excuse for not drawing it; it is a question such as courts must answer in nearly all cases. Whatever may be the difficulties a priori, we have no question on which side of the line this case falls. A comedy based upon conflicts between Irish and Jews, into which the marriage of their children enters, is no more susceptible of copyright than the outline of Romeo and Juliet.

The plaintiff has prepared an elaborate analysis of the two plays, showing a "quadrangle" of the common characters, in which each is represented by the emotions which he discovers. She presents the resulting parallelism as proof of infringement, but the adjectives employed are so general as to be quite useless. Take for example the attribute of "love" ascribed to both Jews. The plaintiff has depicted her father as deeply attached to his son, who is his hope and joy; not so, the defendant, whose father's conduct is throughout not actuated by any affection for his daughter, and who is merely once overcome for the moment by her distress when he has violently dismissed her lover. "Anger" covers emotions aroused by quite different occasions in each case; so do "anxiety," "despondency" and "disgust." It is unnecessary to go through the catalogue for emotions are too much colored by their causes to be a test when used so broadly. This is not the proper approach to a solution; it must be more ingenuous, more like that of a spectator, who would rely upon the complex of his impressions of each character.

We cannot approve the length of the record, which was due chiefly to the use of expert witnesses. Argument is argument whether in the box or at the bar, and its proper place is the last. The testimony of an expert upon such issues, especially his cross-examination, greatly extends the trial and contributes nothing which cannot be better heard after the evidence is all submitted. It ought not to be allowed at all; and while its admission is not a ground for reversal, it cumbers the case and tends to confusion, for the more the court is led into the intricacies of dramatic craftsmanship, the less likely it is to stand upon the firmer, if more naive, ground of its considered impressions upon its own perusal. We hope that in this class of cases such evidence may in the future be entirely excluded, and the case confined to the actual issues; that is, whether the copyrighted work was original, and whether the defendant copied it, so far as the supposed infringement is identical.

The defendant, "the prevailing party," was entitled to a reasonable attorney's fee (section 40 of the Copyright Act [17 U.S.C.A. § 40]).

Decree affirmed.

NOTE

Just as literary works differ from musical works and visual works for purposes of copyright infringement, so pertinent differences may exist between different forms of literary works. Should novels be treated differently from plays? From textbooks? From directories?

In Kepner–Tregoe, Inc. v. Carabio, 203 U.S.P.Q. 124, 131–32 (E.D.Mich.1979), the court took care to distinguish between conventional literary works and instructional materials. One distinction is that "in teaching, a noticeable style is a hindrance. Two simple and straightforward explanations of an economic law or principle must bear a close resemblance, so greater similarity must be allowed." Another distinction is that in a literary work, plot, theme and character are important. "There is an unlimited variety which may be invented. Authors are not confined. In addition, there is no societal interest in many variants on a single theme or plot, nor is there the likelihood that by extending broad protection, entry to the market for literary works will be foreclosed. But with respect to the useful arts, there is a societal interest in having many offer the art in the marketplace. Our economy functions best under competition. And, if many can present variants on the copyrighted material, we hope that advances in its teaching will result. As a consequence, more similarity between two works of a commercial and useful character is required to find infringement than between two literary works." The court concluded that although plaintiff had a "thin" copyright, defendant had infringed it "in certain minor respects."

What if the copyrighted work is a scientific paper from which the accused work—a novel—borrows literary elements? See Musto v. Meyer, 434 F.Supp. 32, 196 U.S.P.Q. 820 (S.D.N.Y.1977), aff'd without opinion, 598 F.2d 609 (2d Cir.1979).

2. MUSIC

Selle v. Gibb

United States Court of Appeals, Seventh Circuit, 1984.
741 F.2d 896, 223 U.S.P.Q. 195.

CUDAHY, Circuit Judge.

The plaintiff, Ronald H. Selle, brought a suit against three brothers, Maurice, Robin and Barry Gibb, known collectively as the popular singing group, the Bee Gees, alleging that the Bee Gees, in their hit tune, "How Deep Is Your Love," had infringed the copyright of his song, "Let It End." The jury returned a verdict in plaintiff's favor on the issue of liability in a bifurcated trial. The district court, Judge George N. Leighton, granted the defendants' motion for judgment notwithstanding the verdict and, in the alternative, for a new trial. Selle v. Gibb, 567 F.Supp. 1173 (N.D.Ill.1983). We affirm the grant of the motion for judgment notwithstanding the verdict.

I

Selle composed his song, "Let It End," in one day in the fall of 1975 and obtained a copyright for it on November 17, 1975. He played his song with his small band two or three times in the Chicago area and sent a tape and lead sheet of the music to eleven music recording and publishing companies. Eight of the companies returned the materials to Selle; three did not respond. This was the extent of the public dissemination of Selle's song. Selle first became aware of the Bee Gees' song, "How Deep Is Your Love," in May 1978 and thought that he recognized the music as his own, although the lyrics were different. He also saw the movie, "Saturday Night Fever," the sound track of which features the song "How Deep Is Your Love," and again recognized the music. He subsequently sued the three Gibb brothers; Paramount Pictures Corporation, which made and distributed the movie; and Phonodisc, Inc., now known as Polygram Distribution, Inc., which made and distributed the cassette tape of "How Deep Is Your Love."

The Bee Gees are internationally known performers and creators of popular music. They have composed more than 160 songs; their sheet music, records and tapes have been distributed worldwide, some of the albums selling more than 30 million copies. The Bee Gees, however, do not themselves read or write music. In composing a song, their practice was to tape a tune, which members of their staff would later transcribe and reduce to a form suitable for copyrighting, sale and performance by both the Bee Gees and others.

In addition to their own testimony at trial, the Bee Gees presented testimony by their manager, Dick Ashby, and two musicians, Albhy Galuten and Blue Weaver, who were on the Bee Gees' staff at the time "How Deep Is Your Love" was composed. These witnesses described in detail how, in January 1977, the Bee Gees and several members of their staff went to a recording studio in the Chateau d'Herouville about 25 miles northwest of Paris. There the group composed at least six new songs and mixed a live album. Barry Gibb's testimony included a detailed explanation of a work tape which was introduced into evidence and played in court. This tape preserves the actual process of creation during which the brothers, and particularly Barry, created the tune of the accused song while Weaver, a keyboard player, played the tune which was hummed or sung by the brothers. Although the tape does not seem to preserve the very beginning of the process of creation, it does depict the process by which ideas, notes, lyrics and bits of the tune were gradually put together.

Following completion of this work tape, a demo tape was made. The work tape, demo tape and a vocal-piano version taken from the demo tape are all in the key of E flat. Lead sheet music, dated March 6, 1977, is in the key of E. On March 7, 1977, a lead sheet of "How Deep Is Your Love" was filed for issuance of a United States copyright, and in November 1977, a piano-vocal arrangement was filed in the Copyright Office.

The only expert witness to testify at trial was Arrand Parsons, a professor of music at Northwestern University who has had extensive professional experience primarily in classical music. He has been a program annotator for the Chicago Symphony Orchestra and the New Orleans Symphony Orchestra and has authored works about musical theory. Prior to this case, however, he had never made a comparative analysis of two popular songs. Dr. Parsons testified on the basis of several charts comparing the musical notes of each song and a comparative recording prepared under his direction.

According to Dr. Parsons' testimony, the first eight bars of each song (Theme A) have twenty-four of thirty-four notes in plaintiff's composition and twenty-four of forty notes in defendants' composition which are identical in pitch and symmetrical position. Of thirty-five rhythmic impulses in plaintiff's composition and forty in defendants', thirty are identical. In the last four bars of both songs (Theme B), fourteen notes in each are identical in pitch, and eleven of the fourteen rhythmic impulses are identical. Both Theme A and Theme B appear in the same position in each song but with different intervening material.

Dr. Parsons testified that, in his opinion, "the two songs had such striking similarities that they could not have been written independent of one another." Tr. 202. He also testified that he did not know of two songs by different composers "that contain as many striking similarities" as do the two songs at issue here. However, on several occasions, he declined to say that the similarities could only have resulted from copying.

Following presentation of the case, the jury returned a verdict for the plaintiff on the issue of liability, the only question presented to the jury. Judge Leighton, however, granted the defendants' motion for judgment notwithstanding the verdict and, in the alternative, for a new trial. He relied primarily on the plaintiff's inability to demonstrate that the defendants had access to the plaintiff's song, without which a claim of copyright infringement could not prevail regardless how similar the two compositions are. Further, the plaintiff failed to contradict or refute the testimony of the defendants and their witnesses describing the independent creation process of "How Deep Is Your Love." Finally, Judge Leighton concluded that "the inferences on which plaintiff relies is not a logical, permissible deduction from proof of 'striking similarity' or substantial similarity; it is 'at war with the undisputed facts,' and it is inconsistent with the proof of nonaccess to plaintiff's song by the Bee Gees at the time in question." ...

III

Selle's primary contention on this appeal is that the district court misunderstood the theory of proof of copyright infringement on which he based his claim. Under this theory, copyright infringement can be demonstrated when, even in the absence of any direct evidence of access, the two pieces in question are so strikingly similar that access can be inferred from such similarity alone. Selle argues that the testimony of his expert witness, Dr. Parsons, was sufficient evidence of such striking similarity that it was permissible for the jury, even in the absence of any other evidence concerning access, to infer that the Bee Gees had access to plaintiff's song and indeed copied it.

In establishing a claim of copyright infringement of a musical composition, the plaintiff must prove (1) ownership of the copyright in the complaining work; (2) originality of the work; (3) copying of the work by the defendant, and (4) a substantial degree of similarity between the two works. See Sherman, *Musical Copyright Infringement: The Requirement of Substantial Similarity*. Copyright Law Symposium, Number 92, American Society of Composers, Authors and Publishers 81–82. Columbia University Press (1977) [hereinafter "Sherman, *Musical Copyright Infringement*"]. The only element which is at issue in this appeal is proof of copying; the first two elements are essentially conceded, while the fourth (substantial similarity) is, at least in these circumstances, closely related to the third element under plaintiff's theory of the case.

Proof of copying is crucial to any claim of copyright infringement because no matter how similar the two works may be (even to the point of identity), if the defendant did not copy the accused work, there is no infringement. However, because direct evidence of copying is rarely available, the plaintiff can rely upon circumstantial evidence to prove this essential element, and the most important component of this sort of circumstantial evidence is proof of access. The plaintiff may be able to introduce direct evidence of access when, for example, the work was sent directly to the defendant (whether a musician or a publishing company) or a close associate of the defendant. On the other hand, the plaintiff may be able to establish a reasonable possibility of access when, for example, the complaining work has been widely disseminated to the public.

If, however, the plaintiff does not have direct evidence of access, then an inference of access may still be established circumstantially by proof of similarity which is so striking that the possibilities of independent creation, coincidence and prior common source are, as a practical matter, precluded. If the plaintiff presents evidence of striking similarity sufficient to raise an inference of access, then copying is presumably proved simultaneously, although the fourth element (substantial similarity) still requires proof that the defendant copied a substantial amount of the complaining work. The theory which Selle attempts to apply to this case is based on proof of copying by circumstantial proof of access established by striking similarity between the two works.

One difficulty with plaintiff's theory is that no matter how great the similarity between the two works, it is not their similarity *per se* which establishes access; rather, their similarity tends to prove access in light of the nature of the works, the particular musical genre involved and other circumstantial evidence of access. In other words, striking similarity is just one piece of circumstantial evidence tending to show access and must not be considered in isolation; it must be considered together with other types of circumstantial evidence relating to access.

As a threshold matter, therefore, it would appear that there must be at least some other evidence which would establish a reasonable possibility that the complaining work was *available* to the alleged infringer. As noted, two works may be identical in every detail, but, if the alleged infringer created the accused work independently or both works were copied from a common source in the public domain, then there is no infringement.

Therefore, if the plaintiff admits to having kept his or her creation under lock and key, it would seem logically impossible to infer access through striking similarity. Thus, although it has frequently been written that striking similarity *alone* can establish access, the decided cases suggest that this circumstance would be most unusual. The plaintiff must always present sufficient evidence to support a reasonable possibility of access because the jury cannot draw an inference of access based upon speculation and conjecture alone.

For example, in Twentieth Century–Fox Film Corp. v. Dieckhaus, 153 F.2d 893 (8th Cir.), cert. denied, 329 U.S. 716, 67 S.Ct. 46, 91 L.Ed. 621 (1946), the court reversed a finding of infringement based solely on the similarities between plaintiff's book and defendant's film. The court stated that the plaintiff herself presented no evidence that the defendant had had access to her book, and the only people to whom the plaintiff had given a copy of her book testified that they had not given it to the defendant. While the court also concluded that the similarities between the book and the film were not that significant, the result turned on the fact that "[t]he oral and documentary evidence in the record ... establishes the fact that the defendant had no access to plaintiff's book unless the law of plagiarism permits the court to draw an inference contrary to such proof from its finding of similarities on comparison of the book with the picture." Id. at 897. Thus, although proof of striking similarity may permit an inference of access, the plaintiff must still meet some minimum threshold of proof which demonstrates that the inference of access is reasonable.

The greatest difficulty perhaps arises when the plaintiff cannot demonstrate any direct link between the complaining work and the defendant but the work has been so widely disseminated that it is not unreasonable to infer that the defendant might have had access to it. In Cholvin v. B. & F. Music Co., 253 F.2d 102 (7th Cir.1958), the plaintiffs' work had been distributed in 2000 professional copies of sheet music and four recordings, of which 200,000 records were sold, and it had been performed on several nationwide broadcasts. The court held that, in light of this circumstantial evidence, it was reasonable to infer, in combination with similarities between the two pieces, that there had been an infringement. In ABKCO Music, Inc. v. Harrisongs Music, Ltd., 722 F.2d 988, 997–99 (2d Cir.1983), the court found that there had been a copyright infringement based on a theory of subconscious copying. The complaining work, "He's So Fine," had been the most popular song in the United States for five weeks and among the thirty top hits in England for seven weeks during the year in which George Harrison composed "My Sweet Lord," the infringing song. This evidence, in addition to Harrison's own admission that the two songs were "strikingly similar," supported the finding of infringement. On the other hand, in Jewel Music Publishing Co. v. Leo Feist, Inc., 62 F.Supp. 596, 598 (S.D.N.Y.1945), almost 10,000 copies of the complaining song had been distributed or sold and the music had also been broadcast on national performances. The court still concluded that the showing of access was insufficient, in combination with the other evidence, to support a reasonable inference of access.

The possibility of access in the present case is not as remote as that in *Dieckhaus* because neither side elicited testimony from the individuals (primarily employees of the publishing companies) to whom the plaintiff had distributed copies of his song. Such evidence might have conclusively disproved access. On the other hand, Selle's song certainly did not achieve the extent of public dissemination existing in *Cholvin, Jewel Music Publishing Co.,* or *Harrisongs Music,* and there was also no evidence that any of the defendants or their associates were in Chicago on the two or three occasions when the plaintiff played his song publicly. It is not necessary for us, given the facts of this case, to determine the number of copies which must be publicly distributed to raise a reasonable inference of access. Nevertheless, in this case, the availability of Selle's song, as shown by the evidence, was virtually *de minimis*.

In granting the defendants' motion for judgment notwithstanding the verdict, Judge Leighton relied primarily on the plaintiff's failure to adduce any evidence of access and stated that an inference of access may not be based on mere conjecture, speculation or a bare possibility of access. Thus, in Testa v. Janssen, 492 F.Supp. 198, 202–03 (W.D.Pa.1980), the court stated that "[t]o support a finding of access, plaintiffs' evidence must extend beyond mere speculation or conjecture. And, while circumstantial evidence is sufficient to establish access, a defendant's opportunity to view the copyrighted work must exist by a reasonable possibility—not a bare possibility."

Judge Leighton thus based his decision on what he characterized as the plaintiff's inability to raise more than speculation that the Bee Gees had access to his song. The extensive testimony of the defendants and their witnesses describing the creation process went essentially uncontradicted, and there was no attempt even to impeach their credibility. Judge Leighton further relied on the principle that the testimony of credible witnesses concerning a matter within their knowledge cannot be rejected without some impeachment, contradiction or inconsistency with other evidence on the particular point at issue. Judge Leighton's conclusions that there was no more than a bare possibility that the defendants could have had access to Selle's song and that this was an insufficient basis from which the jury could have reasonably inferred the existence of access seem correct. The plaintiff has failed to meet even the minimum threshold of proof of the possibility of access and, as Judge Leighton has stated, an inference of access would thus seem to be "at war with the undisputed facts."

IV

The grant of the motion for judgment notwithstanding the verdict might, if we were so minded, be affirmed on the basis of the preceding analysis of the plaintiff's inability to establish a reasonable inference of access. This decision is also supported by a more traditional analysis of proof of access based only on the proof of "striking similarity" between the two compositions. The plaintiff relies almost exclusively on the testimony of his expert witness, Dr. Parsons, that the two pieces were, in fact, "strikingly similar."[3] Yet formulating a meaningful definition of "striking similarity" is no simple task, and the term is often used in a conclusory or circular fashion.

Sherman defines "striking similarity" as a term of art signifying "that degree of similarity as will permit an inference of copying even in the absence of proof of access...." Sherman, *Musical Copyright Infringement,* at 84 n. 15. Nimmer states that, absent proof of access, "the similarities must be so striking as to preclude the possibility that the defendant independently arrived at the same result." Nimmer, *Copyright,* at 13–14.[4]

"Striking similarity" is not merely a function of the number of identical notes that appear in both compositions. An important factor in analyzing the degree of similarity of two compositions is the uniqueness of the sections which are asserted to be similar.

If the complaining work contains an unexpected departure from the normal metric structure or if the complaining work includes what appears to be an error and the accused work repeats the unexpected element or the error, then it is more likely that there is some connection between the pieces. If the similar sections are particularly intricate, then again it would seem more likely that the compositions are related. Finally, some dissimilarities may be particularly suspicious. While some of these concepts are borrowed from literary copyright analysis, they would seem equally applicable to an analysis of music.

The judicially formulated definition of "striking similarity" states that "plaintiffs must demonstrate that 'such similarities are of a kind that can only be explained by copying, rather than by coincidence, independent creation, or prior common source.' " Testa v. Janssen, 492 F.Supp. 198, 203 (W.D.Pa.1980) (quoting Stratchborneo v. Arc Music Corp., 357 F.Supp. 1393, 1403 (S.D.N.Y.1973)). Sherman adds:

> To prove that certain similarities are "striking," plaintiff must show that they are the sort of similarities that cannot satisfactorily be accounted for by a theory of coincidence, independent creation, prior common source, or any theory other than that of copying. Striking similarity is an extremely technical issue—one with which, understandably, experts are best equipped to deal.

Sherman, *Musical Copyright Infringement,* at 96.

---

3. Plaintiff also relies on the fact that both songs were played on numerous occasions in open court for the jury to hear and on the deposition testimony of one of the Bee Gees, Maurice, who incorrectly identified Theme B of Selle's song as the Bee Gees' composition, "How Deep Is Your Love."

4. At oral argument, plaintiff's attorney analyzed the degree of similarity required to establish an inference of access as being in an inverse ratio to the quantum of direct evidence adduced to establish access. While we have found no authoritative support for this analysis, it seems appropriate. In this case, it would therefore appear that, because the plaintiff has introduced virtually no direct evidence of access, the degree of similarity required to establish copying in this case is considerable.

Finally, the similarities should appear in a sufficiently unique or complex context as to make it unlikely that both pieces were copied from a prior common source, or that the defendant was able to compose the accused work as a matter of independent creation. With these principles in mind, we turn now to an analysis of the evidence of "striking similarity" presented by the plaintiff.

As noted, the plaintiff relies almost entirely on the testimony of his expert witness, Dr. Arrand Parsons. The defendants did not introduce any expert testimony, apparently because they did not think Parsons' testimony needed to be refuted. Defendants are perhaps to some degree correct in asserting that Parsons, although eminently qualified in the field of classical music theory, was not equally qualified to analyze popular music tunes. More significantly, however, although Parsons used the magic formula, "striking similarity," he only ruled out the possibility of independent creation; he did not state that the similarities could only be the result of copying. In order for proof of "striking similarity" to establish a reasonable inference of access, especially in a case such as this one in which the direct proof of access is so minimal, the plaintiff must show that the similarity is of a type which will preclude any explanation other than that of copying.

In addition, to bolster the expert's conclusion that independent creation was not possible, there should be some testimony or other evidence of the relative complexity or uniqueness of the two compositions. Dr. Parsons' testimony did not refer to this aspect of the compositions and, in a field such as that of popular music in which all songs are relatively short and tend to build on or repeat a basic theme, such testimony would seem to be particularly necessary. We agree with the Sixth Circuit which explained that "we do not think the affidavit of [the expert witness], stating in conclusory terms that 'it is extremely unlikely that one set [of architectural plans] could have been prepared without access to the other set,' can fill the gap which is created by the absence of any direct evidence of access." Scholz Homes, Inc. v. Maddox, 379 F.2d 84, 86 (6th Cir.1967).

To illustrate this deficiency more concretely, we refer to a cassette tape, Plaintiff's Exhibit 27, and the accompanying chart, Plaintiff's Exhibit 26. These exhibits were prepared by the defendants but introduced into evidence by the plaintiff. The tape has recorded on it segments of both themes from both the Selle and the Gibb songs interspersed with segments of other compositions as diverse as "Footsteps," "From Me To You" (a Lennon–McCartney piece), Beethoven's 5th Symphony, "Funny Talk," "Play Down," and "I'd Like To Leave If I May" (the last two being earlier compositions by Barry Gibb).[5] There are at least superficial similarities among these segments, when played on the same musical instrument, and the plaintiff failed to elicit any testimony from his expert witness about this exhibit which compared the Selle and the Gibb songs to other pieces of contemporary, popular music. These circumstances indicate that the plain-

5. The plaintiff, on cross-examination, admitted that there were some similarities, primarily in melody rather than rhythm, be-tween his song and various other popular tunes, including "From Me To You" and several earlier Bee Gee compositions.

tiff failed to sustain his burden of proof on the issue of "striking similarity" in its legal sense—that is, similarity which reasonably precludes the possibility of any explanation other than that of copying.

The plaintiff's expert witness does not seem to have addressed any issues relating to the possibility of prior common source in both widely disseminated popular songs and the defendants' own compositions. At oral argument, plaintiff's attorney stated that the burden of proving common source should be on the defendant; however, the burden of proving "striking similarity," which, by definition, includes taking steps to minimize the possibility of common source, is on the plaintiff. In essence, the plaintiff failed to prove to the requisite degree that the similarities identified by the expert witness—although perhaps "striking" in a non-legal sense—were of a type which would eliminate any explanation of coincidence, independent creation or common source, including, in this case, the possibility of common source in earlier compositions created by the Bee Gees themselves or by others. In sum, the evidence of striking similarity is not sufficiently compelling to make the case when the proof of access must otherwise depend largely upon speculation and conjecture.

Therefore, because the plaintiff failed both to establish a basis from which the jury could reasonably infer that the Bee Gees had access to his song and to meet his burden of proving "striking similarity" between the two compositions, the grant by the district court of the defendants' motion for judgment notwithstanding the verdict is affirmed. Because of our doubts concerning the defendants' cross-appeal on the denial of the summary judgment, we order that, under Fed.R.App.P. 38, each party shall bear its own costs.

3. VISUAL ARTS

Steinberg v. Columbia Pictures Industries, Inc.

United States District Court, S.D. New York 1987.
663 F.Supp. 706, 3 U.S.P.Q.2d 1593.

STANTON, District Judge.

In these actions for copyright infringement, plaintiff Saul Steinberg is suing the producers, promoters, distributors and advertisers of the movie "Moscow on the Hudson" ("Moscow"). Steinberg is an artist whose fame derives in part from cartoons and illustrations he has drawn for *The New Yorker* magazine. Defendant Columbia Pictures Industries, Inc. (Columbia) is in the business of producing, promoting and distributing motion pictures, including "Moscow." . . .

Artwork Copyright © 1976 Saul Steinberg
Cover Reprinted by Special Permission of Saul Steinberg and *The New Yorker*
All Rights Reserved.

Columbia Pictures' poster
Reproduced with permission of Columbia Pictures

Plaintiff alleges that defendants' promotional poster for "Moscow" infringes his copyright on an illustration that he drew for *The New Yorker* and that appeared on the cover of the March 29, 1976 issue of the magazine, in violation of 17 U.S.C. §§ 101–810. Defendants deny this allegation and assert the affirmative defenses of fair use as a parody, estoppel and laches.

Defendants have moved, and plaintiff has cross-moved, for summary judgment. For the reasons set forth below, this court rejects defendants' asserted defenses and grants summary judgment on the issue of copying to plaintiff. . . .

II

The essential facts are not disputed by the parties despite their disagreements on nonessential matters. On March 29, 1976, *The New Yorker* published as a cover illustration the work at issue in this suit, widely known as a parochial New Yorker's view of the world. The magazine registered this illustration with the United States Copyright Office and subsequently assigned the copyright to Steinberg. Approximately three months later, plaintiff and *The New Yorker* entered into an agreement to print and sell a certain number of posters of the cover illustration.

It is undisputed that unauthorized duplications of the poster were made and distributed by unknown persons, although the parties disagree on the extent to which plaintiff attempted to prevent the distribution of those counterfeits. Plaintiff has also conceded that numerous posters have been created and published depicting other localities in the same manner that he depicted New York in his illustration. These facts, however, are irrelevant to the merits of this case, which concerns only the relationship between plaintiff's and defendants' illustrations.

Defendants' illustration was created to advertise the movie "Moscow on the Hudson," which recounts the adventures of a Muscovite who defects in New York. In designing this illustration, Columbia's executive art director, Kevin Nolan, has admitted that he specifically referred to Steinberg's poster, and indeed, that he purchased it and hung it, among others, in his office. Furthermore, Nolan explicitly directed the outside artist whom he retained to execute his design, Craig Nelson, to use Steinberg's poster to achieve a more recognizably New York look. Indeed, Nelson acknowledged having used the facade of one particular edifice, at Nolan's suggestion that it would render his drawing more "New York-ish." While the two buildings are not identical, they are so similar that it is impossible, especially in view of the artist's testimony, not to find that defendants' impermissibly copied plaintiff's.[1]

To decide the issue of infringement, it is necessary to consider the posters themselves. Steinberg's illustration presents a bird's eye view across a portion of the western edge of Manhattan, past the Hudson River and a telescoped version of the rest of the United States and the Pacific Ocean, to a red strip of horizon, beneath which are three flat land masses labeled China, Japan and Russia. The name of the magazine, in *The New*

---

1. Nolan claimed also to have been inspired by some of the posters that were inspired by Steinberg's; such secondary inspiration, however, is irrelevant to whether or not the "Moscow" poster infringes plaintiff's copyright by having impermissibly copied it.

Yorker's usual typeface, occupies the top fifth of the poster, beneath a thin band of blue wash representing a stylized sky.

The parts of the poster beyond New York are minimalized, to symbolize a New Yorker's myopic view of the centrality of his city to the world. The entire United States west of the Hudson River, for example, is reduced to a brown strip labeled "Jersey," together with a light green trapezoid with a few rudimentary rock outcroppings and the names of only seven cities and two states scattered across it. The few blocks of Manhattan, by contrast, are depicted and colored in detail. The four square blocks of the city, which occupy the whole lower half of the poster, include numerous buildings, pedestrians and cars, as well as parking lots and lamp posts, with water towers atop a few of the buildings. The whimsical, sketchy style and spiky lettering are recognizable as Steinberg's.

The "Moscow" illustration depicts the three main characters of the film on the lower third of their poster, superimposed on a bird's eye view of New York City, and continues eastward across Manhattan and the Atlantic Ocean, past a rudimentary evocation of Europe, to a clump of recognizably Russian-styled buildings on the horizon, labeled "Moscow." The movie credits appear over the lower portion of the characters. The central part of the poster depicts approximately four New York city blocks, with fairly detailed buildings, pedestrians and vehicles, a parking lot, and some water towers and lamp posts. Columbia's artist added a few New York landmarks at apparently random places in his illustration, apparently to render the locale more easily recognizable. Beyond the blue strip labeled "Atlantic Ocean," Europe is represented by London, Paris and Rome, each anchored by a single landmark (although the landmark used for Rome is the Leaning Tower of Pisa).

The horizon behind Moscow is delineated by a red crayoned strip, above which are the title of the movie and a brief textual introduction to the plot. The poster is crowned by a thin strip of blue wash, apparently a stylization of the sky. This poster is executed in a blend of styles: the three characters, whose likenesses were copied from a photograph, have realistic faces and somewhat sketchy clothing, and the city blocks are drawn in a fairly detailed but sketchy style. The lettering on the drawing is spiky, in block-printed handwritten capital letters substantially identical to plaintiff's, while the printed texts at the top and bottom of the poster are in the typeface commonly associated with *The New Yorker* magazine.[2]

III

To succeed in a copyright infringement action, a plaintiff must prove ownership of the copyright and copying by the defendant. There is no substantial dispute concerning plaintiff's ownership of a valid copyright in his illustration. Therefore, in order to prevail on liability, plaintiff need establish only the second element of the cause of action.

---

2. The typeface is not a subject of copyright, but the similarity reinforces the impression that defendants copied plaintiff's illustration.

"Because of the inherent difficulty in obtaining direct evidence of copying, it is usually proved by circumstantial evidence of access to the copyrighted work and substantial similarities as to protectible material in the two works." *Reyher,* 533 F.2d at 90, citing Arnstein v. Porter, 154 F.2d 464, 468 (2d Cir.1946). "Of course, if there are no similarities, no amount of evidence of access will suffice to prove copying." Arnstein v. Porter, 154 F.2d at 468.

Defendants' access to plaintiff's illustration is established beyond peradventure. Therefore, the sole issue remaining with respect to liability is whether there is such substantial similarity between the copyrighted and accused works as to establish a violation of plaintiff's copyright. The central issue of "substantial similarity," which can be considered a close question of fact, may also validly be decided as a question of law.

"Substantial similarity" is an elusive concept. This circuit has recently recognized that

[t]he "substantial similarity" that supports an inference of copying sufficient to establish infringement of a copyright is not a concept familiar to the public at large. It is a term to be used in a courtroom to strike a delicate balance between the protection to which authors are entitled under an act of Congress and the freedom that exists for all others to create their works outside the area protected by infringement.

Warner Bros., 720 F.2d at 245.

The definition of "substantial similarity" in this circuit is "whether an average lay observer would recognize the alleged copy as having been appropriated from the copyrighted work." Ideal Toy Corp. v. Fab–Lu Ltd., 360 F.2d 1021, 1022 (2d Cir.1966); Silverman v. CBS, Inc., 632 F.Supp. at 1351–52. A plaintiff need no longer meet the severe "ordinary observer" test established by Judge Learned Hand in Peter Pan Fabrics, Inc. v. Martin Weiner Corp., 274 F.2d 487 (2d Cir.1960). Under Judge Hand's formulation, there would be substantial similarity only where "the ordinary observer, unless he set out to detect the disparities, would be disposed to overlook them, and regard their aesthetic appeal as the same." 274 F.2d at 489.

Moreover, it is now recognized that "[t]he copying need not be of every detail so long as the copy is substantially similar to the copyrighted work." Comptone Co. v. Rayex Corp., 251 F.2d 487, 488 (2d Cir.1958).

In determining whether there is substantial similarity between two works, it is crucial to distinguish between an idea and its expression. It is an axiom of copyright law, established in the case law and since codified at 17 U.S.C. § 102(b), that only the particular expression of an idea is protectible, while the idea itself is not.

"The idea/expression distinction, although an imprecise tool, has not been abandoned because we have as yet discovered no better way to reconcile the two competing societal interests that provide the rationale for the granting of and restrictions on copyright protection," namely, both rewarding individual ingenuity, and nevertheless allowing progress and improvements based on the same subject matter by others than the original author. *Durham Industries,* 630 F.2d at 912, *quoting Reyher,* 533 F.2d at 90.

There is no dispute that defendants cannot be held liable for using the *idea* of a map of the world from an egocentricly myopic perspective. No rigid principle has been developed, however, to ascertain when one has gone beyond the idea to the expression, and "[d]ecisions must therefore inevitably be ad hoc." Peter Pan Fabrics, Inc. v. Martin Weiner Corp., 274 F.2d 487, 489 (2d Cir.1960) (L. Hand, J.). As Judge Frankel once observed, "Good eyes and common sense may be as useful as deep study of reported and unreported cases, which themselves are tied to highly particularized facts." Couleur International Ltd. v. Opulent Fabrics, Inc., 330 F.Supp. 152, 153 (S.D.N.Y.1971).

Even at first glance, one can see the striking stylistic relationship between the posters, and since style is one ingredient of "expression," this relationship is significant. Defendants' illustration was executed in the sketchy, whimsical style that has become one of Steinberg's hallmarks. Both illustrations represent a bird's eye view across the edge of Manhattan and a river bordering New York City to the world beyond. Both depict approximately four city blocks in detail and become increasingly minimalist as the design recedes into the background. Both use the device of a narrow band of blue wash across the top of the poster to represent the sky, and both delineate the horizon with a band of primary red.[3]

The strongest similarity is evident in the rendering of the New York City blocks. Both artists chose a vantage point that looks directly down a wide two-way cross street that intersects two avenues before reaching a river. Despite defendants' protestations, this is not an inevitable way of depicting blocks in a city with a grid-like street system, particularly since most New York City cross streets are one-way. Since even a photograph may be copyrighted because "no photograph, however simple, can be unaffected by the personal influence of the author," Time Inc. v. Bernard Geis Assoc., 293 F.Supp. 130, 141 (S.D.N.Y.1968), *quoting Bleistein,* supra, one can hardly gainsay the right of an artist to protect his choice of perspective and layout in a drawing, especially in conjunction with the overall concept and individual details. Indeed, the fact that defendants changed the names of the streets while retaining the same graphic depiction weakens their case: had they intended their illustration realistically to depict the streets labeled on the poster, their four city blocks would not so closely resemble plaintiff's four city blocks. Moreover, their argument

---

3. Defendants claim that since this use of thin bands of primary colors is a traditional Japanese technique, their adoption of it cannot infringe Steinberg's copyright. This argument ignores the principle that while "[o]thers are free to copy the original ... [t]hey are not free to copy the copy." Bleistein v. Donaldson Lithographing Co., 188 U.S. 239, 250, 23 S.Ct. 298, 300, 47 L.Ed. 460 (1903) (Holmes, J.). Cf. Dave Grossman Designs, Inc. v. Bortin, 347 F.Supp. 1150, 1156–57 (N.D.Ill.1972) (an artist may use the same subject and style as another "so long as the second artist does not *substantially* copy [the first artist's] specific expression of his idea.")

that they intended the jumble of streets and landmarks and buildings to symbolize their Muscovite protagonist's confusion in a new city does not detract from the strong similarity between their poster and Steinberg's.

While not all of the details are identical, many of them could be mistaken for one another; for example, the depiction of the water towers, and the cars, and the red sign above a parking lot, and even many of the individual buildings. The shapes, windows, and configurations of various edifices are substantially similar. The ornaments, facades and details of Steinberg's buildings appear in defendants', although occasionally at other locations. In this context, it is significant that Steinberg did not depict any buildings actually erected in New York; rather, he was inspired by the general appearance of the structures on the West Side of Manhattan to create his own New York-ish structures. Thus, the similarity between the buildings depicted in the "Moscow" and Steinberg posters cannot be explained by an assertion that the artists happened to choose the same buildings to draw. The close similarity can be explained only by the defendants' artist having copied the plaintiff's work. Similarly, the locations and size, the errors and anomalies of Steinberg's shadows and streetlight, are meticulously imitated.

In addition, the Columbia artist's use of the childlike, spiky block print that has become one of Steinberg's hallmarks to letter the names of the streets in the "Moscow" poster can be explained only as copying. There is no inherent justification for using this style of lettering to label New York City streets as it is associated with New York only through Steinberg's poster.

While defendants' poster shows the city of Moscow on the horizon in far greater detail than anything is depicted in the background of plaintiff's illustration, this fact alone cannot alter the conclusion. "Substantial similarity" does not require identity, and "duplication or near identity is not necessary to establish infringement." *Krofft,* 562 F.2d at 1167. Neither the depiction of Moscow, nor the eastward perspective, nor the presence of randomly scattered New York City landmarks in defendants' poster suffices to eliminate the substantial similarity between the posters. As Judge Learned Hand wrote, "no plagiarist can excuse the wrong by showing how much of his work he did not pirate." Sheldon v. Metro–Goldwyn Pictures Corp., 81 F.2d 49, 56 (2d Cir.), cert. denied, 298 U.S. 669, 56 S.Ct. 835, 80 L.Ed. 1392 (1936).

Defendants argue that their poster could not infringe plaintiff's copyright because only a small proportion of its design could possibly be considered similar. This argument is both factually and legally without merit. "[A] copyright infringement may occur by reason of a substantial similarity that involves only a small portion of each work." Burroughs v. Metro–Goldwyn–Mayer, Inc., 683 F.2d 610, 624 n. 14 (2d Cir.1982). Moreover, this case involves the entire protected work and an iconographically, as well as proportionately, significant portion of the allegedly infringing work.

The process by which defendants' poster was created also undermines this argument. The "map," that is, the portion about which plaintiff is complaining, was designed separately from the rest of the poster. The likenesses of the three main characters, which were copied from a photograph, and the blocks of text were superimposed on the completed map.

I also reject defendants' argument that any similarities between the works are unprotectible *scenes a faire,* or "incidents, characters or settings which, as a practical matter, are indispensable or standard in the treatment of a given topic." *Walker,* 615 F.Supp. at 436. It is undeniable that a drawing of New York City blocks could be expected to include buildings, pedestrians, vehicles, lampposts and water towers. Plaintiff, however, does not complain of defendants' mere use of these elements in their poster; rather, his complaint is that defendants copied his *expression* of those elements of a street scene.

While evidence of independent creation by the defendants would rebut plaintiff's prima facie case, "the absence of any countervailing evidence of creation independent of the copyrighted source may well render clearly erroneous a finding that there was not copying." Roth Greeting Cards v. United Card Co., 429 F.2d 1106, 1110 (9th Cir.1970).

Moreover, it is generally recognized that "... since a very high degree of similarity is required in order to dispense with proof of access, it must logically follow that where proof of access is offered, the required degree of similarity may be somewhat less than would be necessary in the absence of such proof." 2 Nimmer § 143.4 at 634, *quoted in Krofft,* 562 F.2d at 1172. As defendants have conceded access to plaintiff's copyrighted illustration, a somewhat lesser degree of similarity suffices to establish a copyright infringement than might otherwise be required. Here, however, the demonstrable similarities are such that proof of access, although in fact conceded, is almost unnecessary. . . .

VI

For the reasons set out above, summary judgment is granted to plaintiffs as to copying.

Gross v. Seligman

United States Circuit Court of Appeals, Second Circuit, 1914.
212 Fed. 930.

Appeal from the District Court of the United States for the Southern District of New York.

This cause comes here upon appeal from an order of the District Court, Southern District of New York, enjoining defendant from publishing a photograph. The suit is brought under the provisions of the Copyright Act. One Rochlitz, an artist, posed a model in the nude, and therefrom produced a photograph, which he named the "Grace of Youth." A copyright was obtained therefor; all the artist's rights being sold and assigned to complainants. Two years later the same artist placed the same model in the identical pose, with the single exception that the young woman now wears a smile and holds a cherry stem between her teeth. He took a photograph of this pose, which he called "Cherry Ripe,"; this second photograph is published by defendants, and has been enjoined as an infringement of complainant's copyright.

LACOMBE, Circuit Judge (after stating the facts as above). This is not simply the case of taking two separate photographs of the same young woman.

When the Grace of Youth was produced a distinctly artistic conception was formed, and was made permanent as a picture in the very method which the Supreme Court indicated in the Oscar Wilde Case (Burrow–Giles Lithographic Company v. Sarony, 111 U.S. 53, 4 Sup.Ct. 279, 28 L.Ed. 349) would entitle the person producing such a picture to a copyright to protect it. It was there held that the artist who used the camera to produce his picture was entitled to copyright just as he would have been had he produced it with a brush on canvas. If the copyrighted picture were produced with colors on canvas, and were then copyrighted and sold by the artist, he would infringe the purchaser's rights if thereafter the same artist, using the same model, repainted the same picture with only trivial variations of detail and offered it for sale.

Of course when the first picture has been produced and copyrighted every other artist is entirely free to form his own conception of the Grace of Youth, or anything else, and to avail of the same young woman's services in making it permanent, whether he works with pigments or a camera. If, by chance, the pose, background, light, and shade, etc., of this new picture were strikingly similar, and if, by reason of the circumstance that the same young woman was the prominent feature in both compositions, it might be very difficult to distinguish the new picture from the old one, the new would still not be an infringement of the old because it is in no true sense a *copy* of the old. This is a risk which the original artist takes when he merely produces a likeness of an existing face and figure, instead of supplementing its features by the exercise of his own imagination.

It seems to us, however, that we have no such new photograph of the same model. The identity of the artist and the many close identities of pose, light, and shade, etc., indicate very strongly that the first picture was used to produce the second. Whether the model in the second case was posed, and light and shade, etc., arranged with a copy of the first photograph physically present before the artist's eyes, or whether his mental reproduction of the exact combination he had already once effected was so clear and vivid that he did not need the physical reproduction of it, seems to us immaterial. The one thing, viz., the exercise of artistic talent, which made the first photographic picture a subject of copyright, has been used not to produce another picture, but to duplicate the original.

The case is quite similar to those where indirect copying, through the use of living pictures, was held to be an infringement of copyright.

The eye of an artist or a connoisseur will, no doubt, find differences between these two photographs. The backgrounds are not identical, the model in one case is sedate, in the other smiling; moreover the young woman was two years older when the later photograph was taken, and some slight changes in the contours of her figure are discoverable. But the identities are much greater than the differences, and it seems to us that the artist was careful to introduce only enough differences to argue about, while undertaking to make what would seem to be a copy to the ordinary purchaser who did not have both photographs before him at the same time. In this undertaking we think he succeeded.

The order is affirmed.

NOTE

Compare with *Steinberg* and *Gross,* Franklin Mint Corp. v. National Wildlife Art Exchange, Inc., 575 F.2d 62, 197 U.S.P.Q. 721 (3d Cir.1978), cert. denied, 439 U.S. 880, 99 S.Ct. 217, 58 L.Ed.2d 193, 199 U.S.P.Q. 576, where the court observed that "in the world of fine art, the ease with which a copyright may be delineated may depend on the artist's style. A painter like Monet when dwelling upon impressions created by light on the facade of the Rouen Cathedral is apt to create a work which can make infringement attempts difficult. On the other hand, an artist who produces a rendition with photograph-like clarity and accuracy may be hard-pressed to prove unlawful copying by another who uses the same subject matter and the same technique. A copyright in that circumstance may be termed 'weak,' since the expression and the subject matter converge. In contrast, in the impressionist's work, the lay observer will be able to differentiate more readily between the reality of subject matter and subjective effect of the artist's work." 575 F.2d at 65.

Compare with *Steinberg*, *Gross* and *Nichols*, the following observation from Warner Bros., Inc. v. American Broadcasting Cos., 720 F.2d 231, 241–42, 222 U.S.P.Q. 101 (2d Cir.1983):

A story has a linear dimension: it begins, continues, and ends. If a defendant copies substantial portions of a plaintiff's sequence of events, he does not escape infringement by adding original episodes somewhere along the line. A graphic or three-dimensional work is created to be perceived as an entirety. Significant dissimilarities between two works of this sort inevitably lessen the similarity that would otherwise exist between the total perceptions of the two works. The graphic rendering of a character has aspects of both the linear, literary mode and the multi-dimensional total perception. What the character thinks, feels, says, and does and the descriptions conveyed by the author through the comments of other characters in the work episodically fill out a viewer's understanding of the character. At the same time, the visual perception of the character tends to create a dominant impression against which the similarity of a defendant's character may be readily compared, and significant differences readily noted.

See Paul Edward Geller, *Hiroshige vs. Van Gogh*: Resolving the Dilemma of Copyright Scope in Remedying Infringement, 46 J. Copyright Soc'y U.S.A. 39 (1998).

E.   RIGHTS BEYOND COPYRIGHT: MORAL RIGHT

RAYMOND SARRAUTE, CURRENT THEORY ON THE MORAL RIGHT OF AUTHORS AND ARTISTS UNDER FRENCH LAW, 16 AM. J. COMP. L. 465, 465–67, 480–81 (1968).* In French law the concept of literary and artistic rights involves two elements.

The first is analogous to the English-speaking countries' copyright. It is a property right, and consists of a temporary monopoly over the exploitation of protected works. It assures the author of the exclusive right to control the reproduction and the performance or exhibition of his creation.

The second element is the "moral" right. It includes non-property attributes of an intellectual and moral character which give legal expression to the intimate bond which exists between a literary or artistic work and its author's personality; it is intended to protect his personality as well as his work. . . .

Until this moment of disengagement, the work is an expression of the artist's personality and remains strictly his own. No one can claim any right to it whatsoever. It is a rough draft, a design which the artist may modify or destroy at will. He alone can determine from the moment when his plan has been realized, when his work is completed, when he feels that he can, without injuring his reputation, reveal it to the public and surrender his rights over it to a third party.

Once this decision is made, the work is separated from the artist; it falls into commerce, becomes the subject of transactions. It is published, exhibited, performed. But the artist still retains certain rights over the work. In some cases he retains the right to suppress it if he is no longer satisfied with it; in all instances he retains the right to demand that he be recognized as its author, that his name be associated with it, and, above all, that the work be neither abridged nor distorted.

Thus the moral right is generally composed of four aspects:

(1) The right of disclosure (*divulgation*);

Then, after the work has been made public and the author's rights to it have been transferred:

(2) The right to withdraw or disavow;

(3) The right of paternity—i.e., the right to have one's name and authorship recognized;

(4) The right of integrity of the work of art. . . .

---

* Copyright © 1968 The American Association for the Comparative Study of Law, Inc.

As we have seen, Article 6 of the law of March 11, 1957 recognizes the author's right to insist that the integrity of his work be respected. This right has always been acknowledged by the courts. It does not arise until, after completion, the work has been put on the market by the author, has been sold, or has been made the subject of contracts of publication or performance. From that time on the author has the right to insist that its integrity must not be violated by measures which could alter or distort it.

This principle is unquestioned and its practical application presents few theoretical difficulties. A case in point is the recent decision of the Court of Cassation on July 6, 1965, which affirmed a decision rendered by the Paris Court of Appeals of May 30, 1962. Both Courts found in favor of the painter Bernard Buffet, who maintained that the refrigerator he had decorated was an indivisible artistic unit, and opposed the sale of any of the elements of the ornamentation separately from the others.

An extremely delicate problem does, however, arise in one situation. This is the problem of protecting the integrity of a work when the author has authorized its adaptation to a different medium, as in the case of the adaptation of an opera or a ballet for the theatre or the cinema. The problem here is to ascertain to what extent the right of the author of the original work can insist on its integrity, when this claim conflicts with creative freedom of the adapter, as the author of a work which purports to be equally original. How may a conflict between two equally valid moral rights be resolved?

Gilliam v. American Broadcasting Companies, Inc.

United States Court of Appeals, Second Circuit, 1976.
538 F.2d 14, 192 U.S.P.Q. 1.

LUMBARD, Circuit Judge.

Plaintiffs, a group of British writers and performers known as "Monty Python," appeal from a denial by Judge Lasker in the Southern District of a preliminary injunction to restrain the American Broadcasting Company (ABC) from broadcasting edited versions of three separate programs originally written and performed by Monty Python for broadcast by the British Broadcasting Corporation (BBC). We agree with Judge Lasker that the appellants have demonstrated that the excising done for ABC impairs the integrity of the original work. We further find that the countervailing injuries that Judge Lasker found might have accrued to ABC as a result of an injunction at a prior date no longer exist. We therefore direct the issuance of a preliminary injunction by the district court.

Since its formation in 1969, the Monty Python group has gained popularity primarily through its thirty-minute television programs created for BBC as part of a comedy series entitled "Monty Python's Flying Circus." In accordance with an agreement between Monty Python and BBC, the group writes and delivers to BBC scripts for use in the television series. This scriptwriters' agreement recites in great detail the procedure to be followed when any alterations are to be made in the script prior to recording of the program.[2] The essence of this section of the agreement is that, while BBC retains final authority to make changes, appellants or their representatives exercise optimum control over the scripts consistent with BBC's authority and only minor changes may be made without prior consultation with the writers. Nothing in the scriptwriters' agreement entitles BBC to alter a program once it has been recorded. The agreement further provides that, subject to the terms therein, the group retains all rights in the script.

Under the agreement, BBC may license the transmission of recordings of the television programs in any overseas territory. The series has been broadcast in this country primarily on non-commercial public broadcasting television stations, although several of the programs have been broadcast on commercial stations in Texas and Nevada. In each instance, the thirty-minute programs have been broadcast as originally recorded and broadcast in England in their entirety and without commercial interruption.

In October 1973, Time–Life Films acquired the right to distribute in the United States certain BBC television programs, including the Monty Python series. Time–Life was permitted to edit the programs only "for insertion of commercials, applicable censorship or governmental . . . rules and regulations, and National Association of Broadcasters and time segment requirements." No similar clause was included in the scriptwriters' agreement between appellants and BBC. Prior to this time, ABC had sought to acquire the right to broadcast excerpts from various Monty Python programs in the spring of 1975, but the group rejected the proposal for such a disjoined format. Thereafter, in July 1975, ABC agreed with Time–Life to broadcast two ninety-minute specials each comprising three

---

2.   The Agreement provides:

V.   When script alterations are necessary it is the intention of the BBC to make every effort to inform and to reach agreement with the Writer. Whenever practicable any necessary alterations (other than minor alterations) shall be made by the Writer. Nevertheless the BBC shall at all times have the right to make (a) minor alterations and (b) such other alterations as in its opinion are necessary in order to avoid involving the BBC in legal action or bringing the BBC into disrepute. Any decision under (b) shall be made at a level not below that of Head of Department. It is however agreed that after a script has been accepted by the BBC alterations will not be made by the BBC under (b) above unless (i) the Writer, if available when the BBC requires the alterations to be made, has been asked to agree to them but is not willing to do so and (ii) the Writer has had, if he so requests and if the BBC agrees that time permits if rehearsals and recording are to

proceed as planned, an opportunity to be represented by the Writers' Guild of Great Britain (or if he is not a member of the Guild by his agent) at a meeting with the BBC to be held within at most 48 hours of the request (excluding weekends). If in such circumstances there is no agreement about the alterations then the final decision shall rest with the BBC. Apart from the right to make alterations under (a) and (b) above the BBC shall not without the consent of the Writer or his agent (which consent shall not be unreasonably withheld) make any structural alterations as opposed to minor alterations to the script, provided that such consent shall not be necessary in any case where the Writer is for any reason not immediately available for consultation at the time which in the BBC's opinion is the deadline from the production point of view for such alterations to be made if rehearsals and recording are to proceed as planned.

thirty-minute Monty Python programs that had not previously been shown in this country.

Correspondence between representatives of BBC and Monty Python reveals that these parties assumed that ABC would broadcast each of the Monty Python programs "in its entirety." On September 5, 1975, however, the group's British representative inquired of BBC how ABC planned to show the programs in their entirety if approximately 24 minutes of each 90 minute program were to be devoted to commercials. BBC replied on September 12, "we can only reassure you that ABC have [sic] decided to run the programmes 'back to back,' and that there is a firm undertaking not to segment them."

ABC broadcast the first of the specials on October 3, 1975. Appellants did not see a tape of the program until late November and were allegedly "appalled" at the discontinuity and "mutilation" that had resulted from the editing done by Time–Life for ABC. Twenty-four minutes of the original 90 minutes of recording had been omitted. Some of the editing had been done in order to make time for commercials; other material had been edited, according to ABC, because the original programs contained offensive or obscene matter.

In early December, Monty Python learned that ABC planned to broadcast the second special on December 26, 1975. The parties began negotiations concerning editing of that program and a delay of the broadcast until Monty Python could view it. These negotiations were futile, however, and on December 15 the group filed this action to enjoin the broadcast and for damages. Following an evidentiary hearing, Judge Lasker found that "the plaintiffs have established an impairment of the integrity of their work" which "caused the film or program ... to lose its iconoclastic verve." According to Judge Lasker, "the damage that has been caused to the plaintiffs is irreparable by its nature." Nevertheless, the judge denied the motion for the preliminary injunction on the grounds that it was unclear who owned the copyright in the programs produced by BBC from the scripts written by Monty Python; that there was a question of whether Time–Life and BBC were indispensable parties to the litigation; that ABC would suffer significant financial loss if it were enjoined a week before the scheduled broadcast; and that Monty Python had displayed a "somewhat disturbing casualness" in their pursuance of the matter.

Judge Lasker granted Monty Python's request for more limited relief by requiring ABC to broadcast a disclaimer during the December 26 special to the effect that the group dissociated itself from the program because of the editing. A panel of this court, however, granted a stay of that order until this appeal could be heard and permitted ABC to broadcast, at the beginning of the special, only the legend that the program had been edited by ABC. We heard argument on April 13 and, at that time, enjoined ABC from any further broadcast of edited Monty Python programs pending the decision of the court.

I

In determining the availability of injunctive relief at this early stage of the proceedings, Judge Lasker properly considered the harm that would inure to the plaintiffs if the injunction were denied, the harm that defendant would suffer if the injunction were granted, and the likelihood that plaintiffs would ultimately succeed on the merits. We direct the issuance of a preliminary injunction because we find that all these factors weigh in favor of appellants.

There is nothing clearly erroneous in Judge Lasker's conclusion that any injury suffered by appellants as a result of the broadcast of edited versions of their programs was irreparable by its nature. ABC presented the appellants with their first opportunity for broadcast to a nationwide network audience in this country. If ABC adversely misrepresented the quality of Monty Python's work, it is likely that many members of the audience, many of whom, by defendant's admission, were previously unfamiliar with appellants, would not become loyal followers of Monty Python productions. The subsequent injury to appellants' theatrical reputation would imperil their ability to attract the large audience necessary to the success of their venture. Such an injury to professional reputation cannot be measured in monetary terms or recompensed by other relief.

In contrast to the harm that Monty Python would suffer by a denial of the preliminary injunction, Judge Lasker found that ABC's relationship with its affiliates would be impaired by a grant of an injunction within a week of the scheduled December 26 broadcast. The court also found that ABC and its affiliates had advertised the program and had included it in listings of forthcoming television programs that were distributed to the public. Thus a last minute cancellation of the December 26 program, Judge Lasker concluded, would injure defendant financially and in its reputation with the public and its advertisers.

However valid these considerations may have been when the issue before the court was whether a preliminary injunction should immediately precede the broadcast, any injury to ABC is presently more speculative. No rebroadcast of the edited specials has been scheduled and no advertising costs have been incurred for the immediate future. Thus there is no danger that defendant's relations with affiliates or the public will suffer irreparably if subsequent broadcasts of the programs are enjoined pending a disposition of the issues.

We then reach the question whether there is a likelihood that appellants will succeed on the merits. In concluding that there is a likelihood of infringement here, we rely especially on the fact that the editing was substantial, i.e., approximately 27 percent of the original program was omitted, and the editing contravened contractual provisions that limited the right to edit Monty Python material. It should be emphasized that our discussion of these matters refers only to such facts as have been developed upon the hearing for a preliminary injunction. Modified or contrary findings may become appropriate after a plenary trial.

Judge Lasker denied the preliminary injunction in part because he was unsure of the ownership of the copyright in the recorded program. Appellants first contend that the question of ownership is irrelevant because the recorded program was merely a derivative work taken from the script in which they hold the uncontested copyright. Thus, even if BBC owned the copyright in the recorded program, its use of that work would be limited by the license granted to BBC by Monty Python for use of the underlying script. We agree.

Section 7 of the Copyright Law, 17 U.S.C.A. § 7, provides in part that "adaptations, arrangements, dramatizations ... or other versions of ... copyrighted works when produced with the consent of the proprietor of the copyright in such works ... shall be regarded as new works subject to copyright...." Manifestly, the recorded program falls into this category as a dramatization of the script, and thus the program was itself entitled to copyright protection. However, section 7 limits the copyright protection of the derivative work, as works adapted from previously existing scripts have become known, to the novel additions made to the underlying work, and the derivative work does not affect the "force or validity" of the copyright in the matter from which it is derived. Thus, any ownership by BBC of the copyright in the recorded program would not affect the scope or ownership of the copyright in the underlying script.

Since the copyright in the underlying script survives intact despite the incorporation of that work into a derivative work, one who uses the script, even with the permission of the proprietor of the derivative work, may infringe the underlying copyright. See Davis v. E.I. DuPont de Nemours & Co., 240 F.Supp. 612, 145 U.S.P.Q. 258 (S.D.N.Y.1965) (defendants held to have infringed when they obtained permission to use a screenplay in preparing a television script but did not obtain permission of the author of the play upon which the screenplay was based).

If the proprietor of the derivative work is licensed by the proprietor of the copyright in the underlying work to vend or distribute the derivative work to third parties, those parties will, of course, suffer no liability for their use of the underlying work consistent with the license to the proprietor of the derivative work. Obviously, it was just this type of arrangement that was contemplated in this instance. The scriptwriters' agreement between Monty Python and BBC specifically permitted the latter to license the transmission of the recordings made by BBC to distributors such as Time–Life for broadcast in overseas territories.

One who obtains permission to use a copyrighted script in the production of a derivative work, however, may not exceed the specific purpose for which permission was granted. Most of the decisions that have reached this conclusion have dealt with the improper extension of the underlying work into media or time, i.e., duration of the license, not covered by the grant of permission to the derivative work proprietor. Appellants herein do not claim that the broadcast by ABC violated media or time restrictions contained in the license of the script to BBC. Rather, they claim that revisions in the script, and ultimately in the program, could be made only after consultation with Monty Python, and that ABC's broadcast of a program edited after recording and without consultation with Monty Python exceeded the scope of any license that BBC was entitled to grant.

The rationale for finding infringement when a licensee exceeds time or media restrictions on his license—the need to allow the proprietor of the underlying copyright to control the method in which his work is presented to the public—applies equally to the situation in which a licensee makes an unauthorized use of the underlying work by publishing it in a truncated version. Whether intended to allow greater economic exploitation of the work, as in the media and time cases, or to ensure that the copyright proprietor retains a veto power over revisions desired for the derivative work, the ability of the copyright holder to control his work remains paramount in our copyright law. We find, therefore, that unauthorized editing of the underlying work, if proven, would constitute an infringement of the copyright in that work similar to any other use of a work that exceeded the license granted by the proprietor of the copyright.

If the broadcast of an edited version of the Monty Python program infringed the group's copyright in the script, ABC may obtain no solace from the fact that editing was permitted in the agreements between BBC and Time–Life or Time–Life and ABC. BBC was not entitled to make unilateral changes in the script and was not specifically empowered to alter the recordings once made; Monty Python, moreover, had reserved to itself any rights not granted to BBC. Since a grantor may not convey greater rights than it owns, BBC's permission to allow Time–Life, and hence ABC, to edit, appears to have been a nullity.

ABC answers appellants' infringement argument with a series of contentions, none of which seems meritorious at this stage of the litigation. The network asserts that Monty Python's British representative, Jill Foster, knew that ABC planned to exclude much of the original BBC program in the October 3 broadcast. ABC thus contends that by not previously objecting to this procedure, Monty Python ratified BBC's authority to license others to edit the underlying script.

Although the case of Ilyin v. Avon Publications, Inc., 144 F.Supp. 368, 373, 110 U.S.P.Q. 356, 359 (S.D.N.Y.1956), may be broadly read for the proposition that a holder of a derivative copyright may obtain rights in the underlying work through ratification, the conduct necessary to that conclusion has yet to be demonstrated in this case. It is undisputed that appellants did not have actual notice of the cuts in the October 3 broadcast until late November. Even if they are chargeable with the knowledge of their British representative, it is not clear that she had prior notice of the cuts or ratified the omissions, nor did Judge Lasker make any finding on the question. While Foster, on September 5, did question how ABC was to broadcast the entire program if it was going to interpose 24 minutes of commercials, she received assurances from BBC that the programs would not be "segmented." The fact that she knew precisely the length of material that would have to be omitted to allow for commercials does not prove that she ratified the deletions. This is especially true in light of previous assurances that the program would contain the original shows in their entirety. On the present record, it cannot be said that there was any ratification of BBC's grant of editing rights. ABC, of course, is entitled to attempt to prove otherwise during the trial on the merits.

ABC next argues that under the "joint work" theory adopted in Shapiro, Bernstein & Co. v. Jerry Vogel Music Co., 221 F.2d 569, 105 U.S.P.Q. 178 (2d Cir.1955), the script produced by Monty Python and the program recorded by BBC are symbiotic elements of a single production. Therefore, according to ABC, each contributor possesses an undivided ownership of all copyrightable elements in the final work and BBC could thus have licensed use of the script, including editing, written by appellants.

The joint work theory as extended in Shapiro has been criticized as inequitable unless "at the time of creation by the first author, the second author's contribution [is envisaged] as an integrated part of a single work," and the first author intends that the final product be a joint work. Furthermore, this court appears to have receded from a broad application of the joint work doctrine where the contract which leads to collaboration between authors indicates that one will retain a superior interest. In the present case, the screenwriters' agreement between Monty Python and BBC provides that the group is to retain all rights in the script not granted in the agreement and that at some future point the group may license the scripts for use on television to parties other than BBC. These provisions suggest that the parties did not consider themselves joint authors of a single work. This matter is subject to further exploration at the trial, but in the present state of the record, it presents no bar to issuance of a preliminary injunction.

Aside from the question of who owns the relevant copyrights, ABC asserts that the contracts between appellants and BBC permit editing of the programs for commercial television in the United States. ABC argues that the scriptwriters' agreement allows appellants the right to participate in revisions of the script only prior to the recording of the programs, and thus infers that BBC had unrestricted authority to revise after that point. This argument, however, proves too much. A reading of the contract seems to indicate that Monty Python obtained control over editing the script only to ensure control over the program recorded from that script. Since the scriptwriters' agreement explicitly retains for the group all rights not granted by the contract, omission of any terms concerning alterations in the program after recording must be read as reserving to appellants exclusive authority for such revisions.

Finally, ABC contends that appellants must have expected that deletions would be made in the recordings to conform them for use on commercial television in the United States. ABC argues that licensing in the United States implicitly grants a license to insert commercials in a program and to remove offensive or obscene material prior to broadcast. According to the network, appellants should have anticipated that most of the excised material contained scatological references inappropriate for

American television and that these scenes would be replaced with commercials, which presumably are more palatable to the American public.

The proof adduced up to this point, however, provides no basis for finding any implied consent to edit. Prior to the ABC broadcasts, Monty Python programs had been broadcast on a regular basis by both commercial and public television stations in this country without interruption or deletion. Indeed, there is no evidence of any prior broadcast of edited Monty Python material in the United States. These facts, combined with the persistent requests for assurances by the group and its representatives that the programs would be shown intact belie the argument that the group knew or should have known that deletions and commercial interruptions were inevitable.

Several of the deletions made for ABC, such as elimination of the words "hell" and "damn," seem inexplicable given today's standard television fare. If, however, ABC honestly determined that the programs were obscene in substantial part, it could have decided not to broadcast the specials at all, or it could have attempted to reconcile its differences with appellants. The network could not, however, free from a claim of infringement, broadcast in a substantially altered form a program incorporating the script over which the group had retained control.

Our resolution of these technical arguments serves to reinforce our initial inclination that the copyright law should be used to recognize the important role of the artist in our society and the need to encourage production and dissemination of artistic works by providing adequate legal protection for one who submits his work to the public. We therefore conclude that there is a substantial likelihood that, after a full trial, appellants will succeed in proving infringement of their copyright by ABC's broadcast of edited versions of Monty Python programs. In reaching this conclusion, however, we need not accept appellants' assertion that any editing whatsoever would constitute infringement. Courts have recognized that licensees are entitled to some small degree of latitude in arranging the licensed work for presentation to the public in a manner consistent with the licensee's style or standards. That privilege, however, does not extend to the degree of editing that occurred here especially in light of contractual provisions that limited the right to edit Monty Python material.

II

It also seems likely that appellants will succeed on the theory that, regardless of the right ABC had to broadcast an edited program, the cuts made constituted an actionable mutilation of Monty Python's work. This cause of action, which seeks redress for deformation of an artist's work, finds its roots in the continental concept of droit moral, or moral right, which may generally be summarized as including the right of the artist to have his work attributed to him in the form in which he created it.

American copyright law, as presently written, does not recognize moral rights or provide a cause of action for their violation, since the law seeks to vindicate the economic, rather than the personal, rights of authors. Nevertheless, the economic incentive for artistic and intellectual creation that serves as the foundation for American copyright law, cannot be reconciled with the inability of artists to obtain relief for mutilation or misrepresentation of their work to the public on which the artists are financially dependent. Thus courts have long granted relief for misrepresentation of an artist's work by relying on theories outside the statutory law of copyright, such as contract law, Granz v. Harris, 198 F.2d 585 (2d Cir.1952) (substantial cutting of original work constitutes misrepresentation), or the tort of unfair competition, Prouty v. National Broadcasting Co., 26 F.Supp. 265, 40 U.S.P.Q. 331 (D.C.Mass.1939). Although such decisions are clothed in terms of proprietary right in one's creation, they also properly vindicate the author's personal right to prevent the presentation of his work to the public in a distorted form. See Gardella v. Log Cabin Products Co., 89 F.2d 891, 895–96, 34 U.S.P.Q. 145, 148–150 (2d Cir.1937); Roeder, The Doctrine of Moral Right, 53 Harv.L.Rev. 554, 568 (1940).

Here, the appellants claim that the editing done for ABC mutilated the original work and that consequently the broadcast of those programs as the creation of Monty Python violated the Lanham Act § 43(a), 15 U.S.C.A. § 1125(a). This statute, the federal counterpart to state unfair competition laws, has been invoked to prevent misrepresentations that may injure plaintiff's business or personal reputation, even where no registered trademark is concerned. It is sufficient to violate the Act that a representation of a product, although technically true, creates a false impression of the product's origin. See Rich v. RCA Corp., 390 F.Supp. 530, 185 U.S.P.Q. 508 (S.D.N.Y.1975) (recent picture of plaintiff on cover of album containing songs recorded in distant past held to be a false representation that the songs were new).

These cases cannot be distinguished from the situation in which a television network broadcasts a program properly designated as having been written and performed by a group, but which has been edited, without the writer's consent, into a form that departs substantially from the original work. "To deform his work is to present him to the public as the creator of a work not his own, and thus makes him subject to criticism for work he has not done." Roeder, supra, at 569. In such a case, it is the writer or performer, rather than the network, who suffers the consequences of the mutilation, for the public will have only the final product by which to evaluate the work. Thus, an allegation that a defendant has presented to the public a "garbled," distorted version of plaintiff's work seeks to redress the very rights sought to be protected by the Lanham Act, 15 U.S.C.A. § 1125(a), and should be recognized as stating a cause of action under that statute. See Autry v. Republic Productions, Inc., 213 F.2d 667, 101 U.S.P.Q. 478 (9th Cir.1954); Jaeger v. American Int'l Pictures, Inc., 330 F.Supp. 274, 169 U.S.P.Q. 668 (S.D.N.Y.1971), which suggests the violation of such a right if mutilation could be proven.

During the hearing on the preliminary injunction, Judge Lasker viewed the edited version of the Monty Python program broadcast on December 26 and the original, unedited version. After hearing argument of this appeal, this panel also viewed and compared the two versions. We find that the truncated version at times omitted the climax of the skits to which appellants' rare brand of humor was leading and at other times deleted essential elements in the schematic development of a story line.[12] We therefore agree with Judge Lasker's conclusion that the edited version broadcast by ABC impaired the integrity of appellants' work and represented to the public as the product of appellants what was actually a mere caricature of their talents. We believe that a valid cause of action for such distortion exists and that therefore a preliminary injunction may issue to prevent repetition of the broadcast prior to final determination of the issues.[13]

III

We do not share Judge Lasker's concern about the procedures by which the appellants have pursued this action. The district court indicated agreement with ABC that appellants were guilty of laches in not requesting a preliminary injunction until 11 days prior to the broadcast. Our discussion above, however, suggests that the group did not know and had no reason to believe until late November that editing would take place. Several letters between BBC and Monty Python's representative indicate that appellants believed that the programs would be shown in their entirety. Furthermore, the group did act to prevent offensive editing of the second program immediately after viewing the tape of the first edited program. Thus we find no undue delay in the group's failure to institute this action until they were sufficiently advised regarding the facts necessary to support the action. In any event, ABC has not demonstrated how it was prejudiced by any delay.

Finally, Judge Lasker denied a preliminary injunction because Monty Python had failed to join BBC and Time–Life as indispensable parties. We do not believe that either is an indispensable party. ABC argues that joinder of both was required because it acted in good faith pursuant to its

---

12. A single example will illustrate the extent of distortion engendered by the editing. In one skit, an upper class English family is engaged in a discussion of the tonal quality of certain words as "woody" or "tinny." The father soon begins to suggest certain words with sexual connotations as either "woody" or "tinny," whereupon the mother fetches a bucket of water and pours it over his head. The skit continues from this point. The ABC edit eliminates this middle sequence so that the father is comfortably dressed at one moment and, in the next moment, is shown in a soaken condition without any explanation for the change in his appearance.

13. Judge Gurfein's concurring opinion suggests that since the gravamen of a complaint under the Lanham Act is that the origin of goods has been falsely described, a

legend disclaiming Monty Python's approval of the edited version would preclude violation of that Act. We are doubtful that a few words could erase the indelible impression that is made by a television broadcast, especially since the viewer has no means of comparing the truncated version with the complete work in order to determine for himself the talents of plaintiffs. Furthermore, a disclaimer such as the one originally suggested by Judge Lasker in the exigencies of an impending broadcast last December, would go unnoticed by viewers who tuned into the broadcast a few minutes after it began.

We therefore conclude that Judge Gurfein's proposal that the district court could find some form of disclaimer would be sufficient might not provide appropriate relief.

contractual rights with Time–Life in broadcasting edited versions of the programs, and Time–Life, in turn, relied upon its contract with BBC. Furthermore, ABC argues, BBC must be joined since it owns the copyright in the recorded programs.

Even if BBC owns a copyright relevant to determination of the issues in this case, the formalistic rule that once required all owners of a copyright to be parties to an action for its infringement has given way to equitable considerations. In this case, the equities to be considered under Fed.R.Civ.P. 19(a) strongly favor appellants. Monty Python is relying solely on its copyright in the script and on its rights as an author. No claim is being made that Monty Python has rights derived from the copyright held by another. One of the parties is an English corporation, and any action that appellants, a group of English writers and performers, might have against that potential defendant would be better considered under English law in an English court.

Complete relief for the alleged infringement and mutilation complained of may be accorded between Monty Python and ABC, which alone broadcast the programs in dispute. If ABC is ultimately found liable to appellants, a permanent injunction against future broadcasts and a damage award would satisfy all of appellants' claims. ABC's assertion that failure to join BBC and Time–Life may leave it subject to inconsistent verdicts in a later action against its licensors may be resolved through the process of impleader, which ABC has thus far avoided despite a suggestion from the district court to use that procedure. Finally, neither of the parties considered by ABC to be indispensable has claimed any interest in the subject matter of this litigation. See Fed.R.Civ.P. 19(a)(2).

For these reasons we direct that the district court issue the preliminary injunction sought by the appellants.

GURFEIN, Circuit Judge, concurring.

I concur in my brother Lumbard's scholarly opinion, but I wish to comment on the application of Section 43(a) of the Lanham Act, 15 U.S.C.A. § 1125(a).

I believe that this is the first case in which a federal appellate court has held that there may be a violation of Section 43(a) of the Lanham Act with respect to a common-law copyright. The Lanham Act is a trademark statute, not a copyright statute. Nevertheless, we must recognize that the language of Section 43(a) is broad. It speaks of the affixation or use of false designations of origin or false descriptions or representations, but proscribes such use "in connection with any goods or services." It is easy enough to incorporate trade names as well as trademarks into Section 43(a) and the statute specifically applies to common law trademarks, as well as registered trademarks. Lanham Act § 45, 15 U.S.C.A. § 1127.

In the present case, we are holding that the deletion of portions of the recorded tape constitutes a breach of contract, as well as an infringement of a common-law copyright of the original work. There is literally no need to discuss whether plaintiffs also have a claim for relief under the Lanham

Act or for unfair competition under New York law. I agree with Judge Lumbard, however, that it may be an exercise of judicial economy to express our view on the Lanham Act claim, and I do not dissent therefrom. I simply wish to leave it open for the District Court to fashion the remedy.

The Copyright Act provides no recognition of the so-called droit moral, or moral rights of authors. Nor are such rights recognized in the field of copyright law in the United States. If a distortion or truncation in connection with a use constitutes an infringement of copyright, there is no need for an additional cause of action beyond copyright infringement. An obligation to mention the name of the author carries the implied duty, however, as a matter of contract, not to make such changes in the work as would render the credit line a false attribution of authorship.

So far as the Lanham Act is concerned, it is not a substitute for droit moral which authors in Europe enjoy. If the licensee may, by contract, distort the recorded work, the Lanham Act does not come into play. If the licensee has no such right by contract, there will be a violation in breach of contract. The Lanham Act can hardly apply literally when the credit line correctly states the work to be that of the plaintiffs which, indeed it is, so far as it goes. The vice complained of is that the truncated version is not what the plaintiffs wrote. But the Lanham Act does not deal with artistic integrity. It only goes to misdescription of origin and the like.

The misdescription of origin can be dealt with, as Judge Lasker did below, by devising an appropriate legend to indicate that the plaintiffs had not approved the editing of the ABC version. With such a legend, there is no conceivable violation of the Lanham Act. If plaintiffs complain that their artistic integrity is still compromised by the distorted version, their claim does not lie under the Lanham Act, which does not protect the copyrighted work itself but protects only against the misdescription or mislabelling.

So long as it is made clear that the ABC version is not approved by the Monty Python group, there is no misdescription of origin. So far as the content of the broadcast itself is concerned, that is not within the proscription of the Lanham Act when there is no misdescription of the authorship.

I add this brief explanation because I do not believe that the Lanham Act claim necessarily requires the drastic remedy of permanent injunction. That form of ultimate relief must be found in some other fountainhead of equity jurisprudence.

NOTES

1. *Moral Right and the Berne Convention.* Article 6*bis* of the Berne Convention for the Protection of Literary and Artistic Works requires member states to recognize the rights of integrity and paternity. Noting that "Article 6*bis* of Berne has generated one of the biggest controversies surrounding United States adherence to Berne," the House Report on the Berne Implementation amendments concluded that existing state and federal law satisfied the Convention's requirements:

According to this view, there is a composite of laws in this country that provides the kind of protection envisioned by Article 6*bis*. Federal laws include 17 U.S.C. § 106, relating to derivative works; 17 U.S.C. § 115(a)(2), relating to distortions of musical works used under the compulsory license respecting sound recordings; 17 U.S.C. § 203, relating to termination of transfers and licenses, and section 43(a) of the Lanham Act, relating to false designations of origin and false descriptions. State and local laws include those relating to publicity, contractual violations, fraud and misrepresentation, unfair competition, defamation, and invasion of privacy. In addition, eight states have recently enacted specific statutes protecting the rights of integrity and paternity in certain works of art. Finally, some courts have recognized the equivalent of such rights.

H.R.Rep. No. 609, 100th Cong., 2d Sess. 32–34 (1988).

The Berne Implementation Act provides that "[t]he obligations of the United States under the Berne Convention may be performed only pursuant to appropriate domestic law," and that "[t]he amendments made by this Act, together with the law as it exists on the date of the enactment of this Act, satisfy the obligations of the United States in adhering to the Berne Convention and no further rights or interests shall be recognized or created for that purpose." Pub.L. No. 100–568, § 2(2), (3) 102 Stat. 2853 (1988).

2. *The Right of Integrity, Derivative Rights and Parody.* Does *Gilliam* imply that the exclusive right to make an edited version of a work is part of copyright's adaptation right, today secured by section 106(2) of the Copyright Act? The paradox of relying on section 106(2)'s derivative right to secure the integrity of a copyrighted work is that the more completely an unauthorized work distorts the original, the less substantially similar to the original it will be—and the less likely it will be to infringe. Would addition of a discrete right of integrity to U.S. law require an exemption for parody? French law, which offers a robust right of integrity also recognizes a robust privilege of parody.

See generally, Geri Yonover, The Precarious Balance: Moral Rights, Parody, and Fair Use, 14 Cardozo Arts & Ent. L.J. 79 (1996).

3. *Section 43(a) and the Right of Paternity.* Section 43(a) of the Lanham Act secures more than a right against distortion; it may also secure an author's interest in attribution of authorship. In Lamothe v. Atlantic Recording Corp., 847 F.2d 1403, 7 U.S.P.Q.2d 1249 (9th Cir.1988), the court ruled that defendants' failure to identify all of the authors of two musical compositions would violate section 43(a). Relying on its earlier decision in Smith v. Montoro, 648 F.2d 602, 211 U.S.P.Q. 775 (9th Cir. 1981), the court held that defendant's conduct would constitute "express reverse palming off"—"when the wrongdoer removes the name or trademark on another party's product and sells that product under a name chosen by the wrongdoer." 847 F.2d at 1406.

4. *Visual Artists Rights Act.* The Visual Artists Rights Act of 1990, Pub. L. No. 101–650, tit. VI, 603(a) 104 Stat. 5089 (1990) added section 106A to the Copyright Act, giving creators of qualifying "works of visual art" rights of attribution and integrity in their works. The Act essentially equates "works of visual art" with works of fine art—works that exist in only a single copy or works published in signed and numbered editions of no more than 200 copies.

Although section 106A defines attribution and integrity broadly, to include misattribution as well as nonattribution and destruction as well as distortion, it subjects the rights to sweeping limitations. Section 106A's most significant limitation is its exemption from liability of virtually all significant commercial uses of artistic works, including reproduction in books, magazines, newspapers, motion pictures and works made for hire. See, e.g., Carter v. Helmsley–Spear, Inc., 71 F.3d 77, 37 U.S.P.Q.2d 1020 (2d Cir.1995) (vacating injunction against removal of sculpture installed in defendant's building because made as work for hire.)

For a work to enjoy the rights granted by section 106A, it is not enough that it qualifies as a "work of visual art;" the offending work, too, must be a "work of visual art." Thus, section 106A will give the artist a remedy against a gallery owner who fails to attribute a work of visual art to him. But a newspaper that reproduces the same work of art without attribution will escape liability since a newspaper does not itself qualify as a "work of visual art."

For a continental perspective on the Visual Artists Rights Act, see Marina Santilli, United States' Moral Rights Developments in European Perspective, 1 Marq. Int. Prop. L. Rev. 89 (1997).

5. *Artist's Resale Royalty Rights.* As first introduced in Congress, the bill that became the Visual Artists Rights Act gave visual artists not only rights of attribution and integrity, but also a resale royalty right. Just as the attribution and integrity provisions drew on the continental example of *droit moral*, the resale royalty provision drew on legislation, beginning with the 1920 French *droit de suite*, establishing an artist's right to collect a part of the price paid for her work each time it is sold. The premise behind the resale royalty right is that, unlike the typical copyrightable work, which returns economic value to its owner through the dissemination of copies or performances, economically successful works of fine art characteristically realize their value over time not through sale of copies but through appreciation in the value of the original. Copyright, which is designed to capture a work's value through the dissemination of copies or performances, is ill-suited to capture the value of the original, authentic work itself.

The resale royalty provision of the Visual Artists Rights bill provoked a small controversy and was dropped in favor of a provision calling for the Register of Copyrights to study the subject in consultation with the Chair of the National Endowment for the Arts. After holding public hearings, studying the foreign experience with *droit de suite*, as well as California's resale royalty law, Cal. Civ. Code § 986 (1996 Supp.), the Copyright Office found itself "not persuaded that sufficient economic and copyright policy justification exists to establish *droit de suite* in the United States." Copyright Office Report, *Droit de Suite*: The Artist's Resale Royalty, 16 Colum.-VLA J. L & Arts 381, 390 (1992). See Shira Perlmutter, Resale Royalties for Artists: An Analysis of the Register of Copyright's Report, 40 J. Copyright Soc'y 284 (1993).

6. *State Fine Arts Statutes.* Several state legislatures have passed laws to secure artists' interests in works of fine art. See, e.g., Cal.Civ.Code § 987 (West Supp.1996); N.Y.Arts & Cult.Aff.Law § 14.03 (McKinney Supp.1996). California's statute, for example, protects works of fine art—an "original painting, sculpture, or drawing, or an original work of art in glass, of recognized quality"—against any intentional "physical defacement, mutilation, alteration, or destruction." New York's statute protects "works of fine art or limited edition multiples of not more than three hundred copies knowingly displayed in a place accessible to the public, published or reproduced in this state" against publication or display of a mutilated version if the publication or display represents the work as the work of the artist and is reasonably likely to damage the artist's reputation. Both laws give the artist the right to disclaim authorship of a work.

See also La.Rev.Stat.Ann. §§ 2151–2156 (West 1996); Me.Rev.Stat. Ann. tit. 27, § 303 (West Supp.1995); Mass.Ann.Laws ch. 231, § 85S(d) (Law Co-op.1996).

7. *Bibliographic Note.* On moral right generally, see Adolf Dietz, The Moral Right of the Author: Moral Rights and the Civil Law Countries, 19 Colum.-VLA J.L. & Arts 199 (1995); Gerald Dworkin, The Moral Right of the Author: Moral Rights and the Common Law Countries, 19 Colum.-VLA J.L. & Arts 229 (1995); John Henry Merryman, The Refrigerator of Bernard Buffet, 27 Hastings L.J. 1023 (1976).

F. PREEMPTION OF STATE LAW

3 PAUL GOLDSTEIN, COPYRIGHT (2d ed. 1996)*

Section 301(a) of the 1976 Copyright Act prescribes three conditions, all of which must be met, for a state law to be preempted. First, the state right in question must be "equivalent to any of the exclusive rights within the general scope of copyright as specified by section 106." Second, the right must be in a work of authorship that is fixed in a tangible medium of expression. Third, the work of authorship must come within "the subject matter of copyright as specified by sections 102 and 103."

Section 301(a)'s preemptive formula is easily applied to the garden variety common law copyright case. If, before the 1976 Act, an author distributed the manuscript for her novel to a small circle of friends and later discovered that one recipient had published the novel without her permission, the author would have had an action for common law copyright infringement. After the 1976 Act no common law copyright action would lie. The novel is a work of authorship fixed in a tangible medium of expression and the work comes within the subject matter of copyright under section 102(a)(1). Further, the rights sought to be vindicated are rights against reproduction and distribution that are clearly equivalent to the rights prescribed by sections 106(1) and 106(3). Consequently, section 301(a) would bar the state law action and the author would have to rely on federal law for relief. Yet preemption would deprive the author of little since, in this case at least, the Copyright Act would give her the rough equivalent of the protection that she previously enjoyed at common law.

Section 301's application to state law doctrines other than common law copyright may be more problematic. The roots of common law copyright extend deep and wide into state jurisprudence, and related state doctrines are sometimes too entangled in common law copyright to be neatly severed for purposes of preemption. The common law right of privacy, for example, stems in part from common law copyright's right of first publication. If the author in the example just given had written not a novel but a diary, she would, before the 1976 Act, have had an action for common law copyright infringement or for invasion of privacy against a scandal sheet that purloined and published the diary. Section 301 might today bar not only the common law copyright action against the diary's publication, but also the privacy action. Since the diary is fixed in a tangible medium of expression and comes within the subject matter of copyright as a literary work under section 102(a)(1), section 301 would preempt the privacy action if a court held that the right of privacy is equivalent to section 106(1)'s reproduction right. A privacy-minded author would in this case lose something in the exchange of state protection for federal protection since, as a condition to bringing a copyright infringement action, she must register and deposit—and thus publicly expose—the diary.

The House Report on the 1976 Act observes that the declaration of section 301's preemptive principle "is intended to be stated in the clearest and most unequivocal language possible, so as to foreclose any conceivable misinterpretation of its unqualified intention that Congress shall act preemptively, and to avoid the development of any vague borderline areas between State and Federal protection." Although Congress' preemptive purpose is clear, the language that section 301 employs to effectuate this purpose is not. Courts have divided over the precise meaning of two of section 301(a)'s three conditions for preemption—that the state right be equivalent to copyright and that the subject matter of the state right come within the subject matter of copyright. Some confusion also surrounds section 301(b)'s exclusion of certain rights from preemption.

§ 15.2.1 "Equivalent" Rights

As its first condition for preemption, section 301(a) requires that the state right in issue be a "legal or equitable" right that is "equivalent to any of the exclusive rights within the general scope of copyright as specified by section 106." This means that on and after January 1, 1978, a state right will be preempted if it attaches to a tangibly fixed work of authorship coming within the subject matter of copyright and is equivalent to the right to reproduce the work in copies or phonorecords, to prepare derivative works based upon the work, to distribute copies or phonorecords of the work publicly, to perform the work publicly or to display the work publicly.

Congress evidently recognized that the test of equivalence could not be painted with such broad brush-strokes as the "purpose" or "effect" of the state law in issue. To preempt state doctrines because their purpose is equivalent to the purpose of copyright would cut too narrowly, for it is easy to find an independent, noncopyright purpose behind any state law. Common law copyright, for example, may seek to protect personal interests in privacy as well as strictly reputational interests. On the other hand, to preempt state doctrines because their effects are equivalent to copyright would cut too broadly into state doctrines that Congress surely would have wanted to survive preemption. Privacy, trade secret and unfair competition law are only a few of the many state doctrines that, like section 106 of the Copyright Act, prohibit the reproduction, distribution, performance or display of protected subject matter and consequently produce effects equivalent to copyright.

The language and legislative history of section 301, as well as most of the judicial decisions applying the section, support a more discriminating test for equivalence. The mainstream test of equivalence under section 301 focuses on the nature of the state right involved and on the elements required to make out a prima facie case for violation of the right. Courts generally hold that a state law right is equivalent to copyright for the purposes of section 301 if (1) the right encompasses conduct coming within the scope of one or more of section 106's exclusive rights, and (2) if applicable state law requires the plaintiff to prove no more than the elements that the Copyright Act requires for proof of infringement of one or more of section 106's five exclusive rights. The first part of this test would preempt state doctrines that are broader, as well as those that are narrower, than the counterpart statutory right. The second part of the test would exempt state doctrines that require proof of an extra substantive element—beyond the elements required for infringement of a right under the Copyright Act—to make out a prima facie case.

§ 15.2.1.1 State Rights Whose Scope Is Broader Than Statutory Rights

Section 301(a) measures the equivalence of state laws not against section 106's specific exclusive rights, but against "the exclusive rights *within the general scope of copyright* as specified by section 106." The House Report on the 1976 Act explains, "The preemption of rights under State law is complete with respect to any work coming within the scope of the bill, even though the scope of exclusive rights given the work under the bill is narrower than the scope of common law rights in the work might have been."[17]

---

17. House Report, 131.

The "general scope of copyright" means the full scope that Congress could have described for any particular right. For example, the general scope of copyright includes section 106(4)'s exclusive right to perform a work, and any state right that prohibits performance will be considered an equivalent right. Although section 106(4) limits its right to public performances, a state law that prohibited private performances would nonetheless come within the general scope of the right. While the state law right would be broader than the statutory right, it would fall within the general ambit of the performance right and thus be subject to preemption. Similarly, state laws against the private display or private distribution of works would come within the general scope of section 106(3)'s right of public distribution or section 106(5)'s right of public display respectively.

It is less clear that section 301 would treat a state law as coming within the general scope of copyright if instead of filling a gap in the scope of a statutory right—prohibiting private rather than public performances for example—it grants a right that section 106 entirely withholds. For example, section 106(4) gives no performance rights to sound recordings. Does a state law against performance of sound recordings come within the general scope of section 106(4)'s performance right? On the one hand, this might be considered an instance of the federal law being "narrower" than the state law, thus subjecting the state law to preemption. On the other hand, the fact that the Act omits a right against performance of sound recordings may mean that state laws against performance of sound recordings are immune from preemption since a right that does not exist—a performance right in sound recordings—cannot be said to have a "general scope."

Section 301 can be read to save state laws that grant a right to subject matter from which section 106 entirely withholds the same right. Nonetheless, the purposes behind section 301 and Congress' "unqualified intention" to act preemptively[18] suggest that Congress may have intended to treat these state rights as equivalent to copyright. Although Congress could have outlawed the unauthorized performance of sound recordings, it withheld the right in an effort to strike a balance between the need for copyright incentives and competing economic and political pressures for free use in a specific circumstance. Section 301 arguably reflects Congress' belief that this balance should govern not only rights under the Copyright Act but under state law as well. Even if section 301 does exempt state rights from preemption in situations where the Copyright Act withholds particular rights, these state laws may nonetheless be subject to preemption under the Constitution's supremacy clause.

§ 15.2.1.2   State Rights Containing No "Extra Element"

Courts generally hold that a state right is not equivalent to copyright, and thus is not subject to preemption, if the state cause of action contains an operative element that is absent from the cause of action for copyright infringement. To save a state right from preemption, the extra element

---

18. House Report, 130.

must relate to the economic scope of the right and not to the state of mind of the defendant. Because an extra element circumscribes the scope of the property right granted by state law, the extra element test directly serves section 301's central purpose: to bar states from extending property rights that are equivalent to the property rights conferred by the Copyright Act.

Contract law is a good example of a state law that will be immune from preemption under the extra element test. Contract law may be employed to prohibit the unauthorized reproduction, distribution, performance or display of a work. But, in addition to these acts, contract law requires the plaintiff to prove the existence of a bargained-for exchange—something she need not prove in a cause of action for copyright infringement. Similarly, section 301 will not preempt the traditional cause of action for unjust enrichment because to recover under this theory a plaintiff must prove the extra element that the defendant used plaintiff's work under circumstances giving the defendant notice of plaintiff's expectation of payment. An action for unfair competition will not be preempted if the plaintiff can prove the extra element of consumer confusion as to source. An action for trade secret appropriation, and actions based on a confidential relationship generally, will not be preempted if the plaintiff can prove the extra element of breach of confidence. A state law action for conversion will not be preempted if the plaintiff can prove the extra element that the defendant unlawfully retained the physical object embodying plaintiff's work.

Courts applying the extra element test have consistently looked to the substance rather than the form of the state law claim in issue. Simply casting a claim as one for contract breach will not save it from preemption. Courts have held that if a state law claim for tortious interference with contractual relations or prospective business advantage or for unjust enrichment alleges none of the elements that distinguish those causes of action from copyright infringement, the claim will be subject to preemption under section 301. Courts have held that section 301(a) encompasses state unfair competition claims that allege misappropriation, but not the extra element of consumer confusion as to source, and trade secret claims that allege unlawful appropriation, but not breach of confidence. Courts have also held that section 301(a) encompasses claims for conversion in cases where the plaintiff alleges only the unlawful retention of its intellectual property rights and not the unlawful retention of the tangible object embodying its work. . . .

§ 15.2.2 "Fixed in a Tangible Medium of Expression"

Section 301's second requirement for preemption of state law is that the state right be in "works of authorship that are fixed in a tangible medium of expression." Statutory copyright does not extend to works that have not been fixed in a tangible medium of expression. As a consequence, section 301 leaves regulation of unfixed works to the states. The House Report gives several examples of unfixed works that may be protected by state law: "choreography that has never been filmed or notated, an extemporaneous speech, 'original works of authorship' communicated solely through conversations or live broadcasts, and a dramatic sketch or musical composition improvised or developed from memory and without being recorded or written down."[55] State rights in a work will be subject to preemption if the work, though originally unfixed, becomes fixed in a larger copyrightable work with the author's permission. For example, one court held that baseball players' rights of publicity arising from their appearances in ball games were subject to preemption because the ball games were videotaped as they were televised.

§ 15.2.3 "Works of Authorship That ... Come Within the Subject Matter of Copyright"

Section 301's third requirement for preemption is that the work of authorship that is subject to the state right must "come within the subject matter of copyright as specified by sections 102 and 103." The principal ambiguity in the requirement stems from the fact that neither section 102 nor section 103 defines the "subject matter of copyright." At most, section 102(a) defines copyright subject matter obliquely by stating that copyright protection subsists "in original works of authorship fixed in any tangible medium of expression" and by listing seven categories of "works of authorship." Section 102(b) provides that "copyright protection for an original work of authorship does not extend to any idea, procedure, process, system, method of operation, concept, principle, or discovery, regardless of the form in which it is described, explained, illustrated, or embodied in such work." Section 103 adds only that the subject matter of copyright specified by section 102 includes compilations and derivative works.

The thorniest interpretational problem posed by section 301's subject matter test lies in the interplay between sections 301(a) and 102(b). Does section 102(b) say that procedures, processes and similar ideas are not the subject matter of copyright? Or does section 102(b) say that these elements come within the scope of copyright subject matter but that the Act withholds protection from them? The first interpretation would allow states to protect procedures, processes and similar ideas. The second interpretation would prohibit states from protecting these elements, if fixed, through rights equivalent to copyright.

The soundest reading of section 102, supported by the legislative history and case law, is that only works of authorship constitute copyright subject matter and that the ideas, procedures, processes and other elements listed in section 102(b) are not copyrightable subject matter because they are not works of authorship. Just as section 102(b) denies copyright to ideas that appear in otherwise copyrightable works, it implicitly denies copyright to ideas that appear separately, outside the context of an otherwise copyrightable work. As a consequence, section 301 allows states to protect ideas, procedures, processes and methods, whether or not they appear in the context of otherwise copyrightable works. To be sure, states will often decline to protect ideas for the very same reasons that underlay Congress' decision to withhold copyright from ideas. Further, although

---

55. House Report, 131.

state idea protection is exempt from preemption under section 301, it is subject to review under the supremacy clause of the Constitution and the first amendment as incorporated in the fourteenth amendment to the Constitution.

Facts, like ideas, are not copyrightable subject matter. As a consequence, section 301 allows states to protect facts appearing in such forms as "hot news" and uncopyrightable compilations of data, including data compiled in computer databases. The House Report on the 1976 Act observed that "state law should have the flexibility to afford a remedy (under traditional principles of equity) against a consistent pattern of unauthorized appropriation by a competitor of the facts (i.e., not the literary expression) constituting 'hot' news, whether in the traditional mold of International News Service v. Associated Press, 248 U.S. 215, 39 S.Ct. 68, 63 L.Ed. 211 (1918), or in the newer form of data updates from scientific, business, or financial data bases."[64] Courts have indicated that section 301 does not preempt state law protection for facts.

Section 301 will preempt a state law granting a right equivalent to copyright to a tangibly fixed work coming within the scope of copyrightable subject matter if the work is in the public domain because it is not original, because the term of copyright has expired or because publicly distributed copies or phonorecords of the work did not bear the copyright notice required before March 1, 1989, the effective date of the Berne Implementation Amendments. According to the House Report on the 1976 Act, "As long as a work fits within one of the general subject matter categories of sections 102 and 103, the bill prevents the States from protecting it even if it fails to achieve Federal statutory copyright because it is too minimal or lacking in originality to qualify, or because it has fallen into the public domain."[69] One court rejected the argument that section 301 did not preempt the state law right of publicity of baseball players in their on-field performances because the performances lacked sufficient creativity to qualify for copyright.[70] In the court's view, section 301(a) "preempts all equivalent state-law rights claimed in any work within the subject matter of copyright whether or not the work embodies any creativity."[71]

Courts deciding copyright infringement cases do not always distinguish between elements that fall outside the scope of copyright subject matter because they are unprotectible ideas and elements that come within the scope of copyright subject matter but nonetheless fail to meet the copyright law's originality standard. Plots, for example, may be unprotectible because they are akin to ideas or because, though they are akin to expression, they

---

64. House Report, 132. The observation in the House Report is less than definitive, however, since it was evidently addressed to examples of state law, including misappropriation, that section 301(b)(3) had originally declared to be exempt from preemption but that were deleted at the last moment by an amendment introduced on the floor of the House. See § 15.2.1.4, above.

69. House Report, 131.

70. Baltimore Orioles, Inc. v. Major League Baseball Players Assn., 805 F.2d 663, 676, 231 U.S.P.Q. 673 (7th Cir.1986), cert. denied, 480 U.S. 941, 107 S.Ct. 1593, 94 L.Ed.2d 782 (1987).

71. 805 F.2d at 676.

are so common that they probably did not originate with their putative
author. Such line-drawing is unnecessary in the usual infringement case
where the fact, and not the rationale, of unprotectibility is the only
question in issue. But it is necessary to identify the rationale for withholding protection from plots and similar elements where the question in issue
is whether section 301 preempts state law protection for the element. If the
element is uncopyrightable because it is an idea, it may be protected under
state law. If, however, the element is uncopyrightable only because it is not
original—and if section 301's other two conditions are met—the element
may not be protected under state law because it comes within the subject
matter of copyright.

NOTES

1. No state law affecting intellectual property is beyond section 301's
potential reach.

Contract Law. Idea submitters have a hard time recovering under
express or implied contract theories—not because of preemption, but because idea recipients will rarely expose themselves to liability under either
theory. The submitter who has elaborated her idea in detailed, concrete
form has a greater chance of recovery under state law, but also faces a
greater likelihood of preemption under section 301 since her elaborated
submission may constitute the "subject matter of copyright" as described
in section 102(a), and a right against noncontracting parties may be
equivalent to copyright.

Trade Secrets. Does section 301 preempt a state law action against the
misappropriation of secret drawings and specifications? Avco Corp. v.
Precision Air Parts, Inc., 210 U.S.P.Q. 894 (M.D.Ala.1980), aff'd on other
grounds, 676 F.2d 494, 216 U.S.P.Q. 1086 (11th Cir.1982) held that it does:
"The essence of plaintiff's complaint is that Defendant has copied its
drawings and specifications and prepared derivative works based upon
those drawings and specifications. Thus, the complaint fits squarely into
§ 106(1) and (2). It is undisputed that the drawings and specifications are
'fixed in a tangible medium of expression.' Finally, the drawings and
specifications in issue could certainly be characterized as pictorial or
graphic works. Thus, this court is of the opinion that the requirements of
17 U.S.C.A. § 301(a) are satisfied by the facts in this case." The court
added that Congress did not intend to preempt trade secret actions involving elements "such as an invasion of personal rights or a breach of trust or
confidentiality, that are different in kind from copyright infringement."
But plaintiff had not alleged that defendant "has committed any of the
elements that allow the common law rights of 'trade secrets' to avoid
preemption." 210 U.S.P.Q. at 897–98, 898 n. 9.

Unfair Competition. According to the House Report on the 1976
Copyright Act, "[s]ection 301 is not intended to preempt common law
protection in cases involving activities such as false labeling, fraudulent
representation, and passing off even where the subject matter involved

comes within the scope of the copyright statute." H.R.Rep. No. 1476, 94th Cong., 2d Sess. 132 (1976).

Courts have generally held that section 301 does not preempt state law passing off actions because the required proof of consumer confusion represents an "extra element" that distinguishes the right from the exclusive rights granted by section 106 of the 1976 Act. See, e.g., Donald Frederick Evans & Assocs. v. Continental Homes, Inc., 785 F.2d 897, 229 U.S.P.Q. 321 (11th Cir.1986). But, what of misappropriation doctrine, which does not require deception? Would the Illinois Supreme Court's misappropriation decision in Board of Trade v. Dow Jones, page 81, above, withstand preemption analysis under section 301? What of state trademark statutes that protect emblems and insignia apart from any requirement of consumer confusion? State anti-dilution statutes?

Right of Publicity. Names and likenesses—the usual objects of the state right of publicity—fall outside the subject matter of copyright and consequently lie beyond the reach of section 301. What of more original and expressive subject matter, such as voice and singing style? See David E. Shipley, Three Strikes and They're Out at the Old Ball Game: Preemption of Performers' Rights of Publicity Under the Copyright Act of 1976, 20 Ariz.St.L.J. 369 (1988).

Moral Right. To what extent does section 301 preempt state law protection of an author's moral right? Would a state law that prohibited distortion of a work be equivalent to section 106(2)'s provision for derivative rights? Would a state law that permitted authors to recall their copyrighted works be equivalent to section 106(3)'s distribution right as limited by section 109's first sale doctrine?

2. *Constitutional Preemption.* Petitioners in Goldstein v. California, 412 U.S. 546, 93 S.Ct. 2303, 37 L.Ed.2d 163, 178 U.S.P.Q. 129 (1973), had been successfully prosecuted for record piracy under California Penal Code § 653. Appealing their conviction, they argued that "Congress intended to allow individuals to copy any work which was not protected by a federal copyright." Since, at the time, the Copyright Act did not protect sound recordings, and since section 653 prohibited "the copying of works which are not entitled to federal protection ... it conflicts directly with congressional policy and must fall under the Supremacy Clause of the Constitution." Petitioners also argued that "the statute establishes a state copyright of unlimited duration and thus conflicts with Art. I, § 8, cl. 8 of the Constitution" restricting the congressional power to grants of protection for "limited times." 412 U.S. at 551, 93 S.Ct. at 2307.

The Court's answer to the first argument reads like a primer on the federal system. The Court began with Federalist No. 32, defining those areas in which states are considered to have given up their reserved powers:

> [T]his alienation, of State sovereignty, would only exist in three cases: where the Constitution in express terms granted an exclusive authority to the Union; where it granted in one instance an authority

to the Union, and in another prohibited the States from exercising the like authority; and where it granted an authority to the Union to which a similar authority in the States would be absolutely and totally *contradictory* and *repugnant*.

412 U.S. at 553, 93 S.Ct. at 2308. The "first two instances," the Court observed, "present no barrier to a State's enactment of copyright statutes": the Constitution nowhere makes the grant of copyright authority exclusive, and it nowhere withholds the power from the states. Id.

The Court then turned to the formula's third prong. Conceding that the "objective of the Copyright Clause was clearly to facilitate the granting of rights national in scope," the Court concluded that, although "the Copyright Clause thus recognizes the potential benefits of a national system, it does not indicate that all writings are of national interest or that state legislation is, in all cases, unnecessary or precluded." The Court went on: "Since the subject matter to which the Copyright Clause is addressed may thus be of purely local importance and not worthy of national attention or protection, we cannot discern such an unyielding national interest as to require an inference that state power to grant copyrights has been relinquished to *exclusive* federal control." 412 U.S. at 555–558 (emphasis in original). Since Congress had not expressly withdrawn state power over sound recordings, the California statute was valid.

To petitioners' second argument—that the California statute violated the Constitution's "limited times" restriction—the Court answered that "Section 8 enumerates those powers which have been granted *to Congress;* whatever limitations have been appended to such powers can only be understood as a limit on congressional, and not state, action." It added that, in any event, "it is not clear that the dangers to which this limitation was addressed apply with equal force to both the Federal Government and the States. When Congress grants an exclusive right or monopoly, its effects are pervasive; no citizen or State may escape its reach. As we have noted, however, the exclusive right granted by a State is confined to its borders. Consequently, even when the right is unlimited in duration, any tendency to inhibit further progress in science or the arts is narrowly circumscribed." 412 U.S. at 560–61, 93 S.Ct. at 2311 (emphasis in original).

3. *Interplay of Statutory and Constitutional Preemption.* Does section 301 leave any room for constitutional preemption of state laws bordering on copyright? Several courts have treated section 301 and the supremacy clause as discrete sources of preemption. See, e.g., Associated Film Distrib. Corp. v. Thornburgh, 614 F.Supp. 1100, 227 U.S.P.Q. 184 (E.D.Pa.1985), aff'd, 800 F.2d 369, 231 U.S.P.Q. 143 (3d Cir.1986), cert. denied, 480 U.S. 933, 107 S.Ct. 1573, 94 L.Ed.2d 765 (1987). If the Copyright Act—including section 301—is part of the "supreme law of the land," how can any state law that passes muster under section 301 not also pass muster under the supremacy clause? Do the First Amendment's free speech and press guarantees provide an independent basis for preemption?

PART FOUR

INTELLECTUAL PROPERTY PROTECTION OF COMPUTER PROGRAMS

Trade secret, copyright and patent law have been used to protect investment in computer programs since the industry's beginnings. In the early years, when most application software was custom-designed and confidential relationships with business users were easily formed, trade secret law was the most important source of protection. Trade secrets continue to be important in the custom design market and in regulating the software industry's characteristically mobile employees. Copyright, with its low subject matter standards and broadly enforceable rights, emerged as a popular form of protection in the 1980's when consumer oriented, off-the-rack programs began filling computer store shelves. Patent law, with its focus on functionality, might have seemed the better choice, but the Supreme Court's 1972 decision in Gottschalk v. Benson, 409 U.S. 63, 93 S.Ct. 253, 34 L.Ed.2d 273, cast an early, lingering cloud over the prospects for patent protection of computer programs. Only in the 1990's, with the Court's movement away from its previously constrained views— and the increasingly evident limits of copyright in protecting investment in software design—did interest in patent protection revive.

None of these three bodies of intellectual property law comes close to striking the optimal balance for protection of computer programs. The needs of mass distribution and the inroads of reverse engineering make trade secret protection unsatisfactory for off-the-shelf products. Copyright law's systematic exclusion of protection for the functional elements of otherwise copyrightable works may give software producers less protection than their investment in these essentially functional products requires. Patent law, with an examination process that can consume years for a single application, often grinds too slow, and sets its standards of novelty and nonobviousness too high, for this fast-paced and often incremental technology.

Early on, legal writers observed that the shortcomings of existing doctrine made computer programs an ideal candidate for *sui generis* protection—a custom crafted law that could be equally attuned to the needs of mass markets, the essential functionality of software and the level and pace of software innovation. Serious proposals for such legislation were made as early as the 1960's. See Elmer Galbi, Proposal for New Legislation to Protect Computer Programming, 17 Bull. Copyright Soc'y 280 (1970). None, however, even reached the bill-drafting stage in Congress. (Following unsuccessful industry efforts to obtain copyright protection for semiconductor chip designs, Congress did pass a *sui generis* intellectual property law protecting these computer-related products. See page 937, below). At least one major industrial power, Japan, came close to adopting a *sui generis* program protection law for software; the Japanese proposal is the subject of Professor Dennis Karjala's study, Lessons from the Computer Software Protection Debate in Japan, 1984 Ariz. St. L.J. 53, a fascinating examination of the politics—domestic and international—of software protection.

As you read the cases and materials in this part, you may find it useful to reflect on how courts and Congress have shaped copyright, patent and trade secret law—copyright, particularly—to meet software's special needs, and on whether this reshaping of intellectual property law has in fact resulted in *sui generis* laws masquerading as orthodox doctrine. Two articles, which anchor a symposium issue of the Columbia Law Review, elaborate the theory and practice of *sui generis* protection for computer software: Pamela Samuelson, Randall Davis, Mitchell D. Kapor & J. H. Reichman, A Manifesto Concerning the Legal Protection of Computer Programs, and J. H. Reichman, Legal Hybrids Between the Patent and Copyright Paradigms. They appear, together with comments on them, at 94 Colum. L. Rev. 2307 (1994).

I. COPYRIGHT LAW

A. SCOPE OF PROTECTION

1. COMPUTER CODE

Computer Associates International, Inc. v. Altai, Inc.

United States Court of Appeals, Second Circuit, 1992.
982 F.2d 693, 23 U.S.P.Q.2d 1241.

WALKER, J. In recent years, the growth of computer science has spawned a number of challenging legal questions, particularly in the field of copyright law. As scientific knowledge advances, courts endeavor to keep pace, and sometimes—as in the area of computer technology—they are required to venture into less than familiar waters. This is not a new development, though. "From its beginning, the law of copyright has developed in response to significant changes in technology." Sony Corp. v. Universal City Studios, Inc., 464 U.S. 417, 430 (1984)....

Among other things, this case deals with the challenging question of whether and to what extent the "non-literal" aspects of a computer program, that is, those aspects that are not reduced to written code, are protected by copyright. While a few other courts have already grappled with this issue, this case is one of first impression in this circuit. As we shall discuss, we find the results reached by other courts to be less than satisfactory. Drawing upon long-standing doctrines of copyright law, we take an approach that we think better addresses the practical difficulties embedded in these types of cases. In so doing, we have kept in mind the necessary balance between creative incentive and industrial competition.

This appeal comes to us from the United States District Court for the Eastern District of New York, the Honorable George C. Pratt, Circuit Judge, sitting by designation. By Memorandum and Order entered August 12, 1991, Judge Pratt found that defendant Altai, Inc.'s ("Altai"), OSCAR 3.4 computer program had infringed plaintiff Computer Associates' ("CA"), copyrighted computer program entitled CA–SCHEDULER. Accordingly, the district court awarded CA $364,444 in actual damages and apportioned profits. Altai has abandoned its appeal from this award. With respect to CA's second claim for copyright infringement, Judge Pratt found that Altai's OSCAR 3.5 program was not substantially similar to a portion of CA–SCHEDULER called ADAPTER, and thus denied relief. Finally, the district court concluded that CA's state law trade secret misappropriation claim against Altai had been preempted by the federal copyright act. CA appealed from these findings.

Because we are in full agreement with Judge Pratt's decision and in substantial agreement with his careful reasoning, we affirm the judgment of the district court in its entirety.

BACKGROUND

We assume familiarity with the facts set forth in the district court's comprehensive and scholarly opinion. Thus, we summarize only those facts necessary to resolve this appeal.

I.   COMPUTER PROGRAM DESIGN

Certain elementary facts concerning the nature of computer programs are vital to the following discussion. The Copyright Act defines a computer program as "a set of statements or instructions to be used directly or indirectly in a computer in order to bring about a certain result." 17 U.S.C. § 101. In writing these directions, the programmer works "from the general to the specific." Whelan Associates, Inc. v. Jaslow Dental Laboratory, Inc., 797 F.2d 1222, 1229 (3d Cir.1986), cert. denied, 479 U.S. 1031 (1987). See generally, Steven R. Englund, Note, Idea, Process, or Protected Expression?: Determining the Scope of Copyright Protection of the Structure of Computer Programs, 88 Mich.L.Rev. 866, 867–73 (1990) (hereinafter "Englund"); Peter S. Menell, An Analysis of the Scope of Copyright Protection for Application Programs, 41 Stan.L.Rev. 1045, 1051–57 (1989) (hereinafter "Menell"); Mark T. Kretschmer, Note, Copyright Protection For Software Architecture: Just Say No!, 1988 Colum.Bus.L.Rev. 823, 824–27 (1988) (hereinafter "Kretschmer"); Peter G. Spivack, Comment, Does Form Follow Function? The Ideal–Expression Dichotomy In Copyright Protection of Computer Software, 35 U.C.L.A.L.Rev. 723, 729–31 (1988) (hereinafter "Spivack").

The first step in this procedure is to identify a program's ultimate function or purpose. An example of such an ultimate purpose might be the creation and maintenance of a business ledger. Once this goal has been achieved, a programmer breaks down or "decomposes" the program's ultimate function into "simpler constituent problems or 'sub-tasks,'" Englund, at 870, which are also known as subroutines or modules. In the context of a business ledger program, a module or subroutine might be responsible for the task of updating a list of outstanding accounts receivable. Sometimes, depending upon the complexity of its task, a subroutine may be broken down further into sub-subroutines.

Having sufficiently decomposed the program's ultimate function into its component elements, a programmer will then arrange the sub-routines or modules into what are known as organizational or flow charts. Flow charts map the interactions between modules that achieve the program's end goal.

In order to accomplish these intra-program interactions, a programmer must carefully design each module's parameter list. A parameter list, according to the expert appointed and fully credited by the district court, Dr. Randall Davis, is "the information sent to and received from a subroutine." The term "parameter list" refers to the form in which information is passed between modules (e.g. for accounts receivable, the designated time frame and particular customer identifying number) and the information's actual content (e.g. 8/91–7/92; customer No. 3). With respect to form, interacting modules must share similar parameter lists so that they are capable of exchanging information.

"The functions of the modules in a program together with each module's relationships to other modules constitute the 'structure' of the program." Englund, at 871. Additionally, the term structure may include the category of modules referred to as "macros." A macro is a single instruction that initiates a sequence of operations or module interactions within the program. Very often the user will accompany a macro with an instruction from the parameter list to refine the instruction (e.g. current total of accounts receivable (macro), but limited to those for 8/91 to 7/92 from customer No. 3 (parameters)).

In fashioning the structure, a programmer will normally attempt to maximize the program's speed, efficiency, as well as simplicity for user operation, while taking into consideration certain externalities such as the memory constraints of the computer upon which the program will be run. "This stage of program design often requires the most time and investment." Kretschmer, at 826. Once each necessary module has been identified, designed, and its relationship to the other modules has been laid out conceptually, the resulting program structure must be embodied in a written language that the computer can read. This process is called "coding," and requires two steps. First, the programmer must transpose the program's structural blue-print into a source code. This step has been described as "comparable to the novelist fleshing out the broad outline of his plot by crafting from words and sentences the paragraphs that convey the ideas." Kretschmer, at 826. The source code may be written in any one of several computer languages, such as COBAL, FORTRAN, BASIC, EDL, etc., depending upon the type of computer for which the program is intended. Once the source code has been completed, the second step is to translate or "compile" it into object code. Object code is the binary language comprised of zeros and ones through which the computer directly receives its instructions.

After the coding is finished, the programmer will run the program on the computer in order to find and correct any logical and syntactical errors. This is known as "debugging" and, once done, the program is complete.

II. FACTS

CA is a Delaware corporation, with its principal place of business in Garden City, New York. Altai is a Texas corporation, doing business primarily in Arlington, Texas. Both companies are in the computer software industry—designing, developing and marketing various types of computer programs.

The subject of this litigation originates with one of CA's marketed programs entitled CA–SCHEDULER. CA–SCHEDULER is a job scheduling program designed for IBM mainframe computers. Its primary functions are straightforward: to create a schedule specifying when the computer should run various tasks, and then to control the computer as it executes the schedule. CA–SCHEDULER contains a sub-program entitled ADAPTER, also developed by CA. ADAPTER is not an independently marketed product of CA; it is a wholly integrated component of CA–SCHEDULER and has no capacity for independent use.

Nevertheless, ADAPTER plays an extremely important role. It is an "operating system compatibility component," which means, roughly speaking, it serves as a translator. An "operating system" is itself a program that manages the resources of the computer, allocating those resources to other programs as needed. The IBM's System 370 family of computers, for which CA–SCHEDULER was created, is, depending upon the computer's size, designed to contain one of three operating systems: DOS/VSE, MVS, or CMS. As the district court noted, the general rule is that "a program written for one operating system, e.g., DOS/VSE, will not, without modification, run under another operating system such as MVS." ADAPTER's function is to translate the language of a given program into the particular language that the computer's own operating system can understand.

The district court succinctly outlined the manner in which ADAPTER works within the context of the larger program. In order to enable CA–SCHEDULER to function on different operating systems, CA divided the CA–SCHEDULER into two components: a first component that contains only the task-specific portions of the program, independent of all operating system issues, and a second component that contains all the interconnections between the first component and the operating system. In a program constructed in this way, whenever the first, task-specific, component needs to ask the operating system for some resource through a "system call", it calls the second component instead of calling the operating system directly. The second component serves as an "interface" or "compatibility component" between the task-specific portion of the program and the operating system. It receives the request from the first component and translates it into the appropriate system call that will be recognized by whatever operating system is installed on the computer, e.g., DOS/VSE, MVS, or CMS. Since the first, task-specific component calls the adapter component rather than the operating system, the first component need not be customized to use any specific operating system. The second interface component insures that all the system calls are performed properly for the particular operating system in use. ADAPTER serves as the second, "common system interface" component referred to above.

A program like ADAPTER, which allows a computer user to change or use multiple operating systems while maintaining the same software, is highly desirable. It saves the user the costs, both in time and money, that otherwise would be expended in purchasing new programs, modifying existing systems to run them, and gaining familiarity with their operation. The benefits run both ways. The increased compatibility afforded by an ADAPTER-like component, and its resulting popularity among consumers, makes whatever software in which it is incorporated significantly more marketable.

Starting in 1982, Altai began marketing its own job scheduling program entitled ZEKE. The original version of ZEKE was designed for use in conjunction with a VSE operating system. By late 1983, in response to customer demand, Altai decided to rewrite ZEKE so that it could be run in conjunction with an MVS operating system.

At that time, James P. Williams ("Williams"), then an employee of Altai and now its President, approached Claude F. Arney, III ("Arney"), a computer programmer who worked for CA. Williams and Arney were longstanding friends, and had in fact been co-workers at CA for some time before Williams left CA to work for Altai's predecessor. Williams wanted to recruit Arney to assist Altai in designing an MVS version of ZEKE.

At the time he first spoke with Arney, Williams was aware of both the CA–SCHEDULER and ADAPTER programs. However, Williams was not involved in their development and had never seen the codes of either program. When he asked Arney to come work for Altai, Williams did not know that ADAPTER was a component of CA–SCHEDULER.

Arney, on the other hand, was intimately familiar with various aspects of ADAPTER. While working for CA, he helped improve the VSE version of ADAPTER, and was permitted to take home a copy of ADAPTER's source code. This apparently developed into an irresistible habit, for when Arney left CA to work for Altai in January, 1984, he took with him copies of the source code for both the VSE and MVS versions of ADAPTER. He did this in knowing violation of the CA employee agreements that he had signed.

Once at Altai, Arney and Williams discussed design possibilities for adapting ZEKE to run on MVS operating systems. Williams, who had created the VSE version of ZEKE, thought that approximately 30% of his original program would have to be modified in order to accommodate MVS. Arney persuaded Williams that the best way to make the needed modifications was to introduce a "44 common system interface" component into ZEKE. He did not tell Williams that his idea stemmed from his familiarity with ADAPTER. They decided to name this new component-program OSCAR.

Arney went to work creating OSCAR. No one at Altai, including Williams, knew that he had the ADAPTER code, and no one knew that he was using it to design OSCAR/VSE. In three months, Arney successfully completed the OSCAR/VSE project. In an additional month he developed an OSCAR/MVS version. When the dust finally settled, Arney had copied approximately 30% of OSCAR's code from CA's ADAPTER program.

The first generation of OSCAR programs was known as OSCAR 3.4. From 1985 to August 1988, Altai used OSCAR 3.4 in its ZEKE product, as well as in programs entitled ZACK and ZEBB. In late July 1988, CA first learned that Altai may have appropriated parts of ADAPTER. After confirming its suspicions, CA secured copyrights on its 2.1 and 7.0 versions of

CA–SCHEDULER. CA then brought this copyright and trade secret misappropriation action against Altai.

Apparently, it was upon receipt of the summons and complaint that Altai first learned that Arney had copied much of the OSCAR code from ADAPTER. After Arney confirmed to Williams that CA's accusations of copying were true, Williams immediately set out to survey the damage. Without ever looking at the ADAPTER code himself, Williams learned from Arney exactly which sections of code Arney had taken from ADAPTER.

Upon advice of counsel, Williams initiated OSCAR's rewrite. The project's goal was to save as much of OSCAR 3.4 as legitimately could be used, and to excise those portions which had been copied from ADAPTER. Arney was entirely excluded from the process, and his copy of the ADAPTER code was locked away. Williams put eight other programmers on the project, none of whom had been involved in any way in the development of OSCAR 3.4. Williams provided the programmers with a description of the ZEKE operating system services so that they could rewrite the appropriate code. The rewrite project took about six months to complete and was finished in mid-November 1989. The resulting program was entitled OSCAR 3.5.

From that point on, Altai shipped only OSCAR 3.5 to its new customers. Altai also shipped OSCAR 3.5 as a "free upgrade" to all customers that had previously purchased OSCAR 3.4. While Altai and Williams acted responsibly to correct what Arney had wrought, the damage was done. CA's lawsuit remained. . . .

DISCUSSION

While both parties originally appealed from different aspects of the district court's judgment, Altai has now abandoned its appellate claims. In particular, Altai has conceded liability for the copying of ADAPTER into OSCAR 3.4 and raises no challenge to the award of $364,444 in damages on that score. Thus, we address only CA's appeal from the district court's rulings that: (1) Altai was not liable for copyright infringement in developing OSCAR 3.5; and (2) in developing both OSCAR 3.4 and 3.5, Altai was not liable for misappropriating CA's trade secrets.

CA makes two arguments. First, CA contends that the district court applied an erroneous method for determining whether there exists substantial similarity between computer programs, and thus, erred in determining that OSCAR 3.5 did not infringe the copyrights held on the different versions of its CA–SCHEDULER program. CA asserts that the test applied by the district court failed to account sufficiently for a computer program's non-literal elements. Second, CA maintains that the district court erroneously concluded that its state law trade secret claims had been preempted by the federal copyright act, see 17 U.S.C. § 301(a). We shall address each argument in turn.

I.   COPYRIGHT INFRINGEMENT

In any suit for copyright infringement, the plaintiff must establish its ownership of a valid copyright, and that the defendant copied the copyrighted work. The plaintiff may prove defendant's copying either by direct evidence or, as is most often the case, by showing that (1) the defendant had access to the plaintiff's copyrighted work and (2) that defendant's work is substantially similar to the plaintiff's copyrightable material.

For the purpose of analysis, the district court assumed that Altai had access to the ADAPTER code when creating OSCAR 3.5. Thus, in determining whether Altai had unlawfully copied protected aspects of CA's ADAPTER, the district court narrowed its focus of inquiry to ascertaining whether Altai's OSCAR 3.5 was substantially similar to ADAPTER. Because we approve Judge Pratt's conclusions regarding substantial similarity, our analysis will proceed along the same assumption. . . .

A. Copyright Protection for the Non-literal Elements of Computer Programs

It is now well settled that the literal elements of computer programs, i.e., their source and object codes, are the subject of copyright protection. Here, as noted earlier, Altai admits having copied approximately 30% of the OSCAR 3.4 program from CA's ADAPTER source code, and does not challenge the district court's related finding of infringement.

In this case, the hotly contested issues surround OSCAR 3.5. As recounted above, OSCAR 3.5 is the product of Altai's carefully orchestrated rewrite of OSCAR 3.4. After the purge, none of the ADAPTER source code remained in the 3.5 version; thus, Altai made sure that the literal elements of its revamped OSCAR program were no longer substantially similar to the literal elements of CA's ADAPTER.

According to CA, the district court erroneously concluded that Altai's OSCAR 3.5 was not substantially similar to its own ADAPTER program. CA argues that this occurred because the district court "committed legal error in analyzing [its] claims of copyright infringement by failing to find that copyright protects expression contained in the non-literal elements of computer software." We disagree.

CA argues that, despite Altai's rewrite of the OSCAR code, the resulting program remained substantially similar to the structure of its ADAPTER program. As discussed above, a program's structure includes its non-literal components such as general flow charts as well as the more specific organization of inter-modular relationships, parameter lists, and macros. In addition to these aspects, CA contends that OSCAR 3.5 is also substantially similar to ADAPTER with respect to the list of services that both ADAPTER and OSCAR obtain from their respective operating systems. We must decide whether and to what extent these elements of computer programs are protected by copyright law.

The statutory terrain in this area has been well explored. The Copyright Act affords protection to "original works of authorship fixed in any tangible medium of expression." 17 U.S.C. § 102(a). This broad category of protected "works" includes "literary works," id., which are defined by the Act as works, other than audiovisual works, expressed in words, numbers, or other verbal or numerical symbols or indicia, regardless of the nature of the material objects, such as books, periodicals, manuscripts, phonorecords, film tapes, disks, or cards, in which they are embodied. 17 U.S.C. § 101. While computer programs are not specifically listed as part of the above statutory definition, the legislative history leaves no doubt that Congress intended them to be considered literary works.

The syllogism that follows from the foregoing premises is a powerful one: if the non-literal structures of literary works are protected by copyright; and if computer programs are literary works, as we are told by the legislature; then the non-literal structures of computer programs are protected by copyright. We have no reservation in joining the company of those courts that have already ascribed to this logic. However, that conclusion does not end our analysis. We must determine the scope of copyright protection that extends to a computer program's non-literal structure.

As a caveat, we note that our decision here does not control infringement actions regarding categorically distinct works, such as certain types of screen displays. These items represent products of computer programs, rather than the programs themselves, and fall under the copyright rubric of audiovisual works. If a computer audiovisual display is copyrighted separately as an audiovisual work, apart from the literary work that generates it (i.e., the program), the display may be protectable regardless of the underlying program's copyright status. Of course, the copyright protection that these displays enjoy extends only so far as their expression is protectable. In this case, however, we are concerned not with a program's display, but the program itself, and then with only its non-literal components. In considering the copyrightability of these components, we must refer to venerable doctrines of copyright law.

1) Idea vs. Expression Dichotomy

It is a fundamental principle of copyright law that a copyright does not protect an idea, but only the expression of the idea. This axiom of common law has been incorporated into the governing statute. Section 102(b) of the act provides: In no case does copyright protection for an original work of authorship extend to any idea, procedure, process, system, method of operation, concept, principle, or discovery, regardless of the form in which it is described, explained, illustrated, or embodied in such work. See also House Report, at 5670 ("Copyright does not preclude others from using ideas or information revealed by the author's work.").

Congress made no special exception for computer programs. To the contrary, the legislative history explicitly states that copyright protects computer programs only "to the extent that they incorporate authorship in programmer's expression of original ideas, as distinguished from the ideas themselves." Id. at 5667; see also id. at 5670 ("Section 102(b) is intended ... to make clear that the expression adopted by the programmer is the copyrightable element in a computer program, and that the actual processes or methods embodied in the program are not within the scope of copyright law.").

Similarly, the National Commission on New Technological Uses of Copyrighted Works ("CONTU") established by Congress to survey the issues generated by the interrelationship of advancing technology and copyright law, recommended, inter alia, that the 1976 Copyright Act "be amended ... to make it explicit that computer programs, to the extent that they embody the author's original creation, are proper subject matter for copyright." See National Commission on New Technological Uses of Copyrighted Works, Final Report 1 (1979) (hereinafter "CONTU Report"). To that end, Congress adopted CONTU's suggestions and amended the Copyright Act by adding, among other things, a provision to 17 U.S.C. § 101 which defined the term "computer program." CONTU also "concluded that the idea-expression distinction should be used to determine which aspects of computer programs are copyrightable." Lotus Dev. Corp., 740 F.Supp. at 54 (citing CONTU Report, at 44).

Drawing the line between idea and expression is a tricky business. Judge Learned Hand noted that "[n]obody has ever been able to fix that boundary, and nobody ever can." Nichols, 45 F.2d at 121. Thirty years later his convictions remained firm. "Obviously, no principle can be stated as to when an imitator has gone beyond copying the 'idea,' and has borrowed its 'expression,'" Judge Hand concluded. "Decisions must therefore inevitably be ad hoc." Peter Pan Fabrics, Inc. v. Martin Weiner Corp., 274 F.2d 487, 489 (2d Cir.1960).

The essentially utilitarian nature of a computer program further complicates the task of distilling its idea from its expression. In order to describe both computational processes and abstract ideas, its content "combines creative and technical expression." See Spivack, at 755. The variations of expression found in purely creative compositions, as opposed to those contained in utilitarian works, are not directed towards practical application. For example, a narration of Humpty Dumpty's demise, which would clearly be a creative composition, does not serve the same ends as, say, a recipe for scrambled eggs—which is a more process oriented text. Thus, compared to aesthetic works, computer programs hover even more closely to the elusive boundary line described in § 102(b).

The doctrinal starting point in analyses of utilitarian works, is the seminal case of Baker v. Selden, 101 U.S. 99 (1879)*....

While Baker v. Selden provides a sound analytical foundation, it offers scant guidance on how to separate idea or process from expression, and moreover, on how to further distinguish protectable expression from that expression which "must necessarily be used as incident to" the work's underlying concept. In the context of computer programs, the Third Circuit's noted decision in Whelan has, thus far, been the most thoughtful attempt to accomplish these ends.

The court in Whelan faced substantially the same problem as is presented by this case. There, the defendant was accused of making off with the non-literal structure of the plaintiff's copyrighted dental lab

---

* Baker v. Selden appears at page 591, above. [Ed.]

management program, and employing it to create its own competitive version. In assessing whether there had been an infringement, the court had to determine which aspects of the programs involved were ideas, and which were expression. In separating the two, the court settled upon the following conceptual approach: "[T]he line between idea and expression may be drawn with reference to the end sought to be achieved by the work in question. In other words, the purpose or function of a utilitarian work would be the work's idea, and everything that is not necessary to that purpose or function would be part of the expression of the idea.... Where there are various means of achieving the desired purpose, then the particular means chosen is not necessary to the purpose; hence, there is expression, not idea." 797 F.2d at 1236 (citations omitted). The "idea" of the program at issue in Whelan was identified by the court as simply "the efficient management of a dental laboratory." Id. at n. 28.

So far, in the courts, the Whelan rule has received a mixed reception. While some decisions have adopted its reasoning, others have rejected it.

Whelan has fared even more poorly in the academic community, where its standard for distinguishing idea from expression has been widely criticized for being conceptually overbroad. The leading commentator in the field has stated that, "[t]he crucial flaw in [Whelan's] reasoning is that it assumes that only one 'idea,' in copyright law terms, underlies any computer program, and that once a separable idea can be identified, everything else must be expression." 3 Nimmer § 13.03[F], at 13–62.34. This criticism focuses not upon the program's ultimate purpose but upon the reality of its structural design. As we have already noted, a computer program's ultimate function or purpose is the composite result of interacting subroutines. Since each subroutine is itself a program, and thus, may be said to have its own "idea," Whelan's general formulation that a program's overall purpose equates with the program's idea is descriptively inadequate.

Accordingly, we think that Judge Pratt wisely declined to follow Whelan. In addition to noting the weakness in the Whelan definition of "program-idea," mentioned above, Judge Pratt found that Whelan's synonymous use of the terms "structure, sequence, and organization" demonstrated a flawed understanding of a computer program's method of operation. Rightly, the district court found Whelan's rationale suspect because it is so closely tied to what can now be seen—with the passage of time—as the opinion's somewhat outdated appreciation of computer science.

2) Substantial Similarity Test for Computer Program Structure: Abstraction—Filtration—Comparison

We think that Whelan's approach to separating idea from expression in computer programs relies too heavily on metaphysical distinctions and does not place enough emphasis on practical considerations. As the cases that we shall discuss demonstrate, a satisfactory answer to this problem cannot be reached by resorting, a priori, to philosophical first principles.

As discussed herein, we think that district courts would be well-advised to undertake a three-step procedure, based on the abstractions test utilized by the district court, in order to determine whether the non-literal elements of two or more computer programs are substantially similar. This approach breaks no new ground; rather, it draws on such familiar copyright doctrines as merger, scenes a faire, and public domain. In taking this approach, however, we are cognizant that computer technology is a dynamic field which can quickly outpace judicial decisionmaking. Thus, in cases where the technology in question does not allow for a literal application of the procedure we outline below, our opinion should not be read to foreclose the district courts of our circuit from utilizing a modified version.

In ascertaining substantial similarity under this approach, a court would first break down the allegedly infringed program into its constituent structural parts. Then, by examining each of these parts for such things as incorporated ideas, expression that is necessarily incidental to those ideas, and elements that are taken from the public domain, a court would then be able to sift out all non-protectable material. Left with a kernel, or possibly kernels, of creative expression after following this process of elimination, the court's last step would be to compare this material with the structure of an allegedly infringing program. The result of this comparison will determine whether the protectable elements of the programs at issue are substantially similar so as to warrant a finding of infringement. It will be helpful to elaborate a bit further.

Step One: Abstraction

As the district court appreciated, the theoretic framework for analyzing substantial similarity expounded by Learned Hand in the Nichols case is helpful in the present context. In Nichols, we enunciated what has now become known as the "abstractions" test for separating idea from expression: Upon any work . . . a great number of patterns of increasing generality will fit equally well, as more and more of the incident is left out. The last may perhaps be no more than the most general statement of what the [work] is about, and at times might consist only of its title; but there is a point in this series of abstractions where they are no longer protected, since otherwise the [author] could prevent the use of his "ideas," to which, apart from their expression, his property is never extended. Nichols, 45 F.2d at 121.

While the abstractions test was originally applied in relation to literary works such as novels and plays, it is adaptable to computer programs. In contrast to the Whelan approach, the abstractions test "implicitly recognizes that any given work may consist of a mixture of numerous ideas and expressions." 3 Nimmer § 13.03[F] at 13–62.3463.

As applied to computer programs, the abstractions test will comprise the first step in the examination for substantial similarity. Initially, in a manner that resembles reverse engineering on a theoretical plane, a court should dissect the allegedly copied program's structure and isolate each level of abstraction contained within it. This process begins with the code and ends with an articulation of the program's ultimate function. Along the way, it is necessary essentially to retrace the map each of the designer's steps in the opposite order in which they were taken during the program's creation.

As an anatomical guide to this procedure, the following description is helpful: At the lowest level of abstraction, a computer program may be thought of in its entirety as a set of individual instructions organized into a hierarchy of modules. At a higher level of abstraction, the instructions in the lowest-level modules may be replaced conceptually by the functions of those modules. At progressively higher levels of abstraction, the functions of higher-level modules conceptually replace the implementations of those modules in terms of lower-level modules and instructions, until finally, one is left with nothing but the ultimate function of the program. A program has structure at every level of abstraction at which it is viewed. At low levels of abstraction, a program's structure may be quite complex; at the highest level it is trivial.

Step Two: Filtration

Once the program's abstraction levels have been discovered, the substantial similarity inquiry moves from the conceptual to the concrete. Professor Nimmer suggests, and we endorse, a "successive filtering method" for separating protectable expression from non-protectable material. See generally 3 Nimmer § 13.03[F]. This process entails examining the structural components at each level of abstraction to determine whether their particular inclusion at that level was "idea" or was dictated by considerations of efficiency, so as to be necessarily incidental to that idea; required by factors external to the program itself; or taken from the public domain and hence is non-protectable expression. The structure of any given program may reflect some, all, or none of these considerations. Each case requires its own fact specific investigation.

Strictly speaking, this filtration serves "the purpose of defining the scope of plaintiff's copyright." Brown Bag Software v. Symantec Corp., 960 F.2d 1465 (9th Cir.1992). By applying well developed doctrines of copyright law, it may ultimately leave behind a "core of protectable material." 3 Nimmer § 13.03[F][5], at 13–72. Further explication of this second step may be helpful.

(a) Elements Dictated by Efficiency

The portion of Baker v. Selden, discussed earlier, which denies copyright protection to expression necessarily incidental to the idea being expressed, appears to be the cornerstone for what has developed into the doctrine of merger. The doctrine's underlying principle is that "[w]hen there is essentially only one way to express an idea, the idea and its expression are inseparable and copyright is no bar to copying that expression." Concrete Machinery Co. v. Classic Lawn Ornaments, Inc., 843 F.2d 600, 606 (1st Cir.1988). Under these circumstances, the expression is said to have "merged" with the idea itself. In order not to confer a monopoly of the idea upon the copyright owner, such expression should not be protected.

CONTU recognized the applicability of the merger doctrine to computer programs. In its report to Congress it stated that: "[C]opyrighted language may be copied without infringing when there is but a limited number of ways to express a given idea.... In the computer context, this means that when specific instructions, even though previously copyrighted, are the only and essential means of accomplishing a given task, their later use by another will not amount to infringement." CONTU Report at 20. While this statement directly concerns only the application of merger to program code, that is, the textual aspect of the program, it reasonably suggests that the doctrine fits comfortably within the general context of computer programs.

Furthermore, when one considers the fact that programmers generally strive to create programs "that meet the user's needs in the most efficient manner," Menell, at 1052, the applicability of the merger doctrine to computer programs becomes compelling. In the context of computer program design, the concept of efficiency is akin to deriving the most concise logical proof or formulating the most succinct mathematical computation. Thus, the more efficient a set of modules are, the more closely they approximate the idea or process embodied in that particular aspect of the program's structure.

While, hypothetically, there might be a myriad of ways in which a programmer may effectuate certain functions within a program—i.e., express the idea embodied in a given subroutine—efficiency concerns may so narrow the practical range of choice as to make only one or two forms of expression workable options. Of course, not all program structure is informed by efficiency concerns. It follows that in order to determine whether the merger doctrine precludes copyright protection to an aspect of a program's structure that is so oriented, a court must inquire "whether the use of this particular set of modules is necessary efficiently to implement that part of the program's process" being implemented. Englund, at 902. If the answer is yes, then the expression represented by the programmer's choice of a specific module or group of modules has merged with their underlying idea and is unprotected.

Another justification for linking structural economy with the application of the merger doctrine stems from a program's essentially utilitarian nature and the competitive forces that exist in the software marketplace. Working in tandem, these factors give rise to a problem of proof which merger helps to eliminate.

Efficiency is an industry-wide goal. Since, as we have already noted, there may be only a limited number of efficient implementations for any given program task, it is quite possible that multiple programmers, working independently, will design the identical method employed in the allegedly infringed work. Of course, if this is the case, there is no copyright infringement.

Under these circumstances, the fact that two programs contain the same efficient structure may as likely lead to an inference of independent creation as it does to one of copying. Thus, since evidence of similarly efficient structure is not particularly probative of copying, it should be disregarded in the overall substantial similarity analysis.

We find support for applying the merger doctrine in cases that have already addressed the question of substantial similarity in the context of computer program structure. . . .

We agree with the approach taken in these decisions, and conclude that application of the merger doctrine in this setting is an effective way to eliminate non-protectable expression contained in computer programs.

(b) Elements Dictated By External Factors

We have stated that where "it is virtually impossible to write about a particular historical era or fictional theme without employing certain 'stock' or standard literary devices," such expression is not copyrightable. Hoehling v. Universal City Studios, Inc., 618 F.2d 972, 979 (2d Cir.), cert. denied, 449 U.S. 841 (1980). For example, the Hoehling case was an infringement suit stemming from several works on the Hindenberg disaster. There we concluded that similarities in representations of German beer halls, scenes depicting German greetings such as "Heil Hitler," or the singing of certain German songs would not lead to a finding of infringement because they were " 'indispensable, or at least standard, in the treatment of' " life in Nazi Germany. Id. (quoting Alexander v. Haley, 460 F.Supp. 40, 45 (S.D.N.Y.1978)). This is known as the scenes a faire doctrine, and like "merger," it has its analogous application to computer programs.

Professor Nimmer points out that "in many instances it is virtually impossible to write a program to perform particular functions in a specific computing environment without employing standard techniques." 3 Nimmer § 13.03[F][3], at 13–65. This is a result of the fact that a programmer's freedom of design choice is often circumscribed by extrinsic considerations such as (1) the mechanical specifications of the computer on which a particular program is intended to run; (2) compatibility requirements of other programs with which a program is designed to operate in conjunction; (3) computer manufacturers' design standards; (4) demands of the industry being serviced; and (5) widely accepted programming practices within the computer industry.

Courts have already considered some of these factors in denying copyright protection to various elements of computer programs. In the Plains Cotton case [807 F.2d 1256], the Fifth Circuit refused to reverse the district court's denial of a preliminary injunction against an alleged program infringer because, in part, "many of the similarities between the . . . programs [were] dictated by the externalities of the cotton market." 807 F.2d at 1262. . . .

Building upon this existing case law, we conclude that a court must also examine the structural content of an allegedly infringed program for elements that might have been dictated by external factors.

(c) Elements Taken From the Public Domain

Closely related to the non-protectability of scenes a faire, is material found in the public domain. Such material is free for the taking and cannot be appropriated by a single author even though it is included in a copyrighted work. We see no reason to make an exception to this rule for elements of a computer program that have entered the public domain by virtue of freely accessible program exchanges and the like. Thus, a court must also filter out this material from the allegedly infringed program before it makes the final inquiry in its substantial similarity analysis.

Step Three: Comparison

The third and final step of the test for substantial similarity that we believe appropriate for non-literal program components entails a comparison. Once a court has sifted out all elements of the allegedly infringed program which are "ideas" or are dictated by efficiency or external factors, or taken from the public domain, there may remain a core of protectable expression. In terms of a work's copyright value, this is the golden nugget. At this point, the court's substantial similarity inquiry focuses on whether the defendant copied any aspect of this protected expression, as well as an assessment of the copied portion's relative importance with respect to the plaintiff's overall program.

3) Policy Considerations

We are satisfied that the three step approach we have just outlined not only comports with, but advances the constitutional policies underlying the copyright act. Since any method that tries to distinguish idea from expression ultimately impacts on the scope of copyright protection afforded to a particular type of work, "the line [it draws] must be a pragmatic one, which also keeps in consideration 'the preservation of the balance between competition and protection.'" Apple Computer, 714 F.2d at 1253 (citation omitted).

CA and some amici argue against the type of approach that we have set forth on the grounds that it will be a disincentive for future computer program research and development. At bottom, they claim that if programmers are not guaranteed broad copyright protection for their work, they will not invest the extensive time, energy and funds required to design and improve program structures. While they have a point, their argument cannot carry the day. The interest of the copyright law is not in simply conferring a monopoly on industrious persons, but in advancing the public welfare through rewarding artistic creativity, in a manner that permits the free use and development of non-protectable ideas and processes. . . .

Recently, the Supreme Court has emphatically reiterated that "[t]he primary objective of copyright is not to reward the labor of authors. . . ." Feist Publications, Inc. v. Rural Telephone Service Co., Inc., 111 S.Ct. 1282, 1290 (1991) (emphasis added). While the Feist decision deals primarily with the copyrightability of purely factual compilations, its underlying tenets apply to much of the work involved in computer programming. Feist put to rest the "sweat of the brow" doctrine in copyright law. Id. at 1295. The rationale of that doctrine "was that copyright was a reward for the hard work that went into compiling facts." Id. at 1291. The Court flatly rejected this justification for extending copyright protection, noting that it "eschewed the most fundamental axiom of copyright law—that no one may copyright facts or ideas." Id.

Feist teaches that substantial effort alone cannot confer copyright status on an otherwise uncopyrightable work. As we have discussed, despite the fact that significant labor and expense often goes into computer program flow—charting and debugging, that process does not always result in inherently protectable expression. Thus, Feist implicitly undercuts the Whelan rationale, "which allow[ed] copyright protection beyond the literal computer code ... [in order to] provide the proper incentive for programmers by protecting their most valuable efforts." Whelan, 797 F.2d at 1237 (footnote omitted). We note that Whelan was decided prior to Feist when the "sweat of the brow" doctrine still had vitality. In view of the Supreme Court's recent holding, however, we must reject the legal basis of CA's disincentive argument.

Furthermore, we are unpersuaded that the test we approve today will lead to the dire consequences for the computer program industry that plaintiff and some amici predict. To the contrary, serious students of the industry have been highly critical of the sweeping scope of copyright protection engendered by the Whelan rule, in that it "enables first comers to 'lock up' basic programming techniques as implemented in programs to perform particular tasks." Menell, at 1087.

To be frank, the exact contours of copyright protection for non-literal program structure are not completely clear. We trust that as future cases are decided, those limits will become better defined. Indeed, it may well be that the Copyright Act serves as a relatively weak barrier against public access to the theoretical interstices behind a program's source and object codes. This results from the hybrid nature of a computer program, which, while it is literary expression, is also a highly functional, utilitarian component in the larger process of computing.

Generally, we think that copyright registration—with its indiscriminating availability—is not ideally suited to deal with the highly dynamic technology of computer science. Thus far, many of the decisions in this area reflect the court's attempt to fit the proverbial square peg in a round hole. The district court, and at least one commentator has suggested that patent registration, with its exacting up-front novelty and non-obviousness requirements, might be the more appropriate rubric of protection for intellectual property of this kind. In any event, now that more than 12 years have passed since CONTU issued its final report, the resolution of this specific issue could benefit from further legislative investigation—perhaps a CONTU II.

In the meantime, Congress has made clear that computer programs are literary works entitled to copyright protection. Of course, we shall abide by these instructions, but in so doing we must not impair the overall integrity of copyright law. While incentive based arguments in favor of broad copyright protection are perhaps attractive from a pure policy perspective, ultimately, they have a corrosive effect on certain fundamental tenets of copyright doctrine. If the test we have outlined results in narrowing the scope of protection, as we expect it will, that result flows from applying, in accordance with Congressional intent, long-standing principles of copyright law to computer programs. Of course, our decision is also informed by our concern that these fundamental principles remain undistorted.

B. The District Court Decision

... 2) Evidentiary Analysis

The district court had to determine whether Altai's OSCAR 3.5 program was substantially similar to CA's ADAPTER. We note that Judge Pratt's method of analysis effectively served as a road map for our own, with one exception—Judge Pratt filtered out the non-copyrightable aspects of OSCAR 3.5 rather than those found in ADAPTER, the allegedly infringed program. We think that our approach—i.e., filtering out the unprotected aspects of an allegedly infringed program and then comparing the end product to the structure of the suspect program—is preferable, and therefore believe that district courts should proceed in this manner in future cases.

We opt for this strategy because, in some cases, the defendant's program structure might contain protectable expression and/or other elements that are not found in the plaintiff's program. Since it is extraneous to the allegedly copied work, this material would have no bearing on any potential substantial similarity between the two programs. Thus, its filtration would be wasteful and unnecessarily time consuming. Furthermore, by focusing the analysis on the infringing rather than on the infringed material, a court may mistakenly place too little emphasis on a quantitatively small misappropriation which is, in reality, a qualitatively vital aspect of the plaintiff's protectable expression.

The fact that the district court's analysis proceeded in the reverse order, however, had no material impact on the outcome of this case. Since Judge Pratt determined that OSCAR effectively contained no protectable expression whatsoever, the most serious charge that can be levelled against him is that he was overly thorough in his examination.

The district court took the first step in the analysis set forth in this opinion when it separated the program by levels of abstraction. The district court stated: As applied to computer software programs, this abstractions test would progress in order of "increasing generality" from object code, to source code, to parameter lists, to services required, to general outline. In discussing the particular similarities, therefore, we shall focus on these levels. While the facts of a different case might require that a district court draw a more particularized blueprint of a program's overall structure, this description is a workable one for the case at hand.

Moving to the district court's evaluation of OSCAR 3.5's structural components, we agree with Judge Pratt's systematic exclusion of non-protectable expression. With respect to code, the district court observed that after the rewrite of OSCAR 3.4 to OSCAR 3.5, "there remained virtually no lines of code that were identical to ADAPTER." Accordingly, the court found that the code "present[ed] no similarity at all."

Next, Judge Pratt addressed the issue of similarity between the two programs' parameter lists and macros. He concluded that, viewing the conflicting evidence most favorably to CA, it demonstrated that "only a few of the lists and macros were similar to protected elements in ADAPTER; the others were either in the public domain or dictated by the functional demands of the program." Id. As discussed above, functional elements and elements taken from the public domain do not qualify for copyright protection. With respect to the few remaining parameter lists and macros, the district court could reasonably conclude that they did not warrant a finding of infringement given their relative contribution to the overall program. In any event, the district court reasonably found that, for lack of persuasive evidence, CA failed to meet its burden of proof on whether the macros and parameter lists at issue were substantially similar.

The district court also found that the overlap exhibited between the list of services required for both ADAPTER and OSCAR 3.5 was "determined by the demands of the operating system and of the applications program to which it [was] to be linked through ADAPTER or OSCAR." In other words, this aspect of the program's structure was dictated by the nature of other programs with which it was designed to interact and, thus, is not protected by copyright.

Finally, in his infringement analysis, Judge Pratt accorded no weight to the similarities between the two programs' organizational charts, "because [the charts were] so simple and obvious to anyone exposed to the operation of the program[s]." CA argues that the district court's action in this regard "is not consistent with copyright law"—that "obvious" expression is protected, and that the district court erroneously failed to realize this. However, to say that elements of a work are "obvious," in the manner in which the district court used the word, is to say that they "follow naturally from the work's theme rather than from the author's creativity." 3 Nimmer § 13.03[F][3], at 13–65. This is but one formulation of the scenes a faire doctrine, which we have already endorsed as a means of weeding out unprotectable expression.

CA argues, at some length, that many of the district court's factual conclusions regarding the creative nature of its program's components are simply wrong. Of course, we are limited in our review of factual findings to setting aside only those that we determine are clearly erroneous. Upon a thorough review of the voluminous record in this case, which is comprised of conflicting testimony and other highly technical evidence, we discern no error on the part of Judge Pratt, let alone clear error.

Since we accept Judge Pratt's factual conclusions and the results of his legal analysis, we affirm his dismissal of CA's copyright infringement claim based upon OSCAR 3.5. We emphasize that, like all copyright infringement cases, those that involve computer programs are highly fact specific. The amount of protection due structural elements, in any given case, will vary according to the protectable expression found to exist within the program at issue....

[The court's disposition of Computer Associates' trade secret claim, omitted here, is reprinted at page 932, below.]

CONCLUSION

In adopting the above three step analysis for substantial similarity between the nonliteral elements of computer programs we seek to insure two things: (1) that programmers may receive appropriate copyright protection for innovative utilitarian works containing expression; and (2) that non-protectable technical expression remains in the public domain for others to use freely as building blocks in their own work. At first blush, it may seem counter-intuitive that someone who has benefited to some degree from illicitly obtained material can emerge from an infringement suit relatively unscathed. However, so long as the appropriated material consists of non-protectable expression, "[t]his result is neither unfair nor unfortunate. It is the means by which copyright advances the progress of science and art." Feist, 111 S.Ct. at 1290.

Furthermore, while trade secret law may well be an appropriate means by which to secure compensation for software espionage, we conclude that, in order to avoid preemption, it must be employed in a manner that does not encroach upon the exclusive domain of the federal copyright act.

Accordingly, we affirm the judgment of the district court in all respects.

NOTES

1. *Computer Programs as Copyright Subject Matter.* The United States Copyright Office began accepting computer programs as copyrightable subject matter in 1964. See George D. Cary, Copyright Registration and Computer Programs, 11 Bull. Copyright Soc'y 362 (1964). The 1976 Copyright Act, as amended in 1980, defines "computer program" as "a set of statements or instructions to be used directly or indirectly in a computer in order to bring about a certain result." Case law has since established that, so long as it is original and sufficiently expressive, a computer program will be copyrightable whether it is expressed in words, in a flow chart, in source code or object code, and whether it is embodied in paper, magnetic disk, tape or semiconductor chip. See Apple Computer, Inc. v. Franklin Computer Corp., 714 F.2d 1240, 1249, 219 U.S.P.Q. 113 (3d Cir.1983), cert. dismissed, 464 U.S. 1033, 104 S.Ct. 690, 79 L.Ed.2d 158 (1984).

Computer programs exist today that can, without an author's intervention, create such finished works as crossword puzzles and daily weather maps. The day may not be far off when computer programs will be able to create fully realized literary and artistic productions. Should copyright extend to such products? Who would be the "author" of such a product? Does copyright law's originality standard presuppose a human author? The United Kingdom's 1988 Copyright, Designs and Patents Act extends copyright to works, such as drawings and songs, that are generated by a programmed computer and provides that in these cases the author is "the person by whom the arrangements necessary for the creation of the work are undertaken." §§ 9(3), 178.

2. *Infringement.* The first generation of copyright decisions on computer programs, represented by cases like Apple v. Franklin, note 1, above, typically involved literal copies, so that if the program was copyrightable, there was no question but that the copyright was infringed. *Computer Associates* represents the second generation of software copyright cases, testing the scope of rights in admittedly protectible subject matter against nonliteral copying. Virtually every court to face the issue since has followed the *Computer Associates* methodology.

Proof of copying through inferences drawn from access and similarity is much the same in computer program cases as in copyright infringement cases generally. For example, striking similarities may be used to prove copying. In Midway Mfg. Co. v. Strohon, 564 F.Supp. 741, 753, 219 U.S.P.Q. 42 (N.D.Ill.1983), the court found copying where defendant's program embodied 89% of the 16,000 bytes in plaintiff's program and there was "virtually an infinite number of ways to write a set of program instructions." Also, copyists sometimes fall into traps laid by the copyright owner and fail to excise such telltale clues as the programmer's name embedded in object code.

3. *Merger.* As noted in *Computer Associates,* copyright law's merger doctrine will withhold protection from an otherwise protectible expression of an idea if there is only a limited number of ways to express the idea. Should constraints on expression be measured as of the time the copyright claimant wrote the computer code in issue, or as of the time its competitor wrote the allegedly infringing code? From the perspective of system compatibility, the answer to the question is crucial. For example, at the time Apple programmers wrote the operating system for the Apple II line of computers, there were many ways in which they could have written the code. However, by the time a competitor, Franklin, came along, numerous application programs had been independently developed that would run on the Apple II only if they interoperated with the Apple code; for Franklin to compete for customers who had purchased these and future application programs, its machines would have to incorporate code that was functionally identical to Apple's.

In Apple Computer, Inc. v. Franklin Computer Corp., 714 F.2d 1240, 1253, 219 U.S.P.Q. 113 (3d Cir.1983), cert. dismissed, 464 U.S. 1033, 104 S.Ct. 690, 79 L.Ed.2d 158 (1984), the court ruled against Franklin's argument that merger should be measured as of the time the allegedly infringing code was written:

> Franklin claims that whether or not the programs can be rewritten, there are a limited 'number of ways to arrange operating systems

to enable a computer to run the vast body of Apple-compatible software.' This claim has no pertinence to either the idea/expression dichotomy or merger. The idea which may merge with the expression, thus making the copyright unavailable, is the idea which is the subject of expression. The idea of one of the operating system programs is, for example, how to translate source code into object code. If other methods of expressing that idea are not foreclosed as a practical matter, then there is no merger. Franklin may wish to achieve total compatibility with independently developed application programs written for the Apple II, but that is a commercial and competitive objective which does not enter into the somewhat metaphysical issue of whether particular ideas and expressions have merged.

Should the merger test be applied differently when the question of compatibility centers not on a program interface, as in *Apple v. Franklin*, but on a user interface?

4. *Databases.* Anyone who has used a legal research database like LEXIS or WESTLAW knows that the computer offers fast and powerful access to compilations of data. Data in a computerized database are typically arranged in ways that, though imperceptible to the user, make the stored data more readily accessible through the computer, and these arrangements, like the selection, arrangement and coordination that go into compilations of data generally, will usually be the subject matter of copyright.

What of the individual data collected in the database? In Feist v. Rural Telephone, page 606, above, the U.S. Supreme Court ruled that although original compilations of facts and data are constitutionally copyrightable, the facts and data themselves are not. The European Union's 1996 Directive on the Legal Protection of Databases, 96/9/EC, 11 March 1996, O.J. (L77) 20, requires member countries to adopt two tiers of protection for databases. The first tier extends copyright to the original selection or arrangement of the contents of databases, but not the contents themselves. The second, *sui generis,* tier protects against the extraction or reutilization of the contents of a database where the contents are the product of substantial investment by the maker of the database. Protection lasts for a term of fifteen years.

5. *International Protection of Computer Programs.* Other industrialized countries followed the lead of the United States in bringing computer programs within copyright. One notable development was the 1994 TRIPs Agreement which, in Article 10(1) provides that computer programs "whether in source or object code, shall be protected as literary works under the Berne Convention." Another was the European Union's Directive on the Legal Protection of Computer Programs, promulgated on May 14, 1991 and subsequently implemented through legislation in member states. Council Directive 91/250/EEC, 1991 O.J. (L 122) 42. The E.U. Directive definitively brings computer programs within the rubric of "literary works" and, rejecting the high standard of protection applied in at least one E.U. country, Germany, adopts a low originality threshold. On the history of the Directive's evolution, see Bridget Czarnota & Robert J. Hart, Legal Protection of Computer Programs in Europe: A Guide to the EC Directive 3–25 (1991); Alan K. Palmer & Thomas C. Vinje, The E.C. Directive on the Legal Protection of Computer Software: New Law Governing Software Development, 2 Duke J. of Comp. & Int'l L. 65 (1992).

2.   USER INTERFACES

Lotus Development Corp. v. Borland International, Inc.

United States Court of Appeals, First Circuit, 1995.
49 F.3d 807, 34 U.S.P.Q.2d 1014., aff'd by an equally divided Court, 516 U.S. 233, 116 S.Ct. 804, 133 L.Ed.2d 610 (1996).

STAHL, Circuit Judge.

This appeal requires us to decide whether a computer menu command hierarchy is copyrightable subject matter. In particular, we must decide whether, as the district court held, plaintiff-appellee Lotus Development Corporation's copyright in Lotus 1–2–3, a computer spreadsheet program, was infringed by defendant-appellant Borland International, Inc., when Borland copied the Lotus 1–2–3 menu command hierarchy into its Quattro and Quattro Pro computer spread-sheet programs.

I.

Background

Lotus 1–2–3 is a spreadsheet program that enables users to perform accounting functions electronically on a computer. Users manipulate and control the program via a series of menu commands, such as, "Copy," "Print," and "Quit." Users choose commands either by highlighting them on the screen or by typing their first letter. In all, Lotus 1–2–3 has 469 commands arranged into more than 50 menus and submenus.

Lotus 1–2–3, like many computer programs, allows users to write what are called "macros." By writing a macro, a user can designate a series of command choices with a single macro keystroke. Then, to execute that series of commands in multiple parts of the spreadsheet, rather than typing the whole series each time, the user only needs to type the single pre-programmed macro keystroke, causing the program to recall and perform the designated series of commands automatically. Thus, Lotus 1–2–3 macros shorten the time needed to set up and operate the program.

Borland released its first Quattro program to the public in 1987, after Borland's engineers had labored over its development for nearly three years. Borland's objective was to develop a spreadsheet program far superior to existing programs, including Lotus 1–2–3. In Borland's words, "[f]rom the time of its initial release ... Quattro included enormous innovations over competing spreadsheet products."

The district court found, and Borland does not now contest, that Borland included in its Quattro and Quattro Pro version 1.0 programs "*a virtually identical* copy of the entire 1–2–3 menu tree." *Borland III,* 831 F.Supp. at 212 (emphasis in original). In so doing, Borland did not copy any of Lotus's underlying computer code; it copied only the words and structure of Lotus's menu command hierarchy. Borland included the Lotus menu command hierarchy in its programs to make them compatible with Lotus 1–2–3 so that spreadsheet users who were already familiar with Lotus 1–2–3 would be able to switch to the Borland programs without having to learn new commands or rewrite their Lotus macros.

In its Quattro and Quattro Pro version 1.0 programs, Borland achieved compatibility with Lotus 1–2–3 by offering its users an alternate user interface, the "Lotus Emulation Interface." By activating the Emulation Interface, Borland users would see the Lotus menu commands on their screens and could interact with Quattro or Quattro Pro as if using Lotus 1–2–3, albeit with a slightly different looking screen and with many Borland options not available on Lotus 1–2–3. In effect, Borland allowed users to choose how they wanted to communicate with Borland's spreadsheet programs: either by using menu commands designed by Borland, or by using the commands and command structure used in Lotus 1–2–3 augmented by Borland-added commands. . . .

This appeal concerns only Borland's copying of the Lotus menu command hierarchy into its Quattro programs and Borland's affirmative defenses to such copying. Lotus has not cross-appealed; in other words, Lotus does not contend on appeal that the district court erred in finding that Borland had not copied other elements of Lotus 1–2–3, such as its screen displays.

II.

Discussion

On appeal, Borland does not dispute that it factually copied the words and arrangement of the Lotus menu command hierarchy. Rather, Borland argues that it "lawfully copied the unprotectable menus of Lotus 1–2–3." Borland contends that the Lotus menu command hierarchy is not copyrightable because it is a system, method of operation, process, or procedure foreclosed from protection by 17 U.S.C. § 102(b). Borland also raises a number of affirmative defenses.

A. *Copyright Infringement Generally*

To establish copyright infringement, a plaintiff must prove "(1) ownership of a valid copyright, and (2) copying of constituent elements of the work that are original." *Feist Publications, Inc. v. Rural Tel. Serv. Co.,* 499 U.S. 340, 361, 111 S.Ct. 1282, 1296, 113 L.Ed.2d 358 (1991). To show ownership of a valid copyright and therefore satisfy *Feist's* first prong, a plaintiff must prove that the work as a whole is original and that the plaintiff complied with applicable statutory formalities. "In judicial proceedings, a certificate of copyright registration constitutes primary evidence of copyrightability and shifts the burden to the defendant to demonstrate why the copyright is not valid." *Bibbero Sys., Inc. v. Colwell Sys., Inc.*, 893 F.2d 1104, 1106 (9th Cir.1990).

To show actionable copying and therefore satisfy *Feist's* second prong, a plaintiff must first prove that the alleged infringer copied plaintiff's copyrighted work as a factual matter; to do this, he or she may either present direct evidence of factual copying or, if that is unavailable, evidence that the alleged infringer had access to the copyrighted work and that the offending and copyrighted works are so similar that the court may infer that there was factual copying (i.e., probative similarity). The plaintiff must then prove that the copying of copyrighted material was so extensive that it rendered the offending and copyrighted works substantially similar.

In this appeal, we are faced only with whether the Lotus menu command hierarchy is copyrightable subject matter in the first instance, for Borland concedes that Lotus has a valid copyright in Lotus 1–2–3 as a whole and admits to factually copying the Lotus menu command hierarchy. As a result, this appeal is in a very different posture from most copyright-infringement cases, for copyright infringement generally turns on whether the defendant has copied protected expression as a factual matter. Because of this different posture, most copyright-infringement cases provide only limited help to us in deciding this appeal. This is true even with respect to those copyright-infringement cases that deal with computers and computer software.

B.   *Matter of First Impression*

Whether a computer menu command hierarchy constitutes copyrightable subject matter is a matter of first impression in this court. While some other courts appear to have touched on it briefly in dicta, *see, e.g., Autoskill, Inc. v. National Educ. Support, Sys., Inc.*, 994 F.2d 1476, 1495 n. 23 (10th Cir.), cert. denied, 510 U.S. 916, 114 S.Ct. 307, 126 L.Ed.2d 254 (1993), we know of no cases that deal with the copyrightability of a menu command hierarchy standing on its own (i.e., without other elements of the user interface, such as screen displays, in issue). Thus we are navigating in uncharted waters.

Borland vigorously argues, however, that the Supreme Court charted our course more than 100 years ago when it decided *Baker v. Selden*, 101 U.S. 99, 25 L.Ed. 841 (1879). In *Baker v. Selden*, the Court held that Selden's copyright over the textbook in which he explained his new way to do accounting did not grant him a monopoly on the use of his accounting system. Borland argues:

> The facts of *Baker v. Selden* and even the arguments advanced by the parties in that case, are identical to those in this case. The only difference is that the "user interface" of Selden's system was implemented by pen and paper rather than by computer.

To demonstrate that *Baker v. Selden* and this appeal both involve accounting systems, Borland even supplied this court with a video that, with special effects, shows Selden's paper forms "melting" into a computer screen and transforming into Lotus 1–2–3.

We do not think that *Baker v. Selden* is nearly as analogous to this appeal as Borland claims. Of course, Lotus 1–2–3 is a computer spreadsheet, and as such its grid of horizontal rows and vertical columns certainly resembles an accounting ledger or any other paper spreadsheet. Those grids, however, are not at issue in this appeal for, unlike Selden, Lotus does not claim to have a monopoly over its accounting system. Rather, this appeal involves Lotus's monopoly over the commands it uses to operate the computer. Accordingly, this appeal is not, as Borland contends, "identical" to *Baker v. Selden*.

C. *Altai*

Before we analyze whether the Lotus menu command hierarchy is a system, method of operation, process, or procedure, we first consider the applicability of the test the Second Circuit set forth in *Computer Assoc. International, Inc. v. Altai, Inc.*, 982 F.2d 693 (2d Cir.1992). The Second Circuit designed its *Altai* test to deal with the fact that computer programs, copyrighted as "literary works," can be infringed by what is known as "nonliteral" copying, which is copying that is paraphrased or loosely paraphrased rather than word for word. When faced with nonliteral-copying cases, courts must determine whether similarities are due merely to the fact that the two works share the same underlying idea or whether they instead indicate that the second author copied the first author's expression. The Second Circuit designed its *Altai* test to deal with this situation in the computer context, specifically with whether one computer program copied nonliteral expression from another program's code.

The *Altai* test involves three steps: abstraction, filtration, and comparison. The abstraction step requires courts to "dissect the allegedly copied program's structure and isolate each level of abstraction contained within it." *Altai*, 982 F.2d at 707. This step enables courts to identify the appropriate framework within which to separate protectable expression from unprotected ideas. Second, courts apply a "filtration" step in which they examine "the structural components at each level of abstraction to determine whether their particular inclusion at that level was 'idea' or was dictated by considerations of efficiency, so as to be necessarily incidental to that idea; required by factors external to the program itself; or taken from the public domain." *Id*. Finally, courts compare the protected elements of the infringed work (i.e., those that survived the filtration screening) to the corresponding elements of the allegedly infringing work to determine whether there was sufficient copying of protected material to constitute infringement.

In the instant appeal, we are not confronted with alleged nonliteral copying of computer code. Rather, we are faced with Borland's deliberate, literal copying of the Lotus menu command hierarchy. Thus, we must determine not whether nonliteral copying occurred in some amorphous sense, but rather whether the literal copying of the Lotus menu command hierarchy constitutes copyright infringement.

While the *Altai* test may provide a useful framework for assessing the alleged nonliteral copying of computer code, we find it to be of little help in assessing whether the literal copying of a menu command hierarchy constitutes copyright infringement. In fact, we think that the *Altai* test in this context may actually be misleading because, in instructing courts to abstract the various levels, it seems to encourage them to find a base level that includes copyrightable subject matter that, if literally copied, would make the copier liable for copyright infringement. While that base (or literal) level would not be at issue in a nonliteral-copying case like *Altai* it is precisely what is at issue in this appeal. We think that abstracting menu command hierarchies down to their individual word and menu levels and then filtering idea from expression at that stage, as both the *Altai* and the district court tests require, obscures the more fundamental question of whether a menu command hierarchy can be copyrighted at all. The initial inquiry should not be whether individual components of a menu command hierarchy are expressive, but rather whether the menu command hierarchy as a whole can be copyrighted.

D. *The Lotus Menu Command Hierarchy: A "Method of Operation"*

Borland argues that the Lotus menu command hierarchy is uncopyrightable because it is a system, method of operation, process, or procedure foreclosed from copyright protection by 17 U.S.C. § 102(b). Section 102(b) states: "In no case does copyright protection for an original work of authorship extend to any idea, procedure, process, system, method of operation, concept, principle, or discovery, regardless of the form in which it is described, explained, illustrated, or embodied in such work." Because we conclude that the Lotus menu command hierarchy is a method of operation, we do not consider whether it could also be a system, process, or procedure.

We think that "method of operation," as that term is used in § 102(b), refers to the means by which a person operates something, whether it be a car, a food processor, or a computer. Thus a text describing how to operate something would not extend copyright protection to the method of operation itself, other people would be free to employ that method and to describe it in their own words. Similarly, if a new method of operation is used rather than described, other people would still be free to employ or describe that method.

We hold that the Lotus menu command hierarchy is an uncopyrightable "method of operation." The Lotus menu command hierarchy provides the means by which users control and operate Lotus 1–2–3. If users wish to copy material, for example, they use the "Copy" command. If users wish to print material, they use the "Print" command. Users must use the command terms to tell the computer what to do. Without the menu command hierarchy, users would not be able to access and control, or indeed make use of, Lotus 1–2–3's functional capabilities.

The Lotus menu command hierarchy does not merely explain and present Lotus 1–2–3's functional capabilities to the user; it also serves as the method by which the program is operated and controlled. The Lotus menu command hierarchy is different from the Lotus long prompts, for the long prompts are not necessary to the operation of the program; users could operate Lotus 1–2–3 even if there were no long prompts. The Lotus menu command hierarchy is also different from the Lotus screen displays, for users need not "use" any expressive aspects of the screen displays in order to operate Lotus 1–2–3; because the way the screens look has little bearing on how users control the program, the screen displays are not part of Lotus 1–2–3's "method of operation." The Lotus menu command hierarchy is also different from the underlying computer code, because while code is necessary for the program to work, its precise formulation is not. In other words, to offer the same capabilities as Lotus 1–2–3, Borland did not have to copy Lotus's underlying code (and indeed it did not); to allow users to operate its programs in substantially the same way, however, Borland had to copy the Lotus menu command hierarchy. Thus the Lotus 1–2–3 code is not an uncopyrightable "method of operation."

The district court held that the Lotus menu command hierarchy, with its specific choice and arrangement of command terms, constituted an "expression" of the "idea" of operating a computer program with commands arranged hierarchically into menus and submenus. Under the district court's reasoning, Lotus's decision to employ hierarchically arranged command terms to operate its program could not foreclose its competitors from also employing hierarchically arranged command terms to operate their programs, but it did foreclose them from employing the specific command terms and arrangement that Lotus had used. In effect, the district court limited Lotus 1–2–3's "method of operation" to an abstraction.

Accepting the district court's finding that the Lotus developers made some expressive choices in choosing and arranging the Lotus command terms, we nonetheless hold that that expression is not copyrightable because it is part of Lotus 1–2–3's "method of operation." We do not think that "methods of operation" are limited to abstractions; rather, they are the means by which a user operates something. If specific words are essential to operating something, then they are part of a "method of operation" and, as such, are unprotectable. This is so whether they must be highlighted, typed in, or even spoken, as computer programs no doubt will soon be controlled by spoken words.

The fact that Lotus developers could have designed the Lotus menu command hierarchy differently is immaterial to the question of whether it is a "method of operation." In other words, our initial inquiry is not whether the Lotus menu command hierarchy incorporates any "expression." Rather, our initial inquiry is whether the menu command hierarchy is a "method of operation." Concluding, as we do, that users operate Lotus 1–2–3 by using the Lotus menu command hierarchy, and that the entire Lotus menu command hierarchy is essential to operating Lotus 1–2–3, we do not inquire further whether that method of operation could have been designed differently. The "expressive" choices of what to name the command terms and how to arrange them do not magically change the uncopyrightable menu command hierarchy into copyrightable subject matter.

Our holding that "methods of operation" are not limited to mere abstractions is bolstered by *Baker v. Selden*. In *Baker*, the Supreme Court explained that

> the teachings of science and the rules and methods of useful art have their final end in application and use; and this application and use are what the public derive from the publication of a book which teaches them.... The description of the art in a book, though entitled to the benefit of copyright, lays no foundation for an exclusive claim to the art itself. The object of the one is explanation; the object of the other is use. The former may be secured by copyright. The latter can only be secured, if it can be secured at all, by letters-patent.

Baker v. Selden, 101 U.S. at 104–05. Lotus wrote its menu command hierarchy so that people could learn it and use it. Accordingly, it falls squarely within the prohibition on copyright protection established in *Baker v. Selden* and codified by Congress in § 102(b).

In many ways, the Lotus menu command hierarchy is like the buttons used to control, say, a video cassette recorder ("VCR"). A VCR is a machine that enables one to watch and record video tapes. Users operate VCRs by pressing a series of buttons that are typically labelled "Record, Play, Reverse, Fast Forward, Pause, Stop/Eject." That the buttons are arranged and labeled does not make them a "literary work," nor does it make them an "expression" of the abstract "method of operating" a VCR via a set of labeled buttons. Instead, the buttons are themselves the "method of operating" the VCR.

When a Lotus 1–2–3 user chooses a command, either by highlighting it on the screen or by typing its first letter, he or she effectively pushes a button. Highlighting the "Print" command on the screen, or typing the letter "P," is analogous to pressing a VCR button labeled "Play."

Just as one could not operate a buttonless VCR, it would be impossible to operate Lotus 1–2–3 without employing its menu command hierarchy. Thus the Lotus command terms are not equivalent to the labels on the VCR's buttons, but are instead equivalent to the buttons themselves. Unlike the labels on a VCR's buttons, which merely make operating a VCR easier by indicating the buttons' functions the Lotus menu commands are essential to operating Lotus 1–2–3. Without the menu commands, there would be no way to "push" the Lotus buttons, as one could push unlabeled VCR buttons. While Lotus could probably have designed a user interface for which the command terms were mere labels, it did not do so here. Lotus 1–2–3 depends for its operation on use of the precise command terms that make up the Lotus menu command hierarchy.

One might argue that the buttons for operating a VCR are not analogous to the commands for operating a computer program because VCRs are not copyrightable, whereas computer programs are. VCRs may not be copyrighted because they do not fit within any of the § 102(a) categories of copyrightable works; the closest they come is "sculptural work." Sculptural works, however, are subject to a "useful-article" exception whereby "the design of a useful article ... shall be considered a pictorial, graphic, or sculptural work only if, and only to the extent that, such design incorporates pictorial, graphic, or sculptural features that can be identified separately from, and are capable of existing independently of, the utilitarian aspects of the article." 17 U.S.C. § 101. A "useful article" is "an article having an intrinsic utilitarian function that is not merely to portray the appearance of the article or to convey information." *Id.* Whatever expression there may be in the arrangement of the parts of a VCR is not capable of existing separately from the VCR itself, so an ordinary VCR would not be copyrightable.

Computer programs, unlike VCRs, are copyrightable as "literary works." Accordingly, one might argue, the "buttons" used to operate a computer program are not like the buttons used to operate a VCR, for they are not subject to a useful article exception. The response, of course, is that the arrangement of buttons on a VCR would not be copyrightable even without a useful-article exception, because the buttons are an uncopyrightable "method of operation." Similarly, the "buttons" of a computer program are also an uncopyrightable "method of operation."

That the Lotus menu command hierarchy, is a "method of operation" becomes clearer when one considers program compatibility. Under Lotus's theory, if a user uses several different programs, he or she must learn how to perform the same operation in a different way for each program used. For example, if the user wanted the computer to print material, then the user would have to learn not just one method of operating the computer such that it prints, but many different methods. We find this absurd. The fact that there may be many different ways to operate a computer program, or even many different ways to operate a computer program using a set of hierarchically arranged command terms, does not make the actual method of operation chosen copyrightable; it still functions as a method for operating the computer and as such is uncopyrightable.

Consider also that users employ the Lotus menu command hierarchy in writing macros. Under the district court's holding, if the user wrote a macro to shorten the time needed to perform a certain operation in Lotus 1–2–3, the user would be unable to use that macro to shorten the time needed to perform that same operation in another program. Rather, the user would have to rewrite his or her macro using that other program's menu command hierarchy. This is despite the fact that the macro is clearly the user's own work product. We think that forcing the user to cause the computer to perform the same operation in a different way ignores Congress's direction in § 102(b) that "methods of operation" are not copyrightable. That programs can offer users the ability to write macros in many different ways does not change the fact that, once written, the macro allows the user to perform an operation automatically. As the Lotus menu command hierarchy serves as the basis for Lotus 1–2–3 macros, the Lotus menu command hierarchy is a "method of operation."

In holding that expression that is part of a "method of operation" cannot be copyrighted, we do not understand ourselves to go against the Supreme Court's holding in *Feist.* In *Feist* the Court explained:

> The primary objective of copyright is not to reward the labor of authors, but to promote the Progress of Science and useful Arts. To this end, copyright assures authors the right to their original expression, but encourages others to build freely upon the ideas and information conveyed by a work.

Feist, 499 U.S. at 349–50, 111 S.Ct. at 1290. We do not think that the Court's statement that "copyright assures authors the right to their original expression" indicates that all expression is necessarily copyrightable; while original expression is necessary for copyright protection, we do not think that it is alone sufficient. Courts must still inquire whether original expression falls within one of the categories foreclosed from copyright protection by § 102(b), such as being a "method of operation."

We also note that in most contexts, there is no need to "build" upon other people's expression, for the ideas conveyed by that expression can be conveyed by someone else without copying the first author's expression. In the context of methods of operation, however, "building" requires the use of the precise method of operation already employed; otherwise, "building" would require dismantling, too. Original developers are not the only people entitled to build on the methods of operation they create; anyone can. Thus, Borland may build on the method of operation that Lotus designed and may use the Lotus menu command hierarchy in doing so.

Our holding that methods of operation are not limited to abstractions goes against *Autoskill,* 994 F.2d at 1495 n. 23, in which the Tenth Circuit rejected the defendant's argument that the keying procedure used in a computer program was an uncopyrightable "procedure" or "method of operation" under § 102(b). The program at issue, which was designed to test and train students with reading deficiencies, *id.* at 1481, required students to select responses to the program's queries "by pressing the 1, 2, or 3 keys." *Id.* at 1495 n. 23. The Tenth Circuit held that, "for purposes of the preliminary injunction, ... the record showed that [this] keying procedure reflected at least a minimal degree of creativity," as required by *Feist* for copyright protection. *Id.* As an initial matter, we question whether a programmer's decision to have users select a response by pressing the 1, 2, or 3 keys is original. More importantly, however, we fail to see how "a student selec[ting] a response by pressing the 1, 2, or 3 keys," *id.,* can be anything but an unprotectable method of operation.

III.

Conclusion

Because we hold that the Lotus menu command hierarchy is uncopyrightable subject matter, we further hold that Borland did not infringe

Lotus's copyright by copying it. Accordingly, we need not consider any of Borland's affirmative defenses. The judgment of the district court is

Reversed.

BOUDIN, *Circuit Judge,* concurring.

The importance of this case, and a slightly different emphasis in my view of the underlying problem, prompt me to add a few words to the majority's tightly focused discussion.

I.

Most of the law of copyright and the "tools" of analysis have developed in the context of literary works such as novels, plays, and films. In this milieu, the principal problem—simply stated, if difficult to resolve—is to stimulate creative expression without unduly limiting access by others to the broader themes and concepts deployed by the author. The middle of the spectrum presents close cases; but a "mistake" in providing too much protection involves a small cost: subsequent authors treating the same themes must take a few more steps away from the original expression.

The problem presented by computer programs is fundamentally different in one respect. The computer program is a *means* for causing something to happen; it has a mechanical utility, an instrumental role, in accomplishing the world's work. Granting protection, in other words, can have some of the consequences of *patent* protection in limiting other people's ability to perform a task in the most efficient manner. Utility does not bar copyright (dictionaries may be copyrighted), but it alters the calculus.

Of course, the argument *for* protection is undiminished, perhaps even enhanced, by utility: if we want more of an intellectual product, a temporary monopoly for the creator provides incentives for others to create other, different items in this class. But the "cost" side of the equation may be different where one places a very high value on public access to a useful innovation that may be the most efficient means of performing a given task. Thus, the argument for extending protection may be the same; but the stakes on the other side are much higher.

It is no accident that patent protection has preconditions that copyright protection does not—notably, the requirements of novelty and non-obviousness—and that patents are granted for a shorter period than copyrights. This problem of utility has sometimes manifested itself in copyright cases, such as *Baker v. Selden*, 101 U.S. 99, 25 L.Ed. 841 (1879), and been dealt with through various formulations that limit copyright or create limited rights to copy. But the case law and doctrine addressed to utility in copyright have been brief detours in the general march of copyright law.

Requests for the protection of computer menus present the concern with fencing off access to the commons in an acute form. A new menu may be a creative work, but over time its importance may come to reside more in the investment that has been made by *users* in learning the menu and in building their own mini-programs—macros—in reliance upon the menu. Better typewriter keyboard layouts may exist, but the familiar QWERTY keyboard dominates the market because that is what everyone has learned to use. The QWERTY keyboard is nothing other than a menu of letters.

Thus, to assume that computer programs are just one more new means of expression, like a filmed play, may be quite wrong. The "form"—the written source code or the menu structure depicted on the screen—look hauntingly like the familiar stuff of copyright; but the "substance" probably has more to do with problems presented in patent law or, as already noted, in those rare cases where copyright law has confronted industrially useful expressions. Applying copyright law to computer programs is like assembling a jigsaw puzzle whose pieces do not quite fit.

All of this would make no difference if Congress had squarely confronted the issue, and given explicit directions as to what should be done. The Copyright Act of 1976 took a different course. While Congress said that computer programs might be subject to copyright protection, it said this in very general terms; and, especially in § 102(b), Congress adopted a string of exclusions that if taken literally might easily seem to exclude most computer programs from protection. The only detailed prescriptions for computers involve narrow issues (like back-up copies) of no relevance here.

Of course, one could still read the statute as a congressional command that the familiar doctrines of copyright law be taken and applied to computer programs, in cookie cutter fashion, as if the programs were novels or play scripts. Some of the cases involving computer programs embody this approach. It seems to be mistaken on two different grounds: the tradition of copyright law, and the likely intent of Congress.

The broad-brush conception of copyright protection, the time limits, and the formalities have long been prescribed by statute. But the heart of copyright doctrine—what may be protected and with what limitations and exceptions—has been developed by the courts through experience with individual cases. Occasionally Congress addresses a problem in detail. For the most part the interstitial development of copyright through the courts is our tradition.

Nothing in the language or legislative history of the 1976 Act, or at least nothing brought to our attention, suggests that Congress meant the courts to abandon this case-by-case approach. Indeed, by setting up § 102(b) as a counterpoint theme, Congress has arguably recognized the tension and left it for the courts to resolve through the development of case law. And case law development is *adaptive*: it allows new problems to be solved with help of earlier doctrine, but it does not preclude new doctrines to meet new situations.

II.

In this case, the raw facts are mostly, if not entirely, undisputed. Although the inferences to be drawn may be more debatable, it is very hard to see that Borland has shown any interest in the Lotus menu except as a fall-back option for those users already committed to it by prior experience or in order to run their own macros using 1–2–3 commands. At least for the amateur, accessing the Lotus menu in the Borland Quattro or Quattro Pro program takes some effort.

Put differently, it is unlikely that users who value the Lotus menu for its own sake independent of any investment they have made themselves in learning Lotus' commands or creating macros dependent upon them— would choose the Borland program in order to secure access to the Lotus menu. Borland's success is due primarily to other features. Its rationale for deploying the Lotus menu bears the ring of truth.

Now, any use of the Lotus menu by Borland is a commercial use and deprives Lotus of a portion of its "reward," in the sense that an infringement claim if allowed would increase Lotus' profits. But this is circular reasoning: broadly speaking, every limitation on copyright or privileged use diminishes the reward of the original creator. Yet not every writing is copyrightable or every use an infringement. The provision of reward is one concern of copyright law, but it is not the only one. If it were, copyrights would be perpetual and there would be no exceptions.

The present case is an unattractive one for copyright protection of the menu. The menu commands (*e.g.*, "print," "quit") are largely for standard procedures that Lotus did not invent and are common words that Lotus cannot monopolize. What is left is the particular combination and sub-grouping of commands in a pattern devised by Lotus. This arrangement may have a more appealing logic and ease of use than some other configurations; but there is a certain arbitrariness to many of the choices.

If Lotus is granted a monopoly on this pattern, users who have learned the command structure of Lotus 1–2–3 or devised their own macros are locked into Lotus, just as a typist who has learned the QWERTY keyboard would be the captive of anyone who had a monopoly on the production of such a keyboard. Apparently, for a period Lotus 1–2–3 has had such sway in the market that it has represented the *de facto* standard for electronic spreadsheet commands. So long as Lotus is the superior spreadsheet— either in quality or in price—there may be nothing wrong with this advantage.

But if a better spreadsheet comes along, it is hard to see why customers who have learned the Lotus menu and devised macros for it should remain captives of Lotus because of an investment in learning made by the users and not by Lotus. Lotus has already reaped a substantial reward for being first; assuming that the Borland program is now better, good reasons exist for freeing it to attract old Lotus customers: to enable the old customers to take advantage of a new advance, and to reward Borland in turn for making a better product. If Borland has not made a better product, then customers will remain with Lotus anyway.

Thus, for me the question is not whether Borland should prevail but on what basis. Various avenues might be traveled, but the choices are between holding that the menu is not protectable by copyright and devising a new doctrine that Borland's use is privileged. No solution is perfect and no intermediate appellate court can make the final choice.

To call the menu a "method of operation" is, in the common use of those words, a defensible position. After all, the purpose of the menu is not to be admired as a work of literary or pictorial art. It is to transmit directions from the user to the computer, *i.e., to operate* the computer. The menu is also a "method" in the dictionary sense because it is a "planned way of doing something," an "order or system," and (aptly here) an "orderly or systematic arrangement, sequence or the like." *Random House Webster's College Dictionary* 853 (1991).

A different approach would be to say that Borland's use is privileged because, in the context already described, it is not seeking to appropriate the advances made by Lotus' menu; rather, having provided an arguably more attractive menu of its own, Borland is merely trying to give former Lotus users an option to exploit their own prior investment in learning or in macros. The difference is that such a privileged use approach would not automatically protect Borland if it had simply copied the Lotus menu (using different codes), contributed nothing of its own, and resold Lotus under the Borland label.

The closest analogue in conventional copyright is the fair use doctrine. *E.g., Harper & Row, Publishers, Inc. v. Nation Enters.*, 471 U.S. 539, 105 S.Ct. 2218, 85 L.Ed.2d 588 (1985). Although invoked by Borland, it has largely been brushed aside in this case because the Supreme Court has said that it is "presumptively" unavailable where the use is a "commercial" one. *See id.* at 562, 105 S.Ct. at 2231–32. *But see Campbell v. Acuff–Rose Music, Inc.*, 510 U.S. 569, 584, 114 S.Ct. 1164, 1174, 127 L.Ed.2d 500 (1994). In my view, this is something less than a definitive answer; "presumptively" does not mean "always" and, in any event, the doctrine of fair use was created by the courts and can be adapted to new purposes.

But a privileged use doctrine would certainly involve problems of its own. It might more closely tailor the limits on copyright protection to the reasons for limiting that protection; but it would entail a host of administrative problems that would cause cost and delay, and would also reduce the ability of the industry to predict outcomes. Indeed, to the extent that Lotus' menu is an important standard in the industry, it might be argued that any use ought to be deemed privileged.

In sum, the majority's result persuades me and its formulation is as good, if not better, than any other that occurs to me now as within the reach of courts. Some solutions (*e.g.,* a very short copyright period for menus) are not options at all for courts but might be for Congress. In all events, the choices are important ones of policy, not linguistics, and they should be made with the underlying considerations in view.

NOTES

1. Are you convinced by the *Lotus* court's characterization of the Lotus menu command hierarchy as an unprotectible "method of operation"? Are menu commands like the buttons used to control a VCR, as the court suggests, or are they more like the first chapter of a mystery novel that has to be read if the last chapter is to be understood?

2. *Merger.* The *Lotus* facts—an originally arbitrary set of commands becoming a *de facto* standard—raised the difficult question whether the starting point for merger analysis is the time of the copyright owner's creation of its interface, or the time that competitors seek to enter the market. District Judge Robert Keeton had tied merger to the question whether a "reasonable jury could find that the menu command hierarchy was limited to one or even several alternate designs at the time it was created," and concluded on the facts that no reasonable jury could make this finding. 799 F.Supp. 203, 210 (D.Mass.1992). Would the alternative approach to merger doctrine have provided a sounder basis for the circuit court's reversal and a better means for resolving the central problem of program compatibility?

Can merger doctrine for *de facto* standards adequately resolve the compatibility problems raised by a popular graphical user interface, such as Apple's desktop metaphor for its Macintosh computers? In Apple Computer, Inc. v. Microsoft Corp., 799 F.Supp. 1006, 1025, 24 U.S.P.Q. 2d 1081 (N.D.Cal.1992), *aff'd*, 35 F.3d 1435 (9th Cir.1994), *cert. denied*, 513 U.S. 1184, 115 S.Ct. 1176, 130 L.Ed.2d 1129 (1995), Judge Vaughn Walker focussed not on the range of design alternatives available to Apple at the outset, but rather to the range of alternatives available to competitors Microsoft and Hewlett–Packard at the time they designed their Windows and New Wave interfaces. Apple's huge success in marketing its user interface had effectively made the interface a standard and, for others to compete with Apple, they had to conform to this standard: "[O]verly inclusive copyright protection can produce its own negative effects by inhibiting the adoption of compatible standards (and reducing so-called 'network externalities'). Such standards in a graphical user interface would enlarge the market for computers by making it easier to learn how to use them.... While the Macintosh interface may be the fruit of considerable effort by its designers, its success is the result of a host of factors, including the decision to use the Motorola 68000 microprocessor, the tactical decision to require uniform application interfaces, and the Macintosh's notable advertising. And even were Apple able to isolate that part of its interface's success owing to its design efforts, lengthy and concerted effort alone 'does not always result in inherently protectible expression.' *Computer Assoc. Int'l,* 92 Daily Journal DAR at 10121."

Which starting point for merger analysis—the time of the copyright owner's creation of its user interface, or the time that competitors seek to enter the market—will better serve copyright law's goal of promoting consumer welfare? Is it appropriate to compare the costs of designing the original interface with the revenues that can be reaped from excluding, or licensing, competitors? What proofs are relevant in determining whether a user interface has become an industry standard? See generally, Peter Menell, An Analysis of the Scope of Copyright Protection for Application Programs, 41 Stan.L.Rev. 1045 (1989).

3. *Videogames: Subject Matter.* The question of copyright for computer-driven visual displays first arose in the context of videogames. In Stern Electronics, Inc. v. Kaufman, 669 F.2d 852, 855–57, 213 U.S.P.Q. 443 (2d Cir.1982), the court rejected the argument that copyright could protect only the computer program that predetermined the game's audiovisual display. "While that approach would have afforded some degree of protection, it would not have prevented a determined competitor from manufacturing a 'knock-off' of [plaintiff's] 'Scramble' that replicates precisely the sights and sounds of the game's audiovisual display. This could be done by writing a new computer program that would interact with the hardware components of a video game to produce on the screen the same images seen in 'Scramble,' accompanied by the same sounds."

The defendants also argued that plaintiff's display was uncopyrightable because it was neither fixed nor original. The court answered the fixation argument by observing that, while "the entire sequence of all the sights and sounds of the game are different each time the game is played, depending upon the route and speed the player selects for his spaceship and the timing and accuracy of his release of his craft's bombs and lasers ... many aspects of the sights and the sequence of their appearance remain constant during each play of the game."

To the contention that "the audiovisual display contains no originality because all of its reappearing features are determined by the previously created computer program," the court answered that the "visual and aural features of the audiovisual display are plainly original variations sufficient to render the display copyrightable even though the underlying written program has an independent existence and is itself eligible for copyright.... Moreover, the argument overlooks the sequence of the creative process. Someone first conceived what the audiovisual display would look like and sound like. Originality occurred at that point. Then the program was written. Finally, the program was imprinted into the memory devices so that, in operation with the components of the game, the sights and sounds could be seen and heard. The resulting display satisfies the requirement of an original work."

4. *Videogames: Infringement.* Courts have generally applied the same infringement measure to video games as they have to other audiovisual media such as motion pictures. In Atari, Inc. v. North American Philips Consumer Elecs. Corp., 672 F.2d 607, 618, 214 U.S.P.Q. 33 (7th Cir.1982), cert. denied, 459 U.S. 880, 103 S.Ct. 176, 74 L.Ed.2d 145 (1982), the court reversed the lower court's denial of a preliminary injunction to copyright owner, Atari. In the appellate court's view, "North American not only adopted the same basic characters but also portrayed them in a manner which made K.C. Munchkin appear substantially similar to PAC–MAN. The K.C. Munchkin gobbler has several blatantly similar features including the relative size and shape of the 'body,' the V-shaped 'mouth,' its distinctive gobbling action (with appropriate sounds), and especially the way in which it disappears upon being captured. An examination of the K.C. Munchkin ghost monsters reveals even more significant visual similarities. In size, shape, and manner of movement, they are virtually identical to their PAC–MAN counterparts. K.C. Munchkin's monsters, for example, exhibit the same peculiar 'eye' and 'leg' movement. Both games, moreover, express the role reversal and 'regeneration' process with such great similarity that an ordinary observer could conclude only that North American copied plaintiffs' PAC–MAN."

B. LIMITS OF PROTECTION

1. STATUTORY EXEMPTIONS

Vault Corporation v. Quaid Software Limited

United States Court of Appeals, Fifth Circuit, 1988.
847 F.2d 255, 7 U.S.P.Q.2d 1281.

REAVLEY, Circuit Judge:

Vault brought this copyright infringement action against Quaid seeking damages and preliminary and permanent injunctions. The district court denied Vault's motion for a preliminary injunction, holding that Vault did not have a reasonable probability of success on the merits. By stipulation of the parties, this ruling was made final and judgment was entered accordingly. We affirm.

I.

Vault produces computer diskettes under the registered trademark "PROLOK" which are designed to prevent the unauthorized duplication of programs placed on them by software computer companies, Vault's customers. Floppy diskettes serve as a medium upon which computer companies place their software programs. To use a program, a purchaser loads the diskette into the disk drive of a computer, thereby allowing the computer to read the program into its memory. The purchaser can then remove the diskette from the disk drive and operate the program from the computer's memory. This process is repeated each time a program is used.

The protective device placed on a PROLOK diskette by Vault is comprised of two parts: a "fingerprint" and a software program ("Vault's program").[1] The "fingerprint" is a small mark physically placed on the magnetic surface of each PROLOK diskette which contains certain information that cannot be altered or erased. Vault's program is a set of instructions to the computer which interact with the "fingerprint" to

---

[1] A PROLOK diskette contains two programs, the program placed on the diskette by a software company (e.g., word processing) and the program placed on the diskette by Vault which interacts with the "fingerprint" to prevent the unauthorized duplication of the software company's program. We use the term "software program" or "program" to refer to the program placed on the diskette by one of Vault's customers (a computer company) and "Vault's program" to refer to the program placed on the diskette by Vault as part of the protective device. We collectively refer to the "fingerprint" and Vault's program as the "protective device."

prevent the computer from operating the program recorded on a PROLOK diskette (by one of Vault's customers) unless the computer verifies that the *original* PROLOK diskette, as identified by the "fingerprint," is in the computer's disk drive. While a purchaser can copy a PROLOK protected program onto another diskette, the computer will not read the program into its memory from the copy unless the original PROLOK diskette is also in one of the computer's disk drives. The fact that a fully functional copy of a program cannot be made from a PROLOK diskette prevents purchasers from buying a single program and making unauthorized copies for distribution to others.

Vault produced PROLOK in three stages. The original commercial versions, designated as versions 1.01, 1.02, 1.03, 1.04 and 1.06 ("version 1.0") were produced in 1983. Vault then incorporated improvements into the system and produced version 1.07 in 1984. The third major revision occurred in August and September of 1985 and was designated as versions 2.0 and 2.01 ("version 2.0"). Each version of PROLOK has been copyrighted and Vault includes a license agreement with every PROLOK package that specifically prohibits the copying, modification, translation, decompilation or disassembly of Vault's program. Beginning with version 2.0 in September 1985, Vault's license agreement contained a choice of law clause adopting Louisiana law.

Quaid's product, a diskette called "CopyWrite," contains a feature called "RAMKEY" which unlocks the PROLOK protective device and facilitates the creation of a fully functional copy of a program placed on a PROLOK diskette. The process is performed simply by copying the contents of the PROLOK diskette onto the CopyWrite diskette which can then be used to run the software program *without* the original PROLOK diskette in a computer disk drive. RAMKEY interacts with Vault's program to make it appear to the computer that the CopyWrite diskette contains the "fingerprint," thereby making the computer function as if the original PROLOK diskette is in its disk drive. A copy of a program placed on a CopyWrite diskette can be used without the original, and an unlimited number of fully functional copies can be made in this manner from the program originally placed on the PROLOK diskette.

Quaid first developed RAMKEY in September 1983 in response to PROLOK version 1.0. In order to develop this version of RAMKEY, Quaid copied Vault's program into the memory of its computer and analyzed the manner in which the program operated. When Vault developed version 1.07, Quaid adapted RAMKEY in 1984 to defeat this new version. The adapted version of RAMKEY contained a sequence of approximately 30 characters found in Vault's program and was discontinued in July 1984. Quaid then developed the current version of RAMKEY which also operates to defeat PROLOK version 1.07, but does not contain the sequence of characters used in the discontinued version. Quaid has not yet modified RAMKEY to defeat PROLOK version 2.0, and has agreed not to modify RAMKEY pending the outcome of this suit. Robert McQuaid, the sole owner of Quaid, testified in his deposition that while a CopyWrite diskette can be used to duplicate programs placed on all diskettes, whether copy-protected or not, the only purpose served by RAMKEY is to facilitate the duplication of programs placed on copy-protected diskettes. He also stated that without the RAMKEY feature, CopyWrite would have no commercial value.

II.

Vault brought this action against Quaid seeking preliminary and permanent injunctions to prevent Quaid from advertising and selling RAMKEY, an order impounding all of Quaid's copies of CopyWrite which contain the RAMKEY feature, and monetary damages in the amount of $100,000,000. Vault asserted three copyright infringement claims cognizable under federal law, 17 U.S.C. § 101 et seq. (1977 & Supp.1988) (the "Copyright Act"), which included: (1) that Quaid violated 17 U.S.C. §§ 501(a) & 106(1) by copying Vault's program into its computer's memory for the purpose of developing a program (RAMKEY) designed to defeat the function of Vault's program; (2) that Quaid, through RAMKEY, contributes to the infringement of Vault's copyright and the copyrights of its customers in violation of the Copyright Act as interpreted by the Supreme Court in Sony Corp. of Am. v. Universal City Studios, 464 U.S. 417, 104 S.Ct. 774, 78 L.Ed.2d 574 (1984); and (3) that the second version of RAMKEY, which contained approximately thirty characters from PROLOK version 1.07, and the latest version of RAMKEY, constitute "derivative works" of Vault's program in violation of 17 U.S.C. §§ 501(a) & 106(2). Vault also asserted two claims based on Louisiana law, contending that Quaid breached its license agreement by decompiling or disassembling Vault's program in violation of the Louisiana Software License Enforcement Act, La.Rev.Stat. Ann. § 51:1961 *et seq.* (West 1987), and that Quaid misappropriated Vault's program in violation of the Louisiana Uniform Trade Secrets Act, La.Rev. Stat.Ann. § 51:1431 *et seq.* (West 1987).

The district court originally dismissed Vault's complaint for lack of in personam jurisdiction. This court reversed the district court's order of dismissal and remanded the case for further proceedings. On remand, the district court, after a three-day bench trial, denied Vault's motion for a preliminary injunction holding that Vault had not established a reasonable probability of success on the merits. Subsequently, the parties agreed to submit the case for final decision based on the evidence adduced at the preliminary injunction trial. On July 31, 1987 the district court entered final judgment in accordance with its decision on the preliminary injunction.

Vault now contends that the district court improperly disposed of each of its claims.

III. Vault's Federal Claims

An owner of a copyrighted work has the exclusive right to reproduce the work in copies, to prepare derivative works based on the copyrighted work, to distribute copies of the work to the public, and, in the case of certain types of works, to perform and display the work publicly. 17 U.S.C. § 106. Sections 107 through 118 of the Copyright Act limit an owner's exclusive rights, and section 501(a) provides that "[a]nyone who violates any of the exclusive rights of the copyright owner as provided by sections 106 through 118 ... is an infringer of the copyright."

It is not disputed that Vault owns the copyright to the program it places on PROLOK diskettes and is thus an "owner of copyright" under § 106. Therefore, Vault has, subject to the exceptions contained in sections 107 through 118, the exclusive right to reproduce its program in copies and to prepare derivative works based on its program. Vault claims that Quaid infringed its copyright under § 501(a) by: (1) directly copying Vault's program into the memory of Quaid's computer; (2) contributing to the unauthorized copying of Vault's program and the programs Vault's customers place on PROLOK diskettes; and (3) preparing derivative works of Vault's program.

Section 117 of the Copyright Act limits a copyright owner's exclusive rights under § 106 by permitting an owner of a computer program to make certain copies of that program without obtaining permission from the program's copyright owner. With respect to Vault's first two claims of copyright infringement, Quaid contends that its activities fall within the § 117 exceptions and that it has, therefore, not infringed Vault's exclusive rights under § 501(a). To appreciate the arguments of the parties, we examine the legislative history of § 117.

A. Background

In 1974 Congress established the National Commission on New Technological Uses of Copyrighted Works (the "CONTU") to perform research and make recommendations concerning copyright protection for computer programs. Before receiving the CONTU's recommendations, Congress amended the Copyright Act in 1976 to include computer programs in the definition of protectable literary works and to establish that a program copied into a computer's memory constitutes a reproduction. Congress delayed further action and enacted an interim provision to maintain the status quo until the CONTU completed its study and made specific recommendations.

In 1978 the CONTU issued its final report in which it recognized that "[t]he cost of developing computer programs is far greater than the cost of their duplication," CONTU Report at 26, and concluded that "some form of protection is necessary to encourage the creation and broad distribution of computer programs in a competitive market," id. at 27. After acknowledging the importance of balancing the interest of proprietors in obtaining "reasonable protection" against the risks of "unduly burdening users of programs and the general public," id. at 29, the Report recommended the repeal of section 117 (the interim provision) and the enactment of a new section 117 which would proscribe the unauthorized copying of computer programs but permit a "rightful possessor" of a program to make or authorize the making of another copy or adaptation of that computer program *provided:*

> (1) that such a new copy or adaptation is created as an essential step in the utilization of the computer program in conjunction with a machine and that it is used in no other manner, or

> (2) that such new copy or adaptation is for archival purposes only and that all archival copies are destroyed in the event that continued possession of the computer program should cease to be rightful.

Id. at 29–30 (emphasis in original).

Because the act of loading a program from a medium of storage into a computer's memory creates a copy of the program, the CONTU reasoned that "[o]ne who rightfully possesses a copy of a program ... should be provided with a legal right to copy it to that extent which will permit its use by the possessor," and drafted proposed § 117(1) to "provide that persons in rightful possession of copies of programs be able to use them freely without fear of exposure to copyright liability." Id. at 31. With respect to proposed section 117(2), the "archival exception," the Report explained that a person in rightful possession of a program should have the right "to prepare archival copies of it to guard against destruction or damage by mechanical or electrical failure. But this permission would not extend to other copies of the program. Thus one could not, for example, make archival copies of a program and later sell some to another while retaining some for use." Id.

In 1980, Congress enacted the Computer Software Copyright Act which adopted the recommendations contained in the CONTU Report. Section 117 was repealed, proposed section 117 was enacted, and the proposed definition of "computer program" was added to section 101. The Act's legislative history, contained in a short paragraph in a committee report, merely states that the Act, "embodies the recommendations of [the CONTU] with respect to clarifying the law of copyright of computer software." H.R.Rep. No. 1307, 96th Cong., 2d Sess., pt. 1, at 23, *reprinted in* 1980 U.S.Code Cong. & Admin.News 6460, 6482. The absence of an extensive legislative history and the fact that Congress enacted proposed section 117 with only one change have prompted courts to rely on the CONTU Report as an expression of legislative intent. See Micro–Sparc, Inc. v. Amtype Corp., 592 F.Supp. 33, 35 (D.Mass.1984); Atari, Inc. v. JS & A Group, Inc., 597 F.Supp. 5, 9 (N.D.Ill.1983); Midway Mfg. Co. v. Strohon, 564 F.Supp. 741, 750 n. 6 (N.D.Ill.1983).

B. Direct Copying

In order to develop RAMKEY, Quaid analyzed Vault's program by copying it into its computer's memory. Vault contends that, by making this unauthorized copy, Quaid directly infringed upon Vault's copyright. The district court held that "Quaid's actions clearly fall within [the § 117(1)] exemption. The loading of [Vault's] program into the [memory] of a computer is an 'essential step in the utilization' of [Vault's] program. Therefore, Quaid has not infringed Vault's copyright by loading [Vault's program] into [its computer's memory]." *Vault,* 655 F.Supp. at 758.

Section 117(1) permits an owner of a program to make a copy of that program provided that the copy "is created as an essential step in the utilization of the computer program in conjunction with a machine and that it is used in no other manner." Congress recognized that a computer program cannot be used unless it is first copied into a computer's memory, and thus provided the § 117(1) exception to permit copying for this essential purpose. *See* CONTU Report at 31. Vault contends that, due to the inclusion of the phrase "and that it is used in no other manner," this exception should be interpreted to permit only the copying of a computer program for the purpose of using it for *its intended purpose.* Because Quaid copied Vault's program into its computer's memory for the express purpose of devising a means of defeating its protective function, Vault contends that § 117(1) is not applicable.

We decline to construe § 117(1) in this manner. Even though the copy of Vault's program made by Quaid was *not* used to prevent the copying of the program placed on the PROLOK diskette by one of Vault's customers (which is the purpose of Vault's program), and was, indeed, made for the express purpose of devising a means of defeating its protective function, the copy made by Quaid *was* "created as an essential step in the utilization" of Vault's program. Section 117(1) contains no language to suggest that the copy it permits must be employed for a use intended by the copyright owner, and, absent clear congressional guidance to the contrary, we refuse to read such limiting language into this exception. We therefore hold that Quaid did not infringe Vault's exclusive right to reproduce its program in copies under § 106(1).

C.   Contributory Infringement

Vault contends that, because purchasers of programs placed on PRO-LOK diskettes use the RAMKEY feature of CopyWrite to make unauthorized copies, Quaid's advertisement and sale of CopyWrite diskettes with the RAMKEY feature violate the Copyright Act by contributing to the infringement of Vault's copyright and the copyrights owned by Vault's customers. Vault asserts that it lost customers and substantial revenue as a result of Quaid's contributory infringement because software companies which previously relied on PROLOK diskettes to protect their programs from unauthorized copying have discontinued their use.

While a purchaser of a program on a PROLOK diskette violates sections 106(1) and 501(a) by making and distributing unauthorized copies of the program, the Copyright Act "does not expressly render anyone liable for the infringement committed by another." *Sony,* 464 U.S. at 434, 104 S.Ct. at 785. The Supreme Court in *Sony,* after examining the express provision in the Patent Act which imposes liability on an individual who "actively induces infringement of a patent," 35 U.S.C. § 271(b) & (c), and noting the similarity between the Patent and Copyright Acts, recognized the availability, under the Copyright Act, of vicarious liability against one who sells a product that is used to make unauthorized copies of copyrighted material. The Court held that liability based on contributory infringement could be imposed only where the seller had constructive knowledge of the fact that its product was used to make unauthorized copies of copyrighted material, and that the sale of a product "does not constitute contributory infringement if the product is widely used for legitimate, unobjectionable purposes. Indeed, it need merely be capable of substantial noninfringing uses." Id. at 442, 104 S.Ct. at 789.

While Quaid concedes that it has actual knowledge that its product is used to make unauthorized copies of copyrighted material, it contends that the RAMKEY portion of its CopyWrite diskettes serves a substantial noninfringing use by allowing purchasers of programs on PROLOK diskettes to make archival copies as permitted under 17 U.S.C. § 117(2), and thus that it is not liable for contributory infringement. The district court held that Vault lacked standing to raise a contributory infringement claim because "it is not Vault, but the customers of Vault who place their programs on PROLOK disks, who may assert such claims. Clearly the copyright rights to these underlying programs belong to their publishers, not Vault." *Vault,* 655 F.Supp. at 759. Alternatively the court held that CopyWrite is capable of "commercially significant noninfringing uses" because the RAMKEY feature permits the making of archival copies of copy-protected software, and CopyWrite diskettes (without the RAMKEY feature) are used to make copies of unprotected software and as a diagnostic tool to analyze the quality of new computer programs. Id. Therefore, the court held that the sale of CopyWrite did not constitute contributory infringement.

While we hold that Vault has standing to assert its contributory infringement claim, we find that RAMKEY is capable of substantial noninfringing uses and thus reject Vault's contention that the advertisement and sale of CopyWrite diskettes with RAMKEY constitute contributory infringement. . . .

2. *Substantial Noninfringing Uses of RAMKEY*

Vault's allegation of contributory infringement focuses on the RAMKEY feature of CopyWrite diskettes, not on the non-RAMKEY portions of these diskettes. Vault has no objection to the advertising and marketing of CopyWrite diskettes without the RAMKEY feature, and this feature is separable from the underlying diskette upon which it is placed. Therefore, in determining whether Quaid engaged in contributory infringement, we do not focus on the substantial noninfringing uses of CopyWrite, as opposed to the RAMKEY feature itself. The issue properly presented is whether the RAMKEY feature has substantial noninfringing uses.

The starting point for our analysis is with *Sony.* The plaintiffs in *Sony,* owners of copyrighted television programs, sought to enjoin the manufacture and marketing of Betamax video tape recorders ("VTR's"), contending that VTR's contributed to the infringement of their copyrights by permitting the unauthorized copying of their programs. After noting that plaintiffs' market share of television programming was less than 10%, and that copyright holders of a significant quantity of television broadcasting authorized the copying of their programs, the Court held that VTR's serve the legitimate and substantially noninfringing purpose of recording these programs, as well as plaintiffs' programs, for future viewing (authorized and unauthorized time-shifting respectively), and therefore rejected plaintiffs' contributory infringement claim.

Quaid asserts that RAMKEY serves the legitimate purpose of permitting purchasers of programs recorded on PROLOK diskettes to make archival copies under § 117(2) and that this purpose constitutes a substantial noninfringing use. At trial, witnesses for Quaid testified that software programs placed on floppy diskettes are subject to damage by *physical and human mishap* and that RAMKEY protects a purchaser's investment by providing a fully functional archival copy that can be used if the original program on the PROLOK protected diskette, or the diskette itself, is destroyed. Quaid contends that an archival copy of a PROLOK protected program, made without RAMKEY, does not serve to protect against these forms of damage because a computer will not read the program into its memory from the copy unless the PROLOK diskette containing the original undamaged program is also in one of its disk drives, which is impossible if the PROLOK diskette, or the program placed thereon, has been destroyed due to physical or human mishap.

Computer programs can be stored on a variety of mediums, including floppy diskettes, hard disks, non-erasable read only memory ("ROM") chips, and a computer's random access memory, and may appear only as printed instructions on a sheet of paper. Vault contends that the archival exception was designed to permit *only* the copying of programs which are subject to "destruction or damage by *mechanical or electrical failure*." CONTU Report at 31 (emphasis added). While programs stored on all mediums may be subject to damage due to physical abuse or human error, programs stored on certain mediums are not subject to damage by mechanical or electrical failure. Therefore, Vault argues, the medium of storage determines whether the archival exception applies, thus providing only owners of programs, placed on mediums of storage which subject them to damage by mechanical or electrical failure, the right to make back-up copies. To support its construction of § 117(2), Vault notes that one court has held that the archival exception does not apply to the copying of programs stored on ROM chips where there was no evidence that programs stored on this medium were subject to damage by mechanical or electrical failure, *Atari,* 597 F.Supp. at 9–10, and another court has likewise held that the archival exception does not apply to the copying of programs which appear only in the form of printed instructions in a magazine, *Micro–Sparc,* 592 F.Supp. at 35–36.

Vault contends that the district court's finding that programs stored on floppy diskettes are subject to damage by mechanical or electrical failure is erroneous because there was insufficient evidence presented at trial to support it, and, based on this contention, Vault asserts that the archival exception does not apply to permit the unauthorized copying of these programs. Vault performed a trial demonstration to prove that even if a program on an original PROLOK diskette, and Vault's protective program, were completely erased from this diskette, these programs could be restored on the original diskette using a copy made *without* RAMKEY. Therefore, Vault argues that even if a program recorded on a PROLOK diskette is subject to damage by mechanical or electrical failure, the non-operational copy of a PROLOK protected program made without RAMKEY is sufficient to protect against this type of damage. Vault concludes that, in light of the fact that RAMKEY facilitates the making of unauthorized copies and owners of PROLOK protected programs can make copies to protect against damage by mechanical and electrical failure without RAMKEY, the RAMKEY feature is not capable of substantial noninfringing uses.

The narrow construction of the archival exception, advanced by Vault and accepted in the *Atari* and *Micro–Sparc* decisions, has undeniable appeal. This construction would leave the owner of a protected software program free to make back-up copies of the software to guard against erasures, which is probably the primary concern of owners as well as the drafters of the CONTU Report. Software producers should perhaps be entitled to protect their product from improper duplication, and Vault's PROLOK may satisfy producers and most purchasers on this score—*if* PROLOK cannot be copied by the purchaser onto a CopyWrite diskette without infringing the PROLOK copyright. That result does have appeal, but we believe it is an appeal that must be made to Congress. "[I]t is not our job to apply laws that have not yet been written." *Sony,* 464 U.S. at 456, 104 S.Ct. at 796. We read the statute as it is now written to authorize the owner of the PROLOK diskette to copy both the PROLOK program and the software program for any reason so long as the owner uses the copy for archival purposes only and not for an unauthorized transfer. . . .

A copy of a PROLOK protected program made with RAMKEY protects an owner from all types of damage to the original program, while a copy made without RAMKEY only serves the limited function of protecting against damage to the original program by mechanical and electrical failure. Because § 117(2) permits the making of fully functional archival copies, it follows that RAMKEY is capable of substantial noninfringing uses. Quaid's advertisement and sale of CopyWrite diskettes with the RAMKEY feature does not constitute contributory infringement.

D. Derivative Work

Section 106(2) of the Copyright Act provides the copyright owner exclusive rights "to prepare derivative works based on the copyrighted work." Section 101 defines a derivative work as:

> a work based on one or more preexisting works, such as a translation, musical arrangement, dramatization, fictionalization, motion picture version, sound recording, art reproduction, abridgment, condensation,

or any other form in which a work may be recast, transformed, or adapted. A work consisting of editorial revisions, annotations, elaborations or other modifications which, as a whole, represent an original work of authorship is a "derivative work."

To constitute a derivative work, "the infringing work must incorporate in some form a portion of the copyrighted work." Litchfield v. Spielberg, 736 F.2d 1352, 1357 (9th Cir.1984), cert. denied, 470 U.S. 1052, 105 S.Ct. 1753, 84 L.Ed.2d 817 (1985). In addition, the infringing work must be substantially similar to the copyrighted work. Id.

The 1984 version of RAMKEY contained approximately 30 characters of source code copied from Vault's program. Vault's program contained the equivalent of approximately 50 pages of source code, and the 1984 version of RAMKEY contained the equivalent of approximately 80 pages of source code. By all accounts, the 30 character sequence shared by RAMKEY and Vault's program constituted a quantitatively minor amount of source code. In response to Vault's contention that RAMKEY constitutes a derivative work, the district court found that "the copying in 1984 was not significant" and that "there has been no evidence ... that there has been any further duplication." Holding that "RAMKEY is not a substantially similar copy of PROLOK," the court concluded that "RAMKEY is not a derivative work." *Vault,* 655 F.Supp. at 759.

Vault now contends that the district court, in evaluating the 1984 version of RAMKEY, incorrectly emphasized the *quantity* of copying instead of the *qualitative* significance of the copied material, and cites Whelan Assoc's., Inc. v. Jaslow Dental Laboratory, Inc., 797 F.2d 1222 (3d Cir. 1986), cert. denied, 479 U.S. 1031, 107 S.Ct. 877, 93 L.Ed.2d 831 (1987), for the proposition that a "court must make a qualitative, not quantitative, judgment about the character of the work as a whole and the importance of the substantially similar portions of the work." Id. at 1245. See Midway Mfg. Co. v. Artic Int'l, Inc., 704 F.2d 1009, 1013–14 (7th Cir.), cert. denied, 464 U.S. 823, 104 S.Ct. 90, 78 L.Ed.2d 98 (1983). The sequence copied, Vault asserts, constituted the identifying portion of Vault's program which interacts with the "fingerprint" to confirm that the original PROLOK diskette is in the computer's disk drive. Vault contends that, because this sequence was crucial to the operation of Vault's program and RAMKEY's ability to defeat its protective function, the copying was qualitatively significant.

The cases upon which Vault relies, *Whelan* and *Midway,* both involved situations where the derivative work performed essentially the same function as the copyrighted work. In this case, Vault's program and RAMKEY serve opposing functions; while Vault's program is designed to prevent the duplication of its customers' programs, RAMKEY is designed to facilitate the creation of copies of Vault's customers' programs. Under these circumstances, we agree with the district court that the 1984 copying was not significant and that this version of RAMKEY was not a substantially similar copy of Vault's program.

While Vault acknowledges that the latest version of RAMKEY does not contain a sequence of characters from Vault's program, Vault contends that this version is also a derivative work because it "alters" Vault's program. Vault cites *Midway* for the proposition that a product can be a derivative work where it alters, rather than copies, the copyrighted work. The court in *Midway,* however, held that the sale of a product which speeded-up plaintiff's programs constituted contributory infringement because the speeded-up programs were derivative works. The court did not hold, as Vault asserts, that defendant's product itself was a derivative work. We therefore reject Vault's contention that the latest version of RAMKEY constitutes a derivative work.

IV. Vault's Louisiana Claims

Seeking preliminary and permanent injunctions and damages, Vault's original complaint alleged that Quaid breached its license agreement by decompiling or disassembling Vault's program in violation of the Louisiana Software License Enforcement Act (the "License Act"), La.Rev.Stat.Ann. § 51:1961 et seq. (West 1987), and that Quaid misappropriated Vault's program in violation of the Louisiana Uniform Trade Secrets Act, La.Rev. Stat.Ann. § 51:1431 et seq. (West 1987). On appeal, Vault abandons its misappropriation claim, and, with respect to its breach of license claim, Vault only seeks an injunction to prevent Quaid from decompiling or disassembling PROLOK version 2.0.

Louisiana's License Act permits a software producer to impose a number of contractual terms upon software purchasers provided that the terms are set forth in a license agreement which comports with La.Rev. Stat.Ann. §§ 51:1963 & 1965, and that this license agreement accompanies the producer's software. Enforceable terms include the prohibition of: (1) any copying of the program for any purpose; and (2) modifying and/or adapting the program in any way, including adaptation by reverse engineering, decompilation or disassembly. La.Rev.Stat.Ann. § 51:1964. The terms "reverse engineering, decompiling or disassembling" are defined as "any process by which computer software is converted from one form to another form which is more readily understandable to human beings, including without limitation any decoding or decrypting of any computer program which has been encoded or encrypted in any manner." La.Rev. Stat.Ann. § 51:1962(3).

Vault's license agreement, which accompanies PROLOK version 2.0 and comports with the requirements of La.Rev.Stat.Ann. §§ 51:1963 & 1965, provides that "[y]ou may not ... copy, modify, translate, convert to another programming language, decompile or disassemble" Vault's program. Vault asserts that these prohibitions are enforceable under Louisiana's License Act, and specifically seeks an injunction to prevent Quaid from decompiling or disassembling Vault's program.

The district court held that Vault's license agreement was "a contract of adhesion which could only be enforceable if the [Louisiana License Act] is a valid and enforceable statute." *Vault,* 655 F.Supp. at 761. The court noted numerous conflicts between Louisiana's License Act and the Copyright Act, including: (1) while the License Act authorizes a total prohibition on copying, the Copyright Act allows archival copies and copies made as an essential step in the utilization of a computer program; (2) while the License Act authorizes a perpetual bar against copying, the Copyright Act grants protection against unauthorized copying only for the life of the author plus fifty years; and (3) while the License Act places no restrictions on programs which may be protected, under the Copyright Act, only "original works of authorship" can be protected. The court concluded that, because Louisiana's License Act "touched upon the area" of federal copyright law, its provisions were preempted and Vault's license agreement was unenforceable. Id. at 763.

In Sears, Roebuck & Co. v. Stiffel Co., 376 U.S. 225, 84 S.Ct. 784, 11 L.Ed.2d 661 (1964), the Supreme Court held that "[w]hen state law touches upon the area of [patent or copyright statutes], it is 'familiar doctrine' that the federal policy 'may not be set at naught, or its benefits denied' by the state law." Id. at 229, 84 S.Ct. at 787 (quoting Sola Elec. Co. v. Jefferson Elec. Co., 317 U.S. 173, 176, 63 S.Ct. 172, 173, 87 L.Ed. 165 (1942)). See Compco Corp. v. Day–Brite Lighting, Inc., 376 U.S. 234, 84 S.Ct. 779, 11 L.Ed.2d 669 (1964). Section 117 of the Copyright Act permits an owner of a computer program to make an adaptation of that program provided that the adaptation is either "created as an essential step in the utilization of the computer program in conjunction with a machine," § 117(1), or "is for archival purpose only," § 117(2). The provision in Louisiana's License Act, which permits a software producer to prohibit the adaptation of its licensed computer program by decompilation or disassembly, conflicts with the rights of computer program owners under § 117 and clearly "touches upon an area" of federal copyright law. For this reason, and the reasons set forth by the district court, we hold that at least this provision of Louisiana's License Act is preempted by federal law, and thus that the restriction in Vault's license agreement against decompilation or disassembly is unenforceable.

V. Conclusion

We hold that: (1) Quaid did not infringe Vault's exclusive right to reproduce its program in copies under § 106(1); (2) Quaid's advertisement and sale of RAMKEY does not constitute contributory infringement; (3) RAMKEY does not constitute a derivative work of Vault's program under § 106(2); and (4) the provision in Vault's license agreement, which prohibits the decompilation or disassembly of its program, is unenforceable.

The judgment of the district court is AFFIRMED.

NOTES

1. *The "Essential Step" and "Archival Copy" Exemptions.* The key difference between section 117 as passed by Congress and as proposed by CONTU lies in the Act's requirement that the otherwise infringing copy be

made or authorized by "the owner of a copy of the computer program." CONTU had used the term "rightful possessor" rather than "owner." National Comm'n on New Technological Uses of Copyrighted Works, Final Report 12 (1978). This departure complicates application of the provision because section 117 does embody CONTU's proposal that archival copies be destroyed "in the event that continued possession of the computer program should cease to be rightful." For example, if the owner of a copy of a computer program makes an archival copy and leases the original copy to a third party, section 117 requires him to destroy the archival copy since he is no longer entitled to possess the original. At the same time, the third party may not make an archival copy because, though entitled to possess the original, she does not own it.

Section 117's essential step and archival exemptions apply not only to the reproduction right in computer programs, but also to the derivative right. In Aymes v. Bonelli, 47 F.3d 23, 26, 33 U.S.P.Q. 2d 1768 (2d Cir.1995), the court ruled that the adaptation privilege "was intended to apply to modifications for internal use, as long as the adapted program is not distributed in an unauthorized manner." Holding for the defendant, which had regularly altered the copyrighted program to keep it consistent with upgrades in its computer hardware, the court quoted from the CONTU Report:

> The conversion of a program from one higher-level language to another to facilitate use would fall within this right [of adaptation], *as would the right to add features to the program that were not present at the time of rightful acquisition*.... Again, it is likely that many transactions involving copies of programs are entered into with *full awareness that users will modify their copies to suit their own needs*, and this should be reflected in the law.... Should proprietors feel strongly that they do not want rightful possessors of copies of their programs to prepare such adaptations, they could, of course, make such desires a contractual matter.

47 F.3d at 26–27.

See generally, Kreiss, Section 117 of the Copyright Act, 1991 Brig. Young Univ.L.Rev. 1497; Stern, Section 117 of the Copyright Act: Charter of Software Users' Rights or an Illusory Promise?, 7 W.New Eng.L.Rev. 459 (1985).

2. *Software Rental.* The Computer Software Rental Amendments Act of 1990, Pub. L. No. 101–650, tit. VIII, 104 Stat. 5134, (Dec. 1, 1990), amended section 109(b) of the 1976 Copyright Act to carve out an exception from section 109(a)'s first sale doctrine so that the possessor of a copy of a computer program cannot rent the copy for purposes of direct or indirect commercial advantage without permission from the computer program's copyright owner. Section 109(b)'s treatment of computer program rental generally parallels its treatment of phonorecord rental in method and in purpose—to forestall the emergence of a rental marketplace that would facilitate unauthorized home copying of computer programs. Section 109(b) creates expedient exceptions, such as one for programs which are "embodied in a machine or product and which cannot be copied during the ordinary operation or use of the machine or product." The provision "recognizes that many consumer products contain computer programs, including automobiles, calculators, and microwave ovens. Computer programs are typically embodied in electronic circuitry embedded in these products, and cannot be copied by consumers during the ordinary operation or use of the product." H.R. Rep. No. 735, 101st Cong., 2d Sess. 15 (1990).

3. *Shrinkwrap Licenses.* In the computer industry's early years, software producers, uncertain about the legal status of their products under copyright law, used shrinkwrap licenses—their terms printed on a sheet of paper together with the plastic-wrapped diskettes—to define their rights. The introductory language of the *Vault* license is typical: "IMPORTANT! VAULT IS PROVIDING THE ENCLOSED MATERIALS TO YOU ON THE EXPRESS CONDITION THAT YOU ASSENT TO THIS SOFTWARE LICENSE. BY USING ANY OF THE ENCLOSED DISKETTE(S), YOU AGREE TO THE FOLLOWING PROVISIONS. IF YOU DO NOT AGREE WITH THESE LICENSE PROVISIONS, RETURN THESE MATERIALS TO YOUR DEALER, IN ORIGINAL PACKAGING WITHIN 3 DAYS FROM RECEIPT, FOR A REFUND." 847 F.2d at 257 n.2.

Shrinkwrap licenses took a belt and suspenders approach, adding a contractual bar to the underlying prospect of copyright protection. In specificity and scope, these license terms commonly went well beyond copyright law's exclusive rights, prohibiting conduct that the Copyright Act would exempt from liability. The *Vault* language is typical, enjoining the user not to "transfer, sublicense, rent, lease, convey, copy, modify, translate, convert to another programming language, decompile or disassemble the Licensed Software for any purpose without VAULT's prior written consent." Id.

Courts have divided on the enforceability of shrinkwrap licenses. Step–Saver Data Systems, Inc. v. Wyse Technology, 939 F.2d 91 (3d Cir.1991), ruled against enforceability, holding that the applicable contract between a software vendor and its customer was formed when the customer placed its telephone order for the software and the vendor shipped it, not when the customer subsequently opened the shrinkwrap; since the parties did not agree to the additional terms proposed by the shrinkwrap license, these terms could not modify the contract. For an alternative approach, see M.A. Mortenson Co. v. Timberline Software Corp., 140 Wash.2d 568, 998 P.2d 305 (2000)

A proposed revision of Article 2 of the Uniform Commercial Code to validate these licenses ultimately evolved into a discrete Uniform Computer Information Transactions Act promulgated in 1999 by the National Conference of Commissioners on Uniform State Laws. Like the proposed revision of U.C.C. Article 2, U.C.I.T.A. has attracted widespread debate. See Raymond T. Nimmer, Through the Looking Glass: What Courts and UCITA Say About the Scope of Contract Law in the Information Age, 38 Duq. L. Rev. 255 (2000); Pamela I. Samuelson & Kurt Opsahl, How Tensions Between Intellectual Property Policy and UCITA Are Likely to be Resolved,

P.L.I. Patents, Copyrights, Trademarks and Literary Property Course Handbook Series (Aug/Sept. 1999).

4. *Preemption of State Law.* In ProCD v. Zeidenberg, 86 F.3d 1447, 39 U.S.P.Q. 2d 1161 (7th Cir.1996), the court held that a shrinkwrap license prohibiting the commercial use of a database—which the court assumed could not be protected by copyright—was valid and enforceable against a retail purchaser of the database package who sold access to its contents over the Internet. The court overturned both of the lower court's rulings—that the license was unenforceable under the applicable state law and that, even if enforceable, it was preempted by federal law—and held that, under section 301 of the 1976 Copyright Act, contract rights are not "equivalent to any of the exclusive rights within the general scope of copyright," and for this reason are not preempted by the Act.

In the court's view, "[r]ights 'equivalent to any of the exclusive rights within the general scope of copyright' are rights established *by law*—rights that restrict the options of persons who are strangers to the author. Copyright law forbids duplication, public performance, and so on, unless the person wishing to copy or perform the work gets permission; silence means a ban on copying. A copyright is a right against the world. Contracts, by contrast, generally affect only their parties; strangers may do as they please, so contracts do not create 'exclusive rights.' " 86 F.3d at 1454.

Would the court have reached a different result if it had measured preemption not by section 301 of the Copyright Act but rather by the Supremacy Clause of the United States Constitution, as did the court in *Vault*? See I. Trotter Hardy, Contracts, Copyright and Preemption in a Digital World, 1 Rich. J. L. & Tech 2 (1995); Dennis S. Karjala, Federal Preemption of Shrinkwrap and On–Line Licenses, 22 U. Dayton L. Rev. 511 (1997); Maureen A. O'Rourke, Drawing the Boundary Between Copyright and Contract: Copyright Preemption of Software License Terms, 45 Duke L.J. 479 (1995).

2. FAIR USE

Sega Enterprises Ltd. v. Accolade, Inc.

United States Court of Appeals, Ninth Circuit, 1992.
977 F.2d 1510, 24 U.S.P.Q.2d 1561.

REINHARDT, Circuit Judge:

This case presents several difficult questions of first impression involving our copyright and trademark laws. We are asked to determine, first, whether the Copyright Act permits persons who are neither copyright holders nor licensees to disassemble a copyrighted computer program in order to gain an understanding of the unprotected functional elements of the program. In light of the public policies underlying the Act, we conclude that, when the person seeking the understanding has a legitimate reason for doing so and when no other means of access to the unprotected elements exists, such disassembly is as a matter of law a fair use of the copyrighted work. Second, we must decide the legal consequences under the Lanham Trademark Act of a computer manufacturer's use of a security system that affords access to its computers to software cartridges that include an initialization code which triggers a screen display of the computer manufacturer's trademark. The computer manufacturer also manufactures software cartridges; those cartridges all contain the initialization code. The question is whether the computer manufacturer may enjoin competing cartridge manufacturers from gaining access to its computers through the use of the code on the ground that such use will result in the display of a "false" trademark. Again, our holding is based on the public policies underlying the statute. We hold that when there is no other method of access to the computer that is known or readily available to rival cartridge manufacturers, the use of the initialization code by a rival does not violate the Act even though that use triggers a misleading trademark display. Accordingly, we reverse the district court's grant of a preliminary injunction in favor of plaintiff-appellee Sega Enterprises, Ltd. on its claims of copyright and trademark infringement. We decline, however, to order that an injunction pendente lite issue precluding Sega from continuing to use its security system, even though such use may result in a certain amount of false labeling. We prefer to leave the decision on that question to the district court initially.

I. Background

Plaintiff-appellee Sega Enterprises, Ltd. ("Sega"), a Japanese corporation, and its subsidiary, Sega of America, develop and market video entertainment systems, including the "Genesis" console (distributed in Asia under the name "Mega–Drive") and video game cartridges. Defendant-appellant Accolade, Inc., is an independent developer, manufacturer, and marketer of computer entertainment software, including game cartridges that are compatible with the Genesis console, as well as game cartridges that are compatible with other computer systems.

Sega licenses its copyrighted computer code and its "SEGA" trademark to a number of independent developers of computer game software. Those licensees develop and sell Genesis-compatible video games in competition with Sega. Accolade is not and never has been a licensee of Sega. Prior to rendering its own games compatible with the Genesis console, Accolade explored the possibility of entering into a licensing agreement with Sega, but abandoned the effort because the agreement would have required that Sega be the exclusive manufacturer of all games produced by Accolade.

Accolade used a two-step process to render its video games compatible with the Genesis console. First, it "reverse engineered" Sega's video game programs in order to discover the requirements for compatibility with the Genesis console. As part of the reverse engineering process, Accolade transformed the machine-readable object code contained in commercially available copies of Sega's game cartridges into human-readable source code using a process called "disassembly" or "decompilation".[2] Accolade purchased a Genesis console and three Sega game cartridges, wired a decompiler into the console circuitry, and generated printouts of the resulting source code. Accolade engineers studied and annotated the printouts in order to identify areas of commonality among the three game programs. They then loaded the disassembled code back into a computer, and experimented to discover the interface specifications for the Genesis console by modifying the programs and studying the results. At the end of the reverse engineering process, Accolade created a development manual that incorporated the information it had discovered about the requirements for a Genesis-compatible game. According to the Accolade employees who created the manual, the manual contained only functional descriptions of the interface requirements and did not include any of Sega's code.

In the second stage, Accolade created its own games for the Genesis. According to Accolade, at this stage it did not copy Sega's programs, but relied only on the information concerning interface specifications for the Genesis that was contained in its development manual. Accolade maintains that with the exception of the interface specifications, none of the code in its own games is derived in any way from its examination of Sega's code. In 1990, Accolade released "Ishido", a game which it had originally developed and released for use with the Macintosh and IBM personal computer systems, for use with the Genesis console.

Even before Accolade began to reverse engineer Sega's games, Sega had grown concerned about the rise of software and hardware piracy in Taiwan and other Southeast Asian countries to which it exported its products. Taiwan is not a signatory to the Berne Convention and does not recognize foreign copyrights. Taiwan does allow prosecution of trademark counterfeiters. However, the counterfeiters had discovered how to modify Sega's game programs to blank out the screen display of Sega's trademark before repackaging and reselling the games as their own. Accordingly, Sega began to explore methods of protecting its trademark rights in the Genesis and Genesis-compatible games. While the development of its own trademark security system (TMSS) was pending, Sega licensed a patented TMSS for use with the Genesis home entertainment system.

The most recent version of the Genesis console, the "Genesis III", incorporates the licensed TMSS. When a game cartridge is inserted, the microprocessor contained in the Genesis III searches the game program for

---

2. Computer programs are written in specialized alphanumeric languages, or "source code". In order to operate a computer, source code must be translated into computer readable form, or "object code". Object code uses only two symbols, 0 and 1, in combinations which represent the alphanumeric characters of the source code. A program written in source code is translated into object code using a computer program called an "assembler" or "compiler", and then im- printed onto a silicon chip for commercial distribution. Devices called "disassemblers" or "decompilers" can reverse this process by "reading" the electronic signals for "0" and "1" that are produced while the program is being run, storing the resulting object code in computer memory, and translating the object code into source code. Both assembly and disassembly devices are commercially available, and both types of devices are widely used within the software industry.

four bytes of data consisting of the letters "S–E–G–A" (the "TMSS initialization code"). If the Genesis III finds the TMSS initialization code in the right location, the game is rendered compatible and will operate on the console. In such case, the TMSS initialization code then prompts a visual display for approximately three seconds which reads "PRODUCED BY OR UNDER LICENSE FROM SEGA ENTERPRISES LTD" (the "Sega Message"). All of Sega's game cartridges, including those disassembled by Accolade, contain the TMSS initialization code.

Accolade learned of the impending release of the Genesis III in the United States in January, 1991, when the Genesis III was displayed at a consumer electronics show. When a demonstration at the consumer electronics show revealed that Accolade's "Ishido" game cartridges would not operate on the Genesis III, Accolade returned to the drawing board. During the reverse engineering process, Accolade engineers had discovered a small segment of code—the TMSS initialization code—that was included in the "power-up" sequence of every Sega game, but that had no identifiable function. The games would operate on the original Genesis console even if the code segment was removed. Mike Lorenzen, the Accolade engineer with primary responsibility for reverse engineering the interface procedures for the Genesis console, sent a memo regarding the code segment to Alan Miller, his supervisor and the current president of Accolade, in which he noted that "it is possible that some future Sega peripheral device might require it for proper initialization."

In the second round of reverse engineering, Accolade engineers focused on the code segment identified by Lorenzen. After further study, Accolade added the code to its development manual in the form of a standard header file to be used in all games. The file contains approximately twenty to twenty-five bytes of data. Each of Accolade's games contains a total of 500,000 to 1,500,000 bytes. According to Accolade employees, the header file is the only portion of Sega's code that Accolade copied into its own game programs. In this appeal, Sega does not raise a separate claim of copyright infringement with respect to the header file.

In 1991, Accolade released five more games for use with the Genesis III, "Star Control", "Hardball!", "Onslaught", "Turrican", and "Mike Ditka Power Football." With the exception of "Mike Ditka Power Football", all of those games, like "Ishido", had originally been developed and marketed for use with other hardware systems. All contained the standard header file that included the TMSS initialization code. According to Accolade, it did not learn until after the Genesis III was released on the market in September, 1991, that in addition to enabling its software to operate on the Genesis III, the header file caused the display of the Sega Message. All of the games except "Onslaught" operate on the Genesis III console; apparently, the programmer who translated "Onslaught" for use with the Genesis system did not place the TMSS initialization code at the correct location in the program.

All of Accolade's Genesis-compatible games are packaged in a similar fashion. The front of the box displays Accolade's "Ballistic" trademark and states "for use with Sega Genesis and Mega Drive Systems." The back of the box contains the following statement: "Sega and Genesis are registered trademarks of Sega Enterprises, Ltd. Game 1991 Accolade, Inc. All rights reserved. Ballistic is a trademark of Accolade, Inc. Accolade, Inc. is not associated with Sega Enterprises, Ltd. All product and corporate names are trademarks and registered trademarks of their respective owners." ...

III. Copyright Issues

Accolade raises four arguments in support of its position that disassembly of the object code in a copyrighted computer program does not constitute copyright infringement. First, it maintains that intermediate copying does not infringe the exclusive rights granted to copyright owners in section 106 of the Copyright Act unless the end product of the copying is substantially similar to the copyrighted work. Second, it argues that disassembly of object code in order to gain an understanding of the ideas and functional concepts embodied in the code is lawful under section 102(b) of the Act, which exempts ideas and functional concepts from copyright protection. Third, it suggests that disassembly is authorized by section 117 of the Act, which entitles the lawful owner of a copy of a computer program to load the program into a computer. Finally, Accolade contends that disassembly of object code in order to gain an understanding of the ideas and functional concepts embodied in the code is a fair use that is privileged by section 107 of the Act.

Neither the language of the Act nor the law of this circuit supports Accolade's first three arguments. Accolade's fourth argument, however, has merit. Although the question is fairly debatable, we conclude based on the policies underlying the Copyright Act that disassembly of copyrighted object code is, as a matter of law, a fair use of the copyrighted work if such disassembly provides the only means of access to those elements of the code that are not protected by copyright and the copier has a legitimate reason for seeking such access. Accordingly, we hold that Sega has failed to demonstrate a likelihood of success on the merits of its copyright claim. Because on the record before us the hardships do not tip sharply (or at all) in Sega's favor, the preliminary injunction issued in its favor must be dissolved, at least with respect to that claim.

A. Intermediate Copying

We have previously held that the Copyright Act does not distinguish between unauthorized copies of a copyrighted work on the basis of what stage of the alleged infringer's work the unauthorized copies represent. Walker v. University Books, 602 F.2d 859, 864 (9th Cir.1979) ("[T]he fact that an allegedly infringing copy of a protected work may itself be only an inchoate representation of some final product to be marketed commercially does not in itself negate the possibility of infringement."). Our holding in *Walker* was based on the plain language of the Act. Section 106 grants to the copyright owner the exclusive rights "to reproduce the work in copies", "to prepare derivative works based upon the copyrighted work", and to authorize the preparation of copies and derivative works. 17 U.S.C.

§ 106(1)–(2). Section 501 provides that "[a]nyone who violates any of the exclusive rights of the copyright owner as provided by sections 106 through 118 ... is an infringer of the copyright." Id. § 501(a). On its face, that language unambiguously encompasses and proscribes "intermediate copying".

In order to constitute a "copy" for purposes of the Act, the allegedly infringing work must be fixed in some tangible form, "from which the work can be perceived, reproduced, or otherwise communicated, either directly or with the aid of a machine or device." 17 U.S.C. § 101. The computer file generated by the disassembly program, the printouts of the disassembled code, and the computer files containing Accolade's modifications of the code that were generated during the reverse engineering process all satisfy that requirement. The intermediate copying done by Accolade therefore falls squarely within the category of acts that are prohibited by the statute.

Accolade points to a number of cases that it argues establish the lawfulness of intermediate copying. Most of the cases involved the alleged copying of books, scripts, or literary characters. In each case, however, the eventual lawsuit alleged infringement only as to the final work of the defendants. We conclude that this group of cases does not alter or limit the holding of *Walker*.

The remaining cases cited by Accolade, like the case before us, involved intermediate copying of computer code as an initial step in the development of a competing product. In each case, the court based its determination regarding infringement solely on the degree of similarity between the allegedly infringed work and the defendant's final product. A close reading of those cases, however, reveals that in none of them was the legality of the intermediate copying at issue. Sega cites an equal number of cases involving intermediate copying of copyrighted computer code to support its assertion that such copying is prohibited. Again, however, it appears that the question of the lawfulness of intermediate copying was not raised in any of those cases.

In summary, the question whether intermediate copying of computer object code infringes the exclusive rights granted to the copyright owner in section 106 of the Copyright Act is a question of first impression. In light of the unambiguous language of the Act, we decline to depart from the rule set forth in *Walker* for copyrighted works generally. Accordingly, we hold that intermediate copying of computer object code may infringe the exclusive rights granted to the copyright owner in section 106 of the Copyright Act regardless of whether the end product of the copying also infringes those rights. If intermediate copying is permissible under the Act, authority for such copying must be found in one of the statutory provisions to which the rights granted in section 106 are subject.

B.   The Idea/Expression Distinction

Accolade next contends that disassembly of computer object code does not violate the Copyright Act because it is necessary in order to gain access to the ideas and functional concepts embodied in the code, which are not protected by copyright. 17 U.S.C. § 102(b). Because humans cannot comprehend object code, it reasons, disassembly of a commercially available computer program into human-readable form should not be considered an infringement of the owner's copyright. Insofar as Accolade suggests that disassembly of object code is lawful *per se,* it seeks to overturn settled law.

Accolade's argument regarding access to ideas is, in essence, an argument that object code is not eligible for the full range of copyright protection. Although some scholarly authority supports that view, we have previously rejected it based on the language and legislative history of the Copyright Act. . . .

Nor does a refusal to recognize a *per se* right to disassemble object code lead to an absurd result. The ideas and functional concepts underlying many types of computer programs, including word processing programs, spreadsheets, and video game displays, are readily discernible without the need for disassembly, because the operation of such programs is visible on the computer screen. The need to disassemble object code arises, if at all, only in connection with operations systems, system interface procedures, and other programs that are not visible to the user when operating—and then only when no alternative means of gaining an understanding of those ideas and functional concepts exists. In our view, consideration of the unique nature of computer object code thus is more appropriate as part of the case-by-case, equitable "fair use" analysis authorized by section 107 of the Act. Accordingly, we reject Accolade's second argument.

C. *Section 117*

Section 117 of the Copyright Act allows the lawful owner of a copy of a computer program to copy or adapt the program if the new copy or adaptation "is created as an essential step in the utilization of the computer program in conjunction with a machine and . . . is used in no other manner." 17 U.S.C. § 117(1). Accolade contends that section 117 authorizes disassembly of the object code in a copyrighted computer program.

Section 117 was enacted on the recommendation of CONTU, which noted that "[b]ecause the placement of any copyrighted work into a computer is the preparation of a copy [since the program is loaded into the computer's memory], the law should provide that persons in rightful possession of copies of programs be able to use them freely without fear of exposure to copyright liability." CONTU Report at 13. We think it is clear that Accolade's use went far beyond that contemplated by CONTU and authorized by section 117. Section 117 does not purport to protect a user who disassembles object code, converts it from assembly into source code, and makes printouts and photocopies of the refined source code version.

D. *Fair Use*

Accolade contends, finally, that its disassembly of copyrighted object code as a necessary step in its examination of the unprotected ideas and functional concepts embodied in the code is a fair use that is privileged by section 107 of the Act. Because, in the case before us, disassembly is the only means of gaining access to those unprotected aspects of the program, and because Accolade has a legitimate interest in gaining such access (in order to determine how to make its cartridges compatible with the Genesis console), we agree with Accolade. Where there is good reason for studying or examining the unprotected aspects of a copyrighted computer program, disassembly for purposes of such study or examination constitutes a fair use.

1.

As a preliminary matter, we reject Sega's contention that the assertion of a fair use defense in connection with the disassembly of object code is precluded by statute. First, Sega argues that not only does section 117 of the Act *not* authorize disassembly of object code, but it also constitutes a legislative determination that any copying of a computer program *other* than that authorized by section 117 cannot be considered a fair use of that program under section 107. That argument verges on the frivolous. Each of the exclusive rights created by section 106 of the Copyright Act is expressly made subject to all of the limitations contained in sections 107 through 120. Nothing in the language or the legislative history of section 117, or in the CONTU Report, suggests that section 117 was intended to preclude the assertion of a fair use defense with respect to uses of computer programs that are not covered by section 117, nor has section 107 been amended to exclude computer programs from its ambit.

Moreover, sections 107 and 117 serve entirely different functions. Section 117 defines a narrow category of copying that is lawful *per se*. Section 107, by contrast, establishes a *defense* to an otherwise valid claim of copyright infringement. It provides that particular instances of copying that otherwise would be actionable are lawful, and sets forth the factors to be considered in determining whether the defense applies. The fact that Congress has not chosen to provide a *per se* exemption to section 106 for disassembly does not mean that particular instances of disassembly may not constitute fair use.

Second, Sega maintains that the language and legislative history of section 906 of the Semiconductor Chip Protection Act of 1984 (SCPA) establish that Congress did not intend that disassembly of object code be considered a fair use. Section 906 of the SCPA authorizes the copying of the "mask work" on a silicon chip in the course of reverse engineering the chip. The mask work in a standard ROM chip, such as those used in the Genesis console and in Genesis-compatible cartridges, is a physical representation of the computer program that is embedded in the chip. The zeros and ones of binary object code are represented in the circuitry of the mask work by open and closed switches. Sega contends that Congress's express authorization of copying in the particular circumstances set forth in section 906 constitutes a determination that other forms of copying of computer programs are prohibited.

The legislative history of the SCPA reveals, however, that Congress passed a separate statute to protect semiconductor chip products because it believed that semiconductor chips were intrinsically utilitarian articles that were not protected under the Copyright Act. H.R.Rep. No. 781, 98th Cong., 2d Sess. 8–10, *reprinted in* 1984 U.S.C.C.A.N. 5750, 5757–59. Accordingly, rather than amend the Copyright Act to extend traditional copyright protection to chips, it enacted "a sui generis form of protection, apart from and independent of the copyright laws." Id. at 10, 1984 U.S.C.C.A.N. at 5759. Because Congress did not believe that semiconductor chips were eligible for copyright protection in the first instance, the fact that it included an exception for reverse engineering of mask work in the SCPA says nothing about its intent with respect to the lawfulness of disassembly of computer programs under the Copyright Act. Nor is the fact that Congress did not contemporaneously amend the Copyright Act to permit disassembly significant, since it was focusing on the protection to be afforded to semiconductor chips. Here we are dealing not with an alleged violation of the SCPA, but with the copying of a computer program, which is governed by the Copyright Act. Moreover, Congress expressly stated that it did not intend to "limit, enlarge or otherwise affect the scope, duration, ownership or subsistence of copyright protection . . . in computer programs, data bases, or any other copyrightable works embodied in semiconductor chip products." Id. at 28, 1984 U.S.C.C.A.N. at 5777. Accordingly, Sega's second statutory argument also fails. We proceed to consider Accolade's fair use defense.

2.

Section 107 lists the factors to be considered in determining whether a particular use is a fair one. Those factors include:

(1) the purpose and character of the use, including whether such use is of a commercial nature or is for nonprofit educational purposes;

(2) the nature of the copyrighted work;

(3) the amount and substantiality of the portion used in relation to the copyrighted work as a whole; and

(4) the effect of the use upon the potential market for or value of the copyrighted work.

The statutory factors are not exclusive. Rather, the doctrine of fair use is in essence "an equitable rule of reason." Harper & Row, Publishers, Inc. v. Nation Enterprises, 471 U.S. 539, 560 (1985) (quoting H.R.Rep. No. 1476, 94th Cong., 2d Sess. 65, *reprinted in* 1976 U.S.C.C.A.N. 5659, 5679). Fair use is a mixed question of law and fact. "Where the district court has found facts sufficient to evaluate each of the statutory factors," an appellate court may resolve the fair use question as a matter of law. Id.

In determining that Accolade's disassembly of Sega's object code did not constitute a fair use, the district court treated the first and fourth statutory factors as dispositive, and ignored the second factor entirely. Given the nature and characteristics of Accolade's direct use of the copied works, the ultimate use to which Accolade put the functional information it obtained, and the nature of the market for home video entertainment systems, we conclude that neither the first nor the fourth factor weighs in Sega's favor. In fact, we conclude that both factors support Accolade's fair use defense, as does the second factor, a factor which is important to the resolution of cases such as the one before us.

(a)

With respect to the first statutory factor, we observe initially that the fact that copying is for a commercial purpose weighs against a finding of fair use. However, the presumption of unfairness that arises in such cases can be rebutted by the characteristics of a particular commercial use. Further "[t]he commercial nature of a use is a matter of degree, not an absolute. . . ." *Maxtone–Graham,* 803 F.2d at 1262.

Sega argues that because Accolade copied its object code in order to produce a competing product, the *Harper & Row* presumption applies and precludes a finding of fair use. That analysis is far too simple and ignores a number of important considerations. We must consider other aspects of "the purpose and character of the use" as well. As we have noted, the use at issue was an intermediate one only and thus any commercial "exploitation" was indirect or derivative.

The declarations of Accolade's employees indicate, and the district court found, that Accolade copied Sega's software solely in order to discover the functional requirements for compatibility with the Genesis console— aspects of Sega's programs that are not protected by copyright. With respect to the video game programs contained in Accolade's game cartridges, there is no evidence in the record that Accolade sought to avoid performing its own creative work. Indeed, most of the games that Accolade released for use with the Genesis console were originally developed for other hardware systems. Moreover, with respect to the interface procedures for the Genesis console, Accolade did not seek to avoid paying a customarily charged fee for use of those procedures, nor did it simply copy Sega's code; rather, it wrote its own procedures based on what it had learned through disassembly. Taken together, these facts indicate that although Accolade's ultimate purpose was the release of Genesis-compatible games for sale, its direct purpose in copying Sega's code, and thus its direct use of the copyrighted material, was simply to study the functional requirements for Genesis compatibility so that it could modify existing games and make them usable with the Genesis console. Moreover, as we discuss below, no other method of studying those requirements was available to Accolade. On these facts, we conclude that Accolade copied Sega's code for a legitimate, essentially non-exploitative purpose, and that the commercial aspect of its use can best be described as of minimal significance.

We further note that we are free to consider the public benefit resulting from a particular use notwithstanding the fact that the alleged infringer may gain commercially. Public benefit need not be direct or tangible, but may arise because the challenged use serves a public interest. In the case before us, Accolade's identification of the functional requirements for Genesis compatibility has led to an increase in the number of independently designed video game programs offered for use with the Genesis console. It is precisely this growth in creative expression, based on the dissemination of other creative works and the unprotected ideas contained in those works, that the Copyright Act was intended to promote. The fact that Genesis-compatible video games are not scholarly works, but works offered for sale on the market, does not alter our judgment in this regard. We conclude that given the purpose and character of Accolade's use of Sega's video game programs, the presumption of unfairness has been overcome and the first statutory factor weighs in favor of Accolade.

(b)

As applied, the fourth statutory factor, effect on the potential market for the copyrighted work, bears a close relationship to the "purpose and character" inquiry in that it, too, accommodates the distinction between the copying of works in order to make independent creative expression possible and the simple exploitation of another's creative efforts. We must, of course, inquire whether, "if [the challenged use] should become widespread, it would adversely affect the potential market for the copyrighted work," Sony Corp. v. Universal City Studios, 464 U.S. 417, 451 (1984), by diminishing potential sales, interfering with marketability, or usurping the market. If the copying resulted in the latter effect, all other considerations might be irrelevant. The *Harper & Row* Court found a use that effectively usurped the market for the copyrighted work by supplanting that work to be dispositive. 471 U.S. at 567–69. However, the same consequences do not and could not attach to a use which simply enables the copier to enter the market for works of the same type as the copied work.

Unlike the defendant in *Harper & Row,* which printed excerpts from President Ford's memoirs verbatim with the stated purpose of "scooping" a *Time* magazine review of the book, Accolade did not attempt to "scoop" Sega's release of any particular game or games, but sought only to become a legitimate competitor in the field of Genesis-compatible video games. Within that market, it is the characteristics of the game program as experienced by the user that determine the program's commercial success. As we have noted, there is nothing in the record that suggests that Accolade copied any of those elements.

By facilitating the entry of a new competitor, the first lawful one that is not a Sega licensee, Accolade's disassembly of Sega's software undoubtedly "affected" the market for Genesis-compatible games in an indirect fashion. We note, however, that while no consumer except the most avid devotee of President Ford's regime might be expected to buy more than one version of the President's memoirs, video game users typically purchase more than one game. There is no basis for assuming that Accolade's "Ishido" has significantly affected the market for Sega's "Altered Beast", since a consumer might easily purchase both; nor does it seem unlikely that a consumer particularly interested in sports might purchase both Accolade's "Mike Ditka Power Football" and Sega's "Joe Montana Football", particularly if the games are, as Accolade contends, not substantially similar. In any event, an attempt to monopolize the market by making it impossible for others to compete runs counter to the statutory purpose of promoting creative expression and cannot constitute a strong equitable basis for resisting the invocation of the fair use doctrine. Thus, we conclude that the fourth statutory factor weighs in Accolade's, not Sega's, favor, notwithstanding the minor economic loss Sega may suffer.

(c)

The second statutory factor, the nature of the copyrighted work, reflects the fact that not all copyrighted works are entitled to the same level of protection. The protection established by the Copyright Act for original works of authorship does not extend to the ideas underlying a work or to the functional or factual aspects of the work. To the extent that a work is functional or factual, it may be copied, Baker v. Selden, 101 U.S. 99, 102–04 (1879), as may those expressive elements of the work that "must necessarily be used as incident to" expression of the underlying ideas, functional concepts, or facts, id. at 104. Works of fiction receive greater protection than works that have strong factual elements, such as historical or biographical works, or works that have strong functional elements, such as accounting textbooks. Works that are merely compilations of fact are copyrightable, but the copyright in such a work is "thin." *Feist Publications,* 111 S.Ct. at 1289.

Computer programs pose unique problems for the application of the "idea/expression distinction" that determines the extent of copyright protection. To the extent that there are many possible ways of accomplishing a given task or fulfilling a particular market demand, the programmer's choice of program structure and design may be highly creative and idiosyncratic. However, computer programs are, in essence, utilitarian articles—articles that accomplish tasks. As such, they contain many logical, structural, and visual display elements that are dictated by the function to be performed, by considerations of efficiency, or by external factors such as compatibility requirements and industry demands. In some circumstances, even the exact set of commands used by the programmer is deemed functional rather than creative for purposes of copyright. "[W]hen specific instructions, even though previously copyrighted, are the only and essential means of accomplishing a given task, their later use by another will not amount to infringement." CONTU Report at 20.

Because of the hybrid nature of computer programs, there is no settled standard for identifying what is protected expression and what is unprotected idea in a case involving the alleged infringement of a copyright in computer software. We are in wholehearted agreement with the Second Circuit's recent observation that "[t]hus far, many of the decisions in this area reflect the courts' attempt to fit the proverbial square peg in a round hole." Computer Assoc. Int'l, Inc. v. Altai, Inc., 23 U.S.P.Q.2d (BNA) 1241, 1257 (2d Cir.1992) ("CAI"). In 1986, the Third Circuit attempted to resolve the dilemma by suggesting that the idea or function of a computer program is the idea of the program as a whole, and "everything that is not necessary to that purpose or function [is] part of the expression of that idea." Whelan Assoc., Inc. v. Jaslow Dental Laboratory, Inc., 797 F.2d 1222, 1236 (3d Cir.1986) (emphasis omitted). The *Whelan* rule, however, has been widely—and soundly—criticized as simplistic and overbroad. See *CAI*, 23 U.S.P.Q.2d at 1252 (citing cases, treatises, and articles). In reality, "a computer program's ultimate function or purpose is the composite result of interacting subroutines. Since each subroutine is itself a program, and thus, may be said to have its own 'idea,' *Whelan's* general formulation ... is descriptively inadequate." Id. For example, the computer program at issue in the case before us, a video game program, contains at least two such subroutines—the subroutine that allows the user to interact with the video game and the subroutine that allows the game cartridge to interact with the console. Under a test that breaks down a computer program into its component subroutines and sub-subroutines and then identifies the idea or core functional element of each, such as the test recently adopted by the Second Circuit in *CAI*, 23 U.S.P.Q.2d at 1252–53, many aspects of the program are not protected by copyright. In our view, in light of the essentially utilitarian nature of computer programs, the Second Circuit's approach is an appropriate one.

Sega argues that even if many elements of its video game programs are properly characterized as functional and therefore not protected by copyright, Accolade copied protected expression. Sega is correct. The record makes clear that disassembly is wholesale copying. Because computer programs are also unique among copyrighted works in the form in which they are distributed for public use, however, Sega's observation does not bring us much closer to a resolution of the dispute.

The unprotected aspects of most functional works are readily accessible to the human eye. The systems described in accounting textbooks or the basic structural concepts embodied in architectural plans, to give two examples, can be easily copied without also copying any of the protected, expressive aspects of the original works. Computer programs, however, are typically distributed for public use in object code form, embedded in a silicon chip or on a floppy disk. For that reason, humans often cannot gain access to the unprotected ideas and functional concepts contained in object code without disassembling that code—i.e., making copies.

Sega argues that the record does not establish that disassembly of its object code is the only available method for gaining access to the interface specifications for the Genesis console, and the district court agreed. An independent examination of the record reveals that Sega misstates its contents, and demonstrates that the district court committed clear error in this respect.

First, the record clearly establishes that humans cannot *read* object code. Sega makes much of Mike Lorenzen's statement that a reverse engineer can work directly from the zeros and ones of object code but "[i]t's not as fun." In full, Lorenzen's statements establish only that the use of an *electronic* decompiler is not absolutely necessary. Trained programmers can disassemble object code by hand. Because even a trained programmer cannot possibly remember the millions of zeros and ones that make up a program, however, he must make a written or computerized copy of the disassembled code in order to keep track of his work. The relevant fact for purposes of Sega's copyright infringement claim and Accolade's fair use defense is that *translation* of a program from object code into source code cannot be accomplished without making copies of the code.

Second, the record provides no support for a conclusion that a viable alternative to disassembly exists. The district court found that Accolade could have avoided a copyright infringement claim by "peeling" the chips contained in Sega's games or in the Genesis console, as authorized by section 906 of the SCPA, 17 U.S.C. § 906. Even Sega's amici agree that this finding was clear error. The declaration of Dr. Harry Tredennick, an expert witness for Accolade, establishes that chip peeling yields only a physical diagram of the *object code* embedded in a ROM chip. It does not obviate the need to translate object code into source code.

The district court also suggested that Accolade could have avoided a copyright infringement suit by programming in a "clean room". That finding too is clearly erroneous. A "clean room" is a procedure used in the computer industry in order to prevent direct copying of a competitor's code during the development of a competing product. Programmers in clean rooms are provided only with the functional specifications for the desired program. As Dr. Tredennick explained, the use of a clean room would not have avoided the need for disassembly because disassembly was necessary in order to discover the functional specifications for a Genesis-compatible game.

In summary, the record clearly establishes that disassembly of the object code in Sega's video game cartridges was necessary in order to understand the functional requirements for Genesis compatibility. The interface procedures for the Genesis console are distributed for public use only in object code form, and are not visible to the user during operation of the video game program. Because object code cannot be read by humans, it must be disassembled, either by hand or by machine. Disassembly of object code necessarily entails copying. Those facts dictate our analysis of the second statutory fair use factor. If disassembly of copyrighted object code is *per se* an unfair use, the owner of the copyright gains a *de facto* monopoly over the functional aspects of his work—aspects that were expressly denied copyright protection by Congress. In order to enjoy a lawful monopoly over the idea or functional principle underlying a work, the creator of the work must satisfy the more stringent standards imposed by the patent laws. Sega does not hold a patent on the Genesis console.

Because Sega's video game programs contain unprotected aspects that cannot be examined without copying, we afford them a lower degree of protection than more traditional literary works. In light of all the considerations discussed above, we conclude that the second statutory factor also weighs in favor of Accolade.[8]

---

8. Sega argues that its programs are unpublished works and that therefore, under *Harper & Row*, the second statutory factor weighs in its favor. 471 U.S. at 553–55. Re-

(d)

As to the third statutory factor, Accolade disassembled entire programs written by Sega. Accordingly, the third factor weighs against Accolade. The fact that an entire work was copied does not, however, preclude a finding a fair use. In fact, where the ultimate (as opposed to direct) use is as limited as it was here, the factor is of very little weight.

(e)

In summary, careful analysis of the purpose and characteristics of Accolade's use of Sega's video game programs, the nature of the computer programs involved, and the nature of the market for video game cartridges yields the conclusion that the first, second, and fourth statutory fair use factors weigh in favor of Accolade, while only the third weighs in favor of Sega, and even then only slightly. Accordingly, Accolade clearly has by far the better case on the fair use issue.

We are not unaware of the fact that to those used to considering copyright issues in more traditional contexts, our result may seem incongruous at first blush. To oversimplify, the record establishes that Accolade, a commercial competitor of Sega, engaged in wholesale copying of Sega's copyrighted code as a preliminary step in the development of a competing product. However, the key to this case is that we are dealing with computer software, a relatively unexplored area in the world of copyright law. We must avoid the temptation of trying to force "the proverbial square peg in[to] a round hole." *CAI,* 23 U.S.P.Q.2d at 1257.

In determining whether a challenged use of copyrighted material is fair, a court must keep in mind the public policy underlying the Copyright Act. " 'The immediate effect of our copyright law is to secure a fair return for an' author's 'creative labor. But the ultimate aim is, by this incentive, to stimulate artistic creativity for the general public good.' " *Sony Corp.,* 464 U.S. at 432 (quoting Twentieth Century Music Corp. v. Aiken, 422 U.S. 151, 156 (1975)). When technological change has rendered an aspect or application of the Copyright Act ambiguous, " 'the Copyright Act must be construed in light of this basic purpose.' " Id. As discussed above, the fact that computer programs are distributed for public use in object code form often precludes public access to the ideas and functional concepts contained in those programs, and thus confers on the copyright owner a *de facto* monopoly over those ideas and functional concepts. That result defeats the fundamental purpose of the Copyright Act—to encourage the production of original works by protecting the expressive elements of those works while

---

cently, however, this court affirmed a district court holding that computer game cartridges that are held out to the public for sale are published works for purposes of copyright. Lewis Galoob Toys, Inc. v. Nintendo of America, Inc., 964 F.2d 965 (9th Cir.1992, as amended August 5, 1992) (affirming 780 F.Supp. 1283, 1293 (N.D.Cal.1991)). The de-

cision in Association of Am. Medical Colleges v. Cuomo, 928 F.2d 519 (2d Cir.1991), cert. denied, 112 U.S. 184 (1991), is not to the contrary. The Medical College Admission Test is not held out to the public for sale, but rather is distributed on a highly restricted basis.

leaving the ideas, facts, and functional concepts in the public domain for others to build on.

Sega argues that the considerable time, effort, and money that went into development of the Genesis and Genesis-compatible video games militate against a finding of fair use. Borrowing from antitrust principles, Sega attempts to label Accolade a "free rider" on its product development efforts. In *Feist Publications,* however, the [Supreme] Court unequivocally rejected the "sweat of the brow" rationale for copyright protection. 111 S.Ct. at 1290–95. Under the Copyright Act, if a work is largely functional, it receives only weak protection. "This result is neither unfair nor unfortunate. It is the means by which copyright advances the progress of science and art." Id. at 1290; see also id. at 1292 ("In truth, '[i]t is just such wasted effort that the proscription against the copyright of ideas and facts ... [is] designed to prevent.' ") (quoting Rosemont Enterprises, Inc. v. Random House, Inc., 366 F.2d 303, 310 (2d Cir.1966), *cert. denied* 385 U.S. 1009 (1967)). Here, while the work may not be largely functional, it incorporates functional elements which do not merit protection. The equitable considerations involved weigh on the side of public access. Accordingly, we reject Sega's argument.

(f)

We conclude that where disassembly is the only way to gain access to the ideas and functional elements embodied in a copyrighted computer program and where there is a legitimate reason for seeking such access, disassembly is a fair use of the copyrighted work, as a matter of law. Our conclusion does not, of course, insulate Accolade from a claim of copyright infringement with respect to its finished products. Sega has reserved the right to raise such a claim, and it may do so on remand....

[The court's analysis of the Lanham Act issues, omitted here, is summarized in note 5 below.]

AFFIRMED IN PART; REVERSED IN PART; AND REMANDED.

NOTES

1. *Reverse Engineering.* As indicated in *Sega,* software producers commonly disseminate their programs only in the form of object code—a form that is usable in computers but incomprehensible to humans. Source code—the form in which computer programs are initially written—is humanly comprehensible but, for that reason, and because source code would reveal the logical techniques embodied in the program, producers typically withhold source code as a trade secret.

In a report published before the Ninth Circuit Court of Appeals' decision in *Sega,* the Committee on Computer Law of the Association of the Bar of the City of New York examined several examples of reverse engineering against the background of section 107's four factors. Two examples are illustrative: reverse engineering to learn about a program's structure, organization or algorithms as part of a classroom exercise, and reverse engineering in a commercial setting to "develop a directly competing functionally interchangeable program which uses only unprotected features of the first [program], that is, ideas which are not subject to copyright and have not been patented." Reverse Engineering and Intellectual Property Law, 44 The Record 132, 135 (1989).

The report concluded that section 107's first factor—purpose and character of the use—weighs in favor of the classroom use and against the commercial use. The second factor—the nature of the copyrighted work— "strongly" favors a fair use finding in both cases; "[u]nlike a book whose ideas can be discovered by reading it, the nature of a computer program distributed only in object code is such that the ideas embodied in it largely cannot be studied and understood by humans without decompilation. Therefore, prohibiting decompilation could defeat an important societal interest in learning from and improving on the ideas contained in computer programs, by effectively giving the copyright owner a monopoly over the ideas, as well as the expression, in the copyrighted work." Id. at 140.

Since both examples involve the copying of the entire program, the third factor—amount and substantiality of the portion used in relation to the copyrighted work as a whole—weighs against fair use; "[h]owever, even complete verbatim copies may be noninfringing." In the Report's view, the fourth factor—effect of the use upon the potential market for, or value of the copyrighted work—favors the first use, but not the second, "since the effect of the use would be the creation of a competing program." Id. at 140–41. In the usual fair use case, the defendant's work will embody protectible expression appearing in the copyrighted work. Is it relevant that the competing program in the second example embodies no protectible expression drawn from the copyrighted work? Is this fact more relevant than the facts that Judge Reinhardt addressed in his treatment of the fourth factor in *Sega*?

2. *European Software Directive.* The E.C. Directive on the Legal Protection of Computer Programs, 91/250/EEC, 1991 O.J. (L 122) 42, carves out an exemption not only for decompilation, (as in *Sega*, but also for so-called black box analysis—loading), running and storing the object code version of a program to determine its interface specifications. In the case of black box analysis, Article 5(3) entitles one who has the right to use a copy of a computer program to observe, study, or test the functioning of the program in order to determine the ideas and principles that underlie any element of the program, if he does so "while performing any of the acts of loading, displaying, running, transmitting or storing the program which he is entitled to do."

Article 6(1)'s decompilation exception defines the compass of freely discoverable ideas more narrowly than does Article 5(3), but more extensively privileges the conduct, including reproduction and decompilation, aimed at discovering them. Where Article 5(3) excuses observation, study, or testing to determine the ideas and principles that underlie "any element of the program," Article 6(1) excuses the discovery only of "parts of the original program which are necessary to achieve interoperability." But,

Article 6 privileges the competitor's reproduction of code, "and translation of its form," when "indispensable to obtain the information necessary to achieve the interoperability of an independently created computer program with other programs."

Article 9(1) of the Directive specifically nullifies any attempt by software vendors to impose contract conditions that would override the exceptions created by Articles 5(3) and 6(1).

3. *Copying by Independent Service Organizations.* Is it fair use for an independent computer service company to copy a computer program into the random access memory of a customer's computer in the course of maintenance work on the computer, when the terms of the customer's license prohibit such copying and the service company competes with the licensor for maintenance business? In Triad Systems Corp. v. Southeastern Express Co., 64 F.3d 1330, 36 U.S.P.Q.2d 1028 (9th Cir.1995), the court distinguished such copying of operating system and service software from the reverse engineering that was involved in *Sega*: "Southeastern did not make a minimal use of Triad's programs solely to achieve compatibility with Triad's computers for Southeastern's own creative programs. Rather, Southeastern has invented nothing of its own; its use of Triad's software is, in the district court's words, 'neither creative nor transformative and does not provide the marketplace with new creative works.' Southeastern is simply commandeering its customers' software and using it for the very purpose for which, and in precisely the manner in which, it was designed to be used. As a result, the copies made by Southeastern while servicing Triad computers have undoubtedly diminished the value of Triad's copyright." 64 F.3d at 1336–37.

Section 117(c), added to the 1976 Act by the Digital Millennium Copyright Act, Pub. L. No.105–304, 112 Stat. 2860 (Oct. 28, 1998), created a copyright safe harbor for independent service organizations by providing that "it is not an infringement for the owner or lessee of a machine to make or authorize the making of a copy of a computer program if such copy is made solely by virtue of the activation of a machine that lawfully contains an authorized copy of the computer program, for purposes only of maintenance or repair of that machine." The provision imposes two conditions for the exemption to apply: the new copy can be used in no other manner and must be destroyed immediately after the maintenance or repair is completed; and, "with respect to any computer program or part thereof that is not necessary for that machine to be activated, such program or part thereof is not accessed or used other than to make such new copy by virtue of the activation of the machine."

4. *Misuse.* In *Triad Systems*, the Ninth Circuit also rejected Southeastern's defense of copyright misuse on the ground that "Triad did not attempt to prohibit Southeastern or any other ISO from developing its own service software to compete with Triad." 64 F.3d at 1337. By contrast, the Fifth Circuit Court of Appeals upheld a misuse defense in comparable circumstances in DSC Communications Corp. v. DGI Technologies, Inc., 81 F.3d 597, 601, 38 U.S.P.Q.2d 1699 (5th Cir.1996): "DGI may well prevail on the defense of copyright misuse, because DSC seems to be attempting to use its copyright to obtain a patent-like monopoly over unpatented microprocessor cards. Any competing microprocessor card developed for use on DSC phone switches must be compatible with DSC's copyrighted operating system software. In order to ensure that its card is compatible, a competitor such as DGI must test the card on a DSC phone switch. Such a test necessarily involves making a copy of DSC's copyrighted operating system, which copy is downloaded into the card's memory when the card is booted up. If DSC is allowed to prevent such copying, then it can prevent anyone from developing a competing microprocessor card, even though it has not patented the card."

Is it more than coincidence that the first appellate level decision to introduce patent law's misuse defense into decision of a copyright case involved computer programs? See Lasercomb Am., Inc. v. Reynolds, 911 F.2d 970, 15 U.S.P.Q.2d 1846 (4th Cir.1990). Is copyright in computer programs likely to confer greater market power than other forms of copyright subject matter? Is it relevant that the core elements of computer programs, like the elements of patent subject matter, are functional?

5. *Trademark and Unfair Competition.* As part of its strategy to bar use of unlicensed videogames on the company's Genesis consoles, Sega embedded a trademark security system ("TMSS") in the consoles; when activated by a compatible game with the required initialization code—whether Sega's or a competitor's—the system would display the Sega trademark. In its action against Accolade, Sega claimed that, by triggering a display of the Sega mark, Accolade's use of the initialization code in its games misled consumers that the games originated with Sega, and consequently infringed Sega's rights under its trademark registration and under Lanham Act section 43(a). Accolade counterclaimed that Sega's use of the trademark security system constituted a false designation of origin under section 43(a)—that Sega, not Accolade, was the source of Accolade products.

The court of appeals reversed the district court's grant of preliminary trademark relief to Sega, but left decision on Accolade's counterclaim to the remand. "Because the TMSS has the effect of regulating access to the Genesis III console, and because there is no indication in the record of any public or industry awareness of any feasible alternate method of gaining access to the Genesis III, we hold that Sega is primarily responsible for any resultant confusion." 977 F.2d at 1528.

3. FIRST AMENDMENT

Universal City Studios, Inc. v. Corley

United States Court of Appeals, Second Circuit, 2001.
273 F.3d 429, 60 U.S.P.Q.2d 1953.

JON O. NEWMAN, Circuit Judge.

When the Framers of the First Amendment prohibited Congress from making any law "abridging the freedom of speech," they were not thinking about computers, computer programs, or the Internet. But neither were they thinking about radio, television, or movies. Just as the inventions at the beginning and middle of the 20th century presented new First Amendment issues, so does the cyber revolution at the end of that century. This appeal raises significant First Amendment issues concerning one aspect of computer technology—encryption to protect materials in digital form from unauthorized access. The appeal challenges the constitutionality of the Digital Millennium Copyright Act ("DMCA"), 17 U.S.C. § 1201 *et seq.* (Supp. V 1999) and the validity of an injunction entered to enforce the DMCA.

Defendant–Appellant Eric C. Corley and his company, 2600 Enterprises, Inc., (collectively "Corley," "the Defendants," or "the Appellants") appeal from the amended final judgment of the United States District Court for the Southern District of New York (Lewis A. Kaplan, District Judge), entered August 23, 2000, enjoining them from various actions concerning a decryption program known as "DeCSS." *Universal City Studios, Inc. v. Reimerdes,* 111 F.Supp.2d 346 (S.D.N.Y.2000) (*"Universal II"*). The injunction primarily bars the Appellants from posting DeCSS on their web site and from knowingly linking their web site to any other web site on which DeCSS is posted. We affirm.

Introduction

Understanding the pending appeal and the issues it raises requires some familiarity with technical aspects of computers and computer software, especially software called "digital versatile disks" or "DVDs," which are optical media storage devices currently designed to contain movies. Those lacking such familiarity will be greatly aided by reading Judge Kaplan's extremely lucid opinion, *Universal City Studios, Inc. v. Reimerdes,* 111 F.Supp.2d 294 (S.D.N.Y.2000) (*"Universal I"*), beginning with his helpful section "The Vocabulary of this Case," *id.* at 305–09.

This appeal concerns the anti-trafficking provisions of the DMCA, which Congress enacted in 1998 to strengthen copyright protection in the digital age. Fearful that the ease with which pirates could copy and distribute a copyrightable work in digital form was overwhelming the capacity of conventional copyright enforcement to find and enjoin unlawfully copied material, Congress sought to combat copyright piracy in its earlier stages, before the work was even copied. The DMCA therefore backed with legal sanctions the efforts of copyright owners to protect their works from piracy behind digital walls such as encryption codes or password protections. In so doing, Congress targeted not only those pirates who would *circumvent* these digital walls (the "anti-circumvention provisions," contained in 17 U.S.C. § 1201(a)(1)), but also anyone who would *traffic* in a technology primarily designed to circumvent a digital wall (the "anti-trafficking provisions," contained in 17 U.S.C. § 1201(a)(2), (b)(1)).

Corley publishes a print magazine and maintains an affiliated web site geared towards "hackers," a digital-era term often applied to those interested in techniques for circumventing protections of computers and computer data from unauthorized access. The so-called hacker community includes serious computer-science scholars conducting research on protection techniques, computer buffs intrigued by the challenge of trying to circumvent access-limiting devices or perhaps hoping to promote security by exposing flaws in protection techniques, mischief-makers interested in disrupting computer operations, and thieves, including copyright infringers who want to acquire copyrighted material (for personal use or resale) without paying for it.

In November 1999, Corley posted a copy of the decryption computer program "DeCSS" on his web site, http://www.2600.com ("2600.com"). DeCSS is designed to circumvent "CSS," the encryption technology that motion picture studios place on DVDs to prevent the unauthorized viewing and copying of motion pictures. Corley also posted on his web site links to other web sites where DeCSS could be found.

Plaintiffs–Appellees are eight motion picture studios that brought an action in the Southern District of New York seeking injunctive relief against Corley under the DMCA. Following a full non-jury trial, the District Court entered a permanent injunction barring Corley from posting DeCSS on his web site or from knowingly linking via a hyperlink to any other web site containing DeCSS. The District Court rejected Corley's constitutional attacks on the statute and the injunction.

Corley renews his constitutional challenges on appeal. Specifically, he argues primarily that: (1) the DMCA oversteps limits in the Copyright Clause on the duration of copyright protection; (2) the DMCA as applied to his dissemination of DeCSS violates the First Amendment because computer code is "speech" entitled to full First Amendment protection and the DMCA fails to survive the exacting scrutiny accorded statutes that regulate "speech"; and (3) the DMCA violates the First Amendment and the Copyright Clause by unduly obstructing the "fair use" of copyrighted materials. Corley also argues that the statute is susceptible to, and should therefore be given, a narrow interpretation that avoids alleged constitutional objections.

Background

For decades, motion picture studios have made movies available for viewing at home in what is called "analog" format. Movies in this format are placed on videotapes, which can be played on a video cassette recorder ("VCR"). In the early 1990s, the studios began to consider the possibility of distributing movies in digital form as well. Movies in digital form are placed on disks, known as DVDs, which can be played on a DVD player (either a stand-alone device or a component of a computer). DVDs offer advantages over analog tapes, such as improved visual and audio quality, larger data capacity, and greater durability. However, the improved quality of a movie in a digital format brings with it the risk that a virtually perfect copy, *i.e.,* one that will not lose perceptible quality in the copying process, can be readily made at the click of a computer control and instantly distributed to countless recipients throughout the world over the Internet. This case arises out of the movie industry's efforts to respond to this risk by invoking the anti-trafficking provisions of the DMCA.

I.   CSS

The movie studios were reluctant to release movies in digital form until they were confident they had in place adequate safeguards against piracy of their copyrighted movies. The studios took several steps to minimize the piracy threat. First, they settled on the DVD as the standard digital medium for home distribution of movies. The studios then sought an encryption scheme to protect movies on DVDs. They enlisted the help of members of the consumer electronics and computer industries, who in mid–1996 developed the Content Scramble System ("CSS"). CSS is an encryption scheme that employs an algorithm configured by a set of "keys" to encrypt a DVD's contents. The algorithm is a type of mathematical formula for transforming the contents of the movie file into gibberish; the "keys" are in actuality strings of 0's and 1's that serve as values for the mathematical formula. Decryption in the case of CSS requires a set of "player keys" contained in compliant DVD players, as well as an understanding of the CSS encryption algorithm. Without the player keys and the algorithm, a DVD player cannot access the contents of a DVD. With the player keys and the algorithm, a DVD player can display the movie on a television or a computer screen, but does not give a viewer the ability to use the copy function of the computer to copy the movie or to manipulate the digital content of the DVD.

The studios developed a licensing scheme for distributing the technology to manufacturers of DVD players. Player keys and other information necessary to the CSS scheme were given to manufacturers of DVD players for an administrative fee. In exchange for the licenses, manufacturers were obliged to keep the player keys confidential. Manufacturers were also required in the licensing agreement to prevent the transmission of "CSS data" (a term undefined in the licensing agreement) from a DVD drive to any "internal recording device," including, presumably, a computer hard drive.

With encryption technology and licensing agreements in hand, the studios began releasing movies on DVDs in 1997, and DVDs quickly gained in popularity, becoming a significant source of studio revenue. In 1998, the studios secured added protection against DVD piracy when Congress passed the DMCA, which prohibits the development or use of technology designed to circumvent a technological protection measure, such as CSS. The pertinent provisions of the DMCA are examined in greater detail below.

II.   DeCSS

In September 1999, Jon Johansen, a Norwegian teenager, collaborating with two unidentified individuals he met on the Internet, reverse-engineered a licensed DVD player designed to operate on the Microsoft operating system, and culled from it the player keys and other information necessary to decrypt CSS. The record suggests that Johansen was trying to develop a DVD player operable on Linux, an alternative operating system that did not support any licensed DVD players at that time. In order to accomplish this task, Johansen wrote a decryption program executable on Microsoft's operating system. That program was called, appropriately enough, "DeCSS."

If a user runs the DeCSS program (for example, by clicking on the DeCSS icon on a Microsoft operating system platform) with a DVD in the computer's disk drive, DeCSS will decrypt the DVD's CSS protection, allowing the user to copy the DVD's files and place the copy on the user's hard drive. The result is a very large computer file that can be played on a non-CSS-compliant player and copied, manipulated, and transferred just like any other computer file. DeCSS comes complete with a fairly user-friendly interface that helps the user select from among the DVD's files and assign the decrypted file a location on the user's hard drive. The quality of the resulting decrypted movie is "virtually identical" to that of the encrypted movie on the DVD. And the file produced by DeCSS, while large, can be compressed to a manageable size by a compression software called "DivX," available at no cost on the Internet. This compressed file can be copied onto a DVD, or transferred over the Internet (with some patience).

Johansen posted the executable object code, but not the source code, for DeCSS on his web site. The distinction between source code and object code is relevant to this case, so a brief explanation is warranted. A computer responds to electrical charges, the presence or absence of which is represented by strings of 1's and 0's. Strictly speaking, "object code" consists of those 1's and 0's. While some people can read and program in object code, "it would be inconvenient, inefficient and, for most people, probably impossible to do so." *Universal I,* 111 F.Supp.2d at 306. Computer languages have been written to facilitate program writing and reading. A program in such a computer language—BASIC, C, and Java are examples—is said to be written in "source code." Source code has the benefit of being much easier to read (by people) than object code, but as a general matter, it must be translated back to object code before it can be read by a computer. This task is usually performed by a program called a compiler. Since computer languages range in complexity, object code can be placed on one end of a spectrum, and different kinds of source code can be arrayed across the spectrum according to the ease with which they are read and understood by humans. Within months of its appearance in executable form on Johansen's web site, DeCSS was widely available on the Internet, in both object code and various forms of source code.

In November 1999, Corley wrote and placed on his web site, 2600.com, an article about the DeCSS phenomenon. His web site is an auxiliary to the print magazine, *2600: The Hacker Quarterly,* which Corley has been publishing since 1984. As the name suggests, the magazine is designed for "hackers," as is the web site. While the magazine and the web site cover some issues of general interest to computer users—such as threats to online privacy—the focus of the publications is on the vulnerability of computer security systems, and more specifically, how to exploit that vulnerability in order to circumvent the security systems. Representative articles explain how to steal an Internet domain name and how to break into the computer systems at Federal Express.

Corley's article about DeCSS detailed how CSS was cracked, and described the movie industry's efforts to shut down web sites posting DeCSS. It also explained that DeCSS could be used to copy DVDs. At the end of the article, the Defendants posted copies of the object and source code of DeCSS. In Corley's words, he added the code to the story because "in a journalistic world, ... [y]ou have to show your evidence ... and particularly in the magazine that I work for, people want to see specifically what it is that we are referring to," including "what evidence ... we have" that there is in fact technology that circumvents CSS. Writing about DeCSS without including the DeCSS code would have been, to Corley, "analogous to printing a story about a picture and not printing the picture." Corley also added to the article links that he explained would take the reader to other web sites where DeCSS could be found.

2600.com was only one of hundreds of web sites that began posting DeCSS near the end of 1999. The movie industry tried to stem the tide by sending cease-and-desist letters to many of these sites. These efforts met with only partial success; a number of sites refused to remove DeCSS. In January 2000, the studios filed this lawsuit.

III. The DMCA

The DMCA was enacted in 1998 to implement the World Intellectual Property Organization Copyright Treaty ("WIPO Treaty"), which requires contracting parties to "provide adequate legal protection and effective legal remedies against the circumvention of effective technological measures that are used by authors in connection with the exercise of their rights under this Treaty or the Berne Convention and that restrict acts, in respect of their works, which are not authorized by the authors concerned or permitted by law." WIPO Treaty, Apr. 12, 1997, art. 11. Even before the treaty, Congress had been devoting attention to the problems faced by copyright enforcement in the digital age. Hearings on the topic have spanned several years. This legislative effort resulted in the DMCA.

The Act contains three provisions targeted at the circumvention of technological protections. The first is subsection 1201(a)(1)(A), the anti-circumvention provision. This provision prohibits a person from "circumvent[ing] a technological measure that effectively controls access to a work protected under [Title 17, governing copyright]." The Librarian of Congress is required to promulgate regulations every three years exempting from this subsection individuals who would otherwise be "adversely affected" in "their ability to make noninfringing uses." 17 U.S.C. § 1201(a)(1)(B)–(E).

The second and third provisions are subsections 1201(a)(2) and 1201(b)(1), the "anti-trafficking provisions." Subsection 1201(a)(2), the provision at issue in this case, provides:

No person shall manufacture, import, offer to the public, provide, or otherwise traffic in any technology, product, service, device, component, or part thereof, that—

(A) is primarily designed or produced for the purpose of circumventing a technological measure that effectively controls access to a work protected under this title;

(B) has only limited commercially significant purpose or use other than to circumvent a technological measure that effectively controls access to a work protected under this title; or

(C) is marketed by that person or another acting in concert with that person with that person's knowledge for use in circumventing a technological measure that effectively controls access to a work protected under this title.

Id. § 1201(a)(2). To "circumvent a technological measure" is defined, in pertinent part, as "to descramble a scrambled work . . . or otherwise to . . . bypass . . . a technological measure, without the authority of the copyright owner." *Id.* § 1201(a)(3)(A).

Subsection 1201(b)(1) is similar to subsection 1201(a)(2), except that subsection 1201(a)(2) covers those who traffic in technology that can circumvent "a technological measure *that effectively controls access* to a work protected under" Title 17, whereas subsection 1201(b)(1) covers those who traffic in technology that can circumvent "protection afforded by a technological measure *that effectively protects a right of a copyright owner* under" Title 17. *Id.* § 1201(a)(2), (b)(1) (emphases added). In other words, although both subsections prohibit trafficking in a circumvention technology, the focus of subsection 1201(a)(2) is circumvention of technologies designed to *prevent access* to a work, and the focus of subsection 1201(b)(1) is circumvention of technologies designed to *permit access* to a work but *prevent copying* of the work or some other act that infringes a copyright. Subsection 1201(a)(1) differs from both of these anti-trafficking subsections in that it targets the use of a circumvention technology, not the trafficking in such a technology.

The DMCA contains exceptions for schools and libraries that want to use circumvention technologies to determine whether to purchase a copyrighted product, 17 U.S.C. § 1201(d); individuals using circumvention technology "for the sole purpose" of trying to achieve "interoperability" of computer programs through reverse-engineering, *id.* § 1201(f); encryption research aimed at identifying flaws in encryption technology, if the research is conducted to advance the state of knowledge in the field, *id.* § 1201(g); and several other exceptions not relevant here.

The DMCA creates civil remedies, *id.* § 1203 and criminal sanctions, *id.* § 1204. It specifically authorizes a court to "grant temporary and permanent injunctions on such terms as it deems reasonable to prevent or restrain a violation." *Id.* § 1203(b)(1).

IV. Procedural History

Invoking subsection 1203(b)(1), the Plaintiffs sought an injunction against the Defendants, alleging that the Defendants violated the anti-trafficking provisions of the statute. On January 20, 2000, after a hearing, the District Court issued a preliminary injunction barring the Defendants from posting DeCSS.

The Defendants complied with the preliminary injunction, but continued to post links to other web sites carrying DeCSS, an action they termed "electronic civil disobedience." *Universal I,* 111 F.Supp.2d at 303, 312. Under the heading "Stop the MPAA [(Motion Picture Association of America)]," Corley urged other web sites to post DeCSS lest "we ... be forced into submission." *Id.* at 313.

The Plaintiffs then sought a permanent injunction barring the Defendants from both posting DeCSS and linking to sites containing DeCSS. After a trial on the merits, the Court issued a comprehensive opinion, *Universal I,* and granted a permanent injunction, *Universal II.*

The Court explained that the Defendants' posting of DeCSS on their web site clearly falls within section 1201(a)(2)(A) of the DMCA, rejecting as spurious their claim that CSS is not a technological measure that "effectively controls access to a work" because it was so easily penetrated by Johansen, and as irrelevant their contention that DeCSS was designed to create a Linux-platform DVD player. The Court also held that the Defendants cannot avail themselves of any of the DMCA's exceptions and that the alleged importance of DeCSS to certain fair uses of encrypted copyrighted material was immaterial to their statutory liability. The Court went on to hold that when the Defendants "proclaimed on their own site that DeCSS could be had by clicking on the hyperlinks" on their site, they were trafficking in DeCSS, and therefore liable for their linking as well as their posting.

Turning to the Defendants' numerous constitutional arguments, the Court first held that computer code like DeCSS is "speech" that is "protected" (in the sense of "covered") by the First Amendment, but that because the DMCA is targeting the "functional" aspect of that speech, it is "content neutral," and the intermediate scrutiny of *United States v. O'Brien,* 391 U.S. 367, 377, (1968), applies. The Court concluded that the DMCA survives this scrutiny, and also rejected prior restraint, overbreadth, and vagueness challenges.

The Court upheld the constitutionality of the DMCA's application to linking on similar grounds: linking, the Court concluded, is "speech," but the DMCA is content-neutral, targeting only the functional components of that speech. Therefore, its application to linking is also evaluated under *O'Brien,* and, thus evaluated, survives intermediate scrutiny. However, the Court concluded that a blanket proscription on linking would create a risk of chilling legitimate linking on the web. The Court therefore crafted a restrictive test for linking liability (discussed below) that it believed sufficiently mitigated that risk. The Court then found its test satisfied in this case.

Finally, the Court concluded that an injunction was highly appropriate in this case. The Court observed that DeCSS was harming the Plaintiffs, not only because they were now exposed to the possibility of piracy and therefore were obliged to develop costly new safeguards for DVDs, but also because, even if there was only indirect evidence that DeCSS availability actually facilitated DVD piracy, the threat of piracy was very real, particularly as Internet transmission speeds continue to increase. Acknowledging that DeCSS was (and still is) widely available on the Internet, the Court expressed confidence in

> the likelihood ... that this decision will serve notice on others that "the strong right arm of equity" may be brought to bear against them absent a change in their conduct and thus contribute to a climate of appropriate respect for intellectual property rights in an age in which the excitement of ready access to untold quantities of information has blurred in some minds the fact that taking what is not yours and not freely offered to you is stealing.

Id. at 345.

The Court's injunction barred the Defendants from: "posting on any Internet web site" DeCSS; "in any other way ... offering to the public, providing, or otherwise trafficking in DeCSS"; violating the anti-trafficking provisions of the DMCA in any other manner, and finally "knowingly linking any Internet web site operated by them to any other web site containing DeCSS, or knowingly maintaining any such link, for the purpose of disseminating DeCSS." *Universal II,* 111 F.Supp.2d at 346–47.

The Appellants have appealed from the permanent injunction. The United States has intervened in support of the constitutionality of the DMCA. We have also had the benefit of a number of *amicus curiae* briefs, supporting and opposing the District Court's judgment. After oral argument, we invited the parties to submit responses to a series of specific questions, and we have received helpful responses.

Discussion

I. Narrow Construction to Avoid Constitutional Doubt

The Appellants first argue that, because their constitutional arguments are at least substantial, we should interpret the statute narrowly so as to avoid constitutional problems. They identify three different instances of alleged ambiguity in the statute that they claim provide an opportunity for such a narrow interpretation.

First, they contend that subsection 1201(c)(1), which provides that "[n]othing in this section shall affect rights, remedies, limitations or defenses to copyright infringement, including fair use, under this title," can be read to allow the circumvention of encryption technology protecting copyrighted material when the material will be put to "fair uses" exempt from copyright liability. We disagree that subsection 1201(c)(1) permits such a reading. Instead, it clearly and simply clarifies that the DMCA targets the *circumvention* of digital walls guarding copyrighted material (and trafficking in circumvention tools), but does not concern itself with the *use* of those materials after circumvention has occurred. Subsection 1201(c)(1) ensures that the DMCA is not read to prohibit the "fair use" of information just because that information was obtained in a manner made illegal by the DMCA. The Appellants' much more expansive interpretation of subsection 1201(c)(1) is not only outside the range of plausible readings of the provision, but is also clearly refuted by the statute's legislative history.

Second, the Appellants urge a narrow construction of the DMCA because of subsection 1201(c)(4), which provides that "[n]othing in this section shall enlarge or diminish any rights of free speech or the press for activities using consumer electronics, telecommunications, or computing products." This language is clearly precatory: Congress could not "diminish" constitutional rights of free speech even if it wished to, and the fact that Congress also expressed a reluctance to "enlarge" those rights cuts against the Appellants' effort to infer a narrowing construction of the Act from this provision.

Third, the Appellants argue that an individual who buys a DVD has the "authority of the copyright owner" to view the DVD, and therefore is exempted from the DMCA pursuant to subsection 1201(a)(3)(A) when the buyer circumvents an encryption technology in order to view the DVD on a competing platform (such as Linux). The basic flaw in this argument is that it misreads subsection 1201(a)(3)(A). That provision exempts from liability those who would "decrypt" an encrypted DVD with the authority of a copyright owner, not those who would "view" a DVD with the authority of a copyright owner. In any event, the Defendants offered no evidence that the Plaintiffs have either explicitly or implicitly authorized DVD buyers to circumvent encryption technology to support use on multiple platforms.

We conclude that the anti-trafficking and anti-circumvention provisions of the DMCA are not susceptible to the narrow interpretations urged by the Appellants. We therefore proceed to consider the Appellants' constitutional claims.

II.   Constitutional Challenge Based on the Copyright Clause

In a footnote to their brief, the Appellants appear to contend that the DMCA, as construed by the District Court, exceeds the constitutional authority of Congress to grant authors copyrights for a "limited time," U.S. Const. art. I, § 8, cl. 8, because it "empower[s] copyright owners to effectively secure perpetual protection by mixing public domain works with copyrighted materials, then locking both up with technological protection measures." This argument is elaborated in the *amici curiae* brief filed by Prof. Julie E. Cohen on behalf of herself and 45 other intellectual property law professors. For two reasons, the argument provides no basis for disturbing the judgment of the District Court.

First, we have repeatedly ruled that arguments presented to us only in a footnote are not entitled to appellate consideration. Although an *amicus* brief can be helpful in elaborating issues properly presented by the parties, it is normally not a method for injecting new issues into an appeal, at least in cases where the parties are competently represented by counsel.

Second, to whatever extent the argument might have merit at some future time in a case with a properly developed record, the argument is entirely premature and speculative at this time on this record. There is not even a claim, much less evidence, that any Plaintiff has sought to prevent copying of public domain works, or that the injunction prevents the Defendants from copying such works. As Judge Kaplan noted, the possibility that encryption would preclude access to public domain works "does not yet appear to be a problem, although it may emerge as one in the future." *Universal I*, 111 F.Supp.2d at 338 n. 245.

III.   Constitutional Challenges Based on the First Amendment

A.   Applicable Principles

Last year, in one of our Court's first forays into First Amendment law in the digital age, we took an "evolutionary" approach to the task of tailoring familiar constitutional rules to novel technological circumstances, favoring "narrow" holdings that would permit the law to mature on a "case-by-case" basis. *See Name.Space, Inc. v. Network Solutions, Inc.*, 202 F.3d 573, 584 n. 11 (2d Cir.2000). In that spirit, we proceed, with appropriate caution, to consider the Appellants' First Amendment challenges by analyzing a series of preliminary issues the resolution of which provides a basis for adjudicating the specific objections to the DMCA and its application to DeCSS. These issues, which we consider only to the extent necessary to resolve the pending appeal, are whether computer code is speech, whether computer programs are speech, the scope of First Amendment protection for computer code, and the scope of First Amendment protection for decryption code. Based on our analysis of these issues, we then consider the Appellants' challenge to the injunction's provisions concerning posting and linking.

1.   Code as Speech

Communication does not lose constitutional protection as "speech" simply because it is expressed in the language of computer code. Mathematical formulae and musical scores are written in "code," *i.e.,* symbolic notations not comprehensible to the uninitiated, and yet both are covered by the First Amendment. If someone chose to write a novel entirely in computer object code by using strings of 1's and 0's for each letter of each word, the resulting work would be no different for constitutional purposes than if it had been written in English. The "object code" version would be incomprehensible to readers outside the programming community (and tedious to read even for most within the community), but it would be no more incomprehensible than a work written in Sanskrit for those unversed in that language. The undisputed evidence reveals that even pure object code can be, and often is, read and understood by experienced programmers. And source code (in any of its various levels of complexity) can be read by many more. Ultimately, however, the ease with which a work is comprehended is irrelevant to the constitutional inquiry. If computer code is distinguishable from conventional speech for First Amendment purposes, it is not because it is written in an obscure language.

2. Computer Programs as Speech

Of course, computer code is not likely to be the language in which a work of literature is written. Instead, it is primarily the language for programs executable by a computer. These programs are essentially instructions to a computer. In general, programs may give instructions either to perform a task or series of tasks when initiated by a single (or double) click of a mouse or, once a program is operational ("launched"), to manipulate data that the user enters into the computer. Whether computer code that gives a computer instructions is "speech" within the meaning of the First Amendment requires consideration of the scope of the Constitution's protection of speech.

The First Amendment provides that "Congress shall make no law ... abridging the freedom of speech...." U.S. Const. amend. I. "Speech" is an elusive term, and judges and scholars have debated its bounds for two centuries. Some would confine First Amendment protection to political speech. Others would extend it further to artistic expression.

Whatever might be the merits of these and other approaches, the law has not been so limited. Even dry information, devoid of advocacy, political relevance, or artistic expression, has been accorded First Amendment protection. Thus, for example, courts have subjected to First Amendment scrutiny restrictions on the dissemination of technical scientific information and scientific research, and attempts to regulate the publication of instructions.

Computer programs are not exempted from the category of First Amendment speech simply because their instructions require use of a computer. A recipe is no less "speech" because it calls for the use of an oven, and a musical score is no less "speech" because it specifies performance on an electric guitar. Arguably distinguishing computer programs from conventional language instructions is the fact that programs are executable on a computer. But the fact that a program has the capacity to direct the functioning of a computer does not mean that it lacks the additional capacity to convey information, and it is the conveying of information that renders instructions "speech" for purposes of the First Amendment. The information conveyed by most "instructions" is how to perform a task.

Instructions such as computer code, which are intended to be executable by a computer, will often convey information capable of comprehension and assessment by a human being. A programmer reading a program learns information about instructing a computer, and might use this information to improve personal programming skills and perhaps the craft of programming. Moreover, programmers communicating ideas to one another almost inevitably communicate in code, much as musicians use notes. Limiting First Amendment protection of programmers to descriptions of computer code (but not the code itself) would impede discourse among computer scholars, just as limiting protection for musicians to descriptions of musical scores (but not sequences of notes) would impede their exchange of ideas and expression. Instructions that communicate information comprehensible to a human qualify as speech whether the instructions are designed for execution by a computer or a human (or both). . . .

For all of these reasons, we join the other courts that have concluded that computer code, and computer programs constructed from code can merit First Amendment protection, although the scope of such protection remains to be determined.

3. The Scope of First Amendment Protection for Computer Code

Having concluded that computer code conveying information is "speech" within the meaning of the First Amendment, we next consider, to a limited extent, the scope of the protection that code enjoys. As the District Court recognized, the scope of protection for speech generally depends on whether the restriction is imposed because of the content of the speech. Content-based restrictions are permissible only if they serve compelling state interests and do so by the least restrictive means available. A content-neutral restriction is permissible if it serves a substantial governmental interest, the interest is unrelated to the suppression of free expression, and the regulation is narrowly tailored, which "in this context requires ... that the means chosen do not 'burden substantially more speech than is necessary to further the government's legitimate interests.' " *Turner Broadcasting System, Inc. v. FCC,* 512 U.S. 622, 662, (1994) (quoting *Ward v. Rock Against Racism,* 491 U.S. 781, 799, 109 S.Ct. 2746, 105 L.Ed.2d 661 (1989)).

"[G]overnment regulation of expressive activity is 'content neutral' if it is justified without reference to the content of regulated speech." *Hill v. Colorado,* 530 U.S. 703, 720, 120 S.Ct. 2480, 147 L.Ed.2d 597 (2000). "The government's purpose is the controlling consideration. A regulation that serves purposes unrelated to the content of expression is deemed neutral, even if it has an incidental effect on some speakers or messages but not others." *Ward,* 491 U.S. at 791. The Supreme Court's approach to determining content-neutrality appears to be applicable whether what is regulated is expression, conduct, *see O'Brien,* 391 U.S. at 377, or any "activity" that can be said to combine speech and non-speech elements, *see Spence v. Washington,* 418 U.S. 405, 410–11, 94 S.Ct. 2727, 41 L.Ed.2d 842 (1974) (applying *O'Brien* to "activity" of displaying American flag hung upside down and decorated with a peace symbol).

To determine whether regulation of computer code is content-neutral, the initial inquiry must be whether the regulated activity is "sufficiently imbued with elements of communication to fall within the scope of the First ... Amendment[ ]." *Id.* at 409. Computer code, as we have noted, often conveys information comprehensible to human beings, even as it also directs a computer to perform various functions. Once a speech component is identified, the inquiry then proceeds to whether the regulation is "justified without reference to the content of regulated speech." *Hill,* 530 U.S. at 720.

The Appellants vigorously reject the idea that computer code can be regulated according to any different standard than that applicable to pure speech, *i.e.,* speech that lacks a nonspeech component. Although recognizing that code is a series of instructions to a computer, they argue that code is no different, for First Amendment purposes, than blueprints that instruct an engineer or recipes that instruct a cook. We disagree. Unlike a blueprint or a recipe, which cannot yield any functional result without human comprehension of its content, human decision-making, and human action, computer code can instantly cause a computer to accomplish tasks and instantly render the results of those tasks available throughout the world via the Internet. The only human action required to achieve these results can be as limited and instantaneous as a single click of a mouse. These realities of what code is and what its normal functions are require a First Amendment analysis that treats code as combining nonspeech and speech elements, *i.e.,* functional and expressive elements.

We recognize, as did Judge Kaplan, that the functional capability of computer code cannot yield a result until a human being decides to insert the disk containing the code into a computer and causes it to perform its function (or programs a computer to cause the code to perform its function). Nevertheless, this momentary intercession of human action does not diminish the nonspeech component of code, nor render code entirely speech, like a blueprint or a recipe.... The functionality of computer code properly affects the scope of its First Amendment protection.

4. The Scope of First Amendment Protection for Decryption Code

In considering the scope of First Amendment protection for a decryption program like DeCSS, we must recognize that the essential purpose of encryption code is to prevent unauthorized access. Owners of all property rights are entitled to prohibit access to their property by unauthorized persons. Homeowners can install locks on the doors of their houses. Custodians of valuables can place them in safes. Stores can attach to products security devices that will activate alarms if the products are taken away without purchase. These and similar security devices can be circumvented. Burglars can use skeleton keys to open door locks. Thieves can obtain the combinations to safes. Product security devices can be neutralized.

Our case concerns a security device, CSS computer code, that prevents access by unauthorized persons to DVD movies. The CSS code is embedded in the DVD movie. Access to the movie cannot be obtained unless a person has a device, a licensed DVD player, equipped with computer code capable of decrypting the CSS encryption code. In its basic function, CSS is like a lock on a homeowner's door, a combination of a safe, or a security device attached to a store's products.

DeCSS is computer code that can decrypt CSS. In its basic function, it is like a skeleton key that can open a locked door, a combination that can open a safe, or a device that can neutralize the security device attached to a store's products. DeCSS enables anyone to gain access to a DVD movie without using a DVD player.

The initial use of DeCSS to gain access to a DVD movie creates no loss to movie producers because the initial user must purchase the DVD. However, once the DVD is purchased, DeCSS enables the initial user to copy the movie in digital form and transmit it instantly in virtually limitless quantity, thereby depriving the movie producer of sales. The advent of the Internet creates the potential for instantaneous worldwide distribution of the copied material.

At first glance, one might think that Congress has as much authority to regulate the distribution of computer code to decrypt DVD movies as it has to regulate distribution of skeleton keys, combinations to safes, or devices to neutralize store product security devices. However, despite the evident legitimacy of protection against unauthorized access to DVD movies, just like any other property, regulation of decryption code like DeCSS is challenged in this case because DeCSS differs from a skeleton key in one important respect: it not only is capable of performing the function of unlocking the encrypted DVD movie, it also is a form of communication, albeit written in a language not understood by the general public. As a communication, the DeCSS code has a claim to being "speech," and as "speech," it has a claim to being protected by the First Amendment. But just as the realities of what any computer code can accomplish must inform the scope of its constitutional protection, so the capacity of a decryption program like DeCSS to accomplish unauthorized—indeed, unlawful—access to materials in which the Plaintiffs have intellectual property rights must inform and limit the scope of its First Amendment protection.

With all of the foregoing considerations in mind, we next consider the Appellants' First Amendment challenge to the DMCA as applied in the specific prohibitions that have been imposed by the District Court's injunction.

B. First Amendment Challenge

The District Court's injunction applies the DMCA to the Defendants by imposing two types of prohibition, both grounded on the anti-trafficking provisions of the DMCA. The first prohibits posting DeCSS or any other technology for circumventing CSS on any Internet web site. The second prohibits knowingly linking any Internet web site to any other web site containing DeCSS. The validity of the posting and linking prohibitions must be considered separately.

1. Posting.

The initial issue is whether the posting prohibition is content-neutral, since, as we have explained, this classification determines the applicable constitutional standard. The Appellants contend that the anti-trafficking provisions of the DMCA and their application by means of the posting prohibition of the injunction are content-based. They argue that the provisions "specifically target . . . scientific expression based on the particular topic addressed by that expression—namely, techniques for circumventing CSS." We disagree. The Appellants' argument fails to recognize that the target of the posting provisions of the injunction—DeCSS—has both a nonspeech and a speech component, and that the DMCA, as applied to the Appellants, and the posting prohibition of the injunction target only the nonspeech component. Neither the DMCA nor the posting prohibition is concerned with whatever capacity DeCSS might have for conveying information to a human being, and that capacity, as previously explained, is what arguably creates a speech component of the decryption code. The DMCA and the posting prohibition are applied to DeCSS solely because of its capacity to instruct a computer to decrypt CSS. That functional capability is not speech within the meaning of the First Amendment. The Government seeks to "justif[y]," *Hill,* 530 U.S. at 720, both the application of the DMCA and the posting prohibition to the Appellants solely on the basis of the functional capability of DeCSS to instruct a computer to decrypt CSS, *i.e.,* "without reference to the content of the regulated speech," *id.* This type of regulation is therefore content-neutral, just as would be a restriction on trafficking in skeleton keys identified because of their capacity to unlock jail cells, even though some of the keys happened to bear a slogan or other legend that qualified as a speech component.

As a content-neutral regulation with an incidental effect on a speech component, the regulation must serve a substantial governmental interest, the interest must be unrelated to the suppression of free expression, and the incidental restriction on speech must not burden substantially more speech than is necessary to further that interest. *Turner Broadcasting,* 512 U.S. at 662. The Government's interest in preventing unauthorized access to encrypted copyrighted material is unquestionably substantial, and the regulation of DeCSS by the posting prohibition plainly serves that interest. Moreover, that interest is unrelated to the suppression of free expression. The injunction regulates the posting of DeCSS, regardless of whether DeCSS code contains any information comprehensible by human beings that would qualify as speech. Whether the incidental regulation on speech burdens substantially more speech than is necessary to further the interest in preventing unauthorized access to copyrighted materials requires some elaboration.

Posting DeCSS on the Appellants' web site makes it instantly available at the click of a mouse to any person in the world with access to the Internet, and such person can then instantly transmit DeCSS to anyone else with Internet access. Although the prohibition on posting prevents the Appellants from conveying to others the speech component of DeCSS, the

Appellants have not suggested, much less shown, any technique for barring them from making this instantaneous worldwide distribution of a decryption code that makes a lesser restriction on the code's speech component. It is true that the Government has alternative means of prohibiting unauthorized access to copyrighted materials. For example, it can create criminal and civil liability for those who gain unauthorized access, and thus it can be argued that the restriction on posting DeCSS is not absolutely necessary to preventing unauthorized access to copyrighted materials. But a content-neutral regulation need not employ the least restrictive means of accomplishing the governmental objective. *Id.* It need only avoid burdening "substantially more speech than is necessary to further the government's legitimate interests." *Id.* The prohibition on the Defendants' posting of DeCSS satisfies that standard.

2. Linking

In considering linking, we need to clarify the sense in which the injunction prohibits such activity. Although the injunction defines several terms, it does not define "linking." Nevertheless, it is evident from the District Court's opinion that it is concerned with "hyperlinks". A hyperlink is a cross-reference (in a distinctive font or color) appearing on oneweb page that, when activated by the point-and-click of a mouse, brings onto the computer screen another web page. The hyperlink can appear on a screen (window) as text, such as the Internet address ("URL") of the web page being called up or a word or phrase that identifies the web page to be called up, for example, "DeCSS web site." Or the hyperlink can appear as an image, for example, an icon depicting a person sitting at a computer watching a DVD movie and text stating "click here to access DeCSS and see DVD movies for free!" The code for the web page containing the hyperlink contains a computer instruction that associates the link with the URL of the web page to be accessed, such that clicking on the hyperlink instructs the computer to enter the URL of the desired web page and thereby access that page. With a hyperlink on a web page, the linked web site is just one click away.

In applying the DMCA to linking (via hyperlinks), Judge Kaplan recognized, as he had with DeCSS code, that a hyperlink has both a speech and a nonspeech component. It conveys information, the Internet address of the linked web page, and has the functional capacity to bring the content of the linked web page to the user's computer screen (or, as Judge Kaplan put it, to "take one almost instantaneously to the desired destination."). As he had ruled with respect to DeCSS code, he ruled that application of the DMCA to the Defendants' linking to web sites containing DeCSS is content-neutral because it is justified without regard to the speech component of the hyperlink. The linking prohibition applies whether or not the hyperlink contains any information, comprehensible to a human being, as to the Internet address of the web page being accessed. The linking prohibition is justified solely by the functional capability of the hyperlink.

Applying the *O'Brien/Ward/Turner Broadcasting* requirements for content-neutral regulation, Judge Kaplan then ruled that the DMCA, as applied to the Defendants' linking, served substantial governmental interests and was unrelated to the suppression of free expression. We agree. He then carefully considered the "closer call," as to whether a linking prohibition would satisfy the narrow tailoring requirement. In an especially carefully considered portion of his opinion, he observed that strict liability for linking to web sites containing DeCSS would risk two impairments of free expression. Web site operators would be inhibited from displaying links to various web pages for fear that a linked page might contain DeCSS, and a prohibition on linking to a web site containing DeCSS would curtail access to whatever other information was contained at the accessed site.

To avoid applying the DMCA in a manner that would "burden substantially more speech than is necessary to further the government's legitimate interests," *Turner Broadcasting*, 512 U.S. at 662, Judge Kaplan adapted the standards of *New York Times Co. v. Sullivan*, 376 U.S. 254, 283, 84 S.Ct. 710, 11 L.Ed.2d 686 (1964), to fashion a limited prohibition against linking to web sites containing DeCSS. He required clear and convincing evidence

> that those responsible for the link (a) know at the relevant time that the offending material is on the linked-to site, (b) know that it is circumvention technology that may not lawfully be offered, and (c) create or maintain the link for the purpose of disseminating that technology.

Universal I, 111 F.Supp.2d at 341. He then found that the evidence satisfied his three-part test by his required standard of proof.

In response to our post-argument request for the parties' views on various issues, including specifically Judge Kaplan's test for a linking prohibition, the Appellants replied that his test was deficient for not requiring proof of intent to cause, or aid or abet, harm, and that the only valid test for a linking prohibition would be one that could validly apply to the publication in a print medium of an address for obtaining prohibited material. The Appellees and the Government accepted Judge Kaplan's criteria for purposes of asserting the validity of the injunction as applied to the Appellants, with the Government expressing reservations as to the standard of clear and convincing evidence.

Mindful of the cautious approach to First Amendment claims involving computer technology expressed in *Name.Space*, 202 F.3d at 584 n. 11, we see no need on this appeal to determine whether a test as rigorous as Judge Kaplan's is required to respond to First Amendment objections to the linking provision of the injunction that he issued. It suffices to reject the Appellants' contention that an intent to cause harm is required and that linking can be enjoined only under circumstances applicable to a print medium. As they have throughout their arguments, the Appellants ignore the reality of the functional capacity of decryption computer code and hyperlinks to facilitate instantaneous unauthorized access to copyrighted materials by anyone anywhere in the world. Under the circumstances amply shown by the record, the injunction's linking prohibition validly regulates the Appellants' opportunity instantly to enable anyone anywhere to gain unauthorized access to copyrighted movies on DVDs.

At oral argument, we asked the Government whether its undoubted power to punish the distribution of obscene materials would permit an injunction prohibiting a newspaper from printing addresses of bookstore locations carrying such materials. In a properly cautious response, the Government stated that the answer would depend on the circumstances of the publication. The Appellants' supplemental papers enthusiastically embraced the arguable analogy between printing bookstore addresses and displaying on a web page links to web sites at which DeCSS may be accessed. They confidently asserted that publication of bookstore locations carrying obscene material cannot be enjoined consistent with the First Amendment, and that a prohibition against linking to web sites containing DeCSS is similarly invalid.

Like many analogies posited to illuminate legal issues, the bookstore analogy is helpful primarily in identifying characteristics that *distinguish* it from the context of the pending dispute. If a bookstore proprietor is knowingly selling obscene materials, the evil of distributing such materials can be prevented by injunctive relief against the unlawful distribution (and similar distribution by others can be deterred by punishment of the distributor). And if others publish the location of the bookstore, preventive relief against a distributor can be effective before any significant distribution of the prohibited materials has occurred. The digital world, however, creates a very different problem. If obscene materials are posted on one web site and other sites post hyperlinks to the first site, the materials are available for instantaneous worldwide distribution before any preventive measures can be effectively taken.

This reality obliges courts considering First Amendment claims in the context of the pending case to choose between two unattractive alternatives: either tolerate some impairment of communication in order to permit Congress to prohibit decryption that may lawfully be prevented, or tolerate some decryption in order to avoid some impairment of communication. Although the parties dispute the extent of impairment of communication if the injunction is upheld and the extent of decryption if it is vacated, and differ on the availability and effectiveness of techniques for minimizing both consequences, the fundamental choice between impairing some communication and tolerating decryption cannot be entirely avoided.

In facing this choice, we are mindful that it is not for us to resolve the issues of public policy implicated by the choice we have identified. Those issues are for Congress. Our task is to determine whether the legislative solution adopted by Congress, as applied to the Appellants by the District Court's injunction, is consistent with the limitations of the First Amendment, and we are satisfied that it is.

IV. Constitutional Challenge Based on Claimed Restriction of Fair Use

Asserting that fair use "is rooted in and required by both the Copyright Clause and the First Amendment, the Appellants contend that the

DMCA, as applied by the District Court, unconstitutionally '*eliminates* fair use' of copyrighted materials." (Emphasis added). We reject this extravagant claim.

Preliminarily, we note that the Supreme Court has never held that fair use is constitutionally required, although some isolated statements in its opinions might arguably be enlisted for such a requirement. In *Stewart v. Abend*, 495 U.S. 207, 110 S.Ct. 1750, 109 L.Ed.2d 184 (1990), cited by the Appellants, the Court merely noted that fair use " 'permits courts to avoid rigid application of the copyright statute when, on occasion, it would stifle the very creativity which that law is designed to foster.' " In *Campbell v. Acuff–Rose Music, Inc.*, 510 U.S. 569 (1994), the Court observed, "From the infancy of copyright protection, some opportunity for fair use of copyrighted materials has been thought necessary to fulfill copyright's very purpose, '[t]o promote the Progress of Science and useful Arts....' " *Id.* at 575.

We need not explore the extent to which fair use might have constitutional protection, grounded on either the First Amendment or the Copyright Clause, because whatever validity a constitutional claim might have as to an application of the DMCA that impairs fair use of copyrighted materials, such matters are far beyond the scope of this lawsuit for several reasons. In the first place, the Appellants do not claim to be making fair use of any copyrighted materials, and nothing in the injunction prohibits them from making such fair use. They are barred from trafficking in a decryption code that enables unauthorized access to copyrighted materials.

Second, as the District Court properly noted, to whatever extent the anti-trafficking provisions of the DMCA might prevent others from copying portions of DVD movies in order to make fair use of them, "the evidence as to the impact of the anti-trafficking provision[s] of the DMCA on prospective fair users is scanty and fails adequately to address the issues."

Third, the Appellants have provided no support for their premise that fair use of DVD movies is constitutionally required to be made by copying the original work in its original format. Their examples of the fair uses that they believe others will be prevented from making all involve copying in a digital format those portions of a DVD movie amenable to fair use, a copying that would enable the fair user to manipulate the digitally copied portions. One example is that of a school child who wishes to copy images from a DVD movie to insert into the student's documentary film. We know of no authority for the proposition that fair use, as protected by the Copyright Act, much less the Constitution, guarantees copying by the optimum method or in the identical format of the original. Although the Appellants insisted at oral argument that they should not be relegated to a "horse and buggy" technique in making fair use of DVD movies, the DMCA does not impose even an arguable limitation on the opportunity to make a variety of traditional fair uses of DVD movies, such as commenting on their content, quoting excerpts from their screenplays, and even recording portions of the video images and sounds on film or tape by pointing a camera, a camcorder, or a microphone at a monitor as it displays the DVD movie. The fact that the resulting copy will not be as perfect or as manipulable as a digital copy obtained by having direct access to the DVD movie in its digital form, provides no basis for a claim of unconstitutional limitation of fair use. A film critic making fair use of a movie by quoting selected lines of dialogue has no constitutionally valid claim that the review (in print or on television) would be technologically superior if the reviewer had not been prevented from using a movie camera in the theater, nor has an art student a valid constitutional claim to fair use of a painting by photographing it in a museum. Fair use has never been held to be a guarantee of access to copyrighted material in order to copy it by the fair user's preferred technique or in the format of the original.

Conclusion

We have considered all the other arguments of the Appellants and conclude that they provide no basis for disturbing the District Court's judgment. Accordingly, the judgment is affirmed.

Diamond v. Diehr

Supreme Court of the United States, 1981.
450 U.S. 175, 101 S.Ct. 1048, 67 L.Ed.2d 155, 209 U.S.P.Q. 1.

Mr. Justice REHNQUIST delivered the opinion of the Court.

We granted certiorari to determine whether a process for curing synthetic rubber which includes in several of its steps the use of a mathematical formula and a programmed digital computer is patentable subject matter under 35 U.S.C.A. § 101.

I.

The patent application at issue was filed by the respondents on August 6, 1975. The claimed invention is a process for molding raw, uncured synthetic rubber into cured precision products. The process uses a mold for precisely shaping the uncured material under heat and pressure and then curing the synthetic rubber in the mold so that the product will retain its shape and be functionally operative after the molding is completed.[1]

Respondents claim that their process ensures the production of molded articles which are properly cured. Achieving the perfect cure depends upon several factors including the thickness of the article to be molded, the temperature of the molding process, and the amount of time that the article is allowed to remain in the press. It is possible using well-known time, temperature, and cure relationships to calculate by means of the Arrhenius equation[2] when to open the press and remove the cured product. Nonetheless, according to the respondents, the industry has not been able to obtain uniformly accurate cures because the temperature of the molding press could not be precisely measured thus making it difficult to do the necessary computations to determine cure time. Because the temperature *inside* the press has heretofore been viewed as an uncontrollable variable, the conventional industry practice has been to calculate the cure time as the shortest time in which all parts of the product will definitely be cured,

---

1. A "cure" is obtained by mixing curing agents into the uncured polymer in advance of molding, and then applying heat over a period of time. If the synthetic rubber is cured for the right length of time at the right temperature, it becomes a useable product.

2. The equation is named after its discoverer Svante Arrhenius and has long been used to calculate the cure time in rubber molding presses. The equation can be expressed as follows:

$$\ln v = CZ + x$$

wherein ln v is the natural logarithm of v, the total required cure time; C is the activation constant, a unique figure for each batch of each compound being molded, determined in accordance with rheometer measurements of each batch; Z is the temperature in the mold; and x is a constant dependent on the geometry of the particular mold in the press. A rheometer is an instrument to measure flow of viscous substances.

assuming a reasonable amount of mold-opening time during loading and unloading. But the shortcoming of this practice is that operating with an uncontrollable variable inevitably led in some instances to overestimating the mold-opening time and overcuring the rubber, and in other instances to underestimating that time and undercuring the product.

Respondents characterize their contribution to the art to reside in the process of constantly measuring the actual temperature inside the mold. These temperature measurements are then automatically fed into a computer which repeatedly recalculates the cure time by use of the Arrhenius equation. When the recalculated time equals the actual time that has elapsed since the press was closed, the computer signals a device to open the press. According to the respondents, the continuous measuring of the temperature inside the mold cavity, the feeding of this information to a digital computer which constantly recalculates the cure time, and the signaling by the computer to open the press, are all new in the art.

The patent examiner rejected the respondents' claims on the sole ground that they were drawn to nonstatutory subject matter under 35 U.S.C.A. § 101.[5] He determined that those steps in respondents' claims that are carried out by a computer under control of a stored program

---

5. Respondents' application contained 11 different claims. Three examples are claims 1, 2, and 11 which provide:

"1. A method of operating a rubber-molding press for precision molded compounds with the aid of a digital computer, comprising:

"providing said computer with a data base for said press including at least,

"natural logarithm conversion data (ln),

"the activation energy constant (C) unique to each batch of said compound being molded, and

"a constant (x) dependent upon the geometry of the particular mold of the press,

"initiating an interval timer in said computer upon the closure of the press for monitoring the elapsed time of said closure,

"constantly determining the temperature (Z) of the mold at a location closely adjacent to the mold cavity in the press during molding,

"constantly providing the computer with the temperature (Z),

"repetitively calculating in the computer, at frequent intervals during each

cure, the Arrhenius equation for reaction time during the cure, which is

"$\ln v = CZ + x$

"where v is the total required cure time,

"repetitively comparing in the computer at said frequent intervals during the cure each said calculation of the total required cure time calculated with the Arrhenius equation and said elapsed time, and

"opening the press automatically when a said comparison indicates equivalence.

"2. The method of claim 1 including measuring the activation energy constant for the compound being molded in the press with a rheometer and automatically updating said data base within the computer in the event of changes in the compound being molded in said press as measured by said rheometer.

"11. A method of manufacturing precision molded articles from selected synthetic rubber compounds in an openable rubber molding press having at least one heated precision mold, comprising:

"(a) heating said mold to a temperature range approximating a predetermined rubber curing temperature, constituted nonstatutory subject matter under this Court's decision in Gottschalk v. Benson, 409 U.S. 63 (1972). The remaining steps—installing rubber in the press and the subsequent closing of the press—were "conventional in nature and cannot be the basis of patentability." The examiner concluded that respondents' claims defined and sought protection of a computer program for operating a rubber molding press.

The Patent and Trademark Office Board of Appeals agreed with the examiner, but the Court of Customs and Patent Appeals reversed. The court noted that a claim drawn to subject matter otherwise statutory does not become nonstatutory because a computer is involved. The respondents' claims were not directed to a mathematical algorithm or an improved method of calculation but rather recited an improved process for molding rubber articles by solving a practical problem which had arisen in the molding of rubber products.

The Government sought certiorari arguing that the decision of the Court of Customs and Patent Appeals was inconsistent with prior decisions of this Court. Because of the importance of the question presented, we granted the writ.

II.

Last Term in Diamond v. Chakrabarty, 447 U.S. 303, 100 S.Ct. 2204, 65 L.Ed.2d 144 (1980), this Court discussed the historical purposes of the

"(b) installing prepared unmolded synthetic rubber of a known compound in a molding cavity of a predetermined geometry as defined by said mold,

"(c) closing said press to mold said rubber to occupy said cavity in conformance with the contour of said mold and to cure said rubber by transfer of heat thereto from said mold,

"(d) initiating an interval timer upon the closure of said press for monitoring the elapsed time of said closure,

"(e) heating said mold during said closure to maintain the temperature thereof within said range approximating said rubber curing temperature,

"(f) constantly determining the temperature of said mold at a location closely adjacent said cavity thereof throughout closure of said press,

"(g) repetitively calculating at frequent periodic intervals throughout closure of said press the Arrhenius equation for reaction time of said rubber to determine total required cure time v as follows:

"$\ln v = cz + x$

"wherein c is an activation energy constant determined for said rubber being molded and cured in said press, z is the temperature of said mold at the time of each calculation of said Arrhenius equation, and x is a constant which is a function of said predetermined geometry of said mold,

"(h) for each repetition of calculation of said Arrhenius equation herein, comparing the resultant calculated total required cure time with the monitored elapsed time measured by said interval timer,

"(i) opening said press when a said comparison of calculated total required cure time and monitored elapsed time indicates equivalence, and

"(j) removing from said mold the resultant precision molded and cured rubber article."

patent laws and in particular 35 U.S.C.A. § 101. As in *Chakrabarty,* we must here construe 35 U.S.C.A. § 101 which provides:

> Whoever invents or discovers any new or useful process, machine, manufacture, or composition of matter, or any new and useful improvement thereof, may obtain a patent therefor, subject to the conditions and requirements of this Title.

In cases of statutory construction, we begin with the language of the statute. Unless otherwise defined, "words will be interpreted as taking their ordinary, contemporary, common meaning," Perrin v. United States, 444 U.S. 37, 42, 100 S.Ct. 311, 314, 62 L.Ed.2d 199 (1979), and, in dealing with the patent laws, we have more than once cautioned that "courts 'should not read into the patent laws limitations and conditions which a legislature has not expressed.'" Diamond v. Chakrabarty, supra, at 308, 100 S.Ct., at 2207, quoting United States v. Dubilier Condenser Corp., 289 U.S. 178, 199 (1933).

The Patent Act of 1793 defined statutory subject matter as "any new and useful art, machine, manufacture or composition of matter, or any new or useful improvement [thereof]." Act of Feb. 21, 1793, ch. 11, § 1, 1 Stat. 318. Not until the patent laws were recodified in 1952 did Congress replace the word "art" with the word "process." It is that latter word which we confront today, and in order to determine its meaning we may not be unmindful of the Committee Reports accompanying the 1952 Act which inform us that Congress intended statutory subject matter to "include anything under the sun that is made by man." S.Rep. No. 1979, 82d Cong., 2d Sess. 5 (1952); H.R.Rep. No. 1923, 82d Cong., 2d Sess. 6 (1952).

Although the term "process" was not added to 35 U.S.C.A. § 101 until 1952, a process has historically enjoyed patent protection because it was considered a form of "art" as that term was used in the 1793 Act. In defining the nature of a patentable process, the Court stated:

> That a process may be patentable, irrespective of the particular form of the instrumentalities used, cannot be disputed.... A process is a mode of treatment of certain materials to produce a given result. It is an act, or a series of acts, performed upon the subject matter to be transformed and reduced to a different state or thing. If new and useful, it is just as patentable as is a piece of machinery. In the language of the patent law, it is an art. The machinery pointed out as suitable to perform the process may or may not be new or patentable; whilst the process itself may be altogether new, and produce an entirely new result. The process requires that certain things should be done with certain substances, and in a certain order; but the tools to be used in doing this may be of secondary consequence. Cochrane v. Deener, 94 U.S. 780, 787–788 (1876).

Analysis of the eligibility of a claim of patent protection for a "process" did not change with the addition of that term to § 101. Recently, in Gottschalk v. Benson, 409 U.S. 63 (1972), we repeated the above definition recited in Cochrane v. Deener, adding "Transformation and reduction of an article 'to a different state or thing' is the clue to the patentability of a process claim that does not include particular machines." Id., at 70.

Analyzing respondents' claims according to the above statements from our cases, we think that a physical and chemical process for molding precision synthetic rubber products falls within the § 101 categories of possibly patentable subject matter. That respondents' claims involve the transformation of an article, in this case raw uncured synthetic rubber, into a different state or thing cannot be disputed. The respondents' claims describe in detail a step-by-step method for accomplishing such beginning with the loading of a mold with raw uncured rubber and ending with the eventual opening of the press at the conclusion of the cure. Industrial processes such as this are the type which have historically been eligible to receive the protection of our patent laws.

III.

Our conclusion regarding respondents' claims is not altered by the fact that in several steps of the process a mathematical equation and a programmed digital computer are used. This Court has undoubtedly recognized limits to § 101 and every discovery is not embraced within the statutory terms. Excluded from such patent protection are laws of nature, physical phenomena and abstract ideas. See Parker v. Flook, 437 U.S. 584 (1978); Gottschalk v. Benson, 409 U.S. 63, 67 (1972); Funk Bros. Seed Co. v. Kalo Inoculant Co., 333 U.S. 127, 130 (1948). "An idea of itself is not patentable," Rubber–Tip Pencil Co. v. Howard, 20 Wall. 498, 507 (1874). "A principle, in the abstract, is a fundamental truth; an original cause; a motive; these cannot be patented, as no one can claim in either of them an exclusive right." Le Roy v. Tatham, 14 How. 156, 175 (1852). Only last Term, we explained:

> [A] new mineral discovered in the earth or a new plant found in the wild is not patentable subject matter. Likewise, Einstein could not patent his celebrated law that $E=mc^2$; nor could Newton have patented the law of gravity. Such discoveries are "manifestations of . . . nature, free to all men and reserved exclusively to none." Diamond v. Chakrabarty, 447 U.S. at 309, 100 S.Ct., at 2208, quoting Funk Bros. Seed Co. v. Kalo Inoculant Co., 333 U.S. 127, 130 (1948).

Our recent holdings in *Gottschalk v. Benson,* supra, and *Parker v. Flook,* supra, both of which are computer-related, stand for no more than these long established principles. In *Benson,* we held unpatentable claims for an algorithm used to convert binary code decimal numbers to equivalent pure binary numbers. The sole practical application of the algorithm was in connection with the programming of a general purpose digital computer. We defined "algorithm" as a "procedure for solving a given type of mathematical problem," and we concluded that such an algorithm, or mathematical formula, is like a law of nature, which cannot be the subject of a patent.

Parker v. Flook, supra, presented a similar situation. The claims were drawn to a method for computing an "alarm limit." An "alarm limit" is simply a number and the Court concluded that the application sought to protect a formula for computing this number. Using this formula, the updated alarm limit could be calculated if several other variables were known. The application, however, did not purport to explain how these other variables were to be determined, nor did it purport "to contain any disclosure relating to the chemical processes at work, the monitoring of process variables, or the means of setting off an alarm system. All that is provided is a formula for computing an updated alarm limit." 437 U.S. at 586.

In contrast, the respondents here do not seek to patent a mathematical formula. Instead, they seek patent protection for a process of curing synthetic rubber. Their process admittedly employs a well known mathematical equation, but they do not seek to pre-empt the use of that equation. Rather, they seek only to foreclose from others the use of that equation in conjunction with all of the other steps in their claimed process. These include installing rubber in a press, closing the mold, constantly determining the temperature of the mold, constantly recalculating the appropriate cure time through the use of the formula and a digital computer and, automatically opening the press at the proper time. Obviously, one does not need a "computer" to cure natural or synthetic rubber, but if the computer use incorporated in the process patent significantly lessens the possibility of "overcuring" or "undercuring," the process as a whole does not thereby become unpatentable subject matter.

Our earlier opinions lend support to our present conclusion that a claim drawn to subject matter otherwise statutory does not become non-statutory simply because it uses a mathematical formula, computer program or digital computer. In *Gottschalk v. Benson,* supra, we noted "It is said that the decision precludes a patent for any program servicing a computer. We do not so hold." 409 U.S., at 71. Similarly, in *Parker v. Flook,* supra, we stated, "A process is not unpatentable simply because it contains a law of nature or a mathematical algorithm." 437 U.S., at 590. It is now commonplace that an *application* of a law of nature or mathematical formula to a known structure or process may well be deserving of patent protection. As Mr. Justice Stone explained four decades ago:

> While a scientific truth, or the mathematical expression of it, is not a patentable invention, a novel and useful structure created with the aid of knowledge of scientific truth may be. MacKay Radio & Telegraph Co. v. Radio Corp. of America, 306 U.S. 86, 94 (1939).

We think this statement in *MacKay* takes us a long way toward the correct answer in this case. Arrhenius' equation is not patentable in isolation, but when a process for curing rubber is devised which incorporates in it a more efficient solution of the equation, that process is at the very least not barred at the threshold by § 101.

In determining the eligibility of respondents' claimed process for patent protection under § 101, their claims must be considered as a whole. It is inappropriate to dissect the claims into old and new elements and then to ignore the presence of the old elements in the analysis. This is particularly true in a process claim because a new combination of steps in a process may be patentable even though all the constituents of the combination were well known and in common use before the combination was made. The "novelty" of any element or steps in a process, or even of the process itself, is of no relevance in determining whether the subject matter of a claim falls within the § 101 categories of possibly patentable subject matter.[12]

It has been urged that novelty is an appropriate consideration under § 101. Presumably, this argument results from the language in § 101 referring to any "new and useful" process, machine, etc. Section 101, however, is a general statement of the type of subject matter that is eligible for patent protection "subject to the conditions and requirements of this title." Specific conditions for patentability follow and § 102 covers in detail the conditions relating to novelty. The question therefore of whether a particular invention is novel is "fully apart from whether the invention falls into a category of statutory subject matter." In re Bergy, 596 F.2d 952, 961 (CCPA 1979). The legislative history of the 1952 Patent Act is in accord with this reasoning. The Senate Report provided:

> Section 101 sets forth the subject matter that can be patented, "subject to the conditions and requirement of this title." The conditions under which a patent may be obtained follow, and *Section 102 covers the conditions relating to novelty.* S.Rep.No. 1979, 82d Cong., 2d Sess. 5 (1952) (emphasis supplied).

It is later stated in the same report:

> Section 102, in general, may be said to describe the statutory novelty required for patentability, and includes, in effect, the amplification and definition of "new" in Section 101. Id., at 6.

Finally, it is stated in the "Revision Notes":

> The corresponding section of [the] existing statute is split into two sections, Section 101 relating to the subject matter for which patents may be obtained, and Section 102 defining statutory novelty and stating other conditions for patentability. Id., at 17.

In this case, it may later be determined that the respondents' process is not deserving of patent protection because it fails to satisfy the statutory conditions of novelty under § 102 or nonobviousness under § 103. A

---

12. It is argued that the procedure of dissecting a claim into old and new elements is mandated by our decision in *Flook* which noted that a mathematical algorithm must be assumed to be within the "prior art." It is from this language that the Government premises its argument that if everything other than the algorithm is determined to be old in the art, then the claim cannot recite statutory subject matter. The fallacy in this argument is that we did not hold in *Flook* that the mathematical algorithm could not be considered at all when making the § 101 determination. To accept the analysis proffered by the Government would, if carried to its extreme, make all inventions unpatentable because all inventions can be reduced to underlying principles of nature which, once known, make their implementation obvious. The analysis suggested by the Government would also undermine our earlier decisions regarding the criteria to consider in determining the eligibility of a process for patent protection.

rejection on either of these grounds does not affect the determination that respondents' claims recited subject matter which was eligible for patent protection under § 101.

IV.

We have before us today only the question of whether respondents' claims fall within the § 101 categories of possibly patentable subject matter. We view respondents' claims as nothing more than a process for molding rubber products and not as an attempt to patent a mathematical formula. We recognize, of course, that when a claim recites a mathematical formula (or scientific principle or phenomenon of nature), an inquiry must be made into whether the claim is seeking patent protection for that formula in the abstract. A mathematical formula as such is not accorded the protection of our patent laws and this principle cannot be circumvented by attempting to limit the use of the formula to a particular technological environment. Similarly, insignificant post-solution activity will not transform an unpatentable principle into a patentable process. To hold otherwise would allow a competent draftsman to evade the recognized limitations on the type of subject matter eligible for patent protection. On the other hand, when a claim containing a mathematical formula implements or applies that formula in a structure or process which, when considered as a whole, is performing a function which the patent laws were designed to protect (e.g., transforming or reducing an article to a different state or thing), then the claim satisfies the requirements of § 101. Because we do not view respondents' claims as an attempt to patent a mathematical formula, but rather to be drawn to an industrial process for the molding of rubber products, we affirm the judgment of the Court of Customs and Patent Appeals.

Justice STEVENS, with whom Justice BRENNAN, Justice MARSHALL, and Justice BLACKMUN join, dissenting.

The starting point in the proper adjudication of patent litigation is an understanding of what the inventor claims to have discovered. The Court's decision in this case rests on a misreading of the Diehr and Lutton patent application. Moreover, the Court has compounded its error by ignoring the critical distinction between the character of the subject matter that the inventor claims to be novel—the § 101 issue—and the question whether that subject matter is in fact novel—the § 102 issue.

I.

Before discussing the major flaws in the Court's opinion, a word of history may be helpful. As the Court recognized in Parker v. Flook, 437 U.S. 584, 595 (1978), the computer industry is relatively young. Although computer technology seems commonplace today, the first digital computer capable of utilizing stored programs was developed less than 30 years ago. Patent law developments in response to this new technology are of even more recent vintage. The subject of legal protection for computer programs did not begin to receive serious consideration until over a decade after completion of the first programmable digital computer. It was 1968 before the federal courts squarely addressed the subject, and 1972 before this Court announced its first decision in the area.

Prior to 1968, well-established principles of patent law probably would have prevented the issuance of a valid patent on almost any conceivable computer program. Under the "mental steps" doctrine, processes involving mental operations were considered unpatentable. The mental steps doctrine was based upon the familiar principle that a scientific concept or mere idea cannot be the subject of a valid patent. The doctrine was regularly invoked to deny patents to inventions consisting primarily of mathematical formulae or methods of computation. It was also applied against patent claims in which a mental operation or mathematical computation was the sole novel element or inventive contribution; it was clear that patentability could not be predicated upon a mental step. Under the "function of a machine" doctrine, a process which amounted to nothing more than a description of the function of a machine was unpatentable. This doctrine had its origin in several 19th–century decisions of this Court, and it had been consistently followed thereafter by the lower federal courts. Finally, the definition of "process" announced by this Court in Cochrane v. Deener, 94 U.S. 780, 787–788 (1876), seemed to indicate that a patentable process must cause a physical transformation in the materials to which the process is applied.

Concern with the patent system's ability to deal with rapidly changing technology in the computer and other fields led to the formation in 1965 of the President's Commission on the Patent System. After studying the question of computer program patentability, the Commission recommended that computer programs be expressly excluded from the coverage of the patent laws; this recommendation was based primarily upon the Patent Office's inability to deal with the administrative burden of examining program applications. At approximately the time that the Commission issued its report, the Patent Office published notice of its intention to prescribe guidelines for the examination of applications for patents on computer programs. Under the proposed guidelines, a computer program, whether claimed as an apparatus or as a process, was unpatentable. The Patent Office indicated, however, that a programmed computer could be a component of a patentable process if combined with unobvious elements to produce a physical result. The Patent Office formally adopted the guidelines in 1968.

The new guidelines were to have a short life. Beginning with two decisions in 1968, a dramatic change in the law as understood by the Court of Customs and Patent Appeals took place. By repudiating the well-settled "function of a machine" and "mental steps" doctrines, that court reinterpreted § 101 of the Patent Code to enlarge drastically the categories of patentable subject matter. This reinterpretation would lead to the conclusion that computer programs were within the categories of inventions to which Congress intended to extend patent protection.

In In re Tarczy-Hornoch, 397 F.2d 856 (CCPA 1968), a divided Court of Customs and Patent Appeals overruled the line of cases developing and applying the "function of a machine" doctrine. The majority acknowledged that the doctrine had originated with decisions of this Court and that the lower federal courts, including the Court of Customs and Patent Appeals, had consistently adhered to it during the preceding 70 years. Nonetheless, the court concluded that the doctrine rested on a misinterpretation of the precedents and that it was contrary to "the basic purposes of the patent system and productive of a range of undesirable results from the harshly inequitable to the silly." Id., at 867. Shortly thereafter, a similar fate befell the "mental steps" doctrine. In In re Prater, 415 F.2d 1378 (1968), modified on rehearing, 415 F.2d 1393 (CCPA 1969), the court found that the precedents on which that doctrine was based either were poorly reasoned or had been misinterpreted over the years. The court concluded that the fact that a process may be performed mentally should not foreclose patentability if the claims reveal that the process also may be performed without mental operations. This aspect of the original *Prater* opinion was substantially undisturbed by the opinion issued after rehearing. However, the second *Prater* opinion clearly indicated that patent claims broad enough to encompass the operation of a programmed computer would not be rejected for lack of patentable subject matter.

The Court of Customs and Patent Appeals soon replaced the overruled doctrines with more expansive principles formulated with computer technology in mind. In In re Bernhart, 417 F.2d 1395 (CCPA 1969), the court reaffirmed *Prater,* and indicated that all that remained of the mental steps doctrine was a prohibition on the granting of a patent that would confer a monopoly on all uses of a scientific principle or mathematical equation. The court also announced that a computer programmed with a new and unobvious program was physically different from the same computer without that program; the programmed computer was a new machine or at least a new improvement over the unprogrammed computer. Therefore, patent protection could be obtained for new computer programs if the patent claims were drafted in apparatus form.

The Court of Customs and Patent Appeals turned its attention to process claims encompassing computer programs in In re Musgrave, 431 F.2d 882 (CCPA 1970). In that case, the court emphasized the fact that *Prater* had done away with the mental steps doctrine; in particular, the court rejected the Patent Office's continued reliance upon the "point of novelty" approach to claim analysis.[15] The court also announced a new standard for evaluating process claims under § 101: any sequence of operational steps was a patentable process under § 101 as long as it was within the "technological arts." This standard effectively disposed of any vestiges of the mental steps doctrine remaining after *Prater* and *Bernhart.* The "technological arts" standard was refined in In re Benson, 441 F.2d 682 (CCPA 1971), in which the court held that computers, regardless of the

---

15. Under the "point of novelty" approach, if the novelty or advancement in the art claimed by the inventor resided solely in a step of the process embodying a mental operation or other unpatentable element, the claim was rejected under § 101 as being directed to nonstatutory subject matter.

uses to which they are put, are within the technological arts for purposes of § 101.

In re Benson, of course, was reversed by this Court in Gottschalk v. Benson, 409 U.S. 63 (1972). Justice Douglas' opinion for a unanimous Court made no reference to the lower court's rejection of the mental steps doctrine or to the new technological arts standard. Rather, the Court clearly held that new mathematical procedures that can be conducted in old computers, like mental processes and abstract intellectual concepts, are not patentable processes within the meaning of § 101.

The Court of Customs and Patent Appeals had its first opportunity to interpret *Benson* in In re Christensen, 478 F.2d 1392 (CCPA 1973). In *Christensen,* the claimed invention was a method in which the only novel element was a mathematical formula. The court resurrected the point of novelty approach abandoned in *Musgrave* and held that a process claim in which the point of novelty was a mathematical equation to be solved as the final step of the process did not define patentable subject matter after *Benson.* Accordingly, the court affirmed the Board of Patent Appeals' rejection of the claims under § 101.

The Court of Customs and Patent Appeals in subsequent cases began to narrow its interpretation of *Benson.* In In re Johnston, 502 F.2d 765 (CCPA 1974), the court held that a record-keeping machine system which comprised a programmed digital computer was patentable subject matter under § 101. The majority dismissed *Benson* with the observation that *Benson* involved only process, not apparatus, claims. Judge Rich dissented, arguing that to limit *Benson* only to process claims would make patentability turn upon the form in which a program invention was claimed. The court again construed *Benson* as limited only to process claims in In re Noll, 545 F.2d 141 (CCPA 1976), cert. denied, 434 U.S. 875 (1977); apparatus claims were governed by the court's pre-*Benson* conclusion that a programmed computer was structurally different from the same computer without that particular program. In dissent, Judge Lane, joined by Judge Rich, argued that *Benson* should be read as a general proscription of the patenting of computer programs regardless of the form of the claims. Judge Lane's interpretation of *Benson* was rejected by the majority in In re Chatfield, 545 F.2d 152 (CCPA 1976), cert. denied, 434 U.S. 875 (1977), decided on the same day as *Noll.* In that case, the court construed *Benson* to preclude the patenting of program inventions claimed as processes only where the claims would pre-empt all uses of an algorithm or mathematical formula. The dissenting judges argued, as they had in *Noll,* that *Benson* held that programs for general-purpose digital computers are not patentable subject matter.

Following *Noll* and *Chatfield,* the Court of Customs and Patent Appeals consistently interpreted *Benson* to preclude the patenting of a program-related process invention only when the claims, if allowed, would wholly pre-empt the algorithm itself. One of the cases adopting this view was In re Flook, 559 F.2d 21 (CCPA 1977), which was reversed in Parker v. Flook, 437 U.S. 584 (1978). Before this Court decided *Flook,* however, the lower court developed a two-step procedure for analyzing program-related inventions in light of *Benson*. In In re Freeman, 573 F.2d 1237 (CCPA 1978), the court held that such inventions must first be examined to determine whether a mathematical algorithm is directly or indirectly claimed; if an algorithm is recited, the court must then determine whether the claim would wholly pre-empt that algorithm. Only if a claim satisfied both inquiries was *Benson* considered applicable.

In *Flook*, this Court clarified *Benson* in three significant respects. First, *Flook* held that the *Benson* rule of unpatentable subject matter was not limited, as the lower court believed, to claims which wholly pre-empted an algorithm or amounted to a patent on the algorithm itself. Second, the Court made it clear that an improved method of calculation, even when employed as part of a physical process, is not patentable subject matter under § 101. Finally, the Court explained the correct procedure for analyzing a patent claim employing a mathematical algorithm. Under this procedure, the algorithm is treated for § 101 purposes as though it were a familiar part of the prior art; the claim is then examined to determine whether it discloses "some other inventive concept."

Although the Court of Customs and Patent Appeals in several post-*Flook* decisions held that program-related inventions were not patentable subject matter under § 101, in general *Flook* was not enthusiastically received by that court. In In re Bergy, 596 F.2d 952 (CCPA 1979), the majority engaged in an extensive critique of *Flook,* concluding that this Court had erroneously commingled "distinct statutory provisions which are conceptually unrelated." In subsequent cases, the court construed *Flook* as resting on nothing more than the way in which the patent claims had been drafted, and it expressly declined to use the method of claim analysis spelled out in that decision. The Court of Customs and Patent Appeals has taken the position that, if an application is drafted in a way that discloses an entire process as novel, it defines patentable subject matter even if the only novel element that the inventor claims to have discovered is a new computer program. The court interpreted *Flook* in this manner in its opinion in this case. In my judgment, this reading of *Flook*—although entirely consistent with the lower court's expansive approach to § 101 during the past 12 years—trivializes the holding in *Flook,* the principle that underlies *Benson,* and the settled line of authority reviewed in those opinions.

II.

As I stated at the outset, the starting point in the proper adjudication of patent litigation is an understanding of what the inventor claims to have discovered. Indeed, the outcome of such litigation is often determined by the judge's understanding of the patent application. This is such a case.

In the first sentence of its opinion, the Court states the question presented as "whether a process for curing synthetic rubber ... is patentable subject matter." Of course, that question was effectively answered many years ago when Charles Goodyear obtained his patent on the vulcanization process. The patent application filed by Diehr and Lutton, however, teaches nothing about the chemistry of the synthetic rubber-curing process, nothing about the raw materials to be used in curing synthetic rubber, nothing about the equipment to be used in the process, and nothing about the significance or effect of any process variable such as temperature, curing time, particular compositions of material, or mold configurations. In short, Diehr and Lutton do not claim to have discovered anything new about the process for curing synthetic rubber.

As the Court reads the claims in the Diehr and Lutton patent application, the inventors' discovery is a method of constantly measuring the actual temperature inside a rubber molding press. As I read the claims, their discovery is an improved method of calculating the time that the mold should remain closed during the curing process. If the Court's reading of the claims were correct, I would agree that they disclose patentable subject matter. On the other hand, if the Court accepted my reading, I feel confident that the case would be decided differently.

There are three reasons why I cannot accept the Court's conclusion that Diehr and Lutton claim to have discovered a new method of constantly measuring the temperature inside a mold. First, there is not a word in the patent application that suggests that there is anything unusual about the temperature-reading devices used in this process—or indeed that any particular species of temperature-reading device should be used in it. Second, since devices for constantly measuring actual temperatures—on a back porch, for example—have been familiar articles for quite some time, I find it difficult to believe that a patent application filed in 1975 was premised on the notion that a "process of constantly measuring the actual temperature" had just been discovered. Finally, the Board of Patent Appeals expressly found that "the only difference between the conventional methods of operating a molding press and that claimed in [the] application rests in those steps of the claims which relate to the calculation incident to the solution of the mathematical problem or formula used to control the mold heater and the automatic opening of the press." This finding was not disturbed by the Court of Customs and Patent Appeals and is clearly correct.

A fair reading of the entire patent application, as well as the specific claims, makes it perfectly clear that what Diehr and Lutton claim to have discovered is a method of using a digital computer to determine the amount of time that a rubber molding press should remain closed during the synthetic rubber curing process. There is no suggestion that there is anything novel in the instrumentation of the mold, in actuating a timer when the press is closed, or in automatically opening the press when the computed time expires. Nor does the application suggest that Diehr and Lutton have discovered anything about the temperatures in the mold or the amount of curing time that will produce the best cure. What they claim to have discovered, in essence, is a method of updating the original estimated curing time by repetitively recalculating that time pursuant to a well-known mathematical formula in response to variations in temperature within the mold. Their method of updating the curing time calculation is strikingly reminiscent of the method of updating alarm limits that Dale Flook sought to patent.

Parker v. Flook, 437 U.S. 584 (1978), involved the use of a digital computer in connection with a catalytic conversion process. During the conversion process, variables such as temperature, pressure, and flow rates were constantly monitored and fed into the computer; in this case, temperature in the mold is the variable that is monitored and fed into the computer. In *Flook,* the digital computer repetitively recalculated the "alarm limit"—a number that might signal the need to terminate or modify the catalytic conversion process; in this case, the digital computer repetitively recalculates the correct curing time—a number that signals the time when the synthetic rubber molding press should open.

The essence of the claimed discovery in both cases was an algorithm that could be programmed on a digital computer. In *Flook,* the algorithm made use of multiple process variables; in this case, it makes use of only one. In *Flook,* the algorithm was expressed in a newly-developed mathematical formula; in this case, the algorithm makes use of a well-known mathematical formula. Manifestly, neither of these differences can explain today's holding.[32] What I believe does explain today's holding is a misunderstanding of the applicants' claimed invention and a failure to recognize the critical difference between the "discovery" requirement in § 101 and the "novelty" requirement in § 102.

III.

The Court misapplies *Parker v. Flook* because, like the Court of Customs and Patent Appeals, it fails to understand or completely disre-

---

32. Indeed, the most significant distinction between the invention at issue in *Flook* and that at issue in this case lies not in the characteristics of the inventions themselves, but rather in the drafting of the claims. After noting that "[t]he Diehr claims are reminiscent of the claims in *Flook,*" Blumenthal & Riter, 62 J.Pat.Off.Soc'y, at 502–503, the authors of a recent article on the subject observe that the Court of Customs and Patent Appeals' analysis in this case "lends itself to an interesting exercise in claim drafting." Id., at 505. To illustrate their point, the authors redrafted the Diehr and Lutton claims into the format employed in the *Flook* application:

"An improved method of calculating the cure time of a rubber molding process utilizing a digital computer comprising the steps of:

"a. inputting into said computer input values including

"1. natural logarithm conversion data (ln),

"2. an activation energy constant (C) unique to each batch of rubber being molded,

"3. a constant (X) dependent upon the geometry of the particular mold of the press, and

"4. continuous temperature values (Z) of the mold during molding;

"b. operating said computer for

"1. counting the elapsed cure time,

"2. calculating the cure time from the input values using the Arrhenius equation $\ln v = CZ + X$, where v is the total cure time, and

"c. providing output signals from said computer when said calculated cure time is equal to said elapsed cure time." Id., at 505.

The authors correctly conclude that even the lower court probably would have found that this claim was drawn to unpatentable subject matter under § 101.

gards the distinction between the subject matter of what the inventor *claims* to have discovered—the § 101 issue—and the question whether that claimed discovery is in fact novel—the § 102 issue. If there is not even a claim that anything constituting patentable subject matter has been discovered, there is no occasion to address the novelty issue. Or, as was true in *Flook,* if the only concept that the inventor claims to have discovered is not patentable subject matter, § 101 requires that the application be rejected without reaching any issue under § 102; for it is irrelevant that unpatentable subject matter—in that case a formula for updating alarm limits—may in fact be novel.

Proper analysis, therefore, must start with an understanding of what the inventor claims to have discovered—or phrased somewhat differently—what he considers his inventive concept to be. It seems clear to me that Diehr and Lutton claim to have developed a new method of programming a digital computer in order to calculate—promptly and repeatedly—the correct curing time in a familiar process. In the § 101 analysis, we must assume that the sequence of steps in this programming method is novel, unobvious, and useful. The threshold question of whether such a method is patentable subject matter remains.

If that method is regarded as an "algorithm" as that term was used in Gottschalk v. Benson, supra, and in Parker v. Flook, supra, and if no other inventive concept is disclosed in the patent application, the question must be answered in the negative. In both *Benson* and *Flook,* the parties apparently agreed that the inventor's discovery was properly regarded as an algorithm; the holding that an algorithm was a "law of nature" that could not be patented therefore determined that those discoveries were not patentable processes within the meaning of § 101.

As the Court recognizes today, *Flook* also rejected the argument that patent protection was available if the inventor did not claim a monopoly on every conceivable use of the algorithm but instead limited his claims by describing a specific post-solution activity—in that case setting off an alarm in a catalytic conversion process. In its effort to distinguish *Flook* from the instant case, the Court characterizes that post-solution activity as "insignificant," or as merely "token" activity. As a practical matter, however, the post-solution activity described in the *Flook* application was no less significant than the automatic opening of the curing mold involved in this case. For setting off an alarm limit at the appropriate time is surely as important to the safe and efficient operation of a catalytic conversion process as is actuating the mold-opening device in a synthetic rubber curing process. In both cases, the post-solution activity is a significant part of the industrial process. But in neither case should that activity have any *legal* significance because it does not constitute a part of the inventive concept that the applicants claimed to have discovered.

In Gottschalk v. Benson, we held that a program for the solution by a digital computer of a mathematical problem was not a patentable process within the meaning of § 101. In Parker v. Flook, we further held that such a computer program could not be transformed into a patentable process by the addition of post-solution activity that was not claimed to be novel. That holding plainly requires the rejection of Claims 1 and 2 of the Diehr and Lutton application quoted in the Court's opinion. In my opinion, it equally requires rejection of Claim 11 because the presolution activity described in that claim is admittedly a familiar part of the prior art.

Even the Court does not suggest that the computer program developed by Diehr and Lutton is a patentable discovery. Accordingly, if we treat the program as though it were a familiar part of the prior art—as well-established precedent requires—it is absolutely clear that their application contains no claim of patentable invention. Their application was therefore properly rejected under § 101 by the Patent Office and the Board of Patent Appeals.

IV.

The broad question whether computer programs should be given patent protection involves policy considerations that this Court is not authorized to address. As the numerous briefs *amicus curiae* filed in Gottschalk v. Benson, supra, Dann v. Johnston, supra, Parker v. Flook, supra, and this case demonstrate, that question is not only difficult and important, but apparently also one that may be affected by institutional bias. In each of those cases, the spokesmen for the organized patent bar have uniformly favored patentability and industry representatives have taken positions properly motivated by their economic self-interest. Notwithstanding fervent argument that patent protection is essential for the growth of the software industry, commentators have noted that "this industry is growing by leaps and bounds without it."[43] In addition, even some commentators who believe that legal protection for computer programs is desirable have expressed doubts that the present patent system can provide the needed protection.

Within the Federal Government, patterns of decision have also emerged. Gottschalk, Dann, Parker, and Diamond were not ordinary litigants—each was serving as Commissioner of Patents and Trademarks when he opposed the availability of patent protection for a program-related invention. No doubt each may have been motivated by a concern about the ability of the Patent Office to process effectively the flood of applications that would inevitably flow from a decision that computer programs are patentable. The consistent concern evidenced by the Commissioner of Patents and Trademarks and by the Board of Patent Appeals of the Patent and Trademark Office has not been shared by the Court of Customs and Patent Appeals, which reversed the Board in *Benson, Johnston,* and *Flook,* and was in turn reversed by this Court in each of those cases.

Scholars have been critical of the work of both tribunals. Some of that criticism may stem from a conviction about the merits of the broad underlying policy question; such criticism may be put to one side. Other criticism, however, identifies two concerns to which federal judges have a

43. Gemignani, supra, 7 Rut.J.Comp., Tech. & L., at 309.

duty to respond. First, the cases considering the patentability of program-related inventions do not establish rules that enable a conscientious patent lawyer to determine with a fair degree of accuracy which, if any, program-related inventions will be patentable. Second, the inclusion of the ambiguous concept of an "algorithm" within the "law of nature" category of unpatentable subject matter has given rise to the concern that almost any process might be so described and therefore held unpatentable.

In my judgment, today's decision will aggravate the first concern and will not adequately allay the second. I believe both concerns would be better addressed by (1) an unequivocal holding that no program-related invention is a patentable process under § 101 unless it makes a contribution to the art that is not dependent entirely on the utilization of a computer, and (2) an unequivocal explanation that the term "algorithm" as used in this case, as in *Benson* and *Flook,* is synonymous with the term "computer program." Because the invention claimed in the patent application at issue in this case makes no contribution to the art that is not entirely dependent upon the utilization of a computer in a familiar process, I would reverse the decision of the Court of Customs and Patent Appeals.

United States Patent and Trademark Office, Examination Guidelines for Computer–Related Inventions

61 Federal Register 7478 (Feb. 28, 1996).
(Issued, February, 16, 1996; filed, February 27, 1996; Effective Date: March 29, 1996.)

I. Introduction

These "Examination Guidelines for Computer–Related Inventions" ("Guidelines") are to assist Office personnel in the examination of applications drawn to computer-related inventions. The Guidelines are based on the Office's current understanding of the law and are believed to be fully consistent with binding precedent of the Supreme Court, the Federal Circuit and the Federal Circuit's predecessor courts.

These Guidelines do not constitute substantive rulemaking and hence do not have the force and effect of law. These Guidelines have been designed to assist Office personnel in analyzing claimed subject matter for compliance with substantive law. Rejections will be based upon the substantive law and it is these rejections which are appealable. Consequently, any failure by Office personnel to follow the Guidelines is neither appealable nor petitionable.

The Guidelines alter the procedures Office personnel will follow when examining applications drawn to computer-related inventions and are equally applicable to claimed inventions implemented in either hardware or software. The Guidelines also clarify the Office's position on certain patentability standards related to this field of technology. Office personnel are to rely on these Guidelines in the event of any inconsistent treatment of issues between these Guidelines and any earlier provided guidance from the Office. . . .

II. Determine What Applicant Has Invented and Is Seeking To Patent

. . . Prior to focussing on specific statutory requirements, Office personnel must begin examination by determining what, precisely, the applicant has invented and is seeking to patent, and how the claims relate to and define that invention. Consequently, Office personnel will no longer begin examination by determining if a claim recites a "mathematical algorithm." Rather, they will review the complete specification, including the detailed description of the invention, any specific embodiments that have been disclosed, the claims and any specific utilities that have been asserted for the invention.

A. Identify and Understand Any Practical Application Asserted for the Invention.

The subject matter sought to be patented must be a "useful" process, machine, manufacture or composition of matter, i.e., it must have a practical application. The purpose of this requirement is to limit patent protection to inventions that possess a certain level of "real world" value, as opposed to subject matter that represents nothing more than an idea or concept, or is simply a starting point for future investigation or research. Accordingly, a complete disclosure should contain some indication of the practical application for the claimed invention, i.e., why the applicant believes the claimed invention is useful.

The utility of an invention must be within the "technological" arts. A computer-related invention is within the technological arts. A practical application of a computer-related invention is statutory subject matter. This requirement can be discerned from the variously phrased prohibitions against the patenting of abstract ideas, laws of nature or natural phenomena. An invention that has a practical application in the technological arts satisfies the utility requirement.

The applicant is in the best position to explain why an invention is believed useful. Office personnel should therefore focus their efforts on pointing out statements made in the specification that identify all practical applications for the invention. Office personnel should rely on such statements throughout the examination when assessing the invention for compliance with all statutory criteria. An applicant may assert more than one practical application, but only one is necessary to satisfy the utility requirement. Office personnel should review the entire disclosure to determine the features necessary to accomplish at least one asserted practical application.

B. Review the Detailed Disclosure and Specific Embodiments of the Invention To Determine What the Applicant Has Invented.

The written description will provide the clearest explanation of the applicant's invention, by exemplifying the invention, explaining how it relates to the prior art and explaining the relative significance of various features of the invention. Accordingly, Office personnel should begin their evaluation of a computer-related invention as follows:

> Determine what the programmed computer does when it performs the processes dictated by the software (i.e., the functionality of the programmed computer);

> determine how the computer is to be configured to provide that functionality (i.e., what elements constitute the programmed computer and how those elements are configured and interrelated to provide the specified functionality); and

> if applicable, determine the relationship of the programmed computer to other subject matter outside the computer that constitutes the invention (e.g., machines, devices, materials, or process steps other than those that are part of or performed by the programmed computer).

Patent applicants can assist the Office by preparing applications that clearly set forth these aspects of a computer-related invention....

IV.   Determine Whether the Claimed Invention Complies With 35 U.S.C. 101

... 1. Non–Statutory Subject Matter. Claims to computer-related inventions that are clearly non-statutory fall into the same general categories as non-statutory claims in other parts, namely natural phenomena such as magnetism, and abstract ideas or laws of nature which constitute "descriptive material." Descriptive material can be characterized as either "functional descriptive material" or "non-functional descriptive material." In this context, "functional descriptive material" consists of data structures[27] and computer programs which impart functionality when encoded on a computer-readable medium. "Non-functional descriptive material" includes but is not limited to music, literary works and a compilation or mere arrangement of data.

Both types of "descriptive material" are non-statutory when claimed as descriptive material per se. When functional descriptive material is recorded on some computer-readable medium it becomes structurally and functionally interrelated to the medium and will be statutory in most cases. When non-functional descriptive material is recorded on some computer-readable medium, it is not structurally and functionally interrelated to the medium but is merely carried by the medium. Merely claiming non-functional descriptive material stored in a computer-readable medium does not make it statutory. Such a result would exalt form over substance. Thus, non-statutory music does not become statutory by merely recording it on a compact disk. Protection for this type of work is provided under the copyright law.

27. The definition of "data structure" is "a physical or logical relationship among data elements, designed to support specific data manipulation functions." The New IEEE Standard Dictionary of Electrical and Electronics Terms 308 (5th ed. 1993).

Claims to processes that do nothing more than solve mathematical problems or manipulate abstract ideas or concepts are more complex to analyze and are addressed below.

(a) Functional Descriptive Material: "Data Structures" Representing Descriptive Material Per Se or Computer Programs Representing Computer Listings Per Se. Data structures not claimed as embodied in computer-readable media are descriptive material per se and are not statutory because they are neither physical "things" nor statutory processes. Such claimed data structures do not define any structural and functional interrelationships between the data structure and other claimed aspects of the invention which permit the data structure's functionality to be realized. In contrast, a claimed computer-readable medium encoded with a data structure defines structural and functional interrelationships between the data structure and the medium which permit the data structure's functionality to be realized, and is thus statutory.

Similarly, computer programs claimed as computer listings per se, i.e., the descriptions or expressions of the programs, are not physical "things," nor are they statutory processes, as they are not "acts" being performed. Such claimed computer programs do not define any structural and functional interrelationships between the computer program and other claimed aspects of the invention which permit the computer program's functionality to be realized. In contrast, a claimed computer-readable medium encoded with a computer program defines structural and functional interrelationships between the computer program and the medium which permit the computer program's functionality to be realized, and is thus statutory. Accordingly, it is important to distinguish claims that define descriptive material per se from claims that define statutory inventions.

Computer programs are often recited as part of a claim. Office personnel should determine whether the computer program is being claimed as part of an otherwise statutory manufacture or machine. In such a case, the claim remains statutory irrespective of the fact that a computer program is included in the claim. The same result occurs when a computer program is used in a computerized process where the computer executes the instructions set forth in the computer program. Only when the claimed invention taken as a whole is directed to a mere program listing. i.e., to only its description or expression, is it descriptive material per se and hence non-statutory.

Since a computer program is merely a set of instructions capable of being executed by a computer, the computer program itself is not a process and Office personnel should treat a claim for a computer program, without the computer-readable medium needed to realize the computer program's functionality, as non-statutory functional descriptive material. When a computer program is claimed in a process where the computer is executing the computer program's instructions, Office personnel should treat the claim as a process claim. When a computer program is recited in conjunction with a physical structure, such as a computer memory, Office personnel should treat the claim as a product claim.

(b) Non–Functional Descriptive Material. Descriptive material that cannot exhibit any functional interrelationship with the way in which computer processes are performed does not constitute a statutory process, machine, manufacture or composition of matter and should be rejected under § 101. Thus, Office personnel should consider the claimed invention as a whole to determine whether the necessary functional interrelationship is provided.

Where certain types of descriptive material, such as music, literature, art, photographs and mere arrangements or compilations of facts or data, are merely stored so as to be read or outputted by a computer without creating any functional interrelationship, either as part of the stored data or as part of the computing processes performed by the computer, then such descriptive material alone does not impart functionality either to the data as so structured, or to the computer. Such "descriptive material" is not a process, machine, manufacture or composition of matter.

The policy that precludes the patenting of non-functional descriptive material would be easily frustrated if the same descriptive material could be patented when claimed as an article of manufacture. For example, music is commonly sold to consumers in the format of a compact disk. In such cases, the known compact disc acts as nothing more than a carrier for non-functional descriptive material. The purely non-functional descriptive material cannot alone provide the practical application for the manufacture.

Office personnel should be prudent in applying the foregoing guidance. Non-functional descriptive material may be claimed in combination with other functional descriptive material on a computer-readable medium to provide the necessary functional and structural interrelationship to satisfy the requirements of § 101. The presence of the claimed non-functional descriptive material is not necessarily determinative of non-statutory subject matter. For example, a computer that recognizes a particular grouping of musical notes read from memory and upon recognizing that particular sequence, causes another defined series of notes to be played, defines a functional interrelationship among that data and the computing processes performed when utilizing that data, and as such is statutory because it implements a statutory process.

(c) Natural Phenomena Such as Electricity and Magnetism.—Claims that recite nothing but the physical characteristics of a form of energy, such as a frequency, voltage, or the strength of a magnetic field, define energy or magnetism, per se, and as such are non-statutory natural phenomena. However, a claim directed to a practical application of a natural phenomenon such as energy or magnetism is statutory.

2.   Statutory Subject Matter

(a) Statutory Product Claims.—If a claim defines a useful machine or manufacture by identifying the physical structure of the machine or manufacture in terms of its hardware or hardware and software combination, it defines a statutory product.

A machine or manufacture claim may be one of two types: (1) A claim that encompasses any and every machine for performing the underlying process or any and every manufacture that can cause a computer to perform the underlying process, or (2) a claim that defines a specific machine or manufacture. When a claim is of the first type, Office personnel are to evaluate the underlying process the computer will perform in order to determine the patentability of the product.

(i) Claims That Encompass Any Machine or Manufacture Embodiment of a Process. Office personnel must treat each claim as a whole. The mere fact that a hardware element is recited in a claim does not necessarily limit the claim to a specific machine or manufacture. If a product claim encompasses any and every computer implementation of a process, when read in light of the specification, it should be examined on the basis of the underlying process. Such a claim can be recognized as it will:

— Define the physical characteristics of a computer or computer component exclusively as functions or steps to be performed on or by a computer, and

— Encompass any and every product in the stated class (e.g., computer, computer-readable memory) configured in any manner to perform that process.

Office personnel are reminded that finding a product claim to encompass any and every product embodiment of a process invention simply means that the Office will presume that the product claim encompasses any and every hardware or hardware platform and associated software implementation that performs the specified set of claimed functions. Because this is interpretative and nothing more, it does not provide any information as to the patentability of the applicant's underlying process or the product claim.

When Office personnel have reviewed the claim as a whole and found that it is not limited to a specific machine or manufacture, they shall identify how each claim limitation has been treated and set forth their reasons in support of their conclusion that the claim encompasses any and every machine or manufacture embodiment of a process. This will shift the burden to applicant to demonstrate why the claimed invention should be limited to a specific machine or manufacture.

If a claim is found to encompass any and every product embodiment of the underlying process, and if the underlying process is statutory, the product claim should be classified as a statutory product. By the same token, if the underlying process invention is found to be non-statutory, Office personnel should classify the "product" claim as a "non-statutory product." If the product claim is classified as being a non-statutory product on the basis of the underlying process, Office personnel should emphasize that they have considered all claim limitations and are basing their finding on the analysis of the underlying process.

(ii) Product Claims—Claims Directed to Specific Machines and Manufactures. If a product claim does not encompass any and every computer-implementation of a process, then it must be treated as a specific machine or manufacture. Claims that define a computer-related invention as a specific machine or specific article of manufacture must define the physical structure of the machine or manufacture in terms of its hardware or hardware and "specific software." The applicant may define the physical structure of a programmed computer or its hardware or software components in any manner that can be clearly understood by a person skilled in the relevant art. Generally a claim drawn to a particular programmed computer should identify the elements of the computer and indicate how those elements are configured in either hardware or a combination of hardware and specific software.

To adequately define a specific computer memory, the claim must identify a general or specific memory and the specific software which provides the functionality stored in the memory.

A claim limited to a specific machine or manufacture, which has a practical application in the technological arts, is statutory. In most cases, a claim to a specific machine or manufacture will have a practical application in the technological arts. . . .

(b) Statutory Process Claims. A claim that requires one or more acts to be performed defines a process. However, not all processes are statutory under § 101. To be statutory, a claimed computer-related process must either: (1) Result in a physical transformation outside the computer for which a practical application in the technological arts is either disclosed in the specification or would have been known to a skilled artisan or (2) be limited by the language in the claim to be practical application (*sic*) within the technological arts (discussed in (ii) below). The claimed practical application must be a further limitation upon the claimed subject matter if the process is confined to the internal operations of the computer. If a physical transformation occurs outside the computer, it is not necessary to claim the practical application. A disclosure that permits a skilled artisan to practice the claimed invention, i.e., to put it to a practical use, is sufficient. On the other hand, it is necessary to claim the practical application if there is no physical transformation or if the process merely manipulates concept or converts one set of numbers into another. . . .

(c) Non–Statutory Process Claims. If the "acts" of a claimed process manipulate only numbers, abstract concepts or ideas, or signals representing any of the foregoing, the acts are not being applied to appropriate subject matter. Thus, a process consisting solely of mathematical operations, i.e., converting one set of numbers into another set of numbers, does not manipulate appropriate subject matter and thus cannot constitute a statutory process.

In practical terms, claims define non-statutory processes if they:

— Consist solely of mathematical operations without some claimed practical application (i.e., executing a "mathematical algorithm"); or

— Simply manipulate abstract ideas, e.g., a bid or a bubble hierarchy, without some claimed practical application.

A claimed process that consists solely of mathematical operations is non-statutory whether or not it is performed on a computer. Courts have recognized a distinction between types of mathematical algorithms, namely, some define a "law of nature" in mathematical terms and others merely describe an "abstract idea."

Certain mathematical algorithms have been held to be non-statutory because they represent a mathematical definition of a law of nature or a natural phenomenon. For example, a mathematical algorithm representing the formula $E=mc^2$ is a "law of nature"—it defines a "fundamental scientific truth" (i.e., the relationship between energy and mass). To comprehend how the law of nature relates to any object, one invariably has to perform certain steps (e.g., multiplying a number representing the mass of an object by the square of a number representing the speed of light). In such a case, a claimed process which consists solely of the steps that one must follow to solve the mathematical representation of $E=mc^2$ is indistinguishable from the law of nature and would "preempt" the law of nature. A patent cannot be granted on such a process.

Other mathematical algorithms have been held to be non-statutory because they merely describe an abstract idea. An "abstract idea" may simply be any sequence of mathematical operations that are combined to solve a mathematical problem. The concern addressed by holding such subject matter non-statutory is that the mathematical operations merely describe an idea and do not define a process that represents a practical application of the idea.

Accordingly, when a claim reciting a mathematical algorithm is found to define non-statutory subject matter, the basis of the § 101 rejection must be that, when taken as a whole, the claim recites a law of nature, a natural phenomenon, or an abstract idea. . . .

V.   Evaluate Application for Compliance With 35 U.S.C. 112. . . .

A.   Determine Whether the Claimed Invention Complies With 35 U.S.C. 112, Second Paragraph Requirements

1. Claims Setting Forth the Subject Matter Applicant Regards as Invention. Applicant's specification must conclude with claim(s) that set forth the subject matter which the applicant regards as the invention. The invention set forth in the claims is presumed to be that which applicant regards as the invention, unless applicant considers the invention to be something different from what has been claimed as shown by evidence, including admissions, outside the application as filed. An applicant may change what he or she regards as the invention during the prosecution of the application.

2. Claims Particularly Pointing Out and Distinctly Claiming the Invention. Office personnel shall determine whether the claims set out and circumscribe the invention with a reasonable degree of precision and

particularity. In this regard, the definiteness of the language must be analyzed, not in a vacuum, but always in light of the teachings of the disclosure as it would be interpreted by one of ordinary skill in the art. Applicant's claims, interpreted in light of the disclosure, must reasonably apprise a person of ordinary skill in the art of the invention. However, the applicant need not explicitly recite in the claims every feature of the invention. For example, if an applicant indicates that the invention is a particular computer, the claims do not have to recite every element or feature of the computer. In fact, it is preferable for claims to be drafted in a form that emphasizes what the applicant has invented (i.e., what is new rather than old).

A means plus function limitation is distinctly claimed if the description makes it clear that the means corresponds to well-defined structure of a computer or computer component implemented in either hardware or software and its associated hardware platform. Such means may be defined as:

— A programmed computer with particular functionality implemented in hardware or hardware and software;

— A logic circuit or other component of a programmed computer that performs a series of specifically identified operations dictated by a computer program; or

— A computer memory encoded with executable instructions representing a computer program that can cause a computer to function in a particular fashion.

The scope of a "means" limitation is defined as the corresponding structure or material (e.g., a specific logic circuit) set forth in the written description and equivalent. Thus, a claim using means plus function limitations without corresponding disclosure of specific structures or materials that are not well-known fails to particularly point out and distinctly claim the invention. For example, if the applicant discloses only the functions to be performed and provides no express, implied or inherent disclosure of hardware or a combination of hardware and software that performs the functions, the application has not disclosed any "structure" which corresponds to the claimed means. Office personnel should reject such claims under § 112, second paragraph. The rejection shifts the burden to the applicant to describe at least one specific structure or material that corresponds to the claimed means in question, and to identify the precise location or locations in the specification where a description of least one embodiment of that claimed means can be found. In contrast, if the corresponding structure is disclosed to be a memory or logic circuit that has been configured in some manner to perform that function (e.g., using a defined computer program), the application has disclosed "structure" which corresponds to the claimed means.

When a claim or part of a claim is defined in computer program code, whether in source or object code format, a person of skill in art must be able to ascertain the metes and bounds of the claimed invention. In certain circumstances, as where a self-documenting programming code is employed, use of programming language in a claim would be permissible because such program source code presents "sufficiently high-level language and descriptive identifiers" to make it universally understood to others in the art without the programmer having to insert any comments. Applicants should be encouraged to functionally define the steps the computer will perform rather than simply reciting source or object code instructions.

B.   Determine Whether the Claimed Invention Complies With 35 U.S.C. 112, First Paragraph Requirements

1.   Adequate Written Description. The satisfaction of the enablement requirement does not satisfy the written description requirement. For the written description requirement, an applicant's specification must reasonably convey to those skilled in the art that the applicant was in possession of the claimed invention on the date of invention. The claimed invention subject matter need not be described literally, i.e., using the same terms, in order for the disclosure to satisfy the description requirement.

2.   Enabling Disclosure. An applicant's specification must enable a person skilled in the art to make and use the claimed invention without undue experimentation. The fact that experimentation is complex, however, will not make it undue if a person of skill in the art typically engages in such complex experimentation. For a computer-related invention, the disclosure must enable a skilled artisan to configure the computer to possess the requisite functionality, and, where applicable, interrelate the computer with other elements to yield the claimed invention, without the exercise of undue experimentation. The specification should disclose how to configure a computer to possess the requisite functionality or how to integrate the programmed computer with other elements of the invention, unless a skilled artisan would know how to do so without such disclosure.

For many computer-related inventions, it is not unusual for the claimed invention to involve more than one field of technology. For such inventions, the disclosure must satisfy the enablement standard for each aspect of the invention. As such, the disclosure much teach a person skilled in each art how to make and use the relevant aspect of the invention without undue experimentation. For example, to enable a claim to a programmed computer that determines and displays the three-dimensional structure of a chemical compound, the disclosure must

— enable a person skilled in the art of molecular modeling to understand and practice the underlying molecular modeling processes; and

— enable a person skilled in the art of computer programming to create a program that directs a computer to create and display the image representing the three-dimensional structure of the compound.

In other words, the disclosure corresponding to each aspect of the invention must be enabling to a person skilled in each respective art.

In many instances, an applicant will describe a programmed computer by outlining the significant elements of the programmed computer using a functional block diagram. Office personnel should review the specification to ensure that along with the functional block diagram the disclosure provides information that adequately describes each "element" in hardware or hardware and its associated software and how such elements are interrelated. . . .

State Street Bank & Trust Co. v. Signature Financial Group, Inc.

United States Court of Appeals, Federal Circuit, 1998.
149 F.3d 1368, 47 U.S.P.Q.2d 1596, *cert. denied*, 525 U.S. 1093, 119 S.Ct. 851, 142 L.Ed.2d 704 (1999).

[The court's opinion in this case is reproduced beginning at page ____, above.]

AT&T Corp. v. Excel Communications, Inc.

United States Court of Appeals for the Federal Circuit, 1999.
172 F.3d 1352, 50 U.S.P.Q.2d 1447.

PLAGER, Circuit Judge.

This case asks us once again to examine the scope of section 1 of the Patent Act, 35 U.S.C. § 101 (1994). The United States District Court for the District of Delaware granted summary judgment to Excel Communications, Inc., Excel Communications Marketing, Inc., and Excel Telecommunications, Inc. (collectively "Excel"), holding U.S. Patent No. 5,333,184 (the *'184* patent) invalid under § 101 for failure to claim statutory subject matter. AT&T Corp. ("AT&T"), owner of the *'184* patent, appeals. Because we find that the claimed subject matter is properly within the statutory scope of § 101, we reverse the district court's judgment of invalidity on this ground and remand the case for further proceedings.

BACKGROUND

A.

The *'184* patent, entitled "Call Message Recording for Telephone Systems," issued on July 26, 1994. It describes a message record for long-distance telephone calls that is enhanced by adding a primary interexchange carrier ("PIC") indicator. The addition of the indicator aids long-distance carriers in providing differential billing treatment for subscribers, depending upon whether a subscriber calls someone with the same or a different long-distance carrier.

The invention claimed in the *'184* patent is designed to operate in a telecommunications system with multiple long-distance service providers. The system contains local exchange carriers ("LECs") and long-distance service (interexchange) carriers ("IXCs"). The LECs provide local telephone service and access to IXCs. Each customer has an LEC for local service and selects an IXC, such as AT&T or Excel, to be its primary long-distance service (interexchange) carrier or PIC. IXCs may own their own facilities, as does AT&T. Others, like Excel, called "resellers" or "resale carriers," contract with facility-owners to route their subscribers' calls through the facility-owners' switches and transmission lines. Some IXCs, including MCI and U.S. Sprint, have a mix of their own lines and leased lines.

The system thus involves a three-step process when a caller makes a direct-dialed (1+) long-distance telephone call: (1) after the call is transmitted over the LEC's network to a switch, and the LEC identifies the caller's PIC, the LEC automatically routes the call to the facilities used by the caller's PIC; (2) the PIC's facilities carry the call to the LEC serving the call recipient; and (3) the call recipient's LEC delivers the call over its local network to the recipient's telephone.

When a caller makes a direct-dialed long-distance telephone call, a switch (which may be a switch in the interexchange network) monitors and records data related to the call, generating an "automatic message account" ("AMA") message record. This contemporaneous message record contains fields of information such as the originating and terminating telephone numbers, and the length of time of the call. These message records are then transmitted from the switch to a message accumulation system for processing and billing.

Because the message records are stored in electronic format, they can be transmitted from one computer system to another and reformatted to ease processing of the information. Thus the carrier's AMA message subsequently is translated into the industry-standard "exchange message interface," forwarded to a rating system, and ultimately forwarded to a billing system in which the data resides until processed to generate, typically, "hard copy" bills which are mailed to subscribers.

B.

The invention of the *'184* patent calls for the addition of a data field into a standard message record to indicate whether a call involves a particular PIC (the "PIC indicator"). This PIC indicator can exist in several forms, such as a code which identifies the call recipient's PIC, a flag which shows that the recipient's PIC is or is not a particular IXC, or a flag that identifies the recipient's and the caller's PICs as the same IXC. The PIC indicator therefore enables IXCs to provide differential billing for calls on the basis of the identified PIC.

The application that issued as the *'184* patent was filed in 1992. The U.S. Patent and Trademark Office ("PTO") initially rejected, for reasons unrelated to § 101, all forty-one of the originally filed claims. Following amendment, the claims were issued in 1994 in their present form. The *'184* patent contains six independent claims, five method claims and one apparatus claim, and additional dependent claims. The PTO granted the *'184* patent without questioning whether the claims were directed to statutory subject matter under § 101.

AT&T in 1996 asserted ten of the method claims against Excel in this infringement suit. The independent claims at issue (claims 1, 12, 18, and 40) include the step of "generating a message record for an interexchange call between an originating subscriber and a terminating subscriber," and the step of adding a PIC indicator to the message record. Independent claim 1, for example, adds a PIC indicator whose value depends upon the call recipient's PIC:

> A method for use in a telecommunications system in which interexchange calls initiated by each subscriber are automatically routed over the facilities of a particular one of a plurality of interexchange carriers associated with that subscriber, said method comprising the steps of:
>
> > *generating a message record for an interexchange call* between an originating subscriber and a terminating subscriber, and *including, in said message record, a primary interexchange carrier (PIC) indicator* having a value which is *a function of whether or not the interexchange carrier associated with said terminating subscriber is a predetermined one* of said interexchange carriers.

(Emphasis added.) Independent claims 12 and 40 add a PIC indicator that shows if a recipient's PIC is the same as the IXC over which that particular call is being made. Independent claim 18 adds a PIC indicator designed to show if the caller and the recipient subscribe to the same IXC. The dependent claims at issue add the steps of accessing an IXC's subscriber database (claims 4, 13, and 19) and billing individual calls as a function of the value of the PIC indicator (claims 6, 15, and 21).

The district court concluded that the method claims of the *'184* patent implicitly recite a mathematical algorithm. The court was of the view that the only physical step in the claims involves data-gathering for the algorithm. Though the court recognized that the claims require the use of switches and computers, it nevertheless concluded that use of such facilities to perform a non-substantive change in the data's format could not serve to convert non-patentable subject matter into patentable subject matter. Thus the trial court, on summary judgment, held all of the method claims at issue invalid for failure to qualify as statutory subject matter.

DISCUSSION

A.

Summary judgment is appropriate if there are no genuine issues of material fact and the moving party is entitled to judgment as a matter of law. We review without deference a trial court's grant of summary judgment, with all justifiable factual inferences drawn in favor of the party opposing the motion.

The issue on appeal, whether the asserted claims of the *'184* patent are invalid for failure to claim statutory subject matter under 35 U.S.C. § 101, is a question of law which we review without deference. In matters of statutory interpretation, it is this court's responsibility independently to determine what the law is.

B.

Our analysis of whether a claim is directed to statutory subject matter begins with the language of 35 U.S.C. § 101, which reads:

> Whoever invents or discovers any new and useful process, machine, manufacture, or composition of matter, or any new and useful improvement thereof, may obtain a patent therefor, subject to the conditions and requirements of this title.

The Supreme Court has construed § 101 broadly, noting that Congress intended statutory subject matter to "include anything under the sun that is made by man." *See Diamond v. Chakrabarty,* 447 U.S. 303, 309, 100 S.Ct. 2204, 65 L.Ed.2d 144 (1980) (quoting S.Rep. No. 82–1979, at 5 (1952); H.R.Rep. No. 82–1923, at 6 (1952)); *see also Diamond v. Diehr,* 450 U.S. 175, 182 (1981). Despite this seemingly limitless expanse, the Court has specifically identified three categories of unpatentable subject matter: "laws of nature, natural phenomena, and abstract ideas." *See Diehr,* 450 U.S. at 185.

In this case, the method claims at issue fall within the "process" category of the four enumerated categories of patentable subject matter in § 101. The district court held that the claims at issue, though otherwise within the terms of § 101, implicitly recite a mathematical algorithm, and thus fall within the judicially created "mathematical algorithm" exception to statutory subject matter.

A mathematical formula alone, sometimes referred to as a mathematical algorithm, viewed in the abstract, is considered unpatentable subject matter. Courts have used the terms "mathematical algorithm," "mathematical formula," and "mathematical equation," to describe types of nonstatutory mathematical subject matter without explaining whether the terms are interchangeable or different. Even assuming the words connote the same concept, there is considerable question as to exactly what the concept encompasses.

This court recently pointed out that any step-by-step process, be it electronic, chemical, or mechanical, involves an "algorithm" in the broad sense of the term. *See State Street Bank & Trust Co. v. Signature Fin. Group, Inc.,* 149 F.3d 1368, 1374–75, 47 USPQ2d 1596, 1602 (Fed.Cir. 1998), *cert. denied,* 525 U.S. 1093 (1999). Because § 101 includes processes as a category of patentable subject matter, the judicially-defined proscription against patenting of a "mathematical algorithm," to the extent such a proscription still exists, is narrowly limited to mathematical algorithms in the abstract.

Since the process of manipulation of numbers is a fundamental part of computer technology, we have had to reexamine the rules that govern the patentability of such technology. The sea-changes in both law and technology stand as a testament to the ability of law to adapt to new and innovative concepts, while remaining true to basic principles. In an earlier era, the PTO published guidelines essentially rejecting the notion that computer programs were patentable. As the technology progressed, our predecessor court disagreed, and, overturning some of the earlier limiting principles regarding § 101, announced more expansive principles formulated with computer technology in mind. In our recent decision in *State Street,* this court discarded the so-called "business method" exception and reassessed the "mathematical algorithm" exception, both judicially-created "exceptions" to the statutory categories of § 101. As this brief review suggests, this court (and its predecessor) has struggled to make our understanding of the scope of § 101 responsive to the needs of the modern world.

The Supreme Court has supported and enhanced this effort. In *Diehr,* the Court expressly limited its two earlier decisions in *Flook* and *Benson* by emphasizing that these cases did no more than confirm the "long-established principle" that laws of nature, natural phenomena, and abstract ideas are excluded from patent protection. 450 U.S. at 185, 101 S.Ct. 1048. The *Diehr* Court explicitly distinguished Diehr's process by pointing out that "the respondents here do not seek to patent a mathematical formula. Instead, they seek patent protection for a process of curing synthetic rubber." *Id.* at 187, 101 S.Ct. 1048. The Court then explained that although the process used a well-known mathematical equation, the applicants did not "pre-empt the use of that equation." *Id.* Thus, even though a mathematical algorithm is not patentable in isolation, a process that applies an equation to a new and useful end "is at the very least not barred at the threshold by § 101." *Id.* at 188, 101 S.Ct. 1048. In this regard, it is particularly worthy of note that the argument for the opposite result, that "the term 'algorithm' ... is synonymous with the term 'computer program,'" *id.* at 219, 101 S.Ct. 1048 (Stevens, J., dissenting), and thus computer-based programs as a general proposition should not be patentable, was made forcefully in dissent by Justice Stevens; his view, however, was rejected by the *Diehr* majority.

As previously noted, we most recently addressed the "mathematical algorithm" exception in *State Street.* In *State Street,* this court, following the Supreme Court's guidance in *Diehr,* concluded that "[u]npatentable mathematical algorithms are identifiable by showing they are merely abstract ideas constituting disembodied concepts or truths that are not 'useful.' ... [T]o be patentable an algorithm must be applied in a 'useful' way." *Id.* at 1373. In that case, the claimed data processing system for implementing a financial management structure satisfied the § 101 inquiry because it constituted a "practical application of a mathematical algorithm, ... [by] produc[ing] 'a useful, concrete and tangible result.'" *Id.* at 1373.

The *State Street* formulation, that a mathematical algorithm may be an integral part of patentable subject matter such as a machine or process if the claimed invention as a whole is applied in a "useful" manner, follows the approach taken by this court en banc in *In re Alappat,* 33 F.3d 1526, 31 USPQ2d 1545 (Fed.Cir.1994). In *Alappat,* we set out our understanding of the Supreme Court's limitations on the patentability of mathematical subject matter and concluded that:

> [The Court] never intended to create an overly broad, fourth category of [mathematical] subject matter excluded from § 101. Rather, at the core of the Court's analysis ... lies an attempt by the Court to explain a rather straightforward concept, namely, that certain types of mathematical subject matter, *standing alone,* represent nothing more than abstract ideas until reduced to some type of practical application, and thus that subject matter is not, in and of itself, entitled to patent protection.

Id. at 1543. Thus, the *Alappat* inquiry simply requires an examination of the contested claims to see if the claimed subject matter as a whole is a disembodied mathematical concept representing nothing more than a "law of nature" or an "abstract idea," or if the mathematical concept has been reduced to some practical application rendering it "useful." In *Alappat,* we held that more than an abstract idea was claimed because the claimed invention as a whole was directed toward forming a specific machine that produced the useful, concrete, and tangible result of a smooth waveform display.

In both *Alappat* and *State Street,* the claim was for a machine that achieved certain results. In the case before us, because Excel does not own or operate the facilities over which its calls are placed, AT&T did not charge Excel with infringement of its apparatus claims, but limited its infringement charge to the specified method or process claims. Whether stated implicitly or explicitly, we consider the scope of § 101 to be the same regardless of the form—machine or process—in which a particular claim is drafted. Furthermore, the Supreme Court's decisions in *Diehr, Benson,* and *Flook,* all of which involved method (i.e., process) claims, have provided and supported the principles which we apply to both machine—and process-type claims. Thus, we are comfortable in applying our reasoning in *Alappat* and *State Street* to the method claims at issue in this case.

C.

In light of this review of the current understanding of the "mathematical algorithm" exception, we turn now to the arguments of the parties in support of and in opposition to the trial court's judgment. We note that, at the time the trial court made its decision, that court did not have the benefit of this court's explication in *State Street* of the mathematical algorithm issue.

As previously explained, AT&T's claimed process employs subscribers' and call recipients' PICs as data, applies Boolean algebra to those data to determine the value of the PIC indicator, and applies that value through switching and recording mechanisms to create a signal useful for billing purposes. In *State Street,* we held that the processing system there was patentable subject matter because the system takes data representing discrete dollar amounts through a series of mathematical calculations to determine a final share price—a useful, concrete, and tangible result.

In this case, Excel argues, correctly, that the PIC indicator value is derived using a simple mathematical principle (p and q). But that is not determinative because AT&T does not claim the Boolean principle as such or attempt to forestall its use in any other application. It is clear from the written description of the '184 patent that AT&T is only claiming a process that uses the Boolean principle in order to determine the value of the PIC indicator. The PIC indicator represents information about the call recipient's PIC, a useful, non-abstract result that facilitates differential billing of long-distance calls made by an IXC's subscriber. Because the claimed process applies the Boolean principle to produce a useful, concrete, tangible result without pre-empting other uses of the mathematical principle, on its face the claimed process comfortably falls within the scope of § 101.

Excel argues that method claims containing mathematical algorithms are patentable subject matter only if there is a "physical transformation" or conversion of subject matter from one state into another. The physical transformation language appears in *Diehr, see* 450 U.S. at 184, 101 S.Ct. 1048 ("That respondents' claims involve the transformation of an article, in this case raw, uncured synthetic rubber, into a different state or thing cannot be disputed."), and has been echoed by this court in *Schrader,* 22 F.3d at 294, 30 USPQ2d at 1458 ("Therefore, we do not find in the claim any kind of data transformation.").

The notion of "physical transformation" can be misunderstood. In the first place, it is not an invariable requirement, but merely one example of how a mathematical algorithm may bring about a useful application. As the Supreme Court itself noted, "when [a claimed invention] is performing a function which the patent laws were designed to protect (*e.g.,* transforming or reducing an article to a different state or thing), then the claim satisfies the requirements of § 101." *Diehr,* 450 U.S. at 192, 101 S.Ct. 1048. The "e.g." signal denotes an example, not an exclusive requirement.

This understanding of transformation is consistent with our earlier decision in *Arrhythmia* [Research Technology, Inc. v. Corazonix Corp., 958 F.2d 1053 (Fed.Cir.1992)]. Arrhythmia's process claims included various mathematical formulae to analyze electrocardiograph signals to determine a specified heart activity. The *Arrhythmia* court reasoned that the method claims qualified as statutory subject matter by noting that the steps transformed physical, electrical signals from one form into another form—a number representing a signal related to the patient's heart activity, a non-abstract output. The finding that the claimed process "transformed" data from one "form" to another simply confirmed that Arrhythmia's method claims satisfied § 101 because the mathematical algorithm included within the process was applied to produce a number which had specific meaning— a useful, concrete, tangible result—not a mathematical abstraction.

Excel also contends that because the process claims at issue lack physical limitations set forth in the patent, the claims are not patentable subject matter. This argument reflects a misunderstanding of our case law. The cases cited by Excel for this proposition involved machine claims written in means-plus-function language. Apparatus claims written in this manner require supporting structure in the written description that corresponds to the claimed "means" elements. Since the claims at issue in this case are directed to a process in the first instance, a structural inquiry is unnecessary.

The argument that physical limitations are necessary may also stem from the second part of the *Freeman–Walter–Abele* test[4], an earlier test which has been used to identify claims thought to involve unpatentable mathematical algorithms. That second part was said to inquire "whether the claim is directed to a mathematical algorithm that is not applied to or limited by physical elements." *Arrhythmia,* 958 F.2d at 1058. Although our en banc *Alappat* decision called this test "not an improper analysis," we then pointed out that "the ultimate issue always has been whether the claim as a whole is drawn to statutory subject matter." 33 F.3d at 1543 n. 21, 31 USPQ2d at 1557 n. 21. Furthermore, our recent *State Street* decision questioned the continuing viability of the *Freeman–Walter–Abele* test, noting that, "[a]fter *Diehr* and *Chakrabarty,* the *Freeman–Walter–Abele* test has little, if any, applicability to determining the presence of statutory subject matter." 149 F.3d at 1374. Whatever may be left of the earlier test, if anything, this type of physical limitations analysis seems of little value because "after *Diehr* and *Alappat,* the mere fact that a claimed invention involves inputting numbers, calculating numbers, outputting numbers, and storing numbers, in and of itself, would not render it nonstatutory subject matter, unless, of course, its operation does not produce a 'useful, concrete and tangible result.' " *Id.* at 1374, (quoting *Alappat,* 33 F.3d at 1544).

Because we focus on the inquiry deemed "the ultimate issue" by *Alappat,* rather than on the physical limitations inquiry of the *Freeman-Walter-Abele* test, we find the cases cited by Excel in support of its position to be inapposite. For example, in *In re Grams,* the court applied the *Freeman-Walter-Abele* test and concluded that the only physical step in the claimed process involved data-gathering for the algorithm; thus, the claims were held to be directed to unpatentable subject matter. In contrast, our inquiry here focuses on whether the mathematical algorithm is applied in a practical manner to produce a useful result. *In re Grams* is unhelpful because the panel in that case did not ascertain if the end result of the claimed process was useful, concrete, and tangible.

Similarly, the court in *In re Schrader* relied upon the *Freeman–Walter–Abele* test for its analysis of the method claim involved. The court found neither a physical transformation nor any physical step in the claimed process aside from the entering of data into a record. The *Schrader* court likened the data-recording step to that of data-gathering and held that the claim was properly rejected as failing to define patentable subject matter. The focus of the court in *Schrader* was not on whether the mathematical algorithm was applied in a practical manner since it ended its inquiry before looking to see if a useful, concrete, tangible result ensued. Thus, in

---

4. See *In re Freeman,* 573 F.2d 1237, 197 USPQ 464 (CCPA 1978), as modified by *In re Walter,* 618 F.2d 758, 205 USPQ 397 (CCPA 1980), and *In re Abele,* 648 F.2d 902, 214 USPQ 682 (CCPA 1982).

light of our recent understanding of the issue, the *Schrader* court's analysis is as unhelpful as that of *In re Grams*.

Finally, the decision in *In re Warmerdam,* 33 F.3d 1354 (Fed.Cir.1994) is not to the contrary. There the court recognized the difficulty in knowing exactly what a mathematical algorithm is, "which makes rather dicey the determination of whether the claim as a whole is no more than that." *Id.* at 1359, 31 USPQ2d at 1758. Warmerdam's claims 1–4 encompassed a method for controlling the motion of objects and machines to avoid collision with other moving or fixed objects by generating bubble hierarchies through the use of a particular mathematical procedure. The court found that the claimed process did nothing more than manipulate basic mathematical constructs and concluded that "taking several abstract ideas and manipulating them together adds nothing to the basic equation"; hence, the court held that the claims were properly rejected under § 101. Whether one agrees with the court's conclusion on the facts, the holding of the case is a straightforward application of the basic principle that mere laws of nature, natural phenomena, and abstract ideas are not within the categories of inventions or discoveries that may be patented under § 101.

D.

In his dissent in *Diehr,* Justice Stevens noted two concerns regarding the § 101 issue, and to which, in his view, federal judges have a duty to respond:

> First, the cases considering the patentability of program-related inventions do not establish rules that enable a conscientious patent lawyer to determine with a fair degree of accuracy which, if any, program-related inventions will be patentable. Second, the inclusion of the ambiguous concept of an 'algorithm' within the 'law of nature' category of unpatentable subject matter has given rise to the concern that almost any process might be so described and therefore held unpatentable.

Diehr, 450 U.S. at 219, 101 S.Ct. 1048 (Stevens, J., dissenting).

Despite the almost twenty years since Justice Stevens wrote, these concerns remain important. His solution was to declare all computer-based programming unpatentable. That has not been the course the law has taken. Rather, it is now clear that computer-based programming constitutes patentable subject matter so long as the basic requirements of § 101 are met. Justice Stevens's concerns can be addressed within that framework.

His first concern, that the rules are not sufficiently clear to enable reasonable prediction of outcomes, should be less of a concern today in light of the refocusing of the § 101 issue that *Alappat* and *State Street* have provided. His second concern, that the ambiguous concept of "algorithm" could be used to make any process unpatentable, can be laid to rest once the focus is understood to be not on whether there is a mathematical algorithm at work, but on whether the algorithm-containing invention, as a whole, produces a tangible, useful, result.

In light of the above, and consistent with the clearer understanding that our more recent cases have provided, we conclude that the district court did not apply the proper analysis to the method claims at issue. Furthermore, had the court applied the proper analysis to the stated claims, the court would have concluded that all the claims asserted fall comfortably within the broad scope of patentable subject matter under § 101. Accordingly, we hold as a matter of law that Excel was not entitled to the grant of summary judgment of invalidity of the *'184* patent under § 101.

Since the case must be returned to the trial court for further proceedings, and to avoid any possible misunderstandings as to the scope of our decision, we note that the ultimate validity of these claims depends upon their satisfying the other requirements for patentability such as those set forth in 35 U.S.C. §§ 102, 103, and 112. Thus, on remand, those questions, as well as any others the parties may properly raise, remain for disposition.

CONCLUSION

The district court's summary judgment of invalidity is reversed, and the case is remanded for further proceedings consistent with this opinion.

REVERSED & REMANDED.

NOTES

1. *Are Computer Programs Patentable Subject Matter?* For more than a quarter-century, the Patent and Trademark Office treated computer programs as presenting a special case, and set hurdle after hurdle in the way of treating them as patentable subject matter under section 101 of the Patent Act. The Court of Customs and Patent Appeals and its successor, the Court of Appeals for the Federal Circuit, regularly overturned the PTO's rejections of software applications, but the PTO, abetted by ambiguous opinions from the U.S. Supreme Court, persisted in rejecting software as protectible subject matter. One writer has suggested that the main reason for the PTO's intransigence was simply a shortage of trained personnel to examine software applications. See Comment, Computer Program Patentability—The C.C.P.A. Refuses to Follow the Lead of the Supreme Court in *Parker v. Flook*, 58 N.C. L. Rev. 319.

At least two developments accelerated the PTO's decision to help bring computer programs into the mainstream of patentable invention by issuing examination guidelines for them. One was the industry perception following the 1992 decisions in Computer Associates v. Altai and Sega v. Accolade, pages 805 and 855, above, that copyright law offered far narrower protection to computer programs than developers had initially hoped for; patents would have to be more freely available if the industry was to thrive. Second was an intense burst of software decisions coming from the Federal Circuit in 1994, among them: In re Alappat, 33 F.3d 1526, 31 U.S.P.Q.2d

1545 (Fed.Cir.1994) (holding that a patent application that functionally defined a machine by its ability to manipulate data for an oscilloscope display qualified for subject matter protection under section 101); In re Schrader, 22 F.3d 290, 30 U.S.P.Q.2d 1455 (Fed.Cir.1994) (indicating that the addition of a functional step—such as physical display of data—to an otherwise unpatentable algorithm for an auction method could qualify the method for a patent); In re Warmerdam, 33 F.3d 1354, 31 U.S.P.Q.2d 1754 (Fed.Cir.1994) (holding that while a method for generating a data structure does not qualify as statutory subject matter, a machine with the data structure embedded in its memory does qualify); and In re Lowry, 32 F.3d 1579, 32 U.S.P.Q.2d 1031 (Fed.Cir.1994) (holding that, in determining the novelty of a computer memory embodying a novel data structure, the Patent and Trademark Office cannot disregard the data structure on the ground that it constitutes unpatentable "printed matter").

It was the *Lowry* decision that precipitated the Patent Office's about-face on computer programs. Shortly after *Lowry*, an applicant, Beauregard, appealed an Office decision rejecting a software application on similar grounds. The Office, evidently conceding that *Lowry* undercut the *Beauregard* rejection, moved to dismiss the appeal, stating in its motion that "computer programs embodied in a tangible medium, such as floppy diskettes, are patentable subject matter under 35 U.S.C. § 101, and must be examined under 35 U.S.C. §§ 102 and 103." In re Beauregard, 53 F.3d 1583, 1584, 35 U.S.P.Q.2d 1383 (Fed.Cir.1995).

2. *Business Method Patents. State Street*, which held that a general purpose computer programmed to implement a business oriented process constitutes patentable subject matter under section 101 of the Patent Act, represents not only a final chapter in the decades-long judicial struggle over the patentability of computer software, but also an opening chapter in the debate over patent protection for business methods.

In December 1999, Amazon.com, the Internet retailer, won a preliminary injunction against the alleged infringement by its direct competitor, BarnesandNoble.com of Amazon's "one-click" patent on an invention that enables customers to order an item on the Internet with a single click of a computer mouse (avoiding the use of an additional check-out procedure, the so-called "shopping cart model" of Internet purchase). The preliminary injunction—which came in the midst of the 1999 holiday shopping season—attracted substantial press and no little skepticism about the validity of business method patents. One consequence was that in March 2000, the PTO initiated closer review of business method patent applications. In February 2001, the Court of Appeals for the Federal Circuit vacated the preliminary injunction, holding that while Amazon.com had "made a showing that it is likely to succeed at trial on its infringement case," Barnesand-Noble.com had raised "substantial questions" about the patent's validity. Amazon.com, Inc. v. Barnesandnoble.com, Inc., 239 F.3d 1343, 1358, 1366, 57 U.S.P.Q.2d 1747 (Fed.Cir.2001).

3. *Scope of Protection.* Just as the first generation of software copyright cases, such as Apple v. Franklin, established the copyrightability of computer programs and the second generation of cases, such as Computer Associates v. Altai and Sega v. Accolade, established the methodology for determining the scope of protection, the first generation of software patent cases centered on the question of eligibility for protection under section 101, and the next generation of cases can be expected to address the appropriate limitations on patent protection.

In Patent Scope and Innovation in the Software Industry, 89 Calif. L. Rev. 1, 56 (2001), Professors Julie E. Cohen and Mark A. Lemley argue for limitations on the scope of software patents that roughly parallel the limitations carved out for software copyrights in *Sega* (reverse engineering) and *Computer Associates* (abstraction-filtration-comparison): "Because software must be reverse engineered to be understood, the patent law's failure to provide a reverse engineering privilege may pose unique difficulties for software research, and thus may frustrate fundamental patent policies favoring disclosure and competition. Because software innovations tend to be incremental and poorly documented, and because their economic lives tend to be much shorter than the uniform patent term, courts may apply the doctrine of equivalents too broadly in software infringement disputes, and thus may stifle efforts by second-comers to design around existing patents. Further, these problems are linked. Robust competition by improvers requires both that they be able to engage in reverse engineering in order to analyze existing programs, and that they have the freedom to design new products without undue risk of liability for patent infringement."

See also, Richard S. Gruner, Intangible Inventions: Patentable Subject Matter for an Information Age, 35 Loy. L.A. L. Rev. 355 (2002).

III. TRADE SECRET LAW

Computer Associates International, Inc. v. Altai, Inc.

United States Court of Appeals, Second Circuit, 1992.
982 F.2d 693, 715, 23 U.S.P.Q.2d 1241.

[The portion of the court's opinion dealing with copyright issues is reprinted beginning at page 805, above.]

II. TRADE SECRET PREEMPTION

In its complaint, CA alleged that Altai misappropriated the trade secrets contained in the ADAPTER program. Prior to trial, while the proceedings were still before Judge Mishler, Altai moved to dismiss and for summary judgment on CA's trade secret misappropriation claim. Altai argued that section 301 of the Copyright Act preempted CA's state law cause of action. Judge Mishler denied Altai's motion, reasoning that " '[t]he elements of the tort of appropriation of trade secrets' through the breach of contract or confidence by an employee are not the same as the elements of a claim of copyright infringement." *Computer Assocs.*, 775 F.Supp. at 563.

The parties addressed the preemption issue again, both in pre-and post-trial briefs. Judge Pratt then reconsidered and reversed Judge Mishler's earlier ruling. The district court concluded that CA's trade secret claims were preempted because "CA—which is the master of its own case—has pleaded and proven facts which establish that one act constituted both copyright infringement and misappropriation of trade secrets [namely, the] copying of ADAPTER into OSCAR 3.4. . . ." *Id.* at 565. . . .

A. *General Law of Copyright Preemption Regarding Trade Secrets and Computer Programs*

Congress carefully designed the statutory framework of federal copyright preemption. In order to insure that the enforcement of these rights remains solely in the federal domain, section 301(a) of the Copyright Act expressly preempts

> all legal or equitable rights that are equivalent to any of the exclusive rights within the general scope of copyright as specified by section 106 in works of authorship that are fixed in a tangible medium of expression and come within the subject matter of copyright as specified by sections 102 and 103. . . .

17 U.S.C. § 301(a). This sweeping displacement of state law is, however, limited by section 301(b), which provides, in relevant part, that

> nothing in this title annuls or limits any rights or remedies under the common law or statutes of any State with respect to . . . activities violating legal or equitable rights that are not equivalent to any of the

exclusive rights within the general scope of copyright as specified by section 106. . . .

17 U.S.C. § 301(b)(3). Section 106, in turn, affords a copyright owner the exclusive right to: (1) reproduce the copyrighted work; (2) prepare derivative works; (3) distribute copies of the work by sale or otherwise; and, with respect to certain artistic works, (4) perform the work publicly; and (5) display the work publicly.

Section 301 thus preempts only those state law rights that "may be abridged by an act which, in and of itself, would infringe one of the exclusive rights" provided by federal copyright law. But if an "extra element" is "required instead of or in addition to the acts of reproduction, performance, distribution or display, in order to constitute a state-created cause of action, then the right does not lie 'within the general scope of copyright,' and there is no preemption." 1 Nimmer § 1.01[B], at 114–15.

A state law claim is not preempted if the "extra element" changes the "nature of the action so that it is *qualitatively* different from a copyright infringement claim." *Mayer v. Josiah Wedgwood & Sons, Ltd.*, 601 F.Supp. 1523, 1535, (S.D.N.Y.1985). To determine whether a claim meets this standard, we must determine "what plaintiff seeks to protect, the theories in which the matter is thought to be protected and the rights sought to be enforced." 1 Roger M. Milgrim, *Milgrim on Trade Secrets* § 2.06A[3], at 2–150 (1992) (hereinafter "Milgrim"). An action will not be saved from preemption by elements such as awareness or intent, which alter "the action's scope but not its nature. . . ." *Mayer*, 601 F.Supp. at 1535.

Following this "extra element" test, we have held that unfair competition and misappropriation claims grounded solely in the copying of a plaintiff's protected expression are preempted by section 301. We have also preempted a tortious interference with contract claim grounded in the impairment of a plaintiff's right under the Copyright Act to publish derivative works.

However, many state law rights that can arise in connection with instances of copyright infringement satisfy the extra element test, and thus are not preempted by section 301. These include unfair competition claims based upon breaches of confidential relationships, breaches of fiduciary duties and trade secrets.

Trade-secret protection, the branch of unfair competition law at issue in this case, remains a "uniquely valuable" weapon in the defensive arsenal of computer programmers. *See* 1 Milgrim § 2.06A[5][c], at 2–172.4. Precisely because trade secret doctrine protects the discovery of ideas, processes, and systems which are explicitly precluded from coverage under copyright law, courts and commentators alike consider it a necessary and integral part of the intellectual property protection extended to computer programs.

The legislative history of section 301 states that "[t]he evolving common law rights of . . . trade secrets . . . would remain unaffected as long as the causes of action contain elements, such as . . . a breach of trust or confidentiality, that are different in kind from copyright infringement."

House Report, at 5748. Congress did not consider the term "misappropriation" to be "necessarily synonymous with copyright infringement," or to serve as the talisman of preemption. *Id.*

Trade secret claims often are grounded upon a defendant's breach of a duty of trust or confidence to the plaintiff through improper disclosure of confidential material. The defendant's breach of duty is the gravamen of such trade secret claims, and supplies the "extra element" that qualitatively distinguishes such trade secret in claims for copyright causes of action from copyright infringement that are based solely upon copying.

B.   *Preemption in This Case*

The district court stated that:

> Were CA's [trade secret] allegations premised on a theory of illegal *acquisition* of a trade secret, a charge that might have been alleged against Arney, who is not a defendant in this case, the preemption analysis might be different, for there seems to be no corresponding right guaranteed to copyright owners by § 106 of the copyright act.

Computer Assocs., 775 F.Supp. at 565. However, the court concluded that CA's trade secret claims were not grounded in a theory that Altai violated a duty of confidentiality to CA. Rather, Judge Pratt stated that CA proceeded against Altai solely "on a theory that the misappropriation took place by Altai's *use* of ADAPTER—the same theory as the copyright infringement count." *Id.* The district court reasoned that "the right to be free from trade secret misappropriation through 'use', and the right to exclusive reproduction and distribution of a copyrighted work are not distinguishable." *Id.* Because he concluded that there was no qualitative difference between the elements of CA's state law trade secret claims and a claim for federal copyright infringement, Judge Pratt ruled that CA's trade secret claims were preempted by section 301.

We agree with CA that the district court failed to address fully the factual and theoretical bases of CA's trade secret claims. The district court relied upon the fact that Arney—not Altai—allegedly breached a duty to CA of confidentiality by stealing secrets from CA and incorporating those secrets into OSCAR 3.4. However, under a wrongful acquisition theory based on *Restatement (First) of Torts* § 757 (1939), Williams and Altai may be liable for violating CA's right of confidentiality. Section 757 states in relevant part:

> One who discloses or uses another's trade secret, without a privilege to do so, is liable to another if.... (c) he learned the secret from a third person with notice of the fact that it was a secret and that the third person discovered it by improper means or that the third person's disclosure of it was otherwise a breach of his duty to the other....

Actual notice is not required for such a third party acquisition claim; constructive notice is sufficient. A defendant is on constructive notice when, "from the information which he has, a reasonable man would infer [a breach of confidence], or if, under the circumstances, a reasonable man would be put on inquiry and an inquiry pursued with reasonable intelligence and diligence would disclose the [breach]." *Id.*, comment 1.

We agree with the district court that New Jersey's governing governmental interest choice of law analysis directs the application of Texas law to CA's trade secret misappropriation claim. Texas law recognizes trade secret misappropriation claims grounded in the reasoning of *Restatement* section 757(c), and the facts alleged by CA may well support such a claim.

It is undisputed that, when Arney stole the ADAPTER code and incorporated it into his design of OSCAR 3.4, he breached his confidentiality agreement with CA. The district court noted that while such action might constitute a valid claim against *Arney*, CA is the named defendant in this lawsuit. Additionally, the district court found, as a matter of fact, that "[n]o one at Altai, other than Arney, knew that Arney had the ADAPTER code...." *Computer Assocs.*, 775 F.Supp. at 554. However, the district court did not consider fully Altai's potential liability for improper trade secret acquisition. It did not consider the question of Altai's trade secret liability in connection with OSCAR 3.4 under a constructive notice theory, or Altai's potential liability under an actual notice theory in connection with OSCAR 3.5.

The district court found that, prior to CA's bringing suit, Altai was not on actual notice of Arney's theft of trace secrets and incorporation of those secrets into OSCAR 3.4. However, by virtue of Williams' close relationship with Arney, Williams' general familiarity with CA's programs (having once been employed by CA himself), and the fact that Arney used the ADAPTER program in an office at Altai adjacent to Williams during a period in which he had frequent contact with Williams regarding the OSCAR/VSE project, Williams (and through him Altai) may well have been on constructive notice of Arney's breach of his duty of confidentiality toward CA. The district court did not address whether Altai was on constructive notice, thereby placing it under a duty of inquiry; rather the court's finding that only Arney affirmatively knew of the theft of CA's trade secrets and incorporation of those secrets into OSCAR 3.4 simply disposed of the issue of actual notice in connection with the creation of OSCAR 3.4. CA's claim of liability based on constructive notice, never considered in the district court's opinion, must be determined on remand.

With respect to actual notice, it is undisputed that CA's first complaint, filed in August 1988, informed Altai of Arney's trade secret violations in connection with the creation of OSCAR 3.4. The first complaint alleged that Arney assisted in the development of ADAPTER, thereby obtaining knowledge of CA's related trade secrets. It also alleged that Altai misappropriated CA's trade secrets by incorporating them into ZEKE.

In response to CA's complaint, Altai rewrote OSCAR 3.4, creating OSCAR 3.5. While we agree with the district court that OSCAR 3.5 did not contain any expression protected by copyright, it may nevertheless still have embodied many of CA's trade secrets that Arney brought with him to Altai. Since Altai's rewrite was conducted with full knowledge of Arney's prior misappropriation, in breach of his duty of confidentiality, it follows that OSCAR 3.5 was created with actual knowledge of trade secret violations. Thus, with regard to OSCAR 3.5, CA has a viable trade secret claim against Altai that must be considered by the district court on remand. This claim is grounded in Altai's alleged use of CA's trade secrets in the creation of OSCAR 3.5, while on actual notice of Arney's theft of trade secrets and incorporation of those secrets into OSCAR 3.4. The district court correctly stated that a state law claim based *solely* upon Altai's "use," by copying, of ADAPTER's non-literal elements could not satisfy the governing "extra element" test, and would be preempted by section 301. However, where the use of copyrighted expression is simultaneously the violation of a duty of confidentiality established by state law, that extra element renders the state right qualitatively distinct from the federal right, thereby foreclosing preemption under section 301. . . .

Accordingly, we vacate the judgment of the district court and remand for reconsideration of those aspects of CA's trade secret claims related to Altai's alleged constructive notice of Arney's theft of CA's trade secrets and incorporation of those secrets into OSCAR 3.4. We note, however, that CA may be unable to recover damages for its trade secrets which are embodied in OSCAR 3.4 since Altai has conceded copyright liability and damages for its incorporation of ADAPTER into OSCAR 3.4. CA may not obtain a double recovery where the damages for copyright infringement and trade secret misappropriation are coextensive.

However, additional trade secret damages may well flow from CA's creation of OSCAR 3.5. Judge Pratt correctly acknowledged that "[i]f CA's claim of misappropriation of trade secrets did not fail on preemption grounds, it would be necessary to examine in some detail the conflicting claims and evidence relating to the process by which Altai rewrote OSCAR and ultimately produced version 3.5." *Computer Associates.*, 775 F.Supp. at 554–55. Since we hold that CA's trade secret claims are not preempted, and that, in writing OSCAR 3.5, Altai had actual notice of Arney's earlier trade secret violations, we vacate and remand for such further inquiry anticipated by the district court. If the district court finds that CA was injured by Altai's unlawful use of CA's trade secrets in creating OSCAR 3.5, CA is entitled to an award of damages for trade secret misappropriation, as well as consideration by the district court of CA's request for injunctive relief on its trade secret claim. . . .

NOTES

1. On remand to the district court, Judge Pratt held that the applicable Texas statute of limitations barred the trade secret action against Altai. 832 F.Supp. 50 (E.D.N.Y.1993). On appeal by Computer Associates, the Second Circuit certified the question whether the statute of limitations should have been tolled until 1988, when Computer Associates discovered the misappropriation; the Supreme Court of Texas responded that, under Texas law, a discovery rule exception does not apply to the statute of limitations for trade secret actions. 918 S.W.2d 453 (1996). On the basis of the Texas Supreme Court's response, the Second Circuit Court of Appeals affirmed the district court's dismissal of the trade secret claim. 61 F.3d 6, 35 U.S.P.Q.2d 1636 (2d Cir.1995).

2. Computer programs present special problems for trade secret protection. One problem is that a program's innovative elements may embody no more than general, unprotectible concepts. Another is that computer programs are easily reverse-engineered, giving competitors commodious shelter under the reverse engineering privilege. Professor Jerome Reichman has observed that a computer program tends to bear its know-how "on its face" so that "like an artistic work," it is "exposed to instant predation when successful and is likely to enjoy zero lead time after being launched on the market." J. H. Reichman, Computer Programs as Applied Scientific Know–How: Implications of Copyright Protection for Commercialized University Research, 42 Vand.L.Rev. 639, 660 (1989).

NOTE: THE SEMICONDUCTOR CHIP PROTECTION ACT OF 1984

Semiconductor chips are collections of transistors combined into a single structure to process and record information. Semiconductor masks are the intricate stencils used in manufacturing semiconductor chips. Concluding that neither patent nor copyright law offered adequate incentives for investment in chip design, Congress passed the Semiconductor Chip Protection Act of 1984 to protect "mask works" fixed in "semiconductor chip products." For definition of these terms, see 17 U.S.C.A. § 901(a)(1), (2).

Subject Matter. A mask work becomes eligible for protection under the Act when it is fixed in a semiconductor chip product. Under section 901(a)(3), "a mask work is 'fixed' in a semiconductor chip product when its embodiment in the product is sufficiently permanent or stable to permit the mask work to be perceived or reproduced from the product for a period of more than transitory duration...." Section 902(b) withholds protection from any mask work that "(1) is not original; or (2) consists of designs that are staple, commonplace, or familiar in the semiconductor industry, or variations of such designs, combined in a way that, considered as a whole, is not original." Section 902(c) denies protection to "any idea, procedure, process, system, method of operation, concept, principle, or discovery, regardless of the form in which it is described, explained, illustrated, or embodied in such work."

To be protected under the Act, a mask work must meet one of three conditions: (1) it must have been first commercially exploited in the United States; (2) on the date of the work's registration or initial commercial exploitation—whichever occurs first—the work's owner must have been (a) a United States national or domiciliary, (b) a national, domiciliary or sovereign authority of a foreign nation that is party to a mask work treaty to which the United States is also a party, or (c) a stateless person; or (3) the work must come within the scope of a presidential proclamation under the Act. 17 U.S.C.A. § 902(a)(1)(A), (B), (C). Section 902(a)(2) empowers the President to extend mask work protection to foreign works upon finding that the foreign nation protects United States works on substantially the same basis as the Act or "on substantially the same basis as that on which the foreign nation extends protection to mask works of its own nationals and domiciliaries and mask works first exploited in that nation...."

Registration and Notice. Affixation of notice "is not a condition of protection." However, section 909(a) provides that registration is a condition of continued protection under the Act. If a registration application is not made within two years after the date of a mask work's first commercial exploitation, protection for the work will terminate and the work will fall into the public domain. § 908(a). Section 910(b)(1) makes registration a prerequisite to the commencement of an infringement action and section 908(f) makes the certificate of registration prima facie evidence of the facts stated in the certificate and of compliance with the Act's requirements. Section 908(b) vests administrative responsibility in the Register of Copyrights.

Ownership and Rights. Protection under the Act lasts for ten years from the date on which protection began. § 904(b). Section 905 gives a mask work owner "the exclusive rights to do and to authorize any of the following: (1) to reproduce the mask work by optical, electronic, or any other means; (2) to import or distribute a semiconductor chip product in which the mask work is embodied; and (3) to induce or knowingly to cause another person to do any of the acts described in paragraphs (1) and (2)." The Act carves out three limitations from its exclusive rights. Section 906(a) creates a privilege to "reverse engineer" mask works; section 906(b) introduces a first sale defense; and section 907 protects innocent infringers under certain conditions.

The exemption for reverse engineering was one of the Act's most hotly debated provisions. Section 906(a) exempts two forms of reverse engineering. Under section 906(a)(1), it is not an infringement for "a person to reproduce the mask work solely for the purpose of teaching, analyzing, or evaluating the concepts or techniques embodied in the mask work or the circuitry, logic flow, or organization of components used in the mask work." Section 906(a)(2) provides that it is not an infringement for "a person who performs the analysis or evaluation described in paragraph (1) [of section 906(a)] to incorporate the results of such conduct in an original mask work which is made to be distributed." Effectively, this provision permits competitors to imitate protected mask works, and to obtain mask work protection for their "original" imitations, so long as the imitation is not "substantially identical" to the first mask work. According to the House Report, the provision permits "the 'unauthorized' creation of a second mask work whose layout, in substantial part, is similar to the layout of the protected mask work—if the second mask work was the product of substantial study and analysis, and not the mere result of plagiarism accomplished without such study or analysis." H.R.Rep. No. 781, 98th Cong., 2d Sess. 22 (1984).

On the legislative history of the Semiconductor Chip Act, see Robert W. Kastenmeier & Michael J. Remington, The Semiconductor Chip Protection Act of 1984: A Swamp or Firm Ground?, 70 Minn. L. Rev. 417 (1985). The Act generally is examined in Symposium, The Semiconductor Chip Protection Act of 1984 and Its Lessons, 70 Minn. L. Rev. 263 (1985); Richard H. Stern, Semiconductor Chip Protection (1986); David Ladd, David E. Leibowitz & Bruce Joseph, Protection for Semiconductor Chip Masks in the United States (1986).

PART FIVE

INTELLECTUAL PROPERTY PROTECTION OF INDUSTRIAL DESIGN

Works of industrial design may be protected by design patent, copyright, trademark and unfair competition law. The Vessel Hull Design Protection Act, added as Chapter 13 to Title 17 by Pub. L. No. 105–304, 112 Stat. 2860 (Oct. 28, 1998), offers *sui generis* protection to the design of boat and ship hulls and is structured around essentially the same elements as earlier, failed proposals for general design protection legislation. It may be a placeholder for such legislation in the future.

Much of the literature in the field has a strong comparative orientation. See A.L.A.I., The Protection of Designs and Models (1985); Design Protection (Herman Cohen Jehoram, ed. 1976); Christine Fellner, The Future of Legal Protection for Industrial Design (1985). Two articles by Professor Jerome Reichman compare different legal traditions of design protection in their historical setting: Design Protection in Domestic and Foreign Copyright Law: From the Berne Revision of 1948 to the Copyright Act of 1976, 1983 Duke L.J. 1143; Design Protection After The Copyright Act of 1976: A Comparative View of the Emerging Interim Models, 31 J. Copyright Soc'y 267 (1984). A comprehensive symposium on industrial design appears at 24 AIPLA Q.J. 309 (1996).

Anne Marie Greene, Designs and Utility Models Throughout the World (1989) compiles digests of design laws in countries from Abu Dhabi to Zimbabwe. A valuable bibliography appears in U.S. Copyright Office, Bibliography on Design Protection (1955 & Supp.1976).

I. Design Patent Law

In re Nalbandian

United States Court of Customs and Patent Appeals, 1981.
661 F.2d 1214, 211 U.S.P.Q. 782.

NIES, Judge.

This appeal is from the decision of the Patent and Trademark Office (PTO) Board of Appeals (board) affirming the rejection under 35 U.S.C. § 103 by the examiner of appellant's application, serial No. 792,482, filed April 29, 1977, for "Combined Tweezer and Spotlight." We affirm.

Background

The claimed ornamental design is for an implement referred to as an illuminable tweezer. The primary reference on which the examiner and the board relied is U.S. Patent Des. 175,259, issued to Johnson et al. (Johnson) on August 2, 1955, also for an illuminable tweezer. The respective designs are reproduced below:

Appellant's

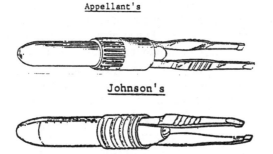

Johnson's

As can be seen from these drawings, appellant's design resembles Johnson's in overall form. The only readily noticeable difference is in the fluting on the cylindrical sleeve which surrounds the body of the implement near the end housing the spotlight. The board agreed with the examiner that secondary references disclosed fluting similar to that in appellant's design, as well as the slight differences in the pincers. However, as we consider it unnecessary to rely on these references, they are not reproduced herein.

The board, in affirming the examiner, stated:

It appears to us that the references are all from reasonably pertinent arts and the claimed design would have been obvious in view of such designs in the prior art. We arrive at this conclusion under Graham et al. v. John Deere Company, 383 U.S. 1, 86 S.Ct. 684, [15 L.Ed.2d 545] 825 OG 24, 148 U.S.P.Q. 459 (1966), whether the test employs a "worker of ordinary skill in the art" or an "ordinary intelligent man."

OPINION

The sole issue on appeal is whether appellant's design would have been obvious within the meaning of 35 U.S.C. § 103. In the words of the statute, are

> ... the differences between the subject matter sought to be patented and the prior art ... such that the subject matter as a whole would have been obvious at the time the invention was made to a person having ordinary skill in the art to which said subject matter pertains[?]

In In re Laverne, 53 CCPA 1158, 356 F.2d 1003, 148 U.S.P.Q. 674 (1966), this court specifically rejected the interpretation generally given to the statutory language "one of ordinary skill in the art" as referring to a designer. The court concluded that this interpretation would not effectuate the intent of Congress to promote progress in designs since it would result in the denial of patent protection for the work of competent designers. Accordingly, it was held that the obviousness of designs over the prior art must be tested by the eyes of the "ordinary intelligent man," who was also referred to as the "ordinary observer."

Since the *Laverne* decision, the Second, Third, Tenth and District of Columbia circuits have specifically considered the "ordinary observer" test set forth therein and rejected it. These circuits continue to interpret "one of ordinary skill" as requiring obviousness to be tested from the viewpoint of the "ordinary designer." Since board decisions may be reviewed by the District of Columbia Circuit as well as this court, the PTO has been faced with two standards in design cases.

We believe it is appropriate to close this schism. Accordingly, with this case we hold that the test of *Laverne* will no longer be followed. In design cases we will consider the fictitious person identified in § 103 as "one of ordinary skill in the art" to be the designer of ordinary capability who designs articles of the type presented in the application. This approach is consistent with Graham v. John Deere Co., 383 U.S. 1, 86 S.Ct. 684, 15 L.Ed.2d 545 (1966), which requires that the level of ordinary skill *in the pertinent art be determined.*

In *Laverne,* this court recognized that the statute does not specifically create a test for nonobviousness of a design which is different from that for inventions defined in 35 U.S.C. § 101. That § 103 applies to designs follows from 35 U.S.C. § 171, which states: "The provisions of this title relating to patents for inventions shall apply to patents for designs...." An ordinary intelligent man was, nevertheless, held to be the person skilled in the art within the meaning of § 103, rather than a designer working in the art, on the following rationale:

> In the mechanical, chemical, and electrical "arts" we have distinguished, since Hotchkiss v. Greenwood, 52 U.S. 248 [11 How 248, 13

L.Ed. 683] (1850), between "an ordinary mechanic acquainted with the business" and the "inventor"; between the craftsman or routineer on the one hand and the innovator on the other, now, by statute, the innovator who makes *unobvious* innovations. With respect to such inventions, these two categories of persons are workers in the same "art."

In the field of design the analysis is not so easy. Design inventing or originating is done by designers. The examiner here has referred to "the expected skill of a competent designer" as the basis of comparison. However, if we equate him with the class of mechanics, as the examiner did, and refuse design patent protection to his usual work product, are we not ruling out, as a practical matter, all patent protection for ornamental designs for articles of manufacture? Yet the clear purpose of the design patent law is to promote progress in the "art" of industrial design and who is going to produce that progress if it is not the class of "competent designers"?

We cannot equate them with the mechanics in the mechanic vs. inventor test for patentability. Correspondingly, we cannot solve the problem here, obviousness, by using for our basis of comparison the inventor class in the field of industrial design. [Id. at 1162, 356 F.2d at 1006, 148 U.S.P.Q. at 676–77. Emphasis in original.]

If an "ordinary designer" test for designs were necessarily equivalent to applying an "ordinary inventor" test for inventions, we would not return to it here. However, the problem thus stated can be viewed as one created by semantics. The "ordinary designer" means one who brings certain background and training to the problems of developing designs in a particular field, comparable to the "mechanic" or "routineer" in non-design arts. We do not have a name for that person in the design field other than "designer" which is also the name we must use for the person who creates a patentable design.

In any event, we do not believe the determination of the level of ordinary skill in the art, as required under *Graham v. John Deere Co.,* supra, cannot be made with respect to designs. Thus, in view of the statutory requirement that patents for designs must be evaluated on the same basis as other patents, the test of *Graham* must be followed.

It is apparent the "ordinary designer" standard has been found helpful to courts in infringement litigation because of the objective evidence which can be brought to bear on the question of obviousness under the tests of *Graham.* We believe it also can be more effectively dealt with by an applicant during patent prosecution than can the "ordinary observer" test. For example, where an examiner selects features from various designs, or relies on common knowledge in the art, the possibility is present of submitting an affidavit from an expert in whose opinion, subjective though it may be, it would not have been obvious to an ordinary designer, despite knowledge (or imputed knowledge) of the prior art to combine features or make modifications as shown in an applicant's design. This possibility is not present using the "ordinary observer" test. No affiant can be qualified as an expert ordinary observer who might, thereby, persuade the person who is deciding the matter that the latter's judgment of the reaction of an ordinary observer is in error.

Rejection of the "ordinary observer" test under 35 U.S.C. § 103 does not preclude its application in other contexts. The "ordinary observer" test was applied in determining whether a claim to a design had been infringed as long ago as Gorham Mfg. Co. v. White, 81 U.S. (14 Wall.) 511, 20 L.Ed. 731 (1871). Further, the "ordinary observer" test has been applied when determining anticipation under § 102 by courts which apply the "ordinary designer" test under § 103.

Conclusion

Applying the "ordinary designer" test of § 103 to the case at bar, the question is whether the changes made by appellant in the Johnson design for an illuminated tweezer would have been obvious to an ordinary design-er of such implements. As noted, the claimed design is substantially identical in overall configuration to the design shown in Johnson for the same type of article. The differences in the finger grips of a slightly different shape and the straight, rather than slightly curved pincers, are de minimis. We also agree that it is well within the skill of an ordinary designer in the art to make the modification of the fluting and that it would have been obvious to do so. Such changes do not achieve a patentably distinct design. We agree, therefore, that the PTO has shown a prima facie case of obviousness.

Once the prima facie case of obviousness was established, the burden shifted to appellant to rebut it, if he could, with objective evidence of nonobviousness. In response, appellant filed a declaration regarding alleged commercial success of his illuminable tweezer. Both the examiner and the board found, and we agree, that the declaration was not persuasive because the alleged commercial success was not shown to be attributable to the design.

In view of the unrebutted prima facie case of obviousness, the rejection of the claimed ornamental design must stand. Accordingly, the decision of the board is *affirmed*.

AFFIRMED.

RICH, Judge, concurring.

A majority of my colleagues choose to swing the court into alignment with the three circuits which have affirmatively rejected the reasoning of our fifteen-year old *In re Laverne* opinion which, until now, this court has always unanimously accepted without question.

Laverne thus being dead, I deem it appropriate, as the father of the so-called "ordinary observer" test (as applied to 35 U.S.C. § 103), to say a few kind words over the corpse.

From the passages quoted from my opinion by the majority, it will be seen that what was written in 1966 was a response to the examiner's reliance on what would be produced by "the expected skill of a competent designer," perhaps an imaginary person of somewhat greater skill than the imaginary "ordinary designer" now enthroned by the majority. I was interested in retaining within the ambit of the patent system the made-for-hire products of "competent designers" so businessmen or corporations would find it economically advantageous to employ them, thus carrying out the objective of 35 U.S.C. § 171, to promote the ornamental design of articles of manufacture.

The majority is not now talking of "competent designers" but of "ordinary designers" from which it follows that there may be extraordinary designers who will produce unobvious designs which ordinary designers will not routinely produce. It is probably true, as the majority says, that all this is just semantics and courts will, with phraseology of their own choosing, continue to find designs patentable or unpatentable according to their judicial "hunches."

The real problem, however, is not whether the § 103 fictitious "person" is an ordinary observer or an ordinary designer but with the necessity under Title 35 of finding unobviousness in a design. The problem long antedates 1952 and its Patent Act and existed from the beginning, the pre–1952 test being the presence of "invention" in a design. The problem was well known to the drafters of the 1952 Act (of which I was one) and it was also known that many prior legislative efforts had been made to solve it. When work on revision of the patent statutes began in 1950, a deliberate decision was made not to attempt any solution of the "controversial design problem" but simply to retain the substance of the existing design patent statute and attack the design problem at a later date, after the new Title 35 had been enacted.

Thus it was that the patentability of designs came to be subject to the new § 103 which was written with an eye to the kinds of inventions encompassed by § 101 with no thought at all of how it might affect designs. Therefore, the design protection problem was in no way made better; perhaps it was made worse.

The intention of the drafters of the 1952 Patent Act to tackle the design protection problem was carried out, by both the private and public sectors, commencing in 1954, by a new "Coordinating Committee" of which I was chairman, and by 1957 new legislation was introduced in the 85th Congress, 1st Session in the form of Willis Bill H.R. 8873. In the 86th Congress, 1st Session, S. 2075 was introduced by Senators O'Mahoney, Wiley, and Hart, being the same bill in substance. From that time on, the legislative effort was continuous until the bill became Title III of the Copyright Revision Bills, later became Title II, and finally was jettisoned to facilitate passage of the main bill, the Act of October 19, 1976, Pub.L. No. 94–553, now 17 U.S.C. § 101 et seq. (1977). Congressmen said they would deal with designs later.

The point of this review is to call attention to the resulting presently pending legislation, H.R. 20, 97th Congress, 1st Session, introduced January 5, 1981, by Mr. Railsback, a bill "To amend the copyright law, title 17 of the United States Code, to provide for protection of ornamental designs of useful articles." The present case and its companion, In re Spreter, 661 F.2d 1220 (Cust. & Pat.App.), concurrently decided, are but the latest examples of the need for a law tailored to the problems of designers, of their employers and clients in the business world, and of the government agencies now concerned. The now-pending legislation is substantially the same bill introduced in 1957, after the refining process of *24 years of legislative consideration. It is time to pass it* and get the impossible issue of obviousness in design patentability cases off the backs of the courts and the Patent and Trademark Office, giving some sense of certainty to the business world of what designs can be protected and how.

Commissioner of Patents and Trademarks Gerald Mossinghoff in his maiden speech to the ABA Patent, Trademark and Copyright Law Section in New Orleans on August 8, 1981, said,

> ... we are *again* urging enactment of an inexpensive and effective form of registration protection for designs and, specifically, we are supporting H.R. 20 introduced by Congressman Railsback last January ... largely because *the concept of unobviousness is not well suited to ornamental designs.* We believe a registration system, such as that contemplated in H.R. 20, would serve industry better at lower cost. [My emphasis.]

The bar would do well to devote its energies to backing this effort of the PTO rather than pursuing appeals such as these which may sometimes result in patents to "extraordinary" designers whose patents, as the Commissioner also pointed out, may then suffer a 70% mortality rate in the courts at the hands of judges reviewing the § 103 unobviousness of the designs.

I have one further comment on the majority opinion, which says that a "determination of the level of ordinary skill in the art" is "required under *Graham v. John Deere Co.*" It is not the Supreme Court that requires such a determination, but the statutory patent law which the Court was simply applying. The *statute* makes that requirement of the courts, all of them, from the highest on down. The Supreme Court said as much. 383 U.S. at 19, 86 S.Ct. at 694.

BALDWIN, Judge, dissenting.

While agreeing with the majority opinion that the "ordinary designer" test of § 103 should be applied, I would reach a different conclusion.

The major difference between the appealed design and the design shown in Johnson is in the fluting on the cylindrical sleeve. This difference is not de minimis but rather creates quite a difference in appearance between the two designs. I cannot agree with the majority that it would have been obvious to the ordinary designer to make the modification of the fluting.

Nor can I agree with the board's conclusion that "the references are all from reasonably pertinent arts and the claimed design would have been obvious in view of such designs in the prior art."

Appellant has taken issue with that board conclusion basically by arguing that the Deibel reference and the Mantelet reference are non-analogous art and that it is improper to use the two references to remedy a deficiency in the Johnson design in order to show a design similar to appellant's illuminable tweezer having a sleeve with longitudinal fluting over a portion of its length.

Even assuming, *arguendo,* that the board did not err by sanctioning utilization of bits and pieces of designs from five references to establish a prima facie case of obviousness of a claimed design, I agree with appellant that the board erred in concluding that all the references are from reasonably pertinent arts. Deibel and Mantelet are not analogous art and should not have been utilized to support the § 103 rejection.

Accordingly, I would reverse the decision of the board.

Avia Group International, Inc. v. L.A. Gear California, Inc.

United States Court of Appeals, Federal Circuit, 1988.
853 F.2d 1557, 7 U.S.P.Q.2d 1548.

NIES, Circuit Judge.

L.A. Gear California, Inc. (LAG) appeals the decision of the United States District Court for the Central District of California, Pensa, Inc. v. L.A. Gear of California, Inc., 4 U.S.P.Q.2d 1016 (C.D.Cal.1987), granting the motion of Avia Group International, Inc. (formerly Pensa, Inc.) for summary judgment holding United States Design Patent Nos. 284,420 ('420) and 287,301 ('301) valid as between the parties and willfully infringed, and the case exceptional under 35 U.S.C. § 285 (1982). We affirm.

I.

BACKGROUND

Avia owns the '420 patent, claiming an ornamental design for an athletic shoe outer sole, and the '301 patent, claiming an ornamental design for an athletic shoe upper, by assignment from the inventor, James Tong. LAG ordered and sold shoes, Model No. 584 "Boy's Thrasher" ("Thrasher") and Model No. 588 "Boy's Thrasher Hi–Top" ("Hi–Top"), designed and manufactured for it by Sheng Chun Chemical Ind. Corp. in Taiwan. Avia filed suit against LAG alleging, *inter alia,* that both of LAG's models infringed its '420 design patent and that LAG's Hi–Top model also infringed the '301 design. LAG counterclaimed for a declaratory judgment that the two patents were not infringed and were invalid because the designs were both obvious and functional. Avia moved for partial summary judgment on the patent validity and infringement issues and for attorney fees.

Finding no bona fide dispute as to any material fact and that Avia had shown entitlement to judgment as a matter of law, the court granted Avia's motion after a hearing. It determined that the infringement was willful and that the case was exceptional within the meaning of 35 U.S.C. § 285 (1982), thus providing the basis for an award of attorney fees. The court also issued a permanent injunction enjoining further infringement by LAG. Because the court reserved decision on the amounts to be awarded as damages and as attorney fees, these matters are not involved in this appeal. . . .

III.

VALIDITY OF '420 AND '301 DESIGN PATENTS

A patent is presumed valid. 35 U.S.C. § 282 (1982). In an infringement action, it is not part of a patent owner's initial burden of going forward with proof of its case to submit evidence supporting validity. Rather, the burden is first on a challenger to introduce evidence which raises the issue of invalidity. Further, a challenger must establish facts, by clear and convincing evidence, which persuasively lead to the conclusion of invalidity. Thus, "[a challenger's] silence leaves untouched at this stage what the statute presumes, namely, that [the] patent is valid." Roper Corp. v. Litton Sys., Inc., 757 F.2d 1266, 1270, 225 U.S.P.Q. 345, 347 (Fed.Cir.1985) (footnote omitted).

With this understanding of the parties' obligations, LAG's argument that Avia unfairly waited for rebuttal to present its evidence regarding validity clearly fails. Avia had no obligation to introduce any evidence initially on validity. Such evidence was required only in response to LAG's evidence.

Where a challenger does put in evidence disputing validity, the presumption of validity is neither eliminated nor undermined by the challenger's evidence, as LAG argues. This is so because the presumption is a procedural device, which assigns the burden of going forward as well as the burden of proof of facts to the challenger. Moreover, the presumption is one of law, not fact, and does not constitute "evidence" to be weighed against a challenger's evidence. Nevertheless, a patent having issued, the challenger bears the burden of persuasion that the established facts lead to a conclusion of invalidity.

The patents in suit are design patents. Under 35 U.S.C. § 171 (1982), a patent may be obtained on the design of an article of manufacture which is "new, original and ornamental" and "nonobvious" within the meaning of section 103, which is incorporated by reference into section 171. LAG attacks the validity of the patents for the subject designs covering parts of shoes on the grounds (1) that the designs are primarily functional rather than ornamental and (2) that the designs would have been obvious from the prior art.

A. *Ornamental versus Functional Designs*

We dispose first of LAG's argument that the record shows genuine issues of material fact with respect to whether the subject designs are ornamental within the meaning of section 171. LAG points only to conclusory, conflicting statements in affidavits, which create no genuine issue for trial, and to evidence of prior art references, none of which is in dispute. LAG's arguments are, thus, misfocused. Rather than arguing that there is a genuine issue of fact, in substance its arguments are that Avia was not entitled to judgment on the basis of the facts established by the record evidence.

LAG correctly asserts that if a patented design is "primarily functional," rather than primarily ornamental, the patent is invalid. When function dictates a design, protection would not promote the decorative arts, a purpose of the design patent statute. There is no dispute that shoes are functional and that certain features of the shoe designs in issue perform functions. However, a distinction exists between the functionality of an article or features thereof and the functionality of the particular design of such article or features thereof that perform a function. Were that not true, it would not be possible to obtain a design patent on a utilitarian article of manufacture, or to obtain both design and utility patents on the same article.

With respect to functionality of the design of the '301 patent, the court stated:

> [LAG] has taken each little aspect of the upper and pointed out that many of the aspects or features of the upper have a function. Even if, arguendo, true that would not make the design primarily functional. If the functional aspect or purpose could be accomplished in many other ways that [sic] is involved in this very design, that fact is enough to destroy the claim that this design is primarily functional. There are many things in the ['301] patent on the upper which are clearly ornamental and nonfunctional such as the location of perforations and how they are arranged, and the stitching and how it's arranged, and the coloration of elements between black and white colors.
>
> The overall aesthetics of the various components and the way they are combined are quite important and are not functional. They are purely aesthetic....

Pensa, Inc., 4 U.S.P.Q.2d at 1019.

On the design of the '420 patent, the court made a similar analysis of various features and concluded:

> But every function which [LAG] says is achieved by one of the component aspects of the sole in this case could be and has been achieved by different components. And that is a very persuasive rationale for the holding that the design overall is not primarily functional. Moreover, there is no function which even defendant assigns to the swirl effect around the pivot point, which swirl effect is a very important aspect of the design.
>
> . . .
>
> ... [T]his is a unique and pleasing design and it's [sic] patentability in my view is not offset or destroyed by the fact that the utility patent is utilized and incorporated in this aesthetically pleasing design.

Plaintiff has given us evidence of other shoes that incorporate the utility patent and its concavity—others of its own shoes—but with a totally different design, and has thus established that the utility patent does not make the design patent invalid in this case.

Pensa, Inc., 4 U.S.P.Q.2d at 1019–20. We agree that the designs in suit have not persuasively been shown to be functional and that no genuine issue of material fact is present with respect to this issue.

B. *Obviousness*

Design patents must meet a nonobvious requirement identical to that applicable to utility patents. Accordingly, 35 U.S.C. § 103 (1982) applies to determine whether the designs of the '420 and '301 patents would have been obvious to one of ordinary skill in the art. The court found no genuine issue of material fact was raised with respect to the four factors to be considered in determining obviousness: the scope and content of the prior art, the differences between the prior art and claims at issue, the level of ordinary skill in the art when the invention was made, and secondary indicia, such as commercial success and copying.

LAG attempts to create a dispute as to the content of the prior art through the court's statement that "all of the shoes referred to as prior art in the record below had come out after the Model 750 [commercial embodiment of the '420 patent] was on the market." LAG mischaracterizes the court's statement. The court restricted that statement to shoes *mentioned by inventor Tong* in deposition answers. The court also noted that LAG's deposition questions were "so generally worded as to be almost meaningless." Neither LAG's failure to ask specific questions during discovery nor its mischaracterization of the court's decision can create a genuine issue of fact.

With respect to a design, obviousness is determined from the vantage of "the designer of ordinary capability who designs articles of the type presented in the application." *In re Nalbandian*, 661 F.2d at 1216, 211 U.S.P.Q. at 784. LAG acknowledges that standard, but asserts that the court is required to defer to its expert testimony. As we have stated, however, an expert's opinion on the legal conclusion of obviousness is neither necessary nor controlling.

Further, a conflict in the legal opinions of experts creates no dispute of fact. LAG argues that the designs would have been obvious because they are "traditional ones consisting of features old in the art." That some components of Avia's designs exist in prior art references is not determinative. "[I]f the combined teachings suggest only components of the claimed design but not its overall appearance, a rejection under section 103 is inappropriate." *In re Cho*, 813 F.2d 378, 382, 1 U.S.P.Q.2d 1662, 1663 (Fed.Cir.1987). There is no evidence that the overall appearances of the '420 and '301 designs would have been suggested to ordinary shoe designers by the references.

LAG does not contest the commercial success of Avia's shoes manufactured according to the patented designs, but argues the success is attributable to factors other than the designs themselves, such as advertising. Although commercial success is relevant only if a nexus is proven between the success of the patented product and the merits of the claimed invention, Avia did present evidence tending to prove nexus and LAG's conclusory statements to the contrary fail to create a genuine factual dispute. In addition, the trial court referred to the accused products as "copies" of the patented designs. Copying is additional evidence of nonobviousness. LAG's conclusory characterization of the evidence as "speculative" is insufficient to create a genuine factual dispute.

On the basis of its evaluation of the four factors outlined above, the court held that the ordinary designer would not have found the '420 or '301 designs, considered as whole designs, obvious in light of the differences between the prior art and the claimed designs. We agree. No genuine issue of material fact or error of law has been shown in the district court's ruling.

IV.

PATENT INFRINGEMENT

The Supreme Court established the test for determining infringement of a design patent in Gorham Mfg. Co. v. White, 81 U.S. (14 Wall.) 511, 20 L.Ed. 731 (1871):

> if, in the eye of an ordinary observer, giving such attention as a purchaser usually gives, two designs are substantially the same, if the resemblance is such as to deceive such an observer, inducing him to purchase one supposing it to be the other, the first one patented is infringed by the other.

Id. at 528. In addition to overall similarity of designs, "the accused device must appropriate the novelty in the patented device which distinguishes it from the prior art." Shelcore, Inc. v. Durham Indus., Inc., 745 F.2d 621, 628 n. 16, 223 U.S.P.Q. 584, 590 n. 17 (Fed.Cir.1984); *Litton Sys.,* 728 F.2d at 1444, 221 U.S.P.Q. at 109. Absent the presence of the novel features in the accused products, a patented design has not been appropriated.

The district court correctly applied the above test for infringement of the subject patented designs, stating:

> I find them as to the ['420] sole virtually identical. In each instance [LAG has] appropriated the novelty of the patented article. One needs only to look at the two soles to see that the infringement exists. But if it is necessary to particularize it we have in the incriminated or accused sole copying of the swirl effect, copying of the separate coloration and configuration of the pivot point, though without the red dot. And we have in the accused sole the whole general appearance, which is almost a direct copy of the patented sole.

> As to the ['301] upper, in my view the same language could be used. It is almost a direct copy. It is much more than the substantially-the-same standard.

Pensa, Inc., 4 U.S.P.Q.2d at 1021. Thus, the court found that LAG's shoes had overall similarity to the patented designs and incorporated the novel features thereof as well. For the '420 patent, those features included the swirl effect and the pivot point; for the '301 patent, the novelty consists, in light of the court's analysis of validity, of the combination of saddle, eyestay, and perforations.

LAG asserts that a patent owner has the burden to prove infringement by preponderant evidence, and that Avia failed to meet that burden. On a motion for summary judgment, however, the question is not the "weight" of the evidence but the presence of a genuine issue of material fact. A patent owner must, of course, present sufficient evidence to make a *prima facie* case. Here, besides its patents and the accused shoes, Avia presented evidence in the form of an expert's declaration analyzing infringement and deposition testimony of LAG's president, in which he confused LAG's Thrasher and Avia's Model 750. In addition, the court performed its own comparison of LAG's shoes to the patented designs. LAG merely challenges the "weight" accorded the expert's declaration and the ultimate finding of infringement. Neither argument raises a genuine issue of material fact which requires a trial.

Finally, LAG points to undisputed evidence that Avia's Model 750 shoe, made in accordance with the patent, and LAG's accused Models 584 and 588, are intended for different customers. The former are for tennis players; the latter are for children. That fact, per LAG, renders the products not "substantially the same," as necessary under *Gorham.* LAG's understanding of *Gorham* is grossly in error. To find infringement, the accused shoes need only appropriate a patentee's protected design, not a patentee's market as well. The products of the parties need not be directly competitive; indeed, an infringer is liable even when the patent owner puts out no product. *A fortiori,* infringement is not avoided by selling to a different class of purchasers than the patentee.

Having considered the above and all other arguments of appellant, LAG, we are unpersuaded of error in the district court's judgment of infringement. . . .

VII.

CONCLUSION

For the foregoing reasons, we affirm the grant of summary judgment to Avia in all respects.

AFFIRMED.

NOTES

1. The incorporation of the design patent provisions, 35 U.S.C. §§ 171–173, in the basic utility patent statute was dictated mainly by expedience.

One reason the design provisions appear in the Patent Act, rather than in the Copyright Act or in a tailor-made statute, is that it was the Commissioner of Patents who first communicated the need for their enactment to Congress. Congress gave little systematic attention to the substantial differences between utility and design subject matter, such as the fact that the Patent Office's lengthy examination procedures may have been out of keeping with the needs of the many designs that enjoy only a short commercial season. Apart from the few specifically stated exceptions from the Act's general application, the Act leaves courts at large in determining the extent to which utility patent principles should govern design patent cases.

On the origins of design patents generally, see Thomas B. Hudson, A Brief History of the Development of Design Patent Protection in the United States, 30 J .Pat. Off. Soc'y 380 (1948). Contemporary efforts to enact a tailor-made industrial design statute along the lines described in Judge Rich's *Nalbandian* concurrence are described at page 997, below.

2. *Ornamentality.* Courts generally treat "ornamentality" as the opposite of "functionality" and construe section 171's requirement that design patent subject matter be "ornamental" to imply the absence of any functional elements in the design patent claims. Does "ornamentality" also require the claimed elements to be aesthetically attractive? Blisscraft of Hollywood v. United Plastics Co., 294 F.2d 694, 696, 131 U.S.P.Q. 55 (2d Cir.1961), read the ornamentality requirement to mean that the design "must be the product of aesthetic skill and artistic conception. Plaintiff's pitcher has no particularly aesthetic appeal in line, form, color, or otherwise. It contains no dominant artistic motif either in detail or in its overall conception. Its lid, body, handle and base retain merely their individual characteristics when used in conjunction with each other without producing any combined artistic effect. The reaction which the pitcher inspires is simply that of the usual, useful and not unattractive piece of kitchenware. The design fails to meet the ornamental prerequisite of the statute."

Consider whether a requirement of aesthetic appeal contradicts the notion, expressed in a leading copyright case, that "[i]t would be a dangerous undertaking for persons trained only to the law to constitute themselves final judges of the worth of pictorial illustrations, outside of the narrowest and most obvious limits." Bleistein v. Donaldson Lithographing Co., page 601, above. Compare *Blisscraft* with the subsequent judicial rejection of an argument that a patented dolly for garbage cans failed the ornamentality test: the argument "overlooks the important point that design patents are concerned with the *industrial* arts, not the fine arts. The statute refers to 'any ... ornamental design for an *article of manufacture.*' 35 U.S.C. § 171. Perhaps it is too much to expect that a trash-can dolly be beautiful. It is enough for present purposes that it is not ugly, especially when compared to prior designs." Contico Int'l, Inc. v. Rubbermaid Commercial Products, Inc., 665 F.2d 820, 825, 212 U.S.P.Q. 741 (8th Cir.1981) (emphasis in original).

3.   During the period 1964–1983, courts held more than 70% of all litigated design patents invalid in cases where validity was in issue. See Thomas B. Lindgren, The Sanctity of the Design Patent: Illusion or Reality? Twenty Years of Design Patent Litigation Since *Compco v. Day–Brite Lighting, Inc.*, and *Sears, Roebuck & Co. v. Stiffel Co.*, 10 Okla. City U.L.Rev. 195 app. II (1985). The Court of Appeals for the Federal Circuit, which has generally loosened the standards for utility patents, see pages 474 to 477, above, may have relaxed the standards for design patents as well. See J.H. Reichman, Computer Programs as Applied Scientific Know–How: Implications of Copyright Protection for Commercialized University Research, 42 Vand. L. Rev. 639, 664 (1989).

II. COPYRIGHT LAW

Mazer v. Stein

Supreme Court of the United States, 1954.
347 U.S. 201, 74 S.Ct. 460, 98 L.Ed. 630, 100 U.S.P.Q. 325.

Mr. Justice REED delivered the opinion of the Court.

This case involves the validity of copyrights obtained by respondents for statuettes of male and female dancing figures made of semivitreous china. The controversy centers around the fact that although copyrighted as "works of art," the statuettes were intended for use and used as bases for table lamps, with electric wiring, sockets and lamp shades attached.

Respondents are partners in the manufacture and sale of electric lamps. One of the respondents created original works of sculpture in the form of human figures by traditional clay-model technique. From this model, a production mold for casting copies was made. The resulting statuettes, without any lamp components added, were submitted by the respondents to the Copyright Office for registration as "works of art" or reproductions thereof under § 5(g) or § 5(h) of the copyright law, and certificates of registration issued. Sales (publication in accordance with the statute) as fully equipped lamps preceded the applications for copyright registration of the statuettes. Thereafter, the statuettes were sold in quantity throughout the country both as lamp bases and as statuettes. The sales in lamp form accounted for all but an insignificant portion of respondents' sales.

Petitioners are partners and, like respondents, make and sell lamps. Without authorization, they copied the statuettes, embodied them in lamps and sold them.

The instant case is one in a series of reported suits brought by respondents against various alleged infringers of the copyrights, all presenting the same or a similar question. Because of conflicting decisions, we granted certiorari.

Petitioners, charged by the present complaint with infringement of respondents' copyrights of reproductions of their works of art, seek here a reversal of the Court of Appeals decree upholding the copyrights. Petitioners in their petition for certiorari present a single question:

Can statuettes be protected in the United States by copyright when the copyright applicant intended primarily to use the statuettes in the form of lamp bases to be made and sold in quantity and carried the intentions into effect?

Stripped down to its essentials, the question presented is: Can a lamp manufacturer copyright his lamp bases?

The first paragraph accurately summarizes the issue. The last gives it a quirk that unjustifiably, we think, broadens the controversy. The case requires an answer, not as to a manufacturer's right to register a lamp base but as to an artist's right to copyright a work of art intended to be reproduced for lamp bases. As petitioners say in their brief, their contention "questions the validity of the copyright based upon the actions of respondents." Petitioners question the validity of a copyright of a work of art for "mass" production. "Reproduction of a work of art" does not mean to them unlimited reproduction. Their position is that a copyright does not cover industrial reproduction of the protected article. Thus their reply brief states:

> When an artist becomes a manufacturer or a designer for a manufacturer he is subject to the limitations of design patents and deserves no more consideration than any other manufacturer or designer.

It is not the right to copyright an article that could have utility under § 5(g) and (h) that petitioners oppose. Their brief accepts the copyrightability of the great carved golden salt-cellar of Cellini but adds:

> If, however, Cellini designed and manufactured this item in quantity so that the general public could have salt cellars, then an entirely different conclusion would be reached. In such case, the salt cellar becomes an article of manufacture having utility in addition to its ornamental value and would therefore have to be protected by design patent.

It is publication as a lamp and registration as a statue to gain a monopoly in manufacture that they assert is such a misuse of copyright as to make the registration invalid.

No unfair competition question is presented. The constitutional power of Congress to confer copyright protection on works of art or their reproductions is not questioned. Petitioners assume, as Congress has in its enactments and as do we, that the constitutional clause empowering legislation "To promote the Progress of Science and useful Arts, by securing for limited Times to Authors and Inventors the exclusive Right to their respective Writings and Discoveries", Art. I, § 8, cl. 8, includes within the term "Authors" the creator of a picture or a statue. The Court's consideration will be limited to the question presented by the petition for the writ of certiorari. In recent years the question as to utilitarian use of copyrighted articles has been much discussed.

In answering that issue, a review of the development of copyright coverage will make clear the purpose of the Congress in its copyright legislation. In 1790 the First Congress conferred a copyright on "authors of any map, chart, book or books already printed". Later, designing, engraving and etching were included; in 1831 musical composition; dramatic compositions in 1856; and photographs and negatives thereof in 1865.

The Act of 1870 defined copyrightable subject matter as:

> ... any book, map, chart, dramatic or musical composition, engraving, cut, print, or photograph or negative thereof, or of a painting, drawing, chromo, *statue, statuary, and of models or designs intended to be perfected as works of the fine arts.* (Emphasis supplied.)

The italicized part added three-dimensional work of art to what had been protected previously. In 1909 Congress again enlarged the scope of the copyright statute. The new Act provided in § 4:

> That the works for which copyright may be secured under this Act shall include all the writings of an author.

Some writers interpret this section as being coextensive with the constitutional grant, but the House Report, while inconclusive, indicates that it was "declaratory of existing law" only. Section 5 relating to classes of writings in 1909 read as shown in the margin with subsequent additions not material to this decision.

Significant for our purposes was the deletion of the fine-arts clause of the 1870 Act. Verbal distinctions between purely aesthetic articles and useful works of art ended insofar as the statutory copyright language is concerned.

The practice of the Copyright Office, under the 1870 and 1874 Acts and before the 1909 Act, was to allow registration "as works of the fine arts" of articles of the same character as those of respondents now under challenge. Seven examples appear in the Government's brief *amicus curiae*. In 1910, interpreting the 1909 Act, the pertinent Copyright Regulations read as shown in the margin.[23] Because, as explained by the Government, this regulation "made no reference to articles which might fairly be considered works of art although they might also serve a useful purpose," it was reworded in 1917 as shown below.[24] The *amicus* brief gives sixty examples selected at five-year intervals, 1912–1952, said to be typical of registrations of works of art possessing utilitarian aspects. The current pertinent regulation, published in 37 CFR, 1949, § 202.8, reads thus:

> Works of art (Class G)—(a)—In General. This class includes works of artistic craftsmanship, in so far as their form but not their mechanical or utilitarian aspects are concerned, such as artistic jewelry, enamels, glassware, and tapestries, as well as all works belonging to the fine arts, such as paintings, drawings and sculpture.

So we have a contemporaneous and long-continued construction of the statutes by the agency charged to administer them that would allow the registration of such a statuette as is in question here.

---

23. "Works of art.—This term includes all works belonging fairly to the so-called fine arts. (Paintings, drawings, and sculpture.)

"Productions of the industrial arts utilitarian in purpose and character are not subject to copyright registration, even if artistically made or ornamented." Rules and Regulations for the Registration of Claims to Copyright, Bulletin No. 15 (1910), 8.

24. "Works of art and models or designs for works of art.—This term includes all works belonging fairly to the so-called fine arts. (Paintings, drawings, and sculpture.)

"The protection of productions of the industrial arts, utilitarian in purpose and character, even if artistically made or ornamented depends upon action under the patent law; but registration in the Copyright Office has been made to protect artistic drawings notwithstanding they may afterwards be utilized for articles of manufacture." 37 CFR, 1939, § 201.4(7).

This Court once essayed to fix the limits of the fine arts. That effort need not be appraised in relation to this copyright issue. It is clear Congress intended the scope of the copyright statute to include more than the traditional fine arts. Herbert Putnam, Esq., then Librarian of Congress and active in the movement to amend the copyright laws, told the joint meeting of the House and Senate Committees:

> The term "works of art" is deliberately intended as a broader specification than "works of the fine arts" in the present statute with the idea that there is subject-matter (for instance, of applied design, not yet within the province of design patents), which may properly be entitled to protection under the copyright law.

The successive acts, the legislative history of the 1909 Act and the practice of the Copyright Office unite to show that "works of art" and "reproductions of works of art" are terms that were intended by Congress to include the authority to copyright these statuettes. Individual perception of the beautiful is too varied a power to permit a narrow or rigid concept of art. As a standard we can hardly do better than the words of the present Regulation, § 202.8, naming the things that appertain to the arts. They must be original, that is, the author's tangible expression of his ideas. Such expression, whether meticulously delineating the model or mental image or conveying the meaning by modernistic form or color, is copyrightable. What cases there are confirm this coverage of the statute.

The conclusion that the statues here in issue may be copyrighted goes far to solve the question whether their intended reproduction as lamp stands bars or invalidates their registration. This depends solely on statutory interpretation. Congress may after publication protect by copyright any writing of an author. Its statute creates the copyright. It did not exist at common law even though he had a property right in his unpublished work.

But petitioners assert that congressional enactment of the design patent laws should be interpreted as denying protection to artistic articles embodied or reproduced in manufactured articles. They say:

> Fundamentally and historically, the Copyright Office is the repository of what each claimant considers to be a cultural treasure, whereas the Patent Office is the repository of what each applicant considers to be evidence of the advance in industrial and technological fields.

Their argument is that design patents require the critical examination given patents to protect the public against monopoly. Attention is called to Gorham Mfg. Co. v. White, 14 Wall. 511, 20 L.Ed. 731, interpreting the design patent law of 1842, 5 Stat. 544, granting a patent to anyone who by "their own industry, genius, efforts, and expense, may have invented or produced any new and original design for a manufacture...." A pattern for flat silver was there upheld. The intermediate and present law differs little. "Whoever invents any new, original and ornamental design for an article of manufacture may obtain a patent therefor, ..." subject generally to the provisions concerning patents for invention. § 171, 66 Stat. 805, 35 U.S.C.A. § 171. As petitioner sees the effect of the design patent law:

If an industrial designer can not satisfy the novelty requirements of the design patent laws, then his design as used on articles of manufacture can be copied by anyone.

Petitioner has furnished the Court a booklet of numerous design patents for statuettes, bases for table lamps and similar articles for manufacture, quite indistinguishable in type from the copyrighted statuettes here in issue. Petitioner urges that overlapping of patent and copyright legislation so as to give an author or inventor a choice between patents and copyrights should not be permitted. We assume petitioner takes the position that protection for a statuette for industrial use can only be obtained by patent, if any protection can be given.

As we have held the statuettes here involved copyrightable, we need not decide the question of their patentability. Though other courts have passed upon the issue as to whether allowance by the election of the author or patentee of one bars a grant of the other, we do not. We do hold that the patentability of the statuettes, fitted as lamps or unfitted, does not bar copyright as works of art. Neither the Copyright Statute nor any other says that because a thing is patentable it may not be copyrighted. We should not so hold.

Unlike a patent, a copyright gives no exclusive right to the art disclosed; protection is given only to the expression of the idea—not the idea itself. Thus, in Baker v. Selden, 101 U.S. 99, 25 L.Ed. 841, the Court held that a copyrighted book on a peculiar system of bookkeeping was not infringed by a similar book using a similar plan which achieved similar results where the alleged infringer made a different arrangement of the columns and used different headings. The distinction is illustrated in Fred Fisher, Inc. v. Dillingham, D.C., 298 F. 145, 151, when the court speaks of two men, each a perfectionist, independently making maps of the same territory. Though the maps are identical each may obtain the exclusive right to make copies of his own particular map, and yet neither will infringe the other's copyright. Likewise a copyrighted directory is not infringed by a similar directory which is the product of independent work. The copyright protects originality rather than novelty or invention—conferring only "the sole right of multiplying copies." Absent copying there can be no infringement of copyright. Thus, respondents may not exclude others from using statuettes of human figures in table lamps; they may only prevent use of copies of their statuettes as such or as incorporated in some other article. Regulation § 202.8 makes clear that artistic articles are protected in "form but not their mechanical or utilitarian aspects." The dichotomy of protection for the aesthetic is not beauty and utility but art for the copyright and the invention of original and ornamental design for design patents. We find nothing in the copyright statute to support the argument that the intended use or use in industry of an article eligible for copyright bars or invalidates its registration. We do not read such a limitation into the copyright law.

Nor do we think the subsequent registration of a work of art published as an element in a manufactured article, is a misuse of the copyright. This is not different from the registration of a statuette and its later embodiment in an industrial article.

"The copyright law, like the patent statutes, makes reward to the owner a secondary consideration." United States v. Paramount Pictures, 334 U.S. 131, 158, 68 S.Ct. 915, 929, 92 L.Ed. 1260. However, it is "intended definitely to grant valuable, enforceable rights to authors, publishers, etc., without burdensome requirements; 'to afford greater encouragement to the production of literary [or artistic] works of lasting benefit to the world.'" Washingtonian Pub. Co. v. Pearson, 306 U.S. 30, 36, 59 S.Ct. 397, 400, 83 L.Ed. 470.

The economic philosophy behind the clause empowering Congress to grant patents and copyrights is the conviction that encouragement of individual effort by personal gain is the best way to advance public welfare through the talents of authors and inventors in "Science and useful Arts." Sacrificial days devoted to such creative activities deserve rewards commensurate with the services rendered.

Affirmed.

Opinion of Mr. Justice DOUGLAS, in which Mr. Justice BLACK concurs.

An important constitutional question underlies this case—a question which was stirred on oral argument but not treated in the briefs. It is whether these statuettes of dancing figures may be copyrighted. Congress has provided that "works of art", "models or designs for works of art", and "reproductions of a work of art" may be copyrighted, 17 U.S.C. § 5, 17 U.S.C.A. § 5; and the Court holds that these statuettes are included in the words "works of art". But may statuettes be granted the monopoly of the copyright?

Article I, § 8 of the Constitution grants Congress the power "To promote the Progress of Science and useful Arts, by securing for limited Times to Authors ... the exclusive Right to their respective Writings...." The power is thus circumscribed: it allows a monopoly to be granted only to "authors" for their "writings." Is a sculptor an "author" and is his statue a "writing" within the meaning of the Constitution? We have never decided the question.

Burrow–Giles Lithographic Co. v. Sarony, 111 U.S. 53, 4 S.Ct. 279, 28 L.Ed. 349, held that a photograph could be copyrighted.

Bleistein v. Donaldson Lithographing Co., 188 U.S. 239, 23 S.Ct. 298, 47 L.Ed. 460, held that chromolithographs to be used as advertisements for a circus were "pictorial illustrations" within the meaning of the copyright laws. Broad language was used in the latter case, " ... a very modest grade of art has in it something irreducible, which is one man's alone. That something he may copyright unless there is a restriction in the words of the act." 188 U.S., at page 250, 23 S.Ct. at page 300. But the constitutional range of the meaning of "writings" in the field of art was not in issue either in the Bleistein case nor in F.W. Woolworth Co. v. Contemporary

Arts, 344 U.S. 228, 73 S.Ct. 222, 97 L.Ed. 276, recently here on a writ for certiorari limited to a question of damages.

At times the Court has on its own initiative considered and decided constitutional issues not raised, argued, or briefed by the parties. . . . We could do the same here and decide the question here and now. This case, however, is not a pressing one, there being no urgency for a decision. Moreover, the constitutional materials are quite meager and much research is needed.

The interests involved in the category of "works of art," as used in the copyright law, are considerable. The Copyright Office has supplied us with a long list of such articles which have been copyrighted—statuettes, book ends, clocks, lamps, door knockers, candlesticks, inkstands, chandeliers, piggy banks, sundials, salt and pepper shakers, fish bowls, casseroles, and ash trays. Perhaps these are all "writings" in the constitutional sense. But to me, at least, they are not obviously so. It is time that we came to the problem full face. I would accordingly put the case down for reargument.

Carol Barnhart Inc. v. Economy Cover Corp.

United States Court of Appeals, Second Circuit, 1985.
773 F.2d 411, 228 U.S.P.Q. 385.

MANSFIELD, Circuit Judge:

Carol Barnhart Inc. ("Barnhart"), which sells display forms to department stores, distributors, and small retail stores, appeals from a judgment of the Eastern District of New York, Leonard D. Wexler, Judge, granting a motion for summary judgment made by defendant Economy Cover Corporation ("Economy"), which sells a wide variety of display products primarily to jobbers and distributors. Barnhart's complaint alleges that Economy has infringed its copyright and engaged in unfair competition by offering for sale display forms copied from four original "sculptural forms" to which Barnhart holds the copyright. Judge Wexler granted Economy's motion for summary judgment on the ground that plaintiff's mannequins of partial human torsos used to display articles of clothing are utilitarian articles not containing separable works of art, and thus are not copyrightable. We affirm.

The bones of contention are four human torso forms designed by Barnhart, each of which is life-size, without neck, arms, or a back, and made of expandable white styrene. Plaintiff's president created the forms in 1982 by using clay, buttons, and fabric to develop an initial mold, which she then used to build an aluminum mold into which the polystyrene is poured to manufacture the sculptural display form. There are two male and two female upper torsos. One each of the male and female torsos is unclad for the purpose of displaying shirts and sweaters, while the other two are sculpted with shirts for displaying sweaters and jackets. All the forms, which are otherwise life-like and anatomically accurate, have hollow backs designed to hold excess fabric when the garment is fitted onto the form.

Barnhart's advertising stresses the forms' uses to display items such as sweaters, blouses, and dress shirts, and states that they come "[p]ackaged in UPS-size boxes for easy shipping and [are] sold in multiples of twelve."

Plaintiff created the first of the forms, Men's Shirt, shortly after its founding in March, 1982, and by the end of July it had attracted $18,000 worth of orders. By December 1982, plaintiff had designed all four forms, and during the first morning of the twice-yearly trade show sponsored by the National Association of the Display Industry ("NADI"), customers had placed $35,000 in orders for the forms. Plaintiff's president maintains that the favorable response from visual merchandisers, Barnhart's primary customers, "convinced me that my forms were being purchased not only for their function but for their artistically sculptured features."

Economy, which sells its wide range of products primarily to jobbers, distributors, and national chain stores, not to retail stores, first learned in early 1983 that Barnhart was selling its display forms directly to retailers. After observing that no copyright notice appeared either on Barnhart's forms or in its promotional literature, Economy contracted to have produced for it four forms which it has conceded, for purposes of its summary judgment motion, were "copied from Barnhart's display forms" and are "substantially similar to Barnhart's display forms." Economy began marketing its product, "Easy Pin Shell Forms," in September 1983. Later in the same month, Barnhart wrote to NADI to complain that Economy was selling exact duplicates of Barnhart's sculptural forms at a lower price and asked it to stop the duplication and underselling. Economy responded with a letter from its counsel dated October 17, 1983 to the Chairman of NADI's Ethics Committee stating that Economy was not guilty of any "underhanded" business practices since Barnhart's forms were not protected by "patent, copyright, trademark, or otherwise."

On the same date (October 17, 1983) Barnhart applied for copyright registration for a number of products, including the four forms at issue here. It identified each of the forms as "sculpture" and sought expedited examination of its applications because of the possibility of litigation over copyright infringement. Copyright registration was granted the same day. Then, on October 18, Barnhart informed Economy that its Easy Pin Shell Forms violated Barnhart's rights and demanded that it discontinue its advertising and sale of the forms. In November 1983, more than 18 months after selling its first form, Barnhart advised its customers that copyright notice had "inadvertently [been] omitted" from the display forms previously distributed and enclosed adhesive stickers bearing a copyright notice, which it asked the customers to affix to unmarked products in inventory.

Barnhart filed this suit in December 1983. Count I charges Economy with violating Barnhart's rights under the Copyright Act, 17 U.S.C. §§ 101–810 (1982), by copying and selling Barnhart's four display forms. Count II alleges that Economy has engaged in unfair competition under the common law of the State of New York. The complaint seeks an adjudication that Economy has infringed Barnhart's copyrights, a preliminary and permanent injunction against Economy's producing, advertising, or selling its forms, damages (consequential, statutory, and punitive), and attorney's fees. Economy moved for summary judgment on the issue of the copyrightability of Barnhart's display forms (and the issue of statutory damages and attorney's fees).

After a hearing on February 3, 1984, Judge Wexler issued an order and opinion on September 12, 1984 granting defendant's motion for summary judgment on the issue of copyrightability. The district court rejected plaintiff's arguments that the issue of copyrightability was an improper subject for summary judgment and that the Copyright Office's issuance of certificates of registration for Barnhart's four forms created an insurmountable presumption of the validity of the copyrights. On the central issue of copyrightability, it reviewed the statutory language, legislative history, and recent case authority, concluding that they all speak with "a single voice," i.e., that a useful article may be copyrighted only to the extent that "there is a physically or conceptually separable work of art embellishing it...." Id. at 370. Applying this test, the district court determined that since the Barnhart forms possessed no aesthetic features that could exist, either physically or conceptually, separate from the forms as utilitarian articles, they were not copyrightable.

On March 6, 1985, 603 F.Supp. 432, Judge Wexler denied Barnhart's motion for reargument. The present appeal followed.

DISCUSSION

Appellant's threshold argument, that the district court erred in ignoring the statutory presumption of validity accorded to a certificate of copyright registration and to the line-drawing expertise of the Copyright Office, can be disposed of briefly. With respect to the prima facie validity of Copyright Office determinations, 17 U.S.C. § 410(c) states:

> In any judicial proceedings the certificate of a registration made before or within five years after first publication of the work shall constitute prima facie evidence of the validity of the copyright and of the facts stated in the certificate. The evidentiary weight to be accorded the certificate of a registration made thereafter shall be within the discretion of the court.

However, "a certificate of registration creates no irrebuttable presumption of copyright validity." Durham Industries, Inc. v. Tomy Corp., 630 F.2d 905, 908 (2d Cir.1980). Extending a presumption of validity to a certificate of copyright registration

> merely orders the burdens of proof. The plaintiff should not ordinarily be forced in the first instance to prove all of the multitude of facts that underline the validity of the copyright unless the defendant, by effectively challenging them, shifts the burden of doing so to the plaintiff.

H.Rep. No. 1476, 94th Cong., 2d Sess. 157, *reprinted in* 1976 U.S.Code Cong. & Ad.News 5659, 5773.

Judge Wexler properly exercised the discretion conferred on him by 17 U.S.C. § 410(c). Once defendant's response to plaintiff's claim put in issue whether the four Barnhart forms were copyrightable, he correctly reasoned that the "mute testimony" of the forms put him in as good a position as the Copyright Office to decide the issue. While the expertise of the Copyright Office is in "interpretation of the law and its application to the facts presented by the copyright application," Norris Industries, Inc. v. I.T. & T., 696 F.2d 918, 922 (11th Cir.), cert. denied, 464 U.S. 818, 104 S.Ct. 78, 78 L.Ed.2d 89 (1983), it is permissible for the district court itself to consider how the copyright law applies to the articles under consideration.

Since the four Barnhart forms are concededly useful articles, the crucial issue in determining their copyrightability is whether they possess artistic or aesthetic features that are physically or conceptually separable from their utilitarian dimension. A "useful article" is defined in 17 U.S.C. § 101 as "an article having an intrinsic utilitarian function that is not merely to portray the appearance of the article or to convey information." Although 17 U.S.C. § 102(a)(5) extends copyright protection to "pictorial, graphic, and sculptural works," the definition of "pictorial, graphic, and sculptural works," at 17 U.S.C. § 101, provides that the design of a useful article

> shall be considered a pictorial, graphic, or sculptural work only if, and only to the extent that, such design incorporates pictorial, graphic, or sculptural features that can be identified separately from, and are capable of existing independently of, the utilitarian aspects of the article.

To interpret the scope and applicability of this language, and the extent to which it may protect useful articles such as the four Barnhart forms, we must turn to the legislative history of the 1976 Copyright Act, which is informative.

Congress, acting under the authority of Art. I, § 8, cl. 8 of the Constitution, extended copyright protection to three-dimensional works of art in the Copyright Act of 1870, which defined copyrightable subject matter as:

> any book, map, chart, dramatic or musical composition, engraving, cut, print, or photograph or negative thereof, or of a painting, drawing, chromo, statue, statuary, and of models or designs intended to be perfected as works of the fine arts.... Act of July 8, 1870, ch. 230, § 86, 16 Stat. 198, 212 (repealed 1916).

The Supreme Court upheld an expansive reading of "authors" and "writings" in Burrow–Giles Lithographic Co. v. Sarony, 111 U.S. 53, 60, 4 S.Ct. 279, 282, 28 L.Ed. 349 (1884), rejecting the claim that Congress lacked the constitutional authority to extend copyright protection to photographs and negatives thereof. The Court further contributed to the liberalization of copyright law in Bleistein v. Donaldson Lithographing Co., 188 U.S. 239, 23 S.Ct. 298, 47 L.Ed. 460 (1903) (Holmes, J.), in which it held that chromo-lithographs used on a circus poster were not barred from protection under the copyright laws. In *Bleistein,* Justice Holmes stated his famous "anti-discrimination" principle:

It would be a dangerous undertaking for persons trained only to the law to constitute themselves final judges of the worth of pictorial illustrations, outside of the narrowest and most obvious limits. At the one extreme some works of genius would be sure to miss appreciation. Their very novelty would make them repulsive until the public had learned the new language in which their author spoke. It may be more than doubted, for instance, whether the etchings of Goya or the paintings of Manet would have been sure of protection when seen for the first time. At the other end, copyright would be denied to pictures which appealed to a public less educated than the judge. Id. at 251–52, 23 S.Ct. at 300–01.

The Copyright Act of 1909 expanded the scope of the copyright statute to protect not only traditional fine arts, but also "[w]orks of art; models or designs for works of art." However, this language was narrowly interpreted by Copyright Office regulations issued in 1910, which stated in part:

> *Works of art.*—This term includes all works belonging fairly to the so-called fine arts. (Paintings, drawings and sculpture).
>
> Productions of the industrial arts utilitarian in purpose and character are not subject to copyright registration, even if artistically made or ornamented. Copyright Office, Rules and Regulations for the Registration of Claims to Copyright, Bulletin No. 15 (1910), 8.

The prospects for a work of applied art obtaining a copyright were enhanced in December 1948, when the Copyright Office changed the definition of a "work of art" in its Regulation § 202.8:

> *Works of art (Class G)—(a) In General.* This class includes works of artistic craftsmanship, in so far as their form but not their mechanical or utilitarian aspects are concerned, such as artistic jewelry, enamels, glassware, and tapestries, as well as all works belonging to the fine arts, such as paintings, drawings and sculpture. 37 C.F.R. § 202.8 (1949).

While this regulation seemed to expand coverage for works of applied art, it did not explicitly extend copyright protection to industrial design objects.

The next significant historical step was taken not by Congress but by the Supreme Court in its 1954 decision in *Mazer v. Stein,* where it upheld § 202.8 as a proper standard for determining when a work of applied art is entitled to copyright protection, in the context of deciding whether lamps which used statuettes of male and female dancing figures made of semi-vitreous china as bases were copyrightable. . . .

The Copyright Office implemented *Mazer v. Stein* by promulgating new regulations interpreting § 5(g) of the 1909 Act, which stated in part:

> (c) If the sole intrinsic function of an article is its utility, the fact that the article is unique and attractively shaped will not qualify it as a work of art. However, if the shape of a utilitarian article incorporates features, such as artistic sculpture, carving, or pictorial representation, which can be identified separately and are capable of existing indepen-

dently as a work of art, such features will be eligible for registration. 37 C.F.R. § 202.10(c) (1959), (as amended June 18, 1959) (revoked 1978).

In an effort to provide some form of protection to "three-dimensional designs of utilitarian articles as such," a number of separate design bills were introduced into Congress. Finally, Title II of a bill passed by the Senate in 1975, S. 22 (The Design Protection Act of 1975), proposed to offer legal protection to the creators of ornamental designs of useful articles. It defined "pictorial, graphic, and sculptural works" to "include two-dimensional and three-dimensional works of fine, graphic, and applied art, photographs, prints and art reproductions, maps, globes, charts, plans, diagrams, and models."

The House, however, responded by passing a strikingly different version. To the text passed by the Senate it added the following:

> Such works shall include works of artistic craftsmanship insofar as their form but not their mechanical or utilitarian aspects are concerned; the design of a useful article, as defined in this section, shall be considered a pictorial, graphic, or sculptural work only if, and only to the extent that such design incorporates pictorial, graphic, or sculptural features that can be identified separately from, and are capable of existing independently of, the utilitarian aspects of the article.

Both of the added clauses were from work of the Copyright Office: the first from its 1948 Regulation § 202.8, approved by the Supreme Court in *Mazer v. Stein;* the second from its post-*Mazer* § 202.10(c). The bill as finally enacted omitted entirely the proposed Title II.

The legislative history thus confirms that, while copyright protection has increasingly been extended to cover articles having a utilitarian dimension, Congress has explicitly refused copyright protection for works of applied art or industrial design which have aesthetic or artistic features that cannot be identified separately from the useful article. Such works are not copyrightable regardless of the fact that they may be "aesthetically satisfying and valuable." H.R.Rep. No. 1476, supra, at 55, 1976 U.S.Code Cong. & Ad.News at 5668.

Applying these principles, we are persuaded that since the aesthetic and artistic features of the Barnhart forms are inseparable from the forms' use as utilitarian articles the forms are not copyrightable. Appellant emphasizes that clay sculpting, often used in traditional sculpture, was used in making the molds for the forms. It also stresses that the forms have been responded to as sculptural forms, and have been used for purposes other than modeling clothes, e.g., as decorating props and signs without any clothing or accessories. While this may indicate that the forms are "aesthetically satisfying and valuable," it is insufficient to show that the forms possess aesthetic or artistic features that are physically or conceptually separable from the forms' use as utilitarian objects to display clothes. On the contrary, to the extent the forms possess aesthetically pleasing features, even when these features are considered in the aggregate, they cannot be conceptualized as existing independently of their utilitarian function.

Appellant seeks to rebut this conclusion by arguing that the four forms represent a concrete expression of a particular idea, e.g., the idea of a woman's blouse, and that the form involved, a human torso, is traditionally copyrightable. Appellant suggests that since the Barnhart forms fall within the traditional category of sculpture of the human body, they should be subjected to a lower level of scrutiny in determining its copyrightability. We disagree. We find no support in the statutory language or legislative history for the claim that merely because a utilitarian article falls within a traditional art form it is entitled to a lower level of scrutiny in determining its copyrightability. Recognition of such a claim would in any event conflict with the anti-discrimination principle Justice Holmes enunciated in Bleistein v. Donaldson Lithographing Co., supra, 188 U.S. at 251–52, 23 S.Ct. at 300.

Nor do we agree that copyrightability here is dictated by our decision in Kieselstein–Cord v. Accessories by Pearl, Inc., 632 F.2d 989 (2d Cir. 1980), a case we described as being "on a razor's edge of copyright law." There we were called on to determine whether two belt buckles bearing sculptured designs cast in precious metals and principally used for decoration were copyrightable. Various versions of these buckles in silver and gold sold wholesale at prices ranging from $147.50 to $6,000 and were offered by high fashion and jewelry stores. Some had also been accepted by the Metropolitan Museum of Art for its permanent collection.

In concluding that the two buckles were copyrightable we relied on the fact that "[t]he primary ornamental aspect of the Vaquero and Winchester buckles is conceptually separable from their subsidiary utilitarian function." Id. at 993. A glance at the pictures of the two buckles, coupled with the description in the text, confirms their highly ornamental dimensions and separability. What distinguishes those buckles from the Barnhart forms is that the ornamented surfaces of the buckles were not in any respect required by their utilitarian functions; the artistic and aesthetic features could thus be conceived of as having been added to, or superimposed upon, an otherwise utilitarian article. The unique artistic design was wholly unnecessary to performance of the utilitarian function. In the case of the Barnhart forms, on the other hand, the features claimed to be aesthetic or artistic, e.g., the life-size configuration of the breasts and the width of the shoulders, are inextricably intertwined with the utilitarian feature, the display of clothes. Whereas a model of a human torso, in order to serve its utilitarian function, must have some configuration of the chest and some width of shoulders, a belt buckle can serve its function satisfactorily without any ornamentation of the type that renders the *Kieselstein–Cord* buckles distinctive.

The judgment of the district court is affirmed.

JON O. NEWMAN, Circuit Judge, dissenting:

This case concerns the interesting though esoteric issue of "conceptual separability" under the Copyright Act of 1976. Because I believe the majority has either misunderstood the nature of this issue or applied an incorrect standard in resolving the issue in this case, I respectfully dissent from the judgment affirming the District Court's grant of summary judgment for the defendant. I would grant summary judgment to the plaintiff as to two of the objects in question and remand for trial of disputed issues of fact as to the other two objects in question.

The ultimate issue in this case is whether four objects are eligible for copyright protection. The objects are molded forms of styrene. Each is a life-size, three-dimensional representation of the front of the human chest. Two are chests of males, and two are chests of females. For each gender, one form represents a nude chest, and one form represents a chest clad with a shirt or a blouse.

Section 102(a)(5) of the Act extends copyright protection to "sculptural works," which are defined to include "three-dimensional works of fine, graphic, and applied art" and "works of artistic craftsmanship insofar as their form but not their mechanical or utilitarian aspects are concerned." 17 U.S.C. § 101 (1982). The definition of "sculptural works" contains a special limiting provision for "useful articles":

> the design of a useful article, as defined in this section, shall be considered a ... sculptural work only if, and only to the extent that, such design incorporates ... sculptural features that can be identified separately from, and are capable of existing independently of, the utilitarian aspects of the article.

Id. Each of the four forms in this case is indisputably a "useful article" as that term is defined in section 101 of the Act, 17 U.S.C. § 101 (1982), since each has the "intrinsic utilitarian function" of serving as a means of displaying clothing and accessories to customers of retail stores. Thus, the issue becomes whether the designs of these useful articles have "sculptural features that can be identified separately from, and are capable of existing independently of, the utilitarian aspects" of the forms.

This elusive standard was somewhat clarified by the House Report accompanying the bill that became the 1976 Act. The Report states that the article must contain "some element that, *physically or conceptually,* can be identified as separable from the utilitarian aspects of that article." H.R.Rep. No. 1476, 94th Cong., 2d Sess. 55, *reprinted in* 1976 U.S.Code Cong. & Ad.News 5668 (emphasis added). In this Circuit it is settled, and the majority does not dispute, that "conceptual separability" is distinct from "physical separability" and, when present, entitles the creator of a useful article to a copyright on its design. . . .

There are several possible ways in which "conceptual separability" might be understood. One concerns usage. An article used primarily to serve its utilitarian function might be regarded as lacking "conceptually separable" design elements even though those design elements rendered it usable secondarily solely as an artistic work. There is danger in this approach in that it would deny copyright protection to designs of works of art displayed by a minority because they are also used by a majority as useful articles. The copyrightable design of a life-size sculpture of the human body should not lose its copyright protection simply because manne-quin manufacturers copy it, replicate it in cheap materials, and sell it in large quantities to department stores to display clothing.

A somewhat related approach, suggested by a sentence in Judge Oakes' opinion in *Kieselstein–Cord,* is to uphold the copyright whenever the decorative or aesthetically pleasing aspect of the article can be said to be "primary" and the utilitarian function can be said to be "subsidiary." 632 F.2d at 993. This approach apparently does not focus on frequency of utilitarian and non-utilitarian usage since the belt buckles in that case were frequently used to fasten belts and less frequently used as pieces of ornamental jewelry displayed at various locations other than the waist. The difficulty with this approach is that it offers little guidance to the trier of fact, or the judge endeavoring to determine whether a triable issue of fact exists, as to what is being measured by the classifications "primary" and "subsidiary."

Another approach, also related to the first, is suggested by Professor Nimmer, who argues that "conceptual separability exists where there is any substantial likelihood that even if the article had no utilitarian use it would still be marketable to some significant segment of the community simply because of its aesthetic qualities." 1 *Nimmer,* supra, § 2.08[B] at 2–96.2. This "market" approach risks allowing a copyright only to designs of forms within the domain of popular art, a hazard Professor Nimmer acknowledges. However, various sculpted forms would be recognized as works of art by many, even though those willing to purchase them for display in their homes might be few in number and not a "significant segment of the community."

Some might suggest that "conceptual separability" exists whenever the design of a form has sufficient aesthetic appeal to be appreciated for its artistic qualities. That approach has plainly been rejected by Congress. The House Report makes clear that, if the artistic features cannot be identified separately, the work is not copyrightable even though such features are "aesthetically satisfying and valuable." H.R.Rep. No. 1476, supra, at 55, 1976 U.S.Code Cong. & Ad.News at 5668. A chair may be so artistically designed as to merit display in a museum, but that fact alone cannot satisfy the test of "conceptual separateness." The viewer in the museum sees and apprehends a well-designed chair, not a work of art with a design that is conceptually separate from the functional purposes of an object on which people sit.

How, then, is "conceptual separateness" to be determined? In my view, the answer derives from the word "conceptual." For the design features to be "conceptually separate" from the utilitarian aspects of the useful article that embodies the design, the article must stimulate in the mind of the beholder a concept that is separate from the concept evoked by its utilitarian function. The test turns on what may reasonably be understood to be occurring in the mind of the beholder or, as some might say, in the "mind's eye" of the beholder. This formulation requires consideration of who the beholder is and when a concept may be considered "separate."

I think the relevant beholder must be that most useful legal personage—the ordinary, reasonable observer. This is the same person the law enlists to decide other conceptual issues in copyright law, such as whether an allegedly infringing work bears a substantial similarity to a copyrighted work. Of course, the ordinary observer does not actually decide the issue; the trier of fact determines the issue in light of the impressions reasonably expected to be made upon the hypothetical ordinary observer. And, as with other issues decided by reference to the reactions of an ordinary observer, a particular case may present undisputed facts from which a reasonable trier could reach only one conclusion, in which event the side favored by that conclusion is entitled to prevail as a matter of law and have summary judgment entered in its favor.

The "separateness" of the utilitarian and non-utilitarian concepts engendered by an article's design is itself a perplexing concept. I think the requisite "separateness" exists whenever the design creates in the mind of the ordinary observer two different concepts that are not inevitably entertained simultaneously. Again, the example of the artistically designed chair displayed in a museum may be helpful. The ordinary observer can be expected to apprehend the design of a chair whenever the object is viewed. He may, in addition, entertain the concept of a work of art, but, if this second concept is engendered in the observer's mind simultaneously with the concept of the article's utilitarian function, the requisite "separateness" does not exist. The test is not whether the observer fails to recognize the object as a chair but only whether the concept of the utilitarian function can be displaced in the mind by some other concept. That does not occur, at least for the ordinary observer, when viewing even the most artistically designed chair. It may occur, however, when viewing some other object if the utilitarian function of the object is not perceived at all; it may also occur, even when the utilitarian function is perceived by observation, perhaps aided by explanation, if the concept of the utilitarian function can be displaced in the observer's mind while he entertains the separate concept of some non-utilitarian function. The separate concept will normally be that of a work of art.

Some might think that the requisite separability of concepts exists whenever the design of a form engenders in the mind of the ordinary observer any concept that is distinct from the concept of the form's utilitarian function. Under this approach, the design of an artistically designed chair would receive copyright protection if the ordinary observer viewing it would entertain the concept of a work of art in addition to the concept of a chair. That approach, I fear, would subvert the Congressional effort to deny copyright protection to designs of useful articles that are aesthetically pleasing. The impression of an aesthetically pleasing design would be characterized by many as the impression of a work of art, thereby blurring the line Congress has sought to maintain. I believe we would be more faithful to the Congressional scheme if we insisted that a concept, such as that of a work of art, is "separate" from the concept of an article's utilitarian function only when the non-utilitarian concept can be entertained in the mind of the ordinary observer without at the same time contemplating the utilitarian function. This temporal sense of separateness permits the designs of some useful articles to enjoy copyright protection, as provided by the 1976 Act, but avoids according protection to every design that can be appreciated as a work of art, a result Congress rejected. The utilitarian function is not truly a separate concept for purposes of "conceptual separateness" unless the design engenders a non-utilitarian concept without at the same time engendering the concept of a utilitarian function.

In endeavoring to draw the line between the design of an aesthetically pleasing useful article, which is not copyrightable, and the copyrightable design of a useful article that engenders a concept separate from the concept of its utilitarian function, courts will inevitably be drawn into some minimal inquiry as to the nature of art. The need for the inquiry is regrettable, since courts must not become the arbiters of taste in art or any other aspect of aesthetics. However, as long as "conceptual separability" determines whether the design of a useful article is copyrightable, some threshold assessment of art is inevitable since the separate concept that will satisfy the test of "conceptual separability" will often be the concept of a work of art. Of course, courts must not assess the *quality* of art, but a determination of whether a design engenders the concept of a work of art, separate from the concept of an article's utilitarian function, necessarily requires some consideration of whether the object *is* a work of art.

Both the trier determining the factual issue of "conceptual separability" and the judge deciding whether the undisputed facts permit a reasonable trier to reach only one conclusion on the issue are entitled to consider whatever evidence might be helpful on the issue, in addition to the visual impressions gained from the article in question. Thus, the fact that an object has been displayed or used apart from its utilitarian function, the extent of such display or use, and whether such display or use resulted from purchases would all be relevant in determining whether the design of the object engenders a separable concept of a work of art. In addition, expert opinion and survey evidence ought generally to be received. The issue need not turn on the immediate reaction of the ordinary observer but on whether visual inspection of the article and consideration of all pertinent evidence would engender in the observer's mind a separate non-utilitarian concept that can displace, at least temporarily, the utilitarian concept.

This approach seems consistent with and may even explain the few cases to have considered the issue, although the language in all of the decisions may not be entirely reconcilable. In *Kieselstein-Cord*, we upheld the copyrightability of the artistic design of two belt buckles. This holding was based upon a conclusion that the design of the buckles was conceptually separate from the utilitarian function of fastening a belt. That view, in turn, was based in part on the undisputed fact that consumers with some frequency wore the buckles as ornamental jewelry at locations other than the waist. The Court apparently concluded that the buckles had created in the minds of those consumers a conception of the design as ornamental jewelry separate from the functional aspect of a belt buckle. Expert testimony supported the view that the buckles "rise to the level of creative art." 632 F.2d at 994. The case was characterized by Judge Oakes as "on a razor's edge of copyright law," id. at 990, as indeed it was; some might have thought that even though some consumers wore the buckle as ornamental jewelry, they still thought of the article as a belt buckle, albeit one so artistically designed as to be appropriate for wearing elsewhere than at the waist. Whether the concept in the mind of the ordinary observer was of a piece of ornamental jewelry separate from the concept of a belt buckle, or only the concept of a belt buckle that could be used either to fasten a belt or decorate clothing at any location was undoubtedly a close question.

In *Trans–World Manufacturing Corp.*, supra, the interesting design of a display case for eyeglasses was deemed to create for the trier of fact a fair question as to whether a concept separable from the utilitarian function existed. By contrast, the designs of the wheel cover in Norris Industries v. I.T. & T., 696 F.2d 918 (11th Cir.), cert. denied, 464 U.S. 818, 104 S.Ct. 78, 78 L.Ed.2d 89 (1983), and the outdoor lighting fixture in *Esquire, Inc. v. Ringer,* supra, were each deemed, as a matter of law, to engender no concept that was separable from the utilitarian function of each article. It evidently was thought that an ordinary observer viewing the articles would have in mind no conception separate from that of a wheel cover (*Norris*) or a lighting fixture (*Esquire*).

Our case involving the four styrene chest forms seems to me a much easier case than *Kieselstein–Cord.* An ordinary observer, indeed, an ordinary reader of this opinion who views the two unclothed forms depicted in figures 1 and 2 below, would be most unlikely even to entertain, from visual inspection alone, the concept of a mannequin with the utilitarian function of displaying a shirt or a blouse. The initial concept in the observer's mind, I believe, would be of an art object, an entirely understandable mental impression based on previous viewing of unclad torsos displayed as artistic sculptures. Even after learning that these two forms are used to display clothing in retail stores, the only reasonable conclusion that an ordinary viewer would reach is that the forms have both a utilitarian function and an entirely separate function of serving as a work of art. I am confident that the ordinary observer could reasonably conclude only that these two forms are not simply mannequins that happen to have sufficient aesthetic appeal to qualify as works of art, but that the conception in the mind is that of a work of art *in addition to and capable of being entertained separately from* the concept of a mannequin, if the latter concept is entertained at all. As appellant contends, with pardonable hyperbole, the design of Michelangelo's "David" would not cease to be copyrightable simply because cheap copies of it were used by a retail store to display clothing.

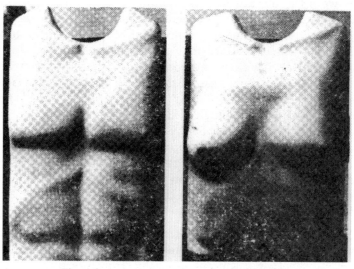

Figure 1   Figure 2

This is not to suggest that the design of every form intended for use as a mannequin automatically qualifies for copyright protection whenever it is deemed to have artistic merit. Many mannequins, perhaps most, by virtue of the combination of the material used, the angular configuration of the limbs, the facial features, and the representation of hair create the visual impression that they are mannequins and not anything else. The fact that in some instances a mannequin of that sort is displayed in a store as an eye-catching item apart from its function of enhancing the appearance of clothes, in a living room as a conversation piece, or even in a museum as an interesting example of contemporary industrial design does not mean that it engenders a concept separate from the concept of a mannequin. The two forms depicted in figures 1 and 2, however, if perceived as mannequins at all, clearly engender an entirely separable concept of an art object, one that can be entertained in the mind without simultaneously perceiving the forms as mannequins at all.

The majority appears to resist this conclusion for two reasons. First, the majority asserts that the appellant is seeking application of a lower level of scrutiny on the issue of copyrightability because the forms depict a portion of the human body. I do not find this argument anywhere in the appellant's briefs. In any event, I agree with the majority that no lower level of scrutiny is appropriate. But to reject a lower level is not to explain why appellant does not prevail under the normal level. Second, the majority contends that the design features of the forms are "inextricably intertwined" with their utilitarian function. This intertwining is said to result from the fact that a form must have "some configuration of the chest and some width of shoulders" in order to serve its utilitarian function. With deference, I believe this approach misapplies, if it does not ignore, the principle of "conceptual separability." Of course, the design features of these forms render them suitable for their utilitarian function. But that fact only creates the issue of "conceptual separability"; it does not resolve it. The question to be decided is whether the design features of these forms create in the mind of an ordinary viewer a concept that is entirely separable from the utilitarian function. Unlike a form that always creates in the observer's mind the concept of a mannequin, each of these unclothed forms creates the separate concept of an object of art—not just an aesthetically pleasing mannequin, but an object of art that in the mind's eye can be appreciated as something other than a mannequin.

Of course, appellant's entitlement to a copyright on the design of the unclothed forms would give it only limited, though apparently valuable, protection. The copyright would not bar imitators from designing human chests. It would only bar them from copying the precise design embodied in appellant's forms.

As for the two forms, depicted in figures 3 and 4 below, of chests clothed with a shirt or a blouse, I am uncertain what concept or concepts would be engendered in the mind of an ordinary observer.

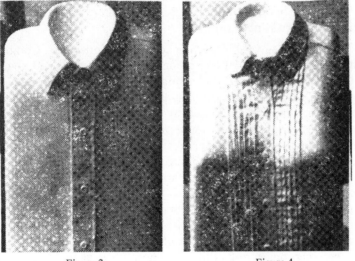

Figure 3   Figure 4

I think it is likely that these forms too would engender the separately entertained concept of an art object whether or not they also engendered the concept of a mannequin. But this is not the only conclusion a reasonable trier could reach as to the perception of an ordinary observer. That observer might always perceive them as mannequins or perhaps as devices advertising for sale the particular style of shirt or blouse sculpted on each form. I think a reasonable trier could conclude either way on the issue of "conceptual separability" as to the clothed forms. That issue is therefore not amenable to summary judgment and should, in my view, be remanded for trial. In any event, I do not agree that the only reasonable conclusion a trier of fact could reach is that the clothed forms create no concept separable from the concept of their utilitarian function.

I would grant summary judgment to the copyright proprietor as to the design of the two nude forms and remand for trial with respect to the two clothed forms.

NOTES

1. Can you reconcile *Barnhart* with Mazer v. Stein? Say that plaintiff had first displayed its works as sculptures in an art gallery and only later marketed them as display forms. What difference, if any, would the court have found between these "sculptures" and the statuettes later used as lamp bases in *Mazer?*

Should the *Barnhart* court have rested its decision on the possibly firmer ground that the works in issue may have been insufficiently original or expressive to qualify for copyright? In Esquire v. Ringer, 591 F.2d 796, 199 U.S.P.Q. 1 (D.C.Cir.1978), cert. denied, 440 U.S. 908, 99 S.Ct. 1217, 59 L.Ed.2d 456 (1979)—where plaintiff unsuccessfully sought copyright registration for the configuration of an outdoor lighting fixture—the Register of Copyrights, Barbara Ringer argued:

> There are several economic considerations that Congress must weigh before deciding whether, for utilitarian articles, shape alone, no matter how aesthetically pleasing, is enough to warrant copyright protection. First, in the case of some utilitarian objects, like scissors or paper clips, shape is mandated by function. If one manufacturer were given the copyright to the design of such an article, it could completely prevent others from producing the same article. Second, consumer preference sometimes demands uniformity of shape for certain utilitarian articles, like stoves for instance. People simply expect and desire certain everyday useful articles to look the same particular way. Thus, to give one manufacturer the monopoly on such a shape would also be anticompetitive. Third, insofar as geometric shapes are concerned, there are only a limited amount of basic shapes, such as circles, squares, rectangles and ellipses. These shapes are obviously in the public domain and accordingly it would be unfair to grant a monopoly on the use of any particular such shape, no matter how aesthetically well it was integrated into a utilitarian article.

591 F.2d at 801 n.15. Would these concerns be better resolved under copyright law's tests of originality and expressive content than under its tests of physical and conceptual separability?

Does the rule denying copyright to utilitarian features of industrial design make sense? Copyright law embraces such patently utilitarian subject matter as computer programs and instruction manuals. What reason is there to distinguish between these works and three-dimensional visual works? If the concern is that copyright for industrial designs will create a monopoly over their functions, would it be better to allow registration—as is done with computer programs and instruction manuals—but to so limit rights that function is not protected?

2. *Separability.* Some courts have required that, to be protected, a design must be "physically separable" from the utilitarian article to which it is attached. See, e.g., Esquire, Inc. v. Ringer, 591 F.2d 796 (D.C.Cir.1978), cert. denied, 440 U.S. 908, 99 S.Ct. 1217, 59 L.Ed.2d 456, reh'g denied, 441 U.S. 917, 99 S.Ct. 2019, 60 L.Ed.2d 389 (1979). Other courts, most notably the Second Circuit Court of Appeals, have followed the suggestion made in the House Report on the 1976 Copyright Act that "conceptually separable" features are also copyrightable. Neither measure is free from difficulty.

Physical Separability. Courts hold that a feature of a useful article is physically separable if the feature can stand alone as a work of art and if separation of the feature will not impair the article's utility. In Ted Arnold Ltd. v. Silvercraft Co., 259 F.Supp. 733 (S.D.N.Y.1966), the court held that a simulated antique telephone that plaintiff used to house a pencil sharpener was copyrightable since the telephone configuration could be physically separated from the pencil sharpener and exist as an independent work of art.

The physical separability test may produce arbitrary distinctions. For example, in Esquire, Inc. v. Ringer, the court held that the configuration of plaintiff's outdoor lighting fixture was not copyrightable because it was not physically separable from the lighting fixture itself. Is the only difference between *Ted Arnold* and *Esquire* that in *Ted Arnold* the copyright claimant had attached its design to a preexisting article, while in *Esquire* it had merged the design into the article itself? If so, could the claimant in *Esquire* have obtained registration for its housing by designing the housing separately, as a work of sculpture, and then welding it to a preexisting lighting fixture?

Conceptual Separability. In Brandir Int'l, Inc. v. Cascade Pacific Lumber Co., 834 F.2d 1142, 5 U.S.P.Q.2d 1089 (2d Cir.1987), a different Second Circuit panel added a new test of conceptual separability to the array explored in *Barnhart's* majority and dissenting opinions. Drawing on an article by Professor Robert Denicola, Applied Art and Industrial Design: A Suggested Approach to Copyright in Useful Articles, 67 Minn.L.Rev. 707 (1983), the court held that "if design elements reflect a merger of aesthetic and functional considerations, the artistic aspects of a work cannot be said to be conceptually separable from the utilitarian elements. Conversely, where design elements can be identified as reflecting the designer's artistic judgment exercised independently of functional influences, conceptual separability exists." 834 F.2d at 1145. Does this test advance analysis of conceptual separability?

Consider whether the following test accurately—or helpfully—synthesizes the prevailing views on conceptual separability: "[A] pictorial, graphic or sculptural feature incorporated in the design of a useful article is conceptually separable if it can stand on its own as a work of art traditionally conceived, and if the useful article in which it is embodied would be equally useful without it." 1 Paul Goldstein, Copyright § 2.5.3.1 (1996).

Under this formulation, the ornamental belt buckle in *Kieselstein–Cord,* discussed in *Barnhart,* would be conceptually separable because the ornamental design could stand on its own as a work of art and the belt buckle would be equally useful without the design; anyone who pays hundreds or even thousands of dollars for an ornamental belt buckle clearly wants something that will do more than hold up his pants. What result would this formulation have produced in *Barnhart?*

3. *"Useful Articles."* Section 101 of the Copyright Act defines "useful article" as "an article having an intrinsic utilitarian function that is not merely to portray the appearance of the article or to convey information. An article that is normally a part of a useful article is considered a 'useful article.' " Is it clear—as the *Barnhart* majority and dissent evidently assumed—that the works in issue there were useful articles? The Venus de Milo can be used as a mannequin for sleeveless blouses, yet few would claim that it is a useful article. Does section 101's use of the adjective "intrinsic" to modify the term "utilitarian function" exclude such marginally useful works from the scope of "useful articles"?

In Superior Form Builders, Inc. v. Dan Chase Taxidermy Supply Co., 74 F.3d 488, 494, 37 U.S.P.Q.2d 1571 (4th Cir.1996), one of the relatively few appellate decisions to explicate the term "useful article," the court ruled that styrofoam mannequins molded in the shape of animals, and used by taxidermists to mount animal skins, did not fit the definition. The court distinguished the mannequins from "ordinary plastic foam pellet animal stuffing": "A mannequin provides the creative form and expression of the ultimate animal display, whereas pellets do not. Even though covered with a skin, the mannequin is not invisible but conspicuous in the final display. The angle of the animal's head, the juxtaposition of its body parts, and the shape of the body parts in the final display is little more than the portrayal of the underlying mannequin." You might consider whether it influenced the court's decision that plaintiff characterized its products as "sculptural works" and had in fact entered several of them in art competitions, where some won awards.

Courts have generally characterized as useful only those articles that have utility as their primary purpose and whose utility lies in their capacity to achieve material ends. One district court held that a toy airplane was a useful article because it possessed "utilitarian and functional characteristics in that it permits a child to dream and to let his or her imagination soar." Gay Toys, Inc. v. Buddy L Corp., 522 F.Supp. 622, 625 (E.D.Mich. 1981). The court of appeals reversed: "[A] toy airplane is to be played with and enjoyed, but a painting of an airplane, which is copyrightable, is to be looked at and enjoyed. Other than the portrayal of a real airplane, a toy airplane, like a painting, has no intrinsic utilitarian function." 703 F.2d 970, 973 (6th Cir.1983).

4. *Should Issuance of a Design Patent Preclude Registration of a Copyright (and Vice-Versa)?* In March 1995, the United States Copyright Office announced that it was dropping the so-called "election doctrine," under which it had for many years refused registration of claims to copyright in pictorial, graphic or sculptural works for which a design patent had previously been issued. 60 Fed. Reg. 15605 (Mar. 24, 1995). Two decades earlier, the Patent Office had dropped a symmetrical rule, following a Court of Customs and Patent Appeals decision, In re Yardley, 493 F.2d 1389, 181 U.S.P.Q. 331 (C.C.P.A.1974), that Congress did not intend to require creators of industrial products to elect between copyright and design patent protection.

The Copyright Office announcement shed little light on the reasons behind the rule change. One reason may have been to obviate the strategic behavior that *Yardley* encouraged—seeking a copyright registration before rather than after the patent issued. It may also reflect a contemporary loosening in Copyright Office registration practices generally.

In re Morton–Norwich Products, Inc.

United States Court of Customs and Patent Appeals, 1982.
671 F.2d 1332, 213 U.S.P.Q. 9.

RICH, Judge.

This appeal is from the ex parte decision of the United States Patent and Trademark Office (PTO) Trademark Trial and Appeal Board (board), in application serial No. 123,548, filed April 21, 1977, sustaining the examiner's refusal to register appellant's container configuration on the principal register. We reverse the holding on "functionality" and remand for a determination of distinctiveness.

Background

Appellant's application seeks to register the following container configuration as a trademark for spray starch, soil and stain removers, spray cleaners for household use, liquid household cleaners and general grease removers, and insecticides:

Appellant owns U.S. Design Patent 238,655, issued Feb. 3, 1976, on the above configuration, and U.S. Patent 3,749,290, issued July 31, 1973, directed to the mechanism in the spray top.

The above-named goods constitute a family of products which appellant sells under the word-marks FANTASTIK, GLASS PLUS, SPRAY 'N WASH, GREASE RELIEF, WOOD PLUS, and MIRAKILL. Each of these items is marketed in a container of the same configuration but appellant varies the color of the body of the container according to the product. Appellant manufactures its own containers and stated in its application (amendment of April 25, 1979) that:

> Since such first use [March 31, 1974] the applicant has enjoyed substantially exclusive and continuous use of the trademark [i.e., the

container] which has become distinctive of the applicant's goods in commerce.

The PTO Trademark Attorney (examiner), through a series of four office actions, maintained an unshakable position that the design sought to be registered as a trademark is not distinctive, that there is no evidence that it has become distinctive or has acquired a secondary meaning, that it is "merely functional," "essentially utilitarian," and non-arbitrary, wherefore it cannot function as a trademark. In the second action she requested applicant to "amplify the description of the mark with such particularity that *any portion* of the alleged mark considered to be non functional [sic] is incorporated in the description." (Emphasis ours.) She said, "The Examiner sees none." Having already furnished two affidavits to the effect that consumers spontaneously associate the package design with appellant's products, which had been sold in the container to the number of 132,502,-000 by 1978, appellant responded to the examiner's request by pointing out, in effect, that it is the overall configuration of the container rather than any particular feature of it which is distinctive and that it was intentionally designed to be so, supplying several pieces of evidence showing several other containers of different appearance which perform the same functions. Appellant also produced the results of a survey conducted by an independent market research firm which had been made in response to the examiner's demand for evidence of distinctiveness. The examiner dismissed all of the evidence as "not persuasive" and commented that there had "still not been one iota of evidence offered that the subject matter of this application has been promoted as a trademark," which she seemed to consider a necessary element of proof. She adhered to her view that the design "is no more than a non-distinctive purely functional container for the goods plus a purely functional spray trigger controlled closure . . . essentially utilitarian and non-arbitrary. . . ."

Appellant responded to the final rejection with a simultaneously filed notice of appeal to the board and a request for reconsideration, submitting more exhibits in support of its position that its container design was not "purely functional." The examiner held fast to all of her views and forwarded the appeal, repeating the substance of her rejections in her Answer to appellant's appeal brief. An oral hearing was held before the board.

Board Opinion

The board, citing three cases, stated it to be "well-settled" that the configuration of a container "may be registrable for the particular contents thereof if the shape is nonfunctional in character, and is, in fact, inherently distinctive, or has acquired secondary meaning as an indication of origin for such goods." In discussing the "utilitarian nature" of the alleged trademark, the board took note of photographs of appellant's containers for FANTASTIK spray cleaner and GREASE RELIEF degreaser, the labels of which bore the words, respectively, "adjustable easy sprayer," and "NEW! Trigger Control Top," commenting that "the advertising pertaining to applicant's goods promotes the word marks of the various products and the desirable functional features of the containers."

In light of the above, and after detailed review of appellant's survey evidence without any specific comment on it, the board concluded its opinion as follows:

After a careful review of the evidence in the case before us, we cannot escape the conclusion that the container for applicant's products, *the configuration* of which it seeks to register, *is dictated primarily by functional (utilitarian) considerations,* and is therefore unregistrable despite any de facto secondary meaning which applicant's survey and other evidence of record might indicate. As stated in the case of In re Deister Concentrator Company, Inc., 48 CCPA 952, 289 F.2d 496, 129 U.S.P.Q. 314 (1961), "not every word or configuration that has a de facto secondary meaning is protected as a trademark." [Emphasis ours.] . . . .

II. Determining "Functionality"

A. In general

Keeping in mind, as shown by the foregoing review, that "functionality" is determined in light of "utility," which is determined in light of "superiority of design," and rests upon the foundation "essential to effective competition," Ives Laboratories, Inc. v. Darby Drug Co., 601 F.2d 631, 643, 202 U.S.P.Q. 548, 558 (2d Cir.1979), and cases cited supra, there exist a number of factors, both positive and negative, which aid in that determination.

Previous opinions of this court have discussed what evidence is useful to demonstrate that a particular design is "superior." In In re Shenango Ceramics, Inc., 53 CCPA 1268, 1273, 362 F.2d 287, 291, 150 U.S.P.Q. 115, 119 (1966), the court noted that the existence of an expired utility patent which disclosed the *utilitarian advantage of the design* sought to be registered as a trademark was *evidence* that it was "functional." It may also be significant that the originator of the design touts its utilitarian advantages through advertising.

Since the effect upon competition "is really the crux of the matter," it is, of course, significant that there are other alternatives available.

It is also significant that a particular design results from a comparatively simple or cheap method of manufacturing the article. In Schwinn Bicycle Co. v. Murray Ohio Mfg. Co., 339 F.Supp. 973, 980, 172 U.S.P.Q. 14, 19 (M.D.Tenn.1971), *aff'd,* 470 F.2d 975, 176 U.S.P.Q. 161 (6th Cir. 1972), the court stated its reason for refusing to recognize the plaintiff's bicycle rim surface design as a trademark:

The evidence is uncontradicted that the various manufacturers of bicycle rims in the United States consider it commercially necessary to mask, hide or camouflage the roughened and charred appearance resulting from welding the tubular rim sections together. The evidence represented indicates that the only other process used by bicycle rim manufacturers in the United States is the more complex and more expensive process of grinding and polishing.

B. *The case at bar*

1. *The evidence of functionality*

We come now to the task of applying to the facts of this case the distilled essence of the body of law on "functionality" above discussed. The question is whether appellant's plastic spray bottle is de jure functional; is it the best or one of a few superior designs available? We hold, on the basis of the evidence before the board, that it is not.

The board thought otherwise but did not state a single supporting reason. In spite of her strong convictions about it, neither did the examiner. Each expressed mere opinions and it is not clear to us what either had in mind in using the terms "functional" and "utilitarian." Of course, the spray bottle is highly useful and performs its intended functions in an admirable way, but that is not enough to render the *design* of the spray bottle—which is all that matters here—functional.

As the examiner appreciated, the spray bottle consists of two major parts, a bottle and a trigger-operated, spray-producing pump mechanism which also serves as a closure. We shall call the latter the spray top. In the first place, a molded plastic bottle can have an infinite variety of forms or designs and still *function* to hold liquid. No one form is *necessary* or appears to be "superior." Many bottles have necks, to be grasped for pouring or holding, and the necks likewise can be in a variety of forms. The PTO has not produced one iota of evidence to show that the shape of appellant's bottle was *required* to be as it is for any de facto functional reason, which might lead to an affirmative determination of de jure functionality. The evidence, consisting of competitor's molded plastic bottles for similar products, demonstrates that the same functions can be performed by a variety of other shapes with no sacrifice of any functional advantage. There is no necessity to copy appellant's trade dress to enjoy any of the functions of a spray-top container.

As to the appearance of the spray top, the evidence of record shows that it too can take a number of diverse forms, all of which are equally suitable as housings for the pump and spray mechanisms. Appellant acquired a patent on the pump mechanism (No. 3,749,290) the drawings of which show it embodied in a structure which bears not the slightest resemblance to the appearance of appellant's spray top. The pictures of the competition's spray bottles further illustrate that no particular housing *design* is necessary to have a pump-type sprayer. Appellant's spray top, seen from the side, is rhomboidal, roughly speaking, a design which bears no relation to the shape of the pump mechanism housed within it and is an arbitrary decoration—no more de jure functional than is the grille of an automobile with respect to its under-the-hood power plant. The evidence shows that even the shapes of pump triggers can and do vary while performing the same function.

What is sought to be registered, however, is no single design feature or component but the overall composite design comprising both bottle and spray top. While that design must be *accommodated* to the functions performed, we see no evidence that it was *dictated* by them and resulted in a functionally or economically superior design of such a container.

Applying the legal principles discussed above, we do not see that allowing appellant to exclude others (upon proof of distinctiveness) from using this trade dress will hinder competition or impinge upon the rights of others to compete effectively in the sale of the goods named in the application, even to the extent of marketing them in *functionally* identical spray containers. The fact is that many others are doing so. Competitors have apparently had no need to simulate appellant's trade dress, in whole or in part, in order to enjoy all of the *functional* aspects of a spray top container. Upon expiration of any patent protection appellant may now be enjoying on its spray and pump mechanism, competitors may even copy and enjoy all of its functions without copying the external appearance of appellant's spray top.[3] . . . .

The decision of the board is *reversed* and the case is *remanded* for further proceedings consistent with this opinion.

REVERSED AND REMANDED.

Two Pesos, Inc. v. Taco Cabana, Inc.

Supreme Court of the United States, 1992.
505 U.S. 763, 112 S.Ct. 2753, 120 L.Ed.2d 615, 23 U.S.P.Q.2d 1081

[The Court's opinion in this case is reproduced beginning at page 368, above.]

Ferrari S.P.A. Esercizio v. Roberts

United States Court of Appeals, Sixth Circuit, 1991.
944 F.2d 1235, 20 U.S.P.Q.2d 1001, cert. denied, 505 U.S. 1219, 112 S.Ct. 3028, 120 L.Ed.2d 899 (1992).

RYAN, Circuit Judge.

This is a trademark infringement action brought pursuant to the Lanham Act, 15 U.S.C. § 1051, et seq. The principal issue is whether the district court correctly concluded that plaintiff Ferrari enjoyed unregistered trademark protection in the exterior shape and appearance of two of its automobiles and, if so, whether defendant Roberts' replicas of Ferrari's designs infringed that protection, in violation of section 43(a) of the Lanham Act. More narrowly focused, the issues are:

3. It is interesting to note that appellant also owns design patent 238,655 for the design in issue, which, at least presumptively, indicates that the design is *not de jure* functional.

— Whether Ferrari's automobile designs have acquired secondary meaning;

— Whether there is a likelihood of confusion between Ferrari's cars and Roberts' replicas;

— Whether the appropriated features of Ferrari's designs are nonfunctional; and

— Whether the injunction granted by the district court is excessively broad.

We must also decide whether the district court properly rejected Roberts' request for a jury trial.

We hold that the district court properly decided all of the issues and, therefore, we shall affirm.

I.

The Facts

Ferrari is the world famous designer and manufacturer of racing automobiles and upscale sports cars. Between 1969 and 1973, Ferrari produced the 365 GTB/4 Daytona. Because Ferrari intentionally limits production of its cars in order to create an image of exclusivity, only 1400 Daytonas were built; of these, only 100 were originally built as Spyders, soft-top convertibles. Daytona Spyders currently sell for one to two million dollars. Although Ferrari no longer makes Daytona Spyders, they have continuously produced mechanical parts and body panels, and provided repair service for the cars.

Ferrari began producing a car called the Testarossa in 1984. To date, Ferrari has produced approximately 5000 Testarossas. Production of these cars is also intentionally limited to preserve exclusivity: the entire anticipated production is sold out for the next several years and the waiting period to purchase a Testarossa is approximately five years. A new Testarossa sells for approximately $230,000.

Roberts is engaged in a number of business ventures related to the automobile industry. One enterprise is the manufacture of fiberglass kits that replicate the exterior features of Ferrari's Daytona Spyder and Testarossa automobiles. Roberts' copies are called the Miami Spyder and the Miami Coupe, respectively. The kit is a one-piece body shell molded from reinforced fiberglass. It is usually bolted onto the undercarriage of another automobile such as a Chevrolet Corvette or a Pontiac Fiero, called the donor car. Roberts marketed the Miami Spyder primarily through advertising in kit-car magazines. Most of the replicas were sold as kits for about $8,500, although a fully accessorized "turn-key" version was available for about $50,000.

At the time of trial, Roberts had not yet completed a kit-car version of the Miami Coupe, the replica of Ferrari's Testarossa, although he already has two orders for them. He originally built the Miami Coupe for the producers of the television program "Miami Vice" to be used as a stunt car in place of the more expensive Ferrari Testarossa.

The district court found, and it is not disputed, that Ferrari's automobiles and Roberts' replicas are virtually identical in appearance.

Ferrari brought suit against Roberts in March 1988 alleging trademark infringement, in violation of section 43(a) of the Lanham Act, and obtained a preliminary injunction enjoining Roberts from manufacturing the replica cars. The injunction was later amended to permit Roberts to recommence production of the two models.

Five months later, Roberts filed a voluntary petition in bankruptcy. Despite the Chapter 11 proceedings, the bankruptcy court, in a carefully limited order, lifted the automatic stay and permitted Ferrari to continue to prosecute this action. Prior to trial, the district court denied Roberts' request for a jury, and the case was tried to the court resulting in a verdict for Ferrari and a permanent injunction enjoining Roberts from producing the Miami Spyder and the Miami Coupe.

II.

Section 43(a) of the Lanham Act creates a civil cause of action for trademark infringement. In relevant part, section 43(a) provides:

> Any person who, on or in connection with any goods or services, or any container for goods, uses in commerce any word, term, name, symbol, or device, or any combination thereof, or any false designation of origin, false or misleading description of fact, or false or misleading representation of fact, which—

> > (1) is likely to cause confusion, or to cause mistake, or to deceive as to the affiliation, connection, or association of such person with another person, or as to the origin, sponsorship, or approval of his or her goods, services, or commercial activities by another person....

> > . . .

> shall be liable in a civil action by any person who believes that he or she is or is likely to be damaged by such act.

The protection against infringement provided by section 43(a) is not limited to "goods, services or commercial activities" protected by registered trademarks. It extends as well, in certain circumstances, to the unregistered "trade dress" of an article. "Trade dress" refers to "the image and overall appearance of a product." Allied Mktg. Group, Inc. v. CDL Mktg., Inc., 878 F.2d 806, 812 (5th Cir.1989). It embodies "that arrangement of identifying characteristics or decorations connected with a product, whether by packaging or otherwise, intended to make the source of the product distinguishable from another and to promote its sale." Mr. Gasket Co. v. Travis, 35 Ohio App.2d 65, 72 n. 13, 299 N.E.2d 906, 912 n. 13 (1973).

Ferrari's Lanham Act claim in this case is a "trade dress" claim. Ferrari charges, and the district court found, that the unique and distinctive exterior shape and design of the Daytona Spyder and the Testarossa are protected trade dress which Roberts has infringed by copying them and marketing his replicas.

Roberts asserts that there has been no infringement under section 43(a) for a number of reasons: (1) the design of Ferrari's vehicles are protected only under design patent law, and not the Lanham Act; (2) there is no actionable likelihood of confusion between Ferrari's vehicles and Roberts' replicas at the point of sale; and (3) the "aesthetic functionality doctrine" precludes recovery.

We shall take up each argument in turn.

III.

To prove a violation of section 43(a), Ferrari's burden is to show, by a preponderance of the evidence:

1) that the trade dress of Ferrari's vehicles has acquired a "secondary meaning,"

2) that there is a likelihood of confusion based on the similarity of the exterior shape and design of Ferrari's vehicles and Roberts' replicas, and

3) that the appropriated features of Ferrari's trade dress are primarily nonfunctional.

A.

Secondary Meaning

> To acquire a secondary meaning in the minds of the buying public, an article of merchandise when shown to a prospective customer must prompt the affirmation, "That is the article I want because I know its source," and not the negative inquiry as to "Who makes that article?" In other words, the article must proclaim its identification with its source, and not simply stimulate inquiry about it.

West Point Mfg. Co. v. Detroit Stamping Co., 222 F.2d 581, 595 (6th Cir.) (citation omitted), cert. denied, 350 U.S. 840, 76 S.Ct. 80, 100 L.Ed. 749 (1955). Arguably, secondary meaning in this case can be presumed from Roberts' admissions that he intentionally copied Ferrari's designs. Roberts told Vivian Bumgardner, an investigator who recorded her conversations with Roberts, that "we put this whole body right on it and it looks just like a real car, I mean they can't tell by looking. . . . We build and sell the same car, reproduce it." The intent to copy was also shown by Roberts' use of the distinctive Ferrari prancing horse logo on the front parking lights of the Daytona Spyder and in advertising brochures. The original Miami Coupe brochure even copied the Ferrari name by referring to the Roberts' car as the "Miami Testarossa." The evidence of intentional copying shows the strong secondary meaning of the Ferrari designs because "[t]here is no logical reason for the precise copying save an attempt to realize upon a secondary meaning that is in existence." Audio Fidelity, Inc. v. High Fidelity Recordings, Inc., 283 F.2d 551, 558 (9th Cir.1960).

Ferrari, however, need not rely on a presumption of secondary meaning because the evidence at trial showed that the exterior design of Ferrari's vehicles enjoyed strong secondary meaning. Lawrence Crane, Art Director of *Automobile* magazine, testified that the shape of a Ferrari "says Ferrari to the general populous (sic)" and that "because it's so instantly recognizable . . . we've used even just portions of Ferraris, the Testarossa, for instance, and people recognize it, and our sales are changed." William Moore, Editor of *Kit Car Illustrated,* and a witness for Roberts, conceded that car replica manufacturers frequently copy Ferraris because the "special image" associated with Ferrari creates a market for cars which look like Ferraris. The testimony of Crane and Moore was supported by survey data which indicated that of survey respondents shown photographs of Ferrari's cars without identifying badges, 73% properly identified a photograph of the Daytona Spyder as manufactured by Ferrari and 82% identified the Testarossa as a Ferrari product. Such survey evidence, combined with intentional copying and the widespread publicity surrounding Ferraris, convinced the court in a separate action brought by Ferrari against Roberts' former partner to enjoin him from producing replicas of the Daytona Spyder identical to those produced by Roberts, that the Ferrari vehicle design has a secondary meaning:

> In light of defendants' close intentional copying, their failure to introduce any evidence to show that such copying was for any purpose but to associate themselves with the reputation and marketability of the Ferrari DAYTONA SPYDER, the large amount of recognition of said design with Ferrari shown in continuous magazine articles and books about the DAYTONA SPYDER long after the cessation of its manufacture, the showings of the Ferrari DAYTONA SPYDER at vintage car shows, the highly publicized sales of said car by Ferrari customers, and the percentages of recognition in both the plaintiff's and the defendants' surveys, . . . the court finds the evidence thorough and convincing that the Ferrari DAYTONA SPYDER design has achieved a strong secondary meaning.

Ferrari S.p.A. v. McBurnie, 11 U.S.P.Q.2d 1843, 1846–47 (S.D.Cal.1989).

Ferrari's vehicles would not acquire secondary meaning merely because they are unique designs or because they are aesthetically beautiful. The design must be one that is instantly identified in the mind of the informed viewer as a Ferrari design. The district court found, and we agree, that the unique exterior design and shape of the Ferrari vehicles are their "mark" or "trade dress" which distinguish the vehicles' exterior shapes not simply as distinctively attractive designs, but as Ferrari creations.

We also agree with the district court that Roberts' admission that he intentionally copied Ferrari's design, the survey evidence introduced by Ferrari, and the testimony of Crane and Moore amount to abundant evidence that the exterior design features of the Ferrari vehicles are "trade dress" which have acquired secondary meaning.

Roberts argues strongly that section 43(a) provides no trademark infringement protection for the exterior design of a product because "automobile designs are to be protected from copying only pursuant to the design patent statute," and Ferrari, during the period relevant to this case, had not protected the Daytona Spyder or the Testarossa with a design patent. We disagree.

Courts have consistently rejected Roberts' argument that the availability of design patent protection precludes applicability of the Lanham Act for products whose trade dress have acquired strong secondary meaning. Actionable harm results from either infringing a design patent or copying a product with secondary meaning. As the court explained in Rolls–Royce Motors, Ltd. v. A & A Fiberglass, Inc., 428 F.Supp. 689, 692–93 (N.D.Ga. 1976):

> There is no doubt that the plaintiffs' Classic Grill and Flying Lady are attractive objects. As such, they may be deserving of copyright or design patent protection. Their entitlement to trademark recognition, however, depends not on their eye appeal but on their characteristic of identifying the manufacturer of Rolls–Royce motor cars.

Likewise, the distinctive appearance of a Ferrari's exterior shape, as evidenced at trial by surveys and the testimony of car magazine editors and others, entitles Ferrari to Lanham Act protection. This trademark protection does not unduly extend the seventeen-year monopoly guaranteed by the patent laws because the two sources of protection are totally separate:

> [T]rademark rights, or rights under the law of unfair competition, which happen to continue beyond the expiration of a design patent, do not "extend" the patent monopoly. They exist independently of it, under different law and for different reasons. The termination of either has no legal effect on the continuance of the other.

Application of Mogen David Wine Corp., 328 F.2d 925, 930, 51 CCPA 1260 (1964). Patent and trademark law are completely distinct fields:

> The protection accorded by the law of trademark and unfair competition is greater than that accorded by the law of patents because each is directed at a different purpose. The latter protects inventive activity which, after a term of years, is dedicated to the public domain. The former protects commercial activity which, in our society, is essentially private.

Truck Equip. Serv. Co. v. Fruehauf Corp., 536 F.2d 1210, 1215 (8th Cir.), cert. denied, 429 U.S. 861, 97 S.Ct. 164, 50 L.Ed.2d 139 (1976)....

Thus, Lanham Act protection is available to designs which also might have been covered by design patents as long as the designs have acquired secondary meaning. Ferrari's designs have clearly acquired secondary meaning and thus were entitled to protection.

B.
Likelihood of Confusion

1.
District Court's Findings

This court has held that in determining likelihood of confusion in a Lanham Act case, the court should consider the following factors: strength of the plaintiff's mark; relatedness of the goods; similarity of the marks; evidence of actual confusion; marketing channels used; likely degree of purchaser care; defendant's intent in selecting the mark; and likelihood of expansion of the product lines. . . .

We conclude that aside from the presumption of likelihood of confusion that follows from intentional copying, Ferrari produced strong evidence that the public is likely to be confused by the similarity of the exterior design of Ferrari's vehicles and Roberts' replicas.

2.

Roberts' Objections

Roberts disagrees with the legal significance of the district court's findings of likelihood of confusion. He argues that for purposes of the Lanham Act, the requisite likelihood of confusion must be confusion at the point of sale—purchaser confusion—and not the confusion of nonpurchasing, casual observers. The evidence is clear that Roberts assured purchasers of his replicas that they were not purchasing Ferraris and that his customers were not confused about what they were buying.

Roberts also argues that actionable confusion may not be inferred from intentional copying when the intentional copying involves the design of a product as opposed to the copying of a trademark, trade name or trade dress. Implicit, of course, is Roberts' related argument that the exterior shape and design of the Ferrari cars is not, and cannot be, a trademark or trade dress. We disagree with these contentions.

a.

Confusion as to Source

Roberts is correct that, for the most part, similarity of products alone is not actionable; there must also be confusion as to the origin of the product. *West Point Mfg.*, 222 F.2d at 589. Similarity of products, however, does become actionable when the similarity leads to confusion as to source and the public cares who the source of the product is. . . .

In contrast to *West Point*, Roberts copied the nonfunctional features of an item having great secondary meaning.

Because consumers care that they are purchasing a Ferrari as opposed to a car that looks like a Ferrari, and because Roberts' replicas look like Ferraris, Ferrari presented an actionable claim as to confusion of source.

b.

Confusion at Point of Sale

Roberts argues that his replicas do not violate the Lanham Act because he informed his purchasers that his significantly cheaper cars and kits were not genuine Ferraris and thus there was no confusion at the point of sale. The Lanham Act, however, was intended to do more than protect consumers at the point of sale. When the Lanham Act was enacted in 1946, its protection was limited to the use of marks "likely to cause confusion or mistake or to deceive purchasers as to the source of origin of such goods or services." In 1967, Congress deleted this language and broadened the Act's protection to include the use of marks "likely to cause confusion or mistake or to deceive." Thus, Congress intended "to regulate commerce within [its control] by making actionable the deceptive and misleading use of marks in such commerce; [and] ... to protect persons engaged in such commerce against unfair competition...." 15 U.S.C. § 1127. Although, as the dissent points out, Congress rejected an anti-dilution provision when recently amending the Lanham Act, it made no effort to amend or delete this language clearly protecting the confusion of goods *in commerce*. The court in *Rolex Watch* explicitly recognized this concern with regulating commerce:

> The real question before this Court is whether the alleged infringer has placed a product *in commerce* that is "likely to cause confusion, or to cause mistake, or to deceive." ... The fact that an immediate buyer of a $25 counterfeit watch does not entertain any notions that it is the real thing has no place in this analysis. Once a product is injected into commerce, there is no bar to confusion, mistake, or deception occurring at some future point in time.

Rolex Watch, 645 F.Supp. at 492–93 (emphasis in original). The *Rolex Watch* court noted that this interpretation was necessary to protect against the cheapening and dilution of the genuine product, and to protect the manufacturer's reputation. As the court explained:

> Individuals examining the counterfeits, believing them to be genuine Rolex watches, might find themselves unimpressed with the quality of the item and consequently be inhibited from purchasing the real time piece. Others who see the watches bearing the Rolex trademarks on so many wrists might find themselves discouraged from acquiring a genuine because the items have become too common place and no longer possess the prestige once associated with them.

Rolex Watch, 645 F.Supp. at 495. Such is the damage which could occur here. As the district court explained when deciding whether Roberts' former partner's Ferrari replicas would be confused with Ferrari's cars:

> Ferrari has gained a well-earned reputation for making uniquely designed automobiles of quality and rarity. The DAYTONA SPYDER design is well-known among the relevant public and exclusively and positively associated with Ferrari. If the country is populated with hundreds, if not thousands, of replicas of rare, distinct, and unique vintage cars, obviously they are no longer unique. Even if a person seeing one of these replicas driving down the road is not confused, Ferrari's exclusive association with this design has been diluted and eroded. If the replica Daytona looks cheap or in disrepair, Ferrari's reputation for rarity and quality could be damaged....

Ferrari, 11 U.S.P.Q.2d at 1848. The dissent argues that the Lanham Act requires proof of confusion at the point of sale because the eight factor test used to determine likelihood of confusion focuses on the confusion of the purchaser, not the public. The dissent submits that three of the factors, marketing channels used, likely degree of purchaser care and sophistication, and evidence of actual confusion, specifically relate to purchasers. However, evidence of actual confusion is not limited to purchasers. The survey evidence in this case showed that members of the public, but not necessarily purchasers, were actually confused by the similarity of the products. Moreover, the other five factors, strength of the mark, relatedness of the goods, similarity of the marks, defendant's intent in selecting the mark, and likelihood of product expansion, do not limit the likelihood of confusion test to purchasers.

Since Congress intended to protect the reputation of the manufacturer as well as to protect purchasers, the Act's protection is not limited to confusion at the point of sale. Because Ferrari's reputation in the field could be damaged by the marketing of Roberts' replicas, the district court did not err in permitting recovery despite the absence of point of sale confusion.

3.

Product Confusion

Roberts argues that the exterior design features of the Ferrari vehicles are not entitled to Lanham Act protection because only packages in which products are marketed, not products themselves, are covered as protected trade dress.... In this case, where the exterior shape and design of the car is a "form of dress ... primarily adopted for purposes of identification and individuality," the interest in free competition of cars would not be impeded by protecting the product itself. We are fortified in this conclusion by the large number of cases extending trademark protection to product designs.

Even if a product cannot be protected, Ferrari is correct in asserting that its exteriors qualify as a trade dress. As the court explained in a replication case involving expensive silver patterns, "A product's trade dress ordinarily consists of its packaging. However, the design given a product by its manufacturer also may serve to distinguish it from the products of other manufacturers and hence be protectible trade dress." Wallace Int'l Silversmiths, Inc. v. Godinger Silver Art Co., 916 F.2d 76, 78–79 (2d Cir.1990), cert. denied, 499 U.S. 976, 111 S.Ct. 1622, 113 L.Ed.2d 720 (1991). In this case, the exterior design is the "packaging" that is the distinctiveness of a Ferrari automobile. The evidence is that Ferraris need no labeling; the shape of the vehicles "says Ferrari."

C.

Nonfunctionality of Appropriated Features

Trademark law does not protect the functional features of products because such protection would provide a perpetual monopoly of features which could not be patented. A product feature is functional "if it is essential to the use or purpose of the article or if it affects the cost or quality of the article." Inwood Laboratories, Inc. v. Ives Laboratories, Inc.,

456 U.S. 844, 850 n. 10, 102 S.Ct. 2182, 2187 n. 10, 72 L.Ed.2d 606 (1982). Functionality is a factual determination reviewed only for clear error.

The district court found that Ferrari proved, by a preponderance of the evidence, that the exterior shapes and features of the Daytona Spyder and Testarossa were nonfunctional. The court based this conclusion on the uncontroverted testimony of Angelo Bellei, who developed Ferrari's grand touring cars from 1964–75, that the company chose the exterior designs for beauty and distinctiveness, not utility. Roberts disagrees that Ferrari established nonfunctionality because he believes that the designs are excluded from protection by the "aesthetic functionality doctrine."

The aesthetic functionality test was developed by the Ninth Circuit in *Pagliero* [v. Wallace China Co.], 198 F.2d 339. In *Pagliero,* the court found that the defendant's copying of the plaintiff's designs for hotel china was not actionable because the designs were functional as "an important ingredient in the commercial success of the product" as opposed to "a mere arbitrary embellishment, a form of dress for the goods primarily adopted for purposes of identification and individuality and, hence, unrelated to basic consumer demands in connection with the product. . . ." Id. at 343. As the court explained:

> [O]ne of the essential selling features of hotel china, if, indeed, not the primary, is the design. The attractiveness and eye-appeal of the design sells the china. Moreover, from the standpoint of the purchaser china satisfies a demand for the aesthetic as well as for the utilitarian, and the design on china is, at least in part, the response to such demand. The granting of relief in this type of situation would render Wallace immune from the most direct and effective competition with regard to these lines of china.

Id. at 343–44.

The broad scope of aesthetic functionality defined in *Pagliero* has been subsequently criticized and limited. Relating functionality to the commercial desirability of the feature regardless of its utilitarian function discourages the development of appealing designs because such designs would be entitled to less protection. Moreover, *Pagliero*'s "important ingredient" formula has been rejected because "[t]rade dress associated with a product that has accumulated goodwill ... will almost always be 'an important ingredient' in the 'saleability' of the product." *LeSportsac* [v. K Mart Corp.], 754 F.2d at 77. In part because of these concerns, the Ninth Circuit itself later rejected the view that "any feature of a product which contributes to the consumer appeal and saleability of the product is, as a matter of law, a functional element of that product." *Vuitton* [v. J. Young Ents., Inc.], 644 F.2d at 773.

Our own circuit seems to have implicitly rejected *Pagliero*'s aesthetic functionality test. In WSM, Inc. v. Tennessee Sales Co., 709 F.2d 1084 (6th Cir.1983), the defendant, who copied plaintiff's amusement park souvenir T-shirts, argued that the design was not protected because of its aesthetic functionality. The court rejected this argument:

TS' assertion that its use of the involved design is "functional," i.e., "ornamental" or "decorative," is unavailing.... That an item serves or performs a function does not mean, however, that it may not at the same time be capable of indicating sponsorship or origin where aspects of the item are nonfunctional. The district court found that WSM's mark served to indicate source in addition to any "ornamental" function it might also serve. No basis exists for upsetting that finding.

Id. at 1087. Thus, the precedent in this circuit suggests that aesthetic functionality will not preclude a finding of nonfunctionality where the design also indicates source.

Other circuits also emphasize identification of source in limiting *Pagliero*. In *Keene Corp.* [v. Paraflex Industries], the Third Circuit suggested that "the inquiry should focus on the extent to which the design feature is related to the utilitarian function of the product or feature." *Keene Corp.*, 653 F.2d at 825. Thus, trademark law would protect designs not significantly related to a product's utilitarian function which had achieved secondary meaning. The court noted that this view had already received acceptance in cases holding that distinctive features used for identification were entitled to protection where such features were only incidentally functional. The Ninth Circuit also seemed to accept this formulation as a legitimate reading of *Pagliero*. In *Vuitton,* the court noted that the designs in *Pagliero* were adopted because of their aesthetic features and only after extensive advertising later became associated with the manufacturer. *Vuitton,* 644 F.2d at 773. That situation differs greatly from this case in which the Ferrari designs were selected for their distinctiveness....

IV.

For the foregoing reasons, the judgment of the district court is AFFIRMED.

[The opinion of **KENNEDY**, Circuit Judge, dissenting, is omitted.]

NOTES

1. Decisions applying section 43(a) of the Lanham Act to product designs have multiplied since the mid–1980s. Many of these decisions have loosened unfair competition law's traditional constraints, including the requirements of secondary meaning and nonfunctionality. The more extended decisions, of which *Ferrari* is typical, have effectively converted section 43(a) into a catch-all misappropriation statute, granting broad copyright-like protection to utilitarian products that copyright law itself will not protect.

Recall the excerpt from the Economides article, The Economics of Trademarks, at page 20, above and consider whether, in slipping section 43(a) from its traditional moorings, courts in contemporary product design cases have effectively given private monopolies over the very objects that least need protection under the economics of unfair competition. Unlike so-called experience goods, such as laundry detergents or canned peas, for which trade dress serves as a signal and indirect guarantor of quality, product designs—the design of a car or a garment, for example—can by their very nature have virtually all of their relevant qualities observed directly in the retail marketplace, so that protection for external, source-identifying trappings is unnecessary to signal quality.

See generally, A. Samuel Oddi, Product Simulation: From Tort to Intellectual Property, 88 Trademark Rep. 101 (1998); J.H. Reichman, Past and Current Trends in the Evolution of Design Protection Law—A Comment, 4 Fordham Intell. Prop. Media & Ent. L.J. 387 (1993); Daniel J. Gifford, The Interplay of Product Definition, Design and Trade Dress, 75 Minn. L. Rev. 769 (1991).

2. *"Distinctiveness" in Industrial Design.* Although, on its facts, the *Two Pesos* case involved only one form of trade dress—building design for food services—the Court's language left little doubt about its intention to include packaging for goods in its holding that, so long as the trade dress in question is inherently distinctive, section 43(a) will protect it even though it may lack secondary meaning. What if the trade dress in issue embodies the design of the product itself and not just its packaging? In Wal–Mart Stores, Inc. v. Samara Brothers, Inc., 529 U.S. 205, 120 S.Ct. 1339, 146 L.Ed.2d 182, 54 U.S.P.Q.2d 1065 (2000), the Court ruled that, unlike the package for a product, the design of a product cannot be inherently distinctive. But, what if the package *is* the product?

In an incisive and scholarly opinion written before the *Wal-Mart* decision, Duraco Products, Inc. v. Joy Plastic Enterprises, Ltd., 40 F.3d 1431, 1434, 32 U.S.P.Q.2d 1724 (3d Cir.1994), Judge Edward Becker essayed the measure of distinctiveness that should be applied to product design in section 43(a) cases after *Two Pesos*. Judge Becker started with the proposition "that traditional trade dress doctrine does not fit a product configuration case because unlike product packaging, a product configuration differs fundamentally from a product's trademark, insofar as it is not a symbol according to which one can relate the signifier (the trademark, or perhaps the packaging) to the signified (the product). In other words, the very basis for the trademark taxonomy—the descriptive relationship between the mark and product, along with the degree to which the mark describes the product—is unsuited for application to the product itself."

Nonetheless, Judge Becker concluded, "there is a proper set of circumstances for treating a product configuration as inherently distinctive. These circumstances are characterized by a high probability that a product configuration serves a virtually exclusive identifying function for consumers—where the concerns over 'theft' of an identifying feature or combination or arrangement of features and the cost to an enterprise of gaining and proving secondary meaning outweigh concerns over inhibiting competition, and where consumers are especially likely to perceive a connection between the product's configuration and its source. We conclude that, to be inherently distinctive, a product feature or a combination or arrangement of features, *i.e.*, a product configuration, for which Lanham Act protection is sought must be (i) unusual and memorable; (ii) conceptually separable from the product; and (iii) likely to serve primarily as a designator of origin of the product." 40 F.3d at 1434.

Is there more than a literal connection between *Duraco's* requirement that a product configuration be "conceptually separable from the product" and copyright law's requirement of "conceptual separability" in the case of useful articles? According to Judge Becker, conceptual separability in the context of trade dress means that consumers will recognize the configuration as a "symbolic (signifying) character. This requirement ensures that consumers unaware of any association of the product with a manufacturer (*i.e.*, where a configuration has no secondary meaning) will not become confused about whether a particular configuration may be trusted as an indicium of origin." 40 F.3d at 1449. It might aid your comparison of these two contexts for applying conceptual separability to compare the easier case for trade dress protection—product packaging—with copyright law's doctrine of physical separability.

3. *Functionality.* Consider whether the following definition of functionality, alluded to in *Ferrari,* is helpful: "In general terms, a product feature is functional if it is essential to the use or purpose of the article or if it affects the cost or quality of the article." Inwood Laboratories, Inc. v. Ives Laboratories, Inc., 456 U.S. 844, 850 n. 10, 102 S.Ct. 2182, 2186 n. 10, 72 L.Ed.2d 606, 214 U.S.P.Q. 1 (1982). What feature that results from investment in artistic design will not affect an article's "cost"? What feature that enhances an article's attractiveness to consumers will not affect its "quality"? Is it any more helpful to hold that a feature is functional if rivals need to employ it to compete effectively? Compete effectively with respect to what? Would it be relevant that, because of plaintiff's success in the marketplace, its configuration has become a standard that competitors must employ if they wish to make products that are interchangeable with plaintiff's? Is genericness rather than functionality the proper touchstone for decision in such cases?

4. *Aesthetic Functionality.* The doctrine of utilitarian functionality guards against giving perpetual monopolies to works that do not meet the standards for a utility patent or on which a utility patent has expired. Does the doctrine of aesthetic functionality, referred to in *Ferrari,* provide a comparable safeguard against perpetual protection of works that do not qualify for a design patent or copyright, or on which the design patent or copyright has expired?

Few intellectual property doctrines have been more mercurial than aesthetic functionality. The Ninth Circuit Court of Appeals, which announced a rigorous version of the aesthetic functionality test in Pagliero v. Wallace China Co., 198 F.2d 339, 95 U.S.P.Q. 45 (9th Cir.1952), substantially, if not entirely, repudiated it twenty-nine years later in Vuitton et Fils S.A. v. J. Young Enters., Inc., 644 F.2d 769, 210 U.S.P.Q. 351 (9th Cir.1981). The Second Circuit Court of Appeals once ruled that any element of a product that is "an important ingredient" in its saleability is unprotectible, Industria Arredamenti Fratelli Saporiti v. Charles Craig Ltd., 725 F.2d 18, 20, 222 U.S.P.Q. 754 (2d Cir.1984), but soon moved off in a different direction: "Where an ornamental feature is claimed as a trademark and trademark protection would significantly hinder competition by limiting the range of adequate alternative designs, the aesthetic functionality doctrine denies such protection"; however, if a plaintiff can show secondary meaning in its precise ornamental expression, "competitors might be excluded from using an identical or virtually identical design." Wallace Int'l Silversmiths, Inc. v. Godinger Silver Art Co., 916 F.2d 76, 81–82 16 U.S.P.Q. 2d 1555 (2d Cir.1990).

5. Does *Ferrari* give industrial designers a blank check for protection, unlimited in time and unconstrained by requirements such as those imposed by design patent and copyright law? Do section 43(a)'s distinctiveness and secondary meaning requirements effectively separate the design protected in *Ferrari* from the designs protected by copyright and patent law?

Judge Cornelia Kennedy dissented in *Ferrari:* "[T]he majority opinion does more than protect consumers against a likelihood of confusion as to the source of goods; it protects the source of goods, Ferrari, against plaintiff's copying of its design even if the replication is accompanied by adequate labelling so as to prevent consumer confusion. I believe the majority commits two errors in reaching this result. The majority first misconstrues the scope of protection afforded by the Lanham Act by misapplying the likelihood of confusion test and reading an anti-dilution provision into the language of section 43(a). The majority then affirms an injunction that is over-broad. The product of these errors is a remedy that provides defendant with absolute protection in perpetuity against copying its unpatented design." 944 F.2d at 1248.

Judge Kennedy also objected that the injunction approved by the majority "runs afoul of Supreme Court precedent"—*Bonito Boats,* page 999, below, and *Sears* and *Compco,* pages 98, 101, above. The Court held in those cases only that federal patent law preempts *state* law protection of unpatented or unpatentable designs. Is there any basis on which laws enacted by Congress under one constitutional power—the copyright-patent clause—can be held to preempt laws enacted under another constitutional power—the commerce clause?

NOTE: PROPOSED INDUSTRIAL DESIGN LEGISLATION

No intellectual property topic has been on the legislative agenda longer than the question of protection for industrial design. Proposals date to H.R. 11321, 63d Cong., 2d Sess. (1914). The constituencies proposing and opposing industrial design bills have shifted over the years. In the early years, dress designers backed the legislation and were opposed by retailers and manufacturers. More recently, industrial and typeface designers have been the principal supporters of design legislation; they have been opposed by automobile insurers worried about the increased cost of replacement parts. See generally, The Industrial Innovation and Technology Act: Hearing on S. 791 Before the Subcomm. on Patents, Copyrights and Trademarks of the

Senate Comm. on the Judiciary, 100th Cong., 1st Sess. 213 (1987) (Statement of Ralph Oman, Register of Copyrights.)

H.R. 3499, 101st Cong., 1st Sess. (1989), typifies contemporary legislative proposals. The bill would have entitled the "designer or other proprietor of an original design of a useful article which makes the article attractive or distinct in appearance to the purchasing or using public" to ten years of protection beginning on the date of publication of registration for the design, or the date the design is first made public, whichever occurs first. The bill contained three definitions:

(1) A "useful article" is an article which in normal use has an intrinsic utilitarian function that is not merely to portray the appearance of the article or to convey information. An article which normally is a part of a useful article shall be deemed to be a useful article.

(2) The "design of a useful article", hereinafter referred to as a "design", consists of those aspects or elements of the article, including its two-dimensional or three-dimensional features of shape and surface, which make up the appearance of the article. The design must be fixed in a useful article to be protectable under this Act.

(3) A design is "original" if it is the independent creation of a designer who did not copy it from another source.

H.R. 3499 would have excluded protection for designs that are "not original;" that are "staple or commonplace, such as standard geometric figures, familiar symbols, emblems, or motifs; or other shapes, patterns, or configurations which have become common, prevalent, or ordinary;" that are "dictated solely by a utilitarian function of the article that embodies it;" or that are "composed of three-demensional [sic] features of shape and surface with respect to men's, women's, and children's apparel, including undergarments and outerwear."

The bill conditioned the recovery of damages or profits on the affixation of a design notice "except on proof that the infringer was notified of the design protection and continued to infringe thereafter, in which event damages or profits may be recovered only for infringement occurring after such notice." Omission of notice would not otherwise affect protection under the bill. But failure to apply for registration within one year after the design was first made public would have forfeited protection.

H.R. 3499 defined infringement to include the unauthorized manufacture, importation, sale or distribution of any "infringing article"—defined as "any article, the design of which has been copied from the protected design, without the consent of the proprietor." The bill authorized injunctive relief, awards of damages—including increased damages—profits and costs, including attorney's fees. The bill would have vested responsibility for administering the Act in the Register of Copyrights.

IV. FEDERAL PREEMPTION

Bonito Boats, Inc. v. Thunder Craft Boats, Inc.

Supreme Court of the United States, 1989.
489 U.S. 141, 109 S.Ct. 971, 103 L.Ed.2d 118, 9 U.S.P.Q.2d 1847.

Justice O'CONNOR delivered the opinion of the Court.

We must decide today what limits the operation of the federal patent system places on the States' ability to offer substantial protection to utilitarian and design ideas which the patent laws leave otherwise unprotected. In Interpart Corp. v. Italia, 777 F.2d 678 (1985), the Court of Appeals for the Federal Circuit concluded that a California law prohibiting the use of the "direct molding process" to duplicate unpatented articles posed no threat to the policies behind the federal patent laws. In this case, the Florida Supreme Court came to a contrary conclusion. It struck down a Florida statute which prohibits the use of the direct molding process to duplicate unpatented boat hulls, finding that the protection offered by the Florida law conflicted with the balance struck by Congress in the federal patent statute between the encouragement of invention and free competition in unpatented ideas. We granted certiorari to resolve the conflict, and we now affirm the judgment of the Florida Supreme Court.

I.

In September 1976, Petitioner Bonito Boats, Inc. (Bonito), a Florida Corporation, developed a hull design for a fiberglass recreational boat which it marketed under the trade name Bonito Boat Model 5VBR. App. 5. Designing the boat hull required substantial effort on the part of Bonito. A set of engineering drawings was prepared, from which a hardwood model was created. The hardwood model was then sprayed with fiberglass to create a mold, which then served to produce the finished fiberglass boats for sale. The 5VBR was placed on the market sometime in September 1976. There is no indication in the record that a patent application was ever filed for protection of the utilitarian or design aspects of the hull, or for the process by which the hull was manufactured. The 5VBR was favorably received by the boating public, and "a broad interstate market" developed for its sale.

In May 1983, after the Bonito 5VBR had been available to the public for over six years, the Florida Legislature enacted Fla.Stat. § 559.94 (1987). The statute makes "[i]t ... unlawful for any person to use the direct molding process to duplicate for the purpose of sale any manufactured vessel hull or component part of a vessel made by another without the written permission of that other person." § 559.94(2). The statute also makes it unlawful for a person to "knowingly sell a vessel hull or component part of a vessel duplicated in violation of subsection (2)." Damages, injunctive relief, and attorney's fees are made available to "[a]ny person who suffers injury or damage as the result of a violation" of the statute. The statute was made applicable to vessel hulls or component parts duplicated through the use of direct molding after July 1, 1983. § 559.94(5).

On December 21, 1984, Bonito filed this action in the Circuit Court of Orange County, Florida. The complaint alleged that respondent here, Thunder Craft Boats, Inc. (Thunder Craft), a Tennessee corporation, had violated the Florida statute by using the direct molding process to duplicate the Bonito 5VBR fiberglass hull, and had knowingly sold such duplicates in violation of the Florida statute. Bonito sought "a temporary and permanent injunction prohibiting [Thunder Craft] from continuing to unlawfully duplicate and sell Bonito Boat hulls or components," as well as an accounting of profits, treble damages, punitive damages, and attorney's fees. Respondent filed a motion to dismiss the complaint, arguing that under this Court's decisions in Sears, Roebuck & Co. v. Stiffel Co., 376 U.S. 225, 84 S.Ct. 784, 11 L.Ed.2d 661 (1964), and Compco Corp. v. Day–Brite Lighting, Inc., 376 U.S. 234, 84 S.Ct. 779, 11 L.Ed.2d 669 (1964), the Florida statute conflicted with federal patent law and was therefore invalid under the Supremacy Clause of the Federal Constitution. The trial court granted respondent's motion, and a divided Court of Appeals affirmed the dismissal of petitioner's complaint.

On discretionary review, a sharply divided Florida Supreme Court agreed with the lower courts' conclusion that the Florida law impermissibly interfered with the scheme established by the federal patent laws. The majority read our decisions in *Sears* and *Compco* for the proposition that "when an article is introduced into the public domain, only a patent can eliminate the inherent risk of competition and then but for a limited time." 515 So.2d, at 222. Relying on the Federal Circuit's decision in the *Interpart* case, the three dissenting judges argued that the Florida anti-direct molding provision "does not prohibit the copying of an unpatented item. It prohibits one method of copying; the item remains in the public domain." 515 So.2d, at 223 (Shaw, J., dissenting).

II.

Article I, § 8, cl. 8, of the Constitution gives Congress the power "[t]o promote the Progress of Science and the useful Arts, by securing for limited Times to Authors and Inventors the exclusive Right to their respective Writings and Discoveries." The Patent Clause itself reflects a balance between the need to encourage innovation and the avoidance of monopolies which stifle competition without any concomitant advance in the "Progress of Science and the useful Arts." As we have noted in the past, the clause contains both a grant of power and certain limitations upon the exercise of that power. Congress may not create patent monopolies of unlimited duration, nor may it "authorize the issuance of patents whose effects are to remove existent knowledge from the public domain, or to restrict free access to materials already available." Graham v. John Deere Co. of Kansas City, 383 U.S. 1, 6, 86 S.Ct. 684, 688, 15 L.Ed.2d 545 (1966).

From their inception, the federal patent laws have embodied a careful balance between the need to promote innovation and the recognition that imitation and refinement through imitation are both necessary to invention itself and the very lifeblood of a competitive economy. . . .

The applicant whose invention satisfies the requirements of novelty, nonobviousness, and utility, and who is willing to reveal to the public the substance of his discovery and "the best mode . . . of carrying out his invention," 35 U.S.C. § 112, is granted "the right to exclude others from making, using, or selling the invention throughout the United States," for a period of 17 years. 35 U.S.C. § 154. The federal patent system thus embodies a carefully crafted bargain for encouraging the creation and disclosure of new, useful, and nonobvious advances in technology and design in return for the exclusive right to practice the invention for a period of years. "[The inventor] may keep his invention secret and reap its fruits indefinitely. In consideration of its disclosure and the consequent benefit to the community, the patent is granted. An exclusive enjoyment is guaranteed him for seventeen years, but upon expiration of that period, the knowledge of the invention inures to the people, who are thus enabled without restriction to practice it and profit by its use." United States v. Dubilier Condenser Corp., 289 U.S. 178, 186–187, 53 S.Ct. 554, 557, 77 L.Ed. 1114 (1933).

The attractiveness of such a bargain, and its effectiveness in inducing creative effort and disclosure of the results of that effort, depend almost entirely on a backdrop of free competition in the exploitation of unpatented designs and innovations. The novelty and nonobviousness requirements of patentability embody a congressional understanding, implicit in the Patent Clause itself, that free exploitation of ideas will be the rule, to which the protection of a federal patent is the exception. Moreover, the ultimate goal of the patent system is to bring new designs and technologies into the public domain through disclosure. State law protection for techniques and designs whose disclosure has already been induced by market rewards may conflict with the very purpose of the patent laws by decreasing the range of ideas available as the building blocks of further innovation. The offer of federal protection from competitive exploitation of intellectual property would be rendered meaningless in a world where substantially similar state law protections were readily available. To a limited extent, the federal patent laws must determine not only what is protected, but also what is free for all to use.

Thus our past decisions have made clear that state regulation of intellectual property must yield to the extent that it clashes with the balance struck by Congress in our patent laws. The tension between the desire to freely exploit the full potential of our inventive resources and the need to create an incentive to deploy those resources is constant. Where it is clear how the patent laws strike that balance in a particular circumstance, that is not a judgment the States may second guess. We have long held that after the expiration of a federal patent, the subject matter of the patent passes to the free use of the public as a matter of federal law. Where the public has paid the congressionally mandated price for disclosure, the States may not render the exchange fruitless by offering patent-like protection to the subject matter of the expired patent. . . .

At the heart of *Sears* and *Compco* is the conclusion that the efficient operation of the federal patent system depends upon substantially free trade in publicly known, unpatented design and utilitarian conceptions. In *Sears,* the state law offered "the equivalent of a patent monopoly," 376 U.S., at 233, 84 S.Ct., at 789, in the functional aspects of a product which had been placed in public commerce absent the protection of a valid patent. While, as noted above, our decisions since *Sears* have taken a decidedly less rigid view of the scope of federal pre-emption under the patent laws, e.g., *Kewanee,* supra, 416 U.S., at 479–480, 94 S.Ct., at 1885–1886, we believe that the *Sears* Court correctly concluded that the States may not offer patent-like protection to intellectual creations which would otherwise remain unprotected as a matter of federal law. Both the novelty and the nonobviousness requirements of federal patent law are grounded in the notion that concepts within the public grasp, or those so obvious that they readily could be, are the tools of creation available to all. They provide the baseline of free competition upon which the patent system's incentive to creative effort depends. A state law that substantially interferes with the enjoyment of an unpatented utilitarian or design conception which has been freely disclosed by its author to the public at large impermissibly contravenes the ultimate goal of public disclosure and use which is the centerpiece of federal patent policy. Moreover, through the creation of patent-like rights, the States could essentially redirect inventive efforts away from the careful criteria of patentability developed by Congress over the last 200 years. We understand this to be the reasoning at the core of our decisions in *Sears* and *Compco* and we reaffirm that reasoning today.

III.

We believe that the Florida statute at issue in this case so substantially impedes the public use of the otherwise unprotected design and utilitarian ideas embodied in unpatented boat hulls as to run afoul of the teaching of our decisions in *Sears* and *Compco*. It is readily apparent that the Florida statute does not operate to prohibit "unfair competition" in the usual sense that the term is understood. The law of unfair competition has its roots in the common-law tort of deceit: its general concern is with protecting *consumers* from confusion as to source. While that concern may result in the creation of "quasi-property rights" in communicative symbols, the focus is on the protection of consumers, not the protection of producers as an incentive to product innovation. Judge Hand captured the distinction well in Crescent Tool Co. v. Kilborn & Bishop Co., 247 F. 299, 301 (C.A.2 1917), where he wrote:

[T]he plaintiff has the right not to lose his customers through false representations that those are his wares which in fact are not, but he may not monopolize any design or pattern, however trifling. The defendant, on the other hand, may copy plaintiff's goods slavishly down to the minutest detail: but he may not represent himself as the plaintiff in their sale.

With some notable exceptions, including the interpretation of the Illinois law of unfair competition at issue in *Sears* and *Compco,* see *Sears,* supra, 376 U.S., at 227–228, n. 2, 84 S.Ct., at 786–787, n. 2, the common-law tort of unfair competition has been limited to protection against copying of nonfunctional aspects of consumer products which have acquired secondary meaning such that they operate as a designation of source. The "protection" granted a particular design under the law of unfair competition is thus limited to one context where consumer confusion is likely to result; the design "idea" itself may be freely exploited in all other contexts.

In contrast to the operation of unfair competition law, the Florida statute is aimed directly at preventing the exploitation of the design and utilitarian conceptions embodied in the product itself. The sparse legislative history surrounding its enactment indicates that it was intended to create an inducement for the improvement of boat hull designs. See Transcript of Meeting of Transportation Committee, Florida House of Representatives, May 3, 1983, reprinted at App. 22. ("[T]here is no inducement for [a] quality boat manufacturer to improve these designs and secondly, if he does, it is immediately copied. This would prevent that and allow him recourse in circuit court"). To accomplish this goal, the Florida statute endows the original boat hull manufacturer with rights against the world, similar in scope and operation to the rights accorded a federal patentee. Like the patentee, the beneficiary of the Florida statute may prevent a competitor from "making" the product in what is evidently the most efficient manner available and from "selling" the product when it is produced in that fashion. The Florida scheme offers this protection for an unlimited number of years to all boat hulls and their component parts, without regard to their ornamental or technological merit. Protection is available for subject matter for which patent protection has been denied or has expired, as well as for designs which have been freely revealed to the consuming public by their creators.

In this case, the Bonito 5VBR fiberglass hull has been freely exposed to the public for a period in excess of six years. For purposes of federal law, it stands in the same stead as an item for which a patent has expired or been denied: it is unpatented and unpatentable. Whether because of a determination of unpatentability or other commercial concerns, petitioner chose to expose its hull design to the public in the marketplace, eschewing the bargain held out by the federal patent system of disclosure in exchange for exclusive use. Yet, the Florida statute allows petitioner to reassert a substantial property right in the idea, thereby constricting the spectrum of useful public knowledge. Moreover, it does so without the careful protections of high standards of innovation and limited monopoly contained in the federal scheme. We think it clear that such protection conflicts with the federal policy "that all ideas in general circulation be dedicated to the common good unless they are protected by a valid patent." Lear, Inc. v. Adkins, 395 U.S., at 668, 89 S.Ct., at 1910.

That the Florida statute does not remove all means of reproduction and sale does not eliminate the conflict with the federal scheme. In essence, the Florida law prohibits the entire public from engaging in a form of reverse engineering of a product in the public domain. This is clearly one of the rights vested in the federal patent holder, but has never been a part of state protection under the law of unfair competition or trade secrets. The duplication of boat hulls and their component parts may be an essential part of innovation in the field of aquadynamic design. Variations as to size and combination of various elements may lead to significant advances in the field. Reverse engineering of chemical and mechanical articles in the public domain often leads to significant advances in technology. If Florida may prohibit this particular method of study and recomposition of an unpatented article, we fail to see the principle that would prohibit a State from banning the use of chromatography in the reconstitution of unpatented chemical compounds, or the use of robotics in the duplication of machinery in the public domain.

Moreover, as we noted in *Kewanee,* the competitive reality of reverse engineering may act as a spur to the inventor, creating an incentive to develop inventions which meet the rigorous requirements of patentability. The Florida statute substantially reduces this competitive incentive, thus eroding the general rule of free competition upon which the attractiveness of the federal patent bargain depends. The protections of state trade secret law are most effective at the developmental stage, before a product has been marketed and threat of reverse engineering becomes real. During this period, patentability will often be an uncertain prospect, and to a certain extent, the protection offered by trade secret law may "dovetail" with the incentives created by the federal patent monopoly. In contrast, under the Florida scheme, the would-be inventor is aware from the outset of his efforts that rights against the public are available regardless of his ability to satisfy the rigorous standards of patentability. Indeed, it appears that even the most mundane and obvious changes in the design of a boat hull will trigger the protections of the statute. See Fla.Stat. § 559.94(2) (1987) (protecting "any manufactured vessel hull or component part"). Given the substantial protection offered by the Florida scheme, we cannot dismiss as hypothetical the possibility that it will become a significant competitor to the federal patent laws, offering investors similar protection without the *quid pro quo* of substantial creative effort required by the federal statute. The prospect of all 50 States establishing similar protections for preferred industries without the rigorous requirements of patentability prescribed by Congress could pose a substantial threat to the patent system's ability to accomplish its mission of promoting progress in the useful arts.

Finally, allowing the States to create patent-like rights in various products in public circulation would lead to administrative problems of no small dimension. The federal patent scheme provides a basis for the public to ascertain the status of the intellectual property embodied in any article in general circulation. Through the application process, detailed information concerning the claims of the patent holder is compiled in a central location. The availability of damages in an infringement action is made contingent upon affixing a notice of patent to the protected article. The notice requirement is designed "for the information of the public," Wine Railway Appliance Co. v. Enterprise Railway Equipment Co., 297 U.S. 387, 397, 56 S.Ct. 528, 531, 80 L.Ed. 736 (1936), and provides a ready means of discerning the status of the intellectual property embodied in an article of manufacture or design. The public may rely upon the lack of notice in exploiting shapes and designs accessible to all.

The Florida scheme blurs this clear federal demarcation between public and private property. One of the fundamental purposes behind the Patent and Copyright Clauses of the Constitution was to promote national uniformity in the realm of intellectual property. Since the Patent Act of 1800, Congress has lodged exclusive jurisdiction of actions "arising under" the patent laws in the federal courts, thus allowing for the development of a uniform body of law in resolving the constant tension between private right and public access. Recently, Congress conferred exclusive jurisdiction of all patent appeals on the Court of Appeals for the Federal Circuit, in order to "provide nationwide uniformity in patent law." H.R.Rep. No. 97–312, p. 20 (1981). This purpose is frustrated by the Florida scheme, which renders the status of the design and utilitarian "ideas" embodied in the boat hulls it protects uncertain. Given the inherently ephemeral nature of property in ideas, and the great power such property has to cause harm to the competitive policies which underlay the federal patent laws, the demarcation of broad zones of public and private right is "the type of regulation that demands a uniform national rule." Ray v. Atlantic Richfield Co., 435 U.S. 151, 179, 98 S.Ct. 988, 1005, 55 L.Ed.2d 179 (1978). Absent such a federal rule, each State could afford patent-like protection to particularly favored home industries, effectively insulating them from competition from outside the State.

Petitioner and its supporting *amici* place great weight on the contrary decision of the Court of Appeals for the Federal Circuit in *Interpart Corp. v. Italia*. In upholding the application of the California "antidirect molding" statute to the duplication of unpatented automobile mirrors, the Federal Circuit stated: "The statute prevents unscrupulous competitors from obtaining a product and using it as the 'plug' for making a mold. The statute does not prohibit copying the design of the product in any other way; the latter if in the public domain, is free for anyone to make, use or sell." 777 F.2d, at 685. The court went on to indicate that "the patent laws 'say nothing about the right to copy or the right to use, they speak only in terms of the right to exclude.'" Ibid., quoting Mine Safety Appliances Co. v. Electric Storage Battery Co., 56 C.C.P.A. (Pat.) 863, 864, n. 2, 405 F.2d 901, 902, n. 2 (1969).

We find this reasoning defective in several respects. The Federal Circuit apparently viewed the direct molding statute at issue in *Interpart* as a mere regulation of the use of chattels. Yet, the very purpose of antidirect molding statutes is to "reward" the "inventor" by offering substantial protection against public exploitation of his or her idea embodied in the product. Such statutes would be an exercise in futility if they did not have precisely the effect of substantially limiting the ability of the public to exploit an otherwise unprotected idea. As *amicus* points out, the direct molding process itself has been in use since the early 1950's. Indeed, U.S. Patent No. 3,419,646, issued to Robert L. Smith in 1968, explicitly discloses and claims a method for the direct molding of boat hulls. The specifications of the Smith Patent indicate that "[i]t is a major object of the present invention to provide a method for making large molded boat hull molds at very low cost, once a prototype hull has been provided." Id., at 15a. In fact, it appears that Bonito employed a similar process in the creation of its own production mold. It is difficult to conceive of a more effective method of creating substantial property rights in an intellectual creation than to eliminate the most efficient method for its exploitation. *Sears* and *Compco* protect more than the right of the public to contemplate the abstract beauty of an otherwise unprotected intellectual creation—they assure its efficient reduction to practice and sale in the marketplace....

Our decisions since *Sears* and *Compco* have made it clear that the Patent and Copyright Clauses do not, by their own force or by negative implication, deprive the States of the power to adopt rules for the promotion of intellectual creation within their own jurisdictions. See *Aronson,* 440 U.S., at 262, 99 S.Ct., at 1099; Goldstein v. California, 412 U.S. 546, 552–561, 93 S.Ct. 2303, 2307–2312, 37 L.Ed.2d 163 (1973); *Kewanee,* 416 U.S., at 478–479, 94 S.Ct., at 1884–1885. Thus, where "Congress determines that neither federal protection nor freedom from restraint is required by the national interest," *Goldstein,* supra, 412 U.S., at 559, 93 S.Ct., at 2311, the States remain free to promote originality and creativity in their own domains.

Nor does the fact that a particular item lies within the subject matter of the federal patent laws necessarily preclude the States from offering limited protection which does not impermissibly interfere with the federal patent scheme. As *Sears* itself makes clear, States may place limited regulations on the use of unpatented designs in order to prevent consumer confusion as to source. In *Kewanee,* we found that state protection of trade secrets, as applied to both patentable and unpatentable subject matter, did not conflict with the federal patent laws. In both situations, state protection was not aimed exclusively at the promotion of invention itself, and the state restrictions on the use of unpatented ideas were limited to those necessary to promote goals outside the contemplation of the federal patent scheme. Both the law of unfair competition and state trade secret law have co-existed harmoniously with federal patent protection for almost 200 years, and Congress has given no indication that their operation is inconsistent with the operation of the federal patent laws.

Indeed, there are affirmative indications from Congress that both the law of unfair competition and trade secret protection are consistent with the balance struck by the patent laws. Section 43(a) of the Lanham Act, 60

Stat. 441, 15 U.S.C. § 1125(a), creates a federal remedy for making "a false designation of origin, or any false description or representation, including words or other symbols tending falsely to describe or represent the same...." Congress has thus given federal recognition to many of the concerns which underlie the state tort of unfair competition and the application of *Sears* and *Compco* to nonfunctional aspects of a product which have been shown to identify source must take account of competing federal policies in this regard. Similarly, as Justice MARSHALL noted in his concurring opinion in *Kewanee,* "[s]tate trade secret laws and the federal patent laws have co-existed for many, many, years. During this time, Congress has repeatedly demonstrated its full awareness of the existence of the trade secret system, without any indication of disapproval. Indeed, Congress has in a number of instances given explicit federal protection to trade secret information provided to federal agencies." *Kewanee,* supra, 416 U.S., at 494, 94 S.Ct., at 1892 (concurring in result) (citation omitted). The case for federal pre-emption is particularly weak where Congress has indicated its awareness of the operation of state law in a field of federal interest, and has nonetheless decided to "stand by both concepts and to tolerate whatever tension there [is] between them." Silkwood v. Kerr–McGee Corp., 464 U.S. 238, 256, 104 S.Ct. 615, 625, 78 L.Ed.2d 443 (1984). The same cannot be said of the Florida statute at issue here, which offers protection beyond that available under the law of unfair competition or trade secret, without any showing of consumer confusion, or breach of trust or secrecy.

The Florida statute is aimed directly at the promotion of intellectual creation by substantially restricting the public's ability to exploit ideas which the patent system mandates shall be free for all to use. Like the interpretation of Illinois unfair competition law in *Sears* and *Compco,* the Florida statute represents a break with the tradition of peaceful co-existence between state market regulation and federal patent policy. The Florida law substantially restricts the public's ability to exploit an unpatented design in general circulation, raising the specter of state-created monopolies in a host of useful shapes and processes for which patent protection has been denied or is otherwise unobtainable. It thus enters a field of regulation which the patent laws have reserved to Congress. The patent statute's careful balance between public right and private monopoly to promote certain creative activity is a "scheme of federal regulation ... so pervasive as to make reasonable the inference that Congress left no room for the States to supplement it." Rice v. Santa Fe Elevator Corp., 331 U.S. 218, 230, 67 S.Ct. 1146, 1152, 91 L.Ed. 1447 (1947).

Congress has considered extending various forms of limited protection to industrial design either through the copyright laws or by relaxing the restrictions on the availability of design patents. Congress explicitly refused to take this step in the copyright laws, and despite sustained criticism for a number of years, it has declined to alter the patent protections presently available for industrial design. It is for Congress to determine if the present system of design and utility patents is ineffectual in promoting the useful arts in the context of industrial design. By offering patent-like protection for ideas deemed unprotected under the present federal scheme, the Florida statute conflicts with the "strong federal policy favoring free competition in ideas which do not merit patent protection." *Lear, Inc.*, 395 U.S., at 656, 89 S.Ct., at 1903. We therefore agree with the majority of the Florida Supreme Court that the Florida statute is preempted by the Supremacy Clause and the judgment of that court is hereby affirmed.

It is so ordered.

QUESTIONS

Was *Bonito Boats* a foregone conclusion after *Sears* and *Compco*, pages 98, 101, above? Did the Court in *Bonito Boats* adequately reconcile the decision with its decision in Kewanee v. Bicron, page 151, above? Aronson v. Quick Point, page 50, above? Goldstein v. California, page 801, above, which *Bonito Boats* nowhere addressed directly, held that states could prohibit copying of sound recordings even though the Copyright Act at the time excluded sound recordings from federal copyright protection. How do the facts in *Bonito Boats* differ from the facts in *Goldstein*? Could the *Bonito Boats* Court have rested its decision on the nonconstitutional ground that section 301 of the 1976 Copyright Act preempted the Florida statute?

The legislative response to *Bonito Boats* was that Pub.L. No. 105–304 (Oct. 28, 1998), added a new Chapter 13 to Title 17 of the United States Code providing *sui generis* protection for original boat hull designs.

See generally, David E. Shipley, Refusing to Rock the Boat: The Sears/Compco Preemption Doctrine Applied to Bonito Boats v. Thunder Craft, 25 Wake Forest L. Rev. 385 (1990); John Wiley, Bonito Boats: Uniformed But Mandatory Innovation Policy, 1989 Sup. Ct. Rev. 283.

APPENDIX

Festo Corporation v. Shoketsu Kinzoku Kogyo Kabushiki Co., Ltd.

Supreme Court of the United States, 2002.
2002 WL 1050479, on writ of certiorari to the United States Court of Appeals for the Federal Circuit.

Justice KENNEDY delivered the opinion of the Court.

This case requires us to address once again the relation between two patent law concepts, the doctrine of equivalents and the rule of prosecution history estoppel. The Court considered the same concepts in *Warner–Jenkinson Co.* v. *Hilton Davis Chemical Co.,* 520 U.S. 17 (1997), and reaffirmed that a patent protects its holder against efforts of copyists to evade liability for infringement by making only insubstantial changes to a patented invention. At the same time, we appreciated that by extending protection beyond the literal terms in a patent the doctrine of equivalents can create substantial uncertainty about where the patent monopoly ends. If the range of equivalents is unclear, competitors may be unable to determine what is a permitted alternative to a patented invention and what is an infringing equivalent.

To reduce the uncertainty, *Warner–Jenkinson* acknowledged that competitors may rely on the prosecution history, the public record of the patent proceedings. In some cases the Patent and Trademark Office (PTO) may have rejected an earlier version of the patent application on the ground that a claim does not meet a statutory requirement for patentability. When the patentee responds to the rejection by narrowing his claims, this prosecution history estops him from later arguing that the subject matter covered by the original, broader claim was nothing more than an equivalent. Competitors may rely on the estoppel to ensure that their own devices will not be found to infringe by equivalence.

In the decision now under review the Court of Appeals for the Federal Circuit held that by narrowing a claim to obtain a patent, the patentee surrenders all equivalents to the amended claim element. Petitioner asserts this holding departs from past precedent in two respects. First, it applies estoppel to every amendment made to satisfy the requirements of the Patent Act and not just to amendments made to avoid pre-emption by an earlier invention, *i.e.,* the prior art. Second, it holds that when estoppel arises, it bars suit against every equivalent to the amended claim element. The Court of Appeals acknowledged that this holding departed from its own cases, which applied a flexible bar when considering what claims of equivalence were estopped by the prosecution history. Petitioner argues that by replacing the flexible bar with a complete bar the Court of Appeals cast doubt on many existing patents that were amended during the application process when the law, as it then stood, did not apply so rigorous a standard.

1009

We granted certiorari to consider these questions.

I

Petitioner Festo Corporation owns two patents for an improved magnetic rodless cylinder, a piston-driven device that relies on magnets to move objects in a conveying system. The device has many industrial uses and has been employed in machinery as diverse as sewing equipment and the Thunder Mountain ride at Disney World. Although the precise details of the cylinder's operation are not essential here, the prosecution history must be considered.

Petitioner's patent applications, as often occurs, were amended during the prosecution proceedings. The application for the first patent, the Stoll Patent (U.S. Patent No. 4,354,125), was amended after the patent examiner rejected the initial application because the exact method of operation was unclear and some claims were made in an impermissible way. (They were multiply dependent.) 35 U.S.C. § 112 (1994 ed.). The inventor, Dr. Stoll, submitted a new application designed to meet the examiner's objections and also added certain references to prior art. 37 CFR § 1.56 (2000). The second patent, the Carroll Patent (U.S. Patent No. 3,779,401), was also amended during a reexamination proceeding. The prior art references were added to this amended application as well. Both amended patents added a new limitation—that the inventions contain a pair of sealing rings, each having a lip on one side, which would prevent impurities from getting on the piston assembly. The amended Stoll Patent added the further limitation that the outer shell of the device, the sleeve, be made of a magnetizable material.

After Festo began selling its rodless cylinder, respondents (whom we refer to as SMC) entered the market with a device similar, but not identical, to the ones disclosed by Festo's patents. SMC's cylinder, rather than using two one-way sealing rings, employs a single sealing ring with a two-way lip. Furthermore, SMC's sleeve is made of a nonmagnetizable alloy. SMC's device does not fall within the literal claims of either patent, but petitioner contends that it is so similar that it infringes under the doctrine of equivalents.

SMC contends that Festo is estopped from making this argument because of the prosecution history of its patents. The sealing rings and the magnetized alloy in the Festo product were both disclosed for the first time in the amended applications. In SMC's view, these amendments narrowed the earlier applications, surrendering alternatives that are the very points of difference in the competing devices—the sealing rings and the type of alloy used to make the sleeve. As Festo narrowed its claims in these ways in order to obtain the patents, says SMC, Festo is now estopped from saying that these features are immaterial and that SMC's device is an equivalent of its own.

The United States District Court for the District of Massachusetts disagreed. It held that Festo's amendments were not made to avoid prior art, and therefore the amendments were not the kind that give rise to estoppel. A panel of the Court of Appeals for the Federal Circuit affirmed. We granted certiorari, vacated, and remanded in light of our intervening decision in *Warner–Jenkinson v. Hilton Davis Chemical Co.*, 520 U.S. 17 (1997). After a decision by the original panel on remand, the Court of Appeals ordered rehearing en banc to address questions that had divided its judges since our decision in *Warner–Jenkinson.*

The en banc court reversed, holding that prosecution history estoppel barred Festo from asserting that the accused device infringed its patents under the doctrine of equivalents. The court held, with only one judge dissenting, that estoppel arises from any amendment that narrows a claim to comply with the Patent Act, not only from amendments made to avoid prior art. More controversial in the Court of Appeals was its further holding: When estoppel applies, it stands as a complete bar against any claim of equivalence for the element that was amended. The court acknowledged that its own prior case law did not go so far. Previous decisions had held that prosecution history estoppel constituted a flexible bar, foreclosing some, but not all, claims of equivalence, depending on the purpose of the amendment and the alterations in the text. The court concluded, however, that its precedents applying the flexible-bar rule should be overruled because this case-by-case approach has proved unworkable. In the court's view a complete-bar rule, under which estoppel bars all claims of equivalence to the narrowed element, would promote certainty in the determination of infringement cases.

Four judges dissented from the decision to adopt a complete bar. In four separate opinions, the dissenters argued that the majority's decision to overrule precedent was contrary to *Warner–Jenkinson* and would unsettle the expectations of many existing patentees. Judge Michel, in his dissent, described in detail how the complete bar required the Court of Appeals to disregard 8 older decisions of this Court, as well as more than 50 of its own cases.

We granted certiorari.

II

The patent laws "promote the Progress of Science and useful Arts" by rewarding innovation with a temporary monopoly. U.S. Const., Art. I, § 8, cl. 8. The monopoly is a property right; and like any property right, its boundaries should be clear. This clarity is essential to promote progress, because it enables efficient investment in innovation. A patent holder should know what he owns, and the public should know what he does not. For this reason, the patent laws require inventors to describe their work in "full, clear, concise, and exact terms," 35 U.S.C. § 112 as part of the delicate balance the law attempts to maintain between inventors, who rely on the promise of the law to bring the invention forth, and the public, which should be encouraged to pursue innovations, creations, and new ideas beyond the inventor's exclusive rights.

Unfortunately, the nature of language makes it impossible to capture the essence of a thing in a patent application. The inventor who chooses to patent an invention and disclose it to the public, rather than exploit it in secret, bears the risk that others will devote their efforts toward exploiting the limits of the patent's language:

"An invention exists most importantly as a tangible structure or a series of drawings. A verbal portrayal is usually an afterthought written to satisfy the requirements of patent law. This conversion of machine to words allows for unintended idea gaps which cannot be satisfactorily filled. Often the invention is novel and words do not exist to describe it. The dictionary does not always keep abreast of the inventor. It cannot. Things are not made for the sake of words, but words for things." *Autogiro Co. of America v. United States*, 384 F.2d 391, 397 (Ct. Cl. 1967).

The language in the patent claims may not capture every nuance of the invention or describe with complete precision the range of its novelty. If patents were always interpreted by their literal terms, their value would be greatly diminished. Unimportant and insubstantial substitutes for certain elements could defeat the patent, and its value to inventors could be destroyed by simple acts of copying. For this reason, the clearest rule of patent interpretation, literalism, may conserve judicial resources but is not necessarily the most efficient rule. The scope of a patent is not limited to its literal terms but instead embraces all equivalents to the claims described. See *Winans v. Denmead*, 15 How. 330, 347 (1854).

It is true that the doctrine of equivalents renders the scope of patents less certain. It may be difficult to determine what is, or is not, an equivalent to a particular element of an invention. If competitors cannot be certain about a patent's extent, they may be deterred from engaging in legitimate manufactures outside its limits, or they may invest by mistake in competing products that the patent secures. In addition the uncertainty may lead to wasteful litigation between competitors, suits that a rule of literalism might avoid. These concerns with the doctrine of equivalents, however, are not new. Each time the Court has considered the doctrine, it has acknowledged this uncertainty as the price of ensuring the appropriate incentives for innovation, and it has affirmed the doctrine over dissents that urged a more certain rule. When the Court in *Winans v. Denmead*, *supra*, first adopted what has become the doctrine of equivalents, it stated that "[t]he exclusive right to the thing patented is not secured, if the public are at liberty to make substantial copies of it, varying its form or proportions." *Id.*, at 343. The dissent argued that the Court had sacrificed the objective of "[f]ul[l]ness, clearness, exactness, preciseness, and particularity, in the description of the invention." *Id.*, at 347 (opinion of Campbell, J.).

The debate continued in *Graver Tank & Mfg. Co. v. Linde Air Products Co.*, 339 U.S. 605 (1950), where the Court reaffirmed the doctrine. *Graver Tank* held that patent claims must protect the inventor not only from those who produce devices falling within the literal claims of the patent but also from copyists who "make unimportant and insubstantial changes and substitutions in the patent which, though adding nothing, would be enough to take the copied matter outside the claim, and hence outside the reach of law." *Id.*, at 607. Justice Black, in dissent, objected that under the doctrine of equivalents a competitor "cannot rely on what the language of a patent claims. He must be able, at the peril of heavy infringement damages, to forecast how far a court relatively unversed in a particular technological field will expand the claim's language...." *Id.*, at 617.

Most recently, in *Warner–Jenkinson*, the Court reaffirmed that equivalents remain a firmly entrenched part of the settled rights protected by the patent. A unanimous opinion concluded that if the doctrine is to be discarded, it is Congress and not the Court that should do so:

"[T]he lengthy history of the doctrine of equivalents strongly supports adherence to our refusal in *Graver Tank* to find that the Patent Act conflicts with that doctrine. Congress can legislate the doctrine of equivalents out of existence any time it chooses. The various policy arguments now made by both sides are thus best addressed to Congress, not this Court." 520 U.S., at 28.

III

Prosecution history estoppel requires that the claims of a patent be interpreted in light of the proceedings in the PTO during the application process. Estoppel is a "rule of patent construction" that ensures that claims are interpreted by reference to those "that have been cancelled or rejected." *Schriber–Schroth Co. v. Cleveland Trust Co.*, 311 U.S. 211, 220–221 (1940). The doctrine of equivalents allows the patentee to claim those insubstantial alterations that were not captured in drafting the original patent claim but which could be created through trivial changes. When, however, the patentee originally claimed the subject matter alleged to infringe but then narrowed the claim in response to a rejection, he may not argue that the surrendered territory comprised unforeseen subject matter that should be deemed equivalent to the literal claims of the issued patent. On the contrary, "[b]y the amendment [the patentee] recognized and emphasized the difference between the two phrases[,] . . . and [t]he difference which [the patentee] thus disclaimed must be regarded as material." *Exhibit Supply Co. v. Ace Patents Corp.*, 315 U.S. 126, 136–137 (1942).

A rejection indicates that the patent examiner does not believe the original claim could be patented. While the patentee has the right to appeal, his decision to forgo an appeal and submit an amended claim is taken as a concession that the invention as patented does not reach as far as the original claim. Were it otherwise, the inventor might avoid the PTO's gatekeeping role and seek to recapture in an infringement action the very subject matter surrendered as a condition of receiving the patent.

Prosecution history estoppel ensures that the doctrine of equivalents remains tied to its underlying purpose. Where the original application once embraced the purported equivalent but the patentee narrowed his claims to obtain the patent or to protect its validity, the patentee cannot assert that he lacked the words to describe the subject matter in question. The doctrine of equivalents is premised on language's inability to capture the essence of innovation, but a prior application describing the precise element at issue undercuts that premise. In that instance the prosecution history has established that the inventor turned his attention to the subject matter in question, knew the words for both the broader and narrower claim, and affirmatively chose the latter.

A

The first question in this case concerns the kinds of amendments that may give rise to estoppel. Petitioner argues that estoppel should arise when amendments are intended to narrow the subject matter of the patented invention, for instance, amendments to avoid prior art, but not when the amendments are made to comply with requirements concerning the form of the patent application. In *Warner–Jenkinson* we recognized that prosecution history estoppel does not arise in every instance when a patent application is amended. Our "prior cases have consistently applied prosecution history estoppel only where claims have been amended for a limited set of reasons," such as "to avoid the prior art, or otherwise to address a specific concern—such as obviousness—that arguably would have rendered the claimed subject matter unpatentable." 520 U.S., at 30–32. While we made clear that estoppel applies to amendments made for a "substantial reason related to patentability," *id.*, at 33, we did not purport to define that term or to catalog every reason that might raise an estoppel. Indeed, we stated that even if the amendment's purpose were unrelated to patentability, the court might consider whether it was the kind of reason that nonetheless might require resort to the estoppel doctrine.

Petitioner is correct that estoppel has been discussed most often in the context of amendments made to avoid the prior art. Amendment to accommodate prior art was the emphasis, too, of our decision in *Warner–Jenkinson*. It does not follow, however, that amendments for other purposes will not give rise to estoppel. Prosecution history may rebut the inference that a thing not described was indescribable. That rationale does not cease simply because the narrowing amendment, submitted to secure a patent, was for some purpose other than avoiding prior art.

We agree with the Court of Appeals that a narrowing amendment made to satisfy any requirement of the Patent Act may give rise to an estoppel. As that court explained, a number of statutory requirements must be satisfied before a patent can issue. The claimed subject matter must be useful, novel, and not obvious. 35 U.S.C. §§ 101–103 (1994 ed. and Supp. V). In addition, the patent application must describe, enable, and set forth the best mode of carrying out the invention. § 112 (1994 ed.). These latter requirements must be satisfied before issuance of the patent, for exclusive patent rights are given in exchange for disclosing the invention to the public. What is claimed by the patent application must be the same as what is disclosed in the specification; otherwise the patent should not issue. The patent also should not issue if the other requirements of § 112 are not satisfied, and an applicant's failure to meet these requirements could lead to the issued patent being held invalid in later litigation.

Petitioner contends that amendments made to comply with § 112 concern the form of the application and not the subject matter of the invention. The PTO might require the applicant to clarify an ambiguous term, to improve the translation of a foreign word, or to rewrite a dependent claim as an independent one. In these cases, petitioner argues, the applicant has no intention of surrendering subject matter and should not be estopped from challenging equivalent devices. While this may be true in some cases, petitioner's argument conflates the patentee's reason for making the amendment with the impact the amendment has on the subject matter.

Estoppel arises when an amendment is made to secure the patent and the amendment narrows the patent's scope. If a § 112 amendment is truly cosmetic, then it would not narrow the patent's scope or raise an estoppel. On the other hand, if a § 112 amendment is necessary and narrows the patent's scope—even if only for the purpose of better description—estoppel may apply. A patentee who narrows a claim as a condition for obtaining a patent disavows his claim to the broader subject matter, whether the amendment was made to avoid the prior art or to comply with § 112. We must regard the patentee as having conceded an inability to claim the broader subject matter or at least as having abandoned his right to appeal a rejection. In either case estoppel may apply.

B

Petitioner concedes that the limitations at issue—the sealing rings and the composition of the sleeve—were made for reasons related to §§ 112, if not also to avoid the prior art. Our conclusion that prosecution history estoppel arises when a claim is narrowed to comply with § 112 gives rise to the second question presented: Does the estoppel bar the inventor from asserting infringement against any equivalent to the narrowed element or might some equivalents still infringe? The Court of Appeals held that prosecution history estoppel is a complete bar, and so the narrowed element must be limited to its strict literal terms. Based upon its experience the Court of Appeals decided that the flexible-bar rule is unworkable because it leads to excessive uncertainty and burdens legitimate innovation. For the reasons that follow, we disagree with the decision to adopt the complete bar.

Though prosecution history estoppel can bar challenges to a wide range of equivalents, its reach requires an examination of the subject matter surrendered by the narrowing amendment. The complete bar avoids this inquiry by establishing a *per se* rule; but that approach is inconsistent with the purpose of applying the estoppel in the first place—to hold the inventor to the representations made during the application process and to the inferences that may reasonably be drawn from the amendment. By amending the application, the inventor is deemed to concede that the patent does not extend as far as the original claim. It does not follow, however, that the amended claim becomes so perfect in its description that no one could devise an equivalent. After amendment, as before, language remains an imperfect fit for invention. The narrowing amendment may demonstrate what the claim is not; but it may still fail to capture precisely what the claim is. There is no reason why a narrowing amendment should be deemed to relinquish equivalents unforeseeable at the time of the amendment and beyond a fair interpretation of what was surrendered. Nor is there any call to foreclose claims of equivalence for aspects of the invention that have only a peripheral relation to the reason the amendment was submitted. The amendment does not show that the inventor suddenly had more foresight in the drafting of claims than an inventor whose application was granted without amendments having been submitted. It shows only that he was familiar with the broader text and with the difference between the two. As a result, there is no more reason for holding the patentee to the literal terms of an amended claim than there is for abolishing the doctrine of equivalents altogether and holding every patentee to the literal terms of the patent.

This view of prosecution history estoppel is consistent with our precedents and respectful of the real practice before the PTO. While this Court has not weighed the merits of the complete bar against the flexible bar in its prior cases, we have consistently applied the doctrine in a flexible way, not a rigid one. We have considered what equivalents were surrendered during the prosecution of the patent, rather than imposing a complete bar that resorts to the very literalism the equivalents rule is designed to overcome.

The Court of Appeals ignored the guidance of *Warner–Jenkinson*, which instructed that courts must be cautious before adopting changes that disrupt the settled expectations of the inventing community. In that case we made it clear that the doctrine of equivalents and the rule of prosecution history estoppel are settled law. The responsibility for changing them rests with Congress. Fundamental alterations in these rules risk destroying the legitimate expectations of inventors in their property. The petitioner in *Warner–Jenkinson* requested another bright-line rule that would have provided more certainty in determining when estoppel applies but at the cost of disrupting the expectations of countless existing patent holders. We rejected that approach: "To change so substantially the rules of the game now could very well subvert the various balances the PTO sought to strike when issuing the numerous patents which have not yet expired and which would be affected by our decision." *Id.*, at 32, n. 6; see also *id.*, at 41 (Ginsburg, J., concurring) ("The new presumption, if applied woodenly, might in some instances unfairly discount the expectations of a patentee who had no notice at the time of patent prosecution that such a presumption would apply"). As *Warner–Jenkinson* recognized, patent prosecution occurs in the light of our case law. Inventors who amended their claims under the previous regime had no reason to believe they were conceding all equivalents. If they had known, they might have appealed the rejection instead. There is no justification for applying a new and more robust estoppel to those who relied on prior doctrine.

In *Warner–Jenkinson* we struck the appropriate balance by placing the burden on the patentee to show that an amendment was not for purposes of patentability:

"Where no explanation is established, however, the court should presume that the patent application had a substantial reason related to patentability for including the limiting element added by amendment. In those circumstances, prosecution history estoppel would bar the application of the doctrine of equivalents as to that element." *Id.*, at 33.

When the patentee is unable to explain the reason for amendment, estoppel not only applies but also "bar[s] the application of the doctrine of equivalents as to that element." *Ibid.* These words do not mandate a complete bar; they are limited to the circumstance where "no explanation is established." They do provide, however, that when the court is unable to determine the purpose underlying a narrowing amendment—and hence a rationale for limiting the estoppel to the surrender of particular equivalents—the court should presume that the patentee surrendered all subject matter between the broader and the narrower language.

Just as *Warner–Jenkinson* held that the patentee bears the burden of proving that an amendment was not made for a reason that would give rise to estoppel, we hold here that the patentee should bear the burden of showing that the amendment does not surrender the particular equivalent in question. This is the approach advocated by the United States, and we regard it to be sound. The patentee, as the author of the claim language, may be expected to draft claims encompassing readily known equivalents. A patentee's decision to narrow his claims through amendment may be presumed to be a general disclaimer of the territory between the original claim and the amended claim. There are some cases, however, where the amendment cannot reasonably be viewed as surrendering a particular equivalent. The equivalent may have been unforeseeable at the time of the application; the rationale underlying the amendment may bear no more than a tangential relation to the equivalent in question; or there may be some other reason suggesting that the patentee could not reasonably be expected to have described the insubstantial substitute in question. In those cases the patentee can overcome the presumption that prosecution history estoppel bars a finding of equivalence.

This presumption is not, then, just the complete bar by another name. Rather, it reflects the fact that the interpretation of the patent must begin with its literal claims, and the prosecution history is relevant to construing those claims. When the patentee has chosen to narrow a claim, courts may presume the amended text was composed with awareness of this rule and that the territory surrendered is not an equivalent of the territory claimed. In those instances, however, the patentee still might rebut the presumption that estoppel bars a claim of equivalence. The patentee must show that at the time of the amendment one skilled in the art could not reasonably be expected to have drafted a claim that would have literally encompassed the alleged equivalent.

IV

On the record before us, we cannot say petitioner has rebutted the presumptions that estoppel applies and that the equivalents at issue have been surrendered. Petitioner concedes that the limitations at issue—the sealing rings and the composition of the sleeve—were made in response to a rejection for reasons under § 112, if not also because of the prior art references. As the amendments were made for a reason relating to patentability, the question is not whether estoppel applies but what territory the amendments surrendered. While estoppel does not effect a complete bar, the question remains whether petitioner can demonstrate that the narrowing amendments did not surrender the particular equivalents at issue. On these questions, respondents may well prevail, for the sealing rings and the composition of the sleeve both were noted expressly in the prosecution history. These matters, however, should be determined in the first instance by further proceedings in the Court of Appeals or the District Court.

The judgment of the Federal Circuit is vacated, and the case is remanded for further proceedings consistent with this opinion.

It is so ordered.

INDEX

References are to Pages

ABANDONMENT
Patent, 427
Trademark, 227–229, 298–299

ACCOUNTING FOR PROFITS
See Profits

ADMINISTRATIVE PROCEDURES
Copyright, 580–587
Patent, 484–505
Trade secrets, 131–133
Trademark, 283–288

ADVERTISING
Ideas, 30–31
Trademark, 20–24
Unfair competition, 63–64

ANTITRUST
Copyright, 735–737

APPEALS
Patent, 207–208, 502–503
Trademark, 286

ARCHITECTURAL WORKS
Copyright, 598

ATTORNEY'S FEES
Copyright, 749
Lanham Act § 43(a), 385
Patent, 540
Right of publicity, 190
Trade secrets, 122–123
Trademark, 337

BERNE CONVENTION
Copyright, 5, 577–578, 790–791

CERTIFICATION MARKS
See Trademark

CHARACTERS
Copyright, 597–598
Unfair competition, 597–598

COLLECTIVE MARKS
See Trademark

COMMON LAW COPYRIGHT
Preemption, 3–5, 56

COMPULSORY LICENSE
Copyright, 677–678
Patent, 524
Trademark, 337–338

COMPUTER PROGRAMS
Copyright,
    Generally, 803–893
    Archival copies, 844–845, 852–853
    Computer Code, 805–826
    Databases, 825
    "Essential step" exemption, 852–853
    Infringement, 824, 840–841
    International protection, 825–826
    Merger, 824–825, 839
    Software rental, 853–854
    Subject matter, 823–824, 840
    User interfaces, 826–841
Patent,
    Generally, 894–931
    Mathematical algorithms, 917, 920–929
Reverse engineering, 870–871
Semiconductor chip protection,
    Generally, 937–939
    Exclusive rights, 938
    Notice, 938
    Registration, 938
    Reverse engineering, 938
    Subject matter, 937–938
    Term, 938
Trade secrets, 870–871, 932–937

CONSTITUTION
Commerce clause, 1–2
Copyright clause, 1–2, 598–599
Federal system, 3–5
Patent clause, 1–2
Preemption, 4–5, 801–802

CONTRIBUTORY INFRINGEMENT
Copyright, 678–685, 717–735
Patent, 518–521
Trademark, 339–347

COPYRIGHT
Administrative procedures, 580–587
Antitrust, 735–737
Architectural works, 598
Attorney's fees, 749
Berne Amendments, 577–578, 790–791

COPYRIGHT—Cont'd
Berne Convention, 5
Characters, 597–598
Compulsory license, 677–678
Computer programs, 803–893
   Rental right, 677, 853–854
Constitutional basis, 1–2
Contributory infringement, 678–685, 717–735
Copyright Clearance Center, 736
Copyright Royalty Tribunal, 678
Criminal sanctions, 734–735
Damages, 748
Deposit, 580–587
Derivative works, 658, 673–674
Display, 659–661, 676
Digital Millennium Copyright Act (DMCA),
   Circumvention, prohibitions against,
    734–735
   Safe Harbors, 732–733
Fact works, 615–617
Fair use,
     Generally, 685–737
    Amount, 711–712
    Classroom photocopying, 713–714
    Computer programs, 855–873
    First Amendment, 715, 873–893
    Market impact, 712
    Nature of work copied, 711
    Parody, 713
    Purpose, 710
    Satire, 713
First Amendment, 715, 873–893
First sale doctrine, 676–677
Formalities, 569–587
Functions of, 6–8
Industrial design, 955–979
Infringement,
     Generally, 750–778
    Audience test, 752
    Common errors, 752–753
    Expert testimony, 753
    Similarities, 751–753
    Strict liability, 753
    Subject matter,
      Instructional materials, 758–759
      Literature, 753–759
      Music, 759–767
      Visual arts, 767–778
Injunctions,
    Permanent, 750
    Preliminary, 749–750
Joint works, 638–639
Jurisdiction, 205–208
Merger, 596–597
Moral right,
     Generally, 778–793
    Integrity, right of, 791
    Paternity, right of, 791
    Preemption, 801
    State law, 793
    Visual Artists Rights Act, 792
Neighboring rights, 600–601
Notice,
     Generally, 569–580

COPYRIGHT—Cont'd
Notice—Cont'd
    Pre–Berne Notice Requirements, 577–578
    Error, 578
    Omission, 578
Notice affixation, 577–578
Novelty, 619–620
Obscene content, 598–599
Ownership, 620–657
Parody, 713
Performing rights societies, 735–736
Phonorecords, 677
Photocopying, 677
Preemption, 793–802
Profits, 748
Public broadcasting, 678
Public performance, 659–661, 674–675
Publication,
    Generally, 579–580
Reasonable royalty, 748
Record Rental Amendment, 677
Registration,
     Generally, 580–587
    Classification, 586
    Condition to suit, 585–586
    Form, 582–583
    Register of Copyrights, 585–586
    "Secure tests," 586–587
Remedies, 737–750
Renewal, 654–656
Requirements,
    Formalities, 569–587
    Originality, 601–620
Royalty payments, 792–793
Satire, 713
Sound recordings, 675–676
Subject matter,
     Generally, 587–591
    Case reports, 618
    Computer programs, 803–893
    Directories, 615–616
    Fact works, 615–617
    Fictional characters, 597–598
    Forms, 600
    Government works, 599–600
    Ideas, 595–596, 600
    Maps, 617–618
    Obscene content, 598–599
    Slogans, 600
    Unlawful content, 598–599
Term, 639–657
Transfers, 639–657
Vicarious liability, 684–685

**COURT OF APPEALS FOR FEDERAL
  CIRCUIT (CAFC)**
Jurisdiction, 207–208
Patent, 207–208, 455–456

COVENANT NOT TO COMPETE
See Trade Secrets

CUSTOMER LIST
See Trade Secrets

DAMAGES
Copyright, 748–749
Ideas, 48
Patent, 539–540
Right of publicity, 190
Trade secrets, 122–123
Trademark, 336
Unfair competition, 64–65, 385

DERIVATIVE WORKS
Copyright, 658, 673–674

DESIGN PATENT
    See also Industrial Design
    Generally, 941–954
Ornamentality, 953

DILUTION
    See also Trademark; Unfair Competition
Common law history, 79–80
Tarnishment, 78–79
Trademark, 299–314
Unfair competition, 72–81

DISTINCTIVENESS
Right of publicity, 188–189
Trademark, 229–256

DOCTRINE OF EQUIVALENTS
See Patent

ESTOPPEL
Collateral, 566–567
File wrapper, 565–566
Licensee, 522–524

FACT WORKS
Copyright, 615–617

FAIR USE
See Copyright; Trademark

FEDERAL TRADE COMMISSION
See Trademark

FILE WRAPPER ESTOPPEL
See Patent

FIRST AMENDMENT
Copyright, 715, 873–893
Right of publicity, 191–204

FUNCTIONALITY
Unfair competition, 96–98, 105

IDEAS
    Generally, 25–56
Advertising, 30–31
Brokers, 31–32
Concreteness, 47–48, 48
Copyright, 595–597, 600
Damages, 48
Novelty, 47–48
Patent protection, 17–19
Preemption, 50–56
Remedies, 48
Submissions,
    Company policies, 30–31

IDEAS—Cont'd
Submissions—Cont'd
    Professional and amateur, 30
Theories of protection, 32–50
    Contract implied in fact, 46–47
    Express contract, 45–46
    Property, 44–45
    Quasi contract, 47
Waiver forms, 31, 49–50

IMMORAL CONTENT
Copyright, 598–599
Trademark, 255–256

INDUSTRIAL DESIGN
    Generally, 940–1008
Copyright,
    Separability,
        Conceptual, 977–978
        Physical, 977
    "Useful articles," 978
Legislative proposals, 997–998
Ornamentality, 953
Patent, 941–954
Preemption, 999–1008
Trademark,
        Generally, 980–998
    Aesthetic functionality, 996–997
    Functionality, 996
Unfair competition, 980–998

INFRINGEMENT
Copyright, 750–778
Patent, 542–567
Trademark, 347–368

INJUNCTIONS
Copyright, 750–778
Patent, 538–539
Right of publicity, 190
Trade secrets, 122
Trademark, 337
Unfair competition, 64

INTERFERENCES
Patent, 427, 503
Trademark, 285

INTERNATIONAL TRADE COMMISSION
Appeals from, 208

JURISDICTION
See Copyright; Patent; Trademark; Unfair
    Competition

MISAPPROPRIATION
Right of publicity, 186–188
Unfair competition, 81–90

MISREPRESENTATION
Common law theory, 383–384
Trademark,
    Federal law, generally, 368–385
    Quality of competitor's goods, 383
    Quality of own goods, 382–383

MORAL RIGHT
See Copyright

NAME AND LIKENESS
See Publicity, Right of

NOTICE
Copyright, 569–580
Patent, 540–541
Semiconductor Chip Protection, 938
Trademark, 336–337

NOVELTY
Copyright, 619–620
Ideas, 47–48
Patent, 407–433

ORIGINALITY
Copyright, 601–620

PARODY
See Satire

PASSING OFF
Generally, 58–65
Federal law, 379–381
Trade dress imitation, 379–381

PATENT
Abandonment, 427
Administrative procedures, 484–505
Alternative systems, 18–19
Anticipation,
　　Generally, 427–428
　　Abroad, 429–430
Antitrust, 519–521
Appeals, 502–503
Application,
　　Generally, 485–488, 501–505
　　Claims, 485–486
　　Co-inventors, 477–479
　　Drawings, 488
　　Fraud, 503–505
　　Judicial review, 496–501
　　Misjoinder, 477–479
　　Nonjoinder, 477–479
　　Prosecution, 489–495
　　Reexamination, 502–503
　　Specification, 486–487
Attorney's fees, 540
Collateral estoppel, 566–567
"Combination" patents, 459
Compulsory licensing, 524
Computer programs, 894–931
Conception, 431–432
Constitutional basis, 1–2
Contributory infringement, 520–521
Court of Appeals for Federal Circuit, 387,
　　455–456
Damages, 539–540
Design patents, 941–954
Doctrine of equivalents, 563–566
Experimental use, 430–431, 517–518
Expert testimony, 457–458
File wrapper estoppel, 565–566
"First-to-file," 432–433

PATENT—Cont'd
Functions of, 6–8, 13–19
History, 386–387
Ideas, 17–18
Infringement,
　　Generally, 542–567
　　Acts abroad, 518–519
　　Contributory infringement, 519–522
　　Inducing infringement, 519–520
Injunctions,
　　Permanent, 538
　　Preliminary, 538–539
Interferences, 427, 503
Jurisdiction, 205–208
Licensee estoppel, 522–524
Microorganisms, 404–405
Modification, 502–503
"New uses," 405–406
Nonobviousness, 434–460
Notice, 540–541
Novelty, 407–433
Ordinary skill, 457, 458
Patent and Trademark Office, 458–459, 477,
　　484–495, 501–505
Patent misuse, 519–521
Pharmaceuticals, 476–478
Plant patents, 406–407
Preemption, 999–1008
Printed publication, 428–429
Prior art, 460–468
Profits, 539–540
Prosecution history estoppel, 565
Reasonable royalty, 539–540
Reconstruction, 516–517
Reduction to practice, 431–432
Relation to trade secrets, 164–166
Relation to trademark, 238–239
Remedies, 525–542
Repair, 516–517
Requirements,
　　Best mode, 483–484
　　Co-inventors, 477–479
　　Enabling disclosure, 479–484
　　Inventorship, 477–479
　　Nonobviousness, 434–460
　　Novelty, 407–434
　　Operability, 475–476
　　Secondary tests, 456–457
　　Statutory bars, 427
　　Utility, 468–479
Subject matter,
　　Generally, 389–407
　　Animals, 404–405
　　Computer programs, 894–931
　　Expired patents, 238–239
　　Foreign Practice, 407
　　Natural principles, 403–404
　　"New uses," 405–406
　　Plants, 406–407
　　Utility patents, 389–407
Suppression, 524
Term, 521–522, 524–525
Treble damages, 540
Utility patents, 389–407

PATENT AND TRADEMARK OFFICE
See also Patent; Trademark
Fraud, 503–505
Nonobviousness, 434–460
Patent applications,
    Generally, 485–488, 501–505
    Claims, 485–486
    Co-inventors, 477–479
    Drawings, 488
    Fraud, 503–505
    Judicial review, 496–501
    Misjoinder, 477–479
    Nonjoinder, 477–479
    Prosecution, 489–495
    Reexamination, 502–503
    Specification, 486–487
Trade secrets, 165–166
Trademark registration, 211–214

PERFORMING RIGHTS SOCIETIES
See Copyright

PERSONAL NAMES
Trademark, 252–253
Unfair competition, 90–96

PHONORECORDS
Copyright, 677

PHOTOCOPYING
Copyright, 677

PLANT PATENT
Generally, 406–407

PLANT VARIETY PROTECTION

PLANTS

PREEMPTION
Common law copyright, 3–5, 56
Constitutional, 801–802
Contract law, 800
Copyright, 793–802
Ideas, 50–56
Industrial design, 999–1008
Moral right, 801
Publicity, right of, 204, 801
Trade secrets, 3–5, 151–166, 166, 800
Unfair competition, 3–5, 96–107, 800–801

PRELIMINARY INJUNCTION
Copyright, 749–750
Patent, 538–539

PRINCIPAL REGISTER
See Trademark

PRODUCT SIMULATION
Trademark, 280–281
Unfair competition, 96–107

PROFITS
Copyright, 748
Lanham Act § 43(a), 385
Patent, 539–540
Right of publicity, 190
Trade secrets, 122–123

PROFITS—Cont'd
Trademark, 336
Unfair competition, 64–65

PUBLICATION
Copyright, 579–580
Printed, patent law, 428–429

PUBLICITY, RIGHT OF
Attorney's fees, 190
Damages, 190
First Amendment, 191–204
Identifiability, 188–189
Injunctions, 190
Misappropriation, 187–188
Name and likeness, 187–188
Newsworthiness exception, 202–203
Preemption, 3–5, 204, 801
Profits, 190
Remedies, 190
States adopting, 185
Theory of protection, 167–190
Unjust enrichment, 185–186
Voice, 187–188

REASONABLE ROYALTY
Copyright, 748
Patent, 539–540

REDUCTION TO PRACTICE
See Patent

REISSUE
See Patent

REMEDIES
See also Damages; Injunctions; Profits
Copyright, 737–750
Ideas, 48
Patent, 525–542
Right of publicity, 190
Trade secrets, 122–123
Trademark, 329–339
Unfair competition, 64–65

RENEWAL
Copyright, 654–656
Trademark, 286

REVERSE ENGINEERING
Copyright,
    Computer programs, 870–871
Trade secrets, 128–129, 938

RIGHT OF PUBLICITY
See Publicity, Right of

SATIRE
Copyright, 713
Trademark, 323–325

SECONDARY LIABILITY
See also Contributory Infringement
Copyright, 678–685, 717–735
Patent, 519–521
Trademark, 339–347

SECONDARY MEANING
Trademark, 229–230, 253
Unfair competition, 61–62

SEMICONDUCTOR CHIP PROTECTION
Generally, 937–939
Exclusive rights, 938
Notice, 938
Registration, 938
Reverse engineering, 938
Subject matter, 937–938
Term, 938

SERVICE MARKS
See Trademark

SHOP RIGHTS
See Trade Secrets

SOUND RECORDINGS
Copyright, 675–676

SUPPLEMENTAL REGISTER
See Trademark

SUPPRESSION
Patent, 524

SURVEYS
Trademark, 367

TERM
Copyright, 639–657
Patent, 521–522, 524–525
Semiconductor chip protection, 938
Trademark, 286

TERRITORIAL RIGHTS
Trademark, 288–299
Unfair competition, 71

TRADE DRESS
Trademark, 313
Unfair competition, 368–385

TRADE SECRETS
Accounting for profits, 122–123
Administrative handling, 131–133, 165–166
Attorney fees, 122–123
Computer programs, 870–871, 932–939
Covenant not to compete, 133–151
Customer lists, 149–150
Damages, 122–123
Departing employees, 150
Freedom of Information Act, 131–132
History, 150–151
Injunctions, 122
Litigation hazards, 130–131
Patent and Trademark Office, 165–166
Preemption, 3–4, 151–166, 800
Relation to patents, 164–166
Remedies, 122–123
Restatement of Torts, 119–120
Reverse engineering, 128–129, 870–871, 938
Secrecy requirement, 120–121
Shop rights, 148–149

TRADE SECRETS—Cont'd
Subject matter, 120
Theory of protection, 108–133

TRADEMARK
Abandonment, 298–299
Generally, 227–229
Consequences, 228–229
Loss of distinctiveness, 228
Non-use, 227–228
Administrative procedures, 283–288
Advertising, 20–24
Appeals, 286
Applications, 211–214
Assignments, 298–299
Attorney fees, 337
Cancellation, 285–286, 287–288
Certification marks, 261–270
Collateral use, 321–323
Collective marks, 261–270
Compulsory license, 337–338
Concurrent registration, 253–254, 285
Concurrent use, 285, 297–298
Constitutional basis, 1–2
Constructive notice, 298
Constructive use, 212–213, 298
Content, 270–282
Contributory infringement, 339–347
Counterfeit goods, 338–339
Cybersquatting, prohibitions against, 313–314, 326–329
Damages, 223, 336
Deceptive terms, 239–242, 254–255
"Deceptively misdescriptive" marks, 245–252, 254–255
Dilution, 299–329
Distinctiveness, 229–256
Domain names, 313–314, 326–329
Examination, 284
Expired patents, 238–239
Fair use, 314–321
"Family" of marks, 279
Federal Trade Commission, 238
Foreign registration, 225–226
Function of, 6–8, 20–24
Generic terms, 235–239
Geographic boundaries, 288–299
Geographic terms, 229–230
History, 209–211
ICANN, 326–329
Immoral content, 255–256
Incontestability, 287–288
Industrial design, 980–998
Infringement, 347–368
Injunctions, 337
"Intent to use" application, 212–213
Interferences, 285
Jurisdiction, 205–208
Licenses, 298–299
Marking, 336–337
"Merely descriptive" marks, 245–248
Metatags, 323
Misrepresentation,
Federal law, generally, 368–385

TRADEMARK—Cont'd
Misrepresentation—Cont'd
    Quality of competitor's goods, 383–834
    Quality of own goods, 382–383
Notice, 336–337
Oppositions, 285
Parody, 323–325
Patent and Trademark Office, 211–214
Personal names, 252–253
Preemption, 106–107
Principal register, 283–286
Priority, 223–226
Profits, 336
Registration, 211–214, 223–226
Relation to patent, 238–239
Remedies, 329–339
Renewal, 286
Requirements,
    Affixation, 226
    Bona fide use, 223–224
    Distinctiveness,
        Generally, 229–256
        Common law, 229–230
        Loss of, 228
        Statutory, 230–256
    Secondary meaning, 229–230
    Token use, 213–214, 223
    Use, 211–229
    Use in commerce, 224–225
Satire, 323–325
Scandalous matter, 255–256
Secondary meaning, 253
Service marks, 256–261
Similarity, 242–245
Subject matter,
    Buildings, 280–281
    Color, 270–277
    Expired utility patents, 238–239
    Fragrance, 277–278
    Location, 278–279
    Packages, 280–281
    Product depictions, 281–282
    Slogan, 279–280
Suggestive terms, 229, 254
Supplemental register, 282–283
Surnames, 252–253
Surveys, 367
Term, 286
Territorial rights, 288–299
Trade dress, 313, 368–385
Transfers, 298–299
UDRP, 326–329
Unfair competition compared, 57–58

TRADEMARK REGISTRATION
See Patent and Trademark Office

TRANSFER
Copyright, 639–657
Trademark, 298–299

UNFAIR COMPETITION
    See also Dilution; Misrepresentation;
        Trademark
Advertising, 63–64
Characters, 597–598
Damages, 64–65
Dilution, 72–81
Federal law,
    Generally, 368–381
    Misrepresentation,
        Quality of competitor's goods, 383–834
        Quality of own goods, 382–383
    Remedies, 385
    Standing, 384–385
Functionality, 96–98, 105
Generally, 57–107
Industrial design, 980–998
Injunctions, 64
International, 65
Jurisdiction, 205–208
Misappropriation, 81–90
Nondeceptive references, 63–64
Passing off, 58–65
Personal names, 90–95
Preemption, 3–5, 96–107, 800–801
Product simulation, 96–107
Profits, 64–65
Remedies, 64–65
Reverse confusion, 70–71
Secondary meaning, 61–62
Territorial rights, 71–72
Trade dress, 379–381
Trademark compared, 57–58
Types of cases, 62–63
Use, 63
Zone of expansion, 65–72

USE
Trademark, 211–229
Unfair competition, 63

UTILITY
Patents,
    Utility patents, 389–407
    Utility requirement, 468–479

VICARIOUS LIABILITY
Copyright, 684–685

VOICE
Right of publicity, 187–188

†

1–58778–166–2